PRESENT-VALUE INTEREST FACTORS FOR ONE DOLLAR, PVIF (continued)

Year	11%	12%	13%	14%	15%	16%	17%	18%	19%	20%
1	.901	.893	.885	.877	.870	.862	.855	.847	.840	.833
2	.812	.797	.783	.769	.756	.743	.731	.718	.706	.694
3	.731	.712	.693	.675	.658	.641	.624	.609	.593	.579
4	.659	.636	.613	.592	.572	.552	.534	.516	.499	.482
5	.593	.567	.543	.519	.497	.476	.456	.437	.419	.402
6	.535	.507	.480	.456	.432	.410	.390	.370	.352	.335
7	.482	.452	.425	.400	.376	.354	.333	.314	.296	.279
8	.434	.404	.376	.351	.327	.305	.285	.266	.249	.233
9	.391	.361	.333	.308	.284	.263	.243	.225	.209	.194
10	.352	.322	.295	.270	.247	.227	.208	.191	.176	.162
11	.317	.287	.261	.237	.215	.195	.178	.162	.148	.135
12	.286	.257	.231	.208	.187	.168	.152	.137	.124	.112
13	.258	.229	.204	.182	.163	.145	.130	.116	.104	.093
14	.232	.205	.181	.160	.141	.125	.111	.099	.088	.078
15	.209	.183	.160	.140	.123	.108	.095	.084	.074	.065
16	.188	.163	.141	.123	.107	.093	.081	.071	.062	.054
17	.170	.146	.125	.108	.093	.080	.069	.060	.052	.045
18	.153	.130	.111	.095	.081	.069	.059	.051	.044	.038
19	.138	.116	.098	.083	.070	.060	.051	.043	.037	.031
20	.124	.104	.087	.073	.061	.051	.043	.037	.031	.026
21	.112	.093	.077	.064	.053	.044	.037	.031	.026	.022
22	.101	.083	.068	.056	.046	.038	.032	.026	.022	.018
23	.091	.074	.060	.049	.040	.033	.027	.022	.018	.015
24	.082	.066	.053	.043	.035	.028	.023	.019	.015	.013
25	.074	.059	.047	.038	.030	.024	.020	.016	.013	.010
30	.044	.033	.026	.020	.015	.012	.009	.007	.005	.004
35	.026	.019	.014	.010	.008	.006	.004	.003	.002	.002
40	.015	.011	.008	.005	.004	.003	.002	.001	.001	.001
45	.009	.006	.004	.003	.002	.001	.001	.001	.000	.000
50	.005	.003	.002	.001	.001	.001	.000	.000	.000	.000

Robert E. Kowalski
865-6936 / 874-7293

W9-BLB-330

Principles of Managerial Finance

SECOND EDITION

HARPER & ROW, PUBLISHERS

PRINCIPLES OF MANAGERIAL FINANCE

LAWRENCE J. GITMAN
SAN DIEGO STATE UNIVERSITY

NEW YORK • HAGERSTOWN • PHILADELPHIA • SAN FRANCISCO • LONDON

Cover photo: Michel Craig

To my wife, Robin, our son, Zachary,
and our daughter, Jessica

Sponsoring Editor: John Greenman
Project Editor: Brigitte Pelner
Designer: Michel Craig
Production Manager: Stefania J. Taflinska
Compositor: Waldman Graphics, Inc.
Printer and Binder: Halliday Lithograph Corporation
Art Studio: J & R Technical Services, Inc.

PRINCIPLES OF MANAGERIAL FINANCE, Second Edition

Library of Congress Cataloging in Publication Data

Gitman, Lawrence J
  Principles of managerial finance.

  Includes bibliographical references and index.
  1. Corporations—Finance. 2. Business enterprises—
Finance. I. Title.
HG4011.G5   1979   658.1′5   78-26083
ISBN 0-06-042339-0

CONTENTS

PREFACE *xiii*

PART ONE: INTRODUCTION 2

Chapter 1: THE ROLE OF FINANCE AND THE FINANCIAL MANAGER 5
FINANCE, ECONOMICS, AND ACCOUNTING 5 / Finance and Economics 5 / Finance and Accounting 7 / AN OVERVIEW OF THE FINANCE FUNCTION 9 / The Role of Finance in the Business Firm 9 / The Functions of the Financial Manager 10 / The Goal of the Financial Manager 11 / AN OVERVIEW OF THE TEXT 15 / Part One: Introduction 15 / Part Two: Financial Analysis and Planning 16 / Part Three: The Management of Working Capital 16 / Part Four: Sources of Short-Term Financing 16 / Part Five: Fixed-Asset Management and Capital Budgeting 16 / Part Six: The Cost of Capital, Capital Structure, and Valuation 17 / Part Seven: Sources of Long-Term Financing 17 / Part Eight: Expansion and Failure 17 / *Summary* 17 / *Questions* 18 / *Selected References* 19

Chapter 2: THE LEGAL, OPERATING, AND TAX ENVIRONMENT OF THE FIRM 21
THE BASIC FORMS OF BUSINESS ORGANIZATION 22 / Sole Proprietorships 22 / Partnerships 24 / Corporations 26 / THE TREATMENT OF CORPORATE INCOME 29 / Depreciation 29 / Interest and Dividends 34 / PERSONAL TAXES 35 / Types of Income and Tax Rates 36 / Determining Taxable Income 38 / Tax Payments 39 / CORPORATE TAXES 40 / Ordinary Income 40 / Capital Gains 42 / Tax Losses 43 / Tax Loss Carrybacks and Carryforwards 44 / The Investment Tax Credit 46 / Subchapter S Corporations 47 / Tax Payment Dates 47 / *Summary* 47 / *Questions* 49 / *Problems* 50 / *Selected References* 53

PART TWO: FINANCIAL ANALYSIS AND PLANNING 54

Chapter 3: THE ANALYSIS OF FINANCIAL STATEMENTS 57
THE USE OF FINANCIAL RATIOS 57 / Interested Parties 58 / Types of Comparisons 58 / Words of Caution 59 / BASIC FINANCIAL STATE-

MENTS *59* / BASIC FINANCIAL RATIOS *62* / Measures of Liquidity and Activity *62* / Measures of Debt *71* / Measures of Profitability *77* / A COMPLETE RATIO ANALYSIS OF PHYLLIS PETROLEUM COMPANY *84* / Liquidity and Activity *85* / Debt *85* / Profitability *85* / *Summary 88* / *Questions 90* / *Problems 91* / *Selected References 97*

Chapter 4: OPERATING, FINANCIAL, AND TOTAL LEVERAGE 99

AN INCOME STATEMENT APPROACH TO LEVERAGE *99* / BREAK-EVEN ANALYSIS *100* / Types of Costs *100* / Determination of the Breakeven Point *101* / Changing Cost Relationships and the Breakeven Point *104* / Other Approaches to Breakeven Analysis *107* / Weaknesses in Breakeven Analysis *109* / OPERATING LEVERAGE *111* / Operating Leverage Illustrated *112* / Measuring the Degree of Operating Leverage (DOL) *113* / Fixed Costs and Operating Leverage *114* / Operating Risk *115* / FINANCIAL LEVERAGE *116* / Financial Leverage Illustrated *116* / Measuring the Degree of Financial Leverage (DFL) *117* / A Graphical Presentation of a Financing Plan *118* / A Graphical Illustration of Different Degrees of Financial Leverage *119* / Financial Risk *121* / TOTAL LEVERAGE: THE COMBINED EFFECT *122* / Total Leverage Illustrated *122* / Measuring the Degree of Total Leverage (DTL) *122* / The Relationship Between Operating, Financial, and Total Leverage *124* / Total Risk *124* / *Summary 125* / *Questions 126* / *Problems 127* / *Selected References 129*

Chapter 5: SOURCES AND USES OF FUNDS AND CASH BUDGETING 131

SOURCE AND USE OF FUNDS STATEMENTS *132* / Classifying Sources and Uses of Cash *132* / Assets, Liabilities, and Stockholders' Equity *134* / Special Adjustments *135* / Preliminaries to the Preparation of a Source and Use Statement *138* / Preparing the Source and Use of Cash Statement *140* / Preparing the Source and Use of Net Working Capital Statement *141* / The Source and Use Statement on a Percentage Basis *142* / Interpreting Source and Use Statements *142* / CASH BUDGETING *143* / The Sales Forecast *144* / The Format of the Cash Budget *145* / Interpreting the Cash Budget *148* / Reducing the Uncertainty in the Cash Budget *150* / Cash Flow Within the Month *150* / *Summary 152* / *Questions 153* / *Problems 154* / *Selected References 158*

Chapter 6: PRO FORMA STATEMENTS 159

BUDGETING INPUTS TO PRO FORMA PREPARATION *159* / A SHORTCUT APPROACH TO PRO FORMA PREPARATION *161* / Background Information *161* / The Pro Forma Income Statement *163* / The Pro Forma Balance Sheet *165* / Weaknesses of Shortcut Approaches *167* / THE LONG APPROACH TO PRO FORMA PREPARATION: PRELIMINARY BUDGETS *168* / Developing Background Information *168* / Developing the Required Plans *171* / THE PRO FORMA INCOME STATEMENT *176* / Preliminary Calculations *176* / The Statement *177* / Comparing the Resulting Income Statement with the Shortcut Approach *177* / THE PRO FORMA BALANCE SHEET *178* / The Cash Budget *179* / Comments on the Cash Budget *180* / The Statement *180* / Comparing the Resulting Balance Sheets with the Shortcut Approach *183* / *Summary 183* / *Questions 184* / *Problems 185* / *Selected References 189*

PART THREE: THE MANAGEMENT OF WORKING CAPITAL 192

Chapter 7: AN OVERVIEW OF WORKING CAPITAL MANAGEMENT 195

NET WORKING CAPITAL *196* / The Common Definition and Its Implications *196* / An Alternate Definition of Net Working Capital *197* / THE TRADE-OFF BETWEEN PROFITABILITY AND RISK *198* / Some Basic Assumptions *199* / The Nature of the Trade-Off Between Profitability and Risk *200* / DETERMINING THE FINANCING MIX *204* / The Aggressive Approach *205* / The Conservative Approach *208* / A Trade-Off Between the Two Approaches *210* / A Summary Comparison of Approaches *212* / *Summary 213* / *Questions 214* / *Problems 215* / *Selected References 218*

Chapter 8: CASH AND MARKETABLE SECURITY MANAGEMENT 219

THE EFFICIENT MANAGEMENT OF CASH *220* / Cash Cycles and Cash Turnovers *220* / Determining a Firm's Minimum Operating Cash *222* / Cash Management Strategies *223* / Combining Cash Management Strategies *228* / REFINEMENTS IN THE CASH MANAGEMENT PROCESS *229* / Collection Procedures *229* / Disbursement Procedures *231* / MOTIVES, CHARACTERISTICS, AND PROPORTION OF MARKETABLE SECURITIES *233* / Motives for Holding Marketable Securities *233* / Characteristics of Marketable Securities *234* / The Optimum Proportion of Marketable Securities in the Firm's Asset Mix *235* / THE BASIC MARKETABLE SECURITIES *235* / Government Issues *236* / Nongovernment Issues *237* / *Summary 239* / *Questions 240* / *Problems 240* / *Selected References 243*

Chapter 9: ACCOUNTS RECEIVABLE MANAGEMENT 245

CREDIT POLICIES *245* / Credit Standards *246* / Credit Analysis *252* / CREDIT TERMS *256* / Cash Discounts *257* / The Cash Discount Period *259* / Credit Period *259* / COLLECTION POLICIES *261* / The Basic Trade-Offs *261* / Types of Collection Techniques *262* / Computerization of Accounts Receivable Management *263* / *Summary 264* / *Questions 265* / *Problems 266* / *Selected References 268*

Chapter 10: INVENTORY MANAGEMENT 269

CHARACTERISTICS OF INVENTORY *269* / Types of Inventory *270* / Functional Viewpoints with Respect to Inventory Levels *273* / A Closer View of Inventory as an Investment *275* / The Relationship Between Inventory and Accounts Receivable *276* / INVENTORY MANAGEMENT AND CONTROL TECHNIQUES *278* / Determining the Type of Control Required: The ABC System *278* / The Basic Economic Order Quantity (EOQ) Model *279* / The Reorder Point *285* / *Summary 285* / *Questions 286* / *Problems 287* / *Selected References 289*

PART FOUR: SOURCES OF SHORT-TERM FINANCING 290

Chapter 11: SOURCES OF UNSECURED SHORT-TERM FINANCING 293

SPONTANEOUS SOURCES OF SHORT-TERM FINANCING *294* / Accounts Payable *294* / Accruals *303* / BANK SOURCES OF UNSECURED SHORT-TERM FUNDS *304* / Notes *304* / Lines of Credit *305* / Revolving Credit Agreements *308* / NONBANK SOURCES OF UNSECURED SHORT-TERM FINANCING *309* / Commerical Paper *309* / Customer Advances *311* / Private Loans *311* / *Summary* *311* / *Questions* *314* / *Problems* *314* / *Selected References* *315*

Chapter 12: SOURCES OF SECURED SHORT-TERM FINANCING 317

CHARACTERISTICS OF SECURED SHORT-TERM LOANS *318* / Types of Security Interest *318* / What Constitutes Acceptable Collateral? *320* / Institutions Extending Secured Short-Term Loans *322* / THE USE OF ACCOUNTS RECEIVABLE AS COLLATERAL *323* / Pledging Accounts Receivable *323* / Factoring Accounts Receivable *327* / THE USE OF INVENTORY AS COLLATERAL *331* / Characteristics of Inventory *332* / Floating Inventory Liens *332* / Trust Receipt Inventory Loans *333* / Warehouse Receipt Loans *333* / OTHER TYPES OF SECURED LOANS *335* / Stock and Bond Collateral *335* / Comaker Loans *338* / *Summary* *338* / *Questions* *339* / *Problems* *340* / *Selected References* *343*

PART FIVE: FIXED-ASSET MANAGEMENT AND CAPITAL BUDGETING 344

Chapter 13: THE MATHEMATICS OF FINANCE 347

COMPOUND INTEREST *348* / Annual Compounding *348* / Intrayear Compounding *351* / The Compound Value of an Annuity *354* / PRESENT VALUE *357* / The Present Value of a Single Amount *357* / Mixed Streams of Cash Flows *360* / Annuities *361* / APPLYING COMPOUND INTEREST AND PRESENT-VALUE TECHNIQUES *364* / Deposits to Accumulate a Future Sum *364* / Loan Amortization *365* / Determining Interest and Growth Rates *366* / Determining Bond Values *367* / Perpetuities *376* / *Summary* *368* / *Questions* *370* / *Problems* *371* / *Selected References* *373*

Chapter 14: FIXED-ASSET MANAGEMENT AND CAPITAL BUDGETING FUNDAMENTALS 375

MANAGING FIXED ASSETS *376* / Capital Expenditures *376* / Authorizing Capital Expenditures *378* / The Origin and Path of Capital Expenditure Proposals *380* / CAPITAL BUDGETING FUNDAMENTALS *380* / Types of Projects *381* / The Availability of Funds *381* / Approaches to Capital Budgeting Decisions *381* / DEVELOPING THE RELEVANT DATA *383* / Types of Cash-Flow Patterns *383* / Initial Investment *385* / Cash Inflows *389* / A Shortcut for Determining Relevant Cash Inflows *392* / *Summary* *395* / *Questions* *396* / *Problems* *397* / *Selected References* *399*

Chapter 15: **CAPITAL BUDGETING CONCEPTS AND TECHNIQUES** *401*

UNSOPHISTICATED CAPITAL BUDGETING TECHNIQUES *402* / Average Rate of Return *403* / Payback Period *405* / SOPHISTICATED CAPITAL BUDGETING TECHNIQUES *407* / Net Present Value (NPV) *408* / Benefit-Cost Ratio (B/C Ratio) *408* / Internal Rate of Return (IRR) *410* / Comparison of NPV and IRR *414* / CAPITAL RATIONING *417* / The Internal Rate of Return Approach *417* / The Net Present-Value Approach *418* / Integer Programming *419* / *Summary 420* / *Questions 422* / *Problems 423* / *Selected References 426*

Chapter 16: **CAPITAL BUDGETING UNDER RISK** *429*

BASIC RISK CONCEPTS *430* / Risk and Uncertainty *430* / Sensitivity Analysis of Risk *431* / Assigning Probabilities to Outcomes *432* / MEASURING PROJECT RISK *433* / Probability Distributions *434* / Using Statistics for Measuring Risk *436* / RISK AND TIME *439* / Risk as a Function of Time *439* / Portfolio Risk *440* / RISK AND RETURN: CAPITAL ASSET PRICING MODEL (CAPM) *444* / Assumptions of the Model *445* / Types of Risk *445* / The Model: CAPM *446* / Some Comments on CAPM *448* / ADJUSTING FOR PROJECT RISK *449* / The Subjective Approach *450* / Decision Trees *450* / Statistical Approaches *450* / Simulation *452* / Certainty Equivalents *453* / Risk-Adjusted Discount Rates *454* / *Summary 457* / *Questions 458* / *Problems 459* / *Selected References 465*

PART SIX: THE COST OF CAPITAL, CAPITAL STRUCTURE, AND VALUATION *468*

Chapter 17: **THE COST OF CAPITAL** *471*

AN OVERVIEW OF THE COST OF CAPITAL *471* / Risk *472* / Taxes *473* / The Key Factor Affecting Financing Costs *474* / THE COST OF SPECIFIC SOURCES OF CAPITAL *475* / The Cost of Long-Term Debt (Bonds) *476* / The Cost of Preferred Stock *479* / The Cost of Common Stock *480* / The Cost of Retained Earnings *487* / MEASURING THE OVERALL OR WEIGHTED AVERAGE COST OF CAPITAL *488* / Historical Weights *489* / Target Weights *491* / Marginal Weights *492* / THE WEIGHTED MARGINAL COST OF CAPITAL (WMCC) *494* / Calculation of the WMCC *494* / Use of WMCC for Decision Making *499* / *Summary 501* / *Questions 503* / *Problems 504* / *Selected References 508*

Chapter 18: **CAPITAL STRUCTURE AND VALUATION** *511*

THE FIRM'S CAPITAL STRUCTURE *511* / Types of Capital *511* / Measures and Considerations of Capital Structure *514* / The Theory of Capital Structure *516* / THE EBIT-eps APPROACH TO CAPITAL STRUCTURE *522* / Presenting a Financing Plan Graphically *523* / Comparing Financing Plans Graphically *525* / Interpreting EBIT-eps Analysis *527* / THE VALUATION OF CORPORATE STOCK *528* / The Book Value of Stock *528* / The Liquidation Value of Stock *529* / The Market Value of Stock *530* / Industry Capitalization and Stock Value *531* / The Gordon Model *531* / Comparing Valuation Techniques *533* / *Summary 533* / *Questions 534* / *Problems 535* / *Selected References 541*

PART SEVEN: SOURCES OF LONG-TERM FINANCING 544

Chapter 19: FINANCIAL INTERMEDIARIES AND MARKETS 547

FINANCIAL INTERMEDIARIES AND MARKETS: AN OVERVIEW 548 /
Financial Intermediaries 548 / Financial Markets 541 / The Relationship
Between Financial Intermediaries and Financial Markets 541 / THE
MONEY MARKET 552 / The Operation of the Money Market 552 / Participants in the Money Market 553 / Money Market Instruments 554 /
THE CAPITAL MARKETS 554 / The Functions of Security Exchanges
554 / Characteristics of Security Exchanges 556 / Special Stock Transactions 559 / Investment Companies 560 / INVESTMENT BANKING
561 / The Functions of the Investment Banker 561 / The Organization of
Investment Banking Activity 562 / The Cost of Investment Banking Services
565 / Direct Placement 565 / Summary 566 / Questions 567 / Problems 568 / Selected References 571

Chapter 20: LEASING 573

CHARACTERISTICS OF LEASES 574 / Basic Types of Leases 574 /
Leasing Arrangements 575 / Legal Requirements of Leases 577 / The
Lease Contract 578 / LEASING AS A SOURCE OF FINANCING 578 /
Lease Costs 579 / The Effect of Leasing on Future Financing 581 / THE
LEASE-PURCHASE DECISION 585 / Lease Payments and After-Tax Cash
Outflows 586 / Borrowing and After-Tax Cash Outflows 587 / Comparing
Lease and Purchase Alternatives 589 / ADVANTAGES AND DISADVAN-
TAGES OF LEASING 590 / Advantages of Leasing 591 / Disadvantages
of Leasing 593 / Summary 594 / Questions 595 / Problems 595 /
Selected References 601

Chapter 21: LONG-TERM DEBT FINANCING 603

CHARACTERISTICS OF LONG-TERM DEBT FINANCING 604 / Stand-
ard Loan Provisions 604 / Restrictive Loan Provisions 605 / The Cost of
Long-Term Financing 608 / TERM LOANS 610 / Characteristics of Term
Loan Agreements 611 / Term Lenders 612 / CHARACTERISTICS OF
CORPORATE BONDS 614 / Legal Aspects of Corporate Bonds 614 / The
General Features of a Bond 615 / Marketing a Bond 616 / Bond
Ratings 617 / TYPES OF BONDS 617 / Unsecured Bonds 618 / Se-
cured Bonds 619 / BOND REFUNDING OPTIONS 622 / Serial
Issues 622 / Refunding Bonds by Exercising a Call Privilege 622 / Sum-
mary 625 / Questions 627 / Problems 628 / Selected References 631

Chapter 22: PREFERRED AND COMMON STOCK 633

THE NATURE OF EQUITY CAPITAL 633 / Ownership Rights 634 /
Claims on Income and Assets 634 / Maturity 635 / PREFERRED
STOCK 635 / Basic Rights of Preferred Stockholders 635 / Special Fea-
tures of Preferred Stock 637 / Advantages and Disadvantages of Preferred
Stock 640 / COMMON STOCK 642 / Characteristics of Common
Stock 642 / Stock Rights 646 / Non-Rights Sale of New Common
Stock 649 / Basic Values of Common Stock 650 / Advantages and Disad-
vantages of Common Stock 650 / Summary 651 / Questions 652 /
Problems 653 / Selected References 656

Chapter 23: CONVERTIBLE SECURITIES AND WARRANTS 659

CHARACTERISTICS OF CONVERTIBLE SECURITIES 660 / Types of Convertible Securities 660 / General Features of Convertibles 660 / Motives for Convertible Financing 663 / Other Considerations 665 / DETERMINING THE VALUE OF CONVERTIBLES 667 / Bond or Preferred Stock Value 667 / Stock or Conversion Value 669 / Market Value 670 / Special Considerations 670 / STOCK PURCHASE WARRANTS 671 / Characteristics of Warrants 671 / The Value of Warrants 673 / *Summary* 675 / *Questions* 676 / *Problems* 677 / *Selected References* 681

Chapter 24: DIVIDENDS AND RETAINED EARNINGS 683

PROCEDURAL AND THEORETICAL CONSIDERATIONS 684 / Retained Earnings as a Source of Financing 684 / Cash Dividend Payment Procedures 686 / Theoretical Viewpoints 688 / FACTORS AFFECTING DIVIDEND POLICY 690 / Legal, Contractual, and Internal Constraints 690 / Growth Prospects 692 / Owner Considerations 693 / Market Considerations 695 / OBJECTIVES AND TYPES OF DIVIDEND POLICIES 696 / Objectives of Dividend Policy 696 / Types of Dividend Policies 697 / NONCASH DIVIDENDS 700 / Stock Dividends 700 / Stock Splits 702 / Stock Repurchases 704 / *Summary* 706 / *Questions* 708 / *Problems* 709 / *Selected References* 713

PART EIGHT: EXPANSION AND FAILURE 716

Chapter 25: CONSOLIDATIONS, MERGERS, AND HOLDING COMPANIES 719

THE FUNDAMENTALS OF BUSINESS COMBINATIONS 719 / Types of Business Combinations 719 / Motives for Business Combinations 721 / Relevant Variables 724 / ANALYZING PROSPECTIVE MERGERS 726 / Cash Purchases of Companies 726 / Stock Exchange Acquisitions 729 / The Merger Negotiation Process 737 / HOLDING COMPANIES 738 / Advantages of Holding Companies 739 / Disadvantages of Holding Companies 741 / *Summary* 741 / *Questions* 743 / *Problems* 743 / *Selected References* 749

Chapter 26: FAILURE, REORGANIZATION, AND LIQUIDATION 751

THE NATURE AND CAUSES OF BUSINESS FAILURE 752 / Types of Business Failure 752 / Major Causes of Business Failure 753 / VOLUNTARY SETTLEMENTS 755 / Initiating a Voluntary Settlement 755 / A Voluntary Settlement to Sustain the Firm 756 / A Voluntary Settlement Resulting in Private Liquidation 757 / REORGANIZATION IN BANKRUPTCY 758 / Bankruptcy 758 / Reorganization Procedures 760 / The Trustee's Responsibilities 762 / LIQUIDATION IN BANKRUPTCY 765 / Legal Aspects 765 / The Priority of Claims 765 / The Discharge of the Firm 768 / *Summary* 768 / *Questions* 770 / *Problems* 771 / *Selected References* 776

Appendix A: FINANCIAL TABLES A-1
Table A-1: Compound-Value Interest Factors for One Dollar, CVIF *A-1* /
Table A-2: Compound-Value Interest Factors for a One-Dollar Annuity, CVIFA
A-6 / Table A-3: Present-Value Interest Factors for One Dollar, PVIF *A-10* /
Table A-4: Present-Value Interest Factors for a One-Dollar Annuity, PVIFA
A-14

Appendix B: ANSWERS TO
**   SELECTED END-OF-CHAPTER PROBLEMS A-19**

Glossary A-31

Index

PREFACE

The field of finance becomes ever more crowded with introductory texts. They vary widely in topic emphasis and depth of quantitative analysis. Only a fortunate few among the dozen or more currently available have attained the degree of market acceptance enjoyed by this book's first edition. Market research indicates that the determining factor in its early success is *teachability*.

The second edition of *Principles of Managerial Finance* was written with the same primary objective as the first: to convey the key concepts of financial management in a way that can be read and comprehended by the student with ease. Although it was designed for the introductory course at the undergraduate level, it may also be used with good results in the core MBA finance course, in management development programs, and in executive reading programs. Feedback from the first edition's use by professors, students, and practitioners has confirmed the text's effectiveness in each of these areas.

The goal of this text remains unchanged; it is to provide the student with a readable narrative that supplies both the breadth and the depth of coverage necessary to obtain an understanding of the underlying principles of managerial finance. The second edition of *Principles* continues to emphasize timely and emerging topics in managerial finance. Two examples of this are the sections on working capital management and on risk and return. Most existing texts have emphasized the long-term implications of financial management without delving into the day-to-day aspects of financial decision making. Recently experienced periods of tight money have made the management of working capital very important. *This text continues to place equal emphasis on short- and long-term financial management.*

Recent theoretical developments concerning the relationship between risk and return have significantly affected such aspects of financial decision making as capital budgeting, cost of capital, and valuation. *The key model that interrelates risk and return—the capital asset pricing model (CAPM)—has been introduced in this edition,* and its applications have been added to discussions of more traditional techniques. I feel that CAPM provides needed linkage between various financial decisions and their probable effects on the wealth of the firm's owners, but I realize that a number of my colleagues prefer not to use CAPM in a first course. Consequently, the CAPM sections are well demarked in this text and may be omitted at the instructor's discretion without loss of continuity.

The second edition of *Principles of Managerial Finance* is intended to make factual material as easily digestible for the student as possible, so that the professor may concentrate on highlighting the theories, concepts, tools, and techniques that will help the student make reasonable real-world financial decisions. I remain committed to the belief that a professor should not have to manufacture examples to simplify concepts or catch student interest; these examples should be liberally included in the text. I also feel that to be truly teachable, a text should be readable; so this one was created and revised with the student constantly in mind. (Yet the payoff of readability accrues not only to the student but to the professor, who finds the job of teaching greatly simplified and considerably more rewarding.) Let me explain the factors that I believe have the greatest effect on the teachability and readability of a finance textbook.

PEDAGOGICAL FEATURES

Organization. This text is structured around the firm's balance sheet, viewed both horizontally and vertically, and the balance sheet is used repeatedly as a reference point. Each part of the text examines aspects of the firm's asset structure, financial structure, or the relationship between them. Part One discusses the financial manager and the legal, operating, and tax environment of the firm; Part Two is devoted to various aspects of financial planning and control; Part Three discusses the management of working capital; Part Four describes the key sources of short-term financing available to the firm; Part Five is devoted to fixed-asset management and capital budgeting; Part Six discusses the cost of capital, capital structure, and valuation; Part Seven describes the various sources of long-term financing available to the firm; and Part Eight is devoted to expansion and failure.

In organizing each chapter, I have tried to adhere to a managerial decision-making perspective. That is, I have not merely described a concept, such as operating leverage or present value; I have always tried to *relate* it to the financial manager's overall goal of owner wealth maximization. Once a particular concept has been developed, I have tried to illustrate its application so that the student is not left with just an abstract definition, but truly senses the decision-making considerations and consequences of *each* financial action. New terms are always defined when first used and sometimes redefined in order to avoid forcing the reader to search for their meaning. Also, the comprehensive glossary at the back of the text makes these terms and definitions accessible in another way.

Principles of Managerial Finance has twenty-six chapters. It was obviously intended to be read as a continuous stream of thought, but almost any chapter may be taken out of sequence and studied as a self-contained unit. Each professor has particular topic preferences, so the topic coverage in this book has deliberately been made both extensive and flexible. The comparatively manageable size of the book, however, makes it suitable for a variety of course lengths, from one quarter to two full semesters, and each professor will want to adjust the breadth of coverage to fit his or her own time parameters.

Examples. Numerous well-marked examples have been inserted throughout the text in order to demonstrate what might otherwise be troublesome concepts for the student to grasp. The examples are detailed, and quite often the reason for using a particular approach is given, along with the demonstration. Reviewers and users of the first edition felt that the content, quality, placement, and method of presentation of the examples are all crucial—both to good teaching and good learning of the material.

Questions and Problems. I am a strong believer in using many good problems in all phases of the first finance course, at whatever level it is taught. Therefore, a comprehensive set of questions and problems at the ends of chapters serves as a review guide with which the student may test his or her understanding of various theories, concepts, tools, and techniques presented within the chapters. More than one problem is provided for each concept to assure the student many self-testing opportunities and to give the professor a wide choice of assignable materials.

MOTIVES FOR REVISION

These were my major objectives in preparing the second edition:

1. To incorporate recent developments in financial management theory and practice, while at the same time citing significant changes in the legal and tax environment.

2. To further enhance the text's teachability through reorganization, improved exposition, and the use of fresh examples.

3. To insert additional topics proposed by a variety of users and critics.

4. To update end-of-chapter questions and replace all end-of-chapter problems with new ones that better reflect the content and aims of this edition.

CHANGES IN THE SECOND EDITION

My publisher and I developed a comprehensive revision plan based upon a large number of written reviews obtained from academicians, plus feedback from other adopters, colleagues, and students, plus observations gleaned from my own use of the text during the past two years. The plan was scrutinized by some on-line financial managers in order to assure that the real-world activities described truly reflect financial management as it is practiced today. The plan called for two kinds of changes: all-encompassing ones and specific ones involving content or structure.

All-Encompassing Changes

1. A 40-percent tax rate on ordinary corporate income is used throughout the text instead of the 50-percent rate used in the first edition; this permits the reader to realistically assess the impact of corporate taxes on a variety of financial decisions.

2. In the spirit of recent legislation and changing attitudes toward sexism, a balance between male-female references has been imposed on the text's exposition.

3. All 400 of the end-of-chapter problems are *new*. Follow-up types of problems have been eliminated; each problem is now completely independent.

4. All end-of-chapter reference lists have been updated to take account of recent additions to the financial literature.

5. Answers to selected end-of-chapter problems have been included in a new appendix (Appendix B); students should find these "check figures" helpful in working homework problems.

Specific Content/Structure Changes

1. An expanded discussion (with examples) of the wealth maximization process was added.

2. The explanation of corporate income taxation was amended to reflect recent tax law changes, and a section on personal taxes was added.

3. Ratio discussions were reorganized and streamlined; the Modified DuPont relationship is introduced; and an illustration and interpretation of a complete ratio analysis, along with a summary table, is now included.

4. The general formulas for various types of leverage—including total leverage—were added.

5. The coverage of cash budgeting was expanded to include sensitivity analysis and a discussion of cash flows within the month.

6. Material on the financing mix was rewritten to eliminate certain conceptual problems found in the first edition.

7. A section illustrating the relationship between inventory and accounts receivable was added.

8. The chapters devoted to the sources of short-term financing were repositioned to directly follow the segment on working capital management.

9. Summary tables of various types, sources, costs, and characteristics of unsecured short-term financing, secured short-term financing, and long-term debt financing are now included at the ends of appropriate chapters.

10. All terminology, including financial table factor abbreviations, is now standardized to agree with the most common usage and notation.

11. A section on direct determination of cash flows (given revenue, expense, and depreciation data) has been integrated into the discussion of capital budgeting fundamentals. It features a shortcut alternative method of determining relevant cash inflows for use in capital budgeting.

12. An example illustrating the diversification process related to portfolio risk was added to the discussion of risk in capital budgeting.

13. A well-demarked, and therefore optional, new section that clearly, concisely, and nonquantitatively develops the basic capital asset pricing model (CAPM) as part of the discussion of risk and return has been added to the chapter on risk in capital budgeting. The model's applicability to capital budgeting decision making is discussed and illustrated.

14. Also added to the section on risk in capital budgeting are discussions of the use of decision trees and the use of certainty equivalents in adjusting for risk in the capital budgeting decision process.

15. Coverage of the measurement of the cost of common stock equity has been reorganized, and the use of the capital asset pricing model as an alternative measurement technique has been appended to it as an optional section.

16. A section describing and illustrating the computation of a firm's weighted marginal cost of capital (WMCC) has been added to the cost-of-capital chapter. The description of using the WMCC function with the firm's investment opportunities schedule (IOS) in making investment decisions comprises a major revision.

17. The valuation discussion now includes another optional section discussing the use of the capital asset pricing model to measure the cost of equity capital.

18. The impacts of recent advances in accounting are now reflected in the discussion of lease financing.

19. The discussions of stock dividends and stock splits are now treated together in the chapter devoted to dividends and retained earnings.

REVISIONS IN THE LEARNING AND TEACHING AIDS

I have completely revised the student review manual, *Study Guide to accompany Principles of Managerial Finance*. Each chapter of the study guide contains a chapter summary, a chapter outline, a programmed self-test, and problems with detailed solutions. Each of these elements has been amended to reflect all text revisions. A completely new companion casebook, *New Cases in Managerial Finance*, in brief paperback form has been written by two *proven expert* financial case writers—Harry R. Kunianky (Allied Plastics Company) and William H. Marsh (College of Charleston). It contains 40 short cases aimed at fostering the student's ability to apply concepts in the main text. These class-tested short cases offer excellent opportunities for the student to develop the ability to solve real financial problems. Several control measures have been used to assure that this casebook is error-free. For those who choose to use it, the earlier casebook, *Cases in Managerial Finance*, coauthored by Timothy E. Johnson (University of Cincinnati), Ross A. Flaherty (The University of Texas at Arlington), and me continues to be available.

ACKNOWLEDGMENTS

Numerous people have made significant contributions to this edition, as well as the first edition. Without their classroom experience, guidance, and advice, this book could not have been written or revised. Only by receiving continual feedback from students, colleagues, and practitioners have I been able to realize my aim of creating a truly teachable textbook. If you or your students are moved to write me about any matters pertaining to this text package, please do. I welcome constructive criticism and suggestions for the book's further improvement. A text should be a reflection of contemporary thought in its discipline. When its author realizes that hundreds of academicians and practitioners have contributed to the body of financial knowledge that he is now attempting to pass on to others, he becomes humbled and most appreciative.

Harper & Row, Publishers, obtained the experienced advice of a large group of excellent reviewers. I appreciate their many suggestions and criticisms, which have had a strong influence on various aspects of this volume. My special thanks go to: Kenneth J. Boudreaux, Glenn Henderson, Kenneth M. Huggins, Terrance E. Kingston, Timothy Hoyt McCaughey, Gene P. Morris, Donald A. Nash, Don B. Panton, Stanley Piascik, Gerald A. Pogue, William L. Sartoris, Richard A. Shick, Gerald Smolen, Gary Tallman, and Richard Teweles. Many of these people, whose affiliations I listed in the first edition, also reviewed parts of all of the second edition manuscript. In addition, the following people provided useful input to the revised edition: David A. Arbeit, Adelphi University; Richard E. Ball, University of Cincinnati; Ron Braswell, The Florida State University; F. Barney English, Southwest Texas State University; Philip W. Glasgo, University of Cincinnati; George T. Harris, The University of Nebraska at Omaha; Roger G. Hehman, Raymond Walters General and Technical College of the University of Cincinnati; William R. Lane, Louisiana State University; Michael A. Lenarcic, Northeastern University; Edward A. Moses, The University of Tulsa; William T. Murphy, Ithaca College; Ronda S. Paul, University of Kentucky; Ron Rizzuto, University of Denver; Carl J. Schwendiman, The University of Texas at Arlington; Carl Schweser, University of Iowa; Robert D. Tollen, The University of Texas at El Paso; John C. Woods, Nichols College; and Joe W. Zeman, Bartlesville Wesleyan College.

I am especially indebted to J. Markham Collins, University of Dayton, not only for his reviews, but for the outstanding job he did in preparing new end-of-chapter materials and the related portions of the instructor's manual. A special word of thanks also goes to my colleague and tax expert, Patrick A. Hennessee, for his assistance in updating and revising the tax discussions; to Harry R. Kuniansky, Allied Plastics Company, Atlanta, and William H. Marsh, College of Charleston, for authoring the accompanying *New Cases in Managerial Finance;* to Timothy E. Johnson, University of Cincinnati, and Ross A. Flaherty, The University of Texas at Arlington, who co-authored the accompanying *Cases in Managerial Finance;* and to my colleagues at The University of Tulsa, particularly Louis E. Boone, Benton E. Gup, William D. Jarnagin, J. Michael Terrell, and Larry E. Wofford, who have provided encouragement, advice, and support throughout this revision.

I would also like to express my appreciation to Kersi P. Damri for his research assistance and to Margaret F. Ferguson, who did an extraordinary job of converting hundreds of my handwritten revisions into typed form. The editorial staff of Harper & Row was cooperative, as usual, and their contributions are sincerely appreciated.

Finally, my wife, Robin, and children, Zachary and Jessica, have played most important parts in patiently providing the support and understanding I needed during the writing of this book. To them I will be forever grateful.

LAWRENCE J. GITMAN

Principles of Managerial Finance

PART ONE

This part of the text presents a general view of the finance function in the business firm. It also focuses on the legal organization of firms and certain key concepts relating to the tax treatment of corporate income. Part One contains two chapters. Chapter 1 provides a description of the role of finance and the financial manager within the firm. Specific attention is given to differentiating finance from economics and accounting. Chapter 1 also presents a brief overview of the text. Chapter 2 discusses the legal and tax environments within which the firm operates. Specific attention is given to the corporate form of business organization. Together, the two chapters in Part One should give the reader an understanding of the importance, the role, and the operating environment of the finance function in the business firm.

Introduction

BALANCE SHEET	
Assets	Liabilities and Stockholders' Equity
Current Assets	Current Liabilities
Fixed Assets	Long-Term Debt
	Stockholders' Equity

CHAPTER 1
The role of finance and the financial manager

This chapter is intended to answer two basic questions—What is finance? and What are the functions of the financial manager? The key points covered in answering these questions will set the stage for a thorough understanding of the important decision areas for the financial manager and the methods he or she uses in resolving problems. This chapter also presents an overview of how the field of financial management is presented in the text. The chapter has three basic sections. The first section answers the question What is finance? by differentiating the finance function from the closely related fields of economics and accounting. The second section provides an overview of the finance function in order to answer the question What are the functions of the financial manager? It discusses the role of finance within the firm and the functions and goal of the financial manager. The final section of the chapter presents an overview of the text, of the approach used to present the key concepts of financial management, and the rationale for that approach.

FINANCE, ECONOMICS, AND ACCOUNTING

Finance is closely allied to economics and accounting. Financial management can be viewed as a form of applied economics that draws heavily on theoretical economic constructs. Financal management also draws certain data from accounting, another area of applied economics. In this section, we shall discuss the relationship between finance and economics and also between finance and accounting. Although these disciplines are related, there are key differences among them.

Finance and economics

The importance of economics to the development of the financial environment and financial theory can best be described in light of the two broad areas of economics—macroeconomics and microeconomics. *Macroeconomics* is concerned with the overall institutional and international environment in which the firm must operate, while *microeconomics* concerns itself with the determination of optimal operating strategies for firms or individuals. Each of these areas, as they relate to financial management, are discussed briefly below.

Macroeconomics. It is from the theories of macroeconomics that the financial environment in which the finance functions are implemented is established. Macroeconomics is concerned with the institutional structure of the banking system, financial intermediaries, the federal treasury, and the economic policies available to the federal government for coping with and controlling the level of economic activity within the economy. It should be obvious that macroeconomic theory and policy know no geographic limits; rather, they are concerned with the establishment of an international framework in which funds flow freely between institutions and countries, economic activity is stabilized, and unemployment is controlled.

Since the business firm must operate in the macroeconomic environment, it is important that the financial manager be aware of the institutional framework it contains. The financial manager must also be alert to the consequences of varying levels of economic activity and changes in economic policy for his or her own decision environment. Without an understanding of the functioning of the broad economic environment within which he or she operates, the financial manager cannot hope to achieve financial success for the firm. The financial manager must recognize the consequences of more restrictive monetary or fiscal policies on the firm's fund-raising and revenue-generating abilities. The financial manager must also be aware of the various financial institutions and their mode of operations to be able to evaluate the potential sources of financing.

Microeconomics. The theories of microeconomics provide for the efficient operation of a business firm. They are concerned with defining actions that will permit the firm to achieve financial success. The concepts involved in supply and demand relationships and profit maximizing strategies are drawn from microeconomic theory. Issues related to the mix of productive factors, "optimal" sales levels, and product pricing strategies are all affected by theories on the microeconomic level. Theories related to the measurement of utility preferences, risk, and the determination of value are rooted in microeconomic theory. The rationale for depreciating assets is also derived from this area of economics. Although not applying the theories of microeconomics directly, the financial manager should operate in a manner consistent with its general principles. The primary principle that applies in financial management is *marginal analysis;* the predominance of this principle suggests that financial decisions should be made and actions taken only when marginal revenues exceed marginal costs. When this condition does exist, a given decision or action should result in an increase in the firm's profits. The importance of marginal analysis in making financial decisions will become apparent in the subsequent chapters of this text.

In summary, a knowledge of economics is necessary in order to understand both the financial environment and the decision theories that underlie contemporary financial management. Macroeconomics provides the financial manager with insight into the policies of the government and private institutions through which various aspects of money flows, credit flows, and general economic activity are controlled. Operating within the "economic ball park" created by these institutions, the financial manager draws on microeconomic theories of the operation of the firm and profit maximization to develop a winning game plan, competing not only against other players in a particular industry but also against prevailing economic conditions, favorable or unfavorable.

Finance and accounting

Many people view the finance and accounting functions within a business firm as virtually the same. Although there is a close relationship between these functions, just as there is a close relationship between finance and economics, the accounting function is best viewed as a necessary input to the finance function—that is, as a subfunction of finance. This view is in line with the traditional organization of the activities of a firm into three basic areas—finance, manufacturing, and marketing. The accounting function is typically viewed as within the control of the financial vice president. However, there are two key differences in viewpoint between finance and accounting—one related to the treatment of funds and the other to decision making.

Treatment of funds. The accountant, whose primary function is to develop and provide data for measuring the performance of the firm, assessing its financial position, and paying taxes, differs from the financial manager in the way he or she views the firm's funds. The accountant, using certain standardized and generally accepted principles, prepares financial statements based on the premise that revenues should be recognized at the point of sale and expenses when they are incurred. This method of accounting is commonly referred to as the *accrual system.* Revenues resulting from the sale of merchandise on credit, for which the actual cash payment has not yet been received, appear on the firm's financial statements as *accounts receivable,* a temporary asset. Expenses are treated in a similar fashion—that is, certain liabilities are established to represent goods or services which have been received but have yet to be paid for. These items are usually listed on the balance sheet as *accounts payable,* or *accruals.*

The financial manager is more concerned with maintaining a firm's solvency by providing the cash flows necessary to satisfy its obligations and acquiring the current and fixed assets needed to achieve the firm's goals. Instead of recognizing revenues at the point of sale and expenses when incurred, as the accountant does, the financial manager recognizes revenues and expenses only with respect to inflows or outflows of cash.

A simple analogy may help to clarify the basic difference in viewpoints between the accountant and the financial manager. If we look on the human body as a business firm in which each pulsation of the heart represents a new sale, the accountant is concerned with each of these pulsations, entering these sales as revenues. The financial manager is concerned with whether the resulting flow of blood through the arteries reaches the right cells and keeps the various organs of the body functioning. It is possible for a body to have a strong heart but cease to function because of the development of blockages or clots in the circulatory system. Similarly, a business firm may have increasing levels of sales but still fail because it has an insufficient inflow of cash to pay its bills.

EXAMPLE

James Thomas, who is in the frisbee business, sold his frisbees for $1 while incurring a production cost of $.75.[1] He extended credit to his customers and required payment within 30 days of the date of sale. He based his level of production in each period on his estimates of the following period's sales. These estimates, which were quite accurate, indicated a steady increase in sales over the next three months. He paid all production costs during the period in which they were incurred. James was quite fortunate in that his customers always paid their accounts within the 30-day credit period. The following events occurred during the period January 1–April 1.

Jan. 1	Cash	$ 750
	Inventory (1500 @ $.75)	1125
	Receivables	1500

During January, he sold 2000 frisbees and produced 2500 more in order to have a 30-day supply as inventory. His profits were $500 ($.25 × 2000 units).

Feb. 1	Cash [$750 begin + $1500 collected − (2500 · $.75) produced]	$ 375
	Inventory [(1500 begin + 2500 produced − 2000 sold) × $.75]	1500
	Receivables (2000 @ $1.00)	2000

During February, sales increased to 2500 units and production increased to 3000 units. James's profits for the period were $625 ($.25 × 2500 units). His profits to date were $1125.

Mar. 1	Cash [$375 begin + $2000 collected − (3000 · $.75) produced]	$ 125
	Inventory [(2000 begin + 3000 produced − 2500 sold) × $.75]	1875
	Receivables (2500 @ $1.00)	2500

During March, sales increased to 3000 units and production to 3500. This time, James's profits for the period were $750 ($.25 × 3000 units). His profits to date were $1875.

Apr. 1	Cash [$125 begin + $2500 collected − (3500 · $.75) produced]	$ 00
	Inventory [(2500 begin + 3500 produced − 3000 sold) × $.75]	2250
	Receivables (3000 @ $1.00)	3000

On April 1, James was out of cash and was therefore unable to produce more frisbees, despite the profits he had recorded in all the preceding periods. ●

---

[1]This example has been adapted from the article "How to Go Broke While Making a Profit," *Business Week*, April 28, 1956, pp. 46–54. In order to provide a clear understanding of the changes in cash, inventory, and accounts receivable, the computations of the account balances for each of the months precede the balance figures.

The lesson of this example is that accounting data do not fully describe the financial circumstances of a firm. The financial manager must look beyond his or her company's financial statements in order to obtain insight into developing or existing problems in its financial position. James's cash shortage resulted from the rapid growth in inventory and accounts receivable required to support his growing level of sales. He should have planned ahead to obtain financing, although he probably could obtain the needed funds on short notice due to his proven profitability.

Decision making. The duties of the corporate financial officer differ from those of the accountant in that the accountant devotes the majority of his or her attention to the collection and presentation of financial data. The financial officer evaluates the accountant's statements, develops additional data, and makes decisions based on subsequent analyses. The accountant's role is to provide consistently developed and easily interpreted data on the firm's past, present, and, possibly, future operations. The financial manager uses these data, either in raw form or after making certain adjustments and analyses, as an important input to the financial decision-making process. Of course, this does not mean that accountants never make decisions and financial managers never gather data; rather, the primary emphases of accounting and finance are on the functions indicated above.

AN OVERVIEW OF THE FINANCE FUNCTION

Since most business decisions are measured in financial terms, it is not surprising that the financial manager plays a key role in the operation of the firm. It is important that persons in all areas of decision making—accounting, manufacturing, marketing, personnel, operations research, and so forth—have a basic understanding of the finance function. Over the past 10 or so years, the trend has been one in which more and more top executives are coming from the finance area.[2] In response to this trend, increased enrollments in finance programs, both undergraduate and graduate, have been experienced by most universities. This trend seems to suggest that a good understanding of financial management is a useful prerequisite for a successful business career. To gain the needed understanding of the finance function, we must look closely at its role within the firm, the key functions of the financial manager, and his or her overall goal.

The role of finance in the business firm

The size and importance of the finance function depends greatly on the size of the business firm. In small firms, the finance function is generally performed by the accounting department. As a firm grows, the importance of

[2]Three relatively recent articles lend support to the belief that finance is currently the most common route to the top. See "The Controller: Inflation Gives Him More Clout with Management," *Business Week*, No. 2496, August 15, 1977, pp. 84–95; C. C. Burke, "A Group Profile of the Fortune 500 Chief Executives," *Fortune*, 93, May 1976, pp. 172–177; and "Why the Financial Man Calls the Plays," *Business Week*, No. 2223, April 8, 1972, pp. 54–57.

the finance function typically results in the evolution of a separate finance department—an autonomous organizational unit linked directly to the company president through a vice president of finance.

Initially, the finance function may be concerned only with the credit function, that is, with evaluating, selecting, and following up on customers to whom credit is extended. As the organization grows, attention is given to the evaluation of the firm's financial position and the acquisition of short-term financing. As the firm takes on a large scale of operations, the finance function expands to include decisions with respect to the acquisition of fixed assets, obtaining funds to finance fixed assets, and the distribution of corporate earnings to owners.

The finance function is necessary for the firm to operate on a large scale. It may be assigned to accounting or to a separate finance department, but it must exist in some form in order to provide the techniques and expertise necessary for the firm to maximize its returns, given the scale of its operations.

The functions of the financial manager

The financial manager's functions within the business firm can be evaluated with respect to the firm's basic financial statements. His three primary functions are (1) financial analysis and planning, (2) the management of the firm's asset structure, and (3) the management of its financial structure.

Financial analysis and planning. This function is concerned with the transformation of financial data into a form that can be used to monitor the firm's financial position, to plan for future financing, to evaluate the need for increased productive capacity, and to determine what additional financing is required. Proper performance of this function is necessary if the financial manager is to carry out the other key functions of managing the firm's asset and financial structures.

Managing the firm's asset structure. The financial manager determines both the mix and the type of assets found on the firm's balance sheet. The *mix* refers to the number of dollars of current and fixed assets. Once the mix is determined, the financial manager must determine and attempt to maintain certain "optimal" levels of each *type* of current asset. He must also decide which are the best fixed assets to acquire and he must know when existing fixed assets become obsolete and need to be replaced or modified. The determination of the best asset structure for the firm is not a simple process; it requires insight into the past and future operations of the firm and an understanding of its long-run objectives.

Managing the firm's financial structure. This function is concerned with the right-hand side of the firm's *balance sheet*. Two major decisions must be made about the firm's financial structure. First, the most appropriate mix of short-term and long-term financing must be determined. This is an important decision since it affects both the firm's profitability and overall liquidity. A second and equally important concern is which individual short-term or long-term sources, or both, of financing are best for the firm at a given point in time. Many of these decisions are dictated by necessity, but some require an in-depth analysis of the available alternatives, their costs, and their long-run implications.

The three functions of the financial manager described above are clearly reflected in the firm's balance sheet, which shows the current financial position of the firm. The financial manager's evaluation of the balance sheet data reflects the overall financial position of the firm. In making this evaluation, he or she must monitor the firm's operations, looking for problem areas and areas in which improvement may be possible. In managing the firm's asset structure, the financial manager is, in effect, determining the construction of the left side of its balance sheet. In managing its financial structure, he or she is constructing the right side of the firm's balance sheet.

The goal of the financial manager

The goal of the financial manager should be to achieve the objectives of the firm's owners. In the case of corporations, the owners of a firm are normally distinct from the managers. The managers' function is not to fulfill their own objectives (which may include increasing their wages, becoming famous, or maintaining their positions). It is, rather, to maximize the owners' (stockholders') satisfaction. Presumably, if the managers are successful in this endeavor, they will also achieve their personal objectives.

Some people believe that the owner's objective is always the maximization of profits; others believe it is the *maximization of wealth*. Wealth maximization is the preferred approach for five basic reasons: it considers (1) the owner's realizable return, (2) a long-run viewpoint, (3) the timing of benefits, (4) risk, and (5) the distribution of returns.

Owner's realizable return. The owner of a share of stock can expect to receive his or her return in the form of periodic cash dividend payments, or through increases in the stock price, or both. The market price of a share of stock reflects a perceived value of expected future dividends as well as actual current dividends; a shareholder's (owner's) wealth in the firm at any point in time is measured by the market price of his or her shares.[3] If a stockholder in a firm wishes to liquidate his ownership, he or she has to sell his or her stock at or near the prevailing market price. Because it is the market price of the stock, and not the profits, that reflect an owner's wealth in a firm at any time, the financial manager's goal should be to maximize this wealth.

EXAMPLE

Four years ago, Harold Jenks purchased one share of Alpha Company and one share of Beta Company stock, each at a price of $100. Both of the companies are in the same line of business. Although their profits have differed over the four-year period, each of the firms has paid an annual dividend of $1 per share. Alpha Company has earned

---

[3] This viewpoint is the generally accepted one with respect to the value of stock. The basic constructs and techniques for valuing common stock are presented in subsequent chapters. At this point, however, the reader should accept this statement as fact.

an annual profit of $2 per share, while the Beta Company's annual profit has been $3 per share. The difference in earnings is attributed to the fact that Alpha Company has spent a great deal of money to develop an innovative new product, thereby lowering its profits. The stock of Alpha Company is currently selling for $130 per share while Beta Company stocks sells for $110 per share. This situation is not uncommon. It reflects the fact that although the profits of Beta Company are greater, Alpha Company has a higher stock price. The higher price of Alpha Company shares can be attributed to the expectation that the successful sale of the new product will provide increased future profits, which will more than compensate for the lower profits experienced during the development period. Harold's wealth in Alpha Company is greater than his wealth in Beta Company in spite of the fact that Beta Company's profits are larger. ●

This example should make it quite clear that profit maximization and wealth maximization are not equivalent. Because the owner's financial position in a firm is reflected by the price at which they can sell their stock, the financial manager must attempt to maximize the owners' wealth as reflected by the share price.

Long-run viewpoint. Profit maximization is a short-run approach while wealth maximization considers the long run. From the preceding example, it should be clear that the higher stock price of Alpha Company has resulted from the fact that its short-term actions related to new-product development, although lowering short-run profits, is expected to result in higher future returns. A firm wishing to maximize profits could purchase low-grade machinery, and use low-grade raw materials, while making a strong sales effort to market its products at a price that yields a high profit per unit. This short-run strategy could result in high profits for the current year, but in subsequent years profits would decline significantly due to (1) the realization by purchasers that the product is of low quality and (2) the high maintenance cost associated with low-grade equipment. The impact of falling sales and rising costs would tend to decrease long-run profits and, if unchecked, could result in the eventual bankruptcy of the firm. The potential consequences of short-run profit maximization are likely to be reflected in the current stock price, which will probably be lower than it would have been if the firm had pursued a longer-run strategy.[4]

Timing of benefits. The profit maximization approach fails to reflect differences in the timing of benefits, while wealth maximization tends to consider such differences. Use of the profit maximization goal places greater value on an investment that returns the highest total profits, while the wealth maximization approach explicitly considers the timing of benefits and their impact upon the stock price.

[4]This expectation is based upon the assumption that investors in the marketplace have perfect knowledge of the firm's short-run posture. This assumption, which underlies the basic theory of value, is discussed in greater detail in subsequent chapters.

EXAMPLE

The Cowell Company is attempting to choose between either of two machines. Both machines will provide benefits over a period of five years and are assumed to cost the same. The expected profits per share directly attributable to each of these machines are shown below.

Year	Machine A	Machine B
1	$ 0	$ 1.75
2	0	1.75
3	0	1.75
4	0	1.75
5	10.00	1.75
Total	$10.00	$ 8.75

Although it appears, based solely upon the profit maximization objective, that machine A would be preferred, it is quite possible that once the differences in timing of benefits are considered, the impact of machine B on the owner's wealth would be greater than that of machine A. If we assume that the owners of the firm can, elsewhere, earn 10 percent on their investments in the machines, certain financial analysis techniques will show that the impact of these investments on the stock price would be a $3.21 per share increase with A and a $3.63 per share increase with B.[5] In other words, the use of the wealth maximization objective considers differences in the timing of benefits. ●

The preceding example illustrates the superiority of wealth maximization over profit maximization in that wealth maximization recognizes that business people, all other things being equal, prefer to receive profits *sooner* as opposed to *later*. This time preference of owners is reflected by the share price, not by the earnings.

Risk. Profit maximization does not consider risk, but wealth maximization does give explicit consideration to differences in risk. A basic premise of financial management is that a trade-off exists between risk and return in that stockholders expect to receive higher returns from investments of higher risk, and vice versa.[6] Financial managers in attempting to maximize wealth must therefore consider risk when evaluating potential investments.

EXAMPLE

Drury Manufacturing is considering expanding its production line into either of two new products, C or D. Product C is considered to be a relatively safe product to invest

[5]The financial analysis techniques alluded to here are fully developed in later chapters of the text. At this point, it is best merely to recognize that quantitative techniques for considering differences in timing are available.

[6]The trade-off between risk and return is discussed in a variety of chapters within this text. It is a concept that underlies nearly all aspects of financial theory.

in, while Product D is considered a highly risky fad item. After considering all costs, the two products are expected to provide the profits per share over their five-year lives as shown:

Year	Product C	Product D
1	$ 2.00	$ 2.20
2	2.00	2.20
3	2.00	2.20
4	2.00	2.20
5	2.00	2.20
Total	$10.00	$11.00

If we ignore any risk differences and use an earnings maximization approach, it would appear the Product D is preferred. However, if one considers that Product D is highly risky while Product C represents a safe investment, the conclusion may not be so straightforward. The firm may only need to earn 10 percent on Product C, while as compensation for the greater risk of Product D it must earn 15 percent. Again by applying certain financial analysis techniques that reflect differences in timing of the earnings receipts, it is found that Product C is likely to increase the share price by $7.58, while Product D is likely to result in a $7.37 increase in share price. It should be clear that the wealth maximization approach reflects differences in the risks associated with the receipt of earnings. ●

Because stockholders require higher returns for greater risks, it is important that the impact of risk upon their returns be adequately considered by the financial manager. The wealth maximization approach considers risk, while profit maximization ignores it. Wealth maximization is therefore the preferred approach.

Distribution of returns.   Use of the profit maximization goal fails to consider that stockholders may wish to receive a portion of the firm's returns in the form of periodic dividends. In the absence of any preference for dividends, the firm could maximize profits from period to period by reinvesting all earnings, using them to acquire new earning assets that will boost its future profits. The wealth maximization strategy takes into consideration the fact that many owners place a value on the receipt of the *regular* dividend, regardless of its size. Financial managers should recognize that the firm's dividend policy affects the attractiveness of its stock for particular types of investors. This "clientele effect" is used to explain the effect of a dividend policy on the market value of shares. Making sure that stockholders receive the return they expect is believed to have a positive effect on stock prices.[7] Since each stockholder's wealth at any time is equal to the market value of

[7]A school of thought does exist suggesting that the payment of cash dividends has no effect on the value of a firm's stock. A discussion of this argument is included in Chapter 24, which is concerned specifically with dividends and retained earnings.

all his assets less the value of his liabilities, an increase in the market price of the firm's shares should increase his wealth. A firm interested in maximizing the owners' wealth may therefore pay dividends on a regular basis. On the other hand, a firm that wishes to maximize profits may opt to pay no dividends. But stockholders would certainly prefer a long-run increase in their wealth to the generation of an increasing flow of profits to the firm without concern for the market value of their holdings.

Because the stock price explicitly reflects the owners' realizable return, considers the firm's long-run prospects, reflects differences in the timing of benefits, considers risk, and recognizes the importance of the distribution of returns, the maximization of wealth as reflected in the share price is viewed as the proper goal of financial management. Profit maximization can be part of a wealth maximization strategy. Quite often, the two objectives can be pursued simultaneously, but maximization of profits should never be permitted to overshadow the broader objective of wealth maximization. This type of sacrifice can only result in the shrinking of the firm's asset values, and an ultimate drop in the value of each owner's interest in the firm.

AN OVERVIEW OF THE TEXT

The text has eight basic parts, each devoted to the explanation of some aspect of the financial manager's functions:

Part One: Introduction
Part Two: Financial Analysis and Planning
Part Three: The Management of Working Capital
Part Four: Sources of Short-Term Financing
Part Five: Fixed Asset Management and Capital Budgeting
Part Six: The Cost of Capital, Capital Structure, and Valuation
Part Seven: Sources of Long-Term Financing
Part Eight: Expansion and Failure

The rationale for this overall organization is a simple balance-sheet approach. Since the balance sheet presents a financial picture of the firm at a given point in time, the logical dissection and investigation of this statement provides the best structure for presenting the key principles of financial management. A brief description of the contents of Parts One through Eight is given below. These descriptions are summarized by Figure 1.1, which relates each part of the text to the firm's balance sheet.

Part One: Introduction

As we indicated earlier, Part One sets the stage for a discussion of the key financial decision areas. This chapter has related finance to economics and accounting and has surveyed the finance function within the firm. Chapter 2 is devoted to a description of the legal organization of firms and a discussion of their operating and tax environments. Special emphasis is placed on the corporate form of business organization.

FIGURE 1.1 An overview of the major parts of the text

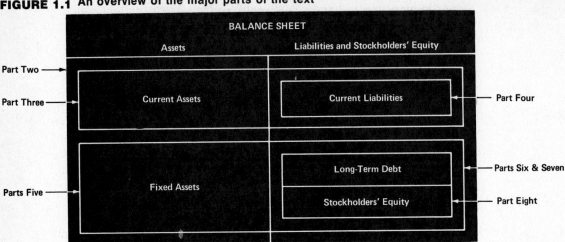

Part Two: Financial analysis and planning

Part Two discusses the basic tools of financial analysis and planning. Special attention is given to the concepts of ratio analysis, leverage, sources and uses of funds, cash budgeting, and pro forma statements. The use, interpretation, and importance of the various financial analysis and planning tools and techniques are presented in this part.

Part Three: The management of working capital

Part Three is devoted to the management of the firm's current accounts, which is referred to as working capital management. Attention is given to the management of the firm's key current assets and liabilities. The relationships between current assets and current liabilities are discussed, and certain strategies aimed at the efficient management of these items are highlighted.

Part Four: Sources of short-term financing

Part Four discusses the key unsecured and secured sources of short-term financing available to the firm. The cost, the availability, and the pros and cons of these sources are discussed. A knowledge of these sources is essential to the successful management of a firm's finances, since the firm cannot operate without short-term funds.

Part Five: Fixed-asset management and capital budgeting

Part Five is concerned with the management of fixed assets and capital budgeting. The primary focus is on the fundamental concepts of capital budgeting, which is concerned with the selection of fixed-asset investments. The mathematics of finance, capital budgeting fundamentals, capital budgeting techniques, and capital budgeting under risk are discussed in this part of the text. A knowledge of each of these areas is necessary for a thorough understanding of the management and selection of fixed-asset investments.

Part Six: The cost of capital, capital structure, and valuation

Part Six is devoted to three important topics—the cost of capital, capital structure, and valuation. These topics are closely related and affect the long-term financing of the firm. The cost of capital is an important input to the capital-budgeting process; capital structure and valuation affect, and are affected by, the firm's cost of capital. An understanding of these topics should provide the reader with a feel for how various suppliers of funds view the business and enable him or her to recognize the key variables the financial manager must consider when attempting to raise money.

Part Seven: Sources of long-term financing

Part Seven describes (1) the various financial intermediaries and markets and (2) the sources of long-term financing available to the firm. It discusses the cost, availability, inherent characteristics, and pros and cons of each of the following: leasing, long-term debt financing, preferred and common stock, convertible securities and warrants, and dividends and retained earnings.

Part Eight: Expansion and failure

Part Eight discusses two topics of interest to the financial manager, who must make decisions with respect to the firm's future: (1) external expansion through consolidations, mergers, and holding companies and (2) the alternatives available to the failed business firm.

SUMMARY

This chapter has described both the finance function and the role of the financial manager within the firm. Financial management is a form of applied economics. Macroeconomics provides an understanding of the institutional structure in which the flow of money and credit takes place. Microeconomics provides various profit maximization guidelines based on the theory of the firm. The financial manager draws on these economic theories to operate the firm efficiently and profitably. He or she draws on the accountant primarily as a source of data on the firm's past, present, and possible future financial position. The two key differences between finance and accounting relate to the recognition of funds and decision making. The financial manager is concerned with cash flows whereas the accountant devotes his attention primarily to accruals. The financial manager also devotes his attention to the analysis of data and decision making. The accountant devotes little of his attention to decision making, since his primary responsibility is for the gathering and presentation of data.

Since most business decisions somehow must be measured in financial terms, the financial manager performs a highly important function within the firm. Of course, the degree of emphasis given to the finance function within a firm depends largely on the size of the firm. In large firms, it may be handled by a separate department; in small firms, the finance function may be performed by the president, who is usually a jack-of-all-trades. The three functions of the financial manager are (1) financial analysis and planning, (2) management of the firm's asset structure, and (3) management of the firm's financial structure. He or she analyzes data in order to monitor the firm's progress. In managing the firm's asset and financial structures, the financial manager makes decisions that greatly affect the health of the firm as reflected in its balance sheet. The financial manager must perform his functions in light of the firm's overall goal of maximizing the owner's wealth, which is a more important strategy than profit maximization. He is expected to consider the owner's realizable return, take a long-run view of the firm, consider the timing of benefits, evaluate the risk-return trade-offs of managerial decisions, decide how returns are to be distributed, and take actions that will generally increase the market price of the firm's shares.

This text is divided into eight major parts. Its organization parallels the organization of a firm's balance sheet. Part One provides an introduction that describes some of the key aspects of the environment in which the financial manager operates. Part Two discusses the tools of financial analysis and planning. Part Three is concerned with the management of the firm's current assets and liabilities; this is referred to as working capital management. Part Four discusses the key unsecured and secured sources of short-term financing. Part Five is devoted to fixed asset management and capital budgeting. Capital budgeting is concerned with the selection and justification of fixed asset investments. Part Six discusses the cost of capital, capital structure, and valuation. These closely related topics are concerned with the firm's long-term financial structure. Part Seven is devoted primarily to the various types of long-term financing available to the firm. Part Eight discusses financial considerations related to business expansion and failure.

QUESTIONS

1-1 Describe the general relationship between finance and economics and explain how the financial manager draws upon the principles of macroeconomics and microeconomics.

1-2 How does the financial manager depend on the accountant? How does the output of accounting act as an input for finance?

1-3 What are the major differences between accounting and finance with respect to
  a The recognition of income and expenses?
  b Decision making?

1-4 a How does the finance function evolve within the business firm?
  b What kind of decisions does the financial manager make in the mature firm?

1-5 What are the three functions of the financial manager with respect to the firm's financial statements?

1-6 What is the goal of financial management? Discuss how one measures achievement of this goal.

1-7 The goal of financial management may conflict with profit maximization for any of five reasons. Briefly discuss these five reasons, showing how they support the goal of financial management.

1-8 Is it true that "if a firm is profitable, its survival is guaranteed"? Explain.

SELECTED REFERENCES

Anthony, Robert N., "The Trouble with Profit Maximization," *Harvard Business Review 38* (November-December 1960), pp. 126–134.

Branch, Ben, "Corporate Objectives and Market Performance," *Financial Management 2* (Summer 1973), pp. 24–29.

Burke, C. C., "A Group Profile of the Fortune 500 Chief Executives," *Fortune 93* (May 1976), pp. 172–177ff.

"The Controller: Inflation Gives Him More Clout with Management," *Business Week*, No. 2496 (August 15, 1977), pp. 84–95.

Dewing, Arthur S., *The Financial Policy of Corporations*, vol. 1, 5th ed. (New York: Ronald, 1953), chap. 1.

Donaldson, Gordon, "Financial Goals: Management vs. Stockholders," *Harvard Business Review 41* (May-June 1963), pp. 116–129.

———, "Financial Management in an Affluent Society," *Financial Executive 35* (April 1967), pp. 52–60.

Findlay, Chapman M., and G. A. Whitmore, "Beyond Shareholder Wealth Maximization," *Financial Management 3* (Winter 1974), pp. 25–35.

Gerstner, Louis V., and Helen M. Anderson, "The Chief Financial Officer as Activist," *Harvard Business Review 54* (September-October 1976), pp. 100–106.

Hill, Lawrence W., "The Growth of the Corporate Finance Function," *Financial Executive 44* (July 1976), pp. 38–43.

Lewellen, Wilbur G., "Management and Ownership in the Large Firm," *Journal of Finance 24* (May 1969), pp. 299–322.

Masson, Robert Tempest, "Executive Motivations, Earnings, and Consequent Equity Performance," *Journal of Political Economy 79* (November-December 1971), pp. 1278–1292.

Moag, Joseph S., Willard T. Carleton, and Eugene M. Lerner, "Defining the Finance Function: A Model-Systems Approach," *Journal of Finance 22* (December 1967), pp. 543–556.

Petty, William J., and Oswald D. Bowlin, "The Financial Manager and Quantitative Decision Models," *Financial Management 5* (Winter 1976), pp. 32–41.

Schmitz, Robert A., "Facing the New Normalcy in Corporate Finance," *Financial Executive 42* (November 1974), pp. 14–21.

Solomon, Ezra, *The Theory of Financial Management* (New York: Columbia University Press, 1963), pp. 15–26.

———, "What Should We Teach in a Course in Business Finance?" *Journal of Finance 21* (May 1966), pp. 411–415.

Weston, J. Fred, "New Themes in Finance," *Journal of Finance 24* (March 1974), pp. 237–243.

———, *The Scope and Methodology of Finance* (Englewood Cliffs, N.J.: Prentice-Hall, 1966).

"Why the Financial Man Calls the Plays," *Business Week*, No. 2223 (April 8, 1972), pp. 54–57.

CHAPTER 2
The legal, operating, and tax environment of the firm

To fully understand many financial decisions, a person must have a good understanding of the legal forms of business organization, their operating environments, and the fund-raising implications and pros and cons of each. The basic assumption of this text is that the firm under study is a corporation. However, other forms of business organization will be mentioned, and it is important to have a thorough understanding of these alternative forms and of their characteristics. An understanding of the taxation of these noncorporate entities is also important. Since the primary emphasis in this book is on the corporate form of organization, it is important for the reader to understand both how corporate income is measured and how it is taxed. Such an understanding makes it easier to see why certain financial variables must be considered by the financial manager in making decisions about the asset or financial structure of the firm. A knowledge of income measurement and tax treatment is also of key importance in financial analysis and planning. Familiarity with the legal organization of firms and the ways of measuring and taxing business income will give the reader a clear picture of the corporation's financial environment, on which subsequent discussions of the various aspects of financial planning and decision making can be based.

This chapter has four major sections. The first section describes the key aspects of the various forms of business organization, placing special emphasis on the corporation. The second section presents a brief discussion of the treatment of corporate income. It covers the important topics of depreciation, interest, and dividends. The third section describes the key aspects of personal taxes. The final section of this chapter presents a general discussion of corporate taxes. Both of the sections concerned with taxes emphasize the various types of income and related tax treatment for the respective entities—individuals and corporations. Examples are used to clarify the analytical portions of the chapter.

THE BASIC FORMS OF BUSINESS ORGANIZATION

The three basic forms of business organization are the *sole proprietorship*, the *partnership*, and the *corporation*. Each of these forms will be evaluated individually in the following pages. Table 2.1 indicates their relative importance. The sole proprietorship is the dominant form of organization, accounting for 73 percent of all business firms. Partnerships and corporations account for only 9 percent and 18 percent, respectively. However, the corporation is by far the dominant form of business organization with respect to both business receipts and profits. Corporations account for 84 percent of all business receipts and 68 percent of net profits. The figures in Table 2.1 strongly indicate that, in general, corporations operate on a much larger scale or achieve considerably greater economies of scale than either sole proprietorships or partnerships. The average business receipts and average net profits for each of these forms of business organization are given in Table 2.2. These figures support the contention that corporations, though less numerous than sole proprietorships or partnerships, operate on a much larger scale and therefore earn larger profits.

Sole proprietorships

A *sole proprietorship* is a business which is owned by one person who operates it for his or her own profit. In essence, the sole proprietor is self-employed. The typical sole proprietorship is a small firm, such as a neighborhood grocery, auto-repair shop, or shoe-repair business. Typically the proprietor, along with a few employees, operates the proprietorship. He normally raises all his capital from personal resources or by borrowing and is responsible for all decisions. The majority of sole proprietorships are in the wholesale, retail, service, and construction industries.

Advantages of a sole proprietorship.

The commonly cited advantages of a sole proprietorship, aside from being one's own boss, are as follows:

Ownership of all profits. Many people do not like the idea of working for someone else and seeing their employer receive the profits from their efforts. The sole proprietorship allows the owner to receive the fruits of his efforts; however, he must also absorb losses.

Low organizational costs. No formal legal documents are required in order to form a sole proprietorship; at the most, the sole proprietor may have to purchase a license from the city or state. Licensing is common in the food service and construction industries.

Tax savings. Typically the sole proprietor is not subject to any special types of taxes. The basic taxes he must pay are those on his income, his property, and his payroll. The income of the sole proprietorship is taxed as personal income of the sole proprietor; in other words, the business is viewed as the job of the individual proprietor. The tax rate applicable to the sole proprietor is typically less than that on corporate income.

TABLE 2.1 **A comparison of the number, business receipts, and net profits of the basic forms of business organization**

Form of business organization[a]	Number of firms	Percent of total	Business receipts		Net profits	
			$ Millions	Percent of total	$ Millions	Percent of total
Sole proprietorship	7,488,734	73.4	$ 261,393	11.0	$ 38,385	23.2
Partnership	939,643	9.2	124,633	5.2	14,974	9.1
Corporation	1,769,786	17.4	1,991,014	83.8	111,937	67.7
All forms	10,198,163	100.0	$2,377,040	100.0	$165,296	100.0

[a]Firms in agriculture, forestry, and fisheries have been omitted.
SOURCE: The data for the Proprietorships and Partnerships were obtained from U.S. Department of the Treasury, Internal Revenue Service, *Statistics of Income, 1974 Business Income Tax Returns* (Washington, D.C.: U.S. Government Printing Office, 1977), pp. 4–11 and 119–126. The data for Corporations were obtained from U.S. Department of the Treasury, Internal Revenue Service, *Statistics of Income, 1972 Corporation Income Tax Returns* (Washington, D.C.: U.S. Government Printing Office, 1977), pp. 10–15.

A possible high credit standing.   If the sole proprietor has any wealth at all, it is quite likely that the proprietorship will have a higher credit standing than a corporation of equal size since the owners' wealth is not considered when a corporation's credit is analyzed.

Other advantages.   Other advantages often cited for sole proprietorships are secrecy and ease of dissolution—secrecy because the owner is not required to disclose his manufacturing processes and so on to others, and ease of dissolution because a sole proprietorship can be dissolved easily by satisfying all the firm's financial obligations.

TABLE 2.2 **Average business receipts and average net profits for the basic forms of business organization**

Item	Form of business organization		
	Sole proprietorship	Partnership	Corporation
Average business receipts	$34,904.80	$132,638.70	$1,125,002.60
Average net profits	$ 5,125.70	$ 15,935.80	$ 63,248.90

NOTE: These figures were obtained by dividing the total business receipts and net profits for each form of business organization from Table 2.1 by the number of firms in each category.

Disadvantages of a sole proprietorship. A number of commonly cited disadvantages of a sole proprietorship exist. In many cases, these may outweigh the advantages of this form of organization.

✓ *Unlimited liability.* The sole proprietor's total wealth, and not merely the amount he originally invested, can be used to satisfy creditors. Since the business is not independent of its proprietor, he may lose many of his personal assets in the process of satisfying the claims of creditors.

✓ *Limitations on size.* The financial fund-raising power of the sole proprietorship is limited to the amount one person can raise. Generally, this is not enough to permit larger-scale operations. The inability of the sole proprietor to raise needed capital often causes him to form a partnership or corporation.

✓ *Other disadvantages.* A number of other disadvantages exist with a sole proprietorship. They are (1) difficulties in management resulting from the need to be a jack-of-all-trades; (2) a lack of opportunity for employees, since, normally, long-run incentives for a good employee to stay in the firm's employ cannot be provided; and (3) a lack of continuity when the proprietor dies.

Partnerships

A *partnership* consists of two or more owners doing business together for a profit. Partnerships are typically larger than sole proprietorships, but they are not generally large businesses. (See Table 2.2). Finance, insurance, and real estate firms are the most common types of partnerships; wholesale and retail firms generate the largest amount of business receipts, and service firms provide the greatest net profits for partnerships. One final (1974) statistic of interest is that the 939,643 partnerships in existence account for 4,265,597 partners, or an average of 4.54 per firm. Since many partnerships consist of only two or three partners, the data indicate that there are a number of large partnerships consisting of a few hundred partners. Public accounting and stock brokerage firms often have large numbers of partners. Recent legislation has permitted the incorporation of such professional organizations in certain cases, but it is not expected to eliminate the majority of these large partnerships.

The partnership contract. Most partnerships are established by a written contract between the partners known as the *articles of partnership*. This contract is important in that, if it is properly executed, it can eliminate many of the possible future problems between partners. Aside from descriptive data, the articles of partnership generally include (1) provisions for salaries, (2) a description of how profits and losses are to be divided, and (3) the procedure to be followed if a partner withdraws from the business or the firm is dissolved.

Limited partnerships. The most common of the special types of partnerships is the limited partnership. In a *general,* or regular, partnership, *all* the partners have unlimited liability; that is, their personal assets can be claimed when the firm defaults on its obligations. In a *limited* partnership, one or more partners can be designated as having limited liability as long as at least *one* partner has unlimited liability. The *limited partner* is normally prohibited from being active in the management of the firm. Limited partnerships are quite common in real estate speculation; their advantage is that an individual can invest money and expect a return without assuming any liability beyond the amount of his or her investment.

Advantages of a partnership. The partnership is similar to the sole proprietorship with respect to taxes and organizational costs. A partner's income is taxed in the same manner as a sole proprietor's; and except for the possible legal cost of having the articles of partnership drawn up, the costs of organization are quite similar to those of the sole proprietorship. However, a partnership does have the following advantages over a sole proprietorship.

A larger amount of capital. The financial resources of more than one individual normally provide higher amounts of capital than the sole proprietor can raise.

A better credit standing. The credit standing of a partnership is higher than that of either a corporation or a sole proprietorship of similar size. This is because the personal assets of all the partners are available to satisfy the claims of creditors.

Other advantages. A partnership is advantageous in the sense that more brainpower and management skills are available than in the sole proprietorship. Also, a partnership is more likely to retain good employees since it can give them the opportunity to become partners.

Disadvantages of a partnership. Partnerships have a number of basic disadvantages which must be weighed against their advantages.

Unlimited liability. Each of the general partners is liable for the partnership's debts. Partners are subject to *joint and several liability*, which means that if an equal partnership with three partners, A, B, and C, fails, with net losses beyond the liquidated value of the firm totaling x dollars, and if neither A nor B has any private resources other than their investment in the business, the entire loss will fall on C if he has the assets to cover it. Partner C will, however, have a legal claim on A and B for the portion of their respective liabilities he has paid.

Limited life. Technically, when a partner dies or withdraws, the partnership is dissolved. The articles of partnership should clearly provide the procedure to be followed when either of these events occurs.

Other disadvantages.   It is difficult for a partner to liquidate or transfer money invested in a partnership. The partnership, although it can grow to a larger size than a sole proprietorship, still has difficulty achieving large-scale operations.

Corporations

As Table 2.2 shows, the corporation is the dominant form of business organization with respect to receipts and net profits. Although only 18 percent of all businesses are corporations, the corporation accounts for 84 percent of business receipts and 68 percent of business net profits. Corporations employ millions of people and many have thousands of shareholders; their activities affect the lives of everyone. The term *corporation* was officially defined by Chief Justice John Marshall of the U.S. Supreme Court in 1819, in the case of *Dartmouth College v. Woodward,* as follows: "A corporation is an artificial being; invisible, intangible, and existing only in contemplation of the law."[1] Because a corporation is an artificial being, it is often referred to as a *legal entity.* It has the powers of a human being in that it can sue and be sued, make and be party to contracts, and acquire property in its own name. Although a large number of corporations are involved in wholesale and retail trade and in finance, insurance, and real estate, manufacturing corporations as a group account for the largest portion of corporate business receipts and net profits.

Corporate organization.   The major parties in a corporation are the *stockholders*, the *board of directors*, and the *officers*. Figure 2.1 depicts the relationship between these three groups. The stockholders are the true owners of the firm. The board of directors is responsible for directing the affairs of the business. Final authority for the actions of the corporation is in the hands of the board of directors. The corporate officers are responsible for day-to-day operations. They are required to report periodically to the board of directors.

Stockholders.   A closer look at the stockholders will aid in analyses of the financial aspects of the corporation. Since the stockholders are the true owners of the firm, they vote periodically to select the board of directors and to make amendments to the corporate charter. The stockholder has the following basic rights:

1. To receive dividends in proportion to his or her ownership
2. To hold or sell his or her stock certificates
3. To share in liquidation
4. To purchase a pro rata portion of any new stock issues[2]
5. To inspect the firm's books and records

[1]*The Trustees of Dartmouth College* v. *Woodward,* 4 Wheaton 636 (1819).
[2]This "preemptive" right is generally provided for in the corporate charter or by state law, although in some instances it may not be offered. It is discussed in greater detail in Chapter 22.

FIGURE 2.1 The general organization of a corporation

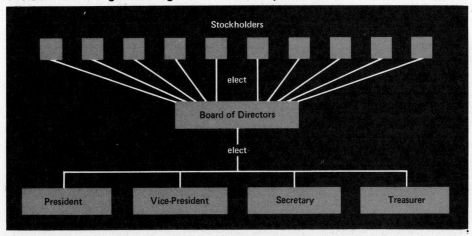

Not all corporations are large. In small corporations, it is quite likely that the board of directors consists of the stockholders, who also manage the business. In a large corporation with thousands of shareholders, the firm's executives do not usually own a large number of shares. Table 2.3 presents a list of the 50 companies on the New York Stock Exchange with the largest number of shareholders. Large numbers of shareholders result in separation of ownership and management. When there are large numbers of shareholders, management is more likely to consider the total operating environment of the firm and attempt to maximize the owners' wealth by satisfying the needs of not only the owners but also employees, customers, suppliers, the general public, and the government. This type of outlook is expected to provide for share price maximization over the long run.

Advantages of a corporation. Since corporations dominate our economy, the corporate form of organization must have certain advantages over the sole proprietorship and the partnership. The principal advantages are listed below.

Limited liability. The owners of a corporation have limited liability, which guarantees that they cannot lose more dollars than they invest. This is one of the major reasons corporate shares are marketable.

Large size. Since corporate shares are readily marketable and can be issued at low per-share prices, capital can be raised from many individuals through the sale of stock.

Transferability of ownership. Corporate ownership is evidenced by stock certificates, which can easily be transferred to new owners. Organized stock exchanges facilitate the sale or purchase of stock and associated transfers of ownership.

TABLE 2.3 NYSE companies with the largest
number of common stockholders of record, early 1978

Company	Stockholders	Company	Stockholders
American Tel. & Tel.	2,897,000	Detroit Edison	210,000
General Motors	1,225,000	du Pont de Nemours	207,000
Exxon Corp.	684,000	Westinghouse Electric	202,000
Int'l Business Machines	582,000	Atlantic Richfield	201,000
General Electric	545,000	Pacific Gas & Electric	198,000
General Tel. & Electronics	443,000	Northeast Utilities	198,000
Texaco Inc.	414,000	Niagara Mohawk Power	196,000
Gulf Oil	357,000	General Public Utilities	176,000
Ford Motor	335,000	BankAmerica	175,000
Southern Company	293,000	Standard Oil (Indiana)	175,000
Sears, Roebuck	291,000	Bethlehem Steel	166,000
International Tel. & Tel.	280,000	Transamerica Corp.	164,000
Consolidated Edison	275,000	Greyhound Corp.	163,000
RCA	273,000	Columbia Gas System	159,000
Standard Oil of Calif.	271,000	Ohio Edison	155,000
Mobil Corp.	265,000	Consumers Power	155,000
Occidental Petroleum	264,000	Union Carbide	154,000
U.S. Steel	249,000	Pan Amer. World Airways	147,000
Eastman Kodak	248,000	Union Electric	147,000
American Electric Power	245,000	Virginia Elec. & Power	142,000
Philadelphia Electric	235,000	Pennsylvania Power	139,000
Tenneco, Inc.	232,000	International Harvester	131,000
Commonwealth Edison	214,000	American Motors	131,000
Public Service Elec. & Gas	214,000	Southern California Edison	130,000
Chrysler Corp.	211,000	American Brands	126,000

SOURCE: *New York Stock Exchange 1977 Fact Book* (New York: New York Stock Exchange, 1977), p. 37.

Other advantages. Corporations also have a few other advantages: (1) they have a long life, since a corporation is not dissolved by the death or withdrawal of an owner; (2) professional managers can be hired to run the corporation, and if they do an unsatisfactory job they can be replaced; and (3) corporations can expand more easily than other types of organizations due to their ready access to capital markets and their large size.

Disadvantages of corporations. Corporations have certain disadvantages, most of which are closely related to their public nature.

Taxes. Tax rates on taxable income in excess of $50,000 is generally higher for corporations than for sole proprietorships and partnerships, which have income taxed as the owners' personal income.[3] In addition, franchise and income taxes are often levied on corporations by the state in which they operate.

Organizational expenses. The costs of incorporation and the issuance of shares often prove to be a drawback to the corporate form of organization, especially for small businesses.

Government regulation. Since the corporation is a legal being, it is subject to regulation by various state and federal government departments. Often, a great deal of paperwork and information gathering is required in order to fulfill the requirements of these regulatory agencies.

Other disadvantages. Other often-cited drawbacks of corporations are (1) a lack of personal interest in the firm by employees due to their often nonowner status and (2) a lack of secrecy, since each stockholder must be provided with an annual report of the corporation's financial performance and financial position.

THE TREATMENT OF CORPORATE INCOME

As indicated in the introduction to this chapter, the emphasis in this text will be on the financial aspects of corporations. There are three basic reasons for this: (1) corporations, due to their generally large size, provide a workshop in which to examine the greatest number of financial concepts; (2) corporations are dominant in our capitalistic economy; and (3) business school graduates will most likely end up working in or with corporations. Since corporate performance is measured with respect to the net income shown on the firm's income statement, it is important to understand the basic concepts used in calculating that income. The key items to be examined are *depreciation, cash flows,* and *interest and dividends.*

Depreciation

Corporations, as well as sole proprietorships and partnerships, are permitted to charge a portion of the cost of fixed assets to the annual revenues they generate. These costs show up as depreciation. For tax purposes, they are based on rules and guidelines established by the Internal Revenue Code. These rules state how certain assets can be depreciated and establish guidelines for the depreciable value and depreciable life of most fixed assets. It should be noted that often a firm will use one method of depreciation for tax purposes and a different method for financial reporting purposes. The student should not jump to the conclusion that the firm is trying to "cook the books" by keeping two different sets of records. The objectives of our tax laws are

---

[3]The federal corporate tax rates are 20 percent on the first $25,000, 22 percent on the next $25,000, and 48 percent on all taxable income over $50,000. At the time of printing (Nov. 1978) it appears likely that President Carter will approve a bill changing these rates to 17 percent on the first $25,000, 20 percent on the second $25,000, 30 percent on the third $25,000, 40 percent on the fourth $25,000, and 46 percent on taxable income above $100,000.

at times distinct from the objectives of financial reporting. For example, tax laws are used to accomplish certain economic goals such as providing economic incentives for firms to invest in certain types of capital goods. This, of course, is not usually the objective of financial reporting. Depreciation that is deducted as an expense on income statements can be calculated in one of three basic ways. However, before discussing the methods of depreciating an asset, we must first understand the relationship between depreciation and cash flows.

Depreciation and cash flows.   Chapter 1 pointed out that the financial manager is concerned with cash flows rather than net profits as indicated by the income statement. To adjust the income statement to show cash flows from operations, all noncash charges must be added back. Noncash charges are expenses that are deducted on the income statement but do not involve an actual outlay of cash. Depreciation, amortization, and depletion allowances are examples of such charges. Since depreciation expenses are the most common noncash charges, we shall focus on their treatment; amortization and depletion charges are treated in the same way.

The general rule for adjusting a firm's net profits after taxes to show cash flows from operations is to add back all noncash charges:

$$\text{Cash flow from operations} = \text{net profits after taxes} + \text{noncash charges} \tag{2.1}$$

Applying Equation 2.1 to the income statement for the ABC Company in Table 2.4 yields a cash flow from operations of $17,000 because of the noncash nature of depreciation.

Net profit after taxes	$12,000
Plus: Depreciation	5,000
Cash Flow from Operations	$17,000

TABLE 2.4 **ABC Company income statement**

Sales		$100,000
Less: Return & allowances		5,000
Net sales		$ 95,000
Less: Cost of goods sold		45,000
Gross profit		$ 50,000
Less: Expenses		
General & administrative	$20,000	
Interest	5,000	
Depreciation	5,000	
Total		$ 30,000
Net profits before taxes		$ 20,000
Less: Federal taxes (40%)		8,000
Net Profit After Taxes		$ 12,000

TABLE 2.5 ABC Company income
statement calculated on a cash basis

Net sales		$95,000
Less: Cost of goods sold		45,000
Gross profit		$50,000
Less: Expenses		
General & administrative	$20,000	
Interest	5,000	
Depreciation	0	
Total		$25,000
Cash flow before taxes		$25,000
Less: Taxes[a]		8,000
Cash Flow from Operations		$17,000

[a]Taxes are based on the inclusion of depreciation, as in Table 2.4.

However, this figure is only approximate, since not all sales are made for cash and not all expenses are paid when they are incurred.

Depreciation and other noncash charges shield the firm from taxes by lowering its taxable income. Many people do not accept depreciation as a source of funds; however, it is a source of funds in the sense that it is a "nonuse" of funds. Table 2.5 shows the ABC Company income statement calculated on a cash basis as an illustration of how depreciation shields income and acts as a nonuse of funds. Ignoring depreciation, except in determining the firm's tax liability, makes the resulting cash flow from operations equal to $17,000—the same figure we obtained earlier. The adjustment of the firm's net profits after taxes by adding back noncash charges such as depreciation will be used on numerous occasions in this text to determine cash flows.

Depreciation methods. The three basic methods of depreciating a fixed asset are (1) the straight-line method, (2) the double-declining balance method, and (3) the sum-of-the-years'-digits method. The double-declining balance and sum-of-the-years'-digits methods are *accelerated* methods of depreciation. The IRS permits firms to switch from an accelerated form of depreciation to the straight-line method, but permission is required when changing from the straight-line to an accelerated method. Each method is illustrated below, using a firm that has acquired a new machine costing $27,000, having a $2000 salvage value, and a depreciable life of 5 years.

The straight-line method. Straight-line depreciation is calculated by dividing the *depreciable value* of an asset, which is its cost less its salvage value, by its depreciable life. The amount of depreciation in each year is therefore equal. For a machine costing $27,000, having a $2000 salvage value, with a depreciable life of five years, the calculations are as follows:

$$\frac{\text{Depreciable value}}{\text{life}} = \frac{\$27,000 - \$2000}{5} = \$5000 \text{ per yr.}$$

The double-declining balance method. Double-declining balance depreciation is calculated by taking twice the normal straight-line rate and multiplying it by the book value of the asset in period t, which is equal to the book value in period t-1 minus the depreciation in period t-1.[4] With the double-declining balance method, the *full* cost of the asset—not cost less salvage value—is depreciated down to its salvage value. Generally, the asset's depreciation in the final period will equal the difference between its book value at the beginning of the period and its salvage value. Thus the depreciable value (cost less salvage value) of the asset must be completely written off at the end of its depreciable life.

For the sample problem, the rate of depreciation is 2/5—twice the straight-line rate of 1/5. Depreciation and book value in each period are as follows:

Period	Book value at beginning of period (1)	Rate of depreciation (2)	Depreciation (1) · (2) (3)	Book value at end of period (1) − (3) (4)
1	$27,000	2/5	$10,800	$16,200
2	16,200	2/5	6,480	9,720
3	9,720	2/5	3,888	5,832
4	5,832	2/5	2,333	3,499
5	3,499	—	1,499	2,000

The total depreciation for the five-year period is, again, $25,000.

The sum-of-the-years'-digits method. With this method, we count the number of years in the life of an asset and add the digits used. If n is the life of the asset in years and S equals the sum of the digits, then in the first year n/S times the depreciable value (cost less salvage value) is written off; in the second year, $(n - 1)/S$ times the depreciable value; in the third year, $(n - 2)/S$ times the depreciable value; and so on. In our example, the asset has a five-year life. The sum of the digits, S, is $5 + 4 + 3 + 2 + 1 = 15$. A shortcut method of finding this sum would be

$$S = \frac{n(n + 1)}{2} = \frac{5(6)}{2} = 15 \tag{2.2}$$

---

[4]Under the double-declining balance method, the firm may switch to straight-line depreciation at any time it chooses during the asset's depreciable life. Of course, such a switch would be made only when such a change would result in larger deductions in the earlier years of the asset's depreciable life.

The factors for years 1 through 5 are 5/15, 4/15, 3/15, 2/15, and 1/15, respectively. The sum of these factors equals 1. For the sample problem, the calculations are as follows:

Year	Factor (1)	Depreciable value (2)	Depreciation (1) · (2) (3)
1	5/15	$25,000	$8,333
2	4/15	25,000	6,667
3	3/15	25,000	5,000
4	2/15	25,000	3,333
5	1/15	25,000	1,667

Again, total depreciation for the five-year period is $25,000.

With both accelerated methods, the depreciation in years 1 and 2 is greater than the $5000 figure obtained using the straight-line method. Although the total amount depreciated is equal to $25,000 with all three methods, the accelerated methods are generally preferable since businessmen would rather receive cash today than in the future.

The advantage of accelerated depreciation can be illustrated using the income statement in Table 2.4 and the values of depreciation calculated in the preceding examples. Assume that the income statement in Table 2.4 will remain the same (except for depreciation) over the next five years. Calculating the firm's net profit after taxes for each of the five years, using each of the three methods of depreciation, yields the values in Table 2.6. These values were obtained by changing *only* the depreciation value in Table 2.4 and finding the resulting after-tax profits.

As expected, each method of depreciation results in the same total net profits for the five-year period. Table 2.6 also shows that the net profits using the accelerated depreciation methods are smaller in the earlier years. How-

TABLE 2.6 Net income after taxes
using varying methods of depreciation

Year	Net income after taxes		
	With straight-line method	With double-declining-balance method	With sum-of-the-years'-digits method
1	$12,000	$ 8,520	$10,000
2	12,000	11,112	11,000
3	12,000	12,667	12,000
4	12,000	13,601	13,000
5	12,000	14,100	14,000
Total	$60,000	$60,000	$60,000

ever, our real concern is not with net profits, but is with the cash flows from operations. Applying the technique described earlier for adjusting net profits to show cash flows from operations results in the figures in Table 2.7. These values were obtained by adding the depreciation obtained using each depreciation method back to the firm's net profits in each year.

The figures in Table 2.7 indicate that with both accelerated depreciation methods the cash flows from operations in the earlier years are greater than the cash flows using straight-line depreciation. The total cash flows generated over the life of the project are the same with each method of depreciation. The important point is the *time* at which the cash flows are received. The firm receives its money earlier using accelerated methods of depreciation.

Though businessmen generally prefer to receive money "sooner as opposed to later," there are times when many firms—especially small ones—may prefer straight-line depreciation to accelerated methods. For example, if tax rates are expected to increase, it may be advantageous for the firm to have as much *income* as possible taxed at current (lower) rates. Straight-line depreciation causes more of the firm's income to be taxed in the current period. A second reason for preferring straight-line depreciation is the ease with which it can be calculated. The examples of various financial concepts in this text will typically assume the use of straight-line depreciation.

Interest and dividends

It is important to have a clear understanding of the difference in the treatment of interest and dividends. *Interest* is shown as an *expense* on the income statement and represents payments made by the firm to its creditors (lenders) for money borrowed. The repayment of a loan itself by a firm to a creditor does not represent interest and is not shown on the firm's income statement. The repayment must be from the firm's cash flows, but it does not affect the company's income since it merely represents the return of something that has been borrowed.

Dividends represent the distribution of earnings to the owners or stock-

TABLE 2.7 Cash flow from
operations for varying methods of depreciation

	Cash flow from operations		
Year	With straight-line method	With double-declining-balance method	With sum-of-the-years'-digits method
1	$17,000	$19,320	$18,333
2	17,000	17,592	17,667
3	17,000	16,555	17,000
4	17,000	15,934	16,333
5	17,000	15,599	15,667
Total	$85,000	$85,000	$85,000

TABLE 2.8 The format
of a general income statement

Sales
− Cost of goods sold
Gross profit
− Expenses other than interest
Operating profit
− Interest expense
Net profits before taxes
− Taxes
Net profits after taxes
− Preferred dividends
Earnings available for common stockholders
− Common stock dividends
To retained earnings

holders of a corporation and are not tax-deductible. They must be paid from the firm's cash flows and are often deducted from the firm's net profits after taxes.[5] Both interest and dividends are payments for funds, but interest is a payment for funds *temporarily* lent to the firm whereas dividends represent payment for *permanent* funds provided by the firm's owners. Moreover, dividend payments received by individuals must be claimed as personal income and are therefore subject to a second tax in the form of a personal income tax. Dividends received by a corporation owning stock in other corporations are 85 percent tax-exempt.

A general income statement format is given in Table 2.8. This basic format will be used frequently throughout the text. One point to note is that before the common stockholders can receive dividends, the preferred stockholders' claims must be satisfied. Although both preferred and common stockholders are owners of the firm, the preferred shareholders are given certain privileges, one of which is preference over common stockholders in the distribution of dividends.

PERSONAL TAXES

The income of individuals is subject to a variety of federal taxes, the primary one being the federal income tax. This tax is levied on wages, salaries, dividends, interest, income from investments, and earnings from a sole proprietorship or partnership. Although the procedures for determining federal taxes owed on personal income can be quite complicated, it is important to gain a basic understanding of the key aspects of personal taxation. Such an understanding should allow the reader to differentiate between the tax treatment given to individuals, which includes sole proprietorships and partner-

---

[5]A firm can pay cash dividends that exceed the current year's earnings, assuming that it has sufficient retained earnings to cover these dividends and the required amount of cash is available. A more in-depth discussion of this topic is included in Chapter 24.

ships, and that given to corporations, which are the primary focus of this text. This section presents a brief overview of personal taxation in three parts: types of income and tax rates, determining taxable income, and tax payments.

Types of income and tax rates

The income of individuals can be classified as either ordinary income or capital-gain income. The method as well as rate of taxation will depend upon which of these types of income is earned.

Ordinary income.   Income from all sources such as salaries, dividends, interest, income from investments, and earnings from a sole proprietorship or partnership are treated as ordinary income. After certain prescribed computations, these forms of income are taxed at *progressive rates*, which are higher the larger the amount of taxable income. Although the applicable tax rates are dependent upon an individual's filing status—single, married filing jointly, married filing separately, or unmarried heads of households—Table 2.9, which is for single taxpayers, clearly illustrates the progressive nature of taxes on individual income.

EXAMPLE
The Smith sisters, June and Jane, wish to calculate their taxes for the current year. They are single individuals; June's taxable income is $11,000 and Jane's taxable income is $22,000. Their taxes are calculated as follows, using Table 2.9:

June: $1590 + .25($11,000 − $10,200) = $1590 + $200 = $\underline{1790}$
Jane: $4510 + .36($22,000 − $20,200) = $4510 + $648 = $\underline{5158}$

The *average tax rate* for June is 16.3 percent ($1790 in taxes ÷ $11,000 taxable income), and Jane's average tax rate is 23.4 percent ($5158 in taxes ÷ $22,000 taxable income). The progressive nature of the tax structure can also be evidenced by the fact that, although Jane's taxable income is twice that of June ($22,000 versus $11,000), her taxes are 2.9 times June's ($5158 versus $1790). ●

The maximum tax rate applicable depends upon the type of ordinary income. Ordinary income that is *earned* includes salaries, wages, and income from proprietorships or partnerships directly attributable to the personal services provided by the proprietor or partner. Examples of earned proprietor or partnership income are fees received by an attorney, doctor, accountant, and so forth, for services provided to clients or patients. The maximum tax rate on earned income is 50 percent. *Unearned* or *passive income* is income received in the form of dividends or interest, or from nonincorporated business interests not fulfilling the requirements mentioned above. The maximum tax rate applicable to unearned income is 70 percent, as can be seen in the tax column in Table 2.9.

Capital gains and losses.   The other major form of income an individual may earn is capital gains. These gains result from the sale of capital assets at prices above the original purchase prices. A *capital asset* is property

TABLE 2.9 1977 tax rates for single taxpayers (Schedule X)

Over	But not over	Tax	Of the amount over	Average tax rate on upper limit
$ 0	$ 2,200	0%	$ 0	0%
2,200	2,700	14	2,200	2.6
2,700	3,200	$ 70+15	2,700	4.5
3,200	3,700	145+16	3,200	6.1
3,700	4,200	225+17	3,700	7.4
4,200	6,200	310+19	4,200	11.1
6,200	8,200	690+21	6,200	13.5
8,200	10,200	1,110+24	8,200	15.6
10,200	12,200	1,590+25	10,200	17.1
12,200	14,200	2,090+27	12,200	18.5
14,200	16,200	2,630+29	14,200	19.8
16,200	18,200	3,210+31	16,200	21.0
18,200	20,200	3,830+34	18,200	22.3
20,200	22,200	4,510+36	20,200	23.6
22,200	24,200	5,230+38	22,200	24.8
24,200	28,200	5,990+40	24,200	26.9
28,200	34,200	7,590+45	28,200	30.1
34,200	40,200	10,290+50	34,200	33.1
40,200	46,200	13,290+55	40,200	35.9
46,200	52,200	16,590+60	46,200	38.7
52,200	62,200	20,190+62	52,200	42.4
62,200	72,200	26,390+64	62,200	45.4
72,200	82,200	32,790+66	72,200	47.9
82,200	92,200	39,390+68	82,200	50.1
92,200	102,200	46,190+69	92,200	51.9
102,200	....	53,090+70	102,200	—

SOURCE: Adapted from U.S. Department of the Treasury, Internal Revenue Service, *1977 Federal Income Tax Forms,* (Washington, D.C.: U.S. Government Printing Office, 1977), p. 41.

owned and used by the taxpayer for personal reasons, pleasure, or investment. The most common types are securities and real estate, including one's home. A *capital gain* represents the amount by which the proceeds from the sale of a capital asset exceeds its original purchase price. Capital gains can be classified as either short-term or long-term, depending upon the length of time they are owned. *Long-term* capital gains result on assets held for more than one year, while gains on assets held for one year or less are considered *short-term.* Although short-term capital gains are taxed as ordinary income, long-term capital gains are taxed at only one-half the ordinary tax rate, since only 50 percent of the gain is shown as taxable income.[6]

[6]The maximum tax rate applicable to long-term gains is 25 percent of the total gain, which means that persons paying taxes on ordinary income at a rate above 50 percent will be taxed on capital gains at a rate of only 25 percent.

EXAMPLE

James McFail, who is in the 30-percent tax bracket, recently sold 100 shares of each of two stocks, A and B, for $10 and $14 per share, respectively. Stock A was originally purchased for $8 per share and held for nine months, while Stock B was purchased fifteen months earlier for $12 per share. The total capital gain on Stock A, therefore, amounted to $200 (100 shares · [$10 per share − $8 per share]) and the total capital gain on Stock B also amounted to $200 (100 shares · [$14 per share − $12 per share]). Since Stock A was held less than one year, the $200 gain on it will be taxed as ordinary income. Since James is in the 30-percent bracket, the tax on the *short-term* capital gain on Stock A would amount to $60 (.30 · $200). The tax on the $200 *long-term* capital gain on Stock B, which was held for longer than one year, would amount to $30 (.30 · ½ · $200). Although James's gain on each of the transactions was the same ($200), the taxes differ since the long-term gain on Stock B is eligible for the more favorable treatment than the tax on the short-term capital gain. ●

Capital losses result when a capital asset is sold for less than its original purchase price. These losses may be either short-term or long-term, depending upon whether or not the asset was held for longer than one year. Before taxes are figured, all gains and losses must be netted out. Up to $3000 of *net* short-term losses can be applied against ordinary income, while one-half of *net* long-term losses up to an annual maximum of $3000 (to $6000 of net long-term losses) can be applied against ordinary income. Losses that cannot be applied in the current year may be carried forward and used to offset future income subject to certain constraints.

Determining taxable income

An individual's taxable income is determined by certain procedures outlined by the Internal Revenue Service (IRS) and computed with a variety of tax forms and schedules. The first step in this process involves the calculation of *gross income,* which is all income subject to federal taxes. Some types of income are *exempt* from gross income. One exemption is the first $100 of dividends received on stocks of domestic corporations. Married persons filing joint returns and jointly owning securities are eligible for a dividend exclusion of $100 each, or a total $200 exemption. A number of deductions can then be made from gross income; these *deductions from gross income* include a variety of trade and business expenses. The resulting balance after making these deductions is called *adjusted gross income.* From adjusted gross income a variety of personal deductions, or *itemized nonbusiness expenses,* can be taken. Actually, the taxpayer may *itemize* these expenses, which include interest expense, medical expenses, property taxes, and so forth, or the taxpayer may take the *zero-bracket amount,* which is a type of blanket deduction. The choice between itemizing and taking the zero-bracket amount depends, of course, upon the level of eligible expenses available. Persons not itemizing expenses can use the tax tables directly, while those itemizing must adjust for any *excess itemized deductions* in order to calculate *tax-table income.*[7]

---

[7]Actually, single individuals with tax-table income below $20,000 and fewer than three exemptions and married persons filing jointly and having less than $40,000 in tax-table income and fewer than nine exemptions can use the tax tables; others have to use the tax schedules.

Computing tax-table income and using tables provided by the IRS, the taxpayer can determine his or her tax liability. The tables consider the *exemptions* and any *credits* available to the taxpayer. The exemptions provide a $750 deduction for the taxpayer and each of his or her dependents; a *tax credit* that is a deduction directly from one's tax liability of $35 per exemption or 2 percent of taxable income (maximum credit—$180) is also provided. From the taxes the taxpayer can deduct any other tax credits such as one for child care.

EXAMPLE

George and Farrah Majors are a married couple with two school-age children. They both work, George as an accountant and Farrah as a medical records technician. During 1977, George earned $22,000 and Farrah earned $13,500. In addition to their salaries, they received $800 in dividends on stock they jointly owned, and $400 interest from their savings accounts. During the year, George paid his own expenses of $400 to attend a special accounting seminar. Their itemized nonbusiness expenses totaled $4300, while their zero-bracket amount was $3200. They will claim four exemptions and are eligible for a $200 tax credit for political contributions. George and Farrah have calculated their tax liability as follows:

Salary and wages		
George		$22,000
Farrah		13,500
Dividends	$800	
Less: Exclusion	(200)	600
Interest earned		400
Gross income		$36,500
Less: George's business expense		(400)
Adjusted gross income		$36,100
Total itemized deductions	$4300	
Less: Zero-bracket amount	3200	
Less: Excess itemized deductions		(1,100)
Tax-Table Income		$35,000
Tax (From tax tables—not shown)[a]		$ 7,242
Less: Credit		200
Total Tax Liability		$7,042

[a]Tax Table B (1977) for 4 exemptions and $35,000 tax-table income was used to find the tax.

Based upon the data given, the Majors' tax liability for 1977 is $7042. ●

Tax payments

The federal tax system is on a *pay-as-you-go basis*. This means that tax payments labeled "withholding taxes" are deducted from the wages and salaries of employees and are paid to the IRS by the employer. Persons who are self-employed, as well as employed persons with outside income from which taxes are not withheld, are required to make *estimated tax payments* on a quarterly basis to the IRS. Failure to make such payments results in a penalty. At the end of the year, once an individual's tax liability has been determined, the amount of taxes already paid through withholding and estimated payments is deducted from his or her tax liability in order to determine the amount of tax due (if the tax liability is greater than amount paid in) or the size of the tax refund (if the paid-in taxes are greater than the tax liability). Individuals must file their tax returns by April 15 immediately following (or by the next business day if that date falls on a weekend or federal holiday) the tax year.

CORPORATE TAXES

In order to have a full understanding of corporate financial decisions, one must have a general understanding of the manner in which corporate income is taxed.[8] Corporations in a fashion similar to individuals may earn either of two types of income, each subject to a different tax rate. By the same token, corporations can experience two types of tax losses—operating and capital losses—which may be carried back or forward and applied against income in other years. The reader should not only understand these aspects of corporate taxes but should also have some familiarity with the investment tax credit, Subchapter S corporations, and tax payment dates. This section of Chapter 2 is divided into seven parts: ordinary income, capital gains, operating and capital tax losses, tax loss carryback and carryforward, investment tax credit, Subchapter S corporations, and tax payment dates.

Ordinary income

For the tax years 1975–1978, the ordinary, or operating, income of a corporation has been taxed at a rate of 20 percent on the first $25,000, 22 percent on the next $25,000, and 48 percent on earnings above $50,000.[9]

EXAMPLE
Jessie's Dry Cleaning, Inc., has before-tax earnings of $60,000. The tax on these earnings can be found by taking .20 ($25,000) + .22($25,000) + .48($60,000 − $50,000), which equals $5000 + $5500 + $4800, or $15,300. The firm's total taxes on its before-tax earnings are therefore $15,300. If the firm had earned only $20,000 before taxes, its total tax liability would have been .20($20,000), or $4000. ●

Average tax rates.
The average tax rate paid on the firm's ordinary income can be found by dividing its taxes by its taxable income. Average tax rates range from 20 to 48 percent. The average tax rate approaches, but never technically reaches, the 48-percent level. The average tax rate paid by Jessie's

---

[8]This section deals only with corporations that are not part of a controlled group of corporations, since controlled groups of corporations have certain additional tax options. For a more detailed discussion of the material in this section of the chapter, see either *Federal Tax Course 1979* (Englewood Cliffs, N.J.: Prentice-Hall, 1978) or *1979 Federal Tax Course* (New York: Commerce Clearing House, 1978).

[9]After 1978, the corporate tax rate *may* be changed to the rates currently (Nov. 1978) being considered by President Carter and cited in footnote 3.

TABLE 2.10 Pretax income, tax liabilities, and average tax rates

Pretax income (1)	Tax liability (2)	Average tax rate (2) ÷ (1) (3)
$ 10,000	$ 2,000	20.00%
25,000	5,000	20.00
40,000	8,300	20.75
50,000	10,500	21.00
100,000	34,500	34.50
200,000	82,500	41.25
500,000	226,500	45.30
1,000,000	466,500	46.65
5,000,000	2,386,500	47.73

Dry Cleaning, Inc. in the preceding example was 25.5 percent (i.e., $15,300 ÷ $60,000). Table 2.10 presents the firm's tax liability and average tax rate for various levels of pretax income. An evaluation of the average tax rates in this table indicates that the average tax rate rapidly approaches 48 percent as the firm's taxable income increases. Figure 2.2 presents the average tax rates associated with various levels of taxable income graphically. Again, although the average tax rate approaches 48 percent, it never quite reaches this level.

Marginal tax rates. The marginal tax rate represents the rate at which additional income is taxed. Due to the nature of the corporate tax structure, the marginal tax rate on income up to $25,000 is 20 percent, from

FIGURE 2.2 Average tax rates vs. pretax income

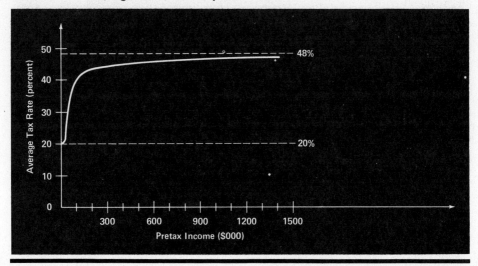

$25,000 to $50,000 it is 22 percent, and for income in excess of $50,000 it is 48 percent.[10]

EXAMPLE

If Jessie's Dry Cleaning's earnings go to $70,000, the marginal tax rate on the additional $10,000 of income will become 48 percent. It will therefore have had to pay additional taxes of $4800 (.48 · $10,000). Total taxes on the $70,000, then, will be $20,100 ($15,300 + $4800). In order to check this figure, we would take, using the ordinary tax rates, 20 percent of $25,000 plus 22 percent of $25,000 plus 48 percent of $20,000 (that is, $70,000 − $50,000). This results in a total tax liability of $20,100— the same value obtained by applying the marginal tax rate to the added income and adjusting the known tax liability. The use of marginal tax rates is quite important in the financial decision process. ●

Capital gains

Corporations in a fashion similar to individuals and unincorporated businesses are given special tax treatment with respect to certain capital gains. As in the case of individuals, if a firm sells certain capital assets for more than the asset's initial purchase price, the difference between the sale price and the purchase price is called a capital gain.[11] Again, a short-term capital gain occurs when an asset held for one year or less is sold for more than its original purchase price; a long-term capital gain occurs when the asset has been held for more than one year. For corporations as well as individuals, only long-term capital gains receive special tax treatment; short-term gains are taxed as ordinary income. The federal tax code provides a tax rate of 30 percent or the ordinary rate, whichever is lower, on long-term capital gains. Taxation of capital gains at the ordinary tax rate is advisable only when a firm's operating income is below $50,000, since the marginal tax rate for earnings over $50,000 is 48 percent. When a firm sells an asset for more than its book value but less than its initial price, the gain, which represents *recaptured depreciation*, is taxed as ordinary income. The 30-percent tax rate applies only to gains *above the initial purchase price* on assets held for longer than one year (i.e., long-term capital gains). If a gain above the purchase price is made on an asset held for one year or less—a short-term capital gain—the total gain is taxed as ordinary income.

EXAMPLE

The Commodore Company has operating earnings of $100,000 and has just sold for $40,000 a machine initially purchased two years ago for $36,000. The machine has been depreciated by the straight-line method over a four-year period and has no salvage value. Because it was purchased two years ago, its current book value is

---

[10]In order to simplify the explanation of certain key concepts in the text, a 40-percent tax rate is assumed to be applicable to ordinary corporate income. This rate is not far out of line with the marginal tax rate of 48 percent and makes the calculations in the various examples easier to follow.

[11]The tax code specifically defines the types of assets eligible for this treatment. See William H. Hoffman, Ed., *West's Federal Taxation: Corporations, Partnerships, Estates and Trusts,* 1979 Edition (St. Paul: West Publishing Company, 1978), pp. 72–74, for an excellent discussion of capital assets and capital gains.

$18,000, that is, $36,000 − [2 · ($36,000 ÷ 4)]. The firm thus makes a capital gain of $4000 ($40,000 − $36,000) and recaptures depreciation of $18,000 ($36,000 − $18,000) on the sale. The ordinary income represents the amount of *recaptured depreciation*, which is depreciation previously taken but recovered as part of the sale price, the firm obtains as a result of the sale. The total gain over the book value of the asset is therefore $22,000 ($40,000 − $18,000); $4000 (i.e., long-term capital gain) of this gain will be taxed at 30 percent since the asset has been held for more than one year, while the remaining $18,000 (i.e., recaptured depreciation) will be taxed as ordinary income. The firm's total tax liability from both its operating earnings and the sale of the machine is as follows:

Taxable income	
Operations	$100,000
Sale of asset	22,000
Total	$122,000
Less: Capital gain (long term)	4,000
Ordinary Income	$118,000
Taxes	
Ordinary income	
.20($25,000) + .22($25,000) + .48($118,000 − $50,000)	
$5000 + $5500 + $32,640 =	$ 43,140
Capital gain (long term)	
.30 ($4000) =	1,200
Total Tax Liability	$ 44,340 ●

In the instance a firm sells certain assets for less than their original purchase price but more than book value, the gain above book value is taxed as ordinary income, as shown in the following example.

EXAMPLE

If the Commodore Company sells the machine described in the preceding example for $30,000, no capital gain will result. But the firm would recapture depreciation of $12,000 ($30,000 − $18,000, the book value). It would therefore have a total taxable income of $112,000 ($100,000 + $12,000), on which the tax liability would be $40,260 [.20($25,000) + .22($25,000) + .48($112,000 − $50,000)].

If the company sells the machine for its exact book value of $18,000, no gain of any type will result and the firm's only taxable income would be its $100,000 of operating income. Its taxes would then be $34,500 [.20($25,000) + .22($25,000) + .48($100,000 − $50,000)]. ●

Tax losses

Three different tax-loss situations may confront the firm.[12] It may have (1) operating losses, (2) capital losses on depreciable assets, or (3) capital losses on nondepreciable assets. The tax treatment of each of these types of losses is described below.

[12]For an in-depth discussion of operating and capital losses, see *Federal Tax Course 1979* (Englewood Cliffs, N.J.: Prentice-Hall, Inc., 1978), Chapter 22.

Operating losses.   An operating loss occurs when a firm has negative before-tax profits. It is permitted to apply this loss to past or future operating gains, or both.

Capital loss on depreciable assets.   If a firm sells a depreciable asset other than buildings used in business or trade for less than its book value, a capital loss equal to the difference between the book value and the sale price results. A capital loss on depreciable assets can be deducted from operating income for tax purposes.

EXAMPLE

If the Commodore Company sells the machine (a depreciable asset) described in the preceding examples for $14,000, it will experience a capital loss equal to the difference between the book value of $18,000 and the sale price of $14,000, or $4000. This loss can be used to offset either past, current, or future operating income. Since the company has operating earnings of $100,000, subtraction of the $4000 loss from this figure would give it a taxable income of $96,000 and a tax liability of $32,580 [.20($25,000) + .22($25,000) + .48($46,000)]. ●

Capital loss on nondepreciable assets.   A firm experiences a capital loss when it sells a nondepreciable asset not used in business or trade for less than its purchase price. A good example of a capital loss of this type would be the sale of marketable securities costing $1,000,000 for $900,000. The firm would thus experience a $100,000 capital loss. A capital loss on nondepreciable assets can be used to offset past, present, or future capital gains only.

Tax loss carrybacks and carryforwards

All three types of tax losses described in the preceding section can be carried back three years; operating losses can be carried forward for seven years, and capital losses five years.[13] The tax laws permit the carryback and carryforward of losses in order to provide a more equitable tax treatment for corporations experiencing volatile patterns of income. The law requires that the firm first net all losses against current gains, if any, and then carry losses back, applying them to the earliest year allowable and progressively moving forward until either the loss has been fully recovered or the carryforward period has passed. Both operating losses and capital losses on the sale of depreciable assets used in business or trade can be applied against operating income, but capital losses on nondepreciable assets may be applied only against capital gains. Carrying tax losses back and forward means using the losses to offset past or future income and recomputing the firm's taxes based on the reduced income. The firm will then receive either a tax refund (on a carryback) or have reduced future tax liabilities (on carryforwards).

---

[13]Financial institutions such as commercial banks, mutual savings banks, savings and loan associations, cooperative banks, business development corporations, and small-business investment companies are given a 10-year tax loss carryback period. See *Federal Tax Course 1979* (Englewood Cliffs, N.J.: Prentice-Hall, Inc., 1978), Chapter 24, for an in-depth discussion of tax-loss carrybacks and carryforwards.

TABLE 2.11 Tax-loss carryback and carryforward adjustments

Year	Item	Before carryback/carryforward (1)	After carryback/carryforward (2)
1975	Earnings	$115,000	$ 0
	Taxes	41,700	0
1976	Earnings	175,000	0
	Taxes	70,500	0
1977	Earnings	85,000	0
	Taxes	27,300	0
1978	Earnings	(500,000)	0
	Taxes	0	0
1979	Earnings	55,000	0
	Taxes	12,900	0
1980	Earnings	80,000	10,000
	Taxes	24,900	2,000
1981	Earnings	100,000	100,000
	Taxes	34,500	34,500
1982	Earnings	110,000	110,000
	Taxes	39,300	39,300
1983	Earnings	120,000	120,000
	Taxes	44,100	44,100
1984	Earnings	130,000	130,000
	Taxes	48,900	48,900
1985	Earnings	150,000	150,000
	Taxes	58,500	58,500

EXAMPLE
The Regal Music Company's before-tax earnings and associated tax liabilities for the years 1975 through 1985 are presented in Table 2.11. Column 1 shows these amounts before any carrybacks or carryforwards have been made. In 1978, the firm had an operating loss of $500,000 as a result of a severe raw-material shortage. Column 2 indicates how this operating loss was carried back and then forward. By carrying the loss back three years and then forward, the firm was able to reduce its before-tax earnings by $115,000 in 1975, $175,000 in 1976, $85,000 in 1977, $55,000 in 1979, and $70,000 in 1980. The total tax savings were $175,300 ($41,700 in 1975, $70,500 in 1976, $27,300 in 1977, $12,900 in 1979, and $22,900 in 1980). ●

As soon as the company recognized the $500,000 loss in 1978, it was able to file for a tax refund for the years 1975–1977. It then carried the portion of the loss not used to offset past income forward to be applied against positive earnings for the next two years, 1979–1980. If the firm does not have sufficient earnings in the 1979–1985 period to permit it to write off fully the 1978 operating loss, it would have had no further tax recourse for recovering it, since such losses can be carried forward only seven years, after which the tax benefit is lost forever. If the loss had been a capital loss instead of an operating loss, the carryback and carryforward procedure would have been similar, but the loss could have been applied against the appropriate type of income and could be carried forward only five instead of seven years.

The investment tax credit

At certain points in time, the Internal Revenue Service, in response to legislative action, has instituted an investment tax credit permitting firms to receive a credit against federal income taxes for the purchase of depreciable property placed in service within the year. All new property purchased during the year plus a limit of $100,000 in used property is eligible for this special treatment.[14] If the property has a useful life of less than or equal to seven years, only two-thirds of its eligible cost can be used as a basis for an investment tax credit. If it has a useful life of greater than three and less than or equal to five years, only one-third of the eligible cost can be used in computing the investment tax credit. Property with a useful life of less than or equal to three years is exempt from the investment tax credit.

The investment tax credit was first enacted by the Kennedy Administration in 1962 to stimulate business investment in machinery and equipment and therefore stimulate economic activity. In 1966, the investment tax credit was suspended for a proposed 15 months due to its expected inflationary effects. After five months, in early 1967, it was reinstituted since inflation had eased. In 1969, the credit was again repealed by the Tax Reform Act because of its presumed inflationary effects and because it was difficult to administer. It was reinstituted again by the Revenue Act of 1971 and has remained in force since that time.

The maximum credit for 7 percent of the cost of an eligible asset remained in force until 1975, when the Tax Reduction Act temporarily increased the credit to 10 percent. The 10-percent credit was extended until January, 1981, by the Tax Reform Act of 1976.

An investment tax credit cannot exceed a firm's tax liability in a given year. For example, when a firm's tax liability exceeds $25,000 in a given year, the investment tax credit cannot exceed $25,000 plus 50 percent of the tax liability over that amount. When the investment tax credit cannot be fully applied in a given year because of these maximum-credit limitations, a three-year carryback and seven-year carryforward are permitted. These carrybacks and carryforwards are similar to those for operating and capital losses.

EXAMPLE
The Precision Milling Company's tax liability from operations for 1978 is $115,000. During 1978, the firm purchased two depreciable assets. One was a new machine, A, having a 10-year life and costing $800,000; the other was a used machine, B, having a six-year usable life and costing $200,000. The total investment tax credit available can be calculated with respect to each machine, A and B.

[14]The property, in order to be eligible, must fall under Section 38 of the Tax Code, which includes, with certain exceptions, only depreciable or amortizable property with lives greater than three years, which includes primarily tangible personal property. See Prentice-Hall, *Federal Tax Course 1979*, pp. 2411–2417, for a more detailed discussion of the technical aspects of this legislation.

Machine A
10% · $800,000   = $80,000.00
Machine B
10% · 2/3 · 100,000   =   6,666.67
    Total Credit $86,666.67

The $6,666.67 figure for machine B is found by multiplying the $100,000 maximum for used property by ⅔ since the usable life of the machine is between five and seven years, and multiplying the result by 10 percent (the amount of the investment tax credit).

    The maximum credit that can be applied to the current year's tax liability is $70,000 [$25,000 + .50($115,000 − $25,000)]. Since the firm is eligible for a credit of $86,666.67, the remaining credit of $16,666.67 ($86,666.67 − $70,000) can be carried back three years and then forward for as many as seven years. ●

Subchapter S corporations

    Subchapter S of the Internal Revenue Code permits corporations with 15 or fewer stockholders, all of whom are individuals—not other corporations—to be taxed as partnerships. That is, income is taxed as direct income of the shareholders, regardless of whether it is actually distributed to them. The key advantage of this form of organization is that the shareholders receive all the organizational benefit of a corporation while escaping the double taxation normally associated with the distribution of corporate earnings to the firm's owners. Subchapter S corporations do not receive certain types of tax advantages accorded other corporations, however.

Tax payment dates

    Corporations that expect to have an annual tax liability of $40 or more are required to make estimated tax payments. These estimated payments are commonly made in four installments, each covering 25 percent of the estimated liability. Estimated tax payments for the calendar year are made on April 15, June 15, September 15, and December 15. Any additional tax payments or refunds resulting from an under- or overpayment of estimated taxes must be settled by March 15 of the following year. Certain penalties may be levied on corporations that significantly underestimate their tax liability.

SUMMARY

This chapter has discussed the basic characteristics, magnitude, and advantages and disadvantages of the basic forms of business organization—the sole proprietorship, the partnership, and the corporation. Although there are more sole proprietorships than any other form of business organization, the corporation is dominant in terms of revenues and profits. Since the corporation is a legal entity, or person, its owners or stockholders have limited liability. They cannot lose more money than they invest. This feature of corporations enables them to raise large sums of money, to grow, and to diversify. Since the corporation is the dominant form of business in our economy, the emphasis in this text is on the corporate form of organization.

An understanding of a number of factors is important in measuring corporate income. Corporations, just as other forms of business, are permitted to allocate the historical cost of certain assets to offset future income. The most common of these allocations are depreciation, amortization, and depletion allowances. Each of these items represents a noncash expenditure and increases the cash flow from operations. Profits after taxes can be adjusted to show cash flows from operations by adding noncash expenditures to them. Depreciation is the most common type of noncash expenditure. The three most common methods of depreciation are the straight-line, double-declining balance, and sum-of-the-years'-digits methods. The double-declining-balance and sum-of-the-years'-digits methods are accelerated methods of depreciation that allow a larger proportion of an asset's value to be deducted in the early years of its life. These accelerated methods are desirable since they increase the firm's cash flows during the early years of the asset's life.

Interest is a tax-deductible payment to lenders for money lent. It does not include return of the principal amount borrowed, which receives no special tax treatment and must be made from the firm's after-tax cash flow. Dividends are payments made by the firm to its owners or stockholders. Dividends differ from interest in that they are not tax-deductible expenses.

The income of individuals, which includes proprietorships and partnerships, is subject to federal income taxes. The income of individuals can be classified as either ordinary or capital-gains—each form is subject to a different tax treatment. On ordinary income, individuals are taxed on a progressive basis such that the higher their taxable income, the higher the rate of taxation. On earned income, the maximum tax rate is 50 percent, and on unearned income the maximum rate is 70 percent. On capital gains, which result when a capital asset is sold for more than its original purchase price, the tax treatment depends upon whether the gain is long-term or short-term. Long-term gains, which result when the asset has been held for longer than one year, are taxed at only one-half the ordinary tax rate up to a maximum rate of 25 percent. Short-term gains are taxed as ordinary income. Depending upon whether capital losses are short-term or long-term, special tax treatment may result. The taxable income of individuals is found by following certain guidelines and using special forms provided by the IRS. Certain income such as the first $100 of dividends received by the taxpayer is exempt from taxes; all interest received is taxable. After trade and business expenses have been deducted from income subject to taxes, tax-table income is found. Using the tax-table income and exemption amounts claimed, the individual's tax is determined with the aid of the tables or schedules provided by the IRS. After any eligible credits are deducted from the tax, the individual's tax liability results. Comparing this value to the total taxes paid through withholding taxes and estimated tax payments, or both, during the tax year, the amount owed or refund due is determined. Individuals must file tax returns by April 15 of the year immediately following the tax year.

The rates for and methods of taxing corporate income differ from the treatment of personal income and are quite complicated. On ordinary income from operations, corporations must pay 20 percent on the first $25,000, 22 percent on the next $25,000, and 48 percent on earnings greater than $50,000. The average tax rate paid by a firm can be found by dividing the taxes it pays by its taxable income. Average tax rates range from 20 percent to 48 percent. The marginal tax rate is 20 percent on income up to $25,000, 22 percent on income between $25,000 and $50,000, and 48 percent on income above $50,000. For classroom purposes, a 40-percent marginal tax rate can be assumed.

If a firm sells certain types of assets for more than their initial price, the amount by which the sale price exceeds the purchase price is considered a capital gain. If the asset has been held for one year or less, it is a short-term capital gain. If held for longer than one year, it is a long-term capital gain. Short-term capital gains are taxed at the firm's ordinary tax rate, while long-term capital gains can be taxed as ordinary income or at a flat 30-percent rate. The 30-percent rate is usually applied on long-term capital gains.

Firms often experience losses that can be used to offset past or future income. Operating losses and capital losses on the sale of depreciable assets used in business or trade can be applied against ordinary income. Capital losses on nondepreciable assets can be applied against only capital gains. Operating losses may be carried back three years and forward seven years, while capital losses can be carried back three years and forward five years. In either case, if the losses cannot be fully applied in the carryforward period, they are lost forever.

In order to stimulate economic activity, the federal government has occasionally instituted an investment tax credit entitling purchasers of new or used depreciable property to special tax deductions. The government also permits certain small businesses to file as Subchapter S corporations, which are taxed as partnerships but have most of the rights of corporations. Corporations make estimated tax payments on the fifteenth of April, June, September, and December each year.

QUESTIONS

2-1   What are the three basic forms of business organization? Which form of business organization is most common? Which form is dominant in terms of business receipts and profits?

2-2   What different types of liability are related to the various forms of business organization? How do the terms "joint and several liability" relate to the business organization?

2-3   Why is a corporation often referred to as a legal entity? Who is responsible for chartering a corporation?

2-4   What are the owners of corporations called? Explain the basic rights of corporate owners. Explain the relationship between owners, directors, and officers of corporations.

2-5   How do the various legal and organizational aspects of corporations facilitate their growth into large businesses?

2-6   In what sense does depreciation act as a cash inflow? How can a firm's after-tax profits be adjusted to show cash flow? What is the rationale for this adjustment?

2-7   How would you explain the basic method of calculating straight-line, double-declining balance, and sum-of-the-years'-digits depreciation? Why are the double-declining balance and sum-of-the-years'-digits methods considered accelerated methods of depreciation?

2-8   How are interest and dividends different? From what instruments do these types of payments arise? What are the tax implications (if any) of each of these types of payments?

2-9   **a** For an individual, what is the difference between *earned or personal service income* and *unearned or passive income?*

   b What differences exist between short-term and long-term capital gains or losses? How are they treated for tax purposes by an individual?

2-10   Discuss the series of computations an individual must complete to determine his or her taxes.

2-11   In view of the progressive structure of personal income taxes, explain the difference between the average and marginal income tax rates for individuals.

2-12   What is the difference between ordinary income and capital gains? What sort of tax treatment occurs in each case?

2-13   How do the average and marginal tax rates on corporate income differ? How are they calculated?

2-14   Can a firm pay both an ordinary tax and a capital gain tax on the sale of an asset at a price
   a Greater than its purchase price?
   b Equal to its purchase price?
   c Equal to its book value?

2-15   Compare the marginal and average tax rates for proprietorships and corporations.

2-16   Discuss and differentiate between the corporation's tax treatment of operating losses, losses on the sale of depreciable assets, and losses on the sale of non-depreciable assets. Explain how losses are carried back and forward.

2-17   What is the rationale for the investment tax credit? What are its tax implications?

2-18   What is a Subchapter S corporation? Why might a firm file under Subchapter S? Explain.

2-19   How and why does a corporation make estimated tax payments?

PROBLEMS

2-1   Marilyn Smith has personal assets with a liquidating value of $125,000 and has invested $25,000 in the Research Marketing Company. The Research Marketing Company has recently become bankrupt and has $60,000 in unpaid debts. Explain the nature of payments (if any) by Ms. Smith in each of the following situations:
   a The Research Marketing Company is a sole proprietorship owned by Ms. Smith.
   b The Research Marketing Company is a 50-50 partnership of Ms. Smith and Arnold Jones. Mr. Jones has personal liquidable assets of $15,000.
   c The Research Marketing Company is a corporation.

2-2   A firm had earnings after taxes of $50,000 in 1977. Depreciation charges were $28,000, and a $2000 charge for amortization on a bond discount was incurred. What was the actual cash inflow?

2-3   A firm expects to have earnings before depreciation and taxes of $160,000. They are considering the purchase of a fixed asset with a depreciable value of

$150,000, a depreciable life of five years, and a zero expected salvage value.

a Calculate the annual depreciation for the asset purchase using the straight-line, double-declining balance, and sum-of-the-years' digits methods.

b Calculate the annual cash flows for the five years using the three methods of depreciation. Assume a 40-percent tax rate.

c Which method of depreciation would you prefer and why?

2-4 The Randy Company expects earnings before interest and taxes to be $40,000 this period. Assuming a tax rate of 40 percent, compare the additional retained earnings the firm will have if

a The firm pays $10,000 in interest, or

b The firm pays $10,000 in preferred dividends.

2-5 Rex Baker had a taxable income of $20,000, and his brother Bob had a taxable income of $12,000.

a Compute the tax liability for each of these single men using Table 2.9.

b Compute the average tax rate for each man.

c What taxation principle is illustrated by your numbers in **b**?

2-6 Patty Clark and Rebecca Collins are equal partners in the American Accounting and Tax Service. Last year, Ms. Clark received $75,000 in taxable income from the firm and no other income. Use Table 2.9 to answer the following (remember the maximum marginal tax rate on earned income is 50 percent):

a Compute Ms. Clark's tax liability if the income is all earned income.

b Compute Ms. Clark's tax liability if the income is all unearned or passive income.

c What conclusions can you draw from your answers?

2-7 Using the corporate tax rates given in the text:

a Calculate the tax liability, after-tax earnings, and average tax rates for the following levels of corporate earnings before taxes: $10,000, $100,000, $1,000,000.

b Plot the average tax rates (measured on the y-axis) against the taxable income levels (measured on the x-axis). What generalization can be made concerning the relationship between these variables?

2-8 Waters Manufacturing purchased a new machine four years ago for $80,000. It is being depreciated over a 10-year life on a straight-line basis with zero expected salvage value at the end of its depreciable life. Assume a 40-percent ordinary tax rate and 30-percent rate on long-term capital gains.

a What is the book value of the machine?

b Calculate the firm's tax liability if they sell the machine for the following: $48,000, $56,000, $100,000, $40,000.

2-9 The Lionel Corporation just sold a four-year-old machine that originally cost $500,000 and was being depreciated by the straight-line method over a 20-year life with a zero expected salvage value. Assume that the firm has a 40-percent tax rate on ordinary income and 30-percent on long-term capital gains. The firm has before-tax operating earnings of $195,000.

a Calculate their taxes due from operating and capital gains income assuming they sell the machine for $550,000.

b Recalculate the taxes due assuming a sale for $450,000.

c Calculate the firm's tax liability if the machine is sold for $300,000.

2-10 The Ordway Shipbuilding Company had operating earnings, ordinary taxes, capital gains, and capital gains taxes for the period 1972 through 1982 as indicated below.

Year	Operating earnings	Ordinary taxes	Capital gains	Capital gains taxes
1972	$600,000	$240,000	$ 0	$ 0
1973	450,000	180,000	60,000	18,000
1974	200,000	80,000	20,000	6,000
1975				
1976	300,000	120,000	0	0
1977	400,000	160,000	0	0
1978	300,000	120,000	40,000	12,000
1979	500,000	200,000	90,000	27,000
1980	600,000	240,000	0	0
1981	300,000	120,000	0	0
1982	450,000	180,000	20,000	6,000

For each of the following cases, (1) calculate the adjusted incomes and taxes for each year and (2) indicate the amount of ordinary and capital gain tax relief, if any. The firm pays taxes of 40 percent on ordinary income and 30 percent on long-term capital gains. Explain your answers.

a In 1975, Ordway had an operating loss of $1,000,000 and no capital gains.
b In 1975, Ordway had operating income of $200,000 and capital gains of $50,000.
c In 1975, Ordway had an operating loss of $2,000,000 and a capital loss of $100,000.
d In 1975, Ordway had operating income of $300,000 and a capital loss of $250,000.

2-11 In 1978, the Comet Manufacturing Company had a tax liability of $100,000. For each of the following purchases calculate (1) the total investment tax credit for which the firm was eligible and (2) the amount of the credit applicable in 1978.

Pur-chase	Price	Usable life (yrs.)	Status of asset when purchased
A	$600,000	4	New
B	$70,000	10	Used
C	$1,000,000	8	New
D	$90,000	2	New
E	$45,000	6	Used

2-12 The Palmer Products Company earns $80,000 before owner's salary and taxes. Mr. Palmer is considering changing his business organization from a sole proprietorship to a corporation. His sole criterion is whether such a move would decrease the level of his tax liability. Currently, he pays himself $45,000 in personal service income from the proprietorship. He has personal deductions of $15,000. If he operated as a corporation, he would receive a $35,000 salary and $10,000 in dividends. Using Table 2.9 and the actual corporate tax rates, which business organization should he select?

SELECTED REFERENCES

Bogen, Jules I., Ed., *Financial Handbook*, 4th ed. (New York: Ronald, 1968), sect. 12.

Boone, Louis E. and David L. Kurtz, *Contemporary Business*, 2nd ed. (Hinsdale, Ill.: Dryden, 1979), chap. 3.

Comiskey, Eugene E., and James R. Hasselback, "Analyzing the Profit-Tax Relationship," *Financial Management 2* (Winter 1973), pp. 57–62.

Dyl, Edward A., "Capital Gains Taxation and Year-End Stock Market Behavior," *Journal of Finance 32* (March 1977), pp. 165-175.

Federal Tax Course 1979 (Englewood Cliffs, N.J.: Prentice-Hall, 1978).

1979 Federal Tax Course (New York: Commerce Clearing House, 1978.)

Fundamentals of Tax Preparation Coursebook (Washington, D.C.: Department of the Treasury, Internal Revenue Service, 1977), Publication 796 (Revised July 1977).

Gitman, Lawrence J., *Personal Finance* (Hinsdale, Ill.: Dryden, 1978), chap. 4.

Hoffman, William H., Ed., *West's Federal Taxation: Corporations, Partnerships, Estates and Trusts* (St. Paul, Minn.: West, 1978).

Howell, Rate A., John R. Allison, and Gaylord A. Jentz, *Business Law: Text and Cases* (Hinsdale, Ill: Dryden, 1978).

Maer, C. M., Jr., and R. A. Francis, "Whether to Incorporate," *Business Lawyer 22* (April 1967), pp. 127–142.

National Industrial Conference Board, *Organizing and Managing the Corporate Finance Function*, Studies in Business Policy, No. 129, New York, 1969.

Phillips, Lawrence C., and William H. Hoffman, Eds., *West's Federal Taxation: Individual Income Taxes* (St. Paul, Minn.: West, 1978).

Shelton, J. R., and C. C. Holt, "The Implications of the Capital Gains Tax for Investment Decisions," *Journal of Finance 16* (December 1961), pp. 559–580.

Smith, Dan Troop, *Tax Factors in Business Decisions* (Englewood Cliffs, N.J.: Prentice-Hall, 1968).

Welsch, Glenn A., and Robert N. Anthony, *Fundamentals of Financial Accounting*, 2nd ed. (Homewood, Ill.: Irwin, 1977).

Welsch, Glenn A., Charles T. Zlatkovich, and John Arch White, *Intermediate Accounting*, 4th ed. (Homewood, Ill.: Irwin, 1976), chap. 23.

PART TWO

This part of the text presents some of the basic tools of financial analysis and planning. Whereas the tools of financial analysis are devoted primarily to a historical evaluation of the firm, financial planning looks ahead to future operations. Both areas are quite important and, as indicated in Chapter 1, together comprise one of the three functions of the financial manager. The four chapters in this part are devoted to the analysis of financial statements, operating, financial, and total leverage, sources and uses of funds and cash budgeting, and pro forma statements. Chapter 3 discusses the key ratios and techniques available for analyzing the firm's performance using data from its income statement and balance sheet. Chapter 4 presents the key concepts of breakeven analysis and defines and discusses operating, financial, and total leverage. Chapter 5 describes how and why sources and uses of funds statements and cash budgets are constructed. Chapter 6 describes both the shortcut and the standard approach for developing pro forma, or projected, financial statements. From this part the reader should gain an understanding of both the importance of financial analysis and planning and the techniques available to the financial manager for this purpose.

Financial analysis and planning

BALANCE SHEET	
Assets	**Liabilities and Stockholders' Equity**
Current Assets	Current Liabilities
Fixed Assets	Long-Term Debt
	Stockholders' Equity

CHAPTER 3
The analysis of financial statements

The analysis of financial statements is typically devoted to the calculation of ratios in order to evaluate the past, current, and projected performance of the business firm. *Ratio analysis* is the most common form of financial analysis. It provides *relative* measures of the company's performance. A number of other techniques for measuring certain aspects of corporate performance are used, but the financial ratio is the one most commonly cited. The basic inputs to financial analysis are the firm's income statement and balance sheet for the period(s) to be examined. Using the data provided by these statements, various ratios can be calculated that permit an evaluation of certain aspects of the firm's performance.

This chapter presents not only definitions of the various financial ratios but also explanations of the implications of certain ratio values. The chapter has four major sections. The first section discusses the use of financial ratios, placing special emphasis on who uses financial ratios and how. The second section briefly describes the basic financial statements that are used to illustrate the calculation of key ratios. The third section describes how to calculate the various financial ratios and discusses their implications. The final section presents a discussion of the complete ratio analysis of the firm, which is used to illustrate the ratio computations in section three of the chapter.

THE USE OF FINANCIAL RATIOS

Before we discuss the methods of calculating and interpreting financial ratios, it is important for the reader to have a basic understanding of the various parties interested in financial ratio analysis, the types of comparisons that are commonly made using financial ratios, and a few words of caution. The first part of this section briefly discusses the parties interested in ratio analysis of the firm and indicates their key areas of interest. The second section describes the two key types of ratio comparisons normally used. The third section offers a few words of caution related to the use of ratio analysis.

Interested parties

Ratio analysis of a firm's financial statements is of interest to a number of parties, especially *current and prospective shareholders, creditors,* and the firm's own *management.* The current and prospective shareholder is interested primarily in the firm's present and projected level of earnings. Although the shareholder's main concern is with profitability which affects share values, he or she also pays close attention to measures of liquidity and activity, and leverage in order to determine the likelihood of the firm's continued existence and to evaluate the probability of receiving any distribution of the firm's earnings.

The firm's creditors are primarily interested in both the short-term liquidity of the firm and the ability of the firm to service its debts over the long run. Existing creditors want to assure themselves that the firm is liquid and that it will be able to make its interest and principal payments when due. Prospective creditors are concerned with determining whether the firm can support the additional debts that would result if they extended credit to the firm. A secondary interest of the present or prospective creditor is the firm's profitability; the creditor wants assurance that the firm is healthy and will continue to be successful.

The firm's management is concerned with all aspects of the firm's financial situation. Since it is aware of the types of things evaluated by owners and creditors, it attempts to operate in a manner that will result in ratios which will be considered favorable by both parties. If the firm is successful, its share price should remain at an acceptable level and its credit-worthiness should be unimpaired. In other words, the firm's ability to raise money through either the sale of stock or the issuance of debt (bonds) should be maintained at a reasonably high level. A collateral objective of the firm's management is to use ratios in order to monitor the firm's performance from period to period. Any unexpected changes are examined in order to isolate developing problems. Financial analysis provides the manager with the tools necessary to check continuously the pulse of the firm in order to implement corrective programs as soon as symptoms of future problems are found.

Types of comparisons

There are two basic ways in which financial ratios are used: (1) in a cross-sectional approach and (2) in time-series analysis. The *cross-sectional approach* involves the comparison of different firms' financial ratios at the same point in time. The typical business firm is interested in how well it has performed in relation to its competitors. If the competitors are also corporations, then their financial statements should be available for analysis. Often the firm's performance will be compared to that of the industry leader. This comparison may allow the firm to uncover major operating differences, which, if changed, will increase its efficiency. Another very popular type of cross-sectional comparison is a comparison of the firm's ratios to industry averages. These figures can be found in *Dun and Bradstreet's Key Business Ratios, The Almanac of Business and Industrial Financial Ratios,* and other sources such as Industry Association publications. A sample of one available source of industry averages is given in Table 3.1.

Time-series analysis is done when the financial analyst measures a firm's performance over time. Comparison of the firm's current performance to past performance utilizing ratio analysis allows the firm to determine whether it is progressing as planned. Developing trends can be seen by using multi-year comparisons; a knowledge of these trends should assist the firm in planning future operations. The theory behind time-series analysis is that the firm must be evaluated in relation to its past performance, any developing trends must be isolated, and appropriate action must be taken to direct the firm toward its immediate and long-term goals. Time-series analysis is often helpful in checking the reasonableness of a firm's projected financial statements. A comparison of current and past ratios to those resulting from an analysis of pro forma statements may reveal discrepancies or overoptimism in the pro forma statements.

Words of caution

Before we discuss specific ratios, four cautions are in order. First, a single ratio does not generally provide sufficient information to judge the overall performance of the firm; only when a group of ratios is used can reasonable judgments concerning the firm's overall financial condition be made. If an analyst is not concerned with a firm's overall financial condition, but only with specific aspects of its financial position, then one or two ratios may be sufficient. Second, an analyst should be sure that the dates of the financial statements being compared are the same. If not, the effects of seasonality may cause erroneous conclusions and decisions. Third, it is best to use audited financial statements for performing ratio analysis; if the statements have not been audited there may be no reason to believe that the data contained in them presents an accurate reflection of the firm's true financial condition. Therefore the resulting ratios may be completely meaningless. Finally, it is important to make sure that the data in the financial statements being compared have been developed in the same way.

BASIC FINANCIAL STATEMENTS

The basic financial statements, the income statement and balance sheet, for the Phyllis Petroleum Company for the years 1977 and 1978 are presented in Tables 3.2 and 3.3. The statements will be used to demonstrate the calculation of the various financial ratios presented in the following sections. Data for the year 1978 will be used for the calculation of most of the ratios.

These financial statements will also be used throughout the remainder of this chapter to demonstrate the use of the ratios defined. In addition, we shall make two basic assumptions:

1. That 95 percent of the firm's sales are on credit and the remaining sales are made for cash
2. That 80 percent of the cost of goods sold represents credit purchases while the remainder represent cash purchases.

These assumptions apply to the operations of the firm in both 1977 and 1978.

TABLE 3.1 Dun and Bradstreet key business ratios for selected industries

Line of business[a] (and number of concerns reporting)		Current assets to current debt	Net profit on net sales	Net profits on tangible net worth	Net profits on net working capital	Net sales to tangible net worth
		Times	Percent	Percent	Percent	Times
Passenger car, truck, and bus bodies		3.69	3.16	15.07	25.65	7.56
		2.25	**2.25**	**9.83**	**12.43**	**4.75**
	(59)	1.46	0.35	4.77	5.11	2.59
Petroleum refining		1.65	5.76	28.47	62.92	8.23
		1.44	**3.13**	**16.94**	**41.82**	**5.46**
	(57)	1.21	1.65	12.16	23.32	3.18
Plastics materials and synthetics		2.93	4.28	11.30	25.64	5.41
		2.23	**3.25**	**8.81**	**13.64**	**3.54**
	(42)	1.68	1.69	5.46	10.86	2.06
Plumbing, heating, and air conditioning		2.66	3.42	18.26	25.44	8.44
		1.81	**1.61**	**9.35**	**11.10**	**5.37**
	(102)	1.48	0.69	3.57	3.64	3.35
Sawmills and planing mills		3.71	7.25	19.74	38.38	4.31
		2.28	**3.28**	**10.35**	**20.52**	**2.59**
	(65)	1.46	1.49	5.06	6.65	1.64
Screw machine products		8.06	8.17	17.10	29.43	3.15
		2.78	**4.63**	**9.65**	**16.38**	**2.58**
	(70)	2.06	2.16	5.16	8.51	1.90
Shirts, underwear, and nightwear, men's and boys'		2.94	4.47	18.28	18.93	6.65
		2.30	**2.78**	**11.28**	**12.33**	**4.42**
	(58)	1.80	0.92	6.59	8.58	3.57
Soap, detergents, perfumes, and cosmetics		3.52	7.13	19.07	24.71	4.89
		2.39	**4.12**	**13.22**	**19.06**	**3.53**
	(76)	1.74	2.10	8.03	11.14	2.58
Soft drinks, bottled and canned		3.45	8.46	29.43	62.45	6.22
		2.23	**5.38**	**19.75**	**50.00**	**3.55**
	(59)	1.48	3.03	13.73	34.70	2.59

SOURCE: *Key Business Ratios* (New York: Dun and Bradstreet, Inc., 1978), p. 11. Adapted by permission.

[a]For each line of business, three values for each of the 14 ratios are given. The center figure in bold type is the median value, while the figures immediately above and below the median are respectively, the upper and lower quartiles.

**Not computed. Building Trades contractors have no inventories in the credit sense of the term. As a general rule, such contractors have no customary selling terms, each contract being a separate job for which individual terms are arranged.

Net sales to net working capital	Collec-tion period	Net sales to inventory	Fixed assets to tangible net worth	Current debt to tangible net worth	Total debt to tangible net worth	Inventory to net working capital	Current debt to inventory	Funded debts to net working capital
Times	Days	Times	Percent	Percent	Percent	Percent	Percent	Percent
12.39	20	8.2	25.0	30.8	46.3	72.0	54.4	9.4
4.99	41	4.5	42.6	62.8	86.4	102.5	83.6	38.3
3.08	53	3.8	57.6	135.5	143.9	150.2	136.4	64.6
21.74	22	35.0	39.3	57.7	84.4	50.0	137.5	20.5
13.87	34	13.6	78.5	94.7	144.6	102.4	205.0	55.7
6.56	54	7.7	139.1	151.9	250.6	165.5	324.4	194.0
8.39	42	11.0	36.9	23.0	54.2	50.3	78.2	26.9
6.40	50	8.3	61.8	47.8	101.5	67.3	116.1	74.8
3.28	64	5.9	101.1	86.5	144.0	101.8	154.4	119.5
11.41	**	**	10.2	39.0	77.2	**	**	8.9
8.16	**	**	22.5	94.6	156.2	**	**	26.1
4.61	**	**	46.3	158.3	232.6	**	**	69.1
8.27	17	14.6	28.4	15.0	49.3	47.5	52.4	36.1
6.57	28	7.1	46.7	38.7	95.3	93.0	100.0	69.2
3.08	43	5.0	89.2	76.2	193.7	137.9	163.0	199.3
6.26	37	11.6	26.8	16.6	39.3	43.0	49.6	13.0
4.36	42	6.7	47.0	34.5	69.8	59.5	81.4	46.7
3.07	52	5.0	64.2	49.0	94.2	94.3	140.7	75.1
6.80	21	7.2	4.5	42.2	55.1	58.0	64.0	7.7
4.85	40	5.4	14.7	71.0	96.6	95.2	87.4	22.4
3.81	68	4.1	26.2	102.4	129.7	133.0	128.4	44.1
8.36	35	13.1	25.8	25.9	39.9	44.2	71.1	8.7
4.68	45	7.8	38.4	47.8	73.2	60.3	110.1	27.6
3.86	60	6.0	62.3	88.4	136.9	84.6	181.9	56.6
15.14	15	20.7	51.2	14.4	32.1	37.1	79.3	10.3
9.48	19	16.8	69.4	30.7	87.5	56.2	125.2	68.6
6.26	27	12.4	122.6	63.3	170.9	107.3	189.9	181.0

TABLE 3.2 Phyllis Petroleum Company income statements

	For the year ending December 31	
	1978	1977
Sales	$3,073,538	$2,567,530
Less: Cost of goods sold	2,088,039	1,711,011
Gross profits	$985,499	$856,519
Less: Operating expenses		
Selling expense	$100,500	$108,089
General and administrative expenses	190,005	190,020
Lease expense	69,011	63,880
Depreciation and depletion charges	238,886	223,099
Total operating expense	$598,402	$585,088
Operating profits	$387,097	$271,431
Less: Interest expense	62,338	58,846
Net profits before taxes	$324,759	$212,585
Less: Taxes (rate = 29%)[a]	94,348	64,157
Net profits after taxes	$230,411	$148,428
Less: Preferred stock dividends	10,000	10,000
Earnings available for common stockholders	$220,411	$138,428
Less: Common stock dividends	98,195	97,598
To Retained Earnings	$122,216	$ 40,830

[a]The 29-percent tax rate for 1978 results from the fact that the firm has certain special tax writeoffs which do not show up directly on its income statement.

BASIC FINANCIAL RATIOS

Financial ratios can be divided into three basic groups: liquidity and activity ratios, debt ratios, and profitability ratios. The first group of ratios relies most heavily on balance sheet data, the second group uses a mix of balance sheet and income statement data, while the third group relies primarily on income statement data. As a rule, the necessary inputs to a good financial analysis include, at minimum, the income statement and the balance sheet. The reader will find greatest emphasis placed on measures of liquidity and profitability, since these areas provide information most critical to the short-run operations of the business firm. If the firm cannot survive in the short run, one need not be concerned with the longer-term financial aspects of the firm. The debt ratios are useful only if one can assure one's self that the firm will successfully weather the short run. A creditor will not provide money if he does not feel the firm will be able to service the resulting debts.

Measures of liquidity and activity

The *liquidity* of a business firm is measured by its ability to satisfy its short-term obligations *as they come due*. Liquidity refers not only to the firm's overall finances but to its ability to convert certain current assets and liabil-

TABLE 3.3 Phyllis Petroleum Company balance sheets

Assets	For the year ending December 31	
	1978	1977
Current assets		
Cash	$ 362,970	$ 287,718
Marketable securities	68,162	50,764
Accounts receivable	502,695	383,854
Inventories	288,883	280,857
Total current assets	$1,222,710	$1,003,193
Property, plant, and equipment (at cost)[a]		
Land and buildings	$2,071,594	$1,902,962
Machinery and equipment	1,743,226	1,692,263
Furniture and fixtures	316,191	286,212
Vehicles	274,704	314,285
Other	98,352	96,183
Total fixed assets (at cost)	$4,504,067	$4,291,905
Less: Accumulated depreciation and depletion	2,172,008	2,056,249
Net property, plant, and equipment	$2,332,059	$2,235,656
Intangible assets	$ 42,004	$ 30,770
Total Assets	$3,596,773	$3,269,619

Liabilities and stockholders' equity		
Current liabilities		
Accounts payable	$ 381,894	$ 270,159
Notes payable and current portion of long-term debt	79,378	58,992
Accruals	159,479	153,786
Total current liabilities	$ 620,751	$ 482,937
Long-term debts[b]	$1,022,437	$ 966,858
Total liabilities	$1,643,188	$1,449,795
Stockholders' equity		
Preferred stock—cumulative 5%, $100 par, 2000 shares authorized and issued	$ 200,000	$ 200,000
Common stock—$2.50 par, 100,000 shares authorized, shares issued and outstanding in 1978: 76,262; in 1977: 76,244	190,655	190,610
Paid-in capital in excess of par on common stock	429,003	417,503
Retained earnings	1,133,927	1,011,711
Total stockholders' equity	$1,953,585	$1,819,824
Total Liabilities and Stockholders' Equity	$3,596,773	$3,269,619

[a]In 1978, the firm has a 6-year operating lease requiring annual beginning-of-year payments of $69,011. Four years of the lease have yet to run. In 1977, the lease payment was $63,880; the upward adjustment in this payment in 1978 is attributable to a number of improvements made to the leased property by the lessor at the company's request.

[b]Annual principal repayments on a portion of the firm's total outstanding debt amount to $71,000.

ities into cash. The discussion of liquidity here will touch on both the overall liquidity of the firm and the liquidity (or activity) of specific current accounts.

Measures of the overall liquidity of the firm. The three basic measures of a firm's overall liquidity are (1) net working capital, (2) the current ratio, and (3) the acid-test (quick) ratio.

Net working capital. The firm's net working capital is calculated by subtracting its current liabilities from its current assets. The net working capital for the Phyllis Petroleum Company in 1978 was as follows:

Net working capital = $1,222,710 − $620,751 = $601,959

This figure is not very useful for comparing the performance of different firms, but it is quite useful for internal control. Quite often the contract under which a long-term debt is incurred specifically states a minimum level of net working capital that must be maintained by the firm. This requirement is intended to force the firm to maintain sufficient operating liquidity and helps protect the creditor's loans. A time-series comparison of the firm's net working capital is often helpful in evaluating the firm's operations.

The current ratio. The current ratio is one of the most commonly cited financial ratios. It is expressed as follows:

$$\text{Current ratio} = \frac{\text{current assets}}{\text{current liabilities}}$$

The current ratio for the Phyllis Petroleum Company is

$$\frac{\$1,222,710}{\$620,751} = 1.97$$

A current ratio of 2.0 is generally considered to be acceptable, but the precise definition of an acceptable ratio is greatly dependent on the industry in which a firm operates. For example, a current ratio of 1.0 would be considered acceptable for a utility, but it might be quite unacceptable for a manufacturing firm. The acceptability of a current ratio is highly dependent on the predictability of the firm's cash flows. The more predictable the cash flows, the lower the current ratio required. The current ratio of 1.97 for the Phyllis Petroleum Company should be quite acceptable.

If the firm's current ratio is divided into 1.0, the resulting quotient subtracted from 1.0 and multiplied by 100 represents the percentage by which the firm's current assets can shrink without making it impossible for the firm to cover its current liabilities. For example, a current ratio of 2.0 means that the firm can still cover its current liabilities even if its current assets shrink by 50 percent $[(1.0 − (1.0 ÷ 2.0)) \cdot 100]$.

The current ratio is much more useful for interfirm comparisons of liquidity than net working capital. For example, assume that there are two firms, A and B, with the following simple balance sheets:

	Firm A		
Current assets	$ 800	Current liabilities	$ 600
Fixed assets	1,200	Long-term debt	600
		Stockholders' equity	800
Total	$2,000	Total	$2,000

	Firm B		
Current assets	$3,000	Current liabilities	$2,400
Fixed assets	2,000	Long-term debt	1,200
		Stockholders' equity	1,400
Total	$5,000	Total	$5,000

Calculating the net working capital and current ratios for both firms yields the following results:

Measure	Firm A	Firm B
Net working capital	$200	$600
Current ratio	1.33	1.25

On the basis of net working capital it appears that firm B is more liquid than firm A, whereas on the basis of the current ratio firm A is more liquid than firm B. The current ratio is the true indicator of liquidity since it considers the overall magnitude of each firm. The inaccurate conclusions that can be drawn from comparisons of net working capital should be clear from this example. A final point worthy of note is that whenever a firm's current ratio is 1.0, its net working capital is zero. If a firm has a current ratio of less than 1.0, it will have a negative net working capital. Net working capital is useful only in comparing the liquidity of the same firm over time and should not be used for comparing that of different firms; instead, the current ratio should be used.

The acid-test (quick) ratio. The acid-test ratio is similar to the current ratio except for the fact that it excludes inventory from the firm's current assets. The basic assumption of the acid-test ratio is that inventory is generally the least liquid current asset and should therefore be ignored. The acid-test ratio is calculated as follows:[1]

[1]Sometimes the acid-test, or quick, ratio is defined as (cash + marketable securities + accounts receivable)/current liabilities. If a firm were to show items other than cash, marketable securities, accounts receivable, and inventory as current assets, its acid-test ratio might vary, depending on which method of calculation is used.

$$\left\{ \text{Acid-test ratio} = \frac{\text{current assets} - \text{inventory}}{\text{current liabilities}} \right\}$$

The acid-test ratio for the Phyllis Petroleum Company in 1978 is

$$\frac{\$1{,}222{,}710 - \$288{,}883}{\$620{,}751} = \frac{\$933{,}827}{\$620{,}751} = 1.50$$

An acid-test ratio of 1.00 or greater is recommended. Again, what is considered an acceptable value depends highly on the industry in which the company operates. This ratio provides a better measure of overall liquidity only when a firm's inventory cannot easily be converted into cash. If inventory is liquid, the current ratio is a preferred measure of overall liquidity.

Measures of the liquidity, or activity,[2] of specific current accounts. Measuring the overall liquidity is generally not enough because the differences in the composition of a firm's current assets and current liabilities can significantly impact the firm's "true" liquidity. For example, consider the current portion of the balance sheets for firms X and Y given below:

Firm X

Cash	$ 0	Accts. pay.	$ 0
Mktble. sec.	0	Notes pay.	10,000
Accts. rec.	0	Accruals	0
Inv.	20,000		
Total C.A.	$20,000	Total C.L.	$10,000

Firm Y

Cash	$ 5,000	Accts. pay.	$ 5,000
Mktble. sec.	5,000	Notes pay.	3,000
Accts. rec.	5,000	Accruals	2,000
Inv.	5,000		
Total C.A.	$20,000	Total C.L.	$10,000

Although both firms appear to be equally liquid since their current ratios are both 2.00 (i.e., $20,000 ÷ $10,000), a closer look at the differences in the composition of current assets and liabilities suggests that firm Y is more liquid than firm X. This results for two reasons: (1) firm Y has generally more liquid assets in the form of cash and marketable securities than firm X, which has only a single and relatively illiquid asset in the form of inventory, and (2)

---

[2]The term "activity" is often used to refer to the liquidity of specific accounts, or the quickness with which these accounts can be converted into cash. The terms "liquidity" and "activity" are used interchangeably to refer to the speed with which specific accounts turn over.

firm Y's current liabilities are in general more flexible than the single current liability—notes payable—of firm X.

It is therefore important to look beyond measures of overall liquidity in order to assess the liquidity (or activity) of specific current accounts. A number of ratios are available for measuring the liquidity of the most important current accounts, which include inventory, accounts receivable, and accounts payable. The most common are discussed in the following pages. A basic simplifying assumption used in many of the calculations is that there are 360 days in the year and 30 days in each month.[3]

Inventory turnover. The liquidity, or activity, of a firm's inventory is quite commonly measured by its turnover. This is calculated as follows:

$$\text{Inventory turnover} = \frac{\text{cost of goods sold}}{\text{average inventory}}$$

Applying this relationship to the Phyllis Petroleum Company yields

$$\text{Inventory turnover} = \frac{\$2,088,039}{\dfrac{\$288,883 + \$280,857}{2}} = \frac{\$2,088,039}{\$284,870} = 7.33$$

The resulting turnover is meaningful only when compared to that of other firms in the same industry or to the firm's past inventory turnover. A ballpark estimate cannot be given. An inventory turnover of 40.0 would not be unusual for a grocery store, whereas a common inventory turnover for an aircraft manufacturer would be 1.0. Differences in turnover rates result from the differing operating characteristics of various industries.

The most acceptable way to calculate average inventory is to use monthly figures rather than the year-end figures given for the Phyllis Petroleum Company. Often, however, the only data available is the year-end inventory figure.

Many people believe that the higher the firm's inventory turnover, the more efficiently it has managed its inventory. This is true up to a point beyond which, a high inventory turnover may signal problems. For example, one way to increase inventory turnover is to carry very small inventories. However, such a strategy could result in a large number of stockouts (lost sales due to insufficient inventory), which could damage the firm's future sales. For each industry, there is a range of inventory turnover that may be considered good. Values below this range may signal illiquid or inactive inventories, while values above this range may indicate insufficient inventories and high stockouts.

[3] Unless otherwise specified, a 360-day year consisting of twelve 30-day months is assumed throughout this text. This assumption allows some simplification of the calculations used to illustrate key principles.

The average age of inventory.   The average age of inventory represents how many days, on the average, an item remains in the firm's inventory. It is calculated as follows:

$$\text{Average age of inventory} = \frac{360}{\text{inventory turnover}}$$

The average age of inventory for the Phyllis Petroleum Company is

$$\frac{360}{7.33} = 49.11 \text{ days}$$

This means that, on the average, an item remains in the firm's inventory for 49.11 days. The shorter the average age of the firm's inventory, the more liquid or active it may be considered. The average age of inventory can be thought of as the amount of time between the purchase of a raw material and the ultimate sale of the finished product. Viewed in this manner, it is useful for evaluating the purchasing, production, and inventory control functions of the firm.

The accounts receivable turnover.   The turnover of a firm's accounts receivable is a measure of their liquidity or activity. It is defined as follows:

$$\text{Accounts receivable turnover} = \frac{\text{annual credit sales}}{\text{average accounts receivable}}$$

In order to apply this ratio to the Phyllis Petroleum Company, the amount of credit sales must be determined. As indicated earlier, 95 percent of its sales are made on credit terms. Ninety-five percent of Phyllis's sales is $2,919,861.10 [.95($3,073,538)]. Financial data quite often require this type of adjustment. The accounts receivable turnover for the Phyllis Petroleum Company is

$$\frac{\$2,919,861.10}{\dfrac{\$502,695 + \$383,854}{2}} = \frac{\$2,919,861.10}{\$443,274.50} = 6.59$$

The higher the firm's accounts receivable turnover, the more favorable it is. A firm can increase its accounts receivable turnover by a very restrictive credit policy, but this strategy would not be recommended due to the lost sales that might result. The financial analyst should question especially high accounts receivable turnovers because they may signal poor credit policies.[4]

---

[4]A discussion of the evaluation and establishment of credit policies is presented in Chapter 9, which is devoted solely to the management of accounts receivable.

The average age of accounts receivable. The average age of accounts receivable, or *average collection period,* is a more meaningful figure to use in evaluating the firm's credit and collection policies. It is found by a simple transformation of the firm's accounts receivable turnover:

$$\left\{ \text{Average age of A/R} = \frac{360}{\text{accounts receivable turnover}} \right\}$$

The average age of the Phyllis Petroleum Company's accounts receivable is

$$\frac{360}{6.59} = 54.63 \text{ days}$$

On the average, it takes the firm 54.63 days to collect an account receivable.

The average age of accounts receivable is meaningful only in light of the firm's credit terms. If, for instance, the Phyllis Petroleum Company extends 30-day credit terms to its customers, an average collection period (age of accounts receivable) of 54.63 days would indicate a poorly managed credit or collection department, or both. If it extended 60-day credit terms, the 54.63 day average collection period would be quite acceptable. The average collection period is much more useful in evaluating a firm's credit policies than is the turnover of accounts receivable. The average age of accounts receivable can be calculated directly with the following formula:

$$\text{Average age of A/R} = \frac{360 \cdot \text{average accounts receivable}}{\text{annual credit sales}}$$

The accounts payable turnover. The turnover of accounts payable is similar to the turnover of accounts receivable. It measures the number of times accounts payable are converted into cash each year. It is defined as follows:

$$\left\{ \text{Accounts payable turnover} = \frac{\text{annual credit purchases}}{\text{average accounts payable}} \right\}$$

Since annual credit purchases do not normally appear on balance sheets or income statements, they must be estimated by determining the percentage of the cost of goods sold that represents credit purchases. As indicated earlier, 80 percent of the Phyllis Petroleum Company's cost of goods sold represents credit purchases. This equals $1,670,431.20 [or .80($2,088,039)]. Using this figure, we can calculate the turnover of the company's accounts payable:

$$\text{A/P turnover} = \frac{\$1,670,431.20}{\dfrac{\$381,894 + \$270,159}{2}} = \frac{\$1,670,431.20}{\$326,026.50} = 5.12$$

This figure indicates how many times during the year the firm turns over its accounts payable. It is not quite as useful a measure as the average age of accounts payable.

The average age of accounts payable.   The average age of accounts payable, or *average payment period,* is calculated in the same manner as the average age of inventory and the average age of accounts receivable:[5]

$$\text{Average age of A/P} = \frac{360}{\text{accounts payable turnover}}$$

The average age of accounts payable for the Phyllis Petroleum Company is

$$\frac{360}{5.12} = 70.31 \text{ days}$$

This figure is meaningful only in light of the average credit terms extended the firm. If the Phyllis Petroleum Company's suppliers, on the average, have extended 30-day credit terms to the firm, an analyst might give it a low credit rating. However, if the firm has been generally extended 60-day credit terms, its credit would certainly be acceptable. Prospective lenders and suppliers of trade credit are especially interested in the average age of accounts payable, since it provides them with a feel for the bill-paying patterns of the firm.

Substituting the formula for the turnover of accounts payable into the denominator of the equation above gives us a one-step formula for determining the average age of accounts payable:

$$\text{Average age of A/P} = \frac{360 \cdot \text{average accounts payable}}{\text{annual credit purchases}}$$

Aging accounts.   *Aging* is a technique for evaluating the composition of *either* accounts receivable or accounts payable. It provides the analyst with information concerning the proportion of each type of account that has been outstanding for a period of time. By highlighting irregularities, it allows him to pinpoint the cause of collection or payment problems.

Aging requires that the firm's accounts receivable or payable be broken down into groups based on their point of origin; this breakdown is typically made on a month-by-month basis, going back three or four months.

EXAMPLE

Assume that a firm extends 30-day credit terms to its customers and on December 31 finds $200,000 of accounts receivable on its books. An evaluation of the $200,000 of accounts receivable results in the following breakdown:

---

[5]At this point, the reader should recognize that the average age of accounts payable can be found by dividing 360 by the turnover. And, of course, given the average age, the turnover can be found by dividing it into 360.

	Days overdue					
Days	Current	0–30	31–60	61–90	Over 90	
Month	December	November	October	September	August	Total
Accounts receivable	$134,000	$16,000	$44,000	$4,000	$2,000	$200,000
Percentage of total	67	8	22	2	1	100

Since it is assumed that the firm gives its customers 30 days after the end of the month in which the sale is made to pay off their accounts, any December receivables still on the firm's books are considered current. November receivables are between zero and 30 days overdue, while October receivables still unpaid are 31–60 days overdue, and so on.

The table shows that 67 percent of the firm's receivables are current, 8 percent are one month late, 22 percent are two months late, 2 percent are three months late, and 1 percent are more than three months late.[6] The only irregularity in these data is the high percentage of accounts receivable represented by October receivables. This indicates that some problem may have occurred in October. Investigation may indicate that the problem can be attributed to the hiring of a new credit manager or the acceptance of a new account that has made a large credit purchase it has not yet paid for. When accounts are aged and such a discrepancy is found, the analyst should determine its cause. ●

The approach illustrated in this example can be applied in aging accounts payable, which would probably be of the most interest to current and prospective creditors. Any discrepancies in the pattern of outstanding payables should be investigated. The benefit of aging lies in its ability to point up specific periods of apparent slowness in the collection or payment of accounts.

Measures of debt

The debt position of the business firm indicates the amount of other people's money that is being used in attempting to generate profits. Typically, the financial analyst is most concerned with the firm's long-term debts, since these debts commit the firm over the long-term to pay interest and eventually repay the sum borrowed. Since the claims of the firm's creditors must be satisfied prior to the distribution of earnings to shareholders,[7] present and

---

[6]The average age of the accounts receivable shown can be estimated using the given data. By weighting the average age—not days overdue—by the percent of accounts with the given age and summing the weighted values, the average age can be approximated. For example, the current (December) accounts would on average have an age of 15 days, the November accounts outstanding would have an average age of 45 days, and so on. Applying the given percentages, the average age is calculated:

$$= .67(15 \text{ days}) + .08(45 \text{ days}) + .22(75 \text{ days}) + .02(105 \text{ days}) + .01(135 \text{ days})$$
$$= 10.05 + 3.60 + 16.50 + 2.10 + 1.35 = \underline{33.60 \text{ days}}$$

This approximation can be applied in a similar fashion to an aging schedule of accounts payable.

[7]The law requires that creditors' claims be satisfied prior to those of the firm's owners. This only makes sense, since the creditor is providing a service (i.e., lending money) to the owners and is not required to bear the risks of ownership. Chapter 4 discusses the precedence of various parties in the distribution of corporate earnings.

prospective shareholders pay close attention to both the degree of indebtedness and ability to repay debts the firm incurs. Lenders are also concerned
about the firm's degree of indebtedness and ability to service debts, since the
more indebtedness present, the higher the probability that the firm will be
unable to satisfy the claims of all its creditors. Management obviously must
be concerned with indebtedness, since it recognizes the attention paid to it
by these other parties and since it certainly does not wish to see the firm
become insolvent.

Measures of the degree of indebtedness.   The degree of indebtedness is typically measured using only balance sheet data. Three of the most
commonly used measures of indebtedness are (1) the debt ratio, (2) the debt-
equity ratio, and (3) the debt-to-total-capitalization ratio.

The debt ratio.   This ratio measures the proportion of total assets provided by the firm's creditors. The higher this ratio, the greater amount of
other people's money that is being used in an attempt to generate profits for
the firm's owners. The ratio is calculated as follows:

$$\left\{ \text{Debt ratio} = \frac{\text{total liabilities}}{\text{total assets}} \right\}$$

The debt ratio for the Phyllis Petroleum Company is

$$\frac{\$1,643,188}{\$3,596,773} = .457 = 45.7\%$$

This indicates that the company has financed 45.7 percent of its assets with
debt. The higher this ratio is, the more financial leverage a firm has.[8]
    The following two ratios differ from the debt ratio in that they focus only
on the firm's long-term debts. Short-term debts, or current liabilities, are
ignored since most of them are spontaneous (that is, they are the natural
result of doing business) and they do not commit the firm to the payment of
fixed charges over a long period of time.

The debt-equity ratio.   This ratio indicates the relationship between
the long-term funds provided by creditors and those provided by the firm's
owners. It is commonly used to measure the degree of financial leverage of
the firm. It is defined as follows:

$$\left\{ \text{Debt-equity ratio} = \frac{\text{long-term debt}}{\text{stockholders' equity}} \right\}$$

---

[8]"Financial leverage" refers to the degree to which a firm uses money requiring fixed
payments to magnify the returns to the owners. This topic is discussed at length in Chapter 4.

The debt-equity ratio for the Phyllis Petroleum Company is

$$\frac{\$1,022,437}{\$1,953,585} = .523 = 52.3\%$$

This indicates that the firm's long-term debts are only 52.3 percent as large as the stockholders' equity. This figure is meaningful only in light of the type of business the firm is in. Firms with large amounts of fixed assets and stable cash flows typically have high debt-equity ratios, while other, less capital-intensive, firms normally have lower debt-equity ratios. An industry average is a good figure to which to compare a debt-equity ratio.

The debt-to-total-capitalization ratio. This commonly used ratio has the same objective as the preceding ratio. It measures the percentage of the firm's *long-term* funds supplied by its creditors. The firm's long-term funds are referred to as its *total capitalization*. They include both long-term debt and the stockholders' equity. The ratio of debt to total capitalization is stated as follows:

$$\text{Debt-to-total-capitalization ratio} = \frac{\text{long-term debt}}{\text{total capitalization}}$$

The value of this ratio for the Phyllis Petroleum Company is

$$\frac{\$1,022,437}{\$1,022,437 + \$1,953,585} = \frac{\$1,022,437}{\$2,976,022} = .344 = 34.4\%$$

The ratio indicates that, of the firm's total long-term funds, 34.4 percent have been supplied by creditors.

Since there is great similarity between the debt-equity ratio and the ratio of debt to total capitalization, the analyst need use only one of these. In either case, the resulting value is meaningful only in light of the nature of the firm's operations and industry averages. The value of either of these ratios will be very different for a utility as compared to a grocery store, and care should be used in making comparisons.

Measures of the ability to service debts. The ability to *service* debts refers to how readily a firm can meet the fixed contractual payments typically required on a scheduled basis over the life of a debt.[9] With debts come scheduled fixed-payment obligations for interest and principal (or sinking fund) payments. Lease payments as well as preferred stock dividend payments also represent scheduled payment obligations, which are quite sim-

---

[9]The term "service" is used throughout this text to refer to the payment of interest and repayment of principal associated with a firm's debt obligations. When a firm services its debts, it pays, or fulfills, these obligations.

ilar to those required as part of many corporate debts. The firm's ability to meet certain fixed charges is measured using *coverage ratios*. Such ratios are of greatest interest to the firm's creditors, who are interested in its ability to service its existing debts or any additional proposed debts, or both. The lower the firm's coverage ratios, the more risky the firm is considered to be. "Riskiness" here refers to the firm's ability to meet its fixed obligations. If a firm is unable to meet these obligations, it will be in default and its creditors may seek immediate repayment. In most instances, this would force a firm into bankruptcy. The ability of coverage ratios to measure this type of risk makes their use quite common.[10] Three ratios of coverage—(1) times interest earned, (2) total debt coverage, and (3) the overall coverage ratio—are discussed below. Actually, only the first two of these ratios devote attention solely to debt; the third ratio considers other fixed payment obligations in addition to debt service.

Times interest earned. This ratio is often called the firm's *total interest coverage ratio*. It measures the firm's ability to pay its contractual interest payments. The higher the value of this ratio, the better able the firm is to fulfill its interest obligations. Times interest earned is calculated as follows:

$$\text{Times interest earned} = \frac{\text{earnings before interest and taxes}}{\text{annual interest expense}}$$

Applying this ratio to the Phyllis Petroleum Company yields the following value:

$$\text{Times interest earned} = \frac{\$387,097}{\$62,338} = 6.21$$

The value of earnings before interest and taxes is the same as the figure for operating profits in Table 3.2. The times interest earned for the Phyllis Petroleum Company is acceptable; as a rule, a value of at least 5.0 and preferably closer to 10.0 is suggested. If the firm's earnings before interest and taxes were to shrink by 84 percent [(6.21 − 1.0) ÷ 6.21], the firm would still be able to pay the $62,338 in interest it owes. Thus it has a good margin of safety. Creditors would probably consider extending a loan to the Phyllis Petroleum Company, since it appears to be easily able to cover its interest charges.

Total debt coverage. This ratio is similar to the interest coverage ratio, except that it measures not only the firm's ability to pay its interest charges but also its ability to repay the *principal* of loans or make scheduled

---

[10]It is important to recognize that coverage ratios use data based upon the application of accrual concepts (discussed in Chapter 1) to measure what in a strict sense should be measured with cash flows. This occurs since debts are serviced using cash flows—not the accounting values shown on the firm's financial statements. But because it is difficult to determine cash flows available for debt service from the firm's financial statements, the calculation of coverage ratios as presented herein is quite common due to the ready availability of financial statement data.

sinking-fund payments. Often, as part of a bond or long-term loan agreement, a firm is required to make periodic payments of principal either to the lender or into a fund that is being accumulated so that the debt can be retired at maturity. Whether one is concerned with an actual principal repayment or a payment into a sinking fund, the procedure for calculating the ratio is the same.

The important point to recognize is that principal repayments are made on an after-tax basis and must be adjusted to a before-tax amount in order to calculate the total debt coverage. Interest is a pretax expenditure, and the interest and principal payments must be measured on a common basis. It is easier to adjust principal payments to pretax equivalents in order to calculate total debt coverage than to adjust both earnings before taxes and interest to after-tax equivalents. Table 3.4 presents a note on the calculation of the before-tax earnings necessary to achieve a stated amount of after-tax earnings. The table also illustrates the resulting relationship. The formula for the firm's total debt coverage is given below:

$$\left\{ \text{Total debt coverage} = \frac{\text{earnings before interest and taxes}}{\text{interest} + \text{principal payments } [1/(1-t)]} \right\}$$

where t = the corporate tax rate applicable to the firm's income.

The term $1/(1-t)$ is included in order to adjust the principal payment back to a pretax amount. If the Phyllis Petroleum Company is required to pay $71,000 annually into a sinking fund and the firm is in a 29-percent tax bracket, its total debt coverage ratio is

$$\frac{\$387,097}{\$62,338 + \$71,000[1/(1-.29)]} = \frac{\$387,097}{\$62,338 + \$100,00} = \frac{\$387,097}{\$162,338} = 2.38$$

A total debt coverage ratio of 2.38 for the Phyllis Petroleum Company appears to be quite good. The firm appears to be able to cover easily its fixed debt service obligations.

It is important to recognize that this ratio, just like the interest coverage ratio, measures risk. The lower the ratio, the more risky the firm is from the lender's viewpoint. Although sinking-fund payments are not always made to the lender, they are usually a contractual requirement. This means that if a firm fails to make a sinking-fund payment it will be considered in default, just as it would be if it failed to repay the principal when it came due. A default normally permits the lender to call in his loan and often results in bankruptcy for the firm. This is why the ability of a firm to cover its interest and principal or sinking-fund payments is viewed as a measure of risk by prospective and existing creditors. An examination of the debt coverage ratio allows creditors to determine whether the firm is capable of handling any additional debts.

The overall coverage ratio. The overall coverage ratio is quite similar to the total debt coverage ratio except that it includes any other fixed

**TABLE 3.4 Calculating the before-tax
earnings necessary to achieve given after-tax earnings**

It is often necessary (especially when calculating coverage ratios) to determine the
amount of before-tax earnings needed to achieve given after-tax earnings.

Let
P = the after-tax earnings desired
B = the before-tax earnings required in order to permit after-tax earnings to equal P
t = the tax rate on income.

Looking at the bottom portion of the income statement, we have

Earnings before taxes	B
Less taxes	$-t \cdot B$
Earnings after taxes	P

It can be seen above that

$$P = B - t \cdot B \tag{1}$$

Factoring B from equation 1 above yields

$$P = B(1 - t) \tag{2}$$

Solving for B yields

$$B = \frac{P}{1 - t} = P \cdot \left[\frac{1}{1 - t}\right] \tag{3}$$

Equation 3 gives the before-tax earnings necessary to have after-tax earnings of P
dollars given a tax rate of t.

Example:

Let P = $120
t = 25%

How much must be earned before taxes to have after-tax earnings of $120.00?

Substituting the data into equation 3, we get

$$B = \frac{\$120}{1 - .25} = \frac{\$120}{.75} = \$120 \cdot \left[\frac{1}{1 - .25}\right] = \$120 \,(1.333) = \$160$$

We can check our answer by the following simple calculation:

Check: Earnings before taxes	$160
Less: Taxes (25 percent)	40
Earnings After Taxes	$120

obligations. Scheduled lease payments as well as preferred stock dividends[11] are often included in this ratio. Since lease payments are tax-deductible expenditures they do not require any tax adjustment; the preferred stock dividends which must be paid from after-tax cash flows, must be adjusted for taxes. The formula for the overall coverage ratio is given below:

$$\text{Overall coverage ratio} = \frac{\text{earnings before lease payments, interest, and taxes}}{\text{interest} + \text{principal payments } [1/(1 - t)] + \text{lease payments} + \text{preferred dividends } [1/(1 - t)]}$$

Applying this formula to the Phyllis Petroleum Company data yields

$$
\begin{aligned}
\text{Overall coverage ratio} &= \frac{\$387{,}097 + \$69{,}011}{\$62{,}338 + \$71{,}000[1/(1 - .29)] + \$69{,}011 + \$10{,}000[1/(1 - .29)]} \\
&= \frac{\$456{,}108}{\$245{,}434} = 1.86
\end{aligned}
$$

The interpretation of this ratio is similar to the interpretation of the firm's total debt coverage ratio, except for the inclusion of lease expense and preferred dividends.

The total coverage ratio is of interest not only to the firm's creditors but also to existing and prospective lessors, preferred stockholders, and common stockholders. It measures the ability of the firm to cover all fixed financial charges. The higher it is, the safer are the interests of creditors, lessor(s), and preferred stockholders in the firm; also, the higher the firm's total coverage ratio, the higher the levels of profit that can be expected by the common stockholders.

Measures of profitability

There are many measures of profitability. Each relates the returns of the firm to its sales, to its assets, or to its equity. As a group, these measures allow the analyst to evaluate the firm's earnings with respect to a given level of sales, a certain level of assets, or the owners' investment. Attention is paid to the firm's profitability since in order to stay in existence it must be profitable. Without profits, a firm could not attract outside capital; moreover, existing creditors and owners would become concerned about the company's future and attempt to recover their funds. Creditors, owners, and, most important, management pay close attention to boosting the firm's profits due to the great importance placed on the earnings of the firm in the marketplace.

[11]Although preferred stock dividends, which are stated at the time of issue, can be "passed" (i.e., not paid) at the option of the firm's directors, it is generally believed that the payment of such dividends is necessary in order to impact favorably the owners' wealth as reflected in the price of their stock. This text therefore treats the preferred stock dividend as if it were a contractual obligation not only to pay a fixed amount but also to make the payments as scheduled.

Percent income statements. A common approach for evaluating profitability in relation to sales is the *percent income statement*.[12] By expressing each item on the income statement as a percentage of sales, the relationship between sales and specific revenues and expenses can be evaluated. Percent income statements are especially useful in comparing a firm's performance for one year with that for another year. Percent income statements for 1977 and 1978 for the Phyllis Petroleum Company are presented in Table 3.5. An evaluation of these statements reveals that the firm's cost of goods sold increased from 66.64 percent of sales in 1977 to 67.94 percent of sales in 1978, resulting in a decrease in the gross profit margin from 33.36 percent to 32.06 percent. However, thanks to a decrease in operating expenses from 22.79 percent in 1977 to 19.47 percent in 1978, the firm's net profit margin rose from 5.78 percent of sales in 1977 to 7.50 percent in 1978. The decrease in expenses in 1978 more than compensated for the increase in the cost of goods sold. A decrease in the firm's 1978 interest expense (2.02 percent of sales as opposed to 2.29 percent in 1977) added to the increase in 1978 profits.

Three commonly cited ratios of profitability can be read directly from the percent income statement: (a) the gross profit margin, (b) the operating profit margin, and (c) the net profit margin.

The gross profit margin. The gross profit margin indicates the percentage of each sales dollar remaining after the firm has paid for its goods. The higher the gross profit, the better, and the lower the relative cost of merchandise sold. Of course, the opposite case is also true, as the Phyllis Petroleum Company example shows.

The gross profit margin is calculated as follows:

$$\text{Gross profit margin} = \frac{\text{sales} - \text{cost of goods sold}}{\text{sales}} = \frac{\text{gross profit}}{\text{sales}}$$

The value for Phyllis Petroleum Company's gross profit margin for 1978 is

$$\frac{\$3,073,538 - \$2,088,039}{\$3,073,538} = \frac{\$985,499}{\$3,073,538} = 32.06\%$$

This value is shown on the percent income statement, Table 3.5.

The operating profit margin. This ratio represents what are often called the *pure profits* earned on each sales dollar by the firm. Operating profits are pure in the sense that they ignore any financial or government charges (interest or taxes) and measure only the profits earned by the firm on its operations. A high operating profit margin is preferred.

The operating profit margin is calculated as follows:

---

[12]This statement is often referred to as a "common-size" statement. The same treatment is often applied to the firm's balance sheet to make it easier to evaluate changes in the asset or financial structure of the firm.

TABLE 3.5 Phyllis Petroleum
Company percent income statements

		For the year ending December 31	
		1978	1977
	Sales	100.00%	100.00%
	Less: Cost of goods sold	67.94	66.64
(a)	Gross profit margin	32.06%	33.36%
	Less: Operating expenses		
	Selling expenses	3.27%	4.21%
	General and admin. expenses	6.18	7.40
	Lease expense	2.25	2.49
	Depreciation and depletion	7.77	8.69
	Total operating expense	19.47%	22.79%
(b)	Operating profit margin	12.59%	10.57%
	Less: Interest expense	2.02%	2.29%
	Net profits before taxes	10.57%	8.28%
	Less: Taxes	3.07%	2.50%
(c)	Net profit margin	7.50%	5.78%

$$\text{Operating profit margin} = \frac{\text{operating profit}}{\text{sales}}$$

The value for Phyllis Petroleum Company's operating profit margin for 1978 is

$$\frac{\$387,097}{\$3,073,538} = 12.59\%$$

This value is shown in the percent income statement, Table 3.5.

The net profit margin. The net profit margin measures the percentage of each sales dollar remaining after all expenses, including taxes, have been deducted. The higher the firm's net profit margin, the better. The net profit margin is a quite commonly cited measure of the corporation's success with respect to earnings on sales. "Good" net profit margins differ considerably across industries. A net profit margin of 1 percent would not be unusual for a grocery store, while a net profit margin of 10 percent would be low for a jewelry store.

The net profit margin is calculated as follows:

$$\text{Net profit margin} = \frac{\text{net profits after taxes}}{\text{sales}}$$

The value of Phyllis Petroleum Company's net profit margin for 1978 is

$$\frac{\$230,411}{\$3,073,538} = 7.50\%$$

This value is shown in the percent income statement, Table 3.5.

The total asset turnover. The total asset turnover indicates the efficiency with which the firm is able to use its assets to generate sales dollars. The higher a firm's total asset turnover is, the more efficiently its assets have been used. The total asset turnover is probably of greatest interest to the firm's management, since it indicates whether the firm's operations have been financially efficient. Other parties, such as creditors and prospective and existing owners, will also be interested in this measure. The firm's total asset turnover is calculated as follows:

$$\text{Total asset turnover} = \frac{\text{annual sales}}{\text{total assets}}$$

The value of the Phyllis Petroleum Company's total asset turnover is

$$\frac{\$3,073,538}{\$3,596,773} = 0.853$$

This indicates that the company turns its assets over only .853 times a year. This value is meaningful only in light of the firm's past performance or an industry average.

The return on investment (ROI) and the DuPont formula. The return on investment, which is often called the firm's *return on total assets*, measures the overall effectiveness of management in generating profits with its available assets. The higher the firm's return on investment, the better. The return on investment is calculated as follows:

$$\text{Return on investment} = \frac{\text{net profits after taxes}}{\text{total assets}}$$

The value of the Phyllis Petroleum Company's return on investment is

$$\frac{\$230,411}{\$3,596,773} = 6.40\%$$

This value appears to be quite acceptable, but only when it is compared to industry averages can meaningful conclusions be drawn.

The firm's return on investment can be calculated in an alternate fashion, utilizing the *DuPont formula*, which is written as follows:

FIGURE 3.1 The DuPont and Modified DuPont formulas

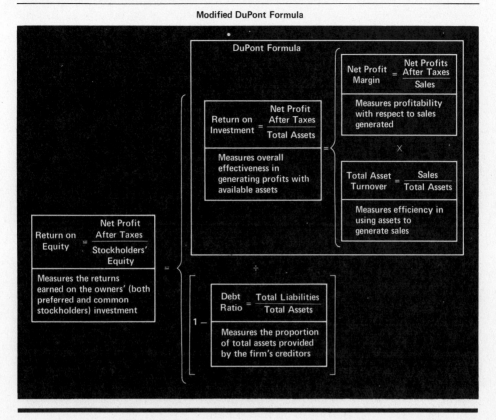

Return on investment = net profit margin · total asset turnover

The upper right-hand portion of Figure 3.1 presents a breakdown of this formula. Substituting the appropriate formulas into the equation and simplifying gives us the same values as those arrived at by the direct method:

$$\frac{\text{Net profits after taxes}}{\text{total assets}} = \frac{\text{net profits after taxes}}{\text{sales}} \cdot \frac{\text{sales}}{\text{total assets}}$$

If the values for the net profit margin and total asset turnover of the Phyllis Petroleum Company, calculated earlier, are substituted into the DuPont formula, the result is

6.40% = 7.50% · 0.853

This result is what would be expected. The DuPont formula allows the firm to break down its return on investment into a profit-on-sales component and an asset efficiency component. Typically, a firm with a low net profit margin has a high total asset turnover, which results in a reasonably good return on investment. Often, the opposite situation exists. The relationship between the two components of the DuPont formula will depend largely on the industry in which the firm operates.

Return on equity (ROE) and the Modified DuPont formula. The return on equity measures the return earned on the owners' (both preferred and common stockholders) investment.[13] Generally the higher this return, the better off are the owners. Return on equity is calculated as follows:

$$\text{Return on equity} = \frac{\text{net profits after taxes}}{\text{stockholders' equity}}$$

The value of this ratio for the Phyllis Petroleum Company is

$$\frac{\$230,411}{\$1,953,585} = 11.79\%$$

This value, which seems to be quite good, could have been calculated using the *Modified DuPont formula*, which is given below:

$$\text{Return on equity} = \frac{\text{net profit margin} \cdot \text{total asset turnover}}{(1 - \text{debt ratio})}$$

Recognizing that the numerator of the right-hand side of the equation is the return on investment, the equation can be rewritten as

$$\text{Return on equity} = \frac{\text{return on investment}}{(1 - \text{debt ratio})}$$

Use of the debt ratio (defined earlier as total liabilities/total assets) to convert the ROI to the ROE reflects the impact of leverage (i.e., use of debt) on the owners' return. Substituting the values for the debt ratio of 45.7 percent and the return on investment of 6.40 percent—both of which were calculated earlier—into the Modified DuPont formula yields the following return on equity:

$$\frac{6.40\%}{(1 - .457)} = \frac{6.40\%}{.543} = 11.79\%$$

The value obtained using the Modified DuPont framework is the same as that calculated directly. The real strength of the Modified DuPont formulation is that it allows the firm to break its return on equity into a profit-on-sales

[13]This ratio includes preferred dividends in the earnings figures and preferred stock in the equity value, but because the amount of preferred stock and its impact on a firm are generally quite small, or nonexistent, this formula is a reasonably good approximation of the true owners', that is, the common stockholders', return.

component (net profit margin), an asset efficiency component (total asset turn-over), and a use-of-leverage component (debt ratio). The relationship between these ratios is clearly depicted in Figure 3.1, which presents a breakdown of the Modified DuPont formula.

The return on common stock equity. This ratio indicates the return earned on the *book value* of the common stockholders' equity. Owners are most concerned with this ratio since it indicates the success of the company in generating earnings on their behalf. The higher this ratio, the better the owners like it. It is calculated as follows:

$$\text{Return on common stock equity} = \frac{\text{net profits after taxes } - \text{ preferred dividends}}{\text{stockholders' equity } - \text{ preferred stock equity}}$$

The value of this ratio for the Phyllis Petroleum Company is

$$\frac{\$230,411 - \$10,000}{\$1,953,585 - \$200,000} = \frac{\$220,411}{\$1,753,585} = 12.57\%$$

The numerator and denominator of this formula are often referred to as "earnings available for common stock" and "common stock equity," respectively. Sometimes more meaningful results can be obtained by substituting the market value of the firm's equity into the denominator. The resulting value can be thought of as the yield, or return, on the current *market value* of the firm. The return on common stock equity is quite useful to the existing or prospective owner interested in comparing the firm's performance to that of other firms.

Earnings per share. The firm's earnings per share are generally of interest to the management and to current or prospective shareholders. The earnings per share represent the number of dollars earned on behalf of each outstanding share of common stock. They are closely watched by the investing public and are considered an important indicator of corporate success. High earnings per share are preferred. Earnings per share are calculated as follows:

$$\text{Earnings per share} = \frac{\text{earnings available for common stock}}{\text{number of shares of common stock outstanding}}$$

The value of the Phyllis Petroleum Company's earnings per share is

$$\frac{\$220,411}{76,262} = \$2.89$$

This figure represents the dollar amount earned on behalf of each share outstanding. It does not represent the amount of earnings actually distributed to shareholders.

Dividends per share.[14]   This figure represents the amount of money distributed to each shareholder. It is calculated as follows:

$$\text{Dividends per share} = \frac{\text{dividends paid}}{\text{number of shares of common stock outstanding}}$$

Since the Phyllis Petroleum Company paid out $98,195 in dividends in 1978, its dividends per share for that year are

$$\frac{\$98,195}{76,262} = \$1.29$$

This figure indicates that owners of the company's 76,262 shares received $1.29 for each share owned. This figure is an important one to present to prospective shareholders. The many facets of dividends and dividend policy will be discussed fully in Chapter 24.

The book value per share.   The book value per share indicates the approximate value of each share of stock based on the assumption that all assets can be liquidated at their book value. Book value as used here represents the accounting value of the common stockholder's equity (i.e., the value shown on the firm's balance sheet). It is useful in estimating the minimum worth of the business firm. The book value per share can be thought of as the amount of money that would be received for each share owned if the firm's assets were sold at their book value and the proceeds remaining after all debts had been settled were distributed to the shareholders. The book value per share is calculated as follows:

$$\text{Book value per share} = \frac{\text{total common stockholders' equity}}{\text{number of shares of common stock outstanding}}$$

The book value per share for the Phyllis Petroleum Company is

$$\frac{\$1,953,585 - \$200,000}{76,262} = \frac{\$1,753,585}{76,262} = \$22.99$$

Normally corporate shares do not sell for less than their book value; typically, they sell for considerably more. The reasons for this are discussed in Chapter 18.

A COMPLETE RATIO ANALYSIS
OF PHYLLIS PETROLEUM COMPANY

As indicated earlier in the chapter, a single ratio is not adequate for assessing all aspects of the firm's financial condition. The 1978 ratio values calculated

[14]Dividends per share and the book value per share are not actually measures of profitability; rather, they measure values that reflect managerial action (in the case of dividends) and historical value (in the case of book value). They have been included here since they are often of interest to prospective and existing stockholders.

in the preceding section of the chapter, and the ratio values calculated for 1976 and 1977 for the Phyllis Petroleum Company, along with the industry average ratios for 1978, are summarized in Table 3.6. The table shows the formula used to calculate each of the ratios. Using these data, the three key aspects of Phyllis's performance—(1) liquidity and activity, (2) debt, and (3) profitability—are discussed separately in the following paragraphs on both a time-series and cross-sectional basis.

Liquidity and activity

The overall liquidity of the firm seems to exhibit a reasonably stable trend and has been maintained at a level that is reasonably consistent with the industry average in 1978. Phyllis's inventory appears to be in good shape. Its inventory management seems to have improved, performing at a level above the industry. The firm may be experiencing some problems with its accounts receivable. The average age of receivables seems to have crept up to a level above that of the industry; therefore, attention should be given to various aspects of the firm's credit management. The firm appears to be a bit slow in paying its bills. Although the trend seems to be towards improvement, Phyllis is paying nearly 14 days slower than the average firm in the industry. The payment procedures should be examined in order to make sure that the company's credit standing is not adversely affected. Overall, the firm's liquidity appears to be in good shape although some attention should be given to the management of accounts receivable and accounts payable.

Debt

The firm's indebtedness seems to have increased over the 1976–1978 period and is currently at a level slightly above the industry average. Although the increase in the ratios of indebtedness could be cause for alarm, a look at the coverage ratios seems to indicate that the firm's ability to meet debt service costs increased from 1977 to 1978 to a level that outperforms the industry. Apparently in 1977, the firm's increased indebtedness caused a deterioration in its ability to adequately service its debts; Phyllis has evidently improved its income in 1978 such that it is able to service its debts in a fashion consistent with the average firm in their industry. The same conclusion results from analysis of Phyllis's overall coverage, which includes not only debt service but also lease payments and preferred stock dividends. In summary, it appears that, although 1977 was an off year, the firm's debt position—both in terms of degree of indebtedness and ability to service debts—is in good shape in 1978.

Profitability

Phyllis's profitability relative to sales in 1978 was better than the average company in their industry, although it does not match its 1976 performance. Although the gross profit margin in 1977 and 1978 was better than in 1976, it appears that higher levels of operating and interest expenses in these latter years have caused the 1978 net profit margin to fall below that of 1976. Phyllis's 1978 net profit margin is certainly quite favorable when viewed in light of the industry average. The firm's return on investment, return on equity,

TABLE 3.6 Summary of Phyllis Petroleum Company ratios (1976–1978, including 1978 industry averages)

Ratio	Formula	Year			1978 industry average[c]
		1976[a]	1977[b]	1978	
I. Liquidity and Activity:					
Overall Firm Liquidity					
Net working capital	current assets − current liabilities	$582,761	$520,256	$601,959	$426,900
Current ratio	$\dfrac{\text{current assets}}{\text{current liabilities}}$	2.04	2.08	1.97	2.05
Acid-test ratio	$\dfrac{\text{current assets} - \text{inventory}}{\text{current liabilities}}$	1.32	1.50	1.50	1.43
Liquidity, or Activity, of Specific Accounts					
Inventory turnover	$\dfrac{\text{cost of goods sold}}{\text{average inventory}}$	5.10	6.00	7.33	6.50
Average age of inventory	$\dfrac{360}{\text{inventory turnover}}$	70.59 days	60.00 days	49.11 days	55.38 days
Accounts receivable turnover	$\dfrac{\text{annual credit sales}}{\text{average accounts receivable}}$	7.67	6.37	6.59	8.12
Average age of accounts receivable	$\dfrac{360}{\text{accounts receivable turnover}}$	46.94 days	56.51 days	54.63 days	44.33 days
Accounts payable turnover	$\dfrac{\text{annual credit purchases}}{\text{average accounts payable}}$	4.75	4.89	5.12	6.37
Average age of accounts payable	$\dfrac{360}{\text{accounts payable turnover}}$	75.79 days	73.62 days	70.31 days	56.51 days
II. Debt					
Degree of Indebtedness					
Debt ratio	$\dfrac{\text{total liabilities}}{\text{total assets}}$	36.8%	44.3%	45.7%	40.0%
Debt-equity ratio	$\dfrac{\text{long-term debt}}{\text{stockholders' eq}}$	44.2%	53.1%	52.3%	50.0%
Debt-to-total capitalization	$\dfrac{\text{long-term debt}}{\text{total capitalization}}$	29.9%	34.7%	34.4%	33.3%

Ability to Service Debts

Ratio	Formula				
Times interest earned	$\dfrac{\text{earnings before interest and taxes}}{\text{interest}}$	6.55	4.61	6.21	5.61
Total debt coverage	$\dfrac{\text{earnings before interest and taxes}}{\text{interest} + \text{principal} \,[1/(1-t)]}$	3.19	1.71	2.38	2.40
Overall coverage ratio	$\dfrac{\text{EBIT} + \text{lease payments}}{\text{int.} + \text{lease pay.} + [\text{prin.} + \text{pref. div}]\,[1/(1-t)]}$	2.65	1.42	1.86	1.54

III. Profitability

Ratio	Formula				
Gross profit margin	$\dfrac{\text{gross profit}}{\text{sales}}$	31.40%	33.36%	32.06%	30.00%
Operating profit margin	$\dfrac{\text{operating profit}}{\text{sales}}$	13.62%	10.57%	12.59%	10.00%
Net profit margin	$\dfrac{\text{net profit after taxes}}{\text{sales}}$	8.76%	5.78%	7.50%	6.40%
Total asset turnover	$\dfrac{\text{sales}}{\text{total assets}}$	.943	.785	.853	.754
Return on investment	$\dfrac{\text{net profit after taxes}}{\text{total assets}}$	8.26%	4.54%	6.40%	4.83%
Return on equity	$\dfrac{\text{net profit after taxes}}{\text{stockholders' equity}}$	13.07%	8.16%	11.79%	8.04%
Return on common stock equity	$\dfrac{\text{earnings available for common}}{\text{common stock equity}}$	12.88%	8.55%	12.57%	8.74%
Earnings per share	$\dfrac{\text{earnings available for common}}{\text{number of shares outstanding}}$	$3.26	$1.82	$2.89	$2.26
Dividends per share	$\dfrac{\text{total dividends paid}}{\text{number of shares outstanding}}$	$1.20	$1.28	$1.29	$1.50
Book value per share	$\dfrac{\text{book value of common}}{\text{number of shares outstanding}}$	$15.74	$21.25	$22.99	$18.75

[a]Calculated from data not included within the chapter.
[b]Calculated using the financial statements presented in Tables 3.2 and 3.3. Where average data is required, data external to the chapter was used.
[c]Obtained from sources external to this chapter.

return on common stock equity, and earnings per share seem to have behaved in a fashion similar to its net profit margin over the 1976 to 1978 period. The firm appears to have experienced either a sizable drop in sales between 1976 and 1977 or a rapid expansion in its assets during that period.

The total asset turnover points to a sizable decline in the efficiency of asset utilization between 1976 and 1977. Although in 1978 this ratio rose to a level considerably above the industry average, it appears that the pre-1977 level of efficiency has not yet been achieved. The owners' return as evidenced by the exceptionally high 1978 levels of the return on equity and return on common stock equity seem to suggest that the firm is performing quite well. The fact that earnings per share are not as far in excess of the industry average as these other measures of profitability suggests that during the 1976–1977 period the firm may have sold additional shares of stock to finance the apparent expansion that took place during that period. The relatively stable level of dividends that are below the industry average suggests that the firm is growing: most growth firms pay out low percentages of dividends. The behavior observed earlier in the 1976–1977 period suggests that, indeed, the firm does seem to reflect a growth posture. The firm's growing and high per-share book value also seems consistent with the firm's asset growth as well as its high level of retained earnings (i.e., low dividends relative to amount earned). In summary, it appears that the firm is growing and has recently gone through an expansion in assets, this expansion being financed through the use of debt as well as the sale of additional shares of stock. The 1977–1978 period seems to reflect a period of adjustment and recovery from the rapid growth in assets which occurred during the 1976–1977 period. The firm's sales, profits, and so forth seem to be growing with the increase in size of the operation. In short, the firm apparently is doing quite well in 1978.

SUMMARY

This chapter has presented a discussion of the importance, techniques, and interpretation of financial ratios. The use of financial ratios allows interested parties to make a relative evaluation of certain aspects of a firm's performance. Interested parties typically include prospective and existing stockholders and lenders as well as the firm's management. Owners and lenders are generally concerned only with certain aspects of the firm, whereas management must monitor many aspects of the firm in order to pinpoint any developing problems. Financial ratios are meaningful only when they are compared to other ratio values. Two types of comparison are common—cross-sectional and time-series. Cross-sectional comparisons involve comparing ratios calculated at a given point in time to similar ratios of another firm or an industry average. Values for industry averages are available from various sources. Cross-sectional comparisons allow the firm to determine how it is doing with respect to another closely related company or the industry as a whole. Time-series, or historical, comparisons merely involve comparing the firm's current performance to its performance at a different point in time to determine whether it is improving or regressing. Time-series comparisons are most useful for internal control purposes.

Certain cautions with respect to the use of ratios are in order. There is no absolutely correct value for any ratio. Each industry has certain characteristics that differentiate it from other industries. Even firms within a given industry may have different types of technology, scales of operations, or stages of distribution. The financial analyst should carefully analyze any differences between firms in attempting to determine which of a group of firms is the most financially sound. Often a company will develop its own ratios, tailored to its specific information requirements. The most important point to keep in mind is that ratios should be consistently applied to similar time periods in order to make the most accurate comparisons. The use of audited financial statements is strongly recommended, since unaudited statements do not offer any assurance of accuracy. Attention should also be given to any recognizable differences in accounting methods.

The most common ratios can be divided into three groups—measures of liquidity and activity, measures of debt, and measures of profitability. The overall liquidity or ability of the firm to pay its bills as they come due can be measured by its net working capital, its current ratio, or its acid-test ratio. The liquidity or activity of inventory can be measured by its turnover or average age, that of accounts receivable by the accounts receivable turnover or average age, and that of accounts payable by the accounts payable turnover or average age. Aging procedures can be applied to either accounts receivable or accounts payable to gain further insight into their liquidity. Debt ratios measure both the degree of indebtedness and the ability to service debts. The commonly used measures of indebtedness include the debt ratio, the debt-equity ratio, and the ratio of debt-to-total-capitalization. In general, the higher these ratios are, the more debt the firm has and the more financially risky it is. Measures of the ability to service debts and other contractual obligations such as interest, principal or sinking fund payments, lease payments, and preferred dividends are provided by coverage ratios such as times interest earned, total debt coverage, and overall coverage. The higher these coverage ratios, the better able the firm is expected to meet its fixed payment obligations.

A number of measures of profitability exist. Using a percent income statement, which shows all items as a percentage of sales, we can readily determine the firm's gross profit margin, operating profit margin, and net profit margin. Other measures of profitability include the total asset turnover, the return on investment, the return on equity, the return on common stock equity, and the earnings per share. The DuPont formula is useful in showing the relationship between a firm's net profit margin, its total asset turnover, and the return on investment. The Modified DuPont formula describes the interaction of leverage—the degree of indebtedness—on the return on investment in order to determine the return on equity. Dividends per share and the book value per share are sometimes calculated and considered important by the firm's shareholders.

3-1   How do the viewpoints held by a firm's current and prospective shareholders, creditors, and management with regard to financial ratio analyses of the firm differ? How can these viewpoints be related to the firm's fund-raising ability?

3-2   How can ratio analysis be used for cross-sectional and time-series comparisons? Which type of comparison would be most common for internal analysis? Why?

3-3   Why may analyses of a firm's ratios calculated at several points within the operating year lead to varying results? How might this problem be overcome?

3-4   Financial ratio analysis is often divided into three areas—measures of liquidity and activity, measures of debt, and measures of profitability. What is the purpose of these measures? Which is of greatest concern to prospective and existing creditors?

3-5   What is the best measure of the overall liquidity of a firm? (Discuss net working capital, the current ratio, and the acid-test ratio in your answer.)

3-6   What ratio can be used to measure the liquidity of a firm having very illiquid inventories and accounts receivable? How does it compare to the acid-test ratio?

3-7   Why does the use of averages in calculating various turnovers help to increase the accuracy of these measures? Can you relate the effect of averaging to the seasonal nature of many businesses?

3-8   What is the general relationship between (1) the turnover of inventory, accounts receivable, and accounts payable and (2) the average ages of these items?

3-9   How can the average age of accounts receivable be used to evaluate the effectiveness of the firm's credit department? How can the average age of accounts payable be used for internal control purposes?

3-10 How does the process of aging either accounts receivable or accounts payable work? In what sense does aging accounts provide more information than calculating their average age?

3-11 What is the difference between the debt ratio, the debt-equity ratio, and the ratio of debt to total capitalization? Would lenders consider high values of these ratios more risky than low values? Why or why not?

3-12 What is the difference between times interest earned, total debt coverage, and the overall coverage ratio? How might the values of these measures and the various debt ratios be related?

3-13 How can one reconcile a firm having a high gross profit margin and a low net profit margin? To what must this situation be attributable?

3-14 What is the significance of the firm's return on investment (ROI)? Why is the ROI often considered a measure of both the firm's ability to generate profits through sales and the efficiency of its use of assets? Can this relationship be explained in light of the DuPont formula?

3-15 There are three areas of analysis or concern which are combined in the Modified DuPont formula. What are these concerns and how are they combined to explain the firm's return on equity (ROE)? Can this formula yield useful information through either cross-sectional or time-series analysis?

3-16 What is the difference between the return on common stock equity and earnings per share? How do each of these measures indicate the owner's returns from operations?

PROBLEMS

3-1 The Houston Corporation's total current assets, net working capital, and inventory for each of the past four years is given below.

Ratio	1975	1976	1977	1978
Total current assets	16,950	21,900	22,500	27,000
Net working capital	7,950	9,300	9,900	9,600
Inventory	6,000	6,900	6,900	7,200

a Calculate the firm's current and acid-test ratios for each year. Compare the resulting time series of each measure of liquidity (i.e., net working capital, the current ratio, and the acid-test ratio).

b Comment on the firm's liquidity over the 1975–1978 period.

c If you were told that the Houston Corporation's inventory turnover for each year in the 1975–1978 period and the industry averages were as follows, would this support or conflict with your evaluation in **b**? Why?

Inventory turnover	1975	1976	1977	1978
Houston Corporation	6.3	6.8	7.0	6.4
Industry average	10.6	11.2	10.8	11.0

3-2 The Davis Company has sales of $4,000,000 and has a gross profit margin of 40 percent. Its end-of-quarter inventories are as follows:

Quarter	Inventory
1	400,000
2	800,000
3	1,200,000
4	200,000

a Calculate the firm's inventory turnover and the average age of inventory.

b Assuming the company is in an industry with an average inventory turnover of 2.0, how would you evaluate the liquidity of Davis' inventory?

3-3 An evaluation of the books of Gordon's Supply Company shows the following end-of-year accounts receivable balance, which is believed to consist of amounts originating in the months indicated. The company had annual sales of $3,000,000 of which 80 percent are on a credit basis. The firm extends 30-day credit terms.

Month of origin	Amounts receivable
July	$ 3,875
August	2,000
September	34,025
October	15,100
November	52,000
December	193,000
Year-End Accounts Receivable	$300,000

a   Use the year-end total to evaluate the firm's collection system.

b   Age the accounts receivable in order to obtain additional information. What other observations can you make about the receivable collection policy?

c   If the firm's peak season is from July to December, how would this affect the validity of your conclusion above? Explain.

3-4   The Center City Bank is evaluating the Graham Corporation, which has requested a $4,000,000 loan, in order to determine its leverage and the financial risk involved.

a   Based on the debt ratios for Graham, along with the industry averages and Graham's recent financial statements (presented below), evaluate and recommend appropriate action on the Graham request.

Income Statement
Graham Corporation
December 31, 1978

Net sales		$30,000,000
Less: Cost of goods sold		21,000,000
Gross profits		$ 9,000,000
Less: Operating expenses		
Selling expense	$3,000,000	
Gen. and admin. expense	2,000,000	
Depreciation expense	1,000,000	
Total operating expense		6,000,000
Earnings before interest and taxes		$3,000,000
Less: Interest		1,000,000
Earnings before taxes		$2,000,000
Less: Taxes (.40)		800,000
Earnings After Taxes		$1,200,000

Balance Sheet
Graham Corporation
December 31, 1978

Assets

Current assets	
Cash	$ 1,000,000
Marketable securities	3,000,000
Accounts receivable	12,000,000
Inventories	7,500,000
Total current assets	$23,500,000
Fixed assets	
Land and buildings	$11,000,000
Machinery and equipment	20,500,000
Furniture and fixtures	8,000,000
Total fixed assets	$39,500,000
Less: Accumulated depreciation	13,000,000
Net fixed assets	$26,500,000
Total Assets	$50,000,000

Graham Corporation
Liabilities and stockholders' equity

Current liabilities	
Accrued liabilities	$ 500,000
Notes payable	8,000,000
Accounts payable	8,000,000
Total current liabilities	$16,500,000
Long-term debts[1]	$20,000,000
Stockholders' equity	
Preferred stock[2]	$ 2,500,000
Common stock	
(1 million shares at $5 par)	5,000,000
Paid-in capital in excess of par value	4,000,000
Retained earnings	2,000,000
Total stockholders' equity	$13,500,000
Total Liabilities and Stockholders' Equity	$50,000,000

[1]Required annual principal payments are $800,000.
[2]25,000 shares of $4.00 cumulative outstanding.

Industry Averages

Debt ratio	0.51
Debt-equity ratio	1.07
Debt-to-total-capital ratio	0.46
Times interest earned	7.30
Total debt coverage	2.00
Overall coverage ratio	1.85

b A percent income statement for the Graham Corporation's 1977 operations is presented below. Develop and compare it to the 1978 year-end percent income statement. Which areas require further analysis or investigation?

Percent Income Statement
Graham Corporation
December 31, 1977

Net sales ($35,000,000)		100.0%
Less: Cost of goods sold		65.9%
Gross profits		34.1%
Less: Operating expenses		
Selling expense	12.7%	
Gen. and admin. expense	6.9%	
Depreciation	3.6%	
Total operating expense		23.2%
Earnings before interest and taxes		10.9%
Less: Interest		1.5%
Earnings before taxes		9.4%
Less: Taxes (40%)		3.8%
Earnings After Taxes		5.6%

3-5 Use the following ratio information for Raimer Industries and the industry averages for Raimer's lines of business to
  a Construct the modified DuPont model for both Raimer and the industry.
  b Evaluate Raimer (and the industry) over the three-year period.
  c For Raimer Industries, which areas require further analysis?

	Raimer		
Ratio	**1976**	**1977**	**1978**
Debt ratio	.43	.43	.46
Net profit margin	.059	.058	.049
Total asset turnover	2.11	2.18	2.34

	Industry Averages		
Debt ratio	.40	.41	.39
Net profit margin	.054	.047	.041
Total asset turnover	2.05	2.13	2.15

3-6 Given the following financial statements, historical ratios, and industry averages, calculate the Baker Company's financial ratios for the most recent year. Analyze its overall financial situation from both a time-series and a cross-sectional viewpoint. Break your analysis into an evaluation of the firm's liquidity, debt, and profitability.

Income Statement
Baker Company
December 31, 1978

Net sales		
Cash		$ 300,000
Credit		9,700,000
Total		$10,000,000
Less: Cost of goods sold		7,500,000
Gross profit		$ 2,500,000
Less: Operating expenses		
Selling expense	$300,000	
General and admin.	700,000	
Depreciation	200,000	1,200,000
Operating profits		$ 1,300,000
Less: Interest expense		200,000
Profits before taxes		$ 1,100,000
Less: Taxes (40%)		440,000
Profits after taxes		$ 660,000
Less: Preferred stock		
dividends		50,000
Earnings available for		
common		$ 610,000
Less: Common stock		
dividends		200,000
To Retained Earnings		$ 410,000

Balance Sheet
Baker Company
December 31, 1978

Assets

Current assets		
Cash		$ 200,000
Marketable securities		50,000
Accounts receivable		800,000
Inventories		950,000
Total current assets		$ 2,000,000
Gross fixed assets	$12,000,000	
Less: Accumulated depreciation	3,000,000	
Net fixed assets		$ 9,000,000
Other assets		$ 1,000,000
Total Assets		$12,000,000

Liabilities and stockholders' equity

Current liabilities	
Accrued liabilities	$ 100,000
Notes payable	200,000
Accounts payable[1]	900,000
Total current liabilities	$1,200,000
Long-term debts[2]	$ 3,000,000
Stockholders' equity	
Preferred stock[3]	$ 1,000,000
Common stock (40,000 shares at $75 par)	3,000,000
Paid-in capital in excess of par value	2,800,000
Retained earnings	1,000,000
Total stockholders' equity	$ 7,800,000
Total Liabilities and Stockholders' Equity	$12,000,000

[1]Annual credit purchases of $6,200,000 were made.
[2]The annual principal payment on the long-term debt is $100,000.
[3]The firm has 25,000 shares of $2.00 preferred outstanding.

Historical Data
Baker Company

Data	Year 1976	1977	Industry Average 1978
Current ratio	1.40	1.55	1.85
Net working capital	$760,000	$720,000	$1,600,000
Acid-test ratio	1.00	.92	1.05
Average age of accounts receivable	45.0 days	36.4 days	35.0 days
Inventory turnover	9.52	9.21	8.60
Average age of accounts payable	58.53 days	60.75 days	45.75 days
Debt ratio	0.20	0.20	0.30
Debt-equity ratio	0.25	0.27	0.39
Debt-to-total-capitalization ratio	0.22	0.22	0.27
Gross profit margin	0.30	0.27	0.25
Operating profit margin	0.12	0.12	0.10
Net profit margin	0.067	0.067	0.058
Total asset turnover	0.74	0.80	0.74
Return on investment	0.049	0.054	0.043
Return on common equity	0.078	0.085	0.084
Earnings per share	$8.65	$11.05	$7.45
Dividends per share	$2.60	$ 3.65	$2.46
Book value per share	$140	$150	$175
Times interest earned	8.2	7.3	8.0
Total debt coverage	4.8	4.5	4.5

SELECTED REFERENCES

Altman, Edward I., "Financial Ratios, Discriminant Analysis and the Prediction of Corporate Bankruptcy," *Journal of Finance 23* (September 1968), pp. 589–609.

Beaver, William H., "Financial Ratios as Predictors of Failure," *Empirical Research in Accounting: Selected Studies in Journal of Accounting Research* (1966), pp. 71–111.

Benishay, Haskell, "Economic Information in Financial Ratio Analysis," *Accounting and Business Research 2* (Spring 1971), pp. 174–179.

Carey, Kenneth J., "Persistence of Profitability," *Financial Management 3* (Summer 1974), pp. 43–48.

Chang, Hui-Shyong, and Cheng F. Lee, "Using Pooled Time-Series and Cross-Section Data to Test the Firm and Time Effects in Financial Analysis," *Journal of Financial and Quantitative Analysis* (September 1977), pp. 457–471.

Helfert, Erich A., *Techniques of Financial Analysis,* 4th ed. (Homewood, Ill.: Irwin, 1976), chap. 2.

Horrigan, James C., "A Short History of Financial Ratio Analysis," *Accounting Review 43* (April 1968), pp. 284–294.

———, "The Determination of Long-Term Credit Standing with Financial Ratios," *Empirical Research in Accounting: Selected Studies in Journal of Accounting Research* (1966), pp. 44–62.

Jaedicke, Robert K., and Robert T. Sprouse, *Accounting Flows, Income, Funds and Cash* (Englewood Cliffs, N.J.: Prentice-Hall, 1965), chap. 7.

Lev, Baruch, *Financial Statement Analysis: A New Approach* (Englewood Cliffs, N.J.: Prentice-Hall, 1974), chaps. 2–5.

Meigs, Walter B., A. N. Mosich, Charles E. Johnson, and Thomas F. Keller, *Financial Accounting*, 3rd ed. (New York: McGraw-Hill, 1974), chap. 24.

Murray, Roger, "Lessons for Financial Analysis," *Journal of Finance 26* (May 1971), pp. 327–332.

O'Conner, Melvin C., "On the Usefulness of Financial Ratios to Investors in Common Stock," *Accounting Review 48* (April 1973), pp. 339–352.

Reiling, Henry B., and John C. Burton, "Financial Statements: Signposts as Well as Milestones," *Harvard Business Review* (November-December 1972), pp. 45–54.

Searby, Frederick W., "Return to Return on Investment," *Harvard Business Review 53* (March-April 1975), pp. 113–119.

Seitz, Neil, *Financial Analysis: A Programmed Approach* (Reston, Va.: Reston Publishing Company, 1976).

Troy, Leo, *Almanac of Business and Industrial Financial Ratios* (Englewood Cliffs, N.J.: Prentice-Hall, 1979).

Viscione, Jerry A., *Financial Analysis: Principles and Procedures* (Boston: Houghton Mifflin, 1977).

Weston, J. Fred, "Financial Analysis: Planning and Control," *Financial Executive 33* (July 1965), pp. 40–48.

Wright, Leonard T., *Financial Management: Analytical Techniques* (Columbus, Ohio: Grid, 1974), chap. 2.

CHAPTER 4
Operating, financial, and total leverage

The term *leverage* is quite commonly used to describe the firm's ability to use fixed-cost assets or funds to magnify the returns to its owners. Increasing leverage increases the uncertainty of returns, and at the same time increases the size of the possible return. Leverage occurs in varying degrees; the higher the degree of leverage, the higher the risk—but the higher the expected return. The term *risk* in this context refers to the degree of uncertainty associated with the firm's ability to cover its fixed-payment obligations. The amount of leverage in the firm's structure greatly reflects the type of risk-return trade-off it makes. There are three types of leverage in most business firms—operating leverage, financial leverage, and total leverage. This chapter is devoted to the discussion of each of these types of leverage.

The chapter has five basic sections. The first section briefly describes the income statement framework used to explain the concepts of operating, financial, and total leverage. The second section is devoted to the quite important topic of breakeven analysis. The third section develops the concept of operating leverage using a breakeven analysis framework: it includes an in-depth discussion of the key aspects of operating leverage. The fourth section discusses financial leverage in both algebraic and graphical contexts and introduces the concept of a financial plan. The final section of this chapter discusses total leverage, which reflects the combined impact of operating and financial leverage on the total risk of the firm.

AN INCOME STATEMENT APPROACH TO LEVERAGE

The two basic types of leverage can best be defined with reference to the firm's income statement. Table 4.1 presents a typical income statement format. The portion of the statement related to the firm's operating leverage and the portion related to its financial leverage are clearly labeled. *Operating leverage* is concerned with the relationship between the firm's sales revenue

TABLE 4.1 A general income statement format

Operating Leverage	Sales revenue
	Less: Cost of good sold
	Gross profits
	Less: Operating expenses
	Earnings before interest and taxes (EBIT)
Financial Leverage	Less: Interest
	Earnings before taxes
	Less: Taxes
	Earnings after taxes
	Less: Preferred stock dividends
	Earnings available for common stockholders

and its earnings before interest and taxes.[1] *Financial leverage* is concerned with the relationship between the firm's earnings before interest and taxes and the earnings available for common stockholders.

BREAKEVEN ANALYSIS

Before developing the concept of operating leverage, it is important to understand various aspects of breakeven analysis. An understanding of the key aspects of breakeven analysis provides the framework from which the fundamental aspects of operating leverage can be described. *Breakeven analysis,* which is sometimes called *cost-volume-profit analysis,* is important to the firm since it allows the firm (1) to determine the level of operations it must maintain to cover all of its operating costs and (2) to evaluate the profitability associated with various levels of sales. In order to understand fully breakeven analysis, it is necessary to analyze further the firm's operating costs. An examination of Table 4.1 reveals that in order to calculate the firm's earnings before interest and taxes, the firm's cost of goods sold and operating expenses must be subtracted from its sales revenue. The upper portion of the income statement can be recast as in Table 4.2.

Types of costs

The firm's cost of goods sold and its operating expenses contain fixed- and variable-operating-cost components. In some cases, specific costs may have both fixed and variable elements. The resulting three types of costs are defined below. Figure 4.1 depicts each type graphically.

Fixed costs. These costs are a function of time, not sales, and are typically contractual. They require the payment of a certain number of dollars each accounting period. Rent is a fixed cost.

---

[1]The firm's earnings before interest and taxes are often referred to as "operating profits." Earnings before interest and taxes are used as the pivotal point in defining operating and financial leverage since they divide the firm's income statement into operating and financial portions.

**TABLE 4.2 Operating
leverage and the income statement**

Operating Leverage	Sales revenue Less: Cost of goods sold Less: Operating expenses Earnings before interest and taxes (EBIT)

Variable costs. These costs vary directly with the firm's sales. They are a function of volume, not time. Production and delivery costs are variable costs.

Semivariable costs. Semivariable costs are partly fixed and partly variable.[2] One example of semivariable costs might be salesmen's commissions. These commissions may be fixed over a certain range of volume and increase to higher levels for higher volumes. Such a commission schedule would have both fixed- and variable-cost characteristics.

Determination of the breakeven point
Using the classification scheme described above, the firm's cost of goods sold and its operating expenses can be grouped into fixed and variable costs.[3] The top portion of Table 4.2 can then be recast as shown in Table 4.3. Using

FIGURE 4.1 Types of costs

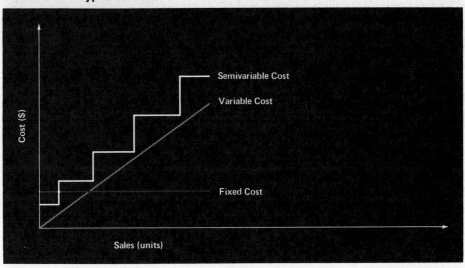

[2]Semivariable costs are sometimes referred to as "semifixed costs." Regardless of how these costs are labeled, they have the characteristics described here.

[3]Semivariable costs are ignored here and in the discussions that follow since they can be broken down into fixed and variable components.

TABLE 4.3 Operating leverage and fixed and variable costs

Operating Leverage	Sales revenue
	Less: Fixed operating costs
	Less: Variable operating costs
	Earnings before interest and taxes (EBIT)

this framework, the firm's breakeven point can be determined either algebraically or graphically.

The algebraic approach. Utilizing the following variable names, the portion of the firm's income statement given in Table 4.3 can be represented as in Table 4.4:

X = sales volume in units
P = sale price per unit
F = fixed operating cost per period
V = variable operating cost per unit

Rewriting the algebraic calculations in Table 4.4 as a formula for earnings before interest and taxes yields Equation 4.1:

$$\text{EBIT} = P \cdot X - F - V \cdot X \tag{4.1}$$

Simplifying Equation 4.1 yields

$$\text{EBIT} = X(P - V) - F \tag{4.2}$$

The firm's *breakeven point* is defined as the level of sales at which all fixed and variable operating costs are covered, that is, the level at which EBIT equals zero.[4] Setting EBIT equal to zero and solving Equation 4.2 for

TABLE 4.4 Algebraic terms in breakeven analysis

Item	Algebraic representation
Sales revenue	$P \cdot X$
Less: Fixed operating costs	$-F$
Less: Variable operating costs	$-V \cdot X$
Earnings before interest and taxes	EBIT

[4] The reader should recognize that the breakeven point defined in this chapter refers to the point at which *all operating costs are covered*, or where EBIT just equals zero. Quite often the breakeven point is calculated so that it represents the point where all operating and financial costs are covered. Our concern in this chapter is not with this overall breakeven point, although its calculation is quite similar.

the firm's sales volume, X, yields

$$X = \frac{F}{P - V} \tag{4.3}$$

This equation is used to find the firm's breakeven volume, X.

EXAMPLE

Assume that a firm has fixed operating costs of $2500, the sale price per unit of its product is $10, and that its variable operating cost per unit is $5. Applying Equation 4.3 to these data yields

$$X = \frac{\$2500}{\$10 - \$5} = \frac{\$2500}{\$5} = 500 \text{ units}$$

At sales of 500 units or $5000 (i.e., $10 · 500 units), the firm's EBIT should just equal zero. ●

In the preceding example, the firm will have positive EBIT for sales greater than 500 units and negative EBIT, or a loss, for sales less than 500 units. The reader can confirm this by substituting values above and below 500 units, along with the other values given, into Equation 4.1.

The graphical approach. The firm's breakeven point can also be calculated graphically. Figure 4.2 presents a graphical breakeven analysis of the data in the preceding example. It has two base-line axes; one represents sales in units, and the other, sales in dollars. Breakeven charts can be presented using either of these axes, but the use of units is the simpler approach.[5]

In Figure 4.2, the firm's breakeven point is the point at which its total operating cost equals its sales revenue. A firm's *total operating cost* is defined as the sum of its fixed and variable operating costs. Using the notation introduced earlier, we can define the equation for the total operating cost as follows:

$$\text{Total operating cost} = F + V \cdot X \tag{4.4}$$

Also depicted in Figure 4.2 are the firm's fixed and variable operating costs. The general cost characteristics defined earlier are exhibited by the lines representing each of these costs.

Figure 4.2 shows that a loss occurs when the firm's sales are below the breakeven point. For sales of less than 500 units ($5000), the firm's total operating costs exceed its sales revenue. For sales levels greater than the breakeven point, EBIT are greater than zero. The absolute amount of the loss increases as the level of sales decreases from the breakeven point; the ab-

[5]A brief discussion of the calculation of breakeven points in terms of dollars is presented in a subsequent part of this section.

FIGURE 4.2 Graphical breakeven analysis

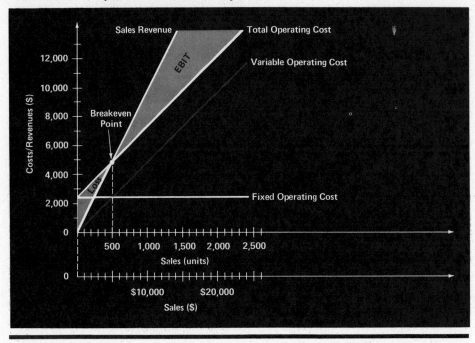

solute amount of EBIT increases as the level of sales increases beyond the breakeven point.

Changing cost relationships and the breakeven point

A firm's breakeven point is sensitive to a number of variables, specifically, fixed operating costs, the sale price per unit, and the variable operating cost per unit. The effects of increases or decreases in each of these variables on the breakeven point are examined below.

Changes in fixed operating costs.

An increase in the firm's fixed operating costs will increase its breakeven point, and a decrease in its fixed operating costs will lower its breakeven point. Consider what would happen if we made some changes in the level of fixed operating costs for the firm described in the preceding example.

If we increased the fixed operating costs to $3000, the breakeven point calculated using Equation 4.3 would be

$$\frac{\$3000}{\$10 - \$5} = 600 \text{ units}$$

If we decreased the fixed operating costs to $2000, the breakeven point would be

FIGURE 4.3 A breakeven graph for increased fixed operating costs

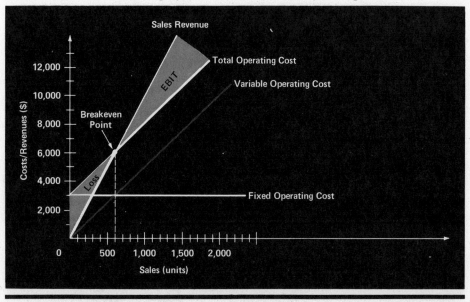

$$\frac{\$2000}{\$10 - \$5} = 400 \text{ units}$$

The effects of an *increase* in fixed operating costs to $3000 on the firm's breakeven point are shown graphically in Figure 4.3.

Changes in the sale price per unit. An increase in the firm's unit sales price will lower the firm's breakeven volume, and a decrease in the firm's unit price will raise the firm's breakeven volume.[6] An increase in the sales price per unit from $10.00 to $12.50 and a decrease from $10.00 to $7.50 would have the following effects on the breakeven point of the firm in our earlier example.

If we increased the sales price to $12.50 per unit, the breakeven point calculated using Equation 4.3 would become

$$\frac{\$2500}{\$12.50 - \$5} = 333\frac{1}{3} \text{ units}$$

If we decreased the sales price to $7.50 per unit, the breakeven point would become

$$\frac{\$2500}{\$7.50 - \$5.00} = 1000 \text{ units}$$

[6]This discussion ignores the effects of changes in the unit sales price on the firm's sales volume. A more in-depth analysis would have to deal with this issue.

FIGURE 4.4 A breakeven graph for increased sale price

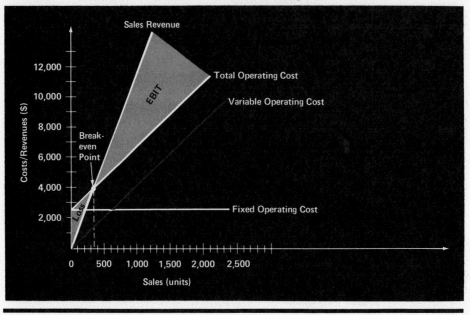

The effects of an *increase* in the sales price to \$12.50 per unit on the firm's breakeven point are shown graphically in Figure 4.4.

Changes in the variable operating cost per unit. An increase in the firm's variable operating cost per unit will raise the firm's breakeven volume, while a decrease in the firm's variable operating cost per unit will lower the firm's breakeven point. The effects of an increase in the variable operating cost per unit from \$5.00 to \$7.50 and a decrease from \$5.00 to \$2.50 per unit on the breakeven point of the firm in the preceding example are calculated below.

If we increased the variable operating cost to \$7.50 per unit, the breakeven point calculated using Equation 4.3 would become

$$\frac{\$2500}{\$10.00 - \$7.50} = 1000 \text{ units}$$

If we decreased variable operating cost to \$2.50 per unit, the breakeven volume would become

$$\frac{\$2500}{\$10.00 - \$2.50} = 333\frac{1}{3} \text{ units}$$

The effects of the *increase* in the variable operating cost per unit to \$7.50 on the firm's breakeven point are illustrated graphically in Figure 4.5.

FIGURE 4.5 A breakeven graph for increased variable operating costs

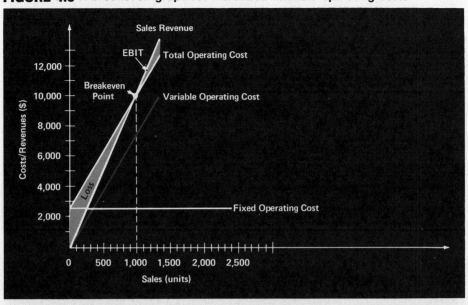

Other approaches to breakeven analysis

Although a wide variety of approaches and techniques can be used to find the breakeven point, space does not permit elaboration of a large number of alternative approaches. Two approaches worthy of attention are (1) measuring the breakeven point in terms of dollars and (2) determining the cash breakeven point. Each of these approaches to breakeven analysis are briefly described below.

Breakeven in dollars. When a firm has more than one product, it is useful to calculate the breakeven point in terms of dollars rather than in terms of units. The use of a dollar breakeven point is especially important for firms that have a variety of products, each selling at a different price. Assuming that the firm's product mix remains relatively constant, the breakeven point can be calculated in terms of dollars by using a contribution margin approach. The *contribution margin* in this case will be defined as the percent of each sales dollar that remains after satisfying the variable costs. Utilizing the following variable names, the firm's dollar breakeven point can be defined.

S = total sales revenue in dollars
TV = total variable operating costs paid to achieve S dollars of sales
F = total fixed operating costs paid during the period in which S dollars of sales are achieved

It is important to recognize that in the case of a single-product firm, using the notation presented earlier, $S = P \cdot X$ and $TV = V \cdot X$.

The variable cost per dollar of sales can be represented as $TV \div S$. Subtracting the variable cost per dollar sold, $TV \div S$, from one will yield the contribution margin, which reflects the per-dollar contribution toward meeting fixed operating costs and profits provided by each dollar of sales.

$$\text{Contribution margin} = 1 - \frac{TV}{S} \tag{4.5}$$

The level of EBIT at any level of sales, D, can be found by multiplying the contribution margin by D, and subtracting the fixed costs, F. The similarity between Equation 4.6 and Equation 4.1 presented earlier

$$\text{EBIT} = D(1 - \frac{TV}{S}) - F \tag{4.6}$$

should be quite clear. To find the dollar breakeven point, we set EBIT equal to zero and solve Equation 4.6 for D. The resulting expression for the dollar breakeven point is given in Equation 4.7 below:

$$D = \frac{F}{(1 - \frac{TV}{S})} \tag{4.7}$$

This equation is used to find a firm's breakeven point in dollars, D.

EXAMPLE
Assume that during a period a firm has fixed operating costs of $100,000, total sales of $800,000, and total variable operating costs of $600,000. Applying Equation 4.7 to these data yields

$$D = \frac{\$100,000}{(1 - \frac{\$600,000}{\$800,000})} = \frac{\$100,000}{.25} = \$400,000$$

Assuming the firm's product mix does not change at a $400,000 sales level, the firm will break even on its operation—its EBIT will just equal zero. ●

Cash breakeven analysis. Because it is quite common for a firm's reported costs to result from the application of accrual concepts rather than a strict cash-flow approach, it is often useful to perform a cash breakeven analysis. This type of analysis recognizes that a firm's cash receipts and payments may not correspond with the recognition of income and expense. Although a variety of differences may result from the existence of accounts receivable and accounts payable, the key items requiring attention in the cash breakeven analysis are noncash charges such as depreciation. Any charges, such as these, that are included as part of the firm's fixed costs must be adjusted in preparing a cash breakeven analysis. The presence of such noncash charges as part of the firm's fixed costs tends to overstate the firm's breakeven point. Assuming that the firm has noncash charges, N, included in its fixed costs, Equation 4.3 can be rewritten for the cash breakeven point as given in Equation 4.8.

$$\text{Cash breakeven point} = \frac{F - N}{P - V} \tag{4.8}$$

EXAMPLE
Assume that the firm presented in the example on page 103 had included in its fixed operating costs of \$2500, \$1500 of depreciation. Substituting this information along with the firm's \$10 per unit sale price and \$5 per unit variable operating cost into Equation 4.8 yields the following:

$$\text{Cash breakeven point} = \frac{\$2500 - \$1500}{\$10 - \$5} = \frac{\$1000}{\$5} = 200 \text{ units}$$

The firm's cash breakeven point would therefore be 200 units, which is considerably below the 500-unit breakeven point calculated earlier using accounting data. This difference can be seen graphically in Figure 4.6, in which point A represents the original breakeven point (500 units) and point B represents the cash breakeven point (200 units). ●

It is important to recognize that while the cash breakeven analysis provides a convenient mechanism for assessing the level of sales necessary to meet the firm's cash operating costs, it is not a substitute for detailed cash plans. Chapter 5 will provide a discussion of the more formal techniques available for analyzing and budgeting the firm's cash flows.

Weaknesses in breakeven analysis

Although breakeven analysis is widely used by business firms, it has a number of inherent weaknesses. The major criticisms of this type of analysis stem from its assumption of linearity, its cost classifications, the difficulty of multi-product applications, and its short-term nature.

The assumption of linearity. Generally, neither the firm's sale price per unit nor its variable cost per unit is independent of sales volume. In most cases, increase in sales beyond a certain point are achieved only by lowering the firm's price per unit. This results in a *curved*, rather than a straight, total revenue function. The firm's variable operating cost per unit normally increases as the firm approaches capacity. This may result from a decrease in the efficiency of labor or an increase in overtime wages. Figure 4.7 shows a graphic breakeven analysis using nonlinear revenue and variable-operating-cost functions. It illustrates that when a firm has nonlinear sales revenue and variable-operating-cost functions, the maximum earnings before interest and taxes may occur at a level of sales below the obtainable maximum. An examination of the breakeven analysis with linear sales revenue and variable-operating-cost functions in Figures 4.2–4.6 indicates that as long as sales increase, profits will also increase; that is, in order to maximize the

FIGURE 4.6 A cash breakeven analysis

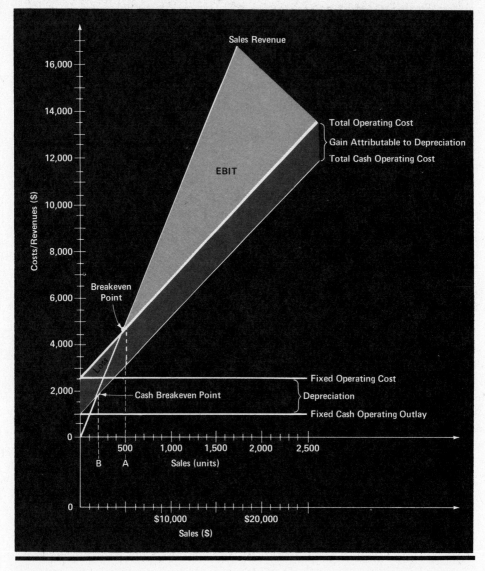

EBIT, sales should be maximized. This relationship does not hold when one evaluates the situation using nonlinear revenue and cost functions.

   Cost classifications.   A second weakness of breakeven analysis is the difficulty of classifying semivariable costs, which are fixed over certain ranges but vary between them. In some cases, it may not be possible to break these costs into fixed and variable components for breakeven analysis.

   Multi-product applications.   A third weakness of breakeven analysis is the difficulty of applying it to multiple-product operations. If each product

FIGURE 4.7 **A nonlinear breakeven analysis**

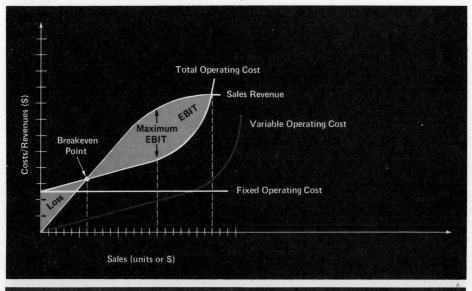

is analyzed separately, it is difficult to divide the costs between products. Although the use of breakeven analysis using dollars instead of units partially overcomes this criticism, it does not allow the firm having a number of products to determine the level of sales required by product in order to cover the related operating costs. More sophisticated multi-product breakeven models do exist, but will not be discussed here.

Short-term nature. A final weakness of breakeven analysis is its short-term nature. It is typically applied to one year's projected operations. If a firm makes a large outlay for advertising or incurs some other major expense whose benefits are not expected to be visible in the current period, these expenses will still add to the current period's total operating costs and raise the breakeven volume. Since the benefits of these outlays are not received in the current period, one may question their inclusion in the breakeven analysis for that period. Items such as advertising and research and development expenditures fall in this category. Care should be exercised when those types of outlays are planned.

OPERATING LEVERAGE

Operating leverage results from the existence of fixed operating costs in the firm's income stream. By definition these fixed operating costs do not vary with sales and therefore must be paid regardless of the amount of revenue available. Using the framework presented in Table 4.3, the firm's *operating leverage* can be defined as the firm's ability to use fixed operating costs to magnify the effects of changes in sales on its earnings before interest and taxes.

FIGURE 4.8 Breakeven analysis and operating leverage

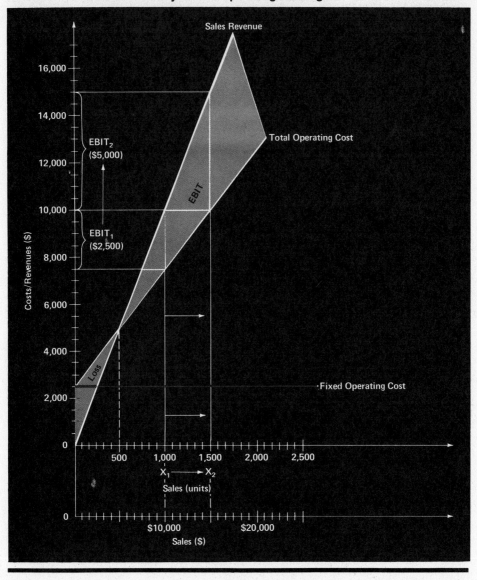

Operating leverage illustrated

Operating leverage can be illustrated conveniently using the data presented earlier (i.e., sale price, $P = \$10$ per unit; variable operating cost, $V = \$5$ per unit; fixed operating costs, $F = \$2500$). Figure 4.8 presents the breakeven chart for these data, which was originally shown in Figure 4.2. It can be seen from the additional notations placed on the chart that as the firm's sales increase from 1000 units to 1500 units (X_1 to X_2), its EBIT increases from $2500 to $5000 (EBIT$_1$ to EBIT$_2$). In order words, a 50-percent increase in sales (i.e., 1000 to 1500 units) results in a 100-percent increase in EBIT

TABLE 4.5 EBIT for various sales levels

	Case 2		Case 1
	−50%		+50%
Sales (in units)	500	1,000	1,500
Sales revenue[a]	$5,000	$10,000	$15,000
Less: Variable operating costs[b]	2,500	5,000	7,500
Less: Fixed operating costs	2,500	2,500	2,500
Earnings before interest and taxes (EBIT)	$ 0	$ 2,500	$ 5,000
	−100%		+100%

[a]Sales revenue = $10/unit · sales in units
[b]Variable operating costs = $5/unit · sales in units

($2500 to $5000). Table 4.5 includes the data relating to Figure 4.8 as well as relevant data associated with a 500-unit sales level. Using the 1000-unit sales level as a reference point, two cases can be illustrated.

CASE 1:
   A 50-percent *increase* in sales (from 1000 to 1500 units) results in a 100-percent *increase* in earnings before interest and taxes (from $2500 to $5000).

CASE 2:
   A 50-percent *decrease* in sales (from 1000 to 500 units) results in a 100-percent *decrease* in earnings before interest and taxes (from $2500 to zero).

These two cases illustrate the fact that operating leverage works in both directions and that when a firm has fixed operating costs, operating leverage is present. An increase in sales results in a greater than proportional increase in earnings before interest and taxes, while a decrease in sales results in a more than proportional decrease in earnings before interest and taxes.

Measuring the degree of operating leverage (DOL)
   The degree of operating leverage can be measured using the following equation.[7]

$$DOL = \frac{\text{percentage change in EBIT}}{\text{percentage change in sales}} \tag{4.9}$$

Whenever the percentage change in EBIT resulting from a given percentage change in sales is greater than the percentage change in sales, operating

[7]The degree of operating leverage is also a function of the base level of sales used. The closer the base sales level used as point of reference is to the breakeven level of sales, the more operating leverage there is. A comparison of the operating-leverage ratio of two firms is valid only when the base level of sales used for each firm is the same.

leverage exists. This means that as long as DOL is greater than one, there is operating leverage. Applying Equation 4.9 to Case 1 and Case 2 yields the following results:[8]

Case 1: $\dfrac{+100\%}{+50\%} = 2.0$

Case 2: $\dfrac{-100\%}{-50\%} = 2.0$

Since the resulting quotient is greater than 1, operating leverage exists. For a given level of sales, the higher the value resulting from applying Equation 4.9, the greater the operating leverage.

A more direct formula for calculating the degree of operating leverage at a base sales level, X, is given by Equation 4.10 using the notation given earlier:

$$\text{DOL at base sales level } X = \frac{X(P - V)}{X(P - V) - F} \tag{4.10}$$

Substituting $X = 1000$, $P = \$10$, $V = \$5$, and $F = \$2500$ into Equation 4.10 yields the following result:

$$\text{DOL at 1000 units} = \frac{1000(\$10 - \$5)}{1000(\$10 - \$5) - \$2500} = \frac{\$5000}{\$2500} = 2.0$$

It should be clear that the use of the formula given in Equation 4.10 provides a more direct method for calculating the degree of operating leverage than the approach illustrated using Table 4.5 and Equation 4.9.[9]

Fixed costs and operating leverage

Changes in a firm's fixed operating costs significantly affect the firm's operating leverage. Assume that the firm discussed in the preceding section is able to exchange a portion of its variable operating costs for fixed operating costs. This exchange results in the variable operating cost per unit being reduced from $5.00 to $4.50 while the fixed operating costs are increased to

---

[8]Because the concept of leverage is *linear*, positive and negative changes of equal magnitude will always result in equal degrees of leverage when the same base sales level is used as a point of reference. This relationship holds for all types of leverage discussed in this chapter.

[9]When total dollar figures—instead of unit sales figures—are available, the following equation in which S = dollar level of base sales and TV = total variable operating costs in dollars can be used.

$$\text{DOL at base dollar sales } S = \frac{S - TV}{S - TV - F} \tag{a}$$

This formula is especially useful for finding the DOL for multiproduct firms. It should be clear that since in the case of a single product firm $S = P \cdot X$ and $TV = V \cdot X$, substitution of these values into Equation 4.10 would result in Equation (a) above.

TABLE 4.6 Operating leverage and increased fixed costs

	Case 2		Case 1
	−50%		+50%
Sales (in units)	500	1,000	1,500
Sales revenue[a]	$5,000	$10,000	$15,000
Less: Variable operating costs[b]	2,250	4,500	6,750
Less: Fixed operating costs	3,000	3,000	3,000
Earnings before interest and taxes (EBIT)	$ −250	$ 2,500	$ 5,250
	−110%		+110%

[a]Sales revenue was calculated as indicated in Table 4.5.
[b]Variable operating costs = $4.50/unit · sales in units.

$3000. Table 4.6 presents an analysis similar to that given in Table 4.5 using these new costs. Although the EBIT of $2500 at the 1000-unit sales level is the same as that before the shift in operating cost structure, it should be clear from Table 4.6 that by shifting to greater fixed costs (and fewer variable costs) the firm has increased its leverage. With the substitution of the appropriate values into Equation 4.10, the degree of operating leverage at the 1000-unit base level of sales becomes

$$\text{DOL at 1000 units} = \frac{1000(\$10 - \$4.50)}{1000(\$10 - \$4.50) - \$3000} = \frac{\$5500}{\$2500} = 2.2$$

Comparing this value to the DOL of 2.0 before the shift to more fixed costs should make it quite clear that the higher the firm's fixed costs relative to its variable costs, the greater the degree of operating leverage.

Since leverage works both ways—it magnifies losses as well as gains—the shift in cost structure toward more fixed costs tends to increase the magnitude of potential losses. This increased risk is quite clear when one compares the breakeven points before and after the shift. Before the shift, the firm's breakeven point is found to be 500 units [i.e., $2500 ÷ ($10 − $5)], while after the shift the breakeven point becomes 545 units [i.e., $3000 ÷ ($10 − $4.50)]. The increased breakeven point reflects the fact that the firm must achieve a higher level of sales in order to meet the increased fixed operating costs.

Operating risk

Operating risk is the risk of being unable to cover operating costs. We have seen that as a firm's fixed operating costs increase the volume of sales necessary for it to cover all its operating costs increases. In other words, as a firm increases its fixed operating costs, the sales volume necessary to break even increases. The breakeven point is a good measure of the firm's operating risk. The higher a firm's breakeven point, the greater degree of operating risk that is present.

In exchange for increasing levels of operating risk, the firm achieves higher operating leverage. The benefit of this is that the firm's EBIT increases at a faster rate for a given increase in unit sales. The financial manager must decide on the level of operating risk that is tolerable. He, or she, must recognize the risk-return trade-off that is in operation. As he increases operating leverage through increased fixed operating costs, the firm's breakeven volume increases; but the degree to which increased sales magnify EBIT also increases. In other words, increased operating risks are justified on the basis of the increased operating returns that are expected to result as sales increase. It is the responsibility of the financial manager to make decisions consistent with the maintenance of a desired level of operating leverage.

FINANCIAL LEVERAGE

Financial leverage results from the presence of fixed *financial* charges in the firm's income stream.[10] These fixed charges do not vary with the firm's earnings before interest and taxes; they must be paid regardless of the amount of EBIT available to pay them. An examination of the lower portion of Table 4.1 indicates that the two financial charges normally found on the firm's income statement are (1) interest on debt and (2) preferred stock dividends. Financial leverage is concerned with the effects of changes in earnings before interest and taxes on the earnings available for the common stockholders. Throughout the following analysis, it is assumed that all preferred stock dividends are paid. This assumption is required in order to measure the amount of money actually available to be distributed to common shareholders.[11]

Financial leverage is defined as the firm's ability to use fixed financial charges to magnify the effects of changes in earnings before interest and taxes on the firm's earnings per share (eps). Earnings per share are commonly considered instead of earnings available *for* common stock because eps measure the returns available to each shareholder; the calculation of earnings per share was discussed in Chapter 3. Taxes, as well as the financial costs of interest and preferred stock dividends, are deducted from the firm's income stream. However, these taxes do not represent a fixed cost, since they change with changes in the level of earnings before taxes (EBT). Since taxes are a variable cost, they have no direct effect on the firm's financial leverage.

Financial leverage illustrated

A firm expects earnings before interest and taxes of $10,000 in the current year. It has a $40,000 bond with a 5-percent coupon and an issue of 600 shares of $4.00 preferred stock outstanding; it also has 1000 shares of common

[10]The term "trading on the equity" is often used interchangeably with "financial leverage."

[11]Preferred stock dividends may be *passed* (unpaid) during a period, but only if no dividends are paid to the common shareholders either. Preferred stock is generally such that unpaid dividends accrue and must be satisfied prior to any distribution of earnings to common stockholders. A more in-depth discussion of the characteristics of preferred stock is included in Chapter 22.

TABLE 4.7 The eps for various EBIT levels

		Case 2		Case 1
		−40%		+40%
EBIT		$6,000	$10,000	$14,000
Less: Interest (I)		2,000	2,000	2,000
Earnings before taxes (EBT)		$4,000	$ 8,000	$12,000
Less: Taxes (T) (40%)		1,600	3,200	4,800
Earnings after taxes (EAT)		$2,400	$ 4,800	$ 7,200
Less: Preferred stock dividends (PD)		2,400	2,400	2,400
Earnings available for common (EAC)		$ 0	$ 2,400	$ 4,800

Earnings per share (eps) $\dfrac{\$0}{1000} = \$0/\text{sh.}$ $\dfrac{\$2400}{1000} = \$2.40/\text{sh.}$ $\dfrac{\$4800}{1000} = \$4.80/\text{sh.}$

−100%   +100%

stock outstanding. The annual interest on the bond issue is $2000 (.05 × $40,000). The annual dividends on the preferred stock are $2400 ($4.00/share × 600 shares). Table 4.7 presents the levels of earnings per share resulting from levels of earnings before interest and taxes of $6000, $10,000, and $14,000 for a firm in the 40-percent tax bracket. Two situations are illustrated in the table.

CASE 1:
A 40-percent *increase* in EBIT (from $10,000 to $14,000) results in a 100 percent *increase* in earnings per share (from $2.40 to $4.80).

CASE 2:
A 40-percent *decrease* in EBIT (from $10,000 to $6000) results in a 100-percent *decrease* in earnings per share (from $2.40 to $0).

Table 4.7 indicates that financial leverage works in both directions and that financial leverage exists when a firm has fixed financial charges. The effect of financial leverage is such that an increase in the firm's EBIT results in a greater than proportional increase in the firm's earnings per share, while a decrease in the firm's EBIT results in a more than proportional decrease in the firm's eps.

Measuring the degree of financial leverage (DFL)

The degree of financial leverage can be measured in a fashion similar to that used to measure the degree of operating leverage. The following equation presents one approach for measuring DFL.[12]

[12]This statement is true only when the base levels of EBIT used in calculating the quotients are the same. The base EBIT must be kept constant in order to compare the leverage associated with different levels of fixed financial costs.

$$\text{DFL} = \frac{\text{percentage change in eps}}{\text{percentage change in EBIT}} \tag{4.11}$$

Whenever the percentage change in eps resulting from a given percentage change in EBIT is greater than the percentage change in EBIT, financial leverage exists. This means that whenever DFL is greater than one, financial leverage exists. Applying Equation 4.11 to Case 1 and Case 2 yields

Case 1: $\dfrac{+100\%}{+40\%} = 2.5$

Case 2: $\dfrac{-100\%}{-40\%} = 2.5$

In both cases, the quotient is greater than 1 and financial leverage exists. The higher this quotient is, the greater the degree of financial leverage a firm has.

A more direct formula for calculating the degree of financial leverage at a base level of EBIT is given by Equation 4.12.

$$\text{DFL for given EBIT} = \frac{\text{EBIT}}{\text{EBIT} - I - PD \cdot [1/(1-t)]} \tag{4.12}$$

Substituting EBIT = $10,000, I = $2000, PD = $2400, and the tax rate ($t$ = .40) into Equation 4.12 yields the following result:

DFL at $10,000 EBIT

$$= \frac{\$10,000}{\$10,000 - \$2000 - \$2400\,[1/(1-.40)]} = \frac{\$10,000}{\$4000} = 2.5$$

It should be apparent that the formula given in Equation 4.12 provides a more direct method for calculating the degree of financial leverage than the approach illustrated using Table 4.7 and Equation 4.11.

Because financial leverage, like operating leverage, works in both directions, magnifying the effects of both increases and decreases in the firm's EBIT, higher levels of risk are again attached to higher degrees of leverage. High fixed financial costs thus increase the firm's financial leverage *and* its financial risk, and the financial manager must keep this in mind when making financing decisions.

A graphical presentation of a financing plan[13]

A financing plan that consisted of $40,000 of 5-percent bonds, 600 shares of $4 preferred stock, and 1000 shares of common stock was used to illustrate financial leverage in Table 4.7. This financing plan can be illustrated graph-

---

[13]*Financing plan* refers to the firm's mix of sources of long-term financing (e.g., long-term debt, preferred stock, and common stock).

ically; like all plans of this type, it can be plotted as a straight line. This is because it is affected only by the deduction of certain fixed dollar costs. Plotting two values of EBIT—$10,000 and $14,000—and associated earnings per share of $2.40 and $4.80 gives us the line in Figure 4.9.

This line shows the earnings per share associated with each level of EBIT. It is interesting to note that the line intersects the EBIT axis at $6000. This value of EBIT represents the level at which the firm's earnings per share are equal to zero. This zero intercept can be verified by looking at Case 2 in Table 4.7. At levels of EBIT below $6000, the firm would have negative eps. This portion of the graph has not been included.

A graphical illustration of different degrees of financial leverage

The type of graphical presentation in Figure 4.9 can be used to illustrate differences in financial leverage. Suppose we want to compare the financing plan in the preceding example with an alternate plan. The alternate plan involves $20,000 of 5-percent debt, 300 shares of $4 preferred stock, and 1750 shares of common stock. The annual interest payment will be $1000 (.05 × $20,000) and the annual preferred dividend payment will be $1200 ($4/sh. × 300 sh.). In order to graph this plan, two sets of EBIT-eps coordinates are required. The eps associated with EBIT values of $10,000 and $14,000 are calculated below.

+40%

EBIT	$10,000	$14,000
−I	1,000	1,000
EBT	$ 9,000	$13,000
−T(40%)	3,600	5,200
EAT	$ 5,400	7,800
−PD	1,200	1,200
EAC	$ 4,200	$ 6,600

eps $\dfrac{\$4200}{1750} = \$2.40/\text{sh.}$ $\dfrac{\$6600}{1750} = \$3.77/\text{sh.}$

+57%

A 40-percent increase in the firm's EBIT will result in a 57-percent increase in eps. Applying Equation 4.12 to these values yields

DFL at $10,000 EBIT

$$= \frac{\$10,000}{\$10,000 - \$1000 - \$1200 \cdot [1/(1 - .40)]} = \frac{\$10,000}{\$7000} = 1.4$$

The value of 1.4, when compared to the financial leverage value of 2.5 calculated earlier, indicates that this plan has a lower degree of financial lever-

FIGURE 4.9 A graphical presentation of a financing plan

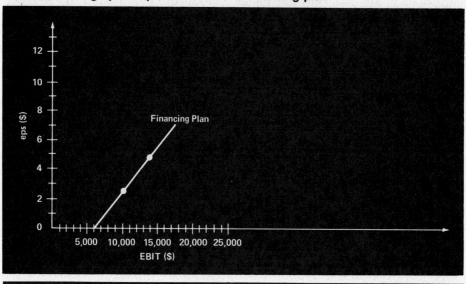

age than the plan presented initially. Each of these plans is graphed in Figure 4.10. The original plan, first graphed in Figure 4.9 is labeled plan A; the current plan is labeled plan B.

As Figure 4.10 illustrates, the slope of plan A is steeper than that of plan B. This indicates that plan A has more financial leverage than plan B. This result is as expected, since the ratio of the degree of financial leverage (DFL) is 2.5 for plan A and 1.4 for plan B. The higher the DFL is, the more leverage a plan has. The reader should recognize from Figure 4.10 that financing plans with higher degrees of leverage have steeper slopes when plotted on EBIT-eps axes.

The point of intersection of each plan with the EBIT axis represents the amount of earnings before interest and taxes necessary for the firm to cover its fixed financial charges, that is, the point at which eps = 0. This point of intersection can be thought of as a *financial breakeven point,* since it represents the level of EBIT necessary for the firm to just cover its fixed financial charges. The breakeven EBIT for plan A is $6000, and for plan B it is $3000. In other words, earnings before interest and taxes of less than $6000 with plan A or less than $3000 with plan B will result in a loss, or negative eps.

The point labeled X in Figure 4.10 represents the point of intersection between plan A and plan B. It indicates that at a level of EBIT of $10,000, eps of $2.40 would result under either plan. At levels of EBIT below $10,000, plan B results in higher levels of eps; while at levels of EBIT above $10,000, plan A results in higher levels of eps. The usefulness of this type of analysis is discussed in Chapter 18, in the section on methods of evaluating financing plans.

FIGURE 4.10 A graphical presentation of alternate financing plans

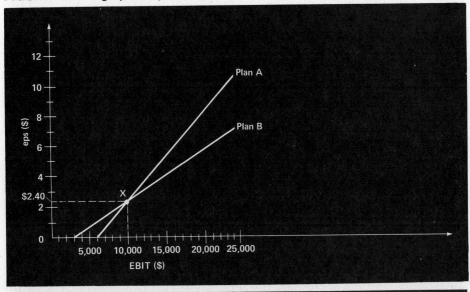

Financial risk

Financial risk is the risk of being unable to cover financial costs. The discussion of financial leverage stressed the fact that as financial charges increase the level of EBIT necessary to cover the firm's financial charges also increases. Increasing financial leverage results in increasing risk, since increased financial payments require the firm to maintain a higher level of EBIT in order to stay in business. If the firm cannot cover these financial payments, it can be forced out of business by creditors whose claims are unsettled.[14]

Financial leverage is often measured by a simple ratio such as the debt-equity ratio, times-interest earned, or the ratio of long-term debt plus preferred stock to total capitalization. Each of these ratios indicates the relationship between the funds on which fixed financial charges must be paid and the total funds invested in the firm. Many analysts calculate these ratios in order to determine how financially "levered" a firm is. As in the case of operating risk, the expected returns to owners normally increase with increases in the degree of financial leverage, but at the same time the risk associated with the returns grows because of the higher levels of EBIT necessary for the firm to survive. Once EBIT greater than the minimum needed for survival are reached, the benefits of financial leverage begin; as long as

---

[14]Preferred stockholders do not have the power to force liquidation if their claims are unpaid. The problem with not paying preferred stock dividends is that the common shareholders can receive no dividends.

the firm meets its fixed financial charges, the rewards to the owners will be greater than they otherwise would have been. It is the responsibility of the financial manager to make decisions consistent with the maintenance of a desired degree of financial leverage.

TOTAL LEVERAGE: THE COMBINED EFFECT

The combined effect of operating and financial leverage on the firm's risk can be assessed using a framework similar to that used to develop the concepts of operating and financial leverage. This combined effect, or *total leverage*, can be defined as the firm's ability to use fixed costs, both operating and financial, to magnify the effect of changes in sales on the firm's earnings per share. Total leverage therefore can be viewed as reflecting the total impact of the fixed costs in the firm's operating and financial structure.

Total leverage illustrated

A firm expects sales of 20,000 units in the coming year and must meet the following: variable operating costs of $2.00 per unit, fixed operating costs of $10,000, interest of $20,000, and preferred stock dividends of $12,000. The firm is in the 40-percent tax bracket and has 5000 shares of common stock outstanding. Table 4.8 presents the levels of earnings per share (eps) associated with the expected sales of 20,000 units and with sales of 30,000 units.

The table illustrates that as a result of a 50-percent increase in sales (20,000 to 30,000 units), the firm would experience a 300-percent increase in earnings per share ($1.20 to $4.80). Although not shown in the table, a 50-percent decrease in sales would, conversely, result in a 300-percent decrease in earnings per share. The linear nature of the leverage relationship accounts for the fact that sales changes of equal magnitude in opposite directions result in earnings per share changes of equal magnitude in the corresponding direction. At this point, it should be quite clear that whenever a firm has fixed costs—operating or financial—in its structure, the total leverage effect will exist.

Measuring the degree of total leverage (DTL)

The degree of total leverage can be measured in a fashion similar to that used to measure operating and financial leverage. The following equation presents one approach for measuring DTL.[15]

$$DTL = \frac{\text{percentage change in eps}}{\text{percentage change in sales}} \qquad (4.13)$$

Whenever the percentage change in eps resulting from a given percentage change in sales is greater than the percentage change in sales, total leverage

---

[15]This statement is true only when the base level of sales used to calculate and compare such quotients are the same. In other words, the base level of sales must be held constant in order to compare the total leverage associated with different levels of fixed costs.

TABLE 4.8 The total leverage effect

	+50%	
Sales (in units)	20,000	30,000
Sales revenue[a]	$100,000	$150,000
Less: Variable operating costs[b]	40,000	60,000
Less: Fixed operating costs	10,000	10,000
Earnings before interest and taxes (EBIT)	$ 50,000	$ 80,000

$$DOL = \frac{60\%}{50\%} = 1.2$$

$$+60\%$$

Less: Interest	20,000	20,000
Earnings before taxes	$30,000	$60,000
Less: Taxes (40%)	12,000	24,000
Earnings after taxes	$18,000	$36,000
Less: Preferred stock dividends	12,000	12,000
Earnings available for common	$ 6,000	$24,000

$$DFL = \frac{300\%}{60\%} = 5.0$$

Earnings per share (eps) $\dfrac{\$6,000}{5,000} = \$1.20/sh.$ $\dfrac{\$24,000}{5,000} = \$4.80/sh.$

$$+300\%$$

[a]Sales revenue = $5/unit · sales in units.
[b]Variable operating costs = $2/unit · sales in units.

exists. This means that, as long as the DTL is greater than one, total leverage exists. Applying Equation 4.13 to the data in Table 4.8 yields

$$DTL = \frac{300\%}{50\%} = 6.0$$

Since this quotient is greater than 1, total leverage exists. The higher this quotient is, the greater the degree of total leverage a firm has.

A more direct formula for calculating the degree of total leverage at a given base level of sales, X, is given by Equation 4.14, which uses the same notation presented earlier:

$$DTL \text{ at base sales } X = \frac{X(P - V)}{X(P - V) - F - I - PD \cdot [1/(1-t)]} \tag{4.14}$$

Substituting $X = 20,000$, $P = \$5$, $V = \$2$, $F = \$10,000$, $I = \$20,000$, and $PD = \$10,000$, and the tax rate ($t = .40$) into Equation 4.14 yields the following result:

DTL at 20,000 units

$$= \frac{20,000(\$5 - \$2)}{20,000(\$5-\$2) - \$10,000 - \$20,000 - \$12,000 \cdot [1/(1-.4)]}$$

$$= \frac{\$60,000}{\$10,000} = 6.0$$

Clearly the formula given in Equation 4.14 provides a more direct method for calculating the degree of total leverage than the approach illustrated using Table 4.8 and Equation 4.13.

Since total leverage, like operating and financial leverage, works in both directions, magnifying the effects of both increases and decreases in the firm's sales, higher levels of risk are attached to higher degrees of total leverage. High fixed costs thus increase the firm's total leverage *and* its total risk; the financial manager must keep this in mind when making both operating and financing decisions.

The relationship between operating, financial, and total leverage

Total leverage merely reflects the combined impact of operating and financial leverage upon the firm. High operating and financial leverage will cause the firm's total leverage to be high. The opposite will also be true. It is important to recognize that the relationship between operating and financial leverage is a multiplicative rather than an additive one. The relationship between the degree of total leverage (DTL) and the degrees of operating (DOL) and financial (DFL) leverage is given by Equation 4.15.

$$DTL = DOL \cdot DFL \tag{4.15}$$

Substituting the values calculated for DOL and DFL, shown in the right-hand column of Table 4.8, into Equation 4.15 yields

$$DTL = 1.2 \cdot 5.0 = 6.0$$

The resulting degree of total leverage of 6.0 is the same value that was calculated directly in the previous section. The fact that the combined effect of operating and financial leverage on the firm's total leverage is multiplicative rather than additive should be quite clear from this illustration.

Total risk

In a relationship similar to operating leverage and operating risk and financial leverage and financial risk, total leverage reflects the total risk of the firm. The firm's *total risk* is therefore the risk associated with the ability to cover the firm's operating and financial costs. With increasing costs—especially fixed operating and financial costs—comes increasing risk since the firm will have to achieve a higher level of sales just to break even. If a firm is unable to meet these costs, it could be forced out of business by its creditors. Although with higher levels of fixed cost comes higher total risk, the magnifying effect of these fixed costs can provide higher levels of return than would otherwise be available. The total risk of the firm is therefore the result of its operating and financial risks. Since the financial manager in the process of making operating and financing decisions affects the level of total risk, it is important that he or she understand the impact of this risk on the risk-return behavior of the firm.

SUMMARY

Breakeven analysis is used to measure the level of sales necessary to cover a firm's total operating costs. The breakeven point can be measured in units or dollars of sales. It may be calculated algebraically or determined graphically. Below the breakeven point, the firm experiences a loss; above the breakeven point, the firm's earnings before interest and taxes are greater than zero. Breakeven points are sensitive to changes in fixed costs, variable costs, and the selling price of the firm's product. As fixed costs increase, the breakeven point increases, and vice versa. As the sale price per unit increases, the breakeven point decreases, and vice versa. Increases in the variable cost per unit increase the breakeven point, and, again, vice versa. Breakeven analysis can be performed on a cash basis by deducting any noncash expenses such as depreciation from the fixed costs and then determining the breakeven point. Breakeven analysis suffers from a number of weaknesses, chief among which are an assumption of linearity, the difficulty of classifying costs as required, the problems caused by multi-product situations, and its short-term nature.

Operating leverage is closely related to breakeven analysis. It is defined as the ability of the firm to use fixed operating costs to magnify the effects of changes in the firm's sales on its earnings before interest and taxes (EBIT). The higher the firm's fixed operating costs, the greater will be its operating leverage. The degree of operating leverage at a specified level of sales can be calculated in either of two ways. Because as the firm's fixed operating costs increase, the volume of sales necessary to cover these costs also increases (and vice versa), the firm's operating risk is directly related to its degree of operating leverage.

Financial leverage is defined as the ability of the firm to use fixed financial costs in order to magnify the effects of changes in earnings before interest and taxes (EBIT) on the firm's earnings per share (eps). The higher the firm's fixed financial costs—typically interest and preferred stock dividends—the greater is its financial leverage. The degree of financial leverage at a given level of earnings before interest and taxes can be calculated in either of two ways. Financial leverage can be viewed graphically, and the level of earnings before interest and taxes necessary to cover all fixed financial charges can be considered a type of financial breakeven point. When various financing plans are graphed on a set of EBIT-eps axes, the differing levels of financial leverage are reflected in the slopes of the plans. The steeper the slope, the higher the financial leverage associated with a given financing plan. With increased fixed financial costs comes increased financial leverage.

The risk associated with covering these financial charges is the firm's financial risk.

The total leverage of the firm is defined as the ability of the firm to use fixed costs—both operating and financial—to magnify the effects of changes in sales on earnings per share. Total leverage reflects the combined effect of operating and financial leverage on the firm. The degree of total leverage at a specified level of sales can be measured in either of two ways. It can also be found by multiplying the degree of operating leverage by the degree of financial leverage. The total risk of the firm, which is associated with its ability to cover fixed operating and financial costs, increases with increasing total leverage, and vice versa. The financial manager must consider the effect of operating and financial leverage on the total risk of the firm when making operating and financing decisions.

QUESTIONS

4-1 What is meant by the term "leverage"? With what type of risk is leverage generally associated?

4-2 What is the difference between operating and financial leverage as reflected in the firm's income statement?

4-3 What is the meaning of the firm's operating breakeven point? Does this breakeven point, as defined, consider financing costs? Does another breakeven concept account for coverage of all costs and, if so, how?

4-4 How can operating breakeven analysis be used to evaluate the feasibility of various types of operations and cost structures?

4-5 How do changes in the selling price of a product, the variable cost per unit, and fixed operating costs affect the firm's operating breakeven point?

4-6 One of the key weaknesses of breakeven analysis is the assumption of linear cost and revenue functions. Why may these functions actually be curvilinear? Can you graphically depict a curvilinear breakeven analysis?

4-7 How is operating leverage related to the firm's fixed and variable costs? Why are earnings before interest and taxes the pivotal variable in leverage analysis?

4-8 Why is increasing operating leverage also indicative of increasing risk? How does the ratio of the percentage change in EBIT to the percentage change in sales reflect this risk?

4-9 What is meant by financial leverage? What items on the firm's income statement affect the degree of financial leverage present in a given firm?

4-10 How can the ratio of the percentage change in earnings per share to the percentage change in EBIT be used to determine and compare the degree of leverage present in a given firm?

4-11 How does a financial manager assess the firm's degree of financial leverage? Why is this measure important in evaluating various financing plans?

4-12 Why must the financial manager keep in mind the firm's degree of financial leverage when evaluating various financing plans?

4-13 What is the meaning of the firm's financial breakeven point? Is this affected by changes in operating costs?

4-14 What is the relationship between the slope of the graph of a financing plan, the financial breakeven point, and the financial leverage ratio? What do these measures reveal about the risk associated with a firm?

4-15 What is the relationship between operating leverage and operating risk? How is each of these related to the firm's breakeven point and risk-return trade-off?

4-16 What is the relationship between financial leverage and financial risk? How is each of these related to the firm's financial breakeven point and risk-return trade-off?

4-17 What is the relationship of total leverage to total risk? How is each of these related to the firm's total breakeven point and overall risk-return trade-off? How does one measure the degree of total leverage?

4-18 What is the general relationship between operating leverage, financial leverage, and the total leverage of the firm? Do both types of leverage complement each other? Why or why not?

PROBLEMS

4-1 The Texas Press publishes the *Annual Texas Almanac*. Last year, the book sold for $8.00 with variable cost per book of $6.00 and fixed costs of $40,000. How many books will they need to sell this year to achieve the breakeven point for their operating expenses given the following different circumstances?

a All figures remain the same as last year.

b Fixed costs increase to $44,000; all other figures remain the same as last year.

c The selling price increases to $8.50; all costs remain the same as last year.

d Variable cost per book increases to $6.50; all other figures remain the same.

e What conclusions about the operating breakeven point can be drawn from your answers?

4-2 Given the following price and cost data for each of the three firms R, S, and T, answer the questions below.

	R	S	T
Sale price per unit	$16	$14	$25
Variable operating cost per unit	$6	$9	$10
Fixed operating cost	$40,000	$20,000	$75,000

a What is the breakeven point in units for each firm?

b Compute the sales dollar breakeven level.

c Assuming $10,000 of each firm's fixed costs are depreciation, compute the cash breakeven point for each firm.

d How would you rank these firms in terms of their risk?

4-3 The Bush Company sells its finished product for $9.00 per unit. Its fixed operating costs are $20,000 and the variable operating cost per unit is $5.00.

a Calculate the firm's earnings before interest and taxes (EBIT) for sales of 10,000 units.

b Calculate the firm's EBIT for sales of 8000 and 12,000 units, respectively.

c Calculate the percentage change in sales and associated percentage changes in EBIT for the shifts in sales indicated in **b**.

4-4 The Fiesta Paper Company has fixed costs of $190,000, variable costs per unit of $8.00, and a selling price of $31.75 per unit.

a Calculate the operating breakeven point in units and sales dollars.

b Calculate the firm's EBIT at 9000, 10,000, and 11,000 units, respectively.

c Using 10,000 units as a base, what are the percentage changes in units sold and EBIT as sales move from the base to the other sales levels used in **b**?

d Use the percentages computed in **c** to determine the degree of operating leverage (DOL).

e Use the degree of operating leverage formula to determine the DOL at 10,000 units.

4-5   Wallace Wigits has fixed operating costs of $60,000, variable operating costs of $5.75 per unit, and a selling price of $8.25 per unit.

    a Calculate the breakeven point in units.

    b Compute the degree of operating leverage (DOL) for the following unit sales levels: 25,000, 30,000, 40,000. Use the formula given in the chapter.

    c Graph the DOL figures you computed in **b** (on the *y*-axis) against sales levels (on the *x*-axis).

    d Compute the degree of operating leverage at 24,000 units; add this point to your graph.

    e What principle is illustrated by your graph and figures?

4-6   The Power Tool Corporation has $120,000 of 8-percent bonds outstanding, 1500 shares of preferred stock paying $5.00 dividends per share, and 4000 shares of common stock outstanding. Assuming the firm has a 40-percent tax rate, compute earnings per share (eps) for the following levels of EBIT:

    a $24,600

    b $30,600

    c $35,000

4-7   United States Barge has 400,000 shares of common stock and $100,000 of bonds outstanding. The firm has a 40-percent tax rate.

    a Calculate the financial breakeven point if the interest rate on the bonds is 10 percent.

    b Calculate the financial breakeven point if the interest rate on the bonds is 8 percent.

    c Using **a** above, also assume the firm has 1000 shares of outstanding preferred stock that pays a $6.00 dividend per share. What is the financial breakeven?

    d Using **a** above, assume the firm has 1000 shares of preferred stock outstanding and the dividend is $5.40 per share. What is the financial breakeven?

4-8   The Wonder Water Company has EBIT of $45,000. Interest costs are $15,000 and the firm has 15,000 shares of common stock. Assume a 40-percent tax rate.

    a Use the degree of financial leverage (DFL) formula to calculate the DFL for the firm.

    b Using a set of EBIT-eps axes, plot the Wonder Water financing plan.

    c Assuming the firm also has 1000 shares of preferred stock paying a $6.00 dividend per share, what is the DFL?

    d Plot the financing plan including the 1000 shares of $6.00 preferred stock on the axes used in **b**.

    e Briefly discuss the graphs of the two financing plans.

4-9   Collins Electronics is considering additional financing of $20,000. They currently have $100,000 of 6-percent bonds and 10,000 shares of common stock outstanding. The firm can obtain the financing through a 6-percent bond issue or a sale of 1000 shares of common stock. If the firm expects EBIT to be $30,000 and has a 40-percent tax rate:

    a What would the degree of financial leverage (DFL) be under each financing plan?

    b Plot the two financing plans on a set of EBIT-eps axes.

    c At what level of EBIT does the bond plan become superior to the stock plan?

4-10 Johnson Manufacturing produces small motors. Their fixed operating costs are $20,000, variable operating costs are $18 per unit, and the motors sell for $23 each. Johnson has $50,000 in 10-percent bonds and 20,000 shares of common stock outstanding. The firm is in the 40-percent tax bracket.

    a What is Johnson's operating breakeven point in units?

    b What is Johnson's financial breakeven point?

    c What is Johnson's total breakeven point?

4-11 Rose Oil Cosmetics produces skin care products, selling 400,000 bottles a year. Each bottle produced has a variable operating cost of $.84, and sells for $1.00. Fixed operating costs are $28,000. The firm has current interest charges of $6000 and preferred dividends of $2000. The firm has a 40-percent tax rate.

    a Calculate operating (units), financial, and total breakeven points.

    b Use the degree of operating leverage (DOL) formula to calculate DOL.

    c Use the degree of financial leverage (DFL) formula to calculate DFL.

    d Use the degree of total leverage (DTL) formula to calculate DTL. Compare this to the product of DOL and DFL calculated in **b** and **c** above.

4-12 Firm A has a contribution margin of $.30 per unit, fixed costs of $6000, and sells 100,000 units. Interest is $10,000 per year. Firm B has a contribution margin of $1.50 per unit, fixed costs of $62,500, and sells 100,000 units. Interest is $17,500 per year. Assume both firms are in the 40-percent tax bracket.

    a Compute the degree of operating, financial, and total leverage for firm A.

    b Compute the degree of operating, financial, and total leverage for firm B.

    c Compare the relative risks of the two firms.

    d Discuss the principles of leverage illustrated in your answers.

SELECTED REFERENCES

Crowingshield, Gerald R., and George L. Battista, "Cost-Volume-Profit Analysis in Planning and Control," *N.A.A. Bulletin 45* (July 1963), pp. 3–15.

Ghandi, J. K. S., "On the Measurement of Leverage," *Journal of Finance 21* (December 1966), pp. 715–726.

Haslem, John A., "Leverage Effects on Corporate Earnings," *Arizona Review 19* (March 1970), pp. 7–11.

Haugen, Robert A., and Dean W. Wichern, "The Intricate Relationship Between Financial Leverage and the Stability of Stock Prices," *Journal of Finance 30* (December 1975), pp. 1283–1292.

Helfert, Erich A., *Techniques of Financial Analysis*, 4th ed. (Homewood, Ill.: Irwin, 1976), chap. 2.

Hugon, J. H., "Break-even Analysis in Three Dimensions," *Financial Executive 33* (December 1965), pp. 22–26.

Jaedicke, R. K., and A. A. Robichek, "Cost-Volume-Profit Analysis under Conditions of Uncertainty," *Accounting Review 39* (October 1964), pp. 917–926.

Kelvie, W. E., and J. M. Sinclair, "New Technique for Break-even Charts," *Financial Executive 36* (June 1968), pp. 31–43.

Krainer, Robert E., "Interest Rates, Leverage, and Investor Rationality," *Journal of Financial and Quantitative Analysis 12* (March 1977), pp. 1–16.

Lev, Baruch, "On the Association Between Operating Leverage and Risk," *Journal of Financial and Quantitative Analysis 9* (September 1974), pp. 627–642.

Percival, John R., "Operating Leverage and Risk," *Journal of Business Research 2* (April 1974), pp. 223–227.

Pfahl, J. K., D. T. Crary, and R. H. Howard, "The Limits of Leverage," *Financial Executive 38* (May 1970), pp. 48–56.

Raun, D. L., "The Limitations of Profit Graphs, Break-Even Analysis, and Budgets," *Accounting Review 39* (October 1964), pp. 927–945.

Shalit, Sol S., "On the Mathematics of Financial Leverage," *Financial Management 4* (Spring 1975), pp. 57–66.

Williams, George E., "The Other Side of Leverage," *Financial Executive 39* (June 1971), pp. 46–48.

CHAPTER 5
Sources and uses of funds and cash budgeting

It is often useful to develop certain financial statements as an aid in evaluating a firm's past or present performance. The *source and use of funds statement* allows the financial manager to analyze the firm's *historical* sources and uses of funds. This statement is often called a "source and application of funds" statement, but for the purposes of this chapter the terms *source* and *use* are more useful. Occasionally, this statement is used for forecasting. Its major strength is its usefulness in evaluating the sources and uses of longer-term funds. A knowledge of the historical patterns of fund usage allows the financial manager to better plan his or her future intermediate and long-term funds requirements.

The *cash budget* is a *forecasting* tool that allows the financial manager to determine the short-term financial needs of the firm. It is often called a "cash forecast," but the term "cash budget" will be used in this chapter. The cash budget is an important tool for evaluating the financial needs of seasonal businesses, since it is typically developed in a manner that permits the analysis of a firm's short-term financing needs on a month-by-month basis. Banks and other lenders often require prospective borrowers of short-term funds to present a cash budget as part of their loan application. The cash budget is a key input to the firm's pro forma balance sheets and income statements, which are discussed in Chapter 6.

This chapter has two major sections. The first section is devoted to the development and interpretation of source and use of funds statements. Attention is given to the classification and adjustment of balance sheet changes in order to prepare both the source and use of cash and the source and use of net working capital statements. A discussion of the interpretation of these statements and the rationale for their preparation is also presented in the first section. The second section of the chapter discusses the importance, preparation, and interpretation of cash budgets. Emphasis is placed on the preparation of the sales forecast, which is the key input to the cash budget. A brief discussion of uncertainty and the cash budget is also included.

SOURCE AND USE OF FUNDS STATEMENTS

The term *funds* can be defined to mean either of two things—cash or net working capital. Both these items are necessary for the firm to function effectively. Cash is needed for the firm to pay bills. Net working capital is necessary, especially in seasonal businesses, to provide a financial cushion for the payment of bills due in the near future. The use of net working capital in the development of the source and use of funds statement is based on the belief that current assets, which by definition can be converted into cash in a short period of time, as well as cash can be utilized to pay the firm's current liabilities. The source and use of cash statement provides much more detailed information than the source and use of net working capital statement.

Figure 5.1 is a diagram of the overall flow of cash through the business firm. It shows (1) operating flows and (2) financial and legal flows. The operating flows relate to the firm's production cycle. Utilizing raw materials, labor, and depreciable assets, and incurring operating and administrative expenses such as salaries and rent, and sales expenses, the firm produces and sells its finished goods. As Figure 5.1 shows, not all purchases are made for cash; rather, many are made on credit through the establishment of an account payable or accrual. Similarly, not all sales are made for cash; many are made on credit, producing accounts receivable.

The financial and legal flows depicted in Figure 5.1 include the payment and receipt of interest, the payment and refund of taxes, the incurrence or repayment of debt, the effect of distributions of equity through the payment of dividends or stock repurchases, and the cash inflow from the sale of stock. These flows differ from operating flows in that they are not directly related to the production and sale of the firm's products, but rather to the financing and tax payments of the firm. No division between operating flows and financial and legal flows will be made in the development of source and use of funds statements, but the reader should recognize the difference between them. The breakdown of financial and operating flows in Figure 5.1 is consistent with the discussion of financial and operating leverage in Chapter 4.

Classifying sources and uses of cash

Sources of cash are items that increase a firm's cash, while *uses* of cash are items that decrease a firm's cash.

Sources. The basic sources of cash are

1. A decrease in an asset
2. An increase in a liability
3. Net profits after taxes
4. Depreciation and other noncash charges
5. Sale of stock

A few points should be clarified with respect to these items.

FIGURE 5.1 The flow of funds through the firm

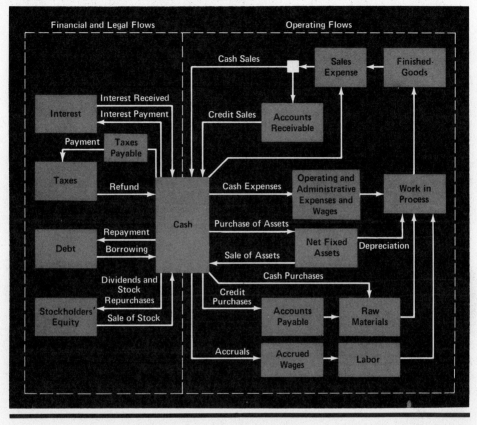

Cash.   The reader may wonder why a decrease in an asset, which would include a decrease in cash, is a source of cash. A decrease in the cash *balance* is a source of cash *flow* in the sense that if the firm's cash balance is decreased the cash flow released must have gone toward some use of cash such as an increase in inventories or the repayment of debt.

Net profits after taxes and noncash charges.   In Chapter 2, Equation 2.1 and the discussion preceding it explained why depreciation and other non-cash charges must be considered cash inflows, or sources of funds. Adding noncash charges back to the firm's net profits after taxes gives us the cash flows from operations:

Cash flow from operations = net profits after taxes + noncash charges

In this chapter, net profits after taxes and noncash charges such as depreciation are treated as separate items in order to increase the informational content of the source and use of funds statement.

Uses.   The most common uses of cash are

1. An increase in an asset
2. A decrease in a liability
3. A net loss
4. Payment of cash dividends
5. The repurchase or retirement of stock

A few points should be clarified with respect to these items.

Cash.   Since all items in the source and use of cash statement attempt to measure changes in cash, it may be hard to understand that an increase in the asset cash can be a use of cash. An increase in the cash *balance* is a use of cash *flow* in the sense that if a firm's cash balance increases this cash flow must come from some source of cash such as a decrease in inventories or an increase in a liability. For example, consider a firm that is confronted with two alternatives: (1) using cash to purchase inventory, or (2) putting the cash in its bank account. Both actions will consume cash, but the purchase of inventory will convert it into another type of asset, whereas the placement of cash in the firm's bank account will not. Both actions will increase the firm's assets and therefore must be considered uses of cash.

Net losses.   If a firm were to experience a net loss, this would result in a use of funds. It is possible for a firm to have a net loss but still have positive cash flows from operations if depreciation in the same period is greater than the net loss. This relationship is consistent with Equation 2.1.

Assets, liabilities, and stockholders' equity

Except for cases described above, increases in assets are uses of funds and decreases in assets are sources of funds. It takes cash to increase assets, and cash is generated through the sale of a fixed asset or the collection of accounts receivable. Increases in liabilities are sources of funds and decreases in liabilities are uses of funds. An increase in a liability represents increased financing, which is expected to generate funds, while a decrease in a liability represents the repayment of a debt, which requires a cash outlay.

One final preliminary point is that no direct stockholders' equity entries have been classified as sources or uses of funds; instead, entries for items that may affect the firm's stockholders' equity have appeared as net profits or losses after taxes, cash dividends, and the result of any sale or repurchase of stock. If the stockholders' equity entries were classified, they would be treated in the same fashion as are the liabilities. An increase in a stockholders' equity account would be treated as a source and a decrease in a stockholders' equity account would be treated as a use. An increase in stockholders' equity represents increased financing that is expected to generate funds, while a decrease in stockholders' equity represents decreased financing, which results in a cash outflow. How stockholders' equity entries are treated on actual source and use of funds statements will be described later.

Special adjustments

A number of special adjustments are often required in making up a source and use of funds statement. Each of these adjustments stems from the nature of the financial statements used. The inputs required for preparing a source and use of funds statement are (1) an income statement for the most recent period, (2) a balance sheet for the most recent period, and (3) a balance sheet for the earlier period being used as a basis for comparisons. Adjustments can be expected relating to the following items.

Changes in fixed assets. Of all the firm's assets, *only* fixed assets require special attention. This is because there are two basic ways in which fixed assets may be shown on the balance sheet. The first way is more detailed and does not require any special attention. Assume that a firm has the following fixed-asset entries on its balance sheet and that depreciation of $500 is shown on the income statement for 19X1.

	19X0	19X1
Fixed assets	$9,500	$10,200
Less: Accumulated depreciation	4,200	4,700
Net fixed assets	$5,300	$ 5,500

In this case, the change in the firm's fixed assets is $700. This figure is easily obtained by taking the difference between the fixed assets for the current year (19X1) and those for the preceding year (19X0), ($10,200 − $9500). The increase in fixed assets of $700 will appear as a use of funds on the firm's source and use statement. The difference between accumulated depreciation in 19X0 and 19X1 ($500) is equal to the depreciation expense on the firm's income statement.

The less detailed way of showing a firm's fixed assets on the balance sheet, which is quite common, is to show only "net fixed assets." Assume that a firm has the net fixed assets indicated below and that $500 in depreciation was written off on its 19X1 income statement.

	19X0	19X1
Net fixed assets	$5300	$5500

To find the change (if any) in the firm's fixed assets when one is given this type of data, the following formula is used:

$$\Delta FA_t = NFA_t + Depr_t - NFA_{t-1} \tag{5.1}$$

where

ΔFA_t = the change in fixed assets in the current period, t
NFA_t = the net fixed assets in the current period, t
$Depr_t$ = the depreciation written off in the current period, t
NFA_{t-1} = the net fixed assets in the preceding period, $t - 1$

Applying Equation 5.1 to the data given above yields

$$\Delta FA_t = \$5500 + \$500 - \$5300 = \underline{\$700}$$

The result is the same as in the first case, but it has been obtained in an indirect fashion.

If the application of Equation 5.1 to the firm's financial statements results in a negative change in fixed assets, the amount of this decrease is entered as a source of funds in the source and use of funds statement. If a change of zero in the firm's fixed assets results, no fixed asset entry is made on its source and use of funds statement. This occurs when the firm's net fixed assets decrease by an amount just equal to the depreciation for the period.

Dividends. Occasionally the firm's cash dividend payments are not shown on the income statement. If they are, of course, they are readily available to be entered on the source and use of funds statement. However, in many instances the last item shown on the firm's income statement is net profits after taxes. In this case the analyst should investigate further to determine whether any cash dividends were paid. Assume that a firm shows net profits after taxes of $5000 for the current year (19X1) and that the stockholders' equity for the past year (19X0) and the current year (19X1) is as follows:

Stockholders' equity	19X0	19X1
Common stock	$40,000	$45,000
Retained earnings	30,000	33,000
Total	$70,000	$78,000

In this case, the firm's retained earnings have increased by $3000, ($33,000 − $30,000). This increase accounts for the disposition of only $3000 of the $5000 of net profits after taxes. The remaining $2000 must therefore represent a dividend payment of $2000. This dividend payment is a use of funds by the firm. Equation 5.2 can be used to calculate the amount of cash dividends paid when they are not shown on the firm's income statement.

$$Div_t = NPAT_t - RE_t + RE_{t-1} \tag{5.2}$$

where

Div_t = the cash dividend paid in period t
$NPAT_t$ = the net profits after taxes in period t
RE_t = the retained earnings at the end of period t
RE_{t-1} = the retained earnings at the end of period $t - 1$

Substituting the data above into Equation 5.2 yields

Div_t = \$5000 − \$33,000 + \$30,000 = $\underline{\$2000}$

If the firm's retained earnings have increased by an amount just equal to its net profits after taxes, it must have paid no dividends. In this case, no dividend entry on the source and use statement is required.

Stock. A firm may sell additional stock, repurchase outstanding shares, or retire existing shares. It may take these actions with regard to both preferred and common stock. Preferred stock is most likely to be retired since it quite often has a call feature,[1] which allows the issuer to buy back shares in the future. In the case of both common and preferred stock, the amount purchased or sold can be determined by calculating the changes in the firm's stockholders' equity account, *other than those* in its retained earnings. An increase in stock is a source of funds, while a decrease is a use of funds. In the example in the preceding section, the firm's common stock increased from \$40,000 in 19X0 to \$45,000 in 19X1. This increase of \$5000 in common stock represents a sale of stock, which is shown as a source of funds on the firm's source and use of funds statement.

The following formula can be used to evaluate whether a sale or purchase of stock has occurred:

$$Stock_t = SE_t - SE_{t-1} - RE_t + RE_{t-1} \tag{5.3}$$

where

$Stock_t$ = the change (if any) in the firm's stock outstanding
SE_t = the firm's stockholders' equity in period t
SE_{t-1} = the firm's stockholders' equity in period $t - 1$
RE_t and RE_{t-1} are defined as before

Although Equation 5.3 may look difficult, it merely represents the calculations described above. Applying Equation 5.3 to the figures given in the preceding section yields

$Stock_t$ = \$78,000 − \$70,000 − \$33,000 + \$30,000 = $\underline{\$5000}$

---

[1]An in-depth discussion of the various types of equity securities is provided in Chapter 22.

The $5000 increase in stock will be shown as a source of funds of $5000 on the source and use statement. If the firm were to repurchase or retire stock, a negative value would result that would be shown as a use of funds. If there were no change in the firm's stock outstanding, no stock entry would be required on the source and use of funds statement.

Preliminaries to the preparation of a source and use statement

The simplified financial statements in Table 5.1 are used to illustrate the actual application of the adjustments discussed above to the preparation of source and use statements. The balance sheet is presented in a *stacked format*, with the assets followed by liabilities and the stockholders' equity, in order to simplify the development of the source and use of cash statement.

Classifying sources and uses.

The suggested procedure for classifying items as sources or uses is illustrated below, using the XYZ Company as an example.

STEP 1:
Using the earliest time period as a base, calculate the balance sheet changes in all assets and liabilities.

STEP 2:
Using the classification scheme presented earlier, classify the changes in all asset and liability accounts, *except* net fixed assets, as either a source (S) or a use (U).

Table 5.2 presents the results of application of Steps 1 and 2 to the XYZ Company's balance sheet. Net fixed assets are not classified as a source or use since a direct entry of this item on the source and use statement is not normally required.

STEP 3:
Calculate the change in XYZ's fixed assets using Equation 5.1:

Change in fixed assets = $1200 + $100 − $1000 = $\underline{\$300}$

Since the firm's fixed assets have increased, a use of funds of $300 results.

STEP 4:
Calculate the cash dividends paid, if they are not shown on the income statement, using Equation 5.2:

Dividends = $180 − $600 + $500 = $\underline{\$80}$

The firm appears to have paid $80 in cash dividends in 19X1. This amount is entered as a use of funds on the source and use of funds statement.

TABLE 5.1 Financial statements for the XYZ Company

Balance sheets

	Year ended	
	19X0	19X1
Assets		
Cash	$ 300	$ 400
Marketable securities	200	600
Accounts receivable	500	400
Inventory	800	500
Prepaid items	100	100
Total current assets	$1,900	$2,000
Net fixed assets	1,000	1,200
Total Assets	$2,900	$3,200
Liabilities and stockholders' equity		
Accounts payable	$ 500	$ 600
Notes payable	700	400
Taxes payable	200	200
Accruals	0	400
Total current liabilities	$1,400	$1,600
Long-term debt	$ 400	$ 600
Preferred stock	$ 100	$ 100
Common stock at par	100	60
Paid in capital in excess of par	400	240
Retained earnings	500	600
Total stockholders' equity	$1,100	$1,000
Total Liabilities and Stockholders' Equity	$2,900	$3,200

Income statement

		19X1
Sales		$1,000
Less: Cost of goods sold		500
Gross profits		$ 500
Less: Expenses		
General and admin. expense	$100	
Depreciation	100	
Total		200
Profits before taxes		$ 300
Less: Taxes (40%)		120
Profits After Taxes		$ 180

TABLE 5.2 A classification of asset
and liability changes for the XYZ Company
as sources (S) or uses (U) of funds

Item	Change ($)	Classification
Cash	+100	U
Marketable securities	+400	U
Accounts receivable	−100	S
Inventory	−300	S
Prepaid items	0	—
Net fixed assets	+200	—*
Accounts payable	+100	S
Notes payable	−300	U
Taxes payable	0	—
Accruals	+400	S
Long-term debt	+200	S

*Not classified at this point in the analysis.

STEP 5:
Calculate the change, if any, in the amount of stock outstanding, using Equation
5.3:

$$\text{Change in stock} = \$1000 - \$1100 - \$600 + \$500 = \underline{-\$200}$$

This decrease in stock of $200 is shown as a use on the source and use
statement. The change in stock could have been calculated directly from the
balance sheet, but the use of Equation 5.3 is suggested since stockholders'
equity items are often grouped together on balance sheets.

Preparing the source and use of cash statement

The source and use of cash statement is prepared by listing all sources
on the left and all uses on the right. The statement for the XYZ Company,
based on the data developed in the preceding section, is presented in Table
5.3.

A number of points should be made about Table 5.3:

1. "Total sources" and "total uses" should be equal; if they are not, the
   analyst must have made an error.
2. Net profits after taxes are normally the first source listed and dividends are normally the first use. Ordering items on the source and
   use of cash statement this way makes it easy to calculate the change
   in the firm's retained earnings.
3. Depreciation and increases in fixed assets are shown second to make
   it easy to compare them. Placing depreciation just below net profits
   after taxes also makes the firm's cash flow from operations easily cal-
   culable.

TABLE 5.3 A source and use of cash statement for the XYZ Company

Sources		Uses	
Net profits after taxes	$ 180	Dividends	$ 80
Depreciation	100	Increase in fixed assets	300
Decrease in accounts receivable	100	Increase in cash	100
Decrease in inventory	300	Increase in marketable securities	400
Increase in accounts payable	100	Decrease in notes payable	300
Increase in accruals	400	Repurchase or retirement of stock	200
Increase in long-term debt	200		
Total Sources	$1,380	Total Uses	$1,380

4. The order of the remaining sources and uses of cash does not matter; the only requirement is that sources appear on the left side of the statement and uses on the right side.

5. The net change in the firm's stockholders' equity can be calculated by adding any sales of stock or subtracting any repurchases or retirements of stock from the difference between the net profits after taxes and cash dividends. For the XYZ Company, the change in stockholders' equity is −$100 ($180 − $80 − $200).

Preparing the source and use of net working capital statement

The source and use of net working capital statement is quite similar to the source and use of cash statement, except that changes in current assets and current liabilities are not entered separately.[2] Instead, they are netted into a single entry—the change in net working capital. Many people prefer the source and use of net working capital statement to the source and use of cash statement because they believe the spontaneous nature of the firm's current accounts makes their inclusion pointless. These people are more concerned with the net change in a firm's liquidity as measured by its net working capital.

It can be seen from the balance sheet for the XYZ Company in Table 5.1 that the firm's current assets, current liabilities, net working capital, and change in net working capital are as given in Table 5.4. The XYZ Company experienced a $100 decrease in net working capital between 19X0 and 19X1. *A decrease in net working capital is a source of funds, whereas an increase in net working capital is a use of funds.* Since XYZ Company's current assets increased by less than its current liabilities, the net result was a source of funds. The increase in current assets, which was a use of funds, was overpowered by the increase in current liabilities, a source of funds.

---

[2]Some authors use the term "working capital" synonymously with what was defined in Chapter 3 as "net working capital." This statement is therefore commonly referred to as the *source and use of working capital* statement.

TABLE 5.4 The change in
net working capital for the XYZ Company

	19X0	19X1
Total current assets	$1900	$2000
Total current liabilities	1400	1600
Net working capital	$ 500	$ 400
Change in net working capital	− $100	

Table 5.5 presents a source and use of net working capital statement for the XYZ Company. The only noticeable difference between the source and use of net working capital statement in Table 5.5 and the source and use of cash statement in Table 5.3 is that the current asset and current liability entries have been replaced in Table 5.5 by a single entry, the change in net working capital. The balancing figures differ in the two types of source and use statements, but this does not have any significance for decision making.

The source and use statement on a percentage basis
It is often useful to present the source and use statement on a percentage basis. When each item is expressed as a percent of the total sources or uses, the statement is easier to interpret. The statement allows the analyst to get a feel for the relative contribution of each source and use to the firm's overall cash flow during the period covered by the statement. Table 5.6 presents the source and use of cash statement in Table 5.3 on a percentage basis.
Both the source and use of cash and source and use of net working capital statements can be prepared on a percentage basis; of course, they must first be prepared in terms of dollars, as illustrated earlier. The presentation of source and use statements on a percentage basis should greatly simplify their interpretation.

Interpreting source and use statements
Source and use of cash and source and use of net working capital statements prepared either on a dollar or on a percentage basis allow the financial

TABLE 5.5 A source and use of net
working capital statement for the XYZ Company

Sources		Uses	
Net profits after taxes	$180	Dividends	$ 80
Depreciation	100	Increase in fixed assets	300
Decrease in net working capital	100	Repurchase or retirement of stock	200
Increase in long-term debt	200		
Total Sources	$580	Total Uses	$580

TABLE 5.6 A percent source and use of cash statement for the XYZ Company

Sources		Uses	
Net profits after taxes	13.1%	Dividends	5.7%
Depreciation	7.2	Increase in fixed assets	21.8
Decrease in accounts receivable	7.2	Increase in cash	7.2
Decrease in inventory	21.8	Increase in marketable securities	29.0
Increase in accounts payable	7.2	Decrease in notes payable	21.8
Increase in accruals	29.0	Repurchase or retirement of stock	14.5
Increase in long-term debt	14.5		
Total Sources	100.0%	Total Uses	100.0%

manager to analyze the firm's past and possibly its future funds flows. He or she will give special attention to the major sources and uses in order to determine whether any developments have occurred that are contrary to the firm's financial policies. Although specific causal relations between sources and uses cannot be determined from an analysis of these statements, they do point out certain types of inefficiencies. For example, large increases in inventories or accounts receivable may signal the existence of certain types of inventory or credit problems. Problems, or symptoms of developing problems, can be recognized and investigation into these problems initiated as a result of the analysis of source and use statements.

Analysis of the XYZ Company's source and use statements does not seem to indicate the existence of any problems. The sources of funds seem to be distributed in a manner consistent with prudent financial management; the same is true of the firm's uses of funds. Analysis of the source and use of cash statement seems to indicate great strength on the part of the firm. The majority of its funds have been generated by decreasing inventory and increasing accruals. Both these strategies are consistent with efficient financial management.[3] The major uses of funds have been an increase in fixed assets, an increase in marketable securities, and a decrease in notes payable. Each of these items reflects financial strength.

As indicated earlier, the financial manager may apply source and use analysis to projected financial statements in order to determine whether a proposed financing plan is feasible in the sense that the financing required to support the projected level of operations will be available.

CASH BUDGETING

The *cash budget,* or *cash forecast,* allows the firm to plan its short-term cash needs. Typically, attention is given both to planning for surplus cash and to planning for cash shortages. A firm expecting a cash surplus can plan short-

---

[3]A thorough discussion of the management of working capital is presented in Chapters 7 through 10. After studying these chapters, the reader should be better able to interpret the source and use statement.

term investments, whereas a firm expecting shortages in cash must arrange for needed short-term financing. The cash budget gives the financial manager a clear view of the timing of both the cash inflows and the cash outflows expected over a given period. This type of information is invaluable in overall planning.

Typically, the cash budget is designed to cover a one-year period, although any time period is acceptable. The period covered is normally divided into intervals. The number and type of intervals depend greatly on the nature of the business. The more seasonal and uncertain a firm's cash flows are, the greater the number of intervals the cash budget is divided into. Since many firms are confronted with a seasonal cash flow pattern, the cash budget is quite often presented on a monthly basis. Firms with very stable patterns of cash flow may use either quarterly or annual intervals. If a cash budget is developed for a period greater than one year, less frequent time intervals may be warranted due to the difficulty and uncertainty of forecasting sales and associated cash items.

The sales forecast

The key input to any cash budget is the sales forecast. This is typically given to the financial manager by the marketing department. On the basis of this forecast, the financial manager estimates the monthly cash flows that will result from projected sales receipts and production- or inventory-related outlays. He also determines how much financing, if any, will be required to support the forecast level of production and sales and whether it can be obtained.

The sales forecast may be based on an analysis of external or internal forecast data.[4]

External forecasts. An external forecast is based on the relationships that can be observed between the firm's sales and certain economic indicators such as the gross national product, new housing starts, and disposable personal income. Typically, forecasts containing these indicators from which the firm can estimate its future level of sales, are readily available. The rationale for this approach is that since the firm's sales are often closely related to some aspect of economic activity, a forecast of economic activity should provide insight into the firm's future sales.

Internal forecasts. Internally generated forecasts are based on a buildup of sales forecasts through the firm's sales channels. Typically, the salespersons in the field are asked to estimate the number of units of each type of product they expect to sell in the coming year. These forecasts are collected by the district sales manager, who may adjust the figures using his own knowledge of specific markets or the salesperson's forecasting ability. Finally, adjustments may be made for additional internal factors such as production capabilities.

---

[4]Forecasting techniques are not discussed in this text. The interested reader is referred to a basic statistics or econometrics text for information on this subject.

TABLE 5.7 The general format of a cash budget

	Jan.	Feb.	. . .	Nov.	Dec.
Cash receipts					
Less: Cash disbursements	——	——	. . .	——	——
Net cash flow					
Add: Beginning cash	—— ↗ ——	↗ ——	↗ . . . ↗ ——	↗ ——	
Ending cash					
Less: Minimum cash balance	——	——	. . .	——	——
Required total financing			. . .		
Excess cash balance			. . .		

Firms generally use both external and internal forecast data in making up the final sales forecast. The internal forecast data provide insight into sales expectations, while the external forecast data provide a way of adjusting these expectations by taking into account general economic factors. Many firms selling necessities are not greatly affected by economic factors, whereas the sales of other firms are highly responsive to changes in economic activity. The nature of the product often affects the mix and types of forecasting methods used.

The format of the cash budget

The general format of the cash budget is presented in Table 5.7. Then each of its components is discussed individually.

Cash receipts. Cash receipts include the total of all items from which cash inflows result in any given month. The most common components of cash receipts are cash sales, collections of credit sales, and other cash receipts.

EXAMPLE

The ABC Company is developing a cash budget for October, November, and December. Sales in August and September were $100,000 and $200,000, respectively. Sales of $400,000, $300,000, and $200,000 have been forecast for October, November, and December, respectively. Historically, 20 percent of the firm's sales have been for cash, 50 percent have generated accounts receivable collected after one month, and the remaining 30 percent have generated accounts receivable collected after two months. Bad-debt expenses have been negligible.[5] In December, the firm will receive a $30,000 dividend from stock in a subsidiary. The schedule of expected cash receipts for the company is given in Table 5.8. It contains the following items.

Forecast sales This initial entry is *merely informational*. It has been provided as an aid in calculating other sales-related items.

Cash sales The cash sales shown for each month represent 20 percent of the sales forecast for that month.

---

[5]Normally it would be expected that the collection percentages would total slightly less than 100% in order to reflect the fact that some of the accounts receivable would be uncollectible. In this example the sum of the collection percentages is 100% (i.e., 20% + 50% + 30%), which reflects the fact that all sales are assumed to be collected since bad debts are said to be negligible.

TABLE 5.8 A schedule of projected cash receipts for the ABC Company ($000 omitted)

	Aug.	Sept.	Oct.	Nov.	Dec.
Forecast sales	$100	$200	$400	$300	$200
Cash sales (.20)	$ 20	$ 40	$ 80	$ 60	$ 40
Collections:					
Lagged one month (.50)		50	100	200	150
Lagged two months (.30)			30	60	120
Other cash receipts					30
Total Cash Receipts			$210	$320	$340

Collection of credit sales These entries represent the collection of accounts receivable resulting from sales in earlier months.

Lagged one month These figures represent sales made in the preceding month that generated accounts receivable collected in the current month. Since 50 percent of the current month's sales are collected one month later, the collections of accounts receivable with a one-month lag shown for September, October, November, and December represent 50 percent of the sales in August, September, October, and November, respectively.

Lagged two months These figures represent sales made two months earlier that generated accounts receivable collected in the current month. Since 30 percent of sales are collected two months later, the collections with a two-month lag shown for October, November, and December represent 30 percent of the sales in August, September, and October, respectively.

Other cash receipts These are cash receipts expected to result from sources other than sales. Items such as dividends received, interest received, proceeds from the sale of equipment, stock and bond sale proceeds, and lease receipts may show up here. For the ABC Company, the only "other cash receipt" is the $30,000 dividend due in December.

Total cash receipts This figure represents the total of all the cash receipt items listed for each month in the cash receipt schedule. In the case of the ABC Company, we are concerned only with October, November, and December; the total cash receipts for these months are shown in Table 5.8. ●

Cash disbursements. Cash disbursements include all outlays of cash in the periods covered. The most common cash disbursements are

    Cash purchases
    Payments of accounts payable
    Payments of cash dividends
    Rent
    Wages and salaries
    Tax payments
    Capital additions

Interest on debt
Repayment of loans and sinking fund payments
Repurchases or retirements of stock

EXAMPLE

The ABC Company discussed in the preceding example has gathered the following data needed for the preparation of a cash disbursements schedule for the months of October, November, and December.

Purchases The firm's purchases represent 70 percent of their sales; 10 percent of this amount is paid in cash, 70 percent is paid in the month immediately following the month of purchase, and the remaining 20 percent is paid two months following the month of purchase.[6]

Cash dividends Cash dividends of $20,000 will be paid in October.

Rent Rent of $5000 will be paid each month.

Wages and salaries The firm's wages and salaries can be calculated by adding 10 percent of its monthly sales to the $8000 fixed-cost figure.

Tax payments Taxes of $25,000 must be paid in December.

Capital additions A new machine costing $130,000 will be purchased and paid for in November.

Interest payments An interest payment of $10,000 is due in December.

Sinking-fund payments A $20,000 sinking-fund payment is also due in December.

Repurchases or retirements of stock No repurchase or retirement of stock is expected to occur during the October–December period.

The firm's cash disbursement schedule, based on the data above, is presented in Table 5.9. Some items in Table 5.9 are explained in greater detail below.

TABLE 5.9 A schedule of projected cash disbursements for the ABC Company ($000 omitted)

	Aug.	Sept.	Oct.	Nov.	Dec.
Purchases (.70 · sales)	$70	$140	$280	$210	$140
Cash purchases (.10)	$ 7	$ 14	$ 28	$ 21	$ 14
Payments					
Lagged one month (.70)		49	98	196	147
Lagged two months (.20)			14	28	56
Cash dividends			20		
Rent expense			5	5	5
Wages and salaries			48	38	28
Tax payments					25
Capital additions				130	
Interest payments					10
Sinking-fund payments					20
Total Cash Disbursements			$213	$418	$305

[6]Unlike the collection percentages for sales, the total of the payment percentages should equal 100% since it is expected that the firm will pay off all of its accounts payable. In line with this expectation, the ABC Company's percentages total 100% (10% + 70% + 20%).

Purchases This entry is merely informational. The figures represent 70 percent of the forecast sales for each month. They have been included at the top of the exhibit to facilitate the calculation of the cash purchases and related payments.

Cash purchases The cash purchases for each month represent 10 percent of the month's purchases.

Payments These entries represent the payment of accounts payable resulting from purchases in earlier months.

Lagged one month These figures represent purchases made in the preceding month that are paid for in the current month. Since 70 percent of the firm's purchases are paid for one month later, the payments lagged one month shown for September, October, November, and December represent 70 percent of the August, September, October, and November purchases, respectively.

Lagged two months These figures represent purchases made two months earlier that are paid for in the current month. Since 20 percent of the firm's purchases are paid for two months later, the payments lagged two months for October, November, and December represent 20 percent of the August, September, and October purchases, respectively.

Wages and salaries These values were obtained by adding $8000 to 10 percent of the *sales* in each month. The $8000 represents the salary component; the rest represents wages.

The remaining items on the cash disbursements schedule are self-explanatory. ●

The net cash flow, ending cash, financing, and excess cash. A firm's *net cash flow* is found by subtracting the cash disbursements from cash receipts in each month. By adding beginning cash to the firm's net cash flow, the ending cash for each month can be found. Finally, subtracting the minimum cash balance from ending cash yields the required total financing or the excess cash. If the ending cash is greater than the minimum cash balance, *excess cash* exists; while, if the ending cash is less than the minimum cash balance, *financing* is required.

EXAMPLE
Table 5.10 presents the ABC Company's cash budget, based on the cash receipt and cash disbursement data already developed for the firm. ABC's end-of-September cash balance was $50,000, and it wishes to maintain a minimum cash balance of $25,000.

In order for the ABC Company to maintain its required $25,000 ending cash balance, it will need to have borrowed $76,000 in November and $41,000 in December. In the month of October the firm will have an excess cash balance of $22,000, which can be placed in some interest earning form. The required total financing figures in the cash budget refer to "how much will have to be owed at the end of month"; they *do not* show the additional borrowing required during the month. In order to clarify the meaning of these financing figures, Table 5.11 presents a different approach to evaluating the firm's required financing. ●

Interpreting the cash budget
The cash budget provides the firm with figures indicating the expected ending cash balance, which can be analyzed to determine whether a cash shortage or cash surplus is expected to result in each of the months covered by the forecast. The ABC Company can expect a surplus of $22,000 in Oc-

**TABLE 5.10 A cash budget for
the ABC Company ($000 omitted)**

	Oct.	Nov.	Dec.
Total cash receipts[a]	$210	$320	$340
Less: Total cash disbursements[b]	213	418	305
Net cash flow	$ (3)	$ (98)	$ 35
Add: Beginning cash	50	47	(51)
Ending cash	$ 47	$ (51)	$ (16)
Less: Minimum cash balance	25	25	25
Required Total Financing[c]	—	$ 76	$ 41
Excess Cash Balance[d]	$ 22	—	—

[a]From Table 5.8.
[b]From Table 5.9.
[c]Values are placed in this line when the "ending cash" is less than the "minimum cash balance" since in this instance financing is required.
[d]Values are placed in this line when the "ending cash" is greater than the "minimum cash balance" since in this instance an excess cash balance exists.

tober, a deficit of $76,000 in November, and a deficit of $41,000 in December. Each of these figures is based on the internally imposed requirement of a $25,000 minimum cash balance.

The excess cash balance in October can be invested in marketable securities. The deficits in November and December will have to be financed by borrowing—typically, short-term borrowing. Since it may be necessary for the firm to borrow up to $76,000 for the three-month period evaluated, the financial manager should be sure that a line of credit is opened or some other arrangement is made to assure the availability of these funds. Typically, the financial manager will request or arrange to borrow more than the maximum financing indicated in the cash budget because of the uncertainty of the ending cash values, which are based on the sales forecast and other forecast values.

**TABLE 5.11 Another view of the
ABC Company's financing requirements ($000 omitted)**

	Oct.	Nov.	Dec.
Net cash flow[a]	$ (3)	$(98)	$ 35
Add: Beginning cash	50	47	25
Less: Minimum cash balance	25	25	25
Less: Excess cash balance	22	0	0
Additional financing (repayment)	$ 0	$ 76	$(35)
Total Financing	$ 0	$ 76	$ 41

[a]From Table 5.10.

Reducing the uncertainty in the cash budget

Aside from care in preparation of sales forecasts and other estimates included in the cash budget, there are two ways of reducing the uncertainty of the cash budget.[7] One is by preparing several cash budgets, one based on a pessimistic forecast, one based on the most likely forecast, and a third based on an optimistic forecast. This type of sensitivity analysis approach allows the financial manager to get an idea of the worst, most likely, and best ending cash flows that can be expected. An evaluation of these ending cash flows will allow him to determine the amount of financing necessary to cover the most adverse situation. The use of a number of cash budgets, each based on differing assumptions, should also give the financial manager a feel for the riskiness of alternatives so that he makes more intelligent short-term financial decisions. The sensitivity analysis approach is commonly used to analyze cash flows under a variety of possible economic circumstances.

EXAMPLE

Table 5.12 presents the summary results of ABC Company's cash budget prepared for each month of concern for a pessimistic, most likely, and optimistic estimate of cash receipts and cash disbursements. The most likely estimate is based upon the expected outcomes presented earlier in Tables 5.8 through 5.11, while the pessimistic and optimistic outcomes are based upon the worst and best possible outcomes respectively. During the month of October, the ABC Company will need at a maximum $15,000 of financing while at best they will have $62,000 excess cash balance available for short-term investment. During November, their financing requirement will be between $0 and $185,000. They could experience an excess cash balance of $5000 during November. The December projections reflect maximum borrowing of $190,000 with a possible excess cash balance of $107,000. By considering the extreme values reflected in the pessimistic and optimistic outcomes, the ABC Company should be better able to plan their cash requirements. For the three-month period, their peak borrowing requirement under the worst circumstances would be $190,000, which happens to be considerably greater than the most likely estimate for this period of $76,000. ●

A second and much more sophisticated way of reducing uncertainty in the cash budget is by *computer simulation*. By simulating the occurrence of sales and other uncertain events, a probability distribution of the firm's ending cash flows for each month can be developed. The financial decision maker can then determine the amount of financing necessary to provide a desired degree of protection against a cash shortage.

Cash flow within the month

Since the cash flows presented in the cash budget are shown only on a total monthly basis, the information it provides is not necessarily adequate

---

[7]The term "uncertainty" is used here to refer to the variability of the outcomes that may actually occur. A thorough discussion of risk and uncertainty and the various techniques available for adjusting for them appears in Chapter 16. Although that chapter discusses uncertainty in light of capital budgeting, many of the techniques covered can easily be applied to cash budgeting.

**TABLE 5.12 A sensitivity analysis of
ABC Company's cash budget ($000 omitted)**

	October			November			December		
	Pessi-mistic	Most Likely	Opti-mistic	Pessi-mistic	Most Likely	Opti-mistic	Pessi-mistic	Most Likely	Opti-mistic
Total cash receipts	$160	$210	$285	$210	$320	$410	$275	$340	$422
Less: Total cash disbursements	200	213	248	380	418	467	280	305	320
Net cash flow	$ (40)	$ (3)	$ 37	$(170)	$ (98)	$ (57)	$ (5)	$ 35	$102
Add: Beginning cash	50	50	50	10	47	87	(160)	(51)	30
Ending cash	$ 10	$ 47	$ 87	$(160)	$ (51)	$ 30	$(165)	$ (16)	$132
Less: Minimum cash balance	25	25	25	25	25	25	25	25	25
Required total financing	$ 15	—	—	$185	$ 76	—	$190	$ 41	—
Excess Cash Balance	—	$ 22	$ 62	—	—	$ 5	—	—	$107

for assuring solvency. A firm must look more closely at its pattern of daily cash receipts and cash disbursements in order to make sure that adequate cash is available for meeting bill payments as they come due. The following example illustrates the importance of monitoring daily cash flows in order to understand another source of variance in cash flow.

EXAMPLE

The ABC Company, presented in the preceding series of examples, found its actual pattern of cash receipt and cash disbursement during the month of October to be as shown in Table 5.13. It can be seen that, although the firm begins the month with $50,000 of cash and ends the month with $47,000 in cash, its cash balance is negative at various times within the month. Table 5.13 reflects negative cash balances during the period October 2 to October 11 and October 17 to October 22. It can be seen that the largest deficit of $72,000 occurs on October 4.

Although based upon the cash budget presented in Table 5.10, it appears that the ABC Company will not require any financing during the month of October since a $22,000 excess cash balance is expected, a look at the firm's daily cash flows during October makes it quite clear that they will need additional financing in order to make payments as they come due. At the maximum, $72,000 is required to meet their daily cash-flow requirements. ●

The preceding example makes it quite clear that while a firm's cash flows as reflected by the cash budget may be synchronized such that at month end receipts exceed disbursements, this still does not insure that the firm can meet its daily cash requirements. Since a firm's cash flows are generally quite variable when viewed on a daily basis, effective cash planning requires a look beyond the cash budget. Although the ABC Company's cash budget (Table 5.10) suggests it does not need to borrow during October, due to the nonsynchronized daily cash flows, the firm needs at the maximum $72,000 in additional funds. The financial manager, in order to maintain the firm's sol-

TABLE 5.13 Daily cash flows during
October for the ABC Company ($000 omitted)

Date	Amount Received	Amount Disbursed	Cash Balance[a]
10/1	Beginning balance		$50
10/2		$100	−50
10/4		22	−72
10/5	$65	15	−22
10/11	74		52
10/12	10	12	50
10/16		40	10
10/17	3	21	−8
10/22	35		27
10/26	20	1	46
10/29	3		49
10/31		2	47
Total	$210	$213	

[a]These figures represent ending cash balances without any
financing.

vency, must therefore plan and monitor its cash flow more frequently than
on a monthly basis. The greater the variability of the firm's cash flows from
day to day, the greater the attention required by this activity.

SUMMARY

This chapter has emphasized two financial statements that are quite helpful
in analyzing the firm's past and future financial needs. The source and use
of funds statement was discussed both on a cash and on a net working capital
basis. In order to make these statements more easily interpreted, they can be
prepared on a percentage basis, in which each source or use is stated as a
percent of the total sources or uses. The importance of this statement lies in
the ability it gives the financial manager to evaluate past or projected sources
and uses of funds. This evaluation should not only indicate the major sources
and uses but also provide insight into them. Analysis of the types and magnitude of sources and uses of funds may uncover problems in some area of
the firm's financing. The existence of high levels of accounts receivable and
inventories or low levels of accounts payable that may not be consistent with
the firm's overall objectives may be recognized.

The cash budget, which is often called the cash forecast, is the second
financial statement discussed in this chapter. The value of developing a cash
budget in order to forecast the firm's short-term financial needs is emphasized. The cash budget relies heavily on the sales forecast as an input. Both
external and internal forecast data are available; the use of both in combination is suggested. The ability to forecast cash flows and therefore financial
needs is important to the business firm—especially the firm with a seasonal

pattern of sales. Typically, the cash budget is prepared for a one-year period divided into monthly intervals. The less seasonal the business, the more infrequent the budget intervals required. The basic format of the cash budget is such that cash receipts and cash disbursements for each period can easily be netted against each other to get the net cash flow in each period. By adding beginning cash to the net cash flow, the ending cash can be estimated. After subtracting the minimum cash balance from the ending cash, the required total financing or excess cash balance can be determined. Any needed financing or surplus funds can therefore be planned for in light of this estimate.

Care is suggested in the preparation of the cash budget, since it is closely tied to forecast data. In order to reduce the uncertainty in the cash budget, the use of sensitivity analysis or computer simulation is suggested. One common sensitivity analysis approach involves preparing separate cash budgets based upon pessimistic, most likely, and optimistic estimates. If it is prepared carefully, the cash budget can be very valuable in determining the need for short-term financing or in planning uses for any excess cash balance. It is important to recognize that the cash budget does not insure that on a day-to-day basis the firm will be able to meet its cash requirements. Only by monitoring daily cash flows can this problem be effectively handled. The major difference between the cash budget and the source and use of funds statement is that the cash budget is a *short-term* financial *planning* tool, whereas the source and use of funds statement is typically a *historical* statement used for evaluating past funds flows to determine whether their pattern is consistent with the firm's long-term financial goals.

QUESTIONS

5-1   What are the key differences between the source and use of funds statement and the cash budget? How does this affect their use by the financial manager?

5-2   What is net working capital? What is the basic premise for using it in evaluating a firm's sources and uses of funds?

5-3   Sometimes the cash flows of a firm are divided into two groups—operating flows and financial and legal flows. What are the key differences between these flows? What are some examples of each type?

5-4   What is meant by "sources of cash"? What are the basic sources of cash for the typical firm?

5-5   Why are depreciation and noncash charges considered sources of cash to the firm?

5-6   What is meant by a "use of cash"? What are the basic uses of cash for the typical business firm?

5-7   Is it possible for a firm to have a net loss but still have positive cash flows from operations? Why or why not?

5-8   What are the three basic inputs for a source and use of funds statement?

5-9   How would the change in the firm's fixed assets be found in each of the following instances?

    a The firm's balance sheets are detailed and include data on its fixed assets, accumulated depreciation, and net fixed assets.

    b The firm's balance sheets include only a net fixed-asset figure.

5-10   How might one determine whether a firm paid cash dividends in the current year when the cash dividend is not shown on the firm's income statement?

5-11 What basic approach should be used in preparing a source and use of cash statement? What steps are required?

5-12 Why do people often argue that the source and use of net working capital statement is just as informative as the source and use of cash statement?

5-13 How is the source and use statement, presented on a percentage basis, prepared and used by the financial manager? Explain why the use of percentages might be especially helpful.

5-14 What is the purpose of the cash budget from the point of view of the financial manager?

5-15 The key input to the cash budget is a sales forecast. What is the difference between external and internal forecast data?

5-16 What general format is used for the cash budget?

5-17 How can the bottom lines of the cash budget be used to determine the firm's short-term borrowing and investment requirements?

5-18 Normally, uncertainty is present in the cash budget. What is the cause of this uncertainty?

5-19 How can sensitivity analysis and computer simulation aid the financial manager and reduce the uncertainty in the cash budget?

5-20 Even with a monthly cash budget, the firm may not be assured of solvency. What actions or analysis beyond preparation of the cash budget should the financial manager undertake to assure cash is available when needed?

PROBLEMS

5-1 Classify the following items as sources or uses of funds, or as neither.

Item	Change ($)	Item	Change ($)
Cash	+100	Accounts receivable	−700
Accounts payable	−1000	Net profits	+600
Notes payable	+500	Depreciation	+100
Long-term debt	−2000	Repurchase of stock	+600
Inventory	+200	Cash dividends	+800
Fixed assets	+400	Sale of stock	+1000

5-2 Using the following balance sheet data for Downing Cushion Company, indicate the change in fixed assets and classify this change as either a source or use of funds. Explain your answer.

a	1977	1978
Fixed assets	$60,000	$62,000
Less: Accumulated depreciation	−18,000	−23,000
Net fixed assets	$42,000	$39,000

b		
Fixed assets	$50,000	$46,000
Less: Accumulated depreciation	−18,000	−23,000
Net fixed assets	$32,000	$23,000

5-3 Given the following balance sheet and income statement data for the Raney Russell Company:

a Prepare and interpret a source and use of cash statement.

b Prepare and interpret a source and use of net working capital statement.
c Prepare and interpret a source and use of cash statement on a percentage basis.

Balance Sheet
Raney Russell Company
Years ending December 31

Assets	1977	1978
Cash	$ 2,200	$ 2,800
Marketable securities	1,000	1,500
Inventory	3,600	3,900
Total current assets	$ 6,800	$ 8,200
Net plant and equipment	$15,000	$14,800
Total	$21,800	$23,000

Liabilities and stockholders' equity

	1977	1978
Accounts payable	$ 1,500	$ 1,600
Notes payable—bank	2,500	3,000
Total current liabilities	$ 4,000	$ 4,600
Long-term debt	$ 5,000	$ 5,000
Common stock	$10,000	$10,000
Retained earnings	2,800	3,400
Total	$21,800	$23,000

Additional data

Depreciation	$1,600
Earnings after taxes	$1,400

5-4 Use the following financial data for the Gold Equipment Company to
a Prepare and interpret a source and use of cash statement.
b Prepare and interpret a source and use of net working capital statement.
c Prepare and interpret a source and use of cash statement on a percentage basis.

Balance Sheet
Gold Equipment Company
Years Ending December 31

Assets	1977	1978
Cash	$ 16,000	$ 15,000
Marketable securities	8,000	7,200
Accounts receivable	40,000	33,000
Inventory	50,000	82,000
Prepaid rent	2,200	1,100
Total current assets	$116,200	$138,300
Net plant and equipment	$285,000	$270,000
Total Assets	$401,200	$408,300

Liabilities and stockholders' equity

Accounts payable	$ 49,000	$ 57,000
Notes payable	16,000	13,000
Accruals	6,000	5,000
Total current liabilities	$ 71,000	$ 75,000
Long-term debt	$160,000	$150,000
Stockholders' equity	$170,200	$183,300
Total Liabilities and Equity	$401,200	$408,300

Income Statement
Gold Equipment Company
Year Ending December 31, 1978

Sales		$600,000
Less: Cost of goods sold		460,000
Gross profit		$140,000
Less: Expenses		
General and administrative	$ 40,000	
Depreciation	30,000	
Total		70,000
Profits before taxes		$ 70,000
Less: Taxes		27,100
Profits after taxes		$ 42,900
Less: Cash dividends		20,000
To Retained Earnings		$ 22,900

5-5 A firm has actual sales of $65,000 in April and $60,000 in May. It expects sales of $70,000 in June and $100,000 in July and August, respectively. Assuming sales are the only source of cash inflows and half of these are for cash while the remainder are collected evenly over the following two months, what are the firm's expected cash receipts for July and August?

5-6 The American Tire Company had sales of $50,000 in March and $60,000 in April. Forecast sales for May, June, and July are $70,000, $80,000, and $100,000, respectively. The firm has a cash balance of $5000 on May 1. Given the following data, prepare and interpret a cash budget for the months of May, June, and July.

   (1) Twenty percent of the firm's sales are for cash, 60 percent are collected in the next month, the remaining 20 percent are collected in the second month following sale.

   (2) The firm receives other income of $2000 per month.

   (3) The firm's actual or expected purchases are $50,000, $70,000, and $80,000 for the months of May through July, respectively.

   (4) Rent is $3000 per month.

   (5) Wages and salaries are 10 percent of the previous month's sales.

   (6) Cash dividends of $3000 will be paid in June.

   (7) Payment of principal and interest of $4000 is due in June.

   (8) A cash purchase of equipment costing $6000 is scheduled in July.

   (9) Taxes of $6000 are due in June.

5-7 Archer Appliance Company's actual sales and purchases for September and October 1977, along with its forecast sales and purchases for the period November 1977 through April of 1978, are presented below.

Year	Month	Sales	Purchases
1977	Sept.	$210,000	$120,000
1977	Oct.	250,000	150,000
1977	Nov.	170,000	140,000
1977	Dec.	160,000	100,000
1978	Jan.	140,000	80,000
1978	Feb.	180,000	110,000
1978	Mar.	200,000	100,000
1978	Apr.	250,000	90,000

The firm makes 20 percent of all sales for cash and collects on 40 percent of its sales in each of the two months following the sale. Other cash inflows are expected to be $12,000 in September, February, and April, and $15,000 in January, February, and March. The firm pays cash for 10 percent of its purchases. It pays for 50 percent of its purchases in the following month and 40 percent of its purchases two months later.

Salaries and wages amount to 20 percent of the preceding month's sales. Rent of $20,000 per month must be paid. Interest payments of $10,000 are due in January and April. A principal payment of $30,000 is also due in April. The firm expects to pay cash dividends of $20,000 in January and April. Taxes of $80,000 are due in April. The firm also intends to make a capital outlay of $25,000 in December.

a Assuming that the firm has a cash balance of $22,000 at the beginning of November, determine the end-of-month cash balances for each month November through April.

b Assuming that the firm wishes to maintain a $15,000 minimum cash balance, determine the monthly borrowing requirements or excess cash.

c If the firm were requesting a line of credit in order to cover needed borrowing for the period of November to April, how large would this line have to be? Explain your answer.

5-8 Patterson's Parts Store expects to sell $100,000 in parts during each of the next three months. It is committed to accept monthly purchases of $60,000 during this time. Wages and salaries are $10,000 per month plus five percent of sales. Patterson's expects to make a tax payment of $20,000 in the next month, a capital expenditure of $15,000 in the second month, and receive $8000 of cash from the sale of an asset in the third month. All sales are for cash. Beginning cash balances are assumed to be zero.

a Construct a cash budget for the next three months.

b Patterson's is unsure of the sales levels, but all other figures are certain. If the most pessimistic sales figure is $80,000 per month and the most optimistic is $120,000 per month, what are the monthly minimum and maximum cash balances the firm can expect for each of the one-month periods?

c Combine a and b into a sensitivity analysis for Patterson's Parts Store. Briefly discuss how these combined data allow the financial manager to plan for his financing needs.

SELECTED REFERENCES

Anthony, Ted F., and Hugh J. Watson, "Probabilistic Financial Planning," *Journal of Systems Management 23* (September 1972), pp. 38–41.

Bogen, Jules I., Ed., *Financial Handbook*, 4th ed. (New York: Ronald, 1968), sect. 15.

Foulke, R. A., *Practical Financial Statement Analysis*, 6th ed. (New York: McGraw-Hill, 1968).

Gitman, Lawrence J., and Thomas M. Cook, "Cash Budgeting: A Simulation Approach," *Journal of the Midwest Finance Association* (1973), pp. 87–100.

Helfert, Erich A., *Techniques of Financial Analysis*, 4th ed. (Homewood, Ill.: Irwin, 1976), chaps. 1 and 5.

Jaedicke, Robert K., and Robert T. Sprouse, *Accounting Flows: Income, Funds, and Cash* (Englewood Cliffs, N.J.: Prentice-Hall, 1965), chaps. 5 and 6.

Lerner, Eugene M., "Simulating a Cash Budget," *California Management Review 11* (Winter 1968), pp. 79–86.

Lynch, Richard M., *Accounting for Management: Planning and Control* (New York: McGraw-Hill, 1967), chap. 6.

Meigs, Walter B., A. N. Mosich, Charles E. Johnson, and Thomas F. Keller, *Financial Accounting*, 3rd ed. (New York: McGraw-Hill, 1974), chaps. 22 and 23.

Moore, Laurence J. and David F. Scott, "Simulation of Cash Budgets," *Journal of Systems Management 24* (November 1973), pp. 28–33.

Packer, Stephen B., "Flow of Funds Analysis—Its Uses and Limitations," *Financial Analysts Journal* (July-August 1964), pp. 117–123.

Pan, Judy, Donald R. Nichols, and O. Maurice Joy, "Sales Forecasting Practice of Large U.S. Industrial Firms," *Financial Management 6* (Fall 1977), pp. 72–77.

Pappas, James L., and George P. Huber, "Probabilistic Short-Term Financial Planning," *Financial Management 2* (Autumn 1973), pp. 36–44.

Seitz, Neil, *Financial Analysis: A Programmed Approach*, (Reston, Va.: Reston Publishing Co., 1976), chaps. 1 and 2.

Stone, Bernell K., and Robert A. Wood, "Daily Cash Forecasting: A Simple Method for Implementing the Distribution Approach," *Financial Management 6* (Fall 1977), pp. 40–50.

Trumbull, Wendell P., "Developing the Funds Statement as the Third Major Financial Statement," *N.A.A. Bulletin 45* (April 1963), pp. 21–31.

Viscione, Jerry A., *Financial Analysis: Principles and Procedures* (Boston: Houghton Mifflin, 1977), chaps. 2 and 3.

Welsch, Glenn A., Charles T. Zlatkovich, and John A. White, *Intermediate Accounting*, 4th ed. (Homewood, Ill.: Irwin, 1976), chap. 25.

Wright, Leonard T., *Financial Management: Analytical Techniques* (Columbus, Ohio: Grid, 1974), chaps. 3 and 4.

CHAPTER 6
Pro forma statements

Pro forma statements are projected financial statements. Typically, data are forecast for one year ahead. The firm's pro forma income statement shows its expected revenues and costs for the coming year, while its pro forma balance sheet shows its expected financial position (i.e., its assets, liabilities, and stockholders' equity) at the end of the forecast period. Pro forma statements are not only useful in the internal financial planning process but are typically required by interested parties such as current and prospective lenders. They provide these parties with an estimate of the firm's financial condition in the coming year. Its actual performance can be evaluated with respect to these estimates in order to determine their accuracy and to make adjustments for discrepancies. Pro forma statements differ from the cash budget in that they provide estimates not just of future cash requirements, but of all assets, liabilities, equities, and income statement items.

This chapter has five major sections. The first section presents an overview of the entire budgeting process and relates the various budgeting inputs to pro forma statements. The second section is devoted to shortcut approaches commonly used in the preparation of pro forma income statements and balance sheets. The third section describes the steps required to develop key budgets, using the same simple two-model-two–raw-materials example illustrated in the preceding section. The development of the sales forecast, the production plan, the raw-material-usage plan, raw material purchases, direct labor requirements, factory overhead, operating expenses, the long-term financing plan, and the capital expenditure plan are described. The fourth section illustrates how the pro forma income statement is prepared. The final section describes how the pro forma balance sheet is developed.

BUDGETING INPUTS TO PRO FORMA PREPARATION

In order to prepare the firm's pro forma income statement and balance sheet correctly, certain preliminary budgets must be developed. The series of budgets begins with the firm's sales forecasts and ends with the cash budget. The

FIGURE 6.1 Budgeting inputs for pro forma statements

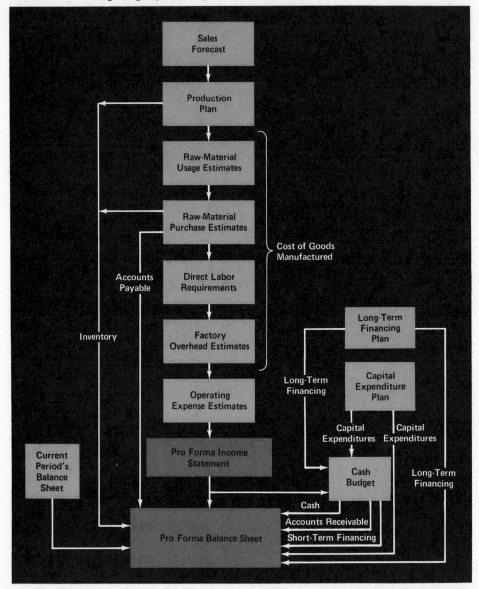

total budgeting process, from the initial sales forecasts through the development of the pro forma income statement and balance sheet, is presented in a flow-chart format in Figure 6.1.

Using the sales forecast as a basic input, a production plan is developed that takes into account the amount of lead time necessary to convert an item from a raw material into a finished good. The types and quantities of raw materials required during the forecast period can be estimated from the production plan. Based on these material usage estimates, a schedule of when and how much of each raw material to purchase can be developed. Also based on the production plan, estimates of the amount of direct labor required, in either man-hours or dollars, can be made. The firm's overhead outlays can also be estimated. Finally, the firm's operating expenses, specifically its sales and administrative expenses, can be estimated based on the level of operations necessary to support forecast sales.

Once this series of plans has been prepared, the firm's pro forma income statement can be developed. The firm's cash budget based on monthly or quarterly breakdowns of cash receipts and disbursements, can also be created. With the pro forma income statement, the cash budget, the long-term financing plan, the capital expenditure plan, and the current period's balance sheet as basic inputs, the firm's pro forma balance sheet can be developed. The pro forma income statement is needed to find the projected change in retained earnings, depreciation, and taxes. Data on the firm's cash balance, notes payable, level of accounts receivable, and level of accounts payable can be obtained from the cash budget. The long-term financing plan provides information on changes in long-term debts and stockholders' equity attributed to the firm's financing decisions. The capital expenditure plan provides information with respect to expected changes in the firm's fixed assets.

The preceding period's balance sheet is necessary in order to have initial values against which to measure changes in various balance sheet items such as fixed assets, common stock, and retained earnings. The values for beginning cash, beginning accounts receivable, beginning inventory, and beginning debts are also derived from the most recent period's balance sheet. It is often quite helpful to compare the pro forma balance sheet to the current balance sheet to check the reasonableness of the forecast statement; a glaring discrepancy may exist that can be reconciled through further analysis.

A SHORTCUT APPROACH TO PRO FORMA PREPARATION

Before treating the theoretically correct method for preparing pro forma statements, it is useful to discuss the commonly used shortcuts for pro forma preparation. Since the procedures outlined by the flow chart in Figure 6.1 are quite tedious and time consuming, shortcut approaches often are used to get a feel for the firm's projected financial condition. Although the use of such shortcuts may not be as accurate as the longer approach, its appeal lies in the ease of application. A variety of shortcut approaches exist for preparing pro forma statements; the most popular are based upon the belief that the financial relationships reflected on the firm's historic financial statements will not change in the coming period. The most common of the shortcut pro forma preparation techniques is presented by way of an example over the next few pages.

Background information

The inputs required for preparing pro forma statements using the shortcut approach are recent financial statements and a sales forecast. A variety of assumptions must also be made when using a shortcut approach. The com-

**TABLE 6.1 An income statement
for the DuBois Manufacturing Company
for the year ended December 31, 1978**

Sales		
Model X	$20,000	
Model Y	81,000	
Total sales		$101,000
Less: Cost of goods sold		
Labor	$28,500	
Material A	8,000	
Material B	5,500	
Overhead	38,000	
Total cost of goods sold		80,000
Gross profits		$ 21,000
Less: Operating expense		10,000
Operating profits		$ 11,000
Less: Interest expense		1,000
Profits before taxes		$ 10,000
Less: Taxes (.20 · $10,000)		2,000
Profits after taxes		$ 8,000
Less: Common stock dividends		4,000
To Retained Earnings		$ 4,000

pany used throughout this chapter is the DuBois Manufacturing Company, which manufactures and sells one basic product, widgets. It has two basic models—model X and model Y. Although each model is produced by the same process, they require different amounts of raw material and labor. The products are produced from two raw materials—A and B.

Recent financial statements. The firm's income statement for the 1978 operations is given in Table 6.1. It indicates that the firm paid $4000 in cash dividends in the most recent period of operation. The firm's balance sheet for the most recent period of operation, 1978, is given in Table 6.2.

The sales forecast. The key input for the development of pro forma statements is the sales forecast. The sales forecast by model for the coming year, 1979, for the DuBois Company is given in Table 6.3. This forecast is based on both external and internal data.[1] The unit sale prices given reflect an increase from $20 to $25 for model X and from $27 to $35 for model Y. These increases are required in order to cover the firm's anticipated increases in labor, overhead, and sales and administrative costs.

---

[1]A discussion of the calculation of the various forecasting techniques, such as regression, moving averages, and exponential smoothing, is not included in this text. The reader is referred to a basic statistics, econometrics, or management science text for a description of the technical side of forecasting. A few references on the subject have been included at the end of this chapter.

TABLE 6.2 A balance sheet for the DuBois Manufacturing Company for the year ended December 31, 1978

Assets		Liabilities and equities	
Cash	$ 6,000.00	Accounts payable	$12,000.00
Marketable securities	4,016.40	Taxes payable	3,740.00
Accounts receivable	13,000.00	Other current liabilities	6,260.00
Inventory	15,983.60	Total current liabilities	$22,000.00
Total current assets	$39,000.00	Long-term debt	$15,000.00
Net fixed assets	51,000.00	Stockholders' equity	
Total Assets	$90,000.00	Common stock	$30,000.00
		Retained earnings	$23,000.00
		Total Liabilities and Stockholders' Equity	$90,000.00

The pro forma income statement

A simple way to develop a pro forma income statement is to use a per-cent-of-sales method, in which one forecasts sales and uses values for the cost of goods sold, operating expense, and interest expense that are a certain percentage of the projected sales. The percentages used are likely to be the percentage of sales these items equaled in a previous year. For the DuBois Manufacturing Company, these percentages are as follows:

$$\frac{\text{cost of goods sold}}{\text{sales}} = \frac{\$80,000}{\$101,000} = 79.2 \text{ percent}$$

$$\frac{\text{operating expenses}}{\text{sales}} = \frac{\$10,000}{\$101,000} = 9.9 \text{ percent}$$

$$\frac{\text{interest expense}}{\text{sales}} = \frac{\$1000}{\$101,000} = 1.0 \text{ percent}$$

The dollar values used are taken from the 1978 income statement (Table 6.1).

TABLE 6.3 1979 sales forecast for the DuBois Manufacturing Company

Unit sales	
Model X	1,500
Model Y	2,800
Dollar sales	
Model X ($25/unit)	$ 37,500
Model Y ($35/unit)	98,000
Total	$135,500

TABLE 6.4 A pro forma income statement, using the shortcut approach, for the DuBois Manufacturing Company for the year ended December 31, 1979

Sales	$135,500.00
Less: Cost of goods sold (79.2%)	107,316.00
Gross profits	$ 28,184.00
Less: Operating expense (9.9%)	13,414.50
Operating profits	$ 14,769.50
Less: Interest expense (1.0%)	1,355.00
Profits before taxes	$ 13,414.50
Less: Taxes (.20 · $13,414.50)	2,682.90
Profits after taxes	$ 10,731.60
Less: Common stock dividends	4,000.00
To Retained Earnings	$ 6,731.60

Applying these percentages to the firm's forecast level of sales of $135,500, developed in Table 6.3, and assuming that the firm will pay $4000 in cash dividends in 1979 results in the pro forma income statement in Table 6.4.

At this point is is difficult to assess the accuracy of the expected contribution to retained earnings since neither the actual outcomes nor the pro forma income statement correctly prepared are available.

Considering types of costs and expenses. It is important to recognize that the technique used to prepare the pro forma income statement in Table 6.4 assumes that all of the firm's costs are variable. This occurs since the use of the historic (i.e., actual 1978) ratios of cost of goods sold, operating expenses, and interest expense to sales assumes that for a given percent increase in sales the same percent increase in each of these cost and expense components will result. For example, as DuBois's sales increased by 34.2 percent (from $101,000 in 1978 to $135,500 projected for 1979), its cost of goods sold also increased by 34.2 percent (from $80,000 in 1978 to $107,316 projected for 1979). Because of this fixed percentage assumption, the firm's profits before taxes also increased by 34.2 percent (from $10,000 in 1978 to $13,414.50 projected for 1979). It should be quite clear that this approach assumes all costs are variable—the firm has no fixed costs. The broader implication is that since the firm has no fixed costs, it has no leverage. Therefore, the use of past cost and expense ratios tends to understate profits since the firm is likely to have certain fixed costs in its operating and financial structure. Of course, for high fixed-cost firms this approach will underestimate profits by more than would be true in the case of firms having lower fixed costs. The best way to adjust for the presence of fixed costs when using the shortcut approach for pro forma income statement preparation is to break the firm's historic costs into fixed and variable components and make the forecast using this relationship.

EXAMPLE

The ABC Company's last and pro forma income statements, which are broken into fixed and variable cost components, are given below:

ABC Company Income Statements		
	Last Year	Pro forma
Sales	$100,000	$120,000
Less: Cost of goods sold		
Fixed cost	20,000	20,000
Variable cost (.40 sales)	40,000	48,000
Gross profit	$ 40,000	$ 52,000
Less: Operating expense		
Fixed expense	5,000	5,000
Variable expense (.15 sales)	15,000	18,000
Operating profit	$ 20,000	$ 29,000
Less: Interest (all fixed)	8,000	8,000
Profit before tax	$ 12,000	$ 21,000
Tax (.20 · profit before tax)	2,400	4,200
Profit after taxes	$ 9,600	$ 16,800

By breaking its costs and expenses into fixed and variable components, the ABC Company's pro forma income is expected to provide a more accurate projection. Had the firm treated all costs as variable, its pro forma profits before taxes would equal 12 percent of sales, just as was the case in the last year ($12,000 profits before tax ÷ $100,000 sales). The profit before taxes would therefore have been $14,400 (12% · $120,000 projected sales) instead of the $21,000 profit before tax value found using the firm's fixed cost-variable cost breakdown. ●

The preceding example should make it clear that when using a shortcut approach to pro forma income statement preparation, it is advisable to consider first the breakdown of costs and expenses into their fixed and variable components. Due to a lack of available data, the pro forma income statement prepared for DuBois Manufacturing Company in Table 6.4 is based upon the assumption that all costs are variable—which is likely *not* to be the case. Therefore, its projected profits may be understated.

The pro forma balance sheet

A short approach for developing the pro forma balance sheet involves estimating the desired levels of certain balance sheet items and calculating the value of other items. When this approach is employed, the firm's required financing is used as a balancing figure. In order to apply this approach to the DuBois Manufacturing Company's balance sheet, a number of assumptions must be made:

1. A minimum cash balance of $6000 is desired.

2. Accounts receivable will average three-fourths of a month's sales (i.e., an average age of accounts receivable of 30 · .75 = 22.5 days). Since DuBois' annual sales are projected to be $135,500, the accounts receivable should average $8468.75 ($1/16$ · $135,000) in any given month. (One-sixteenth represents three-fourths of a month expressed as a fraction of a year.)
3. The ending inventory should remain at a level of about $16,000, of which 25 percent (approximately $4000) should be raw materials, while the remaining 75 percent (approximately $12,000) should consist of finished goods.
4. A new machine costing $20,000, which will be depreciated on a straight-line basis over the next 10 years ($2000 per year) will be purchased. Adding the $20,000 acquisition to the existing fixed assets of $51,000 and subtracting the depreciation of $7000 ($5000 of current depreciation + $2000 on the new machine) will yield net fixed assets of $64,000.
5. Purchases are expected to represent approximately 20 percent of annual sales, which in this case would be approximately $27,000 (.20 · $135,500). The firm believes it can stretch the time it takes to pay its accounts payable to approximately 45 days. Thus accounts payable should equal, on the average, one-eighth (i.e., 45 days ÷ 360 days) of the firm's purchases, or $3375 ($1/8$ · $27,000).
6. Taxes payable are expected to equal the current year's tax liability, which is $2682.90 on the shortcut pro forma income statement found in Table 6.4.
7. No change in other current liabilities is expected. They will remain at the level of the previous year, $6260.
8. The firm's long-term debts and its common stock are expected to remain unchanged, at $15,000 and $30,000, respectively, since no issues, repurchases, or retirements of bonds or stocks are planned.
9. Retained earnings will increase from the beginning level of $23,000 to $29,731.60. The increase of $6731.60 represents the amount of retained earnings calculated in the shortcut pro forma income statement (Table 6.4).

A 1979 pro forma balance sheet for the DuBois Manufacturing Company based on these assumptions is presented in Table 6.5. The approximate nature of the values contained in the pro forma balance sheet is obvious from the fact that a balancing figure of $11,435.65 is needed.

Although the values shown in the pro forma balance sheet prepared using the numerous assumptions may provide a "rough" feel for the firm's financial position one year hence, more reliable estimates are expected to result from application of the procedures reflected in the flow chart in Figure 6.1. The decision maker would certainly have a higher degree of confidence in the balance sheet developed using the long approach, since much more detail and fewer assumptions are required in the development of the values.

TABLE 6.5 **A pro forma balance sheet, using the shortcut approach, for the DuBois Manufacturing Company for the year ended December 31, 1979**

Assets			Liabilities and equities	
Cash		$ 6,000.00	Accounts payable	$ 3,375.00
Marketable securities (unchanged)		4,016.40	Taxes payable	2,682.90
Accounts receivable		8,468.75	Other current liabilities	6,260.00
Inventories			Total current liabilities	$12,317.90
Raw materials	$ 4,000.00		Long-term debt	$15,000.00
Finished goods	12,000.00		Stockholders' equity	
Total		16,000.00	Common stock	$30,000.00
Total current assets		$34,485.15	Retained earnings	$29,731.60
Net fixed assets		64,000.00	Total	$87,049.50
Total Assets		$98,485.15	Plug figure[a]	$11,435.65
			Total Liabilities and Stockholders' Equity	$98,485.15

[a]The plug figure represents financing necessary to force the firm's balance sheet to balance. Due to the nature of the shortcut approach to preparing the pro forma balance sheet, the balance sheet is not expected to balance without some type of adjustment.

While the shortcut approach is based on determining the *effects* desired, developing a balance sheet based on these effects, and balancing it with a *plug figure,* the longer, more accepted approach for pro forma preparation presented in a subsequent section of the chapter is based on determining the *causes* and then calculating the effects.

Weaknesses of shortcut approaches

The basic weaknesses of the shortcut approaches to pro forma statement preparation lie in (1) the assumption that the firm's past financial condition is an accurate predictor of its future financial condition and (2) assuming that the values of certain variables such as cash, inventory, and accounts receivable can be forced to take on certain "desired" values. These assumptions are quite questionable, but due to the ease of the calculations involved, the use of shortcut approaches similar to those illustrated is quite common.

Other shortcut approaches do exist. Most are based on the assumption that certain relationships between income, assets, liabilities, and equities will prevail in the future. For example, in preparing the firm's pro forma balance sheet, the firm's assets, liabilities, and equities are often increased by the percentage increase expected in sales. It is most important for the financial analyst to keep in mind what techniques have been used in preparing pro forma statements. This will give him a feel for the quality of the estimated values and the degree of confidence he can have in them. Subsequent parts of this chapter illustrate the correct approaches for preparing pro forma statements.

TABLE 6.6 1978 sales data for
the DuBois Manufacturing Company

	Model		
	X	Y	Total
Sale price	$ 20	$ 27	—
Units sold	1,000	3,000	—
Sales revenue[a]	$20,000	$81,000	$101,000

[a]Sale price · units sold.

THE LONG APPROACH TO PRO FORMA PREPARATION: PRELIMINARY BUDGETS

In order to prepare pro forma statements using the longer, more correct approach described by Figure 6.1, additional data—both historic and projected—are required. Using the background data along with the past financial statements and sales forecast presented earlier in Tables 6.1 through 6.3, DuBois Manufacturing Company can prepare a variety of plans that act as inputs to the pro forma statements.

Developing background information

As indicated in the preceding part of the chapter, DuBois Manufacturing Company produces and sells one basic product, widgets. It has two basic models of widgets—model X and model Y. Although each model is produced by the same process, they require different amounts of raw material and labor.

Sales data. The sale price of each model also differs. The prevailing market prices, associated unit sales, and sales revenues for each are given in Table 6.6. As the table shows, the firm's total 1978 sales equaled $101,000.

Labor and materials. The labor and material requirements, along with the cost per unit, for each model is given in Table 6.7. As indicated in

TABLE 6.7 1978 labor and
material costs/unit for the DuBois
Manufacturing Company

	Model	
	X	Y
Direct labor	$6.00	$7.50
Raw-materials cost		
A	$2.00	$2.00
B	1.00	1.50
Raw-materials cost/unit	$3.00	$3.50

TABLE 6.8 1978 unit labor and material requirements for the DuBois Manufacturing Company

	Model	
	X	Y
Direct labor (hours)	2.0	2.5
Raw materials (units)		
A	1.0	1.0
B	2.0	3.0

Note: All the unit figures were found by dividing the items in Table 6.7 by the cost per unit, which was $3.00 per labor hour, $2.00 per unit of raw material A, and $0.50 per unit of raw material B.

the table, each model of the product is made from two basic raw materials. Material A costs $2.00 per unit, and B costs $0.50 per unit. Direct labor costs $3.00 per hour. Using these values, Table 6.7 can be recast to show per unit labor and material requirements. This is done in Table 6.8.

Factory overhead. The firm's factory-overhead costs, which represent the outlays necessary to support production, totaled $38,000. These costs are itemized in Table 6.9. Factory-overhead costs are normally applied to each product on the basis of the labor cost per unit, labor hours per unit, or floor space used. The DuBois Manufacturing Company allocated its factory overhead on the basis of direct labor costs. Table 6.10 presents a breakdown of the total overhead costs on a unit-cost basis. The overhead allocation per unit for each of the models is given in Table 6.10 and will be used in the production planning phase of developing the firm's pro forma statements.

TABLE 6.9 A 1978 factory-overhead breakdown for the DuBois Manufacturing Company

Indirect labor	$ 6,000
Factory supplies	5,200
Heat, light, and power	2,000
Supervision	8,000
Maintenance	3,500
Engineering	5,500
Property and payroll taxes and insurance	2,800
Depreciation	5,000
Total Factory Overhead	$38,000

TABLE 6.10 A 1978 breakdown of factory overhead on
the basis of direct labor costs for DuBois Manufacturing Company

	Model	
Item	X	Y
(1) Direct labor cost/unit	$ 6.00	$ 7.50
(2) Number of units produced (sold)	1,000	3,000
(3) Total labor cost/model	$6,000	$22,500
(4) Total labor cost	$28,500	
(5) Percentage of total labor cost/model	21%	79%
(6) Overhead allocation	$7,980	$30,020
(7) Overhead Allocation/Unit	$ 7.98	$ 10.00

SOURCES: Item (1)—from Table 6.7
Item (2)—from Table 6.6
Item (3)—item (1) · item (2)
Item (4)—sum of item (3) for models X and Y
Item (5)—item (3) for each model as a percentage of item (4)
Item (6)—item (5) · total factory overhead ($38,000)
Item (7)—item (6) ÷ item (2)

By adding the labor cost per unit and material cost per unit from Table
6.7 to the overhead allocation per unit from Table 6.10, the total cost per unit
can be found. The total cost per unit for models X and Y is $16.98 and $21.00,
respectively.

Operating expenses. The firm's operating expenses, which consist
of sales and administrative expenses for the most recent year, are given in
Table 6.11.

TABLE 6.11 1978 operating
expenses for the DuBois Manufacturing Company

Selling expense:		
Sales salaries	$3,000	
Freight out	800	
Advertising	1,200	
Total selling expense		$ 5,000
Administrative expense:		
Administrative salaries	$3,100	
Office supplies	700	
Telephone	300	
Professional fees	900	
Total administrative expense		5,000
Total 1978 Operating Expenses		$10,000

TABLE 6.12 1978 inventory breakdown
for the DuBois Manufacturing Company

	Units	Dollars
Raw-materials inventory		
Material A	600	$ 1,200.00
Material B	4,000	2,000.00
Total		$ 3,200.00
Finished-goods inventory		
Model X	320	$ 5,433.60
Model Y	350	7,350.00
Total		$12,783.60
Total Inventory		$15,983.60

The inventory breakdown. The inventory shown on the firm's 1978 balance sheet (Table 6.2) consists only of raw materials and finished goods. No work-in-process inventory remains at the end of the year. Table 6.12 presents the firm's current inventory breakdown based by type of raw material and by model. These figures will be quite helpful in developing the pro forma statements in the following section.

Developing the required plans
The following sections are devoted to the development of the forecasts and plans required as inputs to the pro forma statements. (See Figure 6.1.) They are based upon the forecast sales volumes and increased sales prices presented in Table 6.3.

The production plan. In order to estimate the required level of production for each model, the production plan for the year shown in Table 6.13 was drawn up. The firm's goal is to maintain in its finished-goods inventory 8 percent of the expected sales for the coming year for each model. This

TABLE 6.13 1979 production plan by model
(in units) for the DuBois Manufacturing Company

	Model	
	X	Y
Desired ending inventory of finished goods	120	224
Add: Forecast sales	1500	2800
Total needs	1620	3024
Less: Beginning inventory of finished goods	320	350
Production Required	1300	2674

would provide approximately one month's sales in inventory (since $8\% \cdot 12$ months $= .96$ months). It can be seen from Table 6.13 that the firm will need to produce 1300 model X's and 2674 model Y's in order to fulfill the forecast sales demand while maintaining the desired level of finished goods in inventory.

Raw-materials usage.   Using the production plan as an input, the firm's raw-materials requirements can be estimated. Multiplying the quantity of each raw material needed to produce a unit of each model by the number of units of each model required results in the total raw-materials requirements. The number of units of each raw material required for each product was given in Table 6.8, and the required production was calculated in the production plan, Table 6.13. The raw-materials requirements to the nearest unit can be calculated as follows:

Material A $= 1(1300) + 1(2674)$
$= 3974$ units

Material B $= 2(1300) + 3(2674)$
$= 10,622$ units

The firm's management also wants an ending inventory of raw materials A and B of 500 and 3000 units, respectively. The total purchases of each raw material can be estimated by simple addition, as in Table 6.14.

The required raw-materials purchases calculated in Table 6.14 can easily be converted into dollar figures by multiplying the unit requirements for raw materials A and B by the corresponding unit cost ($2.00 and $0.50, respectively). These are the same unit costs used in 1978; it is assumed that the cost per unit of raw materials A and B will not change.

Multiplying the quantities of each raw material to be purchased by the corresponding unit costs yields the cost of purchase for each raw material, A and B. Adding these costs gives us the total annual raw-materials purchases in dollars.

Purchase cost of material A $= \$2.00\ (3874)$ $=$ $\$\ 7,748.00$
Purchase cost of material B $=\ \ 0.50\ (9622)$ $=$ $\underline{\ \ 4,811.00}$
    Total 1979 raw-materials purchases $=$ $\underline{\underline{\$12,559.00}}$

Raw-materials purchases.   Using the firm's required raw-materials purchases, an estimate of its raw materials-purchase schedule, indicating when and how much of each raw material should be purchased, can be constructed. Since this company is in a relatively stable business, the raw-materials purchases are expected to occur in equal quarterly amounts. This means that one-fourth of the purchase cost of each raw material will be incurred quarterly.

TABLE 6.14 1979 required raw-materials
purchases (in units) for the DuBois Manufacturing Company

	Raw material	
	A	B
Desired ending inventory of raw materials	500	3,000
Add: Required usage	3,974	10,622
Total requirement	4,474	13,622
Less: Beginning raw-materials inventory	600	4,000
Required Raw-Materials Purchases	3,874	9,622

$$
\begin{array}{lll}
\text{Quarterly purchase of material A} & = & \$1937.00 \\
\text{Quarterly purchase of material B} & = & \underline{1202.75} \\
\quad\text{Total quarterly material} & & \\
\quad\quad\text{purchase} & = & \underline{\$3139.75}
\end{array}
$$

The total quarterly purchases of raw materials would therefore cost $3139.75.

Direct labor. In Table 6.7 the direct labor cost per unit of each model, X and Y, was indicated to be $6.00 and $7.50 per unit, respectively. Due to certain labor negotiations that occurred during 1978, the direct labor rate in 1979 will be $4.00 instead of the $3.00. Table 6.8 indicated that models X and Y required 2 and 2.5 direct labor hours, respectively. The new direct labor cost per unit of models X and Y is $8.00 and $10.00, respectively, the labor rate by the required direct labor hours for each model. The per-unit direct labor costs for the current year for each model are as follows:

Model X: 2.0($4.00) = $8.00/unit
Model Y: 2.5($4.00) = $10.00/unit

Applying the per-unit labor costs to the production requirements in Table 6.13 results in the total labor costs associated with the production of each model. Table 6.13 indicated that 1300 and 2674 units of models X and Y, respectively, would have to be produced in the current period. If the direct labor cost per unit of models X and Y is $8.00 and $10.00, respectively, the total direct labor costs for each model, along with the overall total annual direct labor cost, will be as follows:

$$
\begin{array}{lll}
\text{Model X:} \quad \$8.00 \ (1300 \text{ units}) & = & \$10,400 \\
\text{Model Y:} \ \$10.00 \ (2674 \text{ units}) & = & \underline{26,740} \\
\quad\text{Total annual direct labor} & & \\
\quad\quad\text{cost} & = & \underline{\$37,140}
\end{array}
$$

As indicated in the preceding section, the firm produces its products at a constant rate throughout the year. One-fourth of the total annual direct labor cost is expected to be incurred each quarter. Dividing the total annual direct labor cost of $37,140, calculated above, by 4 yields quarterly direct labor costs of $9285.

Factory overhead. The firm's budgeted factory overhead for 1979 is $50,000. This estimate was prepared by the firm's budgeting staff, with the aid of the firm's plant superintendent. The annual and quarterly totals for overhead are shown in Table 6.15. The table indicates (when compared to the 1978 data in Table 6.9) that the cost of most budgeted items is expected to increase in 1979.

A breakdown of these budgeted factory-overhead costs on the basis of direct labor costs can be calculated for the projected level of sales. The technique used is similar to that used in Table 6.10. The calculations are shown in Table 6.16. As the table indicates, the overhead allocation per unit produced is $10.77 and $13.46 for models X and Y, respectively.

Operating expenses. The firm has projected its total operating expenses in 1979 to be $16,000. A detailed breakdown of these expenses is presented in Table 6.17. Comparing the projected operating expenses with those of 1978, given in Table 6.11 shows that the major factors contributing to the increased operating expenses are sales salaries and advertising expenses. Higher levels of these items are projected due to a stiffening of competition. The firm believes that by increasing sales salaries and advertising outlays it can meet the competition head-on and maintain its market share of each of its models.

The long-term financing plan. The firm has not scheduled any changes in its long-term financing during 1979. Any scheduled capital ex-

TABLE 6.15 1979 budgeted factory overhead
cost for the DuBois Manufacturing Company

Item	Annual	Quarterly
Indirect labor	$ 8,000	$ 2,000
Factory supplies	5,600	1,400
Heat, light, and power	3,200	800
Supervision	10,000	2,500
Maintenance	5,000	1,250
Engineering	7,200	1,800
Property and payroll taxes and insurance	4,000	1,000
Depreciation	7,000	1,750
Total Factory Overhead	$50,000	$12,500

TABLE 6.16 1979 allocation of budgeted factory overhead on the basis of direct labor costs for the DuBois Manufacturing Company

	Model	
Item	X	Y
(1) Total labor cost/model	$10,400	$26,740
(2) Total labor cost	$37,140	
(3) Percentage of total labor cost/model	28%	72%
(4) Overhead allocation	$14,000	$36,000
(5) Overhead Allocation/Unit	$ 10.77	$ 13.46

SOURCES: Item (1)—from section on direct labor
Item (2)—sum of item (1) for X and Y
Item (3)—item (1) for each model as a percentage of item (2)
Item (4)—item (3) · budgeted factory overhead ($50,000)
Item (5)—item (4) divided by the corresponding number of units of X and
Y to be produced (1300 and 2674 units, respectively)

penditures are expected to be paid for with funds generated internally from operations. The incurrence or retirement of long-term debt and (or) the sale, repurchase, or retirement of stock is not scheduled for 1979.

The capital expenditure plan. The firm has scheduled one major capital expenditure, the purchase of a new machine costing $20,000. The machine will be depreciated by the straight-line method over a 10-year period with no salvage value. The annual depreciation will therefore be $2000 ($20,000 ÷ 10 years). The machine will be paid for in two equal installments—one in March and one in September.

TABLE 6.17 1979 operating expense forecast for the DuBois Manufacturing Company

Selling expense:		
Sales salaries	$6,000	
Freight out	1,200	
Advertising	1,800	
Total selling expense		$ 9,000
Administrative expense:		
Administrative salaries	$4,000	
Office supplies	1,000	
Telephone	500	
Professional fees	1,500	
Total administrative expense		7,000
Total 1979 Operating Expense Forecast		$16,000

THE PRO FORMA INCOME STATEMENT

Using the preliminary budgets developed in the preceding section, the DuBois Manufacturing Company's pro forma income statement can be developed. First, however, a number of preliminary calculations are necessary.

Preliminary calculations

Since the firm markets two models, each selling for a different price and requiring different cost inputs, both sales and the cost of goods sold require special attention. The cost of goods sold is especially important, since the cost per unit sold has increased from the 1978 level. In our calculations, we shall assume that the firm has a FIFO inventory system; in other words, the oldest units are sold first.

Sales.　The total sales revenue expected from the sale of models X and Y is $135,500. This figure was presented in Table 6.3.

The cost of goods sold.　The calculation of the firm's cost of goods sold is quite complex. Since the per-unit cost of goods is expected to increase between 1978 and 1979, we must consider how much of the goods sold will be from the firm's inventory and how much will be manufactured during the period.

The cost of goods sold from inventory.　Since the firm uses a FIFO (first-in, first-out) inventory system, the first 320 units of model X and first 350 units of model Y sold will cost $5433.60 and $7350.00, respectively. The total of these costs is $12,783.60. These figures can be obtained directly from Table 6.12.

The cost of goods manufactured and sold during the period.　Since the cost of raw materials has not changed since 1978, no special attention need be given to raw-materials costs. The material cost per unit for models X and Y remains $3.00 and $3.50, respectively. These are the values given in Table 6.7, earlier. By adding to these material costs the direct labor cost per unit and the overhead cost per unit, the total cost per unit can be calculated. The total cost per unit for models X and Y is given in Table 6.18.

Table 6.13 indicated that 1500 units of model X and 2800 units of model Y will be sold during the current period. If 320 units of model X and 350 units of model Y come from the firm's beginning inventory, only 1180 units (1500 units − 320 units) and 2450 units (2800 units − 350 units) of models X and Y, respectively, will be produced *and* sold during the year. The cost of these units will be $25,688.60 and $66,052.00 for models X and Y, respectively. These costs can be calculated by multiplying the total unit costs from Table 6.18 by the corresponding number of units produced *and* sold during the period. The total cost of producing and selling both models is $91,740.60.

The cost of goods sold during the period.　The cost of goods sold during the period is the sum of the cost of goods sold from inventory ($12,783.60)

TABLE 6.18 The unit cost of goods manufactured in 1979 for the DuBois Manufacturing Company

	Model	
	X	Y
Raw-materials cost/unit	$ 3.00	$ 3.50
Labor cost/unit	8.00	10.00
Overhead cost/unit	10.77	13.46
Total Cost/Unit	$21.77	$26.96

and the cost of goods manufactured and sold during 1979 ($91,740.60), which is $104,524.20.

The statement

It is assumed that the DuBois Manufacturing Company will pay $1000 in interest and $4000 in dividends during 1979. The interest payment is assumed to be constant since the firm does not plan to either repay or incur any additional long-term debt during 1979. The dividend payment will remain unchanged since the firm has a constant-dollar dividend policy.[2] The remainder of the statement should be self-explanatory. An itemization of sales by model, costs, and expenses is not included in this statement since it was included in the preceding schedules.

The pro forma income statement in Table 6.19 indicates that the company can expect its 1979 profits after taxes to be $11,180.64. These profits seem to be quite good compared to the 1978 profits of $8000.00 indicated in Table 6.1. After paying $4000.00 in cash dividends, the firm still has a sizable amount of funds to reinvest in the business. A meaningful analysis of the pro forma statement can be made by developing a percent income statement based on it and comparing it to the 1978 percent income statement. This type of comparison should reveal any major discrepancies in the pro forma income statement. Other types of ratio analysis may provide additional information.

Comparing the resulting income statement with the shortcut approach

Comparing the amount of profits going to retained earnings of $7180.64 suggested by Table 6.19 to the value of $6731.60 found in Table 6.4, using the shortcut approach, reflects the type of difference resulting from the use of this approach. If we assume the $7180.64 value to be the correct one, then

---

[2]The various types of dividend policies and their justification are thoroughly discussed in Chapter 24. A constant-dollar dividend policy is one that dictates paying out the same dollar amount of dividends each year. Quite often the dollar payment is held constant on a per-share basis, but since the DuBois Manufacturing Company does not anticipate the issuance or retirement of additional shares of common stock, the $4000 in dividends paid causes the per-share dividend to remain constant.

TABLE 6.19 A pro forma income statement for
the DuBois Manufacturing Company for the year
ended December 31, 1979

Sales	$135,500.00
Less: Cost of goods sold	104,524.20
Gross profits	$ 30,975.80
Less: Operating expense	16,000.00
Operating profits	$ 14,975.80
Less: Interest expense	1,000.00
Profits before taxes	$ 13,975.80
Less: Taxes (.20 · $13,975.80)	2,795.16
Profits after taxes	$ 11,180.64
Less: Common stock dividends	4,000.00
To Retained Earnings	$ 7,180.64

the value resulting using the shortcut approach understates the actual value
by $449.04 (i.e., $7180.64 − $6731.60), or 6.3 percent (i.e., $449.04 ÷
$7180.64).[3] If the firm can tolerate this margin of error, the shortcut approach
may be useful; of course, use of the longer approach just illustrated is recommended. The basic advantage of the longer, sophisticated approach is that
it considers changes in costs, prices, and expenses from one year to the next.
The longer approach fits into the firm's overall budgeting and planning process, and key inputs to the firm's cash budget and pro forma balance sheet can
be isolated in preparing the pro forma income statement. The technique chosen by the firm for estimating the pro forma income statement is a function
of the use of the statement, the stability of the firm's operations, and the
expected level of economic activity. If the statement is to be used by a lender
to evaluate the firm's loan application, greater accuracy is required than if the
statement were merely being used for internal control purposes. A lender
will want well-developed figures, and quite often it will examine the procedure used to prepare a statement. If the firm is in a very stable business
and economic activity is expected to remain at current levels, a projected
income statement based on percentages developed from previous statements
is quite likely to be acceptable. The higher the degree of volatility associated
with a firm's operations, the greater the degree of care that should be taken
in developing its pro forma income statement.

THE PRO FORMA BALANCE SHEET

Figure 6.1 presented the basic inputs required for preparing pro forma statements. At this point in the analysis, all the inputs for correctly developing the
firm's pro forma balance sheet, except the firm's cash budget, are available.
The cash budget is necessary since it presents the end-of-year cash and notes

---

[3]This result is consistent with the earlier discussion in which it was suggested that by
using the percent-of-sales method to prepare shortcut pro forma income statements the firm's
profits would be understated in the instance the firm had fixed costs. Since DuBois Manufacturing Company does have fixed costs this result is as expected.

TABLE 6.20 The 1979 cash budget for the DuBois Manufacturing Company

	1st Quarter	2nd Quarter	3rd Quarter	4th Quarter
Sales	$27,500.00	$50,000.00	$35,000.00	$23,000.00
Cash receipts				
75% for current sales	$20,625.00	$37,500.00	$26,250.00	$17,250.00
25% for previous quarter's sales	13,000.00[a]	6,875.00	12,500.00	8,750.00
Total receipts	$33,625.00	$44,375.00	$38,750.00	$26,000.00
Purchases	$ 3,139.75	$ 3,139.75	$ 3,139.75	$ 3,139.75
Cash disbursements				
60% for current purchases	$ 1,833.85	$ 1,883.85	$ 1,883.85	$ 1,883.85
40% for previous quarter's purchases	12,000.00[b]	1,255.90	1,255.90	1,255.90
Payroll—direct labor cost	9,285.00	9,285.00	9,285.00	9,285.00
Factory overhead (excluding depreciation)	10,750.00	10,750.00	10,750.00	10,750.00
Operating expense	4,000.00	4,000.00	4,000.00	4,000.00
Machine purchase	10,000.00		10,000.00	
Interest payment				1,000.00
Cash dividend				4,000.00
Tax payment	935.00	935.00	935.00	935.00
Total disbursements	$48,853.85	$28,109.75	$38,109.75	$33,109.75
Net cash flow	($15,228.85)	$16,265.25	$ 640.25	($7,109.75)
Beginning cash	6,000.00	(9,228.85)	7,036.40	7,676.65
Ending cash	($9,228.85)	$ 7,036.40	$ 7,676.65	$ 566.90
Less: Minimum cash balance	6,000.00	6,000.00	6,000.00	6,000.00
Required Total Financing	$15,228.85	—	—	$ 5,433.10
Excess Cash Balance	—	$1,036.40	$1,676.65	—

[a]Beginning accounts receivable, from Table 6.2.
[b]Beginning accounts payable, from Table 6.2.

payable values. Also, in the process of developing the firm's cash budget, the ending accounts receivable and accounts payable can easily be calculated.

The cash budget

A number of additional facts are required in order to calculate the firm's cash budget (Table 6.20).

1. The firm's projected sales (all on credit) are expected to be $27,500, $50,000, $35,000, and $23,000 in the first through the fourth quarters, respectively.
2. Seventy-five percent of the accounts receivable will be collected during the quarter of the sale; the remaining 25 percent will be collected

during the following quarter. Bad debt expenses are therefore assumed to be negligible.

3. Sixty percent of the purchases of raw materials will be paid for in the current quarter; the remaining 40 percent will be paid for in the following quarter.
4. The payments for direct labor (wages), factory overhead (excluding depreciation), and operating expenses will be divided equally between the quarters.
5. The $1000 interest payment will be made during December.
6. Taxes payable at the beginning of the year will be paid in equal quarterly installments of $935 ($3740.00 ÷ 4).[4]
7. The firm wishes to maintain an ending cash balance of at least $6000.

Comments on the cash budget

Two pro forma balance sheet entries are readily available from the cash budget (Table 6.20).

1. Ending cash—The end-of-year cash balance, based on the various assumptions incorporated in the cash budget, is $6000.00 (i.e., minimum cash balance of $6000 plus excess cash balance of $0).
2. Notes payable—The end-of-year short-term borrowing (the fourth-quarter required total financing in the cash budget) is $5433.10.

Two additional pieces of information, though not directly available on the pro forma balance sheet, can easily be obtained from the preceding analysis. They are the end-of-period accounts receivable and accounts payable.

Accounts receivable.   The end-of-period accounts receivable for the firm's pro forma balance sheet can be calculated by taking 25 percent of the fourth-quarter sales. This is consistent with the analysis used to develop receipts in the preceding section. Ending accounts receivable would therefore be 25 percent of $23,000, or $5750.00.

Accounts payable.   The end-of-period accounts payable can be calculated in much the same way as the accounts receivable. Since 60 percent of the firm's purchases are paid for in the current quarter and the remaining 40 percent are paid for in the following quarter, 40 percent of the fourth quarter's purchases will remain uncollected at the end of the fourth quarter. The fourth-quarter purchases were $3139.75; 40 percent of this amount is $1255.90. The ending accounts payable will therefore be $1255.90.

The statement

The pro forma balance sheet for the DuBois Manufacturing Company for the coming year is presented in Table 6.21. The items in the statement were derived as follows:

[4]The taxes-payable figure represents the end-of-1978 taxes payable shown on the balance sheet in Table 6.2. It is assumed that these taxes of $3740 are paid during the year 1979, whereas the taxes incurred during 1979 are paid in 1980.

TABLE 6.21 The pro forma balance sheet for the DuBois Manufacturing Company for the year ended December 31, 1979

Assets			Liabilities and equities	
(1) Cash (Table 6.20)		$ 6,000.00	(6) Accounts payable	$ 1,255.90
(2) Marketable securities (unchanged)		4,016.40	(7) Taxes payable	2,795.16
(3) Accounts receivable		5,750.00	(8) Notes payable	5,433.10
(4) Inventories			(9) Other current liabilities	6,260.00
(a) Raw materials	$2,500.00			
(b) Finished goods	8,651.44		Total current liabilities	$15,744.16
Total		11,151.44	(10) Long-term debt	$15,000.00
Total current assets		$26,917.84	(11) Stockholders' equity	
(5) Net fixed assets		$64,000.00	(a) Common stock	$30,000.00
Total Assets		$90.917.84[a]	(b) Retained earnings	$30,180.64
			Total Liabilities and Stockholders' Equity	$90,924.80[a]

[a]The total assets should equal the total liabilities and equities. That they do not is due to the rounding off of certain values in the analysis. However, the difference is insignificant; it is $6.96, which represents an error of less than .0077 percent.

1. Cash is obtained from the firm's cash budget (Table 6.20).
2. Marketable securities are assumed to have remained unchanged from the previous period's value, given in Table 6.2.
3. Accounts receivable are based on the cash budget. The derivation of this value was described in the preceding section.
4. Inventories:
   a. Raw materials—The value of the raw-materials inventory has been developed by multiplying the desired ending inventory values for each raw material (given in Table 6.14) by the cost of each raw material, as follows:

Raw material	Ending inventory units	Cost/unit	Total
A	500	$2.00	$1000
B	3000	0.50	1500
Total Raw-Materials Inventory Value			$2500

   b. Finished goods—The value of the finished-goods inventory has been found by multiplying the ending inventories of each model by the total per-unit cost of these items. The per-unit cost is the sum of the raw-materials cost per unit, the labor cost per unit, and the overhead allocation per unit. Values for these items and the per-unit cost of each model have been given in Table 6.18.

Multiplying the ending inventory figures in Table 6.13 by these costs and summing the totals for each product line yields the total finished-goods inventory value.

Finished goods	Ending inventory units	Cost/unit	Total
X	120	$21.77	$2612.40
Y	224	26.96	6039.04
Total Finished Goods Inventory Value			$8651.44

5. Net fixed assets—The firm's net fixed assets have been calculated by adding the $20,000 outlay for a new machine to the firm's beginning-of-period fixed assets of $51,000 (from Table 6.2) and subtracting the current year's depreciation of $7000 (from Table 6.15) from the total. The resulting end-of-1979 net fixed asset value was $64,000.
6. Accounts payable are based on the cash budget. The derivation of this value was discussed in the preceding section.
7. Taxes payable—this figure is the same as the firm's tax liability on the pro forma income statement (Table 6.19), $2795.16.
8. Notes payable—this value is the same as the value for the fourth-quarter borrowing in the cash budget.
9. Other current liabilities—this figure is the same as that given for the preceding year, since the firm's other current liabilities are expected to remain unchanged.
10. Long-term debt—this figure is the same as that given for the previous year. None of the principal will be repaid and the firm does not expect to borrow additional long-term debt; therefore, the value of the debt remains unchanged.
11. Stockholders' equity:
    a. Common stock—This value is the same as that given for the previous year. Since no additional shares of stock are to be sold, repurchased, or retired during the period, the common stockholder's equity in the firm is expected to remain unchanged.
    b. Retained earnings—This value represents the sum of the most recent years' retained earnings (from Table 6.2) and the earnings expected to be retained based on the pro forma income statement (Table 6.19). The $23,000.00 in retained earnings from the 1978 balance sheet (Table 6.2) plus the projected increase in retained earnings of $7180.64 from the 1979 pro forma income statement (Table 6.19) yields total end-of-1979 retained earnings of $30,180.64.

The pro forma balance sheet (Table 6.21) indicates that the firm's total assets are expected to increase by about $900 over the previous year's level of $90,000. The amount of change in the total assets is not nearly as important as the relationships between certain items, that is, the overall construction of the statement. The pro forma balance sheet can be analyzed in the same manner as the historical financial statements described in Chapters 3 and 5. Ratio analysis of both the pro forma income statement and the balance sheet can be performed in order to evaluate the firm's expected liquidity or activity, debt position, and profitability. Source and use of funds statements can be developed using the pro forma balance sheet in order to determine whether the firm will obtain and use funds in a manner consistent with its overall financial policies.

Comparing the resulting balance sheets with the shortcut approach

Comparing the pro forma balance sheet prepared earlier (Table 6.5) using the shortcut approach with the pro forma balance sheet in Table 6.21 reflects a number of differences in account balances. Significant differences in the balances shown for accounts receivable, inventories, accounts payable, and notes payable are seen to exist. Total assets in the long approach are $90,917.84 while in the shortcut approach total assets are $98,485.15. If we assume the longer approach to be the correct one, the $7567.31 ($98,485.15 − $90,917.84) overstatement of total assets using the shortcut approach represents an 8.3 percent error. Since both statements are only forecasts, this discrepancy is not surprising. However, a decision maker would certainly have a higher degree of confidence in the balance sheet developed using the long approach, since much more detail and fewer assumptions are required in the development of values. In sum, the basic difference between the two approaches is that the long approach requires determination of *causes* and calculation of effects, while the shortcut approach determines the *effects* desired, developing a balance sheet based on these effects, and making it balance using a plug figure. Although the approach used to prepare pro forma statements will depend upon the financial manager's need, for convenience, the shortcut approach is recommended, while for accuracy the longer approach should be used.

SUMMARY

This chapter has illustrated procedures to be used in developing projected financial statements. Specific attention has been given to the pro forma income statement and pro forma balance sheet. The most critical input to these statements is a sales forecast. Based on this forecast, a production plan showing raw-material costs and usage, direct labor requirements, factory overhead, and operating expenses is developed. Using this plan, the firm's cost of goods sold can be calculated and a pro forma income statement developed. This statement provides the firm with a projected net income figure from which planned dividend payments can be deducted to obtain an estimate of retained earnings.

The retained earnings figure from the pro forma income statement, the firm's most recent balance sheet, data on any planned long-term financing, planned capital expenditures, and the firm's cash budget, can be used to prepare a pro forma balance sheet using the longer, more sophisticated approach. The cash budget is a quite important input since projections of the firm's ending cash, notes payable, accounts receivable, and accounts payable can easily be obtained from it. The pro forma balance sheet provides the firm with projected values for its various assets, liabilities, and equities, that can be evaluated in light of the firm's overall plans.

Shortcut approaches to developing pro forma income statements and balance sheets exist. A pro forma income statement can be developed using past percentage relationships between certain cost and expense items and the firm's sales and applying these percentages to the firm's forecast sales. Of course, the use of these historic percentages tends to suggest that all costs are variable—a situation that is unlikely to exist. A pro forma balance sheet can be estimated by determining the desired level of certain items and letting additional financing act as a balancing, or plug, figure.

The shortcut approaches to pro forma preparation have appeal since they are more convenient, while the longer approach to pro forma preparation is superior in terms of accuracy. The long approach's superior accuracy is attributed primarily to the use of greater detail, and to the need for fewer assumptions than the shortcut approach. The basic difference between the two can be summed up by saying that the long approach relies on the determination of causes in order to calculate effects while the shortcut approach is based on determining the effects desired and then preparing pro forma statements consistent with them.

Pro forma statements are used for evaluating the firm's future performance. Not only are they useful for internal control, but lenders commonly use them in analyzing a firm before making a loan or deciding to extend a line of credit. Quite often ratio analysis is performed on pro forma statements in order to evaluate the firm's expected financial situation, and source and use of funds statements based on the pro forma statements are prepared.

QUESTIONS

6-1   What are pro forma financial statements? How do the pro forma income statement and the pro forma balance sheet differ?

6-2   What types of budgets are required in order to obtain the data necessary for the preparation of pro forma statements? What is the key input to this budgeting process?

6-3   Which of the pro forma statements must be developed first? Why? What necessary inputs to the pro forma statement preparation process are provided by the cash budget?

6-4   Why may the pro forma income statement prepared using the shortcut method described in the chapter underestimate profits? How would this compare to the resulting statement using the longer method?

6-5   What is the shortcut approach to preparing a firm's pro forma balance sheet described in the chapter? What are the key assumptions necessary in using this approach?

6-6   What is the significance of the "plug figure" used in the preparation of a pro forma balance sheet using the shortcut approach?

6-7 Can you suggest another shortcut approach to preparing pro forma financial statements, knowing that they do exist?

6-8 Why, in order to prepare pro forma statements, is it necessary to have both a unit and a dollar sales forecast by product?

6-9 What person or department of the firm is responsible for the development of each of the following items?
a The sales forecast
b The production plan
c The factory overhead budget
d Historical financial statements
e Pro forma statements

6-10 What items are generally included as part of the firm's manufacturing overhead cost?

6-11 On what basis is a firm's factory overhead cost commonly allocated to the various products produced? How do the three commonly used systems work?

6-12 What are the basic values required to determine the total cost per unit for each of a firm's products?

6-13 Why is it necessary to have a breakdown of the firm's inventory into raw materials (by type), work in process (by product), and finished goods (by product)?

6-14 What critical items used in the preparation of pro forma statements come from the firm's capital expenditure plan?

6-15 Why is the cost-of-good-sold figure the most difficult item to calculate in preparing the pro forma income statement?

6-16 What reasons can be given to support the belief that the long approach to pro forma statement preparation considers both causes and effects whereas the shortcut approach is concerned only with effects?

6-17 How may the financial analyst wish to evaluate pro forma statements? What is his or her objective in evaluating these statements?

PROBLEMS

6-1 The O'Connor Daughters Corporation wishes to apply the shortcut method to prepare their financial plans. Use the operating statements below, and the other information included
a Prepare a pro forma income statement.
b Prepare a pro forma balance sheet.
c Analyze these statements and discuss the financing changes required.

Income Statement
O'Connor Daughters Corporation
December 31, 1978

Sales	$800,000
Less: Cost of goods sold	600,000
Gross profits	$200,000
Less: Operating expense	100,000
Profits before taxes	$100,000
Less: Taxes (40%)	40,000
Profits after taxes	$ 60,000
Less: Cash dividends	20,000
To Retained Earnings	$ 40,000

Balance Sheet
O'Connor Daughters Corporation
December 31, 1978

Assets		Liabilities and equities	
Cash	$ 32,000	Accounts payable	$100,000
Marketable securities	18,000	Taxes payable	20,000
Accounts receivable	150,000	Other current liabilities	5,000
Inventory	100,000	Total current liabilities	$125,000
Total current assets	$300,000	Long term debt	$200,000
Net fixed assets	$350,000	Common stock	$150,000
Total Assets	$650,000	Retained earnings	175,000
		Total Liabilities and Equity	$650,000

The following financial data are also available:

(1) The firm has estimated that its sales for 1979 will be $900,000.
(2) The firm expects to pay $35,000 in cash dividends in 1979.
(3) The firm wishes to maintain a minimum cash balance of $30,000.
(4) Accounts receivable represent approximately 18 percent of annual sales.
(5) The firm's ending inventory will change directly with changes in sales in 1979.
(6) A new machine costing $42,000 will be purchased in 1979. Total depreciation for 1979 will be $17,000.
(7) Accounts payable will change directly in response to changes in sales in 1979.
(8) Taxes payable will equal the tax liability on the pro forma income statement.
(9) Marketable securities, other current liabilities, long-term debt, and common stock will remain unchanged.

6-2 Tucker Tool has 1978 sales of $10 million. They wish to use the shortcut method to analyze their expected performance and financing needs for the next year. Given the information below:

(1) The percent of sales for items which vary directly with sales are
Cash 4%
Receivables 12%
Inventory 18%
Net fixed assets 40%
Accounts payable 14%
Accruals 4%
Net profit margin 3%
(2) No sale of common stock is expected.
(3) The dividend payout of 50% is expected to continue.
(4) Sales are expected to be $11 million in 1979 and $12 million in 1980.
(5) The December 31, 1978, balance sheet follows:

Tucker Tool
Balance Sheet
December 31, 1978
(in thousands)

Cash	$ 400	Accounts payable	$1400
Marketable securities	200	Accruals	400
Accounts receivable	1200	Other current liabilities	80
Inventory	1800	Total current liabilities	$1880
Total current assets	$3600	Long-term debt	$2000
Net fixed assets	$4000	Common equity	$3720
Total Assets	$7600	Total Liabilities and	
		Equity	$7600

a   Prepare a pro forma balance sheet dated December 31, 1980.
b   Discuss the financing changes suggested by the statement prepared in **a**.

6-3   Use the table below to answer the following questions for a firm producing two products, P_1 and P_2, with two raw materials, RM_1 and RM_2.

	P_1	P_2	Total
Selling price per unit	$40.00	$28.00	
Number of units sold	5,000	8,000	
Sales revenue	$200,000	$224,000	$424,000
Direct labor cost per unit	$10.00	$6.00	
Material cost per unit RM_1	$7.00	$4.00	
RM_2	6.00	6.00	
Total Material Cost/Unit	$13.00	$10.00	

Direct labor cost is $5.00 per hour, RM_1 costs $1.00 per unit, RM_2 costs $.50 per unit, factory overhead expense last year was $60,000.

a   What are the firm's historical per unit labor and material requirements for each product?
b   Calculate the firm's overhead allocation per unit for each product. Round percentages and dollars to the nearest whole percentage or cent, respectively.
c   What is the total cost per unit for each product?

6-4   Use the following information for the Morton Materials Company to work this problem as well as problems 6-5 and 6-6.

Morton Materials produces two products, X and Y, with two raw materials, A and B, and direct labor. The production mix is listed below. The firm desires to hold 10 percent of annual sales as year-end finished goods inventory. Overhead estimates for the coming year are $70,000. The firm will maintain raw-material inventories of 3000 and 6000 units of A and B, respectively.

Inputs	Product X	Product Y
Raw material (units)		
A	3.0	1.0
B	4.0	6.5
Labor hours	2.0	1.5
	16.80	14.30

(handwritten: 7.20 + 6 = 13.20 ; 15.80 + 4.50 = 20.30)

Balance Sheet
Morton Materials Company
(Last Year)

Assets		Liabilities and equities	
Cash	$ 20,000	Accounts payable	$ 15,000
Marketable securities	6,534	Taxes payable	8,828
Accounts receivable	25,000	Other current	
Inventory	32,466	liabilities	18,000
Total current assets	$ 84,000	Total current	
Net fixed assets	$116,000	liabilities	$ 41,828
Total Assets	$200,000	Long-term debt	$ 35,000
		Common stock	$ 80,000
		Retained earnings	43,172
		Total Liabilities and Equity	$200,000

Income Statement
Morton Materials Company
(Last Year)

Sales		
Product X	$128,000	
Product Y	200,000	
Total sales		$328,000
Less: Cost of goods sold		
Labor	$ 80,000	
Material A	48,000	
Material B	81,600	
Overhead	60,000	
Total cost of goods sold		269,600
Gross profits		$ 58,400
Less: Operating expense		16,000
Profits before taxes		$ 42,400
Less: Taxes		8,828
Profits after taxes		$ 33,572
Less: Cash dividends		13,000
To Retained Earnings		$ 20,572

Current Inventory Breakdown Morton Materials Company		
Raw-materials inventory	Units	Dollars
Material A	2,000	$ 4,000
Material B	6,000	7,200
Total		$11,200
Finished-goods inventory		
Product X	350	$ 8,680
Product Y	620	12,586
Total		$21,266
Total Inventory		$32,466

24.80 each
20.30 each

Sales Forecast (Coming Year) Morton Materials Company	
Unit sales	
Product X	4,500
Product Y	9,000
Dollar sales	
Product X ($35.00)	$157,500
Product Y ($30.00)	270,000
Total	$427,500

a Calculate the firm's production requirements for the coming year.

b Calculate the firm's raw material usage requirement for the next year, rounded to the nearest unit.

c If direct labor costs are $3.00 per hour, and overhead estimates are $70,000, what is the expected cost per unit for the next period?

6-5 Using the information on Morton Materials given in Problem 6-4, prepare a pro forma income statement for the firm assuming operating expenses will be $25,000, direct labor costs $4.00 per unit, cash dividends will be $15,000, the firm uses FIFO to value inventory, and the actual corporate tax rates apply. Assume the raw-material prices do not change.

6-6 Using the information on Morton Materials given in Problems 6-4 and 6-5, prepare a pro forma balance sheet for the company for the coming year. Use the following information to prepare the balance sheet.

(1) The firm will purchase a new machine for $50,000.

(2) The firm desires to maintain a cash balance of $20,000.

(3) Accounts receivable should equal five percent of annual sales.

(4) Depreciation is expeced to be $14,000.

(5) Taxes payable will equal the coming year's tax liability as indicated on the pro forma income statement.

(6) Accounts payable should be approximately 5.5 percent of annual cost of goods sold.

(7) Assume production and sales occur continuously over the year.

SELECTED REFERENCES

Ansoff, H. Igor, "Planning as a Practical Management Tool," *Financial Executive 32* (June 1964), pp. 34–37.

Bogen, Jules I., Ed., *Financial Handbook,* 4th ed. (New York: Ronald, 1968), sect. 15.

Chambers, J. C., S. D. Mullick, and D. D. Smith, "How to Choose the Right Forecasting Technique," *Harvard Business Review 49* (July-August 1971), pp. 45–74.

Chisholm, R. K., and G. R. Whitaker, Jr., *Forecasting Methods* (Homewood, Ill.: Irwin, 1971).

Gershefski, George W., "Building a Corporate Financial Model," *Harvard Business Review* (July-August, 1969), pp. 61–72.

Francis, Jack Clark, and Dexter R. Rowell, "A Simultaneous Equation Model of the Firm for Financial Analysis and Planning," *Financial Management 7* (Spring 1978), pp. 29–44.

Helfert, Erich A., *Techniques of Financial Analysis,* 4th ed. (Homewood, Ill.: Irwin, 1976), chap. 3.

Jaedicke, Robert K., and Robert T. Sprouse, *Accounting Flows: Income, Funds, and Cash* (Englewood Cliffs, N.J.: Prentice-Hall, 1965), chaps. 3 and 4.

Johnson, Timothy E., and Thomas G. Schmitt, "Effectiveness of Earnings Per Share Forecasts," *Financial Management 3* (Summer 1974), pp. 64–72.

Lynch, Richard M., *Accounting for Management Planning and Control* (New York: McGraw-Hill, 1967), chap. 6.

Merville, Larry J., and Lee A. Tavis, "Long-Range Financial Planning," *Financial Management 3* (Summer 1974), pp. 56–63.

Pappas, James L., and George P. Huber, "Probabilistic Short-Term Financial Planning," *Financial Management 2* (Autumn 1973), pp. 36–44.

Parker, G. C., and E. L. Segura, "How to Get a Better Forecast," *Harvard Business Review 49* (March-April 1971), pp. 99–109.

Preston, Gerald R., "Considerations in Long-Range Planning," *Financial Executive* (May 1968), pp. 44–49.

Ricketts, Donald E., and Michael J. Barrett, "Corporate Operating Income Forecasting Ability," *Financial Management 2* (Summer 1973), pp. 53–62.

Seitz, Neil, *Financial Analysis: A Programmed Approach* (Reston, Va.: Reston Publishing Co., 1976), chap. 2.

Viscione, Jerry A., *Financial Analysis: Principles and Procedures* (Boston: Houghton Mifflin Company, 1977), chap. 3.

Wagle, B., "The Use of Models for Environmental Forecasting and Corporate Planning," *Operational Research Quarterly 22,* No. 3., pp. 327–336.

Weston, J. Fred, "Forecasting Financial Requirements," *Accounting Review 33* (July 1958), pp. 427–440.

Wright, Leonard T., *Financial Management: Analytical Techniques* (Columbus, Ohio: Grid, 1974), chap. 4.

PART THREE

This part of the text is devoted to working capital management. Working capital management is concerned with the management of the firm's current accounts, which include current assets and current liabilities. Efficiency in this area of financial management is necessary in order to assure the firm's long-term success and to achieve its overall goal—the maximization of the owners' wealth. If the financial manager cannot manage the firm's working capital efficiently, these longer-run considerations become irrelevant. Short-term survival is a prerequisite to long-run success. Part Three consists of four chapters. Chapter 7 presents an overview of working capital management that points out some of the key strategies and considerations of the financial manager. Chapter 8 discusses the various aspects of cash and marketable securities management. Chapter 9 describes the key aspects of accounts receivable management, which include credit policies, credit terms, and collection policies. The final chapter in this part, Chapter 10, briefly discusses various inventory considerations and strategies for the financial manager.

The management of working capital

BALANCE SHEET	
Assets	Liabilities and Stockholders' Equity
Current Assets	Current Liabilities
Fixed Assets	Long-Term Debt
	Stockholders' Equity

CHAPTER 7
An overview of working capital management

Working capital management is concerned with the management of the firm's current accounts, which include current assets and current liabilities. The management of working capital is one of the most important aspects of the firm's overall financial management. If the firm cannot maintain a satisfactory level of working capital, it is likely to become insolvent and may even be forced into bankruptcy. The firm's current assets should be large enough to cover its current liabilities in order to ensure a reasonable margin of safety.

The goal of working capital management is to manage each of the firm's current assets and current liabilities in such a way that an acceptable level of net working capital is maintained. The major current assets of concern in this text are cash, marketable securities, accounts receivable, and inventory. Each of these assets must be managed efficiently in order to maintain the firm's liquidity while not keeping too high a level of any one of them. The basic current liabilities of concern are accounts payable, notes payable, and accruals. Each of these short-term sources of financing must be cautiously managed to ensure that they are obtained and used in the best way possible. Individual current assets and current liabilities will not be discussed in this chapter; rather, attention will be given to the basic relationship between current assets and current liabilities. Subsequent chapters will devote attention to individual current assets and current liabilities.

This chapter is divided into three major sections. The first section presents an in-depth discussion of net working capital. Two alternate definitions of net working capital are discussed in light of the firm's financing. The second section develops, discusses, and illustrates the trade-off between profitability and risk associated with a firm's level of net working capital. Examples are used to illustrate the effects of changes in the level of current assets and current liabilities on the firm's profitability-risk configuration. The final section of this chapter evaluates the effects of the firm's short-term–long-term financing mix on its net working capital and profitability-risk trade-off and discusses a number of financing mix strategies.

NET WORKING CAPITAL

The concept of net working capital was discussed in Chapter 3. The drawbacks of using net working capital to compare the liquidity of different firms were emphasized, giving special attention to the use of the current or acid-test ratio. The use of net working capital for evaluating the performance of the same firm over time is generally acceptable, as long as the firm's basic asset structure does not change drastically over the period.

The common definition and its implications

The most common definition of net working capital is the *difference between a firm's current assets and current liabilities.* As long as the firm's current assets exceed its current liabilities, it has net working capital. Most firms must operate with some amount of net working capital; how much depends largely on the industry. Firms with very predictable cash flows, such as electric utilities, can operate with negative net working capital; however, most firms must maintain positive levels of net working capital.

Underlying the use of net working capital (and other liquidity ratios) to measure a firm's liquidity is the belief that the greater the margin by which a firm's current assets cover its short-term obligations (current liabilities) the better able it will be to pay its bills as they come due. This expectation is based on the belief that current assets are sources of *cash receipts,* while current liabilities are sources of *cash disbursements*. However, a problem arises because each current asset and current liability has a different degree of liquidity associated with it. Although the firm's current assets may not be converted into cash precisely when they are needed, the greater the amount of current assets present, the more likely it is that some current asset will be converted into cash in order to pay a debt that is due.

Since for nearly all firms cash inflows and cash outflows are not perfectly synchronized, some level of net working capital is necessary. The firm's cash outflows resulting from payment of current liabilities are relatively predictable. The firm generally learns when bills are due at the time that an obligation is incurred. For instance, when merchandise is purchased on credit, the credit terms extended to the firm require payment at a known point in time. The same predictability is associated with notes payable and accruals, which have stated payment dates. What is difficult to predict are the firm's cash inflows. Predicting when current assets other than cash and marketable securities will be converted into cash is quite difficult. The more predictable these cash inflows are, the less net working capital a firm requires. It is because an electric utility has a very predictable pattern of cash inflows that it can operate with little or no net working capital. Firms with more uncertain cash inflows must maintain levels of current assets adequate to cover current liabilities (scheduled cash outflows). Because most firms are unable to match cash receipts and cash disbursements, sources of cash receipts (current assets) that more than cover cash disbursements (current liabilities) are necessary.

EXAMPLE

For the GHI Company, which has the current position given in Table 7.1, the following situation may exist. All $600 of the firm's accounts payable, plus $200 of its notes

TABLE 7.1 The current position of the GHI Company

Current assets		Current liabilities	
Cash	$ 500	Accounts payable	$ 600
Marketable securities	200	Notes payable	800
Accounts receivable	800	Accruals	200
Inventory	1200	Total	$1600
Total	$2700		

payable and $100 in accruals, are due at the end of the current period. That this $900 in disbursements must be made is certain; how the firm will cover these disbursements is not certain. The firm can be sure that $700 will be available since it has $500 in cash and $200 in marketable securities, which can be easily converted into cash. The remaining $200 must come from the collection of an account receivable, or the sale of inventory for cash, or both.[1] The firm cannot be sure when either a cash sale or the collection of an account receivable will occur. More uncertainty is associated with the collection of accounts receivable than with a cash sale. Although customers who have purchased goods on credit are expected to pay for them by the date specified in the credit arrangement, quite often they will not pay until a later date. Thus the cash flows associated with the sale will not necessarily occur at the point in time they were expected.

Of course, some solution to this dilemma must exist. In order to have a higher probability of having sufficient cash to pay its bills, a firm should attempt to make sales, since in many cases sales will result in the immediate receipt of cash and in other cases they will result in accounts receivable that will eventually be converted into cash. A level of inventory adequate to satisfy the probable demand for the firm's products should be maintained. As long as the firm is generating sales and collecting receivables as they come due, sufficient cash should be forthcoming to satisfy its cash payment obligations. The GHI Company can increase the probability of its being able to satisfy its obligations by maintaining sufficient levels of accounts receivable and inventory to allow the conversion of some of these items into cash. The more accounts receivable and inventories there are on hand, the greater the probability that some of these items will be turned into cash.[2] As a rule, a certain level of net working capital is often recommended in order to ensure that a firm will be able to pay bills. The GHI Company has $1100 of net working capital ($2700 − $1600), which will most likely be sufficient to cover all its bills. Its current ratio of 1.69 ($2700/$1600) should provide sufficient liquidity as long as its accounts receivable and inventories are relatively liquid. ●

An alternate definition of net working capital

An alternate definition of net working capital is *that portion of a firm's current assets financed with long-term funds*. This definition can best be

---

[1] A sale of inventory for credit would show up as a new account receivable, which could not be easily converted into cash. Only a *cash sale* will guarantee the firm that its bill-paying ability during the period of the sale has been enhanced.

[2] It should be recognized that levels of accounts receivable or inventory can be too high, reflecting certain management inefficiencies. Acceptable levels for any firm can be calculated. The efficient management of accounts receivable and inventory is discussed in Chapters 9 and 10, respectively.

FIGURE 7.1 A special balance sheet for the GHI Company

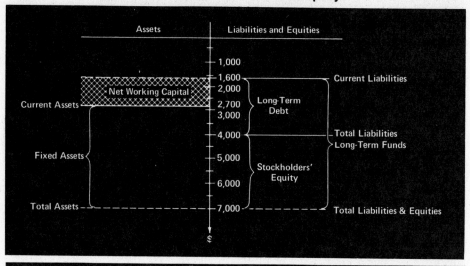

illustrated by a special type of balance sheet, like that for the GHI Company presented in Figure 7.1. The vertical axis of the balance sheet is a dollar scale on which all the major items on the firm's balance sheet are indicated.

Figure 7.1 shows that the firm has current assets of $2700, fixed assets of $4300, and total assets of $7000. It also shows that the firm has current liabilities of $1600, long-term debts of $2400 ($4000 − $1600), and stockholders' equity of $3000 ($7000 − $4000). A firm's long-term debt plus its stockholders' equity represents its sources of long-term funds; the GHI Company's long-term funds equal $5400. The portion of the firm's current assets that have been financed with long-term funds has been labeled "net working capital" in Figure 7.1. Analysis of this figure should enable the reader to understand better why a firm's net working capital can be thought of as the portion of current assets financed with long-term funds. Since current liabilities represent the firm's sources of short-term funds, as long as current assets exceed current liabilities the amount of the excess must be financed with longer-term funds. The usefulness of this alternate definition will become more apparent in a later section of the chapter.

THE TRADE-OFF BETWEEN PROFITABILITY AND RISK

A trade-off exists between a firm's profitability and risk. *Profitability*, in this context, is measured by profits after expenses, while *risk* is measured by the probability that a firm will become *technically insolvent* (i.e., unable to pay bills as they come due). A firm's profits can be increased in two ways: (1) by increasing sales or (2) by decreasing costs. Both methods are discussed in the following pages. Costs can be reduced by paying less for an item or a service or by using existing resources more efficiently. Any reduction in costs should increase a firm's profits. Profits can also be increased by investing in more profitable assets, which are capable of generating higher levels of sales. An understanding of how profits are increased and reduced is critical to grasping the idea of a profitability-risk trade-off.

The risk of becoming technically insolvent is most commonly measured using either the amount of net working capital or the current ratio. In this chapter the amount of net working capital is used as a measure. It is assumed that *the greater the amount of net working capital a firm has, the less risky the firm is*. In other words, the more net working capital, the more liquid the firm, and therefore the less likely it is to become technically insolvent. The opposite is also considered to be true: lower levels of liquidity (i.e., net working capital) are associated with increasing levels of risk on the part of the business firm. The relationship between liquidity, net working capital, and risk is such that if either net working capital or liquidity increases, the firm's risk decreases and vice versa.

Some basic assumptions

In talking about a profitability-risk trade-off, a number of basic assumptions, which are generally true, must be made. The first concerns the nature of the firm being analyzed, the second concerns the basic differences in the earning power of assets, and the third concerns differences in the cost of various methods of financing. Each of these assumptions will be discussed separately.

The nature of the firm. The kind of firm we are talking about in this chapter is a *manufacturing firm*, not some type of merchandising or service organization. As we stated earlier in the text, the emphasis in this book is generally on manufacturing firms since they provide the best laboratory for investigating most of the basic principles of managerial finance.

The earning power of assets. A manufacturing firm is expected to be able to earn more on its fixed assets than on its current assets. Fixed assets represent the true earning assets of the firm. Plants, machines, and warehouses all enable the firm to generate finished products that can ultimately be sold for a profit. The firm's current assets, except for marketable securities, are not generally *earning assets*. Rather, they provide a buffer that allows the firm to make sales and extend credit. The importance of current assets to the firm's operation has been indicated in the preceding section; they are absolutely necessary for the effective operation of the firm. Without fixed assets to generate finished products that can be converted into cash, marketable securities, accounts receivable, and inventory, the firm could not operate. If the firm could earn more money by purchasing its inventory than by producing it or by investing its money in marketable securities, then it should not be in the manufacturing business. In other words, if a firm cannot make more on fixed-asset investments than it makes on current-asset investments, it should sell all its fixed assets and use the proceeds to purchase current assets. In the following discussion, it is assumed that *the firm can earn more on fixed assets than current assets*.

The cost of financing. The firm can obtain its required financing from either of two sources: (1) current liabilities or (2) long-term funds. Current liabilities are sources of short-term funds; long-term debts and equity are sources of long-term funds. Since current liabilities generally consist of accounts payable, notes payable, and accruals, they are typically a cheap source of funds. Of the basic current liabilities, only notes payable normally have a stated cost. This is because notes payable represent the only *negotiated* form of borrowing. Accounts payable and accruals are cheaper sources of funds than notes payable since they do not normally have any type of interest payment directly associated with them.

Historically, in general, short-term funds cost less than long-term funds. In the recent past, interest rates have been increasing and people have expected higher interest rates in the future. Lenders with such expectations will typically provide short-term funds at rates below those charged for longer-term funds.[3] They do this because short-term loans mature in less than a year, and they will get their money back in time to relend it at higher rates if interest rates do increase over the year. If interest rates are expected to increase in the future, a lender will charge a high enough rate of interest on a longer-term loan as compensation for tying up a given amount of money for a long period, thus losing future opportunities to lend the same money at increased rates.

Therefore, whenever lenders believe that future interest rates will rise, short-term borrowing rates are less than long-term rates. When future rates are expected to decline from a currently high level, long-term rates are most often below short-term rates. Since increasing interest rates have prevailed in the most recent past, however, it is assumed in the following discussion that *short-term funds are cheaper than long-term funds*. The fact that short-term sources of funds include not only notes payable but also accounts payable and accruals makes it much easier to accept this assumption, since accounts payable and accruals are virtually interest-free. The cheapest form of financing for the business firm is therefore short-term funds.

The nature of the trade-off
between profitability and risk

If a firm wants to increase its profitability, it must also increase its risk. If it wants to decrease risk, it must decrease profitability. The trade-off between these variables is such that regardless of how the firm increases its profitability through the manipulation of working capital, the consequence is a corresponding increase in risk as measured by the level of net working capital. The effects of changing current assets and changing current liabilities on the firm's profitability-risk trade-off will be discussed separately prior to integrating them into an overall theory of working capital management.

---

[3]There have been periods when short-term interest rates have exceeded long-term rates, but these periods have been exceptions rather than the norm. The second quarter of 1974 through the first quarter of 1975 was a period during which the short-term rates were above long-term rates. This behavior typically occurs during periods of "tight money" or economic recession.

Current assets.   The effects of the firm's level of current assets on its profitability-risk trade-off can be illustrated using a simple ratio—the ratio of the firm's current assets to its total assets. This ratio indicates what percentage of the firm's total assets are current. It may increase or decrease.

Effects of an increase.   As the ratio of current assets to total assets increases, both the firm's profitability and its risk decrease. Its profitability decreases because current assets are less profitable than fixed assets. The risk of technical insolvency decreases because, assuming that the firm's current liabilities do not change, the increase in the firm's current assets will increase its net working capital.

Effects of a decrease.   A decrease in the ratio of current assets to total assets will result in an increase in the firm's profitability since the firm's fixed assets, which increase, generate higher returns than current assets. However, risk will also increase since the firm's net working capital will decrease with the decrease in current assets. The consequences of a decrease in the ratio of current to total assets are exactly the opposite of the results of an increase in the ratio.

EXAMPLE

The balance sheet for the GHI Company presented in Figure 7.1 indicated the following levels of assets, liabilities, and equity:

Assets		Liabilities and equity	
Current assets	$2700	Current liabilities	$1600
Fixed assets	4300	Long-term debts	2400
Total	$7000	Equity	3000
		Total	$7000

If the GHI Company earns approximately 2 percent on its current assets and 12 percent on its fixed assets, the current balance sheet configuration will allow it to earn approximately $570 [(2% · $2700) + (12% · $4300)] on its total assets. The firm's net working capital is currently $1100 ($2700 − $1600). Its ratio of current assets to total assets is approximately .386 ($2700 ÷ $7000).

If the firm *decreases* this ratio by investing $300 more in fixed assets (and thus $300 less in current assets), the new ratio of current to total assets is .343 ($2400 ÷ $7000). The firm's profits on its total assets will then be $600 [2% · ($2400) + 12% · ($4600)]. Its net working capital will be $800 ($2400 − $1600). These results are tabulated in Table 7.2.

As Table 7.2 indicates, as the firm's ratio of current to total assets decreases from .386 to .343 its profits on its total assets increase from $570 to $600. Its risk, measured by the amount of net working capital, increases since its net working capital, and thus its liquidity, is reduced from $1100 to $800. This supports our earlier conclusions concerning the profitability-risk trade-off as related to the firm's current assets. ●

TABLE 7.2 The effects of a
change in GHI's current assets

Item	Initial value	Value after change
Ratio of current to total assets	.386	.343
Profits on total assets	$ 570	$600
Net working capital	$1100	$800

Current liabilities. The effects of changing the level of a firm's current liabilities on its profitability-risk trade-off can also be demonstrated using a simple ratio—in this case, the ratio of the firm's current liabilities to its total assets. This ratio indicates the percentage of the firm's total assets that have been financed by current liabilities. It can either increase or decrease.

Effects of an increase. As the ratio of current liabilities to total assets increases, the firm's profitability increases; but so does its risk. Profitability increases due to the decreased costs associated with using more short-term financing and less long-term financing. Since short-term financing involving accounts payable, notes payable, and accruals is less expensive than long-term financing, the firm's costs decrease, thereby driving its profits higher. Assuming that the firm's current assets remain unchanged, its net working capital will decrease as its current liabilities increase. A decrease in net working capital means an increase in overall risk.

Effects of a decrease. A decrease in the ratio of current liabilities to total assets will decrease the profitability of the firm, since a larger amount of financing must be raised using the more expensive long-term instruments. There will be a corresponding decrease in risk due to the decreased level of current liabilities, which will cause an increase in the firm's net working capital. The consequences of a decrease in the ratio of current liabilities to total assets are exactly the opposite of the results of an increase in this ratio.

EXAMPLE

The balance sheet for the GHI Company in the preceding section can be used to show the effects of an *increase* in the firm's current liabilities. Initially the ratio of current liabilities to total assets is .229 ($1600 ÷ $7000). Assume that the firm's current liabilities cost approximately 3 percent to maintain while the average cost of its long-term funds is 8 percent. Ignoring the changes made in the preceding example, the effect of shifting $300 from long-term funds into current liabilities will increase current liabilities to $1900 ($1600 + $300) and decrease long-term funds to $5100 ($5400 − $300). The new ratio of current liabilities to total assets will be .271 ($1900 ÷ $7000). The result of this change will be a decrease in *costs* from the current level of $480 [(3% · $1600) + (8% · $5400)] to $465 [(3% · $1900) + (8% · $5100)]. The firm's net working capital will decrease from the initial level of $1100 to $800 ($2700 − $1900). These results of the increase in the ratio of current liabilities to total assets are tabulated in Table 7.3.

TABLE 7.3 The effects of a
change in GHI's current liabilities

Item	Initial value	Value after change
Ratio of current liabilities to total assets	.229	.271
Cost of financing[a]	$ 480	$465
Net working capital	$1100	$800

[a]A decrease in any of the firm's costs is equivalent to an *increase in profitability* by the same amount.

Table 7.3 illustrates that as the firm's ratio of current liabilities to total assets increases from .229 to .271, the firm's profits increase by $15 (since its costs drop from $480 to $465). Meanwhile, the firm's risk, measured by the level of net working capital, increases since its net working capital, or liquidity, decreases from $1100 to $800. This example illustrates only the effects of an increase in the ratio of current liabilities to total assets; a decrease would have an opposite effect. ●

Combined effects. The combined effects of changes in current assets and changes in current liabilities can be measured by considering them simultaneously. In the preceding two examples, the effects of a decrease in the ratio of current to total assets and the effects of an increase in the ratio of current liabilities to total assets were illustrated. Both changes, considered independently, were shown to increase the firm's profitability while increasing its risk. Logically, then, the combined effect of these actions should be to increase profits and risk and decrease net working capital. Table 7.4 illustrates the effects of combining the changes in current assets and current liabilities presented in Tables 7.2 and 7.3.

The values in Table 7.4 show that the combined effect of the two changes illustrated earlier is an increase in profits of $45 and a decrease in net working capital (liquidity) of $600. The trade-off here is obvious; the firm has increased its profitability by increasing its risk.

TABLE 7.4 The combined effects of changes
in GHI's current assets and current liabilities

Change	Change in profits	Change in net working capital
Decrease in ratio of current to total assets	+ $30	− $300
Increase in ratio of current liabilities to total assets	+ $15	− $300
Combined Effect	+ $45	− $600

Table 7.4 shows that the firm's net working capital has been reduced from its initial level of $1100 to $500. The firm's *initial net profit* can be thought of as the difference between the initial profits on total assets and the initial cost of financing. The initial profit on total assets was $570, and the initial cost of financing was $480. The initial net profit was therefore $90 ($570 − $480). After the changes in current assets and current liabilities, the firm's profits on its total assets increase to $600 while the cost of financing decreases to $465. Its net profits therefore increase to $135 ($600 − $465).

DETERMINING THE FINANCING MIX

One of the most important decisions that must be made with respect to the firm's current assets and current liabilities is how current liabilities will be used to finance current assets. A number of approaches to this financing decision exist. One of the critical factors the firm must keep in mind is that only a limited amount of short-term financing (current liabilities) is available to any business firm. The amount of current liabilities available is limited by the dollar amount of purchases in the case of accounts payable, by the dollar amount of accrued liabilities in the case of accruals, and by the amount of seasonal borrowing considered acceptable by lenders in the case of notes payable. Lenders make short-term loans only to allow a firm to finance seasonal buildups of inventory or accounts receivable; *they do not lend short-term money for long-term uses.*[4]

The firm's financing requirements can be broken into a permanent and a seasonal need. The permanent need, which consists of fixed assets plus the permanent portion of the firm's current assets, remains unchanged over the year, while the seasonal need, which is attributable to the existence of certain temporary current assets, varies over the year. The relationship between current and fixed assets and permanent and seasonal funds requirements can be illustrated graphically with the aid of a simple example.

EXAMPLE

The GHI Company's estimate of current, fixed, and total asset requirements on a monthly basis for the coming year are given in columns 1, 2, and 3 of Table 7.5. Columns 4 and 5 present a breakdown of the total requirement into its permanent and seasonal components. The permanent component (column 4) is the lowest level of total funds required during the period, while the seasonal portion is the difference between the total funds requirement (i.e., total assets) for each month and the permanent funds requirement.

By comparing the firm's fixed assets found in column 2 to its permanent funds requirement given in column 4, it can be seen that the permanent funds requirement exceeds the firm's level of fixed assets. This result occurs because a portion of the firm's current assets are permanent since they are apparently always being replaced. The size of the permanent component of current assets is $800 for the GHI Company. This value represents the maximum level of current assets that remains on the firm's

---

[4]The rationale for, techniques of, and parties to short-term business loans are discussed in detail in Chapters 11 and 12. The primary source of short-term loans to businesses, the commercial banks, make these loans only for seasonal or self-liquidating purposes such as temporary buildups of accounts receivable or inventory.

TABLE 7.5 Estimated funds requirements for the GHI Company

Month	Current assets (1)	Fixed assets (2)	Total assets[a] (1) + (2) (3)	Permanent requirement (4)	Seasonal requirement (3) − (4) (5)
January	$4,000	$13,000	$17,000	$13,800	$3,200
February	3,000	13,000	16,000	13,800	2,200
March	2,000	13,000	15,000	13,800	1,200
April	1,000	13,000	14,000	13,800	200
May	800	13,000	13,800	13,800	0
June	1,500	13,000	14,500	13,800	700
July	3,000	13,000	16,000	13,800	2,200
August	3,700	13,000	16,700	13,800	2,900
September	4,000	13,000	17,000	13,800	3,200
October	5,000	13,000	18,000	13,800	4,200
November	3,000	13,000	16,000	13,800	2,200
December	2,000	13,000	15,000	13,800	1,200

[a]This represents the firm's total funds requirement.

books throughout the year. This value can also be found by subtracting the level of fixed assets from the permanent funds requirement ($13,800 − $13,000 = $800). The relationships presented in Table 7.5 are depicted graphically in Figure 7.2. ●

There are a number of approaches to determining an appropriate financing mix. The three basic approaches—(1) the aggressive approach, (2) the conservative approach, and (3) a trade-off between the two—are discussed below.[5]

The aggressive approach

The aggressive approach requires that the firm finance its short-term needs with short-term funds and long-term needs with long-term funds.[6] Seasonal variations in the firm's fund requirements are met from short-term sources of funds, while permanent financing needs are met from long-term sources of funds. Short-term borrowing is geared to the actual need for funds. This approach can be illustrated graphically using the GHI Company data developed earlier.

EXAMPLE
The GHI Company's estimate of its total funds requirements (i.e., total assets) on a monthly basis for the coming year has been given in Table 7.5, column 3. Columns

[5]It is important to recognize that the discussions that follow do not explicitly address the various types of financing used and currently found on the firm's books. Rather, they are based upon the assumption that the firm has a flexible financial structure, which can be easily adjusted as required by the financial manager.

[6]The "aggressive" approach is used in this chapter to indicate a process of *matching* maturities of debt with the duration of each of the firm's financial needs.

4 and 5 divide this total funds requirement into permanent and seasonal components.

The aggressive approach requires that the permanent portion of the firm's funds requirement be financed with long-term funds and the seasonal portion be financed with short-term funds. The application of this financing plan to the firm's total funds requirement is illustrated graphically in Figure 7.3. ●

Using the aggressive approach, the firm in this example would have net working capital in an amount equal to the portion of current assets financed using long-term funds. The GHI Company's net working capital would therefore amount to $800, which is the portion of its current assets financed using long-term funds (i.e., $13,800 permanent financing minus $13,000 in fixed assets). This strategy would therefore be quite risky due to the low level of net working capital maintained.

Cost considerations.   If the cost of short-term funds needed by GHI in the example above should be 3 percent and the cost of long-term funds 8 percent, the cost of the financing plan can be estimated as follows:

The cost of the short-term funds.   The cost of the short-term funds can be estimated by calculating the average annual short-term loan and multiplying this amount by the annual cost of short-term funds of 3 percent. The average annual short-term funds requirement can be estimated by dividing the sum of the monthly seasonal funds requirements (column 5 in Table 7.5) by 12.[7] The sum of the seasonal funds requirements is $23,400, and the av-

FIGURE 7.2 GHI Company's estimated funds requirements

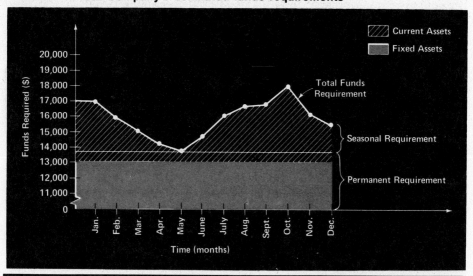

[7]In calculating the average funds requirement, we have merely converted the monthly funds requirements into an equivalent balance for the entire year. In other words, instead of calculating the cost for each month and summing the monthly amounts, we have multiplied the average balance by the annual interest rate in order to find the annual interest cost.

**FIGURE 7.3 Applying the aggressive
approach to the GHI Company's fund requirements**

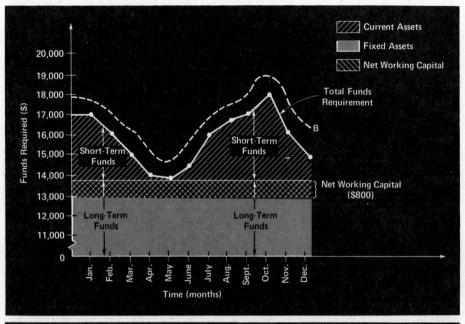

erage short-term funds requirement is $1950 ($23,400 ÷ 12). Thus the cost of short-term funds under this plan is $58.50 (3% · $1950).

The cost of the long-term funds. The cost of the long-term funds can be calculated by multiplying the average annual permanent fund requirement of $13,800 (from column 4 in Table 7.5) by the anual cost of long-term funds of 8 percent. The resulting cost of long-term funds under the aggressive plan is $1,104 (8% · $13,800).

The total cost of the aggressive plan. The total cost of the aggressive plan can be found by adding the cost of the short-term funds ($58.50) and the cost of the long-term funds ($1104). The total cost of the plan is thus $1162.50. This figure will become more meaningful when compared to the cost of various other plans.

Risk considerations. The aggressive plan operates with minimum net working capital since only the permanent portion of the firm's current assets is being financed with long-term funds; none of the firm's short-term seasonal needs are financed using long-term funds. For the GHI Company the level of net working capital is therefore equal to $800, which is the amount of permanent current assets (i.e., $13,800 permanent requirement − $13,000 in fixed assets). The aggressive plan is risky not only from the standpoint of low net working capital but also because the firm is drawing as heavily as possible on its short-term sources of funds to meet seasonal fluctuations in its funds requirements. If its total funds requirement actually turns out to be, say, the level indicated by the dashed line B in Figure 7.3, the firm may find it quite difficult to obtain a sufficient amount of short-term funds. Moreover, it may be impossible to obtain longer-term funds quickly enough to satisfy the firm's short-term needs. This aspect of risk associated with the aggressive approach results from the fact that a firm has only a limited amount of short-term borrowing capacity, and if it draws too heavily on this capacity, unexpected needs for funds may become quite difficult to satisfy. This could have harmful effects on the firm.

The conservative approach

The most conservative approach would be to finance all the firm's projected funds requirements with long-term funds and use short-term funds in the event of an emergency or an unexpected outflow of funds. It is hard to imagine how this approach could actually be implemented, since certain of the firm's short-term financing tools are virtually unavoidable. It would be quite difficult for a firm to keep its accounts payable and accruals low. It would also be unwise, since accounts payable and accruals arise naturally in the process of doing business.

In illustrating this approach, the distinction between payables and accruals will be ignored. For GHI the conservative approach would involve meeting all the forecast funds requirements, even the entire $18,000 needed in October, with long-term funds and reserving the use of short-term financing for contingencies.

EXAMPLE
Figure 7.4 shows graphically the application of the conservative approach to the estimated funds requirements for GHI given in Table 7.5. All the funds required over the one-year period, including the entire $18,000 forecast for October, are financed with long-term funds. The firm's net working capital, defined here as the portion of the firm's current assets financed by long-term funds, amounts to $5000 ($18,000 − $13,000).[8] Any long-term financing in excess of the $13,000 in fixed asset requirements provides net working capital. ●

Cost considerations. The effects of the conservative approach on the firm's profitability can be measured by determining the cost of this financing plan. In the preceding example, the cost of long-term funds was given as 8 percent per year. Since the average long-term financing balance with the conservative financing plan is $18,000, the total cost of this plan is $1440 (8% · $18,000). Comparing this figure to the total cost of $1162.50 using the aggressive approach indicates the more expensive nature of the conservative approach. The reason the conservative approach is so expensive can be

---

[8]The level of net working capital is constant throughout the year since the firm has $5000 in current assets that will be fully financed with long-term funds. Because the portion of the $5000 in excess of the scheduled level of current assets is assumed to be held as cash, the firm's current asset balance will increase to this level.

FIGURE 7.4 Applying the conservative approach to the GHI Company's fund requirements

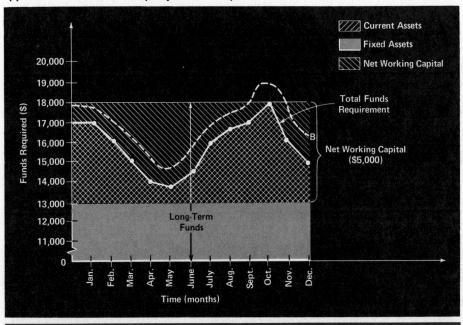

seen by looking at Figure 7.4; the area above the total funds requirement line and below the long-term financing line (shown by diagonal lines going from left to right only) represents the level of funds not actually needed, but on which the firm is paying interest (i.e., the amount of excess funds available).

Risk considerations. The $5000 of net working capital (i.e., $18,000 long-term financing minus $13,000 of fixed assets) associated with this plan should mean a very low level of risk for the firm. The firm's risk should also be lowered by the fact that the plan does not require the firm to use any of its limited short-term borrowing capacity. In other words, if the firm's total required financing actually turns out to be the level represented by the dashed line B in Figure 7.4, sufficient short-term borrowing capacity should be available to cover the unexpected financial needs and avoid technical insolvency.

Comparison with the aggressive approach. Unlike the aggressive approach, the conservative approach requires the firm to pay interest on unneeded funds. The lower cost of the aggressive approach, therefore, makes it more profitable than the conservative approach, but the aggressive is much more risky. The contrast between these two approaches should clearly indicate the trade-off that exists between profitability and risk. The aggressive approach provides high profits but also a high risk, while the conservative approach provides low profits and a low risk. A trade-off between these extremes should result in an acceptable financing strategy for most firms.

A trade-off between the two approaches

Most firms use a financing plan that lies somewhere between the high profit–high-risk aggressive approach and the low-profit–low-risk conservative approach. The exact trade-off made between profitability and risk depends largely on the decision maker's attitudes toward risk. One of many possible trade-offs in GHI Company's case is described below.

EXAMPLE

After careful analysis, the GHI Company has decided on a financing plan based on an amount of permanent financing equal to the midpoint of the minimum and maximum monthly funds requirement for the period. An examination of Table 7.5 reveals that the minimum monthly funds requirement is $13,800 (in May) and the maximum monthly funds requirement is $18,000 (in October). The midpoint between these two values is $15,900 [($13,800 + $18,000) ÷ 2]. Thus, the firm will use $15,900 in long-term funds each month and raise any additional funds required from short-term sources. The breakdown of long- and short-term funds under this plan is given in Table 7.6.

TABLE 7.6 A financing plan based on a trade-off between profitability and risk for the GHI Company

Month	Total assets[a] (1)	Long-term funds (2)	Short-term funds (3)
January	$17,000	$15,900	$1,100
February	16,000	15,900	100
March	15,000	15,900	0
April	14,000	15,900	0
May	13,800	15,900	0
June	14,500	15,900	0
July	16,000	15,900	100
August	16,700	15,900	800
September	17,000	15,900	1,100
October	18,000	15,900	2,100
November	16,000	15,900	100
December	15,000	15,900	0

[a]This represents the firm's total funds requirement from column 3 of Table 7.5.

Column 3 in Table 7.6 shows the amount of short-term funds required each month. These values were found by subtracting $15,900 from total funds required each month, given in column 1. For the months March, April, May, June, and December the level of total funds required is less than the level of long-term funds available; therefore, no short-term funds are needed.

Implementing this plan would result in levels of net working capital as high as $2900 ($15,900 long-term funds − $13,000 fixed assets). This should give the firm a risk position somewhere between the high-risk level of the aggressive approach (which provides $800 of net working capital) and the low-risk position of the conservative approach (which provides $5000 of net working capital). ●

Figure 7.5 presents the trade-off plan described in Table 7.6 along with the plan based on the aggressive approach and the conservative approach, graphically. The area above the total funds requirement line and below the long-term financing line, line 3 (shown by diagonal lines going from left to right only) represents the level of funds not actually needed but on which the firm is paying interest.

Cost considerations. The cost of the trade-off plan can be calculated by finding the average short- and long-term funds required and multiplying these amounts by the short- and long-term financing costs of 3 and 8 percent, respectively. The sum of these two cost components is the overall cost of the plan.

The cost of short-term funds. The cost of the short-term funds can be estimated by calculating the average short-term funds requirement and multiplying this by 3 percent. The average annual short-term funds required can be calculated by dividing the sum of the monthly (seasonal) funds requirements (from column 3 of Table 7.6) by 12. The sum of the seasonal funds requirements is $5400. The average short-term funds requirement is thus $450 ($5400 ÷ 12), and the cost of short-term funds with this plan is $13.50 (3% · $450).

The cost of long-term funds. The cost of long-term funds can be calculated by multiplying the average long-term fund requirement of $15,900 (from column 2 of Table 7.6) by the annual cost of long-term funds of 8 percent. The cost of long-term funds with the trade-off is therefore $1272.

The total cost of the trade-off plan. The total cost of the trade-off plan can be found by adding the cost of short-term funds ($13.50) and the cost of long-term funds ($1272). The total cost of the trade-off plan is therefore $1285.50.

Risk considerations. As Figure 7.5 shows, the trade-off plan is less risky than the aggressive approach but more risky than the conservative approach. With the trade-off plan, if the firm's total funds requirement is actually at the level given by line B in Figure 7.5, the likelihood that it will be able to obtain additional short-term financing is good since a portion of its short-term financial requirements is actually being financed with long-term funds. With respect to cost, the trade-off plan falls between the aggressive approach, which has the lowest cost, and the conservative approach, which has the highest cost.

FIGURE 7.5 Three alternative financing plans for GHI Company

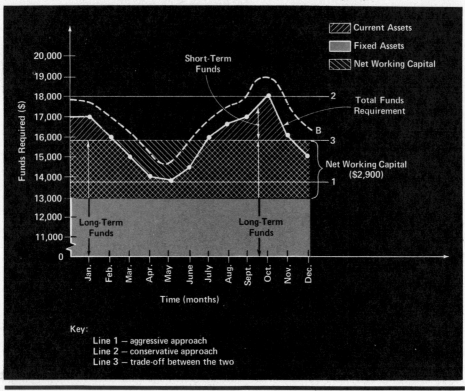

A summary comparison of approaches

Table 7.7 summarizes the results of the analysis of each of the plans. It indicates that the lower the firm's net working capital, the higher the risk present. The table also indicates that the higher the risk of insolvency, the higher the firm's profits are expected to be. The trade-off between the risk and profitability can be demonstrated more clearly by a graph, as in Figure 7.6. Care should be used in analyzing Figure 7.6 since each of the axes meas-

TABLE 7.7 A summary of the results of
the three financing plans for the GHI Company

Financing plan	Net working capital[a]	Degree of risk	Total cost of funds	Level of profits
Aggressive	$ 800.00	Highest	$1162.50	Highest
Trade-off	$2900.00	Intermediate	$1285.50	Intermediate
Conservative	$5000.00	Lowest	$1440.00	Lowest

[a]These values represent the amount of net working capital provided by each financing plan as determined in the preceding examples.

FIGURE 7.6 A graph of the profitability-risk trade-off for the GHI Company

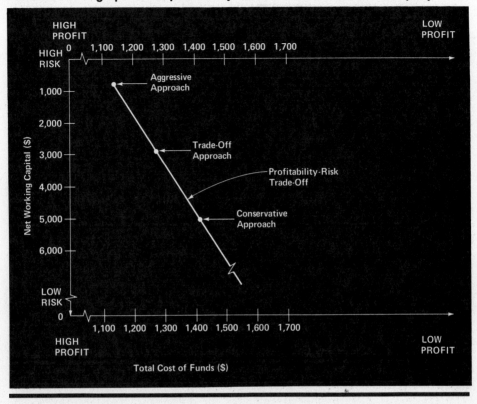

ures two variables. As one moves down the Y axis, risk decreases due to increasing net working capital; unfortunately, profits decrease too, since one is also moving to the right on the X axis, encountering increasing funds costs. The financial manager must determine whether to select a financing plan that places the firm at one or the other ends of the profitability-risk function, or choose a trade-off between profitability and risk. Most financial managers will make some type of trade-off between high profits and high risk.

SUMMARY

This chapter has provided an in-depth look at the broad area of working capital management. Rather than looking at individual current assets and current liabilities it has given specific attention to the relation between the two categories of accounts. The firm's net working capital, which is defined as the difference between its current assets and current liabilities, has been used as a focal point for analysis. The appropriate level of net working capital depends on the firm's cash flow patterns. Firms maintain net working capital to provide a cushion between cash outflows and cash inflows.

Net working capital is often used as a measure of the risk of technical insolvency by the firm. The more liquid a firm is, the less likely it will be unable to satisfy its current obligations as they come due. Since low levels of net working capital indicate a higher probability of insufficient liquidity, and vice versa, net working capital is a very useful measure of risk. An alternative definition of net working capital is that it is that portion of a firm's current assets financed with long-term funds.

In evaluating the profitability-risk trade-off related to the level of a firm's net working capital, we have made three basic assumptions: (1) that we are dealing with a manufacturing firm, (2) that current assets are less profitable than fixed assets, and (3) that short-term funds are less expensive than long-term funds. The higher a firm's ratio of current-to-total assets, the less profitable the firm, and the less risky. The converse is also true. The higher a firm's ratio of current liabilities to total assets, the more profitable and more risky the firm is. The converse of this statement is also true. These trade-offs between profitability and risk must be considered in evaluating a firm's net working capital position.

Since net working capital can be considered the portion of a firm's current assets financed by long-term funds, the mix between long-term and short-term financing is directly related to the profitability-risk trade-off and the firm's net working capital. By forecasting the firm's funds requirements, the financial manager can evaluate the consequences of various financing plans before deciding what portion of the company's current assets should be financed with long-term funds. The firm's financing requirements can be broken into a seasonal and a permanent need. The permanent need is attributable to both fixed assets and the permanent portion of current assets, while the seasonal need is attributable to the existence of certain temporary current assets.

There are a number of approaches for determining an appropriate financing mix. The aggressive approach is a high-profit–high-risk financing plan where seasonal needs are financed with short-term funds and permanent needs are financed with long-term funds. The conservative approach is a low-profit–low-risk financing plan: all funds requirements—both seasonal and permanent—are financed with long-term funds; short-term funds are saved for emergencies. Most firms use a trade-off approach whereby some of the firm's seasonal needs are financed with long-term funds; this approach lies between the high-profit–high-risk aggressive approach and the low-profit–low-risk conservative approach.

QUESTIONS

7-1 Why is working capital management considered so important by stockholders, creditors, and the firm's financial manager? What is the definition of net working capital?

7-2 What relationship would you expect to exist between the predictability of a firm's cash flows and its required level of net working capital?

7-3 Why are a firm's payments considered more predictable than its receipts?

7-4 Given that a firm's net working capital is sometimes defined as the portion of current assets financed with long-term funds, can you show diagrammatically why this definition is valid?

7-5 How are net working capital, liquidity, technical insolvency, and risk related?

7-6 Generally the cost of short-term borrowing is less than that of long-term borrowing. Why is it likely to be cheaper to incur current liabilities than to obtain long-term funds even if the cost of short-term loans is greater than the cost of long-term funds?

7-7 Why is an increase in a firm's ratio of current to total assets expected to decrease both profits and risk as measured by net working capital?

7-8 How can changes in the ratio of a firm's current liabilities to total assets affect its profitability and risk?

7-9 How would you expect both an increase in a firm's ratio of current assets to total assets and a decrease in its ratio of current liabilities to total assets to affect its profits and risk? Why?

7-10 How can the differences between the returns on current and fixed assets and the cost of current liabilities and long-term funds be used to determine how best to change a firm's net working capital?

7-11 What is the basic premise of the aggressive approach for meeting a firm's funds requirements? What are the effects of this approach on the firm's profitability and risk?

7-12 What is the conservative approach to financing a firm's funds requirements? What kind of profitability-risk trade-off is involved?

7-13 Why would a firm using the conservative approach be advised to finance no more than its projected peak financial need with long-term funds?

7-14 If a firm has a constant funds requirement throughout the year, which, if any, of the three financing plans is preferable? Why?

7-15 As the difference between the cost of short-term financing and long-term financing becomes smaller, which financing plan—aggressive or conservative—becomes more attractive? Would the aggressive or the conservative approach be preferable if the costs were equal? Why?

7-16 How would one apply the aggressive approach if one knew that only a certain amount of short-term financing, insufficient to cover the peak short-term need, would be available?

PROBLEMS

7-1 Last year, the NRC Corporation had the following balance sheet:

Assets		Liabilities and equity	
Current assets	$ 6,000	Current liabilities	$ 2,000
Fixed assets	14,000	Long-term funds	18,000
Total	$20,000	Total	$20,000

The firm estimated it earned 3 percent on current assets, current liabilities cost 6 percent, fixed assets earned 18 percent, and long-term funds cost 10 percent.

For the coming year, calculate the expected profits on total assets, financing costs, net profitability, current ratio, and ROI under the following different circumstances:

a There are no changes.

b The firm shifts $1000 from current assets to fixed assets and $500 from long-term funds to current liabilities.

c Discuss the changes in risk and return illustrated by a and b above.

7-2 The Badger Company had the following balance sheet at the end of 1978:

Assets		Liabilities and equity	
Current assets	$ 30,000	Current liabilities	$ 15,000
Fixed assets	90,000	Long-term funds	105,000
Total	$120,000	Total	$120,000

a   Calculate profits on total assets, financing costs, net profits, current ratio, and ROI if the firm (1) expects to earn 1 percent on current assets, 14 percent on fixed assets, current liabilities cost 3 percent, and long-term funds cost 10 percent; and (2) expects to earn 6 percent on current assets, 14 percent on fixed assets, pay 6 percent on current liabilities, and 9 percent on long-term funds.

b   The firm wishes to decrease net working capital by $10,000. This could be accomplished by decreasing current assets, increasing current liabilities, or a combination of the two. Under which circumstances—a(1) or a(2)—would you expect the greater reduction in current assets? Explain.

7-3   What is the average loan balance and the annual loan cost, given an annual interest rate on loans of 8 percent, for a firm with the total monthly borrowings given below?

Month	Amount	Month	Amount
Jan.	$12,000	July	$6,000
Feb.	13,000	Aug.	5,000
Mar.	9,000	Sept.	6,000
Apr.	8,000	Oct.	5,000
May	9,000	Nov.	7,000
June	7,000	Dec.	9,000

7-4   International Tool has forecast its total funds requirements for the coming year to be

Month	Amount	Month	Amount
Jan.	$2,000,000	July	$12,000,000
Feb.	2,000,000	Aug.	14,000,000
Mar.	2,000,000	Sept.	9,000,000
Apr.	4,000,000	Oct.	5,000,000
May	6,000,000	Nov.	4,000,000
June	9,000,000	Dec.	3,000,000

a   Calculate the financing costs of the aggressive approach and the conservative approach if (1) the cost of short-term funds is 5 percent and the cost of long-term funds is 12 percent; and (2) the cost of short-term funds is 6 percent and the cost of long-term funds is 8 percent.

b   Discuss the profitability-risk trade-offs associated with the aggressive plan and the conservative plan.

c   Which plan would more closely approximate your choice in a(1) and a(2)? Why?

7-5   Petro-Gas has forecast its seasonal financing needs for the next year as follows:

Month	Seasonal requirement	Month	Seasonal requirement
Jan.	$2,400,000	July	$ 800,000
Feb.	500,000	Aug.	400,000
Mar.	0	Sept.	0
Apr.	300,000	Oct.	300,000
May	1,200,000	Nov.	1,000,000
June	1,000,000	Dec.	1,800,000

Calculate the financing costs under the aggressive plan and the conservative plan and recommend one of the plans under the following conditions:
a   Short-term funds cost 4 percent and long-term funds cost 12 percent.
b   Short-term funds cost 6 percent and long-term funds cost 8 percent.
c   Both short-term and long-term funds cost 7 percent.

7-6   Stop-and-Shop has seasonal financing needs that vary from zero to $2,000,000. For each separate condition listed below, would the condition tend to move the firm toward an aggressive financing plan or toward a conservative financing plan?
a   The difference between short-term and long-term financing costs has decreased.
b   The average seasonal financing need is $400,000.
c   The average seasonal financing need is $1,800,000.
d   The long-term financing cost is much higher than the short-term cost.
e   The firm has a high proportion of its assets in current assets.
f   Sales are very difficult to predict.

7-7   Mile High Enterprises expects to need the following amounts of funds next year:

Month	Amount	Month	Amount
Jan.	$10,000	July	$10,000
Feb.	10,000	Aug.	9,000
Mar.	11,000	Sept.	8,000
Apr.	12,000	Oct.	8,000
May	13,000	Nov.	9,000
June	11,000	Dec.	9,000

a   What is the average amount of funding needed during the year?
b   If short-term financing costs 4 percent and long-term financing costs 10 percent, what will be the financing costs for the aggressive and conservative financing plans, respectively?
c   If the firm finances $10,000 with long-term financing, what will be the financing cost?

7-8   Snyder Supply has financing needs of $250,000 per month forecast for every month of the coming year. The cost of short-term financing is 6 percent and the cost of long-term financing is 8 percent.
a   What are the costs of the aggressive and conservative financing plans?
b   Which plan is preferable and why?

SELECTED REFERENCES

Aigner, D. J., and C. M. Sprenkle, "On Optimal Financing of Cyclical Cash Needs," *Journal of Finance 28* (December 1973), pp. 1249–1253.

Bean, Virginia L., and Reynolds Griffith, "Risk and Return in Working Capital Management," *Mississippi Valley Journal of Business and Economics 1* (Fall 1966), pp. 28–48.

Beranek, William, *Working Capital Management* (Belmont, Calif.: Wadsworth, 1966).

Bierman, H., K. Chopra, and J. Thomas, "Ruin Considerations: Optimal Working Capital and Capital Structure," *Journal of Financial and Quantitative Analysis 10* (March 1975), pp. 119–128.

Bogen, Jules I., Ed., *Financial Handbook*, 4th ed. (New York: Ronald, 1968), sect. 16.

Cossaboom, Roger A., "Let's Reassess the Profitability-Liquidity Tradeoff," *Financial Executive 39* (May 1971), pp. 46–51.

Glautier, M. W. E., "Towards a Reformulation of the Theory of Working Capital," *Journal of Business Finance 3* (Spring 1971), pp. 37–42.

Jennings, Joseph A., "A Look at Corporate Liquidity," *Financial Executive 39* (February 1971), pp. 26–32.

Knight, W. D., "Working Capital Management—Satisfying versus Optimization," *Financial Management 1* (Spring 1972), pp. 33–40.

Mehta, Dileep R., *Working Capital Management* (Englewood Cliffs, N.J.: Prentice-Hall, 1974), chap. 1.

Merville, L. J., and L. A. Tavis, "Optimal Working Capital Policies: A Chance-Constrained Programming Approach," *Journal of Financial and Quantitative Analysis 8* (January 1973), pp. 47–60.

Smith, Keith V., Ed., *Management of Working Capital: A Reader* (St. Paul, Minn.: West, 1974), readings 1, 30, and 34.

———, "State of the Art of Working Capital Management," *Financial Management 2* (Autumn 1973), pp. 50–55.

Stancill, James McN., *The Management of Working Capital* (Scranton, Pa.: Intext, 1971), chaps. 1, 6, and 7.

Van Horne, James C., "A Risk-Return Analysis of a Firm's Working Capital Position," *Engineering Economist 14* (Winter 1969), pp. 71–89.

Walker, Ernest W., "Towards a Theory of Working Capital," *Engineering Economist 9* (January-February 1964), pp. 21–35.

Walter, James E., "Determination of Technical Solvency," *Journal of Business 30* (January 1959), pp. 39–43.

Welter, Paul, "How to Calculate Savings Possible through Reduction of Working Capital," *Financial Executive* (October 1970), pp. 50–58.

CHAPTER 8
Cash and marketable security management

The management of cash and marketable securities is one of the key areas of working capital management. Since cash and marketable securities are the firm's most liquid assets, they provide the firm with the ability to pay bills as they come due. Collaterally, these liquid assets provide a pool of funds to cover unexpected outlays, thereby reducing the risk of a "liquidity crisis." Since the other major current assets (i.e., accounts receivable and inventory) will eventually be converted into cash through collections and sales, cash is the common denominator to which all liquid assets can be reduced.

Marketable securities represent short-term investments made by the firm to obtain a return on temporarily idle funds. When a firm recognizes that too large an amount of cash has been accumulated, it will often put a portion of the cash into an interest-earning instrument. Idle cash in the firm's checking account does not provide any interest income since commercial banks are currently prohibited by law from paying interest on demand deposits.[1] There are a number of highly liquid interest-earning instruments that allow the firm to make a profit on its idle cash without sacrificing much of its liquidity. The majority of these instruments are referred to as marketable securities.

This chapter has four sections. The first section is concerned with the firm's overall strategy with respect to the payment of accounts payable, the management of inventory, and the collection of accounts receivable. The second section provides a brief discussion of strategies for minimizing the firm's cash requirements. The third section discusses motives for holding marketable securities, aspects of marketability, and certain considerations with respect to the proportion of marketable securities held. The final section is devoted to a description of the characteristics, maturities, yields, and denominations of the most common marketable securities.

---

[1]Pending legislation may soon permit commercial banks to pay interest on demand deposits. Of course, since business firms are already being compensated for the "balances" they hold in commercial banks by receiving reduced activity fees or lower interest rates on loans, or both, the passage of legislation permitting the explicit payment of interest on demand deposits may not significantly affect corporate banking relationships.

THE EFFICIENT MANAGEMENT OF CASH

The basic strategies that should be employed by the business firm in managing its cash are as follows:

1. Pay accounts payable as late as possible without damaging the firm's credit rating, but take advantage of any favorable cash discounts.[2]
2. Turn over inventory as quickly as possible, avoiding stockouts that might result in shutting down the production line or a loss of sales.
3. Collect accounts receivable as quickly as possible without losing future sales because of high-pressure collection techniques. Cash discounts, if they are economically justifiable, may be used to accomplish this objective.

The overall implications of these strategies for the firm can be demonstrated by looking at the cash turnover process.

Cash cycles and cash turnovers

The *cash cycle* of a firm is defined as the amount of time that elapses from the point when the firm makes an outlay to purchase raw materials to the point when cash is collected from the sale of the finished good produced using that raw material. The term *cash turnover* refers to the number of times each year the firm's cash is actually turned over. The relationship between the cash cycle and cash turnover is similar to the relationship between the average age and turnover of inventory, accounts receivable, and accounts payable, discussed in Chapter 3. The concept of cash cycles and cash turnovers can be illustrated by a simple example.

EXAMPLE

The KLM Company currently purchases all its raw materials on a credit basis and sells all its merchandise on credit.[3] The credit terms extended the firm currently require payment within 30 days of a purchase, while the firm currently requires its customers to pay within 60 days of a sale. The firm's calculations of the average age of its accounts payable and accounts receivable indicate that it is taking, on the average, 35 days to pay its accounts payable and 70 days to collect its accounts receivable. Further calculations reveal that, on the average, 85 days elapse between the point a raw material is purchased and the point the finished good is sold. In other words, the average age of the firm's inventory is 85 days.

Cash cycle   The firm's cash cycle can be shown by a simple graph, as in Figure 8.1. There are 120 days between the cash outflow to pay the account payable (on day 35) and the cash inflow from the collection of the account receivable (on day 155). During this period, the firm's money is tied up.

At time zero the firm purchases raw materials, which are initially placed in the

---

[2]A discussion of the variables to consider in determining whether to take cash discounts appears in Chapter 11. A cash discount is often an enticement to pay accounts payable early in order to reduce the purchase price of goods.

[3]This assumption of all credit purchases and credit sales simplifies the cash management model. Although purchases and sales for cash could easily be incorporated into it, they have not been in order to convey the key cash management strategies with a minimum of algebraic complexity.

FIGURE 8.1 The KLM Company's cash cycle

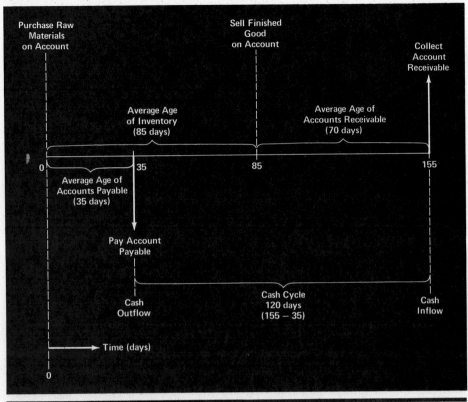

raw-materials inventory. Eventually the raw materials are used in the production process, becoming part of the work-in-process inventory. When the work in process is completed, the finished good is placed in the finished-goods inventory until it is sold. The total amount of time that elapses, on the average, between the purchase of raw materials and the ultimate sale of finished goods is the average age of inventory, 85 days in Figure 8.1.

When the firm initially purchased the raw materials (on day 0), an account payable was established. It remained on the firm's books until it was paid, 35 days later. It was at this point that a *cash outflow* occurred. After the sale of the finished good (on day 85), the firm established an account receivable. This account receivable remained on its books until it was collected 70 days later. It was therefore 70 days after the item was sold, on day 155 (70 days beyond the 85th day, which was the day of sale) that a *cash inflow* occurred.

A firm's cash cycle is calculated by finding the average number of days that elapse between the cash outflows associated with paying accounts payable and the cash inflows associated with collecting accounts receivable. The cash cycle for the KLM Company is 120 days (155 days − 35 days).

Cash turnover   A firm's cash turnover can be calculated by dividing the cash cycle into 360, the assumed number of days in the year. The KLM Company's cash turnover is currently 3 (360 ÷ 120). The higher a firm's cash turnover is, the less cash the firm requires. The firm's cash turnover, like its inventory turnover, should be maximized. However, the firm does not want to run out of cash. The maintenance of a minimum amount of operating cash is discussed in the next section. ●

Determining a firm's minimum operating cash[4]

Because the firm must forego various opportunities to invest or repay debts in order to maintain a cash balance, the objective of the financial manager should be to operate in a fashion that requires minimum cash. The amount of cash that will allow the firm to meet scheduled bill payments as they come due, and provide a margin of safety for making unscheduled payments or making scheduled payments when expected cash inflows are not available, must be planned for by the firm. This "cash," of course, can be held in the form of a demand deposit (i.e., checking account balance) or may be held in some type of interest-earning marketable security. Regardless of the form in which it is held, most firms maintain cash balances in order to meet known outlays as well as to provide a cushion with which to deal with unexpected events.

A variety of quantitative techniques as well as rules of thumb exist for determining "optimum" cash balances. The use of the cash budget, discussed in Chapter 5, presents a method for planning the firm's cash requirements; but does not deal explicitly with the question of the appropriate cash balance level. The optimum level is, of course, dependent upon both expected and unexpected receipts and disbursements of cash. The appropriate balance is often set at a level either sufficient to meet both expected and unexpected requirements, or to meet the requirements established by lenders, whichever is greatest. Another approach is to set the minimum level of cash as a percentage of sales. For example, a firm wishing to maintain a cash balance equal to 8 percent of annual sales, which are expected to be $2,000,000, would maintain a balance of $160,000 (i.e., .08 · $2,000,000). More sophisticated approaches for determining necessary balances are based on the use of techniques such as calculus and statistics. For purposes of illustration, a simple yet appealing and practical technique is used to estimate the minimum liquidity level required. Using the framework already developed, the minimum level of operating cash needed by a firm can be estimated by dividing the firm's total annual outlays by its cash turnover rate.[5]

[4]The phrase "minimum operating cash" as used throughout this part of the chapter can more precisely be viewed as the "level of liquidity," which might be in the form of cash and marketable securities, needed in order to allow the firm to meet its payment obligations as they come due. Although the firm is expected to hold some part of its liquidity in marketable securities instead of cash, the phrase "minimum operating cash" is applicable, since to pay bills any liquidity warehoused in the form of a marketable security first will have to be converted into cash.

[5]The logic of this calculation rests on the existence of the following equation for a firm's cash turnover:

$$\text{Cash turnover} = \frac{\text{total annual outlays}}{\text{average cash balance}}$$

Solving this equation for the average cash balance produces the following equation:

$$\text{Average cash balance} = \frac{\text{total annual outlays}}{\text{cash turnover}}$$

This model assumes that the *average* amount of cash required by the firm in order to operate is the same as the *minimum* amount.

EXAMPLE

If the KLM Company (presented in the preceding example) spends approximately $12,000,000 annually on operating outlays, its minimum cash requirement is $4,000,000 ($12,000,000 ÷ 3). This means that if it begins the year with $4,000,000 in cash, it should have sufficient cash to pay bills as they come due. It should not have to borrow any additional funds in these circumstances. If the opportunity cost of holding cash is 5 percent, then the cost of maintaining a $4,000,000 cash balance will be $200,000 ($4,000,000 · .05) per year. ●

Opportunity cost concept.   The opportunity cost of 5 percent in the example above is based on the fact that the firm, if it were free to use the $4,000,000, could invest it in a riskless investment yielding a return of 5 percent per year or repay a debt costing 5 percent per year. Since there is a cost of maintaining idle cash balances, a firm should attempt to implement policies that will reduce the amount of operating cash it requires.

Analysis of the cash cycle model.   It is important to recognize that the discussion of cash cycles, cash turnover, and minimum operating cash is based on a number of limiting assumptions. One is that the technique explicitly ignores profit—the fact that inflows will actually exceed outflows. The model assumes that outflows equal inflows and therefore no profit exists. Second, the model assumes that *all* outflows occur at the same time that the raw materials are paid for (i.e., payment of account payable). It should be clear that in actuality value will be added to the raw material at various stages throughout the production-sale process. This assumption tends to cause the actual cash requirement to be overestimated. It is also assumed that the firm's purchases, production, and sales occur at a constant rate throughout the year. In situations where this assumption is not valid, a firm's minimum cash balance can be estimated by using the cash turnover rate for the most cash-dependent period of operation. One should also recognize that the amount of uncertainty, or variability, in a firm's cash requirements will certainly affect the minimum level of operating cash maintained. Although, for simplicity, this uncertainty has been ignored here, the reader should be aware of the fact that the amount of cash held by a firm is a function of the uncertainty of its cash inflows and cash outflows. Although these limiting assumptions may subtract from the practical applicabilty of this technique, its use for illustrating the implementation of the recommended cash management strategies warrants its application in the following examples.

Cash management strategies

The effects of implementing each of the strategies for efficient cash management mentioned earlier on the KLM Company are described below.

Stretching accounts payable.   One strategy available to the KLM Company is to "stretch its accounts payable," that is, to pay its bills as late as possible without damaging its credit rating.

EXAMPLE

If KLM company can stretch the age of its accounts payable from the current average of 35 days to an average of 45 days, its cash cycle will be reduced to 110 days. Fig-

FIGURE 8.2 A cash cycle for the KLM Company based on stretching the average age of accounts payable

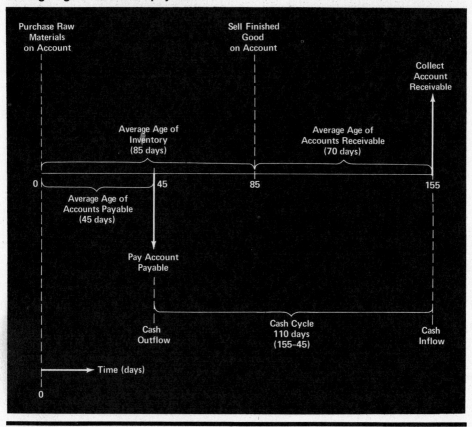

ure 8.2 illustrates this new cash cycle. By stretching its accounts payable 10 additional days, the firm increases its cash turnover rate from 3 to 3.27 (360 ÷ 110). This increased cash turnover rate results in a decrease in the firm's minimum operating cash requirement from $4,000,000 to approximtely $3,670,000 ($12,000,000 ÷ 3.27). The reduction in required operating cash of approximately $330,000 ($4,000,000 − $3,670,000) represents an annual savings to the firm of $16,500 ($330,000 · .05), which is the opportunity cost of tying up that amount of funds. ●

The payoff from stretching accounts payable for the KLM Company should be clear. However, firms are quite often constrained as to the amount of stretching they can do. Only in instances where a firm's suppliers are highly dependent on the firm for a large portion of their business can a firm really capitalize on stretching accounts payable. Many firms offer cash discounts as enticements to their customers to pay their accounts promptly. Had KLM's suppliers offered cash discounts for early payments, the firm might have found that the cheapest overall strategy would be to pay early and take the discount. Occasionally a supplier may let a customer stretch its accounts, recognizing that the customer is a young, growing firm and that the payoff from helping it grow will be increased business in the future. Stretching accounts payable is certainly a strategy to be considered by the business firm that wants to reduce its cash requirements and therefore its operating costs.[6]

Efficient inventory-production management. Another way of minimizing required cash is to increase the inventory turnover rate. This can be achieved in any of the following ways:

Increasing the raw-materials turnover. By using more efficient inventory control techniques, the firm may be able to increase its raw-materials turnover.

Decreasing the production cycle. By initiating better production planning, scheduling, and control techniques, the firm can reduce the length of the production cycle. Reducing the production cycle will cause the firm's work-in-process inventory turnover to increase.

Increasing the finished-goods turnover. The firm can increase its finished-goods turnover by better forecasting of demand and by better planning of production to coincide with these forecasts. More efficient control of the finished-goods inventory will contribute to a faster finished-goods inventory turnover rate. Regardless of which aspect(s) of the firm's overall inventory turnover is (are) adjusted, the result will be a reduction in the amount of operating cash required.

EXAMPLE
If the KLM Company manages to reduce the average age of its inventory from the current level of 85 days to 70 days—a reduction of 15 days—the effects on its minimum operating cash will be as follows. There will be a reduction of 15 days in the cash cycle, from 120 days to 105 days. (See Figure 8.3 for a graph of a new cash cycle.) The decreased average age of inventory for the KLM Company increases the annual cash turnover rate from the initial level of 3 to 3.43 (360 ÷ 105). The increased cash turnover rate results in a decrease in the firm's minimum operating cash requirement from $4,000,000 to approximately $3,500,000 ($12,000,000 ÷ 3.43). The reduction in required operating cash of approximately $500,000 ($4,000,000 − $3,500,000) represents an annual savings to the firm of $25,000 ($500,000 · .05). Since $500,000 less must be tied up, the firm will be able to earn 5 percent on these funds. This savings clearly indicates the importance of efficiency in inventory and production management. ●

Speeding the collection of accounts receivable. Another way of reducing the firm's operating cash requirement is to speed up the collection of accounts receivable. Accounts receivable, just like inventory, tie up dollars that, if they were freed, could be invested in additional earning assets. Accounts receivable are a necessary cost to the firm, since the extension of credit

---

[6]In periods of tight money such as 1974–1975, a firm's ability to stretch payables becomes limited, especially when the supplier can live without the customer's business. In many instances suppliers, during periods of tight money, levy interest charges on a daily basis for payments received after the end of a credit period.

FIGURE 8.3 A cash cycle for the KLM Company based on an increased inventory turnover

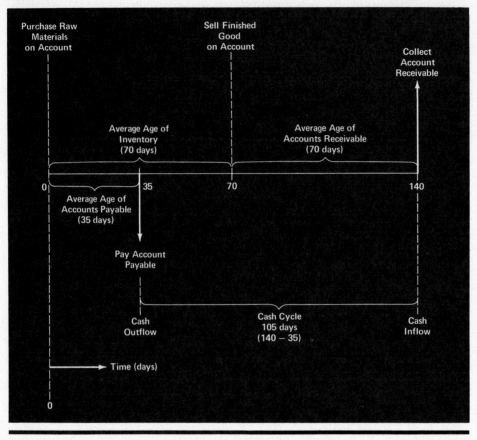

to customers normally allows the firm to achieve higher levels of sales than it could by operating on a strictly cash basis. The actual *credit terms* extended by a firm are normally dictated by the industry in which it operates.[7] Typically, they are related to the nature of the product sold—to the way it is transported and the way it is used. In industries where virtually undifferentiated products are sold, credit terms may be a critical factor in sales. Normally in these industries, all firms match the best credit terms given in order to maintain their competitive position. In industries where relatively differentiated types of products are sold, there may be greater variance in credit terms.

The firm's credit terms affect not only the pattern of collections but also credit policies and collection policies. *Credit policies* are the firm's cri-

---

[7]A discussion of various types of credit terms and their implications is presented in Chapter 9, which is devoted solely to the management of accounts receivable. Credit terms state when payment is due and whether or not and under what conditions a cash discount is offered.

Figure 8.4 A cash cycle for the KLM Company based on speeding the collection of accounts receivable

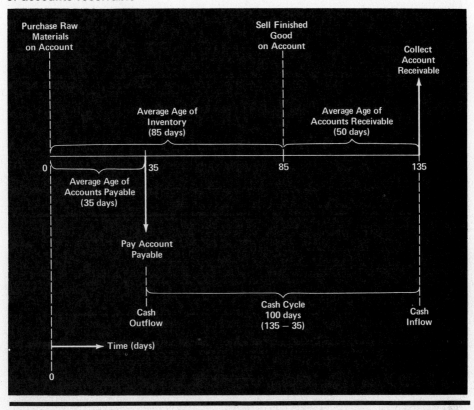

teria for determining to whom credit should be extended; *collection policies* determine the effort put forth by the firm to collect accounts receivable promptly. Changes in credit terms, credit policies, and collection policies can all be used to decrease the average collection period while maintaining or increasing overall profits. Typically the initiation of a cash discount for early payment, the use of more restrictive credit policies, or the initiation of more aggressive collection policies will decrease the average age of the firm's receivables. It is important that the firm consider the consequences of each or all of these actions on sales and profits beforehand. An example will help to clarify the effects of faster collections on the firm's minimum operating cash requirement.

EXAMPLE
If the KLM Company, by changing its credit terms, is able to reduce the average age of its accounts receivable from the current level of 70 days to 50 days, this will reduce its cash cycle by 20 days (70 days − 50 days). Figure 8.4 presents a graph of the new cash cycle. The decrease in the average age of accounts receivable from 70 to 50 days raises the firm's annual cash turnover rate from the initial level of 3 to 3.60 (360 ÷

100). The increased cash turnover results in a decrease in the firm's minimum operating cash requirement from $4,000,000 to approximately $3,333,000 ($12,000,000 ÷ 3.60). The reduction in required operating cash of approximately $667,000 ($4,000,000 − $3,333,000) represents an annual savings to the firm of approximately $33,350 ($667,000 · .05). By speeding the collection of its accounts receivable by 20 days, the firm releases $667,000 in funds, which can be invested in other earning assets or used to repay debts. Again, the efficient management of accounts receivable thus provides the firm with definite financial rewards. ●

Combining cash management strategies

The preceding pages have illustrated the individual effects of implementing each of the suggested cash management strategies on the firm's overall operating cash requirement. The stretching of accounts payable, the speeding of the inventory turnover, and the speeding of the collection of accounts receivable were all shown to have favorable effects on the firm's overall cash turnover. In actuality, firms would not attempt to implement just one of these strategies; rather, they would attempt to use them all to reduce significantly their operating cash requirement. Using a combination of these strategies would have the following effects on the KLM Company.

EXAMPLE
If the KLM Company simultaneously increased the average age of accounts payable by 10 days, decreased the average age of inventory by 15 days, and sped the collection of accounts receivable by 20 days, its cash cycle would be reduced to 75 days (120 days − 10 days − 15 days − 20 days). Figure 8.5 illustrates the results of these actions on KLM's cash cycle. As the graph shows, the firm's total cash cycle is shortened from 120 days to 75 days. Its annual cash turnover rate increases from 3 to 4.8 (360 ÷ 75). The increased cash turnover reduces the firm's minimum operating cash requirement from $4,000,000 to approximately $2,500,000 ($12,000,000 ÷ 4.8). The reduction in required operating cash of approximately $1,500,000 ($4,000,000 − $2,300,000) represents an annual savings to the firm of $75,000 ($1,500,000 · .05). This savings represents a sizable decrease in the firm's opportunity costs, from an initial level of $200,000 ($4,000,000 · .05) to $125,000 ($2,500,000 · .05). ●

The preceding examples have shown clearly the implications of each of the overall strategies for the efficient management of cash. Consciously implementing the basic accounts payable, inventory, and accounts receivable strategies outlined here should maximize a firm's profits with respect to the use of cash. However, when implementing these policies, care should be taken not to damage the firm's credit rating by overstretching accounts payable, to avoid having a large number of stockouts or a production stoppage due to carrying too small an inventory, and to avoid losing sales due to overly restrictive credit terms, credit policies, or collection policies. The financial manager must be aware that he or she does not operate in a vacuum and consider each of his or her decisions in light of their effects on the firm's overall profitability.

FIGURE 8.5 A cash cycle for the KLM Company based on implementing all three strategies simultaneously

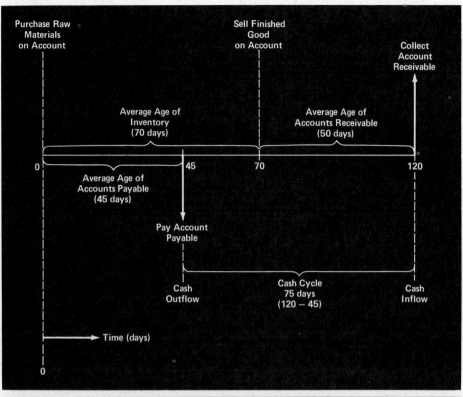

REFINEMENTS IN THE CASH MANAGEMENT PROCESS

A number of more specific techniques for the management of cash are available. These techniques are consistent with the overall strategies presented in the preceding section, but they deal with more obscure areas of cash management. Nevertheless, they can provide the firm with additional cash savings.

Collection procedures

The firm's objective with respect to accounts receivable should be not only to stimulate customers to pay as quickly as possible but to convert customers' payments into a spendable form as quickly as possible. There are ways of reducing the amount of time that elapses between the mailing of a payment by a customer and the point the funds become available to the firm for disbursement. Both the procedures discussed here are based on the idea of geographically dispersed collection centers.

Concentration banking.   Firms with numerous sales outlets throughout the country often designate certain of these offices as collection centers for given geographic areas. Customers in these areas are required to remit their payments to these sales offices, which deposit these receipts in local banks. At certain times or on "a when needed basis," funds are transferred by wire from these regional banks to a *concentration,* or *disbursing, bank,* from which bill payments are dispatched.[8]

Concentration banking is used to reduce the time needed for two aspects of the firm's collection process. The first is the amount of time that elapses between the mailing of a payment by a customer and the receipt of the payment by the firm. Regionally dispersed collection centers should *reduce the mailing time,* since the collecting bank is closer (possibly in the same city or state) to the point from which the check is sent. The time required for the customer's check to clear[9] should also be reduced, since the customer's bank is likely to be in the same federal reserve district, or the same city. It may even be the same bank. A *reduction in clearing time* makes funds available to the firm more quickly.

The net result of concentration banking is a saving of time in both mailing and clearing customer payments. Speeding the receipt of funds so that they can be used to pay bills reduces the firm's operating cash requirement and hence the firm's costs. A savings of only a few days in the collection process may provide significant dollar savings to the firm.

The lock-box system.   Another method of reducing the amount of time that elapses between when a customer pays a bill and when the firm actually has the funds available for disbursement is the lock-box system. The lock-box system differs from concentration banking in that the customer, instead of mailing a payment to a collection center, sends it to a post office box. The post office box is emptied, not by the firm, but by the firm's bank. The bank will normally empty the box at least one or two times each business day. The bank opens the payment envelopes, deposits the checks in the firm's account, and sends a deposit slip indicating the payments received, along with any enclosures, to the collecting firm. The lock boxes are normally geographically dispersed, and funds, when collected, are wired to the firm's disbursing bank.

The lock-box system is better than concentration banking in that one step in the collection process, *processing time*—time involved in the receipt and deposit of checks by the firm—is *greatly reduced* since the payments are received and deposited by the bank. The actual receipt of funds by the firm is recorded once the firm has received notification of the deposits from its lock-box bank. This allows the firm to use the funds as quickly as possible

[8]Most large firms disburse funds, or pay bills, only from certain banks. Normally, separate payroll and general expense accounts are maintained.

[9]This refers to the amount of time it takes for the funds paid to be made available to the firm's bank by the federal reserve system or local clearinghouse. On checks cleared through the federal reserve banking system, clearing time of less than two days is guaranteed to the collecting bank; but of course, this does not assure the depositor that the bank will make the money available within two days.

for disbursing payments. Some savings in mailing time may also result from the lock-box system since payments do not have to be delivered. Instead, the bank picks them up at the post office. Of course, the cost of geographically dispersed lock-boxes must be considered. Each lock-box bank charges the firm a fee or requires the firm to maintain a specified minimum deposit balance, or both. These costs must be evaluated with respect to the volume of checks received and the amount of time saved to determine the economic feasibility of the lock-box system. Lock-box systems are quite prevalent among larger retailers such as oil companies, which bill large numbers of customers throughout the country.

Disbursement procedures

The firm's objective with respect to accounts payable should be not only to pay slowly, but to slow down the availability of funds to suppliers and employees once the payment has been dispatched. In other words, given that a firm has decided to pay certain outstanding obligations (such as those evidenced by accounts payable or employee payrolls), techniques are available for slowing down the withdrawal of funds from the firm's account. These techniques generally are based upon *lengthening mail time* or *lengthening clearing time* associated with the payment process, or both. Although the use of techniques to lengthen mail time are much less common than techniques for lengthening clearing time, each is briefly described below. Accruals also provide a mechanism which allows the firm to delay payments to certain of its suppliers of services and goods. Their use in the cash management process is also briefly discussed below.

Lengthening mail time.

When the date of postmark is considered the effective date of payment by a supplier, the firm may have an opportunity to capitalize on the mail time associated with payments. The basic approach used to lengthen mail time involves placing payments in the mail at a location from which it is known that a great deal of time will likely elapse before the payment is received by the supplier. Typically, small towns that are not close to major highways and cities provide excellent opportunities to slow down mail time. It is not unusual for larger firms to mail batches of payments from a variety of locations—each chosen such that it provides the slowest mail time to the addresses involved. Another approach sometimes suggested is to mail payments to the suppliers' corporate headquarter's address rather than the post office box or collection center specified by the supplier.[10] If the firm can do this without violating the terms of sales specified by the supplier, the mail time may not directly be increased, but because most corporate headquarters cannot process receipts, the entire collection process for the supplier is slowed down thereby slowing down the firm's payment.

[10]A supplier's credit terms as well as any penalties associated with late payment are typically stated in the *invoice* that accompanies the shipment of merchandise. Of course, depending upon the supplier, the terms of the invoice may or may not be enforced. Knowledge of the strictness of enforcement of credit terms by suppliers is often useful for developing the firm's accounts payable strategies.

Lengthening clearing time by playing the float. The term *float* refers to the amount of money tied up in checks that have been written but have yet to be collected or paid on. Due to the presence of float in the banking system, many firms are able to "play the float," that is, to write checks against money not currently in the firm's checking account. Firms are able to play the float because they know that a delay will likely exist between the receipt and deposit of the check by their supplier and the actual withdrawal of funds from their checking account. In spite of the fact that their suppliers' bank may be reimbursed within a few days, it is likely that the firm's bank account will not be drawn down by the amount of the payment for a few additional days. Certain imperfections in the check-clearing system therefore provide for float in the banking system. Playing the float is a method of consciously anticipating the resulting float associated with the payment process. Although this practice is illegal, many firms use it to stretch out their accounts payable.[11] Two ways of playing the float are (1) paying from a distant bank and (2) scientific check-cashing analysis.

Paying from a distant bank. Many firms write their checks for paying bills on a bank that is geographically removed from their supplier's bank in the hope that it will take longer for the checks to clear through the federal reserve system. This strategy allows the firm to keep its money longer. In many cases the firm will keep its money in some interest-earning form such as a marketable security, and not transfer it into a checking account until several days later. Even if a firm does not pay bills from a distant bank, it may play the float for a few days. However, it should be cautious in using this strategy, since "bouncing" checks is not favorably looked on by banks, businesses, or the government.

Scientific check-cashing analysis. Another way of playing the float, which may be used by more sophisticated firms, is to deposit a certain proportion of a payroll or payments in the firm's checking account each day after the actual issuance of a group of payroll checks. For example, if a firm can determine from historical data that only 25 percent of its payroll checks are cashed on the day immediately following the issuance of the checks, then only 25 percent of the value of the payroll needs to be in its checking account one day later. The number of checks cashed on each succeeding day can also be calculated, until the entire payroll is accounted for. Normally, in order to protect itself against any irregularities, a firm will place slightly more in its account than it needs to cover the expected check cashings.

Accruals. Another tool for stretching a firm's payments is accruals. *Accruals* are current liabilities that represent a service or good which has

---

[11]Writing checks against nonexistent funds is considered fraudulent since it entails a misrepresentation of the amount of funds on deposit. If it can be proven that a firm or an individual has intentionally or with knowledge issued a check against a nonexistent balance, the firm or individual could be convicted of breaking the law. Prosecution does not normally result, since the firm or individual either has the money in the account when the check clears or has arranged with its bank for *overdraft privileges* which guarantee that the bank will pay on checks even if the firm has insufficient funds in its account.

been received by the firm but not yet paid for. The most common accruals are wages, rent, and taxes. Just as a firm should stretch its accounts payable as much as possible without damaging its credit rating, so too it should attempt to increase its accruals. In other words, it should attempt to arrange for the payment of wages, rent, taxes, and similar items as infrequently as possible.[12]

Since a firm cannot change the tax laws and most leases require frequent payments, payroll accruals provide the best opportunity for manipulation by the firm. Firms do not pay employees in advance; they pay them on specified dates. The more infrequently a firm pays its employees, the better off it will be from the standpoint of cash flows. An employee extends a service to his or her employer and expects to be paid for this service. Since the firm has received the service in advance of payment, the employee can be thought of as extending credit to the firm and therefore temporarily financing a portion of the firm's assets. The longer after the receipt of service from an employee payment can be deferred, the greater the amount of free financing extended. Accruals allow the firm to obtain credit from employees, lessors, and the government; the more of this type of credit the firm is extended, the less money it will need to operate. The firm should take advantage of opportunities to increase accruals to the extent that the constraints set by unions, the government, lessors, and others allow such action.

MOTIVES, CHARACTERISTICS, AND PROPORTION OF MARKETABLE SECURITIES

Marketable securities are short-term money market instruments that can easily be converted into cash.[13] Marketable securities are often referred to as part of the firm's liquid assets, which also include cash.

Motives for holding marketable securities

There are three basic motives for maintaining liquidity (i.e., cash *or* marketable securities) and therefore for holding marketable securities, which by definition represent a storehouse of liquidity. Each motive is based on the premise that a firm should attempt to earn a return on temporarily idle funds. The type of marketable security a firm purchases will depend greatly on the motive for the purchase. The basic motives, which include the *transactions motive*, *safety motive*, and the *speculative motive*, and the implications of each are as follows.

The transactions motive. Marketable securities that will be converted into cash to make some known future payment are said to be held for transactions purposes. Many firms that must make certain payments in the near future already have the cash with which to make these payments. In

---

[12]A further discussion of accruals, including a numerical example of the usefulness of accruals as a short-term source of financing, is included in Chapter 11.

[13]The *money market* results from an intangible relationship between the demanders and suppliers of short-term funds, i.e., marketable securities. An in-depth description of the organization and operation of the money market is included in Chapter 19.

order to earn some return on these funds, they invest them in a marketable security with a maturity date that coincides with the required payment date. For example, in the cases of quarterly tax payments and outlays for the acquisition of fixed assets, both the amount to be spent and the timing of the expenditure are normally known in advance. Since the exact timing of the payments is known, the firm can invest its cash in an interest-earning instrument until the payment date.

The safety motive.   Marketable securities held for safety are used to service the firm's cash account. These securities must be very liquid, since they are bought with funds that will be needed, though exactly when is unknown. They therefore protect the firm against the possibility of being unable to satisfy unexpected demands for cash.

The speculative motive.   Marketable securities held because the firm currently has no other use for certain funds are said to be held for speculative reasons. Although such situations are not extremely common, some firms occasionally have excess cash (that is, cash not earmarked for any particular expenditures). Until the firm finds a suitable use for this money (say, investment in a new fixed asset, a dividend payment, or a repurchase of stock), it invests it in certain more speculative types of marketable securities. In many cases, these dollars are placed in long-term instruments, which do not fall within the category of marketable securities. This motive is by far the *least common* one for holding marketable securities. Many firms would consider a company with such investments to be in an enviable position.

Characteristics of marketable securities

The basic characteristics of marketable securities affect the degree of their marketability. To be truly marketable a security must have two basic characteristics: (1) a ready market and (2) no likelihood of a loss in value (safety of principal).

A ready market.   The market for a security should have both breadth and depth in order to minimize the amount of time required to convert it into cash. Common definitions of marketable securities suggest that they are securities which can be converted into cash in a short period of time, typically a few days.

The breadth of the market.   The breadth of a market is determined by the number of participants in it. A broad market is one that has many participants. The term breadth is also used to refer to the geographic dispersion of a market. The more scattered the participants (assuming there are many), the more breadth the market is considered to have.

The depth of the market.   The depth of a market is determined by its ability to absorb the purchase or sale of a large dollar amount of securities. Thus it is possible to have a broad market that has no depth. As many as

100,000 participants each willing to purchase one share is less desirable than 1000 participants each willing to purchase 2000 shares. Although both characteristics are desirable, it is much more important for a market to have depth than breadth in order for a security to be marketable.

No likelihood of a loss in value (safety of principal). The second key determinant of marketability is whether the market price received when liquidating a security deviates significantly from the amount invested. There should be little or no loss in the value of a marketable security over time. Consider a security recently purchased for $1000. If it can be sold quickly for $500, does that make it marketable? No. According to the definition of marketability above, not only must the security be salable quickly, but it must be salable for close to the $1000 initially invested. This aspect of marketability is one that many fail to recognize. It is commonly referred to as *the safety of the principal*. The risk associated with a loss in the value of the principal invested in a marketable security is probably the most important aspect of the marketable security selection process. Only those securities that can be easily converted into cash without experiencing any reduction in principal are candidates for short-term investment. It should be clear that the firm would be better off leaving the balances in cash if the alternative were to risk experiencing a significant reduction in principal.

The optimum proportion of marketable securities in the firm's asset mix

A major decision confronting the business firm is exactly what mix of cash and marketable securities should be maintained.[14] This decision is difficult to make because it involves a trade-off between the opportunity to earn interest on idle funds during the holding period and the cost of brokerage fees associated with the purchase and sale of marketable securities. For example, take the case of a firm paying $30 in brokerage fees to purchase and sell $5000 worth of marketable securities yielding an annual return of 6 percent and held for one month. Since the securities are held for $1/12$ of a year, the firm earns interest of 0.5 percent ($1/12 \cdot 6$ percent), or $25 (.005 \cdot $5000). Since this is less than the $30 cost of the transaction, the firm should not have made the investment. This trade-off between interest returns and brokerage costs is a key factor in determining just what proportion of the firm's liquid assets should be held in the form of marketable securities.

THE BASIC MARKETABLE SECURITIES

This section presents a brief description of each of the most commonly held marketable securities. Attention is focused on the types of marketable securities held for transactions and safety motives. Securities held for a specula-

---

[14]Numerous quantitative models for determining the optimum amounts of marketable securities to hold in certain circumstances have been developed. One of the most popular of these models is based on the inventory theory underlying the EOQ model, which is described in Chapter 10. A discussion of these cash-marketable security models is beyond the scope of this text.

TABLE 8.1 Yields on selected securities for
the weeks ending March 8, 1978, and October 4, 1978

Security	Maturity period	Yields (%) March 8, 1978	October 4, 1978
Banker's acceptances	Varies	6.80	8.85
Certificates of deposit	90 days	6.87	8.95
Commercial paper	4–6 months	6.79	8.71
Corporate AAA bonds	Varies	8.50	8.79
Government securities	3–5 years	7.77	8.48
Government securities	Long-term	8.10	8.55
Municipal bonds	Varies	5.63	6.07
Treasury bills	3 months	6.31	8.11

SOURCE: *U.S. Financial Data: Week Ending March 8, 1978* (St. Louis: Federal Reserve Bank of St. Louis, March 10, 1978), pp. 6–7; and *U.S. Financial Data: Week Ending October 4, 1978* (St. Louis: Federal Reserve Bank of St. Louis, October 6, 1978), pp. 6–7.

tive motive are often longer-term, less marketable issues that will not be discussed here. The securities most commonly held as part of the business firm's marketable securities portfolio are divided into two groups; (1) government issues and (2) nongovernment issues. Table 8.1 presents both March 8, 1978, and October 4, 1978, yields on selected securities, some of which are described in the following pages.

Government issues

The short-term obligations issued by the federal government and available as marketable security investments are treasury bills, tax anticipation bills, treasury notes, and federal agency issues.

Treasury bills. These are obligations of the U.S. Treasury and are issued weekly on an auction basis. The most common maturities are 91 and 182 days, although bills with one-year maturities are occasionally sold. Treasury bills are sold by competitive bidding, going to the highest bidder. Because they are issued in bearer form, there is a strong *secondary (resale) market*. The bills are sold at a discount from their face value, the face value being received at maturity. The smallest denomination of treasury bills currently available is $10,000. Since treasury bills are issues of the United States government, they are considered virtually riskless. For this reason, and because of the strong secondary market for them, treasury bills are probably the most popular marketable security. The yields on treasury bills are lower than those on any other marketable securities due to their virtually riskless nature.

Tax anticipation bills. These are issued primarily by the United States government in order to raise funds during a period when tax receipts are not large enough to cover current disbursements. They mature approximately one week after quarterly corporate tax payments are due. The attractiveness of these bills is greatly enhanced by the fact that the government will accept them in payment for taxes at their face value. In effect, the firm can receive its return on these instruments a week early. Because of their riskless nature and the fact that firms often accumulate their tax payments in advance of tax payment dates, tax anticipation bills are a quite attractive marketable security.

Treasury notes. Treasury notes have initial maturities of anywhere between one and seven years, but due to the existence of a strong secondary market they are quite atttractive marketable security investments. A firm that purchases a treasury note which has less than one year left to maturity is in the same position as if it had purchased a marketable security with an initial maturity of less than one year. Due to their virtually riskless nature, treasury notes have a low yield.

Federal agency issues. Certain agencies of the federal government issue their own debt. These issues are not part of the public debt, are not a legal obligation of the U.S. Treasury, and are not even guaranteed by the U.S. Treasury. Nevertheless, regardless of their lack of direct government backing, the issues of government agencies are readily accepted as low-risk securities since most purchasers feel that they are implicitly guaranteed by the federal government.

The agencies that most commonly issue short-term instruments are

1. The Federal Home Loan Bank (FHLB)
2. The Federal Intermediate Credit Bank (FICB)
3. The Federal Land Banks (FLB)
4. The Bank for Cooperatives (BCs)
5. The Federal National Mortgage Association (FNMA)

Most agency issues have short maturities and offer slightly higher yields than Treasury issues. Agency issues have a strong secondary market, which is most easily reached through government security dealers.

Nongovernment issues

A number of additional marketable securities are issued by businesses or banks. These nongovernment issues typically have slightly higher yields than government issues due to the slightly higher risks associated with them. The main nongovernment marketable securities are negotiable certificates of deposit, commercial paper, banker's acceptances, and repurchase agreements.

Negotiable certificates of deposit (CD's). CD's are negotiable instruments evidencing the deposit of a certain number of dollars in a commercial bank. The amounts and maturities are normally tailored to the investor's needs. Minimum maturities of 30 days are quite common. A good secondary market for CD's exists. The maximum initial rates paid on negotiable

CD's are set on the basis of size and maturity by the federal reserve system. Normally the smallest denomination for a negotiable CD is $100,000. The yield on CD's is typically above that on treasury bills and slightly above the yield on commercial paper. Once CD's are in the secondary market, however, their yields are in no way controlled by the federal reserve system.

Commercial paper. Commercial paper is a short-term, unsecured, promissory note issued by a corporation with a very high credit standing.[15] These notes are issued by all types of firms and have maturities of anywhere from three days to 270 days.[16] They can be sold directly by the issuer or through dealers. The yield on commercial paper has historically been higher than that on any other marketable securities, although banking legislation enacted in mid-1973 has changed this relationship by removing interest ceilings on certificates of deposit issued in denominations of $100,000 or more.

Banker's acceptances. Banker's acceptances arise from international trade transactions. An importer, in order to finance a foreign purchase, draws an IOU on his bank. When it is accepted (OK'd) by the bank, the IOU results in an agreement to repay the bank the funds lent, with interest, at a certain point in time. The bank lends the money by paying the foreign exporter for the goods purchased by the importer. If the issuing bank does not wish to hold the acceptance to maturity, it can resell it at a discount to another party who can hold it to maturity or again resell it. In other words, a secondary market exists. The maturities of banker's acceptances are typically between 30 and 180 days. A banker's acceptance is a very safe security because as many as three parties may be liable for its payment at maturity. The yields on banker's acceptances are similar to those on CD's.

Repurchase agreements. A repurchase agreement is not a specific security; rather, it is an arrangement whereby a bank or security dealer sells specific marketable securities to a firm and agrees to repurchase the securities at a specified price at a specified point in time. In exchange for the tailormade maturity date provided by this arrangement, the bank or security dealer provides the purchaser with a return slightly below that obtainable through outright purchase of similar marketable securities. The benefit to the purchaser is the guaranteed repurchase; the tailor-made maturity date assures the purchaser that he or she will have cash at a specified point in time. The actual securities involved may be any government or nongovernment issues. Repurchase agreements are ideal for marketable security investments made to satisfy the transaction motive.

---

[15]An in-depth discussion of commerical paper, from the point of view of the issuer, is deferred until Chapter 11, which is devoted to the various sources of unsecured short-term financing available to business.

[16]The maximum maturity of 270 days exists since the Securities and Exchange Commission requires formal registration of corporate issues having maturities greater than 270 days.

SUMMARY

Cash and marketable securities make up the firm's liquid assets. They give the firm the liquidity it needs to satisfy financial obligations as they come due. Cash is held in the form of a checking deposit at a commercial bank, which earns no interest. There are many forms of marketable securities, each with different characteristics, but all earning some kind of interest.

The efficient management of cash is based on three basic strategies: (1) paying bills as late as possible without damaging the firm's credit rating, (2) managing the inventory-production cycle efficiently in order to maximize the inventory turnover rate, and (3) collecting accounts receivable quickly. Certain constraints are placed on each of these strategies; however, maximizing the firm's cash turnover within these constraints will minimize the level of operating cash (liquid assets, which includes both cash and marketable securities) required and add to the firm's profits.

Although the cash budget is useful for cash planning, decisions with respect to the appropriate cash balance depend upon the magnitude of both expected and unexpected cash receipts and cash disbursements. A variety of rules of thumb as well as sophisticated quantitative models exist for making such decisions. One practical approach is to relate the firm's cash turnover to the annual outlays. Additional refinements in the cash management process such as concentration banking, lock-box systems, lengthening mail time on payments, playing the float in the banking system, and managing accruals intelligently can further increase the efficiency of cash management.

A firm holds marketable securities in order to earn interest on temporarily idle funds. Funds may be held in marketable securities (as well as cash) for a number of motives. They are the transactions motive, the safety motive, and the speculative motive. The transactions and safety motives are the most common. In order for a security to be considered marketable, it must have a ready market which has not only breadth but, more importantly, depth. In addition, the amount that can be realized by selling the security must be close to the amount invested initially. That is, the risks associated with the safety of principal must be quite low. The proportion of a firm's liquid assets made up of marketable securities depends on the trade-off between the interest earned during the holding period and the brokerage costs associated with purchasing and selling marketable securities.

The most commonly held marketable securities are either government issues or nongovernment issues. Government issues include treasury bills, tax anticipation bills, treasury notes, and federal agency issues. The most common nongovernment issues are negotiable certificates of deposit, commercial paper, banker's acceptances, and repurchase agreements. Each has its own risk and yield characteristics. Government issues are the least risky but have the lowest yield; nongovernment issues are more risky but have higher yields.

QUESTIONS

8-1 What is the objective of the financial manager in cash management? What conditions must be satisfied in meeting this objective?

8-2 What role do marketable securities play in fulfilling the firm's overall objective of maximizing its owners' wealth? How does the presence of marketable securities in the firm's asset structure affect the risk associated with the firm?

8-3 What are the key strategies with respect to accounts payable, inventory, and accounts receivable for the firm that wants to manage its cash efficiently?•

8-4 What is a firm's "cash cycle"? How are the cash cycle and cash turnover of a firm related? What should a firm's objectives with respect to its cash cycle and cash turnover be?

8-5 If a firm reduces the average age of its inventories, what effect might this action have on the cash cycle? on the firm's total sales? Is there a trade-off between average inventory and sales? Why?

8-6 "Stretching accounts payable" is often recommended in order to increase a firm's cash turnover. What does "stretching" imply? What two factors may limit the degree to which a firm can stretch its accounts payable?

8-7 How do a firm's credit terms, credit policies, and collection policies affect the minimum level of operating cash it requires?

8-8 What is concentration banking? How does it benefit a firm?

8-9 How does the lock-box system differ from concentration banking? What is the overall objective of both these arrangements?

8-10 How may a firm use "float" to reduce its cash requirements? What cautions are in order when taking advantage of float? Why?

8-11 What are the common types of accruals found on a firm's balance sheet? What is the general rationale for accruing certain items?

8-12 The three commonly cited motives for holding marketable securities are for the safety, transactions, and speculative motives. How do these motives differ?

8-13 What two characteristics are essential in a "marketable" security?

8-14 What are treasury bills? Why are they such attractive marketable securities? What maturities and denominations are common?

8-15 Why are tax anticipation bills attractive to many firms?

8-16 Is there any difference in the "risk" associated with treasury and federal agency issues? Why?

8-17 What is commercial paper? What kind of market is there for this security?

8-18 What are negotiable certificates of deposit and banker's acceptances? Is there any similarity between them?

8-19 Why might a repurchase agreement be attractive to a firm having a temporary excess of liquidity?

PROBLEMS

8-1 Western Supply is concerned about managing cash in an efficient manner. On the average, accounts receivable are collected in 60 days, and inventories have an average age of 90 days. Accounts payable are paid approximately 30 days after they arise. The firm spends $30,000,000 each year, at a constant rate. Assuming a 360-day year,

a Calculate the firm's cash cycle.

b Calculate the firm's cash turnover.

c Calculate the minimum cash balance the firm must maintain to meets its obligations.

8-2 The Denver Company has an inventory turnover ratio of 12, accounts receivable turnover of 8, and an accounts payable turnover ratio of 9. The firm spends $1,000,000 per year. Assuming a 360-day,

    a Calculate the firm's cash cycle.

    b Calculate the firm's cash turnover.

    c Calculate the minimum cash balance the firm must maintain to meet its obligations.

8-3 A firm collects accounts receivable, on the average, after 75 days. Inventory has an average age of 105 days and accounts payable are paid on an average of 60 days after they arise. What changes will occur in the cash cycle and cash turnover with each of the following different circumstances? Assume a 360-day year.

    a The average age of accounts receivable changes to 60 days.

    b The average age of inventory changes to 90 days.

    c The average age of accounts payable changes to 105 days.

    d All the circumstances above (**a** to **c**) occur simultaneously.

8-4 A firm is considering several plans that affect working capital accounts. Given the following five plans and their probable results, which one would you favor? Explain.

	Change in average age of		
Plan	**Inventory**	**Accounts receivable**	**Accounts payable**
A	+30 days	+20 days	+5 days
B	+20 days	−10 days	+15 days
C	−10 days	0 days	−5 days
D	−15 days	+15 days	+10 days
E	+5 days	−10 days	+15 days

8-5 The Watson Manufacturing Company pays accounts payable on the tenth day after purchase. The average age of accounts receivable is 30 days and the average age of inventory is 40 days. Annual cash outlays are approximately $18,000,000. The firm is considering a plan which would stretch its accounts payable by 20 days. If the firm can earn 7 percent on its investments, what annual savings can it realize by this plan. Assume no discount for early payment of trade credit and a 360-day year.

8-6 Consumer Products Corporation sells to a national market and bills all credit customers from the New York City office. Using a continuous billing system, the firm has collections of $1,200,000 per day. Under consideration is a concentration banking system that would require customers to mail payments to the nearest regional office to be deposited in local banks.

    Consumer Products estimates that the collection period for accounts will be shortened an average of 2.5 days under this system. The firm also estimates *annual* service charges and administrative costs of $125,000 will result from the proposed system. The firm can earn 9 percent on its investments.

    a How much cash will be made available for other uses if the firm accepts the proposed concentration banking system?

    b What savings will the firm realize on the 2.5-day reduction in the collection period?

    c Would you recommend the change? Explain your answer.

8-7 Eastern Oil feels a lock-box system can shorten its accounts receivable collection period by 3 days. Credit sales are $3,240,000 per year billed on a continuous basis. The firm has other investments with a return of 10 percent. The cost of the lock-box system is $9000 per year.

    a What amount of cash will be made available for other uses under the lock-box system?

    b What net benefit (cost) will the firm receive if it adopts the lock-box system?

8-8 A large Midwestern firm has annual cash disbursements of $360 million made continuously over the year. Although service and administrative costs would increase by $100,000, the firm is considering writing all disbursement checks on a small bank in Georgia. The firm estimates this will allow them an additional 1.5 days of cash usage. If the firm has a return on other investments of 8 percent, should they change to the distant bank? Why or why not?

8-9 Walter's Window has a weekly payroll of $250,000. The payroll checks are issued on Friday afternoon each week. In examining the check cashing behavior of its employees, it has found the following pattern:

Number of business days[1] since receipt of check	Percentage of checks cleared
1	20
2	40
3	30
4	10

[1]Excludes Saturday and Sunday.

Given this information, what recommendation would you give the firm with respect to managing its payroll account? Explain.

8-10 A firm currently has a weekly payroll of $80,000. Thus, on the average, they have the use of $40,000 in accrued wages ($80,000/2). If the firm changes to payment every two weeks, and can earn an annual rate of 12 percent on other investments, what savings, if any, could be obtained? Explain.

8-11 In order to purchase and sell $25,000 in marketable securities, a firm must pay $500. If the marketable securities have a yield of 9 percent annually, recommend purchasing or not if

    a The securities are held for one month.

    b The securities are held for three months.

    c The securities are held for six months.

    d The securities are held for one year.

8-12 Alice Piper is cash manager for Carousel Corporation. The cash budgets indicate excess cash of $20,000 will be available for the next 90 days. She is considering an investment of this sum in one of the instruments listed below. Calculate the expected rate of return for each and select the best investment. Explain your choice.

    a Common stock costing $40 per share and paying a $2.00 annual dividend ($.50 each quarter).

    b Preferred stock that pays a $6.00 annual dividend ($1.50 each quarter), currently selling for $80 a share.

    c Municipal bonds issued by the city of Houston, Texas, maturing in 2005. These sell at par with an 8-percent annual coupon (2 percent per quarter).

d Ninety-day commercial paper selling at 99 percent of face value (commercial paper sells at a discount).

e A 90-day certificate of deposit paying 6-percent annual interest (1.5 percent per quarter).

SELECTED REFERENCES

Archer, Stephen H., "A Model for Determination of Firm Cash Balances," *Journal of Financial and Quantitative Analysis 1* (March 1966), pp. 1–11.

Baumol, William J., "The Transactions Demand for Cash: An Inventory Theoretic Approach," *Quarterly Journal of Economics 65* (November 1952), pp. 545-556.

Baxter, Nevins D., "Marketability, Default Risk, and Yields on Money-Market Instruments," *Journal of Financial and Quantitative Analysis 3* (March 1968), pp. 75–85.

Calman, Robert F., *Linear Programming and Cash Management/CASH ALPHA* (Cambridge, Mass.: MIT Press, 1968).

Campbell, Tim, and Leland Brendsel, "The Impact of Compensating Balance Requirements on the Cash Balances of Manufacturing Corporations: An Empirical Study," *Journal of Finance 32* (March 1977), pp. 31–40.

DeSalvo, Alfred, "Cash Management Converts Dollars into Working Assets," *Harvard Business Review* (May–June 1972), pp. 92–100.

Gitman, Lawrence J., "Estimating Corporate Liquidity Requirements: A Simplified Approach," *The Financial Review* (1974), pp. 79–88.

———, D. Keith Forrester, and John R. Forrester, Jr., "Maximizing Cash Disbursement Float," *Financial Management 5* (Summer 1976), pp. 15–24.

King, Alfred M., *Increasing the Productivity of Company Cash* (Englewood Cliffs, N.J.: Prentice-Hall, 1969), chaps. 4 and 5.

Kraus, A., C. Janssen, and A. McAdams, "The Lock-Box Location Problem," *Journal of Bank Research 1* (Autumn 1970), pp. 50–58.

Mehta, Dileep R., *Working Capital Management* (Englewood Cliffs, N.J.: Prentice-Hall, 1974), part 3.

Miller, Merton H., and Daniel Orr, "A Model of the Demand for Money by Firms," *Quarterly Journal of Economics 80* (August 1966), pp. 413–435.

Money Market Instruments, 3rd ed. (Cleveland: Federal Reserve Bank of Cleveland, 1970).

Orgler, Yair E., "An Unequal-Period Model for Cash-Management Decisions," *Management Science 16* (October 1969), pp. 77–92.

———, *Cash Management* (Belmont: Wadsworth, 1970).

Pogue, Gerald A., Russell B. Faucett, and Ralph N. Bussard, "Cash Management: A Systems Approach," *Industrial Management Review 2*, No. 2 (1970), pp. 55–74.

Reed, Ward L., Jr., "Profits from Better Cash Management," *Financial Executive 40* (May 1972), pp. 40–56.

Searby, Frederick W., "Use Your Hidden Cash Resource," *Harvard Business Review 46* (March-April 1968), pp. 74–75.

Shanker, Roy J., and Andris A. Zoltners, "The Corporate Payment Problem," *Journal of Bank Research 2* (March 1972), pp. 47–53.

Stancill, James McN., *The Management of Working Capital* (Scranton, Pa.: Intext, 1971), chaps. 2 and 3.

Stone, Bernell K., "The Use of Forecasts and Smoothing in Control-Limit Models for Cash Management," *Financial Management 1* (Spring 1972), pp. 72–84.

CHAPTER 9
Accounts receivable management

Accounts receivable represent the extension of credit on an open account by the firm to its customers. In order to keep current customers and attract new ones, most manufacturing concerns find it necessary to offer credit. Credit terms may differ between industries, but firms within the same industry generally provide similar credit terms. Of course, exceptions do exist, since suppliers often provide more favorable credit terms to attract certain customers. Credit sales, which result in the establishment of accounts receivable, normally have associated credit terms requiring payment within a certain number of days. Although all accounts receivable are not collected within the credit period, most accounts receivable are converted into cash in considerably less than a year; accounts receivable are therefore considered current assets of the firm.

Since most manufacturing firms find that accounts receivable represent a large portion of their current assets, a great deal of attention is normally given to the efficient management of these accounts. In the preceding chapter the benefits of efficient collection policies were illustrated with respect to the firm's cash requirements. It was shown that the more quickly a firm converted its accounts receivable into cash, the less operating cash it required. In this chapter, three aspects of accounts receivable are evaluated with respect to the amount of money tied up. Specific attention is given to credit policies, credit terms, and collection policies. Each of these three areas of accounts receivable management is discussed separately. First, policies with respect to both credit standards and ways of measuring the credit-worthiness of customers are evaluated. Next, cash discounts and credit periods are assessed. Finally, the trade-offs between costs and profits associated with collection policies are analyzed.

CREDIT POLICIES

A firm's credit policy provides the guidelines for determining whether to extend credit to a customer and how much credit to extend. The business firm must concern itself not only with the establishment of credit standards but with the correct use of these standards in making credit decisions. Appropriate sources of credit information and methods of credit analysis must be developed. Each of these aspects of credit policy is important to the successful management of the firm's accounts receivable. Poor implementation of a good credit policy or successful implementation of a poor credit policy will not produce optimal results.

Credit standards

The firm's credit standards define the minimum criteria for the extension of credit to a customer. Such things as credit ratings, credit references, average payment periods, and certain financial ratios provide a quantitative basis for establishing and enforcing credit standards. However, our concern here is not with the individual components of credit standards but is with the restrictiveness or nonrestrictiveness of a firm's overall credit standards. Knowing the key variables that must be considered when a firm is contemplating either relaxing or tightening its credit standards will give the reader a general feel for the kind of decisions involved.

Key variables.   The major variables that should be considered in evaluating proposed changes in credit standards are the clerical expense and investment in receivables involved and the effect of the changes on the firm's bad debt expenses and volume of sales.

Clerical expenses.   If credit standards are relaxed, more credit will be extended and a larger credit department will be required to service the added accounts; if credit standards are tightened, less credit will be extended and a smaller credit department will be required to service accounts. A relaxation of credit standards should increase clerical costs, and a tightening of credit standards should decrease clerical costs. In the analysis of the following sections, these costs are not explicitly identified; rather, they are assumed to be included in the variable cost per unit.[1]

Investment in receivables.   There is a cost associated with carrying accounts receivable. The higher the firm's average accounts receivable are, the more expensive they are to carry, and vice versa. If the firm relaxes its credit standards, the average level of accounts receivable should rise, whereas tightening the firm's credit standards should decrease the average level of accounts receivable. Thus a relaxation of credit standards can be expected to result in higher carrying costs and a tightening of credit standards can be expected to result in lower carrying costs.

The changes in the level of accounts receivable associated with changes in credit standards result from two factors—(a) changes in sales and (b)

---

[1]The reader should recognize that the clerical costs associated with changing credit standards are most likely *semivariable*. This is because the key ingredient of a credit department is people. As the department expands, certain points are reached at which new people must be employed, but between hirings the departmental cost remains fixed.

changes in collections.[2] It is expected that as a firm relaxes its credit standards sales will increase, whereas tightening credit standards will result in decreased sales. Increased sales will result in higher average accounts receivable and decreased sales will result in lower average accounts receivable. When credit terms are relaxed, credit is extended to less credit-worthy customers, who will probably take longer to pay their bills. When credit standards are tightened, the extension of credit will be limited to the more credit-worthy customers, who can be expected to pay their bills more quickly. Since relaxing credit standards results in more slower-paying customers, it raises the average level of accounts receivable; since tightening credit standards means extending credit only to the most credit-worthy, it lowers the average level of accounts receivable.

In short, changes in sales and changes in collections work together to produce higher carrying costs for accounts receivable when credit standards are relaxed, and reduced carrying costs for accounts receivable when credit standards are tightened. These basic reactions also occur when changes in credit terms or collection procedures are made. The effects of these other stimuli are discussed later in the chapter.

Bad debt expenses. Another variable that is expected to be affected by changes in credit standards is bad debt expenses. The probability (or risk) of acquiring a bad debt increases as credit standards are relaxed and decreases as credit standards become more restrictive. Bad debt losses are therefore expected to increase as credit standards are relaxed and decrease as credit standards become more restrictive.

Sales volume. Changing credit standards can be expected to change the volume of sales. As credit standards are relaxed, sales are expected to increase; a tightening of credit standards is expected to reduce sales. The effects of these changes in sales on net profits will depend on their effect on the firm's costs and revenues.

In summary, the basic changes and effects on profits expected to result from the *relaxation* of credit standards are tabulated as follows:

Item	Direction of change [increase (I) or decrease (D)]	Effect on profits [positive (+) or negative (−)]
Sales volume	I	+
Average collection period	I	−
Bad debt expense	I	−

If credit standards were tightened, the opposite effects would be expected.

[2]Due to the forward-looking nature of accounts receivable analysis, certain items such as sales, collections, and bad debts resulting from changes in the management of accounts receivable must be estimated. The need to estimate these future values may introduce a great deal of uncertainty into the decision process. Many of the techniques discussed in Chapter 16 can be applied to these estimates to adjust them for uncertainty.

Evaluating alternative credit standards. The way in which credit standards are evaluated can be illustrated by a simple example.

EXAMPLE

The XYZ Company is currently selling a product for $10 per unit. Sales (all on credit) for the most recent year were 60,000 units. The variable cost per unit is $6, and the average cost per unit, given a sales volume of 60,000 units, is $8. The difference between the average cost per unit and the variable cost per unit of $2 represents the contribution of each of the 60,000 units toward the firm's fixed costs. Working backwards, since each of the 60,000 units sold contributes $2 to fixed costs, the firm's total fixed costs must be $120,000.

The firm is currently contemplating a relaxation of credit standards that is expected to result in a 15-percent increase in unit sales, an increase in the average collection period from its current level of 30 days to 45 days, and no change in bad debt expenses.[3] The increase in clerical expenses is expected to be negligible. The firm's required return on investments is 15 percent.

In order to determine whether the XYZ Company should implement the proposed relaxation in credit standards, the effect on the firm's profit contribution from sales and the cost of the marginal investment in receivables must be calculated.

Additional profit contribution from sales The additional profit contribution from sales expected to result from the relaxation of credit standards can easily be calculated. The firm's profit contribution from sales will increase by an amount equal to the product of the number of additional units sold and the profit contribution per unit. Since the first 60,000 units (i.e., the current level of sales) have absorbed all the firm's fixed costs, any additional units sold will cost only the variable cost per unit.[4] Sales are expected to increase by 15 percent, or 9000 units. The profit contribution per unit will equal the difference between the sale price per unit ($10) and the variable cost per unit ($6). The profit contribution per unit would therefore be $4. The total additional profit contribution from sales will be $36,000 (9000 units · $4).

The approach used above is the quickest way to find the profit contribution from sales. There is also a longer approach, based on calculating the firm's costs and revenues at both the present and the proposed sales levels and finding the difference in profits at each level. This approach is presented in Table 9.1.

The cost of the marginal investment in accounts receivable The cost of the marginal investment in accounts receivable can be calculated by finding the difference between the cost of carrying receivables before and after the introduction of the relaxed credit standards. The cost of investment in accounts receivable can be calculated using the following approach.

---

[3]Although the proposed relaxation in credit standards would likely increase the firm's bad debts, the effect is assumed negligible in this example. This assumption is made solely on the basis of computational convenience. Subsequent analyses will describe the appropriate treatment of bad debt expense changes in the account receivable decision process.

[4]A discussion of the *profit contribution per unit* or *contribution margin* was presented as part of the discussion of breakeven analysis included in Chapter 4. It represents the amount of each sales dollar that is available for meeting fixed costs and profits. Since in the example the firm is assumed to be operating beyond its breakeven point, the amount by which the sale price per unit exceeds the variable cost per unit is viewed as contributing directly toward profits (or reducing losses).

TABLE 9.1 The long method of calculating the additional profit contribution from sales for the XYZ Company

Proposed plan	
Sales revenues	
69,000 units · $10	$690,000
Less: Costs	
Variable (69,000 units · $6)	414,000
Fixed (calculated earlier)	120,000
(1) Profits from sales	$156,000
Current plan	
Sales revenue	
60,000 units · $10	$600,000
Less: Costs	
Variable (60,000 units · $6)	360,000
Fixed (calculated earlier)	120,000
(2) Profits from sales	$120,000
Additional Profit Contribution with New Plan [(1) − (2)]	$36,000

Step 1: Calculate the average accounts receivable Dividing the turnover of accounts receivable into the annual dollar credit sales gives us the average accounts receivable on the firm's books at any time during the year.[5] Currently the firm's accounts receivable turnover is 12 (360/30), and it has credit sales of $600,000 ($10 per unit · 60,000 units). Under the proposed plan, the accounts receivable turnover would be 8 (360/45) and the firm would have credit sales of $690,000 ($10 per unit · 69,000 units). The average accounts receivable in each case are calculated below.

Average accounts receivable:

Present plan: $\dfrac{\$600{,}000}{12} = \$50{,}000$

Proposed plan: $\dfrac{\$690{,}000}{8} = \$86{,}250$

Step 2: Calculate the average investment in accounts receivable The average figure for accounts receivable calculated above represents the average *book value* of receivables. Since accounts receivable reflect the *sales price* of goods, an adjustment must be made to determine how much the firm actually has invested in them (i.e.,

[5]This calculation is based on transposing the expression for the turnover of accounts receivable presented in Chapter 3 as follows:

$$\text{Turnover of accounts receivable} = \frac{\text{annual credit sales}}{\text{average accounts receivable}}$$

$$\text{Average accounts receivable} = \frac{\text{annual credit sales}}{\text{turnover of accounts receivable}}$$

This is the relationship used in Step 1.

the firm's cost of accounts receivable). One way of calculating this cost is to determine what percentage of the sale price represents the firm's costs and multiply the average receivables by this percentage.

In order the calculate the percentage in each case, the average cost per unit must be calculated. The average cost per unit can be calculated by dividing the total cost of sales by the corresponding number of units sold. The average cost per unit under the current plan was given earlier as $8 per unit. The first step in finding average cost per unit under the proposed plan is to find the total cost of producing 69,000 units. This is done by adding to the total cost of producing 60,000 units the marginal cost of producing an additional 9000 units (i.e., $6 per unit).

Proposed plan:

$$\text{Total cost} = \$8 \cdot 60,000 \text{ units} + \$6 \cdot 9000 \text{ units}$$
$$= \$480,000 + \$54,000 = \underline{\underline{\$534,000}}$$

Since the average cost of $8 per unit for the first 60,000 units fully accounts for all fixed costs, only the variable cost per unit is relevant to sales beyond 60,000 units. The reader can be assured of the correctness of the result above by adding the variable and fixed costs for the proposed plan given in Table 9.1.

The average cost per unit for the proposed plan can be calculated by dividing the total cost of $534,000 by 69,000. The resulting value, $7.74, is, as one might expect, less than the $8 average cost per unit given sales of 60,000 units. This makes sense since the fixed cost per unit decreases as the sales volume increases, thereby lowering the average unit cost.

The percentage of each sales dollar representing cost at both the present and proposed sales volume can be calculated simply by dividing the corresponding average cost per unit by the sale price per unit. The percentages for both the present and proposed sales volumes are calculated below.

Percentage of costs in each sales dollar:

Present plan: $\dfrac{\$8/\text{unit}}{\$10/\text{unit}} = 80.0\%$

Proposed plan: $\dfrac{\$7.74/\text{unit}}{\$10/\text{unit}} = 77.4\%$

Multiplying the average accounts receivable calculated earlier by the corresponding cost percentages for each plan results in the firm's average investment in accounts receivable. These calculations are presented below for each plan.

Average investment in accounts receivable:

Present plan: $80.0\% \cdot \$50,000 = \$40,000$
Proposed plan: $77.4\% \cdot \$86,250 = \$66,750$

The values of $40,000 and $66,750 for the average investment in accounts receivable for the present and proposed plans, respectively, represent how many dollars, on the average, the firm must invest in accounts receivable under each plan.

A shorter way of finding the firm's average investment in accounts receivable is available. We simply divide the *cost* of sales by the turnover of accounts receivable for each plan as follows:

Average investment in accounts receivable:

Present plan: $\dfrac{\$480,000}{12} = \$40,000$

Proposed plan: $\dfrac{\$534,000}{8} = \$66,750$

This shortcut approach is recommended since it eliminates the need to find the average cost per unit, thereby greatly simplifying the calculations required.

Step 3: Calculate the cost of the marginal investment in accounts receivable The marginal investment in accounts receivable is the difference between the average investment in accounts receivable under the proposed plan and under the present plan. This is calculated as follows:

Marginal investment in accounts receivable:

Average investment with proposed plan:	$66,750
Average investment with present plan:	−40,000
Marginal Investment:	$26,750

The marginal investment represents the amount of additional dollars the firm will have to tie up in accounts receivable if it relaxes its credit standards. The cost of investing an additional $26,750 in accounts receivable can be found by multiplying this figure by 15 percent (the firm's required return on investment). Multiplying $26,750.00 by 15 percent results in a cost for the marginal investment in accounts receivable of $4012.50. This value is considered a cost because it represents the maximum amount that could have been earned on the $26,750 had it been placed in the best investment alternative available. •

Making the credit standard decision. In order to decide whether the firm should relax its credit standards, the additional profit contribution from sales must be compared to the cost of the marginal investment in accounts receivable. If the additional profit contribution is greater than marginal costs, the credit standards should be relaxed; otherwise, the current credit standards should remain unchanged. Since, for the XYZ Company, the additional profit contribution from the increased sales would be $36,000, which is considerably more than the cost of the marginal investment in accounts receivable of $4012.50, the firm *should* relax its credit standards as proposed. The net addition to total profits resulting from such an action would be $31,987.50 ($36,000.00 − $4012.50).

The technique described here for making a credit standard decision is quite commonly used for evaluating other types of changes in the management of accounts receivable as well. If the firm in the preceding example had been contemplating more restrictive credit terms, the cost would have been a reduction in the profit contribution from sales, and the return would have been a reduction in the cost of the required investment in accounts receivable. Other applications of this analytical technique are described later in the chapter. In the preceding example, it was assumed that the firm's bad debt expenses would be unaffected by the proposed change; in actuality these expenses would most likely change with changing credit standards. The inclusion of changes in bad debt expenses in accounts receivable analysis will be discussed later.

Credit analysis

Once the firm has established its credit standards, it must develop procedures for evaluating credit applicants. Often the firm must not only determine the credit-worthiness of a customer but also must estimate the maximum amount of credit the customer is capable of supporting. Once this is done, the firm can establish a *line of credit,* stating the maximum amount the customer can owe the firm at any time. Lines of credit are established to eliminate the necessity of checking a major customer's credit each time a credit purchase is made.

Regardless of whether the firm's credit department is evaluating the credit-worthiness of a customer desiring credit for a specific transaction or of a regular customer in order to establish a line of credit, the basic procedures are the same. The only difference is in the depth of the analysis. A firm would be unwise to spend $50 to investigate the credit-worthiness of a customer making a one-time $40 purchase, but $50 for a credit investigation may be a good investment in the case of a customer who is expected to make credit purchases of $60,000 annually. The two basic steps in the credit investigation process are (1) obtaining credit information and (2) analyzing the information in order to make the credit decision. Each step is discussed separately here and on the following pages.

Obtaining credit information.   When a firm is approached by a customer desiring credit terms, the firm's credit department typically begins the credit evaluation process by requiring the credit applicant to fill out various forms requesting financial and credit information and credit references. Working from the credit application, the firm then obtains additional credit information from other sources. If the firm has previously extended credit to the applicant, it will have its own historical information on the applicant's payment patterns. The major external sources of credit information are as follows:

Financial statements.   By requiring the credit applicant to provide financial statements for the past few years the firm can analyze the applicant's financial stability, liquidity, debt capacity, and profitability. Although no specific information with respect to past payment patterns is shown on a balance sheet or an income statement, insight into the firm's financial position may indicate the nature of its overall financial management. The willingness of the applicant firm to provide these statements may be indicative of its financial position. Audited financial statements are a must for the analysis of credit applicants desiring to make large credit purchases or to be extended lines of credit.

Dun & Bradstreet.   Dun & Bradstreet, Inc., is the largest mercantile credit-reporting agency. It provides subscribers with a copy of a reference book containing credit ratings and keyed estimates of overall financial strength for approximately 3 million U.S. and Canadian firms. A sample book page along with a key to the ratings is given in Figure 9.1. For an additional charge, subscribers can obtain a Business Information Report on a specific company. This report provides in-depth information on the firm's payments, finances, banking, history, and operations. When applicable, the Business Information Report also includes information on special events in the business, changes in the business, updates in the business's activities, and public filings such as suits, judgments, tax liens, and so forth. A sample report containing only the basic elements is presented in Figure 9.2.

Credit interchange bureaus. Firms may obtain credit information through the National Credit Interchange System, which is a national network of local credit bureaus that exchange credit information on a reciprocal basis. By agreeing to provide credit information to the credit bureau on its present customers, a firm receives the right to make inquiries to the credit bureau concerning prospective customers. The reports obtained through these credit exchange relationships are factual rather than analytical. A fee is usually levied for each inquiry.

Direct credit information exchanges. Another way of obtaining credit information may be through local, regional, or national credit associations. These associations may be organized as part of certain industry or trade organizations. Often, an industry association maintains certain credit information that is available to all its members. Another method of getting information is to contact other suppliers selling to the applicant and ask what its payment patterns are like. Often, cooperation with such requests for information can be obtained with an agreement to reciprocate in the exchange of information.

Bank checking. It may be possible for the firm's bank to obtain credit information from the applicant's bank. However, the type of information obtained is most likely to be vague unless the applicant aids the firm in obtaining it. This is true since the credit applicant's bank cannot disclose specific information such as account balances, loan balances, and so forth, without the consent of the applicant. Typically, an estimate of the firm's cash balance is provided. For instance, it may be found that a firm maintains a "high five-figure" balance.

Analysis of credit information. A credit applicant's financial statements and accounts payable ledger can be used to calculate its "average age of accounts payable." This figure can then be compared to the credit terms currently being extended the firm. A second step may be to age the applicant's accounts payable in order to obtain better insight into its payment patterns. For customers requesting large amounts of credit or lines of credit, a thorough ratio analysis of the firm's liquidity, debt, and profitability should be performed using the firm's financial statements. A time-series comparison (discussed in Chapter 3) of similar ratios for various years should uncover any developing trends.

FIGURE 9.1 An excerpt from the Dun & Bradstreet Reference Book and a Key to Ratings

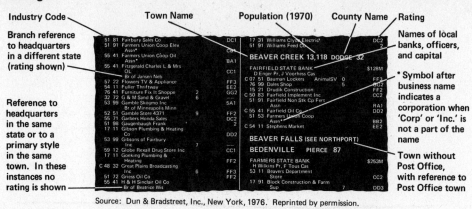

Industry Code

Branch reference to headquarters in a different state (rating shown)

Reference to headquarters in the same state or to a primary style in the same town. In these instances no rating is shown

Town Name

Population (1970)

County Name

Rating

Names of local banks, officers, and capital

* Symbol after business name indicates a corporation when 'Corp' or 'Inc.' is not a part of the name

Town without Post Office, with reference to Post Office town

Source: Dun & Bradstreet, Inc., New York, 1976. Reprinted by permission.

Key to Ratings						
ESTIMATED FINANCIAL STRENGTH		**COMPOSITE CREDIT APPRAISAL**				
		HIGH	GOOD	FAIR	LIMITED	
5A	$50,000,000	and over	1	2	3	4
4A	$10,000,000 to	49,999,999	1	2	3	4
3A	1,000,000 to	9,999,999	1	2	3	4
2A	750,000 to	999,999	1	2	3	4
1A	500,000 to	749,999	1	2	3	4
BA	300,000 to	499,99	1	2	3	4
BB	200,000 to	299,999	1	2	3	4
CB	125,000 to	199,999	1	2	3	4
CC	75,000 to	124,999	1	2	3	4
DC	50,000 to	74,999	1	2	3	4
DD	35,000 to	49,999	1	2	3	4
EE	20,000 to	34,999	1	2	3	4
FF	10,000 to	19,999	1	2	3	4
GG	5,000 to	9,999	1	2	3	4
HH	Up to	4,999	1	2	3	4

**CLASSIFICATION BASED ON BOTH
ESTIMATED FINANCIAL STRENGTH AND COMPOSITE CREDIT APPRAISAL**

FINANCIAL STRENGTH BRACKET
1 $125,000 and over
2 20,000 to $124,999

When only the numeral (1 or 2) appears, it is an indication that the estimated financial strength, while not definitely classified, is presumed to be within the range of the ($) figures in the corresponding bracket and while the composite credit appraisal cannot be judged precisely, it is believed to be "High" or "Good."

"INV." shown in place of a rating indicates that the report was under investigation at the time of going to press. It has no other significance.

"FB" (Foreign Branch). Indicates that the headquarters of this company is located in a foreign country (including Canada). The written report contains the location of the headquarters.

ABSENCE OF RATING, expressed by two hyphens (--), is not to be construed as unfavorable but signifies circumstances difficult to classify within condensed rating symbols. It suggests the advisability of obtaining a report for additional information.

**EMPLOYEE RANGE DESIGNATIONS IN REPORTS ON NAMES NOT LISTED
IN THE REFERENCE BOOK**

Certain business do not lend themselves to a Dun & Bradstreet rating and are not listed in the Reference Book. Information on these names, however, continues to be stored and updated in the D&B Business Information File. Reports are available on such businesses and instead of a rating they carry an Employee Range Designation (ER) which is indicative of size in terms of number of employees. No other significance should be attached.

KEY TO EMPLOYEE
RANGE DESIGNATIONS
ER 1	1000 or more	Employees
ER 2	500 - 999	Employees
ER 3	100 - 499	Employees
ER 4	50 - 99	Employees
ER 5	20 - 49	Employees
ER 6	10 - 19	Employees
ER 7	5 - 9	Employees
ER 8	1 - 4	Employees
ER N		Not Available

Source: Dun & Bradstreet Sales Brochure, Dun and Bradstreet, Inc., 1977.

FIGURE 9.2 A Dun & Bradstreet Business Information Report

Dun & Bradstreet Inc.

Please note whether name, business and street address
correspond with your inquiry.

BUSINESS INFORMATION REPORT

BASE REPORT

SIC	D-U-N-S	© DUN & BRADSTREET, INC.	STARTED	RATING
56 11	04-426-3168	CD 26 MAR 15 197-	1946	DDI
	FRANK'S MEN'S SHOP	MENS CLOTHING		
	SANDERS, FRANK, OWNER			

10 SOUTH BROAD AVE
NEWARK OHIO   43055
TEL 614 206-4555

SUMMARY

PAYMENTS	DISC PPT
SALES	$104,684
WORTH	$40,032 F
EMPLOYS	4
RECORD	CLEAR
CONDITION	STRONG
TREND	UP

PAYMENTS

HC	OWE	P DUE	TERMS	FEB 19 197-	SOLD
3000	1850		2 10 30	Disc	Over 3 yrs
500	200		2 30 60	Disc	Over 3 yrs
3000			1 10 30	Disc Ppt	
7412	1400		30	Ppt	Over 3 yrs

FINANCE

	Dec 31 196-	Dec 31 197-	Dec 31 197-
Curr Assets	$ 42,213	$ 43,312	$ 46,364
Curr Liabs	7,732	8,031	7,383
Working Cap	34,481	35,281	38,981
Worth	34,895	36,902	40,032
Sales	96,890	102,559	104,684

Statement Dec 31 197-

Cash	$ 8,243	Accts Pay	$ 7,101
Accts Rec	7,492	Taxes & Accruals	282
Mdse	30,629		
	— — — — — —		
Current	46,364	Current	7,383
Fixts & Equip	1		
Prepaid Exp	1,050	NET WORTH	40,032
	— — — — — —		— — — — — —
Total Assets	47,415	Total	47,415

Sales 197-, $104,684; gross profit $36,485; drawings by owner $9,463; net profit
$3,130. Annual rent $4,200. Fire insurance on mdse $30,000, fixts $5,000. Fixts
& Equip less depreciation of $6,475.

Prepared from statement signed FRANK'S MEN'S SHOP by Frank Sanders, owner,
Feb 18 197-. Prepared by E. A. Fames, Jr., Independent Accountant.

Mar 15 197-, Sanders said that sales were up 4% so far this year. Profits are
expected also to increase as expenses have remained constant. He estimated
merchandise at $32,000 and owes about $8,000 in accounts payable, all of which
is current.

BANKING   At a local bank balances average medium to high four figures on a routine non-
borrowing basis. Account satisfactory.

HISTORY   Trade name registered July 10, 1946.
SANDERS, born 1917, married. 1935 graduated high school. 1935-43 employed
by Newark Department Store as assistant sales manager, men's wear department.
1943-46 U.S. Navy. 1946 started this business.

OPERATION   Retails medium priced line of men's suits, slacks, shirts, hosiery and accessories.
Features nationally advertised brands, including

(CONTINUED)

Source: Dun & Bradstreet, Inc., New York, 1976. Reprinted by permission.

Dun & Bradstreet's reference book can be used for estimating the maximum line of credit to extend. Dun & Bradstreet itself suggests that 10 percent of a customer's "Estimated Financial Strength" (see Figure 9.1) be the maximum line of credit extended. Additional data providing insight into the credit-worthiness of the customer can be obtained from the "Payments" section of the D & B Business Information Report (see upper portion of Figure 9.2).

Ratios or credit evaluation schemes tailored to its own credit standards can be developed by a firm. There are no established procedures, but the firm must gear its analysis to its needs. This will provide a feeling of confidence that the type of credit risks desired are being taken. One of the key inputs to the final credit decision is the financial analyst's *subjective judgment* of a firm's credit-worthiness. Experience provides a "feel" for the non-quantifiable aspects of the quality of a firm's operations. The analyst will add his or her knowledge of the character of the applicant's management, references from other suppliers, and the firm's historical payment patterns to any quantitative figures developed in order to determine its credit-worthiness. Based on subjective interpretation of his or her firm's credit standards, the analyst will then make the final decision as to whether to extend credit to the applicant, and possibly what amount of credit to extend. Oftentimes these decisions are not made by one individual, but rather a credit review committee.

Thus far, this chapter has been devoted to an analysis of the two major aspects of credit policy—credit standards and credit analysis. We have seen that neither credit standards nor credit analysis are highly quantitative; rather, they rest on the judgment of those involved. However, quantitative techniques are used in making decisions concerning changes in credit standards. The importance of a firm's credit policy cannot be overemphasized.

CREDIT TERMS

A firm's credit terms specify the repayment terms required of all credit customers.[6] Typically, a type of shorthand is used. For example, credit terms may be stated as *2/10 net 30*, which means that the purchaser receives a 2-percent discount if the bill is paid within 10 days after the beginning of the credit period; if the customer does not take the cash discount, the full amount must be paid within 30 days after the beginning of the credit period. Credit terms cover three things: (1) the cash discount, if any (in this case 2 percent), (2) the cash discount period (in this case 10 days), and (3) the credit period (in this case 30 days). Changes in any aspect of the firm's credit terms may have an effect on its overall profitability. The positive and negative factors associated with such changes, and quantitative procedures for evaluating them, are presented in the following sections.

---

[6]An in-depth discussion of credit terms as viewed by the recipient is presented in Chapter 11. The emphasis there is on the analysis of credit terms in order to evaluate trade credit as a source of financing. In this chapter, our concern is with credit terms from the point of view of the offerer.

Cash discounts

When a firm initiates *or increases* a cash discount, the following changes and effects on profits can be expected:

Item	Direction of change [increase (I) or decrease (D)]	Effect on profits [positive (+) or negative (−)]
Sales volume	I	+
Average collection period	D	+
Bad debt expense	D	+
Profit per unit	D	−

The sales volume should increase since, if a firm is willing to pay by day 10, the price per unit decreases. If demand is elastic, sales should increase as a result of this price decrease. The average collection period should decrease, thereby reducing the cost of carrying accounts receivable. The reduction in receivables results from the fact that some customers who did not previously take the cash discount will now take it. The bad debt expense should fall since, as people on the average pay earlier, the probability of a bad debt should decrease.[7] Both the decrease in the average collection period and the decrease in the bad debt expense should result in increased profits. The negative aspect of an increased cash discount is a decreased profit margin per unit as more people take the discount and pay the reduced price. Decreasing or eliminating a cash discount would have opposite effects. The quantitative effects of changes in cash discounts can be evaluated by a method similar to that used to evaluate changes in credit terms.

EXAMPLE

Assume that the XYZ Company, data on which were presented earlier, is contemplating initiating a cash discount of 2 percent for payment prior to day 10 after a purchase. The firm's current average collection period is 30 days, credit sales of 60,000 units are made, the variable cost per unit is $6, and the average cost per unit is currently $8. The firm expects that if the cash discount is initiated 60 percent of its sales will be on discount and sales will increase by 15 percent, to 69,000 units. The average collection period is expected to drop to 15 days. Bad debt expenses are assumed to be unaffected by the decision. The firm requires a 15 percent return on investments.

The advantages of the cash discount plan for the firm are increased sales and a decreased average collection period. An additional 9000 units will be sold, whose contribution to profits will be $36,000 (9000 · $4). This is because the cost of these units is $6, while the sale price is $10. Using the short method of finding the average investment in accounts receivable under both the proposed cash discount plan and

---

[7]This contention is based on the fact that the longer it takes a person to pay, the less likely it is that he will pay. The more time that elapses, the more opportunities there are for a customer to become technically insolvent or bankrupt. Therefore the probability of a bad debt is expected to increase directly with increases in the average collection period.

the present plan produces the following results:[8]

Average investment in accounts receivable:

Present plan: $\dfrac{\$8(60,000 \text{ units})}{12} = \$40,000$

Proposed plan: $\dfrac{\$8(60,000 \text{ units}) + \$6(9,000 \text{ units})}{24} = \dfrac{\$534,000}{24} = \$22,250$

With the cash discount, there is a reduction in the investment in accounts receivable of \$17,750 (\$40,000 − \$22,250). The savings resulting from this reduction is \$2662.50 (15% · \$17,750). The total savings, or addition to profits, is therefore \$38,662.50 (\$36,000 + \$2662.50).

The cost of the proposed cash discount is easily calculated by multiplying it by the dollar amount of sales on which it is taken. Since 60 percent of the sales are expected to be on the discount, the cost of the discount is as follows:

2%(60% · \$690,000) = \$8280

Comparing the savings of \$38,662.50 resulting from the increased sales and re-

---

[8]The calculation of the investment in accounts receivable presented for both the present and proposed plan is not entirely correct. Technically, consideration should be explicitly given to the fact that the proposed action will change the payment pattern of existing customers, which means that not only will cost be recovered in a fashion different from before but the pattern of receipt of profit will also change. In other words, in the example given the old customers, who as a result of the firm offering the cash discount now pay earlier, cause the firm to receive not only its cost but also its profit sooner than would have occurred without such a credit term change. Technically, the analysis should be performed in a fashion that would value the firm's investment in receivables to existing customers that choose to take the cash discount at the *sales price* rather than at cost. Such an approach would more correctly measure the firm's cost or benefits from implementation of a proposed credit term change. If we assume that 54 percent of the XYZ Company's existing customers will take the discount if offered, the *average investment in accounts receivable* would be calculated as follows in each case:

Present plan:
$$\frac{(.54)(\$10)(60,000 \text{ units}) + (1-.54)(\$8)(60,000 \text{ units})}{12} = \frac{\$544,800}{12} = \$45,400$$

Proposed plan:
$$\frac{(.54)(\$10)(60,000 \text{ units}) + (1-.54)(\$8)(60,000 \text{ units}) + (\$6)(9,000 \text{ units})}{24}$$
$$= \frac{\$598,800}{24} = \$24,950$$

The slightly different results from those developed in the preceding example are attributable to the fact that the change in the time-receipt pattern of profits from existing customers is reflected in this analysis while being ignored in the previous one.

Anytime a change in credit terms or some other aspects of accounts receivable is expected to change the payment pattern of existing customers, formal analysis should recognize that the firm's pattern of receipt of both cost *and* profit from these customers is being altered; therefore the investment in receivables for existing customers whose payment patterns have been altered should be measured at the sale price—not cost. For an excellent discussion of this point, the reader is referred to Edward A. Dyl, "Another Look at the Investment in Accounts Receivable," *Financial Management*, Vol. 6. No. 4. (Winter, 1977), pp. 67–70. In order to convey the key concepts throughout the remainder of this chapter without confusing the reader, the account receivable investment is calculated at cost regardless of whether or not the existing customers' payment pattern is altered by the given account receivable action.

duced investment in receivables to the $8280 cost of the discount, indicates that the firm will realize a net profit of $30,382.50 ($38,662.50 − $8280) by implementing the discount. This type of analysis can also be applied to decisions concerning the reduction or elimination of cash discounts. ●

The cash discount period

The net effect of changes in the cash discount period is quite difficult to analyze due to the nature of the forces involved. For example, if the cash discount period were *increased,* the following changes could be expected:

Item	Direction of change [increase (I) or decrease (D)]	Effect on profits [positive (+) or negative (−)]
Sales volume	I	+
Average collection period due to non-discount takers now paying earlier	D	+
Bad debt expense	D	+
Profit per unit	D	−
Average collection period due to discount takers still getting cash discount but paying later	I	−

The problems in determining the exact results of changes in the discount period are directly attributable to the two forces affecting the firm's average collection period. When the cash discount period is increased, there is a positive effect on profits because many people who did not take the cash discount in the past will now take it, thereby reducing the average collection period. However, there is also a negative effect on profits when the discount period is increased because people who already were taking the cash discount will be able to still take it and pay later, slowing the average collection period. The net effect of these two forces on the average collection period is difficult to quantify.

If the firm were to shorten the cash discount period, the effects would be the opposite of those described above. Due to the many assumptions necessary to illustrate changes in the cash discount period analytically, no example of these effects is given.[9] However, the reader should be aware that the basic calculations described earlier can be applied to this decision.

Credit period

Changes in the credit period also affect the firm's profitability. The following effects on profits can be expected from an *increase* in the credit period.

[9]Since changes in the cash discount period may affect the payment pattern of existing customers, the refinement described in footnote 8 would apply to the analysis of proposed cash discount period changes.

Item	Direction of change [increase (I) or decrease (D)]	Effect on profits [positive (+) or negative (−)]
Sales volume	I	+
Average collection period	I	−
Bad debt expense	I	−

Increasing the credit period should increase sales, but both the average collection period and the bad debt expense are likely to increase as well. Thus the net effect on profits of the sales increase is positive while the collection period and bad debt expense increases will negatively impact profits. A decrease in the credit period is likely to have the opposite effects on profits. An example may help to explain the nature of the credit period decision.

EXAMPLE

Assume that the XYZ Company is considering increasing its credit period from 30 to 60 days. The average collection period, currently 45 days, is expected to increase to 75 days. Bad debt expenses, currently 1 percent of sales, are expected to increase to 3 percent due to the higher probability of bad debts associated with a longer credit period. Sales (all on credit) are currently 60,000 units and are expected to increase by 15 percent to 69,000 units.[10] The average cost per unit at the current level of sales is $8. The selling price and variable cost per unit are $10 and $6, respectively. The firm's required return on investment is 15 percent.

Bad debt expense The only difference in the approach used to analyze this decision and the credit standards decision presented earlier is the inclusion of bad debt expenses. The key factor to be recognized when bad debt expenses are included in the analysis is that *the unit cost of a bad debt equals the sale price per unit*. The entire sale price is lost and must be deducted to offset the fact that the additional profit contribution from sales has been calculated on the assumption that the full sale price will be received.

A quantitative approach to the credit period problem Table 9.2 presents a complete analysis of the sample problem. The analysis indicates that the additional profit contribution from sales of $36,000 more than covers the cost of the marginal investment in accounts receivable of $7687.50[11] and the cost of the marginal bad debts of $14,700. The resulting net profit expected from implementation of the proposed change in the credit period is $13,612.50. This suggests that the change should be made. If the firm were contemplating a decrease in its credit period, the analysis would be similar to that presented in Table 9.2, but the negative and positive profit and cost values would be reversed. ●

---

[10]Although all sales have been assumed to be made on credit throughout this chapter, the analytical techniques presented could easily be adapted to situations where only a portion of the firm's sales were made on credit. The simpler all-credit-sale assumption is used in order to avoid confusing the key issues by complicating the analytical procedure.

[11]Because changes in the credit period are likely to affect the payment pattern of existing customers, the refinement described in footnote 8 would apply to the analysis of proposed credit period changes

TABLE 9.2 The effects of an increased credit period on the XYZ Company

Additional profit contribution from sales (9000 units)($10.00 − $6.00)		$36,000.00
Cost of marginal investment in A/R[a]		
Investment with proposed credit period		
$\dfrac{(\$8.00)(60,000) + (\$6.00)(9,000)}{4.8}$	$111,250	
Investment with present credit period		
$\dfrac{(\$8.00)(60,000)}{8.0}$	60,000	
Marginal investment in A/R	$\ 51,250	
Cost of marginal investment in A/R (.15)($51,250)		($ 7,687.50)
Cost of marginal bad debts		
Bad debts with proposed credit period (.03)($690,000)	$ 20,700	
Bad debts with present credit period (.01)($600,000)	6,000	
Cost of marginal bad debts		($14,700.00)
Net Profit from Implementation of Proposed Plan		$13,612.50

[a]The denominators 4.8 and 8.0 in the calculation of the investment in accounts receivable for the proposed and present plans are the accounts receivable turnovers for each of these plans (360/75 = 4.8 and 360/45 = 8.0).

COLLECTION POLICIES

The firm's collection policies are the procedures followed to collect accounts receivable when they are due. The effectiveness of the firm's collection policies can be partially evaluated by looking at the level of bad debt expenses. This level depends not only on the collection policies but on the credit policies on which the extension of credit is based. If one assumes that the level of bad debts attributable to the firm's credit policies is relatively constant, increasing collection expenditures can be expected to reduce the firm's bad debts. This relationship between collection expenditures and bad debts is depicted in Figure 9.3. As the figure indicates, beyond point A additional collection expenditures will not reduce the firm's bad debt losses enough to justify the outlay of funds. The firm must determine the level of collection expenditures that is "optimal" from a cost-benefit viewpoint.

The basic trade-offs

The basic trade-offs expected to result from a *tightening* of collection efforts are tabulated below:

FIGURE 9.3 Collection expenditures and bad debt losses

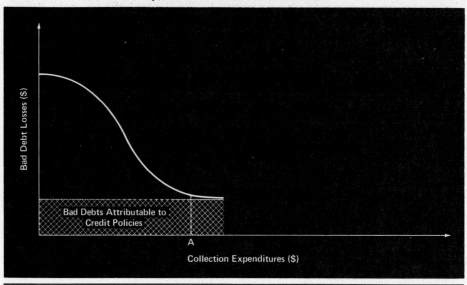

Item	Direction of change [increase (I) or decrease (D)]	Effect on profits [positive (+) or negative (−)]
Bad debt expense	D	+
Average collection period	D	+
Sales volume	0 or D	0 or −
Collection expenditures	I	−

Increased collection expenditures should reduce the bad debt expense and the average collection period, thereby increasing profits. The costs of this strategy may include lost sales in addition to increased collection expenditures if the level of collection effort is too intense. In other words, if the firm pushes its customers too hard to pay their accounts, they may be angered and take their business elsewhere, thereby reducing the firm's sales. The firm should be careful not to be overly aggressive in its collection efforts. If payments are not received on the due date, it should wait a reasonable period of time before initiating collection procedures.

The basic trade-offs described above can be evaluated quantitatively in a manner similar to that used to evaluate the trade-offs for credit standards and credit terms. By calculating the marginal cost of increased efforts and the decreased profit contribution from sales (if any) and comparing this to the savings from both reduced bad debt expenses and decreased investment in accounts receivable,[12] various strategies for increasing the level of collection

[12]Because changes in collection effort are likely to impact the payment patterns of existing customers, the refinement described in footnote 8 would apply to the analysis of proposed collection effort changes.

effort can be assessed. Proposed reductions in the level of collection effort (i.e., expenditures) can be evaluated in a similar manner. An example of such an analysis is not included since the procedures are so similar to those illustrated earlier. All of the analytical approaches discussed in this chapter have been aimed at measuring the benefits and costs of the various proposals and deciding upon the proper strategies to implement.

Types of collection techniques

A number of different collection techniques are typically employed. As an account becomes more and more overdue, the collection effort becomes more personal and more strict. The basic collection techniques used are presented below in the order typically followed in the collection process.

Letters. After an account receivable becomes overdue a certain number of days, the firm normally sends a polite letter reminding the customer about his or her obligation. If the account is not paid within a certain period of time after the letter has been sent, a second, more demanding, letter is sent. This letter may be followed by yet another letter, if necessary. Collection letters are the first step in the collection process for overdue accounts.

Telephone calls. If letters prove unsuccessful, the company's credit manager may call the customer and personally request immediate payment. If the customer has a reasonable excuse, arrangements may be made to extend the payment period. A call from the company's attorney may be used if all else seems to fail.

Personal visits. This technique is much more common at the consumer credit level, but it may be employed by industrial suppliers. Sending a local salesperson, or a collection person, to confront the customer can be a very effective collection procedure. Payment may be made on the spot.

Using collection agencies. A firm can turn uncollectible accounts over to a collection agency or an attorney for collection. The fees for this type of collection effort are typically quite high; the firm may receive less than fifty cents on the dollar for accounts collected in this way.

Legal action. This is the most stringent step in the collection process. It is an alternative to the use of a collection agency. Not only is direct legal action expensive, but it may force the debtor into bankruptcy, thereby reducing the possibility of future business from him without guaranteeing the ultimate receipt of the delinquent charges.

Computerization of accounts receivable management

The use of computers in both the billing and collection of accounts is widespread. A computer is used to bill credit customers at the appropriate time following a purchase. As payments are received, a record of them is keyed into the computer. A computer can be programmed to monitor accounts receivable after a customer has been billed. Periodic checks are automatically made at certain points in time after billing to see if the accounts have been paid. If payment has not been received at certain predetermined points, collection letters are sent. After a prescribed number of these letters have been sent without any receipt of payment, a special notice will be generated, probably as part of a monthly report to the credit manager. At this point, the collection efforts become more directly personal. Actions such as making telephone calls, sending collection persons, and using a collection agency will then be taken. Initiation of legal action is also a possibility.

Currently computers are being used not only to monitor accounts but also as an aid in the credit decision process. Data on each customer's payment patterns are maintained and can be called for as needed to evaluate requests for renewed or additional credit by customers. A computer can also be used to monitor the effectiveness of the collection department by generating data on the status of outstanding accounts. Although the computer cannot carry out the entire accounts receivable management function, it has and will continue to reduce the amount of paperwork required by the credit departments of business firms.

SUMMARY

This chapter has presented discussions and analyses of the important aspects of accounts receivable management. Since accounts receivable represent a sizable investment on the part of most firms, the efficient management of these accounts can provide considerable savings to the firm. The firm's overall objective with respect to the management of accounts receivable should not be merely to collect receivables quickly; attention should also be given to the benefit-cost trade-offs involved in the various areas of accounts receivable management. These areas are the determination of credit policies, credit terms, and collection policies.

Credit policies have two dimensions: credit standards and credit analysis. The firm must determine the appropriate level of risk to accept in order to maximize profits. The basic trade-offs here are the cost of clerical efforts, the cost of investment in accounts receivable, the cost of bad debts, and the profit contribution from sales. Whenever credit standards are relaxed or tightened, these variables must be considered. Credit analysis, although not an exact science, is devoted to the collection and evaluation of credit information on credit applicants in order to determine whether they can meet the firm's credit standards. The subjective judgment of the credit manager is an important input to the credit decision.

Credit terms have three components—the cash discount, the cash discount period, and the credit period. Changes in each of these variables affect the firm's sales, profits, average collection period, and bad debt expenses. The exact effects of a decision to change any of the three credit term components depend on the direction and degree of change. Analytical techniques for evaluating such decisions by assessing the benefit-cost trade-offs are available.

Collection policies determine the type and degree of effort exercised to collect overdue accounts. Decisions with respect to the level of collection effort depend on the cost of collections and the benefits arising from reduced collection periods and fewer bad debts. A point exists beyond which additional collection expenditures do not provide an adequate return; the firm should be aware of this point. Quantitative procedures for evaluating collection policies are available. They are quite similar to those used to evaluate credit standards and credit terms. The basic collection techniques include letters, telephone calls, personal visits, the use of collection agencies, and legal action. The actual methods used depend on the firm. With the widespread use of computers, a large portion of the accounts receivable management process has been automated, thereby eliminating much of the paperwork previously required.

QUESTIONS

9-1 What do the accounts receivable of a firm typically represent? How do credit terms relate to the firm's accounts receivable, and by what are they normally dictated?

9-2 What are a firm's credit standards? Why must a firm have credit standards, and on what basis are they normally established?

9-3 What key variables should be considered in evaluating possible changes in a firm's credit standards?

9-4 Why is a loosening of a firm's credit standards expected to
a Increase clerical expense?
b Increase the receivables investment?
c Increase bad debt expense?
d Increase sales?
Would you expect the opposite events to occur as a result of tightening credit standards? Why?

9-5 What is meant by "the cost of the marginal investment in accounts receivable"? In what sense are accounts receivable viewed as an investment?

9-6 The payment habits of existing customers can affect the results of changes in credit terms and collection policies. Explain how changes in the payment habits of existing accounts can enter into the decision to change each of these.

9-7 How can the firm use the average cost per unit at a given sales volume, along with the corresponding average accounts receivable and sale price per unit, to determine its average investment in accounts receivable?

9-8 How does the firm's required return on investment enter into the evaluation of the effects of changes in credit policy on the firm's accounts receivable? What sort of comparison must be made?

9-9 Once a firm has established its credit standards, it must perform credit analysis of prospective customers for one or both of two possible reasons. What are these motives for credit analyses?

9-10 What are the basic sources of credit information for a business firm? Who is the key provider of mercantile credit information to business? Why?

9-11 What is meant by a firm's credit terms? What do they determine?

9-12 What are the expected effects of a decrease in a firm's cash discount on the firm's sales volume, average collection period, bad debt expense, and per-unit profits?

9-13 What are the expected effects of an increase in the firm's cash discount period? Why may this decision prove quite difficult to quantify?

9-14 What are the expected effects of a decrease in a firm's credit period? What is likely to happen to its sales volume, average collection period, and bad debt expense?

9-15   When considering bad debts in the analysis of a possible change in a firm's credit policy or credit terms, how must the unit cost of a bad debt be viewed? Why?

9-16   Why may there be a point of "saturation" or "diminishing returns" for dollars expended for the collection of accounts receivable?

9-17   How may a computer be used in both the management and collection of accounts receivable? Why is it difficult to use a computer to make credit decisions?

PROBLEMS

9-1   A firm had sales of 30,000 units last year. Variable cost per unit was $23 and average cost per unit was $30. The firm expects to sell the product at $40 this year.
   a   What are the firm's fixed costs?
   b   If the firm expects sales to increase by 20 percent, what change in profits will result?
   c   If the firm offers trade credit at the higher sales level and all customers use credit paying on the thirtieth day, what level of accounts receivable will the firm's balance sheet show (as an average)? Assume a 360-day year.

9-2   Wilson Water Products currently has an average age of accounts receivable of 45 days and annual credit sales of $1 million. Assume a 360-day year.
   a   What is the firm's average accounts receivable balance?
   b   If the average cost of each product is 60 percent of sales, what is the average investment in receivables?
   c   If the opportunity cost of the investment in accounts receivable is 12 percent, what is the total opportunity cost of the investment in accounts receivable.

9-3   Eastinghome Appliance currently has credit sales of $600 million per year and an average collection period of 60 days. Assume the price of Eastinghome's products is $100 per unit, variable costs are $55 per unit, and average costs are $85 per unit at the current level of sales. The firm is considering changing its credit policy. This will result in a 20-percent increase in sales and an equal 20 percent increase in the average collection period. The firm's opportunity cost on its investment in accounts receivable is 14 percent.
   a   What are the firm's fixed costs with and without the policy change?
   b   Calculate the additional profits from new sales the firm will realize if it changes its credit policy.
   c   What additional investment in accounts receivable will result?
   d   Calculate the cost for the marginal investment in receivables.
   e   Should the firm change its credit policy? What other information would be helpful in your analysis?

9-4   Nelson-Hall Menswear feels its credit costs are too high. By raising its credit standards, bad debts will fall from 5 percent of sales to 2 percent of sales. However, sales will fall from $100,000 to $90,000 per year. If the variable cost per unit is 50 percent of the sale price, fixed costs are $10,000, and the average investment in receivables does not change:
   a   What cost will the firm face in a reduced contribution to profits from sales?
   b   Should the firm raise its credit standards? Explain your answer.

9-5   Paul's Products currently makes all sales on credit and offers no cash discount. The firm is considering a 2-percent cash discount for payment within 15 days. The firm's current average collection period is 60 days, sales are 40,000 units, selling price is $45, variable cost per unit is $36, and average cost per unit is $40 at the current sales volume. The firm expects the policy change to result in an increase in sales to 42,000 units, 70 percent of the sales will take the discount, and the average collection period will fall to 30 days. If the firm's required rate of return on investments is 25 percent, should the proposed discount be offered?

9-6 Watson Scott is a financial manager for a large industrial products firm. He has noticed the firm offers a 3-percent discount for payment within 10 days. The average collection period is 28 days. It is Scott's contention that the discount should be dropped. Based on his estimates, the average collection period would only increase to 30 days. And the firm would save 3 percent on all accounts taking the discount (30 percent of the firm's customers currently take the discount). The marketing manager informs him that sales would drop from 21,000 to 20,000. The firm has a 20-percent required rate of return on investments. If the selling price is $22, average cost per unit is $20 at the current sales volume, and variable cost is $17 per unit, should the firm discontinue the discount?

9-7 A firm is evaluating a credit policy change that would increase bad debts from 2 percent to 4 percent of sales. Sales are currently 50,000 units, the selling price is $20, variable cost per unit is $9, and average cost per unit is $11 at the current level of sales. As a result of the change in accounts receivable policy, sales are forecast to increase to 60,000 units.

a What are bad debts in dollars for the present and proposed plans?

b Calculate the cost of the marginal bad debts to the firm.

c Ignoring the profitability from increased sales, if the policy saves $3500 and causes no change in the average investment in accounts receivable, would you recommend the policy change? Explain.

d Considering *all* changes in costs and benefits, would you recommend this policy change? Explain.

e Compare and discuss your answers in **c** and **d** above.

9-8 The Armstrong Equipment company is considering lengthening its credit period from 30 to 60 days. All accounts pay on the net date. The firm currently bills $450,000 for sales, has $345,000 in variable costs, and $45,000 in fixed costs. The change in the credit period is expected to increase sales to $510,000. Bad debt expense will increase from 1 percent to 1½ percent. The firm has a required rate of return on investments of 20 percent.

a What level of additional profitability on sales will be realized by the change?

b What changes in bad debts and costs of financing the investment in accounts receivable will the firm face?

c Rework **a** and **b** above using the method described in footnote 8 of the chapter.

d Why do the two techniques differ? Would you recommend this policy change based on either of these methods of analysis?

9-9 The Rapp Rug Repair Company is attempting to evaluate whether the firm should ease collection efforts. The firm repairs 72,000 rugs per year at an average price of $32 each. Bad debt expenses are 1 percent and collection expenditures are $60,000. The average collection period is 40 days, the average cost per unit is $29 at the current sales level, and the variable cost per unit is $28. By easing the collection efforts, Rapp expects to save $40,000 per year in collection expense. Bad debts will increase to 2 percent of sales, and the average collection period will increase to 58 days. Sales will increase by 1000 repairs per year. If the firm has a required rate of return on its investments of 24 percent, what recommendation would you give the firm? Use your analysis to justify your answer.

SELECTED REFERENCES

Atkins, Joseph C., and Yong H. Kim, "Comment and Correction: Opportunity Cost in the Evaluation of Investment in Accounts Receivable," *Financial Management 6* (Winter 1977), pp. 71–74.

Block, Stanley B., "Accounts Receivable as an Investment," *Credit and Financial Management 76* (May 1974), pp. 32–35, 40.

Dyl, Edward A., "Another Look at the Investment in Accounts Receivable," *Financial Management 6* (Winter 1977), pp. 67–70.

Greer, Carl C., "The Optimal Credit Acceptance Policy," *Journal of Financial and Quantitative Analysis 2* (December 1967), pp. 399–415.

Herbst, Anthony F., "Some Empirical Evidence on the Determinants of Trade Credit at the Industry Level of Aggregation," *Journal of Financial and Quantitative Analysis 9* (June 1974), pp. 377–394.

Kim, Yong H., and Joseph C. Atkins, "Evaluating Investment in Accounts Receivable: A Wealth Maximizing Framework," *Journal of Finance 33* (May 1978), pp. 403–412.

Lewellen, Wilbur G., and Robert O. Edmister, "A General Model for Accounts Receivable Control and Analysis," *Journal of Financial and Quantitative Analysis 8* (March 1973), pp. 195–206.

Lewellen, Wilbur G., and Robert W. Johnson, "Better Way to Monitor Accounts Receivable," *Harvard Business Review 50* (May-June 1972), pp. 101–109.

Long, Michael S., "Credit Screening System Selection," *Journal of Financial and Quantitative Analysis 31* (June 1976), pp. 313–328.

Mao, James C. T., "Controlling Risk in Accounts Receivable Management," *Journal of Business Finance and Accounting 1* (Autumn 1974), pp. 395–403.

Mehta, Dileep R., "The Formulation of Credit Policy Models," *Management Science 15* (October 1968), pp. 30–50.

———, *Working Capital Management* (Englewood Cliffs, N.J.: Prentice-Hall, 1974), part 1.

Oh, John S., "Opportunity Cost in the Evaluation of Investment in Accounts Receivable," *Financial Management 5* (Summer 1976), pp. 32–36.

Poggess, William P., "Screen-Test Your Credit Risks," *Harvard Business Review 45* (November-December 1967), pp. 113–122.

Schwartz, Robert A., "An Economic Model of Trade Credit," *Journal of Financial and Quantitative Analysis 9* (September 1974), pp. 643–658.

Smith, D. W., "Efficient Credit Management with Time Sharing," *Financial Executive 39* (March 1971), pp. 26–30.

Soldofsky, R. M., "A Model for Accounts Receivable Management," *Management Accounting* (January 1966), pp. 55–58.

Stone, Bernell K., "The Payments-Pattern Approach to the Forecasting and Control of Accounts Receivable," *Financial Management 5* (Autumn 1976), pp. 65–82.

Walia, Tirlochan, S., "Explicit and Implicit Cost of Changes in the Level of Accounts Receivable and the Credit Policy Decision of the Firm," *Financial Management 6* (Winter 1977), pp. 75–78.

Welshans, Merle T., "Using Credit for Profit Making," *Harvard Business Review 45* (January-February 1967), pp. 141–156.

Wrightsman, Dwayne, "Optimal Credit Terms for Accounts Receivable," *Quarterly Review of Economics and Business 9* (Summer 1969), pp. 59–66.

CHAPTER 10
Inventory management

Inventory represents a major current-asset investment by most manufacturing firms. Inventory is necessary for the "production-sale" process of the firm to operate with a minimum of disturbances. A stock of both raw materials and work in process is required to ensure that required items are available when needed. Finished-goods inventories must be available to provide a buffer stock that will enable the firm to satisfy sales demands as they arise.

The manufacturing firm typically finds itself operating in an environment that places a major financial constraint on inventories. In Chapter 8 it was indicated that, in order to minimize the firm's cash requirement, inventory should be turned over quickly, since the faster inventory is turned, the smaller the amount the firm must invest in inventory to satisfy a given demand for goods. This financial objective often conflicts with the firm's objective of carrying sufficient inventories to minimize stockouts and satisfy production demands. The firm must determine the "optimal" level of inventories that reconciles these conflicting objectives.

This chapter covers two basic topics. The first portion is devoted to the basic characteristics of inventory. The basic types of inventory, various viewpoints with respect to inventory, the concept of inventory as an investment, and the relationship between inventory and accounts receivable are discussed. The second section of this chapter is devoted to a few basic concepts involved in the management and control of inventory. Attention is given to the types of inventory control and the development of a basic model for inventory control. Although the techniques described may fall in the realm of production management, they are included here because it is important for the financial manager, who is responsible for planning and budgeting for inventory, to understand them.

CHARACTERISTICS OF INVENTORY

A number of aspects of inventory require elaboration. One is the differing types of inventory. Another is the differing viewpoints concerning the appropriate level of inventory held by certain functional areas of the firm. A third is the relationship between the level of inventory and the financial investment it involves. A fourth concerns the relationship between inventory and accounts receivable. Each of these four aspects of inventory will be evaluated separately in this section.

Types of inventory

The basic types of inventory are raw-materials, work-in-process, and finished-goods inventories. Although each type of inventory is not usually shown separately on the firm's balance sheet, an understanding of the nature of each is important.

Raw materials. The raw-materials inventory contains items purchased by the firm, usually basic materials such as screws, plastic, raw steel, or rivets. In some instances when a firm manufactures quite complex products with numerous parts, the raw-materials inventory may consist of manufactured items that have been purchased from another firm or another division of the same corporation. For example, radios, tires, or transmissions might be purchased by a Ford Motor Company assembly plant from other Ford divisions or from outside vendors such as Goodyear (in the case of tires). Actually, there are very few raw materials that are not a finished product of another manufacturer. The only truly "raw" raw materials are basic minerals extracted from the earth and certain agricultural products.

All manufacturing firms have a raw-materials inventory of some kind. The actual level of each raw material maintained depends on the *lead time* it takes to receive orders, the *frequency of use,* the *dollar investment* required, and the *physical characteristics* of the inventory. The lead time must be considered since, if the production process is to operate smoothly, the firm must always have enough raw materials on hand to supply production demands. Due to the lag between placing an order and receiving the raw material, the raw-materials inventory must contain, at minimum, enough merchandise to cover the number of days remaining until additional raw materials will be received.

The frequency of use of inventory also affects the level maintained. The inventory of frequently used raw materials will generally be higher than the inventory of raw materials that are used relatively infrequently. In addition to the lead time and the frequency of use of raw materials, the dollar investment required to maintain a given level of inventory must be considered. In the case of low-cost items such as nails, screws, and bolts, the lead time and frequency of use do not warrant a great deal of attention. Periodic orders of large lots of these items should simplify the inventory process. In the case of expensive raw materials, the lead time and frequency of use are much more important, since frugal management of these raw materials can significantly affect the firm's dollar investment in inventory.

Other factors affecting the level of raw materials are certain physical characteristics such as size or perishability. A cheap item with a long lead time before orders are received but a short "shelf life" would not be ordered in large quantities since, if it were, a portion of the inventory would be likely to spoil or deteriorate before it was used in the production process. It is quite important to consider fully these factors in evaluating the level of inventory that should be maintained. The production demands for each raw material must be satisfied; at the same time, the firm's dollar investment in raw materials must be maintained at a reasonable level (not too high).

The financial, production, and purchasing managers should all be made aware of the possibility of changes in or the elimination of certain items in the product line. This information should induce caution in the production and purchase of raw materials for the uncertain product. The firm does not want to be caught holding high levels of high-cost items that are used solely in the production of a product that is being discontinued. The liquidity (i.e., the quick salability without a high financial loss) of a raw-materials inventory must be considered in making the inventory-level decision.

Work in process.   The work-in-process inventory consists of all items currently being used in the production process. These are normally partially finished goods that are at some intermediate stage of production. Pieces of metal on which some machining has been performed but which will have additional characteristics at the end of the production process are considered work in process. The level of work in process is highly dependent on the length and complexity of the production process. If 50 operations, each requiring approximately two days of production time, are required to convert a raw material into a finished good, an item will remain in the work-in-process inventory for a long period of time. Even if only a few operations are required, their complexity may make the production process long, resulting in a high work-in-process inventory.

A direct relationship exists between the length of the firm's production process and its average level of work-in-process inventory. In other words, the longer the firm's production cycle, the higher the level of work-in-process inventory expected. A higher work-in-process inventory results in higher costs since the firm's money is tied up for a longer period of time. The total inventory cycle was defined in Chapter 8 as the amount of time that elapses from the initial purchase of a raw material to the ultimate sale of a finished good. The firm should try to minimize the length of this cycle while holding stockouts to a minimum. Efficient management of the production process should reduce the work-in-process inventory, which should speed the inventory turnover and reduce the firm's operating cash requirement.

The work-in-process inventory is the least liquid type of inventory. Generally, it is difficult to sell partially finished products. For this reason, the use of work-in-process inventories as collateral for loans is not common. (This aspect of inventory management is discussed in Chapter 12.) One other characteristic of work-in-process inventories is a buildup in value as an item is transformed from a raw material into a finished good through the production process. Raw materials are joined, labor is added, and overhead is allocated to the emerging product, causing the firm's dollar investment in the item to increase. A firm should move items through the work-in-process inventory quickly in order to quickly recover the outlays it has made for raw materials, labor, and overhead. Dollars losses are minimized when errors resulting in scrapping work in process occur early in the production process.

Finished goods.   The finished-goods inventory consists of items that have been produced but not yet sold. Some manufacturing firms that produce to order (i.e., job shops) carry very low finished-goods inventories since virtually all items are sold before they are produced. However, our concern here is with the general manufacturing firm producing and selling a diversified group of products. Most merchandise is produced in anticipation of sales. The level of finished goods is largely dictated by projected sales demands, the production process, and the investment in finished goods required.

The firm's production schedule is geared to make available sufficient finished goods to satisfy the sales demand estimated by the firm's marketing department. If high sales are forecast, the finished-goods inventory should be high; if sales are expected to be low, the finished-goods inventory should be low. Scheduling production in a manner that provides sufficient finished goods to satisfy forecast sales without creating excess inventories should help minimize the firm's overall costs. Firms typically maintain a *safety stock* of finished goods to allow for an unexpected increase in demand for a product or breakdowns in the production cycle. The firm's overall objective of optimizing the level of finished goods can be achieved through realistic sales forecasting and good production scheduling.

There is actually a trade-off between the amount invested in finished goods and the production cost per unit. Often the firm finds that the most efficient production quantities (those with the cheapest production cost per unit) are larger than those needed to satisfy forecast sales demands because of the high level of fixed costs required to set up and schedule machines for production runs of specific items. The firm may find, on investigation, that making fewer but larger production runs results in lower overall costs. Lower production costs per unit may more than compensate for the increased cost of carrying higher finished-goods inventories. The trade-off between these factors must be evaluated in order to determine the optimal production quantities. Quantitative techniques for determining optimal levels of the various types of inventory can be found in most operations and production management texts.

One final consideration with respect to the level of a finished-goods inventory is its degree of liquidity. A firm that sells a staple product in a broad market may be safer carrying high levels of inventory than a firm producing relatively specialized goods. The more liquid and less subject to obsolescence a firm's finished goods are, the higher the levels of inventory it can tolerate. Inventories of high-cost specialized finished goods that are expensive to warehouse (because of the cost of floor space, insurance, and heat) should be scrutinized quite closely in order to keep levels low; inventories of low-cost standard items that are not costly to warehouse can be given less attention. These aspects of inventory management are discussed further in a later section of this chapter.

Functional viewpoints with respect to inventory levels

The preceding discussion concerning the basic types of inventory should have signaled the possibility of conflicting viewpoints concerning the appropriate inventory levels within the business firm. These conflicts between various functional areas must be reconciled in order to fulfill the firm's overall objective of maximizing its owners' wealth. The basic functional areas involved are finance, marketing, production, and purchasing. Each area views inventory levels in light of its own objectives. The basic viewpoints of each of these areas are described below.

Finance. The financial manager's basic responsibility is to make sure that the firm's cash flows are managed efficiently. Efficient management of inventory should contribute toward the maximization of the owners' wealth. The financial manager must monitor the levels of all assets in light of this overall objective, making sure that the firm does not tie up its funds in redundant or excess assets. Inventory, which typically involves a sizable investment by the firm, must be scrutinized closely. The financial manager's general disposition toward inventory levels is to keep them low, thereby keeping down the amount of money that must be tied up in inventory.

The financial manager is concerned with all types of inventory (i.e., raw materials, work in process, and finished goods), actually acting as a kind of watchdog over other functional areas. For instance, the purchasing manager and the production manager are largely concerned with raw materials, the production manager is primarily concerned with work in process, and both the marketing manager and the production manager are concerned with the finished-goods inventory. The financial manager must work with these managers in order to determine what levels of the various inventories are required to keep the production-sales process functioning smoothly. Once these levels are determined, the financial manager must police the inventories, making sure that the firm's money is not being unwisely invested in excess inventory. The opportunity for conflict between various functions arises as a result of the financial manager's watchdog role. He or she must understand the relationship *between* the various inventories.

Marketing. The marketing manager is concerned with the level of finished-goods inventories. He or she would like to have large inventories of each of the firm's finished products. This would ensure that all orders could be filled quickly and eliminate the need for backorders due to stockouts. Since the marketing department's effectiveness is typically evaluated, and the sales force is often compensated, on the basis of the dollar volume of sales generated, they want to make sure that no sales are lost because a product cannot be quickly delivered to a customer. Carrying high inventories should reduce the probability of lost sales due to stockouts.

In Chapter 6, we saw that the key input to the production plan is the sales forecast, which is provided by the firm's marketing department. Emphasis was placed on the fact that both the financial manager and the production manager should analyze and question marketing's forecasts to ensure that the estimates are reasonable. This should guarantee that when the production plan is implemented there will be sufficient inventory to satisfy sales demands. The financial manager should be quite cautious in finalizing the sales forecast, making sure that reasonable estimates of the sales demands are reflected in the figures. It is also important for the financial manager to recognize that, although there is a cost associated with stockouts (i.e., possible lost sales), a certain level of stockouts may be perfectly acceptable in light of the savings that result from a smaller investment in inventory.

Production.   The production manager's main concern is with the level of the raw materials and work-in-process inventories. His or her actions with respect to these inventories directly affect the level of finished-goods inventories. The production manager's major responsibility is to make sure that the production plan is correctly implemented and that it results in the desired level of finished goods. The production manager is evaluated not only on the basis of the efficient delivery of the finished goods, but also on keeping the production cost per unit low.

In order to assure the availability of sufficient finished goods, the production manager would like high raw-materials inventories. This would ensure that there would be no lag in initiating production runs. However, since the financial manager views raw-materials inventories as invested dollars, the production manager will have to keep raw-materials inventories (especially inventories of expensive raw materials) at a level considered reasonable by the financial manager. One way the production manager can lower unit costs is to make large production runs, thereby reducing many of the fixed start-up costs. However, large production runs produce high finished-goods inventories, which may not be looked upon favorably by the financial manager.

The production manager must determine the optimal quantities to produce in order to assure the availability of finished products while keeping production and inventory costs low. Quantitative algorithms using linear programming and other optimization techniques have been developed for making these types of decisions. It is the financial manager's responsibility to make sure that the production manager takes steps to keep not only inventory, but also the cost of production, at an acceptable level. Again, it should be clear to the reader that there are many trade-offs that must be considered in making production decisions.

Purchasing.   The purchasing manager is concerned solely with the raw-materials inventories, having the responsibility to make sure the raw materials required by production are available in the correct quantities at the desired times.[1] The purchasing manager is not only concerned with the *size* and *timing* of raw-materials purchases, but also with buying raw materials at a favorable price. Since raw-material costs are an important component of the

---

[1]Organizationally, the purchasing function is quite often under the control of the plant or production manager rather than being an autonomous function. This arrangement makes sense since the purchasing activity exists primarily to service the production function.

estimated product cost, on the basis of which pricing decisions may be made, it is important for the purchasing manager to buy raw materials wisely.

The purchasing manager is only partially responsible for the level of raw-materials inventories. Although the purchasing manager controls the additions to raw-materials inventories, it is the production manager who dispatches raw materials into the production process and is responsible for reductions in the raw-materials inventories. The joint responsibility of the purchasing manager and the production manager for the level of raw materials inventories should be recognized. The purchasing manager may purchase larger quantities of raw materials than are actually needed by production in order to receive quantity discounts or because of an anticipation of rising prices or a shortage of a certain material. Whatever motive is used to justify large purchases, the financial manager should be aware of any buildups in raw-materials inventories.

It is expected that the purchasing manager, if left on his or her own, would order larger quantities than are actually required. The financial manager must make sure that the cost of carrying higher levels of raw materials than are actually required is justified by the cost savings obtained. One way to do this would be to require purchasing managers to justify larger-than-required purchases by submitting a prepurchase form to the firm's financial management for review. This application of the "exception principle" to the management of raw materials might be quite beneficial.

A closer view of inventory as an investment

On numerous occasions in the preceding discussions, references have been made to inventory as *an investment.* Inventory is an investment in the sense that it requires the firm to tie up its money. The analyses in Chapter 9 illustrated how the average investment in accounts receivable could be calculated using the turnover of accounts receivable and the cost of credit sales. The average investment in inventory can be calculated in a similar manner, as the following example shows.

EXAMPLE

A firm is contemplating making larger production runs in order to reduce the high setup costs associated with production of its only product. The total *annual* reduction in setup costs that can be obtained has been estimated to be $15,000. Currently the firm's inventories turn over 6 times a year; with the proposed larger production runs, the inventory turnover rate is expected to drop to 4. The larger production runs are not expected to have any effect on sales revenues. The cost of goods sold is expected to remain at the current level of $1,200,000. The firm has a required return on investment of 20 percent. Should the firm implement the proposed system?

The first step in determining whether to increase the size of the production runs is to calculate the average investment in inventory under both the proposed and the present system. The value of the firm's average inventory can be calculated, given the cost of goods sold and the inventory turnover, by the following formula:

$$\text{Average inventory} = \frac{\text{cost of goods sold}}{\text{inventory turnover}}$$

Since inventory is carried at cost on the firm's books, this formula can be used to calculate the average investment in inventory under both the proposed and the present system:[2]

Average investment in inventory:

Proposed system: $\dfrac{\$1,200,000}{4} = \$300,000$

Present system: $\dfrac{1,200,000}{6} = \$200,000$

The slower inventory turnover associated with the proposed system is due to the fact that, in the process of running larger lots, the firm must maintain higher average raw-materials, work-in-process, and finished-goods inventories. The result of this slower inventory turnover is a higher average investment in inventory than was previously required. It is the cost of the *marginal* investment in inventory that must be examined. The marginal investment is calculated by subtracting the present average investment ($200,000) from the average investment under the proposed system ($300,000). The marginal investment in inventory is therefore $100,000.

On this additional investment of $100,000 in inventory, the firm must earn 20 percent per year at a minimum, or $20,000. This can be viewed as the annual cost of carrying the higher inventories associated with the proposed system. Comparing the annual $20,000 cost of the system with the annual savings of $15,000 shows that the proposal should be *rejected*, since it results in a net annual loss of $5000. ●

The procedure presented in this example should not be construed as a universal tool to be applied to all inventory decisions. It has been presented to illustrate a way of thinking, especially in the sense of recognizing the relationship between the level of inventory and the number of dollars invested in it. In general, the higher a firm's average inventories, the larger the dollar investment required, and vice versa. The similarity between the approach to evaluating accounts receivable investments and inventory investments should be recognized. The financial manager, in evaluating planned changes in inventory levels, should consider them from a benefit-cost standpoint.

The relationship between inventory and accounts receivable

The level and the management of inventory and accounts receivable are closely related. Generally in the case of manufacturing firms, when an item is sold, it moves from inventory to accounts receivable and ultimately to cash. Because of the close relationship between these current assets, the inventory management and accounts receivable management functions should not be viewed independently of each other. For example, the decision to extend credit to a customer can result in an increased level of sales, which can be

[2]The reader should recall that in determining the firm's investment in accounts receivable it is necessary to take into account the fact that receivables are based on the sale price—not the cost—of the firm's products. Since inventory is carried on the firm's books at cost, no special adjustment is required to estimate the average investment in inventory.

supported only by higher levels of inventory and accounts receivable. The credit terms extended will also impact the investment in inventory and receivables, since longer credit terms may allow a firm to move items from inventory to accounts receivable. Generally there is an advantage to such a strategy since the cost of carrying an item in inventory is greater than the cost of carrying an account receivable. This is true since the cost of carrying inventory includes, in addition to the required return on the invested funds, the costs of storing, insuring, and so forth, the physical inventory. This relationship can be shown using a simple example.

EXAMPLE

The Erker Company estimates that the annual cost of carrying one dollar of merchandise in inventory for a one-year period is 25 cents, while the annual cost of carrying one dollar of receivables is 15 cents. The firm currently maintains average inventories of $300,000 and an average *investment* in accounts receivable of $200,000. The firm believes that by altering its credit terms, it can cause its customers to purchase in larger quantities on the average, thereby reducing its average inventories to $150,000 and increasing the average investment in accounts receivable to $350,000. The altered credit terms are not expected to generate new business, but will result only in a shift in the purchasing and payment patterns of customers. The costs of the present and proposed inventory-account receivable systems are calculated in Table 10.1.

TABLE 10.1 Analysis of inventory-account receivable systems for the Erker Company

	Cost/return	Present		Proposed	
		Ave.	Cost ($)	Ave.	Cost ($)
Item	(%) (1)	Bal. ($) (2)	(1) × (2) (3)	Bal. ($) (4)	(1) × (4) (5)
Average inventory cost	25	$300,000	$75,000	$150,000	$37,500
Average receivable investment	15	200,000	30,000	350,000	52,500
Total		$500,000	$105,000	$500,000	$90,000

This table shows that by shifting $150,000 of inventory cost to accounts receivable investment the Erker Company is able to lower the cost of carrying inventory and accounts receivable from $105,000 to $90,000—a $15,000 ($105,000 − $90,000) addition to profits. This profit is achieved without changing the level of average inventory and account receivable investment from its $500,000 total. Rather, the profit is attributed to a shift in the proportions of these current assets such that a larger portion of them is held in the form of accounts receivable, which is less costly than inventory to hold. ●

The preceding example should make it clear that inventory—especially finished goods—and accounts receivable are closely related. This relationship is affected by decisions made in all areas of the firm—finance, marketing, production, and purchasing. The financial manager should consider the interactions between inventory and accounts receivable when developing strategies and making decisions related to the production-sales process. Explicit recognition of this interaction is especially important when making credit decisions, since the required as well as actual levels of inventory will be directly impacted by them. Although the balance of this chapter is concerned solely with inventory decisions, the reader should recognize that a close relationship always exists between inventory and accounts receivable.

INVENTORY MANAGEMENT AND CONTROL TECHNIQUES

This section of the chapter presents a few production-oriented methods of inventory control. Although the concepts involved are not strictly financial, it is important that the financial manager understand them since they have certain built-in financial costs. Three major areas of inventory control are discussed: (1) the type of control required, (2) the basic economic order quantity, and (3) the reorder point.

Determining the type of control required: The ABC system

Most manufacturing firms find themselves confronted with virtually thousands of different inventory items. Many of these items are relatively inexpensive, while other items are quite expensive and account for a large portion of the firm's dollar investment. Some inventory items, although not especially expensive, turn over slowly and therefore require a high average dollar investment; other items, although they have a high unit cost, turn over rapidly enough to make the required investment relatively low.

A firm having a large number of items of inventory should analyze each item in order to determine its approximate dollar investment in each. Research has indicated that for most firms, the distribution of inventory items is similar to that in Figure 10.1. As the figure shows, approximately 20 percent of the items in the firm's inventory account for approximately 90 percent of its dollar investment in the inventory. The remaining 80 percent of the items account for only 10 percent of the firm's dollar investment in inventory. In response to this general characteristic of inventory, the ABC approach to inventory control has been developed.

A firm using the ABC system of inventory control segregates its inventory into three groups, A, B, and C. The "A" items are the items in which it has the largest dollar investment. In Figure 10.1, this group consists of the 20 percent of the items of inventory that account for 90 percent of the firm's dollar investment. These are the most costly or slowest turning items of inventory. The "B" group consists of the items accounting for the next largest investment. In Figure 10.1, the "B" group consists of the 30 percent of the items accounting for about 8 percent of the firm's dollar investment. The "C" group typically consists of a large number of items accounting for a small dollar investment. In Figure 10.1, the "C" group consists of approximately 50 percent of all the items of inventory but accounts for only about 2 percent of the firm's dollar investment in inventory. Such items as screws, nails, and

FIGURE 10.1 A sample distribution of inventory items

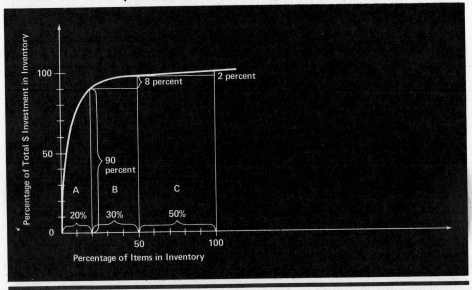

washers would be in this group. A large number of each of these group "C" items would still not require a high dollar investment.

Dividing its inventory into A, B, and C items allows the firm to determine the level and types of inventory control procedures needed. Control of the "A" items of inventory should be most intensive due to the high dollar investments involved; they require the most sophisticated inventory control techniques. The use of the EOQ model, discussed in the next section, would be justifiable for these items. The "B" items can be controlled using less sophisticated techniques, and their level can be reviewed less frequently than "A" items. The "C" items can receive a minimum of attention; they will probably be ordered in large quantities in order to obtain them at the lowest prices.

The reader should recognize that the ABC system of inventory control cannot be universally applied. Certain items of inventory that are inexpensive but are critical to the production process and cannot be easily obtained may require special attention. These types of items must be treated as "A" items even though, using the broad framework described above, they would be "B" or "C" items. Although not perfect, the ABC system is an excellent method for determining the degree of inventory control effort to expend on each item of inventory.

The basic economic order quantity (EOQ) model

One of the most commonly cited sophisticated tools for determining the optimal order quantity for an item of inventory is the economic order quantity (EOQ) model. This model could well be used to control the firm's "A" items. It takes into account various operating and financial costs and determines the order quantity that minimizes the firm's overall inventory costs. The EOQ model is described in the following pages, not only to illustrate a sophisticated technique for controlling inventory, but more importantly to illustrate the financial nature of the order quantity decision. The EOQ model is not only applicable to determining economic order quantities for inventory, but can easily be used to determine the best production quantity as well. However, the emphasis in this section is placed on its use in inventory control.

The EOQ model presented here makes three basic assumptions. The first assumption is that the firm knows with certainty the annual usage of a particular item of inventory. The second assumption is that the rate at which the firm uses inventory is steady over time. The third assumption is that orders placed to replenish inventory stocks are received exactly when inventories reach zero. These highly *restrictive* assumptions are necessary in the most *simplified* version of the EOQ model. In the absence of the certain environment provided for by the three assumptions cited, the firm would have to maintain a *safety stock* of inventory in excess of that necessary to meet expected usage in view of the estimated *lead time* to receive an order. The safety stock would provide a cushion for fulfilling demand in the event that actual usage exceeds the expected, or a delay in receipt of orders occurs. Much more sophisticated EOQ models have been developed.[3] The need for these assumptions will become clearer as the model is described.

The discussion of the economic order quantity model here will cover (1) the basic costs included, (2) a graphical approach, (3) a mathematical approach, and (4) the weaknesses of the model.

Basic costs.   Excluding the actual cost of the merchandise, the costs associated with inventory can be divided into three broad groups—order costs, carrying costs, and total costs. Each has certain key components and characteristics.

Order costs.   Order costs include the fixed clerical costs of placing and receiving an order—the cost of writing a purchase order, of processing the resulting paperwork, and of receiving an order and checking it against the invoice. Order costs are normally stated as dollars per order.

Carrying costs.   Carrying costs are the variable costs per unit of holding an item in inventory for a specified period time. These costs are typically stated as dollars per unit per period. Carrying costs have a number of components such as storage costs, insurance costs, the cost of deterioration and obsolescence, and, most important, the opportunity cost of tying up funds in inventory. The *opportunity cost* is the *financial cost* component; it is the value of the returns that have been foregone in order to have the current

---

[3]Models incorporating probability theory view annual usage, daily usage, and lead time as random variables. These models are quite complex mathematically, though they are built on the general EOQ framework discussed in this chapter. They can be used not only for determining the optimum order quantity, but also to determine the optimum level of safety stock. A discussion of these models is beyond the scope of a basic text.

investment in inventory. A commonly cited rule-of-thumb suggests that the cost of carrying an item in inventory for one year represents approximately 20 percent to 25 percent—and even as much as 30 percent—of the cost (value) of the item.

Total costs. The total cost of inventory is defined as the sum of the order and carrying costs. Total costs are important in the EOQ model since its objective is to determine the order quantity that minimizes them.

EXAMPLE

An example may best illustrate the calculation of order costs, carrying costs, and the total cost for various order sizes. Assume that a firm has order costs of $50 per order and carrying costs of $1 per unit per year for an item. The annual order cost, carrying cost, and total cost if the firm uses 1600 units of this item per year can easily be calculated. Table 10.2 presents the calculations for order quantities of 1600, 800, 400, 200, and 100 units. A few points with respect to these calculations require clarification.

TABLE 10.2 Inventory cost calculations

Order quantity (units) (1)	Number of orders (2)	Cost/order (3)	Annual order cost (2) · (3) (4)	Average inventory (1) ÷ 2 (5)	Carrying cost/unit/yr. (6)	Annual carrying cost (5) · (6) (7)	Total cost (4) + (7) (8)
1600	1	$50	$ 50	800	$1	$800	$850
800	2	$50	$100	400	$1	$400	$500
400	4	$50	$200	200	$1	$200	$400
200	8	$50	$400	100	$1	$100	$500
100	16	$50	$800	50	$1	$ 50	$850

1. The *number of orders* is obtained by dividing the order quantity into 1600, the number of units of the item used annually.

2. The *average inventory* is calculated by dividing the order quantity by 2, since an amount of inventory equal to the order quantity once received is used at a constant rate until the inventory is depleted, at which point a new order is received. A graph of this pattern of inventory usage and replenishment is presented in Figure 10.2. The sawtooth pattern indicates the receipt of an order at each peak, while the negatively sloped lines represent the constantly diminishing inventory level. At t_1, t_2, and t_3 the inventory reaches zero; simultaneously, an order is received raising the inventory by an amount equal to the order quantity. The average inventory is equal to the order quantity divided by 2, since we have assumed that inventory is used at a constant rate.[4] ●

[4]The EOQ methodology is also applied to situations in which the firm wishes to minimize a total cost with fixed and variable components. It is commonly used to determine optimal production quantities when there is a fixed setup cost and a variable operating cost. The EOQ methodology has also been used in the financial cash-marketable security decision process.

FIGURE 10.2 An inventory usage and replenishment cycle

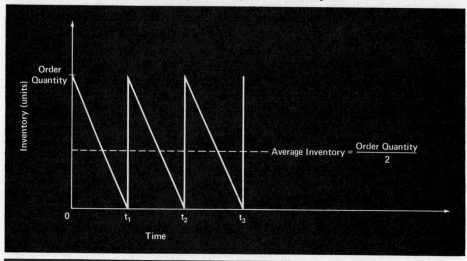

A graphical approach. The stated objective of the EOQ approach is to find the order quantity that minimizes the firm's total inventory cost (i.e., the EOQ). The economic order quantity can be found graphically by plotting order quantities on the x axis and costs on the y axis. Figure 10.3 shows the costs related to the example used in Table 10.2. The minimum total cost occurs at an order quantity of 400 units. Therefore, the economic order quantity is 400 units. It also should be noted that the EOQ occurs at the point where the order cost line and the carrying cost line intersect; since this is always true for this model, the mathematical calculations required to determine the EOQ are quite simple.

It is important to recognize the nature of the cost functions in Figure 10.3. The order cost function varies inversely with the order quantity. In other words, as the order quantity increases, the order cost for the period decreases. This can be explained by the fact that, since the annual usage is fixed, if larger amounts are ordered, fewer orders and therefore lower order costs are incurred. Carrying costs are directly related to order quantities. The larger the order quantity, the larger the average inventory and therefore the higher the firm's carrying cost.

The total cost function exhibits a U shape, which means that a minimum value for the function exists. The total cost line represents the sum of the order costs and carrying costs for each order quantity. It is interesting to note that within a range of plus or minus 20 percent of the EOQ, the total cost function is quite flat, indicating that total cost is relatively insensitive to small shifts away from the EOQ.

A mathematical approach. A formula can be developed for determining the firm's EOQ for a given inventory item. By letting

FIGURE 10.3 A graphical presentation of an EOQ

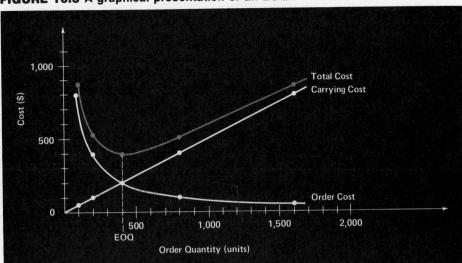

S = the usage in units per period   *Usage*

O = the order cost per order   *cost per order*

C = the carrying cost per unit per period

Q = the order quantity

the firm's total cost equation can be developed. The first step in deriving the total cost equation is to develop an expression for the order cost function and the carrying cost function. The order cost can be expressed as the product of the number of orders and the cost per order. Since the number of orders equals the usage during the period divided by the order quantity (i.e., S/Q), the order cost can be expressed as follows:

$$\text{Order cost} = O \cdot S/Q \qquad (10.1)$$

The carrying cost has been defined as the firm's average inventory (i.e., $Q/2$) multiplied by the cost of carrying a unit per period. The average inventory has been defined as the order quantity divided by 2, since inventory is assumed to be depleted at a constant rate. Thus the carrying cost can be expressed as follows:

$$\text{Carrying cost} = C \cdot Q/2 \qquad (10.2)$$

Analyzing Equations 10.1 and 10.2 shows that as the order quantity, Q, increases, the order cost will decrease while the carrying cost increases proportionately.

The total cost equation is obtained by combining the order cost and carrying cost expressions in Equations 10.1 and 10.2, as follows:

$$\text{Total cost} = O \cdot S/Q + C \cdot Q/2 \tag{10.3}$$

Since the EOQ is defined as the order quantity that minimizes the total cost function, Equation 10.3 must be solved for the EOQ.

Two approaches can be used to find the EOQ. One requires taking the first derivative of Equation 10.3 with respect to Q, setting the resulting expression equal to zero, and solving for Q. A second approach, based on the fact that, as Figure 10.3 shows, the minimum total cost occurs at the point where the order cost and the carrying cost are equal, would be to set Equation 10.1 equal to Equation 10.2 and solve for Q.[5] Using either method, the following equation for the EOQ, represented here by Q^*, results.

$$Q^* = \sqrt{\frac{2SO}{C}} \qquad EOQ = \sqrt{\frac{2 \times \text{usage} \times \text{order cost}}{\text{carrying cost}}} \tag{10.4}$$

EXAMPLE

Substituting the values for S, O, and C given in the earlier example (1600, \$50 and \$1, respectively) into Equation 10.4 yields an EOQ of 400 units:

$$Q^* = \sqrt{\frac{2 \cdot 1600 \cdot \$50}{\$1}} = \sqrt{160{,}000} = \underline{400 \text{ units}}$$

Comparing this result with the EOQ found graphically in Figure 10.3 indicates that both approaches result in the same value of 400 units. If the firm orders in quantities of 400 units, it will minimize its total inventory costs. ●

The weaknesses of the EOQ model. This EOQ model has certain weaknesses that are directly attributable to the assumptions on which it is based. The assumptions of a constant usage rate and the instantaneous replenishment of inventory stocks are quite suspect. Most firms maintain safety stocks as a buffer against an unusual increase in demand or slow deliveries. The assumption of a known annual demand for items is also quite questionable. Actually, a demand forecast is used to make the order quantity decision. If the forecast differs greatly from the actual outcome, the "wrong" EOQ may be used.

Another weakness may become apparent when the model is used. Sub-

---

[5]This solution approach would be carried out as follows:

(1) Multiply both sides by Q	$O \cdot \dfrac{S}{Q} = C \cdot \dfrac{Q}{2}$
(2) Multiply both sides by 2	$O \cdot S = C \cdot \dfrac{Q^2}{2}$
(3) Divide both sides by C	$2OS = C \cdot Q^2$
(4) Take the square root of both sides	$\dfrac{2OS}{C} = Q^2$
	$\sqrt{\dfrac{2OS}{C}} = Q$

The first approach mentioned, which uses simple calculus, requires similar algebraic manipulations once the derivative has been taken.

stituting the appropriate values into the EOQ equation (10.4) may well produce some number such as 325.76 units. Ordering a portion of a unit would be quite difficult; however, this problem is easily solved by rounding the answer. What appears to be a more difficult situation occurs when the number of orders to be placed turns out to be a fraction; 2½ orders may be quite difficult to place in a given period. Since the firm is a "going concern," the problem and need for adjustment is strictly academic. Over a longer period, such as two years, it can be seen that the firm would be able to place five (i.e., 2 yrs. · 2½ orders per yr.) complete orders. Since the total cost function is not actually symmetrical around the EOQ, sensitivity analysis could be used to find the number of complete orders that should be placed over a given period.

Although even the simple EOQ model presented has weaknesses, it certainly provides the decision maker with better grounds for a decision than subjective observations only. Although the financial manager normally is not directly associated with the use of the EOQ model, he or she must be aware of its utility. The financial manager must also provide certain financial inputs, specifically with respect to inventory carrying costs, to permit the use of the EOQ model.

The reorder point

Once the firm has calculated its economic order quantity, it must determine when to place an order. In the preceding EOQ model, it was assumed that orders are received instantaneously when the inventory level reaches zero. Actually, a reorder point is required that considers the lead time needed to place and receive orders.

Assuming, once again, a constant usage rate for inventory, the reorder point can be determined by the following equation:

$$\text{Reorder point} = \text{lead time in days} \cdot \text{daily usage} \qquad (10.5)$$

For example, if a firm knows that it requires ten days to receive an order once the order is placed and it uses 5 units of inventory daily, the reorder point would be 50 units (i.e., 10 days · 5 units per day). As soon as the firm's inventory level reaches 50 units, an order will be placed for an amount equal to the economic order quantity. This order would be received exactly when the inventory level reaches zero. This reorder point formula is based on the assumptions of a fixed lead time and fixed daily usage. However, more sophisticated reorder point formulas, based on less restrictive assumptions, are available.

SUMMARY

This chapter has discussed certain financial aspects of inventory management. Inventory represents a large investment by a manufacturing concern; therefore great emphasis must be placed on its efficient management. The financial manager must be concerned with all types of inventories—raw materials, work in process, and finished-goods. He or she must monitor inventory levels to make sure that excess inventory buildups do not occur.

The financial manager, who views inventory as an investment that consumes dollars, must recognize and consider the interrelationship that exists between inventory and accounts receivable when making production-sale decisions. The financial manager should attempt to make sure that not too many dollars are invested in inventory and that low levels of inventory are maintained. Marketing prefers higher levels, especially of finished-goods inventories, in order to assure quick deliveries and a minimum of stockouts. The production manager, concerned with raw-materials and work-in-process inventories, likes to make sure that sufficient inventory is available to permit continuous production. The production manager's actions directly affect the level of the finished-goods inventory. Purchasing is concerned with raw materials and generally prefers higher levels of inventory. The conflicting viewpoints of all these parties must be resolved in order to have efficient inventory management. The financial manager must act as a watchdog over inventory levels.

Certain production-oriented techniques can be used to keep inventory levels and unit costs low with a minimum of stockouts. The ABC inventory control system is aimed at determining which inventories require the most attention. By dividing inventory into groups according to the dollar investment in various items, control techniques appropriate to each group can be applied.

One of the most common inventory control tools is the economic order quantity model, a sophisticated mathematical technique for estimating appropriate order quantities. The economic order quantity is that order quantity which minimizes the firm's total inventory cost. Although the model described here is based on certain restrictive assumptions, it is quite useful. Once the optimal order quantity has been determined, the firm can set a reorder point, the level of inventory at which an order will be placed.

QUESTIONS

10-1 What trade-off must the financial manager make with respect to the turnover of inventory, the inventory cost, and stockouts?

10-2 How is the level of finished-goods inventories dictated by the firm's production process? What kind of trade-off exists between the production cost per unit, the carrying cost of inventory, and the liquidity of inventory?

10-3 What is the financial manager's role with respect to the management of inventory? With what types of inventories is he or she primarily concerned?

10-4 What are the viewpoints of each of the following managers with respect to the levels of the various types of inventory likely to be?

   a Finance   **c** Production
   b Marketing   **d** Purchasing

10-5 In what sense can inventory be viewed as an investment? How might one calculate a firm's average investment in inventory?

10-6 Why is it important for the financial manager to understand production-oriented inventory control techniques? How does this fit into his or her overall goal of assuring efficient inventory management?

10-7 Explain the relationship between inventory and accounts receivable. What effects on inventory levels are likely to result from easing credit standards and lengthening credit terms? Distinguish between the immediate effects and longer-term effects.

10-8 What is meant by the ABC inventory control system? On what key premise is this system based? When is the system not recommended, and why?

10-9 In what instances may certain items of inventory have to be viewed as outside of the realm of the ABC system? What types of items would these be?

10-10 What is the EOQ model? What are its assumptions and objectives? To what group of inventory items is it most applicable? What costs does it consider? What financial cost is involved?

10-11 When can the average inventory be calculated by dividing the order quantity by two? Graph the depletion and replenishment of inventory and show the average level of inventory.

10-12 What is an EOQ? What are the basic weaknesses of the EOQ model described in the chapter?

10-13 What is the inventory reorder point? What key variables must be known in order to estimate the reorder point? How are these variables related?

PROBLEMS

10-1 Ready Supply has 16 different items in its inventory. The average number of each of these items held, along with their unit costs, is listed below. The firm wishes to introduce an ABC inventory system. Suggest a breakdown of the items into classifications of A, B, and C. Justify your selection and point out items that could be considered borderline cases.

Item	Average number of units in inventory	Average cost per unit
1	1800	$ .54
2	1000	8.20
3	100	6.00
4	250	1.20
5	8	94.50
6	400	3.00
7	80	45.00
8	1600	1.45
9	600	.95
10	3000	.18
11	900	15.00
12	65	1.35
13	2200	4.75
14	1800	1.30
15	60	18.00
16	200	17.50

10-2 What is the firm's average investment in inventory in the following cases?

a The firm has sales of $25,000,000, a gross profit margin of 40 percent, and the average age of inventory is 45 days.

b The firm has an annual cost of goods sold of $200,000 and an inventory turnover ratio of 6.   33,333

c The firm's sales are $2 million, its gross profit margin is 20 percent, and its average age of inventory is 30 days.

10-3 Dayton Truck Parts has a net profit margin of 4 percent, a gross profit margin of 30 percent, and earnings after taxes of $20,000.

   a What is their average investment in inventory if the average age of inventory is 45 days?

   b What is their inventory turnover if the average investment in inventory is $80,000?

   c What is their average age of inventory if the average investment in inventory is $56,000?

10-4 Nieman Brothers has sales of $200,000, a gross margin of 20 percent, and an average age of inventory of 45 days.

   a What will be the change in the average investment in inventory if the firm's inventory turnover ratio changes to 7?

   b If the firm's required rate of return on investments is 18 percent, what additional profits (or losses) result from the change in **a**?

10-5 International Pump is considering a production change that will reduce the average investment in inventory by $60,000. The changeover will cost $10,000 per year, and International's required rate of return on investment is 15 percent. Calculate the additional profits from this change and make a recommendation with respect to the proposed change.

10-6 Franklin Tire estimates the annual cost of carrying a dollar of inventory is $.27, while the carrying cost of an equal investment in accounts receivable is $.17. The firm's current balance sheet reflects its average inventory of $400,000 and average investment in accounts receivable of $100,000. If the firm can convince its customers to purchase in large quantities, the level of inventory can be reduced by $200,000, and the investment in receivables increased by the same amount. Assuming no change in annual sales, what addition to profits will be generated from this shift? Explain your answer.

10-7 Washington Textile uses 10,000 units of a raw material per year on a continuous basis. The firm estimates the cost of carrying one unit in inventory is $.25 per year. Placing and processing an order for additional inventory costs $200 per order.

   a What are annual ordering costs, carrying costs, and total costs of inventory if the firm orders in quantities of 1000, 2000, 3000, 4000, 5000, 6000, and 7000 units, respectively?

   b Graph ordering costs and carrying costs (*y*-axis) relative to quantity ordered (*x*-axis). Label the EOQ.

   c Based on your graph, in what quantity would you order? Is this consistent with the EOQ equation? Explain why or why not.

10-8 Lyons Electronics purchases 100,000 units per month of one component. Monthly carrying costs of the item are 10 percent of the item's $2 cost. Fixed costs per order are $25.

   a Determine the EOQ, average level of inventory, number of orders, and total cost of inventory under the following conditions: (1) no changes, (2) the carrying cost is zero, (3) the ordering cost is zero.

   b What do your answers illustrate about the EOQ model? Explain.

10-9 Columbus Gas and Electric (CG&E) is required to carry 20 days' average coal usage, which is 100 tons of coal. It takes 10 days between order and delivery. At which level of coal would CG&E reorder?

10-10 A firm uses 800 units of a product per year *on a continuous basis*. The product has carrying costs of $2 per unit and fixed costs of $50 per order. It takes five days to receive a shipment after an order is placed, and the firm wishes to hold in inventory 10 days' usage as a safety stock.

   a Calculate the EOQ.

    b Determine the average level of inventory.

    c Determine the reorder point.

    d Which of the following variables change in the event the firm does not hold the safety stock: (1) carrying costs, (2) ordering costs, (3) reorder point, (4) total inventory cost, (5) average level of inventory, (6) number of orders per year, or (7) economic order quantity? Explain.

SELECTED REFERENCES

Beranek, William, "Financial Implications of Lot-Size Inventory Models," *Harvard Business Review 47* (January-February 1969), pp. 72–90.

————, *Working Capital Management* (Belmont, Calif.: Wadsworth, 1966).

Buffa, Elwood S., *Production-Inventory Systems: Planning and Control,* rev. ed. (Homewood, Ill.: Irwin, 1972).

Cook, Thomas M., and Robert A. Russell, *Introduction to Management Science* (Englewood Cliffs, N.J.: Prentice-Hall, Inc., 1977), chap. 11.

Hadley, G., and T. M. Whitin, *Analysis of Inventory Systems* (Englewood Cliffs, N.J.: Prentice-Hall, 1963).

Haley, Charles W., and Robert C. Higgins, "Inventory Control Theory and Trade Credit Financing," *Management Science 20* (December 1973), pp. 464–471.

Hofer, C. F., "Analysis of Fixed Costs in Inventory," *Management Accounting* (September 1970), pp. 15–17.

Magee, John F., "Guides to Inventory Policy, I–III," *Harvard Business Review 34* (January-February 1956), pp. 49–60; (March-April 1956), pp. 103–116; and (May-June 1956), pp. 57–70.

Mao, James C. T., *Quantitative Analysis of Financial Decisions* (New York: Macmillan, 1969), pp. 121–127.

Mehta, Dileep R., *Working Capital Management* (Englewood Cliffs, N.J.: Prentice-Hall, 1974), part 2.

Schiff, Michael, "Credit and Inventory Management—Separate or Together," *Financial Executive 40* (November 1972), pp. 28–33.

Schiff, Michael, and Z. Leiber, "A Model for the Integration of Credit and Inventory Management," *Journal of Finance* (March 1974), pp. 133–140.

Starr, Martin K., and David W. Miler, *Inventory Control—Theory and Practice* (Englewood Cliffs, N.J.: Prentice-Hall, 1962).

Shapiro, Alan, "Optimal Inventory and Credit-Granting Strategies Under Inflation and Devaluation," *Journal of Financial and Quantitative Analysis 7* (January 1973), pp. 37–46.

Snyder, Arthur, "Principles of Inventory Management," *Financial Executive 32* (April 1964), pp. 16–19.

Stancill, James McN., *The Management of Working Capital* (Scranton, Pa.: Intext, 1971), chap. 5.

Thurston, P. H., "Requirements Planning for Inventory Control," *Harvard Business Review 50* (March-April 1972), pp. 67–71.

Vienott, Arthur F., Jr., "The Status of Mathematical Inventory Theory," *Management Science 12* (July 1966), pp. 745–777.

Wagner, Harvey M., *Principles of Operations Research—with Applications for Managerial Decisions* (Englewood Cliffs, N.J.: Prentice-Hall, 1969), chaps. 9 and 19 and appendix 2.

Zink, Karl W., "How to Manage a System of Inventory Control," *Industrial Management* (May 1970), pp. 9–14.

PART FOUR

This part of the text is devoted solely to short-term financing, or current liabilities. Most current liabilities result from the natural course of business; others are the result of negotiated short-term loans. Whereas spontaneous current liabilities are virtually unsecured, negotiated loans may be secured or unsecured, depending on the presence or absence of collateral backing. This section contains two chapters. Chapter 11 discusses the sources of unsecured short-term financing, which include spontaneous forms, such as accounts payable and accruals, and a negotiated form—the bank loan. Chapter 12 discusses the various types of secured short-term loans. These are primarily loans secured by accounts receivable and inventory, although other forms of collateral are occasionally used. In both chapters, the emphasis is on the characteristics, cost, and availability of the various sources of short-term financing available to the business firm.

Sources of short-term financing

BALANCE SHEET	
Assets	**Liabilities and Stockholders' Equity**
Current Assets	Current Liabilities
Fixed Assets	Long-Term Debt
	Stockholders' Equity

CHAPTER 11
Sources of unsecured short-term financing

The availability of short-term financing to the business firm is of key importance to its continued existence. If the firm cannot sustain itself in the short-run, the long run is of no consequence. Short-term financing, which consists of obligations that are expected to mature in one year or less, is required in order to support a large portion of the firm's current assets, such as cash, marketable securities, accounts receivable, and inventory. In Chapter 5 the discussion of cash budgeting emphasized the importance of planning for the firm's short-term financial needs. The discussion of pro forma statements in Chapter 6 also emphasized the importance of short-term financial planning. In Chapters 7 through 10 primary attention was given to the management of specific current assets, again emphasizing the importance of efficient financial management.

In this chapter, we shall discuss the characteristics of unsecured short-term financing. Unsecured short-term financing consists of funds raised by the firm without specifically pledging assets as collateral. These forms of financing show up on the firm's balance sheet as accounts payable, accruals, and notes payable. Accounts payable and accruals are spontaneous sources of short-term funds since they arise from the normal operations of the firm; notes payable, though often unsecured, result from some type of negotiated borrowing by the firm's management. Not all negotiated short-term borrowing by the business firm is unsecured.

This chapter has three basic sections. The first section discusses the spontaneous sources of short-term financing—accounts payable and accruals. Both of these can be manipulated to provide the firm with inexpensive financing. The second section discusses unsecured bank financing. Attention is given to notes, lines of credit, and revolving credit agreements. The third section is devoted to nonbank sources of unsecured short-term financing, which include commercial paper, customer advances, and private loans. A summary table, which presents the key facts related to each of the sources of unsecured short-term financing discussed in this chapter, is included as Table 11.5 at the end of the chapter.

SPONTANEOUS SOURCES OF SHORT-TERM FINANCING

The two major spontaneous sources of short-term financing for the firm are accounts payable and accruals. Each of these sources results from normal business operations. As the firm's sales increase, accounts payable increase in response to the increased purchases required to produce at higher levels. Also in response to increasing sales, the firm's accruals increase as wages and taxes rise as a result of greater labor requirements and the increased taxes on the increased earnings. There is normally no explicit cost attached to either of these current liabilities, although they do have certain implicit costs. The firm should take advantage of these often "interest-free" sources of short-term financing whenever possible.

Accounts payable

Accounts payable are generally created by the purchase of raw materials "on open account." Open-account purchases are the major source of unsecured short-term financing for business firms. They include all transactions in which merchandise is purchased but no formal note is signed evidencing the purchaser's liability to the seller. The purchaser by accepting shipped merchandise in effect agrees to pay the supplier the amount required by the supplier's terms of sale. The credit terms extended in such transactions are normally stated on the supplier's invoice, which often accompanies the goods shipped. These credit terms are of key importance to the purchaser and should be noted in planning all purchases.

Although the obligation of the purchaser to the supplier may not seem as legally binding as it would be if the supplier had required the purchaser to sign a note, there is no legal difference between the two arrangements. If a firm were to become bankrupt, a creditor who sold its goods on open account would have as strong a legal claim on the firm's assets as a creditor who held a note payable. The only advantage of using a note payable is that it gives the holder of the note stronger proof of merchandise sold to the bankrupt firm. In other words, the holder of a note may find the instrument advantageous in a situation where the customer denies having made a given purchase. The use of notes for purchases of raw materials is quite rare; normally they are used only if a supplier has reason to believe that the character or credit-worthiness of a customer is questionable.

In this chapter, we shall deal solely with the use of accounts payable for purchasing raw materials. Among the most important aspects of accounts payable are the types of credit terms offered by suppliers, the costs that result from foregoing cash discounts, and the payoffs that may result from stretching accounts payable. The discussion of accounts payable here is presented from the viewpoint of the purchaser—not the supplier of trade credit. The account payable of a purchaser is an account receivable on the supplier's books.[1]

---

[1]Chapter 9 presented an in-depth discussion of the various aspects of the firm's role as a supplier of credit. It highlighted the key strategies and considerations in extending credit to customers.

Credit terms. The firm's credit terms state the credit period, the size of the cash discount, the cash discount period, and the date the credit period begins. Each of these aspects of a firm's credit terms is concisely stated in such expressions as "2/10 net 30 EOM." The terms contain all the key information concerning the length of the credit period (30 days), the cash discount (2 percent), the cash discount period (10 days), and the time the credit period begins (the end of the month). Although credit terms typically differ among industries, there are a number of commonly used terms, each of which is discussed separately below.

The credit period. The credit period is the number of days until payment in full is required. Regardless of whether a cash discount is offered, the credit period associated with a transaction must be indicated. Credit periods usually range from zero to 120 days, although in certain instances longer credit periods are provided.[2]

No credit period. Often, suppliers do not extend credit to their customers, but instead require payment on delivery. The term COD, indicating "cash on delivery," is normally attached to these credit terms. Generally COD terms are extended only to customers believed to be questionable or unknown credit risks. In some instances, suppliers require payment before delivery. The term CBD, indicating "cash before delivery," is used to designate this type of arrangement. This type of arrangement is used on some contracted manufacturing jobs. For instance, if a firm contracts to have an addition built to its plant, it may agree to make payments at certain predetermined points prior to the completion of the entire project. In essence, the purchaser in this situation is financing the construction of the plant through these periodic payments. COD and CBD terms *do not* actually represent an extension of credit by the supplier to the customer and are *not* evidenced by an account payable on the purchaser's books. They can be thought of as indicating a cash sale, which does not involve the extension of credit.

The net period. Most credit terms include a net period that is typically referred to as "net 30 days," "net 60 days," and so on. The prefix *net* indicates that the face amount of the purchase must be paid within the number of days indicated from the beginning of the credit period. For example, the terms "net 30 days" indicate that the firm must make *full payment* within 30 days of the beginning of the credit period. (Once we have defined the beginning of the credit period, a more detailed example can be given.) A firm that stretches its accounts payable will pay beyond the stated credit period.

Seasonal dating. Seasonal dating is a technique used by suppliers in seasonal businesses, such as clothing and sporting goods firms. It provides a considerably longer credit period than that normally extended, possibly as

---

[2]The credit period is zero days when sales are made for cash.

long as 180 days. The supplier ships finished goods to the purchaser in advance of the selling season, but does not require payment until shortly after the actual demand for the seasonal items is expected. Both parties to the transaction stand to gain from seasonal dating. The seller saves inventory carrying costs, not having to carry as much inventory. Many manufacturers of seasonal merchandise produce at a constant rate throughout the year, and if they could not pass their inventory carrying costs on to their customers, they would have to absorb them.[3] The purchaser gains through assurances of having merchandise available for the peak season, but is not required to pay for it until the actual season arrives. As long as the purchaser has adequate inventory facilities, the use of seasonal dating works to the benefit of both parties concerned.

Cash discounts. If a cash discount is offered as part of the firm's credit terms, it is normally between 1 and 5 percent. It is actually a percentage deduction from the purchase price allowed the purchaser if he pays within the cash discount period. A 2-percent cash discount indicates that the purchaser of $100 of merchandise need pay only $98 if he pays within the discount period. Many purchasers will stretch their cash discounts by taking the discount even when paying after the cash discount period.

From the point of view of the supplier of credit, whose objective it is to collect his accounts receivable quickly, a cash discount provides an incentive for the purchaser to pay early. The reduction in proceeds due to the discount is compensated for by the speeding up of collections. The purchaser, whose objective is to stretch his accounts payable by paying as late as possible, must determine whether it is advantageous to take the cash discount and pay early. Techniques for analyzing the benefits of each alternative will be discussed in a later section.

The cash discount period. The cash discount period specifies the maximum number of days after the beginning of the credit period that the cash discount can be taken. Typically, the cash discount period is between 5 and 20 days. In certain industries, more than one cash discount is offered. The discount period is shortest for the largest discount offered and longest for the smallest discount offered. Often, large customers of smaller firms use their position as key customers as a form of leverage, enabling them to take cash discounts far beyond the end of the cash discount period. This strategy, although ethically questionable, is frequently encountered.

The current trend is toward the elimination of cash discounts. This trend is the result of two basic factors. The first is the widespread use of computers for paying accounts payable. When payments are computerized, most firms take the cash discount regardless of when payment is made. A firm may end

---

[3]As previously noted (p. 281), a commonly cited rule-of-thumb with respect to inventory carrying costs states that the cost of carrying an item in inventory for one year represents approximately 20 to 25—and even as much as 30—percent of the cost (or value) of the item. This suggests that very real savings may result for suppliers using seasonal dating.

up paying 20 days after the end of the discount period but still taking the discount; the United States government is notorious for doing this. The second reason for the trend away from cash discounts is the difficulty of policing the discounts and collecting the amount due when a discount has been incorrectly taken. As a result, firms prefer to offer better prices and no cash discount.

During the tight money period of 1974–1975, many firms began charging interest at a specified rate for each day beyond the credit period it took a customer to pay. This late charge was intended to deter firms from stretching their accounts payable. It appears that along with the trend away from offering cash discounts, an ever-increasing number of firms are simply specifying a relatively short net period and charging daily interest on payments received beyond the net period. This approach is expected to continue into at least the near future.

The beginning of the credit period. The beginning of the credit period is stated as part of the supplier's credit terms. It can be specified in various ways—as the date of the invoice, the end of month, the middle of the month, or on receipt of the goods. The notation used is briefly described below.

The date of the invoice. One of the most common designations for the beginning of the credit period is the date of the invoice. Both the discount period and the net period are then measured with respect to the invoice date.

The end of the month (EOM). The notation EOM indicates that the credit period for all purchases made within a given month begins on the first of the month immediately following. These terms are quite common since they simplify record keeping on the part of the firm extending credit. The date of the invoice is recognized as the date of sale.[4]

The middle of the month (MOM). The notation MOM indicates that the month is broken into two separate credit periods. The credit period for all sales made (i.e., invoices dated) between the first and fifteenth of the current month begins on the sixteenth of the month. The credit period for all sales made between the sixteenth and the thirtieth of the month begins on the first day of the month immediately following. (Thirty-day months are assumed.) These credit terms cause the firm's collections to be speeded up since payments for purchases made prior to the fifteenth of the month are collected earlier than when EOM terms are offered. MOM terms are not commonly used. The following example may help clarify the difference between the various types of credit period beginnings.

---

[4]Occasionally firms receive invoices prior to receiving the actual merchandise purchased. In these situations the beginning of the credit period is not tied to the invoice date, which could be 30 days prior to the receipt of goods.

EXAMPLE

The Grimes Company made two purchases from a certain supplier offering credit terms of 2/10 net 30. One purchase was made on September 10 and the other on September 20. The payment dates for both purchases, based on credit periods that begin at various points, are given in Table 11.1. Both the payment dates if the firm takes the cash discount and the payment dates if it pays the net amount are shown.

TABLE 11.1 Payment dates for the Grimes Company given various assumptions

Beginning of credit period	September 10 purchase		September 20 purchase	
	Discount taken	Net amount paid	Discount taken	Net amount paid
Date of invoice	Sept. 20	Oct. 10	Sept. 30	Oct. 20
EOM	Oct. 10	Oct. 30	Oct. 10	Oct. 30
MOM	Sept. 25	Oct. 15	Oct. 10	Oct. 30

Table 11.1 illustrates that, from the point of view of the recipient of trade credit, a credit period beginning at the end of the month is preferable in all cases since purchases made early in the month can be paid for at a later date than otherwise would have been the case. When the credit period begins on the date of the invoice, the credit recipient must pay earlier regardless of whether it takes the cash discount or pays the net amount. The difference between the MOM and EOM terms can be recognized by noting that, for the September 10 purchase, MOM terms require quicker payment than EOM terms. For the September 20 purchase, MOM and EOM terms result in the same payment dates. ●

Receipt of goods (ROG). Receipt of goods terms are commonly used when goods purchased may be received considerably later than the purchase date. This happens when merchandise is purchased from a geographically distant supplier and the shipping process takes a period of months. A large number of backorders, strikes, and other problems may also delay the receipt of goods. ROG terms indicate that the credit period does not begin until the purchaser has actually received the merchandise. These terms are used when time lags in the receipt of goods are anticipated.

Credit terms are generally standardized within a given industry. This is because credit terms are often viewed as a competitive device adding to the attractiveness of a firm's products. In order to maintain their competitive position, firms within an industry offer the same terms. In many cases the firms' stated credit terms are not the terms actually given to a customer; special arrangements or "deals" are made that provide certain customers with more favorable terms. This is often done in order to attract key accounts or to help a growing firm that is low on working capital. The prospective purchaser is wise to look closely at the credit terms of suppliers when making a purchase decision. In many instances, concessions may be available.

The cost of trade credit. Although no explicit cost is levied on the recipient of trade credit, the firm extending the credit does incur a cost in the sense that its money is tied up for the interim. Extending credit to customers requires the investment of money that could be used elsewhere, and this cost is indirectly passed on to the purchaser in the cost of the merchandise. In the same way that a supplier extends trade credit to a customer, so too the supplier's supplier generally extends trade credit, thereby helping the supplier to absorb a portion of the cost. A more in-depth discussion of trade credit from the point of the issuer (i.e., accounts receivable) was presented in Chapter 9.

Taking or foregoing the cash discount. If a firm is extended credit terms that include a cash discount, it has two options. Its first option is to *take the cash discount.* Taking the cash discount will require the firm to pay earlier than it would have to if the discount were foregone. In many instances, firms take the cash discount regardless of whether payment is made within the cash discount period. If a firm does intend to take a cash discount, it should pay on the last day of the cash discount period. It will be assumed, in subsequent analysis, that this is what happens—that firms that take cash discounts pay on the final day of the cash discount period. There is no implicit cost associated with taking a cash discount.

The second option open to the firm is to *forego the cash discount* and pay at the end of the credit period. Although there is no direct cost associated with foregoing a cash discount, there is an implicit cost. If the cash discount is foregone, the firm should pay on the final day of the credit period. An overall strategy of paying as late as possible was discussed in Chapter 8. A firm should pay its bills as late as it can without damaging its credit rating. In this section, we shall initially assume that if a discount is foregone, payment will be made on the final day of the credit period.

EXAMPLE

The Russell Corporation purchased $1000 worth of merchandise on February 27 from a supplier extending terms of 2/10 net 30 EOM. If the corporation takes the cash discount, it will have to pay $980 [$1000 − .02($1000)] on March 10. If it foregoes the discount, it will have to pay the full $1000 on March 30. The factors involved in deciding whether or not the discount should be foregone are explained in the following section. ●

The cost of foregoing a cash discount. There is an implicit cost in foregoing a cash discount. This is because, in order to delay paying its bill for an additional number of days, the firm must forego an opportunity to pay less for the items it has purchased. The cost of foregoing a cash discount can be illustrated by a simple example. The example below assumes that if the firm takes a cash discount, payment will be made on the final day of the cash discount period, and if the cash discount is foregone, payment will be made on the final day of the credit period.

FIGURE 11.1 Payment options for the Russell Corporation

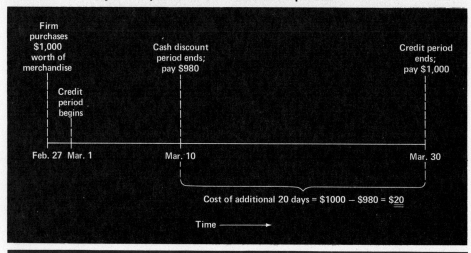

EXAMPLE

The Russell Corporation mentioned in the preceding example, has been extended credit terms of 2/10 net 30 EOM. If it takes the cash discount on its February 27 purchase, payment will be required on March 10. If the cash discount is foregone, payment can be made on March 30. In order to keep its money (i.e., postpone payment) for an extra 20 days (from March 10 to March 30) the firm must forego an opportunity to pay $980 for its $1000 purchase. In other words, it will cost the firm an extra $20 to delay payment for 20 days. Figure 11.1 shows the payment options open to the corporation.

In order to calculate the cost of foregoing the cash discount, the *true purchase price* must be viewed as the discounted cost of the merchandise. For the Russell Corporation, this discounted cost would be $980. In order to avoid paying the $980 for an extra 20 days, the firm must pay $20 ($1000 − $980). The annual percentage cost of foregoing the cash discount can be calculated using Equation 11.1.[5]

$$\text{Cost of foregoing cash discount} = \frac{CD}{1-CD} \cdot \frac{360}{N} \tag{11.1}$$

where

CD = the stated cash discount in percentage terms
N = the number of days payment can be delayed by foregoing the cash discount.

Substituting the values for CD (.02) and N (20 days) into Equation 11.1 and solving results in a cost of foregoing the cash discount of 36.73 percent [(.02 ÷ .98) · (360 ÷ 20)]. A 360-day year is assumed.

---

[5]Equation 11.1 as well as the related discussions are based upon the assumption that there is only one discount period. In the event that multiple discount periods are offered, calculation of the cost of foregoing the discount must be made for each payment alternative.

The same answer could have been obtained by substituting for the first term of Equation 11.1 the quotient obtained by dividing the dollar cash discount ($20) by the price of the merchandise if the cash discount is taken ($980). However, the use of Equation 11.1 is less complicated. A simple way to approximate the cost of a foregone discount is to use the stated cash discount percentage (2 percent for the Russell Corporation) in place of the first term of Equation 11.1. The smaller the cash discount, the closer the approximation of the cost of foregoing the discount is to the actual cost of foregoing the cash discount. Using this simplified approach, the cost of foregoing the cash discount for the Russell Corporation is found to be 36 percent [2% · (360 ÷ 20)]. ●

Using the cost of foregoing a cash discount in decision making. The financial manager must determine whether it is advisable to take a cash discount. There are also a number of other decisions with respect to cash discounts that may confront the financial manager. Each of these decisions can be illustrated by a simple example.

EXAMPLE

The Gup Company has four possible suppliers, each offering different credit terms. Except for the differences in credit terms, their products and services are undifferentiated. Table 11.2 presents the credit terms offered by each supplier, A, B, C, and D and the cost of foregoing the cash discounts. The approximate method of calculating the cost of foregoing a cash discount has been used in order to simplify the analysis. The cost of foregoing the cash discount from supplier A is 36 percent, the cost of foregoing the cash discount from supplier B is 8 percent, the cost of foregoing the cash discount from supplier C is 21.6 percent, and the cost of foregoing the cash discount from supplier D is 28.8 percent. Let us now see how the information in Table 11.2 might be used in a number of decision situations.[6]

TABLE 11.2 Cash discounts and associated costs for the Gup Company

Supplier	Credit terms	Approximate cost of foregoing cash discount
A	2/10 net 30 EOM	36%
B	1/10 net 55 EOM	8%
C	3/20 net 70 EOM	21.6%
D	4/10 net 60 EOM	28.8%

CASE 1: A ONE-BY-ONE ANALYSIS

If the firm needs short-term funds, which are currently available from its commercial bank at 12 pecent, and if each of the suppliers (A, B, C, and D) is viewed *separately,* which (if any) of the suppliers' cash discount will the firm forego? In order to

[6]The analysis of the various decisions implicitly assumes that the firm will continuously make purchases from the given supplier since this permits the term of the loan provided to be aligned with the firm's actual financial need. In actuality, a 20-day loan obtained by foregoing a cash discount may not fulfill a firm's actual funds need.

answer this question, each supplier's terms must be evaluated as they would be if it were the firm's sole supplier. A decision can then be made based on the consequences of the stated credit terms. In dealing with supplier A, the firm will take the cash discount since the cost of foregoing it is 36 percent. The firm will then borrow the funds it requires from its commercial bank at 12-percent interest. In dealing with supplier B, the firm will do better to forego the cash discount since the cost of this action is less than the cost of borrowing money from the bank (8 percent as opposed to 12 percent). In dealing with either supplier C or supplier D, the firm should take the cash discount since in both cases the cost of foregoing the discount is greater than the 12-percent cost of borrowing from the bank.

CASE 2: THE FIRM MUST FOREGO A DISCOUNT

If the Gup Company knows that it must forego cash discounts since it needs money and has no alternate sources of short-term financing, from which of its four alternative suppliers will the purchase be made? In this case, the main concern is not with the cost of foregoing the cash discount, but rather with *which supplier can be paid the latest*. Since the cash discount must be foregone, all suppliers will be paid the full amount for their merchandise. Thus the supplier that can be paid the latest is preferable. In this case, supplier C will be selected since it can be paid on day 70, later than any of the other suppliers.

CASE 3: THE FIRM MUST TAKE A DISCOUNT

If the Gup Company already has sufficient short-term financing, from which supplier should it make the purchase? In this situation, the firm *will* take the cash discount, so the cost of foregoing it is *not* relevant. The chief consideration is *who can be paid the least the latest*. Table 11.3 presents the firm's options with respect to the percentage of the purchase price that must be paid and the payment date if the cash discount is taken. The four alternatives can easily be reduced to two by comparing the terms of suppliers A, B, and D. Each of these suppliers requires payment on day 10, but supplier D is preferable since it requires payment of only 96 percent of the purchase price at that time. In other words, supplier D can be paid less than supplier A or supplier B at the same point in time.

TABLE 11.3 The percentage of the purchase price paid and payment dates when the cash discount is taken for the Gup Company

Supplier	Percentage of purchase price paid	Payment date
A	98	10
B	99	10
C	97	20
D	96	10

The comparison of suppliers C and D is not quite so straightforward. Supplier C can be paid 97 percent on day 20, and supplier D can be paid 96 percent on day 10. In order to delay payment ten days, the firm must pay an additional 1 percent of the purchase price. In order to determine if supplier C is preferable to supplier D the question of whether it is worth this much money (i.e., 1 percent) to delay payment ten days must be answered. The cost of such an action is approximately 36 percent

[1% · (360 ÷ 10)]. Since the firm's cost of borrowing is 12 percent, it seems advisable for the firm to make its purchase from supplier D and avoid the 36 percent marginal borrowing cost. ●

The foregoing examples show that the cost of foregoing a cash discount is relevant only when evaluating a single supplier's credit terms in light of certain bank borrowing costs. In comparing various suppliers' credit terms, the cost of foregoing the cash discount is not the most important input to the decision process.

The effects of stretching accounts payable.   If a firm anticipates stretching accounts payable, the cost of foregoing a cash discount is reduced. Stretching accounts payable is sometimes suggested as a reasonable strategy for a firm as long as it does not damage its credit rating.

EXAMPLE
The Russell Corporation, discussed earlier, was extended credit terms of 2/10 net 30 EOM. The cost of foregoing the cash discount, assuming payment on the last day of the credit period, was found to be approximately 36 percent [2% · (360 ÷ 20)]. If the firm were able to stretch its account payable to 70 days without damaging its credit rating, the cost of foregoing the cash discount would be only 12 percent [2% · (360 ÷ 60)]. Stretching accounts payable reduces the implicit cost of foregoing a cash discount. The length of time a firm can stretch its accounts payable without damage to its credit rating must be kept in mind when developing the firm's cash discount strategy. The firm might find that in view of its ability to stretch accounts payable, foregoing an otherwise nonattractive cash discount may be desirable. ●

Accruals
The second spontaneous source of short-term financing for the business firm is accruals. Accruals are liabilities for services received for which payment has yet to be made. The most common items accrued by a firm are taxes and wages. Since taxes are payments to the government, their accrual cannot be manipulated by the firm. It can, however, manipulate the accrual of wages to some extent.

Although there is no explicit or implicit cost associated with accruals, a firm can save money by accruing as many dollars of wages as possible. Accruals are a virtually free source of financing. Employees provide services for which they normally are not paid until a specified period of time—typically a week, two weeks, or a month—has elapsed. The pay period for hourly employees is often governed by union regulations or state or federal law. However, in other cases the frequency of payment is at the discretion of the company's manager. The following example shows how accruals can be used to increase the firm's financing.

EXAMPLE
The Smith Company currently pays its salaried employees every two weeks. The payroll for two weeks is normally about $3 million. If the firm's opportunity cost is 8 percent, how much would the firm save by changing the pay period from two weeks to one month? If the firm paid monthly, the payroll at the end of each month

would be approximately $6 million. Currently the average amount accured for the salaried payroll is $1.5 million ($3 million ÷ 2), since the accrued payroll is expected to increase at a constant rate until payment is actually made. For the first half of the payroll period, the accrued payroll will be below $1.5 million, and for the second half of the pay period it will be greater than $1.5 million.

Under the new plan, the average amount accrued would be $3 million ($6 million ÷ 2), using the same logic as above. Implementing the proposed plan would therefore increase the average amount of accruals by $1.5 million ($3 million − $1.5 million). This increase in average accrued salaries, in effect, increases the firm's free financing by $1.5 million. This amount of funds can now be used elsewhere at an opportunity cost of 8 percent. The annual savings from this change in the salary payment interval is $120,000 ($1,500,000 · .08). By increasing accruals, the firm can save this amount of funds. ●

The use of accruals as an interest-free source of financing is consistent with the general philosophy of paying bills as late as possible as long as the firm does not damage its credit standing. In the case of accrued wages, the firm must be careful not to damage the morale of its employees by delaying the payment of wages for too long. Since the government requires quarterly tax payments by corporations, tax accruals may be thought of as having an average value of one-half of the quarterly tax liability. Sometimes firms pay rent or lease expenses at the end of a lease period; if they do, these expenditures are accrued. The firm should use accruals as often as possible, keeping in mind any subjective costs associated with their use.

BANK SOURCES OF UNSECURED SHORT-TERM FUNDS

Negotiated unsecured short-term loans are generally obtained from banks. The major type of loan made by banks to business firms is the *short-term self-liquidating loan*. Loans are referred to as self-liquidating when the bank's motive for making them is to provide the firm with financing to meet seasonal needs—for example, to cover seasonal increases in inventories or accounts receivable. Self-liquidating loans are intended merely to carry the firm through seasonal peaks in financing needs attributed primarily to buildups of inventory and accounts receivable. It is expected that as inventories and receivables are converted into cash the funds needed to retire these loans will automatically be generated. In other words, the use to which the borrowed money is put provides the mechanism through which the loan is repaid.

Unsecured short-term loans made by commercial banks represent the primary source of *negotiated* short-term funds to business firms; the primary source of unsecured short-term funds to business in general is trade credit (i.e., accounts payable). Banks lend unsecured short-term funds in three basic ways—(1) through notes, (2) through lines of credit, and (3) through revolving credit agreements. Each of these sources of funds is discussed separately below.

Notes

A *single-payment loan* can be obtained from a commercial bank by a credit-worthy business borrower. Typically, this type of loan is a "one-shot" deal made when a borrower needs additional funds for a short period but does not believe that this need will continue. The instrument resulting from this type of short-term unsecured loan is a *note*, which must be signed by the borrower. The note states the terms of the loan, which include the length of the loan (i.e., the maturity date) and the interest rate charged. This type of short-term note generally has a maturity of 30 to 90 days. The interest charged on the note is generally stated as a fixed percentage, tied in some fashion to the prime interest rate.

The *prime interest rate* is the lowest rate of interest charged on business loans to the best business borrowers by the nation's leading banks. The prime rate fluctuates with changing supply and demand relationships for short-term funds.[7] Banks typically determine the rate charged on loans to various borrowers by adding some type of risk premium to the prime rate to adjust it for the borrower's "riskiness." This riskiness is a composite of the perceived business and financial riskiness of the borrower. The premium may be anything from 0 percent to 4 or more percent, although most unsecured short-term notes carry premiums of less than 2 percent. In general, commercial banks do not make short-term unsecured loans to businesses that are believed to be questionable risks.

Lines of credit

A *line of credit* is an agreement between a commercial bank and a business firm that states the amount of unsecured short-term borrowing the bank will make available to the borrower. A line of credit agreement is typically made for a period of one year and often places certain constraints on the borrower. A line of credit agreement is *not a guaranteed loan*, but indicates that if the bank has sufficient funds available it will allow the borrower to owe it up to a certain amount of money. The major attraction of a line of credit from the bank's point of view is that it eliminates the need to examine the credit-worthiness of a customer each time it borrows money.

In order to obtain a line of credit, a borrower must apply for it. The application may require the borrower to submit such documents as its cash budget, its pro forma income statement, its pro forma balance sheet, and its recent financial statements. The bank will review these statements in order to determine if the firm needs the line of credit it is requesting and, if so, whether it will be able to repay the funds it seeks an option to borrow. If the bank finds the customer acceptable, the line of credit will be extended. A few characteristics of lines of credit require further explanation, which follows.

Interest rates. The interest charge on a line of credit is normally stated as the *prime rate plus x percent*. A line-of-credit agreement is normally for a one-year period, and it is quite likely that the prime rate will change during this period. In order to protect itself, therefore, the bank generally ties the interest charge on a line of credit to the prime rate. Then, if the prime

---

[7]The prime rate typically ranges from 6 to 8 percent, although in the tight money period from 1973 to 1975 it was generally above 8 percent. In mid-1974, it reached a record high of 12 percent. Currently (November 1978), prime is approaching 11 percent.

rate changes, the interest rate charged on new borrowing will automatically change.[8] The amount in excess of the prime interest rate a borrower is charged depends on its credit-worthiness. The more credit-worthy the borrower, the lower the interest differential, and vice versa.

EXAMPLE

The Raine Company is negotiating a line of credit with the First National Bank. After evaluating the Raine Company's financial statements, the bank sets an interest rate for the line of credit that is 2 percent more than the prime rate. The prime rate is currently 7½ percent, so the Raine Company will have to pay 9½ percent for current borrowing. If the prime rate drops to 7 percent in the future, the interest charge on Raine's borrowing will drop to 9 percent. As the prime rate fluctuates, so will the interest rate on the Raine Company's line of credit. ●

Interest rate computations. Once the rate of interest charged a given customer has been established, the method of computing interest should be determined. Interest can be paid when a loan matures or in advance. If interest is paid when a loan matures, the actual rate of interest paid (i.e., the *effective rate of interest*) is equal to the stated interest rate. The effective rate of interest is found by dividing the dollar interest paid by the amount of loan proceeds available to the borrower. When interest is paid in advance, it is deducted from the loan so that the borrower actually receives less money than it requested. Paying interest in advance therefore raises the effective interest rate above the stated rate.

EXAMPLE

The Bressler Company wants to borrow $10,000 at 8 percent for one year. If the interest on the loan is paid at maturity, the firm will pay $800 (.08 · $10,000) for the use of the $10,000 for the year. The effective rate of interest will therefore be

$$\frac{\$800}{\$10,000} = 8.00 \text{ percent}$$

If the money is borrowed at the same rate but interest is paid in advance, the firm will still pay $800 in interest, but it will receive only $9200 ($10,000 − $800). The effective rate of interest in this case is

$$\frac{\$800}{\$9200} = 8.70 \text{ percent}$$

Paying interest in advance thus makes the effective interest rate greater than the stated rate. Loans on which interest is paid in advance are often called *discount loans*. Most commercial bank loans to business require the interest payment at maturity. ●

---

[8]Many banks now not only adjust the interest rate charged on *new borrowing*, but they also adjust the rate charged against *outstanding loans* for changes in the prime rate. In these situations, the borrower is not assured that the rate of interest at the time of borrowing will remain fixed over the maturity of the note; if the prime rate changes, so will the rate of interest charged over the remaining life of the note.

TABLE 11.4 The Holcomb
Company's borrowing against its line of credit

Month	Transaction Borrow	Transaction Repay	Loan balance
January	$ 200,000	0	$200,000
February	$ 600,000	0	$800,000
March	0	$ 200,000	$600,000
April	0	$ 100,000	$500,000
May	$ 400,000	0	$900,000
June	0	$ 900,000	0
Totals	$1,200,000	$1,200,000	

The amount of the line. The amount of a line of credit is *the maximum amount the firm can owe the bank* at any point in time. Technically, it is possible for a firm to *borrow* more than the amount of its line of credit, but at no time can the *loan balance* exceed the line of credit.

EXAMPLE

The Holcomb Company has a line of credit of $1 million with its bank. The borrowing against this line of credit during the first six months of the year, along with cumulative borrowing, is given in Table 11.4. Although Holcomb's loan balance never exceeded its $1 million line of credit, it borrowed a total of $1.2 million during the six-month period.[9] ●

Restrictive provisions. A bank normally includes certain restrictions as part of a line-of-credit agreement. The most common restrictions concern operating changes, compensating balances, and annual clean-ups.

Operating changes. In a line-of-credit agreement, a bank may retain the right to revoke the line if any major changes in the firm's operations occur. Typically, the bank will reserve the right to approve any shifts in key managerial personnel or the nature of the firm's operations before they are initiated. It does this because changes in personnel or operations may affect the future success and debt servicing ability of the firm and could alter its status as an acceptable credit risk.

Compensating balances. In order to ensure that the borrower will be a good customer, most short-term unsecured bank loans require the borrower to maintain a compensating balance in a demand deposit account (i.e., a checking account balance) equal to a certain percentage of the amount bor-

---

[9]If the average loan balance were to exceed the maximum line of credit, it would indicate that at some point during the period the firm borrowed more than the amount permitted by the line of credit. If the firm owed exactly the maximum amount allowed over the entire period, its average borrowing would equal that amount.

rowed. Compensating balances of 10 to 20 percent are normally required. A compensating balance not only forces the borrower to be a good customer of the bank, but it *may* also raise the interest cost to the borrower, thereby increasing the bank's earnings.

EXAMPLE

A company has borrowed $1 million under a line-of-credit agreement. It must pay a stated interest charge of 8 percent and maintain a compensating balance of 20 percent of the funds borrowed, or $200,000, in its checking account. Thus it actually receives the use of only $800,000. In order to use the $800,000 for a year, the firm pays $80,000 (.08 · $1,000,000). The effective interest rate on the funds is therefore 10 percent ($80,000 ÷ $800,000), 2 percent more than the stated rate of 8 percent.

If the firm normally maintains a balance of $200,000 or more in its checking account, then the effective interest cost will equal the stated interest rate of 8 percent. If the firm normally maintains a $100,000 balance in its checking account, then only an additional $100,000 will have to be tied up, leaving it with $900,000 ($1,000,000 − $100,000) of usable funds. The effective interest cost in this case would be 8.89 percent ($80,000 ÷ $900,000). A compensating balance raises the cost of borrowing *only* if it is larger than the firm's normal cash balance. ●

Annual cleanups.   In order to ensure that money lent under a line of credit agreement is actually being used to finance seasonal needs, many banks require an annual cleanup. This means that the borrower must have a loan balance of zero for a certain number of days during the year. Sometimes more than one annual cleanup is required. Forcing the borrower to carry a zero loan balance for a certain period of time ensures that the short-term loans do not turn into long-term loans. A look back at Table 11.4 shows that the Holcomb Company cleaned up its loans during the month of June.

All the characteristics of a line-of-credit agreement are negotiable to some extent. A prospective borrower should attempt to negotiate a line of credit with the most favorable interest rate, for an optimal amount of funds, and with a minimum of restrictive provisions. The lender will attempt to get a good return with maximum safety. The negotiations should produce a line of credit suitable to both parties—the borrower and the lender. Not all lines of credit extended by a given bank have the same terms.

Revolving credit agreements

A revolving credit agreement is nothing more than a *guaranteed line of credit*. It is guaranteed in the sense that the commercial bank making the arrangement guarantees the borrower that a specified amount of funds will be made available regardless of the tightness of money. It is not uncommon for a revolving credit agreement to be for a period greater than a year; two- or three-year agreements may be made.[10] The requirements for a revolving

---

[10]Many authors classify the revolving credit agreement as a form of *intermediate-term financing*, where intermediate-term financing is defined as having a maturity of one to seven years. In this text, the intermediate-term financing classification is not used; only short-term and long-term classifications are made. Since many revolving credit agreements are often for more than one year, they can be classified as a form of long-term financing; however, they are discussed in this chapter due to their similarity to the line-of-credit agreement.

credit agreement are similar to those for a line of credit. Of course, each of these agreements is somewhat negotiable; a standard arrangement does not actually exist.

Since the bank guarantees the availability of funds to the borrower, a *commitment fee* is normally charged on a revolving credit agreement. This fee applies to the average unused balance of the credit agreement.[11] It is normally about one-half percent (i.e., 0.005) of the unused portion of the funds. An example may clarify the nature of commitment fees.

EXAMPLE

The Smith Company has a $2 million revolving credit agreement with its bank. Its average borrowing under the agreement for the past year was $1.5 million. The bank charges a commitment fee of ½ percent. Since the average unused portion of the committed funds was $500,000 ($2 million − $1.5 million), the commitment fee for the year was $2500 (.005 · $500,000). Smith, of course, also had to pay interest on the actual $1.5 million borrowed under the agreement. Although more expensive than a line of credit, a revolving credit agreement can be less risky from the borrower's viewpoint since the availability of funds is guaranteed by the bank. •

NONBANK SOURCES OF UNSECURED SHORT-TERM FINANCING

The three most common nonbank sources of negotiated short-term unsecured loans are the sale of commercial paper, customer advances, and private loans. All these sources are not available to every business firm. The availability of these forms of financing depends largely on the nature, size, and operating environment of the firm.

Commercial paper

Commercial paper consists of short-term, unsecured promissory notes issued by firms having a high credit standing. Generally, only quite large firms of unquestionable financial soundness are able to issue commercial paper. Most commercial paper has maturities ranging from three days to nine months. Although there is no set denomination, most commercial paper is issued in multiples of $100,000 or more. A large portion of the commercial paper issued today is issued by finance companies; manufacturing firms account for a smaller portion of this type of financing.

As was indicated in Chapter 8, business firms often purchase commercial paper, which they hold as marketable securities to provide a reserve of liquidity. Commercial banks, individuals, insurance companies, pension funds, and other types of financial institutions also purchase commercial paper. In each case, the motive for purchasing the paper is the need to find an interest-earning medium in which to place temporarily idle funds.

Because most purchasers of commercial paper hold it to maturity, the secondary market for commercial paper is not well developed. In order to provide investors with the liquidity they desire, the issuing firm or selling dealer will agree to repurchase the paper at a discount price prior to maturity.

---

[11]Some banks not only require payment of the commitment fee, but they also require the borrower to maintain, in addition to the compensating balance against actual borrowings, a ten or so percent compensating balance against the unused portion of the commitment.

Commercial paper is generally considered a quite safe investment, since the issuers are the most credit-worthy of the nation's corporations. However, issues of commercial paper have been known to go sour; Penn Central paper did in 1970 and as a result adversely affected the commercial paper market, causing the paper of Chrysler Corporation to temporarily go into default.

Interest on commercial paper.   The interest paid by the issuer of commercial paper is determined by the size of the discount and the length of time to maturity. Commercial paper is sold at a discount from its face value, and the actual interest earned is determined by certain calculations. These calculations can be illustrated by a simple example.

EXAMPLE
The Howell Corporation has just issued $1 million worth of commercial paper that has a 90-day maturity and sells for $980,000. At the end of 90 days the purchaser of this paper will receive $1 million for his or her $980,000 investment. The interest paid on the financing is therefore $20,000 on a principal of $980,000. This is equivalent to an annual interest rate for the Howell Corporation commercial paper of 8.16 percent [($20,000 ÷ $980,000) · (360 days ÷ 90 days)].   ●

An interesting characteristic of commercial paper is that it *normally* has a yield below the prime bank lending rate. In other words, business firms are able to raise funds through the sale of commercial paper more cheaply than by borrowing from a commercial bank. This is because many suppliers of short-term funds do not have the option of making low risk business loans at the prime rate; they can invest only in marketable securities such as treasury bills and commercial paper. Since commercial paper is an extremely safe marketable security with a higher yield than treasury bills and most other marketable securities, it is a quite attractive investment. Many commercial banks purchase commercial paper that yields less than a prime rate loan. This is generally because of certain limits on bank loans to one customer[12] and the fact that many of the smaller commercial banks do not have many opportunities to lend to business borrowers. Compared to lower-yielding treasury bills, commercial paper is quite attractive to these institutions.

Although the cost of borrowing through the sale of commercial paper is typically lower than the prime bank loan rate (except when interest rates are very high, as in the middle of 1974), one must keep in mind that interest on a bank loan is paid only on the outstanding balance. Since commercial paper, once issued, does not mature for a given period, the firm may pay interest on funds it does not actually need. A second point to recognize is that it is critical for a firm to maintain a good working relationship with its bank. Even if it is slightly more expensive to borrow from a commercial bank, it may be advisable to do so in order to establish the necessary rapport with a banker. This strategy ensures that when money is tight funds can be obtained promptly

[12]Commercial banks are legally prohibited from lending an amount greater than 10 percent of its unimpaired capital and surplus to any one borrower. This restriction is intended to protect depositors by forcing the commercial bank to spread its risk across a number of borrowers.

through the firm's commercial bank. The commercial bank should be the primary source of negotiated unsecured short-term money for the firm, and commercial paper should act as a secondary source of this type of funds.

The sale of commercial paper. Commercial paper is sold either directly to the purchaser or through middlemen known as *commercial paper houses.* For performing the marketing function, the commercial paper house receives a fee. Most commercial paper is directly placed with other corporations, life insurance companies, or pension funds. Dealers in commercial paper purchase the paper from the issuer and place it with banks and other large investors. Direct placement of commercial paper is cheaper from the issuer's viewpoint.

Customer advances

A firm may be able to obtain short-term unsecured funds through customer advances. In other words, customers may pay for all or a portion of what they intend to purchase in advance of their receipt of the goods. In many situations where a large, expensive item is being custom manufactured, the customer may be more than willing to make an advance against the merchandise to finance a portion of its cost of production. In other instances, a customer may be highly dependent on a supplier for a key component and may therefore find it to his or her advantage to assure the supplier's success by providing financing in the form of an advance. In most instances, the supplier must request the advance from the customer.

Private loans

Short-term unsecured loans may also be obtained from stockholders of the firm. Wealthy stockholders in many smaller corporations may be quite willing to lend money to the firm to get it through a period of crisis. This type of arrangement makes sense from the viewpoint of the shareholder, who has a vested interest in the survival of the firm. Another form of private loan can be obtained by temporarily foregoing commissions for salespersons. Each of these types of loans involves the extension of unsecured credit to the firm by an interested or a concerned party.

SUMMARY

This chapter has described the more common sources of unsecured short-term financing for the business firm. Spontaneous sources of short-term unsecured financing result from the firm's normal business operations. Accounts payable, which are created by open-account purchases, are the primary source of short-term funds for the business firm. The terms of trade credit extended a firm may differ with respect to the credit period, cash discount, cash discount period, and the beginning of the credit period. Each of these factors affects the firm's purchase decisions, although typically credit terms are standardized within a given industry.

Although there is no explicit cost associated with trade credit, there is

TABLE 11.5 Summary of sources of unsecured short-term financing

Type of Financing	Source
I. Spontaneous Sources	
Accounts payable	Suppliers of materials
Accruals	Employees and government
II. Bank Sources	
Notes	Commercial banks
Lines of credit	Commercial banks
Revolving credit agreements	Commercial banks
III. Nonbank Sources	
Commercial paper	Other businesses, commercial banks, individuals, insurance companies, and other financial institutions.
Customer advances	Customers having an interest in helping the firm survive.
Private loans	Interested parties such as the firm's stockholders.

an implied cost when a cash discount is offered. The cost of foregoing cash discounts affects the firm's decisions as to which suppliers to patronize as well as whether the discounts should be foregone. Policies with respect to cash discounts must be evaluated in light of the firm's ability to stretch accounts payable. Accruals, typically of wages or taxes, represent another spontaneous source of short-term funds. By accruing wages and taxes, the firm in essence delays payment for certain services. A firm should attempt to accrue as much as possible in light of certain behavioral and legal constraints.

The major source of negotiated short-term unsecured loans to business is the commercial bank. Commercial banks make primarily this type of loan. The unsecured self-liquidating bank loan may take the form of a note, a line-of-credit, or a revolving credit agreement. Each of these arrangements has its own characteristics. The rate of interest charged under each of these arrange-

Cost/Conditions	Characteristics
No explicit cost except when a cash discount is offered for early payment.	Credit extended on open account for 30 to 60 days. The largest source of short-term business financing.
Free	Result from the fact that wages (employees) and taxes (government) are paid at discrete points in time after the service has been rendered. Hard to manipulate this source of financing.
Prime plus 0% to 4% risk premium.	A single-payment note used to meet a funds shortage expected to last only a short period of time.
Prime plus 0% to 4% risk premium. Must maintain 10% to 20% compensating balance and cleanup the line.	A prearranged borrowing limit under which funds, if available, will be lent to allow the borrower to meet seasonal needs.
Prime plus 0% to 4% risk premium. Must maintain 10% to 20% compensating balance and pay a commitment fee of approximately 5% of the average unused balance.	A line of credit agreement under which the availability of funds is guaranteed. They are often two- or three-year agreements.
Slightly below the prime rate of interest.	An unsecured short-term promissory note issued only by the most financially sound companies. It may be placed directly or sold through middlemen known as commercial paper houses.
Negotiable	Customers make advance payments on all or a portion of their planned purchases.
Negotiable	Extension of credit to the firm by an interested or concerned party.

ments is tied to the prime rate of interest; the premium above the prime rate is dependent upon the risk of the borrower as perceived by the bank. The line-of-credit and revolving credit agreement normally require compensating balances. The line of credit normally has an annual clean-up feature, while the revolving credit agreement requires a commitment fee be paid on unused funds. Each of these arrangements must be negotiated between the borrower and the bank.

Nonbank sources of unsecured short-term funds include the sale of commercial paper, customer advances, and private loans. Commercial paper can be issued only by large, financially strong firms. The other alternatives may be available to any firm regardless of its size. The cost of borrowing through the sale of commercial paper is generally lower than any alternate form of negotiated short-term unsecured borrowing.

QUESTIONS

11-1 What are the two key sources of spontaneous short-term financing for the business firm? Why are these sources considered spontaneous, and how are they related to the firm's sales? Do they normally have an explicit cost?

11-2 What are "credit terms"? How are credit periods, cash discounts, cash discount periods, and the beginning of a credit period defined?

11-3 What is a net period? What sort of payment is it concerned with?

11-4 What is meant by seasonal dating? Why is this sometimes considered advantageous to both the vendor and the purchaser of merchandise?

11-5 What are some of the labels used to designate the beginning of a credit period?

11-6 What costs are associated with the extension and use of trade credit? Who pays the cost of trade credit—the vendor or the purchaser? How?

11-7 Is there a cost associated with taking a cash discount? Is there any cost associated with foregoing a cash discount? Why or why not?

11-8 How is the decision whether to take a cash discount affected by the firm's opportunity cost of short-term funds?

11-9 What are accruals? What items are most commonly accrued by the firm? How attractive are accruals as a source of financing to the firm?

11-10 What factors must the firm consider in evaluating the use of accruals to obtain interest-free financing?

11-11 What is the primary source of *negotiated* short-term loans to business? When are loans considered short-term self-liquidating loans?

11-12 What are the basic terms and characteristics of a note? How is the prime interest rate relevant to the cost of borrowing via notes?

11-13 What are line of credit agreements? How does a firm obtain a line of credit? What documents are useful to a banker evaluating an application for a line of credit?

11-14 What is the primary difference between the cost of interest paid at maturity and interest paid in advance?

11-15 What restrictive provisions are commonly included in a line of credit agreement? What are the basic motives for each of these restrictions? Is there any opportunity to negotiate these terms? Why or why not?

11-16 What is meant by a revolving credit agreement? How does this arrangement differ from the line of credit agreement? What is a commitment fee?

11-17 How is commercial paper used for raising short-term funds? Who can issue commercial paper? Who buys commercial paper? How is it sold?

11-18 Why is the cost of financing with commercial paper quite often less than the prime lending rate? Why don't firms raise all their short-term funds through the sale of commercial paper?

PROBLEMS

11-1 Determine when a firm must make payment for purchases made on the 25th day of November under each of the following credit terms.
  a Net 30
  b Net 30 EOM
  c Net 45 MOM
  d COD
  e CBD

11-2 Determine the cost of foregoing discounts under each of the following terms of sale.
  a 2/10 net 30
  b 1/10 net 30

    c 2/10 net 45
    d 3/10 net 45
    e 1/10 net 60
    f 3/10 net 30
    g 4/10 net 180

11-3 Ann Daniels works in accounts payable for Penrod Industries. She has attempted to convince her boss to take advantage of the 3/10 net 45 discounts most suppliers offer, but her boss argues that the 3-percent discount is less costly than a short-term loan at 8 percent. Prove that either Ann or her boss is incorrect.

11-4 Upon accepting the position of chief executive officer and chairman of American Cash Register, Robert Adamson changed the firm's weekly payday from Monday afternoon to the following Friday afternoon. The firm's weekly payroll was $10,000,000, and the cost of short-term funds was 9 percent. If the effect of this change was to delay check clearing by one week, what annual savings, if any, were realized here? Assume a 50-week year for computational purposes.

11-5 Stick Enterprises has obtained a 90-day bank loan at an annual interest rate of 12 percent. If the loan is for $10,000, how much interest (in dollars) will the firm pay?

11-6 Wisconsin Can wishes to establish a prearranged borrowing agreement with its local commercial bank. The banks' terms for a line of credit are 3 percent over the prime rate, and the borrowing must be reduced to zero for a 30-day period. For an equivalent revolving credit account, the rate is 2.80 percent over prime with a commitment fee of .5 percent on the average unused balance. With both loans, the compensating balance is 20 percent. The prime rate is currently 8 percent.
    a What is the effective interest cost of the line of credit?
    b What is the effective cost of the revolving credit account if, on the average, the amount of borrowing is one-half the guaranteed amount?
    c Under what conditions does the revolving credit account have a lower/higher effective interest rate than the line of credit?
    d If the firm does expect to borrow an average of half the prearranged funds, which arrangement would you recommend for the borrower? Explain why.

11-7 Commercial paper is usually sold at a discount. GMAT has just sold an issue of 90-day commercial paper with a face value of $1,000,000. The firm has received $985,222.
    a What effective *annual* rate will the firm pay for financing with commercial paper?
    b If a brokerage fee of $9612 has been charged by an investment banker for selling the issue, what effective interest charge will the firm pay?

11-8 A financial institution lends a firm $10,000 for one year at 10 percent on a discounted basis and requires compensating balances of 20 percent of the face value of the loan. Determine the effective annual interest rate associated with this loan.

SELECTED REFERENCES

Agemian, C. A., "Maintaining an Effective Bank Relationship," *Financial Executive* 32 (January 1964), pp. 24–28.

Baxter, Nevins D., *The Commerical Paper Market* (Princeton, N.J.: Princeton University Press, 1964).

Brosky, John J., *The Implicit Cost of Trade Credit and Theory of Optimal Terms of Sale* (New York: Credit Research Foundation, 1969).

Campbell, Tim S., "A Model of the Market for Lines of Credit," *Journal of Finance 33* (March 1978), pp. 231–244.

Crane, Dwight B., and William L. White, "Who Benefits from a Floating Prime Rate?" *Harvard Business Review 50* (January-February 1972), pp. 121–129.

Gordon, R. L., "Talking Business with a Banker," *Financial Executive 35* (February 1967).

Hayes, Douglas A., *Bank Lending Policies: Domestic and International* (Ann Arbor: University of Michigan, 1971).

Harris, Duane G., "Some Evidence on Differential Lending Practices at Commercial Banks," *Journal of Finance 28* (December 1973), pp. 1303–1311.

Herbst, Anthony F., "A Factor Analysis Approach to Determining the Relative Endogeneity of Trade Credit," *Journal of Finance, 29* (September 1974), pp. 1087–1103.

Keehn, Richard H., "A Note on the Cost of Trade Credit and the Discriminatory Effects of Monetary Policy," *Journal of Finance 29* (December 1974), pp. 1581–1582.

Laffer, Arthur B., "Trade Credit and the Money Market," *Journal of Political Economy 78* (March-April 1970).

Nadler, Paul S., "Compensating Balances and the Prime at Twilight," *Harvard Business Review 50* (January-February 1972), pp. 112–120.

Robichek, Alexander A., and Stewart C. Myers, *Optimal Financing Decisions* (Englewood Cliffs, N.J.: Prentice-Hall, 1965), chap. 7.

——, Teichroew, and J. M. Jones, "Optimal Short-Term Financing Decisions," *Management Science 23* (September 1965), pp. 1–36.

Schwartz, Robert A., "An Economic Analysis of Trade Credit," *Journal of Financial and Quantitative Analysis 9* (September 1974), pp. 643–658.

Stancill, James McN., *The Management of Working Capital* (Scranton, Pa.: Intext, 1971), chap. 6.

Stone, Bernell K., "Allocating Credit Lines, Planned Borrowing, and Tangible Services over a Company's Banking System," *Financial Management 4* (Summer 1975), pp. 65–78.

——, "The Cost of Bank Loans," *Journal of Financial and Quantitative Analysis 7* (December 1972), pp. 2077–2086.

CHAPTER 12
Sources of secured short-term financing

A firm normally has available only a limited amount of unsecured short-term financing. Beyond that point, some type of security is required in order to obtain additional funds. In other words, as a firm incurs greater and greater amounts of unsecured short-term financing, a threshold level is reached beyond which suppliers of short-term funds believe the firm is too risky to be extended additional unsecured credit. This threshold level is closely related to the degree of operating and financial risk present in the firm. Many firms are unable to obtain any unsecured short-term money, and secured financing is therefore their only source of short-term funds. These firms are typically small, growing firms that have yet to establish themselves as financially mature enough to receive unsecured short-term loans.

A firm should always attempt to obtain all the unsecured short-term financing it can before seeking any secured short-term loans. This is important, since unsecured short-term borrowing is normally cheaper than a secured short-term loan. It is also important that the firm use short-term financing, unsecured or secured, to finance seasonal needs for increased accounts receivables or inventories. The importance of this financing strategy to the firm's overall profitability-risk position was emphasized in the overview of working capital management in Chapter 7. Since short-term funds are typically less expensive than long-term funds, consideration of their use for financing seasonal needs, even on a secured basis, is recommended.

This chapter has four basic sections. The first section discusses briefly the nature, characteristics, and suppliers of secured short-term loans to business. The second section discusses how accounts receivable may be used to obtain short-term funds. Both the use of accounts receivable as collateral for a short-term loan and the outright sale—or *factoring*—of accounts receivable are discussed in this section. The third section presents a discussion of the various methods of using inventories as collateral for short-term loans. The final section describes a few other methods of securing short-term loans. A summary table depicting the key information on each of the sources of secured short-term financing is included as Table 12.2, at the end of the chapter.

CHARACTERISTICS OF SECURED SHORT-TERM LOANS

A *secured loan* is a loan for which the lender requires *collateral*.[1] The collateral most commonly takes the form of a physical asset such as accounts receivable or inventory. The lender obtains a security interest in the collateral through the execution of a contract (security agreement) between it and the borrower. The security agreement indicates the collateral held against the loan. A copy of the security agreement is filed in a public office within the state—typically a state or county office. Filing the security agreement provides subsequent lenders with information as to what assets of a prospective borrower are free to be used as collateral. The filing requirement protects the lender by legally establishing his or her security interest.

The terms of the loan against which the security is held are attached to or part of the security agreement. They specify the conditions required for the security interest to be removed, along with the interest rate on the loan, repayment dates, and other loan provisions. Although many people argue that holding collateral as security reduces the risk of the loan, lenders do not usually view loans in this way. Lenders recognize that by having an interest in collateral they can reduce losses in the instance the borrower defaults, but as far as changing the risk that the borrower will default goes, the presence of collateral has no impact. The reason that lenders require collateral is that they feel that the firm is too risky and therefore want to be able to recover some portion of the loan proceeds in the event that default occurs. They do not want to have to administer and liquidate collateral; the lender would like to be repaid as scheduled. In general, they would prefer to make less risky loans at lower rates of interest than to be in a position in which they may have to liquidate collateral.

Due to the additional paperwork and higher degree of risk associated with secured loans, the costs and other factors related to secured short-term loans are generally not as favorable as those of unsecured short-term borrowing. Depending on the exact security arrangement, the borrower may or may not retain control of the loan collateral.

The remainder of this section presents a brief discussion of the common types of security interests, the nature of acceptable collateral for secured short-term loans, and the types of institutions normally extending secured short-term loans to business firms. Each of these topics is discussed in light of the constraints placed on the short-term secured borrower.

Types of security interests

Three basic types of security interest are normally used in secured short-term loans to business borrowers. They are the floating lien, the trust receipt, and the warehouse receipt loan. Each of these arrangements is briefly described below.

---

[1]The terms *security* and *collateral* are used interchangeably to refer to the items used by a borrower to back up a loan. Loan security or collateral may be any assets against which a lender, as a result of making a loan, has a legal claim that is exercisable if the borrower defaults on some provision of the loan. If the borrower defaults, the lender can sell the security or collateral in order to satisfy his claim against the borrower. Some of the more technical aspects of loan defaults are presented in Chapter 26.

Floating liens. A floating lien represents a general claim on a group of assets.[2] In the case of inventory, a floating lien provides the lender with collateral consisting of whatever items are in inventory at a given point in time. Specific items or accounts are not identified by serial number or debtor; rather, the lender has a claim on all items in the collateral grouping specified. Floating liens are useful when the collateral is constantly turning over and the dollar value of the average item of collateral is rather low. In this situation, the cost of specifically identifying and keeping track of each item of collateral would be prohibitive.

From the lender's standpoint, the floating lien is ideal for a firm that maintains, on the average, a fairly constant level of collateral. The collateral under the floating lien remains in the hands of the borrower, who also retains title to it. Since floating liens are so general, lenders typically will not lend heavily against them. Another reason for the small amount lent against this type of collateral is the expense and inconvenience associated with the liquidation of the collateral if the borrower defaults. Nevertheless, the lender *has* a definite legal claim on all items covered by a lien; it is not a casual arrangement.

Trust receipts. A *trust receipt loan* is a loan made against specific collateral that remains in the possession of the borrower. This type of arrangement can be made with respect to any asset, such as inventory or accounts receivable. A trust receipt loan backed by inventory is commonly referred to as *floor planning.* The lender, in this arrangement, takes a lien on the specific assets used as collateral. These assets are specifically identified in the security agreement either by serial numbers or by account names. The borrower normally retains title to or possession of the collateral.

The lender, in this arrangement, places *trust* in the borrower's integrity, and expects the borrower to provide notification immediately upon liquidation of any of the collateral. The borrower, upon the sale of collateral, must remit a certain amount of the proceeds to the lender or give additional collateral for the loan. If the borrower were to collect cash for the collateral and not remit funds to the lender, the lender would be holding *bogus collateral.* In other words, the loan would not actually have the stated collateral backing. In order to police trust receipt loans, the lender normally makes periodic checks on the borrower, taking an inventory of the collateral. If certain items of collateral cannot be found, the borrower is said to have broken the trust and can be considered in default on the loan.

Trust receipt loans are typically made when a borrower has collateral that can be easily identified and each item has a reasonably large dollar value. This situation makes the trust receipt loan feasible; otherwise, a floating lien may have to be used. Since specific collateral can be more easily identified than a general claim (i.e., a floating lien), lenders are apt to lend a larger amount against a given amount of collateral under a trust receipt than under

---

[2]The term "lien" is a legal term meaning a claim on the property of another, such as a security interest against the payment of a legal debt. A lien must be filed by the lender against the collateral in a legal office such as a county or state court.

a floating lien arrangement. The most important consideration from the point of view of the lender is whether the borrower is trustworthy. If the borrower is, and sufficient collateral exists, the loan should be granted; otherwise, alternate lending arrangements might be considered.

Warehouse receipt loans. The *warehouse receipt loan* is typically a loan secured with inventory. This type of loan allows the lender to maintain control over the collateral. The borrower cannot sell any of the collateral without the lender's written permission. Typically, permission to sell an item held as collateral against this type of loan is granted only after the loan has been partially or fully repaid. The warehouse receipt loan provides the lender with the best position with respect to collateral—he has direct control over its disposition. This type of loan involves greater clerical costs than the floating lien; the increased cost is carried by the borrower. A lender is more likely to lend a larger amount against inventory under a warehouse receipt arrangement than under the other forms of security agreements mentioned earlier. Warehouse receipt loans will be discussed in more detail in the discussion of inventory as collateral.

What constitutes acceptable collateral?

A number of factors must be highlighted with respect to the characteristics desirable in collateral for secured short-term loans. These factors include the life of the collateral, the liquidity of collateral, the percentage advance, and the interest rate and fees charged.

The life of the collateral. Lenders of secured short-term funds prefer collateral that has a life closely related to the term of the loan. This requirement assures the lender that the security is sufficiently liquid to satisfy the loan in the event of a default. By tying the life of the collateral closely to the life of the loan, the lender secures reasonable protection. For short-term loans, the likely candidates as collateral are a firm's short-term or current assets. Current assets—accounts receivable, inventories, and marketable securities—are generally the most desirable collateral for short-term loans since they are usually more liquid than fixed assets. The use of fixed assets is better for long-term loans since accounts receivable, inventories, and marketable securities are turned over numerous times in the long run.

The strategy of securing short-term loans with current assets and long-term loans with fixed assets is similar to the aggressive strategy presented in Chapter 7, which suggested financing seasonal needs (primarily current assets) with short-term funds and financing permanent needs (primarily fixed assets) with long-term funds. By the same token, it is normally suggested that short-term loans be secured with current assets and long-term loans be secured with fixed assets. By closely aligning the maturity (i.e., turnover) of the collateral with the loan maturity, the lender is assured of protection throughout the life of the loan and is somewhat assured that his or her funds can be readily recovered through liquidation of the collateral in the event that the borrower defaults on the loan.

The liquidity of the collateral. Another important consideration for the lender in evaluating possible collateral is its liquidity. Although current assets are the most common candidate as collateral for short-term loans, not all current assets are equally desirable. The desirability of various current assets is determined largely by the borrower's line of business. It is the line of business of a firm that largely determines the nature of its accounts receivable and inventories, which are the primary sources of short-term loan collateral. From our previous discussions of ratio analysis, we know that even within a given industry the liquidities of current assets often differ.

The short-term lender of secured funds is more apt than not to find only liquid current assets acceptable as collateral. Accounts receivable or inventories having average ages of 180 days are questionable candidates as security for a 90-day note. The lender often selects only certain current assets as acceptable collateral. Generally, the less acceptable collateral a firm has in the form of current assets, the less short-term money the firm is able to borrow on a secured basis.

Percentage advances. Having determined the acceptable collateral of a given firm, the lender must determine what amount he or she is willing to lend against the book value of this collateral. Typically, the lender determines the desirable *percentage advance* to make against certain collateral. This percentage advance is normally between 30 and 90 percent of the book value of collateral; it varies not only according to the type of collateral, but also according to the type of security interest being taken.

Percentage advances are low for floating liens, and higher for trust receipt and warehouse receipt loans. They are low if the collateral is not very liquid and larger if the collateral is highly liquid. By accepting only a portion of the firm's current assets as collateral, the lender can isolate the faster-turning items, against which to make larger percentage advances. By selecting only acceptable assets and making loans equal to only certain percentages of the collateral's value, the lender adjusts the riskiness of the loan to an acceptable level. The lender can also set the interest rate at a level that provides adequate compensation for the probable risk attached to the loan.

Interest rate and fees. The interest rate charged on secured short-term loans is typically *higher* than the interest rate on unsecured short-term loans. This may be surprising, but it stems from the fact that the primary suppliers of unsecured short-term loans are commercial banks who make loans only to the better business borrowers. If a customer is not a good enough credit risk to warrant an unsecured loan, commercial banks generally prefer to make unsecured loans to other acceptable borrowers than to make a secured loan. Although commercial banks and other institutions do make secured short-term loans, they do not normally look on these loans as being less risky than unsecured loans and therefore require higher interest rates on these loans.

The general rationale for securing a loan is to have a specific claim on assets in case the firm defaults or becomes bankrupt. A lender does not make a secured loan if he or she expects to have to liquidate the collateral; the lender requires the collateral only to reduce losses in the event the borrower defaults. Negotiating and administering secured loans is more troublesome for the lender than negotiating and administering unsecured loans; therefore, the lender normally requires added compensation in the form of a service charge or a higher interest rate, or both. The higher cost of secured as opposed to unsecured borrowing can therefore be attributed to the greater risks of default and the increased loan administration costs.

Institutions extending secured short-term loans

The primary sources of secured short-term loans to business are commercial banks and commercial finance companies. Both of these institutions deal in short-term loans secured by accounts receivable, inventory, and marketable securities. Since the reader is probably familiar with commercial banks, the primary emphasis in this section will be on the commercial finance company.

Commercial banks. As we have seen, although the primary type of loan made by commercial banks to businesses is the short-term unsecured loan, many commercial banks also grant short-term secured loans to businesses. Typically, only the large commercial banks extend these secured loans, due to their ability to achieve certain economies in the administration of these loans. By making a number of loans of this type, the larger banks are able to justify the employment of specialists for analyzing, administering, and policing them. Also, small banks are more constrained with respect to the maximum size loan they can extend to a single borrower.[3]

Commercial finance companies. A *commercial finance company* is a financial institution without a bank charter that makes loans secured with accounts receivable, inventories, or chattel mortgages on fixed assets. Commercial finance companies are also known to finance the installment purchase of commercial and industrial equipment by business firms. Commercial finance companies make only secured loans to business; some of the loans are short-term, while others are long-term arrangements. The leading commercial finance companies include the Commercial Investors Trust Financial Corporation (CIT Financial) and Transamerica Financial Corporation. These firms offer the same basic types of short-term secured financing as commercial banks. The primary type of loan extended by the commercial finance company is the accounts receivable loan, although loans against inventory and other collateral are not uncommon.

Commercial finance companies do not make unsecured business loans, nor are they permitted to hold demand deposits. Thus borrowers in need of short-term financing rely primarily on their commercial bank. Only when

---

[3]A commercial bank is legally prohibited from lending an amount greater than 10 percent of its unimpaired capital and surplus to any one borrower. This restriction is intended to protect depositors by ensuring that the commercial bank spreads its risk across a number of borrowers.

their unsecured and secured short-term borrowing power from the commercial bank is exhausted will they turn to the commercial finance company for additional secured borrowing. Because the commercial finance company typically ends up with higher-risk borrowers, its interest charges on secured short-term loans are generaly higher than the charges levied by commercial banks. Another reason for the slightly higher charges of commercial finance companies is the fact that a portion of their financing is often obtained through commercial bank borrowing at wholesale rates. Since commercial banks are limited with respect to the amount they can lend to a single customer, it is not unusual for a commercial bank to refer certain borrowers to a commercial finance company. It is important to recognize that the commercial finance company actively participates in the market for secured short-term business loans.

THE USE OF ACCOUNTS RECEIVABLE AS COLLATERAL

Two means of obtaining short-term financing with accounts receivable are commonly used by business firms—pledging accounts receivable and factoring accounts receivable. Actually, only a pledge of accounts receivable creates a secured short-term loan; factoring really entails the *sale* of accounts receivable at a discount. Although factoring is not actually a form of secured short-term borrowing, it is discussed in this section since it does involve the use of accounts receivable to obtain needed short-term funds.

Pledging accounts receivable

A pledge or an assignment of accounts receivable is often used to secure a short-term loan. Because accounts receivable are normally quite liquid, they are an attractive form of short-term loan collateral. Both commercial banks and commercial finance companies extend loans against pledges of accounts receivable.

Types of pledges. Accounts receivable are normally pledged on a *selective basis*. The prospective lender analyzes the past payment records of the firm's accounts to determine which accounts represent acceptable loan collateral. A lender will generally advance money only against those accounts determined to be acceptable credit risks. A lender will not extend a loan if he thinks that he will have to liquidate the collateral; the lender can minimize this risk by being selective with respect to those accounts accepted as collateral. A lender is likely to advance as much as 90 percent of the collateral's value against a pledge of selected accounts.

A second method of pledging accounts receivable is to take a lien on all the firm's accounts receivable. This type of *floating lien* arrangement is normally used when a firm has many accounts that, on the average, have only a small dollar value. In this case, the cost of evaluating each account separately in order to determine its acceptability would not be warranted. Instead, the lender places a lien on all the firm's accounts receivable. This arrangement eliminates the need to specifically identify each account. The lender in this situation keeps track of the total dollar amount of pledged accounts. Due to the difficulty of specifically identifying each item of collateral and therefore of policing this arrangement, the percentage advanced against a pledge of accounts receivable in general (a floating lien) is normally less than 50 percent of the book value of the accounts. This situation is more risky from the lender's viewpoint, since the borrower has opportunities to misrepresent accounts.

The pledging process.   The process of pledging accounts receivable will be described with respect to pledging selected accounts, since this situation provides more scope for in-depth analysis. The four major steps in the pledging process are the selection of acceptable accounts, the adjustment of acceptable accounts, the determination of the advance, and the notification of and the collection of pledged accounts.

The selection of acceptable accounts.   When a business firm aproaches a prospective secured lender requesting a loan against accounts receivable, the lender will first evaluate the firm's accounts receivable in order to determine their desirability as collateral. One consideration is whether the accounts are of sufficient size to warrant consideration as specific collateral. If the firm has many small accounts, the lender may extend only a floating lien.

Assuming that the firm has accounts of sufficient size to warrant consideration as specific collateral, the lender will investigate the firm's accounts receivable in order to determine which accounts are acceptable as collateral for a loan. The investigation will involve analyzing the past payment patterns of the various credit customers. The accounts receivable from those customers who appear to be good credit risks will be accepted as collateral. The lender may verify the existence and amount of the accounts by requiring a copy of the invoices. A list of the acceptable accounts, along with the billing dates and amounts, will be made by the lender. Typically a mark of some sort will be placed next to each pledged account in the borrowing firm's accounts receivable ledger.

If the borrowing firm requests a loan for only a fixed amount, the lender will need to select only enough accounts to secure the funds requested. In some instances the borrower may wish the maximum loan available. In this situation the lender will evaluate all the accounts in order to determine the maximum amount of acceptable collateral.

EXAMPLE

The Second National Bank is analyzing the Crowe Company's accounts receivable ledger in order to find acceptable collateral for a pledge of accounts receivable. Each of Crowe's accounts receivable, along with its age and its average payment period, is given in Table 12.1. Since Crowe extends credit terms of 2/10 net 30 EOM, the bank eliminates from further consideration all accounts that are currently overdue (i.e., whose age is greater than 30 days). This immediately eliminates the accounts of customers C, E, and I.

The second step in the bank's evaluation process is to analyze the historical payment patterns of the customers. After calculating the average payment period for each customer (given in the last column of Table 12.1), the Second National Bank

TABLE 12.1 The Crowe
Company's accounts receivable

Customer	Account receivable	Age[a]	Average payment period
A	$10,000	20 days	35 days
B	8,000	5 days	60 days
C	15,000	50 days	45 days
D	4,000	14 days	30 days
E	3,000	70 days	60 days
F	6,000	10 days	20 days
G	14,000	3 days	10 days
H	11,000	23 days	10 days
I	3,000	45 days	45 days

[a]Number of days since beginning of credit period.

decides to eliminate customer B, whose account, although not currently overdue, normally requires 60 days to collect. Having eliminated the accounts of customers B, C, E, and I, the bank is left with $45,000 of acceptable accounts from customers A, D, F, G, and H (who owe $10,000, $4000, $6000, $14,000, and $11,000, respectively). The Crowe Company therefore has $45,000 of acceptable accounts receivable collateral. Each account used as collateral will be marked in the Crowe Company's ledger, and a list of the payment dates and amounts will be kept by the Second National Bank. ●

The adjustment of acceptable accounts. After selecting the acceptable accounts, the lender will normally adjust the dollar value of these accounts for expected returns or allowances. If a customer whose account has been pledged returns merchandise or receives some type of allowance, such as a cash discount for early payment, the amount of the collateral is automatically reduced. For protection from such occurrences, the lender will normally reduce the value of the acceptable collateral by a fixed percentage.

EXAMPLE
The $45,000 of acceptable accounts receivable selected by the Second National Bank from the Crowe Company's books must be adjusted for returns and allowances. The bank decides, after evaluating the company's accounts, that a 5-percent adjustment is appropriate. After this adjustment, the Crowe Company has acceptable collateral of $42,750 [i.e., $45,000 · (1 − .05)]. ●

The determination of the advance. Once the lender has determined the acceptable accounts and made adjustments for returns and allowances, the percentage to be advanced against the collateral must be determined based on the lender's overall evaluation of the quality of the acceptable receivables and the expected cost of their liquidation. For selected accounts receivable, this percentage will range between 50 and 90 percent. The more confident the lender is about the quality of the accounts, the larger the percentage advance that will normally be extended. However, since the lender in the event of default will have to absorb certain paperwork costs and the additional cost of liquidating the pledged accounts, he will rarely advance more than 90 percent of the value of accounts.

EXAMPLE

After a reexamination of the Crowe Company's acceptable accounts receivable *and* general operations, the Second National Bank decides to advance 85 percent of the value of the adjusted acceptable collateral. This means that the bank will lend the company $36,337.50 [i.e., $42,750 · .85] ●

Notification and collection. Pledges of accounts receivable are normally made on a *non-notification* basis. This means that the customer whose account has been pledged is not notified of this action. Instead, the customer continues to remit payments to the firm. If a pledge of accounts receivable is made on a *notification* basis, the customer is notified to remit payments directly to the lender. Non-notification arrangements are preferred by borrowers since their customers may construe the fact that their accounts have been pledged to mean that the firm is in financial difficulty. A notification arrangement is safer from the lender's viewpoint, but the lender is normally willing to trust the borrower and lend on a non-notification basis.

The non-notification arrangement is a type of trust receipt loan, since the borrower still collects the pledged account receivable. In this situation, the borrower is required to remit payments received on pledged accounts to the lender. In essence, the lender *trusts* that the borrower will remit payments on pledged accounts as they are received. If the borrower receives payment and does not remit it to the lender, the trust is broken and part of the collateral held by the lender becomes nonexistent. In order to police a trust arrangement, the lender will frequently check to see if the customers whose accounts have been pledged and are currently listed as uncollected have actually paid any of these accounts. A broken trust arrangement can seriously damage the borrower's future borrowing prospects. As the lender receives payments of accounts, the loan principal is reduced by the amount collected.

The cost of pledges of accounts receivable. The stated cost of a pledge of accounts receivable is normally 2 to 5 percent above the prime rate. It may be even higher on pledges from commercial finance companies. In addition to the stated interest rate, a service charge of up to 3 percent may be levied. Although the interest payment is expected to compensate the lender for loaning the money, the service charge is needed to cover the administrative costs incurred by the lender. These administrative costs result from the need to inspect accounts, keep records of pledged accounts, make entries as collections of accounts are received, and generally police the lending arrangement. The stated cost of a pledge of accounts receivable is normally 1 to 3 percent higher than the cost of an unsecured bank loan.

The effective cost of accounts receivable pledges may not be much greater than the cost of unsecured financing. With unsecured financing, the borrower pays interest on the full amount borrowed for the term of the loan; whereas when accounts receivable are pledged as collateral, the loan principal on which interest is calculated is reduced as accounts are collected. It is possible that with an unsecured note the borrower will be paying interest on funds not actually needed; under a pledge, interest is paid only on the amount needed (i.e., the declining loan balance). In comparing the advantages of unsecured and secured notes, this point is worthy of consideration. Although the stated interest rate is higher for a pledge of accounts receivable than with an unsecured loan, the principal is quite likely to be lower, since the loan balance decreases as payment is received.

Pledges as a continuous source of financing.   Quite often, pledging accounts receivable is used as a continuous source of financing by the firm. As accounts are collected, new accounts acceptable to the lender are substituted, allowing the firm to maintain a relatively constant loan balance with the lender. If the lender finds all the firm's accounts receivable acceptable and continuously takes them as collateral, he ends up financing all the firm's accounts receivable. The firm may find this arrangement quite beneficial from a cost standpoint.

Once the amount of acceptable accounts, the percentage advance (i.e., the loan principal), the interest cost, and other factors have been agreed upon, a note specifying the terms of the pledge is drawn up and signed by both parties. At the same time, a lien is filed on the pledged accounts. A statement of the lien is normally attached to the note. As remittances are received against pledged accounts, the lender records these receipts, thereby reducing both the amount of collateral and the amount of loan principal.

Factoring accounts receivable

Factoring accounts receivable involves the outright sale of accounts receivable to a factor or other financial institution.[4] Although the factor is the primary factoring institution, some commercial banks and commercial finance companies also factor accounts receivable. Factoring accounts receivable does not actually represent a short-term loan, but it is similar to borrowing with accounts receivable as collateral.

The factor.   A *factor* is a financial institution that purchases accounts receivable from business firms. The factor generally accepts all the credit risks associated with the accounts receivable it purchases. Factoring initially began in the textile industry as a result of the long credit period required by

---

[4]The use of bank cards such as Master Charge and VISA by consumers has some similarity to factoring, since the vendor accepting the card is reimbursed at a discount for purchases made using the card. The difference between factoring and bank cards is that the bank cards are nothing more than a line of credit extended by the bank card company, which charges the vendors a fee for accepting the cards. In factoring, the factor does not analyze credit until after the sale has been made; in most cases the initial credit decision is the responsibility of the vendor—not the factor who purchases the account.

purchasers of textiles.[5] There are 15 to 20 firms currently operating in the United States that deal solely in factoring accounts receivable. A factor raises operating funds through the sale of debt and equity capital. Regardless of whether a factor, a commercial bank, or a commercial finance company factors accounts receivable, factoring agreements are normally quite similar.

The factoring agreement.   A factoring agreement is normally drawn up stating the exact conditions, charges, and procedures for factoring.Typically, firms that factor accounts do so on a continuing basis, selling all their accounts receivable to their factor. The factoring agreement covers selection procedures, notification, nonrecourse, factor's reserves, payment dates, advances and surpluses, and factoring costs.

Selection procedures.   A factor, like a lender against a pledge of accounts receivable, chooses accounts for purchase, selecting only those accounts that appear to be acceptable credit risks. Where factoring is to be on a continuing basis, the factor will actually make the firm's credit decisions, since this will guarantee the acceptability of accounts. This situation is quite common in the textile and clothing manufacturing industries.

Notification.   Factoring is normally done on a notification basis. Since the factor is purchasing the accounts, it seems only reasonable that payments be made directly to him. The customers whose accounts have been factored may not be directly advised that their accounts have been factored; they may simply be asked to make checks payable to the factor or to send them to a new address. Regardless of how the fact that an account has been factored is camouflaged, the factor normally receives payment directly from the customer. The degree of secrecy with respect to the arrangement depends largely on the firm's expectations with respect to how its customers may react to the fact that their accounts have been factored. The degree of secrecy required is incorporated in the factoring agreement.

Nonrecourse.   Most sales of accounts receivable to a factor are made on a *nonrecourse* basis. This means that the factor agrees to accept all credit risks; if purchased accounts turn out to be uncollectible, the factor must absorb the loss. Only on rare occasions are factoring agreements made *with recourse*. Pledges of accounts receivable can be likened to a recourse arrangement since, if the borrower were to default and the lender liquidated the pledged accounts receivable for less than the loan principal, the lender would still have recourse to the borrower as a general creditor.

---

[5]Because of the seasonal nature of the sales of clothing and other textile items, textiles must be produced in large quantities well in advance of the selling season. Manufacturers use seasonal datings; they send merchandise to purchasers as soon as it is produced in order to avoid inventory carrying costs, but do not require payment until after the selling season begins. They therefore end up with very high levels of receivables, which they factor in order to get working capital for use in supporting the production and inventory outlays required to meet the next season's demand.

Factor's reserves. After a factor selects the accounts to be included in a factoring agreement, a certain percentage of the total accounts are set aside to cover any returns or allowances against the merchandise sold. If a purchaser finds goods damaged or somehow not as specified, he or she may return the merchandise, thereby eliminating all or part of a factored account receivable. The factor normally holds a reserve of 5 to 10 percent of the amount factored as protection against these situations. The reserve is most important when a factor makes advances against accounts (which will be discussed in a following section).

Payment dates. A factoring agreement is drawn up between the factor and the firm. The agreement not only states the accounts to be factored or the criteria for continuous factoring, but also indicates the payment dates for factored accounts. Typically the factor is not required to pay the firm until either the account is collected or the last day of the credit period arrives, whichever occurs first.

EXAMPLE

The Ross Company has sold five accounts to a factor. All the accounts were due September 30. Each account, its amount, and its status on September 30 are given below.

Account	Amount	Status
A	$10,000	Collected Sept. 20
B	4,000	Collected Sept. 28
C	50,000	Collected Sept. 29
D	8,000	Uncollected
E	12,000	Collected Sept. 20

As of September 30, the factor has received payment from suppliers A, B, C, and E. He therefore has already taken his fee, or discount, on each account and remitted the balance to Ross Company. At September 30, he has to remit the $8000 due on account D, less the factoring fee on this account, even though it has not yet been collected. If account D is uncollectible, the factor will have to absorb the loss. ●

Advances and surpluses. A factor typically sets up an account similar to a bank deposit account for each customer. As the factor receives payment or as due dates arrive, he or she deposits money into the firm's account. The firm is free to withdraw this money as needed. In many cases, if the firm leaves the money in the account, a *surplus* will exist on which the factor will pay interest. In other instances, the firm may need more cash than is available in its account. In order to provide the firm with immediate cash, the factor will make *advances* against the yet uncollected (and not due) accounts. The advances in effect represent a negative balance in the firm's account. Interest, of course, is charged on any advances received from a factor. It is because such advances are common that the factor holds a reserve against factored accounts.[6]

Factoring costs.   Factoring costs include factoring commissions, interest on advances, and interest on surpluses.

Factoring commissions.   Factoring commissions are payments to the factor for the administrative costs of credit checking and collections, as well as for the risk assumed when purchasing accounts without recourse. Factoring commissions are typically stated as a 1 to 3 percent discount from the face value of factored accounts receivable.

Interest on advances.   The interest charge levied on advances is generally 2 to 4 percent above the prime rate. It is levied on the actual amount advanced. The interest is typically paid in advance, thereby raising the effective borrowing cost.

Interest on surpluses.   The interest paid on surpluses or positive account balances left with a factor is generally around ½ percent a month. The inclusion of this feature and the interest rate paid are specified in the factoring agreement.

EXAMPLE

The Graber Company has recently factored a number of accounts. The factor holds an 8-percent reserve, charges a 2-percent factoring commission, and charges 1 percent per month interest (i.e., 12 percent per year) on advances. Graber wishes to obtain an advance on a factored account having a book value of $1000 and due in 30 days. The proceeds to the company are calculated as follows:

Book value of account	$1000
Less: Reserve (8% · $1000)	80
Less: Factoring commission (2% · $1,000)	20
Funds available for advance	$ 900
Less: Interest on advance (1% · $900)	9
Proceeds from Advance	$ 891

The firm receives $891 now and expects to receive eventually the $80 reserve. The exact method used to calculate the amount of the advance will vary depending on the terms of the factoring agreement. Since the Graber Company must pay the interest in advance, the effective annual interest cost is not 12 percent but 12.12 percent $[(\$9 \div \$891) \cdot 12]$. ●

---

[6]If the factor makes an advance against factored accounts and some of the merchandise sold to one of the factored accounts is returned, he could be left with insufficient loan collateral and in effect be extending a partially unsecured loan to the firm. Since this situation is not desirable, the factor maintains a reserve.

Advantages and disadvantages of factoring. Factoring has certain advantages that make it quite attractive to many firms. One advantage is the ability it gives the firm to *turn accounts receivable immediately into cash* without having to worry about repayment. When a firm receives an advance, it does not have to make repayment. Once the factor collects the account or repayment obligation due, it merely retains the money. Another advantage of factoring is that it ensures a *known pattern of cash flows.* A firm that factors its accounts knows that it will definitely receive the cash flows from the accounts (less a factoring fee) by a certain date. This simplifies the firm's cash-flow planning.

If factoring is undertaken on a continuous basis, so that all accounts are sold to the factor, a couple of other advantages result. One is the elimination of the firm's credit department. The factor takes over the firm's credit analysis function when it determines which accounts are acceptable credit risks. Another advantage is the elimination of the firm's collection department. Since the factor normally accepts all credit risks, he must pay any collection costs. The net result of continuous factoring is the elimination of the credit function from the firm. With this function eliminated, many administrative and clerical dollars may be saved.

The disadvantages of factoring are considered to be its cost, the potential sacrifice of liquidity, and the implication of financial weakness associated with it. The stated costs of factoring are obviously higher than unsecured borrowing costs, but in light of the cost savings resulting from the elimination of many administrative and credit outlays, the net cost may not be high for the protection received. The sale of accounts receivable in order to obtain cash for meeting short-term obligations can result in a liquidity squeeze since the sale might represent the sacrifice of the firm's long-run liquidity in order to satisfy its short-term obligations. Such an action could create a gap in the firm's anticipated cash flows since the current accounts receivable could be virtually eliminated from the books. This may not be a valid problem when the firm continuously factors all of its accounts receivable.

The validity of the belief that factoring accounts receivable is a sign of financial weakness that may damage future business if the firm's customers learn about it is quite difficult to assess. Each factoring agreement is unique, and the advantages and disadvantages of factoring for given firms can only be evaluated in light of the terms of the specific agreements drawn up. In general, small firms that cannot afford to carry professional credit and collection people on their payroll often find factoring quite feasible.

THE USE OF INVENTORY AS COLLATERAL

Of the firm's current assets, inventory is generally second to accounts receivable in desirability as short-term loan collateral. Inventory is desirable as collateral since it normally has a market value greater than its book value, which is used to establish its value as collateral. Inventory is carried at cost on a firm's books, and a lender securing a loan with inventory will probably be able to sell it for at least that amount if the firm defaults on its obligations. However, not all inventories are equally desirable as collateral.

Characteristics of inventory

The desirability of inventory as collateral depends on a number of factors—its type, its physical properties, and its marketability. Each of these factors is discussed separately below.

Types of inventory. Chapter 10 gave a description of three basic types of inventory—raw-materials, work-in-process, and finished-goods inventories. All types of inventories may be offered as collateral for a short-term loan, but typically only raw-materials or finished-goods inventories are considered acceptable.

Physical properties. Often inventory has certain physical properties that make it unacceptable as collateral. *Perishability* is one property that may cause inventory to be unacceptable collateral. If an inventory's value declines merely with the passage of time or if it requires special storage conditions, it may not be desirable as collateral. *Specialized* items may also be of questionable use as collateral if the market for them is small. Another property to be considered is the *physical size* of inventory. Very large items may not be desirable as collateral due to the expense associated with their transportation and storage.

Marketability. The most important characteristic of inventory that is being considered as loan collateral is marketability. If an inventory can easily be sold in the future at a price equal to at least current book value, then it is probably desirable as collateral. The marketability of inventory, of course, must be considered in light of its physical properties. A warehouse of peaches may be quite marketable, but if the cost of storing and selling the peaches is high, they may not be desirable collateral. Specialized items such as moon-roving vehicles are not desirable collateral, either, since finding a buyer for them could be quite difficult.

The lender, in evaluating inventory as possible loan collateral, looks for items with very *stable market prices* that can be easily liquidated. Standardized or staple items of a durable nature are generally most desirable. These types of items have prices not subject to fluctuations, they have ready markets, and they have no undesirable physical characteristics. Of course, the lender against inventory as collateral can adjust the percentage advanced against the collateral in order to compensate for expected difficulties in liquidating the inventory.

Floating inventory liens

The use of floating liens as a source of funds was described earlier. A lender may be willing to secure a loan with inventory under a floating lien if the firm has a stable level of inventory that consists of a diversified group of merchandise, no single item of which has an excessively high dollar value.

Since it is difficult for a lender to verify the presence of the inventory, he or she will generally advance less than 50 percent of the book value of the average inventory. Inventories of items such as auto tires, screws and bolts, and shoes are likely candidates for floating lien loans. The interest charge on a floating lien is expected to be 3 to 5 percent above the prime rate. Floating liens are often required by commercial banks as extra security on what would otherwise be an unsecured loan. The floating lien inventory loan may also be available from commercial finance companies.

Trust receipt inventory loans

These loans against inventory are often made by manufacturers' financing subsidiaries to their customers.[7] *Floor planning* of automobile or equipment retailers is done under this arrangement. General Motors Acceptance Corporation (GMAC), the financing subsidiary of General Motors, grants these types of loans to its dealers. Under this type of loan arrangement the inventory, which normally consists of relatively expensive merchandise, remains in the hands of the borrowers.

In the case of a trust receipt loan, the borrower receives the merchandise and the lender advances anywhere from 80 percent to 100 percent of its cost. The lender files a lien on the items financed that contains a listing of each item along with its description and serial number. The borrower is free to sell the merchandise, but is required to remit the amount lent against each item along with accrued interest to the lender immediately after the sale is made; the lender then releases the lien on the item. The lender makes periodic checks of the borrower's inventory in order to make sure that all the required collateral is still in the hands of the borrower. The interest charge to the borrower is normally 2 percent or more above the prime rate; it is generally above that paid on an unsecured loan. Of course, interest is paid only on the declining loan balance, which may cause the overall cost of this type of loan to compare favorably with that of an unsecured short-term loan. Trust receipt loans are available not only from the captive financing subsidiaries of manufacturers, but also through commercial banks and commercial finance companies.

Warehouse receipt loans

A *warehouse receipt loan* is an arrangement whereby the lender, which may be a commercial bank or commercial finance company, receives control of the pledged collateral. This arrangement provides the lender with the ultimate degree of security.

Warehouse receipt lending procedures.

In the case of a warehouse receipt loan, the lender selects the inventory that is acceptable as collateral for the loan. Once the collateral has been selected, the lender hires

---

[7]These manufacturers' subsidiaries are often referred to as *captive finance companies,* since they are wholly owned financing subsidiaries. Captive finance companies are especially popular in industries manufacturing consumer durable goods, since they provide the manufacturer with a useful sales tool as well as certain tax and borrowing advantages.

a warehousing company to physically take possession of the inventory. Two types of warehousing arrangements are possible—terminal warehouses and field warehouses.

Terminal warehouses.   A *terminal warehouse* is one located in the geographical vicinity of the borrower. It is a central warehouse that is used to store the merchandise of various customers. A terminal warehouse is normally used by the lender when the inventory used as security is easily transported and can be delivered to the warehouse relatively inexpensively. When the goods arrive at the warehouse designated by the lender, the *warehouse official* checks the merchandise in, listing each item received on a *warehouse receipt*, noting the quantity, serial or lot numbers, and the estimated value. Once the warehouse official has checked in all the merchandise, he or she forwards the warehouse receipt to the lender, who advances a specified percentage of the collateral value to the borrower and files a lien on all the items listed on the receipt.

Field warehouses.   Under the *field warehouse* arrangement, the lender hires a field warehousing company to actually set up a warehouse on the borrower's premises or lease part of the borrower's warehouse. There are a number of companies in the United States that specialize in establishing field warehouses for a fee. The procedures followed by the field warehouse personnel are quite similar to those followed by the terminal warehouse personnel. Once they have isolated the inventory to be used as collateral, they check it in, listing the items and their characteristics on the warehouse receipt, which is forwarded to the lender. The lender, on receipt of the warehouse receipt, advances a specified percentage of the collateral value to the borrower and files a lien on the pledged collateral. A field warehouse may take the form of a fence around a stock of raw materials located outdoors, it may consist of a roped-off section of the borrower's warehouse, or it may actually be a warehouse constructed by the warehousing company on the borrower's premises, a portion of which may have been leased by the warehousing company.

Regardless of whether a terminal or field warehouse is established, the warehousing company places a guard over the inventory. Public warehouses always have a guard; under a field warehousing arrangement, a guard is stationed nearby the warehoused collateral. The guard or warehouse official is not permitted to release the collateral without authorization from the lender. In other words, the lender has complete control over the inventory used to collateralize the loan. Only upon written approval of the lender can any portion of the secured inventory be released.

The loan agreement.   The actual lending agreement will specifically state the requirements for the release of inventory. As in the case of other secured loans, the lender accepts only collateral believed to be readily marketable and advances only a portion—generally 75 percent to 90 percent—of the collateral's value. The types of collateral normally found most acceptable for warehouse receipt loans are canned foods, lumber, refined products, and basic metal stocks. The loan agreement typically provides for the release of certain pledged items upon receipt of partial repayments of the loan. The lien on the released merchandise is, of course, removed.

Although most warehouse receipts are nonnegotiable, some are *negotiable,* which means that they may be transferred by the lender to other parties. If the lender wants to remove a warehouse receipt loan from his books, he can sell a negotiable warehouse receipt to another party, who then replaces the original lender in the agreement. In some instances, the ability to transfer a warehouse receipt to another party may be desirable.

The cost of warehouse receipt loans. The specific costs of warehouse receipt loans are generally higher than those of any other secured lending arrangements due to the need to hire and pay a third party (the warehousing company) to guard and attend to the collateral. The basic interest charged on warehouse receipt loans is higher than that charged on unsecured loans. It generally ranges from 3 to 5 percent above the prime rate. In addition to the interest charge, the borrower must absorb the costs of warehousing by paying the warehouse fee, which is generally between 1 and 3 percent of the amount of the loan. These charges vary depending upon the size of the loan and other factors. In some instances, the firm's marginal warehousing costs are small since they have to warehouse the inventory anyway. The borrower is normally required to pay the insurance costs on warehoused merchandise.

Whenever warehouse receipt loans are arranged, it is important for the lender to select a reputable warehousing company. The warehousing company as the lender's agent is responsible for seeing that the collateral pledged is actually in the warehouse. There have been instances in the past when warehousing companies have fraudulently issued warehouse receipts against nonexistent collateral. If this happens, and the borrower defaults on the loan, the lender is in the same position as an unsecured creditor.

OTHER TYPES OF SECURED LOANS

Other types of security for short-term loans include stocks and bonds, comaker loans, cash surrender values of life insurance, noncorporate assets, and government-guaranteed loans. The most common of these types of security are stocks and bonds and comaker loans.

Stock and bond collateral

Stocks and certain types of bonds that are issued in bearer form can be assigned as collateral for a loan. *Bearer bonds* are bonds that can be transferred from one owner to another, instead of being issued only in the name of the initial owner like U.S. savings bonds. The lender, which is most commonly a commercial bank, of course is interested in accepting as collateral only those stocks and bonds that have a ready market and a stable market price. Securities listed on the major exchanges are generally preferred. Lenders are likely to advance as much as 90 percent of the market value of the

TABLE 12.2 Summary of sources of secured short-term financing

Type of Financing	Source
I. Accounts Receivable Collateral	
Pledging	Commercial banks and commercial finance companies
Factoring	Commercial banks, commercial finance companies, and factors
II. Inventory Collateral	
Floating liens	Commercial banks and commercial finance companies
Trust receipts	Manufacturer's captive financing subsidiaries, commercial banks, and commercial finance companies
Warehouse receipts	Commercial banks and commercial finance companies
III. Other Collateral	
Stock and bonds	Commercial banks
Comaker	Commercial banks

Cost/Conditions	Characteristics
2% to 5% above prime plus up to 3% in fees. Advance 50% to 90% of collateral value.	Selected accounts receivable are used as collateral; the borrower is trusted to remit to lender upon collection of pledged accounts. Done on a non-notification basis.
1% to 3% discount from face value of factored accounts. Interest on advances of 2% to 4% above prime. Interest on surplus balances left with factor of about .5% per month.	Selected accounts are sold—generally without recourse—at a discount. All credit risks go with the accounts. Factor will loan (i.e., make advances) against accounts sold but not yet scheduled for remittance to seller. Also, they will pay interest on surplus balances left with them. Typically done on a notification basis.
3% to 5% above prime. Advance less than 50% of collateral value.	A loan against inventory in general. Made when firm has stable inventory of a variety of inexpensive items.
2% or more above prime. Advance 80% to 100% of cost of collateral.	Loan against collateral that is relatively expensive and can be identified by serial number. Collateral remains in possession of borrower, who is trusted to remit proceeds to lender upon its sale. Often called "floor planning."
3% to 5% above prime plus a 1% to 3% warehouse fee. Advance 75% to 90% of collateral value.	Inventory used as collateral is placed under control of the lender by putting it in a terminal warehouse or through a field warehouse. A third party—a warehousing company—issues a warehouse receipt that is held by the lender. The warehousing company is an agent of the lender.
2% to 5% above prime. Advance as much as 90% of market value of collateral.	Stocks and bonds issued in bearer form and having a ready market with a stable market price are used as collateral. Lender takes possession and is given power of attorney, which permits liquidation in the event of default.
2% to 5% above prime.	No physical collateral is pledged; rather, the borrowing power of a more financially sound firm or individual that cosigns the loan is used to back up the loan.

securities held as collateral. The lender takes possession of the collateral and receives a power of attorney that allows him to liquidate it if the borrower defaults on the terms of the loan agreement. The interest charges on loans secured with stocks or bonds, or both, is normally between 2 and 5 percent above the prime rate.

Comaker loans

Comaker loans arise when another party, who may have a vested interest in the firm's financial future, *cosigns* for the loan. Although no physical collateral is pledged against the loan, the borrowing power of a more financially sound party is used to back up the loan. If the borrower defaults, the comaker will be liable for the loan. A lender, which is typically a commercial bank, will make comaker loans only when certain of the financial soundness of the comaker. A comaker may be a wealthy stockholder, a supplier, a customer to whom the continued existence of the firm is important, or a friend of the firm. Interest rates charged on comaker loans are comparable to those charged on loans secured by stocks and bonds.

SUMMARY

This chapter has discussed the characteristics and basic types of secured short-term loans available to business. A lender can obtain a legal claim to certain collateral by filing a lien on the collateral, which can be removed only when the terms of the loan agreement have been met. A copy of the security agreement is made available to other lenders so that they will not attempt to secure a loan with collateral already being used as security. A lender can take a number of different types of security interests. A floating lien gives the lender a claim on general collateral. A trust receipt loan is made against specific collateral that remains under the control of the borrower. A warehouse receipt loan allows the lender to control the disposition of the loan collateral, which is typically inventory.

Short-term loan collateral is usually a current asset, such as accounts receivable, inventory, or stocks and bonds whose maturity in effect liquidates the loan. Only a certain percentage of the collateral's value, determined by the lender's assessment of its liquidity and marketability, is advanced by the lender. The interest charges and fees on secured loans are normally higher than those of unsecured loans due to the additional paperwork and higher risks associated with the former. The major secured lenders are commercial banks and commercial finance companies.

Accounts receivable are the most common type of collateral for short-term secured loans. A pledge of accounts receivable is a type of trust arrangement whereby the lender advances a certain percentage of the book value of the accounts found to be acceptable. Accounts of average size are preferable. The borrower collects the pledged accounts and remits the payment to the lender, thereby reducing the loan balance on which interest is calculated. Accounts receivable can be factored, or sold, to a factor, a commercial bank, or a commercial finance company. The accounts are sold at a discount since the factor accepts all types of credit risks and generally can collect nothing from the borrower if an account proves uncollectible. Customers whose accounts have been factored are generally notified to make payments directly to the factor; pledges of accounts receivable do not generally involve notification. The cost of factoring is greater than the cost of pledging accounts receivable since the factor takes the credit risks and performs certain administrative functions.

Inventory can be used as collateral under a floating lien, a trust receipt arrangement, or a warehouse receipt loan. In the case of a warehouse receipt loan, the collateral is placed in either a terminal or a field warehouse chosen by the lender and guarded on his or her behalf. The lender controls the collateral, which only he or she can release. The cost of warehouse receipt loans is high due to the fee that must be paid the warehousing company. This arrangement is quite safe for the lender.

Other types of collateral include stocks and bonds, comaker loans, cash surrender values of life insurance, noncorporate assets, and government guarantees. Regardless of what method of security is used, the lender advances only a percentage of the book value of the collateral and levies interest and other charges as required. All terms and charges are explicitly stated in the loan agreement, which is a legal and binding contract. Liens filed against collateral become part of the loan agreement.

QUESTIONS

12-1 What are the key differences between unsecured and secured forms of short-term borrowing? In what circumstances do firms borrow short-term money on a secured basis?

12-2 Many people argue that secured loans have lower effective interest costs than unsecured loans; they argue that the collateral lowers risk. The text stresses that these two statements are not necessarily complementary. Explain why.

12-3 What are the most common types of short-term loan collateral? How does a lender obtain a security interest in a firm's loan collateral?

12-4 Lenders evaluating the acceptability of short-term loan collateral are often concerned with its liquidity. How can a lender evaluate the liquidity of current assets?

12-5 On what basis is the "percentage advance" against acceptable collateral determined? Within what range is this percentage likely to fall?

12-6 In general, what kind of interest rates and fees are levied on secured short-term loans? Why are these rates generally higher than the rates on unsecured short-term loans?

12-7 What two key institutions provide secured short-term loans to business? Which institution charges the highest interest rates? Why?

12-8 How does a lender determine which accounts receivable are acceptable as pledged collateral for a short-term loan?

12-9 What does the term *notification* refer to? Are pledges of accounts normally on a notification basis? How does the lender collect his money in a pledge arrangement?

12-10 How do the interest charges and effective costs of borrowing differ for loans secured by pledged accounts receivable and unsecured short-term bank loans?

12-11 How is factoring different from a pledge of accounts receivable? What institutions provide factoring services to business?

12-12 What are the commonly cited advantages and disadvantages of factoring? What types of firms are most likely to find factoring a viable source of funds? Why?

12-13 The suitability of inventory as loan collateral generally depends on its type, its physical properties, and its marketability. How do each of these aspects of inventory affect its desirability as collateral?

12-14 What is a floating lien inventory loan? What sort of advances and costs are involved?

12-15 How does a typical trust receipt inventory loan arrangement work? Who makes these types of loans, and how are they policed?

12-16 How does a warehouse receipt lending arrangement work? What is the function of the warehouse personnel, and what types of warehouses are used?

12-17 What types of collateral, other than accounts receivable and inventory, are likely to be used to secure a short-term loan?

PROBLEMS

12-1 The Kansas City Castings (KCC) is attempting to obtain the maximum loan possible using their accounts receivable as collateral. The firm extends net 30-day credit. The amounts owed KCC by its 12 credit customers, the average age of each account, and the customers' average payment period are given:

Customer	Account receivable	Average age of account	Average payment period of customer
A	$37,000	40 days	30 days
B	42,000	25 days	50 days
C	15,000	40 days	60 days
D	8,000	30 days	35 days
E	50,000	31 days	40 days
F	12,000	28 days	30 days
G	24,000	30 days	70 days
H	46,000	29 days	40 days
I	3,000	30 days	65 days
J	22,000	25 days	35 days
K	62,000	35 days	40 days
L	80,000	60 days	70 days

a If the bank will accept all accounts that can be collected in 45 days or less as long as the customer has a history of paying within 45 days, which accounts will be acceptable? What is the total dollar amount of accounts receivable collateral? (Accounts receivable that have an average age greater than the customer's average payment period are also excluded.)

b In addition to the conditions in **a**, the bank recognizes that 5 percent of credit sales will be lost to returns and allowances. Also, the bank will only lend 80 percent of the acceptable collateral (after adjusting for returns and allowances). What level of funds would be made available through this lending source?

12-2 Pottsburg Plate and Glass wishes to borrow $80,000 from the Pottsburg National Bank using its accounts receivable to secure the loan. The bank's policy is to accept as collateral any accounts that are normally paid within 30 days of the end of the credit period so long as the average age of the account is not greater than the customer's average payment period. Pottsburg Plate's accounts receivable, their average ages, and the average payment period for each customer are given below. The company extends terms of net 30 days.

Customer	Account receivable	Average age of account	Average payment period of customer
A	$20,000	10 days	40 days
B	6,000	40 days	35 days
C	22,000	62 days	50 days
D	11,000	68 days	65 days
E	2,000	14 days	30 days
F	12,000	38 days	50 days
G	27,000	55 days	60 days
H	19,000	20 days	35 days

a Calculate the dollar amount of acceptable accounts receivable collateral held by Pottsburg Plate and Glass.
b The bank adjusts collateral by ten percent for returns and allowances; what is the level of acceptable collateral under this condition?
c The bank will advance 75 percent against the firm's acceptable collateral (after adjusting for returns and allowances). What amount can Pottsburg Plate and Glass borrow against these accounts?

12-3 Dynamic Finance factors the accounts of the Russell Allen Company. All eight factored accounts are listed below with the amount factored, the due date, and the status as of May 30. Indicate the amounts which Dynamic should have remitted to Russell Allen as of May 30, and the dates of those remittances. Assume the factor's commission is 2 percent.

Account	Amount	Date due	Status on May 30
A	$200,000	May 30	Collected, May 15
B	90,000	May 30	Uncollected
C	110,000	May 30	Uncollected
D	85,000	June 15	Collected, May 30
E	120,000	May 30	Collected, May 27
F	180,000	June 15	Collected, May 30
G	90,000	May 15	Uncollected
H	30,000	June 30	Collected, May 30

12-4 Duff Duds wishes to receive an *advance* from their factor on an account of $100,000 due in 30 days. The factor holds a 10-percent factor's reserve, charges a 2-percent factoring commission, and charges 16-percent annual interest on advances.
a Calculate the maximum dollar amount of interest to be paid.
b What amount of funds will the firm actually receive?
c What is the effective interest rate on this transaction?

12-5 The Rohio Oil Company factors all of its accounts. The factor charges a 1-

percent factoring commission, holds a 15-percent reserve, and charges 10 percent interest on advances. Rohio wishes to receive an advance against the following accounts as of September 1:

Account	Amount	Date due
A	$ 60,000	September 30
B	100,000	September 30
C	120,000	September 30
D	75,000	September 30
E	40,000	September 30

a Calculate the actual amount the firm can borrow.
b Calculate the maximum dollar amount of interest that must be paid.
c What is the effective interest cost of this advance?
d Why might the actual interest cost be less than the amount calculated in **b**?

12-6 American Manufacturing is considering obtaining funding through advances against receivables. Total credit sales are $12,000,000, terms are net 30 days, and payment is made on the average in 30 days. City State Bank will advance funds under a pledging arrangement for 15-percent annual interest. On the average, 80 percent of credit sales will be accepted as collateral. Friendly Finance offers factoring on a nonrecourse basis for a 2.5-percent factoring commission, charging 1 percent per month on advances, and requiring a 20-percent factor's reserve. Under this plan, the firm would factor all accounts and close its credit and collections department, saving $300,000 per year.

a What is the effective interest rate, and the average amount of funds made available under pledging and under factoring?
b What other effects must be considered in choosing either of these plans?
c Which plan do you recommend and why?

12-7 Prescott Turbine Company faces a liquidity crisis—they need a loan of $100,000 for 30 days. Having no source of additional unsecured borrowing, the firm must find a secured short-term lender. The firm's accounts receivable are quite low, but its inventory is considered liquid and reasonably good collateral. The book value of the inventory is $300,000.

(1) Center City Bank will make a trust receipt loan against the $120,000 finished-goods inventory. This loan costs 6 percent plus a ¼ percent administration fee. The average amount owed over the month is expected to be $75,000.

(2) First Local Bank is willing to lend against a blanket lien on a maximum of one-half of the book value of inventory for the 30-day period at an annual interest rate of 8 percent.

(3) North Mall Bank and Trust will lend an amount equal to 85 percent of the finished-goods balance and charge 9-percent interest on the outstanding loan balance. A one-half percent warehousing fee will be levied against the amount borrowed. The average loan balance is expected to be $60,000.

a Assuming $100,000 is borrowed in each case, calculate the cost of each of the proposed plans.
b Which plan do you recommend? Why?
c If the firm had made a purchase of $100,000 for which it had been given terms of 1/10 net 40, would it increase the firms profitability to forego the discount and not borrow as recommended in **b**? Why or why not?

SELECTED REFERENCES

Abraham, Alfred B., "Factoring—The New Frontier for Commercial Banks," *The Journal of Commercial Bank Lending 53* (April 1971), pp. 32–43.

Addison, Edward, "Factoring: A Case History," *Financial Executive* (November 1963), pp. 32–33.

Adler, M., "Administration of Inventory Loans under the Uniform Commercial Code," *The Journal of Commercial Bank Lending 52* (April 1970), pp. 55–60.

Andrews, Victor L., "Captive Finance Companies," *Harvard Business Review 42* (July-August 1964), pp. 80–92.

Berger, Paul D., and William K. Harper, "Determination of an Optimal Revolving Credit Agreement," *Journal of Financial and Quantitative Analysis 8* (June 1973), pp. 491–498.

Bogen, Jules I., Ed., *Financial Handbook*, 4th ed. (New York: Ronald, 1968), sect. 16.

D'Agostino, R. S., "Accounts Receivable Loans—Worthless Collateral?" *The Journal of Commercial Bank Lending* (March 1970), pp. 34–42.

Daniels, Frank, Sidney Legg, and E. C. Yueille, "Accounts Receivable and Related Inventory Financing," *Journal of Commercial Bank Lending 53* (July 1970), pp. 38–53.

Dennon, Lester E., "The Security Agreement," *Journal of Commercial Bank Lending 50* (February 1968), pp. 32–40.

Edwards, R. E., "Finance Companies and Their Creditors," *Journal of Commercial Bank Lending 54* (October 1971), pp. 2–10.

Fisher, D. J., "Factoring—An Industry on the Move," *The Conference Board Record 9* (April 1972), pp. 42–45.

Holmes, W., "Market Values of Inventories—Perils and Pitfalls," *Journal of Commercial Bank Lending 55* (April 1974), pp. 30–36.

Naitove, Irwin, *Modern Factoring* (New York: American Management Association, 1969).

Phelps, Clyde W., *Accounts Receivable Financing as a Method of Securing Business Loans,* 2nd ed. (Baltimore: Commercial Credit Company, 1961).

Quarles, J. Carson, "The Floating Lien," *Journal of Commercial Bank Lending 53* (November 1970), pp. 51–58.

Rogers, Robert W., "Warehouse Receipts and Their Use in Financing," *Bulletin of the Robert Morris Associates 46* (April 1964), pp. 317–327.

Shay, Robert P., and Carl C. Greer, "Banks Move into High-Risk Commercial Financing," *Harvard Business Review 46* (November-December 1968), pp. 149–153 and pp. 156–161.

Stancill, James McN., *The Management of Working Capital* (Scranton, Pa.: Intext, 1971), chap. 6.

Stone, B., "How Secure Is Secured Financing Under the Code?" *Burroughs Clearing House 50* (April 1966), p. 46.

Wellman, M. T., "Field Warehousing—Protective Measures," *Robert Morris Associates Bulletin 47* (March 1965), pp. 302–312.

Wishner, Maynard, "Coming Significantly Larger Rates for Secured Corporate Financing," *Financial Executive 45* (May 1977), pp. 18–23.

PART
FIVE

This part of the text is devoted to one of the key areas of financial management—fixed-asset management and capital budgeting. The concepts and techniques underlying this topic are often viewed as the backbone of contemporary financial management. Chapter 13 is devoted to the key mathematical concepts of finance. An understanding of many of these concepts is necessary in order to grasp the various capital budgeting techniques; others are used in later parts of the text. Chapter 14 describes certain fixed-asset management strategies and presents the terminology and fundamentals of capital budgeting. Special emphasis is placed upon determination of relevant cash-flow streams. Chapter 15 describes and discusses the key techniques of capital budgeting. The various techniques are illustrated by an ongoing example. Chapter 16 discusses capital budgeting under risk. It covers techniques for evaluating capital budgeting projects under risk and includes a discussion of risk and return which places special emphasis on the Capital Asset Pricing Model (CAPM).

Fixed-asset management and capital budgeting

BALANCE SHEET	
Assets	**Liabilities and Stockholders' Equity**
Current Assets	Current Liabilities
Fixed Assets	Long-Term Debt
	Stockholders' Equity

CHAPTER 13
The mathematics of finance

In order to understand the various techniques of capital budgeting and other interest-related financial concepts, one needs an understanding of certain algebraic relationships associated with interest calculations. The key calculations are the determination of compound interest and the present value of future cash flows. Compound interest calculations are needed to evaluate future sums resulting from an investment in an interest-earning medium. Compound interest techniques are also quite useful in evaluating interest and growth rates of money streams.

Discounting, or the calculation of present values, is inversely related to compounding. It is of key importance in the evaluation of future income streams associated with capital budgeting projects. An understanding of both compound interest and present value is needed to calculate the payments required to accumulate a predetermined future sum or for amortizing loans or calculating loan payment schedules. A thorough knowledge of discounting and present values is also helpful in understanding the techniques for finding internal rates of return and yields to maturity, both of which are discussed in subsequent chapters.

This chapter explains the terminology, concepts, calculations, and tables used in finding compound interest and present values. The reader should not fear these topics, for they are conceptually and algebraically quite simple. Moreover, an understanding of the concepts presented in this chapter will provide the key to understanding the capital budgeting techniques presented in Chapters 14 through 16 as well as the discussions of the cost of capital, capital structure, valuation, leasing, bond refunding, valuing convertible securities, mergers and acquisitions, and business reorganization included in later parts of the text. The importance of these concepts should not be underestimated.

This chapter has three basic sections. The first section discusses compound interest, the second is devoted to present-value calculations, and the final section presents a few important applications of compound interest and present-value techniques.

COMPOUND INTEREST

Compound interest is most commonly thought of in reference to various savings institutions. These institutions quite often advertise the fact that they pay "compound interest at a rate of x percent" or "x-percent interest compounded semiannually, quarterly, weekly, or daily." The principles of compound interest are quite simple, regardless of the period of time involved. In this section, we shall discuss three types of compounding: annual compounding, intrayear compounding, and finding the compound value of an annuity.

Annual compounding

The most common type of compounding is annual compounding. Interest is *compounded* when the amount earned on an initial deposit (the *initial principal*) becomes *part* of the principal at the end of the first compounding period. The term *principal* refers to the amount of money on which *interest* is paid.

The calculation of compound interest.   The actual method by which interest is compounded annually can be illustrated by a simple example.

EXAMPLE
If Steve Saver places $100 in a savings account paying 8-percent interest compounded annually, at the end of one year he will have $108 in the account. This $108 represents the initial principal of $100 plus 8 percent ($8) in interest. The amount of money in the account at the end of the first year is calculated using Equation 13.1:

$$\text{Amount of money at end of year 1} = \$100(1 + .08)$$
$$= \$108 \tag{13.1}$$

If Steve were to leave this money in the account for another year, he would be paid interest at the rate of 8 percent on the new principal of $108. At the end of this second year, there would be $116.64 in the account. This $116.64 would represent the principal at the beginning of year 2 ($108) plus 8 percent of the $108 (i.e., $8.64) in interest. The amount of money in the account at the end of the second year is calculated using Equation 13.2:

$$\text{Amount of money at end of year 2} = \$108(1 + .08)$$
$$= \$116.64 \tag{13.2}$$

Substituting the right side of Equation 13.1 for the $108 figure in Equation 13.2 gives us Equation 13.3:

$$\text{Amount of money at end of year 2} = \$100(1 + .08)(1 + .08)$$
$$= \$100(1.08)^2$$
$$= \$116.64 \ \bullet \tag{13.3}$$

The basic relationship in Equation 13.3 can be generalized to find the amount of money after any number of years. Let

F_n = the amount of money at the end of year n
P = the initial principal
i = the annual rate of interest paid on the account
n = the number of years the money is left in the account

Using this notation, a general equation for the amount of money at the end of year n can be formulated:

$$F_n = P(1 + i)^n \qquad (13.4)$$

The usefulness of Equation 13.4 for finding the amount of money, F_n, in an account paying i-percent interest compounded annually for n years if P dollars were deposited initially can be illustrated by a simple example.

EXAMPLE
James Frugal has placed $800 in a savings account paying 6 percent interest compounded annually. He wishes to determine how much money will be in the account at the end of five years. Substituting P = $800, i = .06, and n = 5 into Equation 13.4 gives him the amount at the end of year 5.

$$F_5 = \$800(1 + .06)^5 = \$800(1.338) = \$1070.40 \qquad (13.5)$$

James will have $1070.40 in the account at the end of year 5. ●

Compound interest tables. Solving Equation 13.5 is quite time consuming, since one must raise 1.06 to the fifth power. In order to simplify compound interest calculations, compound interest tables have been compiled. A table of the amount generated by the payment of compound interest on an initial principal of $1 is given as Appendix Table A-1. This table, labeled "The compound-value interest factors for one dollar," provides a value for $(1 + i)^n$ in Equation 13.4.[1] This portion of Equation 13.4 is called the *compound-value interest factor*. The compound-value interest factor for an initial principal of $1 compounded at i percent for n years is referred to as $CVIF_{i,n}$:

$$\text{Compound-value interest factor} = CVIF_{i,n} = (1 + i)^n \qquad (13.6)$$

By accessing the table with respect to the annual interest rate i, and the appropriate number of years, n, the factor relevant to a particular problem can be found. A sample portion of Table A-1 is given in Table 13.1. An example will illustrate the use of this table.

---

[1]This table is commonly referred to as a "compound interest table" or a "table of the future value of $1." As long as the reader understands the source of the table values, the various names attached to it should not create confusion since one can always make a trial calculation of a value for one factor as a check.

TABLE 13.1 The compound-value interest factors for one dollar, $CVIF_{i,n}$

Year	5.00 percent	6.00 percent	7.00 percent	8.00 percent	9.00 percent	10.00 percent
1	1.050	1.060	1.070	1.080	1.090	1.100
2	1.102	1.124	1.145	1.166	1.188	1.210
3	1.158	1.191	1.225	1.260	1.295	1.331
4	1.216	1.262	1.311	1.360	1.412	1.464
5	1.276	1.338	1.403	1.469	1.539	1.611
6	1.340	1.419	1.501	1.587	1.677	1.772
7	1.407	1.504	1.606	1.714	1.828	1.949
8	1.477	1.594	1.718	1.851	1.993	2.144
9	1.551	1.689	1.838	1.999	2.172	2.358
10	1.629	1.791	1.967	2.159	2.367	2.594

Note. All table values have been rounded to the nearest one-thousandth; thus calculated values may differ slightly from the table values.

EXAMPLE

James Frugal, whom we discussed in the preceding example, has placed $800 in his savings account at 6 percent interest compounded annually. He wishes to find out how much would be in the account at the end of five years and does so by the cumbersome process of raising $(1 + .06)$ to the fifth power. Using the table for the compound value of one dollar (Table 13.1 or Table A-1), he could find the compound-value interest factor for an initial principal of $1 on deposit for five years at 6 percent interest compounded annually without performing any calculations. The appropriate factor, $CVIF_{6\%,5\ yrs}$, for 6 percent and 5 years is 1.338. Multiplying this factor, 1.338, by his actual initial principal of $800 would then give him the amount in the account at the end of year 5, $1070.40. The usefulness of the table should be clear from this example. ●

Three important observations should be made about the table for the compound value of one dollar. The first is that the factors in the table represent factors for determining the compound value of one dollar *at the end of the given year*. Second, *as the interest rate increases for any given year, the compound-value interest factor also increases*. Thus the higher the interest rate, the greater the future sum. The third point is that *for a given interest rate the compound value of a dollar increases with the passage of time*. The relationship between various interest rates, the number of years interest is earned, and compound-value interest factors is illustrated in Figure 13.1. The fact that the higher the interest rate the higher the compound-value interest factor is, and the longer the period of time the higher the compound-value interest factor is, should be clear from this figure. The reader should also note that for an interest rate of 0 percent, the compound-value interest factor always equals 1 and therefore the compound-value always equals the initial principal.

FIGURE 13.1 Interest rates, time, and compound-value interest factors used to find the compound value of one dollar

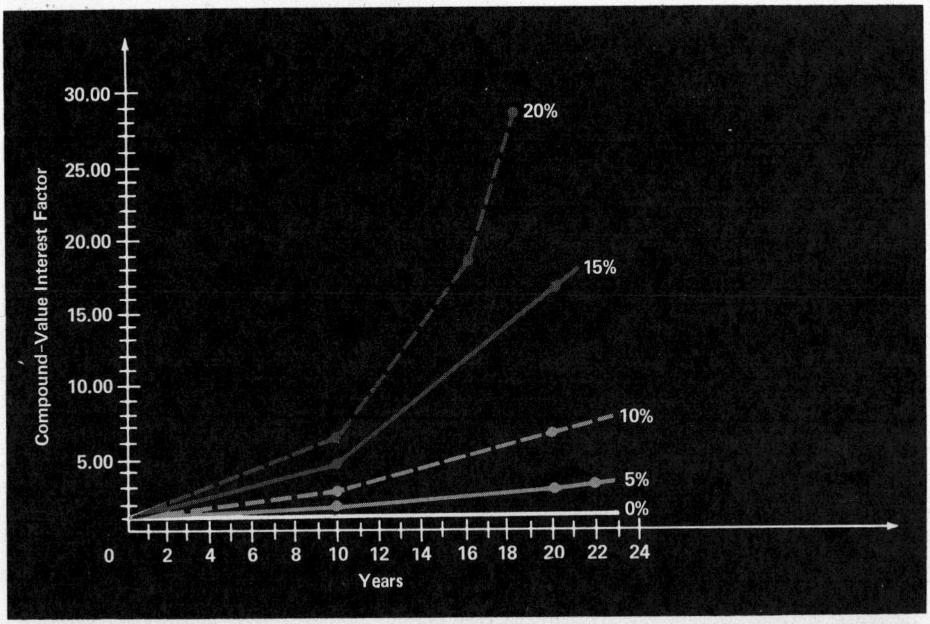

Intrayear compounding

The preceding section was devoted solely to the annual compounding of interest. Quite commonly, interest is compounded more often. This behavior is particularly noticeable in the advertising of savings institutions. Many of these institutions compound interest semiannually, quarterly, monthly, daily, or even continuously. This section first discusses semiannual and quarterly compounding and then presents a general equation for intrayear compounding. It also explains how to use compound-value interest tables in these situations.

Semiannual compounding. When interest is compounded semiannually there are two compounding periods within the year. Instead of being paid the stated interest rate once a year, one is paid one-half of the stated interest rate twice a year.

EXAMPLE

Steve Saver, who was discussed in an earlier example of annual compounding, has decided to place his $100 in a savings account paying 8-percent interest compounded semiannually. If he leaves his money in the account for two years, he will be paid 4-percent interest compounded over four periods—each six months long. Table 13.2 presents the calculations required to determine the amount Steve will have at the end of two years.

TABLE 13.2 The results of investing $100 at 8-percent interest compounded semiannually over two years

Period	Beginning principal (1)	Compound-value interest factor (2)	Amount at end of period (1) · (2) (3)
6 months	$100.00	1.04	$104.00
1 year	104.00	1.04	108.16
18 months	108.16	1.04	112.49
2 years	112.49	1.04	116.99

As the table shows, at the end of one year, when the 8-percent interest is compounded semiannually, Steve will have $108.16; at the end of two years, he will have $116.99. ●

Quarterly compounding. When interest is compounded quarterly, there are four compounding periods within the year. Instead of being paid the stated interest rate once a year, one is paid one-fourth of the stated interest rate four times a year.

EXAMPLE
Steve Saver, after further investigation of his savings opportunities, has found an institution that will pay him 8 percent compounded quarterly. If he leaves his money in this account for two years, he will be paid 2-percent interest compounded over

TABLE 13.3 The results of investing $100 at 8-percent interest compounded quarterly over two years

Period	Beginning principal (1)	Compound-value interest factor (2)	Amount at end of period (1) · (2) (3)
3 months	$100.00	1.02	$102.00
6 months	102.00	1.02	104.04
9 months	104.04	1.02	106.12
1 year	106.12	1.02	108.24
15 months	108.24	1.02	110.40
18 months	110.40	1.02	112.61
21 months	112.61	1.02	114.86
2 years	114.86	1.02	117.16

TABLE 13.4 The results of investing $100 at 8-percent for 1 and 2 years given various compounding periods

End of year	Compounding period		
	Annual	Semiannual	Quarterly
1	$108.00	$108.16	$108.24
2	116.64	116.99	117.16

eight periods—each of which consists of one-fourth of a year. Table 13.3 presents the calculations required to determine the amount Steve will have at the end of two years. As the table shows, at the end of one year, when the 8-percent interest is compounded quarterly, Steve will have $108.24; at the end of two years, he will have $117.16.

Table 13.4 presents comparative values for Steve Saver's $100 at the end of years one and two given annual, semiannual, and quarterly compounding at the 8-percent rate. As the table shows, the *more frequently interest is compounded, the greater the amount of money accumulated.* This is true for any interest rate for any period of time. ●

A general equation for intrayear compounding. It should be clear from the preceding examples of semiannual and quarterly compounding that, if m equals the number of times per year interest is compounded, Equation 13.4 (our formula for annual compounding) can be rewritten as

$$F_n = P \left(1 + \frac{i}{m} \right)^{m \cdot n} \tag{13.7}$$

If $m = 1$, Equation 13.7 reduces to Equation 13.4. Thus if interest is compounded annually (i.e., once a year), Equation 13.7 will provide the same results as Equation 13.4. The general applicability of Equation 13.4 can be illustrated with a simple example.

EXAMPLE
In the preceding examples, the amount that Steve Saver would have at the end of two years if he deposited $100 at 8-percent interest compounded semiannually and quarterly was discussed. For semiannual compounding, m would equal 2 in Equation 13.7, while for quarterly compounding m would equal 4 . Substituting the appropriate values for semiannual and quarterly compounding into Equation 13.7 would yield

1. *For semiannual compounding*

$$F_2 = \$100 \left(1 + \frac{.08}{2} \right)^{2 \cdot 2} = \$100(1 + .04)^4$$
$$= \$116.99$$

2. *For quarterly compounding*

$$F_2 = \$100 \left(1 + \frac{.08}{4} \right)^{4 \cdot 2} = \$100(1 + .02)^8$$
$$= \$117.16$$

If the interest were compound monthly, weekly, or daily, m would equal 12, 52, or 365, respectively. In the case of *continuous compounding*, which implies compounding every microsecond, m would approach infinity and the use of calculus would be required to determine the compound value. The results in the example above agree with the values for F_2, in Table 13.2 and 13.3. ●

Using a table for intrayear compounding. The table of the compound value of one dollar, Table A-1, can be used to simplify the calculations required by Equation 13.7. Instead of indexing the table for i percent and n years, as we do when interest is compounded annually, we index it for $(i \div m)$ percent and $(m \cdot n)$ years. The usefulness of the table is usually somewhat limited since only selected rates for a limited number of years can be found. The table can commonly be used to calculate the results of semiannual and quarterly compounding (i.e., when $m = 2, 4$), but when more frequent compounding is done, the aid of a computer may be necessary to solve Equation 13.7. The following example will clarify the use of the compound interest table for intrayear compounding.

EXAMPLE
In the earlier examples, Steve Saver wished to find the compound value of $100 invested at 8 percent compounded both semiannually and quarterly for two years. The number of compounding periods, m, was 2 and 4 in each of these cases, respectively. The values by which the table for the compound value of one dollar is accessed, along with the compound-value interest factor in each case, are given below.

Compounding period	m	Percentage $(i \div m)$	Years $(m \cdot n)$	Compound-value interest factor from Table A-1
Semiannual	2	.08 ÷ 2 = .04	2 · 2 = 4	1.170
Quarterly	4	.08 ÷ 4 = .02	4 · 2 = 8	1.172

The factor for 4 percent and four years is used for the semiannual compounding, while the factor for 2 percent and eight years is used for quarterly compounding. Multiplying each of the factors by the initial $100 deposit results in a value of $117.00 (i.e., 1.170 · $100) for semiannual compounding and a value of $117.20 (i.e., 1.172 · $100) for quarterly compounding. The corresponding values found by the long method are $116.99 and $117.16, respectively. The discrepancy can be attributed to the rounding of values in the table. ●

The compound value of an annuity
An *annuity* is a stream of equal cash flows. These cash flows can be either received or deposited by an individual in some interest-earning form. The calculations required to find the compound value of an annuity on which interest is paid at a specified rate compounded annually can be illustrated by a simple example.

EXAMPLE

Mary Jones wishes to determine how much money she will have at the end of five years if she deposits $1000 annually in a savings account paying 7-percent annual interest. The deposits will be made at the end of each of the next five years. Table 13.5 presents the calculations required to determine the amount of money she will have. As the table shows, at the end of year 5 Mary will have $5751 in her account. Column 2 of the table indicates that, since the deposits are made at the end of the year, the first deposit will earn interest for four years, the second for three years, and so on. The compound value interest factors in column 3 correspond with these interest-earning periods and the 7-percent rate of interest. ●

TABLE 13.5 The value of a $1000
5-year annuity compounded at 7 percent

End of year	Amount deposited (1)	Number of years compounded (2)	Compound-value interest factor from Table A-1 (3)	Future sum (1) · (3) (4)
1	$1000	4	1.311	$1311
2	1000	3	1.225	1225
3	1000	2	1.145	1145
4	1000	1	1.070	1070
5	1000	0	1.000	1000
	Amount at End of Year 5			$5751

Simplifying the calculations. The calculations required in the preceding example can be simplified somewhat since each of the factors is actually multiplied by the same dollar amount. Of course, this is true only in the case of an annuity. The actual calculations required in the preceding table can be expressed as follows:

$$\text{Amount at end of year 5} = \$1000(1.311) + \$1000(1.225) \\ + \$1000(1.145) + \$1000(1.070) \\ + \$1000(1.000) = \$5751 \qquad (13.8)$$

Factoring out the $1000, Equation 13.8 can be rewritten as

$$\text{Amount at end of year 5} = \$1000(1.311 + 1.225 + 1.145 + 1.070 \\ + 1.000) \\ = \$5751 \qquad (13.9)$$

Equation 13.9 indicates that in order to find the compound value of the annuity, the annual amount must be multiplied by the sum of the appropriate compound-value interest factors.

TABLE 13.6 The compound-value
interest factors for a one-dollar annuity, $CVIFA_{i,n}$

Year	5.00 percent	6.00 percent	7.00 percent	8.00 percent	9.00 percent	10.00 percent
1	1.000	1.000	1.000	1.000	1.000	1.000
2	2.050	2.060	2.070	2.080	2.090	2.100
3	3.152	3.184	3.215	3.246	3.278	3.310
4	4.310	4.375	4.440	4.506	4.573	4.641
5	5.526	5.637	5.751	5.867	5.985	6.105
6	6.802	6.975	7.153	7.336	7.523	7.716
7	8.142	8.394	8.654	8.923	9.200	9.487
8	9.549	9.897	10.260	10.637	11.028	11.436
9	11.027	11.491	11.978	12.488	13.021	13.579
10	12.578	13.181	13.816	14.487	15.193	15.937

Using a compound value of an annuity table. Appendix Table A-2 simplifies even further the calculations required to find the compound value of an annuity. A portion of Table A-2 is given in Table 13.6. The factors in this table are derived by summing the terms in parentheses in equations like Equation 13.9. In the case of Equation 13.9, this results in Equation 13.10.

$$\text{Amount at end of year } 5 = \$1000(5.751) = \$5751 \tag{13.10}$$

The values in the table are based on the assumption that deposits are made at the end of the year. If S_n equals the compound value of an n-year annuity, A equals the amount to be deposited annually at the end of each year, and $CVIFA_{i,n}$ represents the appropriate *compound-value interest factor for an n-year annuity compounded at i percent*, the relationship between these variables can be expressed as follows:

$$S_n = A \cdot (CVIFA_{i,n}) \tag{13.11}$$

Instead of using the equation presented earlier for the compound value of an annuity, we can use Table A-2 and Equation 13.11. In Mary Jones' case, the interest factor for the compound value of a one-dollar annuity with a five-year life at 7 percent can be obtained from Table A-2 and multiplied by the $1000 deposit. Multiplying the table value of 5.751 by $1000 results in a compound value for the annuity of $5751. The following example further illustrates the usefulness of Table A-2.

EXAMPLE
Randa Middleton wishes to determine the sum of money she will have in her savings account, which pays 6-percent annual interest, at the end of ten years if she deposits $600 at the end of each year for the next ten years. The appropriate interest factor $CVIFA_{6\%,10\text{ yrs.}}$ for the compound value of a ten-year annuity at 6 percent is given

in Table A-2 as 13.181. Multiplying this factor by the $600 deposit results in a future sum of $7908.60. The simple calculations required to find the compound value of an annuity using Table A-2 should be clear from this example. ●

PRESENT VALUE

It is often useful to determine the "present value" of a future sum of money. This type of calculation is most important in the capital budgeting decision process, which is discussed in Chapters 14 through 16. The concept of present value, like the concept of compound interest, is based on the belief that the value of money is affected by when it is received. The axiom underlying this belief is that a dollar today is worth more than a dollar that will be received at some future date. In other words, the present value of a dollar that will be received in the future is less than the value of a dollar in hand today. The actual present value of a dollar depends largely on the earning opportunities of the recipient and the point in time the money is to be received. This section explores the present value of single amounts, mixed streams of cash flows, and annuities.

The present value of a single amount

The process of finding present values, or *discounting cash flows,* is actually the inverse of compounding. It is concerned with answering the question "If I can earn *i* percent on my money, what is the most I would be willing to pay for an opportunity to receive F_n dollars *n* years from today?" Instead of finding the future amount (i.e., compound value) of present dollars invested at a given rate, discounting determines the present value of a future amount, assuming that the decision maker has an opportunity to earn a certain return, *i*, on his or her money. This return is often referred to as the *discount rate, the cost of capital,* or *an opportunity cost.*[2] These terms will be used interchangeably in this text. The discounting process can be illustrated by a simple example.

EXAMPLE

Mr. Jones has been given an opportunity to receive $300 one year from now. If he can earn 6 percent on his investments in the normal course of events, what is the most he should pay for this opportunity? To answer this question, we must determine how many dollars must be invested at 6 percent today to have $300 one year from now. Letting *P* equal this unknown amount, and using the same notation as in the compounding discussion, the situation can be expressed as follows:

$$P(1 + .06) = \$300 \tag{13.12}$$

Solving Equation 13.12 for *P* gives us Equation 13.13,

$$P = \frac{\$300}{1.06} \tag{13.13}$$
$$= \$283.02$$

---

[2]The theoretical underpinning of this "cost of capital" as it relates to the business firm's evaluation of capital budgeting proposals is discussed in depth in Chapter 17.

which results in a value of $283.02 for P. In other words, the "present value" of $300 received one year from today, given an opportunity cost of 6 percent, is $283.02. Mr. Jones should be indifferent to whether he receives $283.02 today or $300.00 one year from now. If he can receive either by paying less than $283.02 today, he should, of course, do so. ●

A mathematical expression for present value.　The present value of a future sum can be found mathematically by solving Equation 13.4 for P. In other words, one merely wants to obtain the present value, P, of some future amount, F_n, to be received n years from now, assuming an opportunity rate of i. Solving Equation 13.4 for P gives us Equation 13.14, which is the general equation for the present value of a future sum.

$$P = \frac{F_n}{(1+i)^n} = F_n \left[\frac{1}{(1+i)^n} \right] \tag{13.14}$$

The similarity between this general equation for present value and the equation in the preceding example (Equation 13.13) should be clear. The use of this equation in finding the present value of a future amount can be illustrated by a simple example.

EXAMPLE
Jim McCarthy wishes to find the present value of $1700 that will be received eight years from now. Jim's opportunity cost is 8 percent. Substituting $F_8 = \$1700$, $n = 8$, and $i = .08$ into Equation 13.14 yields Equation 13.15:

$$P = \frac{\$1700}{(1+.08)^8} \tag{13.15}$$

In order to solve Equation 13.15, the term $(1 + .08)$ must be raised to the eighth power. The value resulting from this time-consuming calculation is 1.851. Dividing this value into $1700 yields a present value for the $1700 of $918.42 ●

Present-value tables.　In order to simplify the present-value calculation, tables of present-value interest factors can be used. The table for the *present-value interest factor for one dollar*, $PVIF_{i,n}$, gives values for the expression $1/(1+i)^n$ where i is the discount rate and n is the number of years involved. Table A-3 in the Appendix presents present-value interest factors for various discount rates and years. A portion of Table A-3 is presented in Table 13.7. Since the factors in Table A-3 give the value for the expression $1/(1+i)^n$ for various i and n combinations, we can, by letting $PVIF_{i,n}$ represent the appropriate factor from Table A-3, rewrite Equation 13.14 as follows:

$$P = F_n \cdot (PVIF_{i,n}) \tag{13.16}$$

This expression indicates that in order to find the present value, P, of an amount to be received in a future year, n, we have merely to multiply the future amount, F_n, by the appropriate present value factor from Table A-3. An example should help clarify the use of Equation 13.16.

TABLE 13.7 The present-value interest factors for one dollar, $PVIF_{i,n}$

Year	5.00 percent	6.00 percent	7.00 percent	8.00 percent	9.00 percent	10.00 percent
1	.952	.943	.935	.926	.917	.909
2	.907	.890	.873	.857	.842	.826
3	.864	.840	.816	.794	.772	.751
4	.823	.792	.763	.735	.708	.683
5	.784	.747	.713	.681	.650	.621
6	.746	.705	.666	.630	.596	.564
7	.711	.665	.623	.583	.547	.513
8	.677	.627	.582	.540	.502	.467
9	.645	.592	.544	.500	.460	.424
10	.614	.558	.508	.463	.422	.386

EXAMPLE

Jim McCarthy, whom we met in the preceding example, wishes to find the present value of $1700 to be received eight years from now, assuming an 8-percent opportunity cost. Table A-3 gives us a present-value interest factor for eight percent and 8 years, $PVIF_{8\%,8\ yrs}$, of .540. Multiplying this factor by the $1700 yields a present value of $918. This value is 42 cents less than the value obtained using the long method. This difference is attributable to the fact that the table values have been rounded off to the nearest one-thousandth. ●

A few other points with respect to present-value tables are also important. First, *the present-value interest factor for a single sum is always less than one*; only if the opportunity cost was zero would this factor equal one. Second, Table A-3 shows that *the higher the opportunity cost for a given year, the smaller the present-value interest factor* is. In other words, the greater an individual's opportunity cost, the less an amount to be received in a certain future year is worth today. Finally, observation of the table values for a given discount rate indicates that *the farther in the future a sum is to be received, the less it is worth presently*. The relationship between various discount rates, discount periods, and present-value interest factors is illustrated in Figure 13.2. Everything else being equal, the higher the discount rate, the lower the present-value interest factor, and the longer the period of time, the lower the present-value interest factor. The reader should also note that given a discount rate of 0 percent the present-value interest factor always equals one, and therefore the future value of the funds equals their present value.

Comparing present value and compound interest. A few important observations must be made with respect to present values. One is that the expression for the present-value interest factor for i percent and n years, $1/(1 + i)^n$, is the inverse of the compound-value interest factor for i percent and n years, $(1 + i)^n$. This observation can be confirmed by dividing

FIGURE 13.2 Discount rates, time, and present-value interest factors used to find the present value of one dollar

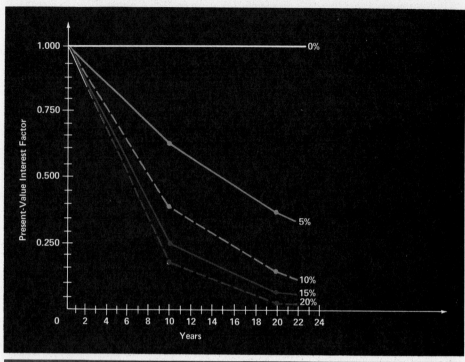

a present-value interest factor for i percent and n years, $PVIF_{i,n}$, into 1 and comparing the resulting value to the compound-value interest factor given in Table A-1 for i percent and n years, $CVIF_{i,n}$. The two values should be equivalent. Because of the relationship between present-value interest and compound-value interest factors, we can find the present-value interest factors given a table of compound-value interest factors and vice versa. The compound-value interest factor from Table A-1 for five years and 10 percent is 1.611. Dividing this value into 1 yields .621, which is the present-value interest factor given in Table A-3 for five years and 10 percent.

Mixed streams of cash flows

Quite often, especially in capital budgeting problems, there is a need to find the present value of a stream of cash flows to be received in various future years. Two basic types of cash-flow streams are possible—the mixed stream and the annuity. A *mixed stream* of cash flows reflects no particular pattern, while an *annuity* is a pattern of equal annual cash flows (i.e., the cash flows are the same each year). Since certain shortcuts are possible in finding the present value of an annuity, mixed streams and annuities will be discussed separately.

In order to find the present value of a mixed stream of cash flows, all that is required is to determine the present value of each future amount in the manner described in the preceding section and then sum all the individual present values to find the present value of the stream of cash flows. A simple example should clarify this process.

EXAMPLE
The CAM Company has been offered an opportunity to receive the following mixed stream of cash flows over the next five years:

Year	Cash flow
1	$400
2	800
3	500
4	400
5	300

If the firm must earn 9 percent, at minimum, on its investments, what is the most it should pay for this opportunity?

In order to solve this problem, the present value of each individual cash flow discounted at 9 percent for the appropriate number of years is determined. The sum of all these individual values is then calculated to get the present value of the total stream. The present-value interest factors required are obtained from Table A-3. Table 13.8 presents the calculations required to find the present value of the cash-flow stream, which turns out to be $1904.60. CAM should not pay more than $1904.60 for the opportunity to receive these cash flows, since paying $1904.60 would provide exactly a 9-percent return. ●

TABLE 13.8 The present value of a mixed stream of cash flows

Year	Cash flow (1)	P.V. interest factor[a] (2)	Present value (1) · (2) (3)
1	$400	.917	$ 366.80
2	800	.842	673.60
3	500	.772	386.00
4	400	.708	283.20
5	300	.650	195.00
	Present Value of Stream		$1904.60

[a]Present-value interest factors at 9 percent are from Table A-3.

Annuities
The present value of an annuity can be found in a manner similar to that used on a mixed stream, but due to the nature of an annuity, a shortcut is possible.

EXAMPLE

The Delco Company is attempting to determine the most it should pay to purchase a particular annuity. The firm requires a minimum return of 8 percent on all investments; the annuity consists of cash inflows of $700 per year for five years. Table 13.9 shows the long way of finding the present value of the annuity, which is the same as the method used for mixed streams. This procedure yields a present value of $2795.10, which can be interpreted in the same manner as for the mixed cash-flow stream in the preceding example. ●

TABLE 13.9 The long method for finding the present value of an annuity

Year	Cash flow (1)	P.V. interest factor[a] (2)	Present value (1) · (2) (3)
1	$700	.926	$ 648.20
2	700	.857	599.90
3	700	.794	555.80
4	700	.735	514.50
5	700	.681	476.70
	Present Value of Annuity		$2795.10

[a]Present-value interest factors at 8 percent are from Table A-3.

Simplifying the calculations.   The calculations used in the preceding example can be simplified by recognizing that each of the five multiplications made to get the individual present values involved multiplying the annual amount ($700) by the appropriate present-value interest factor. This method of finding the present value (P.V.) of the annuity can also be written as an equation:

$$\text{P.V. of annuity} = \$700(.926) + \$700(.857) + \$700(.794) \\ + \$700(.735) + \$700(.681) = \$2795.10 \qquad (13.17)$$

Simplifying Equation 13.17 by factoring out the $700 yields Equation 13.18.

$$\text{P.V. of annuity} = \$700(.926 + .857 + .794 + .735 + .681) \\ = \$2795.10 \qquad (13.18)$$

Thus the present value of an annuity can be found by multiplying the annual amount received by the sum of the present-value interest factors for each year of the annuity's life.

A table of present values for an annuity.   Appendix Table A-4 is a table of *present-value interest factors for a one-dollar annuity* for specified

TABLE 13.10 The present-value
interest factors for a one-dollar annuity, $PVIFA_{i,n}$

Year	5.00 percent	6.00 percent	7.00 percent	8.00 percent	9.00 percent	10.00 percent
1	.952	.943	.935	.926	.917	.909
2	1.859	1.833	1.808	1.783	1.759	1.736
3	2.723	2.673	2.624	2.577	2.531	2.487
4	3.546	3.465	3.387	3.312	3.240	3.170
5	4.329	4.212	4.100	3.993	3.890	3.791
6	5.076	4.917	4.767	4.623	4.486	4.355
7	5.786	5.582	5.389	5.206	5.033	4.868
8	6.463	6.210	5.971	5.747	5.535	5.335
9	7.108	6.802	6.515	6.247	5.995	5.759
10	7.722	7.360	7.024	6.710	6.418	6.145

rates and years. It simplifies even further the calculations required to find the present value of any annuity. A portion of this table is presented in Table 13.10. The interest factors in the table are derived by summing the terms in the parentheses in equations like Equation 13.18. In the case of Equation 13.18, this results in Equation 13.19.

$$\text{P.V. of annuity} = \$700(3.993) = \$2795.10 \tag{13.19}$$

The interest factors in Table A-4 actually represent the sum of the first n present-value interest factors in Table A-3 for a given discount rate. If P_n equals the present value of an n-year annuity, A equals the amount to be received annually at the end of each year, and $PVIFA_{i,n}$ represents the appropriate value for the *present-value interest factor for a one-dollar annuity discounted at i percent for n years*, the present value of the annuity can be found by the following equation:

$$P_n = A \cdot (PVIFA_{i,n}) \tag{13.20}$$

The problem presented earlier involving the calculation of the present value of a five-year annuity of $700 assuming an 8-percent opportunity cost can be easily worked out with the aid of Table A-4 and Equation 13.20. The present-value interest factor for a one-dollar annuity in Table A-4 for 8 percent and 5 years, $PVIFA_{8\%,\,5\,\text{yrs.}}$, is 3.993. Multiplying this factor by the $700 annuity provides a present value for the annuity of $2795.10. A simple example may help clarify the usefulness of Table A-4 in finding the present value of an annuity.

EXAMPLE
The Massachusetts Mining Company expects to receive $160,000 per year at the end of each of the next 20 years from a new mine. If the firm's opportunity cost of funds is 10 percent, how much is the present value of this annuity? The appropriate interest

factor for the present value at 10 percent for a 20-year annuity, $PVIFA_{10\%,20\ yrs}$, is found in Table A-4 to be 8.514. Multiplying this factor by the $160,000 cash flow results in a present value of $1,362,240. ●

APPLYING COMPOUND INTEREST AND PRESENT-VALUE TECHNIQUES

Compound interest and present-value techniques have a number of important applications in addition to those we have discussed. Five of these applications will be presented in this section. They are (1) the calculation of the deposit needed to accumulate a future sum, (2) the calculation of amortization on loans, (3) the determination of interest and growth rates, (4) the determination of bond values, and (5) the calculation of the present value of perpetuities.

Deposits to accumulate a future sum

Often an individual may wish to determine the annual deposit necessary to accumulate a certain amount of money so many years hence. Suppose a person wishes to purchase a house five years from now and recognizes that an initial down payment of $4000 will be required at that time. He wishes to make equal annual end-of-year deposits in an account paying annual interest of 6 percent, so he must determine what size annuity will result in a sum equal to $4000 at the end of year 5. The solution to this problem is closely related to the process of finding the compound value of an annuity.

In an earlier section of this chapter, the compound value of an n-year annuity, S_n, was found by multiplying the annual deposit, A, by the appropriate interest factor from Table A-2, $CVIFA_{i,n}$. The relationship between the three variables has been defined by Equation 13.11, which is rewritten below as Equation 13.21.

$$S_n = A \cdot (CVIFA_{i,n}) \tag{13.21}$$

We can find the annual deposit required to accumulate S_n dollars, given a specified interest rate, i, and a certain number of years, n, by solving Equation 13.21 for A. Isolating A on the left side of the equation gives us

$$A = \frac{S_n}{CVIFA_{i,n}} \tag{13.22}$$

Once this is done, we have only to substitute the known values of S_n and $CVIFA_{i,n}$ into the right side of the equation to find the annual deposit required.

EXAMPLE

In the problem stated earlier in this section, an individual wished to determine the equal annual end-of-year deposits required to accumulate $4000 at the end of five years given an interest rate of 6 percent. Table A-2 indicates that the compound-value interest factor for an annuity at 6 percent for 5 years, $CVIFA_{6\%,\ 5\ yrs.}$, is 5.637. Substituting $S_5 = \$4000$ and $CVIFA_{6\%,\ 5\ yrs.} = 5.637$ into Equation 13.22 yields an annual required deposit, A, of $709.60 (i.e., $4000 ÷ 5.637). If $709.60 is deposited at the end of each year for five years at 6 percent, at the end of the five years there will be $4000 in the account. ●

Loan amortization

The phrase *loan amortization* refers to the determination of the equal annual loan payments necessary to provide a lender with a specified interest return and repay the loan principal over a specified term. The loan amortization process involves finding the future payments (over the term of the loan) whose present value at the loan interest rate just equals the amount of initial principal borrowed. Lenders use loan amortization tables to find these payment amounts. In the case of home mortgages, these tables are used to find the equal monthly payments necessary to amortize or pay off the loan at a specified interest rate over a 20- to 30-year period.

The discussion here will deal only with the amortization of loans on which annual end-of-year payments are made, since the tables in this text are based on annual end-of-year amounts. Amortizing a loan actually involves creating an annuity out of a present sum. For example, an individual may borrow $6000 at 10 percent and agree to make equal annual payments over seven years. In order to determine the size of the payments, the seven-year annuity discounted at 10 percent that has a present value of $6000 must be determined. This process is actually the inverse of finding the present value of an annuity.

Earlier in this chapter the present value, P_n, of an n-year annuity of A dollars was found by multiplying the annual amount, A, by the present-value interest factor for an annuity from Table A-4, $PVIFA_{i,n}$. This relationship, which was originally expressed as Equation 13.20, is rewritten as Equation 13.23 below:

$$P_n = A \cdot (PVIFA_{i,n}) \tag{13.23}$$

To find the equal annual payment, A, required to pay off or amortize the loan, P_n, over a certain number of years at a specified interest rate, we need to solve Equation 13.23 for A. Isolating A on the left side of the equation gives us

$$A = \frac{P_n}{PVIFA_{i,n}} \tag{13.24}$$

Once this is done, we have only to substitute the known values of P_n and $PVIFA_{i,n}$ into the right side of the equation to find the annual payment required.

EXAMPLE

In the problem stated at the start of this section, an individual wished to determine the equal annual end-of-year loan payments necessary to fully amortize a $6000, 10-percent loan over seven years. Table A-4 indicates that the present-value interest factor for an annuity corresponding to 10 percent and 7 years, $PVIFA_{10\%,7\,\text{yrs.}}$, is 4.868. Substituting $P_7 = \$6000$ and $PVIFA_{10\%,7\,\text{yrs.}} = 4.868$ in Equation 13.24 and solving for A yields an annual loan payment of \$1232.54 (i.e., \$6000 ÷ 4.868). In order to repay the principal and interest on a \$6000, 10-percent, seven-year loan, equal annual end-of-year payments of \$1232.54 are necessary. ●

Determining interest and growth rates

It is often necessary to calculate the compound annual interest or growth rate associated with a stream of cash flows. In doing this, either compound, interest or present value tables can be used. The preferred approach, using compound interest tables, is described in this section. The simplest situation is where one wishes to find the rate of interest or growth in a cash-flow stream. This case can be illustrated by a simple example.

EXAMPLE

Tom Richards wishes to find the rate of interest or growth of the following stream of cash flows.[3]

Year	Amount	
1978	$1520	4
1977	$1440	3
1976	$1370	2
1975	$1300	1
1974	$1250	

Interest has been earned (or growth experienced) for four years. In order to find the rate at which this has occurred, the amount received in the latest year is divided by the amount received in the earliest year. This gives us the compound-value interest factor for four years, $CVIF_{i,\,4\,\text{yrs.}}$, which is 1.216 (\$1520 ÷ \$1250). The interest rate in Table A-1 associated with the factor closest to 1.216 for four years is the rate of interest or growth rate associated with the cash flow. Looking across year 4 of Table A-1 shows that the factor for 5 percent is exactly 1.216; therefore the rate of interest or growth rate associated with the cash flows given is 5 percent. ●

Sometimes one wishes to determine the interest rate associated with an equal-payment loan. For instance, if a person were to borrow \$2000 which was to be repaid in equal annual end-of-year amounts of \$514.14 for the next five years, he or she might wish to determine the rate of interest being paid on the loan. Referring back to Equation 13.23 shows that $P_5 = \$2000$ and $A = \$514.14$. Rearranging the equation and substituting these values results in a present-value interest factor for a 5-year annuity, $PVIFA_{i,\,5\,\text{yrs.}}$, of 3.890:

$$PVIFA_{i,\,5\,\text{yrs.}} = \frac{P_5}{A} = \frac{\$2000}{\$514.14} = 3.890 \tag{13.25}$$

---

[3]Since the calculations required for finding interest rates and growth rates, given certain cash flow or principal flow streams, are the same, this section refers to the calculations as those required to find interest *or* growth rates.

The interest rate for five years associated with a factor of 3.890 in Table A-4 is 9 percent; therefore, the interest rate on the loan is 9 percent.

Determining bond values

Corporate bonds, which are discussed in greater detail in Chapter 21, typically pay interest semiannually. Often it is necessary to determine the value, or current worth of a bond. The cash flows from a bond consist not only of the interest inflows every six months, but also of the cash flow resulting from payment of the face value at maturity. Since the interest payments on a bond occur periodically throughout its life, it is easiest to calculate the present value of this annuity-type cash flow separately from the present value of the principal payment at maturity. Since the interest is paid semiannually, the present value is calculated in a manner similar to a compound value when interest is compounded semiannually. In the case of present values of semiannual cash flows, the factors are obtained for one-half the discount rate and twice the number of years.

EXAMPLE

In order to find the value of a 20-year bond with a 10-percent coupon, paying interest semiannually and having a face value of $1000, we must first find the present value of the 40 semiannual interest payments. Since the bond pays $100 (i.e., 10 percent of $1000) in interest per year, the semiannual payments are $50 each (i.e., ½ of $100). In order to find the present value of the 40 semiannual $50 payments, the *market discount rate*, which reflects the return currently available on bonds of similar risk and maturity, must be used. In this case we will assume that the market discount rate equals 10 percent, which happens to be equal to the bond's coupon rate. Since the interest is compounded semiannually over the 20 years, the present-value interest factor for an annuity for 5 percent and 40 years, $PVIFA_{5\%, 40 \text{ yrs.}}$, from Table A-4 is used. This present-value interest factor is 17.159, which when multiplied by $50 gives us a present value for the interest cash flows of $857.95. This value results from viewing the interest payments as a 40-year annuity discounted at 5 percent.

The present value of the $1000 maturity value is found by multiplying the $1000 by the present value interest factor for $1 to be received 40 years from now at 5 percent. The use of 40 years and 5 percent is consistent with the interest treatment described above. The factor in Table A-3 for 5 percent and 40 years, $PVIF_{5\%, 40 \text{ yrs.}}$, is .142. Multiplied by the $1000 maturity value, it gives us a present value for that sum of $142. Adding the present value of the interest ($857.95) to the present value of the maturity value of the bond ($142) gives us a value for the bond of $999.95. Since the market discount rate is assumed to be 10 percent, which equals the coupon rate on the bond, the bond's value of $999.95 is equal (except for a slight rounding error) to its face value of $1000. Should the market discount rate be higher than 10 percent, the bond value would be less than its $1000 face value, and vice versa. ●

Perpetuities

A *perpetuity* is an annuity with an infinite life, or, in other words, an annuity that never stops providing its holder with "*x* dollars" at the end of each year. It is often necessary to find the present value of a perpetuity. The present-value interest factor for a perpetuity discounted at the rate *i* is defined by Equation 13.26.

$$\text{Present-value interest factor for a perpetuity at } i\% = \frac{1}{i} \qquad (13.26)$$

In other words, the appropriate factor is found merely by dividing the discount rate (stated as a decimal) into 1. The validity of this method can be seen by looking at the factors in Table A-4 for 8 percent, 10 percent, and 20 percent. As the number of years approaches 50, the value of these factors approaches 12.500, 10.000, and 5.000, respectively. Substituting .08, .10, and .20 (for i) into Equation 13.26 gives us factors for finding the present value of perpetuities at these rates of 12.500, 10.000, and 5.000. An example may help clarify the application of Equation 13.26.

EXAMPLE

An individual wishes to determine the present value of a $1000 perpetuity discounted at 10 percent. The appropriate present-value interest factor can be found by dividing 1 by .10, as prescribed by Equation 13.26. The resulting factor, 10, is then multiplied by the annual cash inflow of $1000 to get the present value of the perpetuity, $10,000. In other words, the receipt of $1000 every year for an indefinite period is worth only $10,000 today if a person can earn 10 percent on investments. This is because, if the person had $10,000 and earned 10 percent interest on it each year, $1000 a year could be withdrawn indefinitely without affecting the initial $10,000, which would never be drawn down. ●

SUMMARY

This chapter has discussed the key mathematical concepts of finance. Specific attention has been given to compound interest, present value, and certain applications of the techniques for calculating compound interest and present value. Compound interest is an important concept in measuring the value of future sums. When interest is compounded, the initial principal or deposit in one period along with the interest earned on it becomes the beginning principal of the following period, and so on. Interest can be compounded annually, semiannually, quarterly, monthly, weekly, daily, or even continuously. The more frequently interest is compounded, the larger the future sum that will be accumulated. If F_n equals the future sum at the end of year n, P equals the initial principal, m equals the number of times per year interest is compounded, i equals the stated annual rate of interest, and n equals the number of years over which the money earns a return, then

$$F_n = P\left(1 + \frac{i}{m}\right)^{m \cdot n}$$

Whenever interest is compounded annually, m equals 1.

Table A-1 in the Appendix presents the compound-value interest factors used in the annual compounding of interest at various rates for periods from one to 50 years. This table can also be used to evaluate the benefits of compounding interest more frequently than annually. Table A-2 in the Appendix provides a shortcut for finding the compound value of an annuity by multiplying the amount of the annuity by the appropriate factor.

Present value represents the inverse of compounding. When a person finds the present value of a future amount he determines what amount of money today would be equivalent to the given future amount, considering the fact that he can earn a certain return on his money. As long as a person can earn a return at a rate greater than 0 percent, the present value of a future cash flow is less than its future value. If P equals the present value of a future amount, F_n, to be received n years from now and interest can be earned at i percent per year, the formula for present value is

$$P = \frac{F_n}{(1 + i)^n} = F_n \left[\frac{1}{(1 + i)^n} \right]$$

The present-value interest factor is represented by the term in brackets. Table A-3 in the Appendix presents these factors for various discount rates, i, and years, n. Occasionally it is necessary to find the present value of a stream of cash flows. Mixed streams consist of any cash-flow pattern other than an annuity, which is a pattern of equal annual cash flows (i.e., the cash flows are the same each year). For mixed streams, the individual present values must be found and summed. In the case of an annuity, the present value can be found using the present-value interest factor for an annuity from Table A-4 in the Appendix. Multiplying the appropriate interest factor from Table A-4 by the annual cash flow gives us the present value of the annuity.

By manipulating the equations for the compound value and present value of single amounts and annuities in certain ways, the deposits needed to accumulate a future sum, loan amortization payments, interest and growth rates, and bond values can be calculated. Although differing calculations are required in each case, the basic approach is derived from the concepts of compound interest and present value. The present value of a perpetuity, which is an annuity with an infinite life, can be calculated by multiplying the annual cash flow by 1 divided by the appropriate discount rate.

Techniques for calculating compound values and present values are most important in the financial decision-making process. These techniques are not only used in the capital budgeting decision process but also play a major role in analyses of the cost of capital, capital structure, valuation, leasing, bond refunding, valuing convertible securities, mergers and acquisitions, and business reorganization. Subsequent parts of this text will draw on compound-interest and present-value concepts in analyzing decisions in these areas.

QUESTIONS

13-1   How is the compounding process related to the payment of interest on savings? What is the general equation for the future amount, F_n, in year n if P dollars are deposited in an account paying i-percent annual interest?

13-2   How are compound-value interest tables arranged? How may they be used to calculate the future amount generated by a current deposit? Compound-value interest tables are based on the receipt of money *when* in each period?

13-3   What effect would a decrease in the interest rate or an increase in the holding period of a deposit have on the future amount available? Why?

13-4   What effect does compounding interest more frequently than once a year have on the future amount generated by a current sum? Why?

13-5   If interest is compounded m times a year at a stated rate i over n years, what is the expression for the future amount, F_n? Can you explain this equation?

13-6   How may the table for the compound-value interest factor for one dollar be used for calculating the future amount of a present sum when interest is compounded more often than annually?

13-7   What is meant by the term "compound value of an annuity"? How are the factors in the table for the compound value of an annuity developed, and how may the table be used to find the compound value of an annuity?

13-8   What is meant by the phrase "the present value of a future sum"? How are present-value and compound interest calculations related?

13-9   What is the equation for the present value of a future amount, F_n, to be received in year n assuming that the firm's cost of capital is i? How is this equation different from the equation for the compound value of one dollar?

13-10   How may the table of interest factors for the present value of one dollar be used for calculating present values? How could present values be calculated using the table for the compound value of one dollar?

13-11   What effect do increasing (1) costs of capital and (2) increasing time periods have on the present value of a future sum? Why?

13-12   How can the present-value tables be used to find the present value of a mixed stream of cash flows? Why can the present value of an annuity be found by summing the individual present-value interest factors and multiplying the sum by the annual amount received?

13-13   How is the table of interest factors for the present value of an annuity used? How could this table be developed from the table of interest factors for the present value of one dollar?

13-14   How can the size of the equal annual end-of-year deposits necessary to accumulate a certain future amount in a specified future year be determined? How might one of the financial tables discussed in this chapter aid in this calculation?

13-15   How can a loan requiring equal annual end-of-year payments be amortized over its stated life at a given rate? How might one of the financial tables in this chapter be used to simplify this calculation?

13-16   Which financial tables would be used to find (1) the growth rate associated with a stream of cash flows and (2) the interest rate associated with an equal-payment loan? How would each of these be calculated?

13-17   If bond interest is paid semiannually, how can one determine a bond value? Which table(s) are required to calculate this?

13-18   What is a perpetuity? How might the factor for the present value of such a stream of cash flows be determined?

PROBLEMS

13-1 For each of the following cases, calculate the amount of money that will be available at the end of the deposit period if the interest rate is compounded annually for the given period of years.

Case	Amount	Interest rate	Period (years)
A	$ 200	5%	20
B	$ 4,500	8%	7
C	$10,000	9%	10
D	$25,000	10%	12
E	$37,000	11%	5
F	$40,000	12%	9

13-2 An individual borrows $200 to be repaid in 8 years with 14-percent annually compounded interest. The loan may be repaid at the end of any earlier year with no prepayment penalty.

  a What amount would be due if the loan is repaid at the end of year 1?

  b What is the repayment at the end of year 4?

  c What amount is due at the end of the eighth year?

13-3 Using annual, semiannual, and quarterly compounding periods, calculate the future sum if $5000 is deposited

  a At 8 percent for five years.

  b At 12 percent for five years.

  c At 8 percent for twelve years.

13-4 Nancy Jackson has $10,000 that she can deposit in any of three savings accounts for a three-year period. Bank A pays interest on an annual basis; Bank B pays interest twice each year; and Bank C pays interest each quarter. If all banks have a stated annual interest rate of 8 percent, but follow the different payment practices above, what sum would Ms. Jackson have at the end of the third year leaving all interest paid on deposit in

  a Bank A

  b Bank B

  c Bank C

13-5 Jay Martin has been offered a future payment of $500 three years from today. If his opportunity cost is 7 percent compounded annually, what value would he place on this opportunity?

13-6 An Ohio State savings bond can be converted to $25 at maturity six years from purchase. If the state bonds are to be competitive with U.S. Savings Bonds paying 6 percent annual interest (compounded annually), at what price will the state sell its bonds? Assume no cash payments on savings bonds prior to redemption.

13-7 Julio Lopez has $1500 to invest. His investment counselor suggests an investment that pays no explicit interest, but will return $2000 at the end of three years.

  a What annual rate of return will Mr. Lopez earn with this investment?

  b Mr. Lopez is considering another investment, of equal risk, which earns a return of 8 percent. Which investment should he take, and why?

13-8 If one deposits $75 in his or her credit union at the end of each quarter for the next 10 years, and the credit union pays 8-percent interest on the balance on deposit at the end of each year, determine the sum the individual will have if no interest is withdrawn, and:

a The credit union pays interest annually.

b The credit union pays interest semiannually.

c The credit union pays interest quarterly.

13-9 What initial sum would one need to deposit at 10-percent annual interest in order to pay out $85 at the end of each of the next six years, at which time the account would have a zero balance?

13-10 What amount should an individual pay for a bond with a $1000 face value, maturing in six years, paying a coupon yield of 2 percent each six months (4-percent annual interest paid semiannually) if the market rate of interest on equally risky bonds is 10-percent (annual) paid semiannually?

13-11 Calculate the present value of a $500-face-value bond paying quarterly interest at an annual rate of 10 percent and having a 10-year maturity if the market rate of interest is 12 percent (annual) paid quarterly.

13-12 Calculate the value of each of the following bonds, all of which pay interest semiannually.

Bond	Face value	Coupon rate	Maturity	Market rate
A	$ 100	12%	10 years	8%
B	$ 500	10%	15 years	10%
C	$1000	8%	20 years	12%

13-13 Jerry Carney has an opportunity to purchase any of the following cash flows at the prices given. What recommendation would you make assuming that Mr. Carney can earn 10 percent on his investments?

Project	Price	Cash flow	Year of receipt
A	$18,000	$30,000	5
B	$ 600	$ 3,000	20
C	$ 3,500	$10,000	10
D	$ 1,000	$15,000	40

13-14 You are given the following series of cash flows:

	Cash flows		
Year	A	B	C
1	$500	$1500	$2500
2	560	1550	2600
3	640	1610	2650
4	720	1680	2650
5	800	1760	2800
6		1850	2850
7		1950	2900
8		2060	
9		2170	
10		2280	

    a Calculate the compound growth rate associated with each cash-flow stream.

    b If year 1 values represent initial deposits in a savings account paying annual interest, what is the rate of interest on each account?

    c Compare and discuss the growth rates and interest rates found in **a** and **b**, respectively.

13-15 A retirement home at Marineworld Estates now costs $35,000. Inflation is expected to cause this price to increase at 6 percent per year over the 20 years before J. R. Rogers retires. How much will he need to save each year at an annual rate of 10 percent to have the cash to purchase his home upon retirement?

13-16 Young Daniel Markham will be attending Harbard University in 19 years. Total university expenses will be $10,000 per year, payable at the beginning of each of the four years he will attend Harbard. How much will his parents need to save in each of the next 19 years, at 6-percent annual interest, to pay for Daniel's education? Assume a 6-percent annual interest rate throughout and no contribution from the parents after year 19.

13-17 Given the following data, determine for each of the following perpetuities

    a The appropriate present-value interest factor.

    b The present value.

Perpetuity	Annual amount	Discount rate
A	$ 20,000	8%
B	$100,000	10%
C	$ 3,000	6%
D	$ 60,000	5%

13-18 Bob Sherill has been shopping for a loan to finance the purchase of his new car. He has found three possibilities that seem attractive and wishes to select the one having the lowest interest rate. The information available with respect to each of the three $5000 loans follows.

Loan	Principal	Annual payment	Life (years)
A	$5000	$1352.81	5
B	$5000	$1543.21	4
C	$5000	$2010.45	3

    a Determine the interest rate that would be associated with each of the loans.

    b Which loan should Mr. Sherill take?

SELECTED REFERENCES

Bierman, Harold, Jr., Charles P. Bonini, and Warren H. Hausman, *Quantitative Analysis for Business Decisions*, 5th ed. (Homewood, Ill.: Irwin, 1977), chap. 21.

———, and Seymour Smidt, *The Capital Budgeting Decision*, 4th ed. (New York: Macmillan, 1975), chaps. 1 and 4.

Boness, A. James, *Capital Budgeting* (New York: Praeger, 1972).

Cissell, Robert, Helen Cissell, and David C. Flaspohler, *Mathematics of Finance*, 5th ed. (Boston: Houghton Mifflin, 1978).

Clayton, Gary E., and Christopher B. Spivey, *The Time Value of Money* (Philadelphia: W. B. Saunders Company, 1978).

Draper, Jean E., and Jane S. Klingman, *Mathematical Analysis* (New York: Harper & Row, 1967).

Grant, Eugene L., and W. Grant Iverson, *Principles of Engineering Economy*, 6th ed. (New York: Ronald, 1976), pp. 25–61.

Hart, William L., *Mathematics of Investment*, 5th ed. (Lexington, Mass.: Heath, 1975).

Jean, William H., *Capital Budgeting: The Economic Evaluation of Investment Projects* (Scranton, Pa.: Intext, 1969).

Johnson, R. W., *Capital Budgeting* (Dubuque, Iowa: Kendall/Hunt, 1977).

Levy, Haim, and Marshall Sarnat, *Capital Investment and Financial Decisions* (Englewood Cliffs, N.J.: Prentice-Hall, 1978), chap. 2.

Mao, James C. T., *Quantitative Analysis for Financial Decisions* (New York: Macmillan, 1969).

Merrett, A. J., and Allen Sykes, *Capital Budgeting and Company Finance* (London: Longmans, 1966).

Osteryoung, Jerome, *Capital Budgeting: Long-Term Asset Selection*, 2nd ed. (Columbus, Ohio: Grid, 1979), chap. 3.

Peterson, David E., *A Quantitative Framework for Financial Management* (Homewood, Ill.: Irwin, 1969).

Quirin, G. David, *The Capital Expenditure Decision* (Homewood, Ill.: Irwin, 1967).

Solomon, Ezra, "The Arithmetic of Capital-Budgeting Decisions," *Journal of Business* 29 (April 1956), pp. 124–129.

Wright, M. G., *Discounted Cash Flow*, 2nd ed. (London: McGraw-Hill, 1973).

CHAPTER 14
Fixed-asset management and capital budgeting fundamentals

Typically, the largest dollar investment maintained by a manufacturing firm is in fixed assets. Some fixed assets are a necessity for the manufacturing firm, since without them, production would be a virtual impossibility. There are two major classes of fixed assets—plant and equipment. It is possible for a manufacturing firm to operate without any fixed assets on its balance sheet by leasing plant or equipment, or both. However, the emphasis in this chapter will be on owned fixed assets. A discussion of leased fixed assets is presented in Chapter 20.

The level of fixed assets maintained by a manufacturing concern is somewhat dependent on the nature of the firm's production processes. Aside from raw materials, the major inputs to the production process are overhead and labor. The majority of the firm's overhead cost is attributable to its plant and equipment. Some firms require high levels of fixed assets and relatively low labor inputs in order to produce their finished product. This type of firm is often referred to as *capital intensive*. Electric utilities are a good example of capital intensive firms. Other firms require high labor inputs and fewer fixed assets in order to produce a finished good. Manufacturers of electrical equipment that requires a great deal of hand assembly and soldering are examples of *labor intensive* firms. As a rule, the higher the ratio of fixed assets to total assets, the more capital intensive is the firm.

Fixed assets are quite often referred to as *earning assets* since they generally provide the basis for the firm's earning power. Without plant and equipment, the firm could not produce a product. Current assets such as cash, accounts receivable, and inventory do not give the manufacturing firm earning power; only in the case of a merchandising concern could these assets be considered the firm's earning base. The fixed assets of the manufacturing concern provide the finished goods inventories that are ultimately converted into cash. Their importance cannot be overemphasized.

This chapter discusses the key concepts involved in the management of the firm's fixed assets. The first section is devoted to the considerations involved in the acquisition, maintenance, and replacement of fixed assets. The focus is not on the production-oriented aspects of fixed-asset management, but on the financial implications of certain fixed-asset strategies. The second section of the chapter is devoted to basic capital budgeting concepts and terminology. The final section discusses procedures for developing the data needed to evaluate capital expenditure alternatives. The main objective in this chapter is to develop an appropriate "point of view." Chapter 15 will present the basic techniques used to select capital expenditure projects.

MANAGING FIXED ASSETS

Since fixed-asset investments represent sizable outlays to manufacturing firms, a great deal of attention must be given to decisions with respect to not only the initial outlay for purchasing a given asset, but also subsequent outlays associated with the asset. Fixed assets by definition have lives longer than a year and therefore represent a long-term financial commitment by the firm. As time passes, they may become obsolete or require an overhaul. At these points, certain financial decisions are required. This section of the chapter discusses capital expenditures, the authorization of capital expenditures, and the origin and path of capital expenditure proposals, placing special emphasis on their implications for the firm's financial policy.

Capital expenditures

A *capital expenditure* is an outlay made by the firm that is expected to produce *benefits over a period of time greater than one year.* Fixed-asset outlays are capital expenditures, but not all capital expenditures result in the receipt of a fixed asset. A $60,000 outlay for a new machine with a usable life of 15 years is a capital expenditure; so is an outlay for advertising that produces benefits over a long period. However, outlays for advertising are not normally capitalized as an asset on the firm's balance sheet.[1] In this chapter we shall be concerned primarily with capital expenditures for fixed assets.

Capital expenditures can be made for many possible reasons. But although the motives for capital expenditures differ, the techniques for evaluating them remain fixed. The basic motives for capital expenditures are to acquire, replace, or modernize fixed assets or to obtain some less tangible benefit over a long period. Each of these motives is described separately below.

Expenditures to acquire assets.

Probably the most common motive for a capital expenditure is the acquisition of fixed assets. A growing firm often finds it necessary to acquire new fixed assets rapidly. As the firm's growth slows and it reaches maturity, most of its capital expenditures will be

---

[1]Some firms do, in effect, capitalize advertising outlays if there is reason to believe the benefit of the outlay will be received at some future date. The capitalized advertising may appear as a deferred charge such as "deferred advertising expense," which is then amortized over the future. Expenses of this type are often deferred for reporting purposes in order to increase reported earnings, while for tax purposes the entire amount will be expensed in order to reduce the firm's tax liability.

for the replacement of obsolete or worn-out assets. It is important for the reader to keep in mind the fact that fixed assets include both plant and equipment. In other words, the purchase of additional physical facilities, such as an additional plant, is a capital expenditure.

The classic example of a capital expenditure decision involves a firm that is operating at full capacity and unable to fulfill the demand for its products. It must evaluate alternative capital expenditure proposals in order to determine how best to increase its productive capacity. The proposals include the acquisition of an existing facility, an addition to the firm's current facility, or construction of a totally new facility. Techniques for making such a decision are presented in Chapter 15.

Expenditures to replace assets. The replacement decision is quite common in more mature firms. This type of capital expenditure does not always result from the outright failure of a piece of equipment or the inability of an existing plant to function efficiently. The need to replace existing assets must be periodically examined by the firm's financial manager. A machine does not break down and say "Please replace me!"; but each time a machine requires a major repair, the outlay for the repair must be evaluated in light of the outlay that would be needed to replace the machine and the benefits of replacement.

It should not take a breakdown to stir the financial manager to consider the replacement of fixed assets. As machines become less able to hold required tolerances, or become inefficient compared to new-generation machines, the benefits of replacement should be evaluated. Due to electronic advances, numerically and computer-controlled machines have made many existing machines obsolete. New materials also contribute to the obsolescence of machinery. If replacing an existing machine with a new machine would permit the firm to produce the same product at a lower cost, the firm must analyze the costs and benefits of this change. An outlay for a new machine may be quite justifiable in light of the total cost savings that result. Only by keeping abreast of new developments and questioning outlays for repairs can the firm properly manage its fixed assets.

Expenditures for modernization. The modernization of fixed assets is often an alternative to their replacement. Firms needing additional productive capacity may find that both replacing and modernizing existing machinery are suitable solutions to the capacity problem. Modernization may involve rebuilding, overhauling, or adding to an existing machine or facility. Perhaps an existing drill press could be modernized by replacing its motor and adding a numerical control system. Perhaps a physical facility could be modernized by rewiring it, adding air conditioning, and so on.

Modernization decisions must be viewed in light of the relevant costs and benefits. The cost of modernizing a machine or physical facility may well be justified by the benefits. However, the financial manager must be careful in analyzing modernization suggestions to be certain that other alternatives have been considered. He or she may find that the cost of modernizing assets is actually greater than the cost of replacing them. In some cases, although the cost of modernization may be less than the cost of replacement, replacement may be preferable since it results in the receipt of benefits over a longer period of time. Suppose a firm has the following two alternatives: (1) to modernize a machine at a cost of $10,000 and generate savings of $5000 per year for five years or (2) to replace the machine at a cost of $15,000 and generate savings of $5000 a year for ten years. These types of modernization-replacement decisions are difficult to make and must be approached with caution.

Expenditures for other purposes.   Some capital expenditures do not result in the acquisition or transformation of tangible fixed assets that are shown on the firm's balance sheet; rather, they involve a long-term commitment of funds by the firm in expectation of a future return. These types of capital expenditures include outlays for advertising, research and development, management consulting, and new products. Advertising outlays are expected to provide benefits in the form of increased future sales. Research and development outlays are expected to provide future benefits in the form of new product ideas. Management consulting outlays are expected to provide returns in the form of increased profits from an increased efficiency of operation. New products are expected to contribute to a product mix that maximizes the firm's overall returns. Many capital expenditure proposals are hard to evaluate because it is difficult to measure the intangible returns they may generate.

Authorizing capital expenditures

The size of proposed capital expenditures can differ significantly. Some, such as the purchase of a hammer, do not require large outlays. The purchase of a hammer that will provide benefits for three years is by definition a capital expenditure, even if it costs only $8.[2] The purchase of a new machine costing $20,000 is also a capital expenditure since the machine is also expected to provide long-run returns. The actual dollar outlay and the importance of a capital item determine the organizational level at which the capital expenditure decision is made.

Dollar outlay.   Firms typically delegate capital expenditure authority on the basis of certain dollar limits. Typically, the board of directors reserves the right to make final decisions on capital expenditures requiring outlays beyond a certain dollar limit, while the authority for making smaller expen-

---

[2]Even though purchases of items such as hammers are known to provide benefits over a period greater than a year, they are treated as expenditures in the year of purchase. There is a certain dollar limit beyond which outlays are capitalized and depreciated rather than expensed. This dollar limit depends largely on what the Internal Revenue Service will permit. In accounting, the issue of whether to expense or capitalize an outlay is resolved using the *principle of materiality*, which suggests that any outlays that are deemed material (i.e., large) relative to the firm's scale of operations should be capitalized; others should be expensed in the current period. Of course, the firm, by expensing instead of capitalizing outlays, avoids the clerical work required to set up and maintain a depreciation schedule for the item, while at the same time receiving the maximum tax relief.

TABLE 14.1 A scheme for
delegating capital expenditure decision authority

Size of expenditure	Decision-making authority
Over $100,000	Board of directors or specified top management committee
$50,000–$100,000	President and/or chairman of board of directors
$20,000–$50,000	Vice president in charge of division
$5000–$20,000	Plant manager
Under $5000	Persons chosen by plant manager

ditures is delegated to other organizational levels. An example of a scheme for delegating capital expenditure decision authority is presented in Table 14.1. The table illustrates that as the dollar value of outlays decreases, the decision-making authority moves to lower levels within the organization. The actual breakdown of decision-making authority may differ from one organization to the next.

The top management committee mentioned in Table 14.1 generally consists of high-level officers and members of the board of directors. This special committee, which is sometimes called an executive committee, an advisory committee, an operations committee, or a planning committee, often has the final authority for approving proposals concerning plant expansion, subsidiary acquisitions, and any other actions that would require a major financial commitment by the firm. The actual dollar limit on outlays that can be authorized at various organizational levels depends directly on the size of the operation. In a small firm, expenditures over a few hundred dollars may have to be OK'd by the company president, whereas in larger firms a procedure similar to that shown in Table 14.1 may be used.

Critical expenditures. Firms operating under critical time constraints with respect to production often find it necessary to provide for exceptions to a dollar outlay scheme for making capital expenditure decisions. The plant manager is often given the power to make capital expenditure decisions necessary to keep the production line moving even though they entail larger outlays than he or she would normally be allowed to authorize. These types of exceptions must be allowed because of the high cost of interrupting the flow of production. Certain expenditure decisions must be made immediately, and, in cases where many dollars would be lost should a shutdown occur, the authority to make these decisions must be given to those directly involved. It is wise to put some dollar limit on these critical expenditures, but it can be set somewhat above the normal limit at that organizational level.

Large critical expenditures must be evaluated from a cost-benefit standpoint. If a critical machine breaks and the cost of its repair is found to be high, it is advisable for the decision maker to evaluate the possibility of replacing the machine. These types of decisions must be made in light of the lost dollars that would result from a shutdown, the cost of repairs versus the cost of replacement, and the duration and dollar amount of the benefits that would result from replacement. Critical expenditures must be allowed for in the firm's overall capital expenditure decision-making policies.

The origin and path of capital expenditure proposals

Proposals for capital expenditures are made by people at all levels within a business organization. Many firms require the originator of a capital expenditure proposal to fill out certain forms indicating the estimated costs and benefits. The actual path the proposal follows as it travels from the originator to the ultimate decision maker(s) differs from one organization to another. Two patterns are quite common.

Minor expenditures. Proposals for minor expenditures typically go from the originator to a reviewer at some higher level in the firm. The reviewer's function is to check the accuracy and utility of the proposal, making sure that the information it contains is correct. If the reviewer is satisfied with the accuracy of the proposal, he or she passes it on to a decision maker, who may be a department head or plant manager. The decision maker then determines whether the proposed expenditure should be made. In the case of outlays critical to the continuation of production, the proposal-review process may be bypassed.

Major expenditures. Proposals for major expenditures go from the originator to a reviewer at a top management level. These proposals are quite often originated by top management and reviewed by a high-level committee. More than one reviewing process is often required in order to assure the accuracy of the data, and the proposal is screened to ensure that all of the information necessary to evaluate it has been included. A higher level of scrutiny is required in the case of major proposals because of the large outlays involved.

The screening process assures the decision maker or decision-making committee that the proposal being considered meets the minimum standards of the firm, that estimates of cost and benefits are reasonable and conclusive, and that the calculations are accurate. The review of proposals saves a great deal of time for the decision maker(s). The decision whether a proposal should be implemented is made by the decision maker(s) on the basis of the figures submitted, relevant subjective factors, and any financial constraints present. Various decision-making criteria and financial constraints are discussed in Chapter 15.

CAPITAL BUDGETING FUNDAMENTALS

Capital budgeting refers to the total process of generating, evaluating, selecting, and following up on capital expenditure alternatives. Quite often the capital budgeting process is constrained by the amount of money available for investment. The preceding section of this chapter described the generation and flow of proposals. This section of the chapter is devoted to the basic concepts and terminology used in the capital budgeting decision environment. Attention is given to the basic types of projects, the availability of funds, and the approaches to capital budgeting decisions. Actual techniques for evaluating capital expenditure alternatives will be discussed in Chapter 15.

Types of projects

The firm may be confronted with a number of different types of decision-making situations, depending on the types of projects it is considering. The two most common types are (1) independent and (2) mutually exclusive projects.

Independent projects. Independent projects are projects that compete with one another in such way that the acceptance of one *does not eliminate* the others from further consideration. If a firm has unlimited funds to invest, all the independent projects that meet its minimum investment criteria can be implemented.

Mutually exclusive projects. Mutually exclusive projects are projects that have the same function. The acceptance of one of a group of mutually exclusive projects *eliminates* all other projects in the group from further consideration. For example, if a firm is confronted with three ways to achieve its goal of increasing its productive capacity, the three alternatives would be considered mutually exclusive. If each of these alternatives meet the firm's minimum acceptance criteria, some technique will have to be used to determine the "best" one. Acceptance of this "best" alternative will eliminate the need for either of the other two alternatives.

The availability of funds

The availability of funds for capital expenditures affects the firm's decision environment.

Unlimited funds. If a firm has unlimited funds for investment, making capital budgeting decisions is quite simple. All independent projects that provide returns greater than some predetermined level can be accepted. Most firms are not in such a situation. Typically only a certain number of dollars are allocated for making capital expenditures. Normally the amount is specified in the firm's annual budget.

Capital rationing. Most firms find they have only a fixed number of dollars available for making capital expenditures. Numerous projects may compete for these limited dollars. The firm must therefore ration its funds, allocating them to projects in a manner that maximizes the long-run returns. Techniques for *capital rationing* are briefly discussed at the end of Chapter 15. Quite often, firms confronted with serious capital rationing are able to raise additional money in order to ease the budget constraint.

Approaches to capital budgeting decisions

Two basic approaches to capital budgeting decisions are available. These approaches are somewhat dependent on whether the firm is confronted with capital rationing. They are also affected by the type of project involved.

The two basic decision approaches are the *accept-reject approach* and the *ranking approach*.

The accept-reject approach.   The accept-reject approach involves evaluating capital expenditure proposals to determine whether they are acceptable. This is a simple approach since it requires merely applying predetermined criteria to a proposal and comparing the resulting return to the firm's minimum acceptable return. This approach can be used if the firm has unlimited funds available. An accept-reject decision is also a preliminary step in evaluating mutually exclusive projects or in a situation where capital must be rationed. If a mutually exclusive project does not meet the firm's basic acceptance criteria, it shoud be eliminated from consideration. If the firm is evaluating projects with a view to capital rationing, only acceptable projects should be considered.

The ranking approach.   A second approach to evaluating capital expenditure alternatives involves ranking projects on the basis of some predetermined criterion such as the rate of return. The project with the highest return is ranked first and the project with the lowest acceptable return last. Only acceptable projects should be ranked. Ranking is useful in selecting the "best" of a group of mutually exclusive projects and in evaluating projects with a view to capital rationing.

When the firm is confronted with a number of projects, some of which are mutually exclusive and some of which are independent, the proper approach is to determine the best of each group of mutually exclusive alternatives, and therefore reduce the mixed group of projects to a group of independent projects. The best of the acceptable independent projects can then be selected. All acceptable projects can be implemented if the firm has unlimited funds. If capital rationing is necessary, the mix of projects that maximizes the firm's overall return should be accepted. Various decision-making techniques applicable in these situations are presented in Chapter 15.

EXAMPLE

A firm with unlimited funds must evaluate eight projects—A through H. Projects A, B, and C are mutually exclusive; projects G and H are also mutually exclusive; and the remaining projects D, E, and F are independent of each of the other projects. The projects are listed below along with their returns:

Project	Status	Return
A	} Mutually exclusive	16%
B		19%
C		11%
D	Independent	15%
E	Independent	13%
F	Independent	21%
G	} Mutually exclusive	20%
H		17%

In order to evaluate these projects, the best of the mutually exclusive groups must first be determined. On the basis of the given return figures, project B would be selected from mutually exclusive projects A, B, and C since it has the highest return of this group; and project G would be preferred to project H since it has the higher return. After the selection of the best of the two groups of mutually exclusive projects, the five (three projects—A, C, and H—will have been eliminated) remaining independent projects can be ranked on the basis of their returns as shown:

Rank	Project	Return
1	F	21%
2	G	20%
3	B	19%
4	D	15%
5	E	13%

Given the firm has unlimited funds, and assuming that all projects are acceptable, the ranking would not be especially useful. If the firm were operating, instead, in an environment of capital rationing, the rankings would be useful in choosing which projects to accept. ●

DEVELOPING THE RELEVANT DATA[3]

In order to evaluate capital expenditure alternatives, the *after-tax cash outflows* and *inflows* associated with each project must be determined. *Cash flows* are measured rather than using accounting figures because it is these flows that directly affect the firm's ability to pay bills or purchase assets. Accounting figures and cash flows are not necessarily the same due to the presence of certain noncash expenditures on the firm's income statement. When a proposed purchase is intended to replace an existing asset, the *incremental* cash outflows and inflows that will result from the investment must be measured.

The remainder of this chapter is devoted to the development of procedures for measuring the *relevant* cash outflows and cash inflows associated with proposed capital expenditures. Cash-flow patterns are discussed, the concept of "initial investment" is examined, and two alternative techniques for determining the incremental, after-tax cash inflows associated with a capital expenditure project are illustrated.

Types of cash-flow patterns

Cash-flow patterns associated with capital investment projects can be classified as conventional or nonconventional. Another classification is as an annuity or mixed stream.

---

[3]The term "relevant" is used throughout this and the following chapters to refer to the cash flows that must be considered in analyzing various capital budgeting decision alternatives. The term is used to mean the "incremental after-tax cash flows" associated with a capital expenditure alternative.

FIGURE 14.1 A conventional cash-flow pattern

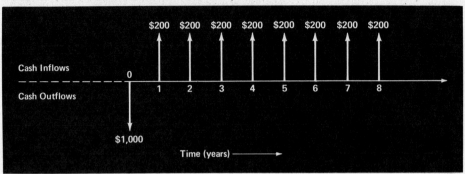

Conventional cash flows. The conventional cash-flow pattern consists of an initial cash outflow followed by a series of cash inflows. This pattern is associated with many types of capital expenditures. For example, a firm may spend $1000 today and as a result expect to receive cash inflows of $200 at the end of each year for the next eight years. This conventional cash-flow pattern is diagrammed in Figure 14.1. All conventional cash-flow patterns can be diagrammed in this way.

Nonconventional cash flows. A nonconventional cash-flow pattern is any cash-flow pattern in which an initial outlay is not followed by a series of inflows. Alternating inflows and outflows and an inflow followed by outflows are examples of nonconventional cash-flow patterns. A common type of nonconventional cash-flow pattern results from the purchase of an asset that generates cash inflows for a period of years, is overhauled, and again generates a stream of cash inflows for a number of years. For example, the purchase of a machine may require an initial cash outflow of $2000 and generate cash inflows of $500 each year for four years. In the fifth year after the purchase, an outlay of $800 may be required in order to overhaul the machine, after which it generates inflows of $500 each year for five years. This nonconventional pattern of cash flows is illustrated in Figure 14.2.

Serious difficulties arise in evaluating projects involving a nonconventional pattern of cash flows. The discussions in the remainder of this chapter and in the following chapters will be limited to the evaluation of conventional cash-flow patterns.

Annuity or mixed stream. The term *annuity* is commonly used to describe a pattern of cash inflows that are the same every year. In other words, an annuity is a series of *equal annual* cash inflows. A stream of cash inflows that is not an annuity is referred to as a *mixed stream* of cash inflows. The cash inflows of $164,000 per year associated with the new machine in Table 14.4 (see p. 391) are inflows from an annuity, while the unequal pattern of inflows generated by the present machine are a mixed stream. As pointed out

FIGURE 14.2 A nonconventional cash-flow pattern

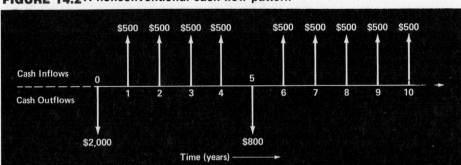

in Chapter 13, the techniques required to evaluate cash inflows are much simpler to use when the pattern of inflows is an annuity. An annuity is a conventional cash-flow pattern, while mixed streams may be conventional or nonconventional cash-flow patterns.

Initial investment

The term *initial investment* as used here refers to the relevant cash outflow to be considered in evaluating a prospective capital expenditure. It is calculatd by netting out all outflows and inflows occurring at time zero (the time the expenditure is made) to get the initial outlay at time zero. Since our discussion of capital budgeting is concerned only with investments exhibiting conventional cash flows, a net outflow or initial investment must occur at time zero.

The basic variables that must be considered in determining the initial investment associated with a project are the cost of the new project, the installation costs (if any) associated with it, the proceeds (if any) from the sale of assets, and the taxes (if any) resulting from the sale of assets. The basic format for determining initial investment is given in Table 14.2. Each component of initial investment is discussed separately on the following pages.

The cost of a new project. The *cost* of a new project is the outlay it requires. Typically we are concerned with the acquisition of a fixed asset

TABLE 14.2 The basic format
for determining initial investment

Cost of new project
+ Installation cost
− Proceeds from sale of assets
± Taxes on sale of assets

Initial investment

for which a definite purchase price is paid. If the firm is not replacing an existing asset, and there are no installation costs, the purchase price of the asset is equal to the initial investment. Each capital expenditure decision should be closely analyzed in order to make sure that installation costs have not been overlooked.

Installation costs.   The cost of installing a new asset once it has been acquired is considered part of the capital expenditure for it, since the Internal Revenue Service requires the inclusion of this cost in calculating the assets' depreciable value, which is written off over a period of years. *Installation costs are defined as any added costs necessary to get a machine into operation.*[4] The IRS frowns on firms expensing these costs since they actually should be capitalized.

Proceeds from the sale of assets.   If a new asset is intended to replace existing assets which are being sold, the proceeds from the sale are considered a cash inflow. If costs are incurred in the process of removing the old assets, the proceeds from the sale of the old assets are reduced by these *removal costs.* Some firms expense removal costs, but the IRS requires that they be deducted from the proceeds received on the sale of the asset. The proceeds from the sale of a replaced asset are often referred to as the *liquidation value* of the asset. These proceeds help to reduce the cost of the new asset, thereby reducing the firm's initial investment.

Taxes.   Taxes must be considered in calculating the initial investment whenever a new asset replaces an old asset that has been sold.[5] The proceeds from the sale of the replaced asset are normally subject to some type of tax. The amount of taxes and the way the proceeds are taxed depends directly on the relationship between the proceeds, the initial purchase price, and the book value of the asset being replaced. There are four possibilities: (1) the asset is sold for more than its initial purchase price, (2) the asset is sold for more than its book value but less than its initial purchase price, (3) the asset is sold for its book value, and (4) the asset is sold for less than its book value.

EXAMPLE

Let us assume that a firm purchased an asset four years ago for $100,000. The asset is being depreciated on a straight-line basis over 10 years with no salvage value; therefore, the annual depreciation is $10,000 ($100,000 ÷ 10). The book value of the asset today is $60,000 [$100,000 − (4 · $10,000/year)]. What will happen if the firm now decides to sell the asset and replace it with a new asset. Since the old

---

[4]The IRS only requires the firm to charge to the cost of the new asset all material installation costs. Even if a firm uses its in-house maintenance department to install the asset, if the cost of this installation is greater than a few hundred dollars, the installation cost should be added to the cost of the asset and depreciated over its life. If the installation cost is not greater than a few hundred dollars, it should be expensed in the current period rather than capitalized and depreciated.

[5]A detailed discussion of the tax treatment of ordinary income and losses, and capital gains income and losses by corporations was presented at the end of Chapter 2.

asset has been held for longer than one year, certain gains (if there are any) from the sale will be long-term and therefore subject to capital gains taxes. (See Chapter 2.) If the asset had not been held for longer than one year, all gains would be short term and therefore taxed at the firm's ordinary tax rate. The firm's ordinary tax rate is assumed to be 40 percent,[6] and the tax rate on long-term capital gains is 30 percent. Let us consider each of the situations that may exist.

The sale of the asset for more than its initial purchase price If the firm sells the old asset for $110,000, it realizes a long-term capital gain of $10,000 (the amount by which the sale price exceeds the initial purchase price of $100,000). The firm also experiences an ordinary gain in the form of recaptured depreciation of $40,000 (i.e., $100,000 − $60,000), taxable at the ordinary rate. The taxes on the total gain of $50,000 are calculated as follows:

> *Total taxes*
> Capital gains (long-term): $10,000(.30)   = $ 3,000
> Ordinary gains: $40,000(.40)   =   16,000
> $19,000

These taxes should be used in calculating the initial investment in the new machine being purchased, using the format in Table 14.2. In effect, they raise the amount of the firm's initial investment in the new asset by reducing the proceeds from the sale of the old asset.

The sale of the asset for more than its book value but less than its initial purchase price If the firm sells the old asset for $80,000, which is less than its original purchase price but more than its book value, there is no capital gain. However, the firm still experiences a gain in the form of recaptured depreciation of $20,000 (i.e., $80,000 − $60,000), which is taxed as part of its ordinary income. Since the firm is assumed to be in the 40-percent tax bracket, the taxes on the $20,000 gain are $8000. This $8000 in taxes should be used in calculating the firm's initial investment in the new machine.

The sale of the asset for its book value If the asset is sold for $60,000, which is its book value, the firm experiences neither a gain nor a loss on the sale. It breaks even. Since no tax results from selling an asset for its book value, there is no effect on the firm's initial investment in the new machine.

The sale of the asset for less than its book value If the firm sells the asset for $40,000, an amount less than its book value, it experiences a loss of $20,000 (i.e., $60,000 − $40,000). If it was a depreciable asset used in business, or trade, the loss may be used to offset ordinary operating income. If the asset was not used in business or trade, the (capital) loss can only be used to offset capital gains. Both types of loss can be applied currently or carried back three years, while depreciable asset losses can be carried forward seven years and capital losses can be carried forward only five years, if necessary.[7] In this case, there are two possibilities:

---

[6] In order to emphasize better the tax effects on various aspects of the initial investment and subsequent cash flows, a 40-percent ordinary income tax rate is used throughout this and following chapters.

[7] The reader is referred to Chapter 2 for a more detailed discussion of tax loss carrybacks and carryforwards.

1. If the asset is used in business or trade and there are operating earnings which the depreciable asset loss can be used to offset, the firm will save $8000 in taxes (i.e., $20,000 · .40).
2. If the asset was *not* used in business or trade but there are capital gains that the capital loss of $20,000 can be used to offset, the firm will save $6000 in taxes (i.e., $20,000 · .30).

In either case, if current operating earnings or capital gains are not sufficient to offset the loss, the firm can carry portions of it back or forward. Losses treated in this way may affect the initial investment in the new machine. The impact of a carryback provides a refund that will effectively reduce the firm's initial investment while carryforwards of tax losses will only impact the subsequent years' cash flows. ●

We have now seen the various tax situations that may result from selling an asset that is being replaced.[8] A final example of how the initial investment associated with capital expenditures is calculated is given below.

EXAMPLE
The Ajax Company is trying to determine the initial investment required to replace an old machine with a newer, much more sophisticated model. The proposed machine's purchase price is $380,000, and an additional $20,000 will be required to install it. It will be depreciated on a straight-line basis over five years with no salvage value. The old machine was purchased three years ago at a cost of $240,000 and was being depreciated on a straight-line basis (no salvage value) over its eight-year life (i.e., $30,000/yr. depreciation). The firm has found a buyer willing to pay $280,000 for the old machine and remove it at his own expense. The firm is in the 40-percent tax bracket and long-term capital gains are taxed at a rate of 30 percent.

The only component of the initial investment required by the proposed purchase that is difficult to obtain is taxes. Since the firm is planning to sell the old machine for $40,000 more than its purchase price, it will realize a long-term capital gain of $40,000. The book value of the old machine is $150,000 [$240,000 − (3 yrs. · $30,000/year)]. An ordinary gain of $90,000 ($240,000 − $150,000) in recaptured depreciation is also realized on the sale. The total taxes on the gain are $48,000 [($40,000 · .30) + ($90,000 · .40)]. Substituting these taxes, along with the purchase price and installation cost of the new machine and the proceeds from the sale of the old machine, into the format in Table 14.2 results in an initial investment of $168,000.

Cost of proposed machine	$380,000	Depreciable
+ Installation cost	20,000	outlay
− Proceeds from sale of old machine	280,000	
+ Taxes on sale of old machine	48,000	
Initial Investment	$168,000	

This represents the net cash outflow required at time zero. ●

---

[8]Throughout the discussion of capital budgeting in this section, all assets evaluated as candidates for replacement are assumed to be depreciable assets that are directly used in the business, so that any losses on the sale of these assets can be applied against ordinary operating income. The decisions are also structured in order to assure that the life remaining on the old asset is just equal to the life of the new asset; this assumption permits the avoidance of the problem of unequal lives.

In the example above, the *net* proceeds from the sale of the old machine ($232,000) could have been found by subtracting the taxes from the sale price ($280,000 − $48,000). This is, in essence, the net amount that has been deducted from the sum of the purchase price and installation cost of a new machine. Regardless of which approach is used, the resulting initial investment figure is the same.

Cash inflows

The benefits expected from a capital expenditure are measured as *incremental after-tax cash inflows*. The major emphasis in this section will be on developing clear definitions of the terms *after-tax*, *cash inflows*, and *incremental*. Examples will be included as necessary.

Interpreting the term *after-tax*.   Benefits expected to result from proposed capital expenditures must be measured on an after-tax basis, since the firm will not have the use of any benefits until it has satisfied the government's tax claims. Since these claims depend on the firm's taxable income, the deduction of taxes *prior to* making comparisons between proposals is necessary for consistency. Consistency is required in evaluating capital expenditure alternatives since the intention is to compare "like benefits."

Interpreting the term *cash inflows*.   All benefits expected from a proposed project must be measured on a cash-flow basis. Cash inflows represent dollars that can be spent, not merely "accounting profits," which, as indicated in Chapter 1, are not necessarily available for paying the firm's bills. A simple technique for converting the firm's after-tax net profits into cash inflows was illustrated in Chapter 2. The basic calculation requires adding any noncash charges that are deducted as expenses on the firm's income statement back to the net profits after taxes. Probably the most common noncash charge found on income statements is depreciation. It is the only noncash charge that will be considered in this section. The following example shows how after-tax cash inflows can be calculated for both a present and a proposed project.

EXAMPLE

The Ajax Company has estimated its revenues, expenses (excluding depreciation), and earnings before depreciation and taxes, with and without the capital expenditure—machine purchase—proposed in the preceding example, to be as given in Table 14.3. The amount to be depreciated with the proposed machine is calculated by summing the purchase price of $380,000 and the installation cost of $20,000. No salvage value is expected for the proposed machine at the end of its depreciable life.[9] Since the machine is to be depreciated on a straight-line basis over a five-year

---

[9]If a salvage value were expected at the end of the asset's depreciable life, the salvage value would be deducted from the purchase price plus the installation cost to get the machine's depreciable value. In other words, if a salvage value is expected, this portion of the purchase price should not be depreciated. Where no salvage value is expected, the sum of the purchase price and any installation cost is the depreciable value of the asset.

period, the annual depreciation will be $80,000 (i.e., $400,000 ÷ 5). The annual depreciation on the present machine was given earlier as $30,000.

TABLE 14.3 Ajax Company's revenues, expenses (excluding depreciation), and earnings before depreciation and taxes

Year	Projected revenue (1)	Projected expenses (excl. depr.) (2)	Projected earnings before depreciation and taxes (1) − (2) (3)
With proposed machine			
1	$2,520,000	$2,300,000	$220,000
2	2,520,000	2,300,000	220,000
3	2,520,000	2,300,000	220,000
4	2,520,000	2,300,000	220,000
5	2,520,000	2,300,000	220,000
With present machine			
1	$2,200,000	$1,990,000	$210,000
2	2,300,000	2,110,000	190,000
3	2,400,000	2,230,000	170,000
4	2,400,000	2,250,000	150,000
5	2,250,000	2,120,000	130,000

The cash inflows in each year can be calculated as follows using the projected earnings before depreciation and taxes.[10]

Projected earnings before depreciation and taxes
− Depreciation
_____
Projected earnings before taxes
− Taxes
_____
Projected earnings after taxes
+ Depreciation
_____
Projected Cash Inflows

Treating the projected earnings before depreciation and taxes in Table 14.3 in this way results in the projected cash inflows in Table 14.4. A 40-percent tax rate is used, with an annual depreciation of $80,000 and $30,000 for the proposed and present machines, respectively. ●

[10]Sometimes it is not necessary to relate the effects of a proposed expenditure directly to the firm's after-tax profits. In these cases, the incremental after-tax cash flows can be estimated directly by netting additional after-tax cash inflows and after-tax cash outflows for each period and adding the tax rate times the amount of additional depreciation expected to the net cash flows. This approach is discussed in greater detail and illustrated in a subsequent section of this chapter.

TABLE 14.4 Projected cash inflows
for the Ajax Company

	Projected cash inflows	
Year	With proposed machine (1)	With present machine (2)
1	$164,000	$138,000
2	164,000	126,000
3	164,000	114,000
4	164,000	102,000
5	164,000	90,000

Interpreting the term *incremental*. The final step in estimating the cash inflows to be used in evaluating a proposed project is to calculate the *incremental* or *relevant* cash inflows. Incremental cash inflows are needed since our concern is *only* with how much more or less cash will flow into the firm as a result of the proposed project.

EXAMPLE
The figures given for each year in column 2 of Table 14.4 represent the amount of cash inflows the Ajax Company will receive without the proposed expenditure. If the proposed machine replaces the present machine, the firm's cash inflows for each year will be those shown in column 1 of Table 14.4. Just as, earlier, we were concerned only with the firm's initial investment, so here we are concerned only with its incremental, or relevant, cash inflows.

Subtracting the cash inflows with the present machine from the cash inflows with the proposed machine in each year results in the incremental cash inflows for each year given in Table 14.5. These incremental after-tax cash inflows are the relevant cash inflows to be considered in evaluating the benefits of making a capital expenditure for the proposed machine. ●

Now that both the initial investment and the relevant or incremental cash inflows have been determined, the Ajax Company's proposed expenditure can be evaluated. A diagram of the relevant cash flows is given in Figure

TABLE 14.5 Relevant or incremental
cash inflows for the Ajax Company

Year	Relevant cash inflow
1	$26,000
2	38,000
3	50,000
4	62,000
5	74,000

FIGURE 14.3 The Ajax Company's relevant (or incremental) cash flows with the new machine

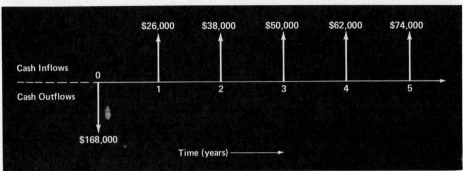

14.3. As the figure shows, they follow a conventional pattern (i.e., an initial outlay followed by a series of inflows). Techniques for analyzing this type of cash inflow pattern to determine whether to undertake a proposed capital investment are discussed in Chapter 15. Only projects generating a conventional pattern of cash flows are considered.

A shortcut for determining relevant cash inflows

The cash inflows calculated in the preceding section can be determined more directly by finding the changes in revenues, changes in expenses (excluding depreciation), and changes in depreciation; adjusting these changes for taxes in order to determine the cash flows resulting from them; and adding the cash flows together in order to get the relevant cash inflow for each year. The factors for converting changes in revenues, expenses, and depreciation to (after-tax) cash flow changes are given in Table 14.6.

By multiplying the change in each of the items listed above by the respective factors given in Table 14.6, the cash-flow change caused by these items will result. By summing the individual cash flow changes for each year, one can determine the relevant cash inflow for the year.

The tax-adjustment factors for revenues and expenses are quite straightforward, but the depreciation adjustment may be a little less clear since

TABLE 14.6 Factors for converting changes in revenues, expenses (excluding depreciation), and depreciation into changes in cash flow

Change in	Tax-adjustment factor
Revenue	(1-tax rate)
Expense (excluding depreciation)	−(1-tax rate)
Depreciation	tax rate

the reader may feel that cash flows should be increased by the full amount of depreciation since, to find cash flows from operations, the amount of depreciation is added back to the after-tax profits. The following example should clarify why the depreciation tax-adjustment factor is defined as the tax rate times the change in depreciation.

EXAMPLE

A firm is contemplating whether or not to purchase an asset that is *not* expected to impact the firm's earnings in any way other than by increasing depreciation from its current level of zero to $10,000. The firm expects its earnings before depreciation and taxes to remain at $100,000 as a result of the proposed purchase. The firm, which is in the 40-percent tax bracket, has determined the cash flows resulting in each case as shown below:

	Without purchase	With purchase
Earnings before depreciation and taxes	$100,000	$100,000
Less: Depreciation	0	10,000
Earnings before taxes	$100,000	$90,000
Less: Taxes (.40)	40,000	36,000
Earnings after taxes	$60,000	$54,000
Plus: Depreciation	0	10,000
Cash flow	$60,000	$64,000
Difference in cash flow attributable to depreciation (.40)($10,000)		$4000

It should be clear from this data that the presence of depreciation causes the firm's cash flows with depreciation ($64,000) to exceed the cash flows resulting without the depreciation deduction ($60,000) by an amount ($4000) equal to the product of the tax rate (.40) and the difference in depreciation ($10,000). In other words, a change in depreciation will increase a firm's cash flow by an amount equal to the tax rate times the amount of the change. ●

Using the data presented earlier in the Ajax Company example, the application of the shortcut approach for determining relevant cash inflows using the factors given in Table 14.6 for converting changes in revenues, expenses (excluding depreciation), and depreciation into changes in cash flows is illustrated in the following example.

EXAMPLE

Using the Ajax Company data given in Table 14.3, the changes in revenues and expenses excluding depreciation are calculated in Table 14.7. Since the annual depreciation on the proposed machine is $80,000 (i.e., $400,000 ÷ 5 yrs.) and on the present machine it is $30,000 (i.e., $240,000 ÷ 8 yrs.), the change in depreciation for each year will be $50,000 (i.e., $80,000 − $30,000). Using the change data developed for revenues, expenses (excluding depreciation), and depreciation, the relevant cash inflows are determined in Table 14.8 by applying the tax adjustment factors presented earlier in Table 14.6.

TABLE 14.7 Determination of annual changes in revenue and expenses (excluding depreciation) for the Ajax Company

Year	Revenue			Expense (excluding depr.)		
	Proposed (1)	Present (2)	Change (1) − (2) (3)	Proposed (4)	Present (5)	Change (4) − (5) (6)
1	$2,520,000	$2,200,000	$320,000	$2,300,000	$1,990,000	$310,000
2	2,520,000	2,300,000	220,000	2,300,000	2,110,000	190,000
3	2,520,000	2,400,000	120,000	2,300,000	2,230,000	70,000
4	2,520,000	2,400,000	120,000	2,300,000	2,250,000	50,000
5	2,520,000	2,250,000	270,000	2,300,000	2,120,000	180,000

Note: The data in columns (1), (2), (4), and (5) are from Table 14.3.

TABLE 14.8 Determination of the relevant cash inflows for the Ajax Company using the shortcut approach

Year	Item	Amount (1)	Factor (2)	Cash flow (1) × (2) (3)
1	Change in revenues	$320,000	(1 − .4)	$192,000
	Change in expenses	310,000	− (1 − .4)	− 186,000
	Change in depreciation	50,000	.4	20,000
	Relevant Cash Inflow			$26,000
2	Change in revenues	$220,000	(1 − .4)	$132,000
	Change in expenses	190,000	− (1 − .4)	− 114,000
	Change in depreciation	50,000	.4	20,000
	Relevant Cash Inflow			$38,000
3	Change in revenues	$120,000	(1 − .4)	$72,000
	Change in expenses	70,000	− (1 − .4)	− 42,000
	Change in depreciation	50,000	.4	20,000
	Relevant Cash Inflow			$50,000
4	Change in revenues	$120,000	(1 − .4)	$72,000
	Change in expenses	50,000	− (1 − .4)	− 30,000
	Change in depreciation	50,000	.4	20,000
	Relevant Cash Inflow			$62,000
5	Change in revenues	$270,000	(1 − .4)	$162,000
	Change in expenses	180,000	− (1 − .4)	− 108,000
	Change in depreciation	50,000	.4	20,000
	Relevant Cash Inflow			$74,000

A comparison of the relevant cash inflows calculated in Table 14.8 above with the cash inflows calculated earlier using the longer approach and presented in Table 14.5 confirms the accuracy of the shortcut approach for determining relevant cash inflows. •

Although the shortcut approach illustrated in the preceding example does not present the calculations in a fashion that is as readily understandable as using the more detailed approach, which involves calculation of each year's cash flows using an income statement format, it provides the same results in a more direct fashion. The use of the shortcut approach, which involves three basic steps: (1) determining the changes in revenues, expenses (excluding depreciation), and depreciation for each year; (2) adjusting these changes using the specified factors in order to get their cash-flow effects; and (3) adding the cash-flow effects in order to determine the net effect on cash flows resulting from a proposed change, is recommended due to its computational efficiency.

SUMMARY

This chapter has been devoted to certain key concepts with respect to the management and analysis of fixed assets. Various motives were discussed for capital expenditures, which are outlays that generate benefits over a period greater than a year. Some capital expenditures are made in order to acquire new assets for expansion; others result from the need to replace or modernize existing facilities. Another group of capital expenditures, the results of which do not necessarily show up as fixed assets on the firm's balance sheet, are those made for advertising campaigns, research and development projects, and the like. Regardless of the motive for making a capital expenditure, the basic format for analyzing capital expenditure proposals remains the same.

The authority to make capital expenditures is typically delegated on the basis of the dollar outlays involved. Generally there is a maximum dollar amount a given manager can expend. Procedures for the review of all capital expenditures are a normal part of the capital expenditure process. Often capital expenditure decisions involving large dollar outlays are made by a committee of top executives. Proposals for capital expenditures must be closely scrutinized because of the long-term commitments they entail.

Capital expenditure proposals may be either independent or mutually exclusive. Proposals are mutually exclusive if the acceptance of one eliminates the other proposals from consideration. Independent proposals are not eliminated from consideration due to the acceptance of a given project. Most firms have only limited funds for capital investments and must ration them between carefully selected projects. In order to make investment decisions when capital must be rationed or proposals are mutually exclusive, projects must be ranked. Independent project decisions can be made using an accept-reject criterion when funds are unlimited.

The relevant data necessary for making capital budgeting decisions are the initial investment and the incremental after-tax cash inflows associated with a given proposal. The initial investment is the initial outlay required, taking into account all installation costs, liquidation values, and taxes. Incremental after-tax cash inflows are the additional cash flows received as a result of implementing a proposal. Cash flows are used instead of after-tax profits since cash, not paper profits, pays the bills and permits additional investments. Two basic approaches exist for determining the relevant cash inflows. One approach uses the income statement format to estimate the relevant cash inflows; the other is a shortcut approach that directly adjusts changes in revenues, expenses (excluding depreciation), and depreciation for tax effects in order to determine the relevant cash inflows. Only conventional cash flows, which consist of an initial outlay followed by cash inflows, are dealt with in this book. Annuities, which provide conventional patterns of equal annual cash inflows, simpify the analysis of capital expenditures. The following two chapters are devoted to the description of capital budgeting techniques and their application to relevant cash-flow patterns in the capital expenditure decision process.

QUESTIONS

14-1   What does the fact that a firm is described as "capital intensive" reveal about its production process and level of fixed assets? Why?

14-2   What is a capital expenditure? How does the definition of a capital expenditure suggest that all fixed-asset outlays are capital expenditures?

14-3   What are the key motives for capital expenditures? Which motive is most commonly cited?

14-4   What sort of expenditure might be referred to as a "critical capital expenditure"? Why might the decision authority with respect to these outlays bypass the traditional decision channels?

14-5   How does the term "capital budgeting" relate to capital expenditures? What are key aspects of this process?

14-6   What two situations with respect to the availability of funds may be faced by the firm attempting to make capital budgeting decisions? Which of these situations is most common? Why?

14-7   What is the "accept-reject" approach for evaluating capital budgeting projects? For what sort of projects and in what situations is it used?

14-8   What is the "ranking approach" to evaluating capital budgeting projects? How does it differ from the accept-reject approach?

14-9   Why is it important to evaluate capital budgeting projects on the basis of *incremental after-tax cash flows?* Why not use accounting data instead of cash flows?

14-10 What is the difference between conventional and nonconventional cash-flow patterns? Can you diagram a conventional and a nonconventional pattern of cash flows? Which of these patterns is easiest to work with?

14-11 What is meant by the term "initial investment" in talking about the capital budgeting decision? With conventional cash-flow patterns, when does the initial investment occur?

14-12 What is the difference between annuities and mixed streams of cash flows? Why is it important to recognize the existence of an annuity?

14-13 Why are installation costs included in the cost of a new asset? What is the IRS's rationale for forcing a firm to include installation costs as part of the purchase price and forcing a firm to deduct any removal costs from the proceeds from sale of an old asset?

14-14 What four tax situations may result from sale of an asset that is being replaced?

14-15 In what situations can a firm benefit from a loss on the sale of an asset? Can any future benefit result from this loss? Why?

14-16 Using the framework for calculating initial investment given in this chapter, explain how a firm would calculate the value of depreciation needed to find cash flows. How is the depreciation of an asset that has a salvage value calculated?

14-17 Given the earnings before depreciation and taxes associated with an existing asset and a proposed replacement for it, how would the projected cash inflows associated with the decision be calculated?

14-18 Aside from its treatment as an adjustment for calculating depreciation, where else must salvage value be considered when evaluating the cash flows from a proposed project? Why?

14-19 Two methods of calculating future cash flows are presented in this chapter. Explain how the shortcut approach that uses tax-adjustment factors can yield the same result as the more detailed approach. Why does the shortcut approach use a different tax-adjustment factor for depreciation?

PROBLEMS

14-1 Given the following list of outlays, indicate whether each would normally be considered a capital or a current expenditure. Explain your answers.
  a An initial lease payment of $5000 for electronic point-of-sale cash register systems.
  b An outlay of $20,000 to purchase patent rights from the inventor.
  c An outlay of $80,000 for a large research and development program.
  d An $80,000 investment in a portfolio of marketable securities.
  e A $300 outlay for an office machine.
  f An outlay of $2000 for a new machine tool.
  g An outlay of $240,000 for a new building.
  h An outlay of $1000 for a marketing research report.

14-2 For each of the following cases, describe the various taxable components of the funds received through sale of the asset and determine the total taxes resulting from the transaction. Assume a 30-percent (long-term) capital gains tax and a 40-percent ordinary tax rate. The asset was purchased for $80,000 three years ago and is being depreciated straight-line over a five-year life to zero salvage value.
  a The asset is sold for $75,000.
  b The asset is sold for $85,000.
  c The asset is sold for $25,000.
  d The asset is sold for $32,000.

14-3 For each of the following projects, determine the cash flows for each year, classify the cash-flow pattern, and diagram the pattern.
  a A project requiring an initial investment of $120,000 that generates annual cash inflows of $25,000 for the next 18 years. In each of the 18 years, maintenance of the project will require a $5000 outflow.
  b A project requiring an initial outlay of $85,000 to purchase a machine. Sale of the old machine will yield $30,000. Cash inflows generated by the replacement will amount to $20,000 in each year of an eight-year period. At the end of eight years, the new machine will be sold for $15,000.

    c A project requires an intial investment of $2,000,000 and will yield annual inflows of $300,000 for each of the next 10 years. Operating outlays will be $20,000 for each year except year 6, when an overhaul requiring an additional outlay of $100,000 will be required. The asset will be sold for $250,000 at the end of year 10.

14-4 American Castings Corporation is considering replacement of one machine with another. The old machine was purchased five years ago for $10,000. The firm is depreciating the machine on a straight-line basis over a 10-year life to a zero salvage value. The new machine costs $14,000. Assume the firm has a 40-percent marginal tax rate on ordinary income and a 30-percent tax rate on long-term capital gains. What is the initial investment of the replacement if

    a The American Castings Company (ACC) sells the old machine for $5000.

    b ACC sells the old machine for $6000.

    c ACC sells the old machine for $4000.

    d ACC sells the old machine for $11,000.

    e ACC must pay $2000 to have the old machine removed.

14-5 A firm is evaluating the acquisition of an asset costing $64,000, having $4000 in installation costs, and having an expected salvage value of $8000 at the end of its six-year life. If the firm uses the straight-line depreciation method,

    a Determine the annual depreciation charge.

    b If the firm has a 48-percent tax rate on ordinary income, what effect does this depreciation have on the firm's cash inflows? Explain your answer.

14-6 The Dennis Tool Company has been considering replacement of a fully depreciated lathe that will last six years. The replacement is expected to have a six-year life and a $2000 depreciation charge each year. The firm estimates the following earnings *before depreciation and taxes* without and with the proposed replacement. The firm has a 48-percent tax rate on ordinary income.

Year	Without	With
1	10,000	10,000
2	10,000	11,000
3	10,000	12,000
4	10,000	13,000
5	10,000	14,000
6	10,000	15,000

    a Calculate the after-tax cash inflows associated with each machine.

    b Calculate the incremental cash inflows resulting from the acquisition of the new machine.

    c Diagram the relevant cash inflows associated with the replacement decision.

14-7 Tex-Tube Corporation is considering replacement of a machine. The replacement will reduce operating expenses by $8000 per year for each of the 10 years the new machine is expected to last. Although the old machine has zero book value, it will last 10 more years. If the depreciable value of the new machine is $48,000, the firm uses straight-line depreciation (no salvage value), and is subject to a 40-percent tax rate on ordinary income,

    a What incremental cash inflows are generated by the replacement?

    b Diagram these cash inflows.

14-8 A firm is considering opening a new plant to meet increased demand for their product. Total depreciable value of new plant and equipment will be $2,000,000 and the firm will apply straight-line depreciation over a 19-year life with an expected salvage value of $100,000. Sales from the expansion should amount to $300,000 per year, and operating expenses and other costs will amount to 40 percent of sales. The firm has an ordinary tax rate of 40 percent.

    a What incremental profit before depreciation and taxes will result from the expansion?

    b What incremental earnings after taxes will result from the expansion?

    c What incremental cash inflow will result from the expansion?

14-9 Gulf Coast Drydock is considering replacement of an existing hoist with one of two newer, more efficient, pieces of equipment. The old hoist is three years old, cost $32,000, and is being depreciated on a straight-line basis to a zero expected salvage value at the end of its eight-year life. Hoist A, one of the two possible replacement hoists, costs $40,000 to purchase and $8000 to install. It has a five-year life and expected salvage value of $8000. The other hoist, Hoist B, costs $54,000 to purchase and $6000 to install. It also has a five-year life but only a $5000 expected salvage value. Both hoists would be depreciated on a straight-line basis. The projected *profits before depreciation and current taxes* with each alternative hoist are tabulated below. The old hoist can currently be sold for $18,000, and will not incur any removal costs. The firm is subject to a 40-percent tax rate on ordinary income and a 30-percent rate on long-term capital gains.

Year	With present hoist	With hoist A	With hoist B
1	$14,000	$21,000	$22,000
2	14,000	21,000	24,000
3	14,000	21,000	26,000
4	14,000	21,000	26,000
5	14,000	21,000	26,000

    a Calculate the initial investment associated with each alternative.

    b Calculate the incremental cash inflows associated with each alternative.

    c Diagram the relevant cash flows associated with each of the alternatives.

SELECTED REFERENCES

Abdelsamad, Maustafa, *A Guide to Capital Expenditure Analysis* (New York: American Management Association, 1973).

Aplin, Richard D., and George L. Casler, *Capital Investment Analysis* (Columbus, Ohio: Grid, 1973), chap. 5.

Bierman, Harold, Jr., and Seymour Smidt, *The Capital Budgeting Decision*, 4th ed. (New York: Macmillan, 1975), chaps. 1, 5, 6, and 7.

Bogen, Jules I., Ed., *Financial Handbook*, 4th ed. (New York: Ronald, 1968), sect. 17.

Cooley, Phillip L., Rodney L. Roenfeldt, and It-Keong Chew, "Capital Budgeting Procedures Under Inflation," *Financial Management 4* (Winter 1975), pp. 18–27.

Federal Tax Course 1979 (Englewood Cliffs, N.J.: Prentice-Hall, 1978).

1979 Federal Tax Course (New York: Commerce Clearing House, 1978).

Hastie, K. Larry, "One Businessman's View of Capital Budgeting," *Financial Management 3* (Winter 1974), pp. 36–44.

Horngren, Charles T., *Accounting for Management Control: An Introduction*, 4th ed. (Englewood Cliffs, N.J.: Prentice-Hall, 1978), chaps. 12 and 13.

Hunt, Pearson, *Financial Analysis in Capital Budgeting* (Boston: Harvard University Graduate School of Business Administration, 1964).

Johnson, Robert W., *Capital Budgeting* (Dubuque, Iowa: Kendall/Hunt, 1977).

Mayer, Raymond R., *Capital Expenditure Analysis for Managers and Engineers* (Prospect Heights, Ill.: Waveland, 1978).

Meyers, Stephen L., "Avoiding Depreciation Influences on Investment Decisions," *Financial Management 1* (Winter 1972), pp. 17–24.

Murdick, Robert G., and Donald D. Deming, *The Management of Corporate Expenditures* (New York: McGraw-Hill, 1968).

Oakford, Robert V., *Capital Budgeting* (New York: Ronald, 1970).

Osteryoung, Jerome S., *Capital Budgeting: Long-Term Asset Selection*, 2nd ed. (Columbus, Ohio: Grid, 1979), chaps. 1 and 2.

Petty, J. William, David F. Scott, Jr., and Monroe M. Bird, "The Capital Expenditure Decision-Making Process of Large Corporations," *Engineering Economist 20* (Spring 1975), pp. 159–172.

Porterfield, James T. S., *Investment Decisions and Capital Costs* (Englewood Cliffs, N.J.: Prentice-Hall, 1965), chap. 2.

Schnell, James S., and Roy S. Nicolosi, "Capital Expenditure Feedback: Project Reappraisal," *Engineering Economist 19* (Summer 1974), pp. 253–261.

Spies, Richard R., "The Dynamics of Corporate Capital Budgeting," *Journal of Finance 29* (June 1974), pp. 829–845.

Weaver, James B., "Organizing and Maintaining a Capital Expenditure Program," *Engineering Economist 20* (Fall 1974), pp. 1–36.

Westfall, Othel D., "Evaluation of the Equipment Replacement Alternative," *Financial Executive* (August 1963), pp. 29–32.

CHAPTER 15
Capital budgeting concepts and techniques

The two preceding chapters, Chapters 13 and 14, have provided the necessary background for a discussion of capital budgeting concepts and techniques. Chapter 13 presented the key mathematical concepts used in various interest-related aspects of finance. It discussed the meaning and methods of calculating compound interest and present values. Chapter 14 presented a general approach to finding the relevant cash flows associated with a given project so that capital budgeting decision criteria can be applied. Emphasis was placed on conventional cash-flow patterns, which consist of an initial outlay followed by a series of cash inflows. The initial investment in capital projects was calculated by measuring the after-tax cash outflows required. The relevant cash inflows were defined as the incremental after-tax cash inflows expected to result from the investment. The application of present-value techniques to relevant project cash flows in order to evaluate capital expenditure proposals for decision-making purposes will receive a great deal of attention in this chapter.

In discussing the basic techniques for evaluating capital expenditure alternatives, this chapter will draw heavily on the material in Chapters 13 and 14. All capital investment projects will be assumed to exhibit conventional cash-flow patterns. The emphasis here will be on the presentation and illustration of basic capital budgeting techniques. One area that is not discussed in this chapter is how to measure the relative benefits of assets with different lives. Comparisons of investment projects involving assets with unequal lives often entail interesting questions. However, since the objective of this chapter is to provide a general understanding of capital budgeting techniques and concepts, such technical refinements will be ignored.

The chapter is divided into three major sections. The first section presents the "unsophisticated" capital budgeting techniques that are commonly used today. The second section presents more "sophisticated," or more theoretically sound, capital budgeting techniques that consider the time factor in the value of money. The final section presents a brief discussion of capital rationing, a situation that must commonly be considered when evaluating proposed capital expenditures. Examples are used to illustrate all these topics.

UNSOPHISTICATED CAPITAL BUDGETING TECHNIQUES

There are two basic unsophisticated techniques for determining the acceptability or nonacceptability of capital expenditure alternatives. One is to calculate the average rate of return and the other is to find the payback period.

We shall use the same basic problem to illustrate the application of all the techniques described in this chapter. The problem concerns the Bosco Company, which is currently contemplating two projects, project A, which requires an initial investment of $60,000, and project B, which requires an initial investment of $72,000. The profits after taxes (PAT) and relevant cash inflows (CI) associated with each of these projects for each year of their six-year lives are presented in Table 15.1. The average PAT and CI for each project are also indicated in the table.

Both projects A and B are to be depreciated on a straight-line basis with no salvage value. The annual depreciation for project A will be $10,000 (i.e., $60,000 ÷ 6); for project B, it will be $12,000 (i.e., $72,000 ÷ 6). Since these projects do not involve the replacement of existing assets, the initial investment in each project and the cost of the project are the same and the depreciation is based on the initial investment alone.

Another point to note is the difference between the profits after taxes (PAT) and cash inflows (CI) for each of the projects. As the discussions of the relationship between cash flows and profits after taxes in Chapters 2 and 14 have indicated, cash inflows are equal to profits after taxes plus depreciation. This relationship can be shown as a simple equation. If we let

CI = the cash inflows
PAT = profits after taxes
D = depreciation

then

$$CI = PAT + D \qquad (15.1)$$

This relationship can be checked by adding the depreciation of $10,000 and $12,000 to each year's profits after taxes for projects A and B, respectively. The resulting cash-inflow values are the same as those in Table 15.1.

The analysis of these alternatives on the following pages is approached with a view to both making an "accept-reject" decision and "ranking" the alternatives. The analysis of project A is simpler than the analysis of project B since the cash inflows for project A are an "annuity" while those for project B are a "mixed stream." Shortcuts in applying both the unsophisticated and the sophisticated capital budgeting techniques to project A are pointed out in the analysis.

TABLE 15.1 Capital expenditure data for the Bosco Company

Initial investment	Project A $60,000		Project B $72,000	
Year	PAT	CI	PAT	CI
1	$10,000	$20,000	$33,000	$45,000
2	10,000	20,000	10,000	22,000
3	10,000	20,000	8,000	20,000
4	10,000	20,000	1,000	13,000
5	10,000	20,000	1,000	13,000
6	10,000	20,000	1,000	13,000
Averages	$10,000	$20,000	$ 9,000	$21,000

Average rate of return

Finding the average rate of return is a quite popular approach for evaluating proposed capital expenditures. Its appeal stems from the fact that the average rate of return is typically calculated from accounting data (i.e., profits after taxes). This measure is sometimes called the *accounting rate of return*. The most common definition of the average rate of return is as follows:

$$\text{Average rate of return} = \frac{\text{average profits after taxes}}{\text{average investment}} \qquad (15.2)$$

The average profits after taxes. Average profits after taxes are found by adding up the after-tax profits expected for each year of the project's life and dividing the total by the number of years. In the case of an annuity, the average after-tax profits are equal to any year's profits. The average profits expected for projects A and B (given in Table 15.1) are $10,000 and $9000, respectively.

The average investment. The average investment is found by dividing the initial investment by 2. This averaging process assumes that the firm is using straight-line depreciation with no salvage value, in which case the book value of the asset declines at a constant rate from its purchase price to zero at the end of its depreciable life. This means that, on the average, the firm will have one-half of the assets' initial purchase price on the books. The logic of this averaging process is the same as that used in the EOQ inventory model in Chapter 10. The average investment for each project is as follows:

Average investment

Project A: $\dfrac{\$60,000}{2} = \$30,000$

Project B: $\dfrac{\$72,000}{2}$ = \$36,000

Project A requires an average investment of \$30,000, while project B requires an average investment of \$36,000.

The ratio of the two.   Dividing the average profits after taxes by the average investment results in the average rate of return for each project:

Average rate of return

Project A: $\dfrac{\$10,000}{\$30,000}$ = 33.33%

Project B: $\dfrac{\$\,9,000}{\$36,000}$ = 25.00%

The results indicate that project A is preferable to project B since project A has a higher average rate of return. The actual percentages can be interpreted as the annual accounting rate of return expected on the average investment.

Variations in methods of calculation.   A number of alternate methods of calculating the average rate of return are available. One approach involves using average annual *cash inflows* instead of average annual accounting profits as the numerator. This approach has an appeal since using returns measured as cash flows as opposed to accounting figures is in line with the basic financial viewpoint. Another variation is to use the initial investment instead of the average investment as the denominator of the ratio. This in effect cuts the calculated values in half. Thus the average rates of return for projects A and B, respectively, would be 16.67 percent and 12.50 percent. It is up to the decision maker to determine which method provides him or her with the most useful information. In order to make investment decisions based on an average rate of return, the decision maker must compare the average rate of return to a predetermined cutoff rate or minimum acceptable average rate of return.

Pros and cons of using the average rate of return.   The most favorable aspect of using the average rate of return to evaluate projects is its ease of calculation. The only input required is projected profits, a figure that should be easily obtainable. The major weaknesses of this approach are twofold. The first weakness stems from the use of accounting instead of cash inflow data. This weakness can be overcome by using average cash inflows in the numerator in Equation 15.2, as suggested in the preceding section. The second major weakness of this method is that it ignores the time factor in the value of money. Firms generally prefer to receive cash inflows today as opposed to in the future. This technique does not consider time preference. The indifference to the time factor can be illustrated using Table 15.2. Each project for which data are given has an average rate of return of 40 percent.

TABLE 15.2 Calculation of the average rate
of return for three alternate capital expenditure projects

	Project		
	X	Y	Z
(1) Initial investment	$20,000	$20,000	$20,000
(2) Average investment (1) ÷ 2	$10,000	$10,000	$10,000
Year	Profits after taxes		
1	$ 2,000	$ 4,000	$ 6,000
2	3,000	4,000	5,000
3	4,000	4,000	4,000
4	5,000	4,000	3,000
5	6,000	4,000	2,000
(3) Average profits after taxes	$ 4,000	$ 4,000	$ 4,000
(4) Average rate of return [(3) ÷ (2)]	40%	40%	40%

Although the average rates of return are the same for each project, the financial manager would not be indifferent between these projects. He or she would prefer project Z to project Y and project Y to project X since project Z has the most favorable profit-flow pattern, project Y has the next most favorable pattern, and project X has the least attractive profit-flow pattern. Businesspersons like to receive returns as quickly as possible, and the average rate of return criterion fails to consider this viewpoint.

Payback period

Payback periods are commonly used to evaluate proposed investments. The payback period is the number of years required to recover the initial investment. It is calculated by figuring *exactly* how long it takes to recover the initial investment.[1] For instance, in the case of project A, $60,000 must be recovered. After one year, $20,000 will be recovered; after two years, a total of $40,000 will be recovered (i.e., $20,000 in year 1 plus $20,000 in year 2). At the end of the third year, exactly $60,000 will be recovered (i.e., $40,000 total from years 1 and 2 plus the $20,000 recovered in year 3). The payback period for project A is therefore exactly 3 years. In the case of any *annuity*, such as project A, the payback period can be found by merely dividing the initial investment by the annual cash inflow. The result for project A would be 3.00 years (i.e., $60,000 ÷ $20,000).

---

[1]An alternate and less exact approach for calculating the payback period is available. The so-called "average" payback period is found by merely dividing the initial investment by the average cash inflows. Since this approach only approximates the firm's actual payback period, it does not warrant attention in this text; instead only the "actual" payback period is described herein.

Since project B generates a *mixed stream* of cash inflows, the calculation of the payback period is not quite as clearcut. In year 1, the firm will recover $45,000 of its $72,000 initial investment. At the end of year 2, $67,000 ($45,000 from year 1 plus $22,000 from year 2) will be recovered. At the end of year 3, $87,000 ($67,000 from years 1 and 2, plus the $20,000 from year 3) will be recovered. Since the amount received by the end of year 3 is more than the initial investment of $72,000, the payback period is somewhere between two and three years. Only $5000 ($72,000 − $67,000) must be recovered during year 3. Actually, $20,000 is recovered; but only 25 percent of this cash inflow ($5000 ÷ $20,000) is needed to complete the payback of the initial $72,000.[2] The payback period for project B is therefore 2.25 years (2 years + 25 percent of year 3). Project B would be preferred to project A since the former has a shorter payback period (i.e., 2.25 years versus 3.00 years). In general, shorter payback periods are preferred. Often companies establish a maximum payback period such that projects with longer paybacks are rejected; other projects will either be accepted or further evaluated using some type of more sophisticated capital budgeting technique. In other words the payback period is commonly used as an initial screening device for projects.

The pros and cons of using payback periods.   The payback period is a better measure than the average rate of return since it considers cash flows rather than accounting profits. Only cash inflows can pay the firm's bills. The payback period is also a superior measure (compared to the average rate of return) in that it gives *some* implicit consideration to the timing of cash flows and therefore the time factor in the value of money. A final reason many firms use the payback period as a decision criterion, or as a supplement to sophisticated decision criteria, is that it is a measure of risk. The payback period reflects the liquidity of a project and thereby the risk of recovering the investment.[3] The more liquid an investment is, the less risky it is assumed to be, and vice versa. Companies making international investments in countries having high inflation rates, unstable governments, or other problems, use the payback period as a primary decision criterion because of their inability to forecast or measure such risks.

There are two primary disadvantages of using the payback period as a basis for decisions. One as we have noted, is that this approach fails to take *fully* into account the time factor in the value of money; by measuring how quickly the firm recovers its initial investment, it only implicitly considers the timing of cash flows. A second weakness of this approach is its failure to recognize cash flows that occur after the payback period. This weakness can

[2]This method of finding fractional payback periods implicitly assumes that the cash inflows from the project are received at a constant rate instead of discretely throughout a year. Although this may not be the case, this method is believed to provide the best estimate of payback periods.

[3]The liquidity of a capital project is determined by the speed with which the firm recovers the initial investment. The reader may recall the discussion in Chapter 7, which indicated that liquidity and risk are somewhat related. The more liquid a project (i.e., the quicker the payback) the less risk, and vice versa. The longer one must wait to recover an investment, the higher the possibility of a calamity, and vice versa.

TABLE 15.3 Calculation of the payback period for two alternative investment projects

	Project X	Project Y
Initial investment	$10,000	$10,000
Year	Cash inflows	
1	$ 5,000	$ 3,000
2	5,000	4,000
3	1,000	3,000
4	100	4,000
5	100	3,000
Payback period	2 yrs.	3 yrs.

be illustrated using the two investment opportunities given in Table 15.3. The payback period for project X is two years; for project Y, it is three years. Strict adherence to the payback approach suggests that project X is preferable to project Y. However, if we look beyond the payback period, we see that project X returns only an additional $1200 ($1000 in year 3, $100 in year 4, and $100 in year 5), while project Y returns an additional $7000 ($4000 in year 4 and $3000 in year 5). Based on this information it appears that project Y is preferable to X. The payback approach ignores the cash inflows in years 3–5 for project X and years 4–5 for project Y and therefore is subject to criticism. The use of the payback period is probably the better of the two unsophisticated approaches for evaluating investment alternatives discussed here since it implicitly considers the *timing* of *cash flows*.

SOPHISTICATED CAPITAL BUDGETING TECHNIQUES

Sophisticated capital budgeting techniques give explicit consideration to the time factor in the value of money. In one way or another, they all discount the firm's cash flows at a specified rate. Thus far, the rate used has been referred to as the *discount rate* or *opportunity cost*. The rate used to discount cash flows is also referred to as the firm's *cost of capital*, which is the topic of Chapter 17. The terms *discount rate, opportunity cost*, and *cost of capital* will be used interchangeably to refer to the minimum return that must be earned on a project in order to leave the firm's market value (i.e., the owners' wealth) unchanged. A second assumption in the following discussions will be that the projects evaluated are equally risky—in other words, that the probability of receiving projected cash flows is known with certainty. The issue of risk and uncertainty will be dealt with in Chapter 16.[4]

---

[4]The discussion of risk and uncertainty and, specifically, the use of certainty equivalents and risk-adjusted discount rates in Chapter 16 will explain how projects involving different degrees of risk must be evaluated (i.e., how the cash inflows should be adjusted or discounted, or both). Assuming in this example that projects A and B are equally risky lets us use the same discount rate or cost of capital in evaluating each of them.

This section is divided into four major parts. The first three parts are devoted to an explanation of the three basic sophisticated capital budgeting techniques—the calculation of net present value, the benefit-cost ratio, and the internal rate of return. The final part is devoted to a comparison of the net present value and internal rate of return techniques.

Net present value (NPV)

The calculation of the net present value (NPV) of projects is one of the most commonly used sophisticated capital budgeting techniques. The definition of net present value (NPV) is given in Equation 15.3.

$$\text{NPV} = \text{present value of cash inflows} - \text{initial investment} \tag{15.3}$$

It is found by subtracting the initial investment in a project from the present value of the cash inflows discounted at a rate equal to the firm's cost of capital. Only if all cash flows, both inflows and outflows, are measured in terms of present dollars can valid comparisons between them be made. Since we are dealing with conventional investments, the initial investment is automatically stated in terms of today's dollars. If it were not, the present value of a project would be found by subtracting the *present value of outflows* from the present value of inflows.

The decision criterion. The decision-making criterion when the net present-value approach is used to make "accept-reject" decisions is as follows: *If* NPV $\geq$ 0, *accept the project; otherwise, reject the project.* If the NPV is greater than or equal to zero, the firm will earn a return greater than or equal to its required return, or cost of capital. Such action should enhance (i.e., if NPV > 0) or maintain (i.e., if NPV = 0) the wealth of the firm's owners, which is the objective of the financial manager.

EXAMPLE

The net present-value approach can be illustrated using the Bosco Company data presented in Table 15.1. If the firm has a 10-percent cost of capital, the net present values for projects A and B can be calculated as in Table 15.4. These calculations are based on the application of the techniques presented in Chapter 13. The results show that the net present value of projects A and B is, respectively, $27,100 and $26,381. The reader should note the use of the shortcut approach to find the present value for project A, which is an annuity. Both projects are acceptable since their net present values are greater than zero. If the projects were being ranked, project A would be considered superior to B since it has a higher net present value (i.e., $27,100 vs. $26,381). ●

Benefit-cost ratio (B/C ratio)

The benefit-cost ratio (B/C ratio) is sometimes called a *profitability index*. The benefit-cost ratio approach to capital budgeting does not differ greatly from the net present value approach. The only difference is the fact that the B/C ratio measures the present-value return per dollar invested while the net present-value approach gives the dollar difference between the pres-

TABLE 15.4 The calculation of NPV's for the Bosco Company's capital expenditure alternatives

Project A		Project B			
		Year	Cash inflow (1)	P.V. interest factor, PVIF[b] (2)	Present value (1) · (2) (3)
Annual inflow	$20,000	1	$45,000	.909	$40,905
× P.V. annuity interest factor, PVIFA[a]	4.355	2	22,000	.826	18,172
P.V. of inflows	$87,100	3	20,000	.751	15,020
− Initial investment	60,000	4	13,000	.683	8,879
Net Present Value	$27,100	5	13,000	.621	8,073
		6	13,000	.564	7,332
		P.V. of inflows			$98,381
		− Initial investment			72,000
		Net Present Value			$26,381

[a]From Table A-4, for 6 years and 10 percent.
[b]From Table A-3, for given year and 10 percent.

ent value of returns and the initial investment. The B/C ratio is defined by the following equation:

$$\text{B/C ratio} = \frac{\text{present value of cash inflows}}{\text{initial investment}} \qquad (15.4)$$

It gives the dollar return for each dollar invested.

The decision criterion. The decision criterion when B/C ratios are used to make "accept-reject" decisions is as follows: *If B/C ratio* ≥ 1, *accept the project; otherwise, reject the project.* When the B/C ratio is greater than or equal to 1, the net present value is greater than or equal to zero. Therefore, the NPV and B/C ratio approaches give the same solution to "accept-reject" decisions. In a fashion similar to that described for NPV, the acceptance of projects having B/C ratios greater than or equal to 1 will enhance or maintain, respectively, the wealth of the owners as reflected in the share price.

EXAMPLE
Benefit-cost ratios for the Bosco Company can be easily determined using the present values calculated in Table 15.4 The B/C ratios for projects A and B, respectively, are 1.45 ($87,100 ÷ $60,000) and 1.37 ($98,381 ÷ $72,000). Since both these ratios are greater than one, the projects are both acceptable. Ranking the projects on the basis of their B/C ratios indicates that project A is preferable to project B since A returns $1.45 present value for each dollar invested while B returns only $1.37 present value for each dollar invested. This ranking is the same as that obtained using NPV's; however, *the condition of conflicting rankings by these two techniques is not unusual.* ●

The following example illustrates the possibility of conflicting rankings using net present values and benefit-cost ratios as decision criteria.

EXAMPLE

The Sargent Mills Company, in the process of evaluating two mutually exclusive projects, X and Y, developed the information given below.

	Project X	Project Y
(1) Present value of cash inflows	$30,000	$60,000
(2) Initial investment	20,000	45,000
(3) Net present value [(1) − (2)]	$10,000	$15,000[a]
(4) Benefit-cost ratio [(1) ÷ (2)]	1.50[a]	1.33

[a]Preferred project using respective technique shown.

The results of the analysis indicate that both the projects are acceptable since their NPV's are greater than zero and their B/C ratios are greater than one. If the projects were ranked on the basis of NPV's, project Y would be preferable; but if the projects were ranked on the basis of B/C ratios, project X would be preferable. Such conflicting rankings are not unusual. Which investment is actually preferable may then depend upon the amount of funds available to the firm. If a firm has unlimited funds, the NPV ranking would probably be preferred, whereas in cases of capital rationing the ranking based on B/C ratios would probably be most useful since B/C ratios indicate the per-dollar return from a project ●

Internal rate of return (IRR)

The internal rate of return (IRR), or *yield criterion*, is probably the most used technique for evaluating investment alternatives, but it is considerably more difficult to calculate than are NPV and B/C ratios. The IRR is defined as *the rate of discount that equates the present value of cash inflows with the initial investment associated with a project.* The IRR, in other words, is the discount rate that equates the NPV of an investment opportunity with zero (since the P.V. of inflows equals the initial investment).

The decision criterion.   The decision criterion when the IRR is used in making "accept-reject" decisions is as follows: *If IRR ≥ cost of capital, accept the project; otherwise, reject the project.* In order for a project to be acceptable, the IRR must exceed or at least equal the firm's cost of capital or opportunity rate. This guarantees that the firm is earning more than its required return, and assures that the market value of the firm will increase (i.e., IRR greater than the cost of capital) or will remain unchanged (i.e., IRR equals the cost of capital). Such decisions will of course be consistent with the financial manager's goal of owners' wealth maximization.

Calculating the IRR. The IRR must be calculated using a trial and error technique. Calculating the IRR for an annuity is considerably easier than calculating one for a mixed stream of cash inflows. The steps involved in calculating the IRR in each case are described below. The Bosco Company data are used in the examples.

For annuities. Finding the IRR for an annuity involves the following steps:

Step 1: Calculate the payback period[5] for the project.

Step 2: Use Table A-4 (the present-value interest factors for a one-dollar annuity, PVIFA) and find, for the life of the project, the factor closest to the payback value. This is the IRR to the nearest 1 percent.

EXAMPLE
Steps 1 and 2 can be illustrated by applying them to project A of the Bosco Company, cash flows for which were given in Table 15.1. The payback (or present-value annuity factor, PVIFA) for the Bosco Company is 3.000 years ($60,000 ÷ $20,000). According to Table A-4, the factors closest to 3.000 for six years are 3.020 (for 24 percent) and 2.951 (for 25 percent). The value closest to 3.000 is 3.020; therefore, the IRR for project A, to the nearest 1 percent, is *24 percent*. The actual value, which is between 24 and 25 percent, could be found by interpolation;[6] it is 24.29 percent. For our purposes, however, values rounded to the nearest 1 percent are acceptable.

Since the Bosco Company has a cost of capital of 10 percent, project A, with an IRR of approximately 24 percent, is quite acceptable (i.e., 24 percent IRR > 10 percent cost of capital. ●

For a mixed stream of cash inflows. Calculating the IRR for a mixed stream of cash inflows is considerably more difficult. One way to simplify the process is to use a "fake annuity" as a starting point. A series of suggested steps for calculating the IRR for a mixed stream of cash inflows is given below. There are other approaches.

Step 1: Calculate the average annual cash inflow to get a "fake annuity."

Step 2: Divide the average annual cash inflow into the initial outlay in order to get a "fake payback period" (or present-value interest factor for an annuity, PVIFA). The fake payback is needed in order to estimate the IRR for the fake annuity.

---

[5]The payback period calculated actually represents the factor for the present value of an annuity (PVIFA), for the given life discounted at an unknown rate, which once determined represents the IRR for the project.

[6]*Interpolation* is a mathematical technique used to find intermediate or fractional values when only integer data are provided. Since interest factors only for whole percentages are included in the financial tables in Appendix A of this text, interpolation is required in order to calculate more precisely the internal rate of return.

Step 3: Use Table A-4 (PVIFA) and the fake payback period in the same manner as described in Step 2 for finding the IRR of an annuity. The result will be a *very rough* approximation of the IRR, based on the assumption that the mixed stream of cash inflows is an annuity.

Step 4: Subjectively adjust the IRR obtained in Step 3 by comparing the pattern of average annual cash inflows (calculated in Step 1) to the actual mixed stream of cash inflows. If the actual cash-flow stream seems to have higher cash inflows in the earlier years than the average stream, adjust the IRR up a few percentage points. If the early year actual cash inflows are below the average, adjust the IRR down a few percentage points. If the average cash inflows seem fairly close to the actual pattern, make no adjustment in the IRR

Step 5: Using the IRR from Step 4, calculate the net present value of the mixed-stream project. Be sure to use Table A-3 (the present-value interest factors for one dollar, PVIF) treating the estimated IRR as the discount rate.

Step 6: If the resulting NPV is greater than zero, subjectively raise the discount rate; if the resulting NPV is less than zero, subjectively lower the discount rate.

Step 7: Calculate the NPV using the new discount rate. Repeat Step 6. Stop once two *consecutive* discount rates that cause the NPV to be positive and negative, respectively, have been found.[7] Whichever of these two rates causes the NPV to be closest to zero is the IRR to the nearest 1 percent.

In a number of steps described above the use of subjective estimates was suggested. A subjective feel for the amount of adjustment needed in the estimated IRR cannot be taught, but as one works a number of these mixed-stream problems, one does tend to develop such a feel. Another point with respect to the preceding approach that should be clarified is that Step 4 can actually be skipped. The only advantage of Step 4 is that it should provide a more accurate first estimate of the firm's IRR.

EXAMPLE

The application of the seven-step procedure for finding the internal rate of return of a mixed stream of cash inflows can be illustrated using the Bosco Company's project B. The cash flows associated with the project were presented in Table 15.1.

Step 1: Summing the cash inflows for years 1 through 6 results in total cash inflows of $126,000, which, when divided by the number of years in the project's life (i.e., 6) results in an average annual cash inflow or "fake annuity" of $21,000.

Step 2: Dividing the initial outlay of $72,000 by the average annual cash inflow of $21,000 (calculated above) results in a "fake" payback period (or present value of an annuity factor, PVIFA) of 3.429 years.

---

[7]A shortcut method is merely to find a discount rate that results in a positive NPV and another that results in a negative NPV. Using only these two values one can interpolate in order to find the IRR. This approach, which may be nearly as accurate as that described above, can guarantee an answer after only two NPV calculations (i.e., one resulting in a positive NPV and one resulting in a negative NPV).

Step 3: In Table A-4, the factor (PVIFA) closest to 3.429 for six years is 3.410, the factor for a discount rate of 19 percent. The starting estimate of the IRR is therefore 19 percent.

Step 4: Since the actual early year cash inflows are greater than the average cash inflows of $21,000, a *subjective* increase of 3 percent is made in the discount rate. This makes the estimated IRR now 22 percent.

Step 5: Using the present-value interest factors (PVIF) for 22 percent and the correct year from Table A-3, the present value of the mixed stream is calculated:

Year	Cash inflow (1)	P.V. interest factor (PVIF) @ 22% (2)	Present value (1) · (2) (3)
1	$45,000	.820	$36,900
2	22,000	.672	14,784
3	20,000	.551	11,020
4	13,000	.451	5,863
5	13,000	.370	4,810
6	13,000	.303	3,939
P.V. of cash inflows			$77,316
− Initial investment			72,000
Net Present Value			$ 5,316

Steps 6 and 7: Since the net present value of $5316 calculated in Step 5 is greater than zero, the discount rate should be subjectively increased. Since the NPV is not even close to zero, let's try an increase to 26 percent.

Year	Cash inflow (1)	P.V. interest factor (PVIF) @ 26% (2)	Present value (1) · (2) (3)
1	$45,000	.794	$35,730
2	22,000	.630	13,860
3	20,000	.500	10,000
4	13,000	.397	5,161
5	13,000	.315	4,095
6	13,000	.250	3,250
P.V. of cash inflows			$72,096
− Initial investment			72,000
Net Present Value			$ 96

The calculations above indicate that the NPV of $96 for an IRR of 26 percent is reasonably close to, but still greater than, zero. Thus a higher discount rate should be tried. Since we are so close, let's try 27 percent. As the calculations below show, the net present value from an IRR of 27 percent is −$1160.

Year	Cash inflow (1)	P.V. interest factor (PVIF) @ 27% (2)	Present value (1) · (2) (3)
1	$45,000	.787	$35,415
2	22,000	.620	13,640
3	20,000	.488	9,760
4	13,000	.384	4,992
5	13,000	.303	3,939
6	13,000	.238	3,094
P.V. of cash inflows			$70,840
−Initial investment			72,000
Net Present Value			−$ 1,160

Since 26 and 27 percent are consecutive discount rates that give positive and negative net present values, the trial and error process can be terminated. The IRR we are seeking is the discount rate for which the NPV is closest to zero. For this project, 26 percent causes the NPV to be closer to zero than 27 percent, so 26 percent is the IRR we shall use. Had interpolation been used, the exact IRR would be 26.08 percent; as indicated earlier, for our purposes the IRR rounded to the nearest 1 percent will suffice. Therefore, the IRR of project B is approximately *26 percent*.

Project B is acceptable since its IRR of approximately 26 percent is greater than the Bosco Company's 10-percent cost of capital. This is the same conclusion reached using the NPV and B/C ratio as criteria. It is interesting to note that the IRR suggests that project B is preferable to A, which has an IRR of approximately 24 percent. This conflicts with the rankings of the projects obtained using NPV and B/C ratios. Such conflicts are not unusual; there is no guarantee that these three techniques (i.e., using NPV, the B/C ratio, and the IRR) will rank projects in the same order.[8]

However, all the methods should reach the same conclusion about the acceptability or nonacceptability of projects. ●

Comparison of NPV and IRR

The key difference between the NPV and IRR approaches that often causes conflicting rankings is that the NPV approach assumes that all intermediate cash flows are reinvested at the firm's cost of capital, whereas the IRR approach assumes reinvestment at the IRR. If the firm believes that its cash flows once received can realistically be reinvested at the IRR, then the IRR approach is best. Typically, this assumption would be rather bold, and the firm should use the NPV criterion. Techniques are available for resolving these conflicts. The most common is to find the IRR of the incremental cash flows resulting from two projects and compare this IRR to the firm's cost of capital to determine which project to accept.

---

[8]A discussion of the theoretical implications of these conflicts is beyond the scope of this text. The basic causes of the conflicting rankings are differences in one or more of a number of factors related to the projects being compared, such as their size, their patterns of cash flow, and the length of their lives.

FIGURE 15.1 Present-value profiles for projects A and B

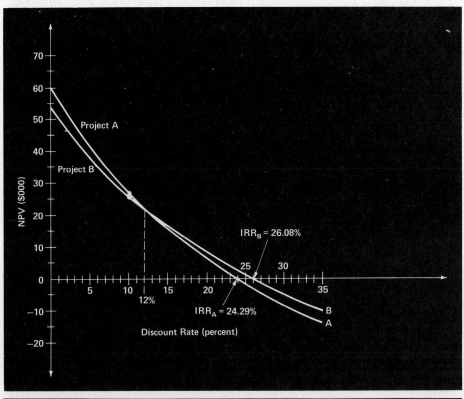

Graphical presentations. Projects can be compared graphically by constructing *net present-value profiles* that depict the net present value for various discount rates. The IRR, as we have seen, is the discount rate for which the NPV equals zero. Figure 15.1 presents net present-value profiles for projects A and B, which were described in Table 15.1. An analysis of Figure 15.1 indicates that for any discount rate less than approximately 12 percent the NPV for project A is greater than the NPV for project B. Beyond this point, the NPV for B is greater than that for A. Since the present-value profiles for projects A and B cross at a positive NPV, the IRR's for the projects cause conflicting rankings whenever they are compared to NPV's calculated at discount rates below 12 percent. In such cases, the use of the NPV for evaluating projects is preferable since the assumption that intermediate cash flows will be reinvested at the IRR is avoided.

Ranking revisited. The possibility of conflicts in ranking projects by different methods should be clear. The ranking of projects is an important consideration when projects are mutually exclusive or when capital rationing is necessary. When projects are mutually exclusive, ranking enables the firm to determine the "best" project from a financial viewpoint. When capital rationing is necessary, ranking projects may not completely determine the group of projects to accept, but it will provide a logical starting point. Care must be used when ranking projects.

Which approach is better: NPV or IRR?   On a purely theoretical basis, the use of NPV is best. Its theoretical superiority is attributed to a number of factors. Most important, the use of NPV implicitly assumes that any intermediate cash flows generated by an investment are reinvested at the firm's cost of capital, while the use of IRR assumes reinvestment at the often unrealistic rate specified by the IRR. A second theoretical problem with the IRR is that it is not unusual for nonconventional patterns of cash flows to have more than one IRR. The multiple IRR problem results from certain mathematical properties of the calculations involved. Due to the technical nature of this problem, suffice it to say that a project may have more than one IRR. When this occurs, difficult problems of interpretation result. A third criticism of IRR results from the fact that certain projects may have mathematical properties such that an IRR does not even exist. Again, this technical problem may cause theoretical difficulties that will not occur when one uses the NPV approach.

Because the NPV approach does not suffer from any of the deficiencies described with respect to IRR, it is the theoretically preferred approach. In spite of this fact, evidence suggests[9] that financial managers (of large corporations) prefer to use IRR over NPV. This preference for IRR is believed attributable to the general disposition of business persons toward *rates* of return rather than pure *dollar* returns. Because interest rates, profitability measures, and so on, are most often cited as annual rates of return, the use of IRR makes sense to corporate decision makers. They tend to find NPV harder to relate to since, as was pointed out in the discussion of B/C ratios, the NPV does not really measure the benefits relative to the amount invested. The IRR on the contrary, by providing the decision maker with data on the returns relative to the initial investment, gives him or her much greater information from which to make an investment decision as well as to compare returns to the cost of capital.

In summary, the reader should understand that although NPV is theoretically preferable, the IRR is more popular due to the fact that financial decision makers can more readily relate it to the available decision data. To answer the question of which technique is best, one can only respond *theoretically the NPV, but on a practical basis the IRR.* Because a variety of methods and techniques are available for avoiding the theoretical pitfalls of the IRR, its widespread use should not be viewed as reflecting a lack of sophistication on part of financial decision makers. Of course, on a purely academic or theoretical basis one can only suggest that the NPV is the superior technique.

[9]For example, see Lawrence J. Gitman and John R. Forrester, Jr., "A Survey of Capital Budgeting Techniques Used by Major U.S. Firms," *Financial Management*, Vol. 6, No. 3 (Fall, 1977), pp. 66–71, for a discussion of evidence with respect to capital budgeting decision-making practices in major U.S. firms.

CAPITAL RATIONING

Firms commonly find that there are more *acceptable* projects than they have the money to undertake. The objective of capital rationing is to select the group of projects that will maximize the owners' wealth. This is generally done by selecting the group of acceptable projects that provides the *highest overall net present value* and does not require more dollars than are budgeted. A number of capital rationing approaches are available. Whichever approach is used, it should be remembered that all the projects considered must be independent; if there are any mutually exclusive projects, the best of these should be chosen and placed in the group of independent projects.[10] Three basic approaches to project selection under capital rationing are discussed in this section. They are the internal rate of return approach, the net present-value approach, and the use of integer programming.

The internal rate of return approach

This approach involves plotting IRR's, or yields, against total dollars on the basis of decreasing yields.[11] By drawing an acceptable-project line and then imposing a budget constraint, the group of acceptable projects can be determined. The problem with this technique is that it does not guarantee the maximum dollar return to the firm; it merely provides a satisfactory solution to capital rationing problems.

EXAMPLE

The Zink Fuel Company is confronted with six projects competing for the firm's fixed budget of $250,000. The IRR and initial investment for each project are given below:

Project	Initial investment	IRR
A	$ 80,000	12%
B	70,000	20%
C	100,000	16%
D	40,000	8%
E	60,000	15%
F	110,000	11%

The firm has a cost of capital of 10 percent. Figure 15.2 presents a graph of the six projects ranked in descending order according to their IRR's. According to the graph, only Projects B, C, and E should be accepted. Together they will absorb $230,000 of the $250,000 budget. Project D is not even worthy of consideration, since its IRR is

[10]When more sophisticated mathematical programming and statistical techniques are applied to capital rationing problems, the mutually exclusive projects are grouped in various ways and the mutually exclusive project that is best in light of the total portfolio of projects is chosen. Due to the basic level of this text, this approach is not described in detail.

[11]The schedule of investment opportunities plotted on a set of financing-return axes beginning with the largest IRR and continuing in order of decreasing IRR's is often called the firm's *investment opportunities schedule*. This schedule is developed in greater detail in Chapter 17 as part of the discussion of the cost of capital.

FIGURE 15.2 IRR's for the Zink Fuel Company's Projects

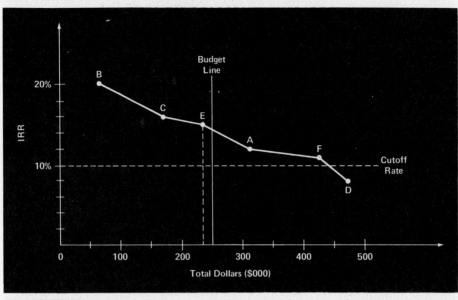

less than the firm's 10-percent cost of capital, or opportunity rate. The drawback of this approach is that there is no guarantee that acceptance of projects B, C, and E will maximize the firm's total dollar returns. ●

The net present-value approach

This approach is based on the use of present values and IRR's to determine the group of projects that will maximize the firm's owners' wealth. It involves ranking projects on the basis of IRR's and then evaluating the present value of the benefits from each project in order to determine the combination of projects with the highest overall present value. This is the same as maximizing net present value, since whether the entire budget is used or not it is viewed as the total initial investment for which maximum present value of benefits must be obtained. It is important to recognize that *the portion of the firm's budget that is not used does not increase firm value.* At best, the unused money can be invested in marketable securities or returned to the owners in the form of cash dividends. In either case the wealth of the owners would not likely be enhanced.

EXAMPLE
The group of projects described in the preceding example are ranked in Table 15.5 on the basis of IRR's. The present value of the cash inflows associated with the projects is also included in the table. Projects B, C, and E, which together require $230,000, yield a return of $336,000. However, if projects B, C, and A were implemented, the total budget of $250,000 would be used and the present value of the cash inflows would be $357,000. This is greater than the return expected from se-

TABLE 15.5 **Rankings for the Zink Fuel Company projects**

Project	Initial investment	IRR	P.V. of inflows at 10 percent	
B	$ 70,000	20%	$112,000	
C	100,000	16%	145,000	
E	60,000	15%	79,000	
A	80,000	12%	100,000	
F	110,000	11%	126,500	
D	40,000	8%	36,000	Cutoff point

lecting the projects with the highest IRR's. Implementing B, C, and A is preferable since it maximizes the present value of the firm's overall return for the given budget. It is important to keep in mind that if a portion of the budget is not used, it likely will not enhance the owners' wealth. Our *objective is to use the budget to generate the highest present value of inflows or net present value*.[12] Assuming that any unused portion of the budget does not gain or lose money, the total NPV for projects B, C, and E would be $106,000 (i.e., $336,000 − $230,000);[13] while for projects B, C, and A the total NPV would be $107,000 (i.e., $357,000 − $250,000). In light of this comparison, it is clear that of the available acceptable projects the optimal selection would be B, C, and A, since they generate the highest NPV from the available budget. Selecting projects B, C, and A will therefore maximize NPV. The technique described above is probably the best trial and error method for selecting projects when capital rationing is necessary. ●

Integer programming

Integer programming, which is a quantitative technique for optimizing some objective subject to certain constraints, is quite useful in solving capital rationing problems. Capital rationing problems represent situations of constrained maximization since the objective is to select the group of projects that maximizes the present-value cash inflows subject to a budget (or financial) constraint. Integer programming is used instead of linear programming so that the results will all be in terms of whole projects.[14] It would be quite difficult to implement .6 of a project. Computer programs are available for solving integer programming problems.

[12]It may be conceptually difficult for the reader to understand why any unused portion of the budget actually loses money. One must view the situation as one in which the firm has a fixed amount of money available for which the firm is paying an annual cost equal to the cost of capital. Any unused portion of this money can, at best, be invested in marketable securities or paid out as cash dividends. Both of these alternatives will likely not enhance the owners' wealth.

[13]It is important to note that because it is likely the firm will lose money on the $20,000 excess (i.e., $250,000 available less $230,000 used) with projects B, C, and E (since they are paying more for the money than they earn on it), the NPV from this selection will be less than the $106,000 calculated above.

[14]The integer programming algorithm described here is a form of zero-one integer programming, which permits the decision variable to take values of only 0 or 1. Since at most we want to accept a project only once, this integer programming algorithm is used to solve capital rationing problems.

The basic integer programming problem can be stated as follows:[15]

Maximize $b_1X_1 + b_2X_2 + \cdots + b_nX_n$

when

$c_1X_1 + c_2X_2 + \cdots + c_nX_n \leq C \qquad X_i = 0, 1 \text{ (for all } i = 1, n)$

where

b_i (for $i = 1, n$) = the present value of the cash inflows from project i
X_i (for $i = 1, n$) = a decision variable which can have a value of either
0 or 1 depending on whether the project is accepted
(if $X_i = 1$) or rejected (if $X_i = 0$)
c_i (for $i = 1, n$) = the initial investment required for project i
C = the amount of budget available for investment
n = the number of projects considered

Using certain integer programming algorithms, the acceptable projects (those for which $X_i = 1$) can be determined. The following example shows how integer programming problems are set up.

EXAMPLE
Using the Zink Fuel Company data in Table 15.5 and the stated budget constraint of $250,000, and labeling project A as X_1, B as X_2, C as X_3, E as X_4, and F as X_5, the integer programming problem posed by the need to select the project that maximizes the firm's overall return can be stated as follows:

Maximize $100{,}000X_1 + 112{,}000X_2 + 145{,}000X_3 + 79{,}000X_4 + 126{,}500X_5$

when

$80{,}000X_1 + 70{,}000X_2 + 100{,}000X_3 + 60{,}000X_4 + 110{,}000X_5 \leq 250{,}000$
$X_i = 0, 1 \text{ (for } i = 1, 5)$

It should be noted that since project D is unacceptable, it has been eliminated from consideration. The solution to this problem is $X_1 = 1$, $X_2 = 1$, $X_3 = 1$, $X_4 = 0$, and $X_5 = 0$. Thus projects A, B, and C should be accepted and projects E and F should be rejected. This is the same result obtained using the net present-value approach. ●

SUMMARY
This chapter has been devoted to a description of the basic capital budgeting concepts and techniques. Unsophisticated capital budgeting techniques use the average rate of return or the payback period to evaluate the attractiveness

---

[15]Because the full amount of the capital budget, C, is assumed to represent the initial investment, by maximizing the present value of cash inflows resulting from projects, the firm is providing for maximum net present value.

of capital investment projects. The average rate of return is calculated by dividing the average profits after taxes by the average investment. The drawback of using the average rate of return is that it relies on accounting—not cash flow—data and it does not reflect the time factor in the value of money. The payback period on the other hand is calculated by determining the amount of time it will take the firm to recover its initial investment. The payback method implicitly considers cash-flow patterns, though it fails to consider directly the time factor in the value of money and it ignores profits. The payback method is the best of the unsophisticated approaches to capital budgeting; it is commonly used as a supplement to the more sophisticated techniques due to its ability to measure risk.

Sophisticated techniques for capital budgeting consider the time factor in the value of money and their use is consistent with the objective of maximizing stockholders' wealth. The net present-value (NPV) approach measures the difference between the present values of inflows and the initial investment, or present value of outflows, in order to determine the desirability of a project. It is a popular approach. If the net present value of a project is greater than or equal to zero, it is considered acceptable; if the net present value is less than zero, the project must be rejected. Benefit-cost ratios (B/C ratio) are similar to net present values, but they measure the ratio of the present value of inflows to the initial investment, thereby indicating the present-value return per dollar invested. Projects are acceptable if their benefit-cost ratios are greater than or equal to one; otherwise they should be rejected. The internal rate of return (IRR), the discount rate that equates the net present value of a project with zero, is also used as a basis for capital budget decision making. If this rate is greater than or equal to the firm's cost of capital, a project is acceptable; otherwise it must be rejected.

Each of the sophisticated capital budgeting techniques somehow uses the cost of capital in its decision criterion. In the case of the net present-value and benefit-cost ratio approaches, the cost of capital is used to discount the cash flows in order to calculate these measures. In the case of the internal-rate-of-return method, the cost of capital is compared to the project's internal rate of return in order to determine its acceptability. Each of these sophisticated capital budgeting techniques provides the same accept-reject decision for a given project, but there are quite often conflicts between the rankings of projects using these various techniques. The basic conflict in ranking between net present value and internal rate of return results from the internal rate of return's implicit assumption that intermediate cash flows are reinvested at the internal rate of return. Although the net present-value technique is the theoretically most sound when compared to the internal rate of return, the internal rate of return is more commonly used by major firms since this approach reflects the disposition of financial decision makers, that is, toward rates of return.

Capital rationing situations are not uncommon since most firms have a large number of acceptable projects competing for a portion of their fixed budget. Under capital rationing, the firm must select the projects that maximize its overall net present value. A number of techniques for solving capital rationing problems are available. They include the internal rate of return approach, the net present-value approach, and the use of integer programming. The most desirable of these approaches are the net present-value approach and the use of integer programming, since these approaches recognize that the firm must maximize net present value by selecting acceptable projects while not spending more money than is available in the budget. The objective, therefore, is to use the budget to maximize the overall net present value resulting from selection of a group of acceptable projects.

QUESTIONS

15-1 What adjustment is required to convert a stream of cash inflows into an after-tax profit figure? What is the rationale for this adjustment?

15-2 How does the average rate of return measure project desirability? What are some alternate approaches for calculating this measure of an investment's worth?

15-3 What weaknesses are associated with use of the average rate of return for measuring an investment's worth? How can a tie in ranking be resolved?

15-4 What is the payback period? Is it calculated using after-tax profits or cash flows? What are the pros and cons of using the payback period to measure an investment's attractiveness?

15-5 How are the capital budgeting techniques based on the payback period and the average rate of return different?

15-6 What weaknesses are commonly associated with the use of the payback period to measure an investment's worth? What factors are usually used to justify the use of the payback period? In what situations is it justifiable?

15-7 How can either the average rate of return or the payback period of an investment be used to make accept-reject decisions? What additional data is required?

15-8 How does the passage of time affect the value of money? How are compound interest and discounting related?

15-9 What is meant by the phrase "the present value of $X to be received n years from now"? How is the present value of a future sum related to compounding?

15-10 How can the present value of a mixed stream of cash flows be determined?

15-11 What is the one thing the so-called "sophisticated" capital budgeting techniques have in common that the unsophisticated techniques do not do? What are the names commonly used to describe the rate at which cash flows are discounted in order to find present values?

15-12 What is meant by the phrase "net present value"? How may it be used in making accept-reject decisions? How is NPV calculated?

15-13 How are benefit-cost ratios calculated? What is the criterion for judging the acceptability of investments when using B/C ratios? What do B/C ratios signify? What is an investment's B/C ratio when its net present value equals zero?

15-14 Do the benefit-cost ratio and the net present-value approaches to capital budgeting always agree with respect to both the acceptability and ranking of investments? Why or why not?

15-15 What is the internal rate of return of an investment? How is it used to determine the acceptability of a project?

15-16 In attempting to find the internal rate of return for a project, what must one do if the present value of inflows discounted at a given rate is greater than the initial investment? Why?

15-17 Do the NPV and IRR approaches to capital budgeting always agree with respect to the acceptability and ranking of projects? Can you explain your answer graphically?

15-18 There is disagreement with respect to the theoretical and practical superiority of the NPV and IRR methods of evaluating capital expenditures. Briefly discuss the arguments favoring each of these techniques.

15-19 When mutually exclusive projects have different rankings using NPV and IRR, which project would be preferred? Explain your answer.

15-20 What assumption inherent in the use of internal rates of return for ranking projects suggests that the net present-value approach is superior?

15-21 What is meant by "capital rationing"? Is it unusual for a firm to ration capital? Why or why not?

15-22 What are the internal rate of return, net present value, and integer programming approaches to capital rationing? Which method, if any, is preferable?

PROBLEMS

15-1 A firm is considering the acquisition of an asset that requires an initial investment of $10,000 and will provide after-tax profits of $2000 per year for five years.
  a Calculate the average rate of return using the most common formula.
  b Calculate the average rate of return using the *initial* investment instead of the average investment in the denominator.
  c Calculate the average rate of return using the after-tax cash inflow instead of the after-tax profit in the numerator and using the average investment in the denominator. Assume the firm uses straight-line depreciation with no expected salvage value and that the initial investment represents the total depreciable value of the asset.

15-2 Durotool is considering two fixed-asset purchases. Asset A has an initial cost of $5000 and generates after-tax profits of $1000 per year for six years. Asset B has an initial cost of $8000 and generates after-tax profits of $1600 per year for 25 years.
  a Determine the average rate of return for each asset using the most common formula.
  b Which asset seems preferable for the firm? Why?

15-3 The Lee Corporation is considering a capital expenditure that requires an initial investment of $42,000 and returns after-tax cash inflows of $7000 per year for 10 years. The company has established a maximum payback standard of 8 years.
  a Determine the payback period for this project?
  b Should the company accept the project? Why or why not?

15-4 Walter's Sporting Equipment Company is evaluating a new machine. The initial investment, which equals the depreciable value of the machine, is $20,000. The machine will generate earnings after taxes of $6000 per year for each of the five years it will operate. The firm's ordinary income is taxed at a 40-percent rate and there is zero expected salvage value on the machine.
  a Determine the average rate of return for the machine, using the most common formula.
  b Determine the after-tax cash inflows associated with the machine.
  c Determine the payback period for the machine.

15-5 Houston Tool uses a five-year maximum payback standard. The firm is considering the purchase of a new machine and must choose between two. The first machine requires an initial investment of $14,000 and generates annual after-tax cash inflows of $3000 for each of the next seven years. The second machine requires an initial investment of $21,000 and provides an annual cash inflow after taxes of $4000 for 20 years.

a Determine the payback period for each machine.

b Comment on the acceptability of the machines assuming they are independent projects.

c Which machine should the firm accept, and why?

d Do the machines in this problem illustrate any of the criticisms of using payback? Discuss.

15-6 Bonnie's Beauty Aids is evaluating a new fragrance mixing machine. The asset requires an initial investment of $24,000 and will generate after-tax cash inflows of $5000 per year for eight years. For each of the required rates of return listed below (1) calculate the net present value, (2) indicate whether to accept or reject the machine, and (3) explain your decision.

a The required rate of return is 12 percent.

b The required rate of return is 10 percent.

c The required rate of return is 14 percent.

15-7 A firm can purchase a fixed asset for a $13,000 initial investment. If the project yields an annual after-tax cash inflow of $4000 for four years,

a Determine the maximum required rate of return the firm can have and still accept the project (closest whole percentage rate).

b Determine the net present value of the project assuming the firm has a 10-percent cost of capital.

c Determine the benefit-cost ratio assuming the firm has a 10-percent cost of capital.

15-8 Calculate the net present value and benefit-cost ratio for the following 20-year projects. Assume the firm has an opportunity cost of 14 percent.

a Initial investment is $10,000; cash inflows are $2000 per year.

b Initial investment is $25,000; cash inflows are $3000 per year.

c Initial investment is $30,000; cash inflows are $5000 per year.

15-9 Metropolitan Manufacturing Enterprises has been given the following figures for a long-term project it is considering. The initial investment will be $18,250 and the project is expected to yield after-tax cash inflows of $4000 per year for seven years. The firm has a 10-percent required rate of return.

a Determine the net present value of the project.

b Determine the benefit-cost ratio for the project.

c Determine the internal rate of return for the project.

d Would you recommend that Metropolitan accept or reject the project? Explain your answer.

Cincinnati Machine Tool (CMT) accepts projects earning more than the firm's 15-percent cost of capital. CMT is currently considering a 10-year project that provides annual cash inflows of $10,000 and requires an initial investment of $61,450.

a Determine the IRR of this project.

b How many years of cash inflows would it take to make this project just acceptable (i.e., have an IRR of 15 percent)?

c With the given life, initial investment, and cost of capital, what is the minimum annual cash inflow the firm should accept?

15-11 The Comfort Chair Company is attempting to select the best of three mutually exclusive proposals for increasing its aluminum extrusion capacity. The initial investment and after-tax cash inflows associated with each proposal are given in the table below. Assume the initial investment equals total depreciable value, depreciation is straight-line, and the firm is subject to a 40-percent tax rate on ordinary income.

| | Project | | |
Cash flow	A	B	C
Initial investment	$60,000	$100,000	$110,000
Cash inflow, years 1–5	$20,000	$ 31,500	$ 32,500

a Calculate the average rate of return for each project using the most common formula.
b Calculate the payback period for each project.
c Calculate the net present value of each project assuming the firm has a required rate of return equal to 13 percent.
d Calculate the internal rate of return for each project.
e Assuming the cost of capital is 13 percent, which project would you recommend and why?

15-12 Yellow Springs Cash Register is considering opening a new plant in Pryor, Oklahoma. The total cost of land, construction, and equipment would be $2,200,000. This outlay would be partially offset by the sale of an existing facility in Tacoma, Washington. The Tacoma site has zero book value, cost $1,000,000 in 1952, and can be sold for $250,000. As a result of the new facilities, sales are expected to increase by $800,000 but product costs will represent 50 percent of sales. The firm will use straight-line depreciation and a zero salvage value over the project's 25-year-life. The firm is subject to a 40-percent tax rate on ordinary income and a 30-percent tax rate on long-term capital gains. Yellow Springs Cash Register's cost of capital is 11 percent.
a Determine the initial investment required by the new plant.
b Determine the change in earnings after taxes attributable to the new plant.
c Determine the change in after-tax cash inflows attributable to the new plant.
d Determine the average rate of return and payback period applying the most common formulas to the data developed above.
e Determine the net present value and the internal rate of return related to the proposed new plant.
f Make a recommendation to accept or reject the new plant and justify your answer.

15-13 Kannon Textile is considering the replacement of an existing machine. The new machine costs $1,200,000 and requires installation costs of $150,000. The existing machine can be sold for $185,000. It is five years old, cost $800,000 new, and is being depreciated straight-line over a 15-year life to a $50,000 salvage value. Over its 10-year life, the new machine should reduce operating costs by $200,000 per year. The firm has a 14-percent cost of capital, a 40-percent tax rate on ordinary income, and a 30-percent tax rate on long-term capital gains. The new machine will be depreciated on a straight-line basis with no salvage value.
a Develop the relevant cash-flow data needed for capital budgeting analysis.
b Determine the net present value of the proposal.
c Determine the internal rate of return on the proposal.

d Make a recommendation to either accept or reject the replacement proposal and justify your answer.

e What is the highest cost of capital the firm could have and still accept the project?

15-14 A firm must select the optimal group of projects from those in the table below, given its capital budget of $1,000,000.

Project	Initial investment	NPV
A	$300,000	$ 84,000
B	200,000	10,000
C	100,000	25,000
D	900,000	90,000
E	500,000	70,000
F	100,000	50,000
G	800,000	160,000

a Calculate the benefit-cost ratios associated with each project.

b Select the optimal group of projects, keeping in mind that unused funds are costly.

c Express this capital rationing situation as an integer programming problem.

SELECTED REFERENCES

Bacon, Peter W., "The Evaluation of Mutually Exclusive Investments," *Financial Management 6* (Summer 1977), pp. 55–58.

Bernhard, Richard H., "Mathematical Programming Models for Capital Budgeting—A Survey, Generalization and Critique," *Journal of Financial and Quantitative Analysis 4* (June 1969), pp. 111-158.

Bernardo, John S., and Howard P. Lanser, "A Capital Budgeting Decision Model with Subjective Criteria," *Journal of Financial and Quantitative Analysis 12* (June 1977), pp. 261–275.

Bierman, Harold, Jr., "A Reconciliation of Present Value Capital Budgeting," *Financial Management 6* (Summer 1977), pp. 52–54.

Bierman, Harold, Jr., and Seymour Smidt, *The Capital Budgeting Decision*, 4th ed. (New York: Macmillan 1975), chaps. 2, 3, and 8.

Brigham, Eugene F., "Hurdle Rates for Screening Capital Expenditure Proposals," *Financial Management 4* (Autumn 1975), pp. 17–26.

Doenges, R. Conrad, "The Reinvestment Problem in Practical Perspective," *Financial Management 1* (Spring 1972), pp. 85–91.

Donaldson, Gordon, "Strategic Hurdle Rates for Capital Investment," *Harvard Business Review 50* (March-April 1972), pp. 50–58.

Fogler, H. Russell, "Overkill in Capital Budgeting Techniques?," *Financial Management 1* (Spring 1972), pp. 92–96.

———, "Ranking Techniques and Capital Rationing," *Accounting Review 47* (January 1972), pp. 134–143.

Fremgen, James M., "Capital Budgeting Practices: A Survey," *Management Accounting* (May 1973), pp. 19–25.

Gitman, Lawrence J., and John R. Forrester, Jr., "A Survey of Capital Budgeting Techniques Used by Major U.S. Firms," *Financial Management 6* (Fall 1977), pp. 66–71.

Jean, William H., "On Multiple Rates of Return," *Journal of Finance 23* (March 1968), pp. 187–192.

Klammer, Thomas, "Empirical Evidence of the Adoption of Sophisticated Capital Budgeting Techniques," *Journal of Business 45* (July 1972), pp. 387–397.

Levy, Haim, and Marshall Sarnat, *Investment and Financial Decisions* (Englewood Cliffs, N.J.: Prentice-Hall, 1978).

Lewellen, Wilbur G., H. P. Lanser, and J. J. McConnell, "Payback Substitutes for Discounted Cash Flow," *Financial Management 2* (Summer 1973), pp. 17–25.

Mao, James C. T., "The Internal Rate of Return as a Ranking Criterion," *Engineering Economist 11* (Winter 1966), pp. 1–13.

Merville, L. J., and L. A. Tavis, "A Generalized Model for Capital Investment," *Journal of Finance 28* (March 1973), pp. 109–118.

Nelson, Charles R., "Inflation and Capital Budgeting," *Journal of Finance 31* (June 1976), pp. 923–931.

Osteryoung, Jerome, *Capital Budgeting: Long-Term Asset Selection*, 2nd ed. (Columbus, Ohio: Grid, 1979).

Robichek, Alexander A., Donald G. Ogilivie, and John D. C. Roach, "Capital Budgeting: A Pragmatic Approach," *Financial Executive 37* (April 1969), pp. 26–38.

Rychel, Dwight F., "Capital Budgeting with Mixed Integer Linear Programming: An Application," *Financial Management 6* (Winter 1977), pp. 11–17.

Sarnat, M., and H. Levy, "The Relationship of Rules of Thumb to the Internal Rate of Return: A Restatement and Generalization," *Journal of Finance 24* (June 1969), pp. 479–489.

Schwab, Bernhard, and Peter Lustig, "A Comparative Analysis of the Net Present Value and the Benefit-Cost Ratios as a Measure of the Economic Desirability of Investments," *Journal of Finance 24* (June 1969), pp. 507–516.

Van Horne, James C., "A Note on Biases in Capital Budgeting Introduced by Inflation." *Journal of Financial and Quantitative Analysis 6* (January 1971), pp. 653–658.

Weingartner, H. Martin, *Mathematical Programming and the Analysis of Capital Budgeting Problems*, (Englewood Cliffs, N.J.: Prentice-Hall, 1963).

————, "Some New Views on the Payback Period and Capital Budgeting Decisions," *Management Science 15* (August 1969), pp. 594–607.

CHAPTER 16
Capital budgeting under risk

In Chapter 15, the key concepts and techniques of capital budgeting were discussed. A key assumption implicit in the discussions was that the project cash inflows were known with certainty. In actuality, there are very few capital budgeting projects for which the cash inflows are perfectly certain. Only where the cash inflows associated with a project are contractual or somehow guaranteed by the federal government can the decision maker consider them certain. An example of a capital budgeting decision made under conditions of perfect certainty would be the decision by a firm to purchase (i.e., make an initial cash outlay for) an asset and then to lease the asset to the federal government for a contracted number of annual lease payments. The lease-purchase decision, which is discussed in Chapter 20, is also viewed as being made under conditions of certainty.

Since most capital budgeting problems actually do contain some degree of "risk" or "uncertainty," it is important to have a basic understanding of the problems in dealing with risk and uncertainty. There are certain techniques for adjusting for varying degrees of project risk or uncertainty. This chapter presents some of the key considerations in, and techniques for, dealing with risk in capital budgeting projects. Attention is focused on the basic risk concepts, the measurement of a project's risk, the risk-time relationship, the risk-return relationship, or capital asset pricing model (CAPM), and the practical approaches to risk adjustment.

These topics are presented in five separate sections. The first section discusses the basic concepts of risk and uncertainty, sensitivity analysis of risk, and the use of probabilities. The second section discusses the risk measurement process from both visual and statistical viewpoints. The third section discusses the risk-time relationship. It describes the risk-time function and the nature of portfolio risk. The fourth, and possibly most important, section briefly describes the relationship between risk and return as it relates to proposed asset acquisitions. It presents a brief description of the capital asset pricing model (CAPM), which is used to explain the risk-return tradeoff. The last section presents a number of risk-adjustment techniques, including the subjective approach, the use of "decision trees," the use of statistics, simulation, the use of certainty equivalents, and the application of risk-adjusted discount rates. Examples are used to clarify key concepts.

BASIC RISK CONCEPTS

In order to have some appreciation of the basic problems associated with project risk, it is useful to understand the basic risk-related concepts. An understanding of the similarities and differences between risk and uncertainty provides a feel for the nature of the risk problem. An appreciation of some elementary approaches aimed at providing a very rough feel for project risk also aids in gaining an understanding of why differences in project risk must be considered in capital budgeting. In this section, the terms risk and uncertainty are discussed, and two techniques—sensitivity analysis and the use of probabilities—that should provide some appreciation for the risk problem are presented.

Risk and uncertainty

Throughout this text the terms *risk* and *uncertainty* are used interchangeably to refer to the variability of expected returns associated with a given project. For instance, a capital budgeting project in which the government contractually guarantees the firm $1000 per year for ten years has no risk, since there is no variability associated with the returns; on the other hand a capital budgeting project that may return anywhere from $0 to $2000 per year is very risky due to the high variability of the returns. The more certain the returns of a project, the less variability and therefore the less risk. Projects with uncertain returns that may take on any one of numerous values are more risky.

The difference between risk and uncertainty as defined by the statistician is related to the decision maker's knowledge of the probabilities, or chances, of certain outcomes or cash flows occurring. *Risk* exists when the decision maker is able to estimate the probabilities associated with various outcomes (i.e., a probability distribution). *Objective probability distributions* are normally based on historical data. For instance, if a person wishes to determine the probabilities associated with various occupancy rates in an apartment complex, he or she can develop a distribution of probabilities based on historical data on other projects of the same type. *Uncertainty* exists when the decision maker has no historical data from which to develop a probability distribution and must make educated guesses in order to develop a *subjective probability distribution*. For example, if the proposed project is completely new to the firm, the decision maker, through research and consultation with others, may be able subjectively to assign probabilities to various outcomes. Throughout this section, the terms risk and uncertainty will be used interchangeably to refer to risky decision situations.

Sensitivity analysis of risk

One of the simplest ways of considering the risk of a project is to use sensitivity analysis. *Sensitivity analysis* involves using a number of possible outcomes in evaluating a project. It is probably most useful in truly uncertain decision situations. The basic procedure is to evaluate a project using a number of possible cash inflow estimates to get a "feel" for the variability of the associated outcomes. One of the most common sensitivity approaches is to estimate the worst (i.e., most pessimistic), the expected (i.e., most likely) and the best (i.e., most optimistic) outcomes associated with a project. In this case the risk of a project is reflected by the *range*, which is the most basic measure of risk. The range can be found by subtracting the pessimistic outcome from the optimistic outcome. The larger the range for the given project, the more variability or risk it is said to have.

EXAMPLE

The Goodwear Tire Company is attempting to evaluate two mutually exclusive projects, A and B, each requiring an initial investment of $10,000 and both having *most likely* annual cash inflows of $2000 per year for the next 15 years. The firm's cost of capital is 10 percent. In order to obtain some insight into the riskiness of these projects, management has made *pessimistic* and *optimistic* estimates of the annual cash inflows associated with each one. The three cash inflow values for each project along with their ranges are given in Table 16.1. Comparing the ranges of project cash inflows, it can be seen that project A appears to be less risky than project B since its range of $1000 (i.e., $2500 − $1500) is less than the range of $4000 (i.e., $4000 − $0) for project B.

TABLE 16.1 Goodwear Tire's projects A and B

	Project A	Project B
Initial investment	$10,000	$10,000
Cash inflow estimates		
Pessimistic	$ 1,500	$ 0
Most likely	$ 2,000	$ 2,000
Optimistic	$ 2,500	$ 4,000
Range	$ 1,000	$ 4,000

Using the techniques presented in Chapter 15, the net present value of each project at the 10-percent cost of capital can be calculated for each of the possible cash inflows. The results are presented in Table 16.2, which is a *payoff matrix* indicating, for each possible outcome of *state of nature*, the associated payoff.

Table 16.2 illustrates that sensitivity analysis can produce some useful information about projects that appear equally desirable on the basis of the most likely estimates of their cash inflows. Comparing the range of net present value for project A ($7606) with that of project B ($30,424) it should be clear that project A is less risky (i.e., has a smaller range) than project B. Depending on the decision maker's attitude toward risk he or she may choose either project. If conservative, the decision maker

TABLE 16.2 A payoff matrix of NPV's for projects A and B

Outcomes (states of nature)	Net present value	
	Project A	Project B
Possible cash inflows (outcomes)		
Pessimistic	$1,409	− $10,000
Most likely	$5,212	$ 5,212
Optimistic	$9,015	$20,424
Range	$7,606	$30,424

will take project A, thereby eliminating the possibility of loss; if, instead, a risk taker, he or she may take project B due to the possibility of receiving a return with a high net present value. Although sensitivity analysis and the use of the range are still rather crude, it does provide the decision maker with more than one estimate of the project's outcome, which can be used to assess roughly the risk involved. The same type of sensitivity analysis could have, of course, been applied more directly to the cash inflows themselves, as was illustrated in Table 16.1. ●

Assigning probabilities to outcomes

Probabilities are used to assess more accurately the risk involved in a project. The *probability* of an event occurring may be thought of as the *percentage chance* of a given outcome. In other words, if it has been determined that an outcome has an 80-percent probability of occurrence, it is expected that the given outcome will occur eight out of ten times. If an outcome has a probability of 100 percent, it is certain to occur; outcomes having a probability of zero will never occur. By assigning probabilities to its outcomes, the *expected value* of the return on a project can be calculated.

The expected value of a project is a weighted average return, in which the weights used are the probabilities of the various outcomes. Although the expected value may never be realized, it is indicative of the likely return if the project is repeated a large number of times. The most difficult aspect of determining expected values is the estimation of the probabilities associated with the various outcomes. Regardless of whether these probabilities are estimated *objectively* or *subjectively*, the expected value is calculated in the same manner. The expected value calculation can be illustrated using the cash inflows[1] for projects A and B, which were presented in Table 16.1.

[1] Throughout the remainder of this chapter, attention will be devoted to risk as reflected in a project's cash inflows rather than its associated net present value. This approach is preferred since the risk of most projects is introduced through their cash inflows rather than through their initial investments, which are often known with certainty. The only difference between using cash inflows rather than net present value is that the initial investment has not been subtracted from the present value of the cash inflows in order to determine the net present value. Since the projects used throughout the next few pages require the same initial investment of $10,000 and are discounted at the same rate (10 percent), conclusions relating to project risk can be drawn more directly using the cash inflow data. Had the probabilities been attached to the NPV's from Table 16.2, the same answers for expected NPV as those found using cash inflows in Table 16.3 would have resulted.

EXAMPLE

An evaluation of the Goodwear Tire's past pessimistic, most likely, and optimistic estimates indicates that 25 out of 100 times, or 25 percent of the time, the pessimistic outcome occurred; 50 out of 100 times, or 50 percent of the time, the most likely outcome occurred; and 25 out of 100 times, or 25 percent of the time, the optimistic outcome occurred. Thus the probabilities of the pessimistic, most likely, and the optimistic outcomes occurring this time are 25 percent, 50 percent, and 25 percent, respectively. The sum of these probabilities must equal 100 percent; that is, they must be based upon all the alternatives considered. Table 16.3 presents the calculations required to find the expected values of the cash inflows and NPV's for projects A and B.

TABLE 16.3 **Expected values of cash inflows and NPV'S for projects A and B**

Possible outcomes	Probability (1)	Cash inflows (2)	Weighted value (1) · (2) (3)
Project A			
Pessimistic	0.25	$ 1500	$ 375
Most likely	0.50	2000	1000
Optimistic	0.25	2500	625
	1.00	Expected Cash Inflows	$ 2000

Expected NPV = 7.606[a] ($2,000) − $10,000 = $5,212

Project B			
Pessimistic	0.25	$ 0	$ 0
Most likely	0.50	2000	1000
Optimistic	0.25	4000	1000
	1.00	Expected Cash Inflows	$ 2000

Expected NPV = 7.606[a] ($2000) − $10,000 = $5212

[a]The present-value interest factor for an annuity (PVIFA) with a 15-year life discounted at 10 percent is 7.606.

A number of important points should be recognized in Table 16.3. First, the probabilities in each case sum to one, which must be true when calculating expected values. Second, since the states labeled "possible outcomes" are the same for projects A and B, the associated probabilities are the same in each case. Finally, the expected cash inflow values are equivalent to the most likely estimate in each case. This does not generally happen when expected cash inflow values are calculated.[2] ●

MEASURING PROJECT RISK

The measurement of project risk is quite important in the overall evaluation of capital budgeting projects. Being able to measure the risk of capital budg-

[2]As the reader may imagine, this example has been designed in order to highlight certain aspects of risk. For this reason the expected cash inflow values for the differing projects are the same.

Figure 16.1 **Bar charts for project A and B's cash inflows**

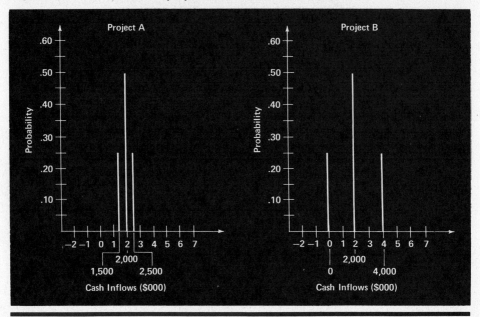

eting projects lets one somehow differentiate between those projects having similar returns. One's ability to compare projects with different returns is also greatly enhanced, since one can get some feel for the type of risk-return trade-offs offered by the projects. In order to measure project risk, a decision maker must be able to differentiate between the variability of project returns. In this section, two related methods of measuring project risk are discussed. The first method is a visual one that requires the development of probability distributions. The second method uses statistical measures to get a more concrete index of project variability, or risk.

Probability distributions

Although the calculation of expected value does provide the decision maker with better inputs than the use of a single point estimate or sensitivity analysis, it still does not allow him or her to get a handle on risk. If one were to compare the expected values of cash inflows for projects A and B, from Table 16.3, they would again be the same. Comparing the probability distribution associated with each project allows the decision to get some "feel" for differing degrees of project risk. A probability distribution can be graphed by plotting possible outcomes and associated probabilities on a set of outcome-probability axes.

The simplest type of probability distribution is the *bar chart*, or *discrete probability distribution*, which shows only a limited number of outcome-probability coordinates. The bar charts for projects A and B are shown in Figure 16.1. A comparison of the two charts shows that although both projects

Figure 16.2 Continuous probability distributions for project A and B's cash inflows

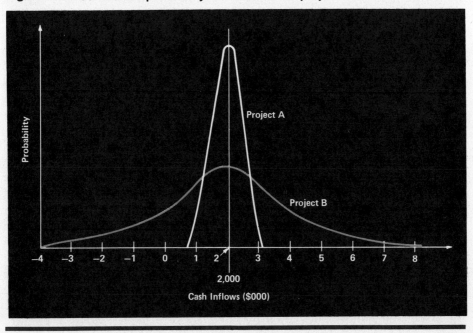

have the same expected value of cash inflows, the range of cash inflows is much more dispersed for project B than for project A—$4000 versus $1000.

A more descriptive probability distribution for a project can be developed if the decision maker obtains the probabilities associated with every possible outcome. In the preceding example, we had only three possible cash inflow outcomes and associated probabilities; if we knew all of the possible cash inflow outcomes and their associated probabilities, a *continuous probability distribution* could be developed. This type of distribution can be thought of as a bar chart for a very large number of outcomes. Figure 16.2 presents a graph of continuous probability distributions for projects A and B. In order to actually draw these curves, a large number of outcomes would be required.[3]

In the bar charts in Figure 16.1, projects A and B had the same probability (i.e., 50 percent) of cash inflows of $2000. In the continuous distribution, these probabilities change due to the large number of additional outcomes considered. The area under each of the curves is equal to 1, which means that 100 percent of the outcomes, or all the possible outcomes, have been

---

[3]In order to develop a continuous probability distribution, one must have data on a large number of historical occurrences of the event. Then, by developing a frequency distribution indicating how many times each outcome has occurred over the given time horizon, one can convert this data into a probability distribution. Probability distributions for risky events can also be developed using simulation—a process that is briefly discussed in a latter part of this chapter.

considered. Often probability distributions such as those in Figure 16.2 are converted into *cumulative probability distributions*, which allow the decision maker to determine easily the probability of obtaining at least some value.[4] It is important to note in Fig. 16.2 that, although projects A and B have the same expected cash inflow value ($2000), the distribution of cash inflows for project A is much tighter, or closer to the expected value, than that for project B. The distribution of cash inflows for project B would be said to have much greater *dispersion* than the distribution of cash inflows for project A.

Using statistics for measuring risk

Figure 16.2 shows that the variability of possible cash inflows for project A is much less than that for project B since the probability distribution for project A is much tighter than that for project B. Given the initial statement that the more variable the possible returns from a project the more risky it is, the cash inflows associated with project B are more risky than those associated with project A. Instead of visually observing the variability of project returns, we can use certain statistical measures of risk. These measures provide the decision maker with a concrete value indicative of project variability and therefore risk.[5] The most common statistical measure of project risk is the *standard deviation* from the mean or expected value of the return. Dividing the associated standard deviation by the *mean* or expected value of a return provides the *coefficient of variation*, which allows the risk associated with projects of different size to be compared.

The standard deviation.   The standard deviation of a distribution of project returns represents the square root of the average squared deviations of the individual observations from the expected value. The first step in calculating the standard deviation of a distribution is to find the expected value, $\overline{E}$, which is given by Equation 16.1.

$$\overline{E} = \sum_{i=1}^{n} E_i \cdot P_i \qquad\qquad (16.1)$$

where

E_i = the outcome for the ith case
P_i = the probability of occurrence of ith outcome
n = the number of outcomes considered

[4] A probability distribution can be converted into a cumulative probability distribution by determining the probability associated with obtaining at least each given value and plotting the cumulative probability of all occurrences less than or equal to the given value against the associated outcome.

[5] Although risk is typically viewed as determined by the variability, or dispersion, of values around an expected value, many people believe that it should be said to be present only when outcomes are below the expected value, since only returns below the expected value are considered bad. Nevertheless, the common approach is to view risk as determined by the variability on either side of the expected value since the greater this variability the less confident one can be of the outcomes associated with a project.

The calculation of the expected value of cash inflows, $\bar{E}$, for projects A and B were presented in Table 16.3. Column 1 gave the P_i's and column 2 gave the E_i's, n equaling 3 in each case. The expected value for each project's cash inflows was found to be $2000.

The expression for the standard deviation of the probability distribution, σ, is given by Equation 16.2.[6]

$$\sigma = \sqrt{\sum_{i=1}^{n} (E_i - \bar{E})^2 \cdot P_i} \tag{16.2}$$

It can be seen from this equation that the standard deviation represents the square root of the sum of the product of each deviation from the expected value, $\bar{E}$, squared and the associated probability of occurrence. Table 16.4 presents the calculation of the standard deviations for the cash inflows for projects A and B, based on the data presented earlier. The standard deviation of the cash inflows for project A is found to be $353.55, and the standard deviation for project B to be $1414.21. Statistically, if the probability distribution is *normal*, 68 percent of the outcomes will lie between ± 1 standard deviation from the expected value, 95 percent of all observations will lie between ± 2 standard deviations from the expected value, and 99 percent of all observations will lie between ± 3 standard deviations of the expected value.[7]

Our primary concern with standard deviations lies in their use to compare project risk. One must be careful in using the standard deviation to compare risk since it is only an absolute measure of dispersion and does not consider the dispersion of outcomes in relationship to an expected value. Since projects A and B have the same expected values (i.e., $2000), it would be safe to say that project A is less risky than project B since A has a smaller standard deviation than B (i.e., $353.55 vs. $1414.21). In comparisons of projects with differing expected values, the use of the standard deviation can easily be improved upon by converting the standard deviation into a *coefficient of variation*.

The coefficient of variation. The coefficient of variation, V, is calculated simply by dividing the standard deviation, σ, for a project by the

---

[6]The formula commonly used to find the standard deviation, σ, in a situation where all of the outcomes are known, but their related probabilities have not been determined, is

$$\sigma = \sqrt{\sum_{i=1}^{n} \frac{(E_i - \bar{E})^2}{n}}$$

where n is the number of observations. Because when analyzing capital budgeting proposals, outcomes and related probabilities are often available, the formula given in Equation 16.2 is emphasized in this chapter.

[7]A probability distribution that is *normal* is symmetrical around the expected value. This type of distribution is best viewed graphically, in which case it resembles a bell-shaped curve. Tables of values indicating the probabilities associated with various deviations from the expected value of a normal distribution can be found in any basic statistics text.

TABLE 16.4 The calculation of the standard deviation of the cash inflows for projects A and B

Project A

i	E_i	$\overline{E}$	$E_i - \overline{E}$	$(E_i - \overline{E})^2$	P_i	$(E_i - \overline{E})^2 \cdot P_i$
1	$1500	$2000	− $500	$250,000	.25	$62,500
2	2000	2000	0	0	.50	0
3	2500	2000	500	250,000	.25	62,500

$$\sum_{i=1}^{3} (E_i - \overline{E})^2 \cdot P_i = \$125,000$$

$$\sigma_A = \sqrt{\sum_{i=1}^{3} (E_i - \overline{E})^2 \cdot P_i} = \sqrt{\$125,000} = \underline{\$353.55}$$

Project B

i	E_i	$\overline{E}$	$E_i - \overline{E}$	$(E_i - \overline{E})^2$	P_i	$(E_i - \overline{E})^2 \cdot P_i$
1	$ 0	$2000	− $2000	$4,000,000	.25	$1,000,000
2	2000	2000	0	0	.50	0
3	4000	2000	2000	4,000,000	.25	1,000,000

$$\sum_{i=1}^{3} (E_i - \overline{E})^2 \cdot P_i = \$2,000,000$$

$$\sigma_B = \sqrt{\sum_{i=1}^{3} (E_i - \overline{E})^2 \cdot P_i} = \sqrt{\$2,000,000} = \underline{\$1,414.21}$$

expected value, $\overline{E}$, for the project. Equation 16.3 presents the equation for the coefficient of variation.

$$V = \frac{\sigma}{\overline{E}} \tag{16.3}$$

The coefficients of variation for projects A and B are 0.177 ($353.55 ÷ $2000) and 0.707 ($1414.21 ÷ $2000.00). The higher the coefficient of variation, the more risky the project; project B is therefore more risky than project A. Since both these projects have the same expected value, the coefficient of variation has not provided any more information than the standard deviation.

The real utility of the coefficient of variation is in comparing projects having different expected values. A simple example will illustrate this point.

EXAMPLE
A firm is attempting to select the least risky of two mutually exclusive projects—X and Y. The expected value, standard deviation, and coefficient of variation for each of these project's cash inflows is given below.

Statistics with respect to cash inflows	Project X	Project Y
(1) Expected value	$12,000	$20,000
(2) Standard deviation	$ 9,000[a]	$10,000
(3) Coefficient of variation (2) ÷ (1)	0.75	0.50[a]

[a]Preferred project using the given risk measure.

If the firm were to compare the projects solely on the basis of their standard deviations, they would prefer project X to project Y since project X has a lower standard deviation than Y ($9000 vs. $10,000). Comparing the coefficients of variation of the projects shows that management would be making a serious error in accepting project X in preference to project Y, since the relative dispersion or risk of the projects as reflected in the coefficient of variation is lower for project Y than for project X (0.50 vs. 0.75). This example should make it clear that as a rule the use of the coefficient of variation for comparing project risk is best since it does consider the relative size, or expected value, of projects.[8] ●

RISK AND TIME

Time is an important consideration in evaluating the risk in a capital budgeting project. When capital budgeting projects were originally defined in Chapter 14, the key factor said to differentiate capital expenditures from operating expense was the amount of time over which the benefits from the expenditure were expected to be received. Capital expenditures have benefits received over a period greater than one year and quite often greater than five years. In order to evaluate these capital expenditures, consideration must be given to the fact that future industry and economic factors may greatly affect the project outcomes. In this section, the time-related aspects of risk will be discussed. The first part will discuss the general risk-time relationship; the second part will discuss portfolio risk, which is indirectly tied to the time-related risk associated with projects.

Risk as a function of time

Risk must be viewed not only with respect to the current time period, but *as an increasing function of time*. Although the cash inflows associated with a given project may be expected to resemble an annuity, and therefore have similar expected values, it is not unusual to find that they have differing degrees of risk. Even where the expected values are not believed to be equal in each year, the probability distributions of cash inflows will probably become more dispersed with the passage of time due to the difficulty of accurately forecasting future outcomes. Generally, the *farther into the future one forecasts cash flows, the more variable* and therefore the more risky the forecast values are.

---

[8]The only situation in which the standard deviation is sufficient is when the risks of two projects having the same expected value are being compared, since in this case risk rankings based on the standard deviation and coefficient of variation will agree.

Figure 16.3 Risk as a function of time

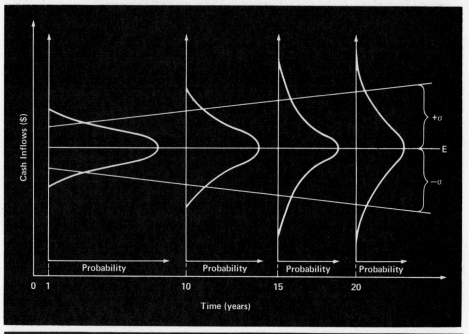

Figure 16.3 depicts increasing dispersion with the passage of time, assuming that the expected value of each year's cash inflows are equal. A band representing ±1 standard deviation, σ, from the expected value, $\overline{E}$, is indicated in the figure. It can be seen that the variability of the returns, and therefore the risk associated with the project, increases with the passage of time. Generally, the longer-lived a capital budgeting project, the greater the risk due to the increasing variability of returns resulting from increased forecasting errors for distant years.[9] Of course, where returns have been guaranteed contractually or otherwise, the standard deviation and therefore the risk is likely to be constant over time. Where the expected values of returns in each year differ, the coefficient of variation should be used to highlight the differences in risk.

Portfolio risk

Thus far attention has been devoted only to the evaluation of the time-related risk for a single project. Unfortunately, the risk of proposed capital budgeting projects cannot be viewed independently of other projects. The firm should be viewed as having a *portfolio* of projects (i.e., assets) selected in a fashion consistent with the goal of maximization of the owners' wealth.

---

[9]These forecast errors are only normal since, in most situations, there are many uncontrollable factors such as labor strikes, inflation, and wars that are difficult, if not impossible, to predict but can have a very real effect on the firm's future cash inflows and therefore on net present values.

Figure 16.4 The correlation between series M and N

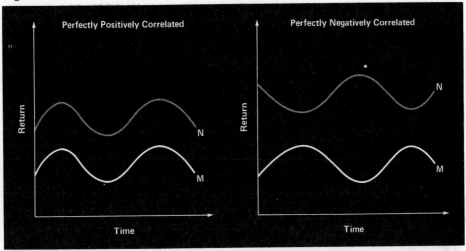

New capital budgeting proposals must be considered in light of both existing projects and other proposed projects, and the projects selected must be those that best *diversify*, or reduce, the firm's risk while generating an acceptable return. Successful diversification may make the risk of a group, or *portfolio*, of projects less than the sum of the risk of the individual projects.

In order to diversify risk in order to create an *efficient portfolio*, which is one that allows the firm to achieve the maximum return for a given level of risk or to minimize risk for a given level of return, the concept of correlation must be understood. *Correlation* is a statistical measure that indicates the relationship, if any, between series of numbers representing anything from cash flows to test data. If two series move together, they are *positively correlated*; if the series are countercyclical, or move in opposite directions, they are *negatively correlated*. The statistical measure of correlation, the *correlation coefficient* has a range of +1 for perfectly positively correlated series and −1 for perfectly negatively correlated series. These two extremes are depicted for series *M* and *N* in Figure 16.4. The perfectly positively correlated series move exactly together, while the perfectly negatively correlated series move in exactly opposite directions. The existence of perfectly correlated— especially negatively correlated—projects is quite rare.

In order to diversify project risk and thereby reduce the firm's overall risk, the projects that are best combined or added to the existing portfolio of projects are those that have a negative (or low positive) correlation with existing projects. By combining negatively correlated projects, the overall variability of returns or risk, σ, can be reduced. The result of diversifying to reduce risk is illustrated in Figure 16.5. Figure 16.5 shows that a portfolio containing the negatively correlated projects F and G, both having the same expected return, $\overline{E}$, also has the return, $\overline{E}$, but less risk (i.e., less variability of returns) than either of the projects taken separately. The benefits of diver-

Figure 16.5 Combining negatively correlated projects to diversify risk

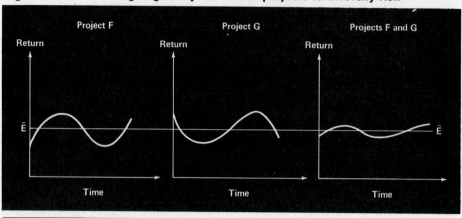

sifying risk by combining negatively correlated projects in order to build an efficient portfolio of assets should be clear from this discussion. The reader should recognize that even if projects are not negatively correlated, the lower the positive correlation between them the lower the resulting risk.[10]

The creation of a portfolio by combining two perfectly positively correlated projects can not reduce the portfolio's overall risk below the risk of the least risky project, while the creation of a portfolio by combining two projects that are perfectly negatively correlated can reduce the portfolio's total risk to a level below that of either of the component projects, which in certain situations may be zero. Combining projects with correlations falling between perfect positive correlation (i.e., a correlation coefficient of +1) and perfect negative correlation (i.e., a correlation coefficient of −1) can therefore reduce the overall risk of a portfolio. An example of perfect positive correlation might be a meat packer acquiring another meat packer; perfect negative correlation might result from the meat packer acquiring a flour mill, since when meat sales increase flour sales decrease and vice versa. Often a firm must consider the correlation of a proposed project with its existing portfolio of assets in order to make an investment decision; the procedure for this is no different than that required when creating a portfolio of two new projects.

EXAMPLE

Table 16.5 presents the expected cash inflows from three different projects — X, Y, and Z — over the next five years along with their expected values and standard deviations. It can be seen that each of the projects has an expected value of 30 and a standard deviation of 14.14. The projects therefore have equal risk and equal return although their cash-inflow patterns are not necessarily identical. A comparison of the cash-inflows patterns of projects X and Y should disclose that they are perfectly neg-

---

[10]Some projects are *uncorrelated*, that is, they are completely unrelated in the sense that there is no interaction between their returns. Combining uncorrelated projects can reduce risk— not as effectively as combining negatively correlated projects, but more effectively than combining positively correlated projects. The correlation coefficient for uncorrelated projects is close to zero and acts as the midpoint between perfect positive and perfect negative correlation.

TABLE 16.5 Cash inflows, expected values, and standard deviations for projects X, Y, and Z and portfolios XY and XZ

Year	Projects			Portfolios	
				XY[a]	XZ[b]
	X	Y	Z	(50%X plus 50%Y)	(50%X plus 50%Z)
1979	10	50	10	30	10
1980	20	40	20	30	20
1981	30	30	30	30	30
1982	40	20	40	30	40
1983	50	10	50	30	50
Statistics:					
Expected value	30	30	30	30	30
Standard deviation[c]	14.14	14.14	14.14	0	14.14

[a]Portfolio XY, which consists of 50 percent of project X and 50 percent of project Y, illustrates *perfect negative correlation*, since these two cash-inflow streams behave in completely opposite fashions over the five-year period.

[b]Portfolio XZ, which consists of 50 percent of project X and 50 percent of project Z, illustrates *perfect positive correlation*, since these two cash-inflow streams behave identically over the five-year period.

[c]Since the probabilities associated with the returns are not given, the formula given earlier in Equation 16.2 could not be used to calculate the standard deviations, σ. Instead the more general formula,

$$\sigma = \sqrt{\frac{\sum_{i=1}^{n} (E_i - \bar{E})^2}{n}}$$

where E_i = return i, $\bar{E}$ = expected value of the returns, and n = the number of observations, was used.

atively correlated since they move in exactly opposite directions over time. Comparing projects X and Z, it should be clear that they are perfectly positively correlated since they move in precisely the same direction (note that the cash inflows for X and Z are identical).[11]

Portfolio XY By combining equal portions of projects X and Y—the perfectly negatively correlated projects—portfolio XY (shown in Table 16.5) is created.[12] The risk in the portfolio created by this combination as reflected in the standard deviation is reduced to zero, while the expected cash inflow remains at 30. Since both of the projects had the same expected cash-inflow values, are combined in equal parts, and are perfectly negatively correlated, the combination results in the complete elimination of risk. Whenever projects are perfectly negatively correlated, an optimum combination (similar to the 50-50 mix in the case of projects X and Y) exists for which the resulting standard deviation will equal zero.

Portfolio XZ By combining equal portions of projects X and Z—the perfectly positively correlated projects—portfolio XZ (shown in Table 16.5) is created. The risk

[11]It is *not* necessary for cash inflow streams to be identical in order for them to be perfectly positively correlated. Identical cash inflow streams are used in this example in order to permit the concepts to be illustrated in the simplest, most straightforward fashion available. Any cash inflow streams that move (i.e., vary) exactly together—regardless of the relative magnitude of the cash inflows—are perfectly positively correlated.

[12]Although the projects are not in actuality divisible, for illustrative purposes it has been assumed that each of the projects—X, Y, and Z—can be divided up and combined with other projects in order to create portfolios. This assumption is made only to permit the concepts, again, to be illustrated in the simplest, most straightforward fashion.

in this portfolio as reflected by its standard deviation, which remains at 14.14, is unaffected by this combination; and the expected cash inflow remains at 30. Whenever perfectly positively correlated projects such as X and Z are combined, the standard deviation of the resulting portfolio cannot be reduced below that of the least risky project; the maximum portfolio standard deviation will be that of the riskier project. Since projects X and Z have the same standard deviation (14.14), the minimum and maximum standard deviations are both 14.14, which is the only value that could be taken on by a combination of these projects. This result can be attributed to the existence of the unlikely event that X and Z are identical projects. ●

Although detailed statistical explanations can be given for the behaviors illustrated in Table 16.5 and discussed in the preceding example, the important point to recognize is that projects can be combined so that the resulting portfolio has less risk than that of either of the projects viewed independently. This often can be achieved without any loss of return. Portfolio XY in the preceding example has illustrated such behavior. The greater the risk-reducing benefits of diversification, the more negative (or less positive) the correlation is between project returns. In no case will the result of creating portfolios of projects be such that the risk of the resulting portfolio is greater than that of the riskiest project included in the portfolio. In summary, it should be clear that by carefully constructing portfolios of projects, the financial manager can create efficient portfolios of assets that contribute positively to the achievement of the firm's overall goal of owners' wealth maximization.

RISK AND RETURN: CAPITAL ASSET PRICING MODEL (CAPM)

Over the past fifteen or so years,[13] a great deal of theory has been developed with respect to risk-return trade-offs. In Chapter 7, this type of trade-off was discussed as it related to the management of the firm's working capital. It was shown that a firm's profitability would be expected to increase as the firm decreased its liquidity, which would increase the risk of technical insolvency, and vice versa. The broader and equally important aspect of risk is the overall risk of the firm as perceived by investors in the marketplace. An understanding of this risk is important since it significantly impacts the firm's investment opportunities—and even more importantly, the owners' wealth. The basic theory with respect to risk and return is commonly referred to as the *capital asset pricing model (CAPM)*. It was developed primarily to explain the behavior of security prices and provide a mechanism whereby investors could readily assess the impact of a proposed security investment on their overall portfolio risk and return. Although the theory cannot be readily applied to the internal capital-budgeting project-selection process,[14] it does provide use-

[13]The key development of this theory is generally attributed to William F. Sharpe, "Capital Asset Prices: A Theory of Market Equilibrium Under Conditions of Risk," *Journal of Finance 19* (September 1964), pp. 425–442. A variety of authors have significantly advanced, refined, and tested this theory.

[14]Although research on the application of the capital asset pricing model to "real assets" continues, the CAPM cannot be readily applied to these decisions due to their indivisibility, relatively large size, small number, and lack of an efficient market.

ful insights into the nature of risk-return tradeoffs that must be considered as part of the capital budgeting process. This section of the chapter describes the basic CAPM in order to provide an intuitive understanding of the risk-return trade-offs involved, not only in capital budgeting decisions, but also in all types of financial decisions.

Assumptions of the model

The capital asset pricing model relies on a number of assumptions that create a nearly perfect world in which the model can be most clearly defined. Although they appear to be unrealistic, empirical studies have confirmed their reasonableness and have provided support for the existence of the relationships described by CAPM. The basic assumptions are related to the efficiency of the markets and the investor preferences.

Efficient markets. The marketplace in which investors make transactions in securities (or assets) is assumed to be highly efficient. This means that investors all have the same information with respect to securities and that this information is accurate. The investors are assumed to all view securities in light of a common ownership (or holding) period that is typically one year. There are no restrictions on investment, no taxes, and no transactions cost. None of the investors are assumed to be large enough to impact significantly the market price of the stock.

Investor preferences. Investors are assumed to prefer to earn higher (vs. lower) returns, while, at the same time, they are averse to risk, preferring lower (vs. higher) risk. In general, they will prefer to invest in securities offering the highest return for a given level of risk or the lowest risk for a given level of return. They are assumed to measure return using the expected value and measure risk using the standard deviation.

Types of risk

A security (or assets) risk is said to consist of two components—diversifiable and nondiversifiable risk. *Diversifiable risk,* which is sometimes referred to as *unsystematic risk,* represents the portion of an asset's risk that can be eliminated through diversification. It results from the occurrence of uncontrollable or random events such as labor strikes, lawsuits, regulatory actions, loss of a key account, and so forth. The events that cause firms to have diversifiable risk vary from firm to firm; they are therefore unique to the given firm. *Nondiversifiable risk,* which is also called *systematic risk,* is attributed to forces that affect all firms and are therefore not unique to the given firm. Factors such as war, inflation, international incidents, and political events account for an asset's nondiversifiable risk. This risk can be assessed relative to the risk of a diversified portfolio of securities, which is commonly referred to as the *market portfolio* or *the market*. The market portfolio commonly contains all securities listed on a given exchange or included in a major index such as Standard & Poor's 500 Stock Composite Index.

Because any investor can create a portfolio of assets that will diversify away all diversifiable risk, the only *relevant risk* is the nondiversifiable risk.[15] Any investor (or firm) therefore must be concerned solely with the non-diversifiable risk, which reflects the contribution of an asset to the risk of the portfolio. This risk is not the same for each asset, but rather different assets will affect the portfolio differently. In other words, the nondiversifiable risk of each asset depends upon how it behaves relative to changes in the market environment in which it exists. As pointed out earlier, certain factors such as war, inflation, etc. affect all assets and are inescapable. The degree of their effect, or nondiversifiable risk, of course will not be the same for all assets. Because the relevant risk differs from asset to asset, its measurement is important in order to allow investors to select assets offering the desired risk-return characteristics to be included in their portfolios. The capital asset pricing model provides a mechanism that can be used to relate risk and return.

The model: CAPM

The capital asset pricing model (CAPM) links together the relevant risk and return for all assets; it is discussed in three parts below. The first part defines and describes the beta coefficient, which is an index of nondiversifiable risk. The second part presents an equation of the model, and the final part graphically describes the relationship between risk and return.

Beta coefficient.   In order to assess an asset's nondiversifiable risk, its *beta coefficient, b,* must be determined. The beta coefficient for an asset can be found by examining an asset's historic returns relative to the returns for the market (i.e., market portfolio).[16] The market returns typically are meas-

---

[15]Empirical studies have found that portfolios of eight to twelve randomly selected securities will allow the firm to diversify fully the diversifiable risk. Two interesting studies are that of W. H. Wagner and S. C. Lau, "The Effect of Diversification on Risk," *Financial Analysts Journal 26* (November-December 1971), pp. 48–53, and Jack Evans and Stephen H. Archer, "Diversification and the Reduction of Dispersion: An Empirical Analysis," *Journal of Finance 23* (December 1968), pp. 761–767.

[16]The empirical measurement of beta is approached using regression analysis in order to find the regression coefficient (b_j) in the equation

$$k_j = a_j + b_j k_m + e_j$$

where:

k_j = the required return on security j
a_j = the intercept that equals the risk-free rate R_F
b_j = the beta coefficient, which equals

$$\frac{Cov\ (k_j, k_m)}{\sigma_m^2}$$

where

$Cov\ (k_j, k_m)$ = covariance of the return on security j, k_j, and the market portfolio, k_m
   σ_m^2 = variance of the market portfolio
   k_m = the required rate of return on the market portfolio of securities
   e_j = random error term, which reflects the diversifiable or unsystematic risk of security j

Because of the somewhat rigorous calculations involved in finding betas, the interested reader is referred to an advanced managerial finance or investments text for a more detailed discussion of this topic. Published security betas can be found in a variety of sources such as *Value Line,* as well as in the "Beta Books" now published by many of the leading stock brokerage firms such as Paine, Webber, Jackson, and Curtis, Inc.

TABLE 16.6 Selected betas and their associated interpretations

Beta	Comment	Interpretation[a]
2.0 ⎫	Move in same	Twice as responsive, or risky, as the market.
1.0 ⎬	direction as market	Same response or risk as the market (i.e., average risk).
.5 ⎭		Only half as responsive as the market.
0		Unaffected by market movement.
−.5 ⎫	Move in opposite	Only half as responsive as the market.
−1.0 ⎬	direction to	Same response or risk as the market.
−2.0 ⎭	market	Twice as responsive as the market.

[a]A stock that is twice as responsive as the market will experience a 2-percent change in its return for each 1-percent change in the return of the market portfolio; while the return of a stock that is half as responsive as the market will change by ½ of 1 percent for each 1 percent change in the return of the market portfolio.

ured by the average return on all (or a large sample of) assets. The Standard & Poor's 500 Stock Composite Index or some other stock index is commonly used to measure the market return. The beta coefficient can be viewed as an *index* of the degree of responsiveness or comovement of the asset return with the market return. The beta for the market is equal to 1; all other betas are viewed relative to this value. Asset betas may take on values that are either positive or negative; positive betas are much more common than negative betas. The majority of betas fall between .2 and 2.0. Table 16.6 gives some selected beta values and their associated interpretations. Because negative betas are not commonly found, primary attention is given to only the positive beta assets.

The equation. Using beta as our index of nondiversifiable (relevant) risk, the capital asset pricing model, which relates risk and return for all assets, is given in Equation 16.4. It should be clear from the equation

$$k_j = R_F + b_j \cdot (k_m - R_F) \tag{16.4}$$

where

k_j = the required (or expected) return on asset j

R_F = the rate of return required on a risk-free security, which is commonly measured by the yield on a U.S. government security such as a treasury bill

b_j = the beta coefficient or index of nondiversifiable (relevant) risk for asset j

k_m = the required rate of return on the market portfolio of assets that can be viewed as the average rate of return on all securities

that the required return on an asset, k_j, is an increasing function of beta, b_j, which reflects the relevant risk. In other words, the higher the risk, the higher the required return, and vice versa. The model can be broken into two parts: (1) the risk-free rate, R_F; and (2) the *risk premium*, $b_j \cdot (k_m - R_F)$. The portion of the risk premium, $(k_m - R_F)$, could be called the *market risk premium* since it represents the premium that the investor must receive for taking the average amount of risk associated with holding the market portfolio of assets.

EXAMPLE

Alter Corporation wishes to determine the required return on an asset that has a beta of 1.5. The risk-free rate of interest is found to be 7 percent, while the return on the market portfolio of assets is 11 percent. Substituting $b = 1.5$, $R_F = 7\%$, and $k_m = 11\%$ into the capital asset pricing model given in Equation 16.4 yields a required return,

$$k = 7\% + 1.5 \cdot (11\% - 7\%) = 7\% + 6\% = \underline{13\%.}$$

It can be seen that the market risk premium of 4 percent (i.e., 11 percent − 7 percent) when adjusted for the assets index of risk (beta) of 1.5 results in a risk premium of 6 percent (i.e., $4\% \cdot 1.5$) which, when added to the 7-percent rate of return expected on a risk-free security, results in a 13-percent required return. It should be clear that other things being equal the higher the beta, the greater the required return, and vice versa. ●

The graph: The security market line (SML). When the capital asset pricing model (Equation 16.4) is depicted graphically, it is called the *security market line (SML).* It should be clear from Equation 16.4 that the SML will, in fact, be a straight line. It reflects for each level of nondiversifiable risk (i.e., beta) the required return in the marketplace. In the graph, risk as measured by beta, b, is plotted on the x-axis and required returns, k, are plotted on the y-axis.

EXAMPLE

In the preceding example for the Alter Corporation, the risk-free rate, R_F, was 7 percent and the required return on the market portfolio, k_m, was 11 percent. Since the betas associated with R_F and k_m, b_{RF} and b_m, are by definition zero and one, respectively, the SML can be plotted using these two sets of coordinates. Figure 16.6 presents the security market line (SML) resulting from plotting the coordinates given. As traditionally shown, the security market line in Figure 16.6 presents the required or expected returns associated with all positive betas. The market risk premium of 4 percent (i.e., k_m of 11 percent minus R_F of 7 percent) has been highlighted. Using the beta for the Alter Corporation, b_{AC}, of 1.5, its corresponding required return, k_{AC}, has also been noted as 13 percent. Also shown in the figure is the Alter Corporation's risk premium of 6 percent (k_{AC} of 13 percent minus R_F of 7 percent). It should be clear from the figure that for assets with betas greater than one, the risk premium is greater than that for the market; while for assets with betas less than one, the risk premium is less than that for the market. ●

Some comments on CAPM

Although the capital asset pricing model (CAPM) was developed primarily for use in creating efficient portfolios of securities, it can also be adapted to making capital budgeting and other types of internal financial decisions. The use of the model's basic constructs in capital budgeting is

Figure 16.6 The security market line (SML) with Alter Corporation (AC) data shown

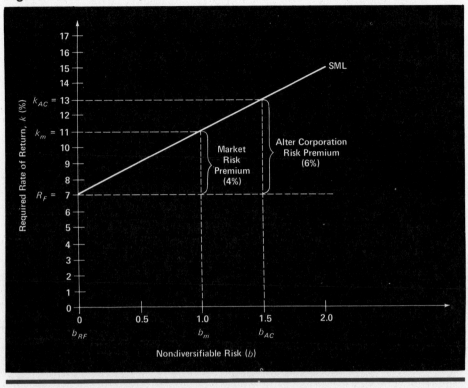

discussed in the following section. The key concept that should result from the preceding discussion is that a risk-return trade-off, which sometimes may be difficult to quantify, exists. When making financial decisions, an awareness to this risk-return trade-off and an attempt to somehow capture and consider the risk involved should provide for better financial decisions that help to achieve the firm's goal of owners' wealth maximization.

It is important to remember that the model relies on expectational data to estimate required (or expected) returns. The betas, which are developed by using historical data for the given asset as well as for the market, may or may not actually reflect the future variability of returns relative to the market. Therefore the required returns specified by the model can only be viewed as rough approximations. It is interesting to note that analysts and other users of betas commonly make subjective adjustments to the historically determined betas in order to reflect their expectations of the future when such expectations differ from the actual risk-return behaviors of the past.

ADJUSTING FOR PROJECT RISK

The discussion thus far has been devoted primarily to the problems of measuring risk and evaluating certain risk-related considerations. In this section, some actual techniques that may be used to adjust for project risk in capital budgeting are presented. The key techniques discussed are the subjective approach, decision trees, statistical approaches, simulation, the use of certainty equivalents, and the use of risk-adjusted discount rates.

The subjective approach

The subjective approach to risk adjustment involves calculating the net present value of a project and then making the capital budgeting decision on the basis of the decision maker's subjective evaluation of the project risk in light of the calculated return. Projects having similar net present values but believed to have differing degrees of risk can easily be selected, whereas projects exhibiting differing net present values are much more difficult to select. The use of sensitivity techniques such as pessimistic, most likely, and optimistic estimates of project returns is also somewhat subjective, but these techniques enable the decision maker to make a somewhat more educated "guess" as to the comparative risk of projects.

Decision trees

An expected value-based approach commonly used when making capital budgeting decisions is the *decision tree*. Decision trees are diagrams that permit the various decision alternatives and payoffs as well as their probabilities of occurrence to be mapped out in a clear and easy-to-analyze fashion. They get their name from their resemblance to trees with a number of branches (see Figure 16.7). Although decision trees provide a mechanism that allows the decision maker to analyze choices more clearly and select courses of action, they are not especially sophisticated methods for dealing with risk.[17] They rely on estimates (normally subjective) of the probabilities associated with the outcomes (or payoffs) of competing courses of action. The payoffs associated with each course of action are weighted by the associated probability; the weighted payoffs for each course of action are summed; and the expected value of each course of action is then determined. The alternative providing the highest expected value would then be selected.

EXAMPLE

Elroy's Inc. wishes to choose between two projects, I and J. To make this decision, Elroy's management has gathered the necessary data, which are depicted in the decision tree given in Figure 16.7. Project I requires an initial investment of $120,000; the calculation in column 4, based on the present values of cash inflow in column 3 and associated probabilities in column 2, gives an expected present value of cash inflows of $130,000. Project I's expected net present value, which is calculated below the decision tree, is therefore $10,000. Since the $15,000 expected net present value of project J, which is determined in a similar fashion as for project I, is greater than that for I, project J would be preferred. ●

Statistical approaches

Techniques for measuring project risk using the standard deviation and coefficient of variation were presented earlier. Also presented was a discus-

---

[17]Decision trees are most useful when a series of sequential decisions must be made. In such cases, conditional probabilities must be determined, and in general the analysis is much more sophisticated than that described herein. Even in the case of sequential decisions, the technique does not really capture risk; it instead relies on the use of expected values.

Figure 16.7 Decision tree for Elroy Inc.'s choice between projects I and J

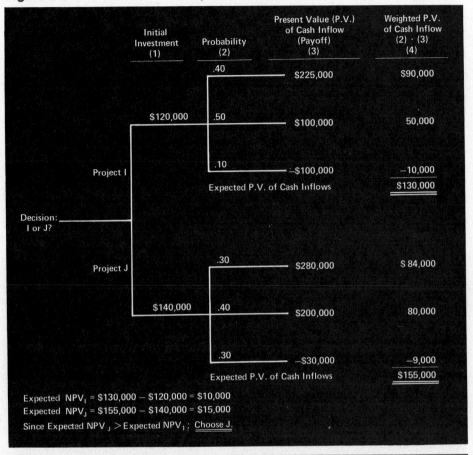

	Initial Investment (1)	Probability (2)	Present Value (P.V.) of Cash Inflow (Payoff) (3)	Weighted P.V. of Cash Inflow (2) · (3) (4)
		.40	$225,000	$90,000
	$120,000	.50	$100,000	50,000
Project I		.10	–$100,000	–10,000
			Expected P.V. of Cash Inflows	$130,000
Decision: I or J?				
		.30	$280,000	$ 84,000
Project J	$140,000	.40	$200,000	80,000
		.30	–$30,000	–9,000
			Expected P.V. of Cash Inflows	$155,000

Expected NPV_I = $130,000 – $120,000 = $10,000
Expected NPV_J = $155,000 – $140,000 = $15,000
Since Expected NPV_J > Expected NPV_I; Choose J.

sion of correlation between projects, which was related to the concept of a portfolio of assets. Correlation is a statistical measure that, when combined with other statistical measures such as the standard deviation and expected value of returns, provides a framework within which the decision maker can view the risk-return trade-offs associated with various projects in order to select those that align best with his or her (or the firm's) risk-return disposition. The capital asset pricing model (CAPM) provides a mechanism whereby the contribution of a project to the firm's overall risk and return can be assessed. Highly sophisticated statistical techniques have been combined into a body of knowledge referred to as *portfolio theory*, which provides techniques for selecting the best of a group of available projects in light of the firm's risk-return disposition or *utility function*. A more in-depth discussion of portfolio theory is beyond the scope of this text. The important point is that these approaches explicitly—not subjectively—consider expected values, standard deviations, and correlations between projects in order to select the projects that best fulfill the firm's objectives.

Figure 16.8 **A flowchart of a net present-value simulation**

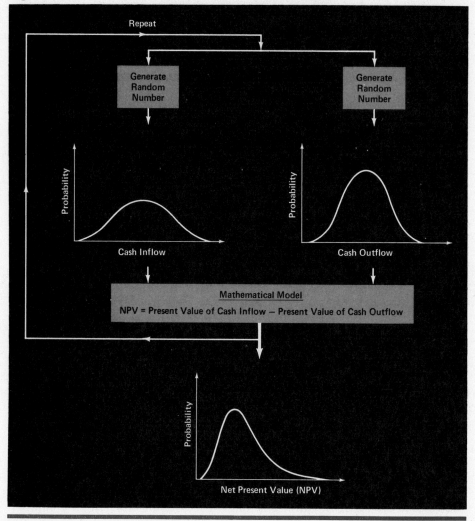

Simulation

Simulation is a sophisticated and statistically based approach for dealing with risk. Applying it to capital budgeting requires the generation of cash flows using predetermined probability distributions and random numbers. By tying the various cash flow components together in a mathematical model and repeating the process numerous times, a probability distribution of project returns can be developed. Figure 16.8 presents a flow chart of the simulation of the net present value of a project. The process of generating random numbers and using the probability distributions for cash inflows and cash outflows allows values for each of these variables to be determined. Substituting these values into the mathematical model results in a net present value.

By repeating this process maybe 1000 times, a probability distribution of net present values is created. The key to simulating successfully the distribution of returns is to identify accurately the probability distributions for the input variables and to formulate a mathematical model that truly reflects the existing relationships.

By simulating the various cash flows associated with a project and then calculating the NPV or IRR on the basis of these simulated cash flows, a probability distribution of each project's returns based upon either the NPV or the IRR criterion can be developed. Although only gross cash inflows and outflows are simulated in Figure 16.8, more sophisticated simulations in which each cash inflow and cash outflow component is simulated are quite common.[18] From the distribution of returns, regardless of how they are measured, the decision maker can determine not only the expected value of the return but also the probability of achieving a given return, or better, and so on. The use of computers has made this approach quite feasible since the extensive calculations need not be done by hand. The output of simulation provides an excellent basis for decision making since the decision maker can view a continuum of risk-return trade-offs instead of a single-point estimate.

Certainty equivalents

One of the most direct and theoretically preferred approaches for project risk adjustment is the use of *certainty equivalents*, which are factors that reflect the percent of a given cash flow the financial decision maker would accept in exchange for the expected cash flow. The project is therefore adjusted for risk by first converting the expected cash flows to certain amounts using the certainty equivalents and then discounting the cash flows at a risk-free rate.[19] The risk-free rate, R_F, is used to discount the certain cash flows since, if a risk-adjusted rate were used, the risk would in effect be double-counted. Although the process of converting the risky cash flows to certain cash flows is somewhat subjective, this technique is believed to be theoretically sound. The fact that the decision maker by converting the risky cash flows to certain cash flows introduces his or her own risk preferences into the analysis is viewed as a quite positive aspect of the use of certainty equivalents.

EXAMPLE

Spalding Sporting Goods is attempting to choose the best of two possible advertising campaigns—S and T. Both campaigns require initial investments of $200,000; Campaign S is quite conservative while campaign T is rather innovative and bold. The theory underlying campaign T is such that either people will be offended and not purchase the product or they will be pleased and purchase the product. Each cam-

---

[18]The cash inflow components are such things as the number of units sold, the sale price per unit, and collection patterns of receivables. The cash outflow components include such items as maintenance costs, payments for raw materials, and wages. Sophisticated simulation models for capital budgeting consider the probability distribution of these and other cash flow components.

[19]Alternately, the internal rate of return could be calculated for the risk-adjusted cash flows and then compared to the risk-free rate in order to make the accept-reject decision.

TABLE 16.7 Cash inflows, certainty equivalents, and certain cash inflows for Campaigns S and T for Spalding Sporting Goods

	Campaign S			Campaign T		
Year	Cash inflows (1)	Certainty equivalents[a] (2)	Certain cash inflows (1) · (2) (3)	Cash inflows (4)	Certainty equivalents[a] (5)	Certain cash inflows (4) · (5) (6)
1	$75,000	1.00	$75,000	$80,000	.90	$72,000
2	75,000	1.00	75,000	80,000	.80	64,000
3	75,000	.90	67,500	80,000	.70	56,000
4	75,000	.90	67,500	80,000	.60	48,000
5	75,000	.80	60,000	80,000	.50	40,000
	NPV @ 6% = $92,455			NPV @ 6% = $39,792		

[a]These values were estimated by management; they reflect the risk they perceive in the cash inflows.

paign is expected to provide equal annual benefits over a five-year period. Campaign S has expected benefits of $75,000 per year while campaign T has expected benefits of $80,000 per year. Table 16.7 presents the cash inflows, the certainty equivalents the firm believes applicable to each of them, and the resulting certain cash inflows, which are found by multiplying the cash inflow for each of the five years by the associated certainty equivalent. The certain cash inflows for campaigns S and T are given in columns 3 and 6, respectively, of the table.

Upon investigation, Spalding's management estimated the prevailing risk-free rate of return, R_F, to be 6 percent. Using the 6-percent risk-free rate to discount the certain cash inflows for each of the campaigns (S and T) results in the net present values of $92,455 for campaign S and $39,792 for campaign T. Therefore campaign S is preferred to campaign T. It is interesting to note that had the cash inflows not been adjusted for risk using the certainty equivalent approach, campaign T would have been preferred to campaign S because of its higher annual inflows for the same initial investment. The usefulness of the certainty equivalent approach for risk-adjustment should be quite clear; the only difficulty lies in the need to make subjective estimates of the certainty equivalents. ●

Risk-adjusted discount rates

Another direct approach for risk adjustment involves the use of risk-adjusted discount rates. Instead of adjusting the cash inflows for risk as was done using the certainty equivalent approach, the risk-adjusted discount rate approach instead adjusts the discount rate.[20] To adjust the discount rate, it is necessary to develop a function that expresses the return required for each

[20]The risk-adjusted discount rate approach can be applied when using the internal rate of return as well as net present value. If the IRR is used, the risk-adjusted discount rate becomes the cutoff rate that must be equaled or exceeded by the IRR for the project to be accepted. When using net present value, the projected cash inflows are merely discounted at the risk-adjusted discount rate.

Figure 16.9 A hypothetical market indifference curve

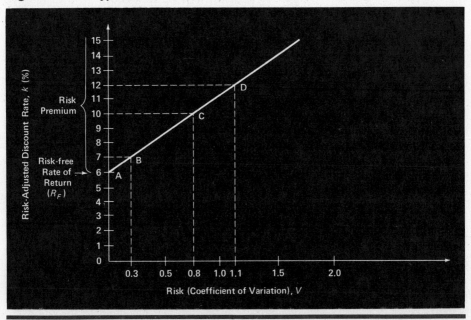

level of project risk in order to at least maintain the firm's value. Because the market for the assets of the firm is not an efficient one in which all firms have the same correct knowledge about an asset, the capital asset pricing model (CAPM) cannot be applied directly to these capital budgeting decision situations. Instead, the firm must develop a relationship between risk and return for real assets. One method of relating real asset risk and return is to measure an asset's contribution to the portfolio owned by the firm, and then relate for various degrees of risk the return required by prospective and existing shareholders as adequate compensation for the risks taken.

Using the coefficient of variation[21] as a measure of project risk, the firm can develop some type of *risk-return function,* or *market indifference curve.* An example of such a function is given in Figure 16.9, which relates the risk-adjusted discount rates, k, to the project risk as measured by the coefficient of variation, V. In a fashion similar to CAPM, the relationship is assumed to be linear. The market indifference curve in Figure 16.9 indicates that project cash inflows associated with a riskless event (i.e., $V = 0$) should be discounted at a 6-percent rate. This rate therefore represents the risk-free rate of return, R_F (point A in the figure). For all levels of risk greater than certainty ($V > 0$),

[21]The use of beta as prescribed by the capital asset pricing model (CAPM) is not feasible for nonsecurity types of investments due to the lack of an efficient market for such assets. The assumptions of CAPM are completely violated in the world of real corporate assets and therefore more practical techniques are required for relating risk and return. Although the coefficient of variation is a project-specific measure, it is assumed to represent a reasonable measure of the relative risk of real asset projects.

the associated required rate of return is indicated. Points *B*, *C*, and *D* indicate that rates of return of 7, 10, and 12 percent will be required on projects with coefficients of variation of 0.3, 0.8, and 1.1, respectively. Investors will be indifferent as to a choice of any of these risk-return combinations.

Figure 16.9 is a *market* indifference curve, which means that investors will discount cash inflows with the given levels of risk at the corresponding rates; therefore, in order not to damage its market value, the firm must use the correct discount rate for evaluating a project. If a firm discounts a risky project's cash inflows at too low a rate and accepts the project, the firm's market price may drop as investors recognize that the firm itself has become more risky.[22] The amount by which the required discount rate exceeds the risk-free rate is referred to as the *risk premium*; this definition is consistent with that given in the earlier discussion of the capital asset pricing model. The risk premium increases directly with increasing project risk. A simple example may help clarify how the risk-adjusted rate of return, *k*, can be used to evaluate capital budgeting projects.

EXAMPLE

Spalding Sporting Goods (presented in the preceding example) wishes to use the risk-adjusted discount rate approach in order to determine whether to increase its sales by accepting either of two advertising campaigns—S and T. In addition to the data presented earlier, Spalding's management has estimated that the standard deviation of campaign S's benefits is $22,500, while the standard deviation of benefits for campaign T is $64,000. Figure 16.9 represents the current market indifference curve.

The first step in evaluating the campaigns is to calculate their coefficients of variation. The coefficient of variation for campaign S is 0.30 (i.e., $22,500 ÷ $75,000) while the coefficient of variation for campaign T is 0.80 (i.e., $64,000 ÷ $80,000). According to Figure 16.9, the risk-adjusted discount rate for campaign S is 7 percent; for campaign T, it is 10 percent. Due to the more certain nature of campaign S, its risk premium is only 1 percent (i.e., 7 percent − 6 percent); for campaign T the risk premium is 4 percent (i.e., 10 percent − 6 percent). The net present value of each campaign at its risk-adjusted discount rate is calculated below:

Campaign S

$$\text{NPV} = \$75,000(\text{P.V. of an annuity, 5 years at 7\%}) - \$200,000$$
$$= \$75,000(4.100) - \$200,000$$
$$= \underline{\$107,500}$$

Campaign T

$$\text{NPV} = \$80,000(\text{P.V. of an annuity, 5 years @ 10\%}) - \$200,000$$
$$= \$80,000(3.791) - \$200,000$$
$$= \underline{\$103,280}$$

Apparently, campaign S is preferable to campaign T since it has a higher net present value. This is the same result obtained earlier using the certainty equivalent approach.

---

[22]It is also true that if the firm discounts a project's cash inflows at too high a rate, resulting in the rejection of an acceptable project, the firm's market price may drop because investors believe it is being overly conservative and sell their stock, putting downward pressure on the firm's market value.

Had the discount rates not been adjusted for risk, campaign T would have been preferred to campaign S because of its higher annual inflows for the same initial investment. The usefulness of risk-adjusted discount rates should now be clear; the real difficulty with this approach lies in estimating the market indifference curve. •

SUMMARY

This chapter has presented a discussion of capital budgeting under risk. Because the cash inflows associated with capital budgeting projects are future cash inflows, an understanding of risk is most important to making good capital budgeting decisions. The terms risk and uncertainty are often used interchangeably to refer to the variability of project returns. Statistically, risk is present when the probability distribution of outcomes is known, while uncertainty is present when the probability distributions are unknown. The terms are used interchangeably in this text. Two approaches often used to get a "feel" for project risk are sensitivity analysis and the use of probabilities. Sensitivity analysis involves evaluating various estimates of project outcomes such as the most pessimistic, most likely, and most optimistic. The range is often used to quantify risk by measuring the dispersion of these potential outcomes. This approach gives the decision maker a feel for the sensitivity of the project to various changes. A more sophisticated approach would be to assign probabilities to the various outcomes either objectively or subjectively in order to determine the expected value of the project returns.

Risk can be assessed visually by drawing either a bar graph or the entire probability distribution (if sufficient data are available) associated with a project's outcomes. To obtain a more concrete measure of project risk, statistical measures of variability can be used. Two statistics that provide a measure of project risk are the standard deviation and the coefficient of variation. The coefficient of variation, which is the standard deviation from the mean (or expected value of the project return) divided by the expected value of the project return, is most useful in obtaining a relative measure of project risk.

The timing of returns also affects project risk. In general, the farther into the future cash inflows are to be received, the greater the variability of these cash inflows. Another time-related consideration is portfolio risk, which is concerned with the time-related relationship between project cash inflows. The correlation between projects in a portfolio, which is the degree to which their returns vary together, greatly affects the overall risk of the portfolio. Capital budgeting projects whose returns are negatively correlated provide the best combination for minimizing overall risk. The best strategy is to diversify the firm's risk across projects in order to either maximize the return for a given level of risk or minimize the risk for a given level of return.

One of the key considerations in financial decision making involves the trade-off between risk and return. In a perfect world of efficient markets, the only relevant risk is the nondiversifiable risk, which is inescapable since it is attributed to changes in the economy. The diversifiable risk, which is attributed to the firm itself and results from the occurrence of uncontrollable or random events, can be eliminated through diversification. The nondiversifiable risk can be measured by beta, which is an index that relates the responsiveness or comovement of an asset's return to that of the market. Betas may be positive or negative; most are positive and less than 2.0. The capital asset pricing model (CAPM) uses beta to relate an asset's risk relative to the market to the asset's required return. Letting k_j = the required (or expected) return on an asset j, R_F = the risk-free rate of return, b_j = the index of non-diversifiable risk (or beta) for asset j, and k_m = the required return on the market portfolio, the capital asset pricing model is given by the following equation:

$$k_j = R_F + b_j \cdot (k_m - R_F)$$

The required return on asset j, k_j can be viewed as the sum of the return on a risk-free asset, R_F, plus a risk premium, $b_j \cdot (k_m - R_F)$, which reflects the asset's (relevant) risk relative to the market. Graphically, the capital asset pricing model is referred to as the security market line (SML), which depicts for each level of nondiversifiable risk (i.e., beta) the associated required return. Although the model is difficult to apply to real assets, the type of risk-return relationship depicted by the capital asset pricing model must be considered when making capital budgeting decisions in order to provide for owners' wealth maximization.

A number of techniques for adjusting projects for risk exist. Subjective approaches based on "educated guesses" or sensitivity analysis are quite common. The use of decision trees, which rely on expected values, is somewhat better than subjective approaches. Statistical techniques for measuring project risk and for determining efficient portfolios are also available. Simulation, which provides a probability distribution of project returns, is a quite sophisticated approach that usually requires the use of a computer. Certainty equivalents provide a mechanism whereby risky cash flows can be adjusted to certain amounts and then discounted at a risk-free rate in order to evaluate a project. Because the cash flows once adjusted for certainty are risk-free, the discount rate is accordingly one that does not consider risk. Risk-adjusted discount rates, which are the discount rates required in the marketplace in order to compensate for project risk, are quite useful. By discounting cash flows at the appropriate risk-adjusted rate, project risk is automatically accounted for.

QUESTIONS

16-1　Why is it important for a decision maker to have some feel for the risk or uncertainty associated with capital budgeting projects? What kind of capital budgeting project would have perfectly certain returns?

16-2　What is the difference between the terms "risk" and "uncertainty" as defined by a statistician? What kind of probability distributions are associated with each of these states?

16-3　What is the sensitivity approach for dealing with project risk? What is one of the most common methods used to evaluate projects using sensitivity analysis? Define and describe the role of the *range* as an aid in sensitivity analysis.

16-4　What is a payoff matrix? What are the two dimensions of this matrix? How can a payoff matrix be used to evaluate risk?

16-5   What is meant by "the probability of an event occurring"? What do probabilities of zero and one indicate about outcomes? Why?

16-6   How does a plot of the probability distribution of outcomes allow the decision maker to get a "feel" for project risk? What is the difference between a bar chart and a continuous probability distribution?

16-7   What does the standard deviation of a distribution of project returns indicate? What relationship exists between the size of the standard deviation and the degree of project risk?

16-8   What is the coefficient of variation? How is it calculated? Why may the coefficient of variation be a better basis for comparing the risk associated with different projects than the standard deviation?

16-9   What general relationship is expected to exist between project risk and time? To what factor(s) is this behavior attributable? Why?

16-10   Why should the firm be viewed as having a portfolio of projects? Why is the correlation between project returns important?

16-11   What are correlation coefficients? When do perfect positive and perfect negative correlation exist? Which is more desirable for effective diversification? Why?

16-12   How does diversification of risk in the project selection process allow the firm to combine risky projects in such a fashion that the risk of the portfolio is less than the risk of the individual projects in it? What is an efficient portfolio?

16-13   What is the basic theory with respect to risk and return? Upon what assumptions is this theory based?

16-14   Explain the difference between nondiversifiable and diversifiable risk. Why would one argue that nondiversifiable risk is the only *relevant* risk?

16-15   What is a *beta coefficient*? How can a beta coefficient be measured or estimated?

16-16   Using the beta coefficient as the measure of nondiversifiable risk, what is the equation for the *capital asset pricing model* (CAPM)? Explain the meaning of each variable.

16-17   What graphical representation is used to depict the risk-return trade-off given by the CAPM? Define the axes and construct a graph for a risk-free rate of 5 percent and a market rate of return of 10 percent.

16-18   How may decision trees be used in considering project risk? Do they provide for the measurement of risk? Explain.

16-19   What is the basic simulation approach for dealing with project risk? How does simulation provide the decision maker with useful decision-making inputs?

16-20   Explain the concept of *certainty equivalents*.

16-21   Using the NPV framework, what changes are necessary to utilize the certainty equivalent approach to evaluate risky capital expenditures?

16-22   What is a risk-return function, or market indifference curve? On what axes is it plotted?

16-23   How can a risk-return function be used to determine the risk-adjusted discount rate used in evaluating a project? What must be known in order to determine the risk-adjusted discount rate? Why?

PROBLEMS

16-1   Klauer Pharmaceutical is in the process of evaluating two mutually exclusive additions to their processing capacity. The firm's financial analysts have developed pessimistic, most likely, and optimistic estimates of the annual cash inflows associated with each project. These estimates are given in the table:

	Project A	Project B
Initial investment	$8000	$8000
Cash inflow estimates		
Pessimistic	$ 200	$ 900
Most likely	1000	1000
Optimistic	1800	1100

a Determine the range of annual cash inflows for each of the two projects.
b Assume the cost of capital for the firm is 10 percent, and the projects should have 20-year lives. Construct a sensitivity table for the *net present values* of the estimates. Include the range of NPV's for each project.
c Do a and b give consistent views of the risk of the two projects? Explain.
d Which project would you recommend and why?

16-2 Micro-Pub, Inc., is considering the purchase of one of two new microfilm cameras—R or S. Both should provide benefits over a 10-year period, and each has a required investment of $3000. Management has constructed the following table of estimates of probabilities and cash inflows for pessimistic, most likely, and optimistic results:

	Camera R		Camera S	
	Amount	Probability	Amount	Probability
Initial investment	$3000	1.00	$3000	1.00
Cash Inflow				
Pessimistic	$ 500	.25	$ 400	.20
Most likely	750	.50	750	.55
Optimistic	1000	.25	1200	.25

a Determine the range of cash inflows for each camera.
b Determine the expected cash inflow for each camera.
c Which camera do you consider the more risky? Discuss the nature of the risk-return trade-off associated with these cameras.

16-3 Whitney's Western-Wear, a clothing manufacturer, is considering a new line of female headwear. The table summarizes the cash inflows and probabilities for the two lines under consideration:

Market		Cash inflow	
acceptance	Probability	Line A	Line B
Very poor	.05	$ 100	$ 75
Poor	.15	250	125
Average	.60	800	850
Good	.15	1350	1475
Excellent	.05	1500	1625

Use the table to
a Construct a bar chart for each line's cash inflows.

    b Calculate the expected value of each line's cash inflows.

    c Evaluate the relative riskiness of each clothing line's cash inflows using the bar charts.

16-4 Using the net present values (NPV) and associated probabilities for two projects—X and Y—summarized in the table,

    a Prepare bar charts for the two projects' net present values.

    b Calculate and compare the expected net present values of the projects.

    c Compare the riskiness of the two projects.

Project X		Project Y	
NPV ($)	Probability	NPV ($)	Probability
−15,000	.01	−20,000	.00
0	.03	−10,000	.02
15,000	.03	0	.04
25,000	.05	10,000	.06
30,000	.15	20,000	.08
35,000	.50	30,000	.15
40,000	.15	40,000	.35
45,000	.05	50,000	.20
55,000	.03	60,000	.05
70,000	.00	70,000	.03
		80,000	.01
		90,000	.01
		100,000	.00

16-5 A firm is considering two projects; their cash inflow probability distributions are summarized:

Project A		Project B	
Cash inflow	Probability	Cash inflow	Probability
$100	.10	$100	.10
200	.20	300	.80
300	.40	500	.10
400	.20		
500	.10		

    a Determine the range for each distribution of project cash inflows.

    b Determine the expected cash inflow from each project.

    c Determine the standard deviation of each project's probability distribution of cash inflow.

    d Discuss the information the financial manager gains from each of the measures calculated above.

16-6 Robin Parker must decide which of two projects is best for her firm. By using probability estimates, she has determined the following information:

Statistic	Project I	Project II
Expected NPV	$24,000	$18,000
Standard deviation	$36,000	$32,000

a Complete the table by computing the coefficient of variation for each project.

b Explain to Ms. Parker why the standard deviation and coefficient of variation give different rankings of risk. Which method is superior and why?

16-7 Weber Tool must choose between two asset purchases. The cash-inflow data and related probabilities given below summarize the firms' analysis to this point.

Project 473		Project 297	
Cash inflow ($)	Probability	Cash inflow ($)	Probability
100	.05	−100	.01
150	.10	100	.04
200	.10	200	.05
250	.15	300	.10
300	.20	400	.15
350	.15	450	.30
400	.10	500	.15
450	.10	600	.10
500	.05	700	.05
		800	.04
		1000	.01

a For each project, compute
  (1) The range of cash inflow.
  (2) The expected value of cash inflow.
  (3) The standard deviation of cash inflow.
  (4) The coefficient of variation of cash inflow.

b Construct a bar chart of each distribution of cash inflow.

c Which project would you consider least risky and why?

16-8 The project cash inflows for four projects—A through D—forecast for the period 1979–1986 are given in the table below:

Year	A	B	C	D
1979	$2,000	$ 7,000	$15,000	$18,000
1980	3,000	8,000	15,000	17,000
1981	4,000	9,000	15,000	16,000
1982	5,000	6,000	15,000	15,000
1983	4,000	5,000	15,000	17,000
1984	3,000	7,000	15,000	18,000
1985	2,000	9,000	15,000	19,000
1986	5,000	10,000	15,000	20,000

a Indicate for each of the project combinations AB, AC, AD, BC, BD, and CD whether the returns are positively correlated, negatively correlated, or not correlated.

b Calculate the average cash inflows and standard deviation of cash inflows for each project. Hint: to calculate the standard deviation, σ, with these data, employ the formula found in footnote 6 in the chapter, which uses the same notation that was used in Equation 16.2 of the chapter:

$$\sigma = \sqrt{\dfrac{\sum\limits_{i=1}^{n}(E_i - \overline{E})^2}{n}}$$

   c Calculate the average cash inflows and standard deviation of cash inflows for project combinations AB and AD. (See hint in **b**).

   d What conclusions about the portfolio effects of combinations of projects can be drawn from your preceding work? Explain.

16-9 The Jenkins Box Company must consider several investment projects using the capital asset pricing model (CAPM) and its graphical representation, the security market line (SML). Using the table below,

   a Calculate the rate of return and risk premium each project must produce given its level of nondiversifiable risk.

   b Graph the security market line (required rate of return relative to non-diversifiable risk) for all projects listed in the table.

   c Discuss the relative nondiversifiable risk of projects A–E.

Project	Rate of return	b value
Risk-free asset	5%	0
Market portfolio	12%	1.00
Asset A	—	1.50
Asset B	—	.75
Asset C	—	2.00
Asset D	—	0
Asset E	—	− .50

16-10 The Emory Board-Games Company can bring out one of two new games this season. The *Signs Away* game has a higher initial cost but also has a higher expected return. *Monopolistic Competition,* the alternative, has a slightly lower initial cost but also has a lower expected return. The probabilities and present values associated with each game are listed in the following table.

Game	Initial investment	PV of Cash inflows	Probabilities
Signs Away	$140,000		1.00
		$320,000	.30
		220,000	.50
		−80,000	.20
Monopolistic Competition	$120,000		1.00
		$260,000	.20
		200,000	.45
		−50,000	.35

   a Construct a decision tree to analyze the two games.

   b Which game would you recommend (following a decision-tree analysis)?

   c Has your analysis captured the differences in project risk? Explain.

16-11 Creighton Castings has compiled the following information on a capital expenditure proposal:

(1) The projected cash inflows are normally distributed with a mean of $36,000 and a standard deviation of $9000.

(2) The projected cash outflows are normally distributed with a mean of $30,000 and a standard deviation of $6000.

(3) The firm has an 11-percent cost of capital.

(4) The probability distributions of cash inflows and cash outflows are not expected to change over the project's 10-year life.

a Describe how the preceding data could be used to develop a simulation model for finding the net present value of the project.

b Discuss the advantages of using a simulation to evaluate the proposed project.

16-12 Westchester Ball Valve has constructed a table, shown below, that gives expected cash inflows and certainty equivalents for these cash inflows. These measures are for a new machine that lasts five years and requires an initial investment of $100,000. The firm has a 10-percent cost of capital and its risk-free rate is 7 percent.

a What is the unadjusted net present value?

b What is the certainty equivalent net present value?

c Should the firm accept the project? Explain.

Year	Cash inflow	Certainty equivalent
1	$35,000	1.0
2	35,000	.8
3	35,000	.6
4	35,000	.6
5	35,000	.2

16-13 A firm is considering a risky project that requires an initial investment of $1,000,000 and will have expected after-tax cash inflows of $200,000 per year for the next 10 years. The firm uses a 10-percent cost of capital for projects of average risk, but feels this project requires an additional premium of 4 percent.

a Should the firm accept the project? Why or why not?

b At what risk premium (above the average risk of the firm) would the project be acceptable?

16-14 Preston Tire has recently investigated market risk-return trade-offs and has assembled the following data:

Coefficient of variation	Market discount rate
0.0	6.5%
0.2	7.5%
0.4	8.5%
0.6	9.5%
0.8	10.5%
1.0	11.5%
1.2	12.5%
1.4	13.5%
1.8	15.5%
2.2	17.5%

a   Construct a graph of the market indifference curve. Be sure to clearly label the axes and indicate the area of risk premiums.

b   The firm is evaluating the two following projects. Both have four-year lives and require initial investments of $4000.

Project I		Project II	
Annual cash inflow ($)	Probability	Annual cash inflow ($)	Probability
−2000	.25	−1000	.20
2000	.50	1600	.50
6000	.25	3000	.30

(1) Determine the expected value, standard deviation, and coefficient of variation for each of the two projects' cash inflows.

(2) Use the market indifference curve to determine the appropriate risk-adjusted discount rate for each project. (Adjust to the nearest one-half percent.)

(3) Which project do you recommend and why?

SELECTED REFERENCES

Bierman, Harold Jr., and Jerome E. Hass, "Capital Budgeting Under Uncertainty: A Reformulation," *Journal of Finance 28* (March 1973), pp. 119–130.

Blume, Marshall, E., "On the Assessment of Risk," *Journal of Finance 26* (March 1971), pp. 95–117.

Carter, E. Eugene, *Portfolio Aspects of Corporate Capital Budgeting* (Lexington, Mass.: Heath, 1974).

Evans, Jack, and Stephen H. Archer, "Diversification and the Reduction of Dispersion: An Empirical Analysis," *Journal of Finance 23* (December 1968), pp. 761–767.

Findlay, M. Chapman III, Arthur E. Gooding, and Wallace Q. Weaver, Jr., "On the Relevant Risk for Determining Capital Expenditure Hurdle Rates," *Financial Management 5* (Winter 1976), pp. 9–16.

Gitman, Lawrence J., "Capturing Risk Exposure in the Evaluation of Capital Budgeting Projects," *Engineering Economist 22* (Summer 1977), pp. 261–276.

Grayson, C. Jackson, "The Use of Statistical Techniques in Capital Budgeting," in Alexander A. Robichek, Ed., *Financial Research and Management Decisions* (New York: Wiley, 1967), pp. 90–132.

Greer, Willis R., "Theory versus Practice in Risk Analysis: An Empirical Study," *Accounting Review 49* (July 1974), pp. 496–505.

Harvey, R. K., and A. V. Cabot, "A Decision Theory Approach to Capital Budgeting Under Risk," *Engineering Economist 20* (Fall 1977), pp. 37–49.

Hertz, David B., "Investment Policies That Pay Off," *Harvard Business Review 46* (January-February 1968), pp. 96–108.

———, "Risk Analysis in Capital Investment," *Harvard Business Review 42* (January-February 1964), pp. 95–106.

Hillier, Frederick S., "A Basic Model for Capital Budgeting of Risky Interrelated Projects," *Engineering Economist 17* (Fall 1971), pp. 1–30.

Jensen, M. C., Ed., *Studies in the Theory of Capital Markets* (New York: Praeger, 1972).

Lessard, Donald R., and Richard S. Bower, "Risk-Screening in Capital Budgeting," *Journal of Finance 28* (May 1973), pp. 321–338.

Lewellen, Wilbur G. and Michael E. Long, "Simulation versus Single-Value Estimates in Capital Expenditure Analysis," *Decision Sciences 3* (1972), pp. 19–33.

Magee, John F., "Decision Trees for Decision-Making," *Harvard Business Review* (July-August 1964), pp. 126–136.

———, "How to Use Decision Trees in Capital Investment," *Harvard Business Review* (September-October 1964), pp. 79–96.

Markowitz, H., *Portfolio Selection* (New York: Wiley, 1959).

Miller, Robert B., and Dean W. Wichern, *Intermediate Business Statistics: Analysis of Variance, Regression and Time Series* (New York: Holt, Rinehart, and Winston, 1977).

Modigliani, Franco, and Gerald A. Pogue, "An Introduction to Risk and Return," *Financial Analysts Journal* (March-April 1974), pp. 68–80 and (May-June 1974), pp. 69–86.

Myers, Stewart C., and Stuart M. Turnbull, "Capital Budgeting and Capital Asset Pricing Model: Good News and Bad News," *Journal of Finance 32* (May 1977), pp. 321–333.

Osteryoung, Jerome S., Elton Scott, and Gordon S. Roberts, "Selecting Capital Projects with the Coefficient of Variation," *Financial Management 6* (Summer 1977), pp. 65–70.

Porter, R. Burr, Roger P. Bey, and David C. Lewis, "The Development of a Mean-Semi-Variance Approach to Capital Budgeting," *Journal of Financial and Quantitative Analysis 10* (November 1975), pp. 639–650.

Robichek, Alexander A., and Stewart C. Myers, "Conceptual Problems in the Use of Risk-Adjusted Discounted Rates," *Journal of Finance* (December 1966), pp. 727–730.

Sharpe, William F., "Capital Asset Prices: A Theory of Market Equilibrium Under Conditions of Risk," *Journal of Finance 19* (Sept. 1964), pp. 425–442.

———, *Portfolio Theory and Capital Markets* (New York: McGraw-Hill, 1970).

Stapleton, R. C., "Portfolio Analysis, Stock Valuation and Capital Budgeting Decision Rules for Risky Projects," *Journal of Finance 26* (March 1971), pp. 95–117.

Van Horne, James C., "Capital Budgeting Decisions Using Combinations of Risky Investments," *Management Science 13* (October 1966), pp. 84–92.

Wagner, Wayne H., and Sheila Lau, "The Effect of Diversification on Risk," *Financial Analysts Journal 26* (November-December 1971), pp. 48–53.

Weston, J. Fred, "Investment Decisions Using the Capital Asset Pricing Model," *Financial Management 2* (Spring 1973), pp. 25–33.

PART SIX

This part of the text covers three important and closely related topics—the cost of capital, capital structure, and valuation. The cost of capital, which represents the firm's average cost of money, is an important input to the capital budgeting process; the firm's capital structure and valuation affect, and are affected by, its cost of capital. The first chapter in this part, Chapter 17, is devoted to the cost of capital. It presents an in-depth discussion of the underlying theory, methods of calculation, and application of the cost of capital for a hypothetical firm. Chapter 18 discusses both capital structure and valuation. It describes the basic theories and some of the mathematical techniques for evaluating the mix of long-term debt and equity financing of a firm. It also presents, compares, and contrasts the key methods of determining the worth of a firm.

The cost of capital, capital structure, and valuation

BALANCE SHEET	
Assets	Liabilities and Stockholders' Equity
Current Assets	Current Liabilities
Fixed Assets	Long-Term Debt
	Stockholders' Equity

CHAPTER 17
The cost of capital

In the preceding chapters we developed various techniques and concepts for evaluating investment alternatives. In discussions of the so-called sophisticated techniques of capital budgeting, the term *cost of capital* was commonly used. When net present values or benefit-cost ratios are used to evaluate a firm's cash flows, they are discounted at the firm's cost of capital. Although the cost of capital is not needed to calculate the internal rate of return of an investment project, it is needed to make accept-reject decisions. If a project's IRR is greater than or equal to the firm's cost of capital, the project is considered acceptable.

This chapter is divided into four sections. The first section discusses the definition and implications of the firm's cost of capital. The second section presents the various components of the cost of capital—the cost of debt, the cost of preferred stock, the cost of common stock, and the cost of retained earnings. The third section of the chapter describes how the firm's overall or weighted average cost of capital is determined. The final section describes the weighted marginal cost of capital and explains how it can be used in the financial decision-making process.

AN OVERVIEW OF THE COST OF CAPITAL

The *cost of capital* is the rate of return a firm must earn on its investments for the market value of the firm to remain unchanged.[1] It can also be thought of as the rate of return required by the market suppliers of capital in order to attract needed financing at a reasonable price. Acceptance of projects with a rate of return below the cost of capital will decrease the value of the firm; acceptance of projects with a rate of return above the cost of capital will

---

[1]The value of the firm can be viewed as the present value of the firm's expected earnings. The cost of capital is the rate at which the firm's future earnings are discounted in the marketplace. The relationship between cost of capital and the value of a firm will become clearer after the discussion of valuation in Chapter 18.

increase the value of the firm. The objective of the financial manager is to maximize the wealth of the firm's owners. Using the cost of capital as a basis for accepting or rejecting investments is consistent with this goal.

Risk

A basic assumption of traditional cost of capital analysis is that *the firm's operating and financial risk are generally unaffected* by the acceptance and financing of projects.[2]

Operating risk.　*Operating risk*, which was briefly described as part of the discussion of operating leverage in Chapter 4, is related to the response of the firm's earnings before interest and taxes, or operating profits, to changes in sales. When the cost of capital is used to evaluate investment alternatives, it is assumed that acceptance of the proposed projects will not affect the firm's *operating* risk. The types of projects accepted by a firm can greatly affect its *operating* risk.

If a firm accepts a project that is considerably more risky than average, suppliers of funds to the firm are quite likely to raise the cost of funds. This is because of the decreased probability of the fund suppliers' receiving the expected returns on their money. A long-term lender will charge higher interest on loans if the probability of receiving periodic interest from the firm and ultimately regaining the principal is decreased.[3] Common stockholders will require the firm to increase earnings as compensation for increases in the uncertainty of receiving dividend payments or any appreciation in the value of their stock.

In analyzing the cost of capital, it is assumed that the operating risk of the firm remains unchanged (i.e., that the projects accepted do not affect the variability of the firm's sales revenues). This assumption tends to suggest that the firm's asset structure, which is its mix of assets, remains unchanged, thereby resulting in an unchanging level of operating risk. This assumption also eliminates the need to consider changes in the cost of specific sources of financing resulting from changes in operating risk. The definition of the cost of capital developed in this chapter is valid only for projects that do not change the firm's operating risk.

Financial risk.　*Financial risk* is affected by the mixture of long-term financing, or the capital structure, of the firm. Firms with high levels of long-term debt in proportion to their equity are more risky than firms maintaining lower ratios of long-term debt to equity. It is the contractual fixed-payment

---

[2]Although the acceptance of projects is independent of their financing, such a decision may or may not affect the operating and financial risk of the firm. In fact, the use of the weighted marginal cost of capital—a topic discussed in the final section of this chapter—recognizes that by increasing the amount of financing, the firm's weighted average cost of capital is likely to increase. At this point in the analysis it is best to assume the complete independence of operating and financial risk from the acceptance and financing of projects.

[3]There obviously would be a point at which, regardless of the amount of interest the borrower would be willing to pay, the lender would not make the loan. The firm would be *too risky*.

obligations associated with debt financing that make a firm financially risky. The greater the amount of interest and principal (or sinking-fund) payments a firm must make in a given period, the higher the operating profits required to cover these charges.[4] If a firm fails to generate sufficient revenues to cover financial charges, it may be forced into bankruptcy. As we indicated in the discussion of financial leverage in Chapter 4, the higher the firm's financial leverage, the greater the firm's financial risk.

As a firm's financial structure shifts toward a more highly levered position, the increased financial risk associated with the firm is recognized by suppliers of funds. They compensate for this increased risk by charging higher rates of interest or requiring greater returns. In short, they react in much the same way as they would to increasing operating risks.

Frequently the funds supplied to a firm by lenders will change its financial structure, and the charge for the funds will be based on the changed financial structure. In the analysis of the cost of capital in this chapter, however, the firm's financial structure is assumed to remain fixed. This assumption is necessary in order to isolate the costs of the various forms of financing. If the firm's capital structure were not held constant, it would be quite difficult to find its cost of capital, since the selection of a given source of financing would change the costs of alternate sources of financing. The assumption of a constant capital structure implies that when a firm raises funds to finance a given project these funds are raised in the same proportions as the firm's existing financing. The awkwardness of this assumption is obvious since in reality a firm raises funds in "lumps"; it does not raise a mixture of small amounts of various types of funds.[5] For example, in order to raise $1 million a firm may sell either bonds, preferred stock, or common stock in the amount of $1 million; or, it may sell $400,000 worth of bonds, $100,000 worth of preferred stock, and $500,000 worth of common stock. Most firms will use the former strategy, but our analysis of cost of capital is based on the assumption that the firm will follow the latter type of strategy. More sophisticated approaches for measuring the cost of capital when a firm's capital structure is changing are available.

Taxes

In the discussion of capital budgeting in the preceding chapters, all cash flows were evaluated on an after-tax basis. In order to be consistent with this capital budgeting framework, the cost of capital, which is used to discount cash flows in determining net present values and benefit-cost ratios and as the cut-off rate for internal rates of return, must also be measured on an after-

---

[4]The financial risk, or the likelihood that a firm will be able to meet its fixed charges, is often measured by a debt ratio such as the debt-equity ratio or a coverage ratio such as times interest earned. All these measures are rough indicators of the firm's ablity to service its debts.

[5]The discussion of capital structure in Chapter 18 will shed light on the fact that many firms determine their optimum capital structure and then attempt to maintain this structure over the *long run*. In other words, they raise money in lumps in the short run but do this in a fashion consistent with some long-run capital structure goal. A reading of Chapter 18 should clarify the relationship between the pattern of fund raising, the cost of capital, and capital structure.

tax basis. The only specific cost of capital that actually requires any type of tax adjustment is the cost of debt.

The key factor affecting financing costs

Since the cost of capital is measured under the assumption that both the firm's asset structure and its capital (financial) structure are fixed, the only factor that affects the various specific costs of financing is the supply-and-demand forces operating in the market for long-term funds. In other words, as a firm raises long-term funds at different points in time, the only factor affecting their cost is the risk-free cost of the particular type of financing. Regardless of the type of financing used, the following relationship should prevail:

$$k_l = r_l + op + fp \qquad (17.1)$$

where

k_l = the specific cost of the various types of long-term financing, l
r_l = the risk-free cost of the given type of financing, l
op = the operating risk premium
fp = the financial risk premium

Equation 17.1 indicates that the cost of each type of capital depends on the risk-free cost of that type of funds, the operating risk of the firm, and the financial risk of the firm.[6]

Since the firm's operating and financial risk are assumed to be constant, the changing cost of each type of capital, l, over time should be affected only by changes in *the supply of and demand for* each type of funds, l. The cost of each type of capital to a given firm compared to the cost to another firm (i.e., the *interfirm* comparison) can differ because of differences in the degree of operating and financial risk associated with each firm, since the risk-free cost of the given type of funds remains constant.[7] Different operating and financial risk premiums, op and fp, respectively, are associated with different levels of operating and financial risk. These premiums are a function of the operating risk, op, and financial risk, fp, of a firm. For *intrafirm* (i.e., time-series) comparisons, the only differentiating factor is the risk-free cost of the

[6]Although the relationship between r_l, op, and fp is presented as linear in Equation 17.1, this is only for simplicity; the actual relationship is likely to be much more complex mathematically. The only definite conclusion that can be drawn is that the cost of a specific type of financing for a firm is somehow functionally related to the risk-free cost of that type of financing adjusted for the firm's operating and financial risk (i.e., that $k_l = f(r_l, op, fp)$). In a latter part of this chapter, the cost of equity capital is discussed using the capital asset pricing model (CAPM), which relates the nondiversifiable risk, which in turn may contain components of both operating and financial risk, to the required returns for investors in the marketplace.

[7]The reader should recognize that the risk-free cost of each type of financing, r_l, may differ considerably. In other words, at a given point in time the risk-free cost of debt may be 6 percent while the risk-free cost of common stock may be 9 percent. The risk-free cost is expected to be different for each type of financing, l. The risk-free cost of different *maturities* of the same type of debt may differ, since longer-term issues are generally viewed as more risky than short-term issues.

given type of financing, since operating and financial risk are assumed to be constant. An example may help to clarify these points.

EXAMPLE

The W. T. L. Company's cost of long-term debt two years ago was 8 percent. This 8 percent was found to represent a 4-percent risk-free cost of long-term debt, a 2-percent operating risk premium, and a 2-percent financial risk premium. Currently, the risk-free cost of long-term debt is 6 percent. How much would you expect the W. T. L.'s cost of debt to be today, assuming that the risk structure of the firm's assets (operating risk) and its capital structure (financial risk) have remained unchanged? The previous operating risk premium of 2 percent and financial risk premium of 2 percent will still prevail, since neither of these risks has changed in two years. Adding the 4-percent total risk premiums (i.e., the 2-percent operating risk and the 2-percent financial risk premium) to the 6-percent risk-free cost of long-term debt results in a cost of long-term debt to the W. T. L. Company of 10 percent. In this time-series comparison, where operating risk and financial risk are assumed to be constant, the cost of the long-term funds changes only in response to changes in the risk-free cost of a given type of funds.

Let us now suppose that there is another company, the Plato Company, for which the risk-free cost of long-term debt is the same as it is for W. T. L. The Plato Company has a 2-percent operating risk premium and a 4-percent financial risk premium because of the high degree of leverage in its financial structure. Although both companies are in the same type of business (and thus have the same operating risk premium of 2 percent), the cost of long-term debt to the Plato Company is 12 percent (i.e., the 6-percent risk-free cost of money plus a 2-percent operating risk premium plus a 4-percent financial risk premium). This is greater than the 10-percent cost of long-term debt for the W. T. L. Company. The difference is attributable to the greater financial risk associated with the Plato Company. ●

In summary, if we hold operating and financial risk constant for a given firm, the cost of a given type of capital for the firm will change over time only in response to changes in the risk-free cost of that source of financing. The cost of a given type of capital for two firms at the same point in time will differ only as a result of differences in the firms' risk configurations. In making this statement, however, we are assuming that the various suppliers of funds in the marketplace perceive the risk associated with each firm in the same way. Different perceptions of risk by particular suppliers of funds could result in different financial costs.

THE COST OF SPECIFIC SOURCES OF CAPITAL

The ultimate objective of this chapter with respect to cost of capital is to analyze the specific sources of capital in order to show the basic inputs for determining the firm's overall cost of capital. This section describes the procedures for measuring the costs of specific sources of capital. Our concern is only with the long-term sources of funds available to a business firm, since these sources supply the permanent financing of the firm. Long-term financing supports the firm's fixed-asset investments, which, so it is assumed, have been selected using appropriate capital budgeting techniques. As we indicated in Chapter 7, it is generally advisable for a firm to finance a portion of its short-term financial needs with long-term funds, and at minimum to finance its fixed assets with long-term funds.

There are four basic sources of long-term funds for the business firm. The right side of a balance sheet can be used to illustrate these sources.

Balance sheet

Assets	Current liabilities	
	Long-term debt	
	Stockholders' equity Preferred stock Common stock Retained earnings	Sources of long-term funds

The basic sources of long-term funds, then, are long-term debt, preferred stock, common stock, and retained earnings. Although all firms will not necessarily use each of these methods of financing, each firm is expected to have funds from some of these sources in its financial structure. It is important to recognize that the specific cost of each source of financing is the *after-tax* cost of obtaining the financing *today* (i.e., new funds)—not the historically based cost reflected by the existing financing on the firm's books. Techniques for determining the specific costs of each of these sources of financing are presented on the following pages. Although the techniques presented in this and later parts of the chapter tend to develop precisely calculated values of specific as well as weighted average costs, it is important to recognize that the resulting values are at best *rough approximations* due to the numerous assumptions and forecasts that underlie them.

The cost of long-term debt (bonds)

The cost of long-term debt has two basic components. One is the annual interest; the other arises from the amortization of discounts or premiums paid or received when the debt is initially issued. In order to simplify the calculations in this section, *annual* interest payments on debt issues are assumed.[8]

Net proceeds.   Most corporate long-term debts are incurred through the sale of bonds. The net proceeds from the sale of a bond are the funds received from the sale after all underwriting and brokerage fees have been paid. Sometimes the net proceeds from the sale of a bond are greater than the bond's *face*, or *maturity, value*. This is generally true when the stated interest on the bond (the *coupon rate*) is greater than interest associated with other, similar-risk debt instruments. The bond is sold for a *premium* (more

---

[8]Interest on bonds is typically paid *semiannually*. The assumption of annual payments is made in order to simplify the required calculations, while still conveying the key concepts. A discussion of how to treat bonds paying semiannual interest was included in Chapter 13.

than its face value) in order to align the actual interest yield with the yields prevailing in the market. Bonds sold for less than their face value, or at a *discount*, have stated interest rates (coupon rates) below the prevailing rates for similar-risk debt instruments. Selling bonds at a discount puts the effective yield to the purchaser on a par with yields of similar-risk debt instruments. Underwriting and brokerage costs reduce the net proceeds from the sale of a bond at a premium, at a discount, or at its par (i.e., face) value.

EXAMPLE

The Zero Company is contemplating selling $10 million worth of 20-year 9-percent bonds, each with a face value of $1000. Since similar-risk debt instruments are yielding more than 9 percent, the firm must sell the bonds for $980 in order to compensate for the low coupon rate. The firm underwriting the bond issue receives a fee of 2 percent of the face value of the bond (i.e., 2% · $1000, or $20).[9] The net proceeds to the firm from the sale of each bond are therefore $960 ($980 − $20). ●

Calculating the cost of debt.   The before-tax cost of debt can be found by determining the internal rate of return on the bond cash flows. From the issuer's point of view this value can be referred to as the *cost to maturity* of the cash flows associated with the debt.[10] The cost to maturity is calculated using the techniques presented in Chapter 15. It represents the annual before-tax percentage cost of the debt to the firm.

EXAMPLE

In the preceding example the net proceeds of a $1000, 9-percent, 20-year bond were found to be $960. Although the cash flows from the bond issue do not have a conventional cash-flow pattern, the calculation of the annual cost is quite simple. Actually, the cash-flow pattern is exactly the opposite of a conventional pattern since it consists of an initial inflow (the net proceeds) followed by a series of annual outlays (the interest payments). In the final year, when the debt is retired, an outlay representing the repayment of the principal also occurs. The cash flows associated with the Zero Company's bond issue are as follows:

End of year(s)	Cash flow
0	$ 960
1–20	− $ 90
20	− $1000

[9]An investment banker "underwrites" a bond issue when he or she buys it at a discount from the issuer and sells it on behalf of the issuer. The discount compensates the underwriter for acting as a middleman. An in-depth discussion of the underwriting function is included in Chapter 19.

[10]The internal rate of return on a bond investment when viewed by a purchaser—not issuer—is referred to as *yield to maturity* since it would represent the investor's return from purchasing the bond at a given price and holding it until maturity. Since our concern is from the viewpoint of the issuer, emphasis is placed on cost to maturity.

The initial $960 inflow is followed by annual interest outflows of $90 (i.e., 9% of $1000) over the 20-year life of the bond. In year 20 an outflow of $1000, representing the repayment of the principal, occurs. The before-tax cost of the debt can be determined by finding the discount rate that equates the present value of the outflows with the initial inflow. Applying the trial and error techniques of Chapter 15 results in an approximate before-tax cost, or cost to maturity, of 9.47 percent.[11] ●

As we indicated earlier, the cost of debt must be stated on an after-tax basis, and since interest charges are tax deductible, a tax adjustment is required. The before-tax debt cost, k_b, can be converted to an after-tax debt cost, k_i, by the following equation:

$$k_i = k_b(1 - t) \tag{17.2}$$

The t represents the firm's marginal tax rate.

EXAMPLE

The before-tax debt cost for the Zero Company, which has a 40-percent marginal tax rate, is 9.47 percent. Applying Equation 17.2 results in an after-tax debt cost of 5.68 percent [i.e., 9.47% (1 − .40)]. Typically, the cost of debt is considerably less than the cost of any of the alternate forms of long-term financing. This is because the interest expense is tax deductible. ●

A shortcut for approximating the cost of debt. The cost of debt can be approximated using a shortcut approach that bypasses the need to find the internal rate of return (i.e., cost) for the cash flows associated with borrowing. This approach involves determining the average annual outflow, which consists of the annual interest plus the amortization of any premium or discount, and dividing this outflow by the average amount borrowed. If

I = the annual interest payment in dollars
N_b = the net proceeds from the sale of a bond
n = the term of the bond in years

---

[11]In Chapter 15 an explanation was given of how to approximate internal rates of return to the nearest 1 percent. To get the 9.47 percent cost to maturity, *interpolation*, which is a simple technique for estimating a value more accurately, must be used. In order to interpolate a more precise value for the internal rate of return, or cost to maturity, for the Zero Company's bond issue, the following steps are necessary:

(a) Find the present value of the outflows at the two consecutive rates that cause the initial inflow to be straddled. In this case the present value of the outflows at 9 percent is $999.61; at 10 percent it is $915.26. The initial inflow is $960, which is between these values.

(b) Find the difference between the present value of the two outflows, which in this case is $84.35 (i.e., $999.61 − $915.26).

(c) Find the difference between the present value of the outflow at the lower rate (i.e., $999.61 at 9%) and the desired value, or initial inflow ($960), which in this case is $39.61 ($999.61 − $960.00).

(d) Divide the result from (c) which is $39.61, by the result from (b), which is $84.35. This results in a value rounded to the nearest one-hundredth of 0.47.

(e) Add the fraction from (d) to the lower of the two rates developed in (a), 9 percent. This results in an approximate cost to maturity of 9.47 percent (0.47 + 9.00).

the approximate before-tax debt cost for a bond with a $1000 face value[12] can be found by the following equation:

$$\text{Approximate before-tax debt cost} = \frac{I + \dfrac{\$1000 - N_b}{n}}{\dfrac{N_b + \$1000}{2}} \tag{17.3}$$

The first term in the numerator of Equation 17.3 represents the annual interest, the second term in the numerator represents the annual amortization of any premium or discount, and the denominator represents the average amount borrowed.

EXAMPLE
Substituting the appropriate values from the Zero Company example into Equation 17.3 results in an approximate before-tax debt cost of 9.39 percent. Converting this value to an after-tax basis using Equation 17.2 results in an approximate after-tax debt cost of 5.63 percent. The accuracy of this approximation can be seen by comparing the approximate value of 5.63 percent to the actual after-tax debt cost of 5.68 percent calculated earlier. The reader may want to use this approximation in making rough calculations of the after-tax cost of debt. •

The cost of preferred stock
Preferred stock represents a special type of ownership interest in the firm. Preferred shareholders must receive their *stated* dividends prior to the distribution of any earnings to common shareholders. Since preferred stock is a form of ownership, and a business firm is viewed as a "going concern," the proceeds from the sale of preferred stock are expected to be held for an infinite period of time. A complete discussion of the various characteristics of preferred stock will be presented in Chapter 22. However, one aspect of preferred stock that requires clarification at this point is preferred stock dividends.

Preferred stock dividends. The amount of preferred stock dividends that must be paid each year before earnings can be distributed to common stockholders may be stated either in dollars or as a percentage of the stock's *par,* or *face, value.*

Dollar amounts. Most preferred stock dividends are stated as "*x* dollars per year." When dividends are stated this way, the stock is often referred to as "*x*-dollar preferred stock." A $4 preferred stock is expected to pay preferred shareholders $4 in dividends each year on each share of preferred stock owned.

---

[12]This formula can be used to find yields to maturity by considering all cash flows from the point of view of an investor. For bonds with face values in an amount other than $1000, the face value can be substituted into Equation 17.3 for $1000 in order to apply the formula.

Percentage amounts. Sometimes preferred stock dividends are stated as an annual percentage rate. This rate represents the percentage of the stock's par, or face, value that equals the annual dividend. For instance, a 4-percent preferred stock with a $100 par value would be expected to pay an annual dividend of $4 a share. Before calculating the cost of preferred stock, any dividends stated as percentages should be converted into annual dollar dividends.

Calculating the cost of preferred stock. The cost of preferred stock, k_p, is found by dividing the annual preferred stock dividend, d_p, by the net proceeds from the sale of the preferred stock, N_p. The net proceeds represent the amount of money to be received net of any underwriting or sales expenses required to market the stock. For example, if a preferred stock is sold for $100 per share but a $3 per share underwriting fee is incurred, the net proceeds from the sale are $97. Equation 17.4 gives the cost of preferred stock k_p, in terms of the annual dollar dividend, d_p, and the net proceeds from the sale of the stock, N_p:

$$k_p = \frac{d_p}{N_p} \tag{17.4}$$

Since preferred stock dividends are paid out of the firm's *after-tax* cash flows, a tax adjustment is not required.

EXAMPLE

The Zero Company is contemplating issuance of a 9-percent preferred stock that is expected to sell for $85 per share. The cost of issuing and marketing the stock is expected to be $3 per share. The firm would like to determine the cost of the stock. The first step in finding this cost is to calculate the dollar amount of preferred stock dividends, since the dividend is stated as a percentage of the stock's $85 face value. The annual dollar dividend is $7.65 (i.e., 9% of $85). The net proceeds from the proposed sale of stock can be found by subtracting the underwriting costs from the sale price. This gives us a value of $82 per share. Substituting the annual dividend, d_p, of $7.65 and the net proceeds, N_p, of $82 into Equation 17.4 gives us the cost of preferred stock, which is 9.33 percent (i.e., $7.65 ÷ $82). ●

Comparing the 9.33-percent cost of preferred stock to the 5.68-percent cost of debt shows that the preferred stock is more expensive. This is generally true since the cost of debt (interest) is tax-deductible. If the dividends on the preferred stock of the Zero Company had been stated in dollars, the calculations would have been greatly simplified since the dollar dividend could have been substituted directly into Equation 17.4.

The cost of common stock

The cost of common stock is not nearly as easy to calculate as either the cost of debt or the cost of preferred stock. The difficulty arises from the definition of the cost of common stock, which is based on the premise that the value of a share of stock in a firm is determined by the present value of all future dividends expected to be paid on the stock. The rate at which these expected dividends are discounted to determine their present value represents the cost of common stock. The theory underlying this definition is rooted in one of the more sophisticated share-price valuation models, which will be discussed in the following chapter.

The definition itself is based on a few key assumptions with respect to the behavior of individuals and their ability to forecast future values.

Share values.   The basic assumption on which the cost of common stock is calculated is that the value of a share of stock is equal to the present value of all future dividends expected to be paid on the stock over an infinite period of time. Not all earnings are paid out as dividends, but it is expected that those earnings which are retained and reinvested will boost future dividends. At infinity a *liquidating*, or final, dividend is expected, which actually represents the distribution of the firm's assets. Since the firm is viewed as a going concern with an infinite life, the liquidating dividend does not have to be specified.

Growth rates.   Another necessary assumption is that the rate of growth in dividends and earnings is *constant* over the infinite time horizon. This assumption implies a constant dividend payout (i.e., dividends per share that are a constant percentage of earnings per share) by the firm. The growth rate expected is assumed to be measurable, typically on the basis of the past growth in earnings demonstrated by the firm.

Risk classes.   A final assumption made in defining the cost of common stock concerns the riskiness of a business firm as viewed by both existing and prospective shareholders. Earlier in the chapter, a general expression for the relationship between risk and financing costs was presented that showed that the cost of a specific type of funds is virtually the same for firms viewed by investors as having equivalent levels of operating and financial risk. In the case of common stock, it is assumed that firms perceived by investors as being equally risky (i.e., having the same degree of operating and financial risk) will have their expected earnings discounted at the same rate. This same assumption underlies the capital asset pricing model (CAPM), which relates risk and required return on common stock, discussed in Chapter 16. Common stockholders, just like bondholders and preferred stockholders, expect larger returns for higher levels of risk. As the risk increases, so does the required return and vice versa. In the case of bonds, if the firm becomes more risky the returns to bondholders are increased by virtue of the fact that the bond sells at a discount in the marketplace. This is similar to what happens to preferred stocks. In the case of common stocks, increased risk must result in increased returns to the owners *or* the market price of their shares will fall. Of course, implicit in the assumption that firms of equivalent risk have their earnings discounted at the same rate, is the assumption that prospective and existing investors can accurately measure the riskiness of the firm and thereby agree on the rate at which to discount the firm's earnings.

Finding the cost of common stock equity. The cost of common stock equity can be generally stated as the rate at which investors discount the expected dividends of the firm in order to determine the market price of an ownership interest in the firm. As mentioned earlier, the rate of discount is a function of the riskless return on money adjusted for the operating and financial risk associated with the firm. Two techniques for measuring the cost of common stock equity capital are available. One is the use of the *Gordon model*, while the other relies on the *capital asset pricing model (CAPM)*. The use of each of these techniques to find the cost of common stock equity is described and illustrated in this section.

Gordon model. The Gordon model is a valuation equation that, based upon a variety of theoretical considerations, can be used to estimate the owners' required return, or cost, of common stock equity capital. The model is based upon the widely accepted premise that the value of a share of stock is the present value of all anticipated dividends it will provide over an infinite time horizon. The basic model is given in Equation 17.5.

$$P = \frac{D_1}{(1 + k_e)^1} + \frac{D_2}{(1 + k_e)^2} + \cdots + \frac{D_\infty}{(1 + k_e)^\infty} \tag{17.5}$$

where

P = the current price per share of common stock
$D_t \, (t = 1, \infty)$ = the per share dividend expected in year t
k_e = the cost of common stock equity capital (i.e., the required return or rate at which investors discount future dividends)

This valuation model is discussed in greater detail in Chapter 18. We mentioned earlier that one of the assumptions on which the analysis in this chapter is based is that investors expect dividends to grow at a constant rate, g. If we let D_0 represent the most recent dividend, Equation 17.5 can be rewritten as follows:

$$P = \frac{D_0(1 + g)^1}{(1 + k_e)^1} + \frac{D_0(1 + g)^2}{(1 + k_e)^2} + \cdots + \frac{D_0(1 + g)^\infty}{(1 + k_e)^\infty} \tag{17.6}$$

Simplifying Equation 17.6 and solving for k_e results in the following expression for the cost of common stock equity, k_e.[13]

$$k_e = \frac{D_1}{P} + g \tag{17.7}$$

---

[13]For the interested reader, the calculations necessary to derive Equation 17.7 from Equation 17.6 follow.

The first step is to multiply each side of Equation 17.6 by $(1 + k_e)/(1 + g)$ and subtract Equation 17.6 from the resulting expression. This yields

$$\frac{P(1 + k_e)}{1 + g} - P = D_0 - \frac{D_0(1 + g)^\infty}{(1 + k_e)^\infty} \tag{1}$$

Equation 17.7 indicates that the cost of common stock equity can be found by dividing the dividend expected at the end of period 1 by the current price of the stock and adding the expected growth rate. The first term, D_1/P, represents the expected *dividend yield* on the stock. Since common stock dividends are paid from after-tax income, no tax adjustment is required.

EXAMPLE

The Zero Company wishes to determine its cost of common stock equity capital, k_e. The prevailing market price, P, of its common stock is $50 per share. The firm expects to pay a dividend, D_1, of $4 at the end of the coming year. The dividends paid on the outstanding common stock over the past six years (i.e., 1973–1978) are given below.

Year	Dividend
1978	$3.80
1977	3.62
1976	3.47
1975	3.33
1974	3.12
1973	2.97

The firm has maintained a fixed dividend payout ratio from 1973 to 1978. Using the table for the compound-value interest factor, CVIF (i.e., Table A-1) in conjunction with the technique described for finding growth rates in Chapter 13, the annual growth rate of dividends, g, can be calculated.[14] It turns out to be approximately 5 percent. Substituting $D_1 = \$4.00$, $P = \$50$, and $g = 5$ percent into Equation 17.7 results in the cost of common stock equity, calculated below.

$$k_e = \frac{\$4}{\$50} + .05 = .08 + .05 = .13 = \underline{\underline{13.00\%}}$$

Since k_e is assumed to be greater than g, the second term on the right side of Equation 1 should be zero. Thus,

$$P\left(\frac{1 + k_e}{1 + g} - 1\right) = D_0 \tag{2}$$

Equation 2 is simplified as follows:

$$P\left(\frac{(1 + k_e) - (1 + g)}{1 + g}\right) = D_0 \tag{3}$$

$$P(k_e - g) = D_0(1 + g) \tag{4}$$

$$P = \frac{D_1}{k_e - g} \tag{5}$$

$$k_e = \frac{D_1}{P} + g \tag{6}$$

Equation 6 equals Equation 17.7 above.

[14]The technique involves two basic steps. First, dividing the most recent dividend ($3.80) by the earliest dividend ($2.97), a factor for the compound value of one dollar of 1.279 (i.e., $3.80 ÷ $2.97) results. Although six dividends are shown, they reflect only five years of growth. Looking across the table for the compound-value interest factors, CVIF (i.e., Table A-1), for five years, the factor closest to 1.279 occurs at 5 percent (i.e., 1.276). Therefore the growth rate of the dividends rounded to the nearest whole percentage is 5 percent.

The 13.00-percent cost of common stock equity capital represents the return required by existing shareholders on their investment in order to leave the market price of the firm's outstanding shares unchanged. ●

Using CAPM to measure the cost of common stock equity. Another approach for measuring the cost of common stock equity involves use of the capital asset pricing model, CAPM, which was developed and described in Chapter 16. The model describes the relationship between the required return or cost of common stock equity capital, k_e, and the nondiversifiable or relevant risks of the firm as reflected by its index of nondiversifiable risk, b. The basic CAPM is given in Equation 17.8.[15]

$$k_e = R_F + b \cdot (k_m - R_F) \qquad\qquad (17.8)$$

where

R_F = the required rate of return on a risk-free security, which is commonly measured by the yield on a U.S. government security such as a treasury bill.

k_m = the expected rate of return on the market portfolio of assets that can be viewed as an average rate of return on all securities

The use of CAPM to measure the cost of common stock equity capital relies on the securities market to reflect the returns required by a firm having a specified level of nondiversifiable or relevant risk. This risk is measured by the firm's security beta, b, which is an index of the degree of responsiveness or co-movement of the stocks' return with the return of the market, which is a portfolio of a large number of stocks.

EXAMPLE

The Zero Company, which calculated its cost of common stock equity capital, k_e, using the Gordon model in the preceding example, also wishes to calculate this cost using the capital asset pricing model, CAPM. From information provided the firm by its investment advisors along with the firm's own analyses, it is found that the risk-free rate, R_F, equals 7.00 percent; the firm's beta, b, equals 1.50; and the return on the market k_m, equals 11.00 percent. Substituting these values into the CAPM (i.e., Equation 17.8) they have estimated the cost of common stock equity capital, k_e, calculated below.

$$k_e = 7.00\% + 1.50(11.00\% - 7.00\%) = 7.00\% + 6.00\% = \underline{13.00\%}$$

The 13.00-percent cost of common stock equity capital represents the required return of investors in Zero Company common stock. This return, which is the same as that

[15]For a more complete development and discussion of CAPM, the reader should refer back to the discussion of risk and return in Chapter 16. Comparison of Equation 17.8 and Equation 16.4 in Chapter 16 reveals a few minor differences in notation. These were made merely to simplify the current discussion of cost of capital; they do not alter the model in any way.

found using the Gordon model in the preceding example,[16] represents the return that must be earned by investors in order to adequately compensate them for the nondiversifiable or relevant risk involved. The 13.0-percent cost of common stock equity capital can be viewed as consisting of a 7.00% risk-free rate plus a 6.00-percent risk premium, which reflects the fact that Zero Company's stock price is 1.50 times more responsive than the market portfolio to the factors affecting nondiversifiable or relevant risk. ●

Use of the CAPM to measure the cost of common stock equity capital is expected to become better accepted by practitioners over the next few years. The use of CAPM differs from the use of the Gordon model described in the preceding section in that it directly considers the firm's risk as reflected by beta in order to determine the *required* return or cost of common stock equity capital, while the Gordon model does not look at risk but rather uses the market price, *P*, as a reflection of the *expected* risk-return preference of investors in the marketplace. Although both of these techniques are theoretically sound, the use of the Gordon model is preferred by many due to the more readily available data required (i.e., D_1, P, and g). Obtaining the data required to apply the CAPM (i.e., R_F, b, and k_m—especially b) is currently a bit more time-consuming.

Another difference lies in the fact that when the Gordon model is used to find the cost of common stock equity capital, it can be readily adjusted for flotation costs to find the cost of *new* common stock; the CAPM does not provide a mechanism for such an adjustment. The inability to adjust the cost of common stock equity capital calculated using CAPM for flotation costs stems from the fact that the model does not include the market price, P, a variable that is needed in order to make such an adjustment. This process will become clearer in a subsequent section of the chapter.

Until the problems in application and definition associated with the use of CAPM to measure the costs of common stock equity capital and new common stock are dealt with, the apparent preference for use of the valuation-based Gordon model is expected to continue. The better availability of data accompanied with a better understanding and additional refinements of CAPM may result in more widespread use of the model for estimating these costs in the future. Throughout the remainder of this text, the traditional Gordon model approach will be used for measuring both the cost of common stock equity capital and the cost of new common stock. The use of the Gordon model to determine the cost of new common stock is described in the following section.

The cost of new issues of common stock. Since our purpose in finding the firm's overall cost of capital is to determine the after-tax cost of

---

[16]The agreement between the cost of common stock equity capital, k_e, of 13.00 percent calculated using CAPM and the 13.00-percent cost found earlier using the Gordon model has been intentionally so arranged in order to avoid any problems that may arise from differing values. In actual situations, the cost of common stock equity capital, calculated using these alternate approaches, will not necessarily agree due to certain underlying differences in the models.

new funds required for financing projects, attention must be given to the cost of *new* issues of common stock. Two methods for finding the current cost of existing common stock were described in the preceding parts; assuming that new funds are raised in the same proportions as the current capital structure, the only additional data required for finding the cost of new common stock issues are the underwriting and selling costs associated with them. It is quite likely that, in order to sell a new common stock issue, the sale price will have to be below the current market price (i.e., *underpriced*), thereby reducing the proceeds below the current market price, *P*. The stock must be underpriced by an amount that will result in a "fair price" in light of the dilution of ownership that will take place. Another factor that may reduce these proceeds is an underwriting fee paid for marketing the new issue.

The cost of new issues of common stock can easily be calculated by determining the percentage reduction in the current market price attributable to *flotation costs*, which consist of underpricing and underwriting fees, and using the Gordon model expression for the cost of existing common stock, k_e, as a starting point.[17] If we let f represent the *percentage* reduction in the current market price expected as a result of underpricing and underwriting charges on a new stock issue, the cost of the new issue, k_c, can be expressed as follows:[18]

$$k_c = \frac{D_1}{(1-f)P} + g \tag{17.9}$$

It is quite important that the cost of common stock equity be adjusted for any underpricing or underwriting costs in determining the cost of new issues of common stock. The cost of new issues will be greater than the cost of existing issues as long as f in Equation 17.9 is greater than zero.

EXAMPLE

In the example using the Gordon model, an expected dividend, D_1, of $4.00, a current market price, P, of $50, and an expected growth rate of dividends, g, of 5 percent, were used to calculate Zero Company's cost of common stock equity capital, k_e, which was found to be 13.00 percent. In order to determine its cost of new common stock, k_c, the Zero Company with the aid of its advisors have estimated that on average new shares can be sold for $49.00. The $1.00 per-share (i.e., $50.00 per-share market price – $49.00 per-share average sale price) underpricing is necessary due to the competitive nature of the market for securities. A second cost associated with a new issue is an underwriting fee of $0.75 per share that would have to be paid in order to cover the costs of selling the new issue of common stock. The total flotation costs

---

[17]As indicated in the preceding section, because the CAPM model does not include a price variable, which can be adjusted for flotation costs, the model cannot be readily adapted for finding the cost of new issues of common stock. Attention here is therefore devoted solely to the use of the Gordon model.

[18]It should be clear from an examination of Equation 17.9 that the denominator of the first term right of the equal sign "$(1 - f)P$" merely represents the *net proceeds* from the sale of a new issue of common stock. It is sometimes more convenient to substitute the amount of net proceeds into the denominator rather than calculate the flotation percentage, f.

per share are therefore expected to be $1.75 (i.e., $1.00 per-share underpricing plus $0.75 per-share underwriting).

Expressing the dollar flotation cost of $1.75 per share as a percentage of the current market price of $50.00 per share results in a flotation percentage, f, of 3.50 percent (i.e., $1.75 per share ÷ $50.00 per share). Substituting f = 3.50 percent, D_1, = $4, P = $50, and g = 5 percent into Equation 17.9 results in a cost of new common stock, k_c, shown below.

$$k_c = \frac{\$4.00}{(1 - .0350) \cdot (\$50.00)} + .0500 = \frac{\$4.00}{\$48.25} + .0500 = .0830 + .0500 = .1330$$
$$= \underline{\underline{13.30\%}}$$

Zero Company's relevant cost of new common stock, k_c, is therefore 13.30 percent. This is the value to be used in the subsequent calculation of the firm's overall cost of capital. The cost of new common stock is normally greater than any other long-term financing cost. Since the common stock dividends are paid from after-tax cash flows, no tax adjustment is required. ●

The cost of retained earnings

The cost of retained earnings is closely related to the cost of common stock. If earnings were not retained they would be paid out to the common stockholders as dividends. Retained earnings are often looked on as a *fully subscribed issue of new common stock*, since they increase the stockholders' equity in the same way that a new issue of common stock would. The cost of retained earnings must therefore be viewed as the opportunity cost of the forgone dividends to the existing common stockholders.

If the firm is unable to earn as much on its retained earnings as other firms with a comparable level of risk, it is assumed that shareholders will prefer to receive these earnings in the form of dividends, so that they can invest in the other firms. When the company retains earnings, it assumes that the shareholders cannot earn as much on the money elsewhere as the firm can through reinvestment. (The reader should keep in mind that it is assumed the firm takes actions that will maximize the owners' wealth.)

If retained earnings are viewed as a fully subscribed issue of new common stock, the firm's cost of retained earnings, k_r, can be assumed to be equal to the firm's cost of common stock equity as given by Equations 17.7 and 17.8. That is,

$$k_r = k_e \qquad\qquad (17.10)$$

It is not necessary to adjust the cost of retained earnings for either underwriting or underpricing costs. By retaining earnings, the firm bypasses these costs and still raises the equity capital.

EXAMPLE

The cost of retained earnings for the Zero Company was actually calculated in the preceding examples, since it is equal to the cost of common stock equity when underwriting or underpricing costs are ignored. Thus k_r equals 13.00 percent. The cost of retained earnings is always lower than the cost of a new issue of common stock, which in this case is 13.30 percent. This is because of the absence of underwriting and underpricing costs in financing projects with retained earnings. ●

Actually, the cost of retained earnings is less than Equation 17.10 indicates. We have chosen to view retained earnings as a fully subscribed issue of common stock. However, if a stockholder is paid dividends out of these earnings and wanted to invest them in additional shares of the firm's stock, he or she would have to first pay taxes on the dividends and then pay brokerage fees in order to acquire the added shares. If pt is the average shareholder's personal tax rate and bf represents the average brokerage fees stated as a percentage, the cost of retained earnings is actually

$$k_r = k_e \,(1 - pt)(1 - bf) \tag{17.11}$$

The value of k_r is thus less than the value of k_e.

EXAMPLE
If the average tax rate of stockholders in the Zero Company is 20 percent, the average brokerage fees are 3 percent, the cost of retained earnings for the Zero Company can be found by substituting the appropriate values into Equation 17.11, as follows:

$$k_r = (.1300)(1 - .20)(1 - .03) = (.1300)(.80)(.97) = .1009 = \underline{\underline{10.09\%}}$$

The resulting cost of retained earnings of 10.09 percent is greater than the 9.33-percent cost of preferred stock, but less than the 13.30-percent cost of new common stock. This type of cost relationship generally prevails. ●

For the purposes of this text, the simpler definition of the cost of retained earnings given by Equation 17.10 is preferable. Due to the difficulty of estimating the average tax rate of stockholders and the percentage of brokerage fees, Equation 17.11 is quite hard to apply. The cost of retained earnings is a very real cost to the firm, since paying these earnings out to the owners is an ever-present alternative.

MEASURING THE OVERALL OR
WEIGHTED AVERAGE COST OF CAPITAL
Now that methods for calculating the cost of specific sources of capital have been developed, techniques can be presented for determining the overall cost of capital to be used to evaluate prospective investments. The *weighted average cost of capital* is found by weighing the cost of each specific type of capital by the *historical, target,* or *marginal* proportions of each type of capital used. Historical weights are based on the firm's existing capital structure, target weights are based upon the proportions of the various types of capital the firm wishes to maintain, whereas marginal weights consider the actual proportions of each type of capital expected to be used in financing a given project.

Historical weights

The use of historical weights for calculating the firm's weighted average cost of capital is quite common. The use of these weights is based on the assumption that the firm's existing mix of funds (i.e., capital structure) is optimal and therefore should be maintained in the future. Two types of historical weights can be used—book value weights and market value weights.

Book value weights. The use of book value weights in calculating the firm's weighted average cost of capital assumes that new financing will be raised using exactly the same proportion of each type of financing as the firm currently has in its capital structure. The calculations involved can be illustrated by a simple example.

EXAMPLE

Earlier in the chapter the cost of the various types of capital for the Zero Company were found to be as follows:

Cost of debt = 5.68 percent
Cost of preferred stock = 9.33 percent
Cost of new common stock = 13.30 percent
Cost of retained earnings = 13.00 percent

Using these costs and the appropriate book value weights gives us the weighted average cost of capital for the Zero Company, calculated in Table 17.1. The resulting weighted average cost of capital based on book value weights is 10.190 percent. The book values in column 1 of Table 17.1 are taken from the lower right-hand side of the Zero Company's balance sheet. In view of the 10.190-percent cost of capital, the firm should accept all projects whose internal rate of return is greater than 10.190 percent, whose net present value discounted at 10.190 percent is greater than zero, or whose benefit-cost ratio calculated using a discount rate of 10.190 percent is greater than 1. ●

TABLE 17.1 Calculation of the weighted average cost of capital for the Zero Company using book value weights

Source of capital	Book value (1)	Percentage of total book value of capital (2)	Cost (3)	Weighted cost (2) · (3) (4)
Long-term debt	$15,000,000	30%	5.68%	1.704%
Preferred stock	10,000,000	20	9.33	1.866
Common stock	20,000,000	40	13.30	5.320
Retained earnings	5,000,000	10	13.00	1.300
Totals	$50,000,000	100%		10.190%

Weighted average cost of capital = 10.190%

Market value weights. The use of market value weights for calculating the firm's weighted average cost of capital is theoretically more appealing than the use of book value weights since the market values of the securities closely approximate the actual dollars to be received from their sale. Moreover, since the costs of the various types of capital are calculated using prevailing market prices, it seems only reasonable to use market value weights too. However, it is more difficult to calculate the market values of a firm's sources of equity financing (i.e., preferred stock, common stock, and retained earnings) than to use book values. It is particularly difficult to allocate a market value to the firm's retained earnings. The weighted average cost of capital based on market value weights is typically greater than the weighted average cost based on book value weights, since it is not unusual for preferred and common stocks to have market values that are above their book values.[19] Since these sources of long-term funds have higher specific costs than debt, the overall cost of capital normally increases when market value instead of book value weights are used.

EXAMPLE

Using the Zero Company data presented earlier, along with the market value of the firm's equity components, gives us the firm's weighted average cost of capital, which is developed in Table 17.2. The resulting weighted average cost of capital, 10.789 percent, is greater than the weighted average cost of capital calculated using book value weights. If the book value weighted average cost of capital were used, projects would be accepted that would be unacceptable based on the market value approach. For example, a project with a 10.50 percent internal rate of return would be accepted (i.e., 10.50% > 10.19%) using the weighted average cost of 10.19 percent found using book values, while the same project would be rejected (i.e., 10.50% < 10.79%) using the weighted average cost of 10.79 percent found using market value weights. The use of market value weights is suggested since market values are believed to be a better indicator of the firm's true capital structure.[20] ●

Target weights

Another approach for weighting the various components of a firm's capital structure in order to calculate the weighted average cost of capital is the use of target capital structure weights. If the firm has determined the capital structure they believe most consistent with their goal of owner wealth maximization, and they are directing their financing toward achievement of this "optimal" capital structure, then the use of these target capital structure

---

[19]In situations where a preferred or especially common stock is selling below its book value, it is presumed that the shareholders do not have much confidence in the firm's future success. In many cases this situation would be viewed as one in which the firm might be worth more dead than alive. A more detailed discussion of book values and the valuation of the firm is presented in Chapter 18.

[20]Some authors suggest that, because market values are not stable at all times, it is probably preferable to use book values since they will add stability to the firm's capital structure as reflected in the calculation of the weighted average cost of capital at various times.

TABLE 17.2 Calculation of the weighted average
cost of capital for the Zero Company using market value weights

Source of capital	Market value (1)	Percentage of total market value of capital (2)	Cost (3)	Weighted cost (2) · (3) (4)
Long-term debt	$15,000,000	21.4%	5.68%	1.216%
Preferred stock	15,000,000	21.4	9.33	2.000
Common stock	32,000,000	45.7	13.30	6.078
Retained earnings[a]	8,000,000	11.5	13.00	1.495
Totals	$70,000,000	100.0%		10.789%

Weighted average cost of capital = 10.789%

[a] The market value of common stock and retained earnings was found by allocating to each of these items a percentage of the total $40,000,000 market value of common stock equal to their percentage share of the total common stock equity based on the book value of $25,000,000.

Source of capital	Book value	Percentage of book value	Market value
Common stock	$20,000,000	$\frac{\$20,000,000}{\$25,000,000} = .80 = 80\%$	.80($40,000,000) = $32,000,000
Retained earnings	5,000,000	$\frac{\$5,000,000}{\$25,000,000} = .20 = 20\%$	.20($40,000,000) = $8,000,000
Total Book Value of Common Stockholders' Equity	$25,000,000	Total Market Value of Common Stock	$40,000,000

weights may be appropriate. Because of the fluctuations expected in the market values of the capital components, these target weights are typically based upon historic book values rather than market values. Although, in theory, the use of market value weights makes more sense, the practical difficulty associated with their use causes them to be operationally impractical; target weights based upon historic book values are therefore much more commonly utilized. Often, firms believing that the existing capital structure is optimal, will use existing book value proportions as target capital structure proportions. Unless a firm's existing capital structure significantly differs from the optimal capital structure, the weighted average cost of capital using historic book value weights is not expected to differ greatly from the weighted average cost of capital calculated using target capital structure proportions. When one considers the somewhat approximate nature of these calculations, the choice of weights may not be as "critical" as was believed initially.

EXAMPLE:

The Zero Company presented in the earlier examples believes that the optimal capital structure is one consisting of 40-percent debt, 10-percent preferred stock, 35-percent common stock, and 15-percent retained earnings. Comparing these target proportions to the actual book value proportions in column 2 of Table 17.1, it should be clear that the target proportions only differ slightly from the book value proportions. Using the target proportions and the specific costs calculated earlier, the weighted average cost of capital for the Zero Company is calculated in Table 17.3. Comparing the weighted average cost of 9.810 percent to the weighted average costs of 10.190 percent and 10.789 percent resulting from use of historic book value and market value proportions respectively, it can be seen that the use of target proportions results in a lower cost. Of course, such a relationship would be expected since the fact that the target proportions differ from the historic ones implies that a better capital structure exists. The achievement of such a structure would be expected to reduce the firm's weighted average cost of capital since it reflects a more nearly optimal mix of financing. ●

TABLE 17.3 Calculation of the weighted average cost of capital for the Zero Company using target weights

Source of capital	Target proportions (1)	Cost (2)	Weighted cost (1) · (2) (3)
Long-term debt	40%	5.68%	2.272%
Preferred stock	10	9.33	.933
Common stock	35	13.30	4.655
Retained earnings	15	13.00	1.950
Totals	100%		9.810%

Weighted average cost of capital = 9.810%

Marginal weights

An alternative to the use of historical weights based on the firm's current capital structure as measured by either book values or market values or target weights based upon the desired capital structure proportions is to use marginal weights. The use of marginal weights involves weighting the specific costs of various types of financing by the percentage of the total financing expected to be raised via each method. In using historical weights we have assumed that the proportion of each type of financing in the firm's capital structure would remain the same. In using target weights we have assumed that the firm is trying to develop what is believed to be an optimal capital structure reflected by certain desired proportions of capital. In using marginal weights, we are concerned with the *actual* amounts of each type of financing used. Only over the long run can a firm maintain certain historical or target proportions of the various types of capital. The use of marginal weights is more attuned to the actual process of financing projects. It recognizes that funds are actually raised in discrete amounts, using the various sources of long-term funds. The use of marginal weights also reflects the fact that the firm does not have a great deal of control over the amount of financing obtained through retained earnings. In any given year there will be only so many dollars available for retention.

One of the major criticisms of the use of marginal weights is that this approach does not consider the long-run implications of the firm's current financing. Since capital expenditures are long-term investments of the firm, attention should be given to the long-run ramifications of a certain financing strategy. Using cheaper sources of funds to finance a given project may place the firm in a position where more expensive equity financing will have to be raised to finance a future project. For example, a firm may be able to sell debt at an after-tax cost of 5 percent. If the best investment project currently available returns 6 percent and the weighted average cost of capital based on marginal weights is used as a decision criterion, the project will be accepted. If next year the firm must raise equity at a cost of 12 percent, it will end up rejecting a project returning 11 percent. The fact that today's financing affects tomorrow's costs is not considered in using marginal weights. If the weighted average cost of the firm's overall financing is used as a decision criterion, the future is not penalized; rather, a long-run view is taken. If the weighted average cost of capital to the firm is 9 percent, and this cost is used as a criterion for capital budgeting, the 6-percent project available this year will be rejected and the 11-percent project available next year will be accepted. Although firms actually raise funds in lumps, the use of historical or target weights to calculate the overall weighted average cost of a firm's existing or desired capital structure is more consistent with the firm's long-term goal of maximizing its owners' wealth. The reason many analysts prefer to use *historical book value weights* or *target capital structure weights,* or both, should now be clear. The following example illustrates how using marginal weights affects the cost of capital.

EXAMPLE

The Zero Company, whose specific capital costs have already been calculated, is contemplating raising $10 million for plant expansion. They estimate that $2 million in retained earnings will be available and intend to sell $6 million worth of long-term debt and $2 million worth of preferred stock to raise the remaining $8 million. Table 17.4 presents the firm's weighted average cost of capital when the marginal weights

TABLE 17.4 Calculation of the weighted average cost of capital for the Zero Company using marginal weights

Source of capital	Amount (1)	Percent of total (2)	Cost (3)	Weighted cost (2) · (3) (4)
Long-term debt	$ 6,000,000	60%	5.68%	3.408%
Preferred stock	2,000,000	20	9.33	1.866
Retained earnings	2,000,000	20	13.00	2.600
Totals	$10,000,000	100%		7.874%

Weighted average cost of capital = 7.874%

are used. The resulting value of 7.874 percent is less than the weighted average cost of capital calculated using either type of historical weights or target capital structure weights. This is because of the small amount of the more expensive preferred stock and retained earnings financing used. Since only a given amount of debt financing can be raised for a given equity base, it is quite likely the Zero Company will have to use primarily expensive equity financing for future projects. ●

In using marginal weights to calculate the cost of capital, a firm fails to consider the interrelationship between the various methods of financing. Thus it may, as we indicated earlier, accept a project with an internal rate of return of 6 percent one year and reject a project with an internal rate of return of 11 percent the next year. Obviously this situation is not desirable. The use of historical book or market value weights or target capital structure weights, or both, in calculating the cost of capital is much more likely to lead to an optimal selection of capital investment projects in the long run.

THE WEIGHTED MARGINAL COST OF CAPITAL (WMCC)

The weighted average cost of capital may vary at any time depending on the volume of financing the firm plans to raise. As the volume of financing increases, the costs of the various types of financing will increase, thereby raising the firm's weighted average cost of capital. A schedule or graph relating the firm's weighted average cost of capital to the level of new financing is called the *weighted marginal cost of capital* (WMCC).[21] These increasing costs are attributable to the fact that suppliers of capital—long-term debt, preferred stock, and common stock equity—will require greater returns in the form of interest, dividends, or growth in order to compensate them for the increased risk introduced as larger volumes of *new* financing are incurred. A second factor contributing to the increased cost relates to the use of common stock equity financing. The portion of new financing provided by common stock equity will be taken from available retained earnings until exhausted, and then obtained through new common stock financing. Since retained earnings are a less expensive form of common stock equity financing than the sale of new common stock, it should be clear that once retained earnings have been exhausted, the weighted average cost of capital will rise with the addition of more expensive new common stock. Because firms will first utilize all retained earnings financing available prior to selling new common stock, it is best to view the firm as having three types of capital: (1) long-term debt, (2) preferred stock, and (3) common stock equity, which includes both retained earnings and new common stock financing.

Calculation of the WMCC

In order to calculate its weighted marginal cost of capital, the firm must first determine the cost of each source of financing at various levels of total financing. To do this, the firm must take the following steps:

---

[21]Some authors refer to this function as the marginal cost of capital (MCC), but in order to avoid confusing this relationship with the marginal weights presented earlier, the relationship herein is called the weighted marginal cost of capital (WMCC).

STEP 1

The cost of each source of financing for various levels of use of that type of financing must be determined through an analysis of current market conditions.

STEP 2

Using the historic or target capital structure proportions of debt, preferred stock, and common stock equity, the levels of *total new financing* at which the cost of the new components change must be determined. The levels at which the component costs increase are called *breaking points*. They can be calculated using the relationship given in Equation 17.12:

$$BP_i = \frac{TF_i}{Pr_i} \qquad (17.12)$$

where

BP_i = breaking point for financing source i
TF_i = total new financing from source i at the breaking point
Pr_i = capital structure proportion—historic or target—for financing type i

EXAMPLE

A firm expects to have available $200,000 of retained earnings for investment in the coming year. The cost of these earnings has been calculated as 12 percent. Once the retained earnings have been exhausted, the firm's common stock equity financing will have to be obtained through the sale of new common stock; the firm's cost of new common stock is 13 percent. The firm's target capital structure contains 40-percent common stock equity, which consists of retained earnings and common stock. To find the breaking point, or level of total financing, at which their cost of common equity will rise, the firm applies Equation 17.12 as follows:

$$BP_{\substack{common \\ equity}} = \frac{\$200,000}{.40} = \$500,000$$

This result indicates that, at levels of *total* financing up to $500,000, the firm's cost of common stock equity would be 12 percent; while at a level of total financing greater than $500,000 the cost of equity would increase to 13 percent since the firm's retained earnings would be exhausted and the more expensive new common stock would have to be utilized. As a check to this conclusion, it should be clear that, in order to maintain 40-percent common equity at a total new financing level of $500,000, $200,000 (i.e., .40 × $500,000) of common equity is needed. Since only $200,000 of retained earnings will be available, more expensive new common stock financing will be required to obtain more than $500,000 in total financing in order to maintain the required target capital structure. Therefore, the $500,000 level of total new financing is a breaking point for common stock equity. ●

STEP 3

Once the breaking points have been determined, the weighted average cost of capital over the range of total financing between breaking points must be determined. First, the weighted average cost of capital for a level of total new financing between zero and the first breaking point is found. Next, the weighted average cost of capital for a level of total new financing between the first and second breaking points is found, and so on. It is important to recognize that, by definition, for each of the ranges of total new financing between breaking points, certain component capital costs will increase, thereby causing the weighted average cost of capital to increase to a higher level than over the preceding range.

STEP 4

Once the weighted average cost of capital for each range of total new financing has been determined, a schedule of these results is prepared. The schedule shows for each range of new financing the related weighted average cost of capital. As indicated earlier, this relationship is called the *weighted marginal cost of capital (WMCC)* since it shows the weighted average cost of capital for each level of total new financing. This function, which is commonly presented graphically, provides a mechanism whereby the firm can more readily choose from available investment opportunities those that would maximize the owners' wealth.

The use of these steps to find a firm's weighted marginal cost of capital can best be demonstrated by using a simple example:

EXAMPLE

The Zero Company, which has been presented in a number of earlier examples, wishes to determine its weighted marginal cost of capital. In making the required calculations, the firm wishes to use the target capital structure proportions given earlier in column 1 of Table 17.3. Grouping the common stock and retained earnings as

---

TABLE 17.5 Data for use in calculating the weighted marginal cost of capital (WMCC) for the Zero Company

Source of capital	Target proportion (1)	Range of new financing[a] (2)	Cost (3)
Long-term debt	40%	$0 to $400,000	5.68%
		$400,000 to $800,000	6.50%
		Greater than $800,000	7.10%
Preferred stock	10%	$0 to $100,000	9.33%
		Greater than $100,000	10.60%
Common stock equity	50%	$0 to $300,000	13.00%[b]
		$300,000 to $750,000	13.30%[c]
		Greater than $750,000	15.50%

[a]These ranges are for the corresponding sources of capital. They do *not* represent levels of total new financing.

[b]The firm expects that it will have $300,000 available from earnings after paying cash dividends. This amount of common equity will therefore have a cost of 13.00 percent, which is the cost of retained earnings calculated earlier.

[c]The 13.30-percent cost assigned to this range of new financing is the cost of new common stock calculated earlier in the chapter. This cost applies since once the $300,000 of expected retained earnings are exhausted, new common stock must be sold in order to obtain additional common stock equity.

common stock equity,[22] the target proportions for each of the three sources of capital are given in column 1 of Table 17.5. Using these data, the steps presented above can be followed in order to find Zero Company's weighted marginal cost of capital.

Step 1: After consulting a variety of sources, the Zero Company finds the cost of each of its three capital sources over various ranges of the respective types of new financing. Columns 2 and 3 of Table 17.5 present this information for each of the three sources of financing. The specific costs given in column 3 are calculated using the applicable techniques presented earlier in this chapter.

Step 2: Using the target capital structure proportions given in column 1 of Table 17.5 and the financing ranges given in column 2 of the table, the breaking points for each source of capital are calculated in column 3 of Table 17.6. The resulting ranges of total new financing are given in column 4 of the latter table.

TABLE 17.6 Determination of breaking points for Zero Company's capital sources

Source of capital	Cost (1)	Range of new financing (2)	Breaking point (3)	Range of total new financing (4)
	5.68%	$0 to $400,000	$\dfrac{\$400,000}{.40} = \$1,000,000$	$0 to $1,000,000
Long-term debt	6.50%	$400,000 to $800,000	$\dfrac{\$800,000}{.40} = \$2,000,000$	$1,000,000 to $2,000,000
	7.10%	Greater than $800,000	—	Greater than $2,000,000
Preferred stock	9.33%	$0 to $100,000	$\dfrac{\$100,000}{.10} = \$1,000,000$	$0 to $1,000,000
	10.60%	Greater than $100,000	—	Greater than $1,000,000
	13.00%	$0 to $300,000	$\dfrac{\$300,000}{.50} = \$600,000$	$0 to $600,000
Common stock equity	13.30%	$300,000 to $750,000	$\dfrac{\$750,000}{.50} = \$1,500,000$	$600,000 to $1,500,000
	15.50%	Greater than $750,000	—	Greater than $1,500,000

Key:
Column 1: these costs are strictly notational; they were initially given in column 3 of Table 17.5.
Column 2: ranges of new financing from column 2 of Table 17.5.
Column 3: breaking points calculated by dividing the upper limit of the financing ranges by the appropriate target capital structure proportion from column 1 of Table 17.5. The breaking point is calculated using Equation 17.12.
Column 4: using the breaking point calculated in column 3, the range of *total* new financing corresponding to each financing range given in column 2 is determined.

[22]As indicated earlier, because only a finite amount of retained earnings will be available in any period, and since retained earnings will be utilized prior to the sale of new common stock, it is best to view both common stock and retained earnings as common stock equity.

**TABLE 17.7 Weighted average cost of capital
for ranges of total new financing for the Zero Company**

Range of total new financing	Type of capital (1)	Target proportion (2)	Cost[a] (3)	Weighted cost (2) · (3) (4)
$0 to $600,000	Debt	.40	5.68%	2.272%
	Preferred	.10	9.33	.933
	Common	.50	13.00	6.500
	Weighted Average Cost of Capital			9.705%
$600,000 to $1,000,000	Debt	.40	5.68%	2.272%
	Preferred	.10	9.33	.933
	Common	.50	13.30	6.650
	Weighted Average Cost of Capital			9.855%
$1,000,000 to $1,500,000	Debt	.40	6.50%	2.600%
	Preferred	.10	10.60	1.060
	Common	.50	13.30	6.650
	Weighted Average Cost of Capital			10.310%
$1,500,000 to $2,000,000	Debt	.40	6.50%	2.600%
	Preferred	.10	10.60	1.060
	Common	.50	15.50	7.750
	Weighted Average Cost of Capital			11.410%
Greater than $2,000,000	Debt	.40	7.10%	2.840%
	Preferred	.10	10.60	1.060
	Common	.50	15.50	7.750
	Weighted Average Cost of Capital			11.650%

[a]The costs given for each range of total new financing were obtained from a comparison of Columns (1) and (4) of Table 17.6.

**TABLE 17.8 Weighted marginal
cost of capital for the Zero Company**

Range of total new financing	Weighted average cost of capital
$0 to $600,000	9.705%
$600,000 to $1,000,000	9.855
$1,000,000 to $1,500,000	10.310
$1,500,000 to $2,000,000	11.410
Greater than $2,000,000	11.650

Step 3: An examination of columns 3 and 4 of Table 17.6 indicates that the firm's weighted average cost of capital will change at levels of total new financing of $600,000, $1,000,000, $1,500,000, and $2,000,000. These are the breaking points listed in increasing order. In Table 17.7, the weighted average cost of capital over the ranges of total new financing between increasing breaking points is calculated. It is important to note that only the costs change as the total new financing increases from one breaking point to the next. The effect of these increases in component costs is to raise the firm's weighted average cost of capital as the range of total new financing increases.

Step 4: A schedule of the weighted average cost of capital associated with each range of total new financing is given in Table 17.8. This schedule represents the weighted marginal cost of capital (WMCC). The increasing nature of this relationship should be quite evident from the data presented. Figure 17.1 presents the WMCC graphically. Frame **a** shows a plot of the actual data; while frame **b** presents a smoothed function that more realistically depicts the firm's WMCC. Again, it is quite clear that the WMCC of capital is an increasing function of the amount of total new financing raised. ●

Use of WMCC for decision making

The WMCC should be used in conjunction with the firm's available investment opportunities in order to choose investments to be implemented. As long as a project's internal rate of return[23] is greater than the weighted marginal cost of new financing to be used to finance the project, the project should be accepted. As a firm increases the amount of money available for investment in capital projects, the return (IRR) on the projects will decrease

FIGURE 17.1 Weighted marginal cost of capital functions for the Zero Company

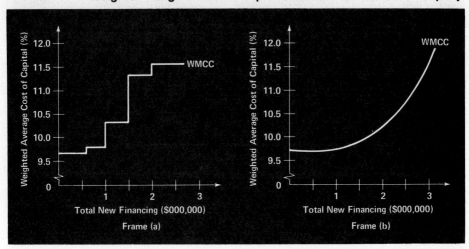

Frame (a)

Frame (b)

[23]Although other sophisticated measures of project acceptability could be used to make these decisions, the internal rate of return is used in this illustration due to the ease of comparison it offers.

since generally the first project accepted would have the highest return, the next project selected would have the second highest return, and so on. In other words, the return on investments will decrease as the firm accepts additional projects. At the same time, as more projects are accepted the weighted marginal cost of capital will increase since greater amounts of new financing will be required. The firm would therefore accept projects up to the point where the marginal return on its investment just equals its weighted marginal cost of capital, since beyond that point its investment return will be less than its capital cost.[24] An example should clarify this relationship.

EXAMPLE

The Zero Company's current investment opportunities schedule (IOS), which lists from the best (i.e., highest internal rate of return) to the worst (i.e., lowest internal rate of return) investment opportunities is given in column 1 of Table 17.9. In column 2 of the table, the initial investment required by the project is given, and in column 3 the cumulative total invested funds required to finance all projects better than (i.e., higher IRR) and including the corresponding investment opportunity is given. Plotting the project IRR's against the cumulative investment (i.e., column 1 against column 3 in Table 17.9 on a set of new financing/investment–cost/IRR axes), the firm's investment opportunity schedule (IOS) results. A graph of the IOS for Zero Company is given in Figure 17.2. The firm's WMCC is also shown in Figure 17.2. Using these two functions in combination, the firm's optimal capital budget ("X" in Figure 17.2)

TABLE 17.9 Investment opportunities schedule (IOS) for the Zero Company

Investment opportunity	Internal rate of return (IRR) (1)	Initial investment (2)	Cumulative investment[a] (3)
A	16%	$ 200,000	$ 200,000
B	15	400,000	600,000
C	14	1,000,000	1,600,000
D	13	100,000	1,700,000
E	12	300,000	2,000,000
F	11	500,000	2,500,000
G	10	200,000	2,700,000
H	9	400,000	3,100,000
I	8	100,000	3,200,000
J	7	300,000	3,500,000

[a]The cumulative investment represents the total amount invested in projects with higher IRR's plus the investment required for the given investment opportunity.

---

[24]In order not to confuse the discussion presented here, the fact that the use of the IRR for selecting projects may not provide optimum decisions is ignored. The problems associated with the IRR and its use in capital rationing were discussed in greater detail in Chapter 15.

is determined. By raising $2,000,000 of new financing and investing these funds in projects A, B, C, D, and E, the wealth of the firm's owners should be maximized since the 12-percent return on the last dollar invested (in project E) exceeds its 11.410-percent weighted average cost. Investment in project F is not feasible since its 11-percent return is less than the 11.650-percent cost of funds available for investment. The importance of the IOS and WMCC for investment decision making should now be quite clear. ●

SUMMARY

This chapter has presented the basic concepts and techniques needed for calculation of the cost of capital, which is the rate of return required by the market suppliers of capital in order to allow the firm's market price to remain unchanged. The basic factors underlying the cost of capital for a firm are the degree of risk associated with the firm, the taxes it must pay, and the supply of and demand for various types of financing. Two basic types of risk are associated with the business firm—operating risk and financial risk. Operating risk depends on the stability of a firm's sales revenues. It is closely related to the firm's operating leverage. Financial risk is affected by a firm's capital structure (i.e., its mix of long-term financing). The concept of financial leverage somehow reflects financial risk. In evaluating the cost of capital in this chapter, we have assumed (1) that firms are acquiring assets that do not

FIGURE 17.2 Using the IOS and WMCC to select projects

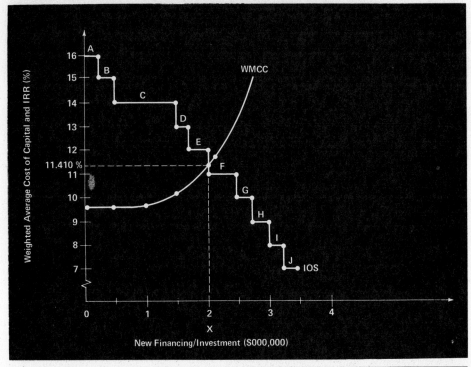

change their operating risk and (2) that these acquisitions are financed using the same proportion of each of the various types of financing as in the existing capital structure.

Since investment opportunities are evaluated on an after-tax basis, a firm must measure its cost of capital on an after-tax basis in order to be consistent. The cost of capital is used to discount project cash flows in finding net present values or calculating benefit-cost ratios and to determine the acceptability of project internal rates of return. Since operating risk and financial risk are assumed to be fixed, the only factor differentiating the cost of various types of financing is the supply of and demand for each type of funds.

The specific costs of the basic types of capital (i.e., long-term debt, preferred stock, common stock, and retained earnings) can be calculated individually. Only the cost of debt must be adjusted for taxes since the costs of the other forms of long-term financing are paid from after-tax cash flows. The calculation of the cost of common stock equity is rooted in the theory of the value of the firm. It can be calculated using either the Gordon model or the capital asset pricing model (CAPM). The cost of retained earnings is equal to the cost of common stock equity. The cost of new common stock incorporates an adjustment in the cost of common stock equity in order to reflect underwriting or underpricing costs, or both. Retained earnings can, in fact, be viewed as a fully subscribed new issue of common stock. Adjustments in the cost of retained earnings are sometimes made for stockholders' personal taxes and brokerage fees.

A firm's weighted average cost of capital can be determined by combining the costs of specific types of capital after weighting each cost using historical book or market value weights, target weights based on a desired capital structure, or marginal weights based on the actual percentage of each type of financing to be used for a project. The use of marginal weights is not recommended since it does not reflect the firm's true financing costs over the long run. Although theoretically preferable, market value weights are difficult to use due to the fluctuating nature of market prices. The most popular weighting alternatives are the use of either book value weights or target weights based upon a desired capital structure that is believed to be optimal.

A firm's weighted marginal cost of capital (WMCC) function can be developed by finding the weighted average cost of capital for various levels of new financing. The function relates the weighted average cost of capital to each level of total new financing. The weighted marginal cost of capital is determined by first finding the cost of each source of financing for various levels of use. Next, the breaking points in total financing must be calculated and the weighted average cost of capital associated with each range of total financing determined. Because the firm will first exhaust its available retained earnings before selling new common stock, one breaking point is attributable to the shift from lower-cost retained earnings to the more expensive new common stock financing. The weighted marginal cost of capital is quite useful since it recognizes that as the firm raises more new capital, the cost of the various sources of capital will increase, thereby raising the weighted average cost of capital. The firm can use this function to select the group of acceptable investment opportunities while recognizing that the weighted average cost of capital is not independent of the level of financing. Using its investment opportunities schedule (IOS), the firm should accept all projects for which the internal rate of return on its investment exceeds the weighted marginal cost of capital. Such action will not only determine the optimal capital budget but it will add to the wealth of the firm's owners—the overriding goal of all financial decisions.

QUESTIONS

17-1 How is the cost of capital used in the capital budgeting process? Specifically, how is it connected with the net present-value, benefit-cost ratio, and internal rate-of-return techniques for determining a project's acceptability?

17-2 What is meant by the cost of capital for a firm? What effect will accepting projects earning less than the cost of capital have on the firm's value?

17-3 Why, in using the cost of capital for evaluating investment alternatives, was it assumed that the acceptance of proposed projects would not affect the operating risk of the firm?

17-4 What is financial risk? Why is it necessary to assume that the firm's financial structure remains unchanged when evaluating the firm's cost of capital? Why is this assumption awkward?

17-5 Why is the cost of capital most appropriately measured on an after-tax basis? What effect, if any, does this have on specific cost components?

17-6 What factors are likely to cause differences in the cost of a given type of financing for different firms?

17-7 What are the four key sources of long-term funds for the business firm? Why is the cost of capital dependent only on the cost of long-term funds?

17-8 What is meant by the net proceeds from the sale of a bond? In what circumstances is a bond expected to sell at a discount or premium?

17-9 How is the cost of debt generally related to the cost of other types of capital? Why is this relationship generally true?

17-10 What sort of general approximation is used to find the before-tax cost of debt? What do the numerator and denominator of this expression represent?

17-11 How would one calculate the cost of preferred stock? Why do we concern ourselves with the net proceeds from the sale of the stock instead of the sale price?

17-12 What assumptions underlie the Gordon model for the cost of common stock equity, k_e? What does each component of the equation represent?

17-13 What does the assumption made about growth rates in this chapter imply about the firm's dividend policy? What assumption about risk is made by the share-price valuation model?

17-14 What is meant by *underwriting* and *underpricing*? How does the cost of each affect the firm's cost of equity capital? How is the firm's cost of equity capital adjusted for these two factors?

17-15 How is the cost of retained earnings defined? What theoretical underpinnings suggest the validity of this definition?

17-16 Why, if retained earnings are viewed as a fully subscribed issue of new common stock, is the cost of financing a project with retained earnings technically less than the cost of using a new issue of common stock?

17-17   What basic assumption is made in using historical weights in evaluating the cost of capital? How does the weighted average approach for finding a firm's overall cost of capital work?

17-18   Discuss and differentiate between the two basic historical capital structure weights—book value and market value.

17-19   Describe the logic underlying the use of target capital structure weights and compare and constrast this approach to the use of historic weights.

17-20   What are the pros and cons of using marginal as opposed to historical or target weights for calculating the weighted average cost of capital? Why is the use of historical or target weights more consistent with the firm's goal of owner's wealth maximization?

17-21   Outline the basic steps involved in calculating the weighted marginal cost of capital (WMCC). Be sure to discuss the significance and computations involved in determining the *breaking points*.

17-22   What does the weighted marginal cost of capital function represent? Why does this function increase, and how can it be used in conjunction with the investment opportunities schedule (IOS) to select acceptable investments?

PROBLEMS

17-1   The Three N Company's cost of long-term debt last year was 10 percent. This rate was attributable to a 7-percent risk-free cost of money, a 2-percent operating risk premium, and a 1-percent financial risk premium. The firm currently desires a long-term loan.

   a   If the firm's operating and financial risk are unchanged from the previous period, and the risk-free cost of money is now 8 percent, at what rate would you expect the firm to obtain a long-term loan?

   b   If, as a result of borrowing, the firm's financial risk will increase enough to raise the financial risk premium to 3 percent, how much would you expect the firm's borrowing cost to be?

   c   One of the firm's competitors has a 1-percent operating risk premium and a 2-percent financial risk premium. What is that firm's cost of long-term debt likely to be?

17-2   For each of the following $1000 bonds, assuming annual interest payment and a 40-percent tax rate, calculate the *after-tax* cost to maturity using

   a   The long approach, and

   b   The shortcut method.

   c   Compare the costs calculated for each bond in **a** and **b**.

Bond	Life	Underwriting fee	Discount (−) or premium (+)	Coupon rate
A	20 years	$25	$−20	8%
B	16 years	$40	$+10	10%
C	15 years	$30	$−15	7%
D	25 years	$15	par	6%
E	22 years	$20	$−60	5%

17-3   The Flat Free Tire Company has just issued preferred stock. The stock has an 8-percent annual dividend, a $100 par value, and was sold at $97.50 per share.

    a Calculate the after-tax cost of the preferred stock.

    b If the firm had sold the preferred stock with a 6-percent annual dividend and a $90 net price, what would its after-tax cost have been?

17-4 Determine the after-tax cost for each of the following preferred stocks.

Preferred stock	Par value	Underwriting cost	Annual dividend
A	$100	$5.00	7%
B	$ 80	$3.50	8%
C	$ 75	$4.00	$5.00
D	$ 60	5%	$3.00
E	$ 40	$2.50	9%

17-5 Tasty Meat Packing wishes to measure its cost of new common equity capital. The firm's stock is currently selling for $57.50. The firm expects to pay a $2 dividend at the end of the year. The dividends for the past five years are summarized:

Year	Dividend
1978	$1.96
1977	1.88
1976	1.82
1975	1.76
1974	1.73

After flotation costs, the firm expects to net $52 per share on a new issue.

    a Determine the growth rate of dividends.

    b Determine the percentage of market price the firm actually receives.

    c Using the Gordon model, determine the after-tax cost of retained earnings.

    d Using the Gordon model, determine the after-tax cost of new common stock equity.

17-6 For the following firms, calculate the cost of retained earnings and the cost of new common stock equity using the Gordon model.

Firm	Current market price per share	Dividend growth rate	Projected dividend per share next year	Cost of underwriting per share	Underpricing per share
A	$100	8%	$2.25	$1.00	$2.00
B	$ 40	4%	$1.00	$1.50	$ .50
C	$ 85	6%	$2.00	$2.00	$1.00
D	$ 38	2%	$2.10	$1.70	$1.30

17-7 Tucker and Tucker (T & T) common stock has a measure of responsiveness to the overall market of 1.2 (i.e., $b = 1.2$). If the risk-free rate is 6 percent, and the average return in the market is 11 percent:

    a Determine the premium for risk on T&T common stock.

    b What rate of return should T&T common provide?

    c Determine T & T's after-tax cost of common equity using the CAPM.

17-8 Ohio Tire has on its books the following amounts and specific after-tax current costs for each type capital:

Type of capital	Book value	Specific cost
Long-term debt	$700,000	4.25%
Preferred stock	50,000	5.85%
Common stock equity	650,000	9.75%

    a Calculate the firm's weighted average cost of capital.

    b Explain how the firm can use this cost in the capital budgeting decision-making process.

17-9 The Cool Airconditioning Company has compiled the following information:

Type of capital	Book value	Market value	After-tax cost
Long-term debt	$4,000,000	$3,840,000	4.50%
Preferred stock	40,000	60,000	8.25%
Common stock equity	1,060,000	3,000,000	12.50%
	$5,100,000	$6,900,000	

    a Calculate the weighted average cost of capital using book value weights.

    b Calculate the weighted average cost of capital using market value weights.

    c Compare the answers obtained in **a** and **b**. Explain the differences.

17-10 Keystone Pump has charged Martin Drywater, its financial manager, with measuring the cost of each specific type of capital as well as the weighted average cost of capital. The weighted average cost is to be measured using the firm's target capital structure weights. The firm wishes to finance projects using 40-percent long-term debt, 10-percent preferred stock, and 50-percent common stock equity (retained earnings or common stock, or both). The firm's average tax rate is 40 percent on ordinary income.

Debt: The firm can sell a 10-year $1000-face-value bond having a 6-percent annual coupon for $980. A fee of 3 percent of the face value would be required in addition to the discount of $20 per bond.

Preferred Stock: Eight-percent preferred stock having a par value of $100 can be sold for $98. An additional fee of $2 per share must be paid to the underwriters.

Common Stock: The firm's common stock is currently selling for $90 per share. The dividend expected to be paid at the end of the coming year is $4. Its dividend payments, which have been approximately 60 percent of earnings per share in each of the past five years, are given:

Year	Dividend
1978	$3.75
1977	3.50
1976	3.30
1975	3.15
1974	2.85

It is expected that, to sell, new common stock must be underpriced $5 per share, and the firm will also pay a $3-per-share underwriting fee. Dividend payments are expected to continue at 60 percent of earnings.

a Calculate the specific cost of each source of financing.

b If earnings available to common shareholders are expected to be $7,000,000, what is the breaking point associated with the exhaustion of retained earnings?

c Determine the weighted average cost of capital between zero and the breaking point given in **b**.

d Determine the weighted average cost of capital just beyond the breaking point calculated in **b** above.

17-11 The H. Grimmer Company has compiled the following data relative to the current costs of its three basic sources of external capital—long-term debt, preferred stock, and common stock equity—for various ranges of financing.

Source of capital	Range of financing	After-tax cost
Long-term debt	$0 to $200,000	6%
	$200,000 to $300,000	7%
	$300,000 and above	9%
Preferred stock	$0 to $100,000	8%
	$100,000 and above	10%
Common stock equity	$0 to $220,000	12%
	$220,000 to $320,000	13%
	$320,000 and above	14%

The firm's current earnings, of which 40 percent will be retained, amount to $200,000. The cost of these retained earnings to the firm has been estimated to be 11 percent. The company's target capital structure proportions that are used in calculating its weighted average cost of capital are shown on the following table:

Type of capital	Target capital structure
Long-term debt	40%
Preferred stock	20%
Common stock equity	40%

a Determine the breaking points and ranges of *total* new financing associated with each source of capital. Hint: Be sure to recognize that any available retained earnings would be exhausted prior to using new common stock equity.

b Using the data developed in **a**, determine the levels of *total* new financing at which the firm's weighted average cost of capital will change.

c Calculate the weighted average cost of capital for each range of total new financing found in **b**.

d Using the results of **c** along with the following information on the available investment opportunities given below, draw the firm's weighted marginal cost of capital (WMCC) function and investment opportunities schedule (IOS) on the same set of new financing/investment (*x*-axis)–cost/IRR (*y*-axis) axes.

Investment	Amount of capital required	Internal rate of return
A	$200,000	14%
B	300,000	10
C	100,000	17
D	600,000	9
E	200,000	18
F	100,000	8
G	300,000	16
H	100,000	12
I	400,000	11

e. Which, if any, of the available investments would you recommend the firm accept? Explain your answer.

SELECTED REFERENCES

Ang, James S., "Weighted Average versus True Cost of Capital," *Financial Management 2* (Autumn 1973), pp. 56–60.

Arditti, Fred D., "Risk and the Required Return on Equity," *Journal of Finance 22* (March 1967), pp. 19–36.

———, "The Weighted Average Cost of Capital: Some Questions on Its Definition, Interpretation and Use," *Journal of Finance 28* (September 1973), pp. 1001–1008.

Arditti, Fred D., and Haim Levy, "The Weighted Average Cost of Capital as a Cutoff Rate: A Critical Analysis of the Classical Textbook Weighted Average," *Financial Management 6* (Fall 1977), pp. 24–34.

Arditti, Fred D., and Milford S. Tysseland, "Three Ways to Present the Marginal Cost of Capital," *Financial Management 2* (Summer 1973), pp. 63–67.

Beranek, William, "The Cost of Capital, Capital Budgeting, and the Maximization of Shareholder Wealth," *Journal of Financial and Quantitative Analysis 10* (March 1975), pp. 1–21.

———, "The Weighted Average Cost of Capital and Shareholder Wealth Maximization," *Journal of Financial and Quantitative Analysis 12* (March 1977), pp. 17–32.

Brennan, Michael J., "A New Look at the Weighted Average Cost of Capital," *Journal of Business Finance 5* (No. 1, 1973), pp. 24–30.

Brigham, Eugene F., and Myron J. Gordon, "Leverage, Dividend Policy, and the Cost of Capital," *Journal of Finance 23* (March 1968), pp. 85–103.

Brigham, Eugene F., Myron J. Gordon, and Keith V. Smith, "The Cost of Capital and the Small Firm," *Engineering Economist 13* (Fall 1967), pp. 1–26.

Elton, Edwin J., and Martin J. Gruber, "The Cost of Retained Earnings—Implications of Share Repurchase," *Industrial Management Review 9* (Spring 1968), pp. 87–104.

Ezzell, John R., and R. Burr Porter, "Floatation Costs and the Weighted Average Cost of Capital," *Journal of Financial and Quantitative Analysis 11* (September 1976), pp. 403–414.

Gordon, Myron J., and Paul J. Halpern, "Cost of Capital for a Division of a Firm," *Journal of Finance 29* (September 1974), pp. 1153–1163.

Grinyer, John R., "The Cost of Equity, the C.A.P.M. and Management Objectives Under Uncertainty," *Journal of Business Finance and Accounting 3* (Winter 1976), pp. 101–121.

Haley, Charles W., "Taxes, the Cost of Capital, and the Firm's Investment Decisions," *Journal of Finance 20* (September 1971), pp. 901–917.

Henderson, Glenn V., "Shareholder Taxation and the Required Rate of Return on Internally Generated Funds," *Financial Management 5* (Summer 1976), pp. 25–31.

Keane, Simon M., "Some Aspects of the Cost of Debt," *Accounting and Business Research* (Autumn 1975), pp. 298–304.

Lawrenz, David W., "The Effects of Corporate Taxation on the Cost of Equity Capital," *Financial Management 5* (Spring 1976), pp. 53–57.

Lewellen, Wilbur G., *The Cost of Capital* (Dubuque, Iowa: Kendall/Hunt, 1976).

———, "A Conceptual Reappraisal of Cost of Capital," *Financial Management 3* (Winter 1974), pp. 63–70.

Lintner, John, "The Cost of Capital and Optimal Financing of Corporate Growth," *Journal of Finance 18* (May 1963), pp. 292–310.

Melnyk, Z. Lew, "Cost of Capital as a Function of Financial Leverage," *Decision Sciences* (July-October 1970), pp. 327–356.

Modigliani, Franco, and Merton Miller, "The Cost of Capital, Corporation Finance and the Theory of Investment," *American Economic Review 48* (June 1958), pp. 261–296.

Nantell, Timothy J., and C. Robert Carlson, "The Cost of Capital as a Weighted Average," *Journal of Finance 30* (December 1975), pp. 1343–1355.

Petry, Glenn H., "Empirical Evidence on Cost of Capital Weights," *Financial Management 4* (Winter 1975), pp. 58–65.

Porterfield, James T. S., *Investment Decisions and Capital Costs* (Englewood Cliffs, N.J.: Prentice-Hall, 1965).

Reilly, Raymond R., and William E. Wecker, "On the Weighted Average Cost of Capital," *Journal of Financial and Quantitative Analysis 8* (January 1973), pp. 123–126.

Robichek, Alexander A., and Stewart C. Myers, *Optimal Financing Decisions* (Englewood Cliffs, N.J.: Prentice-Hall, 1965).

Solomon, Ezra, "Measuring a Company's Cost of Capital," *Journal of Business 28* (October 1955), pp. 240–252.

Taggart, Robert A., Jr., "Capital Budgeting and the Financing Decision: An Exposition," *Financial Management 32* (Summer 1977), pp. 59–64.

Vickers, Douglas, "The Cost of Capital and the Structure of the Firm," *Journal of Finance 25* (March 1970), pp. 35–46.

CHAPTER 18
Capital structure and valuation

Capital structure and valuation are topics closely related to the firm's long-term financial position. Capital structure was referred to on numerous occasions in the preceding chapter. Basically, it is determined by the mixture of long-term debt and equity used by the firm to finance its operations. We shall examine in this chapter the basic capital structure concepts and theory, the relationship between a firm's capital structure and its cost of capital, and a simple approach for analyzing alternative financing plans.

Valuation was also referred to in the preceding chapter, in the discussion of the cost of common stock. Valuation is concerned with the determination of the "worth" or "value" of a business enterprise. Numerous techniques for valuing a firm are available. Some are based on superficial data, while others have deep theoretical underpinnings. The value of a firm is important not only to its existing and prospective shareholders, but also to its management and creditors. Valuation techniques are also quite useful when a firm is considering acquiring or merging with another firm. The application of valuation techniques will become clearer in the discussion of consolidations, mergers, and holding companies presented in Chapter 25.

This chapter is divided into three basic sections. The first section defines the types of capital and various measures of capital structure, and discusses capital structure theory. The second section presents a graphical method of evaluating various financing plans in light of the returns received by the firm's owners. The final section of the chapter is devoted to various methods for valuing the stock of a business firm. Common valuation techniques are presented, beginning with the most naive and ending with one of the more sophisticated valuation approaches.

THE FIRM'S CAPITAL STRUCTURE
Types of capital

The two basic types of capital are *debt capital* and *equity capital*. Although both represent sources of funds to the business firm, they have certain characteristic differences. The term *capital* denotes the long-term funds of the firm. In the preceding chapter, the cost of capital from various sources was evaluated. All the items on the right side of the firm's balance sheet, excluding the firm's current liabilities, are sources of capital.

The simplified balance sheet below indicates the basic breakdown of the firm's long-term financing into its debt and equity components.

Balance sheet

Assets	Current liabilities	} Debt capital	} Capital
	Long-term debt		
	Stockholders' equity	} Equity capital	
	Preferred stock		
	Common stock		
	Retained earnings		

Debt capital. Debt capital includes any type of long-term funds obtained by borrowing. There are various types of long-term debt. It can be unsecured or secured, senior or subordinated, raised by the sale of bonds or through a negotiated long-term loan. Many large manufacturing firms have more than one type of debt on their books. Probably the most common type of long-term debt instrument is the corporate bond, which is typically sold in $1000 denominations and made available to numerous long-term lenders.

In the preceding chapter, the cost of debt capital was found to be considerably less than the cost of any other forms of long-term financing. The "cheapness" of debt capital is attributable to the fact that as creditors, holders of such debt have the least risk of any long-term contributors of capital: they, first, have a higher priority of claim against any earnings or assets available for payment; second, they have a legal pressure against the company to make payment far stronger than that of preferred or common stock; and, third, the treatment of interest payments as tax-deductible expenses lowers the cost substantially. The stated interest associated with each type of long-term debt will vary depending on the timing and specific characteristics of the issue and issuer. A firm can only use a given amount of debt financing because of the fixed payments associated with it. The characteristics of the various types of long-term debt are discussed in greater detail in Chapter 21.

Equity capital. Equity capital consists of the long-term funds provided by the firm's owners. Unlike borrowed funds that must be repaid at a specified date, equity capital is expected to remain in the firm for an infinite period of time. The three basic sources of equity capital to the firm are preferred stock, common stock, and retained earnings. It is important to note that most corporate financial managers think of preferred stock not as equity but as a substitute for debt that does not have a fixed maturity date. As far as common stockholders are concerned, preferred stock is a senior claim that hangs over their right to receive income from earnings through cash dividends. As we saw in Chapter 17, the cost of each of these sources of equity capital differs. Common stock is typically the most expensive, followed by retained earnings and preferred stock, respectively.

Our concern in this chapter is not with the specific types of equity capital but rather with the gross relationship between debt and equity capital. A detailed discussion of the characteristics of the various types of equity is presented in Chapters 22 through 24. All equity capital takes a secondary position to debt capital with respect to the distribution of earnings and the liquidation of assets in the event of bankruptcy. This generally makes the returns on equity capital more uncertain than returns on debt capital, and thus more risky. However, the higher risk must be compensated for with higher expected returns.

Differences between debt and equity capital. There are three basic differences between debt and equity capital. These differences concern the length of time the funds are available to the firm, the claims on income and assets of lenders and shareholders, and the voice of each in management.

Maturity. Long-term debts have a stated maturity date on which the principal amount borrowed must be repaid. Equity has no maturity; its life is assumed to be infinite. An equity holder can sell his or her ownership to an interested buyer if one can be found, but he or she has no guarantee that the original investment can be recouped.

Claims on income and assets. The debt holder has a prior claim on both the income and the assets of the firm. However, a prior claim on assets is meaningful only if the assets are liquidated. The periodic payments to debt holders are fixed and must be paid prior to the distribution of income to equity holders. Certain types of equity do have stated returns, but the receipt of these returns in a given period is not guaranteed.[1] Payments to equity holders are not mandatory.

Voice in management. The long-term lender typically has no voice in the management of the firm or in the election of the board of directors. Normally, the true owners of the firm (i.e., the common stockholders) have the only voice in management through their voting power. In certain instances, preferred stockholders may be given some voting power. Debt holders may receive a voice in management or representation on the firm's board if the firm has defaulted on the terms of the debt issue.

Financial leverage. Financial leverage was discussed in Chapter 4, where it was defined as the use of fixed-cost financing to magnify the effects of changes in the firm's earnings before interest and taxes (EBIT) on the

---

[1]As we briefly mentioned in Chapter 4, the holders of preferred stock expect to receive a fixed dividend payment. Since this payment to preferred shareholders must be made prior to distributing any earnings to common stockholders, the preferred stock dividend is generally expected to be paid. This strategy is consistent with the firm's overall objective of owners' wealth maximization. Paying preferred shareholders somewhat enhances both the actual and the expected returns to the common stockholders.

firm's earnings per share (eps). In general, financial leverage can be viewed as determined by the relationship between the firm's debt and equity capital since the only fixed financial charge the firm *must* pay is interest on debt. As the amount of debt increases, so do the fixed payments required, and so does financial risk. However, in order to get a better feel for the firm's true financial leverage, it may be necessary to take into account preferred stock, which has a fixed dividend payment. Thus the distinction between debt and equity capital as opposing forces in determining financial leverage cannot always be maintained.

Measures and considerations of capital structure

In Chapter 3, certain ratio measures of debt were presented. These ratios indicate both directly and indirectly, the degree of financial leverage confronting the firm. The direct measures considered the degree of indebtedness; the measures of the ability to service debts indirectly provided information concerning the firm's financial leverage. Since the firm's capital structure directly affects these ratios, we shall briefly review them here. In addition, a new ratio, the *market* debt-equity ratio, will be presented.

The debt-equity ratio.   The debt-equity ratio indicates the relationship between long-term debt and stockholders' equity. The higher this ratio, the higher the firm's financial leverage.

The debt-to-total-capitalization ratio.   This ratio is similar to the debt-equity ratio, except that the firm's long-term debt is given as a percentage of the firm's total capitalization (i.e., long-term debt plus stockholders' equity). Higher levels of this ratio indicate higher degrees of financial leverage, and vice versa.

Times interest earned.   This ratio measures the ability of the firm to cover its fixed interest charges. The better able a firm is to cover these charges, the less financially risky it is considered to be. A firm can have high leverage and also high interest coverage, but typically firms with high degrees of indebtedness have low abilities to service their debts. In this situation the ratios support each other, both indicating high financial risk.

Total debt coverage.   This ratio measures the firm's ability to cover not only its interest obligations but also any required principal or sinking-fund payments. It measures financial risk in the sense that the less able the firm is to cover these charges (i.e., the lower the ratio), the more financially risky it is.

A new ratio.   A new ratio that will be used later in this chapter is the *market debt-equity ratio*. The debt-equity ratio presented earlier considered only the book values of debt and equity. This ratio measures the market value of the firm's debt and equity. In equation form, it is as follows:

$$\text{Market debt-equity ratio} = \frac{\text{market value of debt}}{\text{market value of equity}} \qquad (18.1)$$

This ratio measures the firm's leverage in the same manner that prospective and existing lenders do.

In the preceding chapter, in the discussion of the approaches for calculating the firm's weighted average cost of capital, we concluded that the use of market value (as opposed to book value) weights was theoretically preferable, although in a practical sense book value or target capital structure weights (or both) are commonly used. This conclusion was based on the fact that when a firm raises additional financing, the cost of this financing depends on the price at which the financial instrument is sold. In the same sense, suppliers of funds are more apt to view the firm's financial position in light of its financial structure as measured in the marketplace. This belief is based on the premise that if the firm were to obtain its existing financing today, receiving current market prices, its financial structure would be reflected by the market—not book or target—proportions of its existing financial instruments.

Suppliers of long-term funds are expected to consider the firm's market debt-equity ratio in determining the firm's cost of financing. Viewing the firm's costs of various forms of financing in light of the firm's financial risk as measured by the market debt-equity ratio gives us a more realistic idea of the relationship between financial risk and financial costs. The market approach to risk valuation, along with the market view of financial costs, provides a good framework for evaluating the theory of capital structure, which will be discussed later.

Industry differences. A final consideration with respect to the measurement of corporate financial structure concerns industry differences. An acceptable degree of financial leverage for one industry could be very highly risky in another industry. This is because of differing operating characteristics between industries. The stability of the firm's sales revenues, which depends on its line of business, is the key factor determining what is an acceptable degree of financial leverage. Firms such as electric utilities, which have very stable and predictable patterns of revenues, can operate with high degrees of financial leverage; firms with volatile sales revenues must operate with lower levels of financial leverage. A sample of financial leverage ratios (based on book values) for firms operating in a variety of lines of business for a cross-section of industries is given in Table 18.1.

The key factor affected by the degree of volatility of sales revenues is the firm's ability to service debt (i.e., pay the interest and the principal when due). If a firm does not meet these obligations, it can be forced into bankruptcy. Typically, the degree of volatility of sales revenues is assumed to be constant within a given industry. However, differences in financial risk, resulting from differing capital structures, are still likely to exist within an industry. The amount of financial leverage (i.e., risk) in a given firm is largely

TABLE 18.1 Selected industry
total-liability-to-net-worth ratios

Industry	Ratio
Retailers	
Auto and truck dealers	1.81
Department stores	.73
Grocery stores	1.51
Household appliance stores	1.34
Wholesalers	
Dairy products	1.25
Lumber and construction materials	1.10
Petroleum products	1.06
Manufacturers	
Agricultural chemicals	.57
Book publishing and printing	.61
Building contractors	1.96
Car and truck bodies	.86
Communication equipment	1.04
Household appliances	1.02
Office, computing, and accounting machines	1.21
Petroleum refining	1.45
Surgical, medical, and dental instruments	.51

SOURCE: Compiled from data in *Key Business Ratios,* 1976 statistics. (New York: Dun and Bradstreet, Inc., 1978).
  Note: The ratio of total liabilities to net worth was used instead of the market debt-equity ratios because of problems in obtaining data. The ratio of total liabilities to net worth is believed to be a reasonable substitute for the market debt-equity ratio.

the result of the financial decision maker's attitude toward risk. The more risk a firm wishes to take, the greater the amount of financial leverage that will be employed.[2] Theoretically, the firm should let its financial leverage be the result of maintaining a capital structure that minimizes its weighted average cost of capital.

The theory of capital structure

The theory of capital structure is closely related to the firm's cost of capital. Many debates over whether an "optimal" capital structure exists are found in the financial literature. Arguments between those who believe that there is an optimal capital structure for each firm and those who believe that no such optimum exists began in the late 1950s, and there is as yet no resolution of the conflict in sight. Those who assert the existence of an optimal

---

[2]Generally, a firm determines the level of return it desires and then evaluates various financial schemes to find one that will provide the desired return. The key variable evaluated is the risk or uncertainty associated with the receipt of the target return. Evaluation of the financial risk involved may cause the firm to change its financial goals.

capital structure are said to take a *traditional approach,* while those who believe an optimal capital structure does not exist are referred to as supporters of the *M and M approach,* named for its initial proponents, Franco Modigliani and Merton H. Miller.

In order to provide the reader with some insight into what is meant by an "optimal capital structure," we shall examine a number of assumptions and cost functions that are part of the traditional theory of capital structure. The material presented here represents only a fraction of the developments in capital structure theory. More sophisticated theories have eliminated the need for many of the highly restrictive assumptions cited. The selected references at the end of the chapter include materials on some of these theories.

Assumptions. There are a number of simplifying assumptions on which the traditional capital structure model is based. Each of these assumptions is described briefly.

Financing through bonds and stocks. The traditional capital structure model assumes that the sources of financing available to the firm are bonds and stocks. Specific types of bonds or stocks are not isolated by the traditional model. This assumption simplifies graphical representation of the analysis, since only two dimensions are required.

A 100-percent dividend payout. The firm is assumed to pay out *all* earnings in the form of dividends. This assumption supports the preceding assumption by eliminating retained earnings as a source of financing.

No income taxes. Income taxes will be ignored here to simplify the analysis, but the absence of taxes does not detract from the general relationships. Without taxes the after-tax cost of debt, k_i, and the before-tax cost of debt, k_b, are equal.

Constant earnings before interest and taxes (EBIT). The distributions of future EBIT are known and the mean value of each annual EBIT distribution is constant. This provides for the determination of an optimal capital structure. Changes in expected EBIT would therefore result in a different "optimum" capital structure for each level of EBIT.

Constant operating risk. Operating risk is held constant by assuming that all assets acquired are such that the line of business of the firm remains unchanged. Holding operating risk constant lets us isolate the effects of financial risk (i.e., financial leverage).

Changes in financial leverage. The firm decreases its financial leverage by selling stock and using the proceeds to retire bonds. The firm's leverage is increased by issuing bonds and using the proceeds to retire stock. In other words, the firm's total book financing (i.e., stock plus bonds) remains fixed over the period being considered. The second assumption also supports this

FIGURE 18.1 The cost of debt function

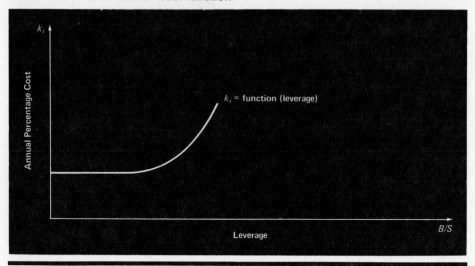

strategy. Keeping the total financing constant makes it easier to isolate the effects of a changing capital structure on the firm's value.

All these assumptions are restrictive, but they are necessary in order to present a simple model that provides some feel for capital structure theory. Models based on less restrictive assumptions are too complex for a basic text.[3]

Cost functions needed to find the value of the firm.   The value of the firm, in the *traditional approach to capital structure,* is determined by adding the market value of the firm's debt to the market value of its equity. Once the firm's market value has been determined, its overall cost of capital, or overall capitalization rate, can be found. The calculation of each of these items is described below, using simple examples.

The market value of debt.   The market value of the firm's debt for a given amount of leverage can be estimated. Since the firm's total financing is assumed to be constant, the cost of debt will remain fixed as leverage increases until a point is reached where lenders feel the firm is becoming financially risky. At this point, the cost of debt, k_i, will increase. This cost of debt function is presented graphically in Figure 18.1. Leverage is measured on the x-axis by the ratio of the market value of debt, B, to the market value of equity, S; B and S represent bonds and stock, respectively.

The market value of debt is merely the dollar value of debt outstanding.

---

[3]The reader may wonder why attention is given solely to development of the traditional approach and not also to the Modigliani and Miller approach. The chief reason is that the M and M model is algebraically somewhat rigorous, and it is more important at this level to familiarize the reader with the key concepts that affect managerial decisions than to delve deeply into the theory of finance.

FIGURE 18.2 The cost of equity function

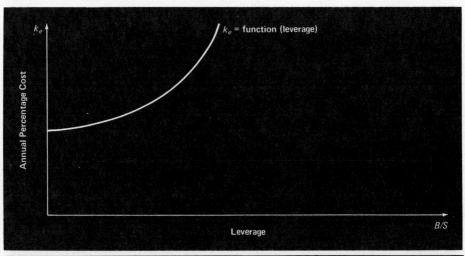

As this amount increases, so, eventually, will the cost of debt. In Figure 18.1, the k_i function represents the *average* cost of debt for various degrees of leverage.

The market value of equity. The market value of the firm's equity is not as easy to determine as the market value of debt due to the large discrepancy that normally exists between a firm's book and market value. The general relationship between leverage and the cost of equity, k_e, is presented in Figure 18.2. The cost of equity also increases with increasing leverage, but much more rapidly than the cost of debt. The faster increase in the cost of equity occurs because market participants recognize that the earnings of the firm must be discounted at a higher rate as leverage increases in order to compensate for the higher degree of financial risk associated with the firm.

The market value of the firm's equity is calculated by *capitalizing* (discounting at the firm's cost of equity) the earnings available for common stockholders (EAC), which are expected to be received annually over an infinite time horizon.[4] Due to certain mathematical properties of infinite series, an *infinite* stream of equal earnings can be capitalized at a given rate by dividing the annual earnings by the capitalization rate, k_e (in this case, the cost of equity).[5] The basic format for calculating the market value of the firm's equity is given in Table 18.2. The absence of taxes, and the technique used to

[4]The term *capitalize* is commonly used to refer to the process of converting a future stream of cash flows into its present value. This is done merely by discounting the cash flows at the appropriate cost, or *capitalization rate*. The capitalization rate is largely a function of how the market views the risk of the firm. It is similar to the required return and risk-adjusted discount rate discussed in Chapter 16.

[5]This approach, which was discussed in Chapter 13, is merely a mathematical technique for finding the present value of a *perpetuity*, which is an annuity with an infinite life.

**TABLE 18.2 A format for
calculating the market value of equity**

EBIT	Earnings before interest and taxes
$-I$	Interest on debt $(B \cdot k_i)$
EAC	Earnings available for common stockholders
$\dfrac{EAC}{k_e}$ = The market value of equity, S	

capitalize earnings available for common stockholders, should be clear from the table.

The overall cost of capital.   The overall cost of capital, or overall capitalization rate, k_o, is found by first determining the total value of the firm, V, and then using V and the firm's EBIT to determine at what rate the EBIT must have been capitalized in order for the firm's value to equal V. Equation 18.2 presents a simple expression for the total value of the firm, V.

$$V = B + S \qquad\qquad (18.2)$$

The value of the firm is equal to the sum of the market values of the firm's bonds, B, and stock, S. The expression for the overall capitalization rate of the firm is

$$k_o = \frac{\text{EBIT}}{V} \qquad\qquad (18.3)$$

Since the firm's EBIT is assumed to be constant, Equation 18.3 provides the rate at which the firm's EBIT would have to have been discounted over an infinite time horizon in order to end up with the market value V.

Figure 18.3 shows the function for the firm's overall (or weighted average) cost of capital.[6] It also shows the firm's cost of debt and cost of equity functions. The point labeled "M" represents the "optimal" leverage for the firm, since it is at this point that the firm's overall capitalization rate, k_o, reaches a minimum. At the point where the firm's weighted average cost of capital (i.e., its overall capitalization rate, k_o) reaches a minimum, the value of the firm reaches a maximum. This can be shown by rearranging Equation 18.3 as follows:

$$V = \frac{\text{EBIT}}{k_o} \qquad\qquad (18.4)$$

Since EBIT are held constant, the lower the value of k_o the higher the value of the firm. *The optimal capital structure is therefore that at which the*

---

[6]The overall and weighted average cost of capital are one and the same. The term "overall cost of capital" is used here since it is used in the theoretical literature.

FIGURE 18.3 The overall cost of capital function

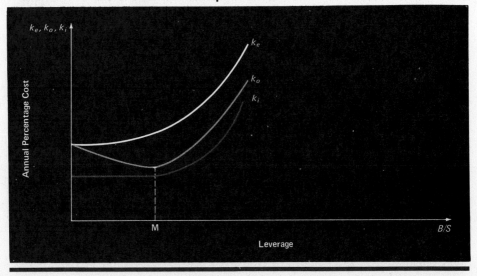

overall cost of capital, k_o, is minimized. However, the reader *must* keep in mind that this traditional approach for determining the "optimal" capital structure is only one of many approaches.[7] It is also important to recall the numerous restrictive assumptions used to develop this analytical framework. An example may help to clarify this approach.

EXAMPLE

The Butler Company currently has earnings before interest and taxes, EBIT, of $16,000. The firm has $50,000 of outstanding debt with an average cost, k_i, of 8 percent, and its equity capitalization rate, k_e, is 12 percent. The current value of the firm, V, can be found as follows:

EBIT		$ 16,000
−I	($50,000 · .08)	4,000
EAC		$ 12,000
	$S = \dfrac{\$12,000}{.12} =$	$100,000
	$B =$	50,000
	$V = S + B$	$150,000

Substituting the value of the firm, $150,000, in Equation 18.3, gives us the overall capitalization rate, 10.67 percent ($16,000 ÷ $150,000). The debt-equity ratio (B/S) in this case equals 0.50 ($50,000 ÷ $100,000).

[7]In the Modigliani and Miller approach, the firm's overall cost of capital, when plotted on a graph similar to Figure 18.3, is represented by a horizontal line parallel to the x-axis. In other words, the M and M approach suggests that there is no optimal capital structure since the method by which the firm finances itself has no effect on its overall cost of capital. These conclusions are logically sound, given M and M's assumptions, but their assumptions are highly unrealistic.

The firm is considering increasing its leverage by issuing an additional $20,000 in bonds and using the proceeds to retire that amount of stock. If it does sell these additional bonds, the firm will have $70,000 worth of bonds outstanding at an average debt cost, k_i, of 9 percent. The increased average cost will result from the increased leverage. (Figure 18.1 presented the general relationship between leverage and the cost of debt.) The cost of equity, k_e, will increase to 14 percent, as a result of the increased leverage. (Figure 18.2 presented the general relationship between leverage and the cost of equity.) The value of the firm will drop to $139,285.71:

EBIT		$ 16,000.00
$-I$	($70,000 $\cdot$ .09)	$ 6,300.00
EAC		$ 9,700.00
	$S = \dfrac{\$9,700}{.14} =$	$ 69,285.71
	$B =$	70,000.00
	$V = S + B$	$139,285.71

The overall capitalization rate will rise to 11.49 percent ($16,000 $\div$ $139,285.71), and the debt-equity ratio will rise to 1.01 ($70,000 $\div$ $69,285.71). ●

Although we did not attempt to find the optimal capital structure for the firm in the example above, we know that the optimal debt-equity ratio must be less than 1.01, since at that ratio the value of the firm is $139,285.71 while at a debt-equity ratio of 0.50 it is $150,000.[8] However, the nature of the relationship between the cost of debt, k_i, the cost of equity, k_e, and the resulting overall cost of capital, k_o, should now be clear. Referring to Figure 18.3 may help the reader to relate this example to traditional capital structure theory. This section should also have given the reader an appreciation of the relationship between the firm's cost of capital and the owners' returns. The lower the firm's overall, or weighted average cost of capital, the higher are the expected returns to the owners. Given a fixed capital budget, the less the firm's money costs, the greater the difference between the return on a project and the cost of money and the greater the profits from the project. Reinvesting these increased profits will increase the firm's expected future earnings and therefore its value. The stated objective of the firm is to maximize the owners' wealth. The selection of a capital structure that minimizes the overall, or weighted average, cost of capital is consistent with fulfillment of this objective.

THE EBIT-eps APPROACH TO CAPITAL STRUCTURE

In Chapter 4, a brief discussion of techniques for evaluating financing plans containing differing degrees of financial leverage was presented. The discussion was devoted basically to a graphical presentation of the financing

---

[8]One way to find the optimal capital structure would be to find, through trial and error, the debt-equity ratios on either side of a given debt-equity ratio that result in lower valuations than the middle ratio. The optimum debt-equity ratio would be somewhere between the two outside ratios. More sophisticated mathematical or graphical techniques could also be used to estimate the optimal capital structure.

plans. In this section, the "EBIT-eps" approach for evaluating various capital structures (i.e., financing plans) will be examined in greater detail. The main emphasis will *not* be on measuring the effects of various financial structures on the firms' average cost of capital but rather on the effects of various financial structures on the owners' returns. The overall goal of the firm is to maximize the owners' wealth; this goal is fulfilled by increasing the value of the firm's shares. Since one of the key variables affecting the market value of the firm's shares is its earnings, earnings per share (eps) can be used to measure the effect of various financial structures on the shareholders' investment.[9]

Presenting a financing plan graphically

In analyzing the effects of a firm's financial structure on the returns to the firm's owners, we need to be concerned only with the effects of earnings before interest and taxes (EBIT) on the firm's earnings per share (eps). Expected earnings before interest and taxes are assumed to be constant, since an analysis of a firm's financial structure is concerned only with the effects of financing costs, such as interest and preferred stock dividends, on the owners' investment. This assumption implies a constant operating risk (i.e., that the firm's line of business and operating cost structure remain unchanged). As indicated earlier, earnings per share are used as a measure of the effects of operations on the owners' wealth, since a close relationship is expected between the firm's eps and share prices.[10]

The data required.   In order to graph a financing plan, at least two EBIT-eps coordinates are required. There are two ways of obtaining these coordinates—a long and a shortcut approach. These approaches can be illustrated by a simple example.

EXAMPLE

The Shlitz Corporation's current financial structure is as follows:

Type of financing	Amount of financing (1)	Stated annual cost (2)	Annual payment required (1) · (2) (3)
Bonds	$500,000	8%	$40,000
Preferred stock	5,000 shares	$3.00	$15,000
Common stock	10,000 shares	—	—

[9]In the event that investors did not require risk premiums (i.e., additional returns) as the firm increases its proportion of debt in its capital structure, a strategy involving maximizing earnings per share would also maximize the owners' wealth. Since risk premiums are increasing functions of financial leverage, the maximization of eps does not assure owners' wealth maximization.

[10]The relationship expected to exist between earnings per share and the owners' wealth is not one of cause and effect. As was indicated in Chapter 1, the maximization of profits does not necessarily assure the firm that the owners' wealth is also being maximized. Profit maximization is a very short-run approach, while wealth maximization is a long-run approach. Nevertheless, it is expected that the movement of earnings per share will have some effect on the owners' wealth since earnings per share data is one of the few pieces of information investors receive, and they bid the firm's share prices up or down in response to the level of these earnings.

The company is in the 40-percent tax bracket. The EBIT-eps coordinates can be found by either of two methods.

The long approach. The EBIT-eps coordinates can be found by assuming two different levels of EBIT and calculating the firm's eps at each level. Using EBIT values of $80,000 and $100,000, the calculations are as follows:

	Case 1	Case 2
Earnings before interest and taxes (EBIT)	$80,000	$100,000
− Interest (*I*)	40,000	40,000
Earnings before taxes (EBT)	$40,000	$ 60,000
− Taxes (*T*) [(.40) EBT]	16,000	24,000
Earnings after taxes (EAT)	$24,000	$ 36,000
− Preferred dividends (*PD*)	15,000	15,000
Earnings available for common stockholders (EAC)	$ 9,000	$ 21,000

$$\text{Earnings per share (eps)} = \frac{\text{EAC}}{\text{number of shares of common }(N)}$$

$$\text{Case 1: eps} = \frac{\$9,000}{10,000 \text{ sh.}} = \$0.90$$

$$\text{Case 2: eps} = \frac{\$21,000}{10,000 \text{ sh.}} = \$2.10$$

The notation used to represent the various values needed in calculating the eps is the same as that used in Chapter 4. The two EBIT-eps coordinates resulting from these calculations are (1) $80,000 and $.90 per share and (2) $100,000 and $2.10 per share.

The shortcut approach. The shortcut approach for finding EBIT-eps coordinates involves determining one coordinate by the long method described above and then finding a second coordinate representing the firm's financial breakeven point. The *financial breakeven point* is the level of EBIT for which the firm's eps just equals zero. It is the level of EBIT necessary to satisfy all fixed financial charges (i.e., interest and preferred stock dividends). Equation 18.5 expresses the firm's financial breakeven point in terms of its annual interest payment, *I*, its preferred stock dividends, *PD*, and its tax rate, *t*.

$$\text{Financial breakeven point} = I + \frac{PD}{1-t} \tag{18.5}$$

Solving Equation 18.5 gives us the before-tax earnings necessary to cover the firm's fixed financial obligations. Since preferred stock dividends are paid after taxes, the division by $1 - t$ converts this obligation to a before-tax amount.[11] Substituting the appropriate values for the Shlitz Corporation into Equation 18.5 yields a financial breakeven point of $65,000 ($40,000 + [$15,000 ÷ (1 − .40)]). ●

Plotting the data.   The data developed for the Shlitz Corporation's current financing plan in the preceding example can now be plotted on a set of EBIT-eps axes, as in Figure 18.4. All three available coordinates are used to plot the financing plan, but any two of the points could have been used.

[11]A discussion of the conversion of after-tax figures to before-tax amounts was included as part of the discussion of measures of the ability to service debts in Chapter 3. See Table 3.4.

FIGURE 18.4 The current financing plan for the Shlitz Corporation

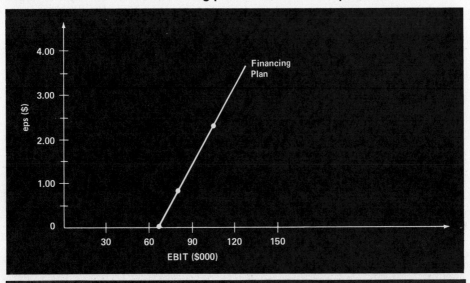

Since our concern is only with positive levels of eps, the graph has not been extended below the x-axis. Figure 18.4 shows the level of eps that can be expected for each level of EBIT. If the level of EBIT is less than $65,000 (the firm's financial breakeven point) a loss (i.e., negative eps) will result.

Comparing financing plans graphically

The graph presented above is most useful as a mechanism for comparing various financing plans, as in the following simple example.

EXAMPLE

The Shlitz Corporation, whose current financial position was described in the preceding example, is contemplating changing its capital structure. Two plans appear most attractive. Plan A involves selling additional debt in order to retire preferred stock. Plan B involves the sale of additional common stock in order to eliminate preferred stock. One hundred thousand dollars is required to retire the preferred stock. It can be obtained either through the sale of an additional $100,000 of 8-percent bonds (plan A), or the sale of 2500 shares of common stock, which is currently selling for $40 per share (plan B). The capital structures that would result from each plan are given below:

Capital structure with plan A

Type of financing	Amount of financing (1)	Stated annual cost (2)	Annual payment required (1) · (2) (3)
Bonds	$600,000	8%	$48,000
Common stock	10,000 shares	—	—

Capital structure with plan B

Type of financing	Amount of financing (1)	Stated annual cost (2)	Annual payment required (1) · (2) (3)
Bonds	$500,000	8%	$40,000
Common stock	12,500 shares	—	—

The coordinates necessary to plot plans A and B can be determined. One coordinate for each plan can be calculated by assuming EBIT of $100,000. The calculations are given below.

	Plan A	Plan B
EBIT	$100,000	$100,000
−*I*	48,000	40,000
EBT	$ 52,000	$ 60,000
−*T* (.40)	20,800	24,000
EAT	$ 31,200	$ 36,000
−*PD*	0	0
EAC	$ 31,200	$ 36,000
eps	$\dfrac{\$31{,}200}{10{,}000 \text{ sh.}} = \$3.12$	$\dfrac{\$36{,}000}{12{,}500 \text{ sh.}} = \$2.88$

A second coordinate can be found by calculating the financial breakeven points for each plan using Equation 18.5. These breakeven points are $48,000 (i.e., $48,000 + [0 ÷ (1 − .40)]) and $40,000 (i.e., $40,000 + [0 ÷ (1 − .40)]) for plans A and B, respectively.

Using the two sets of coordinates developed above, the two financing plans under consideration, as well as the current financing plan, can be compared graphically. This is done in Figure 18.5. Figure 18.5 reveals that plans A and B are both superior to the current plan for all the levels of EBIT shown, since they provide higher levels of eps. The current plan would be superior to plan B only at some point beyond a level of EBIT of $165,000.[12] Plan A is always superior to the current plan and is superior to plan B for levels of EBIT greater than approximately $80,000 (point I in Figure 18.5). If the firm is fairly certain that its EBIT will be greater than $80,000, plan A should be implemented; otherwise, plan B should be used, since the objective is to select the financing plan that maximizes the firm's eps for the expected range of EBIT. ●

[12]Algebraic techniques for finding the points of indifference between various financing plans are available. These techniques involve expressing each financing plan as an equation stated in terms of earnings per share (eps), setting the equations for two financing plans equal to each other, and solving for the level of EBIT that causes the equations to be equal. Using the notation above and letting N equal the number of shares of common stock outstanding, the general equation for the earnings per share (eps) from a financing plan is

$$\text{eps} = \frac{(1 - t)(\text{EBIT} - I) - PD}{N}$$

FIGURE 18.5 A graphical comparison of financing plans for the Shlitz Corporation

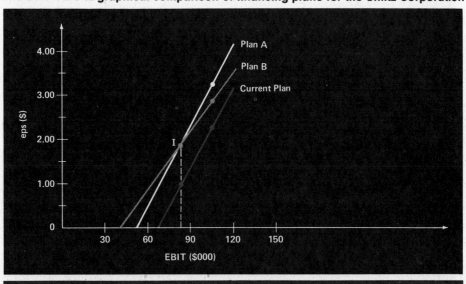

Interpreting EBIT-eps analysis

The usefulness of EBIT-eps analysis for determining the effects of *re-capitalization* or raising new funds on the returns to the firm's owners should be clear.[13] When interpreting EBIT-eps analysis, it is important to accurately assess the risks involved with each of the financing alternatives. It is also important to recognize certain weaknesses associated with the use of this approach.

Risk assessment. The riskiness of each financing plan can be viewed in light of both the firm's financial breakeven point and the degree of financial leverage (i.e., the slope of the financing plan line) that result. Plan A in Figure 18.5 is more risky than plan B since it has both a higher financial breakeven point and more financial leverage (a steeper slope). Plan A has a lower financial breakeven point than the current plan and has the same degree of financial leverage (since the lines are parallel). It is far superior to the current plan since it is less risky and provides greater return for all levels of EBIT.

The risk of the plans can also be evaluated using a ratio measure of the firm's ability to service its interest and preferred stock dividend obligations. Using the ratio of coverage of these two fixed charges given in Equation 18.6,

$$\text{Coverage of interest and preferred stock dividends} = \frac{\text{EBIT}}{I + PD\,[1/(1 - t)]} \qquad (18.6)$$

---

[13]The term *recapitalization* indicates that the firm is changing the mix of its existing capital, or its capital structure.

the risk of each plan can be assessed. Substituting the appropriate interest and preferred stock dividend values into Equation 18.6, assuming EBIT of $100,000, results in coverage ratios of 1.54 (i.e., $100,000 ÷ ($40,000 + ($15,000 ÷ (1 − .4)))) for the current plan, 2.08 (i.e., $100,000 ÷ ($48,000 + ($0 ÷ (1 − .4)))) for plan A, and 2.50 (i.e., $100,000 ÷ ($40,000 + ($0 ÷ (1 − .4)))) for plan B. Since the higher this ratio, the less risky, it can be seen that the financial risk of plan B is lowest, followed by plan A, and the current plan. The use of a coverage ratio such as that in Equation 18.6 therefore tends to permit the risk as well as the return to be measured as part of the EBIT-eps analysis of alternative financing plans.

A word of caution. The most important point to keep in mind in using EBIT-eps analysis is that each of the financing plans must be feasible in the sense that the stated amount of dollars can be raised at the specified cost. The approach described in this section only evaluates financing plans in light of the resulting capital structure and its effect on the owners' returns as measured by eps. It completely ignores the effects of various feasible financing plans on the firm's future cost of financing. The points made in the discussions of the theory of capital structure and the firm's cost of capital should also be considered when making capital structure decisions. Whenever the firm is considering recapitalization or raising new funds, the effects of these changes on the firm's future funds costs, as well as the returns to its owners, should receive consideration. Unfortunately, there is no magic formula for determining what the most beneficial changes in a firm's capital structure would be.

THE VALUATION OF CORPORATE STOCK

A number of techniques are available for measuring the value of the stock of a firm. It is important for both the firm's management and its current and prospective owners to know the value of the firm so that they can determine how well its objective of maximization of the owners' wealth is being met. Existing and prospective stockholders are also concerned with whether the actual market price of the firm's stock is more or less than their valuation so that they can make intelligent purchase or sale decisions. The valuation of corporate stock is also of interest to financial analysts, whose function it is to analyze the quality of prospective security investments in order to make recommendations with respect to their purchase.

The importance of security valuation should not be underestimated. An in-depth discussion of this subject can be found in security analysis and investments texts. In this section we shall consider only five basic valuation techniques. These techniques are based on book value, liquidation value, market value, industry capitalization, and the Gordon model, which was briefly described in the discussion of the cost of capital in Chapter 17.

The book value of stock

The book value per share is one of the simplest measures of the value of a firm. It is simply the value of the common stockholder's per share ownership if all the firm's assets are liquidated for their exact book value. The book value per share is calculated by dividing the common stock equity by the number of shares of common stock outstanding. It can be thought of as the amount of money that would be received by each shareholder if the firm were to sell its assets for their exact book values. The equation for the firm's book value per share is simply

$$\text{Book value per share} = \frac{\text{common stock equity}}{\text{number of shares of common stock outstanding}} \qquad (18.7)$$

This valuation method lacks sophistication and can easily be criticized on the basis of its heavy reliance on balance sheet data. It totally ignores the expected earnings or dividend potential of the firm. A simple example will clarify the calculations involved.

EXAMPLE

The Swanson Company's most recent balance sheet is given in Table 18.3. It can be used to determine the company's book value per share. The firm's common stock equity is $15,000, since it has $10,000 of common stock outstanding, paid-in capital in excess of par of $3000, and retained earnings of $2000. Substituting this value into Equation 18.7 results in a *book value per share of $15* (i.e., $15,000 ÷ 1000 shares). If the firm were to sell all its assets for their book value and pay off all its creditors and preferred stockholders from the proceeds, the amount left over for each holder of common stock would be $15. However, the implied assumption that assets are liquidated for their book value is somewhat questionable. ●

TABLE 18.3 **Balance sheet for the Swanson Company**

Assets		Liabilities and Stockholders' equity	
Cash	$ 1,000	Accounts payable	$ 4,000
Marketable securities	2,000	Notes payable	4,000
Inventory	5,000	Accruals	4,000
Accounts receivables	12,000	Total current liabilities	$12,000
Total current assets	$20,000	Long-term debt	$28,000
Fixed assets	40,000	Preferred stock	$ 5,000
Total Assets	$60,000	Common stock (1,000 shares)	10,000
		Paid-in capital in excess of par	3,000
		Retained earnings	2,000
		Total Liabilities and Stockholders' Equity	$60,000

The liquidation value of stock

The liquidation value per share is the *actual* amount expected to be received by each shareholder if the firm's assets are sold, creditors and preferred stockholders are paid, and the remaining money (if any) is divided between the common stockholders.[14] It is a more realistic indicator of the value of a firm than the book value of shares since it takes into account the fact that the firm's assets cannot normally be liquidated for their book value. Typically, they are liquidated for less than their book value. Thus the liquidation value of the firm's shares most often represents their lowest value.

EXAMPLE

The Swanson Company, whose balance sheet was given in Table 18.3, has estimated that it can liquidate its noncash assets for the following percentages of their book value:

Inventory	80 percent of book value
Accounts receivable	90 percent of book value
Fixed assets	80 percent of book value

The firm's liabilities, of course, must be liquidated at their face value. The actual liquidation value of the assets, is therefore

Cash	$ 1,000
Marketable securities	2,000
Inventory (.80)($5000)	4,000
Accounts receivable (.90)($12,000)	10,800
Fixed assets (.80)($40,000)	32,000
Liquidation value of assets	$49,800

Subtracting the firm's liabilities and payments due preferred stockholders from the liquidation value of the firm's assets yields the amount of money available for common stockholders.

Liquidation value of assets	$49,800
− Current liabilities	−12,000
− Long-term debt	−28,000
− Preferred stock (book value)	− 5,000
Funds available to common stockholders	$ 4,800

Dividing the number of shares of common stock into the amount available for common stockholders yields a *liquidation value per share of $4.80.* This is considerably less than the book value per share of $15. It is possible for the liquidation value to be greater than book value if assets are undervalued; however, normally, the liquidation value of assets is less than their book value. ●

The market value of stock

The simplest way to measure the value of a publicly held firm is to go into the marketplace and find the price at which the most recent transaction in the firm's common stock occurred.[15] Market price quotations for many se-

---

[14]In the event of liquidation, creditors' claims must be satisfied first, then those of the preferred shareholders. Anything left over goes to the common stockholders. A more detailed discussion of liquidation proceedings is presented in Chapter 26.

[15]The reader should recognize that the market price is a marginal price per share—not an average. The total market price of the common equity will be greater than the market price per share times the number of shares if there is a downward sloping demand curve for shares. As evidence one can observe the premiums over market price paid in a merger or acquisition.

curities are published daily in *The Wall Street Journal* and most local newspapers. Prices of less actively traded stocks can be obtained from a stockbroker. The value of shares of small, closely held companies, for which there is no actual market, cannot be measured in this manner. However, the market value of similar firms that have publicly traded shares may act as a very rough approximation of the firm's share value. Publicly traded stocks normally sell above their book value, though in some cases the market price may be less than the book value.

Industry capitalization and stock value

The average price-earnings ratio (P/E) in an industry can be used as a guide to a firm's value if it is assumed that investors value the earnings of a given firm in the same way (i.e., discount them at the same rate) as they do the earnings of the average firm in the industry. The average P/E for an industry can be obtained from a source such as *Standard & Poors Industrial Ratios.* Multiplying the forecast annual earnings per share of a firm by this ratio gives us an estimate of the value of the firm's shares. This measure of value, like the preceding ones, lacks any deep theoretical roots. It is best looked on as a tool for forecasting a firm's future share price. The accuracy of the forecast depends greatly on "how average" the company is since the use of the industry average price-earnings ratio assumes the firm to be average. This technique is especially useful for valuing firms that are not publicly traded; the use of market price may be preferable in the case of a publicly traded firm. Regardless, the industry capitalization approach is believed to be superior to the use of book or liquidation values since it implicitly considers *expected* earnings.

EXAMPLE

The Swanson Company is expected to earn $1.58 per share next year. This expectation is based on an analysis of the firm's historical earnings trend and certain industry factors expected to be operating in the coming year. The average price-earnings ratio for firms in the same industry is 12.5. Multiplying Swanson's expected earnings per share of $1.58 by this ratio gives us *a value for the firm's shares of $19.75*, assuming that investors will continue to capitalize the value of the firm at 12.5 times its earnings. The actual rate at which an investor is assumed to capitalize the earnings is found by taking the inverse of the price-earnings ratio (i.e., 1/12.5, or .08). Dividing this into the firm's expected earnings of $1.58 would give us, once again, a figure of $19.75 for the value of the firm's shares.[16] It is easier to use the P/E ratio directly. ●

The Gordon model

The Gordon model is a theoretical model based on the assumption that the value of the firm is equal to the present value of all future dividends paid over the life of the firm, which is assumed to be infinite. The basic expression

---

[16]The industry capitalization approach to valuation, when viewed in this manner, does have a theoretical explanation. If we view one divided by the price-earnings ratio, or the earnings-price ratio, as the rate at which investors capitalize the firm's earnings and assume that the projected earnings per share will be earned indefinitely, the industry-capitalization approach can be looked on as a method of capitalizing a perpetuity of projected earnings per share at a rate equal to the earnings-price ratio.

for the firm's value, which was presented in Chapter 17 as Equation 17.6, is repeated below as Equation 18.8.

$$P = \frac{D_0(1 + g)^1}{(1 + k_e)^1} + \frac{D_0(1 + g)^2}{(1 + k_e)^2} + \cdots + \frac{D_0(1 + g)^\infty}{(1 + k_e)^\infty}$$ (18.8)

where

P = the current price per share of common stock
D_0 = the most recent per share dividend (i.e., the dividend at time zero)
$D_t(t = 1, \infty)$ = the per share dividend expected in year t
k_e = the equity capitalization rate (or required return)
g = the expected annual earnings and dividend growth rate[17]

Simplifying Equation 18.8 by assuming a constant growth rate and applying certain mathematical techniques gives us an expression for the theoretical value of a share of stock:[18]

$$P = \frac{D_1}{k_e - g}$$ (18.9)

The problem in using this model lies in the difficulty of estimating k_e and g. The equity capitalization rate, k_e, can be estimated by using the earnings yield, which is the inverse of the price-earnings ratio (i.e., the earnings per share divided by the market price per share). Another way of estimating k_e is to substitute *historical* dividend data, share prices, and growth rates into Equation 17.7, and use the resulting historically based capitalization rate in solving the Gordon model for the stock price. A third method for finding the equity capitalization rate, or required return, k_e, is to use the capital asset pricing model (CAPM). By estimating and substituting values for the risk-free rate, the firm's beta coefficient, and the expected market return into the model presented in Chapter 16 (see Equation 16.4), the value of k_e can be estimated. The dividend growth rate, g, can be estimated by using historical dividend per share values to calculate the compound annual growth rate. The Gordon model is one of the most commonly cited valuation models and is theoretically superior to the other measures of a firm's value presented in this section.

EXAMPLE

The Swanson Company has estimated that its dividend, D_1, next year will be $.52 per share. On the basis of past data and certain expectations, the growth rate, g, in dividends is expected to be 6.2 percent per year. The rate at which investors capitalize

---

[17]One of the assumptions of the Gordon model as presented is that earnings and dividends grow at the same rate. This assumption is true only in cases where a firm pays out a fixed percentage of its earnings each year (i.e., has a fixed payout ratio).

[18]See footnote 13 in Chapter 17 for the algebraic derivation of the Gordon model.

the earnings of similar-risk firms within the industry, k_e, is estimated as 8.2 percent. Substituting these values into Equation 18.9 results in a *stock value of $26 per share* [$.52 ÷ (.082 − .062)]. This is the theoretical, or "intrinsic," value of the firm's stock. The basis of this projection is the assumption that the firm's dividend of $.52 will grow at a rate of 6.2 percent per year and that investors will discount these future dividends at a rate of 8.2 percent per year. ●

Comparing valuation techniques

The valuation techniques mentioned each provide an estimate of the per share worth of the business firm. The first two techniques discussed (i.e., measuring book value and liquidation value) do not actually view the firm as a going concern; rather, they value the firm on the basis of its assets. The market value approach accepts the value of the firm as measured in the marketplace as correct. Although this approach views the firm as a going concern, it ignores behavioral factors in the marketplace. The market value of a stock sometimes reflects the whims of large investors and not the stock's true economic worth. The industry capitalization approach assumes that the performance of the firm in the future will be the same as it was in the past and that investors will discount the earnings of the firm at the same rate over time. This approach, since it uses market price, does reflect behavioral factors in the marketplace to some extent. The Gordon model, which capitalizes the future returns of the firm over an assumed infinite life, is the most theoretically correct approach since it views the firm as a going concern and does not use asset values or market price as inputs to the valuation process. Instead, it assumes that the value of the firm is equal to the discounted value of all future dividends or returns. The Gordon model is believed to be theoretically superior to the other valuation approaches presented above.

SUMMARY

In this chapter, we have discussed two important topics related to the firm's long-term position—capital structure and valuation. A firm's capital structure is determined by the mix of long-term funds it maintains. The basic sources of long-term funds are long-term debt, preferred stock, common stock, and retained earnings. Sometimes the firm's long-term funds are divided into debt and equity capital—long-term debt being debt capital and the remaining funds representing equity capital. The simplest way to view a firm's capital structure is as a mix of debt and equity capital rather than as a mix of individual types of capital. The basic differences between debt and equity capital are related to the length of time the funds are available to the firm, the claim on income and assets of the providers of each type of capital, and their voice in management.

The firm's capital structure directly affects its financial leverage and therefore the financial risk associated with the firm. Common ratios for measuring the degree of financial leverage are the debt-equity ratio, the debt-to-total-capitalization ratio, times interest earned, and the total debt coverage. In analyzing the firm's capital structure, the ratio of the market value of debt to the market value of equity is most useful. What constitutes an acceptable degree of financial leverage differs between industries since the degree of operating leverage greatly affects the level of acceptable financial risk.

The controversy over the existence of an optimal capital structure for firms is as yet unresolved in the literature of finance. The "traditional approach" to capital structure is based on a number of restrictive assumptions, and suggests that the optimal capital structure for a firm is that for which the firm's overall cost of capital is minimized. Both the cost of debt and the cost of equity are increasing functions of leverage. The cost of debt typically increases only beyond a certain level of leverage. There are other theories of capital structure, but the traditional approach is most popular.

The EBIT-eps approach can be used to evaluate various capital structures in light of the degree of financial risk they entail and the returns to the firm's owners. This approach does not directly consider the long-run financial consequences of certain capital structures, but concerns itself with the returns to owners. It can be used for making decisions about recapitalization and raising new funds. By using a ratio measure of the firm's ability to cover its interest and preferred stock dividends in conjunction with the EBIT-eps analysis, the risk as well as the return associated with various financing plans can be evaluated.

The second major topic discussed in this chapter is how to determine the worth of a business firm. The approaches discussed use the book value, liquidation value, and market value of stock, industry capitalization rates, and the Gordon model. Book value and liquidation value do not actually view the firm as a going concern; rather, they value the firm solely on the basis of its assets. The market value, industry capitalization, and Gordon model approaches view the firm as a going concern; the Gordon model is the theoretically superior technique for use in valuation. It requires estimates of dividends, the equity capitalization rate, and dividend growth rate. The earnings-price ratio, a historical approach, or the capital asset pricing model (CAPM) can be used to estimate the equity capitalization rate; the dividend growth rate can be estimated using historic dividend data. Since the objective of the firm is to maximize the owners' wealth, the financial manager should continuously monitor the value of the firm in order to make sure this goal is being fulfilled.

QUESTIONS

18-1 How are debt and equity capital different?

18-2 What is financial leverage? How is it related to the firm's debt and equity capital? Why is it difficult to estimate the firm's financial leverage accurately using a debt-capital–equity-capital breakdown?

18-3 What traditional ratios reflect the firm's financial leverage and capital structure? How do they change as the firm's capital structure changes?

18-4 What is the *market debt-equity ratio?* Why might it be quite useful for evaluating the firm's capital structure? How is this measure consistent with the weighted average cost of capital calculation and the way fund suppliers view the firm?

18-5 Why do differences in the stability of sales revenues between industries in a sense dictate what is an acceptable degree of financial leverage for a firm?

18-6 What two schools of thought exist with respect to an optimal capital structure? Which theory makes the fewest restrictive assumptions?

18-7 What is the relationship between increasing leverage and the firm's cost of debt? How is leverage measured in this case?

18-8 What is the relationship between leverage and the firm's cost of equity? How does this relationship differ from the debt-leverage relationship?

18-9 How can the market value of the firm's stock be found using the firm's cost of equity capital and the earnings available for common stockholders? On what assumption is this calculation based?

18-10 How is the total value of the firm determined? If this value is known, along with the firm's EBIT, how can the firm's overall capitalization rate be calculated? What is the significance of the overall capitalization rate?

18-11 How might a firm go about determining its "optimal capital structure"?

18-12 What general concepts underlie the use of the EBIT-eps approach for evaluating capital structures? Does this approach reflect the firm's overall goal of owner wealth maximization?

18-13 In evaluating capital structures using the EBIT-eps approach, why is the level of EBIT considered constant?

18-14 What is meant by a "financial breakeven point"? How can it be determined? Graph a financing plan, indicating the financial breakeven point and labeling the axes.

18-15 Discuss the calculation and interpretation of the *coverage of interest and preferred stock dividends ratio*. How can use of this measure enhance the EBIT-eps analysis of alternative financing plans?

18-16 Why is it important to be able to measure the value of corporate stock? What parties might be interested in the value of corporate stock, and why?

18-17 How can the book value per share of a corporation's stock be calculated? Of what use is this measure of stock value?

18-18 What is meant by the liquidation value per share? How is this calculated? How is it different from the book value per share?

18-19 What are the theoretical underpinnings of the *Gordon model*? What difficulties may be encountered in using this approach? How does it compare to valuation techniques using book value, liquidation value, market value, and industry capitalization rates?

18-20 Why, according to the Gordon model, would firms paying small dividends but having high growth expectations have a high stock value?

PROBLEMS

18-1 The earnings before interest and taxes (EBIT), interest (I), equity capitalization rate (k_e), and overall cost of capital (k_o) are tabulated below for firms A through E. Assume that taxes are zero.

Firm	EBIT	I	k_e	k_o
A	$ 110,000	$11,000	6.7%	6.0%
B	$ 880,000	$10,000	8.2%	7.2%
C	$ 230,000	$20,000	7.4%	6.6%
D	$1,200,000	$33,000	10.2%	8.5%
E	$ 660,000	$40,000	9.8%	7.0%

a Determine the market value of each firm's stock.

    b Determine the total market value of each firm.

    c Determine the market value of each firm's bonds.

18-2 Graphically depict the cost of debt, cost of equity, and overall cost of capital for a business firm as functions of leverage (i.e., B/S) using the *traditional* approach to capital structure.

18-3 Collins Equipment has a current level of EBIT of $96,000. The firm has $360,000 of outstanding 7-percent bonds. The firm's equity capitalization rate is 10 percent. Use the traditional approach to answer the following. Note: Ignore taxes.

    a What is the current value of the firm?

    b Calculate the firm's overall or weighted average cost of capital, k_o.

    c Determine the firm's market debt-equity ratio.

    d The firm is considering an increase in its financial leverage. The plan is to sell $120,000 in bonds and retire an equal amount of stock. The increase in leverage will increase the average cost of debt to 8 percent and the cost of equity to 12 percent. Should the firm adopt this plan? Explain your answer.

    e Using the original capital structure and the one implied by **d** as bench marks, approximately where is the firm's optimal debt-equity structure?

18-4 The Big Red Cup Company has earnings before interest and taxes of $700,000. The firm currently has outstanding debt of $4,200,000 at a cost of 6 percent. Its cost of equity is estimated to be 11 percent. Use the traditional approach to answer the following. Note: Ignore taxes.

    a What is the current value of the firm?

    b Calculate the firm's overall or weighted average cost of capital.

    c Determine the firm's market debt-equity ratio.

    d If the firm reduces its leverage by selling $1,000,000 in stock and retiring an equal amount of debt, the cost of debt will not change, but the cost of equity is expected to fall to 9.5 percent. Would you recommend the reduction in leverage? Why or why not?

18-5 A company with earnings before interest and taxes, EBIT, of $80,000 is attempting to evaluate a number of possible capital structures. Although the firm recognizes that it cannot determine its optimal capital structure, there are five possible capital structures it wishes to consider. These capital structures, along with their associated debt and equity capital costs, are given below. Note: ignore taxes.

Capital structure	Debt in capital structure	Cost of debt	Cost of equity
A	$100,000	5%	8.00%
B	$200,000	5%	8.25%
C	$300,000	6%	8.50%
D	$400,000	7%	9.00%
E	$500,000	9%	10.50%

    a Calculate the firm's value for each of the capital structures.

    b Calculate the debt-equity ratio and overall capitalization rate for each structure.

    c Tabulate the results of **a** and **b**.

    d Using this data, graph the firm's debt, equity, and overall cost functions.

    e Which capital structure would you recommend? Why?

18-6   Western Oil Corporation has a current financial structure consisting of $500,000 of 8-percent debt, 1000 shares of 7-percent, $100-par-value preferred stock, and 2000 shares of common stock. The firm pays taxes at the rate of 40 percent on ordinary income.

    a Using EBIT values of $80,000 and $120,000, determine the associated earnings per share (eps).

    b Calculate the financial breakeven point for this financial structure.

    c Graph the firm's current financial structure on a set of EBIT-eps axes.

18-7   Parker Petroleum is considering two financing plans. The key information follows. Assume a 40-percent tax rate on ordinary income.

Sources of funds	Plan A	Plan B
Long-term debt	$200,000 @ 8%	$400,000 @ 8.5%
Preferred stock	2000 shares,	1000 shares,
	9%, $100 par	9%, $100 par
Common stock	4000 shares	2000 shares

    a Calculate two EBIT-eps coordinates for each of the plans.

    b Determine the financial breakeven point for each plan.

    c Plot the two financing plans on a set of EBIT-eps axes.

    d Indicate over what EBIT range, if any, each plan is preferred.

    e Discuss the leverage and risk aspects of each plan.

    f If the firm is fairly certain its EBIT will exceed $75,000, which plan would you recommend? Why?

18-8   Wonder Diaper is considering two possible financing plans, A and B:

Source of funds	Plan A	Plan B
Long-term debt	$150,000 @ 8%	$100,000 @ 7.5%
Preferred stock	$ 20,000 @ 9%	$ 30,000 @ 9%
Common stock	8,000 shares @ $20	10,000 shares @ $20

    a Calculate the financial breakeven point for each plan. Assume a 40-percent tax rate on ordinary income.

    b Graph the two financing plans on the same set of EBIT-eps axes.

    c Discuss the leverage and risk associated with each of the plans.

    d Over what range of EBIT would each plan be preferred?

    e Which plan would you recommend if the firm expects its EBIT to be $35,000? Explain.

18-9   The General Telephone Company wishes to evaluate three proposed financing plans in order to determine the best way to raise a needed $400,000. Due to the relatively small amount of money being raised, the firm believes that its financing cost and share price will be unaffected by the selection of a particular plan. Long-term debt is expected to cost 7 percent, 9-percent preferred stock can be issued, and common stock can be sold for $40 per share. The firm is subject to a 40-percent tax rate on ordinary income. The three financing plans are given:

Source of funds	Plan A	Plan B	Plan C
Long-term debt	0%	60%	30%
Preferred stock	0%	10%	20%
Common stock	100%	30%	50%

    a Calculate the financial breakeven point for each plan.

    b Graph each of the plans on a set of EBIT-eps axes.

    c If the firm expects its EBIT to be $50,000, what is the interest and preferred dividends coverage ratio for each plan? Evaluate the leverage and risk associated with each plan at an EBIT of $50,000.

    d Discuss the conditions or levels of EBIT that would cause you to prefer each plan.

18-10 The Hot Drop Forge Company is attempting to evaluate four possible financing plans in order to determine which is most likely to maximize its earnings per share. The firm is subject to a 40-percent tax rate on ordinary income. The details of each plan are as follows:

Plan	Debt	Preferred stock	Common stock
A	$300,000 @ 9%	0	10,000 shares
B	$200,000 @ 8.5%	3,000 shares of $75 par @ 8%	7,500 shares
C	$0	2,000 shares of $75 par @ 8%	15,000 shares
D	$500,000 @ 9.5%	0	5,000 shares

    a Calculate the financial breakeven point for each plan.

    b Graph the four plans on the same set of EBIT-eps axes.

    c Discuss the leverage and financial risk associated with each plan.

    d Discuss the circumstances, if any, in which each plan would be preferred.

18-11 Using the balance sheet of the National Steel Company below:

Balance Sheet
National Steel Company
Year Ending December 31

Assets		Liabilities and stockholders' equity	
Cash	$ 90,000	Accounts payable	$180,000
Marketable securities	20,000	Notes payable	60,000
Accounts receivable	200,000	Accruals	40,000
Inventory	210,000	Total current	
Total current assets	$ 520,000	liabilities	$280,000
Fixed assets	$1,680,000	Long-term debt	$800,000
Total Assets	$2,200,000	Preferred stock ($100	
		par)	$300,000
		Common stock (20,000	
		shares)	500,000
		Paid-in capital in	
		excess of par	200,000
		Retained earnings	120,000
		Total Liabilities and	
		Stockholders'	
		Equity	$2,200,000

    a Determine the firm's book value per share. Comment on the usefulness of the book value figure.

    b If the firm believes it can sell various assets and receive for them the percentages of book value:

Accounts receivable	95% of book value
Inventory	65% of book value
Fixed assets	80% of book value

(1) Determine the liquidation value of each asset and the firm.
(2) Determine the liquidation value per share of common stock.
(3) Compare the book value per share to the liquidation value per share, and discuss the relevance of the two.

18-12 The balance sheet for the Imperial Mill Company follows:

Balance Sheet
Imperial Mill Company
Year Ending December 31

Assets		Liabilities and stockholders' equity	
Cash	$ 20,000	Accounts payable	$ 50,000
Marketable securities	30,000	Notes payable	15,000
Accounts receivable	60,000	Accrued wages	15,000
Inventory	80,000	Total current liabilities	$80,000
Total current assets	$190,000	Long-term debt	$ 90,000
Fixed assets	$200,000	Preferred stock	$ 40,000
Total Assets	$390,000	Common stock (1,000 shares)	180,000
		Total Liabilities and Stockholders' Equity	$390,000

The following additional information with respect to the firm is available:
(1) Preferred stock can be liquidated for its book value.
(2) Accounts receivable and inventory can be liquidated at 90 percent of book value.
(3) The firm has 1000 shares of common stock outstanding.
(4) All dividends and interest are currently paid up.
(5) Fixed assets can be liquidated at 70 percent of book value.
(6) Cash and marketable securities can be liquidated at book value.
Given this information, answer the following:
a How large is Imperial Mill's book value per share?
b How large is their liquidation value per share?
c Compare, contrast, and discuss the values found in **a** and **b**.

18-13 Given the forecast earnings for each of five firms in the same industry, estimate their values using the industry capitalization approach assuming that the average price-earnings ratio for the industry is 12.

Company	Forecast eps
A	$3.00
B	$4.50
C	$1.80
D	$2.40
E	$5.10

18-14   For each of the five firms in the following table, determine the historical growth rate of earnings.

Year	A	B	Earnings C	D	E
1978	$3.40	$.80	$4.25	$1.00	$7.00
1977	3.00	.80	4.00	.98	6.40
1976	2.80	.78	3.80	.97	5.00
1975	2.50	.76	3.65	.90	5.80
1974	2.40	.75	3.53	.85	4.50

18-15   The Baxter Boiler Company has paid the following dividends over the past six years:

Year	Dividend per share
1978	$2.87
1977	3.76
1976	2.60
1975	2.46
1974	2.37
1973	2.25

The firm's dividend per share next year is expected to be $3.02. If you can earn 13 percent on similar-risk investments, what is the most you would pay per share for this firm? Explain your answer.

18-16   Jackson Steel Company wishes to determine the value of Acme Foundry, a firm that it is considering acquiring for cash. Jackson wishes to use the capital asset pricing model (CAPM) to determine the applicable discount rate to use as an input to the Gordon valuation model. Because Acme's stock is not publicly traded, Jackson, after studying the betas of similar firms (to Acme) that are publicly traded, believes that an appropriate beta for Acme's stock would be 1.25. The risk-free rate is currently 7 percent and the market return is 11 percent. Acme's historic dividend per share for each of the past six years is given below:

Year	Dividend per share
1978	$3.44
1977	3.28
1976	3.15
1975	2.90
1974	2.75
1973	2.45

a   Given that Acme is expected to pay a dividend of $3.68 per share next year, determine the maximum cash price that Jackson should pay for each share of Acme.

   b Discuss the use of the CAPM for estimating the cost of equity and describe the effect on the resulting value (of Acme) of
   (1) An increase in the risk-free rate to 8 percent.
   (2) A decrease in the beta to 1.0.
   (3) An increase in the market return to 12 percent.
   (4) All of the above changes.

SELECTED REFERENCES

Barges, Alexander, *The Effect of Capital Structure on the Cost of Capital* (Englewood Cliffs, N.J.: Prentice-Hall, 1963).

Basu, Sanjoy, "The Information Content of Price-Earnings Ratios," *Financial Management 4* (Summer 1975), pp. 53–64.

Beranek, William, *The Effects of Leverage on the Market Value of Common Stocks* (Madison: University of Wisconsin School of Commerce, 1964).

Bower, Richard S., and Dorothy M. Bower, "Risk and the Valuation of Common Stock," *Journal of Political Economy 77* (May-June 1969), pp. 349–362.

Durand, David, "Cost of Debt and Equity Funds for Business: Trends and Problems of Measurement," reprinted in *The Management of Corporate Capital*, Ezra Solomon, Ed. (New York: Free Press, 1959), pp. 91–116.

Gordon, Myron J., *The Investment, Financing, and Valuation of the Corporation* (Homewood, Ill.: Irwin, 1962).

Hamada, Robert S., "The Effect of the Firm's Capital Structure on the Systematic Risk of Common Stocks," *Journal of Finance 27* (May 1972), pp. 435–452.

Haugen, Robert A., and Dean W. Wichern, "The Intricate Relationship Between Financial Leverage and the Stability of Stock Prices," *Journal of Finance 30* (December 1975), pp. 1283–1292.

Hubbard, Charles L., and Clark A. Hawkins, *Theory of Valuation* (Scranton, Pa.: Intext, 1969).

Kraft, John, and Arthur Kraft, "Determinants of Common Stock Prices: A Time Series Analysis," *Journal of Finance 33* (May 1977), pp. 417–425.

Krouse, Clement G., "Optimal Financing and Capital Structure Programs for the Firm," *Journal of Finance 27* (December 1972), pp. 1057–1072.

Lerner, Eugene M., and Willard T. Carleton, *A Theory of Financial Analysis* (New York: Harcourt Brace Jovanovich, 1966).

Lewellen, Wilbur G., and John J. McConnell, "Tax Reform, Firm Valuation, and Capital Costs," *Financial Management 6* (Winter 1977), pp. 59–66.

Malkiel, Burton G., *The Debt-Equity Combination of the Firm and the Cost of Capital: An Introductory Analysis* (New York: General Learning Press, 1971).

Martin, John D., and David F. Scott, Jr., "A Discriminant Analysis of the Corporate Debt-Equity Decisions," *Financial Management 3* (Winter 1974), pp. 71–87.

Modigliani, Franco, and Merton H. Miller, "The Cost of Capital, Corporation Finance, and the Theory of Investment," *American Economic Review 48* (June 1958), pp. 261–296.

——, "Dividend Policy, Growth and the Valuation of Shares," *Journal of Business 34* (October 1961), pp. 411–432.

Olsen, I. J., "Valuation of a Closely Held Corporation," *Journal of Accountancy 128* (August 1969), pp. 35–47.

Pfahl, John K., David T. Crary, and R. Hayden Howard, "The Limits of Leverage," *Financial Executive 38* (May 1970), pp. 48–56.

Porterfield, James T. S., *Investment Decisions and Capital Costs* (Englewood Cliffs, N.J.: Prentice-Hall, 1965).

Pringle, John J., "Price/Earnings Ratios, Earnings per Share, and Financial Management," *Financial Management 2* (Spring 1973), pp. 34–40.

Robichek, Alexander A., "Risk and the Value of Securities," *Journal of Financial and Quantitative Analysis 4* (December 1969), pp. 513–538.

Senchack, Andrew J., "The Firm's Optimal Financial Policies: Solution, Equilibrium, and Stability," *Journal of Financial and Quantitative Analysis 10* (November 1975), pp. 543–555.

Schwartz, Eli, and J. Richard Aronson, "Some Surrogate Evidence in Support of the Concept of Optimal Capital Structure," *Journal of Finance 22* (March 1967), pp. 10–18.

Scott, David F., Jr., "Evidence on the Importance of Financial Structure," *Financial Management 1* (Summer 1972), pp. 45–50.

Scott, David F., and John D. Martin, "Industry Influence on Financial Structure," *Financial Management 4* (Spring 1975), pp. 67–73.

Scott, J. H., "A Theory of Optimal Capital Structure," *Bell Journal of Economics and Management Science 7* (Spring 1976), pp. 33–54.

Sloane, William R., and Arnold Reisman, "Stock Evaluation Theory: Classification, Reconciliation, and General Model," *Journal of Financial and Quantitative Analysis 3* (June 1968), pp. 171–204.

Solomon, Ezra, *The Theory of Financial Management* (New York: Columbia University Press, 1963).

Taggart, Robert A., Jr., "A Model of Corporate Financing Decisions," *Journal of Finance 32* (December 1977), pp. 1467–1484.

Wippern, Ronald F., "Financial Structure and the Value of the Firm," *Journal of Finance 21* (December 1966), pp. 615–634.

PART SEVEN

This part of the text discusses the various types of long-term financing available to the business firm. These include leasing, debt, preferred and common stock, convertible securities and warrants, and dividends and retained earnings. There are six chapters. Chapter 19 describes the types and functions of financial intermediaries and the markets for short- and long-term financing. It sets the stage for the following five chapters by its description of the market for long-term funds. Chapter 20 describes leasing as a form of long-term financing. Chapter 21 discusses long-term debt financing, including long-term loans and the sale of bonds. Chapter 22 discusses the key aspects of preferred and common stock. Chapter 23 describes the nature and uses of convertible securities and warrants that are often used to enhance the firm's ability to obtain long-term funds. Finally, Chapter 24 discusses dividends and retained earnings, two closely related factors in financing decisions. The key emphasis in this part of the text is on the various forms of long-term financing as viewed by the corporate fund raiser.

Sources of long-term financing

BALANCE SHEET	
Assets	Liabilities and Stockholders' Equity
Current Assets	Current Liabilities
Fixed Assets	Long-Term Debt
	Stockholders' Equity

CHAPTER 19
Financial intermediaries and markets

A corporation does not operate in a financial vacuum; on the contrary, it operates in close contact with the various financial intermediaries and markets. This close relationship to the various financial media allows the firm to obtain needed financing and also to invest idle funds in various financial instruments. Large corporations find it necessary to frequent the financial marketplace, while small corporations may visit these markets relatively infrequently. Regardless of the size of the firm, the various financial media act as clearing mechanisms, matching the suppliers and demanders of funds and giving a structure to the fund-raising and investing process.

The emergence of strong financial intermediaries and markets is greatly responsible for the existence of large-scale business firms. Without some mechanism through which idle funds could be attracted by firms needing funds for investment in current and fixed assets, companies such as General Motors and American Telephone and Telegraph would have been unable to reach their current size. Not only do these financial media make funds available, but they allocate funds through the pricing mechanism. Firms that have uncertain future prospects must compensate suppliers of funds by providing higher returns; firms with quite predictable futures, such as public utilities, do not have to offer such high returns.

In this chapter, we shall discuss the key aspects of both financial intermediaries and financial markets. A broad understanding of the nature and role of these financial media will give the reader a better understanding of the firm's financing decisions. The chapter has four basic sections. The first section discusses the broad framework of financial intermediaries and markets and their role in our economy. The second section is devoted solely to a discussion of the money market. The third section presents a brief discussion of the key aspects of capital markets. Finally, the last section presents a discussion of the function and importance of the investment banker in capital markets.

FINANCIAL INTERMEDIARIES
AND MARKETS: AN OVERVIEW

There are three external ways by which available funds can be transmitted to firms requiring funds. One way is through a *financial intermediary*, which is an institution that accepts savings and transfers them to those needing funds. Another way is through *financial markets*, organized forums where the suppliers and demanders of various types of funds can make transactions. A third way in which funds can be transferred from a saver to an investor is through a direct placement arrangement. Due to the unstructured nature of direct placements, in this section we shall focus primarily on financial intermediaries and financial markets. However, the direct placement of funds is not unusual—especially in the case of debt instruments and preferred stock.

Financial intermediaries

Financial intermediaries, or *financial institutions*, channel the savings of various parties into loans or investments.[1] The process by which savings are accumulated by financial institutions and then lent or invested is generally referred to as *intermediation*.[2] Many financial institutions directly or indirectly pay savers interest on deposited funds; others provide services for which they charge depositors. (For example, commercial banks levy service charges on checking accounts, thereby indirectly charging depositors in these accounts.) Some financial intermediaries accept savings and lend this money to their customers, others accept savings and then invest the funds in earning assets such as real estate or stocks and bonds, and still others both lend and invest money. In most instances, a financial intermediary must operate within certain legal constraints on the type of loans or investments, or both, that can be made. A brief discussion of the key participants in financial transactions and the key institutions acting as intermediaries follows.

Key participants in financial transactions.
The key suppliers and demanders of funds are individuals, businesses, and governments. The role of each of these in financial transactions is discussed separately below.

Individuals. The savings of individual consumers placed in certain financial institutions provide these institutions with a large portion of the funds they lend or invest. Individual savings may be kept in a checking or a savings account in a commercial bank, or in savings accounts in a savings and loan association or a credit union. They may be used to purchase life insurance, contributed to pension funds, or used to make other types of deposits. Indi-

---

[1]When a financial institution receives deposits or borrows money, it can either lend the money out directly or invest it in other types of earning assets such as real estate or stocks and bonds. Some institutions primarily make loans, while others primarily invest their money. In this chapter the terms "loans" and "investments" are used interchangeably to mean the placement of funds in some type of earning instrument.

[2]Often during inflationary periods as a result of the high interest rates available from media other than financial institutions, the process of *disintermediation* takes place. This process is one in which depositors withdraw their funds from financial institutions and invest them in the higher yielding marketable securities.

viduals not only act as suppliers of funds to intermediaries, but they also obtain funds in the form of loans from various intermediaries. Individuals may borrow money from commercial banks, savings and loan associations, credit unions, life insurance companies and other institutions. In summary, individuals can be viewed as both suppliers of funds to and demanders of funds from financial intermediaries. The important point to recognize is that individuals as a group are *net suppliers*. They save more money than they borrow, thereby providing funds for use by others.

Businesses.   Business firms also place some of their funds with financial intermediaries, primarily in checking accounts with various commercial banks. Firms, like individuals, also obtain funds from various financial institutions. They borrow primarily from commercial banks, commercial finance companies, life insurance companies, and pension funds. Business firms as a group are *net demanders* of funds. They borrow more money than they save.

Governments.   The federal government maintains deposits of temporarily idle funds, certain tax payments, and social security payments in commercial banks. It does not borrow funds directly from financial institutions, but does obtain needed financing through the financial markets. State and local governments behave similarly by maintaining bank deposits and raising needed financing in the financial markets. When one considers the savings and borrowings of various levels of government in the financial marketplace, the government, like business firms, is typically a *net demander* of money since it borrows more than it saves.

Key financial intermediaries.   The key financial intermediaries in the United States economy are commercial banks, mutual savings banks, savings and loan associations, credit unions, life insurance companies, and pension funds. These institutions attract funds from individuals, business, and government, combine them into large amounts, and perform certain services to make attractive loans available to individuals and businesses. They may also make some of these funds available to fulfill various government demands for funds through the financial markets. The key financial intermediaries are briefly described below.

Commercial banks.   The *commercial bank* is an important financial intermediary. It accepts both demand (checking) and time (savings) deposits, which it then loans out directly to borrowers or through the financial markets.[3] The primary type of loan made by a commercial bank is a short-term unse-

---

[3]Prior to mid-November 1975, business firms (except certain charitable organizations) were legally prohibited from maintaining savings deposits in commercial banks. A change in the law at that time now permits businesses to maintain savings deposits of up to $150,000 at a commercial bank. This change in the law was made in order to provide the small business with a mechanism whereby some return could be conveniently earned on temporarily idle funds; large businesses were not significantly impacted by this change.

cured business loan. A discussion of short-term commercial bank loans to business was included in Chapters 11 and 12. Commercial banks also make some installment and mortgage loans to individuals. The commercial bank is an important financial intermediary, especially in accumulating funds from individuals and lending them to business.

Mutual savings banks. *Mutual savings banks* are similar to commercial banks except that they may not hold demand (checking) deposits.[4] They get their funds from savings deposits, and they make these funds available to various business firms. They generally lend or invest funds through financial markets rather than through negotiated loans, although they do make some residential real estate loans to individuals. Mutual savings banks are located primarily in New York, New Jersey, and the New England states.

Savings and loan associations. *Savings and loan associations* are similar to mutual savings banks in that they hold only savings deposits, which they lend out primarily to individuals for real estate mortgage loans. Some savings and loan funds are channeled into investments in the financial markets. Savings and loan associations also raise some of their capital through the sale of securities in the financial markets. Since savings and loan associations are quite dominant in the mortgage lending area, certain federal agencies often become involved in lending money to them to finance certain types of real estate mortgages. Business firms, in their day-to-day fund-raising activities, do not generally become involved with savings and loan associations.

Credit unions. A *credit union* is a financial intermediary that deals primarily in transfers of funds between consumers. Membership in a credit union is generally based on some common bond such as working for the same employer or attending the same church. Credit unions accept members' savings deposits and then lend the majority of these funds to other members, who typically use the money to purchase automobiles or appliances or make home improvements. If the demand for loans is not great enough to absorb all the available funds, the credit union may channel some of its funds into short-term investments through the financial markets. When a credit union needs additional funds, it generally borrows them directly from a commercial bank.

Life insurance companies. Insurance companies, specifically life insurance companies, are the largest financial intermediary handling individual savings. Although a person generally purchases life insurance to provide for his or her beneficiaries after death, most life insurance (i.e., whole life and endowment policies) has a savings function. A portion of each premium payment goes to cover the death benefit, but the remainder is invested in order

---

[4]Commercial banks are the only financial institutions that are legally permitted to hold checking accounts (demand deposits).

to cover death losses in later years. In other words, life insurance companies receive large amounts of premium payments that must be invested to accumulate funds to cover future claims. Thus they act as financial intermediaries that transfer the savings of individuals into loans and investments. Some life insurance money is lent directly to individuals, business, and government; another portion is channeled through the financial markets to those who demand funds.

Pension funds. *Pension funds* are set up so that employees of various institutions can receive income after retirement. There are numerous types of pension plan arrangements. Quite often employers contribute to a pension fund, matching in some way the contributions of their employees; occasionally employer contributions are based on a profit-sharing arrangement. In essence, pension funds represent an accumulation of savings that will be disbursed in future years. Pension fund dollars are loaned or invested in numerous areas. Some of the money is transferred directly to various borrowers, but the majority of it is lent or invested via the financial markets. The largest pension fund is the federal Old Age Survivors and Disability Insurance System, or Social Security Plan, to which nearly all of us belong. Most Social Security funds are lent to other agencies of the federal government.

The financial intermediaries described above are the key financial institutions in the United States economy, although other institutions such as charitable organizations, small business investment companies, and commercial finance companies also act as financial intermediaries. Of the key financial intermediaries, commercial banks, life insurance companies, and pension funds are the major suppliers of loans and investments to business firms. Most of the dollars provided are not channeled directly to business firms but pass through the financial markets. Without these institutions, the funds available for business financing would be significantly reduced.

Financial markets

Financial markets permit the demanders and suppliers of short-term and long-term loans and investments to transact business directly. Whereas the loans and investments of financial intermediaries are made without the direct knowledge of the fund suppliers (i.e., savers), suppliers in the financial marketplace know exactly where their funds are being lent or invested. The two key financial markets are the *money market* and the *capital market*. Transactions in short-term debt instruments or marketable securities take place in the money market. Long-term securities (stocks and bonds) are traded in the capital market.

The relationship between financial intermediaries and financial markets

Financial intermediaries and financial markets are not independent of each other; on the contrary, it is quite common to find financial intermediaries actively participating in both the money market and the capital market, as both suppliers and demanders of funds. Figure 19.1 depicts the general flow

FIGURE 19.1 Financial intermediaries and markets

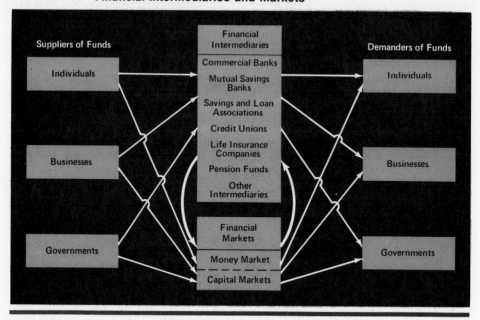

of funds through and between financial intermediaries and financial markets. The individuals, businesses, and governments that supply and demand funds may be domestic or foreign. In some instances there may be legal constraints on the operations of certain institutions in the financial marketplace. Because of the key importance of the money and capital markets to the business firm, the next two sections of this chapter will be devoted solely to these topics.

THE MONEY MARKET

The money market is created by an intangible relationship between the suppliers and demanders of short-term funds. It is not an actual organization housed in some central location, such as a stock market, although the majority of money market transactions culminate in New York City. Except for certain types of bank-to-bank transactions, money market transactions are made in marketable securities. The money market exists because certain individuals, businesses, governments, and financial intermediaries have temporarily idle funds that they wish to place in some type of liquid asset or short-term interest-earnings instrument, while other individuals, businesses, governments, and financial intermediaries find themselves in situations where they need additional seasonal or temporary financing. The money market brings together these suppliers and demanders of short-term funds.

The operation of the money market

Since the money market is intangible, one may wonder how the suppliers and demanders of short-term funds are brought together to engage in transactions. Typically, suppliers and demanders of short-term funds are matched through the facilities of large New York banks, through government security dealers, or through the federal reserve banks. The federal reserve banks typically become involved only in loans from one commercial bank to another; these loans are commonly referred to as transactions in *federal funds*. A number of stock brokerage firms purchase various money market instruments for resale to customers. If a brokerage firm does not have an instrument demanded by a customer, it will attempt to acquire it.

Most money market transactions are negotiated by telephone. A firm wishing to purchase a certain marketable security may call its bank, which will then attempt to buy the securities by contacting a New York bank or another bank known to "make a market" or deal in the given security. The bank or the firm itself may also go directly to a government security dealer, a type of intermediary that primarily purchases for resale various government securities and other money market instruments, in order to negotiate a transaction. Regardless of whether a business or government is issuing a money market instrument (demanding short-term funds) or purchasing a money market instrument (supplying short-term funds), one party must go directly to another party or use a middleman such as a commercial bank, government security dealer, or brokerage firm to make a transaction.

The key to successful transactions in the money market is knowing *who* is willing to buy or sell a given instrument at a certain time. Firms that make frequent transactions in the money market become aware of the dealers in the market, while firms that make less frequent transactions generally have to pay a bank, brokerage firm, or government security dealer to facilitate a transaction. Individuals wishing to purchase money market instruments (i.e., marketable securities) generally must go through a dealer firm. Purchasers of marketable securities must sell these securities to get their money back before the securities mature. The *secondary* (or *resale*) *market* for marketable securities is no different from *the primary* (or *initial issue*) *market* with respect to the basic transactions that are made.

Participants in the money market

As Figure 19.1 indicated, the key participants in the money market include individuals, businesses, governments, and financial intermediaries. Individuals participate both as purchasers and sellers of money market instruments. Their purchases are somewhat limited due to the large denominations— typically $100,000 or more—of money market instruments traded. Of course, certain banks and stock brokerage firms will "break down" marketable securities and make them available in smaller denominations than the initial issue. Individuals sell marketable securities in the money market not as issuers, but in order to liquidate the securities prior to maturity. Individuals do not initially issue marketable securities.

Business firms, governments, and financial institutions both buy and sell marketable securities. They may be the primary issuers of marketable securities, or they may sell securities they have purchased and wish to liquidate prior to maturity. They therefore may act as either primary or secondary sellers of these securities. Of course, each of these parties can issue only certain money market instruments; a business firm, for example, cannot issue a treasury bill. Some financial institutions purchase marketable securities specifically for resale, while others purchase these securities as short-term investments. Businesses and governments purchase marketable securities solely to earn a return on temporarily idle funds.

Money market instruments

The key money market instruments include treasury bills, tax-anticipation bills, treasury notes, federal agency issues, negotiable certificates of deposit, commercial paper, banker's acceptances, and repurchase agreements. These marketable securities were briefly described in the second half of Chapter 8. It is important for the reader to have a general understanding of the key characteristics of these instruments. One characteristic common to all of them is their liquidity. The yields on these securities reflect directly the "tightness" or "looseness" of money. Differences in yield between various instruments result from the different degrees of "risk" associated with the issuers. Although the list of securities given above is not all-inclusive, it does contain the key money market instruments available to the corporate purchaser. The only money market instrument actually issued by a nonfinancial corporate business is commercial paper.

THE CAPITAL MARKETS

Capital markets are created by a number of institutions and arrangements that allow the suppliers and demanders of *long-term funds* to make transactions. Included among these transactions are transactions in the debt and equity issues of businesses and the debt issues of local, state, and federal governments. Capital markets are of key importance to the long-run growth and prosperity of business and government organizations since they provide the funds needed to acquire fixed assets and implement programs aimed at insuring the organizations' continued existence. The backbone of the capital markets is the various security exchanges, which provide a marketplace for debt and equity transactions.

The functions of security exchanges

Capital markets are necessary for the stock of capital goods in the economy to grow. They permit those segments of the economy that need capital to acquire plant and equipment to obtain funds from the numerous savers in the economy. Just as financial intermediaries collect savings from numerous parties and lend them to acceptable borrowers, so too do the capital markets permit the conversion of savings into investment, either through loans or through the sale of ownership interests. They permit individuals, businesses, governments, and financial institutions to channel their savings into long-term loans or purchases of equity in businesses, government, and financial institutions.

The key factor differentiating money and capital markets is that the capital markets provide permanent or long-term funds for the firm while the money market provides short-term debt financing. Although both markets are important to the longevity of business and government, the capital markets provide the mechanism whereby large sums of money can be raised to increase the productive capability of the economy. The organized security exchanges that make up the capital markets actually perform a number of important functions, such as creating a continuous market, allocating scarce capital, determining and publicizing security prices, and aiding in new financing.

Creating a continuous market. The key function of a securities market is to create a continuous market for securities at a price that is not very different from the price at which they were previously sold. The continuity of security markets provides securities with the *liquidity* necessary to attract investors' funds. Without securities markets, investors might have to hold debt securities to maturity and equity securities indefinitely. It is doubtful that many people would be willing to invest under such conditions. A continuous market also reduces the volatility of security prices, further enhancing their liquidity.

Allocating scarce capital. The securities markets help allocate scarce funds to the best uses. That is, by disclosing the price behavior of various securities and requiring the disclosure of certain corporate financial data, they allow prospective and existing investors to assess risk-return trade-offs and to move their funds into the most promising investments. An *efficient market* is one that allocates funds to the most productive uses. Although they are not truly efficient, security markets are a step in the direction of market efficiency.

Determining and publicizing security prices. Security exchanges both determine and publicize security prices. The price of an individual security is determined by what is bought and sold, or the demand of and supply for the security. A capital market brings together buyers and sellers from all geographic areas while still affording them some anonymity. This helps to ensure a price that reflects the true value of the security. Changing evaluations of a firm, of course, cause changes in the supply of and demand for its securities and ultimately result in a new price for the securities. Since the prices of securities are readily available to interested parties, they can use this information to make better purchase and sale decisions.

Aiding in new financing. Security markets also provide firms with a method of obtaining new financing. Since the markets are continuous, thereby ensuring investor liquidity, new capital can be raised through new security issues. Of course, not all firms have access to those markets in order to raise new capital, but the presence of organized markets does give certain firms direct access to the savings of individuals, other firms, and financial institutions in order to finance new capital expenditures. Without these markets, new capital could be obtained only through direct negotiations with holders of large amounts of money. This obviously would be quite tedious.

Characteristics of security exchanges

Security exchanges are the key institutions making up capital markets. Many people refer to these exchanges as "stock markets"; however, this phrase is somewhat misleading since both stocks and bonds are traded on these exchanges. There are two key types of security exchange—organized exchanges and the over-the-counter exchange.

Organized security exchanges. *Organized security exchanges* are tangible organizations on whose premises securities are traded. The key exchanges are the New York Stock Exchange (NYSE) and the American Stock Exchange (AMEX), both headquartered in New York City and accounting for approximately 65 and 25 percent, respectively, of the total annual volume of shares traded. Each of these exchanges has its own building, membership, and trading rules. Other regional exchanges, such as the Midwest Stock Exchange, the Pacific Coast Stock Exchange, and the Boston Stock Exchange, account for only about 7 percent of the annual share volume on organized exchanges. In all, there are 11 regional exchanges that deal primarily in the trading of securities with local or regional appeal. Since most of the exchanges are modeled after the New York Stock Exchange, a brief discussion of its membership, its policies with respect to listing securities, trading activity, and reporting market activity is in order.

Membership. Membership in the New York Stock Exchange is expensive. In order to become a member, an individual or firm must own a "seat" on the exchange. The word "seat" is used only figuratively, since members trade securities standing up. There are a total of 1366 seats on the NYSE. Seats on the exchange have sold for as much as $125,000 (in 1929) and as little as $4000 (in 1876 and 1878), although most recently they have gone for about $100,000. Most seats are owned by brokerage firms, and many brokerage firms own more than one seat. The largest brokerage firm, Merrill Lynch, Pierce, Fenner & Smith, owns seven seats. Firms such as Merrill Lynch designate officers to occupy a seat. Only designated seat holders are permitted to make transactions on the floor of the exchange. The membership of the exchange is often divided into broad classes based on the members' activities. Membership on the American and other stock exchanges is obtained in a similar manner, but the cost of a seat is generally less and the other requirements are not as strict.

Listing policies. In order to become listed on an organized stock exchange, a firm must file an application for listing. Some firms are listed on more than one exchange. The New York Stock Exchange has the most stringent listing requirements. Currently over 1500 firms, accounting for over 2100 stocks, and over 1050 issuers, accounting for over 2600 bonds, are listed on the NYSE. In order to be eligible for listing on the NYSE, a firm must have at least 2000 stockholders owning 100 shares (i.e., a *round lot*) or more. It must have a minimum of 1 million shares of stock outstanding that is publicly held; it must have a demonstrated earning power of $2.5 million before taxes at the time of the listing; it must have a total of $16 million in market value of publicly traded shares; and, finally, it must pay a listing fee. Once a firm's stock has been accepted for listing, it must meet certain requirements of the Securities and Exchange Commission (SEC), which regulates certain aspects of listed securities. If listed firms do not continue to meet certain requirements, they may be *de-listed* from the exchange. The listing requirements of other exchanges are more lenient than those of the NYSE.

Trading activity. Trading is carried out on the floor of an exchange. The floor of the NYSE is an area about the size of a football field. On the floor are 18 trading posts and around the perimeter are telephones and telegraphs, which are used primarily to transmit buy and sell orders from brokers' offices to the exchange floor and back again once an order has been executed. Certain *stocks* are traded at each of the 18 trading posts. At the NYSE, there is an annex where *bonds* and less active stocks are traded. All trades are made on the floor of the exchange by the occupants of seats. Only these people can make transactions on the floor. Trades are made primarily in *round lots* (lots of 100 shares) not *odd lots* (lots of less than 100 shares). Certain specialists known as *odd-lot brokers* make odd-lot transactions. The general procedure for placing and executing an order can be described by a simple example.

EXAMPLE
Sally Jones, who has an account with Merrill Lynch, Pierce, Fenner & Smith (MLPF & S), wishes to purchase 200 shares of the Cities Service Company at the prevailing market price. Sally calls her account executive, Abe Cohen of Merrill Lynch, and places her order.[5] Abe immediately has the order transmitted to the New York headquarters of Merrill Lynch, which immediately forwards the order to the Merrill Lynch clerk on the floor of the exchange. The clerk dispatches the order to one of the firm's seat holders, who goes to the appropriate trading post, executes the order at the best possible price, and returns to the clerk, who then wires the execution price and confirmation of the transaction back to the brokerage office. Abe is then given the relevant information and passes it along to Sally. Abe then has certain paperwork to do. ●

Only a matter of minutes are required for an order, once placed, to be executed, thanks to sophisticated telecommunication devices. A sale of securities would have been handled in a similar manner.

All transactions on the floor of the exchange are made through an *auction process*. The goal is to fill all *buy orders* at the lowest price and to fill all *sell orders* at the highest price, thereby giving both purchasers and sellers the best possible deal. The actual auction process is quite complicated. New security issues of listed firms are generally handled in a special way, so that the market can absorb them at a reasonable price.

---

[5]The title "account executive" is often used to refer to an individual who traditionally has been called a "stockbroker." The account executive title is believed to add respectability to the position and change the image of the stockbroker from that of a salesperson to that of a personal financial manager who provides diversified financial services to his or her clients.

FIGURE 19.2 New York Stock Exchange stock price quotations

52 Weeks High	52 Weeks Low	Stocks	Div.	Yld %	P-E Ratio	Sales 100s	High	Low	Close	Net Chg.
29⅞	21½	ChiPrieT	2	6.8	16	53	29⅜	29⅛	29¼	− ¼
7⅜	3⅛	ChkFull		..	..	155	u 7½	7⅛	7½	+ ⅛
10⅝	4⅜	ChrisCft		..	24	131	9⅜	9⅛	9¼	.....
20⅜	14⅜	Chromal	1	5.1	6	146	20⅛	19½	19½	.....
79	61	Chroma	pf5	6.6	..	12	77	75½	75½	−1½
17½	10¾	Chrysler	1	8.5	..	1006	12	11¾	11¾	.....
44⅛	20⅛	ChurCh	.84	2.0	12	61	43¼	42½	42½	− ⅜
30¼	26¼	CinBell	1.92	6.8	6	35	28¾	28⅜	28⅜	− ⅝
25⅞	20	CinGE	1.84	8.9	8	82	20¾	20½	20¾	+ ¼
50	42½	CinG	pf 4	9.2	..	z250	43⅝	43½	43½	.....
110½	101½	CinG	pf 9.30	8.9	..	z500	104	104	104	+1½
109½	102	CinG	pf 9.28	9.0	..	z10	103¼	103¼	103¼	.....
112	104	CinG	pf 9.52	9.0	..	z1050	105¾	105½	105½	.....
30⅜	17⅝	CinMil	.90	3.0	9	285	30⅜	30	30⅛	+ ⅛
30½	18⅞	Citicrp	1.16	4.4	8	3328	26⅛	25¾	26⅛	+ ¼
63	45⅛	CitiesSv	3	5.7	7	244	52½	51⅞	52¼	+ ¼
16¼	11⅜	CityInv	1	6.5	5	216	15⅝	15¼	15⅜	− ⅛
1½	1-64	CityInv	wt	..	..	220	1½	1¼	1¼	− ⅛
33	26⅛	CityIn	pf1.31	4.1	..	1	32	32	32	−1
27⅞	22⅜	CityIn	pf 2	7.4	..	98	27	26⅝	26⅞	+ ⅛
12⅛	10⅞	Cityh	pf1.10	10.	..	70	11	10⅞	10⅞	− ⅛
42⅝	28⅝	ClarkE	1.80	4.6	8	217	39⅜	38¾	38¾	− ¾
17⅝	11	ClarkOil	.60	4.6	7	36	13⅜	13⅛	13⅛	− ⅛
65⅝	47⅝	ClvClf	2	3.4	14	28	59¼	58⅝	59¼	+ ¼
23⅛	18⅜	ClevEl	1.84	9.6	8	134	19⅞	18¾	19⅛	+ ¼
92½	82	ClvEl	pf7.40	8.9	..	z300	83	83	83	+ ½
130½	112	ClvEl	pf 12	11.	..	z80	113⅞	113⅞	113⅞	+ ⅛
14¾	8⅜	Clevepk	.60	5.9	9	47	10¼	10	10⅛	− ⅜
15⅞	11⅜	Clorox	.68	4.6	10	698	15	14⅝	14¾	− ⅛

Source: *The Wall Street Journal*, May 19, 1978

Reporting market activity. Information with respect to the trading of listed securities on organized exchanges is reported in various financial and nonfinancial media. Most big city newspapers report the daily activity on major exchanges, although the key source of stock price information on listed securities is *The Wall Street Journal*. Figure 19.2 presents an example of some NYSE listings from *The Wall Street Journal*. Reporting these data daily enhances investor confidence in the continuity of the security markets.

To see exactly what stock price information is reported, suppose we take a closer look at the data on Cities Service Company (CitiesSv) stock outlined in Figure 19.2. The first two columns, labeled "High" and "Low," contain the highest and lowest price at which the stock sold during the latest 52-week period. The figure immediately following the company name is the cash dividend expected to be paid in 1978, \$3.00. The "yield %" figure, which immediately follows the dividend, represents the dividend yield, which has been calculated by dividing the expected dividend (\$3.00) by the stock's current or closing price (\$52¼) and rounding the answer to the nearest tenth of a percent (5.7%). The next entry is the price-earnings ratio, the current market price divided by the previous year's per share earnings. The P-E ratio is believed to reflect investor expectations concerning the firm's future activities. The daily volume follows the P-E ratio; 24,400 shares of Cities Service Company were traded on May 18, 1978.[6] The "High," "Low," and "Close" columns contain the highest, lowest, and last (closing) price, respectively, at

[6]There is a one-day lag in reporting, which means that the May 19, 1978, *The Wall Street Journal* reported the May 18, 1978, transactions.

which the stock sold on May 18. The prices of stocks are quoted and traded in eighths of a dollar.[7] The final column shows the net change between the current day's closing price and the closing price on the preceding day. Cities Service Company closed at 52¼, up ¼ on May 18, 1978, which means that it must have closed at 52 (i.e., ¼ point lower) on May 17. Not all price quotations are as easy to read as this example, since quite often a number of footnotes are included in the listing.

The over-the-counter exchange. The over-the-counter exchange is not a specific institution; rather, it is a way of trading securities other than on an organized security exchange. The over-the-counter exchange (OTC) is the result of an intangible relationship among the purchasers and the sellers of securities. Active traders in this market are linked by a telecommunications network. The prices at which securities are traded over the counter are determined by both competitive bids and negotiation. The actual process depends on the general activity of a security. A numerical majority of stocks are traded over the counter, as are most government and corporate bonds. Some traders, known as *broker-dealers, make markets* in certain securities by offering to either buy or sell them at stated prices. Over 90 percent of all corporate bonds are traded in this market. Many of these bonds are listed on the New York Stock Exchange.

The *bid* and *ask* prices quoted on the OTC market represent, respectively, the highest price offered to purchase a given stock and the lowest price at which it is offered for sale. The OTC market today is linked through the National Association of Security Dealers Automated Quotation System (NASDAQ), which is an automated system that provides up-to-date bid and ask prices on thousands of securities. NASDAQ has provided a great deal of continuity in the OTC market because it allows buyers and sellers to locate each other in order to consummate a transaction. In order to trade in securities not quoted in NASDAQ, purchasers and sellers must find each other through references or through known *market makers* in the securities. The OTC market is quite important and most useful, especially for transactions involving large blocks of securities.

Special stock transactions

Two special types of stock market transactions often made by a purchaser of common stock are *margin purchases* and *short selling*.[8] These transactions are aimed at stimulating market activity and adding additional continuity to the securities markets.

Margin purchases. The Federal Reserve Board sets *margin requirements* that specify how much of the dollar price of a security purchase the

---

[7]Although the smallest divisor of security prices is one-eighth, the fractions are rounded off whenever possible. In other words, two-eighths, four-eighths, and six-eighths are expressed as one-fourth, one-half, and three-fourths.

[8]There are numerous other types of orders and trades that can be made on the security exchanges. For information on them, the reader is referred to an elementary investments text. A few of these texts are referenced at the end of this chapter.

purchaser must have and how much he or she is permitted to borrow. By raising or lowering margin requirements, the Fed can depress or stimulate activity in the security markets. Margin purchases must be approved by a broker. The brokerage firm then lends the purchaser the needed funds and retains the securities purchased as collateral. Some brokerage firms have "in-house" margin requirements that are more restrictive than those of the Fed. Margin requirements most recently have been around 50 percent. Margin purchasers, of course, must pay interest at a specified rate on the amount they borrow.

EXAMPLE

Stan Washington wishes to purchase on margin 200 shares of Cities Service at $52.25 per share. If the margin requirement is 50 percent, Stan will have to pay 50 percent of the total purchase price of $10,450 ($52.25/share · 200 shares), or $5225. The remaining $5225 of the purchase price will be lent to Stan by his brokerage firm. Stan will, of course, have to pay interest to his broker on the $5225 he borrows, along with the appropriate brokerage fee. ●

Short selling. Most people, when they think of security purchases, think of "buying low and selling high." These types of *long* transactions are most common; but there are some individuals who engage in *short selling,* which can be thought of as "selling high and buying low." Long transactions are made in anticipation of price increases, whereas *short transactions are made in anticipation of price decreases.* When an individual sells a security short, his or her broker borrows the security from someone else and then sells it on the short seller's behalf. These borrowed shares must be replaced by the short seller in the future. If he can repurchase the shares at a lower price in the future and then return them to their owner, his profit will be the difference between the proceeds of the initial sale and the repurchase price. If the short seller ends up repurchasing the shares at a higher price than he sold them for, he sustains a loss. There are numerous rules and regulations that govern short sales.

EXAMPLE

Stan Washington wishes to sell short 100 shares of Cities Service at $52.25 per share. His broker borrows the shares and sells them, receiving proceeds of $5225 ($52.25/share · 100 shares). If the price of the stock drops as Stan expects it to and he repurchases the stock at $39.00 per share, Stan will make a profit, since the cost of replacing the stock, $3900 ($39.00/share · 100 shares) is less than his initial proceeds of $5225. Stan's profit will be $1,325 ($5225 − $3900). If the stock prices rises above $52.25 per share and Stan repurchases it at, say, $56.00 per share, he will sustain a loss of $375 [($56.00/share · 100 shares) − ($52.25/share · 100 shares)]. When Stan, or any person, sells short he is betting on a price decline; if wrong, the short seller will suffer a loss. Stan, of course, will have to pay brokerage fees on his short sale transaction. ●

Investment companies

An investment company is a peculiar kind of financial organization that can be considered either a financial intermediary or a business firm. Investment companies pool funds of investors and invest them in a portfolio of securities. They are financial intermediaries in the sense that they channel individual savings into investments, but they are similar to business firms in that they sell both debt and equity, the proceeds from which they invest in certain earning assets—in this case, stocks and bonds of other companies. There are numerous types of investment companies, each specializing in certain types of securities. A *mutual fund* is a common form of investment company.[9]

The attractiveness of investment companies lies in their ability to provide the small investor with the benefits of diversification, professional portfolio management, and skilled timing of purchases and sales. By purchasing a broad group of securities, the investment company attempts to maximize the return for a given level of risk. An individual owning one share in an investment company would probably be unable to obtain so diversified an investment in any other way, since it would require a large amount of money for him or her to assemble a portfolio similar to that of the investment company. An investment company allows the investor to buy a small portion of a diversified portfolio of securities for a modest outlay.

INVESTMENT BANKING

Investment banking plays a most important role in aiding firms to raise money in capital markets. The investment banker is responsible for finding buyers for new security issues. The name "investment banker" is somewhat misleading, since an investment banker is neither an investor nor a banker, since he or she neither makes long-term investments nor guards the savings of others. Instead, acting as a middleman between the issuer and seller of new security issues, the investment banker purchases securities from corporations and governments and markets them to the public. The First Boston Corporation and Merrill Lynch, Pierce, Fenner & Smith are two of the largest of the few thousand investment banking firms in existence. Many investment banking firms operate in other financial areas as well; for example, Merrill Lynch is also the nation's largest stock brokerage firm.

The functions of the investment banker

The investment banker performs a number of important functions; his or her primary function is underwriting security issues. The investment banker also performs the secondary functions of advising clients and bearing risk.

Underwriting. When an investment banker agrees to underwrite a security issue, he or she guarantees the issuer that he will receive at least a specified minimum amount from the issue. The banker buys the securities at a lower price than he plans to sell them for, thereby making a profit. However, the banker runs the risk of being unable to actually sell the issue.

---

[9]A *mutual fund*, or *open-end investment company*, as it is often called, sells its shares to the public and redeems these shares at a value representing their claim on the firm's total portfolio. Mutual funds are attractive in that they are open-ended. New shares can be sold, so that the size of the fund increases.

EXAMPLE

The First Big Corporation has agreed to underwrite a new $50 million common stock issue for the Taxaco Oil Company. It has agreed to purchase the stock for $48 million. Since First Big must pay Taxaco $48 million for the stock, it must attempt to sell the stock for net proceeds of at least $48 million. Actually, it will attempt to sell the stock for at least $50 million, thereby obtaining a $2 million commission. If it is unable to raise $50 million, the investment banking firm will lose its $2 million commission and possibly part of the $48 million spent for the stock initially. In some cases, a security issue can be sold in a few days; in other, less fortunate, situations months are required to negotiate a sale. The investment banker therefore bears the risk of unfavorable price changes before the issue is sold as well as the risk of being unable to sell the issue at all. ●

Many security issues are not underwritten; rather, they are *privately placed* or sold on a *best efforts* basis. These functions are also handled by investment bankers.

Private placement.   Private placement occurs when an investment banker arranges for the direct purchase of a new security issue by an individual, several individuals, a firm, or a group of firms. The investment banker is then paid a commission for acting as a middleman in the transaction.

Best efforts.   In the case of some public offerings, the investment banker may not actually underwrite the issue; rather, the banker may use his or her resources to sell the securities on a *best efforts* basis. In this case, the banker does not take on the risk associated with underwriting and his or her compensation is based on the number of securities sold.

Advising.   The investment banker performs an advisory function by analyzing the firm's financial needs and recommending appropriate means of financing. Since an investment banker has a feel for the pulse of the securities markets, he or she can provide useful advice on mergers, acquisitions, and refinancing decisions.

Risk bearing.   As we indicated in the discussion of the underwriting function, the investment banker accepts the risk of price changes and a market collapse between the time of purchase and the time of sale of securities. There is always the possibility that he or she will be "stuck" with a large amount of the securities. In some instances, he or she may be able to sell the securities only at a price lower than the initial purchase price.

The organization of investment banking activity

The investment banker's functions of underwriting security issues, advising clients, and bearing risks come into play as a result of a quite logical sequence of events. The process begins with a firm needing additional financing selecting an investment banking firm, which then confers with the issuer, syndicates the underwriting, forms the selling group, fulfills legal requirements for a sale, sets a price, distributes the security, and stabilizes the price. Each of these activities is briefly described below.

Selecting an investment banker. A firm needing additional financing through the capital markets initiates the fund-raising process by selecting an investment banker to advise, underwrite, and therefore bear the risk of the new issue. The investment banker may be selected through *competitive bidding* or chosen by the issuing firm. In the case of competitive bidding, the investment banker or group of investment bankers bidding the highest price for the issue receives it. If the investment banker is chosen by the issuing firm, the security issue is termed a *negotiated offering.*

Conferring with the issuer. Once selected, the investment banker that will take a leading role in underwriting the issue aids the firm in determining how much capital should be raised and in what form—debt or equity. The investment banker analyzes the firm's financial position and proposed disposition of the funds to be raised in order to make sure that the firm is financially sound and that the proposed expenditures are justifiable. After an examination of certain legal aspects of the firm and its proposed offering, a tentative underwriting agreement is drawn up.

Syndicating the underwriting. Due to the size of most new security issues, it is necessary for the investment banker to form a *purchase syndicate,* which is generally a group of 10 to 60 investment banking firms. The use of a purchase syndicate lessens the risk of loss to any single firm. Each underwriter in the syndicate must sell his or her portion of the issue. This is likely to result in a wider distribution of the new securities.

Forming a selling group. Each of the underwriters in the syndicate forms a selling group to sell the securities once they have been purchased. These *selling groups* consist of other investment bankers and stock brokerage firms. Members of the selling group are paid a certain amount for each security sold.[10] Figure 19.3 depicts the distribution channels for a new security issue.

Fulfilling legal requirements. Prior to a new security issue, the issuer must obtain the approval of the Securities and Exchange Commission (SEC). According to the Securities Exchange Act of 1933, which was passed to ensure the full disclosure of information with respect to new security issues and prevent a stock market collapse similar to that which occurred in 1929–1932, the issuer is required to file a registration statement with the SEC containing certain information with respect to a new issue. The firm cannot sell the security until the SEC approves the registration statement. This usually requires 20 days.

One portion of the registration statement is called the *prospectus*. This prospectus may be issued to potential buyers during the waiting period between filing the registration statement and its approval as long as a *red her-*

---

[10]The selling group is usually compensated in the same fashion as the underwriter. In other words, the selling group buys the securities at a discount from the sale price and profits from the *spread* between the price at which it purchases and the price at which it sells the security.

FIGURE 19.3 Distribution channels for a new security issue

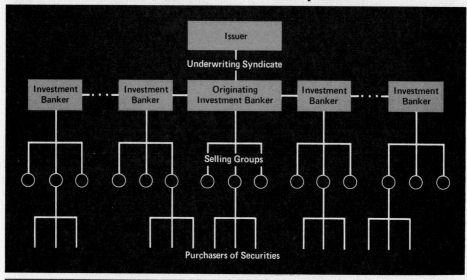

ring, which is a statement indicating the tentative nature of the offer, is stamped in red on the prospectus. Once the registration statement has been approved, the new security can be offered for sale if the prospectus is made available to all interested parties. If the registration statement is found to be fraudulent, the SEC will not only reject the issue, but can sue the directors and others responsible for the misrepresentation. Approval of the registration statement by the SEC does not mean that the security is a good investment; it indicates only that the facts presented in the statement accurately reflect the firm's true position.

Although not directly related to new issues, another important piece of legislation regulating the security markets is the Securities Exchange Act of 1934, which is aimed at controlling the secondary trading of securities by providing for the regulation of securities exchanges, listed securities, and the general activities of the security markets. The act provides for the disclosure of information on and accurate representation of securities traded. This piece of legislation and the Securities Exchange Act of 1933 are the key acts protecting participants in the capital markets. Many states also have laws aimed at regulating the sale of securities within their borders. These *"blue sky laws"* protect investors by preventing the sale of securities that provide nothing but "blue sky."

Pricing the issue.   Underwriting syndicates generally wait until the end of the registration period to price securities, so that they will have a feel for the current mood of the market. The pricing decision is quite important since it affects the ease with which the issue can be sold and also the issuer's proceeds. The investment banker's "feel" for the market should result in a price that achieves the optimum mix of marketability and financial return.

Distributing the issue. Prior to the actual offering of a new security for sale, the issue is publicized. This can be done only after the registration statement has been approved. Publicity is obtained through advertising and personal contacts through the brokerage firms handling the issue. When the security is formally placed on the market, orders are accepted both from the selling groups and from outsiders. If the issue is sold out, it is considered *oversubscribed;* if all the shares are not sold immediately, it is said to be *undersubscribed.*

Stabilizing the price. Once an issue has been offered for sale, the original underwriter attempts to stabilize the price of the issue so that the entire issue can be sold at the initial offering price. By placing orders to buy the security, the original investment banker can keep the demand for the issue and therefore the price at the desired level. This activity, sometimes referred to as *price-pegging,* is legal as long as the intent is disclosed in the registration statement filed with the SEC. Price-pegging is in the best interests of both the issuer and the underwriting syndicate, since it reduces the syndicate's risk, thereby lowering the issuance cost charged the issuer.

The cost of investment banking services

The investment banker is compensated by purchasing the security issue at a discount from the proposed sale price. The discount on an individual per-bond or per-share basis is referred to as the *spread.* The size of the spread depends on the cost of investigations, printing, registration, the discount to the underwriting syndicate, and the discount given to the selling group. The cost of an issue is a function of two basic components—administrative cost and underwriting cost. Generally, the larger the issue, the lower the overall cost in percentage terms. It is also generally true that the overall flotation cost for common stock is highest, with preferred stock and bonds following in that order. The overall flotation cost ranges from as little as 1 percent of the total proceeds on a large bond issue to as much as 20 percent of proceeds on a small common stock issue. The size of an issue affects the cost in that large issues have a lower percentage cost due to economies of scale. The type of security issued affects the cost because it affects the ease with which large blocks can be placed with one purchaser. The firm contemplating a security issue must therefore weigh the cost of public sale against the cost and feasibility of direct placement, which is briefly described in the next section.

Direct placement

The direct placement of a security issue in the hands of a purchaser can sometimes be negotiated by a business firm. Typically direct placements are used only for bonds or preferred stock; common stock is rarely placed directly, except when it is believed that the existing shareholders might purchase the issue through an arrangement known as a *rights offering*, which is described in detail in Chapter 22. Direct placement usually reduces issuance and administrative costs and provides the issuer with a great deal of flexibility since the firm need not file certain registration statements and is not required to obtain the approval of the Securities and Exchange Commission. Often, even in the case of a direct placement, the advice of an investment banker is required to price the issue correctly.

Direct placement of common stock is sometimes made through stock options or stock purchase plans. *Stock options* are generally extended to management and permit it to purchase a certain number of shares of their firm's common stock at a specified price over a stated period of time. These options are intended to stimulate managerial actions that increase the long-run success of the firm. *Stock-purchase plans* are a fringe benefit occasionally offered to a firm's employees. They allow the employees to purchase the firm's stock at a discount or on a matching basis with the firm absorbing part of the cost. Both of these plans provide equity capital and at the same time increase employee motivation and interest in the company.

SUMMARY

This chapter has presented a discussion of the institutions and markets that allow the funds of savers to be channeled into the hands of those who need funds for investment purposes. The forums in which this activity takes place are the financial intermediaries and markets. Financial intermediaries, or institutions, channel the savings of various individuals, businesses, and governments into the hands of demanders of these funds. The key financial intermediaries include commercial banks, mutual savings banks, savings and loan associations, credit unions, life insurance companies, and pension funds. These intermediaries either lend out their funds directly to individuals, businesses, and governments or channel them to these same parties via loans and investments made in the financial markets. These intermediaries sometimes go into the financial markets to raise money in order to supplement their funds from savings deposits.

There are two components of the financial market. The short-term market is known as the money market. It is created by the intangible relationship between suppliers and demanders of short-term funds. The key instruments of the money market include all the so-called marketable securities such as treasury bills, tax-anticipation bills, treasury notes, federal agency issues, negotiable certificates of deposit, commercial paper, banker's acceptances, and repurchase agreements. Participants in the money market include individuals, businesses, government, and financial institutions.

The capital market is the market where long-term debt and equity capital is raised. This market is of key importance to new capital formation in our economy. It is made up of both the organized security exchanges and the over-the-counter exchange. These exchanges create a continuous market, allocate scarce capital, determine and publicize security prices, and aid firms in obtaining new financing. There are a number of organized exchanges, the largest of which is the New York Stock Exchange. Each of these exchanges allows only members to make transactions in listed securities, which are securities that have met some predefined standards. The results of trading activity in securities listed on the major exchanges is reported daily in financial news media such as *The Wall Street Journal*. The over-the-counter exchange is not a specific institution, but there is a telecommunication network between active participants in this market. The NASDAQ system has provided a great deal of continuity in this market. Securities can be traded in the capital markets not only by normal purchase and sale transactions but by margin purchases and short selling. These are only two of the special types of stock market transactions that can be made. Investment companies enable individuals to purchase ownership in a portfolio of securities.

Investment bankers make it easier for firms to raise long-term debt and equity funds in the capital markets. The investment banker underwrites or sells total issues of securities, receiving compensation in the form of a spread between the price at which he or she purchases and sells a security issue. Occasionally the investment banker does not accept all the risk of an issue, instead being paid a commission for privately placing an issue or selling whatever is possible. Investment bankers also provide advice to the issuer of new securities. Generally the original investment banker contacted by a firm will syndicate a large issue with other investment bankers. Before a new security can be sold, the Securities and Exchange Commission must approve the issue. The investment banker aids in pricing an issue and usually forms selling groups to market the issue. The cost of investment banking services is a function of the size of the issue and the type of security being sold. The investment banker's knowledge of the market is quite important to the issuer. An alternative to the use of an investment banker is the direct placement of a security—typically a debt or preferred stock—in the hands of a single or small group of purchasers. Even in the case of a direct placement, though, an investment banker is often used in an advisory capacity.

QUESTIONS

19-1 What are financial intermediaries and financial markets? What is the fund-raising alternative to these media?

19-2 Who are the key participants in the financial intermediation process? Indicate which are net savers and which are net borrowers.

19-3 How does a savings and loan association operate? How does it differ from a commercial bank?

19-4 What role do life insurance companies and pension funds play in lending and investing funds? Are these institutions important sources of funds to business?

19-5 What relationship exists between financial intermediaries and financial markets? Why does it exist?

19-6 What is the money market? Where is it housed? How does it differ from the capital markets?

19-7 What are the capital markets? What role do securities exchanges play in this market? How is membership on these exchanges obtained, and how do they operate?

19-8 How does the over-the-counter market operate? How does it differ from the organized security exchanges? How is it linked? What are *bid* and *ask* prices?

19-9 What are margin purchases and short sale transactions? Who controls margin requirements? When is an individual likely to make a short sale?

19-10 What is an investment company? Is it a financial intermediary or a business firm? Why are these companies attractive to investors?

19-11 What is an investment banker, and what are his or her functions in the financial marketplace?

19-12 What events occur between the time an issuer decides to raise capital and the ultimate sale of the securities by the investment banker?

19-13 What legal requirements are imposed on issuers and securities exchanges by the Securities Exchange Acts of 1933 and 1934?

19-14 How does an investment banker attempt to stabilize the market price of a new issue? Are there any legal requirements with respect to this activity?

19-15 How is an investment banker compensated for his or her services? How are underwriting costs affected by the size and type of an issue?

19-16 Explain the *direct placement* of a security issue. What securities typically would be considered for direct placement? Under what conditions would the firm decide on using direct placement rather than an investment banker?

PROBLEMS

19-1 Given the following quotations for Mobil Corporation and NCR, from the Tuesday, June 13, *The Wall Street Journal*, answer questions **a** through **j** for Mobil and NCR, respectively.

| 70½ | 58⅛ | MOBIL | 4.20 | 6.4 | 7 | 254 | 65¾ | 64⅞ | 65⅝ | +¼ |
| 58⅝ | 34½ | NCR | 1 | 1.7 | 10 | 600 | 58¾ | 57¼ | 57½ | −¼ |

    a On what day did the trading activity occur?

    b At what price did the stock sell at the end of the day on Friday, June 9?

    c What are the highest and lowest prices at which the stock sold on the day quoted?

    d How much is the firm's price-earnings ratio? What does it indicate?

    e What is the firm's percentage dividend yield? What does it signify?

    f What was the last price (or closing price) at which the stock was traded on the day quoted?

    g How large a dividend is expected in the current year?

    h What are the highest and lowest prices at which the stock has traded in the past 52 weeks?

    i How many shares of the stock were traded on the day quoted?

    j How much, if any, of a change in the stock price took place between the day quoted and the preceding trading day?

19-2 For each of the following cases, indicate how much money Paula Lipski would have to put up in order to make the given transaction with the stated margin requirements.

Case	Number of shares	Price per share ($)	Margin requirement
A	100	23¼	55%
B	80	41½	40%
C	900	94	60%
D	100	22⅛	35%
E	250	14⅞	65%
F	400	62	20%

19-3 Wayne Marcotti is considering purchasing stock on margin. He has the following information. Use it to answer the questions below.

Security	Number of shares	Price per share ($)	Margin requirement	Interest on margin	Holding period of stock
A	100	25	20%	10%	3 months
B	50	28½	40%	9%	6 months
C	200	37¼	60%	12%	1 month
D	450	16⅞	55%	8%	4 months

    a How much money will he have to put up in each case?
    b For each case, what amount of interest would he owe if he sells at the end of the given holding period?

19-4 Winston Ross, on February 2, 1979, purchased 400 shares of CBA at $23½ and 300 shares of DZC at $44⅞. The margin requirement at the time was 40 percent and the interest rate on margin purchases was 9 percent.

    a If Winston used the maximum amount of margin available, how much of his own money would he need for the purchase?
    b If he sold the stocks on June 2, 1979, how much interest would he pay on the transaction?
    c If the total brokerage fees for the purchase and sale were $62.50, and he sold CBA for $23 and DZC for $49⅜, considering all costs, how much did Winston net from his purchases?
    d What was his rate of return on his *invested capital*?
    e What would his net return have been if he had not bought on margin?
    f What would his return on *invested capital* have been if he had *not* bought on margin?

19-5 Consider each of the following cases:

	Case			
	A	**B**	**C**	**D**
Number of shares purchased	300	150	150	80
Price per share ($)	31	62½	62½	254
Brokerage fees (total)	$60	$100	$100	$90
Margin requirement	65%	55%	55%	45%
Margin interest rate	9%	8%	8%	9%
Holding period	6 months	9 months	9 months	12 months
Sale price per share ($)	37¼	55	70	302

    a Calculate the amount of money the purchaser must put up in each case assuming he or she uses the full amount of margin available.
    b Calculate the margin interest charged for the specified holding period.
    c Calculate the net profit (i.e., the proceeds after brokerage and margin costs) in each case.
    d Determine the return on *invested capital* earned by the purchaser in each case.
    e Calculate the net profit in each case assuming margin is *not* used.

f Determine the return on *invested capital* assuming margin was *not* used.

g What conclusions can you draw with respect to the risk-return trade-off provided by the use of margin? Explain this in light of cases B and C.

19-6 Chung Li is considering the purchase of the common stock of Mountain Pass Food Processing, Incorporated. She has $8000 to invest and the stock is currently selling at $50 per share.

    a How many shares can she purchase if the margin requirement is
        (1) 100 percent?
        (2) 50 percent?
        (3) 10 percent?

    b From **a** above, what conclusions with respect to the effects of changes in the margin requirements on the ability to purchase securities can be drawn?

19-7 For each of the following cases indicate

    a The short profit or loss made (prior to brokerage fees).

    b The net profit after all costs.

Case	Number of shares	Price ($) at which shares sold short	Price ($) at which shares repurchased	Broker's commission
A	100	50	55	$ 25
B	700	80	70	$280
C	300	23⅞	32¼	$120
D	1000	32½	32¼	$180

19-8 Ray Glaser, who is a real gambler, cannot decide whether to take a long or a short position in a given security. The stock is currently selling for $48 per share.

    a How much would Ray lose or gain if he bought 200 shares of the stock and later sold it for $54 per share?

    b How much would he have lost or gained had he taken a short position if the stock was repurchased at $54 per share?

    c Answer **a** and **b** above, assuming that the stock was sold or repurchased at $38 per share.

    d If Mr. Glaser does some research into future stock price movements, what expectation will cause him to take a long position and what expectation will justify selling short? Explain.

19-9 Given the following securities and expected prices now and six months from now, indicate whether you would take a long or short position in each stock, and how much per share would be earned in each case if the expected prices matched the actual prices.

Stock	Current price per share ($)	Expected price per share ($) 6 months from now
A	44	50
B	37	32½
C	14¼	18½
D	19⅛	22
E	47	47

19-10 The Gray Company is interested in selling common stock in order to raise capital for plant expansion. The firm has consulted the First Omaha Company, a large underwriting firm, which believes the stock can be sold for $80 per share. The underwriter, on investigation, has found that its administrative costs will be 2 percent of the sale price and its selling costs will be 1½ percent of the sale price. If the underwriter requires a profit of 1 percent of the sale price, how much will the *spread* have to be in *dollars* in order to cover the underwriter's costs and profit?

19-11 The Philip-Marrow Company wishes to raise $100 million to be used in the acquisition of Unsoda Soft Drinks. The company has estimated that the $100 million should provide an amount sufficient to make the acquisition after paying the underwriter. The underwriter, Morris Lunch & Co., believes it can sell the 100,000 bonds at their $1000 face value. The underwriter estimates that its administrative costs will be $3.5 million. It also must sell the bonds at a ¾ of one percent discount from their face value to members of the selling group. Morris Lunch's required return on the sale price is 1 percent.

    a Calculate the per-bond spread required by the underwriter in order to cover its costs.

    b How much will Philip-Marrow Company net from the issue?

    c How much will the selling group receive? How much will the underwriter receive?

    d Describe the nature of the underwriter's risk assuming that this is *not* a private placement or best efforts offering.

SELECTED REFERENCES

Amling, Frederick, *Investments: An Introduction to Analysis and Management,* 4th ed. (Englewood Cliffs: N.J.: Prentice-Hall, 1978).

Coates, C. Robert, *Investment Strategy* (New York: McGraw-Hill, 1978).

D'Ambrosio, Charles A., *Principles of Modern Investments* (Chicago, Ill.: Science Research Associates, 1976).

Dougall, Herbert E., and Jack E. Gaumnitz, *Capital Markets and Institutions,* 3rd ed. (Englewood Cliffs, N.J.: Prentice-Hall, 1975).

Ederington, Louis H., "Negotiated versus Competitive Underwriting of Corporate Bonds," *Journal of Finance 31* (March 1976), pp. 17–28.

Francis, Jack Clark, *Investments: Analysis and Management* (New York: McGraw-Hill, 1972).

Friend, Irwin, *Investment Banking and the New Issues Market* (Cleveland: World, 1967).

Gup, Benton E., *Financial Intermediaries: An Introduction* (Boston: Houghton Mifflin Company, 1976).

Hamilton, James L., "Marketplace Organization and Marketability: NASDQ, the Stock Exchange, and the National Market System," *Journal of Finance 33* (May 1978), pp. 487–503.

Hayes, Samuel III, "Investment Banking Power Structure in Flux," *Harvard Business Review* (March-April 1971), pp. 136–152.

Henning, Charles N., William Pigott, and Robert H. Scott, *Financial Markets and the Economy* (Englewood Cliffs, N.J.: Prentice-Hall, 1975).

Jacobs, Donald P., Loring C. Farwell, and Edwin H. Neave, *Financial Institutions,* 5th ed. (Homewood, Ill.: Irwin, 1972).

Johnson, Keith B., T. Gregory Morton, and M. Chapman Findlay III, "An Empirical

Analysis of the Floatation Cost of Corporate Securities, 1971–1972," *Journal of Finance 30* (June 1975), pp. 1129–1133.

Johnson, Timothy E., *Investment Principles* (Englewood Cliffs, N.J.: Prentice-Hall, 1978).

Logue, Dennis E., and John R. Lindvall, "The Behavior of Investment Bankers: An Econometric Investigation," *Journal of Finance 29* (March 1974), pp. 203–215.

Loll, L. M., Jr., and J. G. Buckley, *The Over-the-Counter Securities Markets: A Review Guide*, 3rd ed. (Englewood Cliffs, N.J.: Prentice-Hall, 1973).

Polakoff, Murray E., et al., *Financial Institutions and Markets* (Boston: Houghton Mifflin, 1970).

Robinson, Roland I., and Dwayne Wrightsman, *Financial Markets: The Accumulation and Allocation of Wealth* (New York: McGraw-Hill, 1974).

Shapiro, Eli, and Charles R. Wolf, *The Role of Private Placements in Corporate Finance* (Boston: Division of Research, Graduate School of Business Administration, Harvard University, 1972).

Sharpe, William F., *Investments* (Englewood Cliffs, N.J.: Prentice-Hall, 1978).

Smith, Paul, *Money and Financial Intermediation: The Theory and Structure of Financial Systems* (Englewood Cliffs, N.J.: Prentice-Hall, 1978).

Stevenson, Richard A., and Edward H. Jennings, *Fundamentals of Investments* (St. Paul., Minn.: West, 1976).

Stoll, Hans R., and Anthony J. Curley, "Small Business and the New Issues Market for Equities," *Journal of Financial and Quantitative Analysis 5* (September 1970), pp. 309–322.

Taft, R. W., "The Greening of the Red Herring Prospectus," *Financial Executive 39* (November 1971), pp. 73–76.

Van Horne, James C., *The Function and Analysis of Capital Market Rates* (Englewood Cliffs, N.J.: Prentice-Hall, 1970).

Wiesen, Jeremy L., *Regulating Transactions in Securities* (St. Paul, Minn.: West, 1975).

CHAPTER 20
Leasing

Leasing involves obtaining the use of specific fixed assets, such as land and equipment, without actually receiving title to them. The *lessee* receives the services of the assets *leased* to him or her (or "it" in the case of a firm) by the *lessor*, who owns the assets. In exchange for the use of the assets, the lessee pays the lessor a fixed periodic payment, which is normally made in advance of each lease period. The lease payment is treated as a tax-deductible expenditure by the lessee; lease receipts are treated as revenues by the lessor. The popularity of leasing has increased over the past 20 years as a result of the growing awareness of businesspeople of the financial power of leasing.

The uses of leasing as a source of financing can best be understood by comparing the lease to the purchase of a specific asset. If a firm wishes to obtain the service of a specific asset, it has two basic alternatives: to purchase the asset or to lease it. To purchase the asset, the firm must pay out a lump sum or agree to some type of installment purchase plan that in essence involves incurring a long-term liability. Both the asset purchased and the associated long-term debt will show up on the firm's balance sheet. Leasing the desired asset provides the firm with the asset's service without necessarily increasing any balance sheet accounts.[1] Leasing is a source of financing in that it enables the firm to obtain the use of a fixed asset without directly incurring any fixed debt obligation.

Leasing is discussed in this section of the text because it has many of the characteristics of long-term financing. The discussion of leasing is divided into four basic sections. The first section discusses the important characteristics of leases. Emphasis is given to the various types of leases and lease arrangements, the legal requirements of leases, and the lease contract. The

---

[1]Recent rulings by the Financial Accounting Standards Board (FASB) have made it mandatory that certain types of lease commitments be shown as an asset and corresponding liability on the firms' balance sheet. This treatment as well as other aspects of lease commitment disclosure are discussed in a later section of this chapter.

second section looks more deeply into the use of leasing as a source of financing. Emphasis is placed on both the costs and capital structure implications of leasing. The third section discusses the lease-purchase decision in light of quantitative capital budgeting techniques. The final section points out certain advantages and disadvantages commonly cited with respect to the use of leasing as a source of financing.

CHARACTERISTICS OF LEASES

Leasing arrangements can take a number of different forms. This section discusses both the most common types of leases and various leasing arrangements. Special emphasis is placed on the effects of leasing on the corporation. The common provisions of a lease, such as maintenance clauses, are discussed here. Also emphasized in this section are the legal requirements of leases. A final portion of this section is devoted to a brief discussion of the lease contract.

Basic types of leases

The two basic types of leases available to the business firm are *operating* and *financial* leases, the latter of which are often called *capital leases* by accountants. Operating leases generally represent a short-term arrangement in which the service of certain assets is obtained by the firm. The primary difference between operating and financial leases is that a financial lease is a long-term arrangement that cannot be canceled at the option of the lessee.

Operating leases.

An operating lease is normally a contractual arrangement whereby the lessee agrees to make periodic payments to the lessor for five or fewer years for an asset's services. Such leases are generally *cancelable* at the option of the lessee, who may be required to pay a predetermined penalty for cancellation. Operating leases are most commonly used for leasing such things as computer hardware, heavy equipment, automobiles, and cash registers. Assets leased under an operating lease generally have a usable life *longer* than the term of the lease. Usually, they would become less efficient and technologically obsolete if they were leased for a longer period of years. Computer systems are prime examples of assets whose relative efficiency is expected to diminish with new technological developments; the operating lease is therefore a commonly used leasing arrangement for computers.

Operating leases are generally written for periods of time shorter than the life of the leased asset. In other words, if an operating lease is held to maturity, the lessee at that time returns the leased asset to the lessor, who may either lease it again or sell the asset. Normally the asset has a positive market value at the termination of the lease. In some instances, the lease contract will give the lessee the opportunity to purchase the leased asset. Generally under the operating lease, the total payments made by the lessee to the lessor are *less* than the initial cost of the leased asset paid by the lessor. Since the operating lease is normally for a period less than the asset's usable life, the lessor expects to be able to sell the asset (for an amount greater than its unrecovered cost)[2] when the lease matures.

Financial (or capital) lease.   A financial (or capital) lease is a *longer-term* lease than an operating lease. Financial leases are *noncancelable* and therefore obligate the lessee to make payments for the use of an asset over a predefined period of time. Even if the lessee does not require the service of the leased asset, it is contractually obligated to make payments over the life of the lease contract. Financial leases are commonly used for leasing land, buildings, and large pieces of fixed equipment. The noncancelable feature of the financial lease makes it quite similar to certain types of long-term debt.[3] The lease payment becomes a fixed, tax-deductible expenditure that must be paid at predefined dates over a definite period. Failing to make the contractual payments may mean bankruptcy for the lessee.

Another distinguishing characteristic of the financial lease is that the total payments over the lease period are *greater* than the cost of the leased assets to the lessor. The lease period therefore is generally closely aligned with the productive life of the asset. If the salvage value of the asset is expected to be negligible, the lessor must receive more than the asset's purchase price in order to earn its required return on the dollars it has invested in the leased asset. The emphasis in this chapter will be primarily on financial leases, since this type of lease results in an inescapable financial commitment by the business firm. Because of the binding nature of financial leases, a firm must be very careful in making financial lease commitments. Some financial leases give the lessee a purchase option at maturity.

Leasing arrangements

Certain options are available as part of any lease. One of these options is concerned with the manner in which leased assets are acquired by the lessor. A second is related to the maintenance of the leased assets. A third is related to the renewability of the lease contract. A final option is related to the types of lessors available. Each of these options is discussed separately below.

The acquisition of leased assets.   Two primary techniques for obtaining assets to be leased are used by lessors. In essence, the method of acquiring assets depends largely on the desires of the prospective lessee. The two most common techniques are direct leases and sale-leaseback arrangements.

---

[2]This implies that generally the original cost of the leased asset to the lessor, along with the financial charges incurred less the costs recovered through the lease payments received from the lessee, results in an end-of-lease investment by the lessor that is below the asset's market value at that time. The lessor therefore usually gains on the sale of the asset at termination of the lease.

[3]Some authors classify financial leases as *intermediate-term financing*, where the intermediate term is assumed to represent a period of one to seven years. In this text the intermediate-term classification is not used; rather, any debt having maturity of greater than one year is classified as *long term*.

Direct leases. A direct lease results when a lessor either owns or acquires the assets that are leased to a given lessee. In other words, the lessee did not previously own the assets it is leasing. The lessor may be the actual manufacturer of the asset, or it may be a leasing firm or subsidiary that acquires the assets from the manufacturer and then leases them to the lessee. A lessee will normally specify the manufacturer, model number, and other relevant characteristics of the asset it wishes to lease.

Sale-leaseback arrangements. A second type of technique used by lessors to acquire leased assets is to purchase assets already owned by the lessee and lease them back. This type of arrangement is quite common. A sale-leaseback arrangement is normally initiated by a firm that needs funds for operations. By selling an existing asset to a lessor and then leasing it back, the lessee receives cash for the asset immediately while at the same time obligating himself to make fixed periodic payments for the services of the leased asset. The sale-leaseback of an existing old asset provides the firm with a mechanism whereby the firm's liquidity can be increased. Certain other advantages that may also accrue to the lessee under the sale-leaseback arrangement will be discussed later. The periodic lease payments charged the lessee will be set by the lessor at a level that allows the lessor to recover its investment in the leased assets and obtain some required return on the dollars invested.

Maintenance provisions. A lease agreement normally specifies whether the lessee is responsible for maintenance of the leased assets. *Operating leases* normally include maintenance clauses requiring the lessor to maintain the leased assets. Maintenance normally includes not only repairs, but also includes insurance and tax payments on leased assets. The lessor, of course, will include in the lease payment sufficient compensation for the expected maintenance costs of the leased assets. Since operating leases are relatively short-term agreements, the lessor is generally able to accurately estimate the maintenance outlays expected for the duration of the lease.

Financial leases almost always require the lessee to pay maintenance costs. In other words, the lease payment under a financial lease is a payment for the use of the asset only. Since the term of a financial lease is normally closely aligned with the life of the leased asset (except in the case of land), the lessee's position is quite similar to that of an owner; therefore, the responsibility and cost of maintaining the asset is placed in its hands. Since a financial lease is a long-term agreement, it would be quite difficult, if not impossible, for the lessor to estimate maintenance costs for the asset's life so that they could be fairly reflected in the lease payment. The costs of maintenance are therefore borne by the lessee.

Renewability. Generally the lessee is given the option to renew a lease at its expiration. Renewal options are especially common in operating leases, since they have shorter lives and the chance that the leased assets will become obsolete is reduced. Lease payments are normally lower after the renewal of the lease than during the initial lease period. The renewal option, of course, does not come into play until the term of the original lease has expired.

Types of lessors.   The lessor can be one of a number of parties. In operating lease arrangements, the lessor is quite likely to be the manufacturer of the leased item. Generally manufacturers such as IBM and Telex have their own leasing divisions, which are responsible for negotiating leases for their products. Independent leasing companies also exist. Companies such as Hertz and Avis provide operating leases. Financial leases are often offered by large financial institutions such as commercial banks and life insurance companies. Life insurance companies are especially active in real estate leasing. A large amount of life insurance investments are currently being placed in land and buildings that are leased to various business concerns. Commercial banks, although not a dominant force in leasing, have been increasing their leasing activities in an attempt to provide a full range of financial services to their business customers. Pension funds have also been moving into the general area of leasing, although to date their penetration has been negligible.

Legal requirements of leases

In order to prevent business firms from using leasing arrangements as a disguise for what is actually an installment loan, the Internal Revenue Service Code, Section 1031, "Exchange of Property Held for Productive Use or Investment," specifies certain conditions under which lease payments are tax deductible. If a lease arrangement does not meet these basic requirements, the lease payments are not completely tax-deductible.[4] In order to comform with the IRS Code, a leasing arrangement must meet the following requirements:

1. The term of a lease must be less than 30 years. A lease with a life greater than 30 years is considered a sale by the IRS.
2. The premium paid to the lessor must be "reasonable"—that is, equal to the premium being paid on leases of similar assets. A premium between 8 and 15 percent would currently be considered reasonable.
3. No preferential purchase option is permitted. The lessee can be given an opportunity to purchase the asset only at a price equal to or above any other offers received by the lessor.
4. The renewal option payment must also be "reasonable." If an outsider is willing to pay a higher amount to obtain the lease, the lease cannot be renewed with the original lessee at a lower rate. This is an application of the "fair market value" concept, which is also applied to purchase options.

[4]The IRS's concern stems from the fact that the full lease payment is tax-deductible, while in the case of an installment loan only the interest component of the payment is tax-deductible. In order to obtain high current tax deductions, the firm could therefore lease the asset over a specified period at the end of which it could purchase the asset for a nominal amount. Such a scheme would permit the firm to maximize its tax deductions, while still ultimately owning the asset.

The lease contract

The key items in the lease contract normally include the term of the lease, provisions for its cancellation, lease payment amounts and dates, renewal features, purchase clauses, maintenance and associated cost provisions, and other provisions specified in the lease negotiation process. As we indicated in the preceding discussion, many provisions are optional. A lease can be cancelable or noncancelable, but if cancellation is permitted the penalties must be clearly specified. The lease may be renewable. If it is, the renewal procedures and costs should be specified. The lease agreement may provide for the purchase of the leased assets either during the contract period or at the termination of the lease. The costs and conditions of the purchase must be clearly specified. In the case of operating leases, it is likely that maintenance costs, taxes, and insurance will be paid by the lessor. In the case of a financial lease these costs will generally be borne by the lessee. The bearer of these costs must be specified in the lease agreement.

The leased assets, the terms of the agreement, the lease payment, and the payment interval must be clearly specified in all lease agreements. The consequences of missing a payment or violating any other lease provisions must also be clearly stated in the lease contract. The consequences of violation of the agreement by the lessor must also be specified in this contract. Once the lease contract has been drawn up and agreed to by the lessor and lessee, the notarized signatures of these parties binds them both to the terms of the contract.

LEASING AS A SOURCE OF FINANCING

Leasing is considered a source of financing provided by the lessor to the lessee. The lessee receives the service of a certain fixed asset for a specified period of time, while in exchange for the use of this asset the lessee commits himself to a fixed periodic payment. It is the fixed financial obligation of the lessee to the lessor that forces us to consider a lease—specifically a financial lease—as a form of financing. The only other way the lessee could obtain the services of the given asset would be to purchase it outright, and the outright purchase of the asset would require financing. Again, fixed—most likely periodic—payments would be required. The lessee might have sufficient funds to purchase the asset outright without borrowing, but the funds used would not be free since there is an opportunity cost associated with the use of cash. It is the fixed payment obligation for a set period that forces us to view the financial lease as a source of long-term financing. Although at this point the rationale for leasing may seem no different than that for borrowing when a cash purchase cannot be made, certain other considerations with respect to the lease-purchase decision do exist.

The two major topics discussed in this section are the cost of leasing and the effect of leasing on future financing. An understanding of these aspects of leasing should help to clarify some of the subjective considerations in the leasing decision.

Lease costs

In order to discuss the lease cost as viewed by both the lessee and lessor, tax considerations, payment timing, and lease payment calculations must be evaluated. Each of these items is briefly discussed below.

Tax considerations. Lease payments are treated as tax-deductible expenditures on the firm's income statement. A lease payment can be deducted from the firm's before-tax income in the *period in which the service for which the payment is made is received*. The tax-deductibility of lease payments makes leasing quite competitive with the alternatives of borrowing to purchase an asset. Many financial leases involve the leasing of land, which cannot be depreciated. The tax-deductibility of the total lease payment may make it more advantageous to lease rather than to buy land. The lease payment received by the lessor must be treated as taxable income; however, our concern here is primarily with the lessee's position.

Advance payments. A lessor normally requires lease payments in advance. In the case of yearly payments, the lessee will be required to make its lease payment at the beginning of the year, although the benefits from the leased asset will not yet have been received. In evaluating lease-purchase decisions, it is important to clearly specify when lease payments are to be made. Since the tax laws permit the deduction of lease expenses only in the period in which the lease benefits have been received, making a lease payment in advance may cause the actual tax benefits of the payment to lag as much as one year behind the actual outlay.

EXAMPLE

The Kulsrud Corporation has recently entered into a leasing agreement with the First National Leasing Company. The agreement requires Kulsrud to make annual beginning-of-year payments of $39,535.88 for the next 12 years. In exchange, Kulsrud will receive the use of a 20,000-square-foot warehouse. Kulsrud is in the 40-percent tax bracket. The payment pattern required, the tax benefits, and the cash outflows for the Kulsrud Corporation over the life of the lease are given in Table 20.1. The

TABLE 20.1 Lease-related
cash flows for the Kulsrud Corporation

End of Year(s)	Lease payment (1)	Tax benefit[a] (2)	After-tax cash outflow (1) − (2) (3)
0	$39,535.88	$ 0	$39,535.88
1-11	39,535.88	15,814.35	23,721.53
12		15,814.35	(15,814.35)

[a]40% tax rate.

lag in the tax benefits resulting from the advance payment can be clearly seen in the table. The effect of this lag must be considered in the lease evaluation process. ●

Lease payment calculations.   The lessor charges the lessee a lease payment that will provide it (the lessor) with a certain required return. In determining these payments, the lessor takes into account its required return, the lease period, and the expected salvage value (if any) of the leased asset at the termination of the lease. The calculations required are based on the present-value concepts developed in Chapter 13. These calculations can be illustrated by a simple example.

EXAMPLE

The First National Leasing Company is attempting to determine the annual lease payment to be paid at the start of each year by the Kulsrud Corporation. Kulsrud is leasing a warehouse that was purchased by First National for $300,000 and is expected to have a salvage value of $100,000 at the end of the 12-year lease period. First National wishes to determine the annual lease payment it must charge Kulsrud at the start of each year in order to earn a 12-percent return on the leasing arrangement.[5]

Step 1: Calculating the initial investment (net of salvage) The first step in the analysis is to determine First National's initial investment (net of salvage) in the warehouse. Since the warehouse can be sold for its $100,000 book value at the end of year 12, subtracting the present value of the $100,000 discounted at the 12-percent required rate of return from the $300,000 outlay gives us the initial investment (net of salvage):

Current outlay to purchase warehouse	$300,000
Less: Present value of salvage value	
$100,000 (.257)	−25,700
Initial Investment in Warehouse (net of salvage)	$274,300

The initial investment (net of salvage) in the warehouse is $274,300.

Step 2: Calculating the payments The second step is to determine the 12 equal payments that will amortize the initial investment (net of salvage) while providing a 12-percent return to First National. Since the lease payment is made at the start of each of the 12 years, the 12 payments actually consist of an initial (beginning of year 1) payment followed by 11 end-of-year payments. The beginning of any year is considered equivalent to the end of the immediately preceding year. Equation 20.1 equates the initial investment (net of salvage) of $274,300 with the present value of the annual lease payment, x, discounted at the required return of 12 percent:

$$\$274,300 = 1.000x + 5.938x \tag{20.1}$$

---

[5]It is important to note that the payment value calculated in this example actually represents the *after-tax cash inflow* that the lessor must receive annually in order to provide its required return. In actuality, the lessor would adjust this cash flow for the benefit of depreciation and the investment tax credit, any administrative or maintenance expenses associated with the lease, and the tax effects of each of the aforementioned items as well as any other expenses borne by the lessor. Rather than confuse the issue at this time, it is assumed that the after-tax lessor cash-inflow requirement represents the amount of the lease payment charged the lessee in order to provide the lessor with its required return.

Since present-value tables are based on year-end cash flows, the present value factor for the end of the year zero (the beginning of year 1) payment is 1.000. The remaining 11 payments can be viewed as an 11-year annuity, since they are made at the end of years 1 through 11. The present-value interest factor for an annuity, PVIFA, with an 11-year life discounted at 12 percent is 5.938 (the coefficient of the second term on the right side of Equation 20.1).

Simplifying Equation 20.1 and solving for x, the annual lease payment, yields a lease payment, x, of \$39,535.88. By requiring the lessee to make this payment at the beginning of each year for the next 12 years, and selling the warehouse for \$100,000 at the end of this period, the First National Leasing Company will earn its required 12-percent return on the lease to the Kulsrud Corporation. The only "tricky" step in the calculation of the lease payments is due to the fact that payments are made at the beginning of each year. ●

The effect of leasing on future financing

Since leasing can be considered a type of financing, its effects on the firm's future financing must be discussed. Since lease payments are tax deductible, they are shown as an expense on the firm's income statement. Anyone analyzing the firm's income statement would probably recognize that an asset is being leased, although the actual details as to the amount and term of the lease would still be unclear. This section will discuss the lease disclosure requirements established by the Accounting Principles Board (APB) (today, the Financial Accounting Standards Board, FASB)[6] of the American Institute of Certified Public Accounts (AICPA), the effects of leases on financial ratios, and how both existing and prospective creditors view a lessee firm.

APB and FASB opinions. The initial opinion of the Accounting Principles Board was Opinion No. 5—"Reporting of Leases in Financial Statements of Lessee"—issued in September 1965. This opinion suggested that the financial statements of the lessee should disclose a sufficient amount of information concerning noncancelable (i.e., financial) leases, which are not recorded as assets or liabilities, to provide those concerned with the statements with sufficient information on the lease. Anyone reading the statements would then be able to assess the effects of the lease on the lessee's financial position. As a result of this statement by the board, financial leases were to be disclosed in a footnote to the firm's audited financial statements.

Accounting Principles Board Opinion No. 7—"Accounting for Leases in Financial Statements of Lessors"—issued in May 1966, reaffirmed the general statement made in Opinion No. 5 with respect to disclosures by the lessee. Accounting Principles Board Opinion No. 31—"Disclosure of Lease Commitments by Lessee"—issued in June 1973, suggested that disclosure of the present value of lease commitments (i.e., the capitalization of leases) would be helpful in evaluating the lessee's credit capacity and comparing it with

[6]Beginning on April 1, 1973, the name of the Accounting Principles Board (APB) was changed to the Financial Accounting Standards Board (FASB). The reorganization and renaming of the board was initiated to make it more responsive to the needs of the profession. The name Accounting Principles Board is used in this text when referring to any opinions rendered by the original APB.

that of firms using other means of financing property. Although this opinion did not require the capitalization of financial leases, it was indicative of the most recent decision on leasing. Guidelines were included in the opinion for the capitalization of leases, but until January 1, 1977, the disclosure of leases in a footnote to financial statements was all that was required. When leases are *capitalized*, the present value of all lease payments is shown as an asset and the total lease payment obligation is included as a liability on the firm's balance sheet. Most lessees find it advantageous *not* to capitalize lease payment obligations.

After many years of debate and controversy, the Financial Accounting Standards Board (FASB) in November 1976 in Standard No. 13, "Accounting for Leases," finally established requirements for the explicit disclosure of certain types of lease obligations on the firm's balance sheet. Standard 13 established criteria for classifying various types of leases and set reporting standards for each class. The requirements outlined in this standard applied initially only to leases entered into after January 1, 1977, and will apply retroactively after December 31, 1980, to any leases that were already in operation on January 1, 1977. The Standard defines a capital (i.e., financial) lease as one having *any* of the following four elements: (1) the lease transfers ownership of the property to the lessee by the end of the lease term; (2) the lease contains an option to purchase the property at a "bargain" price; (3) the lease term is equal to 75 percent or more of the estimated economic life of the property; or (4) the present value of the lease payments is equal to 90 percent or more of the fair market value of the leased property less any investment tax credit received by the lessor. If a lease meets any of these four criteria, it must be capitalized by the lessee on its balance sheet as an asset captioned "Lease Property Under Capital Lease" and a corresponding obligation (i.e., liability) captioned "Obligation Under Capital Lease." If it does not meet any of these criteria, it is an operating lease and need not be capitalized but its basic features must be disclosed in a footnote to the financial statements. The Standard, of course, establishes detailed guidelines to be used in capitalizing leases in order to reflect them as an asset and corresponding liability on the firm's balance sheet. In addition to requirements placed on the lessee, Standard 13 also provides explicit guidelines for the disclosure of leases by the lessor.

Leases and financial ratios.   The effect of leasing on financial ratios related to the balance sheet is quite interesting if leases are viewed as an alternative to borrowing. If a firm were to borrow to acquire assets, its assets would increase but so would its long-term debts. Prior to passage of FASB No. 13, leasing the same assets would create no changes in balance sheet accounts. Because FASB No. 13 will not be in full effect until December 31, 1980, certain financial commitments in the form of lease payments may still be camouflaged on the firm's balance sheet. An example will illustrate the effect of not capitalizing financial leases (as per FASB No. 13) on financial ratios.

EXAMPLE

In 1976 (i.e., prior to FASB No. 13) the Graber Company was considering either leasing or purchasing a machine costing $100,000 in order to replace an existing machine that was no longer useful.[7] If it had purchased the machine, the machine would have been depreciated straight-line over its ten-year life (it had no salvage value); a $100,000 9-percent loan would have been used to finance it. If the machine had been leased, the firm would have taken on a ten-year lease requiring annual beginning-of-year payments of $15,000. Table 20.2 presents the firm's 1976 income statement and balance sheet. The last two columns reflect the changes in various accounts that would have occurred had the proposed borrowing or leasing arrangements been made. Note particularly the difference in total assets values:

TABLE 20.2 Financial statements for the Graber Company (1976)

Income statement	1976	With borrow-ing	With leasing[a]
Sales	$500,000	$500,000	$500,000
Less: Cost of goods sold	−300,000	−300,000	−300,000
Gross profits	$200,000	$200,000	$200,000
Less: Operating expenses excluding interest, depreciation, and lease expense	− 80,000	− 80,000	− 80,000
Less: Depreciation expense	− 40,000	− 50,000	− 40,000
Lease expense	− 0	− 0	− 15,000
Interest expense	− 16,000	− 25,000	− 16,000
Profits before taxes	$ 64,000	$ 45,000	$ 49,000
Less: Taxes (.40)	− 25,600	− 18,000	− 19,600
Profits After Taxes	$ 38,400	$27,000	$ 29,400
Balance sheet			
Current assets	$ 60,000	60,000	$ 60,000
Fixed assets (net)	240,000	340,000	240,000
Total assets	$300,000	$400,000	$300,000
Current liabilities	$ 30,000	$ 30,000	$ 30,000
Long-term debt	120,000	220,000	120,000
Total liabilities	$150,000	$250,000	$150,000
Stockholders' equity	150,000	150,000	150,000
Total Liabilities and Stockholders' Equity	$300,000	$400,000	$300,000

[a]The firm has a ten-year lease on machinery requiring beginning-of-year payments of $15,000 for the next ten years. The lease is noncancelable.

[7]By assuming that an existing machine is being replaced, one can analyze the effects of the lease-purchase decision on various financial ratios without concerning oneself with the effects of the decision on the firm's revenues. The firm's sales revenues are assumed to be unaffected by this lease-purchase decision.

TABLE 20.3 A comparison of borrowing and leasing alternatives for the Graber Company, using ratio analysis

Ratio	With borrowing	With leasing
Debt-equity	1.47	0.80
Times-interest earned	2.80	4.06
Total asset turnover	1.25	1.67
Return on investment	6.75%	9.80%

Table 20.3 presents a number of ratios calculated from the data in Table 20.2.[8] The debt-equity ratios indicate that the firm would have been more highly levered and therefore financially more risky if it had chosen to borrow to purchase the new machine. The times-interest earned ratio for borrowing is below the same ratio for leasing, again indicating a higher financial risk associated with borrowing. The lower total asset turnover ratio for the borrowing alternative indicates a less efficient use of assets when the machine was purchased instead of leased. Finally, the lower return on investment if funds had been borrowed indicates that the firm's overall earning power would have been less if the asset had been purchased rather than leased. ●

The preceding example illustrates the effects leasing, as opposed to borrowing, has had on some standard financial ratios prior to implementation of FASB No. 13. By using leasing as opposed to borrowing to acquire the use of assets the firm, prior to FASB No. 13, was able to appear less financially risky, more efficient in its use of assets, and more profitable with respect to its return on assets than the firm that borrowed. However, these differences were the result of the accounting procedures used, and did not reflect true financial differences. Today (with the passage of FASB No. 13) prospective and existing creditors can more directly assess the *true* consequences of leasing on the firm's financial status; they should no longer be misled as the ratios in Table 20.3 illustrate.

Creditors' view. Existing and prospective creditors must closely evaluate a firm's financial statements. The creditor's analysis is now somewhat routine, even where a firm is committed to certain financial leases. Since the AICPA now requires the disclosure of financial leases directly on the firm's balance sheet, adjustments to financial statements for noncapitalized leases in order to get a true picture of a firm's financial position are no longer necessary. The firm's balance sheet now (after passage of FASB No. 13) includes the capitalized value of lease payments as an asset and the present value of lease payments as a liability. By applying ratio analysis to the financial statement, the creditor can obtain a more accurate picture of the firm's financial position than would have been the case prior to passage of FASB

---

[8]An in-depth discussion of the methods of calculation and the interpretation of these and various other ratios was presented in Chapter 3.

No. 13 (effective January 1, 1977, and retroactive at December 31, 1980). Existing and prospective shareholders and management are also now better able to use balance sheet data directly for doing financial analysis, since the capitalized value of lease payments is shown as an asset and corresponding liability.

EXAMPLE

The Graber Company lease described in the preceding example can be capitalized merely by determining the present value of the lease payments over the life of the lease. However, the rate at which the payments should be discounted is difficult to determine.[9] If 10 percent were used, the present value (i.e., the capitalized value) of the lease would be approximately $100,000 [$15,000 · (1.000 + 5.759)]. The methodology used is similar to that given in Equation 20.1, except that now the "x's" are known and their present value must be determined. If the capitalized value of the lease is added to both the firm's assets and its long-term liabilities, the ratios calculated for both the borrowing and leasing alternatives will be approximately equal. This provides a more accurate reflection of the firm's true financial position. ●

Since the consequences of missing a financial lease payment are the same as those of missing an interest or principal payment on debt, a financial analyst must view the lease as a long-term financial commitment by the lessee. With the passage of FASB No. 13, the inclusion of financial (capital) leases as an asset and corresponding liability provides for a balance sheet that more accurately reflects the firm's true financial status and thereby permits various types of financial ratio analyses to be performed directly on the statement by any interested party.

THE LEASE-PURCHASE DECISION

The lease-purchase, or lease-buy, decision is a decision that commonly confronts firms contemplating the acquisition of new fixed assets. The basic alternatives available are (1) to lease the assets, (2) to borrow in order to purchase the assets, or (3) to purchase the assets using available liquid cash. Alternatives (2) and (3), although they differ, can be analyzed in a similar fashion. Even if the firm has liquid resources with which to purchase the assets, the use of these dollars should be viewed as a form of borrowing. This is true since the opportunity cost of the funds is at minimum equal to the prevailing interest rate on borrowing, which the firm is assumed always to have available by having the ability to retire outstanding debt. Because the cash purchase and borrowing alternatives can be viewed as much the same, we need to compare only the leasing and borrowing alternatives here. Most firms, in any event do not generally have sufficient cash on hand to make cash purchases of fixed assets.

---

[9]The rate at which a financial lease is capitalized should be closely related to the cost of financing associated with the outright purchase alternative. The Financial Accounting Standards Board in Standard No. 13 established certain guidelines with respect to the appropriate rate for capitalizing leases. The interested reader is referred to that standard for a detailed description of these guidelines.

This section presents the analytical framework for comparing leasing and purchasing alternatives. Basically, what is needed is an *after-tax, incremental, present-value comparison.* As in the earlier discussions of capital budgeting, all costs will be measured on an after-tax cash-flow basis. The required analysis is presented in three sections. The first section is devoted to converting lease payments to after-tax cash outflows. The second is concerned with determining the after-tax cash outflows associated with the borrowing alternative. The final section presents the techniques required for comparing the lease and borrowing (i.e., purchase) outflows in order to make the lease-purchase decision. The description of these analytical manipulations will be aided using a simple example.

Lease payments and after-tax cash outflows

The after-tax cash outflows associated with leasing are relatively easy to calculate. If the periods in which lease payments are made are aligned with the periods in which the resulting tax benefits occur, the after-tax cash outflows for each period of the lease's life can be found simply by determining the difference between the lease payment and the tax savings in each period. An example will clarify the calculations required.

EXAMPLE

The Moore Company is contemplating acquiring a new machine tool costing $24,000. Discussions with various financial institutions have shown that either leasing or borrowing arrangements can be made to obtain the use of the machine. The leasing alternative would require the firm to sign a five-year financial lease requiring annual lease payments made in advance, although, for tax purposes, the payments could not be deducted until the services of the asset had actually been received. The annual payments would be set at a level that would give the lessor a 14-percent return on its investment. The machine is expected to have no salvage value at the end of its life. All maintenance, insurance, and other costs would be borne by the lessee.[10] The firm pays a 40-percent tax on its ordinary income.

Step 1: Finding the annual lease payment Substituting the appropriate values for this problem into Equation 20.1 results in Equation 20.2.

$$\$24{,}000 = 1.000x + 2.914x \tag{20.2}$$

The coefficient 2.914 represents the present-value interest factor for an annuity, PVIFA, from Table A-4 for four years discounted at 14 percent. Simplifying the equation and solving for x yields an annual lease payment of approximately $6132.[11]

---

[10]If maintenance, insurance, and other costs were to be borne by the lessor, the lessor in calculating the required lease payments in order to earn a specified return would have to include the present value of the after-tax cash outflows associated with these items as part of its initial investment. The present value of these cash outflows would be calculated using the lessor's required rate of return.

[11]As pointed out earlier in footnote 5, the value referred to here as the lease payment would actually represent the lessor's cash-inflow requirement, which is likely to be smaller than this amount. In order to simplify this discussion, the payment calculated is assumed to represent the actual lease payment.

**TABLE 20.4 The cash outflows
associated with leasing for the Moore Company**

Year ended	Lease payment (1)	Tax savings from lease payment[a] (2)	Cash outflow (1) − (2) (3)
0	$6,132	$ 0	$6,132
1	6,132	2,453	3,679
2	6,132	2,453	3,679
3	6,132	2,453	3,679
4	6,132	2,453	3,679
5	0	2,453	(2,453)

[a]Tax savings are calculated by multiplying the tax rate (.40) by the lease expense deductible in the year indicated.

Step 2: Finding the cash outflows Table 20.4 presents the after-tax cash outflows associated with each of the five years of the lease agreement.[12] Column 3 of the table presents the relevant cash outflows associated with the lease. The cash inflow of $2453 shown for year 5 is due to the fact that no actual lease payment is made in year 5 and the tax savings from the year 4 lease payment are realized in that year. ●

Borrowing and after-tax cash outflows

The cash outflows associated with borrowing are more difficult to obtain due to the need to identify both the interest on the loan and the depreciation expense associated with borrowing to purchase the asset. The calculation of the cash outflows associated with borrowing has two steps. The first step is to determine the annual interest component; the second is to calculate the depreciation and aggregate the cash outflows.

Step 1: Calculating the interest

Since the Internal Revenue Service allows the deduction of interest only—not the principal of a loan—from income for tax purposes, it is often necessary to split a loan payment into its interest and principal components. The technique used to do this can be illustrated by continuing the Moore Company example.

EXAMPLE

The purchase of the machine tool needed by the Moore Company could be financed by a 9-percent five-year loan requiring equal end-of-year installment payments of $6170.[13] These payments include both interest and principal. Table 20.5 presents the

[12]Although other cash outflows such as maintenance, insurance, taxes, and operating expenses may be relevant here, they are ignored in order to simplify the concepts being presented.

[13]The annual loan payment on the 9-percent, five-year loan of $24,000 is calculated using the loan amortization techniques described in Chapter 13. Dividing the present-value interest factor for an annuity, PVIFA, from Table A-4 for five-years at 9 percent (3.890) into the loan principal of $24,000 results in the annual loan payment of $6170. For a more detailed explanation of loan amortization, see Chapter 13.

TABLE 20.5 Determining the interest and principal components of the Moore Company loan payments

Year	Loan payment (1)	Beginning-of-year principal (2)	Payments Interest .09 · (2) (3)	Payments Principal (1) − (3) (4)	End-of-year principal (2) − (4) (5)
1	$6,170	$24,000	$2,160	$4,010	$19.990
2	6,170	19,990	1,799	4,371	15,619
3	6,170	15,619	1,406	4,764	10,855
4	6,170	10,855	977	5,193	5,662
5	6,170	5,662	510	5,660	—[a]

[a]The values in this table have been rounded to the nearest dollar, which results in a slight difference ($2) between the beginning-of-year-5 principal (in col. 2) and the principal payment (in col. 4).

calculations required to split the loan payments into their interest and principal components. Columns 3 and 4 show the annual interest and principal paid in each of the five years. ●

Step 2: Finding the cash outflows

The cash outflows[14] associated with borrowing to purchase the machine can be calculated once the loan payment has been broken into the interest and principal components. Again, we can continue the Moore Company example.

EXAMPLE

The only pertinent information we still need on the Moore Company is its depreciation schedule. The company intends to depreciate the $24,000 machine purchase price by the straight-line method over the asset's five-year life. No salvage value is expected. The annual depreciation is therefore $4800 ($24,000 ÷ 5). Table 20.6 presents the calculations required to determine the cash outflows associated with borrowing to purchase the new machine. Column 6 of the table presents the cash outflows associated with the borrowing alternative. A few points should be clarified with respect to the calculations in Table 20.6. The major cash outflow is the total loan payment for each year given in column 1. This outflow is reduced by the tax savings from writing off the depreciation and interest associated with the new machine and its financing, respectively. The resulting cash outflows are the after-tax cash outflows associated with the borrowing alternative. ●

[14]Although other cash outflows such as maintenance, insurance, taxes, and operating expenses may be relevant, here they have been ignored in order to simplify the concepts being presented.

TABLE 20.6 The cash outflows
associated with borrowing for the Moore Company

Year	Loan payment (1)	Deprecia-tion (2)	Interest (3)[a]	Total deductions (2) + (3) (4)	Tax shield .40 · (4) (5)	Cash outflow (1) − (5) (6)
1	$6,170	$4,800	$2,160	$6,960	$2,784	$3,386
2	6,170	4,800	1,799	6,599	2,640	3,530
3	6,170	4,800	1,406	6,206	2,482	3,688
4	6,170	4,800	977	5,777	2,311	3,859
5	6,170	4,800	510	5,310	2,124	4,046

[a]From Table 20.5, column 3.

Comparing lease and purchase alternatives

In order to compare lease and purchase alternatives, the present value of the stream of cash outflows associated with each alternative must be calculated. This is because the cash outflows occur at different points in time. The discount rate used to evaluate the cash flows should be the *after-tax cost of debt*,[15] since both alternatives may be considered equally risky and are contractual—not guaranteed—arrangements similar to long-term debt. If the after-tax cost of debt, which was discussed in Chapter 17, is used to evaluate the alternative cash outflows, only the cost of a riskless contractual obligation—not risk—is considered. The procedure for comparing the two alternatives can be illustrated using the Moore Company example.

EXAMPLE

At the time the Moore Company must make the lease-purchase decision, its after-tax cost of debt is approximately equal to 6 percent.[16] By comparing the present value of the cash outflows associated with each of the alternatives, the decision whether to lease or purchase the machine can be made. The alternative for which the present value of the cash outflows is the lowest will be the most acceptable, since it will be the cheapest alternative in terms of today's dollars. Table 20.7 presents the calculations required.

[15]Although a great deal of controversy surrounds the appropriate discount rate, the after-tax cost of debt is used to evaluate the lease-purchase decision because the decision itself involves the choice between two contractual alternatives having very low risk. If we were evaluating whether a given machine should be acquired, the appropriate risk-adjusted rate or cost of capital would be used, but in this type of analysis we are attempting only to determine the best *financing* techniques—leasing or borrowing.

[16]Ignoring any flotation costs, the firm's after-tax cost of debt would be 5.4 percent (i.e., 9% debt cost × (1 − .40 tax rate)). In order to reflect both the flotation costs associated with selling new debt and the need to sell the debt at a discount, the use of an after-tax debt cost of 6 percent was believed to be the applicable discount rate. A more detailed discussion of techniques for calculating a firm's after-tax cost of debt can be found in Chapter 17.

**TABLE 20.7 A comparison of the cash outflows
associated with leasing and borrowing for the Moore Company**

	Leasing			Borrowing		
Year	Cash outflows[a] (1)	Present value factors[b] (2)	Present value of outflows (1) · (2) (3)	Cash outflows[c] (4)	Present value factors[b] (5)	Present value of outflows (4) · (5) (6)
0	$6,132	1.000	$ 6,132	$ 0	1.000	$ 0
1	3,679	.943	3,469	3,386	.943	3,193
2	3,679	.890	3,274	3,530	.890	3,142
3	3,679	.840	3,090	3,688	.840	3,098
4	3,679	.792	2,914	3,859	.792	3,056
5	(2,453)	.747	(1,832)	4,046	.747	3,022
	P.V. of Cash Outflows		$17,047	P.V. of Cash Outflows		$15,511

[a]From column 3, Table 20.4.
[b]From Table A-3, PVIF, for 6 percent and the corresponding year.
[c]From column 6, Table 20.6.

The sum of the present values of the cash outflows for leasing and borrowing (the totals of columns 3 and 6, respectively, in Table 20.7) indicates that borrowing is preferable. This is because the present value of the borrowing cost is less than the present value of the leasing cost ($15,511 vs. $17,047). The *incremental* savings achieved by borrowing rather than leasing would be $1536 ($17,047 − $15,511). Thus borrowing and purchasing the machine will save the firm $1536 in today's dollars. Had the present value of the cash outflows associated with the lease been less than the present value of the cash outflows associated with borrowing, leasing would have been preferable. ●

The techniques described in the preceding pages for comparing lease and borrowing alternatives may be applied in different ways. The approach illustrated here using the Moore Company data is one of the most straightforward. Some of the factors to be considered in making lease-purchase decisions are the effects of accelerated depreciation, inexpensive borrowing opportunities, high required lessor returns, and a low risk of obsolescence. All these would increase the attractiveness of borrowing. Subjective factors must also be included in the decision-making process. Like most financial decisions, the lease-purchase decision requires a certain degree of judgment or intuition.

ADVANTAGES AND DISADVANTAGES OF LEASING

Leasing has a number of nonquantifiable advantages and disadvantages that should be considered in making a decision between leasing and borrowing.

Although not all these advantages and disadvantages hold in every case, it is not unusual for a number of them to be relevant to a given lease-purchase decision.

Advantages of leasing

The basic advantages commonly cited for leasing are the ability it gives the lessor to, in effect, depreciate land, its effects on financial ratios, its effect on the firm's liquidity, the ability it gives the firm to obtain 100-percent financing, the limited claims of lessors in the event of bankruptcy or reorganization, the fact that the firm may avoid assuming the risk of obsolescence, the lack of many restrictive covenants, and the flexibility provided. Each of these often cited advantages is described and critically evaluated below.

Effective depreciation of land. Leasing allows the lessee to, in effect, depreciate land, which is prohibited under a purchase of land. Since the lessee who leases land is permitted to deduct the total lease payment as an expense for tax purposes, the effect is the same as it would be if he or she purchased the land and then depreciated it. The larger the amount of land included in a lease agreement, the more advantageous this factor becomes from the point of view of the lessee. However, this advantage is somewhat tempered by the fact that land generally has a salvage value for its purchaser, which it does not for a lessee.

Effects on financial ratios. Earlier in the chapter we described the effect leasing could have on certain financial ratios involving balance sheet data. Leasing, since it results in the receipt of service from an asset possibly without increasing the assets or liabilities on the firm's balance sheet, may be camouflaged on the balance sheet. With the passage of FASB No. 13 this advantage no longer applies to financial leases, although in the case of operating leases it remains a potential advantage. Of course, even in the case of operating leases, the American Institute of Certified Public Accountants requires disclosure of the lease in a footnote to the firm's statements. Today, most analysts are aware of the significance of leasing for the firm's financial position and will not view the firm's financial statements strictly as presented; instead, they will make certain adjustments to these statements that will more accurately reflect the effect of any existing operating leases on the firm's financial position.

Increased liquidity. The use of sale-leaseback arrangements may permit the firm to increase its liquidity by converting an *existing* asset into cash, which can be used as working capital. A firm short of working capital or in a liquidity squeeze can sell an owned asset to a lessor and lease the asset back for a specified number of years. Of course, this action binds the firm to making fixed payments over a period of years. The benefits of the increase in current liquidity are therefore tempered somewhat by the added fixed financial payments incurred through the lease.

100-percent financing.   Another advantage of leasing is that is provides 100-percent financing. Most loan agreements for the purchase of fixed assets require the borrower to pay a portion of the purchase price as a down payment. As a result, the borrower receives only 90 to 95 percent of the purchase price of the asset. In the case of a lease, the lessee is not required to make any type of down payment; he or she must make only a series of periodic payments. In essence, a lease permits a firm to receive the use of an asset for a smaller initial out-of-pocket cost than borrowing. However, since large initial lease payments are often required in advance, it is possible to view the initial advance payment as a type of down payment.[17]

Limited claims in the event of bankruptcy or reorganization. When a firm becomes bankrupt or is reorganized, the maximum claim of lessors against the corporation is three years of lease payments.[18] If debt is used to purchase an asset, the creditors have a claim equal to the total amount of unpaid financing. Of course, in such a case an owned asset may have a salvage value that can be used to defray the firm's obligations to its creditors.

Avoidance of the risk of obsolescence.   In a lease arrangement, the firm may avoid assuming the risk of obsolescence if the lessor in setting the lease payments fails to anticipate accurately the obsolescence of assets. This is especially true in the case of operating leases, which generally have relatively short lives. However, most lessors are perceptive enough to require sufficient compensation in both the term and the amount of lease payments to protect themselves against obsolescence.

Lack of many restrictive covenants.   A lessee avoids many restrictive covenants that are normally included as part of a long-term loan.[19] Requirements with respect to subsequent financing, minimum working capital, changes in management, and so on are *not* normally found in a lease agreement; the only restrictive covenant occasionally included in the lease relates to subsequent lease commitments. The general lack of restrictive covenants allows the lessee much greater flexibility in its operations. This may be viewed as a quite important advantage by the lessee.

Flexibility provided.   In the case of low-cost assets that are infrequently acquired, leasing—especially operating leases—may provide the firm with needed financing flexibility. This flexibility is attributable to the fact

---

[17]Since lease payments are normally made in advance, there is no guarantee that leasing a given asset provides more financing than borrowing; in many instances it may provide less financing than borrowing.

[18]This limitation is specified in Chapter X of the Bankruptcy Act. A description of the key aspects of the Bankruptcy Act, along with a discussion of the various bankruptcy and reorganization procedures, is included in Chapter 26.

[19]An in-depth discussion of the various *restrictive covenants,* which are certain financial and operating constraints contractually placed upon the firm included in long-term loan agreements, is presented in Chapter 21. It is possible that even under a lease certain contractual constraints may be placed upon the firm as part of the lease agreement.

that the firm does not have to arrange other financing for these assets and can somewhat conveniently obtain them through a lease, thereby preserving its fund-raising power for the acquisition of more costly assets; the firm also retains its ability to raise funds in economically preferred quantities at the right time, thereby, again helping to lower its overall capital costs. Flexibility is also provided in the sense that with a short-term operating lease the firm can buy time to shop around for an owned asset that may be more advantageous from the standpoint of long-run owners' wealth maximization.

Disadvantages of leasing

The commonly cited disadvantages of leasing include high interest costs, the lack of salvage value, the difficulty of making property improvements, and obsolescence considerations. Though not relevant in every case, they may bear importantly on the lease-purchase decision in certain instances. Each of the often cited disadvantages is described and critically evaluated below.

High interest costs.   As we pointed out earlier, a lease does not have an explicit interest cost; rather, the lessor builds a return for itself into the lease payment. In many leases the implicit return to the lessor is quite high, so that the firm might be better off borrowing to purchase the asset. The lessee should estimate this return in the manner illustrated earlier, using Equation 20.1, in order to determine whether it is reasonable.

Lack of salvage value.   At the end of the term of the lease agreement, the salvage value of assets, if any, is realized by the lessor. If the firm had purchased the assets, it could have realized their salvage value. If assets are expected to appreciate over the life of a lease agreement, it may be wiser to purchase them, although various other factors must be considered in making this decision. Appreciation in the value of assets is especially likely when land or buildings, or both, are involved. If the lease contains a purchase option, this disadvantage may not exist.

Difficulty of property improvements.   Under a lease, the lessee is generally prohibited from making improvements on the leased property without the approval of the lessor. If the property were owned, this difficulty would not arise. Related to this disadvantage is the fact that it is often hard to obtain financing for improvements on leased property since it is difficult for the lender to obtain a security interest in the improvements. On the other hand, the lessor may agree in the initial lease contract to finance or make certain leasehold improvements specified by the lessee.

Obsolescence considerations.   If a lessee leases (under financial lease) an asset that subsequently becomes obsolete, it still has to make lease payments over the remaining life of the lease. This is true even if it is unable to use the leased assets. In many instances, a lessee will continue to use obsolete assets since it must pay for them. This type of situation can weaken a firm's competitive position by raising (or failing to lower) production costs and therefore forcing the sale price of its products to be increased in order to earn a profit.

SUMMARY

This chapter has discussed a number of important aspects of leasing. The basic types of leases are operating and financial leases. The noncancelability and generally longer term of financial leases makes them a source of financing to the business firm. Since the basic alternative to a financial lease is an outright purchase of assets, which normally requires borrowing, leasing can be viewed as a source of financing to the firm. A financial lease can be initiated in two ways—as a direct lease or as a sale-leaseback arrangement. Under a direct lease, the lessor purchases specified assets from an outsider and leases them to the firm. Under a sale-leaseback arrangement, the lessor purchases the assets from the lessee and then leases them back to the same firm.

Most financial leases require the lessee to maintain, insure, and pay taxes on leased assets; operating leases, on the other hand, normally include maintenance clauses whereby the lessor absorbs these costs. Leases may be renewable, although most financial leases are not. The IRS provides guidelines specifying which lease payments are tax-deductible. A lease is a contractual arrangement with a specified term, series of lease payments, payment dates, penalties, and other important features.

Since lease payments are tax-deductible, the cost of leasing is reduced by the tax shield provided. Most lease payments are made in advance, although the tax deduction cannot be taken until the service provided by the lease has been received. The amount of the annual lease payment is determined by the lessor, who seeks to assure itself of a certain return over the term of the lease. In calculating lease payments, present values must be taken into account. The lessee firm is required by certain opinions of the Financial Accounting Standards Board (formerly known as the Accounting Principles Board) of the AICPA to disclose the existence of leases on its financial statements. In the case of financial (or capital) leases, Standard No. 13 (effective January 1, 1977, and retroactive after December 31, 1980) requires and outlines detailed procedures for capitalization of the lease commitment as an asset and corresponding liability. In the case of operating leases, only a footnote to the firm's statements indicating the key features of the lease is required. In the instance a lease obligation is not capitalized, traditional financial ratios can be misleading. Therefore, the capitalization of financial leases required by Standard No. 13 provides for a balance sheet that more accurately reflects the true financial condition of the firm. This disclosure permits financial ratio analysis to be performed on the unadjusted financial statements.

A lease-purchase decision can be evaluated by calculating the after-tax cash outflows associated with the lease and purchase alternatives. By discounting the cash outflows at the after-tax cost of debt, the most desirable alternative (i.e., to lease or to borrow and purchase) can be determined. The most desirable alternative is one that has the minimum present value of after-tax cash outflows associated with it. However, the results of all such quantitative analyses should be viewed in light of a variety of subjective advantages and disadvantages of leasing. Commonly cited advantages of leasing include the ability to depreciate land, potential favorable ratio effects, increased liquidity, the ability to obtain 100-percent financing, limited claims of lessors in bankruptcy or reorganization, the avoidance of obsolesence risk, lack of many restrictive covenants, and the flexibility provided. Disadvantages include high interest costs, lack of salvage value, difficulty of property improvements, and obsolesence considerations.

QUESTIONS

20-1 What is leasing? What roles are played by the lessor and lessee? How are lease payments treated for tax purposes?

20-2 Why is leasing often viewed as a source of financing? Why was it often referred to as a form of "off-balance-sheet financing" prior to FASB No. 13?

20-3 What is an operating lease? What are its key characteristics? What is the market value (at the termination of the lease) of a leased asset?

20-4 What is a financial lease? How is it different from an operating lease?

20-5 What is the difference between a *direct lease* and a *sale-leaseback arrangement*? Which of these is a quick source of cash for the firm? Why?

20-6 What sort of companies may act as lessors of assets? Do these lessors generally provide for the renewal of a lease? Under what conditions may a renewal be offered?

20-7 How are lease payments timed? What effect might advance payments have on the tax benefits of a lease arrangement and the after-tax cash outflows associated with the lease?

20-8 What were the requirements for lease disclosure as outlined by the Accounting Principles Board in its Opinions 5, 7, and 31? What did most lessees do with respect to disclosure?

20-9 According to FASB No. 13, certain types of leases must be *capitalized* and reflected on the balance sheet. What types of leases must be capitalized? How does a financial manager capitalize a lease?

20-10 What cash flows are used in evaluating leasing and purchase alternatives? How are they calculated?

20-11 Why are the cash outflows associated with both leasing and borrowing discounted at the after-tax cost of debt in evaluating a lease-purchase decision?

20-12 What are the key advantages and disadvantages of leasing as a source of financing? Which of these advantages and disadvantages are most important in a subjective lease-buy evaluation?

20-13 What are the major similarities and the major differences between lease and debt financing? In what circumstances may leasing be most attractive?

PROBLEMS

20-1 The Lima Company's lease on a warehouse requires annual lease payments of $40,000 to be made at the beginning of each year for the next 12 years. Determine the after-tax cash outflows each year, assuming the firm is in the 40-percent tax bracket.

20-2 Given the following lease payments and terms, determine the yearly after-tax cash outflows in each case assuming that lease payments are made at the start of each year and the firm is in the 40-percent tax bracket.

Firm	Annual lease payment	Term of lease
A	$100,000	4 years
B	$ 80,000	14 years
C	$150,000	8 years
D	$ 60,000	25 years
E	$ 20,000	10 years

20-3 The American Leasing Company is attempting to determine the initial investment (net of salvage value) it must make in a number of leases. The firm's required rate of return is 16 percent. Given the following costs, salvage values, and lives, determine the initial investment required under each of the leasing alternatives.

Leasing alternatives	Cost of leased asset	Salvage value	Life of lease
A	$100,000	$ 25,000	14 years
B	$150,000	$ 30,000	18 years
C	$400,400	$ 40,000	8 years
D	$440,000	$100,000	16 years
E	$ 38,000	$ 3,000	7 years

20-4 For each of the following initial investments (net of salvage), required returns, and lease lives, determine the annual beginning-of-period lease payments required to justify the lease.

Lease	Initial investment	Required return	Life of lease
A	$400,000	10%	15 years
B	$320,000	12%	8 years
C	$180,000	13%	13 years
D	$ 65,000	9%	7 years
E	$ 13,000	15%	4 years
F	$723,000	11%	19 years

20-5 The Confederated Financial Corporation is considering leasing a facility costing $280,000 to the Klink-Klenke Aviation Company. K-K wants a 10-year lease and is in the 40-percent tax bracket. Confederated has estimated a $40,000 salvage value at the end of 10 years. Confederated wishes to earn 15 percent on each leasing deal. The lease payment will be made at the start of each year.
a Determine the required initial investment (net of salvage) if Confederated accepts the lease.
b Determine the annual lease payments that K-K must make to Confederated to justify the arrangement.

c Determine the annual after-tax cash outflow for K-K resulting from the lease.

20-6 The Big Warehouse Company is in need of cash and is considering a sale-leaseback arrangement involving one of its warehouse buildings. Three different leasing companies have been approached and, as a result of industrial espionage, Big Warehouse has obtained certain information with respect to each of the prospective lessors—R, S, and T. Each lessor is expected to require beginning-of-year lease payments and a 10-year lease commitment. Each is willing to purchase the firm's warehouse for its current $120,000 book value. Big Warehouse is currently in the 40-percent tax bracket. The lessors' required returns and the salvage value they estimate for the building are tabulated below.

Lessor	Expected salvage value of building	Required rate of return
R	$12,000	11%
S	$30,000	12%
T	$20,000	13%

a Calculate the initial investment (net of salvage) required of each lessor.
b Determine the annual lease payments that would be charged by the three lessors, respectively, if each just receives its required rate of return.
c Determine the annual after-tax cash outflow for Big Warehouse under each of the leasing arrangements.
d Which of the lessors should Big Warehouse do business with? Why?

20-7 The Rapid American Company is considering either leasing or purchasing a new machine costing $60,000. If the machine is purchased, it will be depreciated straight-line (no salvage value) over a 20-year life. A $60,000, 10-percent loan will be used to finance the purchase. The leasing arrangement would entail a 20-year lease requiring annual beginning-of-year payments of $6300. The firm's most recent financial statements are given.

Financial Statements
Rapid American Company
Year Ending December 31

Income statement

Sales	$200,000
Less: Cost of goods sold	140,000
Gross profits	$ 60,000
Less: Operating expenses excluding interest, depreciation, and	
lease expense	$ 10,000
Depreciation expense	10,000
Lease expense	0
Interest expense	15,000
Profits before taxes	$ 25,000
Less: Taxes (.40)	10,000
Profits After Taxes	$15,000

Balance sheet

Current assets	$ 30,000
Fixed assets (net)	120,000
Total Assets	$150,000
Current liabilities	$ 20,000
Long-term debt	50,000
Total Liabilities	$ 70,000
Stockholders' equity	$ 80,000
Total Liabilities and Stockholders' Equity	$150,000

a Recast the Rapid American Company's *income statement* on the assumption that, as a result of acquiring the new machine, sales increased to $280,000, the cost of goods sold to $196,000, and operating expenses excluding interest, depreciation, and lease expense to $40,000.
   (1) Show the income statement if borrowing is used to purchase the asset.
   (2) Show the income statement if the asset is leased.
b Recast the Rapid American Company's *balance sheet* assuming that all items will remain unchanged other than those affected by the new machine.
   (1) Show the balance sheet if the borrowing alternative is selected.
   (2) Show the balance sheet if the leasing alternative is selected.
c Based on the income statements and balance sheets generated for the borrowing and leasing alternatives, calculate the following ratios in each case.
   (1) The debt-equity ratio.
   (2) The times interest earned ratio.
   (3) The total asset turnover.
   (4) The return on investment.
d Discuss the effects of each of the alternatives (borrowing or leasing) on the firm's financial picture as indicated by the ratios calculated in c. Explain why leasing was often considered a form of "off-balance-sheet financing" prior to FASB No. 13.

20-8 Rocky Smith, a credit analyst for Winger City Bank, has been charged with analyzing the financial statements of the Wayne Corporation. An abbreviated income statement and balance sheet for the company are presented below.
a Calculate the firm's cash outflow resulting from the lease for each year, assuming that the firm pays taxes of 40-percent on ordinary income.
b Calculate the following ratios, using the data in the financial statements presented above.
   (1) The debt-equity ratio.
   (2) The times-interest earned ratio.
   (3) The total asset turnover.
   (4) The return on investment.
c If the capitalization rate was 11 percent, what would the capitalized value of the lease be?
d Using the result of c, prepare a balance sheet for the firm showing the capitalized lease value.
e Using the new balance sheet, calculate the ratios indicated in b.

Financial Statements
Wayne Corporation
Year Ending December 31

Income statement

Sales		$400,000
Less: Cost of goods sold		260,000
Gross profit		$140,000
Less: Expenses		
General and admin.	$80,000	
Lease[a]	20,000	
Interest	12,000	
Depreciation	8,000	
Total		120,000
Profits before taxes		$ 20,000
Less: Taxes (40%)		8,000
Profits after Taxes		$ 12,000

Balance sheet

Current assets	$120,000	Current liabilities	$ 60,000
Fixed assets (net)	360,000	Long-term debt	240,000
Total Assets	$480,000	Total liabilities	$300,000
		Stockholders' equity	$180,000
		Total Liabilities and Stockholders' Equity	$480,000

[a]A lease requiring annual beginning-of-year payments of $20,000 for the next 15 years is held by the firm.

f Compare the ratios derived in **b** and **e**. Which do you believe are most indicative of the firm's true financial position? Explain.

20-9 Given the following lease payments, years remaining until the lease terminates, and capitalization rates, calculate the capitalized value of each lease, assuming that lease payments are made annually at the beginning of each year.

Lease	Lease payment	Remaining life	Capitalization rate
A	$ 40,000	12 years	10%
B	$120,000	8 years	12%
C	$ 9,000	18 years	14%
D	$ 16,000	3 years	9%
E	$ 47,000	20 years	11%

20-10 The Walker Company wishes to purchase an asset costing $117,000. The full amount needed to finance the asset can be borrowed at 11-percent interest.

The terms of the loan require equal end-of-year payments for the next six years. Determine the total annual loan payment, the amount of interest, and the amount of principal paid for each year.

20-11 For each of the following loan amounts, loan payments, and loan lives, calculate the interest rate and interest paid each year over the life of the loan, assuming loan payments are made at the end of each year.

Loan	Amount	Payment	Life
A	$ 30,000	$11,641	3 years
B	$ 80,000	$24,691	4 years
C	$ 40,000	$10,018	5 years
D	$150,000	$60,313	3 years
E	$100,000	$24,325	6 years

20-12 For each of the following loan amounts, interest rates, and loan lives, calculate the annual loan payment and annual interest paid each year over the life of the loan, assuming the payments are made at the end of each year.

Loan	Amount	Interest rate	Life
X_1	$14,000	10%	4 years
X_2	$17,500	7%	2 years
X_3	$ 2,400	13%	3 years
X_4	$49,000	14%	5 years
X_5	$26,500	11%	6 years

20-13 The Haunted House Restaurant wishes to evaluate two plans, borrowing to purchase and leasing, for financing an oven.
Purchase: The oven costs $20,000 and will have a five-year life. The asset will be depreciated straight-line to a zero salvage value. The total purchase price will be financed by a five-year, 12-percent loan requiring equal annual end-of-year payments. The firm is in the 40-percent tax bracket.
Leasing: The restaurant could lease the asset under a five-year lease requiring annual beginning-of-year payments of $5000.
a For the purchase plan, calculate the following:
   (1) The annual end-of-year payment.
   (2) The annual interest expense deductible for tax purposes for each of the five years.
   (3) The after-tax cash outflows resulting from the purchase for each of the five years.
   (4) Using a 4-percent *discount* rate, the present value of the cash outflows.
b For the leasing plan, calculate the following:
   (1) The after-tax cash outflows each year.
   (2) The present value of the cash outflows using a 4-percent *discount* rate.
c Compare the present value of each of the cash-flow streams (from each plan) and determine which would be preferable. Explain your answer.
20-14 The Tony Corporation is attempting to determine whether to lease or purchase a new plating mill. The firm is in the 40-percent tax bracket and its after-tax cost of debt is currently 5 percent. The terms of the lease and the purchase are given below.

Purchase: The mill, costing $60,000, can be financed entirely with an 8-percent loan requiring annual end-of-year payments of $23,282 for three years. The firm in this case would depreciate the asset with the straight-line method to a zero salvage value at the end of its three-year life.

Lease: Annual advance lease payments of $21,930 are required over the three-year life of the lease. The lease payment is not deductible for tax purposes until the end of each year.

a Calculate the after-tax cash outflows associated with each alternative.

b Calculate the present value of each cash-flow stream.

c Which alternative would you recommend and why?

20-15 The Tucson Taxi Company needs to expand its facilities. In order to do so, the firm must acquire land and improvements costing $80,000. These assets can be leased or purchased. The firm is in the 40-percent tax bracket and its after-tax cost of debt is 6 percent. The terms of the lease and purchase plans are given:

Lease: The leasing arrangement would require beginning-of-year payments which for tax purposes could not be deducted until the end of the year. The lease would be for five years, and the facility is expected to have a salvage value of $10,000 at the end of that period. The lessor intends to charge equal annual lease payments that would allow a return of 16-percent on the investment.

Purchase: If the firm purchases the facility, the purchase would be financed with a five-year 10-percent loan requiring equal end-of-year payments of $21,103. The facility would be depreciated straight-line over its life. The Tucson Taxi Company anticipates a zero salvage value for the facility at that time.

a Calculate the annual lease payment required in order to provide the lessor with a 16-percent rate of return.

b Determine the after-tax cash outflows of the lessee under each alternative.

c Find the present value of the after-tax cash outflows using the after-tax cost of debt.

d Which alternative (i.e., lease or purchase) would you recommend? Why?

SELECTED REFERENCES

Anderson, Paul F., and John D. Martin, "Lease versus Purchase Decisions: A Survey of Current Practice," *Financial Management 6* (Spring 1977), pp. 41–47.

Bierman, H., Jr., "Accounting for Capitalized Leases: Tax Considerations," *Accounting Review 48* (April 1973), pp. 421–424.

Blum, James D., "Accounting and Reporting for Leases by Lessees: The Interest Rate Problems," *Management Accounting 59* (April 1978), pp. 25–28.

Bower, Richard S., "Issues in Lease Financing," *Financial Management 2* (Winter 1973), pp. 25–34.

Bower, Richard S., Frank C. Herringer, and J. Peter Williamson, "Lease Evaluation," *Accounting Review 41* (April 1966), pp. 257–265.

Cooper, Kerry, and Robert H. Strawser, "Evaluation of Capital Budgeting Projects Involving Asset Leases," *Financial Management 4* (Spring 1975), pp. 44–49.

Doenges, R. Conrad, "The Cost of Leasing," *Engineering Economist 17* (Fall 1971), pp. 31–44.

Ferrara, William L., "The Case for Symmetry in Lease Reporting," *Management Accounting 59* (April 1978), pp. 17–24.

Ferrara, William L., and Joseph F. Wodjak, "Valuation of Long-term Leases," *Financial Analysts Journal 25* (November-December 1969), pp. 27–32.

Financial Accounting Standards Board, *Financial Accounting Standards: Original Pronouncements as of July 1, 1978* (Stamford, Conn.: Financial Accounting Standards Board, 1978), Standard No. 13—"Accounting for Leases."

Franks, Julian, and Stewart D. Hodges, "Valuation of Financial Lease Contracts: A Note," *Journal of Finance 33* (May 1978), pp. 657–669.

Gordon, Myron J., "A General Solution to the Buy or Lease Decision: A Pedagogical Note," *Journal of Finance 29* (March 1974), pp. 245–250.

Gritta, Richard D., "The Impact of the Capitalization of Leases on Financial Analysis," *Financial Analysts Journal 30* (March-April 1974), pp. 1–6.

Honing, Lawrence E., and Stephen C. Coley, "An After-Tax Equivalent Payment Approach to Conventional Lease Analysis," *Financial Management 4* (Winter 1975), pp. 18–27.

Jackson, James F., Jr., *An Evaluation of Lease Financing* (Austin: Bureau of Business Research, University of Texas, 1967).

Jenkins, David O., "Purchase or Cancelable Lease," *Financial Executive 38* (April 1970), pp. 26–31.

Johnson, Robert W., and Wilbur G. Lewellen, "Analysis of the Lease-or-Buy Decision," *Journal of Finance 27* (September 1972), pp. 815–823.

Levy, L. E., "Off Balance Sheet Financing," *Management Accounting* (May 1969), pp. 12–14.

Lewellen, Wilbur G., Michael S. Long, and John J. McConnell, "Asset Leasing in Competitive Capital Markets," *Journal of Finance 31* (June 1976), pp. 787–798.

Long, Michael S., "Leasing and the Cost of Capital," *Journal of Financial and Quantitative Analysis 12* (November 1977), pp. 579–586.

Miller, Merton H., and Charles W. Upton, "Leasing, Buying, and the Cost of Capital Services," *Journal of Finance 31* (June 1976), pp. 761–786.

Mitchell, G. B., "After-Tax Cost of Leasing," *Accounting Review 45* (April 1970), pp. 308–314.

Myers, Stewart C., David A. Dill, and Alberto J. Bautista, "Valuation of Financial Lease Contracts," *Journal of Finance 31* (June 1976), pp. 799–819.

Nantell, Timothy J., "Equivalence of Lease versus Buy Analyses," *Financial Management 2* (Autumn 1973), pp. 61–65.

Ofer, Aharon R., "The Evaluation of the Lease versus Purchase Alternatives," *Financial Management 5* (Summer 1976), pp. 67–72.

Roenfeldt, Rodney L., and Jerome S. Osteryoung, "Analysis of Financial Leases," *Financial Management 2* (Spring 1973), pp. 74–87.

Sartoris, William L., and Ronda S. Paul, "Lease Evaluation—Another Capital Budgeting Decision," *Financial Management 2* (Summer 1973), pp. 46–52.

Schall, Lawrence D., "The Lease-or-Buy and Asset Acquisition Decisions," *Journal of Finance 29* (September 1974), pp. 1203–1214.

Vancil, Richard F., "Lease or Borrow: New Method of Analysis," *Harvard Business Review 39* (September-October 1967), pp. 68–83.

CHAPTER 21
Long-term debt financing

This chapter is devoted to the long-term debt financing (debt capital) of the business firm. The importance of long-term debt to the firm's capital structure was emphasized in earlier discussions of financial leverage, the cost of capital, and capital structure. The presence of debt in the firm's capital structure provides financial leverage, which tends to magnify the effects of increased operating profits on the owners' returns. Since debt is normally the cheapest form of long-term financing, due to the tax deductibility of interest, it is a quite desirable component of the firm's capital structure. The presence of long-term debt in the firm's capital structure generally lowers the firm's cost of capital,[1] thereby permitting the firm to select from a larger group of acceptable investment alternatives.

Long-term debt financing can be obtained in two ways. One way is to borrow the money directly. These *term loans* with varying requirements are available from a number of major financial institutions. A second method of raising long-term debt funds is to sell marketable debt in the form of *bonds*. By selling bonds, the firm can sell small parts of the total debt financing to various purchasers.

This chapter is divided into five major sections. The first section discusses the general characteristics of long-term debt financing. The second section describes the various types of term loans available to the business borrower and identifies the major suppliers of term loans. The third section discusses the characteristics of corporate bonds. The fourth section discusses common types of bonds. The final section of this chapter discusses bond-refunding options; special emphasis is placed on the early retirement of outstanding bonds.

---

[1]This is commonly the case due to the tax deductibility of interest, which causes the explicit cost of debt (discussed in Chapter 17) to be quite low. Of course, as was pointed out in Chapter 18, the introduction of large quantities of debt into the firm's capital structure can result in high levels of financial risk, which can cause the firm's weighted average cost of capital to rise.

CHARACTERISTICS OF LONG-TERM DEBT FINANCING

Long-term debt is defined as debt having a maturity of greater than one year.[2] The long-term debts of business firms typically have maturities of between five and twenty years. When a long-term debt is within a year of its maturity, many accountants will move the debt balance from the "long-term debt" account to the current liabilities account since at that point the long-term debt has actually become a short-term obligation. Similar treatment is given to portions of long-term debts that are payable in the coming year. These entries are normally captioned the "Current Portion of Long-Term Debt."

Standard loan provisions

A number of standard provisions are included in long-term loan agreements. These provisions are intended to assure the lender that the firm continues to exist and operates in a respectable and businesslike manner. They should not place a burden on the financially sound business firm. The borrower is required to maintain satisfactory accounting records, render financial statements, pay its taxes and other liabilities, maintain all its facilities in good condition, and not sell its accounts receivable.

The maintenance of satisfactory accounting records.
The borrower is required to maintain satisfactory accounting records in accordance with generally accepted accounting principles. This guarantees the lender that the financial data of the borrower is accurately presented and permits the easy interpretation of operating results.

The rendering of financial statements.
The borrower is required to supply, at certain dates, audited financial statements that provide the lender with a yardstick for enforcing certain restrictive covenants and enable it to monitor the firm's progress. Often, the lender requires the firm's bank account statements in order to evaluate its spending behavior.

The payment of taxes and other liabilities.
The borrower is required to pay taxes and other liabilities when due. The lender is not only concerned with receiving its required payments; it must also make sure that the borrower does not default on any of its other payment obligations, since default on any payment could result in bankruptcy. If the borrower does not pay its bills, the lender can force repayment of the loan.

Repair and maintenance requirements.
The lender requires the borrower to maintain all its facilities in good working order. This ensures the lender that the borrower will not let its assets deteriorate to the point where

---

[2]Some texts classify debts with maturities of one to seven years as *intermediate-term debt*. This text uses a strict short-term–long-term classification. Debts with maturities of less than one year are considered short term, and debts with maturities greater than one year are considered long term. This type of classification is more in line with the firm's balance sheet classification of current liabilities and long-term debts.

their market value is negligible. In a sense, it forces the borrower to act like a "going concern."

Sale of accounts receivable.

Borrowers are prohibited from selling accounts receivable to generate cash, since this could result in a long-run liquidity squeeze—especially when the firm must use the proceeds to meet current obligations. Selling accounts receivable is viewed as a sacrifice of the firm's long-run liquidity in order to satisfy short-term obligations. From a long-term lender's viewpoint, this behavior is not desirable.

Restrictive loan provisions

Long-term lending agreements, whether resulting from a negotiated term loan or a bond issue, normally include certain "restrictive covenants," contractual clauses placing certain financial and operating *constraints* on the borrower. Since the lender is committing its funds for a long period, it seeks to protect itself against adverse financial developments affecting the borrower. Restrictive covenants generally require the firm to maintain a specified financial condition and managerial structure. These covenants stay in force for the life of the loan agreement. Generally, they include working capital restrictions, fixed-asset restrictions, constraints with respect to subsequent borrowing, prohibition on leases, combination restrictions, salary restrictions, management restrictions, constraints on security investment, constraints on the use of loan proceeds, and dividend restrictions.

Working capital restrictions.

One of the most common restrictions placed on the long-term borrower by the lender requires the borrower to maintain a minimum level of net working capital at all times. The level required is determined through negotiations between the borrower and the lender. If the net working capital of the firm falls below the predetermined level, this is construed as an indicator of a deteriorating financial position and entitles the lender to *call* the loan prior to the firm's downfall.[3] Although a firm whose net working capital falls below the predetermined level may not be on the road to bankruptcy, this provision gives the lender the opportunity to evaluate the borrower's financial position and decide whether to continue the established lending arrangement.

In addition to a net working capital requirement, many loan agreements contain provisions specifying minimum levels of current assets or minimum current ratios, or both. These provisions are also aimed at forcing the firm to maintain its liquidity, since a failure to maintain short-run solvency makes the firm's long-run success rather questionable. If the firm cannot survive in

---

[3]When a loan is "called," the lender demands immediate repayment. Violation of any standard or restrictive loan covenants generally gives the lender the right to call a loan. In other words, violation of the covenants means the borrower has failed to abide by the terms of the loan contract. The lender's recourse is to require the immediate return of its money along with any accrued interest. Sometimes the lender will merely request some type of concession such as representation on the borrower's board of directors as an alternative to calling the loan; of course, the acceptance of such a concession is controlled by the lender—not the borrower.

the short run, there will be no long run. However, the working capital requirements should not be so restrictive that they impede the firm's ability to achieve reasonable profits.

Fixed-asset restrictions. Long-term lenders often place constraints on the firm with respect to the liquidation, acquisition, and encumbrance of fixed assets.

The liquidation of fixed assets. Lenders often prohibit the liquidation of fixed assets. A firm that does not have sufficient liquidity to make required payments can sell fixed assets in order to get cash. However, this is a dangerous strategy that may damage the firm's ability to repay a term loan. Some firms sell fixed assets because they are no longer useful; if this is the case, the lender may find the liquidation of assets acceptable. By including a restrictive covenant, the lender at least retains the right to pass judgment in such a situation. The lender may merely require the borrower to get its "OK" prior to liquidating any fixed assets. In some cases, the working capital provision specifically restricts the sale of fixed assets to obtain liquidity.

The acquisition of fixed assets. Lenders sometimes prohibit the borrower from making capital expenditures to acquire new fixed assets. They may specify a maximum dollar capital expenditure per year. The purpose of this restriction is to require the firm to maintain liquidity by keeping its dollars in current as opposed to fixed assets. A lender normally permits a level of capital expenditures sufficient to allow for adequate maintenance and repair of assets. It may waive the capital expenditure restriction if a large capital expenditure is shown to be justifiable.

The encumbrance of fixed assets. Quite often lenders will prohibit the use of fixed assets as collateral for a loan. By forcing the borrower to leave fixed assets unencumbered, the lender protects itself in case of liquidation. If the assets were used as collateral for another loan and the firm failed, the proceeds from the sale of the encumbered assets would be unavailable to satisfy the term lender's claims.

Constraints on subsequent borrowing. Many lending agreements prohibit the borrower from incurring any additional long-term debt. Short-term borrowing, which is a necessity for a seasonal business, is not usually limited in the lending agreement. The restriction on long-term borrowing may require only that additional borrowing be *subordinated* to the original loan. Subordination of subsequent debts means that the subordinated creditors agree to wait until all the claims of the existing or *senior debt* are satisfied prior to receiving any distribution of assets in the event of liquidation.[4] The

---

[4]Debts are quite often subordinated in such a way that the senior debt's recovery in liquidation is greater than that of the general creditors. An example of how the subordination feature works in liquidation is given later in this chapter.

lender may require only that all subsequent long-term loans be unsecured. Any restrictive provisions placed on subsequent borrowing are aimed at protecting the long-term lender(s)' loan(s) by assuring the recovery of its accrued interest and principal if the borrower becomes bankrupt.

Prohibition on leases. Borrowers may be prohibited from entering into financial leases. Often a certain dollar limit is placed on the amount of lease liability acceptable to the lender. If the firm were permitted to make unlimited lease agreements, the effectiveness of restrictive provisions with respect to debt and capital expenditures would be minimal. The similarity between a lease and a long-term debt obligation was discussed in Chapter 20. The lender's objective is to ensure that financial lease commitments, which also are a form of long-term financing, are kept under control.

Combination restrictions. Occasionally, the lender requires the borrower to agree not to merge or consolidate or combine in any way with another firm. Such an action could completely change the firm's financial and operating structure, and the changed structure could make the firm more financially risky than it was when the loan was initially negotiated. The lender may also prohibit the firm from changing its line of business by internally diversifying into new areas. The lender may permit the borrower to make certain changes if it has the lender's approval.

Salary restrictions. In order to prevent the firm's liquidation through large salary payments, the lender may prohibit salary increases for specified employees. The clause may permit salary increases up to a certain annual percentage. Restrictions on salary increases are intended to prevent the firm from paying out dollars that could be used to increase its liquidity and decrease its financial risk by increasing its operating profits (earnings before interest and taxes). Normally included in this provision is a statement prohibiting employee loans or advances since the effect of either is similar to that of a large salary payment.

Management restrictions. The lender may require the borrower to maintain certain "key employees" without whom the future success of the firm is uncertain. The lender may also retain the privilege of calling the loan or taking part in the selection of a new executive if a key executive were to resign. In order to protect itself in the event of the death of a key executive, the lender may also require the firm to maintain a "key man" life insurance policy on specified executives. The policies may be payable to the company or directly to the lender to retire the loan. These management-related provisions are needed only when the presence of certain individuals is critical to the future success of the firm.

Constraints on security investment. Occasionally the lender includes a covenant limiting the borrower's security investment alternatives. For example, the firm may be limited to highly liquid securities such as treasury bills and negotiable certificates of deposit. By limiting the borrower's alternatives, the lender protects itself and prohibits the firm from making investments in securities of questionable liquidity. This increases the probability that the borrower will survive a liquidity crisis.

Constraints on the use of loan proceeds.   Occasionally a covenant specifically requiring the borrower to spend the borrowed funds on certain items is included in the loan agreement. This restriction assures the lender that the funds lent will not be diverted outside the company or to some less productive use than that for which the money was initially borrowed. It forces the borrower to act in a manner consistent with its proven financial need.

Dividend restrictions.   A relatively common provision in long-term loan agreements limits the firm's cash dividend payout to a maximum of 50 to 70 percent of its net earnings. Occasionally the dividend restriction is stated as a maximum dollar amount per year. Many lenders also place restrictions on the *repurchase* of stock, which in essence is merely a roundabout method of distributing corporate earnings.

The preceding list of restrictive covenants should not be construed as all-inclusive; it contains merely the more common loan restrictions. In the process of negotiating the terms of long-term borrowing, the borrower and lender must ultimately agree to acceptable restrictive covenants; if agreement is not reached, the loan will not be made. Normally the lender is in control since it is the one who has been approached for the loan. It includes those restrictions it believes are necessary to protect itself.

It is important to recognize that the violation of any standard or restrictive provisions by the borrower gives the lender the right to demand the immediate repayment of accrued interest and the principal of the loan. The lender will not normally demand immediate repayment, but it will evaluate the situation in order to determine whether the violation is serious enough to jeopardize the loan. On the basis of this evaluation it may call the loan, waive the violation and continue the loan, or waive the violation but alter the terms of the initial loan agreement.

The cost of long-term financing

The cost of long-term financing is generally higher than short-term financing costs due to the high degree of uncertainty associated with the future. The long-term financing agreement specifies the actual interest rate charged to the borrower, the timing of the payments, and the dollar amount of the payments. An important consideration for the borrower is the rate of interest, or the cost of borrowing the funds. The major factors affecting the cost of money for a given borrower are the maturity date, the size of the loan, the financial riskiness of the borrower, and the basic cost of money.

The maturity of the loan.   Generally, long-term loans have higher interest rates than short-term loans. The difference in rates is attributable to the fact that lenders cannot accurately predict the future behavior of interest rates. The longer the term of a loan, the less accuracy is possible in predicting interest rate patterns to maturity and therefore the greater the uncertainty associated with the loan. In order to compensate it for both the uncertainty of future interest rates and the fact that the longer the term of a loan the higher the probability that the borrower will default, the lender typically charges a higher interest rate on long-term loans.

If a lender expects the future interest rates to be higher than current (i.e., short-term) interest rates, it will definitely charge more for long-term as opposed to short-term loans. In certain instances when short-term rates are quite high (the 1974–1975 period, for example), lenders will make long-term loans at rates below the prevailing short-term rate. Even in these situations, the lender does not make long-term loans at rates far from the prevailing short-term borrowing rate. If the lender knows it can currently lend its money at 9 percent for a short-term loan and believes that long-term rates do not accurately reflect future interest rate movements, it may be wise to lend its money for the short term, since at the end of the short-term loan period it can again evaluate future interest rate expectations to determine whether they accurately reflect future interest rate movements. An evaluation of the lender's own expectations in light of those reflected in the rates charged by other long-term lenders aids the lender in determining the best disposition of its loanable funds.

A firm needing funds is advised to use an alternate form of financing (short-term debt, preferred stock, or common stock) when long-term rates are high. There is obviously a trade-off between these alternative forms of financing and long-term debt. The borrower should attempt to quantify the differences and determine whether an alternate form of financing (assuming it is available) would be preferable. The long-term commitment resulting from a long-term debt financing decision suggests the need for careful study by both the lender and the borrower before a long-term loan agreement is signed.

The size of the loan. The size of the loan affects the interest cost of borrowing in an inverse manner. Loan administration costs are likely to decrease with increasing loan size, but the risk to the lender increases, since the more long term the debt incurred by the borrower, the greater the risk of default. The size of the loan sought by each borrower must be evaluated to determine the net administrative cost-risk trade-off. The size of the loan with respect to the lender's total funds also affects the interest cost. If a lender lends 50 percent of its money to one borrower, it will charge a rate reflecting the riskiness of the loan to it. This risk will be high because of the lender's failure to diversify its loans.

The financial riskiness of the borrower. This is closely related to the size of the loan. The higher the borrower's ratio of long-term debt to equity, the more financially risky it is considered. A low times-interest-earned ratio also reflects this financial risk. The lender's main concern is with the ability of the borrower to repay the loan requested. If the lender's assessment of the borrower's financial riskiness indicates that the requested loan would make it unable to service all its debt, the loan will not be made. The overall assessment of the borrower's financial risk, along with information on past payment patterns, is used by the lender in setting the interest rate on any term loan. In the case of bonds, ratings by independent services reflect their financial risk and thereby impact the associated interest rate.[5] It should be clear that a careful credit analysis of a borrower by the lender or potential bondholder is necessary in order to assess the riskiness of the prospective borrower.

The basic cost of money. The cost of money is the basis for determining the actual interest rate charged a prospective borrower. It is defined as the interest rate on long-term debt issues that are virtually risk-free. Generally, the rate on government bonds with equivalent maturities is used as the basic cost of money. Each lender will add premiums related to such factors as the maturity date of the loan, the size of the loan, or the financial riskiness of the borrower. If the lender agrees that the prevailing rate of interest on equal-maturity government issues accurately reflects interest rate expectations, it may not need to make any adjustment for the maturity of the loan. Adjustments for the size of the loan and financial risk are much more common. Generally, the basic cost of long-term money adjusted for certain specific factors determines the rate of interest charged.

Some lenders determine a prospective borrower's "risk class"[6] and find the rates charged on similar-maturity loans to firms believed to be in the same risk class. Instead of having to determine a risk premium, the lender can use the risk premium prevailing in the marketplace for similar loans. A key to the successful use of this approach is to be able to accurately measure and classify the financial riskiness of a given firm. Regardless of which approach is actually used for determining the interest rate on a long-term loan, it is important that both the borrower and the lender feel comfortable with the interest rate, since both commit themselves to it for a long period of time.

TERM LOANS

Long-term loans are made by various financial institutions to business firms. These loans generally have maturities of five to twelve years; shorter maturities are available, but minimum five-year maturities are most common. These loans are most often made to finance *fixed* working capital needs, to purchase machinery and equipment, or to liquidate other loans—either to change their maturities or to lower the interest cost. This section discusses both the specific characteristics of term loan agreements and the various suppliers of term loans to business.

---

[5] A brief discussion of bond ratings is included in a later section of this chapter.

[6] A *risk class* reflects the firm's overall risk profile. One must envision a continuum of risk, break it into discrete classes, and place the firm in an appropriate class. Looking at other firms perceived to be in the same risk class will help the lender to make certain decisions with respect to the appropriate rate of interest. For publicly traded firms, betas (see Chapter 16) are often used to classify firms into homogeneous risk classes.

Characteristics of term loan agreements

The actual term loan agreement is a formal contract containing anywhere from a few to a few hundred pages. These agreements are normally prepared by the lender's attorneys. The following items are normally specified in the loan agreement: the amount and maturity of the loan, payment dates, the interest rate, standard provisions, restrictive provisions, the collateral (if any), the purpose of the loan, the action to be taken in the event of default, and stock purchase options. Of these basic factors only payment dates, collateral requirements, and stock purchase options require further discussion. The remaining factors were discussed earlier in the chapter.

Payment dates. Term loan agreements generally require quarterly, semiannual, or annual payments. Generally, these equal payments fully amortize the principal and interest over the life of the loan. Occasionally a term loan agreement will require periodic payments over the life of the loan followed by a large lump-sum payment at maturity. This lump-sum, or *balloon payment*, in some instances represents the entire loan principal since the periodic payments represent only interest. If the lending agreement specifies a large balloon payment, the borrower often is required to make periodic payments into a *sinking fund*, which is a type of deposit or investment that at maturity is equal to the required balloon payment. The use of sinking funds is much more common in the case of bond financing. Term loan agreements normally include prepayment penalties of 2 to 10 percent of the outstanding loan balance. This is because term lenders generally prefer to have their loans held to maturity.

Collateral requirements. Term lending arrangements may be unsecured or secured in a fashion similar to short-term loans. Whether collateral is required depends on the lender's evaluation of the borrower's financial condition. Common types of collateral include machinery and equipment, plant, pledges of accounts receivable, and pledges of securities. The lender can obtain a security interest in any of these assets by filing certain documents that become part of the term loan agreement in a public office. When fixed assets are used as collateral, the lender files a mortgage on them; in many instances the loan is actually made to finance the purchase of these fixed assets. If current assets such as accounts receivable and marketable securities are used as collateral, the lender requires continuous pledges of acceptable accounts and securities.

Stock-purchase options. A recent trend in term lending is for the lender to require the borrower to provide stock-purchase options in addition to the required interest payments. Stock-purchase options are *warrants* that allow the holder to purchase a stated amount of common stock in the firm at a specified price over a certain period of time. These options can be made available only by corporate borrowers. They are used to entice institutional lenders to make term loans. Warrants are discussed in greater detail in Chapter 23.

Term lenders

The primary financial institutions making term loans to business are commercial banks, insurance companies, pension funds, regional development companies, the Small Business Administration, small business investment companies, commercial finance companies, and equipment manufacturers. Although the characteristics and provisions of term lending agreements made by these institutions are quite similar, a number of basic differences exist. Since the common characteristics of such agreements have already been discussed, only differentiating factors will be presented in this section.

Commercial banks.   Large commercial banks make some term loans to business. These loans are generally for periods of no more than 12 years except in the case of real estate loans, which may have maturities of as long as 25 years. Since commercial banks are limited as to the amount they can lend to a single borrower (i.e., no more than 10 percent of the bank's capital and surplus), many commercial banks are unable to make loans requested by credit-worthy borrowers. Often a commercial bank will syndicate a large loan by forming a credit group made up of a number of banks. Each bank provides a certain percentage of the total loan. Sometimes loans are syndicated not because of a constraint on lending but in order to spread, or diversify, the risk of a large loan. Commercial banks generally require collateral for term loans.

The advantages of commercial bank term loans include the establishment of a working relationship with a banker, advice and counsel from experts in business loans, a source of credit information on customers, and the establishment of a possible source of information on mergers and acquisitions. Their disadvantages include the need to divulge confidential information and the general control given the lender by the provisions of the loan agreement. Many of these advantages and disadvantages are present in term loans from other financial institutions as well.

Insurance companies.   Insurance companies—especially life insurance firms such as the Prudential Insurance Company—make term loans with maturities of 10 to 20 years. Insurance company loans are generally for much larger amounts than commercial bank loans. Insurance companies make term loans to large firms, while commercial banks generally make term loans to smaller firms. Insurance companies make both mortgage (i.e., secured) loans and unsecured term loans. The mortgage loans are generally made for not more than two-thirds to three-fourths of the value of the collateral. The basic covenants and terms of insurance company loans are the same as for bank loans. The major advantages of insurance company loans over bank loans are the longer terms and larger amounts of money available from insurance companies. The basic disadvantage of insurance company loans is that the rate of interest charged is in many cases slightly higher than that charged on commercial bank loans.

Pension funds.   Employee pension funds invest a small portion of their funds in term loans to business. These loans are generally mortgage loans to large firms. The terms and costs of pension fund loans to business firms are similar to those of life insurance company loans. This similarity is largely attributable to the fact that many pension funds are managed by life insurance companies.

Regional development companies.   Term loans to business are often made by *regional development companies*, which are associations generally attached to local or regional governments that attempt to promote business development in specific geographic areas. These associations attempt to make it possible for businesses with good prospects of success and companies desiring to expand to fulfill these objectives. Regional development companies obtain funds from various governmental bodies and from the federal government. By making long-term loans at competitive rates, they attract new and expanding businesses into an area. Their long-run objective is to increase the economic base and promote favorable economic conditions in the given geographic area.

The Small Business Administration.   The Small Business Administration, which is an agency of the federal government, makes loans to business firms fulfilling certain eligibility requirements. Most SBA loans are long-term loans that cannot exceed $350,000, although under exceptional circumstances, they can be increased to $500,000. The SBA often joins with a private lending institution in making these loans. It either lends a portion of the principal or guarantees repayment of a portion of a privately made loan. The SBA makes loans, rather than providing guarantees, only when a qualified borrower cannot obtain financing elsewhere. The rates charged on SBA loans are equal to or below commercial bank rates. Generally, SBA loans are for between $50,000 and $100,000. The SBA makes some loans to regional development companies.

Small business investment companies.   A *small business investment company* is an institution licensed by the government that makes both debt and equity investments in small firms. The small business investment company raises its capital by borrowing from the Small Business Administration or from other sources. The owners of an SBIC are primarily interested in placing their money in companies with high growth potential. An SBIC loan to a company normally provides the SBIC with an opportunity to receive an equity interest in the borrowing firm. The payoff to the SBIC is expected to result from capital gains on the SBIC's equity interest. Term loans made by SBIC's have maturities of from 5 to 20 years and interest rates slightly higher than those for bank term loans.

Commercial finance companies.   Commercial finance companies make secured long-term loans (i.e., mortgages) to business firms. CFC's are generally involved in the financing of equipment purchases by manufacturing firms. Often the commercial finance company is a subsidiary of the manufacturer of the equipment. The term of CFC loans is generally less than ten years. The borrower is generally required to make a specified down payment followed by equal installment payments over the life of the loan. Title to the equipment may or may not initially pass to the borrower. The cost of term loans from CFC's is generally high in comparison with the cost of long-term loans from other sources.

Equipment manufacturers. The manufacturer or seller of equipment may finance long-term installment sales to business firms directly. The characteristics of manufacturers' loans to customers are similar to those of loans made by commercial finance companies. Many manufacturers have their own commercial financing subsidiaries.

CHARACTERISTICS OF CORPORATE BONDS

A *bond* is a certificate indicating that a corporation has *borrowed* a certain amount of money and promises to repay it at a future date. The issuing corporation agrees to pay bondholders a stated amount of interest at specified time intervals (usually semiannually). Most bonds are issued with maturities of 10 to 30 years and in denominations of $1000. However, maturities of less than 10 years and denominations of anywhere from $100 to $10,000 are not uncommon. Bonds with face values of less than $500 are referred to as *baby bonds*. The stated interest rate on a bond represents the percentage of the bond's face value that will be paid out annually. A bond is another form of long-term debt financing available to the corporation. Purchasers of bonds (i.e., bondholders) are creditors who expect to receive specified periodic interest and repayment of the principal amount (i.e., the face value of the bond) at maturity.

Legal aspects of corporate bonds

Since a corporate bond issue may be for millions of dollars that are obtained by selling portions of the debt to numerous unrelated persons, certain legal arrangements are required to protect purchasers of the bond. Bondholders are legally protected primarily through the indenture and the trustee.

Bond indenture. A *bond indenture* is a legal document stating the conditions under which a bond has been issued. It specifies both the rights of the bondholders and the duties of the issuing corporation. The actions that may be taken by bondholders if the issuer violates any of the clauses in the indenture are also clearly specified. An indenture is normally a quite complex and lengthy legal document. In addition to specifying the interest and principal payments and dates, it contains various standard and restrictive provisions, sinking fund requirements, and provisions with respect to a security interest (if the bond is secured).

Standard and restrictive provisions. The standard and restrictive provisions of a bond issue are virtually the same as those found in a term loan agreement. These were briefly discussed in an earlier section of the chapter.

Sinking-fund requirements. One other restrictive provision that is normally included in a bond indenture is a *sinking-fund* requirement. The objective of this requirement is to provide for the systematic retirement of the outstanding bonds prior to maturity. Bondholders generally favor this activity since it reduces the firm's debt and thereby its financial riskiness as the bond approaches maturity. In order to simplify the sinking fund retirement of bonds, a *call* feature is normally included in the indenture. This feature permits the issuer to repurchase outstanding bonds at a specified price. The firm may be required to make fixed or variable sinking-fund payments. *Fixed sinking-fund payments* represent prespecified annual dollar repurchases; *variable sinking-fund payments* require the firm to repurchase an amount of bonds equal to a certain percentage of earnings. Since the variable plan requires that few or no bonds be repurchased in a lean year, bondholders prefer fixed sinking-fund requirements. Even the fixed payment plans sometimes provide for a "balloon payment" in order to retire outstanding bonds at maturity. Most bond issues require fixed-dollar sinking-fund payments.

Under a sinking-fund requirement, the issuer can either purchase the bonds in the marketplace or "call" them at the specified call price. It will call bonds only when sufficient bonds cannot be purchased directly in the marketplace or when the market price of the bond is above the call price. When the market price is above the call price, random selection procedures are normally used to determine which bonds to call.

Security interest. The bond indenture is similar to a loan agreement in that any collateral pledged against the bond is specifically identified in the document. Generally the title to the collateral is attached to the indenture and the disposition of the collateral in various circumstances is specifically described. The protection of bond collateral is quite crucial in order to increase the safety and thereby enhance the marketability of a bond issue.

Trustee. A *trustee* is a third party to a bond indenture. The trustee can be an individual, a corporation, or a commercial bank trust department. Most often, the trustee is a trust department of a commercial bank. It is the trustee's responsibility to make sure that the issuer lives up to the provisions in the bond indenture. The trustee acts as a watchdog on behalf of the bondholders, making sure that the issuer does not default on its contractual responsibilities; it takes specified actions on behalf of the bondholders if the terms of the indenture are violated. The trustee also normally participates in the actual creation of the indenture, making sure that all necessary legal protections have been provided in the agreement. Bond indentures not only specify the provisions of the issue, but they also indicate the duties, rights, responsibilities, and conditions for removal of a trustee. In other words, the bondholders retain the right to hire trustees and fire them when they fail to fulfill their responsibilities. A trustee is paid a fixed fee for its services.

The general features of a bond
Three general features quite often found in a bond issue are a conversion feature, a call feature, and warrants. These features provide both the issuer (borrower) and the purchaser (lender) with certain opportunities for replacing, retiring, and (or) supplementing the bond with some type of equity issue.

The conversion feature.   The conversion feature of certain so-called convertible bonds allows the creditor (bondholder) to convert the bonds into a certain number of shares of preferred or common stock. The creditor will convert his or her bond only if the market value of stock becomes greater than the conversion price. Since Chapter 23 will discuss convertible bonds in great detail, no further discussion of these bonds is necessary here. The conversion feature is generally considered attractive by both the issuer and the purchaser of corporate bonds.

The call feature.   The call feature is included in almost all corporate bond issues. It gives the issuer the opportunity to repurchase bonds at a stated price prior to maturity. Often the *call price* will vary over time, decreasing at discrete predefined points in time. Sometimes the call privilege is exercisable only during a certain period. The call price is set above the bond's face value in order to provide some compensation to holders of called bonds. As a rule, the call price exceeds the face value of a bond by an amount equal to one year's interest. For example, a $1000 8-percent bond would be callable for around $1080 (i.e., $1000 + 8\% \cdot \$1000$). The amount by which the call price exceeds the bond's face value is commonly referred to as the *call premium*. The call feature is generally advantageous to the issuer, since it permits it to retire outstanding debt prior to maturity. When interest rates fall, an issuer can call an outstanding bond and reissue a new bond at a lower interest rate. When interest rates rise, the call privilege will not be exercised, except possibly to meet sinking-fund requirements.

In order to sell a callable bond, the issuer must pay an interest rate higher than that on noncallable bond issues of equal risk. The interest premium required to sell a callable bond depends directly on the expectations of both the issuer and the purchaser with respect to future interest rates. The call feature is helpful in forcing the conversion of convertible bonds when the conversion price of the stock is below the market price.[7]

Warrants.   Warrants are occasionally attached to bonds as "sweeteners" to make them more attractive to prospective buyers. A *warrant* is a certificate giving its holder the right to purchase a certain number of shares of common stock at a specified price. An in-depth discussion of stock-purchase warrants is included in Chapter 23.

Marketing a bond
Primary or new issues of corporate bonds can be made in two ways—through direct placements or public offerings.

Direct placements.   The direct placement of bonds involves the sale of a bond issue directly to one purchaser or a group of purchasers, normally

---

[7]A discussion of how the call feature can be used to force conversion of a convertible security has been included in Chapter 23. Once the reader has obtained a feel for the various aspects of the conversion feature, the use of the call to force conversion will be better understood.

large financial institutions such as life insurance companies and pension funds. Directly placed bond issues do not differ significantly from a long-term loan; there is virtually no secondary market for them. Since the bonds are placed directly with the purchasers, registration of the issue with the Securities and Exchange Commission is not required. Interest rates on directly placed bonds are slightly above those for similar public issues since certain administrative and underwriting costs are avoided.

Public offerings. Bonds sold to the public are generally sold by investment bankers, who are in the business of selling corporate securities.[8] The investment banker is compensated by the issuer for its services. Its fee may range from .5 to 10 percent of the principal amount sold. The rate charged is largely dependent on the size of the issue and the reputation of the issuer. Bonds issued through public offerings must be registered with the SEC. Many of these issues become listed on security exchanges and have an active secondary market. The price at which bonds are publicly offered often differs from the bonds' stated, or *face value*. If similar-risk debt instruments currently yield a higher interest rate than the bond's stated, or *coupon rate*, the bond will have to be sold at a discount (i.e., below its face value); if the prevailing rate on similar-risk instruments is below the bond's coupon rate, the bond will be sold at a premium (i.e., above its face value). This is generally true with respect to both new and existing bond issues.

Bond ratings

The riskiness of publicly traded bond issues is assessed by certain financial services such as Moody's and Standard & Poor's. These firms provide ratings with respect to the overall quality of bonds as measured by the safety of the principal and interest. Moody's has nine ratings while Standard & Poor's has twelve ratings. Table 21.1 summarizes these ratings along with a brief interpretation of each group of ratings. There is normally an inverse relationship between the quality or rating of a bond and its interest rate or yield to maturity. High-quality (high-rated) bonds have lower yields than lower-quality (low-rated) bonds. This reflects a type of risk-return trade-off for the lender. When considering bond financing, the financial manager must therefore concern him or herself with the expected bond ratings since these ratings can significantly impact the bonds' saleability and cost to maturity.

TYPES OF BONDS

Bonds can be classified according to whether or not they are secured by pledges of specific assets. The following two sections discuss the various types of unsecured and secured bond issues. A summary of the key characteristics and priority of lenders' claims against the major types of bonds is included in Table 21.2, presented at the end of this section.

---

[8]A more detailed discussion of the investment banking function was presented in Chapter 19. Also included in Chapter 19 was a description of the capital markets in which both corporate stocks and bonds may be traded.

TABLE 21.1 Moody's and Standard & Poor's bond ratings

Moody's	Interpretation	Standard & Poor's	Interpretation
Aaa	Prime quality	AAA	Bank investment
Aa	High grade	AA	quality
A	Upper medium grade	A	
Baa	Medium grade	BBB	
		BB	
Ba	Lower medium grade or speculative	B	Speculative
B	Speculative	CCC	
		CC	
Caa	From very speculative	C	
Ca	to near or in default		
C		DDD	In default (rating
		DD	indicates the relative
		D	salvage value)

Source: Moody's Investors Service, Inc., and Standard & Poor's N.Y.S.E. Reports.

Unsecured bonds

Unsecured bonds are issued without the pledge of collateral. They therefore represent a claim on the firm's earnings, not its assets. There are three basic types of unsecured bonds—debentures, subordinated debentures, and income bonds.

Debentures. *Debentures* have a claim on any of the firm's assets remaining once the claims of all secured creditors have been satisfied. The indenture under which a debenture is issued may contain restrictions on the issuance of future debentures and secured debt. Since the debenture holder is only a general creditor, these clauses may be quite important. Only quite credit-worthy firms are able to issue debentures. Convertible bonds are normally debentures.

Subordinated debentures. *Subordinated debentures* are debentures that are made specifically subordinate to other types of debt. Although the subordinated-debt holders rank below all other long-term creditors with respect to both liquidation and the payment of interest, their claims must be satisfied prior to those of common or preferred stockholders. Some people view subordinated debentures as a type of equity. The higher risk of subordinated debentures generally makes them a more expensive method of financing for the issuer. If the subordinated debentures are convertible, they might have a lower yield than debentures. The existence of subordinated debentures is to the advantage of regular (senior) debenture holders in the event of liquidation. An example will clarify this point.

EXAMPLE

The Bell Company has $3 million worth of debentures, $3 million worth of subordinated debentures, and $4 million worth of general creditors' claims outstanding. The total claims—all unsecured—against the firm are therefore $10 million dollars. The firm has just gone bankrupt and has been liquidated for only $6 million. All unsecured creditors do *not* receive their 60-percent (i.e., $6 million available ÷ $10 million in claims) share of the $6 million. Instead, the debenture holder has a claim on both its and the subordinated-debenture holder's portion. Together, these amount to 60 percent (i.e., since each of them has a $3 million claim out of total claims of $10 million) of the $6 million, or $3.6 million. Since it needs $3 million to satisfy its claim, the debenture holder receives this amount. The subordinated-debenture holder receives $600,000 (i.e., $3.6 million − $3.0 million), and the general creditors receive $2.4 million (i.e., 40% × $6 million). Rather than receiving its proportionate share of $1.8 million (30 percent of $6 million), the debenture holder receives full satisfaction of its claim.[9] Without the subordinated debentures, the senior debt holder would have received only a little more than half this amount (i.e., $1.8 million instead of $3.0 million). ●

Income bonds.   An *income bond* requires the payment of interest only when earnings are available from which to make the payment. These bonds are commonly issued during the reorganization of a failed or failing firm. The unpaid interest generally accumulates and must be paid prior to any distribution of funds to stockholders. Due to the weak claim of the income bondholder on the firm's assets, the stated rate of interest is generally quite high.

Secured bonds

A variety of secured bonds are available for raising long-term funds. The basic types are mortgage bonds, collateral trust bonds, and equipment trust certificates. Secured bonds, like secured short-term loans, have specific assets pledged against them as collateral. If the issuer defaults on any provisions of the secured bond indenture, the trustee can liquidate the collateral to satisfy the bondholder's claim. If the bondholder's full claim is not satisfied through liquidation of collateral, it becomes a general creditor.

Mortgage bonds.   A *mortgage bond* is a bond secured with a lien on real property or buildings. Normally the market value of the security is greater than the amount of the mortgage bond issue. Some mortgage bonds are secured by *blanket mortgages* such that all the assets of the firm act as collateral. A *first-mortgage bond* gives the holder the first claim on secured assets. A *second-mortgage bond* gives the holder a secondary claim on assets already secured by the first mortgage. The first-mortgage bond is obviously the most secure since the holder has the first claim on the pledged assets. Although first and second mortgages are most common, subsequent mortgages can be

---

[9]A more detailed example of the place of senior and subordinated debt holders in the liquidation process is included in Chapter 26. The example illustrates the rights of both debt and equity holders in the liquidation process.

filed. The claims of first-mortgage bondholders must be satisfied prior to the payment of any subsequent mortgage claims. A number of features may be included in a mortgage bond indenture.

Open-end mortgages.   An *open-end mortgage* permits the issuance of additional bonds under the same mortgage contract. This arrangement provides the issuer with some flexibility in its financing. Creditors are usually protected under this arrangement by restrictions on the amount of additional borrowing.

Limited open-end mortgages.   A *limited open-end mortgage* allows the firm to issue additional bonds for up to a specified maximum, which is typically stated as a percentage of the original cost of the pledged property. This arrangement provides more protection to existing bondholders than the open-end mortgage.

Closed-end mortgages.   A *closed-end mortgage* does not permit additional borrowing on a given mortgage. The only way additional funds can be raised is through a new or subsequent mortgage. Creditors are well protected under this arrangement.

After-acquired clauses.   Many mortgages, especially open-end mortgages, contain an *after-acquired clause*. This clause provides that all property acquired after the first mortgage be added to the property already pledged as security under the first mortgage. The clause in effect protects the claim of

TABLE 21.2 Summary of characteristics and priority of claim of bonds

Bond type	Characteristic	Priority of lender's claim
I. Unsecured		
Debentures	Only creditworthy firms can issue them. Convertible bonds are normally debentures.	Claims are same as those of any general creditor. May have other unsecured bonds subordinated to them.
Subordinated debentures	Claims are not satisfied until those of the creditors holding certain (senior) debts have been fully satisfied.	Claim is that of general creditor but not as good as senior debt claim.
Income bonds	Payment of interest required only when earnings are available from which to make such payment. Commonly issued in reorganization of a failed or failing firm.	Claim is that of a general creditor. Not in default when interest payments are missed since they are contingent only on earnings being availabe.

TABLE 21.2 (continued)

Bond type	Characteristic	Priority of lender's claim
II. Secured		
Mortgage bonds	Secured by a lien on real property. Can be open-end (other bonds issued against collateral), limited open-end (a specified amount of additional bonds can be issued against collateral), closed-end, or may contain an after-acquired clause (property subsequently acquired becomes part of mortgage collateral).	Claim on proceeds from sale of mortgaged assets; if not fully satisfied, they become a general creditor. The first-mortgage claim must be fully satisfied prior to distribution of proceeds to second-mortgage holders, and so on. A number of mortgages can be issued against the same collateral.
Collateral trust bonds	Secured by stock and (or) bonds that are owned by the issuer. Collateral value is generally 25 to 35% greater than bond value.	Claim on proceeds from stock and (or) bond collateral; if not fully satisfied, they become general creditors.
Equipment trust certificates	Used to finance "rolling stock"—airplanes, trucks, boats, railroad cars. A mechanism whereby a trustee buys equipment with funds raised through the sale of trust certificates and then leases the asset to the firm, which, after the final scheduled lease payment receives title to the asset. It is a type of leasing.	Claim is on proceeds from sale of asset; if proceeds do not satisfy outstanding debt, trust certificate holders become general creditors.

current mortgage holders by giving them a lien on any additional property acquired.

Collateral trust bonds. If the security held by a trustee consists of stock and (or) bonds of other companies, the secured bonds issued against this collateral are called *collateral trust bonds*. Since the assets of *holding companies* generally consist of stocks and bonds of their subsidiaries, holding companies are the primary issuers of collateral trust bonds.[10] Many of these

---

[10]A *holding company* is a corporation having a controlling interest in one or more other corporations. In order to maintain this controlling interest, ownership of between 10 and 25 percent of the outstanding shares of the firm's stock is normally required. A discussion of holding companies is included in Chapter 25.

bonds provide for the substitution of fixed assets as collateral as long as a predefined collateral premium over the amount borrowed is maintained. The value of the collateral generally must be 25 to 35 percent greater than the value of the bonds it supports.

Equipment trust certificates. Equipment trust certificates originally were used primarily by railroads to finance the purchase of equipment. Today they are commonly used by airlines, truck lines, and barge lines to finance their "rolling stock"—planes, trucks, or boats. In order to obtain the equipment, a down payment of 20 to 25 percent is made by the purchaser (borrower) to the trustee, which is normally a bank. The trustee sells certificates to raise the additional funds required to purchase the equipment from the manufacturer. The purchaser makes periodic lease payments to the trustee, which then pays dividends to the trust certificate holders. The trust certificates mature serially and are retired by the trustee, using the balance of the lease payments. The final lease payment is used to retire any remaining trust certificates. After the final payment, the trustee passes title of the equipment to the borrower. The annual lease payment to the trustee is set to cover the cost of dividends, retiring certificates, and the expenses of the trust in each period of the trust agreement's life. Although discussed in this chapter, it should be clear that equipment trust certificates are essentially a form of leasing.

BOND REFUNDING OPTIONS

A firm wishing to refund a bond prior to maturity has two basic options. Both require some foresight on the part of the issuer. Each of these options is discussed below.

Serial issues

The borrower can issue *serial bonds*, a certain proportion of which come due each year. When serial bonds are issued, a schedule showing the yields, interest rates, and prices associated with each maturity is given. An example would be a $30 million, 20-year bond issue for which $1.5 million of the bonds mature each year. The interest rate associated with the shorter maturities would, of course, be lower than the rates associated with the longer maturities. Although serial bonds cannot necessarily be retired at the option of the issuer, they do permit the issuer to refund the debt over its life. Not only does this type of bond have appeal to the firm, it also can attract purchasers, since such an issue offers a variety of yields and maturities from which the investor can select. This type of bond is issued primarily by various governmental bodies.

Refunding bonds by exercising a call privilege

If interest rates drop after the issuance of a bond, the issuer may wish to refund the bond and issue new bonds at the lower interest rate. If a call feature has been included in the bond issue, the issuer can easily retire it. The desirability of such an action is not necessarily obvious, but can be determined by a type of cost-benefit analysis using present-value techniques. The actual process used to make these types of decisions can be illustrated by a simple example. However, a few tax-related points should be clarified first.

Bond discounts and premiums. When bonds are sold either at a discount (i.e., for less than their face value) or at a premium (i.e., for more than their face value), the firm is required to amortize the discount or *premium* over the life of the bond. The amortized discount is treated as a tax-deductible expenditure, while the amortized premium is treated as income. If a bond is retired prior to maturity, any unamortized portion of a discount or premium is deducted or treated as income, respectively, at that time.

Call premiums. The amount by which the call price exceeds the face value of the bond is the *call premium*. It is paid by the issuer to the bond-holder in order to buy back outstanding bonds prior to maturity. The call premium is treated as a tax-deductible expense in the year of the call.

Flotation or issuing costs. Any costs incurred in the process of issuing a bond must be amortized over the life of the bond. The annual writeoff is therefore a tax-deductible expenditure. If a bond is retired prior to maturity, any unamortized portion of this cost is deducted at that time.

EXAMPLE
The Flaherty Company is contemplating calling $30 million of 30-year, $1000 bonds that were issued five years ago at a coupon rate of 9 percent. The bonds have a call price of $1090 and initially netted proceeds of $29.1 million due to a discount of $30 per bond. The initial flotation cost was $360,000. The Flaherty Company intends to sell $30 million of 7-percent, 25-year bonds in order to net proceeds for retiring the old bonds.[11] The firm intends to sell the new bonds at their face value for $1000. The underwriting costs on the new issue are estimated to be $440,000. The firm is currently in the 40-percent tax bracket and estimates its after-tax cost of debt to be 5 percent.[12] It expects a four-month period of overlapping interest, during which interest must be paid on both the old and the new bonds.

The first step is to calculate the incremental initial outlay, or initial investment, involved in implementing the proposed plan. Table 21.3 presents the calculations required, which indicate that the Flaherty Company must pay out $2,180,000 now in order to implement the refunding plan. The second step in the analysis is to determine the annual cash savings that will result from the new bond. The annual cash savings each year are the same since the old bond has 25 years remaining to maturity and the

[11]In order to simplify this analysis, the maturity of the new bonds has been set equal to the number of years to maturity remaining on the old bonds. The interested reader is referred to more advanced texts for a discussion of the situation in which new and old bonds have unequal maturities remaining.

[12]Ignoring any flotation costs, the firm's after-tax cost of debt would be 4.2 percent (i.e., (7 percent debt cost × (1 − .40 tax rate))). In order to reflect the flotation costs associated with selling new debt, the use of an after-tax debt cost of 5 percent was believed to be the applicable discount rate. A more detailed discussion of techniques for calculating a firm's after-tax cost of debt can be found in Chapter 17.

TABLE 21.3 Calculating the incremental initial outlay for the Flaherty Company

Initial cash outflows	
Cost of calling old bonds ($1,090 · 30,000)	$32,700,000
Cost of issuing new bonds	440,000
Interest on old bonds during overlap period	
$(.09 \cdot \frac{4}{12} \cdot \$30,000,000)$	900,000
Total Cash Outflows	$34,040,000

Initial cash inflows	
Proceeds from new bond	$30,000,000
Tax shields[a]	
Call premium (.40 · $.90 · 30,000)	1,080,000
Unamortized discount on old bond	
$(\$900,000 \cdot \frac{25}{30} \cdot .40)$	300,000
Unamortized issue cost of old bond	
$(\$360,000 \cdot \frac{25}{30} \cdot .40)$	120,000
Overlapping interest	
$(.09 \cdot \frac{4}{12} \cdot \$30,000,000 \cdot .40)$	360,000
Total Cash Inflows	$31,860,000
Incremental Initial Outlay	$ 2,180,000

[a]These are treated as a cash inflow, although they actually represent a negative cash outflow.

life of the new bond is 25 years. Table 21.4 shows how the annual savings are calculated by subtracting the annual cash outflows of the new bond from the annual cash outflows of the old bond. The new bond results in cash savings of $350,240 per year.

The final step in the analysis is to compare the initial outlay of $2,180,000 required to retire the old bond and issue the new bond to the annual cash savings of $350,240 resulting from the new bond. Because of the difference in the timing of these cash flows, the present value of the 25-year annuity of $350,240 must be found using the after-tax cost of debt. (The *after-tax cost of debt* is used since the alternatives are equally risky contractual—not guaranteed—obligations that have very low risk.[13] The same logic was used in Chapter 20 in the lease-purchase decision.) The present value of the $350,240 25-year annuity, discounted at 5 percent, is $4,936,283

[13]Although a great deal of controversy surrounds the appropriate discount rate, the after-tax cost of debt is used to evaluate the bond refunding proposal because the decision itself involves the choice between two contractual alternatives having very low risk. If we were deciding whether a new bond should be sold—not making a refunding decision—the appropriate risk-adjusted rate, or cost of capital, would be used. In the bond refunding decision, we are only attempting to evaluate a possible replacement for an existing financing instrument. This is a very low-risk decision.

TABLE 21.4 Calculating the annual cash flows for the Flaherty Company

Old bond	Annual cash outflow
Annual interest (.09 · $30,000,000)	$2,700,000
Less: Tax savings[a]	
Interest (.09 · $30,000,000 · .40)	(1,080,000)
Amortization of issuing cost [($360,000 ÷ 30).40]	(4,800)
Amortization of discount [($900,000 ÷ 30).40]	(12,000)
Annual Cash Outflows with Old Bond	$1,603,200
New bond	
Annual interest (.07 · $30,000,000)	$2,100,000
Less: Tax savings[a]	
Interest (.07 · $30,000,000 · .40)	($840,000)
Amortization of issuing cost [($440,000 ÷ 25).40]	(7,040)
Annual Cash Outflows with New Bond	$1,252,960
Annual Cash Flow Savings from New Bond	$ 350,240

[a]Tax savings are treated as cash inflows because of the tax shield they provide.

(14.094 · $350,240). Comparing the present value of the cash savings ($4,936,283) to the initial outlay of $2,180,000 shows that there is a net savings of $2,756,283 ($4,936,283 − $2,180,000). Since a net cash savings does result, the proposed refunding plan is recommended. ●

The analytical approach illustrated for bond refunding decisions can be applied to all refunding problems. Certain modifications may be required, but the basic process of finding the incremental initial outlay and annual cash flow savings and comparing the present value of the savings to the initial outlay in order to make the decision is always the same. Care is required in the treatment of bond discounts or premiums, interest, interest overlaps, issuance costs, and call premiums since these items are tax-deductible.

SUMMARY

This chapter has discussed the various characteristics and types of long-term debt financing available to the business firm. Certain standard and restrictive loan provisions are common to all long-term borrowing arrangements. The standard provisions are generally concerned with the maintenance of satisfactory accounting records, the rendering of financial statements, the payment of obligations, the repair and maintenance of assets, and the sale of accounts receivable. Restrictive provisions are generally concerned with working capital minimums, the disposition of fixed assets in the event of liquidation, subsequent borrowing, financial lease commitments, business combinations, executive salaries, management, security investments, the disposition of loan proceeds, and dividend payments. The intension of all loan provisions is to protect the lender by permitting it to break the loan agreement and demand immediate repayment when the firm's financial position appears to be weakening as indicated by violation of one or more loan provisions.

The cost of long-term loans is normally higher than the cost of short-term borrowing. The difference depends on future interest rate expectations, the loan's maturity, the loan's size, the financial riskiness of the borrower, and the basic cost of money. Generally the key factor differentiating the rates on similar loans is the financial position of the borrower.

Long-term loans generally require quarterly, semiannual, or annual installment payments. Some loans provide for balloon payments at maturity; others require that sinking-fund payments be made to retire the loan. Term loans may be unsecured or secured; secured term loans are normally collateralized with fixed assets. Some term lenders require stock purchase options, which give them an opportunity to take an equity interest in the borrowing company. These loans can be obtained directly from a number of financial institutions. The primary term lenders are commercial banks and life insurance companies, but term loans are also available from pension funds, regional development companies, the Small Business Administration, small business investment companies, commercial finance companies, and equipment manufacturers.

Bonds, which are certificates carrying a promise to pay interest and principal at specified future dates, can be issued by large corporations. The agreement under which the bond is issued is called an indenture, and the enforcement of the indenture is placed in the hands of a trustee. Bonds are typically in $1000 denominations and have 20- to 30-year maturities. Many bonds have a conversion feature, a call feature, or stock-purchase warrants attached. Bonds are sold either through direct placements or public offerings; investment bankers are quite active in public offerings. Bond ratings, which are issued by independent companies such as Moody's and Standard & Poor's, are important indicators of the risk of a proposed or existing bond. The higher the risk the lower the rating, and therefore the higher the interest cost, and vice versa.

Bonds may be unsecured or secured. Unsecured bonds are referred to as debentures. Some debentures are subordinated to other types of debt. Income bonds are another type of unsecured bond which pay interest only when earnings are available. The types of secured bonds include mortgage bonds, collateral trust bonds, and equipment trust certificates. The mortgage bond is the most common type of secured bond.

Bond refunding is an important consideration for a firm. When serial bonds are issued, the refunding is on a planned basis since the bonds' maturities are originally set so as to provide for their orderly retirement. The inclusion of a call feature in a bond allows the issuer to refund a bond prior to maturity. Refunding is done when there is a drop in interest rates great enough to provide savings if the old bond is called and new bonds are issued at the lower rate. Analytical techniques using present values should be used in making bond refunding decisions. The basic approach involves comparing the present value of the annual savings (discounted at the after-tax cost of debt) with the initial outlay required to initiate the refunding. The key variables considered include amortization of issue costs and discounts and (or) premiums, interest, interest overlaps, and the call premium. A variety of tax adjustments are also required. If the present value of the savings exceeds the initial outlay, the refunding is made; otherwise it is rejected.

QUESTIONS

21-1 Why is long-term debt an important component of a firm's capital structure? What are the two key methods of raising long-term debt?

21-2 How do long-term debts differ from current liabilities? When will a long-term debt be reclassified as a current liability?

21-3 What motive does the lender have for including certain restrictive provisions in a loan agreement? How do these covenants differ from the so-called standard loan provisions?

21-4 What sort of working capital requirements are specified in loan agreements? What protection are they intended to provide for the long-term lender?

21-5 What sort of restrictions on fixed assets are included in loan agreements? How do these restrictions affect the liquidation, acquisition, or encumbrance of fixed assets?

21-6 What sort of negotiation process is required in settling on a set of restrictive covenants? What generally are the consequences of violation of a standard or restrictive loan covenant?

21-7 What is the general relationship between the cost of short-term and long-term borrowing? Why are long-term rates generally higher than short-term rates? How may interest rate expectations affect financing decisions?

21-8 How do the size of a loan, the financial riskiness of the borrower, and the basic cost of money affect the cost of long-term financing?

21-9 What types of interest and principal payment dates are generally associated with a term loan agreement? What are balloon payments? How do they differ from lump-sum payments?

21-10 What sort of term loans are secured? What types of collateral are commonly used as security for term loans?

21-11 What role do commercial banks play in term lending to business? What are some of the "extras" that may result from borrowing through a commercial bank?

21-12 What role do insurance companies, pension funds, regional development companies, the Small Business Administration, small business investment companies, commercial finance companies, and equipment manufacturers play in lending long-term funds to business?

21-13 What sort of maturities, denominations, interest payments, and types of purchasers are associated with a typical corporate bond?

21-14 What is a bond indenture? What role does a trustee play with respect to a bond indenture?

21-15   What does it mean if a bond has a conversion feature? A call feature? Warrants?

21-16   How may a primary bond issue be sold? Which method is more expensive? How are bonds rated, and why?

21-17   What are the basic types of unsecured bonds? What can happen to the subordinated-debt holder in the instance of bankruptcy?

21-18   What are the various types of mortgage bonds? What is an after-acquired clause?

21-19   What two options may be available to a firm wishing to retire an outstanding bond issue prior to maturity? Must these options be provided for in advance of issuance? Why might the issuer wish to retire a bond prior to maturity?

21-20   What are (a) bond discounts and premiums and (b) call premiums? How are they treated for tax purposes? How are flotation or issuing costs of bonds treated for tax purposes?

PROBLEMS

21-1   Thompson and Thompson have $25 million of debentures currently outstanding; $15 million are straight debentures and the remaining $10 million are subordinated. The firm has recently become bankrupt; the assets have been liquidated for $15 million and there are $15 million of general creditor claims.
   a Determine how much of the $15 million will be distributed to each creditor.
   b Calculate the percentage of each debt recovered by each creditor.
   c Explain why debenture holders may permit the issuance of only subordinate debt when the firm raises new capital.

21-2   The Shoestring Company currently has $10 million of unsecured debt oustanding. The unsecured debt has the following components:

Debt	Amount	Subordinated
General creditors' claims	$1,000,000	No
Debenture A	2,000,000	No
Debenture B	3,000,000	No
Debenture C	2,000,000	Yes, to debenture A
Debenture D	2,000,000	Yes, to debentures A and B
Total	$10,000,000	

The firm has just become bankrupt and has no secured debt outstanding. The liquidation of the firm has produced $5 million.
   a Determine the amount each debt holder would have gotten if all the creditors had been general creditors.
   b Given the actual nature of the firm's indebtedness, how much money, if any, will each creditor receive?
   c Determine the percentage of claims recovered by each creditor.
   d Discuss the advantage to debenture holders of subordinating subsequent indebtedness.

21-3   For each of the bond issues in the table below, calculate the dollar amount of interest that must be paid during the interest overlap period.

Bond	Principal	Coupon rate	Interest overlap period
A	$ 2,000,000	9%	2 months
B	$60,000,000	8%	4 months
C	$40,000,000	10%	3 months
D	$10,000,000	8.5%	4 months
E	$25,000,000	9.5%	1 month

Also calculate the tax shield resulting from the overlapped interest if the firm is in the 40-percent tax bracket.

21-4 The initial proceeds per bond, the size of the issue, the life of the bond, and the years remaining to maturity are given for a number of bonds below. In each case the firm is in the 40-percent tax bracket and the bond has a $1000 face value.

Bond	Proceeds per bond	Size of issue	Life of bond	Years remaining to maturity
A	$ 980	20,000 bonds	25 years	20
B	$1020	14,000 bonds	20 years	12
C	$1000	10,500 bonds	10 years	8
D	$ 950	9,000 bonds	30 years	21
E	$1030	3,000 bonds	30 years	15

a Indicate whether each bond was sold at a discount or a premium or at its face value.

b Determine the total discount or premium for each issue.

c Determine the annual amount of discount or premium amortized in each case.

d Calculate the unamortized discount or premium in each case.

e Determine the after-tax cash outflow associated with the retirement now of each of these bonds, using the values developed in **d**.

21-5 For each of the callable bond issues below, calculate the after-tax cost of calling the issue. Each bond has a $1000 face value; the various issue sizes and call prices are summarized in the table. The firm is in the 40-percent tax bracket.

Bond	Size of issue	Call price
A	8,000 bonds	$1080
B	10,000 bonds	$1060
C	6,000 bonds	$1010
D	3,000 bonds	$1050
E	9,000 bonds	$1040
F	13,000 bonds	$1090

21-6 The initial issuance cost, the life, and the number of years remaining to maturity are given below for a number of bonds. The firm is in the 40-percent tax bracket.

Bond	Initial issuance cost	Bond life	Years remaining to maturity
A	$500,000	30 years	24
B	$200,000	20 years	5
C	$ 40,000	25 years	10
D	$100,000	10 years	2
E	$ 80,000	15 years	9

    a Calculate the annual amortization of the issuance cost for each bond.

    b Determine the after-tax cash inflow, if any, expected to result from the unamortized issuance cost if the bond is called today.

21-7 The Hunt Company is contemplating calling an outstanding $30 million bond issue and replacing it with a new $30 million bond issue. The firm wishes to do this in order to take advantage of the decline in interest rates that has occurred since the initial bond issuance. The old and new bonds are described below. The firm is in the 40-percent tax bracket.

Old bonds: The outstanding bonds have a $1000 face value and a 10-percent coupon rate. They were initially issued five years ago with a 25-year maturity. They were initially sold for their face value of $1000, and the firm incurred $250,000 in issuance costs. They are callable at $1060.

New Bonds: The new bonds would have a $1000 face value and an 8-percent coupon. They would have a 20-year maturity and could be sold at their face value. The issuance cost of the new bonds would be $400,000. The firm does not expect to have any overlapping interest.

    a Calculate the after-tax cash inflow expected from the unamortized portion of the old bonds' issuance cost.

    b Calculate the annual after-tax cash inflow from the issuance cost of the new bonds assuming the 20-year amortization.

    c Calculate the after-tax cash outflow from the call premium required to retire the old bonds.

    d Determine the incremental initial outlay required to issue the new bonds.

    e Calculate the annual after-tax cash savings, if any, expected from the bond refunding and reissue.

    f If the firm has a 5-percent after-tax cost of debt, would you recommend the proposed refunding and reissue? Why or why not?

21-8 Lawrence Furniture is considering calling an outstanding bond issue of $10 million and replacing it with a new $10 million issue. The firm wishes to do this to take advantage of the decline in interest rates that has occurred since the original issue. The two bond issues are discussed below; the firm is in the 40-percent tax bracket.

Old bonds: The outstanding bonds have a $1000 face value and a 12-percent coupon rate. They were issued five years ago with a 20-year maturity. They were initially sold at a $20 discount for a $120,000 issuance cost. They are callable at $1080.

New bonds: The new bonds would have a 15-year maturity, a face value of $1000, and a 9-percent coupon rate. It is expected that these bonds can be sold at face value for a flotation cost of $200,000. The firm expects the two issues to overlap by two months.

    a Calculate the incremental initial outlay required to issue the new bonds.

    b Calculate the annual after-tax cash savings, if any, expected from the bond refunding and reissue.

    c If the firm uses its after-tax cost of debt of 6 percent to evaluate its least risky decisions, would you recommend refunding? Explain your answer.

21-9 The Korrect Copy Company is considering the calling of an outstanding bond issue of $14 million and replacing it with a new $14 million issue. The details of both bond issues are outlined below. The firm has a 40-percent marginal tax rate.

Old bond: Korrect's old issue has a coupon rate of 10-percent, was issued six years ago, and had a 30-year maturity. The bonds sold at a $15 discount from their $1000 face value, flotation costs were $120,000, and their call price is $1080.

New bond: The new issue is expected to sell at face value ($1000), have a 24-year maturity, and have a flotation cost of $360,000. The firm will have a three-month period of overlapping interest while it retires the old bond.

    a What is the initial outlay required to issue the new bonds?

    b What are the annual after-tax cash savings, if any, from refunding and reissuing if:

        (1) The new bonds have an 8.5-percent coupon.

        (2) The new bonds have a 9.0 percent coupon.

    c Construct a table showing the net benefits of refunding under the two circumstances given in **b**, when

        (1) The firm has an after-tax cost of debt of 5 percent.

        (2) The firm has an after-tax cost of debt of 7 percent.

    d Discuss the set(s) of circumstances when the reissue is favorable and when it is not.

    e If the four circumstances were equally probable (i.e., each had .25 probability), would you recommend the refunding and reissue? Why or why not?

SELECTED REFERENCES

Ang, James S., "The Two Faces of Bond Refunding," *Journal of Finance 30* (June 1975), pp. 869–874.

Bierman, Harold, "The Bond Refunding Decision," *Financial Management 1* (Summer 1972), pp. 22–29.

Black, Fischer, and John C. Cox, "Valuing Corporate Securities: Some Effects of Bond Indenture Provisions," *Journal of Finance 31* (May 1976), pp. 351–367.

Boot, John C. G., and George M. Frankfurter, "The Dynamics of Corporate Debt Management, Decision Rules and Some Empirical Evidence," *Journal of Financial and Quantitative Analysis 7* (September 1972), pp. 1957–1966.

Bowlin, Oswald D., "The Refunding Decision: Another Special Case in Capital Budgeting," *Journal of Finance 21* (March 1966), pp. 55–68.

Brown, Bowman, "Why Corporations Should Consider Income Bonds," *Financial Executive 35* (October 1967), pp. 74–78.

Donaldson, Gordon, *Corporate Debt Capacity* (Boston: Division of Research, Harvard Business School, 1961).

Emery, Douglas R., "Overlapping Interest in Bond Refunding: A Reconsideration," *Financial Management 7* (Summer 1978), pp. 19–20.

Everett, Edward, "Subordinated Debt—Nature and Enforcement," *Business Lawyer 20* (July 1965), pp. 953–987.

Handorf, William C., "Flexible Debt Financing," *Financial Management 3* (Summer 1974), pp. 17–23.

Jen, Frank C., and James E. Wert, "The Deferred Call Provision and Corporate Bond Yields," *Journal of Financial and Quantitative Analysis 3* (June 1968), pp. 157–169.

Johnson, Rodney, and Richard Klein, "Corporate Motives in Repurchases of Discounted Bonds," *Financial Management 3* (Autumn 1974), pp. 44–49.

Karna, Adi S., "The Cost of Private versus Public Debt Issues," *Financial Management 1* (Summer 1972), pp. 65–67.

Laber, Gene, "Repurchase of Bonds through Tender Offers: Implications for Shareholder Wealth," *Financial Management 7* (Summer 1978), pp. 7–13.

Litzenberger, Robert H., and David P. Rutenberg, "Size and Timing of Corporate Bond Floatations," *Journal of Financial and Quantitative Analysis 8* (January 1972), pp. 1343–1359.

Mayor, Thomas H., and Kenneth G. McCoin, "The Rate of Discount in Bond Refunding," *Financial Management 3* (Autumn 1974), pp. 54–58.

Morris, James R., "On Corporate Debt Maturity Strategies," *Journal of Finance 31* (March 1976), pp. 29–37.

Ofer, Aharon R., and Robert A. Taggart, Jr., "Bond Refunding: A Clarifying Analysis," *Journal of Finance 32* (March 1977), pp. 21–30.

Pinches, George E., "The Role of Subordination and Industrial Bond Ratings," *Journal of Finance 30* (March 1975), pp. 201–206.

Pogue, Thomas F., and Robert M. Soldofsky, "What's in a Bond Rating?" *Journal of Financial and Quantitative Analysis 4* (July 1969), pp. 201–228.

Reilly, Frank K., and Michael D. Joehnk, "The Association Between Market-Determined Risk Measures for Bonds and Bond Ratings," *Journal of Finance 31* (December 1976), pp. 1387–1402.

Sibley, A. M., "Some Evidence on the Cash Flow Effects of Bond Refunding," *Financial Management 3* (Autumn 1974), pp. 50–53.

Van Horne, James C., "A Linear-Programming Approach to Evaluating Restrictions under a Bond Indenture or Loan Agreement," *Journal of Financial and Quantitative Analysis 1* (June 1966), pp. 68–83.

Weingartner, H. Martin, "Optimal Timing of Bond Refunding," *Management Science* (March 1967), pp. 511–524.

White, William L., "Debt Management and the Form of Business Financing," *Journal of Finance 29* (May 1974), pp. 565–577.

Winn, Willis J., and Arleigh Hess, Jr., "The Value of the Call Privilege," *Journal of Finance 14* (May 1959), pp. 182–195.

Zinbarg, Edward D., "The Private Placement Loan Agreement," *Financial Analysts Journal 31* (July-August 1975), pp. 33–35.

CHAPTER 22
Preferred and common stock

This chapter is devoted to the two sources of negotiated equity capital for the business firm—preferred and common stock. Retained earnings, another source of equity capital, are discussed in Chapter 24. The use of preferred and especially common stock to raise equity capital is necessary for a corporation's continued existence.

Chapters 17 and 18 discussed the firm's cost of capital and capital structure. The cost of capital discussion indicated that preferred stock is generally a less expensive source of financing than common stock. The lower cost of preferred stock was attributed primarily to the fact that preferred stock dividends are fixed. The cost of common was found to depend primarily on the riskiness of the firm as perceived by investors and the historical pattern of dividend payments. The discussion of capital structure emphasized the need for an equity base large enough to allow the firm to raise sufficient low-cost debt to build an optimal capital structure.

In this chapter, we shall discuss the characteristics, types, and advantages and disadvantages of preferred and common stock issues. The chapter is designed to provide insight into these forms of long-term financing which are available to corporations. It has three basic sections. The first section is devoted to a discussion of equity capital as an alternative to debt capital. The second section presents the basic rights, special features, and advantages and disadvantages of preferred stock. The final section discusses the characteristics, stock rights, non-rights sale, values, and advantages and disadvantages of common stock as a source of long-term financing.

THE NATURE OF EQUITY CAPITAL

Equity capital differs from debt capital in a number of key ways. These differences are considered by the financial manager in contemplating the use of equity as opposed to debt capital for raising funds. Various differences between debt and equity capital were discussed at the beginning of Chapter 18. In this section, only the key differences between these two types of long-term capital will be emphasized. The three basic differences between debt and equity capital relate to the ownership of the firm, the claims on its income and assets, and the maturity of the two types of capital.

Ownership rights

Unlike creditors, holders of equity capital (i.e., preferred and common stockholders) are owners of the business firm. The dollars invested by equity holders do not mature at some future date; they represent permanent capital that is expected to remain on the firm's books indefinitely. Holders of equity capital often receive voting rights that permit them to select the firm's directors and to vote on special issues. Debt holders receive voting privileges only when the firm has defaulted or violated the terms of a loan agreement or bond indenture. As long as the firm meets all the requirements of a loan agreement, only certain equity holders are given a voice in management (voting rights). It is only when the firm is approaching or in financial difficulty that creditors may receive some voice in management.

Claims on income and assets

Holders of equity capital receive a claim on both income and assets that is secondary to the claims of the firm's creditors. Each of these claims is discussed briefly below.

Claims on income. The claims of equity holders on income cannot be paid until the claims of all creditors have been satisfied. These claims include both interest and principal, regardless of whether the principal payment is in the form of a sinking-fund payment. Once these claims have been satisfied, the firm's board of directors can decide whether to distribute any of the remaining funds to the firm's owners. Certain owners may have preference over other owners with respect to the distribution of the firm's earnings. It is important to recognize that a firm's ability to make these payments may be constrained due to its cash position or certain loan covenants. The firm may have sufficient earnings, but no cash; it is the availability of cash that permits the firm to distribute earnings to owners.

Claims on assets. The claim of equity holders on the firm's assets is secondary to the claims of its creditors. The stockholders' claim on assets is relevant primarily when the firm becomes bankrupt.[1] When this happens, the assets are liquidated and the proceeds are distributed first to the government, then to secured creditors, then to general creditors, and finally to equity holders. Since the liquidation value of the firm's assets is generally below their book value, the equity holders rarely receive the book value of their equity in the event of liquidation. Because equity holders are the last to receive any distribution of assets during bankruptcy proceedings, they expect greater compensation in the form of dividends or rising market prices on their holdings.

Chapter 17 indicated that the cost of equity capital (i.e., common stock,

---

[1]The various procedures followed in bankruptcy proceedings are described in Chapter 26.

preferred stock, and retained earnings) is generally greater than the cost of debt. The lower cost of debt capital was attributed primarily to the tax-deductibility of interest payments to debt holders. If one were to disregard the tax-deductible feature of interest, the cost of the various forms of equity financing would still be generally higher than debt costs. The firm must compensate suppliers of equity more than suppliers of debt capital because the suppliers of equity capital take a higher risk. This higher risk results from the secondary claims of equity holders on the firm's income and assets. Although more costly, equity capital is necessary for the firm to grow and mature. Almost all business firms must initially be capitalized with some form of equity.

Maturity
Unlike debt, equity capital is a permanent form of financing. It does not mature, and therefore the repayment of the initial capital is not required. However, holders of equity capital are often able to liquidate their holdings through the various security exchanges. Even equity in closely held corporations can be sold, although the process of finding a suitable buyer may be a bit more difficult than in the case of large publicly held equity issues. Since equity does not mature and will be liquidated only during bankruptcy proceedings, the holder of equity must recognize that, although a ready market may exist for his or her shares, the price that can be realized may fluctuate with the level of the firm's current and expected earnings.[2] The fluctuating market price of equity makes the overall returns to owners even more risky.

PREFERRED STOCK
Preferred stock gives its holders certain privileges that make them senior to the common stockholders. Firms generally do not issue large quantities of preferred stock; the ratio of preferred stock to a firm's stockholders' equity is normally quite small. Preferred stockholders are promised a fixed periodic return, which is stated either as a percentage or in dollars. In other words, 5-percent preferred stock or $5 preferred stock can be issued. The way the dividend is stated depends on whether the preferred stock has a par value. The *par value* of a stock is the face amount of the stock specified in the corporate charter. It is important for certain legal purposes. The annual dividend is stated as a percentage on par-value preferred stock and in dollars on *no-par* preferred stock. A 5-percent preferred stock with a $100 par value is expected to pay $5 (5 percent of $100) in dividends per year.

Basic rights of preferred stockholders
The basic rights of preferred stockholders with respect to voting, the distribution of earnings, and the distribution of assets are somewhat more

---

[2]The market price of the publicly traded shares of a firm's stock is affected not only by *fundamental* factors such as the firm's current and expected earnings, but also by a number of *technical* factors. These technical factors include things such as economic activity, the time of year, and investor confidence. Technical or behavioral factors are often responsible for the fact that shares of firms with high earnings expectations sometimes sell at a low price.

favorable than the rights of common stockholders. Since preferred stock is a form of ownership and has no maturity date, its claims on income and assets come behind those of the firm's creditors.

Voting rights.   Preferred stockholders have many of the characteristics of both creditors and owners. Because preferred stockholders are promised a fixed periodic return similar to the interest paid creditors, but do not expect to have their invested capital repaid by the firm at maturity, they are often considered a *quasi-debt* supplier. The fixed return characteristic of debt coupled with the permanent nature of the preferred stock investment suggests a *hybrid* type of security. Since the preferred stock investment is permanent, it does represent ownership; but because the preferred stockholders' claim on the firm's income is fixed and takes precedence over the claim of common shareholders, they do not expose themselves to the same degree of risk as common stockholders. Preferred stockholders are therefore *not* normally given the right to vote. In certain instances, they may receive voting rights.

The distribution of earnings.   Preferred stockholders are given preference over common stockholders with respect to the distribution of earnings. If the stated preferred stock dividend is *passed* (i.e., not declared) by the board of directors, the payment of dividends to common stockholders is prohibited. It is this preference in dividend distributions that makes common stockholders the true risk takers with respect to expected returns. Since the stated objective of the firm's financial manager is to maximize the wealth of the firm's owners, the presence of preferred stock adds an additional constraint to the owners' wealth maximization objective. Preferred stock is *not* issued unless the directors are reasonably certain that funds will be available to pay preferred stock dividends. This ensures that there is at least a possibility that some earnings will be distributed as dividends to common stockholders, also. The payment of dividends to common stockholders is necessary in order to sustain the market price of the firm's common stock; thus without dividend payments to preferred stockholders, the market price of common stock may be damaged.

The distribution of assets.   Preferred stockholders are usually given preference over common stockholders in the liquidation of assets as a result of bankruptcy. Although the preferred stockholders must wait until the claims of all creditors have been satisfied, their claims are normally given preference over those of the common stockholders. The amount of the claim of preferred stockholders in liquidation proceedings is normally equal to the *par* or stated book value of the preferred stock. Preferred stockholders may be given a slight premium above the stock's book value, depending on the initial agreement under which the stock had been issued. Just as in the case of earnings, the preferred stockholder is usually given preference over the common stockholder, therefore placing the common stockholders in the most risky position with respect to the recovery of their investment.

Special features of preferred stock

A number of features are generally included as part of a preferred stock issue. These features, along with a statement of the stock's par value, the amount of dividend payments, and the dividend payment dates, are specified in an agreement similar to a long-term loan agreement or bond indenture. Certain restrictive covenants similar to long-term debt covenants may also be included in this agreement. The various items commonly covered by preferred stock agreements are discussed below.

Preferred stock covenants. The restrictive covenants commonly found in a preferred stock issue are aimed at assuring the continued existence of the firm and, most important, the regular payment of the stated preferred stock dividends. They include provisions concerning passing preferred dividends; the sale of senior securities; mergers, consolidations, and sale of assets; working capital requirements; and the payment of common stock dividends or common stock repurchases.

Passing preferred dividends. Since the directors of the corporation make preferred dividend payment decisions, there may be a provision stating that if preferred stock dividends are passed for a certain number of quarters (i.e., assuming quarterly payments are required), the preferred stockholders are entitled to elect a certain number of directors. In other words, when the preferred stockholders are not receiving their dividends, they are given a voice in management. As indicated earlier, preferred stock normally confers no voting power.

The sale of senior securities. Quite often, a preferred stock issue will prohibit the issuance of any additional securities senior to the preferred stock. Constraints may be placed on added preferred stock issues, also. The issuance of additional common stock is not viewed negatively by preferred stockholders since added funds are raised without impairing the preferred stockholders' claims on earnings and assets. If a clause does not prohibit new issues of debt and preferred stock, there may be a constraint on the amount of new funds that can be raised with senior securities. Sometimes, subsequent but subordinate issues of preferred stock are permitted.

Mergers, consolidations, and sale of assets. Often, preferred stock issues prohibit the firm from merging or consolidating with any other firm. The sale of all or a portion of the firm's assets may be specifically prohibited. Mergers, consolidations, or sales of assets may change the firm's asset and capital structures in a fashion believed detrimental to the interest of preferred stockholders.[3]

[3]In other words, if a firm were to merge with or acquire a firm that had very high levels of debt, the post-merger firm would have more debt claims, which are senior to the preferred stockholders' claims, and therefore the preferred stockholders would be in a more risky position with respect to the distribution of income and assets than they were prior to the merger.

Working capital requirements. Working capital requirements similar to those for long-term debt are not uncommon in preferred stock issues. The firm may be required to maintain a minimum amount of net working capital or a minimum current ratio. The motive for this requirement is to cause the firm to maintain sufficient liquidity to perpetuate itself over the long run.

Dividends and stock repurchases. Preferred stock issues may prohibit or limit the amount of common stock cash dividends or common stock repurchases the firm can make in any year. The reason for this prohibition is to prevent the firm from using a large portion of its cash to pay dividends or repurchase stock, which has an effect similar to a large dividend payment. The objective is to maintain adequate cash to provide a continuing stream of preferred stock dividends.

These are not the only covenants that may occur in preferred stock issues, but they illustrate the types of restrictions preferred stock issues can place on the firm. The violation of restrictive covenants usually permits the preferred stockholders to force the retirement of their stock at its stated value plus a possible premium. When the firm defaults, the initiative is placed in the hands of the preferred stockholder.

Cumulation. Most preferred stock is *cumulative* with respect to any dividends passed. That is, all dividends in arrears must be paid prior to the payment of dividends to common stockholders. If preferred stock is *noncumulative,* passed dividends do not accumulate. Only the most recent dividend must be paid prior to distributing earnings to common stockholders. Since the common stockholders, who are the firm's true owners, can receive dividends only by first satisfying the dividend claims of preferred stockholders, it is in the firm's best interest to pay preferred stock dividends when they are due.[4] A simple example may help clarify the distinction between cumulative and noncumulative preferred stock:

EXAMPLE

The Morgan Company currently has outstanding an issue of $6 preferred stock on which quarterly dividends of $1.50 are to be paid. Due to the cash shortage, the last two quarterly dividends were passed. The directors of the company have been receiving a large number of complaints from common stockholders, who have of course not received any dividends in the past two quarters either. If the preferred stock is cumulative, the company will have to pay the preferred shareholders $4.50 per share ($3.00 of dividends in arrears plus the current $1.50 dividend) prior to paying out any earnings to the common stockholders. If the preferred stock is noncumulative, the firm would have to pay only the current $1.50 dividend to the preferred stockholders prior to paying out funds to the common stockholders. This example should make it quite clear why most preferred stock issues are cumulative and why the dividends on cumulative preferred stock are normally paid when they are due. ●

---

[4]Most preferred stock is cumulative since it is difficult to market noncumulative stock. The common stockholders will obviously prefer noncumulative preferred to be issued since it does not place them in quite as poor a position, but they must recognize that it is often in the best interest of the firm to raise needed funds by selling cumulative preferred stock.

Participation. Most issues of preferred stock are *nonparticipating,* which means that the preferred stockholders receive only the required dividend payments. Occasionally, *participating* preferred stock is issued. This type of preferred stock provides for dividend payments based on certain formulas that allow the preferred stockholders to participate with common stockholders in the receipt of dividends beyond a specified amount. This feature is included only when the firm considers it absolutely necessary in order to obtain badly needed funds.

The call feature. Preferred stock is generally callable, which means that the issuer can retire outstanding stock within a certain period of time at a specified price. The call option generally cannot be exercised until a period of years has elapsed since the issuance of the preferred stock. The call price is normally set above the initial issuance price, but it is quite likely to decrease according to a predetermined schedule as time passes. Making preferred stock callable provides the issuer with a method of bringing the fixed-payment commitment of the preferred stock issue to an end.

The conversion feature. Preferred stock quite often contains a conversion feature that permits its conversion into a specified number of shares of common stock. Sometimes the conversion ratio or time period for conversion changes according to a prespecified formula. The call option is a useful tool for forcing the conversion of convertible preferred stock. A more in-depth discussion of conversion is presented in Chapter 23.

Retirement, refinancing, and recapitalization. There are a number of ways of providing for the retirement of preferred stock either for the purpose of refinancing or in order to recapitalize (i.e., change the capital structure of) the firm.

Planned retirement. One uncommon method of retiring preferred stock is to provide a sinking fund to retire shares at a specified rate over a given period of time. This type of planned retirement makes the preferred stock quite similar to long-term debt except that if the firm is unable to make a sinking-fund payment for preferred stock, bankruptcy will not result. It is this feature that sometimes makes preferred stock issued with planned retirement in mind more attractive than debt. A missed preferred stock dividend or sinking-fund payment also does not have the same consequences as a missed interest or sinking-fund payment on a long-term debt.

Refinancing. By including a call feature in a preferred stock, the issuer can replace an outstanding issue with a less expensive form of financing. The stock could be retired by purchasing it outright in the marketplace, but due to the difficulty and expense of this approach, the use of the call feature is almost a necessity. Whether refinancing is justified depends on the present value of the cost of maintaining the preferred stock as opposed to the cost of an alternate source of financing. This decision is quite similar to the bond refunding decision discussed in Chapter 21.

Recapitalization. A firm may want to retire preferred stock to change its capital structure. This can be accomplished by purchasing the preferred stock in the market, calling the preferred stock, or forcing its conversion.

Advantages and disadvantages of preferred stock

It is difficult to generalize about the advantages and disadvantages of preferred stock due to the various features that may or may not be incorporated in a preferred stock issue. The attractiveness of preferred stock is also affected by current interest rates and a firm's existing capital structure. Nevertheless, some key advantages and disadvantages can be discerned.

Advantages. The basic advantages of preferred stock are its ability to increase leverage, the flexibility of the obligation, and its use in mergers and acquisitions.

Increased leverage. Since preferred stock obligates the firm to pay only fixed dividends to its holders, its presence helps to increase the firm's financial leverage; the effects of preferred stock on a firm's financial leverage were discussed in Chapters 4 and 18. It is the fixed payment obligation of preferred stock that allows the firm's common stockholders to receive increased returns when earnings on total capital are greater than the cost of preferred stock. An example will help to illustrate this point.

EXAMPLE

The Robin Company has the following capital structure.

Type of capital	Amount	Percentage of total capital
Long-term debt @ 8%	$ 30,000	30%
Preferred stock @ 10%	30,000	30
Common stock equity	40,000	40
Total capital	$100,000	100%

In the most recent period, the firm earned $10,000 *before interest and after taxes,* or 10 percent on its total capital. Since the firm is in the 40-percent tax bracket, the after-tax cost of debt is only 4.8 percent (i.e., 8 percent × (1 − .40)).[5] The firm must therefore pay its long-term creditors $1440 (.048 · $30,000) and its preferred stockholders $3000 (.10 · $30,000), leaving $5560 ($10,000 − $1440 − $3000) available for the common stockholders. The return on the common stock equity is therefore 13.9 percent ($5560 ÷ $40,000). The presence of the preferred stock increases the firm's leverage and magnifies the return to the common stockholders since the return on the total capital is greater than the cost of fixed financing.

---

[5]The reader should recall from Chapter 17, which was concerned with the cost of capital, that since interest is tax-deductible the after-tax cost of debt to the firm is calculated by multiplying the stated cost by one minus the tax rate. In this example, since the $10,000 represents earnings measured *before interest and after taxes,* in order to get earnings *after* interest and taxes, the interest cost times one minus the tax rate [interest · (1 − tax rate)] must be subtracted from the earnings before interest and after taxes.

If the Robin Company had earned the same amount but had $30,000 worth of bonds, no preferred stock, and $70,000 worth of common stock, the earnings available for the common stockholders would have amounted to $8560 ($10,000 − $1440). The return on the common stock equity would thus have been only 12.2 percent ($8560 ÷ $70,000). The decreased return to the common stockholders is due to the decreased leverage resulting from the replacement of the $30,000 worth of preferred stock with an additional $30,000 worth of common stock. It should be clear from this example how preferred stock can be used to increase the firm's leverage, thereby magnifying the effects of increased earnings on the common stockholders' returns. ●

Flexibility. Although preferred stock does provide added leverage in much the same way as a bond, it differs from a bond in that the issuer can pass a dividend payment without suffering consequences that result when an interest payment is missed. Preferred stock allows the issuer to keep its levered position without running as great a risk of being forced out of business in a lean year as it might if it missed interest payments on debt.

Use in mergers and acquisitions. Preferred stock has been successfully to either merge or acquire firms. Often preferred stock is exchanged for the common stock of an acquired firm; the preferred dividend is set at a level equivalent to the historical dividend of the acquired firm. This lets the acquiring firm state at the time of the acquisition that only a fixed dividend will be paid. All other earnings can be reinvested to perpetuate the growth of the merged enterprise. This approach also permits the owners of the acquired firm to be assured of a continuing stream of dividends equivalent to that which may have been provided prior to its acquisition. Quite often, preferred stock used for mergers and acquisitions is convertible. The use of preferred stock in mergers and acquisitions is discussed in greater depth in Chapter 25.

Disadvantages. The two major disadvantages of preferred stock are the seniority of the holders' claims and its cost.

Seniority of the holders' claims. Since holders of preferred stock are given preference over the common stockholders with respect to the distribution of both earnings and assets, the presence of preferred stock in a sense jeopardizes the common shareholders' returns. Adding preferred stock to the firm's capital structure creates additional claims prior to those of the common stockholders. If the firm's after-tax earnings are quite variable, its ability to pay at least token dividends to its common stockholders may be seriously impaired with the addition of preferred stock to the firm's capital structure.

Cost. The cost of preferred stock financing is generally higher than the cost of debt financing. This is because the payment of dividends to preferred stockholders is not guaranteed, whereas interest on bonds is. Since the preferred shareholders are willing to accept the added risk of purchasing preferred stock rather than long-term debt, they must be compensated with a higher return. Another factor causing the cost of preferred stock to be significantly greater than that of long-term debt is the fact that interest on long-term debt is tax-deductible, while preferred dividends must be paid from earnings after taxes.[6]

In summary, the desirability of using preferred stock to raise funds depends not only on the firm's current financial structure and the state of the financial markets, but on the trade-offs among the cost, risk, and control of the alternate forms of long-term financing. The firm must weigh the long-run costs and benefits of preferred stock financing against the advantages and disadvantages of both long-term debt and common stock financing. Consideration must also be given to whether the stock will be cumulative or noncumulative, participatng or nonparticipating, callable or noncallable, and convertible or nonconvertible. In many instances, the preferred stock financing decision is a quite difficult one. Of the major external sources of long-term funds, preferred stock financing is the least commonly used.

COMMON STOCK

The true owners of the business firms are the common stockholders, who invest their money in the firm only because of their expectations of future returns. A common stockholder is sometimes referred to as a *residual owner*, since in essence he or she receives what is left after all other claims on the firm's income and assets have been satisfied. It is the common stockholder whose wealth it should be the objective of the firm's financial manager to maximize. Since the common stockholder accepts what is left after all other claims have been satisfied, he or she is placed in a quite uncertain or risky position with respect to return on his or her invested capital. As a result of this generally uncertain position, the common stockholder expects to be compensated with adequate dividends and capital gains.

This section of the chapter discusses the characteristics of common stock, how stock rights can be used to raise additional capital, the non-rights sale of new common stock, the basic values of common stock, and some of the chief advantages and disadvantages of common stock financing.

Characteristics of common stock

An issue of common stock has a number of basic characteristics. An understanding of these characteristics will provide the reader with a better grasp of the nature of common stock financing. In this section we shall discuss par value; authorized, outstanding, and issued stock; voting rights; dividends; stock repurchases; and the distribution of earnings and assets.

Par value. Common stock may be sold either with or without a par value. A *par value* is a relatively useless value arbitrarily placed on the stock in the corporate charter. It is generally quite low, since in many states the

[6]From time to time, discussion of making preferred stock dividends tax-deductible occurs in Congress and other legal forums. Tax reform recommendations made by President Ford to Congress during his term in office included such a proposal. Currently, no legislation relative to the tax deductibility of preferred stock dividends is under congressional consideration.

firm's owners can be held legally liable for an amount equal to the difference between the par value and the price paid for the stock if the price paid for the stock is less than the par value. Setting the par value quite low, in the range of $1, reduces the possibility that the stock will sell for less than its par value. Firms often issue *no-par* stock, in which case they may assign it a value or place it on the books at the price at which it is sold.

A low par value may also be advantageous in states where certain corporate taxes are based on the par value of stock; if a stock has no par value, the tax may be based on an arbitrarily determined per-share figure. The accounting entries resulting from the sale of common stock can be illustrated by a simple example:

EXAMPLE

The Nixon Company has issued 1000 shares of $2 par-value common stock, receiving proceeds of $50 per share. This results in the following entries on the firm's books.

Common stock (1000 shares @ $2 par)	$ 2,000
Paid-in capital in excess of par	48,000
Common stock equity	$50,000

Sometimes the entry labeled "paid-in capital in excess of par," above, may be labeled "capital surplus." Firms are usually prohibited by state law from distributing any of their paid-in capital as dividends.[7] ●

Authorized, outstanding, and issued stock. A corporate charter must state the number of shares of common stock the firm is *authorized* to issue. Not all authorized shares will necessarily be *outstanding*. Since it is often difficult to amend the corporate charter to authorize the issuance of additional shares, firms generally attempt to authorize more shares than they plan to issue. A possible disadvantage of this approach is the fact that in some states certain corporate taxes are based on the number of shares authorized. It is possible for the corporation to have *issued* more shares of common stock than are currently outstanding if it has repurchased stock. Repurchased stock is referred to as *treasury stock*. The amount of treasury stock is therefore found by subtracting the number of outstanding shares from the number of shares issued.

Voting rights. Generally, each share of common stock entitles the holder to one vote in the election of directors or in other special elections. Votes are generally assignable and must be cast at the annual shareholders' meeting. Occasionally, *nonvoting common stock* is issued when the firm's present owners wish to raise capital through the sale of common stock, but do not want to give up any voting power. When this is done, the common stock will be classed. Class A common is typically designated as nonvoting,

---

[7]The various legal and internal considerations with respect to the payment of cash dividends are discussed in detail in Chapter 24. A firm can pay out more dollars in cash dividends than it earns in a given period if sufficient cash and retained earnings are available.

while class B common would have voting rights. Because class A shares are not given voting rights, they typically are given preference over class B shares in the distribution of earnings and (or) assets (in the event of liquidation). Three aspects of voting require special attention—proxies, majority voting, and cumulative voting.

Proxies.   Since most small stockholders often cannot attend the annual meeting in order to vote their shares, they may sign a proxy statement giving their votes to another party. The solicitation of proxies from shareholders is closely controlled by the Securities and Exchange Commission since there is a possibility that proxies will be solicited on the basis of false or misleading information. The existing management generally receives the stockholders' proxies, since it is able to solicit them at company expense. Occasionally, when the ownership of the firm is widely disseminated, outsiders may attempt to gain control by waging a *proxy battle*. This requires soliciting a sufficient number of votes to unseat the existing management. In order to win a corporate election, votes from a majority of the shares voted—not outstanding—is required. Proxy battles generally occur when the existing management is performing poorly; however, the odds of a nonmanagement group winning a proxy battle are generally slim.

Majority voting.   In the majority voting system, each stockholder is entitled to one vote for each share of stock owned. The stockholders vote for each position on the board of directors separately and each stockholder is permitted to vote all of his or her shares for *each* director he or she favors. The directors receiving the majority of the votes are elected. It is impossible for minority interests to select a director, since each shareholder can vote his or her shares for as many of the candidates as he or she wishes. As long as management controls a majority of the votes, it can elect all the directors. An example will clarify this point.

EXAMPLE

The Baker Company is in the process of electing three directors. There are 1000 shares of stock outstanding, of which management controls 60 percent. The management-backed candidates are A, B, and C; the minority candidates are D, E, and F. By voting its 600 shares (60 percent of 1000) for *each* of its candidates, management can elect A, B, and C; the minority shareholders, with only 400 votes for each of their candidates, cannot elect any directors. Management's candidates will receive 600 votes each, and other candidates will receive 400 votes each. ●

Cumulative voting.   Some states require and others permit the use of a cumulative voting system to elect corporate directors. This system gives a number of votes equal to the number of directors to be elected to each share of common stock. The votes can be given to *any* director(s) the shareholder desires. The advantage of this system is that it provides the minority shareholders with an opportunity to elect at least some directors.

EXAMPLE

The Able Company, like the Baker Company, is in the process of electing three directors. In this case, however, each share of common entitles the holder to three votes, which may be voted in any manner desired. Again, there are 1000 shares outstanding, and management controls 600. It therefore has a total of 1800 votes (3 · 600), while the minority shareholders have 1200 votes (3 · 400). In this situation, the majority shareholders can elect only two directors, and the minority shareholders can select at least one director. The majority shareholders can split their votes evenly between their three candidates (i.e., give them 600 votes each); but if the minority shareholders give all their votes to one of their candidates, he or she will win. ●

A commonly cited formula for determining the number of shares necessary to elect a certain number of directors, *NE*, is given by Equation 22.1:

$$NE = \frac{O \cdot D}{T + 1} + 1 \tag{22.1}$$

where

NE = the number of shares needed to elect a certain number of directors
O = the total number of shares of common stock outstanding
D = the number of directors desired
T = the total number of directors to be elected

Substituting the values in the example above for O and T and letting $D = 1$, 2, and 3 yields values of *NE* equal to 251, 501, and 751. Since the minority stockholders control only 400 shares, they can elect only one director. The advantage of cumulative voting from the point of view of minority shareholders should be clear from this example. However, even with cumulative voting, certain election procedures such as staggered terms for directors can be used to prevent minority representation on a firm's board of directors. Also, the majority shareholders may control a large enough number of shares and (or) the total number of directors to be elected may be small enough to prevent minority repesentation.

Dividends. The payment of corporate dividends is at the discretion of the board of directors. Most corporations pay these dividends quarterly as a result of the quarterly dividend meeting of the board of directors. Dividends may be paid in cash, stock, or merchandise. Cash dividends are most common, and merchandise dividends are least common. Stock splits, which have some similarity to stock dividends are sometimes used to enhance the trading activity of a stock. The common stockholder is not promised a dividend, but he or she grows to expect certain dividend payments from the historical dividend pattern of the firm. Before dividends are paid to the common stockholders, the claims of all creditors, the government, and preferred stockholders must be satisfied. Because of the great importance of the dividend decision to the growth and valuation of the firm, Chapter 24 is devoted solely to a discussion of dividends and retained earnings.

Stock repurchases. Another characteristic of common stock, alluded to earlier in the discussion of authorized, outstanding, and issued stock, is the repurchase of stock. As stated earlier, stock that has been repurchased by a firm is called *treasury stock*. Firms occasionally repurchase stock in order to change their capital structure or to increase the returns to the owners. The effect of repurchasing common stock is similar to that of the payment of cash dividends to stockholders. The repurchase of stock has become quite popular among firms that are in a very liquid position with no attractive investment opportunities. Since stock repurchases are similar to cash dividend payments, they too are given in-depth coverage in Chapter 24.

The distribution of earnings and assets. As we have mentioned in previous sections, the holders of common stock have no guarantee of receiving any periodic distribution of earnings in the form of dividends, nor are they guaranteed anything in the event of liquidation. The common stockholders are likely to receive nothing as a result of bankruptcy proceedings. However, one thing they are assured of is that as long as they pay more than the par value for the stock they cannot lose any more than they have invested in the firm. Moreover, the common stockholder can receive unlimited returns both through the distribution of earnings and through appreciation in the value of their holdings. To them nothing is guaranteed, but the possible rewards for providing risk capital can be great. The common stockholders must view the firm as a going concern; and if their feelings change, opportunities to sell or divest themselves of their holdings do exist.

Stock rights

Stock rights, which provide certain common stock purchase privileges to existing shareholders, are an important tool of common stock financing. Without them, the shareholders run the risk of losing their proportionate control of the corporation. Certain aspects of rights financing are discussed below.

Preemptive rights. Most issues of common stock provide shareholders with *preemptive rights*, which allow the stockholders to maintain their proportionate ownership in the corporation when new issues are made. Most states require that shareholders be extended this privilege unless it is explicitly prohibited by the corporate charter. Preemptive rights permit existing shareholders to maintain their voting control and protect against the dilution of their ownership and earnings. *Dilution* of ownership usually results in the dilution of earnings since each shareholder will have a claim on a smaller part of the firm's earnings—more shares own the same basic enterprise. Of course, if earnings simultaneously increase, the long-run effect may be an overall increase in earnings per share. From the firm's viewpoint, the use of preemptive rights offerings to raise new equity capital may be cheaper than a public issue of stock. An example may help clarify the use of rights.

EXAMPLE
The Maverick Company currently has 100,000 shares of common stock outstanding and is contemplating issuing an additional 10,000 shares through a rights offering. Each existing shareholder will receive one right per share, and each right will entitle the shareholder to purchase $1/10$ of a share of new common stock (10,000 ÷ 100,000). Therefore 10 rights will be required to purchase one share of the stock. The holder of 1000 shares of existing common stock will receive 1000 rights, each permitting the purchase of $1/10$ of a share of new common stock. Thus he or she can purchase 100 shares of new common stock. If the shareholder exercises his or her rights, he or she will end up with a total of 1100 shares of common stock, or 1 percent of the total number of (110,000) shares outstanding. This is the same proportion the shareholder had prior to the rights offering. ●

The mechanics of rights offerings. When a company makes a rights offering, the board of directors must set a *date of record,* which is the last date on which the recipient of a right must be the legal owner indicated in the company's stock ledger. Due to the lag in bookkeeping procedures, stocks are usually sold *ex rights* (i.e., without rights) four business days prior to the date of record. Prior to this point, the stock is sold *cum rights* or *rights on,* which means that purchasers of the stock will receive the rights.

The issuing firm sends rights to holders of record, who are free to exercise them, sell them, or let them expire. Rights are transferable, and many are traded actively enough to be listed on the various stock exchanges. They are exercisable for a specified period of time, generally not more than a few months, at a price, which is called the *subscription price,* set somewhat below the prevailing market price. Since fractions of shares are not always issued, it is sometimes necessary to either purchase additional rights or sell any extra rights. The value of a right depends largely on the number of rights needed to purchase a share of stock and the amount by which the right-subscription price is below the current market price. If the rights have a very low value and an individual owns only a small number of shares, the rights may be permitted to expire.

Management decisions. A firm's financial management must make two basic decisions when preparing for a rights offering. The first is the price at which the right holders can purchase a new share of common stock. The subscription price must be set *below* the current market price, but how far below this it is set depends on management's evaluation of the sensitivity of the market to a price change, the degree of dilution in ownership and earnings expected, and the size of the rights offering. Management will consider the rights offering successful if approximately 90 percent of the rights are exercised.

Once management has determined the subscription price, it must determine the number of rights required to purchase a share of stock. Since the amount of funds to be raised is known in advance, the subscription price can be divided into this figure to get the total number of shares that must be sold. Dividing the total number of shares outstanding by the total number of shares to be sold will give management the number of rights required to purchase a share of stock.

EXAMPLE

The Boone Company intends to raise $1 million through a rights offering. The firm currently has 160,000 shares outstanding, which have been most recently trading for $53 to $58 per share. The company has consulted an investment banking firm, which has recommended setting the subscription price for the rights at $50 per share. It believes that at this price the offering will be fully subscribed. The firm must therefore sell an additional 20,000 shares ($1,000,000 ÷ $50 per share). This means that 8 rights (i.e., 160,000 ÷ 20,000) will be needed to purchase a new share at $50. Therefore each right will entitle its holder to purchase ⅛ of a share of common stock. ●

The value of a right.   Theoretically the value of a right should be the same if the stock is selling *with rights on (cum rights)* or *ex rights*. However, the market value of a right may differ from its theoretical value.

With rights on.   Once a rights offering has been declared, shares will trade for only a few days with rights on. Equation 22.2 is used to find the value of a right when the stock is trading with rights on, R_o.

$$R_o = \frac{M_o - S}{N + 1}$$
(22.2)

where

R_o = the theoretical value of a right when stock is selling rights on
M_o = the market value of the stock with rights on
S = the subscription price of the stock
N = the number of rights needed to purchase a share of stock

EXAMPLE

The Boone Company's stock is currently selling with rights on at a price of $54.50 per share, the subscription price is $50 per share, and 8 rights are required to purchase a new share of stock. According to Equation 22.2, the value of a right is $0.50 [($54.50 − $50.00) ÷ (8 + 1)]. A right should therefore be worth $0.50 in the marketplace. ●

Ex rights.   When a share of stock is traded ex rights, meaning that the value of the right is no longer included in the stock's market price, the share price is expected to drop by the value of a right. Equation 22.3 is used to find the market value of the stock trading ex rights, M_e. The same notation is used as in Equation 22.2.

$$M_e = M_o - R_o$$
(22.3)

The value of a right when the stock is trading ex rights, R_e, is given by Equation 22.4.

$$R_e = \frac{M_e - S}{N} \hspace{4cm} (22.4)$$

The use of these equations can be illustrated by returning to the Boone Company example.

EXAMPLE
According to Equation 22.3, the market price of the Boone Company stock selling ex rights is $54 ($54.50 − $0.50). Substituting this value into Equation 22.4 gives us the value of a right when the stock is selling ex rights, which is $0.50 [($54.00 − $50.00) ÷ 8]. The theoretical value of the right when the stock is selling with rights on or ex rights is therefore the same. ●

The market behavior of rights. As indicated earlier, stock rights are negotiable instruments that are traded on security exchanges. The market price of a right will generally differ from its theoretical value. The extent to which it will differ will depend on how the firm's stock price is expected to behave during the period when the right is exercisable. By buying rights instead of the stock itself, investors can achieve much higher returns on their money when stock prices advance.

Under- and oversubscribed offerings. Rights offerings may be made through underwriters or directly by the issuing company. Most rights offerings are made through investment bankers, who underwrite and issue the rights. In most underwriting agreements, the investment banker agrees to a *standby arrangement,* which is a formal guarantee that any shares not subscribed to or sold publicly will be purchased by the investment banker. This guarantee assures the firm that the entire issue will be sold; it will not be *undersubscribed.* The investment banker, of course, requires an additional fee for making this guarantee.

Most rights offerings include an *oversubscription privilege,* which provides for the distribution of shares the rights to which were not exercised to interested shareholders on a pro rata basis at the stated subscription price. This privilege is a method of restricting ownership to the same group, although ownership proportions may change slightly. Shares that cannot be sold through the oversubscription privilege may be offered to the public. If an investment banker is used, the disposition of unsubscribed shares may be left up to it.

Non-rights sale of new common stock
Aside from the sale of new common stock through a rights offering, the firm may be able to place directly new shares of common stock through some type of stock option or stock purchase plan. As pointed out in Chapter 19,

stock options are generally extended to management and permit it to purchase a certain number of shares at a specified price over a certain period of time, while *stock-purchase plans* are fringe benefits occasionally offered to employees that allow them to purchase the firm's stock at a discount or on a matching basis, with the firm absorbing part of the cost. New issues of common stock, of course, can also be sold publicly through an investment banker. This approach is commonly used in situations in which rights offerings are not required or are unsuccessful. The sale of common stock through an investment banker is generally more expensive than any type of direct placement, but the investment banker does provide a convenient mechanism for selling new common stock. Since a detailed discussion of the functions, organization, and operation of the investment banker in selling corporate securities was presented in Chapter 19, further discussion is not included here.

Basic values of common stock

The value of a share of common stock may be measured in a number of ways. It has a book value, a liquidation value, a market value, and a theoretical value. The book value and the liquidation value do not reflect the value of the firm as a going concern, but rather view the firm as a conglomeration of assets and liabilities without any earning power. The book value measures the firm's common stock value as the per-share amount of common stock equity recorded on the firm's balance sheet. The liquidation value is based on the fact that the book value of the firm's assets is not generally equal to their market value. It is calculated by taking the *market* value of the firm's assets, subtracting its liabilities and the claims of preferred stockholders from this figure, and dividing the result by the number of shares of common stock outstanding.

The most accepted way of determining the true (or theoretical) value of a share is to find the present value of all future per-share dividends expected over the firm's assumed infinite life. This approach is theoretically superior to the use of market values since a firm's stock may be over- or underpriced in the market. An in-depth discussion of common stock valuation was presented in Chapter 18.

Advantages and disadvantages of common stock

Common stock has a number of basic advantages and disadvantages. Some of the factors to be reckoned with in considering common stock financing are discussed below.

Advantages.   The basic advantages of common stock stem from the fact that it is a source of financing that places a minimum of constraints on the firm. Since dividends do not *have* to be paid on common stock and their nonpayment does not jeopardize the receipt of payment by other security holders, common stock financing is quite attractive. The fact that common stock has no maturity, thereby eliminating any future repayment obligation, also enhances the desirability of common stock financing. Another advantage of common stock over other forms of long-term financing is its ability to increase the firm's borrowing power. The more common stock the firm sells, the larger the firm's equity base and therefore the more easily and cheaply long-term debt financing can be obtained.

Disadvantages. The disadvantages of common stock financing include the potential *dilution* of voting power and earnings. Only when rights are offered and exercised by their recipients can this be avoided. Of course, the dilution of voting power and earnings resulting from new issues of common stock may go unnoticed by the small shareholder. Another disadvantage of common stock financing is its high cost. In Chapter 17 common stock equity was shown to be, normally, the most expensive form of long-term financing. This is because dividends are not tax-deductible and because common stock is a riskier security than either debt or preferred stock.

SUMMARY

Both preferred and common stock are instruments for raising long-term equity funds. Both these securities represent forms of ownership and therefore the payment of dividends is not mandatory. These securities also have no maturity. Preferred stock is considered a security senior to common stock since the holders of preferred stock are given preference over common stockholders with respect to the distribution of both income and assets. Before dividends are paid or assets are distributed to the common stockholders, the claims of the preferred shareholders must be satisfied. In liquidation proceedings, the claims of preferred stockholders are paid immediately after the creditors' claims have been satisfied.

Preferred stock is similar to debt in that it has a fixed annual dividend. Since the preferred stockholders' claims are given preference over the claims of common stockholders, they do not run the same risks as the common stockholders, who are the firm's true owners. They therefore do not receive any voting privileges. Preferred stock issues may have certain restrictive covenants similar to those of bond issues. They may also have such features as cumulative dividends, participation in earnings, a call feature, a conversion feature, and certain retirement options. The basic advantages cited for the use of preferred stock financing include its ability to increase leverage, the flexibility of the obligation, and its use in mergers and acquisitions. Disadvantages include its preference over the common stockholders, who are the firm's true owners, and its relatively high cost.

Common stockholders are the true owners of the firm because they subordinate their claims to those of all other parties. Some firms issue various classes of common stock, such as class A and class B. Class A stock may have no voting rights, but is given preference over class B voting shares with respect to the receipt of distributions of earnings or assets, or both. Various voting systems are available for providing minority representation on the firm's board of directors. Purchasers of common stock normally expect to receive some type of dividend; sometimes common stock is repurchased in order to meet any of a variety of objectives. Holders of common stock generally receive a preemptive right that gives them an opportunity to purchase any new common stock issues on a pro rata basis in order to maintain their proportion of votes and earnings. Stock rights are used to pass a purchase option to the owners. A certain number of rights are required to purchase shares at a reduced price, which causes the rights to have a value. Rights may be sold, exercised, purchased, or allowed to expire. Common stock may be placed directly with the purchaser by the issuer or sold by an investment banker. In addition to the use of rights offerings, direct placement can be achieved through the use of stock options and (or) stock-purchase plans. Additional administrative expense must also be absorbed when a public issue of securities is made through an investment banker. The worth of a share of common stock may be judged by its book value, liquidation value, market value, or theoretical value.

The basic advantages of common stock stem from the fact that it is a source of financing that places a minimum of constraints on the firm with respect to periodic payments and retirement. Common stock also allows the firm to enhance its borrowing power. Disadvantages often cited for common stock include the potential dilution of voting power and earnings, and the high cost of this form of financing.

QUESTIONS

22-1   How do debt and equity capital differ? What are the key differences between them with respect to ownership, claims on income and assets, and maturity?

22-2   What is preferred stock? What claims do preferred stockholders have on the firm's income and assets? How are dividends on preferred stock stated?

22-3   What is cumulative and noncumulative preferred stock? Which is most common? Why?

22-4   What is participating and nonparticipating preferred stock? How is the degree of participation specified? In what circumstance would you expect participating preferred to be issued?

22-5   What is a call feature in a preferred stock issue? When and at what price does the call usually take place? What benefit does the call offer the issuer of preferred stock?

22-6   What are the advantages of raising funds through issues of preferred stock? Are there any disadvantages to preferred stock as a source of financing?

22-7   Why is the common stockholder considered the true owner of a business firm? What risks do common stockholders take that other suppliers of long-term capital do not?

22-8   What is the difference between the number of shares of common stock *authorized* and the number of shares actually *outstanding*? Why are firms likely to authorize more shares than they initially intend to issue?

22-9   What are proxies? How are they used? What are proxy battles, and why are they initiated? Why is it difficult for minority shareholders to win such a battle?

22-10   How do majority and cumulative voting systems differ? Which of these voting systems would be preferred by the small shareholder? Why?

22-11   Common stock is sometimes issued in classes. What differences exist between class A and class B common stock? Why might a firm issue two classes of stock?

22-12   What are stock rights? How are they related to *preemptive rights*? Why might the issuance of stock rights on a preemptive basis be an attractive and fast method of raising new equity capital?

22-13   What is a date of record for stock rights? What do the terms *ex rights* and *cum rights* or *rights on* mean? Are stock rights marketable?

22-14   What is a right subscription price? How is it determined? Given the subscription price, what must the firm know in order to determine the number of rights to offer?

22-15   What are the key advantages and disadvantages of using common stock financing as a source of new capital funds?

PROBLEMS

22-1   Sinderson, Schaefer, and Schloff has an outstanding issue of preferred stock with an $80 par value and an 11-percent annual dividend.

  a What is the annual dollar dividend? If it is paid quarterly, how much will be paid each quarter?

  b If the preferred stock is *noncumulative* and the board of directors has passed the preferred dividend for the last three years, how much must the preferred stockholders be paid prior to paying dividends to common stockholders?

  c If the preferred stock is *cumulative* and the board of directors has passed the preferred dividend for the last three years, how much must be paid to the preferred stockholders prior to paying dividends to common stockholders?

22-2   In each case below, how many dollars of preferred dividends per share must be paid to preferred stockholders prior to paying common dividends?

Case	Cumulative-noncumulative provision	Par value	Dividend per share	Periods of dividends passed
A	Cumulative	$ 80	$5	2
B	Noncumulative	$110	8%	3
C	Noncumulative	$100	$11	1
D	Cumulative	$ 60	8.5%	4
E	Cumulative	$ 90	9%	0

22-3   The Korrect Kan Company has outstanding an issue of 3000 shares of participating preferred stock, having a $100 par value and an 8-percent annual dividend. The preferred stockholders participate fully with common shareholders in dividends of more than $9 per share for common stock. The firm has 5000 shares of common stock outstanding.

  a If the firm pays the preferred stockholders their dividends and then declares an additional $100,000 of dividends, how much will be the total dividend per share for preferred and common stock, respectively?

  b If the firm pays the preferred stockholders their dividends and then declares an additional $40,000 in dividends, what is the total dividend per share for each type of shareholder?

  c If the firm's preferred stock is cumulative and the past two years' dividends have been passed, what dividends will be received by each type of shareholder if the firm declares a *total* dividend of $30,000?

    d Rework **c** assuming the total dividend payment is $20,000.

    e Rework **a** and **b** assuming the preferred stock is nonparticipating.

22-4 The Great Plains Corporation had *earnings before interest and after taxes* of $300,000 last year. The firm has a marginal tax rate of 40 percent, and currently has the following capital structure:

Type of capital	Amount	Percent of capital
Long-term debt @ 10%	$ 600,000	25%
Preferred stock @ 11%	600,000	25
Common stock equity	1,200,000	50
Total capital	$2,400,000	100%

    a Calculate the firm's *before-interest and after-tax* return on its total capital.

    b Calculate the firm's after-tax return on common equity.

    c If the firm had raised the $600,000 of preferred stock capital through the sale of $600,000 of additional common stock, what would its after-tax return on common equity have been?

    d If the firm had shifted the preferred stock financing to debt (at the same 10-percent cost), what effect would this have had on the after-tax return on common equity?

    e Use the answers in **b** through **d** above to evaluate the effects of preferred stock on the firm's financial leverage.

22-5 Zesto-Presto currently has the following capital structure:

Type of capital	Amount	Percent of capital
Long-term debt @ 10%	$100,000	20%
Preferred stock @ 8%	50,000	10
Common stock equity	350,000	70
Total capital	$500,000	100%

The firm had earnings *before interest and after taxes* of $80,000 in the past year and has a 40-percent tax rate.

    a What was the firm's after-tax return on common equity?

    b What effect on the after-tax return on common equity would result from a $50,000 shift from long-term debt to preferred stock?

    c What effect on the after-tax return on common equity would result from a $50,000 shift from common equity to preferred equity?

    d What information concerning preferred stock leverage is illustrated by **b** and **c** above?

22-6 What accounting entries on the firm's balance sheet would result from the following cases?

    a A firm sells 10,000 shares of $1-par common stock at $13 per share.

    b A firm sells 20,000 shares of $2-par common and receives $100,000.

    c A firm sells 200,000 shares of no-par common stock for $8,000,000.

    d A firm sells 14,000 shares of common stock for the par value of $5 per share.

22-7 Max-an'-Maud's, a fast-food franchise, is electing five new directors to the board. The company has 1000 shares of common stock outstanding. The management, which controls 54-percent of the common shares outstanding, backs candidates A–E, while the minority shareholders are backing candidates F–J.

   a If the firm uses a majority voting system, how many directors will each group elect?

   b If the firm uses a cumulative voting system, how many directors will each group elect?

   c Discuss the differences between these two approaches and the resulting election outcomes.

22-8 Determine the number of directors that can be elected by the minority shareholders using (1) majority voting and (2) cumulative voting in each of the following cases.

Case	Number of shares outstanding	Percentage of shares held by minority	Number of directors to be elected
A	140,000	20%	3
B	100,000	40%	7
C	175,000	30%	4
D	880,000	40%	5
E	1,000,000	18%	9

22-9 Indicate (1) how many shares of stock one right is worth and (2) the number of shares a given stockholder, X, can purchase in each of the following situations:

Case	Number of shares outstanding	Number of new shares to be issued	Number of shares held by stockholder X
A	900,000	30,000	600
B	1,400,000	35,000	200
C	800,000	40,000	2,000
D	60,000	12,000	1,200
E	180,000	36,000	1,000

22-10 Utah Gas wishes to raise $1 million in common equity financing using a rights offering. The company has 500,000 outstanding shares of common stock, which have recently traded for $25 to $28 per share. The firm believes if the subscription price is set at $25, the shares will be fully subscribed.

   a Determine the number of new shares the firm must sell in order to raise the desired amount of capital.

   b How many shares will each right entitle a holder of one share to purchase?

   c Rework **a** and **b** assuming the subscription price is $10.

   d What is the theoretical value of a right if the current market price is $27 and the subscription price is $25? Answer for both the *rights-on* and *ex-rights* situations.

   e Rework **d** assuming the subscription price is $10.

   f Which subscription price ($10 or $25) will be more likely to assure complete subscription? Why?

22-11   Determine the theoretical value of a right when the stock is selling (1) rights on and (2) ex rights in the following cases:

Case	Market value of stock, rights on	Subscription price of stock	Number of rights needed to purchase one share of stock
A	$20.00	$17.50	4
B	$56.00	$50.00	3
C	$41.00	$30.00	6
D	$50.00	$40.00	5
E	$92.00	$82.00	8

22-12   The Flint Paper Corporation is interested in raising $600,000 of new equity capital through a rights offering. The firm currently has 300,000 shares of common stock outstanding. It expects to set the subscription price at $25 and that the stock will sell for $29 with rights on.

  a   Calculate the number of new shares the firm must sell in order to raise the desired amount of funds.

  b   How many rights will be needed to purchase one share of stock at the subscription price?

  c   Cogburn Jones holds 48,000 shares of Flint Paper common stock. If he exercises his rights, how many additional shares can he purchase?

  d   Determine the theoretical value of a right when the stock is selling (1) rights on and (2) ex rights.

  e   Approximately how much could Jones get for his rights immediately after the stock goes ex rights?

  f   If the date of record for the Flint Paper Company was Monday, March 15, on what days would the stock sell (1) rights on and (2) ex rights?

SELECTED REFERENCES

Bacon, Peter W., "The Subscription Price in Rights Offerings," *Financial Management 1* (September 1972), pp. 59–64.

Bear, Robert M., and Anthony J. Curley, "Unseasoned Equity Financing," *Journal of Financial and Quantitative Analysis 10* (June 1975), pp. 311–325.

Bildersee, John S., "Some Aspects of the Performance of Non-Convertible Preferred Stocks," *Journal of Finance 28* (December 1973), pp. 1187–1202.

Bogen, Jules I., Ed., *Financial Handbook,* 4th ed. (New York: Ronald, 1968), sec. 13.

Brown, Michael J., "Post-Offering Experience of Companies Going Public," *Journal of Business* (January 1970), pp. 10–18.

Donaldson, Gordon, "In Defense of Preferred Stock," *Harvard Business Review 40* (July-August 1962), pp. 123–136.

Duvall, Richard M., and Douglas V. Austin, "Predicting the Results of Proxy Contests," *Journal of Finance 20* (September 1965), pp. 467–471.

Elsaid, Hussein H., "The Function of Preferred Stock in the Corporate Financial Plan," *Financial Analysts Journal* (July-August 1969), pp. 112–117.

Evans, G. H., Jr., "The Theoretical Value of a Stock Right," *Journal of Finance 10* (March 1955), pp. 55–61.

Fewings, David R., "The Impact of Corporate Growth on the Risk of Common Stocks," *Journal of Finance 30* (May 1975), pp. 525–531.

Fischer, Donald E., and Glenn A. Wilt, Jr., "Nonconvertible Preferred Stock as a Financing Instrument, 1950–1965," *Journal of Finance 23* (September 1968), pp. 611–624.

Flink, S. J., *Equity Financing for Small Business* (New York: Simmons-Boardman, 1962).

Furst, Richard W., "Does Listing Increase the Market Price of Common Stocks?" *Journal of Business 43* (April 1970), pp. 174–180.

Johnson, Keith B., "Stock Splits and Price Change," *Journal of Finance 21* (December 1966), pp. 675–686.

Keane, Simon M., "The Significance of Issue Price in Rights Issues," *Journal of Business Finance 4* (September 1972), pp. 40–45.

Livingston, Miles, "Industry Movement of Common Stocks," *Journal of Finance 32* (June 1977), pp. 861–874.

Loll, Leo M., and Julian G. Buckley, *The Over-the-Counter Securities Markets: A Review Guide*, 3rd ed. (Englewood Cliffs, N.J.: Prentice-Hall, 1973), chaps. 6 and 7.

Lynch, J. E., "Accounting for Equity Securities," *Financial Management 2* (Spring 1973), pp. 41–47.

McDonald, J. G., and A. K. Fisher, "New-Issue Stock Price Behavior," *Journal of Finance 27* (March 1972), pp. 97–102.

Nelson, J. Russell, "Price Effects in Rights Offerings," *Journal of Finance 20* (December 1965), pp. 647–660.

O'Neal, F. H., "Minority Owners Can Avoid Squeeze-Outs," *Harvard Business Review 41* (March-April 1963), pp. 150–152.

Pinches, George E., "Financing with Convertible Preferred Stock, 1960–1967," *Journal of Finance 25* (March 1970), pp. 53–63.

Reilly, Frank K., "A Three Tier Stock Market in Corporate Financing," *Financial Management 4* (Autumn 1975), pp. 7–16.

Soldofsky, Robert M., "Classified Common Stock," *The Business Lawyer* (April 1968), pp. 899–902.

Soldofsky, Robert M., and Craig R. Johnson, "Rights Timing," *Financial Analysts Journal 23* (July-August 1967), pp. 101–104.

Sprecher, C. Ronald, "A Note on Financing Mergers with Convertible Preferred Stock," *Journal of Finance 26* (June 1971), pp. 683–686.

Stevenson, Richard A., "Retirement of Non-Callable Preferred Stock," *Journal of Finance 25* (December 1970), pp. 1143–1152.

Thompson, Howard E., "A Note on the Value of Rights in Estimating the Investor Capitalization Rate," *Journal of Finance 28* (March 1973), pp. 157–160.

CHAPTER 23
Convertible securities and warrants

The last two chapters presented the various methods of raising long-term funds externally. They discussed term loans, bonds, preferred stock, and common stock, emphasizing primarily the general characteristics of each of these financing sources. In this chapter, we shall focus on two optional features of security issues—conversion options and stock purchase warrants.

Both conversion features and warrants allow the firm to shift its future capital structure automatically. The conversion feature, which may be attached to either a bond or preferred stock permits the firm's capital structure to be changed without increasing the total financing. Stock purchase warrants may be attached to a long-term debt, a bond, or preferred stock. They permit the firm to raise added funds at some point in the future by selling common stock. The use of warrants shifts the firm's capital structure toward a less highly levered position since new equity capital is obtained. Both conversion features and warrants are commonly used today. Bonds that can be converted into common stock are the most common type of convertible security; warrants attached to corporate bond issues are the most common type of warrants. Both convertible securities and warrants may be listed and traded on organized security exchanges and over the counter.

The major goal of this chapter is to present the key characteristics and considerations the financial manager must be aware of when contemplating the use of convertible securities or warrants as part of a financing package. The chapter has three major sections. The first section discusses the characteristics of convertible securities, the motives for their issuance, and other managerial considerations. The second section discusses the various values that can be assigned to convertible securities. The final section is devoted to the general characteristics and values of stock purchase warrants. Examples are used throughout this chapter in order to clarify sometimes difficult concepts.

CHARACTERISTICS OF CONVERTIBLE SECURITIES

A *conversion feature* is an option included as part of either a bond or pre-ferred stock issue that permits the holder of the bond or stock to convert his or her security into a different type of security. Bonds can be convertible into preferred or common stock, but preferred stock can be convertible only into common stock. A conversion feature often adds to the marketability of an issue. This section discusses the types of convertible securities, the general features of convertibles, motives for convertible financing, and certain other considerations.

Types of convertible securities

Either corporate bonds or preferred stocks may be convertible. These securities are most commonly convertible into common stock, although in the case of bonds conversion into preferred stock occurs in rare instances.[1] The most common type of convertible security is the bond. Both convertible bonds and convertible preferred stock normally have a *call feature* accompanying the conversion feature. The call feature permits the issuer to force conversion if it so desires.

Convertible bonds. A convertible bond is almost always a debenture or an unsecured bond with a call feature. It is most commonly convertible into a predefined number of shares of common stock. Because the conversion feature provides the purchaser of a convertible bond with the possibility of becoming a stockholder on quite favorable terms, convertible bonds are generally a less expensive form of financing than nonconvertible or *straight bonds*. A conversion feature adds a degree of speculation to a bond issue, though the issue still maintains its value as a bond.

Convertible preferred stock. Occasionally a preferred stock will contain a conversion feature. Often this feature is included in order to enhance the marketability of the issue. Convertible preferred stock can normally be sold with a lower stated dividend than a similar-risk nonconvertible or *straight preferred stock*. This is because the convertible preferred holder is assured of the fixed dividend payment associated with a preferred stock and also may receive the appreciation resulting from increases in the market price of the common stock. Convertible preferred stocks are usually convertible over an unlimited time horizon; convertible bonds normally are convertible only for a specified period of years.

General features of convertibles

The general features of convertible securities include the conversion ratio, the conversion period, the conversion value, and the conversion premium. Each of these items is discussed separately below.

---

[1]It is quite uncommon for a bond to be convertible into preferred stock. The discussion throughout this chapter deals only with the near-universal case of convertible securities convertible into common stock.

The conversion ratio. The conversion ratio is the ratio in which the convertible security can be exchanged for common stock. (Bonds could be convertible into preferred stock, but for the purposes of explanation this possibility can be ignored.) The conversion ratio can be stated in two ways.

1. Sometimes the conversion ratio is stated by indicating that the security is convertible into x shares of common stock. In this situation the conversion ratio is *given*, and in order to find the *conversion price* the face value (not the market value) of the convertible security must be divided by the conversion ratio.

EXAMPLE
International Widget Company has outstanding two convertible security issues—a bond with a $1000 face value convertible into 25 shares of common stock and preferred stock with a par value of $114 convertible into 3 shares of common stock. The conversion ratios for the bond and the preferred stock are 25 and 3, respectively. The conversion price for the bond is $40 ($1000 ÷ 25), and the conversion price for the preferred stock is $38 ($114 ÷ 3). ●

2. Sometimes, instead of the conversion ratio, the conversion price is given. The conversion ratio can then be obtained by dividing the face value of the convertible by the conversion price. Often the conversion price is not constant, changing in response to the length of time the issue has been outstanding or the proportion of the issue that has been converted. A convertible security could have a conversion price of $30 for the first ten years and $35 after ten years. Or, the conversion price could be $30 for the first 30 percent of the securities converted and $35 for all subsequent conversions. These types of acceleration features are often included in a bond indenture or preferred stock covenants in order to give the issuer the power to force conversion.

EXAMPLE
The Ginsberg Company has outstanding a convertible 20-year bond with a face value of $1000. The bond is convertible at $50 per share into common stock for the next five years and at $55 for the remainder of its life. The conversion ratio for the first five years is 20 ($1000 ÷ $50), and for the remainder of the bond's life it is 18.18 ($1000 ÷ $55). ●

When a conversion ratio indicates the issuance of *fractional shares*, the issuer may: issue the fractional shares; permit the converter to purchase the balance of a fractional share in order to get a full share; or pay the converter the fractional share price upon conversion. The treatment of fractional shares on conversion must be specified in the initial bond indenture or preferred stock covenants.

The issuer of a convertible security normally establishes a conversion price or conversion ratio that makes the conversion price per share at the time of issuance of the security somewhere between 10 and 20 percent above the current market price of the firm's stock. The premium above the market price at the time of issuance must be set at a level realistic enough so that at some point during the convertible's life conversion will become feasible. In other words, the conversion price must be a price that the firm's common stock can realistically be expected to fetch in the market at some time prior to the maturity of the convertible. If prospective purchasers do not expect conversion ever to be feasible, they will purchase a straight bond or a different convertible issue. A predictable chance of conversion must be provided for in order to enhance the marketability of a convertible security.

The conversion period.   Convertible securities are often convertible only within or after a certain period of time. Sometimes conversion is not permitted until two to five years have passed. In other instances, conversion is permitted only for a limited number of years, say for five or ten years after issuance of the convertible. Other issues are convertible at any time during the life of the security. Convertible preferred stocks are generally convertible for an unlimited time. Time limitations on conversion are imposed by the issuer to suit the firm's forecast long-run financial needs.

The conversion value.   The conversion value of a convertible security is the value of the security measured in terms of the market value of the security into which it may be converted. Since most convertible securities are convertible into common stock, the conversion value can generally be found simply by multiplying the conversion ratio by the current market price of the firm's common stock.

EXAMPLE
The Krohn Electronics Company has outstanding a $1000 bond that is convertible into common stock at $62.50 a share. The conversion ratio is therefore 16 ($1000 ÷ $62.50). Since the current market price of the common stock is $65 per share, the conversion value is $1040 (16 · $65). Since the conversion value is above the bond value of $1000, conversion is a viable option for the owner of the convertible security. Of course, the security holder may anticipate a still greater conversion value and therefore maintain his or her present position if the issuer does not force conversion by using its call privilege. ●

The conversion premium.   The *conversion premium* is the percentage difference between the conversion price and the issuance price of a security. As pointed out earlier, the conversion premium is normally set initially in the 10- to 20-percent range. The actual size of the premium depends largely on the nature of the company. If the company's stock is not expected to appreciate greatly over the coming years, a low premium will be used; if considerable appreciation in the price of the stock is expected, the conversion premium may be in the 15- to 20-percent range. The conversion premium given to a convertible security can greatly affect the future success of the security.

EXAMPLE
The Oliver Book Company, a high-growth book publisher, has just issued a $1000 convertible bond. The bond is convertible into 20 shares of the firm's common stock

at a price of $50 per share. Since the firm's common stock is currently selling at $42 per share, the conversion premium is $8 per share ($50 − $42), or $160 ($8 per share · 20 shares). The conversion premium can be stated as a percentage by dividing the difference between the conversion price per share and the market price per share by the market price per share. For the Oliver Book Company, the conversion premium is approximately 19 percent ($8 ÷ $42), which would not be unusual for a high-growth company like Oliver. ●

Motives for convertible financing

There are a number of basic motives for the use of convertible financing to raise long-term funds. The motives or advantages associated with convertible security financing are generally consistent with the long-run view of the firm's financial structure discussed in Chapters 17 and 18. A basic theme is the importance of timing security issues in order to best capitalize on varying financial costs, which are dictated to some extent by activity in the capital markets. This section discusses the use of convertibles as a form of deferred common stock financing, as a sweetener for debt or preferred stock financing, and for raising temporarily cheap financing.

Deferred common stock financing.   The use of convertible securities in essence provides for future common stock financing. When a convertible security is issued, both the issuer and the purchaser expect the security to be converted into common stock at some point in the future. If the purchaser did not have this expectation, he or she would not accept the lower return normally associated with convertible issues. However, since the convertible security is sold with a conversion premium that sets the conversion price above the current market price of the firm's stock, conversion is initially not feasible.

The issuer of a convertible could sell common stock instead, but it could be marketed only at the current market price or below. By selling the convertible, the issuer in effect makes a deferred sale of common stock. As the market price of the firm's common stock rises to a higher level, conversion may occur voluntarily or be forced. By deferring the issuance of new common stock until the market price of the stock has increased, the firm is able to decrease the dilution of both earnings and control. This benefit of using convertible securities as a form of deferred common stock financing can be illustrated by a simple example.

EXAMPLE

The Green Manufacturing Company needs $1 million of new long-term financing. The firm is considering the sale of either common stock or a convertible bond. The current market price of the common stock is $20 per share. In order to sell the new issue, the stock would have to be underpriced by $1 and sold for $19 per share. This means that approximately 52,632 shares ($1 million ÷ $19 per share) would have to be sold. The alternative would be to issue 30-year 9-percent, $1,000 face-value convertible bonds. The conversion price would be set at $25 per share and the bond could be sold at par (i.e., for $1000). Thus 1000 bonds ($1 million ÷ $1000 per bond) would have to be sold. The firm currently has outstanding 200,000 shares of common stock. Most recently, the earnings available for common stock were $400,000 or $2 per share (i.e., $400,000 ÷ 200,000 shares).

If we assume that the earnings available for common stock will remain at the $400,000 level, the dilution benefit of using a convertible security to defer common stock financing can easily be illustrated. The earnings per share with both the common stock financing and a convertible bond are given below.

Financing alternative	Number of shares outstanding	Earnings per share
Common stock	252,632	$1.58
Convertible bond		
Before conversion	200,000	$2.00[b]
After conversion[a]	240,000	$1.67

[a]Assuming all bonds are converted.
[b]In order to simplify this example, the additional interest expense on the convertible bond has been ignored. If we assumed a 40-percent tax rate, the $400,000 should be reduced by the after-tax cost of debt of $54,000 [i.e., .09 · $1,000,000 · (1 − .40)], thereby resulting in earnings available for common stock of $346,000 (i.e., $400,000 − $54,000). Dividing the $346,000 of available earnings by the 200,000 shares outstanding, the correct earnings per share value of $1.73 results.

After conversion of the convertible bond, 40,000 additional shares of common stock are outstanding. ●

A convertible security is a useful tool for deferring common stock financing to when the price of the stock is higher and the dilution of earnings is reduced. In the foregoing example, the use of the convertible bond has not only resulted in a smaller dilution of earnings per share ($1.67 per share vs. $1.58 per share) but also in a smaller number of shares outstanding (240,000 vs. 252,632), thus better preserving the voting control of the owners. In actuality, the firm's earnings would be expected to increase as a result of the new financing, thereby providing some per-share earnings increase in both cases. The per-share earnings increase would be larger with the convertible bond due to the smaller number of owners.

A sweetener for financing. A second common motive for the use of convertible securities is the fact that the conversion feature often makes the bond or preferred stock issue more attractive to the purchaser. The holder of debt or preferred stock is given an opportunity to become a common stockholder and share in the potential growth of the firm. Since the purchaser of the convertible security is given the opportunity to share in the firm's future success, *convertibles can normally be sold with lower interest rates than nonconvertibles.* Therefore, from the firm's viewpoint, including a conversion feature as part of a bond or preferred stock issue reduces the effective interest cost or preferred dividend, whichever is applicable. The purchaser of the issue sacrifices a portion of his or her fixed return in order to have the opportunity to become a common stockholder in the future. The conversion feature acts as a sweetener in the sense that the security becomes a more attractive investment to prospective purchasers.

Raising temporarily cheap funds. The discussion of the cost of capital in Chapter 17 indicated that the cost of both debt and preferred stock financing is normally less than the cost of common stock. Thus by using convertible securities the firm can raise temporarily cheap funds. Funds raised in this way are technically cheaper than a straight issue of debt or preferred stock. When a firm raises funds to finance a specific project that is expected to boost future earnings, the use of low-cost financing during the start-up period can minimize the financial pressures on the firm. Once the project is on line, the firm may wish to shift its capital structure to a less highly levered position. A conversion feature gives the issuer of a security the opportunity to shift its capital structure automatically at a future point in time.

The general pattern for a growing firm is to sell convertible securities to finance its expansion, thereby minimizing its financial costs. Once expansion has been achieved and a higher level of revenues is being generated, the fixed payment obligations can be shifted to common stock equity, assuming that conversion is feasible.[2] With a larger equity base, the firm can obtain new low-cost debt funds for further expansion. Quite often a conversion feature may be the key factor that makes the sale of debt or preferred stock feasible during a period of tight money. This too must be considered as a possible advantage of the use of convertible security financing.

Other considerations

Two other considerations with respect to convertible security issues require discussion—forcing conversion and overhanging issues.

Forcing conversion. A firm issues a convertible security with the expectation that the price of its common stock will rise by enough to make conversion attractive. It hopes that once the market price of the common stock exceeds the conversion price the purchaser will convert the security into the common stock. This expectation on the part of the issuer is only logical, since one of the motives for issuing a convertible security is to provide for a change in the firm's capital structure when the firm's stock price becomes higher.

When the price of the firm's common stock rises above the conversion price, the market price of the convertible security will normally rise to a level close to its conversion value. When this happens, many convertible security holders will not convert the security. There are two major reasons a convertible security holder may not act in such a situation. The first is that it already has the market price benefit obtainable from conversion and still receives fixed periodic interest or dividend payments. The second reason for nonconversion is generally a lack of confidence in the current market price of the common stock. If the stock price has not exhibited some stability or there is no reason to believe that it will stay above the conversion price, the con-

---

[2]The option to convert is actually placed in the hands of the purchaser of the security—not the issuing firm. The *call* feature can be used by the issuer to force conversion, although as we shall see later, sometimes the economics of the situation result in an "overhanging issue." If the stock price appreciates sufficiently above the conversion price, conversion should be automatic.

vertible security holder may feel safer holding the convertible.[3] Once there is reason to believe that the common stock price will remain stable at a sufficiently high level, the holder may convert the security.

As indicated earlier, virtually all convertible securities have a call feature that enables the issuer to force their conversion. The call price of the security is generally 5 to 10 percent above the face value of the security. Quite commonly the call price exceeds the security's face value by an amount equal to one year's stated interest on the security. Since the issuer must pay a premium for calling a security, the call privilege is generally not exercised until the conversion value of the security is 10 to 15 percent above the call price. This type of premium above the call price helps to assure the issuer that when the call is made the holders of the convertible will convert it instead of accepting the call price. When the convertible holders believe the stock price to be quite volatile, the conversion value must be considerably above the call price for the call to be effective in forcing conversion.

EXAMPLE

The Felix Catfood Company currently has outstanding a 9-percent $1000 convertible bond. The bond is convertible into 50 shares of common stock at $23 per share and callable at $1090. Since the bond is convertible into 50 shares of common stock, calling it would be equivalent to paying each common stockholder $21.80 per share ($1090 ÷ 50 shares). If the firm issues the call when the stock is selling for $23 per share, a convertible security holder is likely to take the $1090 instead of converting the security even though he or she realizes only $21.80 per share instead of $23. This is because the security holder recognizes that the stock price is likely to drop as soon as the conversion occurs. Also, if the security holder wishes to sell the stock after conversion, he or she will have to pay taxes and brokerage fees on the transaction.

If the Felix Catfood Company waited until the market price exceeded the call price by 10 to 15 percent—if, say, the call was made when the market price of the stock reached $24.50—most of the convertible holders would probably convert the security. The conversion price of $24.50 per share would be approximately 12.4 percent above the call price per share of $21.80—high enough to cover any movements in the stock price or brokerage fees associated with conversion. At least 30 days advance notice is normally given prior to a call. ●

When a call privilege is exercised it is likely that a small percentage of the convertibles will be called and not converted. As indicated in an earlier discussion, the conversion price or conversion quantity often changes at certain intervals in order to decrease the conversion ratio and make conversion of the securities more likely. Prior to a scheduled decrease in the conversion ratio, the conversion of securities is likely. Since these changes are determined at the time of issuance, it is difficult to force conversion at a chosen point in time; the superiority of the call feature in this respect should be obvious. Increasing common stock dividends in order to raise the common

---

[3]Of course the holder of the convertible could convert the security and then sell the stock, but he or she would have to pay both brokerage fees and taxes on the sale. By converting and holding the stock or not converting at all, he or she delays or avoids these expenses.

stock price and thereby the conversion value is sometimes effective in forcing conversion.

Overhanging issues.   There are instances when the market price of a security does not reach a level sufficient to stimulate the conversion of associated convertibles. In some cases the market price may not exceed the conversion price; in other cases the market price may rise to within a few percentage points of the call price per share. In either of these cases, conversion is not a viable alternative for the holders of the security. A convertible security that cannot be forced into conversion is called an *overhanging issue.*

An overhanging issue can be quite detrimental to a firm. If the firm were to call the issue, not only would it have to pay the call premium, but additional financing would be required to raise the money for the call. If the firm raised these funds through the sale of equity, a great deal of dilution would result due to the low market price. The firm might actually have been better off selling equity initially instead of selling the convertible. Another source of financing would be the use of debt or preferred stock, but this would leave the firm's capital structure at least as levered or more highly levered than prior to the call. In short, an overhanging issue places the firm in a quite undesirable position with respect to new financing.

Although convertible securities are an attractive type of deferred equity financing, the issuer must have confidence in its ability to use the funds to stimulate increases in the value of its common stock in order to make conversion feasible. The issuer must recognize the possibility that the convertible securities may not be converted and new equity financing may not be automatically forthcoming. Ways of handling an overhanging convertible should be planned in advance; if not, the firm may find itself unable to obtain future long-term financing on favorable terms.

DETERMINING THE VALUE OF CONVERTIBLES

The key characteristic of convertible securities that greatly enhances their marketability is their ability to minimize the possibility of a loss while providing a possibility of capital gains. Closely related to this characteristic is the fixed pattern of interest or dividend income from convertible securities. In order to understand these characteristics, an understanding of the basic values of convertible securities is needed. This section discusses the three values of a convertible security—the bond or preferred stock value, the stock or conversion value, and the market value. Also discussed are a few special considerations.

Bond or preferred stock value

The *bond,* or *preferred stock, value* of a convertible security is the price at which it would sell in the market without the conversion feature. It is found by determining the value of a *straight* bond or preferred stock issued by a firm having the same operating and financial risk. As indicated earlier, a convertible security's value will normally be greater than that of a straight bond or preferred stock. The bond or preferred stock value is typically the *floor*, or minimum, price at which a convertible bond or preferred stock will be traded.

Calculating the straight bond value. The straight value of a convertible bond can be found by discounting the bond interest payments and maturity value at the rate of interest that would have to be charged on a straight bond issued by the company. In other words, the bond value of a convertible bond is equal to the present value of its interest and principal payments discounted at the straight bond interest rate.

EXAMPLE

The Rich Company has just sold a $1000, 20-year convertible bond with an 8-percent coupon. The bond interest will be paid at the end of each year and the principal will be repaid at maturity.[4] A straight bond could have been sold with a 10-percent coupon, but the addition of the conversion feature compensates for the lower rate on the convertible. The straight bond value of the convertible is calculated as follows:

Year(s)	Payment (1)	Present value factor @ 10% (2)	Present value (1) · (2) (3)
1-20	$ 80[a]	8.514[b]	$681.12
20	1,000	.149[c]	149.00
		Straight Bond Value	$830.12

[a]$1,000 @ 8% = $80 interest per year.
[b]Present-value interest factor for an annuity, PVIFA, for 20 years discounted at 10%, from Table A-4.
[c]Present-value interest factor, PVIF, for $1 to be received at the end of year 20 discounted at 10%, from Table A-3.

This value, $830.12, is the minimum price at which the convertible bond is expected to sell. Generally, only in certain instances where the stock price is below the conversion price will the bond be expected to sell at this level. ●

Calculating the straight preferred stock value. The minimum price at which a convertible preferred stock can be expected to sell can be found in a similar manner. Since the preferred stock is a form of ownership, its life is assumed to be infinite and therefore the present-value factor used to find its value is not readily available. The straight preferred stock value of a convertible preferred stock is assumed to equal the present value of preferred dividends over an infinite life discounted at the yield on a straight preferred stock. The present-value factor for an infinite-lived annuity is given

---

[4]As indicated earlier, bond interest is typically paid semiannually, which means that in order to calculate a bond value a process using semiannual discounting to find the present value is required. Although the techniques for finding a bond value for a bond paying semiannual interest were described in Chapter 13, the technique will not be applied here in order not to complicate the concepts being presented.

by Equation 23.1.[5]

$$d = \frac{1}{r} \tag{23.1}$$

where

   d = the present-value interest factor for an infinite-lived annuity
   r = the appropriate discount rate

An example will clarify the calculations required to find the straight value of convertible preferred stock.

EXAMPLE
The Rich Company has just issued a 9-percent convertible preferred stock with a $100 par value. If the firm had issued a nonconvertible preferred stock, the annual dividend would probably have been 11 percent. Dividends are paid annually at the end of each year. Multiplying the annual dividend of $9 (9 percent of $100) by the factor for the present value of an infinite-lived annuity discounted at 11 percent, which is 9.09 (1 ÷ .11), yields a value for the preferred stock of $81.81 ($9 · 9.09). In other words, the straight value of the preferred stock is $81.81. If the market price of common stock fell below the conversion price, the preferred stock would be expected to sell for no less than $81.81. ●

Stock or conversion value

   The *stock,* or *conversion, value* of a convertible security was defined earlier as the value of the convertible measured in terms of the market price of the common stock into which the security can be converted. When the market price of the common stock exceeds the conversion price, the stock, or conversion, value is expected to exceed the straight bond or preferred stock value of the convertible. An example will clarify the nature of the stock or conversion value.

EXAMPLE
The Rich Company convertible bond described earlier is convertible at $50 per share. This means that it can be converted into 20 shares, since it has a $1000 face value. The conversion value of the bond when the stock is selling at $40, $50, $60, $70, and $80 per share is shown below.

Market price of stock	Conversion value
$40	$ 800
$50	$1000
$60	$1200
$70	$1400
$80	$1600

---

[5]The factor for the present value of an infinite-lived annuity, or *perpetuity,* as it is called, was discussed in some detail in Chapter 13.

Since the straight value of this bond is $830.12, it will never sell for less than this amount, regardless of how low its conversion value is. If the market price per share were $40, the bond would still sell for $830.12—not $800—since its value as a bond would dominate. ●

Market value

The market value of a convertible is likely to be greater than either its straight value or its conversion value. The amount by which the market value exceeds the straight or conversion value is often designated the *market premium*. The market premium is larger the closer the straight value is to the conversion value. Even when the conversion value is below the straight value, a premium based on expected stock price movements exists. The same type of premium exists when the conversion value is above the straight value; this premium is also attributed to the convertible security purchaser's expectations. The general relationship between the straight value, the conversion value, the market value, and the market premium of the Rich Company's convertible bond, described in the preceding examples, is shown in Figure 23.1.[6] As Figure 23.1 shows, the straight bond value acts as a floor for the security's value, and when the market price of the stock exceeds a certain value the conversion value of the bond exceeds the straight bond value. Also, due to the expectations of investors about movements in the price of the firm's common stock, the market value of the convertible often exceeds both the straight and the conversion value of the security, resulting in a market premium on the security.

Special considerations

Unfortunately, the behavior of convertible security values—specifically the straight value of a convertible—is not precisely as described. The straight value of a bond or preferred stock is not necessarily fixed over a long period of time. It can be affected by a number of firm and capital market factors. If the firm runs into operating or financial difficulties, it is quite possible that its credit-worthiness will deteriorate and the risk associated with its securities will increase. Due to this increase in risk, the rate at which the payments associated with its bonds or preferred stock are discounted will rise, thereby lowering their straight value. It is also possible for the firm's credit rating to rise, so that the straight value of its convertible securities rises also.

The second factor affecting straight values is interest rate movements in the capital markets. If money becomes tighter, interest rates will rise, causing the present value of the cash flows associated with a bond or a preferred stock to decline. If money loosens up and capital market rates decline, the straight value of a convertible bond or preferred stock can be expected to increase.

Regardless of which factor causes a decline in the straight value of a convertible, the conversion value, although it may also decline, will act as a

---

[6]We have discussed the method of finding the market value, conversion value, straight value, and market premium associated with a convertible bond. The values of a convertible preferred stock would be found in a similar fashion. Bond examples are used throughout the chapter because convertible bonds are more common than convertible preferred stock.

**FIGURE 23.1 The values and market
premium for the Rich Company's convertible bond**

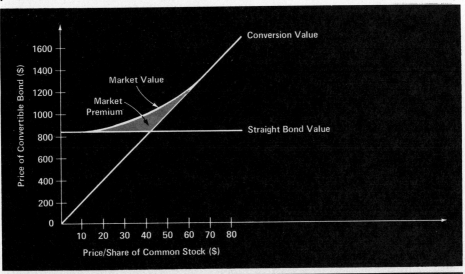

floor for the convertible security's value. The market value of the stock into
which a convertible may be converted is thus the absolute minimum value
of the convertible. Only if a firm were to go bankrupt with no liquidable
assets would the market value of its convertible securities approach zero.
However, when the firm's financial riskiness increases or the cost of money
rises, the alleged attraction of the floor price as a downside protection for
purchasers of convertibles may deteriorate significantly.

STOCK PURCHASE WARRANTS

Stock purchase warrants are quite similar to stock rights, which were described in detail in Chapter 22. A *warrant* gives the holder an option to
purchase a certain number of shares of common stock at a specified price.
Warrants also bear some similarity to convertibles, since they provide for the
injection of additional equity capital into the firm at·some future date.

Characteristics of warrants

An understanding of the basic characteristics of stock purchase warrants
should provide the reader with a feel for their usefulness. This part is devoted
to the use of warrants as sweeteners, exercise prices, the life of a warrant,
warrant trading, a comparison of warrants and convertibles, and a comparison
of warrants and rights.

Warrants as sweeteners.   Warrants are often attached to debt or
preferred stock issues as sweeteners. When a firm makes a large issue of debt
or preferred stock, the attachment of stock purchase warrants may add to the

marketability of the issue while lowering the required interest or preferred dividend rate. As sweeteners, warrants are quite similar to conversion features. When money is tight, the attachment of warrants may be the key factor enabling the firm to raise needed funds. Also, when a firm is believed to be financially risky, warrants may be the key factor enabling it to obtain debt or preferred stock financing. Often, when a new firm is being capitalized, suppliers of debt or preferred stock will require warrants in order to permit them to share in whatever success the firm achieves. Since the initial capital is generally considered risk capital, its suppliers expect an opportunity to share in the rewards that (hopefully) will result from the use of the funds they supply. Warrants are quite often used to pay for the services acquired in mergers and to compensate investment bankers for underwriting services.

Exercise prices. The price at which holders of warrants can purchase the specified number of shares is normally referred to as the *exercise price* or the *option price*. This price is normally set 10 to 20 percent above the market price of the firm's stock at the time of issuance. Until the market price of the stock exceeds the exercise price, holders of warrants would not be advised to exercise warrants, since they could purchase the stock more cheaply in the market place. Occasionally the exercise price of a warrant is not fixed, but changes at certain predefined points in time. An exercise price will rise in order to give holders of warrants an incentive to exercise them. The exercise price of a warrant is automatically adjusted for stock splits and stock dividends.

The life of a warrant. Warrants normally have a life of no more than ten years, although some warrants do have infinite lives. Although warrants cannot be called like convertible securities, their finite life acts as an impetus for their holders to exercise them if the exercise price is below the market price of the firm's stock.

Warrant trading. Warrants are usually *detachable,* which means that the recipient of a warrant may sell it without selling the security to which it is attached. Many detachable warrants are listed and actively traded on the stock exchanges and in the over-the-counter market. The majority of actively traded warrants are listed on the American Stock Exchange, although the New York Stock Exchange began listing certain warrants in 1970. Warrants quite often provide investors with better opportunities for gain than the underlying securities themselves. This characteristic of warrants will be further discussed later in the chapter.

A comparison of warrants and convertibles. The potential effects on the firm's capital structure of the exercise of warrants is best explained in light of the use of convertibles. One effect of the exercise of stock purchase warrants is a dilution of earnings and control, since a number of new shares of common stock are automatically issued. Of course, the conversion of a convertible security generally results in a greater dilution of earnings and control due to the considerably larger number of shares of common stock issued.

The exercise of a warrant shifts the firm's capital structure to a less highly levered position, since new equity capital is created without any change in the firm's debt capital. If a convertible issue were converted, the reduction in leverage would be even more pronounced, since the new common equity would be created through a corresponding reduction in either debt or preferred stock. The exercise of warrants reduces the firm's leverage, but not to the degree that the conversion of a convertible security issue does.

The key difference between the result of exercising a warrant and converting convertibles is that the warrants provide an influx of new capital. When a warrant is exercised, new common stock is issued. The firm's total capital is increased through an increase in equity funds. The conversion of a convertible security does not change the firm's total capital; it merely shifts debt or preferred stock into common stock. The influx of new equity capital resulting from the exercise of a warrant does not occur until the firm has achieved a certain degree of success that is reflected in an increased price for its stock. At that time, new equity capital is created automatically, without a public issue. This is a very simple way for the firm to obtain needed funds.

A comparison of warrants and rights. The similarity between a warrant and a right should be clear. Both result in new equity capital, although the warrant provides for deferred equity financing. The right provides for the maintenance of pro rata ownership by existing owners, while the warrant has no such feature; rather, the warrant is generally used to make other forms of financing more attractive. The life of a right is typically less than a few months, whereas a warrant is generally exercisable for a period of years. Also, rights are issued with a subscription price below the prevailing market price of the stock, while warrants are generally issued at an exercise price 10 to 20 percent above the prevailing market price.

The value of warrants

Like a convertible security, a warrant has both a theoretical and a market value. The difference between these values, or the *warrant premium*, depends largely on investor expectations and the ability of the investors to get more leverage from the warrants than the underlying stock.

The theoretical value of a warrant. The theoretical value of a stock purchase warrant is the amount one would expect the warrant to sell for in the marketplace if investors were "perfectly rational." Equation 23.2 gives the theoretical value of a warrant:

$$TV = (P - E)N \qquad (23.2)$$

where

TV = the theoretical value of a warrant
P = the market price of a share of common stock
E = the exercise price of the warrant
N = the number of shares of common stock obtainable with one warrant

The use of Equation 23.2 can be illustrated by a simple example.

EXAMPLE
The Classic Car Company has outstanding warrants that are exercisable at $40 per share and entitle the holders to purchase three shares of common stock. The warrants were initially attached to a bond issue in order to sweeten the bond. The common stock of the firm is currently selling for $47 per share. Substituting $P = \$47$, $E = \$40$, and $N = 3$ into Equation 23.2 yields a theoretical warrant value of $21 [(\$47 - \$40) \cdot 3]$. If investors are perfectly rational and have no expectations about the future price of the stock, Classic's warrants should sell for $21 in the marketplace. ●

The market value of a warrant.   The market value of a stock purchase warrant is generally above the theoretical value of the warrant. Only when the theoretical value of the warrant is very high are the market and theoretical values of a warrant quite close. The general relationship between the theoretical and market value of the Classic Car Company's warrants is presented graphically in Figure 23.2. The market value of the warrants generally exceeds the theoretical value by the greatest amount when the stock's market price is close the the warrant exercise price per share.

Warrant premium.   The *warrant premium,* or amount by which the market price of the Classic Car Company's warrants exceeds the theoretical value of these warrants, is also shown in Figure 23.2. This premium results from a combination of investor expectations and the ability of the investor to obtain much larger potential returns by trading in warrants rather than stock. If an investor has a fixed amount of money to spend, the potential returns from trading warrants are typically greater than those obtainable from trading the underlying stock. An example will clarify the effect of expectations of stock price movements on warrant market values.

EXAMPLE
John J. Investor has $2430 he is interested in investing in the Classic Car Company. Classic's stock is currently selling for $45 per share and its warrants are selling for $18 per warrant. Each warrant entitles the holder to purchase three shares of Classic's common stock at $40 per share. Since Classic's stock is selling for $45 per share, the theoretical warrant value, according to Equation 23.2, is $15 [(\$45 - \$40) \cdot 3]$.

The warrant premium is believed to result from investor expectations and leverage opportunities. John J. Investor could spend his $2430 in either of two ways. Ignoring brokerage costs, he could purchase either 54 shares of common stock at $45 per share or 135 warrants at $18 per warrant. If Mr. Investor purchases the stock, its price rises to $48, and he then sells the stock, he will gain $162 ($3 per share $\cdot$ 54 shares). If, instead of purchasing the stock, he purchases the 135 warrants and the stock price increases by $3 per share, Mr. Investor will make approximately $1215. Since the price of a share of stock rises by $3, the price of each warrant can be expected to rise by $9, since each warrant can be used to purchase three shares of common stock. A gain of $9 per warrant on 135 warrants means a total gain of $1215 on the warrants. ●

The greater leverage associated with warrants should be clear from the example above. Of course, leverage works both ways. If the market price fell by $3, the loss on the stock would be $162, while the loss on the warrants

**FIGURE 23.2 The values and warrant premium
of the Classic Car Company's stock purchase warrants**

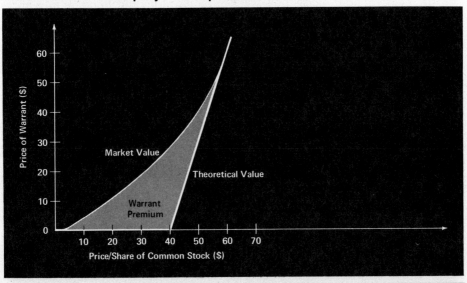

would be close to $1215. The leverage effect is not perfectly symmetrical, since the warrant premium varies depending on the price of the common stock as depicted in Figure 23.2. Other factors affecting the warrant premium are the stability of common stock prices, the nearness to the warrant's maturity or expiration date, and the dividend policies of the firm. Stock rights, which were discussed in the preceding chapter, also give their purchasers the same opportunity to achieve a more highly levered position, although their life is generally limited to a short period of time (i.e., a few months).

SUMMARY

This chapter has presented an in-depth discussion of two optional features of long-term debt or preferred stock—convertibles and warrants. Both features are attractive due to their usefulness as sweeteners and as forms of deferred equity financing. Corporate bonds or preferred stocks may be convertible into common or preferred stock, although the conversion of bonds into preferred stock is relatively uncommon. Most convertibles have a call feature. A convertible's conversion ratio indicates the number of shares it can be converted into. A conversion privilege may have a limited life, or the conversion ratio may decrease at predefined points in time. Conversion is not an attractive alternative when a security is initially issued.

The major motives for the use of convertibles are to obtain deferred common stock financing, to sweeten security issues, and(or) to raise temporarily cheap funds. When the value of a stock rises to a level at which conversion becomes attractive, the firm may use the call feature in order to force conversion. Usually conversion is not forced until the conversion value of the security is 10 to 15 percent above the call price. Sometimes the predefined decreases in the conversion ratio or changes in dividends on common stock can force conversion. Occasionally, conversion does not become attractive and the firm cannot force it. An overhanging issue is quite difficult to cope with and may place the firm in an undesirable financial position.

The value of a convertible can be measured in a number of ways. Generally the minimum value at which a convertible will trade is the value of a straight (i.e., nonconvertible) security of the same company. The conversion value of a convertible is its value measured in terms of the securities into which it may be converted. The market value of a convertible is generally above these values, especially when the straight security value and conversion value are quite close. The amount by which the market value exceeds the straight or conversion value is called the market premium. The straight value of the convertible may fluctuate in response to changes in the firm's financial risk and capital market activity.

Stock purchase warrants are generally attached to debt or preferred stock issues to enhance their attractiveness and possibly lower their cost. Sometimes warrants are used in mergers or to compensate underwriters. A warrant provides the holder with the privilege of purchasing a certain number of shares of common stock at a specified price, called the exercise price. Warrants generally have limited lives, although infinite-lived warrants do exist. They are generally detachable, and many are traded on organized security exchanges and in the over-the-counter market. Warrants are quite similar to convertibles, but they have a less pronounced effect on the firm's leverage and bring in new funds. They are also similar to stock rights, except that their exercise generally results in a dilution of ownership control and earnings. The life of a warrant is also generally longer than that of a right. The exercise price of a warrant is initially set above the underlying stock's current price, while the subscription price of a right is set below the prevailing market price of the stock.

The market value of a warrant is usually greater than its theoretical value due to market price expectations and the ability of investors to obtain considerably more leverage from trading warrants than from trading the underlying stock. The warrant premium, or amount by which the market value of a warrant exceeds its theoretical value, generally declines as the warrant approaches maturity or in response to certain internal firm factors.

QUESTIONS

23-1 What are the key similarities and differences between *convertible securities* and *stock purchase warrants?* What effect do these instruments have on the firm's capital structure?

23-2 What is a conversion ratio? How may it be stated? Is a conversion ratio always fixed over the conversion period?

23-3 What is the conversion value of a convertible security? How can the conversion value be calculated if one knows the conversion ratio and the current market value of the firm's stock?

23-4 Why is convertible security financing often viewed as a form of deferred common stock financing? Do issuers of convertibles expect them to be converted?

23-5   Why is a conversion feature often considered a type of sweetener to be used in raising debt or preferred stock capital? What sort of compensation does the issuer receive in exchange for this sweetener?

23-6   When the stock price of a convertible security rises above the conversion price, why may the security *not* be converted?

23-7   What is a call feature? Why do virtually all convertible securities have a call feature? At what level is the call price generally set, and how far above the call price must the conversion value be before the call is exercised?

23-8   What is an overhanging issue? Why is it often considered problematic? Can it be avoided? How might the payment of cash dividends help a firm with an overhanging issue?

23-9   What is meant by the bond or preferred stock value of a convertible security? How is this *straight value* calculated, and why is it often viewed as a floor for the convertible's value?

23-10   What is meant by the stock or conversion value of a convertible security? In what circumstances will a convertible sell for its stock or conversion value?

23-11   Can you graphically depict the general relationship between the straight value, conversion value, market value, and the market premium associated with a convertible security?

23-12   Why may the straight value of a convertible not be constant over a long period of time?

23-13   What are *stock purchase warrants?* How do they differ from stock rights? How are warrants issued, and how are they similar to convertibles?

23-14   What is the exercise or option price of a warrant? What relationship does this price have to the stock price at the time of issue?

23-15   What are the similarities and key differences between the effects of convertibles and warrants on the firm's ownership, its earnings per share, its capital structure, and its ability to raise new capital?

23-16   What is the general relationship between the theoretical and market value of a warrant? In what circumstances are these values quite close?

23-17   What factors other than the price of the associated common stock affect the warrant premium?

PROBLEMS

23-1   Calculate the conversion price for each of the following convertible issues.
  a   A $1000-face-value bond convertible into 20 shares of common stock.
  b   Preferred stock with a $104 par value and convertible into 13 shares of common stock.
  c   A $1000-face-value bond convertible into 50 shares of common stock.
  d   A $90-par-value preferred stock convertible into 6 shares of common stock.

23-2   What is the conversion ratio for each of the following securities?
  a   A $115-par-value preferred convertible into common at $20 per share.
  b   A $1000-face-value bond convertible into common stock at $25 per share.
  c   An $80-par-value preferred stock convertible into common stock at $5 per share.
  d   A $600 bond convertible into common stock at $30 per share.

23-3   What is the conversion value for each of the following convertible securities?
  a   A $1000 bond convertible into 25 shares of common stock. The stock is currently selling at $50 per share.
  b   A $1000 bond convertible into 12.5 shares of preferred stock. The stock is currently selling for $42 per share.

    c A $1000 bond convertible into 100 shares of common stock. The common stock is currently selling for $10.50 per share.

    d A $60 preferred convertible into 2 shares of common stock. The common stock is currently selling for $30 per share.

23-4 Market Manufacturing Company has two convertible issues outstanding. One is an $85-par-value convertible preferred, convertible into common stock at $40 per share for the next year, after which it is convertible at $42.50 per share for the next three years. After four years, the conversion feature expires. The other convertible issue is a bond with a $1000 face value. It is convertible into 20 shares of common stock in the first year, and 18 shares of common stock thereafter.

    a Calculate the conversion ratio for the preferred issue in the first year and in the following three years.

    b Calculate the conversion price for the convertible bond in the first year and thereafter.

    c Explain the rationale for increases in the conversion price (decreases in the conversion ratio) with the passage of time.

    d If the current market price of common stock is $35, which issue would you expect to be converted first? Explain your answer.

23-5 The Hoben Medical Supply Corporation has just issued a convertible bond with a face value of $1000. The bond may be converted into 12.5 shares of common stock. The stock is currently selling at $73 per share.

    a What is the per share conversion premium associated with this issue?

    b Calculate the total conversion premium for the bond.

    c State the conversion premium as a percentage of the current share price.

    d If the market price increased to $80, $85, and $100 per share of common stock, what would be the conversion value of the bond in each case?

23-6 Give the conversion value, conversion premium, and the conversion premium in percentage terms (of the current share price) for the following convertibles.

Convertible	Face value	Conversion ratio	Current market price of stock
A	$1000	25	$42.25
B	$ 800	16	$50.00
C	$1000	20	$44.00
D	$ 100	5	$19.50

23-7 The Glen Watkins Company is considering two alternatives for raising a needed $1,000,000. Option A involves a sale of common stock at $37 per share, a $3 underprice relative to the current market price of $40. The alternative, option B, would be to sell $1000-face-value convertible bonds. These carry a 10-percent interest coupon and can be sold at face value. The conversion ratio would be 22. The firm currently has 150,000 shares of common stock outstanding. The earnings available for common stockholders are expected to be $600,000 per year for each of the next several years.

    a Determine the number of shares of common stock outstanding and the earnings per share under the common stock financing alternative.

    b Determine the number of shares of common stock outstanding and the earnings per share associated with the bond prior to its conversion under the convertible bond financing alternative. (Ignore bond interest.)

    c Determine the number of shares outstanding and the earnings per share associated with the bond alternative once all bonds have been converted.

    d Discuss which of the two alternatives is preferable in terms of maximizing earnings per share.

23-8 Atlanta Ice must decide whether to obtain a needed $2,000,000 of financing by selling common stock at its currently depressed price or selling convertible bonds. The firm's common stock is currently selling for $32 per share; new shares can be sold for $30 per share, an underpricing of $2 per share. The firm currently has 100,000 shares of common stock outstanding. Convertible bonds can be sold for their $1000 par value and would be convertible at $34. The firm expects its earnings available for common stockholders to be $200,000 each year over the next several years.

    a Calculate the earnings per share of common stock resulting from

      (1) The sale of common stock.

      (2) The sale of the convertible bonds prior to conversion. (Ignore bond interest.)

      (3) The sale of convertible bonds after all bonds have been converted.

    b Which of the two financing alternatives would you recommend the company adopt? Why?

23-9 Calculate the straight value for each of the following:

Case	Face or par value	Coupon or dividend	Coupon or dividend on equal-risk straight instruments	Years to maturity (bonds)
Bond A	$1000	10%	11%	20
Preferred R	$ 80	8%	9%	—
Bond B	$ 800	8%	10%	14
Preferred S	$ 60	6%	7%	—
Bond C	$1000	11%	13%	30
Preferred T	$ 50	7%	9%	—
Bond D	$1000	10%	13%	25

23-10 The Western Clock Company has an outstanding issue of convertible bonds with a $1000 face value. These bonds are convertible into 40 shares of common stock. They have an 8-percent coupon and a 20-year maturity. The interest rate on a straight bond of similar risk would be 10 percent.

    a Calculate the conversion value of the bond when the market price of the common stock is $20, $25, $28, $35, and $50 per share.

    b Calculate the straight value of the bond.

    c For each of the stock prices given in **a**, at what price would you expect the bond to sell? Why?

    d What is the least you would expect the bond to sell for regardless of the common stock price behavior?

23-11 Mrs. Tom Fish Company has an outstanding issue of convertible preferred with a $50 par value. These preferred stocks are convertible into four shares of common stock. They have a 9-percent dividend while the coupon on straight preferred of similar risk is 10 percent.

    a Calculate the conversion value of the preferred stock when the market price is $15, $12.50, $11.00, $13.00, and $20.00 per share of common stock.

    b Calculate the straight value of this preferred stock.

    c For each of the common stock prices given in **a**, at what price would you expect the preferred stock to sell? Why?

    d Graph the conversion value and straight value of the preferred stock for each common stock price given. Plot the common stock prices on the *x*-axis and the preferred prices on the *y*-axis. Use this graph to indicate minimum market price associated with each common stock price.

23-12 Elmer's Electronics has warrants that allow the purchase of three shares of its outstanding common stock at $50 per share. The stock price per share and the warrant value associated with that stock price are summarized:

Common stock price per share	Market value of warrant
$42	$ 2
46	8
48	9
54	18
58	28
62	38
66	48

    a For each of the values given, calculate the theoretical warrant value.

    b Graph on a set of common stock price—warrant price axes the theoretical and market values of the warrant.

    c If the warrant value is $12 when the market price of common stock is $50, does this contradict or support the graph you have constructed? Explain why or why not.

    d Specify the area of warrant premium. Why does this premium exist?

    e If the expiration date of the warrants is quite close, would you expect your graph to look different? Explain.

23-13 Gayle Graham is evaluating the Ever-On Battery Company's stock and warrants in order to choose the best investment. The firm's stock is currently selling for $50 per share; its warrants to purchase three shares for $45 are selling for $20. Ignoring transactions costs, Ms. Graham has $8000 to invest. She is quite optimistic with respect to Ever-On because she has certain "inside information" about the firm's prospects with respect to a large government contract.

    a How many shares of stock and how many warrants can Ms. Graham purchase?

    b Suppose Ms. Graham purchased the stock, held it one year, then sold it for $60 per share. Ignoring broker's fees and taxes, what return would she realize? What would be her rate of return on this investment?

    c Suppose Ms. Graham purchased warrants, held them for one year, and the market price of the stock increased to $60. Ignoring brokerage fees and taxes, what return would she realize if the market value of warrants increased to $45 and she sold out?

    d What benefit, if any, would the warrants provide? Are there any differences in the risk of these two alternative investments? Explain.

23-14 Mark Christian can invest $5000 in either the common stock or the warrants of Kettering Engineering Center, Inc. The common stock is currently selling for $30 per share; its warrants, which provide for the purchase of two shares of common stock at $28 per share, are currently selling for $7. The stock is expected to rise to a market price of $32 within the next year, so the expected value of a warrant over the next year is $8. The expiration date of the warrant is one year from the present.

   a If Mr. Christian purchases the warrant, and converts to common stock in one year, what rate of return would he earn if the market price of common shares is actually $32 then? (Ignore brokerage fees and taxes.)

   b If he purchases the stock, holds it for one year and then sells it for $32, what is his rate of return? (Ignore brokerage fees and taxes.)

   c Repeat **a** and **b** assuming the market price of the stock in one year is (1) $30 and (2) $28.

   d Discuss the two alternatives and the trade-offs associated with them.

SELECTED REFERENCES

Alexander, Gordon J., and Roger D. Stover, "Pricing in the New Issue Convertible Debt Market," *Financial Management 6* (Fall 1977), pp. 35-39.

Bacon, Peter W., and Edward L. Winn, Jr., "The Impact of Forced Conversion on Stock Prices," *Journal of Finance 24* (December 1969), pp. 871-874.

Baumol, William J., Burton G. Malkiel, and Richard E. Quandt, "The Valuation of Convertible Securities," *Quarterly Journal of Economics 80* (February 1966), pp. 48-59.

Bond, F. M., "Yields on Convertible Securities: 1969-1974," *Journal of Business Finance and Accounting 3* (Summer 1976), pp. 93-114.

Brennan, M. J., and E. S. Schwartz, "Convertible Bonds: Valuation and Optimal Strategies for Call and Conversion," *Journal of Finance 32* (December 1977), pp. 1699-1715.

Brigham, Eugene F., "An Analysis of Convertible Debentures: Theory and Some Empirical Evidence," *Journal of Finance 21* (March 1966), pp. 35-54.

Chen, Andrew H. Y., "A Model of Warrant Pricing in a Dynamic Market," *Journal of Finance 25* (December 1970), pp. 1041-1059.

Frank, Werner G., and Charles O. Kroncke, "Classifying Conversions of Convertible Debentures Over Four Years," *Financial Management 3* (Summer 1974), pp. 33-42.

Frank, Werner G., and Jerry J. Weygandt, "Convertible Debt and Earnings per Share: Pragmatism vs. Good Theory," *Accounting Review 45* (April 1970), pp. 280-289.

Frankle, A. W., and C. A. Hawkins, "Beta Coefficients for Convertible Bonds," *Journal of Finance 30* (March 1975), pp. 207-210.

Hayes, Samuel L., III, and Henry B. Reiling, "Sophisticated Financing Tool: The Warrant," *Harvard Business Review 47* (January-February 1969), pp. 137-150.

Horrigan, James O., "Some Hypotheses on the Valuation of Stock Warrants," *Journal of Business Finance and Accounting 1* (Summer 1974), pp. 239-247.

Ingersoll, Jonathan, "An Examination of Corporate Call Prices on Convertible Securities," *Journal of Finance 32* (May 1977), pp. 463-478.

Jennings, Edward H., "An Estimate of Convertible Bond Premiums," *Journal of Financial and Quantitative Analysis 9* (January 1974), pp. 33-56.

Leabo, Dick A., and Richard L. Rogalski, "Warrant Price Movements and the Efficient Market Model," *Journal of Finance 30* (March 1975), pp. 163-178.

Lewellen, Wilbur G., and George A. Racette, "Convertible Debt Financing," *Journal of Financial and Quantitative Analysis 7* (December 1973), pp. 777-792.

Mehta, Dileep R., "The Impact of Outstanding Convertible Bonds on Dividend Policy," *Journal of Finance 31* (May 1976).

Meyer, Anthony H., "Designing a Convertible Preferred Issue," *Financial Executive 36* (April 1968), pp. 48 ff.

Miller, Alexander B., "How to Call Your Convertible," *Harvard Business Review 49* (May-June 1971), pp. 66-70.

Pinches, George E., "Financing with Convertible Preferred Stocks, 1960-1967," *Journal of Finance 25* (March 1970), pp. 53-64.

Rush, David F., and Ronald W. Melicher, "An Empirical Examination of Factors Which Influence Warrant Prices," *Journal of Finance 29* (December 1974), pp. 1449-1466.

Samuelson, P. A., and R. C. Merton, "A Complete Model of Warrant Pricing That Maximizes Utility," *Industrial Management Review 10* (Winter 1969), pp. 17-46.

Schwartz, Eduardo S., "The Valuation of Warrants: Implementing a New Approach," *Journal of Financial Economics 4* (January 1977), pp. 79-94.

Shelton, John P., "The Relation of the Price of a Warrant to the Price of Its Associated Stock," *Financial Analysts Journal 23* (May-June and July-August 1967), pp. 143-151 and 88-89.

Soldofsky, Robert M., "Yield-Rate Performance of Convertible Securities," *Financial Analysts Journal 27* (March-April 1971), pp. 61-65.

Stevenson, Richard A., and Joe Lavely, "Why a Bond Warrant Issue?" *Financial Executive 38* (June 1970), pp. 16-21.

Stone, Bernell K., "Warrant Financing," *Journal of Financial and Quantitative Analysis 11* (March 1976), pp. 143-154.

Van Horne, James C., "Warrant Valuation in Relation to Volatility and Opportunity Costs," *Industrial Management Review 10* (Spring 1969), pp. 19-32.

Walter, James E., and Augustin V. Que, "The Valuation of Convertible Bonds," *Journal of Finance 28* (June 1973), pp. 713-732.

Weil, Roman L., Jr., Joel E. Segall, and David Green, Jr., "Premiums on Convertible Bonds," *Journal of Finance 23* (June 1968), pp. 445-463.

CHAPTER 24
Dividends and retained earnings

Retained earnings are the primary internally generated source of long-term funds for the business firm. Like financial leases, long-term loans, bonds, preferred stock, and common stock, they provide capital to the firm. And like capital from other sources, funds from retained earnings are not "free." Since the alternative to the retention of earnings is the payment of them to the firm's owners in the form of cash dividends, there is a reciprocal relationship between retained earnings and cash dividends.

Once a firm has satisfied its obligations to its creditors, the government, and its preferred stockholders (if any), any remaining earnings can be retained, paid out as cash dividends, or split between retained earnings and cash dividends. Retained earnings can be invested in assets that will help the firm to expand or to maintain its present rate of growth. If earnings were not retained, additional funds would have to be raised through one of the other sources of long-term financing. The owners of the firm generally desire some payment or current return on their equity investment, and the payment of a cash dividend, which reduces the amount of earnings retained, generally fulfills this requirement. A difficult and quite critical decision affecting the firm's overall objective of owners' wealth maximization revolves around the firm's retained earnings-dividend decision.

This chapter is devoted to both retained earnings and dividends. The primary emphasis is on the dividend decision since, in actuality, it is made in order to produce a desired level of retained earnings while satisfying the current requirements of the firm's shareholders. The chapter has four major sections. The first section delves into certain procedural and theoretical considerations with respect to retained earnings and cash dividends. The second section presents the key factors affecting the firm's cash dividend policy. Certain of these factors act as constraints on the corporate dividend decision. The third section discusses the objectives and types of dividend policies commonly in use. The final section of the chapter discusses two noncash methods of paying dividends—declaring stock dividends (and the related topic of stock splits) or making stock repurchases.

PROCEDURAL AND THEORETICAL CONSIDERATIONS

In order to understand the mechanics and importance of the dividend decision, the reader must understand how retained earnings act as a source of long-term funds for the business firm, the procedures for paying cash dividends, and, most important, certain theoretical viewpoints on the importance of dividend payments. This section discusses retained earnings as a source of financing, cash dividend payment procedures, and the key theoretical viewpoints on the relevance of dividend policies.

Retained earnings as a source of financing

Retained earnings are viewed as a source of financing since paying out earnings as cash dividends to common stockholders results in the reduction of the asset cash. In order to increase the firm's assets back to the level that would have prevailed had dividends not been paid, the firm must obtain additional debt or equity financing. By forgoing dividend payments and retaining earnings, the firm can avoid having to raise a given amount of funds or can eliminate certain existing sources of financing. In either case, the retention of earnings is a source of funds to the firm. A simple example will clarify this point.

EXAMPLE

The Miller Flour Company's financial statements, presented in Table 24.1, have been constructed on the assumption that the company has paid out all its earnings as dividends. Miller had $40,000 of earnings available after paying all claims other than those of common stockholders, and it decided to distribute the entire $40,000 as cash dividends to these owners, reinvesting none of these earnings in the firm. Had Miller gone to the other extreme and retained all $40,000 of its earnings available for common, the bottom portion of its income statement would be as follows:

TABLE 24.1 The Miller Flour Company's financial statements when all earnings are paid out as dividends

Balance sheet			
Assets		**Liabilities and stockholders' equity**	
Cash	$ 20,000	Accounts payable	$ 30,000
Marketable securities	30,000	Notes payable	150,000
Accounts receivable	100,000	Accruals	20,000
Inventory	200,000	Total current liabilities	$ 200,000
Prepaid items	10,000	Long-term debt	$ 300,000
Total current assets	$ 360,000	Common stock at par	$ 100,000
Fixed assets (net)	640,000	Paid-in capital in excess of par	200,000
Total Assets	$1,000,000	Preferred stock @ 8%	100,000
		Retained earnings	100,000
		Total stockholders' equity	$ 500,000
		Total Liabilities and Stockholders' Equity	$1,000,000

TABLE 24.1 (continued)

Income statement

Sales	$1,500,000
Less cost of goods sold	1,000,000
Gross profits	$ 500,000
Less: Expenses	420,000
Profits before taxes	$ 80,000
Less: Taxes (.40)	32,000
Profits after taxes	$ 48,000
Less: Preferred stock dividends	8,000
Earnings available for common	$ 40,000
Less: Common stock dividends	40,000
To Retained Earnings	$ 0

Earnings available for common	$40,000
Less: Common stock dividends	0
To Retained Earnings	$40,000

Table 24.2 presents the firm's balance sheet when it retains the $40,000 in earnings. Comparing the balance sheet in Table 24.2 to that in Table 24.1 shows that Miller has available an added $40,000 of financing as a result of retaining (instead of paying out in common stock dividends) the $40,000 of earnings available to be paid out to the common stockholders.[1]

TABLE 24.2 The Miller Flour Company's balance sheet when all earnings are retained

Assets		Liabilities and stockholders' equity	
Cash	$ 60,000	Accounts payable	$ 30,000
Marketable securities	30,000	Notes payable	150,000
Accounts receivable	100,000	Accruals	20,000
Inventory	200,000	Total current liabilities	$ 200,000
Prepaid items	10,000	Long-term debt	$ 300,000
Total current assets	$ 400,000	Common stock at par	$ 100,000
Fixed assets (net)	640,000	Paid-in capital in excess of par	200,000
Total Assets	$1,040,000	Preferred stock @ 8%	100,000
		Retained earnings	140,000
		Total stockholders' equity	$ 540,000
		Total Liabilities and Stockholders Equity	$1,040,000

[1]Firms can pay out in cash dividends more than the current period's earnings. The two items that may act as constraints are the amount of cash available and the total amount of retained earnings. The maximum amount of cash dividends a firm can pay in a given period is discussed later in the chapter.

Regardless of how Miller disposes of the $40,000 in financing provided by the current period's operation, the firm, by retaining earnings, has raised $40,000 in long-term funds. Had it paid out these earnings as dividends, it would have to borrow or sell common or preferred stock to attain the asset and financial structure shown in the balance sheet in Table 24.2. Retained earnings are actually funds obtained from the common stockholders. Since another way to obtain funds from this source is to sell new shares of common stock, retained earnings are often viewed as a fully subscribed new issue of common stock. The implications of this fact for the firm's cost of capital were discussed in Chapter 17. ●

The example above should make it clear to the reader that *the dividend decision is actually a financing decision* since paying a dividend directly affects the firm's financing. The discussion in the remainder of the chapter is devoted primarily to the dividend decision, but the reader must also bear in mind the financial consequences of the payment of cash dividends.

Cash dividend payment procedures

The payment of cash dividends to corporate stockholders is decided upon by the board of directors. The directors normally hold a quarterly or semiannual dividend meeting at which they evaluate the past period's financial performance in order to determine whether and in what amount dividends should be paid. The payment date of the cash dividend (if one is declared) must also be established.

The amount of dividends. Whether dividends should be paid and, if they are, how large they should be are important decisions that depend largely on the firm's dividend policy. Dividend policy will be investigated in much greater detail in a later section. It is safe to say that most firms pay some cash dividends each period. The amount is generally fixed, although significant increases or decreases in earnings may justify changing it. Although most firms have a set policy with respect to the amount of the periodic dividend, the firm's directors can change the amount at their periodic dividend meeting.

Relevant dates. If the firm's directors declare a dividend, they will also indicate the record and payment dates associated with the dividend. Typically, the directors issue a statement indicating their dividend decision, the record date, and the payment date. This statement is generally quoted in *The Wall Street Journal, Barrons*, and other financial news media.

The record date. All persons whose names appear as stockholders in the firm's stock ledger on the *date of record,* which is set by the directors, will receive a declared dividend.[2] These stockholders are often referred to

---

[2]The *stock ledger* is the official book in which the records of the current owners of the firm's outstanding shares are kept. All state corporation laws require firms to maintain a stock ledger. *Transfer agents,* which are generally large commercial banks, maintain the stock ledgers for large corporations. Of course, they are paid by the firms for their services.

as *holders of record*. Because of the time needed to make bookkeeping entries when a stock is traded, the stock will sell *ex dividend* for four business days prior to the date of record. The NYSE and other stock exchanges allow four business days for recording changes of ownership. When a stock sells ex dividend, purchasers do not receive the dividends. When a stock is selling prior to the ex dividend date, it is said to be selling with *dividends on* or *cum dividends*.

The payment date. The payment date is also set by the directors. It is generally set a few weeks after the record date. The payment date is the actual date on which the company will mail the dividend payment to the holders of record. An example will clarify the various dates and accounting entries associated with the payment of cash dividends.

EXAMPLE

At the quarterly dividend meeting of the Wiseley Gun Company, held June 10, the directors declared an $0.80 per share cash dividend for holders of record on Monday, July 1. The firm has 100,000 shares of common stock outstanding. The payment date for the dividend is August 1. Before the dividend was declared, the key accounts of the firm were as follows.

Cash	$200,000	Dividends payable	$ 0
		Retained earnings	1,000,000

When the dividend was announced by the directors, $80,000 (i.e., $.80 per share · 100,000 shares) of the retained earnings was transferred to the dividends payable account. The key accounts thus became

Cash	$200,000	Dividends payable	$ 80,000
		Retained earnings	920,000

The Wiseley Company stock sold ex dividend for four business days prior to the date of record, which is June 25. Purchasers of Wiseley's stock on June 24 or earlier received the rights to the dividends, and those purchasing the stock on or after June 25 did not.[3] When the August 1 payment date arrived, the firm mailed dividend checks to the holders of record as of July 1. This produced the following balances in the key accounts of the firm:

Cash	$120,000	Dividends payable	$ 0
		Retained earnings	920,000

Thus the net effect of declaration and payment of the dividend was to reduce the firm's total assets (and stockholders' equity) by $80,000. ●

---

[3]A simple way to determine the first day on which the stock sells ex dividend is to subtract four from the date of record; if a weekend intervenes, subtract two additional days. One business day prior to the first ex dividend day is the last day the stock will sell with dividends on. This, of course, will be five business days prior to the date of record. The relationship between the record date and ex dividend date is the same for stock dividends. In the case of rights offerings, the ex rights date is similar to the ex dividend date.

Theoretical viewpoints

The two key theoretical views concerning the importance of dividend policy differ with respect to the relevance of dividends. One point of view is that dividends are irrelevant and the amount of dividends paid does not affect the value of the firm. The other is that dividends are relevant and that the amount of dividends paid does affect the value of the firm as measured in the marketplace.

The irrelevance of dividends.   The major argument indicating that dividends are irrelevant was first propounded by Franco Modigliani and Merton Miller in 1961. Modigliani and Miller (M and M) built their argument on a number of assumptions, the most critical of which were

1. No flotation or brokerage costs.[4]
2. No taxes
3. No uncertainty.

Using these three key assumptions, M and M argued that the value of the firm was not determined by the amount of dividends paid, but rather by the earning power of the projects in which the firm invested its money. They claimed that how the firm split its earnings between dividends and reinvestment had no direct effect on its value since in a world without taxes there was no difference between dividends and capital gains. The argument used by M and M to support this key assumption is referred to as the *clientele effect*. The clientele effect states that a firm will attract stockholders whose preferences with respect to the payment pattern and stability of dividends corresponds to the firm's payment pattern and stability of dividends. Since the shareholders, or the clientele, of the firm get what they expect, the value of the firm's stock is unaffected by changes in its dividend policy.

The key to M and M's theory is the belief that since the retention of earnings is a form of equity financing, the sale of common stock is an alternate source of equity financing. They argue that the negative effect of the dilution of earnings and ownership resulting from the sale of common stock on the stock's value is just offset by the positive effect of the dividends paid.[5] Since M and M assume that there are no flotation or brokerage costs, the cost of raising common equity through the retention of earnings or the sale of new stock is in effect assumed to be the same. Their conclusion is that, given

---

[4]It should be recalled from Chapter 17 that flotation costs are borne by the issuer of a security. This cost consists of two components: (1) underpricing costs, which reflect the fact that in a competitive market the price of stock must be reduced in order to sell additional shares, and (2) underwriting costs, which include administrative and sales fees. This assumption also implies that prospective and existing shareholders do not have to pay any brokerage fees on purchase and sale transactions.

[5]Since retained earnings are not used to raise common stock equity, then new shares of common stock must be sold. The sale of new shares of common stock may decrease the proprotionate ownership and earnings claim of existing shareholders. M and M argue that since this dilution is the cost associated with paying higher cash dividends (i.e., retaining less earnings) the impact of the increased dividend payment just compensates existing shareholders for any dilution they might experience. The stock price is therefore unaffected by the dividend decision.

certain "restrictive" assumptions, dividend policy is irrelevant since it has no effect on the market value of the firm.

However, recognizing that dividends do somehow affect stock prices, M and M suggest that the positive effects of dividend increases on stock prices are attributable not to the dividend itself, but rather to the *informational content* of dividends with respect to future earnings. The information provided by the dividends causes owners to bid up the price of the stock based on their expectations of future earnings. M and M's arguments lead one to believe that when acceptable investment opportunities are not available the firm should distribute the unneeded funds to the owners, who can invest the money in other firms having acceptable investment alternatives. This residual theory of dividends is consistent with M and M's dividend irrelevance theory.[6] It suggests that since, given certain assumptions, dividends are irrelevant to the firm's value, the firm does not need to have a "dividend policy."

The relevance of dividends.   Another school of thought suggests that without M and M's restrictive assumptions, their argument collapses. They assert that since, in actuality, investors operate in a world of flotation costs, brokerage costs, taxes, and uncertainty, it is better to view the firm in light of these factors. If one removes the assumption of no uncertainty, it can be seen that most investors prefer some current payment in the form of cash dividends to an eventual return in the form of a capital gain. It is the uncertainty associated with the future financial outcomes of the firm that prompts owners to prefer some current payment as compensation for their invested capital. Because current dividend payments reduce investor uncertainty, the investors discount the firm's earnings at a lower rate, thereby placing a higher value on the firm's stock. If dividends are not paid, investor uncertainty will increase, raising the rate at which the firm's earnings are discounted and lowering the value of its stock.

The preceding argument with respect to the reduction of uncertainty is closely allied to M and M's argument that the value of the firm's shares may increase only because of the informational content of dividends. However, M and M do not concede that the increased stock price results from an increase in the value placed on earnings due to a reduction in the uncertainty of returns. Rather, they suggest that the increased value placed on the earnings is based only on the expectation that they will be higher in the future. The real difficulty in disproving M and M's theory of the irrelevance of dividends is in countering M and M's use of the clientele effect argument to suggest that the firm's shareholders are indifferent to whether they receive dividends or capital gains.

Removing M and M's assumption of no taxes makes it obvious that stockholders will not be indifferent as to whether they receive dividends or capital

---

[6]In the case of small firms, the treatment of dividends as a residual remaining after all acceptable investments have been initiated is quite common. This occurs since small firms do not normally have comparatively ready access to capital markets. The use of retained earnings therefore acts as a key source of financing for the firm's growth, which is generally an important goal of a small firm.

gains since the tax rates on capital gains are lower. However, this does not necessarily disprove the clientele effect. Both the effect of taxes favoring capital gains and the uncertainty of returns must be considered by the firm establishing a dividend policy. Although the reduction of uncertainty suggests the need for dividend payments and the presence of taxes indicates an advantage of retaining earnings, both these factors suggest that the cash dividend decision is an important one and that dividends are relevant.

M and M use the assumptions of no flotation or brokerage costs and no taxes to argue that if the internal investment opportunities of the firm are greater than the firm's cost of equity funds it should retain all its earnings, since, if the earnings were paid out as dividends, the recipients would use the dividends to purchase added shares of the firm's stock. Since the firm would not have to pay any flotation costs and the stockholders would have to pay neither brokerage costs nor taxes, their proportion of the firm's equity would be no different than if the firm had retained the earnings. This argument, like the other arguments presented by M and M, is valid given their highly restrictive and unrealistic assumptions.

The dividend relevance school's leading proponent, Myron J. Gordon, suggests that stockholders do have a preference for current dividends—that, in fact, there is a direct relationship between the dividend policy of a firm and its market value. Gordon argues that investors are generally risk averters and attach less risk to current as opposed to future dividends or capital gains. This "bird-in-the-hand" argument suggests that a firm's dividend policy is relevant since investors prefer some dividends now in order to reduce their uncertainty. When investors are less uncertain about their returns, they discount the firm's future earnings at a lower rate—therefore placing a higher value on the firm. Gordon's arguments with respect to dividend relevance are much more acceptable than M and M's arguments. Since our concern in this text is with the real-world behavior of business firms, the remainder of this chapter incorporates the general belief that dividends *are relevant*—that each firm must develop a dividend policy that fulfills the goals of its owners and maximizes their wealth in the long run.

FACTORS AFFECTING DIVIDEND POLICY

It is important for the firm to establish a general policy with respect to the payment of cash dividends. Before discussing the common types of dividend policies, we should consider the factors involved in formulating dividend policy. These factors include certain legal, contractual, and internal constraints, the firm's growth prospects, owner considerations, and market considerations.

Legal, contractual, and internal constraints

The firm's dividend policy is often constrained by certain legal, contractual, and internal factors. The legal factors result from certain state and federal laws, the contractual constraints typically result from certain loan covenants, and the internal constraints are the result of the firm's liquid-asset position.

Legal constraints. There are four basic legal constraints confronting the corporation with respect to cash dividend payments. They concern capital impairment, net profits, insolvency, and the accumulation of excess profits.

Capital impairment. Most states prohibit corporations from paying out as cash dividends any portion of the firm's capital stock as measured by the par value of common stock. Other states define capital to include not only the par value of the common stock, but also any capital paid-in in excess of par. Capital impairment restrictions are generally established in order to provide a sufficient equity base to protect creditors' claims on the firm's assets. An example will clarify the different definitions of capital.

EXAMPLE
The Miller Flour Company balance sheet presented in Table 24.2 indicated that the firm has common stock with a par value of $100,000, paid-in capital in excess of par of $200,000, and retained earnings of $140,000. In states where the firm's capital is defined as the par value of its common stock, the firm could pay out $340,000 ($200,000 + $140,000) in cash dividends without impairing its capital. In states where the firm's capital includes all paid-in capital, the firm could pay out only $140,000 in cash dividends. ●

Net profits. The net profits requirement is similar to the capital impairment requirement in that it limits the amount of dividends to the sum of the firm's present and past earnings. In other words, the firm cannot pay more in cash dividends than the sum of its most recent and past retained earnings. This requirement has the same effect as the capital impairment rule where capital is defined as all paid-in capital. The reader should recognize, however, that *the firm is not prohibited from paying more in dividends than its current earnings.*[7]

EXAMPLE
The Miller Flour Company's income statement, presented in Table 24.1, indicates that the firm currently has $40,000 in earnings available for common stock dividends. An analysis of the balance sheet in Table 24.1 indicates that the firm has past retained earnings of $100,000. Thus it could pay dividends of up to $140,000. ●

Insolvency. If a firm has overdue liabilities or is legally insolvent or bankrupt (i.e., if the fair value of its assets is less than its liabilities), most states prohibit the payment of cash dividends. This restriction is intended to protect the firm's creditors by prohibiting the liquidation of a near-bankrupt firm through the payment of cash dividends to owners. The payment of cash dividends by an insolvent firm could seriously impair its creditors claims in bankruptcy.

The accumulation of excess profits. The Internal Revenue Service prohibits firms from accumulating excess profits. A firm's owners must pay in-

---

[7]A firm having an operating loss in the current period could still pay cash dividends as long as sufficient retained earnings were available and, of course, as long as it had the cash with which to make the payments.

come taxes on dividends when received, but the owners are not taxed on capital gains in market value until the stock is sold. A firm may retain a large portion of earnings in order to provide capital gain opportunities to the owners. If the IRS can determine that a firm has accumulated an excess of earnings in order to avoid ordinary income taxes, it may levy an *excess profits tax* on the firm's retained earnings. A firm that has paid low or no cash dividends, has high retained earnings, and has a great deal of cash and marketable securities is a likely candidate for an IRS investigation. The federal government takes a dim view of a firm retaining earnings so that its owners can avoid ordinary income taxes. This is an impetus for firms to pay dividends if attractive internal investment opportunities do not exist.

Contractual constraints.   Often the firm's ability to pay cash dividends is constrained by certain restrictive covenants in a lease contract, term loan agreement, a bond indenture, or a preferred stock agreement. Generally these constraints either prohibit the payment of cash dividends until a certain level of earnings has been achieved or limit the amount of dividends paid to a certain amount or percentage of earnings. Since cash is required to pay dividends, constraints on dividend payments help to protect lessors, creditors, and preferred stockholders from losses due to insolvency on part of the firm. Contractual constaints on dividend payments are quite common, and their violation is generally grounds for a request for immediate repayment by the funds supplier affected.

Internal constraints.   The firm's ability to pay cash dividends is generally constrained by the amount of excess cash available. Of course it is possible for a firm to borrow funds to pay dividends; but, if borrowing were necessary, the minimum dividend would most likely be paid. Lenders are not especially interested in lending money for dividend payments, since they produce no tangible or operating benefits that will help the firm repay the loan. It is important to keep in mind that, although a firm may have high earnings, its ability to pay dividends may be constrained by a low level of liquid assets (cash and marketable securities).

EXAMPLE
The Miller Flour Company's financial statements, presented in Table 24.1, indicate that if the firm's capital is defined as all paid-in capital, the firm can pay $140,000 in dividends (since it has $100,000 in past retained earnings plus $40,000 in current earnings available for common stock). The firm has total liquid assets of $50,000 ($20,000 in cash plus marketable securities worth $30,000), but $35,000 of this is needed for operations. Therefore the maximum dividend the firm can pay is $15,000. It is important to recognize internal liquidity constraints when making the cash dividend decision. ●

Growth prospects
The growth prospects of the firm must be evaluated in establishing a dividend policy. The firm must plan its needed financing in light of its forecast growth prospects. The availability of outside financing and the exact

timing of funds needs will greatly affect the need for retained earnings to finance growth. Two factors related to growth—financial requirements and the availability of funds—are discussed separately below.

Financial requirements. The firm's financial requirements are directly related to the degree of asset expansion anticipated. If the firm is in a growth stage, it may need all the funds it can get to finance capital expenditures. A growing firm also requires funds to maintain and improve its assets. High-growth firms typically find themselves constantly in need of funds. Their financial requirements may be characterized as large and immediate. Other firms exhibiting little or no growth may not have a constant need for new funds, but they may need funds to replace or modernize assets. In many instances these outlays may not be required immediately, but rather two or three years in the future. These types of mature firms' funds requirements can be considered periodic, since they are only for specific projects. The nature of the firm's funds need has a large effect on the disposition of its earnings.

The availability of funds. A firm must evaluate its financial position from both a profitability and a risk standpoint in order to develop insight into its ability to raise capital externally. It must determine not only its ability to raise funds, but also the cost and quickness with which financing can be obtained. Generally the large mature firm has greater access to new capital than the firm in a state of rapid growth. For this reason, the funds available to the rapidly growing firm may not be sufficient to support the numerous acceptable projects. A growth firm is likely to have to depend heavily on internal financing through retained earnings in order to take advantage of the profitable projects available to it. It is therefore quite likely to pay out only a very small percentage of its earnings as dividends. However, not all growth firms are small, struggling enterprises; IBM is considered a growth firm with a low dividend payout.

The more stable firm that needs capital funds only for planned outlays is better advised to pay out a large proportion of its earnings, especially if it has ready sources of financing, instead of retaining these earnings and investing them in marketable securities until the planned outlay must be made. The firm's owners, it is assumed, can earn a greater return on other investments. When funds are needed, the firm should obtain them externally. Only when the firm's external sources of funds are limited should it retain earnings for a planned future outlay. If funds are needed currently, the retention of earnings may also be justifiable. The important point for the financial manager to keep in mind, regardless of whether the firm is a growing or a mature firm, is that his or her actions with respect to the retention or payout of earnings should be aimed at maximizing the owners' wealth.

Owner considerations

As noted, in establishing a dividend policy, the primary concern should be how to maximize the firm's owners' wealth over the long run. Although it is impossible to establish a policy that will maximize each owner's wealth, the firm must establish a policy that has a favorable effect on the wealth of the majority of the owners. Three factors that must be considered are the tax status of the owners, their other investment opportunities, and the dilution of ownership.

The tax status of the firm's owners. The tax status of a firm's owners can have a significant effect on the firm's dividend policy. If a firm has a large percentage of wealthy stockholders who are in a high tax bracket, it may pay out a lower percentage of its earnings in order to provide its owners with income in the form of capital gains as opposed to dividends.[8] Since the capital gains tax rate is considerably less than the ordinary tax rate, these wealthy owners would find their tax liability reduced. On the other hand, a firm may have mostly lower-income shareholders who need dividend income and are in a low tax bracket. These owners will prefer a higher payout of earnings since their tax status is not a source of concern.

It is quite difficult for the financial manager of a large, diversely held firm to know the tax status of the owners; he or she can base assessments only on feedback from directors and data obtained in the marketplace. If the directors believe a low dividend payout is preferable, any owners disagreeing with this strategy can divest themselves of their holdings and purchase the stock of a firm paying out a high percentage of earnings. Although, as we indicated in the previous section, the tax status of owners may not be the primary factor in the dividend decision, it should be given some attention.

Owner investment opportunities. A firm should not retain funds for investment in projects yielding lower returns than the owners could obtain from external investments. The firm should evaluate the returns expected on its investment opportunities and determine whether greater returns are obtainable from external investments such as government securities or other corporate stocks. If it appears the owners have better opportunities externally, the firm should pay out a high percentage of its earnings. If the firm's investment opportunities are at least as good as similar-risk external investments, a low payout of earnings is justifiable. A firm should not retain funds in the form of marketable securities in order to make some future outlay; rather, it should pay out these earnings now and raise the needed funds later when the outlay must be made. The external investment opportunities of owners must be appraised and considered when dividend policy decisions are formulated; otherwise, the goal of maximization of owners' wealth may not be achieved.

The dilution of ownership. Since the most comparable alternative to the use of retained earnings as a source of equity financing is the sale of

---

[8]The consideration of the owners' tax status in making dividend policy decisions is illegal, although it is quite difficult for the IRS to police this law. Rather, the IRS will look for high retained earnings and high liquidity. Firms in this situation are penalized through an excess profits tax. It is quite difficult, if not impossible, to determine the extent to which the tax status of a firm's owners affects dividend policy decisions.

new common stock, consideration must be given to the dilution of ownership interests that may result from a high-payout dividend policy. If a firm pays out a high percentage of earnings, new equity capital will have to be raised with common stock, which may result in the dilution of both control and earnings for the existing owners. By paying out a low percentage of its earnings (i.e., retaining a high percentage of its earnings), the firm can minimize the possibility of dilution of control. High percentage payouts increase the likelihood that the firm will experience dilution in the future.

It is most important that the stockholders recognize the firm's motives for retaining or paying out a large percentage of earnings. Although the ultimate dividend policy depends on numerous factors, the avoidance of shareholder discontent is important. If the shareholders become dissatisfied with the existing dividend policy, they may sell their shares, increasing the possibility that control of the firm will be seized by some outside group. The "takeover" of a firm by outsiders is more likely when owners are dissatisfied with its dividend policy. It is the financial manager's responsibility to keep in touch with the owners' general attitude toward dividends.

Market considerations

In establishing dividend policy, it is important to consider certain behavioral aspects of the securities market. Since the wealth of the firm's owners is reflected in the market price of the firm's shares, an awareness of the market's probable response to certain types of dividend policies is helpful in formulating a suitable dividend policy. The probable market response to fixed-dollar or increasing dividends, continuous dividend payments, and the informational content of dividends are discussed in this section.

Fixed-dollar or increasing dividends. Stockholders are believed to value a fixed or increasing level of dividends as opposed to a fixed payout ratio. If the *payout ratio,* which is found by dividing the dividends per share by the earnings per share, is held constant, the shareholders may receive no dividends in lean periods and high dividends when earnings are high. Since paying a fixed or increasing dividend eliminates uncertainty about the magnitude of dividends, the earnings of the firm are likely to be discounted at a lower rate and the value of the firm's stock is likely to remain at a reasonably high level. In short, stable or gradually increasing dividends are considered preferable to the variable dividends that may result from a fixed payout ratio. The policy implications of this are discussed further in the section on dividend policy.

Continuous dividend payments. The marketplace generally not only values a fixed or increasing dividend level, but also values a policy of continuous dividend payment. A firm may pay $0.50 per share whenever dividends are paid, but if dividends are not paid each quarter the shareholders will still have to live with a degree of uncertainty. In order to reduce owners' uncertainty about returns, not only must the amount of the dividend payment be predictable but also its frequency of receipt. The continuous payment of cash dividends, regardless of their magnitude, reduces shareholder uncertainty and lowers the rate at which earnings are discounted. The net effect should therefore be an increase in the market value of the firm's stock and therefore increased owners' wealth.

The informational content of dividends.   A final market consideration, alluded to earlier, is the informational content of dividends. Shareholders often view the firm's dividend payments as an indicator of the future success of the firm. A stable, continuous dividend conveys to the firm's owners that the firm is OK and there is no reason for concern. If the firm passes a dividend payment in a given period due to a loss or very low earnings, shareholders are quite likely to react unfavorably. The nonpayment of the dividend creates uncertainty about the firm's future success, and this uncertainty is likely to result in lower stock values. Even if current earnings are low, a firm should continue its dividend payment in order to avoid conveying negative information to owners and prospective investors. Owners and investors generally construe a dividend payment during a period of losses as an indication that the loss is temporary.

In summary, the marketplace views the firm's dividends as a source of information. The firm should attempt to develop a dividend policy that provides owners and prospective investors with positive information, therefore reducing their uncertainty about the firm's future success. By paying fixed or increasing dividends on a continuous basis, the firm gives its owners a feeling of confidence in its continued success. It is quite important for the firm to consider the views and reactions of the marketplace to dividends when formulating a dividend policy.[9]

OBJECTIVES AND TYPES OF DIVIDEND POLICIES

The preceding section presented a number of factors that must be considered in establishing a dividend policy. Because these factors conflict, it is the responsibility of the financial manager and the board of directors to establish a dividend policy that best fulfills the firm's overall objectives. This section discusses the basic objectives of dividend policy and the most common types of dividend policies.

Objectives of dividend policy

The firm's dividend policy represents a plan of action to be followed whenever the dividend decision must be made. The dividend policy must be formulated with two basic objectives in mind—maximizing the wealth of the firm's owners and providing for sufficient financing. These objectives are not mutually exclusive but, rather, are interrelated. They must be fulfilled in light

---

[9]The marketplace must be considered since the wealth of owners is best measured by the market value of their ownership. By considering the market reaction in setting a dividend policy, the financial manager is operating in a manner consistent with his or her stated goal of maximizing the wealth of the firm's owners. The policy, of course, must be established in light of its long-run effect, not merely a transitory one, on the stock price.

of a number of constraints—legal, contractual, internal, owner-related, and market-related—that limit the alternatives available to the decision maker when establishing dividend policy.

Wealth maximization.   The firm's dividend policy should be one that supports the general objective of maximizing the wealth of the firm's owners over the long run. It must be designed not merely to maximize the share price in the coming year, but to maximize wealth in the *long run,* since the firm is assumed to have an infinite life. Of course, theoretically, we expect that shareholders and prospective investors will recognize the long-run effects of a dividend policy on their ownership and that this recognition will be reflected in the level of future returns they forecast. In actuality, owners are often not fully aware of the implications of certain dividend policies and, as a result, their actions may cause the stock price to drop. It is the responsibility of the firm's management to make the owners aware of the objectives and implications of dividend policy, so that the market reaction is favorable.

Providing for sufficient financing.   Making provision for sufficient financing can be considered a secondary objective of dividend policy. Without sufficient financing to implement acceptable projects, the wealth maximization process cannot be carried out. The firm must forecast its future funds needs and, taking into account the external availability of funds and certain market considerations, determine both the amount of retained earnings financing needed and the amount of retained earnings available *after* the minimum dividends have been paid. In other words, *dividend payments should not be viewed as a residual, but rather as a required outlay,* after which any remaining funds can be reinvested in the firm. If the firm were to view its dividend payments as a residual, it would be supporting the dividend-irrelevance theory described earlier. In investing retained earnings in profitable projects and paying out only "extra," or residual, retained earnings, the financial manager is attaching no importance to the cash dividend. If the cash dividend is as relevant to the valuation of the firm, as it seems to be, treating dividends as a residual instead of an active decision variable is inconsistent with the objective of owners' wealth maximization. Only in rare instances should the firm cut its dividend in order to obtain funds. The important point to remember here is that the amount of retained earnings financing available must be forecast on an *after-dividends basis,* since the market can be expected to react adversely to the nonpayment of cash dividends.

Types of dividend policies

Although there are an infinite number of possible dividend policies available to the business firm, most of them have one of a number of basic features. In this section, three of the more commonly used dividend policies are briefly described—a constant-payout-ratio dividend policy, a regular dividend policy, and a low regular-and-extra-dividend policy. A particular firm's cash dividend policy may incorporate elements of each of these policies.

A constant-payout-ratio dividend policy. One type of dividend policy often adopted by firms is the use of a constant payout ratio.[10] The firm simply establishes a certain percentage of earnings to be paid out each period. The problem with this type of policy is that if the firm's earnings drop or a loss occurs in a given period, the dividends will be low or even nonexistent. Since dividends are looked on as supplying certain information about the firm's future, the firm's stock will most likely be adversely affected by this type of action. An example will clarify the problems stemming from a constant-payout-ratio dividend policy.

EXAMPLE

The Nader Motor Company has a policy of paying out 40 percent of earnings in cash dividends. In periods when a loss occurs the firm's policy is to pay no cash dividends. Nader's earnings per share, dividends per share, and average price per share for the past six years are given:

Year	Earnings/share	Dividends/share	Av. price/share
1973	$4.50	$1.80	$50.00
1974	2.00	.80	46.00
1975	−1.50	.00	38.00
1976	1.75	.70	48.00
1977	3.00	1.20	52.00
1978	− .50	.00	42.00

Dividends increased in 1975–1976 and 1976–1977 and decreased in 1973–1974, 1974–1975, and 1977–1978. It can be seen that in years of decreased dividends the firm's stock price dropped; when dividends increased, the price of the stock increased. Nader's sporadic dividend payments appear to make its owners very uncertain about the returns they can expect from their investment in the firm and therefore generally depress the stock's price. Although a constant-payout-ratio dividend policy is used by some firms, it is not recommended. ●

A regular dividend policy. Another type of dividend policy is based on the payment of a fixed-dollar dividend in each period. This policy does not provide the owners with either good or bad information; instead, it minimizes their uncertainty. Often, firms using this policy will increase the regular dividend once a *proven* increase in earnings has occurred. Under this policy, dividends are almost *never* decreased. An example will clarify how a regular dividend policy works.

EXAMPLE

The Tulsa Oil Company's dividend policy is to pay annual dividends of $1.00 per share until per-share earnings have exceeded $4.00 for three consecutive years, at which time the annual dividend will be raised to $1.50 per share and a new dividend

[10]The *payout ratio*, by definition, is the firm's cash dividend per share divided by its earnings per share. It indicates the percentage of each dollar earned that is distributed to the owners in the form of cash.

plateau established. The firm does not anticipate decreasing its dividend unless its liquidity is in jeopardy. Tulsa's earnings per share, dividends per share, and average price per share for the past 12 years are given:

Year	Earnings/share	Dividends/share	Av. price/share
1967	$3.00	$1.00	$35.00
1968	2.80	1.00	33.50
1969	.50	1.00	33.00
1970	.75	1.00	33.00
1971	3.00	1.00	36.00
1972	6.00	1.00	38.00
1973	2.00	1.00	38.50
1974	5.00	1.00	42.00
1975	4.20	1.00	43.00
1976	4.60	1.50	45.00
1977	3.90	1.50	46.50
1978	4.50	1.50	47.50

It can be seen that, regardless of the level of earnings, Tulsa paid dividends of $1.00 per share through 1975. In 1976 the dividend was raised to $1.50 per share, since earnings of $4.00 per share had been achieved for three years. In 1976, the firm would also have had to establish a new earnings plateau for further dividend increases. It can be seen that Tulsa Oil Company's average price per share exhibited a stable, increasing behavior in spite of their somewhat volatile pattern of earnings. ●

Often, a regular dividend policy, such as that of the Tulsa Oil Company, is built around a *target dividend-payout ratio*. The firm attempts to pay out a certain percentage of earnings; but, rather than let the dividends fluctuate, it pays a stated dollar dividend and adjusts it toward the target payout as proven increases in earnings occur. For instance, the Tulsa Oil Company appears to have a target payout ratio of around 35 percent. The payout was about 33 percent ($1.00 ÷ $3.00) when the dividend policy was set in 1967 and the dividend was raised to $1.50 (about a 38-percent payout ratio) when per-share earnings exceeded $4.00. The use of a target payout ratio with a regular dividend policy is not unusual.

A low regular-and-extra-dividend policy. Some firms establish a policy of a low regular dividend accompanied by an additional dividend when earnings warrant it. If earnings are higher than normal in a given period, the firm may pay this additional dividend, which will be designated an *extra dividend*. By designating the amount by which the dividend exceeds the regular payment as an extra dividend, the firm avoids giving existing and prospective shareholders false hopes of increased dividends in coming periods. The use of the low regular-extra designation is especially common among companies that experience cyclical shifts in earnings.

By establishing a low regular dividend that is paid each period, the firm gives investors the stable dividend income necessary to build their confidence in the firm, while the extra dividend permits them to share in the spoils if the firm experiences an especially good period. Firms using this type of dividend policy must raise the level of the regular dividend once proven increases in earnings have been achieved. The extra dividend should not be allowed to become a regular event, or it becomes meaningless. The use of a target payout ratio in establishing the regular dividend level is advisable.

The three dividend policies described in this section are only some of the basic plans available to the firm; the interrelationship of these plans has been emphasized. The reader should keep in mind the importance of the establishment of a dividend policy which is known not only by the directors but also by the firm's owners. The policy should be geared to the various constraints placed on the firm and should be consistent with achieving the firm's long-run objective of maximizing the owners' wealth.

NONCASH DIVIDENDS

Attention thus far in this chapter has been devoted to the payment of cash dividends. A number of alternatives or supplements to the payment of cash dividends are available to the firm. One uncommon approach, which will not be discussed in the text, is the payment of dividends in merchandise produced by the firm. However, two noncash methods of paying dividends—stock dividends and stock repurchases—as well as a closely related topic—stock splits—are discussed in this section. Stock dividends are easily recognizable as a dividend payment. Stock splits, although not strictly a form of dividend payment, result in a similar effect on the firm as a stock dividend. The repurchase of stock also has an effect similar to the payment of cash dividends since it can be viewed as an alternate method of distributing funds to the firm's owners.

Stock dividends

Often, firms pay stock dividends either as a replacement for or a supplement to the payment of cash dividends. Although stock dividends do not have a real value, the firm's stockholders are likely to believe that they represent something they did not have before and therefore have value. By definition, a *stock dividend* is a payment of stock to the existing owners. The accounting aspects, the shareholder's viewpoint, and the company's viewpoint of stock dividends are discussed in this section.

Accounting aspects.

In an accounting sense, the payment of a stock dividend is a shifting of funds between capital accounts rather than a use of funds. When a firm declares a stock dividend, the general procedures with respect to its announcement and distribution are the same as those described earlier for a cash dividend. The difference is that the owner receives additional stock, which in actuality represents something he or she already owns. It does not change the shareholders proportional ownership or increase the assets of the firm. An example of the accounting entries associated with the payment of stock dividends is given below.

EXAMPLE

The J and L Company's current stockholders' equity on its balance sheet is as follows:

Preferred stock	$ 300,000
Common stock (100,000 shares @ $4 par)	400,000
Paid-in capital in excess of par	600,000
Retained earnings	700,000
Stockholders' Equity	$2,000,000

If J and L declares a 10-percent stock dividend and the market price of its stock is $15 per share, $150,000 (10% · $15 per share · 100,000 shares) of retained earnings will be capitalized. The $150,000 will be distributed between the common stock and paid-in capital in excess of par accounts based on the par value of the common stock. The resulting account balances are given:

Preferred stock	$ 300,000
Common stock (110,000 shares @ $4 par)	440,000
Paid-in capital in excess of par	710,000
Retained earnings	550,000
Stockholders' Equity	$2,000,000

Obviously, the owner's equity has not changed as a result of the payment of a 10-percent stock dividend. Since 10,000 (10 percent of 100,000) new shares have been issued and the prevailing market price is $15 per share, $150,000 ($15 per share · 10,000 shares) has been shifted from retained earnings to the common stock and paid-in capital accounts. A total of $40,000 ($4 par · 10,000 shares) has been added to common stock, and the remaining $110,000 [($15 − $4) · 10,000 shares] has been added to the paid-in capital in excess of par. The reader should recognize that the firm's stockholders' equity has not changed; funds have only been redistributed between the stockholders' equity accounts. ●

Since certain legal constraints relating to capital impairment and net profits (discussed earlier in this chapter) may limit the firm's cash dividend payment, it is important to recognize that since the payment of stock dividends reduces the firm's retained earnings, it reduces the aggregate amount of cash dividends that can be paid out. Because the availability of cash is typically more binding on the firm's ability to pay cash dividends, the reduction of retained earnings as the result of stock dividend payments generally does not unfavorably impact the firm.

The shareholders' viewpoint. The shareholder receiving a stock dividend receives nothing of value. After the stock dividend is paid, the per-share value of the shareholder's stock will decrease in proportion to the stock dividend in such a way that the market value of his or her total holdings in the firm will remain unchanged. The shareholder's proportion of ownership in the firm will also remain the same, and as long as the firm's earnings remain unchanged, so too will his or her proportion of earnings. An example will clarify this point.

EXAMPLE

Mr. X owned 10,000 shares of the J and L Company's stock. The company's most recent earnings were $220,000, and earnings are not expected to change in the near future. Before the stock dividend, Mr. X owned 10 percent (10,000 shares ÷ 100,000 shares) of the firm's stock, which was selling for $15 per share. Earnings per share were $2.20 ($220,000 ÷ 100,000 shares). Since Mr. X owns 10,000 shares, his earnings were $22,000 ($2.20 per share · 10,000 shares). After receiving the 10-percent stock dividend, Mr. X has 11,000 shares, which again is 10 percent (11,000 shares ÷ 110,000 shares) of the ownership. The market price of the stock can be expected to drop to $13.64 per share [$15 · (1.00 ÷ 1.10)], which means that the market value of Mr. X's holdings will be $150,000 (11,000 shares · $13.64 per share). This is the same as the initial value of his holdings ($10,000 shares · $15 share). The future earnings per share will drop to $2 ($220,000 ÷ 110,000 shares), since the same $220,000 in earnings must now be divided between 110,000 shares. Since Mr. X still owns 10 percent of the stock, his share of the total earnings is still $22,000 ($2 per share · 11,000 shares). In summary, if the firm's earnings remain constant and its cash dividends decrease, a stock dividend may result in a lower market value for the firm's stock. ●

Sometimes when a firm issues a stock dividend, it will maintain the cash dividend per share, thereby increasing the dividends paid out since more shares are outstanding. This type of action actually represents an increase in dividends and may result in an increased market value for the firm's stock. The effect of this increased dividend is somewhat dependent on the existing investment opportunities and the firm's funds needs. Another plus for the stock dividend is its informational content. Although it has no current value, the stock dividend may indicate to owners that if the firm retains and reinvests its earnings, its earnings will grow enough to more than offset the decreased market value and per-share earnings resulting from the payment of the stock dividend.

The company's viewpoint.   Stock dividends are more costly to issue than cash dividends, but the advantages of using them generally outweigh these costs. Firms find the stock dividend a means of giving owners something without having to use cash. Generally, when a firm is growing rapidly and needs internal financing to perpetuate this growth, a stock dividend is used. As long as the investors recognize that the firm is reinvesting its earnings in a manner that should tend to maximize their future earnings, the market price of the firm's stock should not be adversely affected. If the stock dividend is paid so that cash can be retained to satisfy past due bills, the market reaction may be less favorable.

Stock splits

Although not a type of dividend, *stock splits* have a similar effect upon a firms share price as do stock dividends. Therefore stock splits are briefly described here. Stock splits are commonly used to lower the market price of a firm's stock. Quite often, the firm believes its stock is too high-priced and that lowering the market price will enhance its trading activity. Stock splits are often made prior to new issues of a stock in order to enhance the marketability of the stock and stimulate market activity. A stock split has no effect on the firm's financial structure. It most commonly increases the number of shares outstanding and reduces the stock's par value. In other words, when a stock is split, a specified number of new shares are exchanged for a given number of outstanding shares. In a 2-for-1 split, two new shares are exchanged for each old share; in a 3-for-2 split three new shares are exchanged for each two old shares, and so on.

EXAMPLE

The Krantz Company had 200,000 shares of $2 par-value common stock and no preferred stock outstanding. Since the stock is selling at a high market price, the firm has declared a 2-for-1 stock split. The before-and-after stockholders' equity is given below.

Before	
Common stock (200,000 shares outstanding with a $2 par value)	$ 400,000
Paid-in capital in excess of par	4,000,000
Retained earnings	2,000,000
Stockholders' Equity	$6,400,000

After	
Common stock (400,000 shares outstanding with a $1 par value)	$ 400,000
Paid-in capital in excess of par	4,000,000
Retained earnings	2,000,000
Stockholders' Equity	$6,400,000

The insignificant effect of the stock split on the firm's books should be obvious. ●

Stock can be split in any way desired. Sometimes *reverse stock splits* are made; that is, a certain number of outstanding shares are exchanged for a new share. For example in a 1-for-2 split, one new share is exchanged for two old shares; in a 2-for-3 split, two new shares are exchanged for three old shares, and so on. Reverse stock splits are initiated when a stock is selling at too low a price to appear respectable.[11] It is not unusual for a stock split to cause a slight increase in the market value of the firm's stock. This is attributable to both the informational content of stock splits and the fact that *total* dividends paid commonly increase slightly after a stock split.

The stock dividend, since it does tend to lower the price of a firm's shares, has an effect similar to a stock split. A lower per-share price may mean increased trading activity in the stock. However, the use of stock dividends

[11]If a firm's stock is selling at a low price—possibly less than a few dollars—many investors are hesitant to purchase it because they believe it is "cheap." These somewhat unsophisticated investors correlate cheapness and quality, and they feel that a low-priced stock is a low-quality investment. A reverse stock split raises the stock price and increases per share earnings.

to lower the market price of shares must be considered as only a collateral objective. The primary use of stock dividends, from the firm's viewpoint, is as a means of avoiding paying out cash while still giving owners a type of psychological or informational income; the primary objective of a stock split is somehow to stimulate trading activity in the firm's shares. It should be clear that although a stock dividend impacts the firm's retained earnings, a stock split has no effect on retained earnings and therefore does not have any impact on the aggregate amount of cash dividend payments a firm may legally make.

Stock repurchases

In the recent past, firms have increased their repurchasing of shares of outstanding common stock in the marketplace. Common stock is repurchased for a number of reasons, such as to obtain shares to be used in acquisitions, to have shares available for stock option plans, or merely to retire outstanding shares. This section is concerned with the repurchase of shares for retirement, since this type of repurchase may be used as a substitute for the payment of cash dividends. It covers the accounting entries resulting from repurchases, motives for the retirement of shares, and the repurchase process.

Accounting entries.   The accounting entries resulting when common stock is repurchased are a reduction in cash and the establishment of an asset account called "treasury stock," which is typically shown as a deduction from stockholders' equity. The label *treasury stock* is used to indicate the presence of repurchased shares on the firm's balance sheet. The repurchase of stock can be viewed as a cash dividend, since it involves the distribution of cash to the firm's owners, who are the sellers of the shares.

Motives for the retirement of shares.   When common stock is repurchased for retirement, the underlying motive is to distribute excess cash to the firm's owners. Retiring stock means that the owners receive cash for their shares. The general rationale for this action is that as long as earnings remain constant the repurchase of shares reduces the number of outstanding shares, raising the earnings per share and therefore the market price per share. The retirement of common stock can be viewed as a type of reverse dilution since the earnings per share and the market price of stock are increased by reducing the number of shares outstanding. A simple example will clarify this point.

EXAMPLE
The Terrell Company has released the following financial data:

Earnings available for common	$1,000,000
Number of shares outstanding	400,000
Earnings per share ($1,000,000 ÷ 400,000)	$2.50
Market price per share	$50
Price-earnings ratio ($50 ÷ $2.50)	20

The firm is contemplating paying cash dividends of $2 per share, which will raise the price of the stock to $52 (since the market price is currently $50) while the stock is selling with dividends on. The total amount of dividends to be paid by the firm will be $800,000 (400,000 shares · $2 per share). However, instead of paying $800,000 in cash dividends, the firm could repurchase stock at $52 per share. With $800,000, it could repurchase approximately 15,385 shares ($800,000 ÷ $52 per share). As a result of this repurchase, 384,615 shares (400,000 shares − 15,385 shares) of common stock would remain outstanding. Earnings per share would rise to $2.60 ($1,000,000 ÷ 384,615), and if the stock still sold at 20 times earnings, its market price would rise to $52 per share. It should be noted that the market price per share would be the same, $52, regardless of whether the cash dividend was paid[12] or stock was repurchased.

The impact of the stock repurchase illustrated is attributable to two key assumptions—(1) the shares could be repurchased at $52 each, and (2) the price-earnings ratio remains at 20 in either case (i.e., cash dividend or stock repurchase). If the firm were to buy the shares for less than $52, the remaining shareholders would gain; while at more than $52, the remaining shareholders would lose. If the price-earnings ratio rose as a result of repurchase, the remaining shareholders would gain, and if it were to drop they would lose. In other words, the assumptions made with respect to both the repurchase price and the price-earnings ratio significantly impact the analysis of a proposed stock repurchase in lieu of paying cash dividends. ●

The advantages of stock repurchases are an increase in per-share earnings and certain tax benefits. The increase in per-share earnings for the Terrell Company has been illustrated above. The tax advantage stems from the fact that if the cash dividend is paid the owners will have to pay ordinary income taxes on it, while the $2 increase in the market value of the stock due to the stock repurchase will be taxable at the capital gains rate (assuming the stock has been held for at least one year). The IRS closely watches firms that regularly repurchase stock and levies a penalty if it believes that the stock repurchases have been made in order to shield the stockholders from taxes on cash dividends.

Although the use of stock repurchases to retire shares is most commonly viewed as a dividend decision, some people view it as an investment or a financing decision. A stock repurchase is an investment decision in the sense that the firm has excess cash but no acceptable investment opportunities except to repurchase shares. This can be thought of as an investment in the company's own shares, which in the long run should help to maximize the remaining owners' wealth, although no specific return can be attached to the investment. The retirement of stock through repurchases may be considered a financing decision in the sense that it enables the firm to shift its debt-equity ratio to a more highly levered position. When debt or preferred stock is used to raise funds for a repurchase of shares, it is more likely to be viewed

---

[12]When the stock is selling with dividends on, its price would be $52; once the dividend is paid, the stock price would drop by the $2-per-share dividend to $50. Of course, the shareholders would have gained the $2-per-share dividend, while in the case of the stock repurchase, the remaining shareholders would have experienced a $2-per-share increase in the market price (i.e., from $50 per share to $52 per share).

as a financing decision. However, our basic concern in this chapter is with the use of stock repurchases as a form of cash dividend.

The repurchase process.   When a company intends to repurchase a block of outstanding shares, it should make shareholders aware of its intentions. Specifically, it should advise them of the purpose of the repurchase (i.e., acquisitions, stock options, retirement, and so forth) and the disposition (if any) planned for the repurchased shares (i.e., traded for shares of another firm, distribution to executives, held in the treasury, and so forth). Three basic methods of repurchase are commonly used. One is to purchase shares on the *open market.* This places upward pressure on the price of shares if the number of shares being repurchased is reasonably large in comparison to the total number of shares outstanding. It is quite important, when open-market repurchases of sizable blocks of shares are made, that owners of the stock be made fully aware of the repurchase objectives. If they are not, they may sell their shares when the price increases—not recognizing that an increase in per-share earnings will result that is likely to raise the stock price even higher.

The second method of repurchasing stock is through *tender offers.*[13] A tender offer is a formal offer by the firm to purchase a given number of shares at a specified price. The price at which a tender offer is made is set above the current market price in order to attract sellers. If the number of shares desired cannot be repurchased through the tender offer, open-market purchases can be used to obtain the additional shares. Tender offers are preferred when large numbers of shares are repurchased since the company's intentions are clearly stated and each stockholder has an opportunity to sell his or her shares at the tendered price.

The third method sometimes used to repurchase shares involves arranging to purchase on a *negotiated basis* a large block of shares from one or more large stockholders. Again in this case, the firm would have to clearly state its intentions and make certain that the purchase price is fair and equitable in view of the interests and opportunities of the remaining shareholders in the firm.

SUMMARY

This chapter has discussed two closely related topics—dividends and retained earnings. The cash dividend decision is normally a quarterly decision made by the corporate board of directors. Any earnings remaining after cash dividends have been paid become retained earnings, which represent reinvested funds to the firm. Retained earnings are a source of long-term financing to the business firm. Since they are a source of capital, they are an alternative to financial leases, long-term debt, bonds, preferred stock, or the sale of new common stock. Retained earnings may be viewed as a fully subscribed new issue of common stock since they represent new ownership capital.

---

[13]Tender offers are discussed in greater detail in Chapter 25. The motive for these offers may be to acquire control of another firm rather than to tender the firm's own shares.

Theoretical arguments have been made suggesting the irrelevance of dividends with respect to the market value of a firm. The major proponents of this belief are Modigliani and Miller, who base their proof on very unrealistic and restrictive assumptions. Another school of thought suggests that, in the absence of M and M's restrictive assumptions, dividends are relevant and are an important factor in maximizing the wealth of the firm's owners. Paying dividends reduces the owners' uncertainty concerning the future success of the firm, causing them to discount its earnings at a lower rate. The effect of this lower discount rate is to raise the market value of the firm's stock.

The firm must consider certain factors in setting its dividend policy. State laws prohibit it from paying out capital, which is defined either as the par value of the stock or all paid-in capital. Some laws limit dividends to an amount equal to current and past retained earnings only. Most states prohibit insolvent firms from paying cash dividends. Lease contracts, loan covenants, bond indentures, and preferred stock agreements quite often limit dividends to a certain amount. The amount of cash and marketable securities a firm has often acts as an internal dividend constraint. Other factors that require consideration by the firm are its growth prospects, the owners' tax status, the owners' other investment opportunities, dilution, and certain market considerations.

The firm must establish a dividend policy that maximizes the wealth of its owners in the long run while allowing it sufficient financing to perpetuate itself. A cash dividend should not be viewed as a residual payment to owners; it should be established and then any remaining earnings reinvested. Common dividend policies include a constant payout ratio, regular dividends, or low regular and extra dividends. A firm's dividend policy is often a combination of these policies. Firms commonly establish a target payout ratio, which they attempt to maintain by making discrete increases in dividends with proven increases in earnings. Most firms try to establish dividend policies that will not require them to decrease their dividends.

Occasionally, firms cannot pay cash dividends or can only pay low cash dividends. In order to provide owners with some indication that the firm is doing well, they may pay stock dividends. Stock dividends result from capitalizing retained earnings, and they do not actually have a value to the recipient. However, the psychological effect of stock dividends on owners is generally favorable. Although not a type of dividend, stock splits, which are used to enhance trading activity in a firm's shares, are sometimes initiated. They tend to have effects similar to a stock dividend since they most often (except in the case of a reverse stock split) increase the number of shares outstanding while not providing any inflow of new capital. In an accounting sense, the stock split does not affect retained earnings; it merely results in a notational entry.

Another method of paying noncash dividends is to repurchase stock. Firms having excess cash can repurchase and retire stock in order to increase their earnings and market price per share. These increases occur if the firm can repurchase shares at a price equal to or below the stock price with dividends on, and if the firm's post-repurchase price-earnings ratio remains unchanged or improves over the pre-repurchase price earnings ratio. The actual repurchase decision would of course depend upon the reasonableness of such assumptions. Making stock repurchases in lieu of cash dividend payments may provide tax benefits to the firm's owners by providing them with capital gain income, instead of ordinary income, which would be taxed at a higher rate. Some firms repurchase stock for acquisitions, for stock options, or for retirement. Stock repurchases can be made either directly in the marketplace, through tender offers, or on a negotiated basis from holders of large blocks of shares.

QUESTIONS

24-1   How are retained earnings a source of funds to the business firm? If earnings were not retained, what might the financial consequences for the firm be?

24-2   Why must the firm view its dividend decision as a financing decision?

24-3   How do the date of record and the holders of record relate to the payment of cash dividends? What do the terms *ex dividend* and *dividends on,* or *cum dividends,* mean? Who sets the dividend payment date?

24-4   What assumptions and arguments are used by Modigliani and Miller in support of the irrelevance of dividends? What is the key to M and M's argument?

24-5   What do M and M say about the effect of dividends on stock prices? Do they believe dividends affect stock prices?

24-6   What effects do brokerage fees and taxes have on the relevance of dividends?

24-7   What are some contractual and internal constraints on the firm's ability to pass dividends? Why do contractual constraints exist?

24-8   Why must the firm's dividend policy be based somehow on its growth prospects?

24-9   Why is the primary consideration with respect to dividend policy its effect on the firm's owners? How may the tax status of the owners affect a firm's dividend policy?

24-10   What effect do outside investment opportunities and the possible dilution of ownership have on the firm's determination of an acceptable dividend policy?

24-11   What are the two broad objectives of dividend policies? Are these two objectives mutually exclusive? Why or why not?

24-12   What are (1) a constant-payout-ratio policy, (2) a regular dividend policy, and (3) a low regular-and-extra-dividend policy? What are the ramifications of these policies?

24-13   What is a stock dividend? Do stock dividends have any value in and of themselves? Why are they issued?

24-14   What is a stock split? Compare a stock split with a stock dividend. What is a reverse stock split?

24-15   Explain how stock dividends and stock splits affect the firm's balance sheet and the firm's ability to pay dividends.

24-16   If it is more costly to issue stock than to pay cash dividends, why do firms issue stock dividends? Are there any similarities between stock dividends and stock splits? What are they?

24-17   What motives prompt firms to repurchase their shares? What effect on balance sheet accounts does the repurchase of shares have?

24-18   What is the logic behind repurchasing shares of common stock in order to redistribute excess cash to the firm's owners? How might this raise the per-share earnings and market price of outstanding shares?

24-19 How may stock be repurchased by a firm? Why is it important that the firm's shareholders be made aware of the purpose of a repurchase and the planned disposition of repurchased shares?

PROBLEMS

24-1 Wisconsin Widget, at the quarterly dividend meeting, declared a cash dividend of $1.10 per share for holders of record on Monday, July 10. The firm has 300,000 shares of common stock outstanding and has set a payment date of July 31. Prior to the dividend declaration, the firm's key accounts were as follows:

| Cash | $500,000 | Dividends payable | $ 0 |
| | | Retained earnings | $2,500,000 |

   a Show the entries after the meeting adjourned.
   b When is the ex dividend date?
   c After the July 31 payment date, what would the key accounts be?
   d What effect, if any, will the dividend have on the firm's total assets?

24-2 The Big D Company's stockholders' equity account is as follows:

Preferred stock	$ 500,000
Common stock (400,000 shares @ $4 par value)	1,600,000
Paid-in capital in excess of par	1,000,000
Retained earnings	1,900,000
Total Stockholders' Equity	$5,000,000

The earnings available for common stockholders from this period's operations are $100,000, which have been included as part of the $1.9 million retained earnings. Capital is defined to include *all* paid-in capital.

   a What is the maximum dividend per share the firm can pay?
   b If the firm has $160,000 in cash, what is the largest per-share dividend it can pay without borrowing?
   c Indicate what accounts, if any, will be affected if the firm pays the dividends indicated in **a** and **b** above. What changes would result from the dividends indicated in **a** and **b**?
   d Indicate the effects of an $80,000 cash dividend on the firm's stockholders' equity.

24-3 A firm has $800,000 in paid-in capital, retained earnings of $40,000 (including the current year's earnings), and 25,000 shares of common stock outstanding. It earned $29,000 after taxes and preferred stock dividends in the most recent year.

   a What is the most the firm can pay in cash dividends to each common shareholder? (Assume capital includes *all* paid-in capital.)
   b What effect would a cash dividend of $.80 have on the firm's balance sheet entries?
   c If the firm cannot raise any new funds from external sources, what do you consider the key constraint with respect to the magnitude of the firm's dividend payments? Why?

24-4 A firm has had the indicated earnings per share over the past 10 years:

Year	Earnings per share
1978	$ 4.00
1977	3.80
1976	3.20
1975	2.80
1974	3.20
1973	2.40
1972	1.20
1971	1.80
1970	−.50
1969	.25

  a If the firm's dividend policy was based on a constant payout ratio of 40 percent for all years with positive earnings and a zero payout otherwise, determine the annual dividend for each year.

  b If the firm had a dividend payout of $1.00 per share, increasing by $.10 per share whenever the dividend payout fell below 50 percent for two consecutive years, what annual dividend did the firm pay each year?

  c If the firm's policy was to pay $.50 per share each period except when earnings per share exceed $3.00, when an extra dividend equal to 80 percent of earnings beyond $3.00 would be paid, what annual dividend did the firm pay each year?

  d Discuss the pros and cons of each dividend policy described in **a** through **c**.

24-5 Given the following earnings per share over the 1971-1978 period, determine the annual dividend per share under each of the policies set forth in **a** through **d**.

Year	Earnings per share
1978	$ 1.40
1977	1.56
1976	1.20
1975	−.85
1974	1.05
1973	.60
1972	1.00
1971	.44

  a Pay out 50 percent of earnings in all years with positive earnings.

  b Pay $.50 per share except when earnings exceed $1.00 per share, when there would be an extra dividend of 60 percent of earnings above $1.00 per share.

  c Pay $.50 per share and increase to $.60 per share whenever earnings per share rise above $.90 per share for two consecutive years.

  d Combine policies in **b** and **c**. When the dividend is raised (in **c**), raise the excess dividend base (in **b**) from $1.00 to $1.10 per share.

e Compare and contrast each of the dividend policies described in **a** through **d**.

24-6 FMA has a stockholders' equity account, given below. The firm's common stock has a current market price of $30 per share.

Preferred stock	$100,000
Common stock (10,000 shares @ $2 par)	20,000
Paid-in capital in excess of par	280,000
Retained earnings	100,000
Stockholders' Equity	$500,000

a Show the effects on FMA of a 5-percent stock dividend.
b Show the effects of (1) a 10-percent and (2) a 20-percent stock dividend.
c In light of your answers to **a** and **b**, discuss the effects of stock dividends on the firm's stockholders' equity.

24-7 Hadley-Walsh Steel has a stockholders' equity account as given below. The firm's common stock currently sells for $4 per share.

Preferred stock	$100,000
Common stock (400,000 shares @ $1 par)	400,000
Paid-in capital in excess of par	200,000
Retained earnings	320,000
Stockholders' Equity	$1,020,000

a Show the effects on the firm of a $.01, $.05, $.10, and $.20-per-share *cash* dividend.
b Show the effects on the firm of a 1-percent, 5-percent, 10-percent, and 20-percent *stock* dividend.
c Compare the effects in **a** and **b**. What are the significant differences in the two methods of paying dividends?

24-8 Alfred Clark currently holds 400 shares of Mountain Grown Coffee. The firm has 40,000 shares outstanding. The firm most recently had earnings available for common shareholders of $80,000 and its stock has been selling for $22 per share. The firm intends to retain its earnings and pay a 10-percent stock dividend. The retention of earnings is deemed necessary to finance a planned expansion. The firm expects the rate of return on the expansion to equal the rate of return the firm now earns on stockholders' equity.
a How much does the firm currently earn per share?
b What proportion of the firm does Alfred Clark currently own?
c What porportion of the firm will Mr. Clark own after the stock dividend? Explain your answer.
d At what market price would you expect the stock to sell after the stock dividend?
e Discuss what effect, if any, the payment of stock dividends will have on Mr. Clark's share of the ownership and earnings of Mountain Grown Coffee.

24-9 The Mission Company has outstanding 50,000 shares of common stock currently selling at $40 per share. The firm most recently had earnings available for common stockholders of $120,000, but it has decided to retain these funds and is considering either a 5-percent or a 10-percent stock dividend in lieu of a cash dividend.

a Determine the firm's current earnings per share.

b If Jack Frost currently owns 500 shares of the firm's stock, determine his proportion of ownership currently and under each of the proposed dividend plans. Explain your findings.

c Calculate and explain the market price per share under each of the stock dividend plans.

d For each of the proposed stock dividends, calculate the earnings per share after payment of the stock dividend.

e How much would the value of Mr. Frost's holdings be under each of the proposals? Explain.

f As Mr. Frost, would you have any preference with respect to the proposed stock dividends? Why or why not?

24-10 The U.S. Oil Company's current stockholders' equity account is as follows:

Preferred stock (5% cumulative, $100 par)	$ 400,000
Common stock (600,000 shares @ $3 par)	1,800,000
Paid-in capital in excess of par	200,000
Retained earnings	800,000
Stockholders' Equity	$3,200,000

a Indicate the change, if any, expected if the firm declares a 2-for-1 stock split.

b Indicate the change, if any, expected if the firm declares a 1-for-1½ reverse stock split.

c Indicate the change, if any, expected if the firm declares a 3-for-1 stock split.

d Indicate the change, if any, expected if the firm declares a 6-for-1 stock split.

e Indicate the change, if any, expected if the firm declares a 1-for-4 reverse stock split.

24-11 The Big Company is considering a 3-for-2 stock split. They currently have the stockholders' equity position shown below. The current stock price is $120 per share. The most recent period's earnings available for common is included in retained earnings.

Preferred stock	$ 1,000,000
Common stock (100,000 shares @ $3 par)	300,000
Paid-in capital in excess of par	1,700,000
Retained earnings	10,000,000
Stockholders' Equity	$13,000,000

a What effects on Big Company would result from the stock split?

b What change in stock price would you expect to result from the stock split?

c What is the maximum cash dividend per share the firm could pay before and after the stock split? (Assume capital includes *all* paid-in capital.)

    d Contrast your answers to **a** through **c** with the circumstances surrounding a 50-percent stock dividend.

    e Explain the differences between stock splits and stock dividends.

24-12 The following financial data on the Victor Stock Company are available:

Earnings available for common stockholders	$800,000
Number of shares of common outstanding	400,000
Earnings per share ($800,000 ÷ 400,000)	$2
Market price per share	$20
Price-earnings ratio ($20 ÷ $2)	10

The firm is currently contemplating paying cash dividends of $1 per share, which will raise the stock price to $21 per share while dividends are on.

    a Approximately how many shares of stock can the firm repurchase at the $21 per share price using the funds that would have gone to pay the cash dividend?

    b Calculate earnings per share after the repurchase. Explain your calculations.

    c If the stock still sells at 10 times earnings, how much will the market price be after the repurchase?

    d Compare and contrast the pre- and post-repurchase earnings per share. Discuss the tax implications of this action.

    e Compare and contrast the pre- and post-repurchase market price. Discuss your findings.

24-13 The Off Shore Steel Company has earnings available for common stockholders of $2 million and 500,000 shares of common stock outstanding at $60 per share. The firm is currently contemplating the payment of $2 per share in cash dividends.

    a Calculate the firm's current earnings per share and price-earnings multiple.

    b If the firm's stock is expected to sell at $62 per share with dividends on and the firm can repurchase shares at this price, how many shares can be purchased in lieu of making the proposed cash dividend payment?

    c How much will the earnings per share be after the proposed repurchase? Why?

    d If the stock will sell at the old price-earnings multiple, how much will the market price be after repurchase?

    e Compare and contrast the earnings per share and market price per share before and after the proposed stock repurchase.

    f Describe and discuss the differences, if any, in balance sheet entries resulting from the payment of cash dividends and the proposed stock repurchase. Be specific.

    g What recommendations and cautions might you offer Off Shore with respect to the proposed stock repurchase? Why?

SELECTED REFERENCES

Arditti, Fred D., Haim Levy, and Marshall Sarnat, "Taxes, Uncertainty, and Optimal Dividend Policy," *Financial Management* 5 (Spring 1976), pp. 46-53.

Black, Fischer, and Myron Scholes, "The Effects of Dividend Yield and Dividend Policy on Common Stock Prices and Returns," *Journal of Financial Economics* 1 (May 1974), pp. 1-22.

Brennan, Michael, "A Note on Dividend Irrelevance and the Gordon Valuation Model," *Journal of Finance 26* (December 1971), pp. 1115–1121.

Brigham, Eugene F., "The Profitability of a Firm's Repurchase of Its Own Common Stock," *California Management Review 7* (Winter 1964), pp. 69–75.

Brigham, Eugene F., and Myron J. Gordon, "Leverage, Dividend Policy, and the Cost of Capital," *Journal of Finance 23* (March 1968), pp. 85–104.

Elton, Edwin J., and Martin J. Gruber, "Marginal Stockholder Tax Rates and the Clientele Effect," *Review of Economics and Statistics 52* (February 1970), pp. 68–74.

———, "The Effect of Share Repurchases on the Value of the Firm," *Journal of Finance 23* (March 1968), pp. 135–150.

Fama, Eugene F., and Harvey Babiak, "Dividend Policy: An Empirical Analysis," *Journal of the American Statistical Association 63* (December 1968), pp. 1132–1161.

Finnerty, Joseph E., "Corporate Stock Issue and Repurchase," *Financial Management 4* (Autumn 1975), pp. 62–71.

Friend, Irwin, and Marshall Puckett, "Dividends and Stock Prices," *American Economic Review 54* (September 1964), pp. 656–682.

Gordon, Myron J., "Dividends, Earnings and Stock Prices," *Review of Economics and Statistics 41* (May 1959), pp. 99–105.

Higgins, Robert C., "The Corporate Dividend-Savings Decision," *Journal of Financial and Quantitative Analysis 7* (March 1972), pp. 1527–1541.

Johnson, Keith B., "Stock Splits and Price Changes," *Journal of Finance 21* (December 1966), pp. 675–686.

Keane, Simon M., "Dividends and the Resolution of Uncertainty," *Journal of Finance and Accounting 1* (Autumn 1974), pp. 389–393.

Krainer, Robert E., "A Pedagogic Note on Dividend Policy," *Journal of Financial and Quantitative Analysis 6* (September 1971), pp. 1147–1154.

Laub, P. Michael, and Ross Watts, "On the Informational Content of Dividends," *Journal of Business 49* (January 1976).

Lintner, John, "Distribution of Income of Corporations Among Dividends, Retained Earnings, and Taxes," *American Economic Review 46* (May 1956), pp. 97–113.

———, "Dividends, Earnings, Leverage, Stock Prices, and the Supply of Capital to Corporations," *Review of Economics and Statistics 44* (August 1962), pp. 243–269.

———, "Optimal Dividends and Corporate Growth Under Uncertainty," *Quarterly Journal of Economics 78* (February 1964), pp. 49–95.

Millar, James A., and Bruce D. Fielitz, "Stock Split and Stock Dividend Decisions," *Financial Management 2* (Winter 1973), pp. 35–45.

Miller, Merton H., and Franco Modigliani, "Dividend Policy, Growth and the Valuation of Shares," *Journal of Business 34* (October 1961), pp. 411–433.

Norgaard, Richard and Corine Norgaard, "A Critical Examination of Share Repurchase," *Financial Management 3* (Spring 1974), pp. 44–50.

Pettit, R. Richardson, "The Impact of Dividend and Earnings Announcements: A Reconciliation," *Journal of Business 49* (January 1976), pp. 86–96.

Smith, Keith V., "Increasing Stream Hypothesis of Corporate Dividend Policy," *California Management Review 14* (Fall 1971), pp. 56–64.

Stewart, Samuel S., Jr., "Should a Corporation Repurchase Its Own Stock?," *Journal of Finance 31* (June 1976), pp. 911–921.

Van Horne, James C., and John J. McDonald, "Dividend Policy and New Equity Financing," *Journal of Finance 26* (May 1971), pp. 507–519.

Walter, James E., "Dividend Policies and Common Stock Prices," *Journal of Finance 11* (March 1956), pp. 29–41.

———, *Dividend Policy and Enterprise Valuation* (Belmont, Calif.: Wadsworth, 1967).

———, "Dividend Policy: Its Influence on the Value of the Enterprise," *Journal of Finance 18* (May 1963), pp. 280–291.

Watts, Ross, "The Information Content of Dividends," *Journal of Business 46* (April 1973), pp. 191–211.

West, Richard R., and Harold Bierman, Jr., "Corporate Dividend Policy and Preemptive Security Issues," *Journal of Business 42* (January 1968), pp. 71–75.

West, Richard R., and Alan B. Brouilette, "Reverse Stock Splits," *Financial Executive 38* (January 1970), pp. 12–17.

Whittington, G., "The Profitability of Retained Earnings," *Review of Economics and Statistics 54* (May 1972), pp. 152–160.

Woods, Donald H., and Eugene F. Brigham, "Stockholder Distribution Decisions: Share Repurchase or Dividends," *Journal of Financial and Quantitative Analysis 1* (March 1966), pp. 15–28.

Wrightsman, Dwayne, and James O. Horrigan, "Retention, Risk of Success, and the Price of Stock," *Journal of Finance 30* (December 1975), pp. 1357–1359.

PART EIGHT

This part of the text is concerned with two areas of interest to the financial manager, who must make decisions with respect to the firm's future. The topics of consolidations, mergers, and holding companies are discussed in order to provide a basic understanding of the principles of these types of external expansion. Often, firms seeking either to obtain additional capacity, to diversify, or to use excess liquidity will find external growth a viable alternative. Another area in which the financial manager unfortunately may become involved is business failure and reorganization. An understanding of the key concepts related to failure and reorganization may be of benefit not only when the firm itself is failing, but also when a customer or creditor of the firm is failing. Chapter 25 discusses the common types of business combinations, motives for combining, and the procedures used. Chapter 26, the final chapter of the text, describes the key concepts and legal procedures related to business failures, reorganizations, and liquidations. Both chapters are primarily concerned with the firm's equity position.

Expansion
and failure

BALANCE SHEET	
Assets	**Liabilities and Stockholders' Equity**
Current Assets	Current Liabilities
Fixed Assets	Long-Term Debt
	Stockholders' Equity

CHAPTER 25
Consolidations, mergers, and holding companies

Often, for one or a number of motives, business firms find external expansion through a business combination a viable alternative. Typically, these firms wish to increase rapidly their productive capacity, their earnings, or the market price of their stock, or take advantage of certain liquidity benefits. The most common forms of business combination are consolidations, mergers, and holding companies. Consolidations and mergers are similar to each other, while the holding company arrangement is quite distinct. These business combinations differ not only with respect to the procedures involved, but also with respect to their objectives.

In this chapter, the primary emphasis will be on viewing business combinations from the standpoint of the acquiring firm, although some considerations on the part of the acquired firm will be highlighted. The chapter has three major sections. The first section presents certain fundamental information about the types of business combinations, motives for forming business combinations, and the relevant variables to be considered in contemplating combinations. The second section discusses certain aspects of consolidations and mergers, including the negotiations involved in completing a merger. The final section discusses holding companies by placing primary emphasis on their key advantages and disadvantages.

THE FUNDAMENTALS OF BUSINESS COMBINATIONS
Types of business combinations

The key forms of business combinations are *consolidations*, *mergers*, and *holding companies*. These arrangements have certain basic similarities and differences.

Consolidations. A *consolidation* involves the combination of two or more companies to form a completely new corporation. The new corporation normally absorbs the assets and liabilities of the companies from which it is formed. The old corporations merely cease to exist. Consolidations normally occur when the firms to be combined are of similar size. They are normally carried out by issuing to shareholders in the old firms a certain number (or fraction) of shares of stock in the new firm in exchange for each share of the old firm. The number of shares issued for each old share may differ depending on differences in the size of the firms to be consolidated.

Mergers.   A *merger* is quite similar to a consolidation except that, when one or more firms are merged, the resulting firm maintains the identity of one of the merger firms. Mergers are generally confined to combinations of two firms that are unequal in size; the identity of the larger of the two firms is normally maintained. Usually, the assets and liabilities of the smaller firm are consolidated into those of the larger firm. The merger may be used by a larger firm to obtain either the assets or the common stock of a smaller company. The larger firm pays for its acquisition either with cash or with preferred or common stock.

The similarity of consolidations and mergers should be clear at this point. There are two key differences between consolidations and mergers. One is that consolidations result in the creation of a new corporation, while in mergers one of the merged companies remains in existence. The second key difference is that in consolidations common stock is exchanged for common stock, while mergers may involve the exchange of cash or stock for the assets or common stock of the second party to the merger. Because of the great similarity between consolidations and mergers, the remainder of this chapter will not differentiate between these forms of combination. *The term "merger" will be used to refer to both consolidations and mergers.*

Holding companies.   A *holding company* is a corporation having a controlling interest in one or more other corporations. Having a controlling interest in large, widely held companies generally requires the ownership of between 10 and 25 percent of the outstanding stock. A holding company must own enough shares to have *voting* control of the firms it holds. The companies controlled by a holding company are normally referred to as *subsidiaries*. The reader should recall from the discussion of common stock voting in Chapter 22 that ownership of the majority of outstanding shares is not necessary in order to control a company. A holding company obtains control of a subsidiary by purchasing (generally for cash) a sufficient number of shares of its stock.

The holding company, as a form of business combination, differs significantly from consolidations and mergers. A holding company consists of a group of subsidiary firms, each operating as a separate corporate entity, while a consolidated or merged firm is a single corporation. The holding company arrangement permits a firm greater asset control per dollar than a consolidation or merger. This is because the holding company does not acquire the entire firm, whereas in consolidations and mergers the entire firms are acquired. Other key differences between these forms of business combination will be discussed later in the chapter.

Motives for business combinations

Firms combine through mergers or holding company arrangements in order to fulfill certain objectives. Although the maximization of owners' wealth is their long-run objective, firms may have one or more of a number of possible motives for combining with other firms. The more common motives for combination, which include growth, synergistic effects, fund raising, increased managerial skills, tax considerations, and increased ownership liquidity, are discussed in this section.

Growth. Companies desiring rapid growth either in *size* or in *the range of their products* may find that some form of business combination will fulfill this objective. Instead of going through the time-consuming process of internal growth, the firm may achieve the same growth objective in a short period of time by acquiring or combining with an existing firm. If a firm wishing to expand operations in existing or possibly new product areas can find a suitable combination partner, it may avoid many of the risks inherent in achieving the same objective through internal growth. The risks associated with the design, construction, and sale of new products or more products are eliminated if the firm can acquire a proven concern. Moreover, when a firm expands or extends its product line by acquiring another firm, it also removes a potential competitor.[1]

Mergers and holding companies may be used to achieve either horizontal, vertical, or conglomerate growth. Each of these types of growth is briefly described below.

Horizontal growth. Horizontal growth occurs when firms in the same line of business are combined. For example, the merger of two machine tool manufacturers is a form of horizontal growth. This type of growth allows the firm to expand its operations in an existing product line and at the same time eliminate a competitor. Certain economies result from this type of growth due to the elimination of certain staff and support functions in order to avoid duplication. For example, two vice presidents of finance or two purchasing agents may no longer be required. Economies are also expected to result through the purchase of merchandise in larger quantities and the elimination of duplicate sales channels. Often, a horizontal combination of firms increases sales by increasing the diversity of styles and sizes of the finished products. Horizontal growth is commonly referred to as *horizontal integration.*

Vertical growth. Vertical growth occurs when a firm grows by acquiring suppliers of its raw materials or purchasers of its finished products. If the firm is already the first element in the production process or if it sells to the ultimate consumer, then only forward or backward growth, whichever is ap-

---

[1]The reader may recognize that certain legal constraints on growth—especially where the elimination of competition is expected—exist. The various antitrust laws, which are closely enforced by the Federal Trade Commission, prohibit business combinations which eliminate competition, especially when the resulting enterprise would be a monopoly.

propriate, can occur. In other words, vertical growth involves expansion either backward toward the firm's suppliers or forward toward the ultimate consumer. The economic benefits of vertical growth, which is commonly referred to as *vertical integration,* stem from the firm's greater control over the acquisition of raw materials or the distribution of finished goods. A firm that is *totally integrated* controls the entire production process from the extraction of raw materials to the sale of finished goods. An example of vertical growth would be the merger of a machine tool manufacturer with a supplier of castings.

Conglomerate growth.   Conglomerate growth involves the combination of firms in unrelated businesses. This type of growth was quite popular in the late 1960s when, for example, Jimmy Ling built the LTV empire, which subsequently faced financial difficulties. This conglomerate consisted of firms as diverse as sporting goods companies and manufacturers of aircraft components. Since a conglomerate consists of firms in unrelated businesses, no real operating economies are expected from this type of growth. The key benefit of conglomerates lies in their ability to diversify risk by combining firms in a manner that provides a minimum risk and a maximum return. Conglomerate growth should be most attractive to firms having quite seasonal or cyclical patterns of earnings. Diversification is one way to stabilize their earnings. The theory of conglomerate diversification is drawn directly from the portfolio theory used for asset or security selection.[2]

Synergistic effects.   The synergistic effects of business combinations are certain economies of scale resulting from the firms' lower overhead. Synergistic effects are said to be present when a whole is greater than the sum of the parts, or 1 and 1 equals 3. The economies of scale that generally result from the combination of business firms lowers their combined overhead, thereby increasing their earnings to a level greater than the sum of their earnings as independent firms. Synergistic effects are most obvious when firms grow horizontally, since many redundant functions and employees can be eliminated. Staff functions such as purchasing and sales are probably most greatly affected by this type of combination.

Synergistic effects also result when firms are combined vertically, since certain administrative functions can be eliminated. For example, two presidents making $60,000 per year may not be required; the elimination of one of these salaries will provide a considerable savings. Conglomerate growth also results in some slight synergistic effects, especially in the area of fund raising.

Fund raising.   Often firms combine in order to enhance their fund-raising ability. A firm may be unable to obtain funds for internal expansion, but able to obtain funds for external business combinations. Quite often,

---

[2]A brief discussion of the key concepts underlying the portfolio-type approach to the diversification of risk was presented in Chapter 16.

especially in the case of conglomerates, a firm may combine with a firm having high liquid assets and low levels of liabilities. The acquisition of this type of "cash-rich" company immediately increases the firm's borrowing power and decreases its financial riskiness. This should enable it to raise funds externally at more favorable rates. Both mergers and holding company arrangements may enhance the firm's fund-raising ability when it combines with a low-leverage–high-liquidity firm.

Increased managerial skills. Occasionally a firm will become involved in a business combination in order to obtain certain key management personnel. A firm may have quite a bit of potential that it finds itself unable to develop fully due to deficiencies in certain areas of management. If the firm cannot hire the management it needs, it may find combination with a compatible firm having the needed managerial personnel a viable solution. Of course, any combination, regardless of the specific motive for it, should contribute to the long-run maximization of the owners' wealth. Combination with a firm having a competent manager but possessing a poor financial record is certainly not recommended.

Tax considerations. Quite often, especially in the case of conglomerate mergers, tax considerations are a key motive. Generally the tax benefit stems from the fact that one of the firms has a tax-loss carryforward, which can be applied against future income for up to seven years.[3] Two situations could actually exist. A company with a tax-loss carryforward could acquire a profitable company in order to utilize the tax-loss carryforward. In this case, the acquiring firm would boost the combination's earnings by reducing the taxable income of the acquired firm. If the profitable firm had not been acquired, the tax-loss carryforward might not have been used. A tax-loss carryforward may also be useful when a profitable firm acquires a firm having such a carryforward. In either of these two situations, however, the merger must be justified not only on the basis of the tax benefits, but also on the basis of future operating benefits or on grounds consistent with the goal of long-run maximization of the owners' wealth. Moreover, the tax benefits described are useful only in mergers—not in the formation of holding companies—since only in the case of mergers are the operating results reported on a consolidated basis. An example will clarify the use of the tax-loss carryforward.

EXAMPLE
The Perkins Company has a total of $450,000 in tax-loss carryforwards resulting from operating tax losses of $150,000 a year in each of the past three years. In order to use these losses and diversify its operations, the C. B. Company has acquired Perkins Company through a merger. C. B. expects to have *earnings before taxes* of $300,000 per year. Assuming these earnings are realized, the Perkins portion of the merged

---

[3]A seven-year carryforward is permitted on operating losses, while capital losses can only be carried forward five years. A detailed discussion of tax-loss carrybacks and carryforwards was presented in Chapter 2. The reader should review this material if greater clarification is required.

firm just breaks even, and C. B. is in the 40-percent tax bracket, the total taxes paid by the two firms without and with the merger are calculated.

Total taxes without merger			
	Year		
	1	2	3
Profits before taxes	$300,000	$300,000	$300,000
Taxes (.40)	$120,000	$120,000	$120,000

Total taxes with merger			
	Year		
	1	2	3
Profits before taxes	$300,000	$300,000	$300,000
Less: Tax-loss carryforward	300,000	150,000	0
Taxable income	$ 0	$150,000	$300,000
Taxes (.40)	$ 0	$ 60,000	$120,000

With the merger, the total tax payments are less. The combination is able to deduct the tax-loss carryforward until either seven years have elapsed since the loss or the total tax losses have been exhausted, which happens at the end of year 2. The tax advantages resulting from a merger of, or with, a company with a tax-loss carryforward should be clear from this example. ●

Increased ownership liquidity. In the case of mergers, the combination of a small and a larger firm, or two small firms, into a larger corporation may provide the owners of the small firm(s) with greater liquidity. This is because of the higher marketability associated with the shares of larger firms. Instead of holding shares in a small firm having a very "thin" market, the owners will receive shares that are traded in a broader market and can be liquidated more readily. Not only does the ability to convert shares into cash quickly have appeal, but owning shares for which market price quotations are readily available provides owners with a better feel for the value of their holdings. Especially in the case of small, closely held firms, the increase in the liquidity of shares obtainable through a merger with an acceptable firm may have considerable appeal.

Relevant variables

In evaluating possible business combinations, the financial manager must consider not only the goals mentioned in the preceding section as motives for combinations, but also the primary goal of the firm—to maximize the wealth of its owners over the long run. If achieving one or more of the goals mentioned above will contribute to the achievement of this primary goal, the business combination should be made. In order to forecast the effects of a proposed combination on the firm's future financial performance, the financial manager must quantitatively evaluate certain key financial variables. The primary variables of concern are earnings per share, dividends per share, the market price of shares, the book value of shares, and financial leverage. As the discussion of capital structure and valuation in Chapter 18 stressed, each of these variables is related to the valuation of corporate shares.

Earnings per share.   The effects of a merger on earnings per share must be forecast and evaluated by the financial manager in order to determine the desirability of the proposed combination. Normally, the financial manager is looking for a reduction in the variability of earnings per share or some type of long-run increase in per-share earnings that will increase the market value of the firm's shares.

Dividends per share.   The financial manager must also be concerned with the dividends per share to be paid after the combination. He or she must recognize and consider the importance of a suitable dividend policy. At the least, the precombination dividend will have to be maintained to stabilize the market price of the firm's shares.

The market price of shares.   The market price per share of the merged firm is the key variable that the financial manager attempts to maximize in selecting a suitable merger partner. The resulting earnings and dividends will directly affect the market price of the firm's shares. Only if the market price of shares in the combined enterprise increases over the long run will the firm's overall objective of owner's wealth maximization be achieved. The value of the owners' holdings is most easily measured by the market price of their stock.

The book value of shares.   In certain situations, firms are acquired for fund-raising purposes. In these types of combinations the amount paid for the stock of the acquired firm must be considered in light of the book value of the firm, since the firm is not being acquired for its earnings potential, but for its favorable financial and asset structure. Since the book value of firms does not directly reflect their valuation, it is not a key variable in the analysis of prospective acquisitions.

Financial leverage.   The effects of a proposed merger on the financial leverage or structure of the resulting enterprise is of key importance in the valuation process. Investors in a firm's shares determine their value by discounting expected dividends at a rate highly dependent on the riskiness of the firm. If the firm becomes more highly levered as the result of a merger, its expected earnings and dividends will be discounted by investors at a higher rate. The net effect will be to lower the value of the owners' holdings if earnings are not expected to increase sufficiently to offset the increased financial risk associated with the firm. Of course, it is possible that an increase in earnings will be sufficient to compensate for the increased financial risk, thereby causing the market value of the firm to increase. Valuation and financial risk were discussed in Chapter 18.

Although the factors described above are not equally easy to measure or predict, the financial manager must attempt to quantify and forecast them in order to get a better feel for the long-run effects of a proposed business combination on the owners' wealth as measured in the marketplace. His or her primary concern should be the effect on earnings and the market price of the firm's shares; dividends, book values, and financial leverage considerations are of lesser importance.

ANALYZING PROSPECTIVE MERGERS

This portion of the chapter is devoted to the various analytical decision-making techniques commonly used in evaluating and negotiating mergers. As indicated earlier, the term *merger* is used here to mean both mergers and consolidations. As the preceding section pointed out, the two key variables of concern are earnings per share and market price per share. An important ratio in analyzing prospective mergers is the *price-earnings (P/E) ratio.*

The key topics in this section are cash purchases of companies, stock exchange acquisitions, and the negotiation of mergers.

Cash purchases of companies

When a firm is acquiring another firm for cash (debt is assumed to be the same as cash here), the use of simple capital budgeting procedures is required. Regardless of whether the firm is being acquired for its assets or as a going concern, the basic approach is quite similar.

Acquisitions of assets.

In some instances a firm is acquired not for its income-earning potential, but as a conglomeration of assets (generally fixed assets) needed by the acquiring firm. The cash price paid for this type of acquisition depends largely on which assets are being acquired. If the entire firm is acquired, the liquidation value of the firm is a reasonable price; if only certain key assets are purchased, no more than the market value of these assets should be paid. If the entire firm is purchased as a nongoing concern, consideration must also be given to the value of any tax losses.

In order to determine whether the purchase of assets is financially justifiable, the firm must estimate both the costs and the benefits of the assets. This, in effect, is the classic capital budgeting problem. A cash outlay is made to acquire assets and, as a result of their acquisition, certain future cash benefits are expected.

EXAMPLE

The VW Company is interested in acquiring certain fixed assets of the Bug Manufacturing Company. Bug, which has had some losses over the past five years, is interested in selling out; but it wishes to sell out entirely, not just to get rid of certain fixed assets. A condensed balance sheet for the Bug Company is given below.

Assets		Liabilities and stockholders' equity	
Cash	$ 2,000		
Marketable securities	0	Total liabilities	$ 80,000
Accounts receivable	8,000	Stockholders' equity	120,000
Inventory	10,000	Total Liabilities	
Machine A	10,000	and Stockholders'	
Machine B	30,000	Equity	$200,000
Machine C	25,000		
Land and buildings	115,000		
Total Assets	$200,000		

VW Company needs only machines B and C and the land and buildings. However, it has made some inquiries and has arranged to sell the accounts receivable, inventory, and machine A for $23,000. Since there is also $2000 in cash, VW will get $25,000 for the excess assets. Bug wants $20,000 for the entire company, which means that VW will have to pay the firm's creditors $80,000 and its owners $20,000. The actual outlay required by VW after liquidating the unneeded assets will be $75,000 [($80,000 + $20,000) − $25,000]. In other words, in order to obtain the use of the desired assets (machines B and C and the land and buildings) and the benefits of Bug's tax losses, VW must pay $75,000. The *after-tax cash inflows* expected to result from the new equipment and tax losses are $14,000 per year for the next five years and $12,000 per year for the following five years. The desirability of this acquisition can be determined by calculating the net present value of this outlay using the VW Company's 9-percent cost of capital, as shown in Table 25.1.

TABLE 25.1 An analysis of the Bug Company acquisition by the VW Company

Years	Cash flow (1)	P.V. factor @ 9% (2)	Present value (1) · (2) (3)
0	($75,000)	1.000[a]	$(75,000)
1–5	14,000	3.890[b]	54,460
6	12,000	0.596[a]	7,152
7	12,000	0.547[a]	6,564
8	12,000	0.502[a]	6,024
9	12,000	0.460[a]	5,520
10	12,000	0.422[a]	5,064
		Net Present Value	$ 9,784

[a]The present-value interest factors, PVIF, for $1 discounted at 9 percent for the corresponding years obtained from Table A-3.

[b]The present-value interest factor for an annuity, PVIFA, with a five-year life discounted at 9 percent obtained from Table A-4.

Since the net present value of $9784 is greater than zero, VW should find acquisition of the Bug Company an acceptable investment. Of course, if VW has alternate ways of obtaining similar assets or must ration its capital, the acquisition may not be made. The importance of capital budgeting techniques in evaluating cash acquisitions of assets should be clear from this example. As long as the firm makes acquisitions having positive net present values, the market value of the firm should be enhanced. ●

Acquisitions of going concerns.   Cash acquisitions of going concerns are best analyzed using capital budgeting techniques like that described for asset acquisitions. The basic difficulty in applying the capital budgeting approach to the cash acquisition of a going concern is in the *estimation of cash flows* and certain *risk considerations that may result from the changed financial structure*. The methods of estimating the cash flows expected from an acquisition are no different than the methods used in estimating cash flows in any capital budgeting decision. Prudent forecasting, along with the use of probability techniques, may be required.

If a firm acquires a company having a considerably different financial structure than itself, the effects of the new financial structure on the firm's overall cost of capital must be estimated. As the discussion of capital structure in Chapter 18 showed, a shift in its capital structure may affect the firm's overall financial risk, thereby causing a change in its overall cost of capital. Only when a firm acquires another firm having the same financial structure is its cost of capital expected to remain fixed. Therefore, whenever a firm considers acquiring for cash another firm having a different capital structure, it should adjust the cost of capital appropriately prior to applying capital budgeting techniques. An example will clarify the application of capital budgeting techniques when the cash acquisition of a going concern is being considered.

EXAMPLE

The Stockade Company is contemplating the acquisition of the Wall Company, which can be purchased for $60,000 in cash. Stockade currently has a high degree of leverage, which is reflected in its 13-percent cost of capital. Because of the low leverage of the Wall Company, Stockade estimates its overall cost of capital will drop to 10 percent after the acquisition. Since the effect of the less risky capital structure resulting from the acquisition of Wall Company cannot be reflected in the expected cash benefits, the post-acquisition cost of capital (i.e., 10 percent) must be used to evaluate the cash flows expected from the acquisition. The incremental cash inflows expected from the proposed acquisition are expected over a 30-year time horizon. These estimated cash inflows are $5000 for years 1 through 10, $13,000 for years 11 through 18, and $4000 for years 19 through 30. The net present value of the acquisition is calculated in Table 25.2.

Since the net present value of the acquisition is greater than zero ($2357), the acquisition is acceptable. It is interesting to note that had the effect of the changed capital structure on the cost of capital not been considered, the acquisition would have been found unacceptable since the net present value at a 13-percent cost of capital is −$11,864, which is less than zero. ●

**TABLE 25.2 An analysis of the
Wall Company acquisition by the Stockade Company**

Years	Cash flow (1)	P.V. factor @ 10%[a] (2)	Present value (1) · (2) (3)
0	($60,000)	1.000	($60,000)
1–10	5,000	6.145	30,725
11–18	13,000	$(8.201 - 6.145)^b$	26,728
19–30	4,000	$(9.427 - 8.201)^b$	4,904
		Net Present Value	$ 2,357

[a]Present-value interest factors for annuities, obtained from Table A-4.

[b]These factors are found using a shortcut technique that can be applied to annuities for periods of years beginning at some point in the future. By finding the appropriate factor for the present value of an annuity given for the last year of the annuity and subtracting the present value of an annuity factor for the year immediately preceding the beginning of the annuity, the appropriate interest factor for the present value of an annuity beginning sometime in the future can be obtained. The interested reader can check this shortcut by using the long approach and comparing the results.

Stock exchange acquisitions

Quite often a firm is acquired through the exchange of common stock. The acquiring firm will exchange its shares for shares of the firm being acquired according to a predetermined ratio. The *ratio of exchange* of shares is determined in the merger negotiations. This ratio is quite important because it affects the various financial yardsticks that are used by existing and prospective shareholders in valuing the merged firm's shares. This section discusses the ratio of exchange and its effect on key financial variables.

The ratio of exchange. When a firm trades its stock for the shares of another firm, the number of shares of the acquiring firm to be exchanged for each share of the acquired firm must be determined. The first requirement, of course, is that the acquiring company have sufficient authorized and unissued and (or) treasury stock available to complete the transaction. Often the repurchase of shares, which was discussed in Chapter 24, is necessary in order to obtain sufficient shares for the transaction. Since the acquiring firm is *generally* larger and has a market for its shares, while the smaller acquired firm may have closely held shares, the acquiring firm offers a certain amount for each share of the acquired firm. This amount is generally greater than the current market price of publicly traded shares. Because of the difficulty of placing a value on and explaining the results of acquisitions of closely held firms, the discussion in this section assumes that the acquired firm's shares are publicly traded. *The actual ratio of exchange is merely the ratio of the amount paid per share of the acquired firm to the market price of the ac-*

quiring firm's shares. It is calculated in this manner since the acquiring firm pays the acquired firm in stock, which has a value equal to its market price. An example will clarify the calculation of the ratio of exchange.

EXAMPLE

The Huge Company, whose stock is currently selling for $80 per share, is interested in acquiring the Tiny Company in order to integrate its operation vertically. To prepare for the acquisition, Huge has been repurchasing its shares over the past three years. Tiny's stock is currently selling for $50 per share, but in the merger negotiations, Huge has found it necessary to offer $56 per share for it. Since Huge does not have sufficient financial resources to purchase the firm for cash, nor does it wish to raise these funds, Tiny has agreed to accept Huge's stock in exchange for its shares. Since Huge's stock currently sells for $80 per share, and it must pay $56 per share for Tiny's stock, the ratio of exchange is .7 ($56 ÷ $80). This means that the Huge Company must give .7 shares of its stock for each share of Tiny's stock. ●

The effect of the ratio of exchange on key financial variables. Owners of both the acquiring and acquired firm are concerned with the effect of the acquisition on certain financial variables. The *key* focus is on the resulting earnings and market price per share, but attention is sometimes given to dividends per share, book value per share, and the operating and financial riskiness of the merged company. Each of these financial variables will be briefly discussed in this section. The effect of the ratio of exchange on these variables will be illustrated by a simple example.

The effect on earnings per share. The earnings per share of the firm are likely to change as a result of a merger. Generally the resulting earnings per share differ from the premerger earnings per share for both the acquiring and the acquired firm. They depend largely on the ratio of exchange and the premerger earnings of each firm. It is best to view the initial and long-run effects of the ratio of exchange on earnings per share (eps) separately.

The initial effect. When the ratio of exchange is equal to 1 and both the acquiring and the acquired firm have the same premerger earnings per share, the merged firm's earnings per share will initially remain constant. In this rare instance, both the acquiring and the acquired firms would have equal price-earnings ratios. In actuality, the earnings per share of the merged firm are generally above the premerger earnings per share of one firm and below the premerger earnings per share of the other firm, after making the necessary adjustment for the ratio of exchange. These differences can be illustrated by a simple example.

EXAMPLE

The Huge Company is contemplating acquiring the Tiny Company by exchanging .7 shares of its stock for each share of Tiny's stock. The current financial data related to the earnings and market price for each of these companies are given in Table 25.3. Although Tiny's stock currently has a market price of $50 per share, Huge has offered it $56 per share. As we saw in the preceding example, this results in a ratio of exchange of .7.

TABLE 25.3 Huge Company and Tiny Company financial data

Item	Huge Company	Tiny Company
Earnings available for common	$500,000	$100,000
Number of shares of common outstanding	125,000	20,000
Earnings per share	$4	$5
Market price per share	$80	$50
Price-earnings ratio	20	10

In order to complete the merger and retire the 20,000 shares of Tiny Company stock outstanding, Huge will have to issue and (or) use treasury stock totaling 14,000 shares (.70 · 20,000 shares). Once the merger is completed, Huge will have 139,000 shares of common stock (125,000 + 14,000) outstanding. If the earnings of each of the firms remain constant, the merged company will be expected to have earnings available for the common stockholders of $600,000 ($500,000 + $100,000). The earnings per share of the merged company should therefore equal approximately $4.32 per share ($600,000 ÷ 139,000 shares). At first, it would appear that the Tiny Company's shareholders have sustained a decrease in per-share earnings (from $5 to $4.32); but, since each share of the Tiny Company's original stock is equivalent to .7 shares of the merged company, the equivalent earnings per share are $3.02 ($4.32 · .70). In other words, as a result of the merger, the Huge Company's original shareholders experience an increase in earnings per share from $4 to $4.32 at the expense of the Tiny Company's shareholders, whose earnings per share drop from $5 to $3.02. These results are summarized in Table 25.4.

TABLE 25.4 A summary of the effects on earnings per share of a merger between the Huge Company and the Tiny Company at $56 per share

Stockholders	Earnings per share	
	Before merger	After merger
Huge Company	$4.00	$4.32
Tiny Company	5.00	3.02[a]

[a]Based on .70 of the Huge Company's earnings per share.

The easiest way to explain the increased eps for the original Huge Company shareholders and the decreased eps for the original Tiny Company shareholders is to compare the price-earnings ratio of the original company to that based on the price paid for the acquired company. The possible outcomes are presented in Table 25.5. The usefulness of the relationships in Table 25.5 can be illustrated by comparing the P/E ratios associated with the Huge-Tiny merger. The Huge Company's P/E ratio is

TABLE 25.5 The effect of P/E ratios on earnings per share

	Effect on eps	
Relationship between P/E paid and P/E of acquiring company	Acquiring company	Acquired company
P/E paid > P/E of acquiring company	Decrease	Increase
P/E paid = P/E of acquiring company	Constant	Constant
P/E paid < P/E of acquiring company	Increase	Decrease

20, while the P/E ratio based on the share price paid the Tiny Company was 11.2 ($56 ÷ $5). Since the P/E based on the share price paid for the Tiny Company was less than the P/E of the Huge Company (11.2 vs. 20), the effect was to increase the eps for original holders of shares in the Huge Company (from $4.00 to $4.32) and to decrease the effective eps to original holders of shares in the Tiny Company (from $5.00 to $3.02).

TABLE 25.6 A summary of the effects on earnings per share of a merger between the Huge Company and the Tiny Company at $110 per share

	Earnings per share	
Stockholders	Before merger	After merger
Huge Company	$4.00	$3.93[a]
Tiny Company	5.00	5.40[b]

[a] $\dfrac{\$500{,}000 + \$100{,}000}{(1.375 \cdot 20{,}000) + 125{,}000} = \$3.93$

[b] $\$3.93 \cdot 1.375 = \$5.40$

Had Huge paid the Tiny Company $110 per share, which would result in a ratio of exchange of 1.375 ($110 ÷ $80), the effects on eps would be as shown in Table 25.6. The original holders of Huge Company stock would experience a drop in eps (from $4.00 to $3.93), while the original holders of Tiny Company's stock would experience an increase in eps (from $5.00 to $5.40). This is because the P/E ratio based on the share price paid for Tiny's stock was 22 ($110 ÷ 5), while the P/E of Huge Company stock was 20. As indicated in Table 25.5, whenever the P/E ratio based on the share price paid is greater than the P/E of the acquiring company, the earnings per share of the original owners of the acquring company will decrease while the effective eps of the original holders of the acquired company increases. ●

The long-run effect. The long-run effect of a merger on the earnings per share of the merged company depends largely on whether the earnings of the merged firm grow. It is generally expected that the earnings of either or both of the component firms will grow. Especially when mergers to achieve horizontal or vertical integration are made, increases in earnings are likely. Combining the two firms may make it possible for the sum of their earnings to exceed the total earnings of the firms when viewed separately. Often, although a decrease in the per-share earnings of the stock held by original owners of the acquiring firm is expected initially, the long-run effects of the merger on earnings per share are quite favorable.

Since growth in earnings is generally expected by a business firm, the key factor enabling the acquiring company, which initially experiences a decrease in eps, to experience higher future eps than it would have without the merger is the fact that the earnings of the acquired company grow at a faster rate than those of the acquiring company. An example will clarify this point.

EXAMPLE

In 1978, the Huge Company acquired the Tiny Company by exchanging 1.375 shares of its common stock for each share of the Tiny Company. Other key financial data and the effects of this exchange ratio were discussed in the preceding example. The total earnings of the Huge Company are expected to grow at an annual rate of 3 percent without the merger, while the Tiny Company's earnings are expected to grow at a 7 percent annual rate without the merger. No synergistic effects are expected from the merger, and the same growth rates are expected to apply to the component earnings streams with the merger. Table 25.7 shows the future effects on the eps for the Huge Company without and with the proposed Tiny Company merger, based on these growth rates.

TABLE 25.7 The effects of earnings growth on eps for the Huge Company without and with the Tiny Company merger

Year	Without merger		With merger	
	Total earnings[a]	Earnings per share[b]	Total earnings[c]	Earnings per share[d]
1978	$500,000	$4.00	$600,000	$3.93
1979	515,000	4.12	622,000	4.08
1980	530,450	4.24	644,940	4.23
1981	546,364	4.37	668,868	4.39
1982	562,755	4.50	693,835	4.55
1983	579,638	4.64	719,893	4.72

[a]Based on a 3-percent compound growth rate.
[b]Based on 125,000 shares outstanding.
[c]Based on a 3-percent growth in the Huge Company's earnings and a 7-percent growth in the Tiny Company's earnings.
[d]Based on 152,500 shares outstanding (i.e, (1.375 · 20,000 shares) + 125,000 shares).

Table 25.7 indicates that the earnings per share without the merger will be greater than the eps with the merger for the years 1978 through 1980; after 1980, the eps will increase above what they would have been without the merger as a result of

FIGURE 25.1 Future eps without and with the Huge-Tiny merger

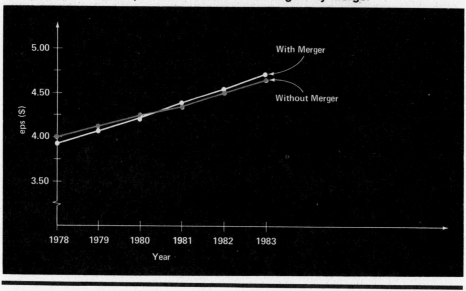

the faster earnings growth rate of the Tiny Company (7 percent vs. 3 percent). Although a few years are required for this difference in the growth rate of earnings to pay off, it can be seen that in the future the Huge Company will receive a payoff from merging with the Tiny Company at a 1.375 ratio of exchange. The relationships in Table 25.7 are graphed in Figure 25.1. The long-run advantage of the merger is clearly depicted by this graph. ●

The type of analysis in the preceding example should provide the financial manager with useful information for making the merger decision. The presence of synergistic effects or differential growth rates of earnings may suggest that, even though the initial effect of the merger will be to lower eps, the long-run effect may be an increase in eps. Since the financial manager must view the firm as a going concern attempting to maximize its shareholders' wealth, a long-run view is necessary. The use of various assumptions to test the sensitivity of the long-run effects of a proposed merger should reduce the uncertainty associated with the merger decision.

The market price per share. The market price per share does not necessarily remain constant after an acquisition; rather, adjustments take place in the marketplace in response to changes in expected earnings, the dilution of ownership, changes in operating and financial risk, and certain other financial and managerial changes. Using the ratio of exchange discussed in the preceding section, a *ratio of exchange in market price* can be calculated. This ratio, the MPR, is defined by Equation 25.1:

$$MPR = \frac{MP_{acquiring} \cdot RE}{MP_{acquired}}$$

(25.1)

where

MPR = market price ratio of exchange
MP_i = the market price for firm i
i = the acquiring or acquired firm
RE = the ratio of exchange

A simple example can be used to illustrate the calculation of this ratio.

EXAMPLE
In the Huge-Tiny Company example used earlier, the market price of the Huge Company's stock was $80 and that of the Tiny Company's stock was $50. The ratio of exchange was 1.375. Substituting these values into Equation 25.1 yields a market price ratio of exchange of 2.2 [($80 · 1.375) ÷ $50]. This means that $2.20 of the market price of the Huge Company is given for every $1.00 of the market price of the Tiny Company. ●

The ratio of exchange of market prices is normally greater than one, which indicates that in order to acquire a firm a premium over its market price must be paid. It would be unusual for a firm to acquire another firm by paying less than the firm's market price per share. Even so, however, the original owners of the acquiring firm may still gain because of differences in the two firms' price-earnings ratios. If a firm with a high P/E ratio acquires a firm with a low P/E ratio and the merged company maintains the higher P/E ratio, a rise in the market price of its shares may result. This can be illustrated by a simple example.

EXAMPLE
The Huge Company and Tiny Company financial data in Table 25.3 can be used to explain the market price effects of a merger. If we assume that the ratio of exchange between the two stocks was .7, which means that $56 of the Huge Company's stock was given for each share of the Tiny Company's stock, substituting into Equation 25.1 gives us a ratio of exchange of market prices of 1.12 [($80 · .70) ÷ $50]. If the earnings of the merged companies remain at the premerger levels, and if the stock of the merged companies sells at the Huge Company's premerger multiple of 20 times earnings, the values in Table 25.8 can be expected. Not only will the original company have higher earnings per share, but the market price of its shares will increase. ●

TABLE 25.8 Postmerger market price of the Huge Company using a .7 ratio of exchange and a P/E ratio of 20

Item	Merged company
Earnings available for common	$600,000
Number of shares of common outstanding	139,000
Earnings per share	$4.32
Price-earnings ratio	20
Expected market price per share (20 · $4.32)	$86.40

Although the kind of behavior exhibited in the preceding example is not unusual, the financial manager must recognize that only with proper management of the merged enterprise will he or she be able to sustain its market value. Part of the boost in market price can justifiably be attributed to the fact that the acquired firm's stock may have been selling at a low P/E due to the thin market in which it was traded.[4] If the merged firm cannot achieve sufficiently high earnings while maintaining its current risk configuration, there is no guarantee that its market price will reach or maintain the forecast value. Nevertheless, a policy of acquiring firms with low P/E's can produce quite favorable results for the owners of the acquiring firm. Acquisitions are especially attractive when the acquiring firm's stock price is high since fewer shares must be exchanged to acquire a given firm.

Dividends per share. The dividend per share does not normally enter into the merger decision since the payment of dividends is a discretionary decision based on numerous firm and market factors. The primary concern of the acquiring firm is earnings per share, since earnings are believed to be a prerequisite to the payment of dividends. Once an acquisition has been consummated, the dividend decision must be made; but this decision is not a prerequisite to acquisitions.

The book value per share. The book value per share, like the dividend per share, is irrelevant when a firm is acquiring a going concern. If the firm being acquired is being obtained only for its assets, then the book value per share may be helpful in determining the purchase price per share. When this type of acquisition is made, there is a great deal of concern about the liquidity in the form of working capital provided by the acquired firm. In this case, both the book value per share and the *working capital per share* are relevant. The post-merger book value depends to some extent on the accounting procedures used in consolidating the firm's statements. Explanation of the accounting techniques used in mergers can be found in most intermediate accounting texts.

The operating and financial risk. The operating and financial risk resulting from a merger must be considered in analyzing a merger candidate. Generally operating risk, which reflects the stability of sales, is considered in making the initial merger inquiry. Since the nature of the business being acquired is studied by the acquiring firm, the operating risk is implicitly considered. The financial risk, which depends on the firm's financial structure, must normally be evaluated through a study of the post-merger financial structure. Occasionally, a desire to change the firm's financial risk is the primary motive for a merger. An accurate estimation of the changes in risk is important because of its effect on the post-merger market valuation of the

---

[4]A *thin market* exists when a firm's stock is not actively traded due to the small number of owners or the small size of the enterprise. The stocks of such firms are usually traded over the counter and, as a result of their relative inactivity, the price at which they are traded may not reflect their true value or potential.

firm's shares. If the combined risk (operating and financial) increases as a result of a merger, investors will discount the firm's earnings at a higher rate, thereby lowering its market price. The increased market price will be reflected in a lower P/E ratio. If the combined risk decreases, an increase in the market price of the firm's shares and its P/E ratio can be expected. An awareness of these effects is important in forecasting the post-merger market price per share. Failure to recognize these effects could result in an incorrect merger decision.

The merger negotiation process

A merger can normally be initiated in either of two ways. When the management of an acquiring firm has found a suitable merger candidate, it can negotiate either with the firm's management or directly with its stockholders. Typically, negotiation with the management is preferred, although if such negotiations fall through the acquiring firm may make a direct appeal to the other firm's shareholders through tender offers.

Management negotiations. The acquiring firm must make an offer based on a certain exchange ratio in order to initiate the merger negotiation process. The merger candidate must then review the offer and, in light of alternate offers, agree or disagree with the terms offered. A desirable merger candidate normally receives more than a single offer. Normally, certain nonfinancial questions must be answered in the negotiations. These usually relate to the disposition and compensation of the existing management, product line policies, financing policies, and the autonomy of the acquired firm.

The key factor will be largely the price per share offered, which is reflected by the ratio of exchange. If the acquired firm is offered a good premium over its market price along with certain other guarantees, the merger may be consummated. Occasionally there are lengthy negotiations in which the merger candidate plays one offer against another in order to obtain the best possible terms. Although the merger negotiations are generally based on the expectation of a merger, sometimes the negotiations will break down. Both parties must agree to the various financial and nonfinancial terms prior to merging.

Occasionally, in order to satisfy the management of the acquired firm, certain *contingent payments* are built into the merger contract. In a cash transaction, *stock purchase warrants* may be given to the management of a closely held company which is to be operated by its management[5] as a subsidiary. The warrants may be exercisable once the market price of the acquiring firm reaches a certain level; more commonly, however, they are tied somehow to the earnings of the subsidiary. The terms of this type of warrant generally state that if the subsidiary's accumulated earnings exceed a specified amount within a certain period of time, the management will be paid a certain percentage of earnings or will receive or be able to purchase at a prespecified price a certain number of shares of the firm's stock. The level of

---

[5]Stock purchase warrants were described in detail in Chapter 23. The reader should review this material if greater clarification is desired.

performance necessary to receive the contingency payment may be geared to average annual earnings or some other financial value. The contingency payments in a stock exchange transaction are quite similar except that there is a greater likelihood that the payment will be made in stock instead of cash.

The use of contingency payments as a *sweetener* to stimulate the existing management of the acquired company to operate the firm, once it has been acquired, in a manner that will benefit the merged company is an attractive feature from both the acquiring and the acquired firm's viewpoint. Sometimes a contingency payment is included as an undefined portion of the initial purchase price; in other cases it is used merely as an incentive for the subsidiary's management, which has been paid in full for the acquisition, to operate the firm efficiently and in the best interests of all. Here the contingency payment represents a type of profit-sharing for the subsidiary management. When these types of payments are included, the acquiring firm in effect is providing a financial incentive to the management of the subsidiary to operate the subsidiary successfully.

Tender offers. When management negotiations for an acquisition break down, tender offers may be used in an attempt to negotiate a merger directly with the firm's stockholders. As we saw in Chapter 24, a tender offer is made at a premium above the market price and is offered to all the stockholders of the firm. The stockholders are advised of the offer either through announcements in financial newspapers or through direct communications from the offering firm. Sometimes a tender offer is made in order to add pressure to existing merger negotiations; in other cases the tender offer may be made without warning to catch the management off guard.

If the management is not desirous of a merger or believes that the premium in a projected tender offer is too low, it is likely to take certain defensive actions in order to ward off the tender offer. Common strategies include declaring an attractive dividend, informing stockholders of alleged damaging effects of being taken over, or attempting to sue the acquiring firm on even the slightest point of law. These actions may deter or delay a tender offer. Deterring the tender offer by filing suit gives the management that is fearful of a takeover time to find and negotiate a merger with a firm they would prefer to be acquired by. It is the management's responsibility to make sure that any action it takes is consistent with the firm's overall objective of long-run owner's wealth maximization.

HOLDING COMPANIES

A *holding company* is a company that has voting control of one or more other companies. In order to have this voting control, the holding company may need to own only a small percentage of the outstanding shares. The number of shares required depends on the dispersion of ownership of the company. In the case of companies with a relatively small number of shareholders, as much as 30 to 40 percent of the stock may be required; in the case of firms having a widely dispersed ownership, 10 to 20 percent of the shares may be sufficient to gain voting control. A holding company desirous of obtaining voting control of a firm may use either direct market purchases or tender offers to obtain needed shares.

Advantages of holding companies

The key advantages of the holding company arrangement are the leverage effect, protection from risk, legal benefits, and the fact that control can be obtained without negotiations.

The leverage effect. A holding company arrangement permits a firm to control a large amount of assets with a relatively small dollar investment. In other words, the owners of a holding company can *control* significantly larger amounts of assets than they could acquire through mergers. A simple example may help illustrate the leverage effect.

EXAMPLE

The Moses Company currently holds voting control of two subsidiaries—Company X and Company Y. The balance sheets for the Moses Company and its two subsidiaries are presented in Table 25.9. It owns approximately 17 percent ($10 ÷ $60) of Company X and 20 percent ($14 ÷ $70) of Company Y. It is assumed that these holdings are sufficient for voting control.

**TABLE 25.9 Balance sheets for
the Moses Company and its subsidiaries**

Moses Company			
Assets		Liabilities and stockholders' equity	
Common stock holdings		Long-term debt	$ 6
Company X	$10	Preferred stock	6
Company Y	14	Common stock equity	12
Total	$24	Total	$24

Company X			
Current assets	$ 30	Current liabilities	$ 15
Fixed assets	70	Long-term debt	25
Total	$100	Common stock equity	60
		Total	$100

Company Y			
Current assets	$ 20	Current liabilities	$ 10
Fixed assets	140	Long-term debt	60
Total	$160	Preferred stock	20
		Common stock equity	70
		Total	$160

The owners of the Moses Company's $12 worth of equity have control over $260 worth of assets (Company X's $100 worth and Company Y's $160 worth). This means that the owners' equity represents only about 4.6 percent ($12 ÷ $260) of the total assets controlled. From the discussions of ratio analysis, financial leverage, and capital structure in Chapters 3, 4, and 18, respectively, the reader should recognize that this is quite a high degree of leverage. If an individual stockholder or even another holding company owns $3 of Moses Company's stock, which is sufficient for its control, it will in actuality control the whole $260 of assets. The investment in this case would represent only 1.15 percent ($3 ÷ $260) of the assets controlled. ●

The high leverage obtained through a holding company arrangement greatly magnifies earnings (and losses) for the holding company. Quite often a *pyramiding* of holding companies occurs when one holding company controls other holding companies. This type of arrangement causes an even greater magnification of earnings and losses. It is important to recognize that the greater the leverage, the greater the risk involved. The risk-return trade-off is a key consideration in the holding company decision.

Risk protection.   Another advantage commonly cited for the holding company arrangement is that the failure of one of the companies held does not result in the failure of the entire holding company. Since each subsidiary is a separate corporation, the failure of one company should cost the holding company, at a maximum, no more than its investment in that subsidiary. Often, lenders to subsidiaries of holding companies will require the holding company to guarantee the subsidiaries' loans in order to protect themselves in the event that the subsidiary goes bankrupt.

Legal benefits.   Many states provide certain tax breaks to corporations chartered within the state. If a company were to merge with several other companies located in different states, the surviving company would receive these special tax benefits in its state of incorporation. If, instead of merging, a holding company arrangement was used whereby the subsidiaries still maintained their corporate identities, each of the subsidiaries would benefit from more favorable tax treatment since they would be operating in their respective states of incorporation. Another legal benefit of the holding company is the fact that since each subsidiary is a separate corporation, any lawsuits or legal actions filed against the subsidiary will not threaten the remaining companies.

Lack of negotiations.   Another major advantage of the holding company arrangement is the relative ease with which control of a subsidiary can be acquired. The holding company can gain control of a company simply by purchasing enough shares of its stock in the marketplace. If the holding company makes these purchases discretely over a period of time, its seizure of control may go unnoticed. Stockholder or management approval is not generally required for a holding company to acquire control of a firm, whereas it usually is required for a merger.

Disadvantages of holding companies

The key disadvantages commonly cited with respect to the holding company arrangement include multiple taxation, the magnification of losses, and high administrative expenses.

Multiple taxation. Since the income to the holding company from its subsidiaries is in the form of cash dividends, a portion of it is doubly taxed. The subsidiary, prior to paying dividends, must pay federal and state taxes on its earnings; when the holding company receives these earnings as dividends, it must claim 15 percent of them for taxes. In other words, although an 85-percent tax exemption on dividends is permitted, the remaining 15 percent received by the holding company is considered taxable income. When a large proportion—currently 80 percent or more—of the subsidiaries' stock is held, the IRS will give the holding company a 100-percent dividend exemption. If a subsidiary were part of a merged company, there would also be *no* multiple taxation.

Magnification of losses. As the discussion of the leverage resulting from the holding company arrangement indicated, both earnings and losses are magnified. The magnification of losses when general economic conditions are unfavorable may result in the collapse of the holding company. The degree of risk is to some extent a function of the degree of pyramiding and the general stability of the subsidiaries' earnings. However, since in general most business persons are risk averters, increased risk must be recognized as a very real disadvantage of holding companies.

High administrative expenses. A holding company is generally a more expensive form of business organization to administer than a single company created by a merger. The increased cost is generally attributable to the cost of maintaining each company as a separate entity and therefore not achieving all the economies available through a merger. Also, coordination between the holding company and its subsidiaries normally requires additional staff to maintain channels of communication. These diseconomies of administration can be viewed as a type of negative synergistic effect.

SUMMARY

This chapter has discussed the common types of business combinations, which are consolidations, mergers, and holding companies. A consolidation involves the combination of two firms of similar size to form a completely new corporation. A merger involves combining two firms of unequal size in such a way that the larger of the firms maintains its corporate identity. Due to the similarity of consolidations and mergers, the term "merger" is used to describe either of these types of combinations. A holding company is a corporation that has a controlling interest in one or more other corporations.

The motives for business combinations include growth, synergistic effects, fund raising, increased managerial skills, tax considerations, and increased ownership liquidity. A firm can grow horizontally, vertically, or as a conglomerate. Horizontal growth involves acquiring firms in the same line of business, while vertical growth involves acquiring another firm in the same channel of production or distribution. Conglomerates are the result of acquiring unrelated firms in order to diversify risk. Synergistic effects are economies of scale resulting from the lower overhead of merged firms. Managerial skill can be acquired, tax benefits through tax-loss carryforwards may be acquired, the marketability of stock may be increased, and the firm's fund-raising ability may be enhanced through the acquisition of another firm. These motives for merging are not mutually exclusive; generally a mixture of them provides justification for a business combination.

In establishing the ratio of exchange, the effects of the key financial variables—the earnings per share and the market price per share of the merged firm—must be forecast for both the immediate future and the long run. Attention is sometimes given to the dividends per share, book value per share, and the operating and financial riskiness of the merged firm. A key relationship affecting the merged firm's earnings per share and market price per share is the relationship between the price-earnings ratio paid for the acquired firm and the price-earnings ratio of the acquiring firm. Analytical schemes for evaluating these relationships are available.

Mergers can be transacted either by paying cash or through the exchange of stock. In either case, the firm being acquired may be acquired for its assets or as a going concern. If cash is paid, traditional capital budgeting procedures using net present value can be applied to determine the economic feasibility of the purchase. If the merger will significantly change the capital structure of the acquiring firm, the cost of capital should be adjusted to take this into account. If an exchange of stock is used to acquire a firm, a ratio of exchange of stock must be established. The ratio of exchange can be stated as the ratio of the price paid for the acquired firm's shares to the acquiring firm's market price. The price paid must normally be greater than the acquired firm's market price in order to make the merger attractive.

A merger can be negotiated either with the firm's management or directly with the firm's stockholders. Not only do negotiations with management require a favorable cash price or exchange ratio, but certain nonfinancial factors must be agreed upon. Often the management is given certain sweeteners as part of the payment price or to stimulate positive future performance. If a merger cannot be negotiated, tender offers can be used to purchase stock directly from the owners. Often merger negotiations become quite competitive and cutthroat.

A holding company can be created by gaining control of other companies with as little as 10 to 20 percent of the stock. The chief advantages of holding companies are leverage effects, risk protection, legal benefits, and the fact that negotiations are not required to gain control of a subsidiary. The disadvantages commonly cited include multiple taxation, the magnification of losses, and high administrative expenses.

QUESTIONS

25-1 What are consolidations and mergers? How are they different? How is the acquisition transacted in each case?

25-2 What is a holding company? What are the companies held by a holding company called? How does the holding company arrangement differ from both mergers and consolidations?

25-3 What is the difference between horizontal, vertical, and conglomerate growth? In which case could "total integration" result? Why?

25-4 How may business combinations increase the firm's fund-raising capability or its managerial skill? What broader justification must a business combination have?

25-5 Often in mergers—especially in conglomerate mergers—tax considerations are a key motive for a business combination. Why and in what situations may the acquisition of a firm with a tax-loss carryforward be quite acceptable?

25-6 Why may consolidations and mergers be made to increase the liquidity of a firm's ownership? What types of firms are likely to combine for this motive?

25-7 What should be the financial manager's overriding concern in evaluating possible business combinations? What should his viewpoint be with respect to (1) the earnings per share, (2) the dividends per share, (3) the market price per share, (4) the book value per share, and (5) the financial leverage of the firm?

25-8 What is the justification for the acquisition of companies not as going concerns, but rather for all or part of their assets? What other benefit may result from such acquisitions?

25-9 How should one evaluate the acquisition of a going concern? What difficulties are often encountered?

25-10 What is a ratio of exchange? Is it based on the current market prices of the shares of the acquiring and acquired firm? Why or why not?

25-11 When a stock exchange type of acquisition is being evaluated, what is normally the key variable considered? Why?

25-12 What are the important considerations in evaluating the long-run impact of a merger on the combined firm's earnings per share? Why may a long-run view change a merger decision?

25-13 What consideration, if any, should be given to dividends per share, book value per share, working capital per share, and operating and financial risk in evaluating prospective mergers?

25-14 What is a tender offer? How might it be used to arrange a merger? Are tender offers the primary tool used to arrange mergers?

25-15 In order to discourage shareholders from accepting tender offers, what actions might the firm's management take?

25-16 In order to obtain voting control in other companies, how many shares of stock must a company control? On what does this depend?

25-17 What are the key advantages cited for the holding company arrangement? What leverage effect is involved?

25-18 What disadvantages are commonly cited for the holding company arrangement? What is pyramiding?

PROBLEMS

25-1 The Whitower Watch Company is contemplating the acquisition of the Sport-Watch Company, a firm that has shown large operating losses over the past few years. As a result of the acquisition, Whitower believes the total pretax profits of the consolidation will not change from their present level for seven years. The total tax loss of Sport-Watch is $500,000, while Whitower projects annual earnings before taxes to be $280,000 per year for each of the next seven years. The firm is in the 40-percent tax bracket.

a If Whitower does not make the acquisition, what is the company's tax liability each year over the next seven years?

b If the acquisition were made, how much would the company owe in taxes each year over the next seven years?

c If Sport-Watch can be acquired for $225,000 in cash, should Whitower make the acquisition based on tax considerations? (Ignore timing.)

25-2 The General Restaurant Corporation is evaluating the acquisition of Student Prince Hot Dog Stands. Student Prince has a tax-loss carryforward of $1.8 million. The tax loss resulted from earlier operations of Student Prince and can be broken down into the following schedule:

Years remaining	Amount
1	$ 400,000
2	200,000
3	600,000
4	100,000
5	500,000
Total	$1,800,000

General can purchase the Student Prince for $2.1 million. They can sell the assets for $1.6 million—their book value. General Restaurant expects their earnings before taxes in the five years following the acquisition to be as follows:

Year	Earnings before taxes
1	$150,000
2	400,000
3	450,000
4	600,000
5	600,000

If General Restaurant is in the 40-percent tax bracket:

a Calculate the firm's tax payments for each of the next five years without the acquisition.

b Calculate the firm's tax payments for each of the next five years with the acquisition.

c What are the total benefits associated with the tax losses from the acquisition? (Ignore timing.)

d Discuss whether you would recommend the proposed acquisition. Support your decision with figures.

25-3 Peterson's Pants has experienced losses in the past two years of $400,000 per year. Two firms are interested in acquiring Peterson's for the tax loss advantage. Stud Duds has expected income before taxes of $200,000 per year and a cost of capital of 15 percent. Glitter Threads has expected income before taxes for the next seven years as indicated:

Year	Glitter Threads Earnings before taxes
1	$ 80,000
2	120,000
3	200,000
4	300,000
5	400,000
6	400,000
7	500,000

Glitter Threads has a cost of capital of 15 percent. Both firms are subject to 40-percent tax rates on ordinary income.

a What is the tax advantage of the acquisition each year for Stud Duds?

b What is the tax advantage of the acquisition each year for Glitter Threads?

c What is the maximum cash price each interested firm would be willing to pay for Peterson's Pants?

d Use your answers in a through c to explain why a potential acquisition can have different values to different potential acquiring firms.

25-4 The Gray Printing Company is considering the acquisition of the Multi-Color Press at a cash price of $60,000. The Multi-Color Press has liabilities of $90,000. Multi-Color has a large press that Gray needs; the remaining assets would be sold to net $65,000. As a result of acquiring the press, Gray would experience an increase in cash inflow of $20,000 per year over the next 10 years. The firm has a 14-percent cost of capital.

a What is the effective or net cost of the large press?

b If this is the only way Gray can obtain the large press, should the firm go ahead with the acquisition? Explain your answer.

c If the firm could purchase a press which would provide slightly better quality, and $26,000 annual cash inflow for 10 years, for a price of $120,000, which alternative would you recommend? Explain your answer.

25-5 The Toma Fish Company is contemplating acquisition of the Seaside Packing Company for a cash price of $180,000. Toma currently is quite highly levered and therefore has a cost of capital of 14 percent. As a result of acquiring the Seaside Packing, which is financed entirely with equity, the firm expects its capital structure to be improved and its cost of capital therefore to drop to 11 percent. The acquisition of Seaside Packing is expected to increase Toma's cash inflows by $20,000 per year for the first 3 years and by $30,000 per year for the following 12 years.

a Determine whether the proposed cash acquisition is desirable. Explain your answer.

b If the firm's capital structure would actually remain unchanged as a result of the proposed acquisition, would this alter your recommendation? Support your answer with numerical data.

25-6 Elkheart Oil is being considered for acquisition by Onagonda Oil. The combination, Onagonda believes, would increase its cash inflows by $25,000 for each of the next five years and $50,000 for the following five years. Elkheart has a heavily levered position, and Onagonda can expect its cost of capital to increase from 12 to 15 percent if the acquisition is made. The cash price of Elkheart is $125,000.

a Would you recommend the acquisition?

b Would you recommend the acquisition if the Onagonda firm could use the $125,000 to purchase equipment returning cash inflows of $40,000 per year for each of the next ten years?

c If the cost of capital does not change with the acquisition, would your decision in **b** be different? Explain.

25-7 Flannagan's Public House is attempting to acquire the Moon Bar and Semi-Private Club. Certain financial data on these corporations are summarized below:

Item	Flannagan's Public House	Moon Bar and Semi-Private Club
Earnings available for common	$20,000	$8,000
Number of shares of common outstanding	20,000	4,000
Market price per share	$12	$24

Flannagan's has sufficient authorized but unissued shares to carry out the proposed acquisition.

a If the ratio of exchange is 1.8, what will be the earnings per share based on the original shares of each firm?

b If the ratio of exchange is 2.0, what will be the earnings per share based on the original shares of each firm?

c If the ratio of exchange is 2.2, what will be the earnings per share based on the original shares of each firm?

d Discuss the principle illustrated by your answers to **a** through **c**.

25-8 United Manufacturing Company is interested in acquiring the Boren Machine Company by exchanging four-tenths shares of its stock for each share of Boren's stock. Certain financial data on these companies are given below.

Item	United Manufacturing	Boren Machine
Earnings available for common	$200,000	$50,000
Number of shares of common outstanding	50,000	20,000
Earnings per share	$4.00	$2.50
Market price per share	$50.00	$15
Price-earnings ratio	12.5	6

United has sufficient authorized but unissued shares to carry out the proposed acquisition.

a How many new shares of stock will United have to issue in order to make the proposed acquisition?

b If the earnings for each firm remain unchanged, what will the post-merger earnings per share be?

    c How much, effectively, has been earned on behalf of each of the original shares of Boren's stock?

    d How much, effectively, has been earned on behalf of each of the original shares of United Stock?

25-9 Calculate the ratio of exchange of (1) shares and (2) the market price in each of the following cases.

	Current market price per share		Price per share
Case	Acquiring	Acquired	offered
A	$50	$25	$ 30
B	$80	$80	$100
C	$40	$60	$ 70
D	$50	$10	$ 12.50
E	$25	$20	$ 25

    What does each ratio signify? Explain

25-10 Gordo Enterprises, at the end of 1978, had 80,000 shares of common stock outstanding and most recently had net income of $160,000. The Potut Company, at the end of 1978, had 10,000 shares of common stock outstanding and earned $20,000 for common shareholders last year. Gordo's earnings are expected to grow at an annual rate of 5 percent, while Potut's growth rate in earnings should be 10 percent per year.

    a Calculate earnings per share for Gordo Enterprises for the next five years assuming there is no merger.

    b Calculate the next five years' earnings per share for Gordo assuming it acquires Potut at a ratio of exchange of 1.3.

    c Calculate the next five years' earnings per share for Gordo assuming it acquires Potut at a ratio of exchange of 1.1.

    d Graph the earnings-per-share figures from **a**, **b**, and **c**. Explain the differences.

    e Which plan—**b** or **c**—is preferable from the viewpoint of each of the firms? Why?

25-11 B. S. Books wishes to evaluate a proposed merger with Plain Cover Publications. B. S. had 1978 earnings of $200,000, has 100,000 shares of common stock outstanding, and expects earnings to grow at an annual rate of 7 percent. Plain Cover had 1978 earnings of $800,000, has 200,000 shares of common stock outstanding, and its earnings are expected to grow at 3 percent per year.

    a Calculate the expected earnings per share for B. S. Books for the next five years without the merger.

    b What would the B. S. Books stockholders earn over the next five years on each of their B. S. Books shares converted into Plain Cover shares at a ratio of (1) .6 and (2) .8 shares of Plain Cover for one share of B. S. Books?

    c Graph the pre- and post-merger earnings-per-share figures developed in **a** and **b**.

    d If you were a financial manager, what would you recommend from **b**, (1) or (2)? Explain your answer.

25-12 Data for both the Merwin Company and the Lyle Company are given. The Merwin Company is considering the acquisition of the Lyle Company by exchanging 1.25 shares of its stock for each share of Lyle Company stock. The

Merwin Company expects to sell at the same price-earnings multiple after the merger as before merging.

Item	Merwin Company	Lyle Company
Number of shares of common stock outstanding	90,000	15,000
Earnings available for common	$225,000	$50,000
Market price per share	$45	$50

a Calculate the ratio of exchange of market prices.
b Calculate the earnings per share and price-earnings ratio for each company.
c Calculate the price-earnings ratio used to purchase the Lyle Company.
d Calculate the post-merger earnings per share for the Merwin Company.
e Calculate the expected market price per share of the merged firm. Discuss this result in light of your findings in a.

25-13 The Magna Company holds stock in company A and company B. For the companies, a simplified balance sheet is presented below. Magna has voting control over both company A and company B.

Magna Company

Assets		Liabilities and stockholders' equity	
Common stock holdings		Long-term debt	$ 40,000
Company A	$ 40,000	Preferred stock	25,000
Company B	60,000	Common stock equity	35,000
Total	$100,000	Total	$100,000

Company A

Assets		Liabilities and stockholders' equity	
Current assets	$100,000	Current liabilities	$100,000
Fixed assets	400,000	Long-term debt	200,000
Total	$500,000	Common stock equity	200,000
		Total	$500,000

Company B

Assets		Liabilities and stockholders' equity	
Current assets	$180,000	Current liabilities	$100,000
Fixed assets	720,000	Long-term debt	500,000
Total	$900,000	Common stock equity	300,000
		Total	$900,000

    a What percentage of the total assets controlled by the Magna Company does its common stock equity represent?

    b If another company owns 15 percent of the common stock of the Magna Company and by virtue of this fact has voting control, what percentage of the total assets controlled does the outside company's equity represent?

    c How does a holding company effectively provide a great deal of control for a small dollar investment?

    d Given the following additional facts, answer questions **a** and **b**.

        (1) Company A's fixed assets consist of $20,000 of common stock in company C. This provides voting control.

        (2) Company C, which has total assets of $400,000, has voting control of company D, which has $50,000 of total assets.

        (3) Company B's fixed assets consist of $60,000 of stock in both company E and Company F. In both cases, this gives it voting control. Companies E and F have total assets of $300,000 and $400,000, respectively.

SELECTED REFERENCES

Ackerman, Robert W., and Lionel L. Fray, "Financial Evaluaton of a Potential Acquisition," *Financial Executive* (October 1967), pp. 34–54.

Austin, Douglas V., "The Financial Management of Tender Offer Takeovers," *Financial Management 3* (Spring 1974), pp. 37–43.

Cheney, Richard E., "Remedies for Tender-Offer Anxiety," *Financial Executive 43* (August 1975), pp. 16–19.

Cunitz, Jonathan H., "Valuing Potential Acquisitions," *Financial Executive 39* (April 1971), pp. 16–28.

Goudzwaard, Maurice B., "Conglomerate Mergers, Convertibles, and Cash Dividends," *Quarterly Review of Business and Economics* (Spring 1969), pp. 53–62.

Haugen, Robert A., and Terence E. Langetieg, "An Empirical Test for Synergism in Merger," *Journal of Finance 39* (June 1975), pp. 1003–1014.

Heath, John, Jr., "Valuation Factors and Techniques in Mergers and Acquisitions," *Financial Executive 49* (April 1972), pp. 34–44.

Hogarty, Thomas F., "The Profitability of Corporate Mergers," *Journal of Business 43* (July 1970), pp. 317–327.

Kelly, Eamon M., *The Profitability of Growth Through Mergers* (State College, Pa.: Pennsylvania State University, 1967).

Larson, Kermit D., and Nicholas D. Gonedes, "Business Combinations: An Exchange Ratio Determination Model," *Accounting Review 44* (October 1969), pp. 720–728.

Lewellen, Wilbur G., "A Pure Financial Rationale for the Conglomerate Merger," *Journal of Finance 26* (May 1971), pp. 521–537.

MacDougal, Gary E., and Fred V. Malek, "Master Plan for Merger Negotiations," *Harvard Business Review 48* (January-February 1970), pp. 71–82.

Mandelker, Gershon, "Risk and Return: The Case of Merging Firms," *Journal of Financial Economics 1* (December 1974), pp. 303–336.

Mason, R. Hal., and Maurice B. Goudzwaard, "Performance of Conglomerate Firms: A Portfolio Approach," *Journal of Finance 31* (March 1976), pp. 39–48.

Melicher, Ronald W., and David F. Rush, "Evidence on the Acquisition-Related Performance of Conglomerate Firms," *Journal of Finance 29* (March 1974), pp. 141–149.

Melicher, Ronald W., and Thomas R. Harter, "Stock Price Movements of Firms Engaging in Large Acquisitions," *Journal of Financial and Quantitative Analysis 7* (March 1972), pp. 1469–1475.

Nielsen, James F., and Ronald W. Melicher, "A Financial Analysis of Acquisiton and Merger Premiums," *Journal of Financial and Quantitative Analysis 8* (March 1973), pp. 139–148.

Reilly, Frank K., "What Determines the Ratio of Exchange in Corporate Mergers?" *Financial Analysts Journal 18* (November-December 1972), pp. 47–50.

Reinhardt, Uwe E., *Mergers and Consolidations: A Corporate-Finance Approach* (Morristown, N.J.: General Learning Press, 1972).

Rockwell, Willard F. Jr., "How to Acquire a Company," *Harvard Business Review 46* (May-June 1968), pp. 121–132.

Schwartz, G. B., and E. J. Kelly, "Bank Financing of Corporate Acquisitions: The Cash Tender Offer," *Journal of Commercial Bank Lending 53* (August 1971), pp. 19–29.

Scott, James H., Jr., "On the Theory of Conglomerate Mergers," *Journal of Finance 32* (September 1977), pp. 1235–1250.

Shad, John S. R., "The Financial Realities of Mergers," *Harvard Business Review 47* (November-December 1969), pp. 133–146.

Shick, Richard A., "The Analysis of Mergers and Acquisitions," *Journal of Finance* (May 1972), pp. 495–502.

Shick, Richard A., and Frank C. Jen, "Merger Benefits to Shareholders of Acquiring Firms," *Financial Management 3* (Winter 1974), pp. 45–53.

Stapleton, R. C., "The Acquisition Decision as a Capital Budgeting Problem," *Journal of Business Finance and Accounting 2* (Summer 1975), pp. 187–202.

Stevens, Donald L., "Financial Characteristics of Merged Firms: A Multivariate Analysis," *Journal of Financial and Quantitative Analysis 8* (March 1973), pp. 149–158.

Woods, Donald H., and Thomas A. Caverly, "Development of a Linear Programming Model for the Analysis of Merger/Acquisition Situations," *Journal of Financial and Quantitative Analysis 4* (January 1970), pp. 627–642.

Wyatt, Arthur R., and Donald E. Kieso, *Business Combinations: Planning and Action* (Scranton, Pa.: Intext, 1969).

CHAPTER 26
Failure, reorganization, and liquidation

The preceding 25 chapters of this text have presented various concepts, tools, and techniques for efficiently managing the finances of the business firm. Unfortunately, not all business firms, even if they use these techniques, are able to sustain themselves indefinitely; many firms fail each year as a result of one or a group of causes. In some instances, the failure of the firm may be due to temporary phenomena that can be overcome with the cooperation of outsiders. In other instances, certain legal procedures can be employed to reorganize the failed firm and eliminate its recognized weaknesses. If the weaknesses that caused the firm to fail cannot be eliminated, there are legal procedures for the liquidation of the firm.

Although financial managers do not like to think of the reorganization or liquidation of the firm, it is important that they be aware of the consequences of failure and the remedies available to the failed firm. This knowledge is important not only when the firm itself fails, but also when the firm is a creditor of a failed firm. The procedures for collecting (if possible) at least a portion of the outstanding account when a customer of the firm that owes it money for the purchase of merchandise fails should be understood. A knowledge of the possible consequences of a business failure is important not only from the viewpoint of a failed or failing firm, but also from the viewpoint of the failing firm's suppliers of credit.

This chapter presents the fundamental concepts related to business failure. Attention is given to the remedies available to the failed firm and the satisfaction of creditor claims associated with a business failure. The chapter has four major sections. The first section presents a brief discussion of the nature and possible causes of business failure. The second section discusses the voluntary actions that can be taken to settle the claims of creditors. The third and fourth sections discuss legal remedies for the failed firm—reorganization and liquidation.

TABLE 26.1 Business failure statistics 1966–1976

Year	Number of failures	No. of failures per 10,000 businesses	Average liability per failure[a]
1966	13,061	52	106,000
1967	12,364	49	102,000
1968	9,636	39	98,000
1969	9,154	37	125,000
1970	10,748	44	176,000
1971	10,326	42	186,000
1972	9,566	38	209,000
1973	9,345	36	246,000
1974	9,915	38	308,000
1975	11,432	43	383,000
1976	9,628	35	313,000

[a]Values rounded to the nearest $1000.
SOURCE: U.S. Bureau of the Census, *Statistical Abstract of the United States: 1977*, 98th ed. (Washington, D.C.: U.S. Government Printing Office, 1977), Table 935, p. 570.

THE NATURE AND CAUSES OF BUSINESS FAILURE

A business failure is an unfortunate circumstance that may confront a firm. In order to provide the reader with a feel for the frequency and magnitude of business failure, some statistics on business failure have been given in Table 26.1. Although the frequency of failures did not change significantly over the period shown, the average debt of the failed firms certainly increased between 1966 and 1976. It is interesting to note the unusually large number of failures shown for 1975. These are obviously attributable to the severe recession experienced in the 1974–1975 period. Although the majority of firms that fail do so within the first year or two of their life, other firms grow, mature, and eventually fail. The failure of a business firm can be viewed in a number of ways and may be the result of one or more causes. This section presents both the types and major causes of business failure.

Types of business failure

Business firms may fail in a number of ways—if their returns are too low, if they become technically insolvent, or if they become bankrupt.

Low returns. A firm may fail in the sense that its returns are low or negative. A firm that consistently reports operating losses has failed to earn at a level that permits it to cover all its costs. From the point of view of prospective and existing shareholders, this type of performance is not desirable, and it will probably result in the deterioration of the value of the firm in the marketplace. If the firm has negative before-tax earnings, the owners' return is technically less than zero. If it cannot earn a return on its assets greater than its cost of capital, it may be viewed as having failed. Thus, a firm that just breaks even each period may be considered a failure by its owners, for whose gain it is being operated. The consequences in the marketplace of failure due to low returns can be great, although outsiders cannot pressure the firm to liquidate. When returns are low, corrective action must be initiated and carried out by the owners and directors. Low returns, unless remedied, are likely to result eventually in a more serious type of failure.

Technical insolvency. Technical insolvency occurs when a firm is unable to pay its liabilities as they come due. When a firm is technically insolvent, its assets are still greater than its liabilities, but it is confronted with a *liquidity crisis*. If some of its assets can be converted into cash within a reasonable period, the firm may be able to escape complete failure. Though it cannot pay its bills, the firm's assets have not deteriorated and its liabilities have not increased to a point where they exceed the fair value of the assets. Nevertheless, a technically insolvent firm is illiquid and cannot continue to conduct business without certain changes.

Bankruptcy. Bankruptcy occurs when a firm's liabilities exceed the fair value of its assets. A bankrupt firm has a negative stockholders' equity.[1] This means that the claims of its creditors cannot be satisfied unless the firm's assets can be liquidated for more than their book value. Although bankruptcy is an obvious form of failure, the *courts treat technical insolvency and bankruptcy in the same way*. They are both considered to indicate the financial failure of the business firm.

Although poor returns to the firm's owners may not be in line with the financial manager's goal of long-run owners' wealth maximization, they are not considered legal evidence of business failure. The law defines business failure as either technical insolvency or bankruptcy. Though poor returns are not desirable, as long as a firm pays its obligations as they come due and does not allow its liabilities to exceed the fair value of its assets, it is legally considered OK. The laws relating to business failures are aimed primarily at protecting creditors. If the creditors' claims against a firm are jeopardized, the law allows the creditors certain recourse to the firm. Our concern in this chapter is with what the law—not the owners or management of a firm—considers to be business failure.

Major causes of business failure

The major causes of business failure are a lack of managerial skill, economic activity, and corporate maturity.

Lack of managerial skill. The primary cause of business failure is mismanagement, which indeed accounts for more than 50 percent of all busi-

---

[1]Since on a balance sheet the firm's assets equal the sum of its liabilities and stockholders' equity, the only way a firm having more liabilities than assets can balance its balance sheet is to have a *negative* stockholders' equity.

PART EIGHT: EXPANSION AND FAILURE

ness failures. Numerous specific managerial faults can cause the firm to fail. Overexpansion, poor financial advice, a poor sales force, and high production costs are the types of factors that may result in the ultimate failure of the business firm. Since a firm is generally organized in a hierarchical form, the top manager, president, and board of directors all must share the responsibility for the failure of a firm as a result of mismanagement. It is the responsibility of the board of directors to monitor the president's activities, and, of course, the top managers normally report to the firm's president. Each of these parties therefore contributes to the firm's overall success or failure. Since all major corporate decisions are eventually measured in terms of dollars, the financial manager may play a key role in avoiding or causing a business failure. It is his or her role to keep in touch with the firm's financial pulse.

Economic activity. Economic activity—especially economic downturns—can contribute to the failure of a business firm. If the economy goes into a recession, the firm's sales may decrease abruptly, leaving it with high fixed costs and insufficient revenues to cover these fixed operating and financial outlays. If the recession is prolonged, the likelihood of survival decreases. The impact of a recent recession (i.e., 1974–1975) on the number of business failures in 1975 can be seen in Table 26.1, presented earlier.

Not all firms are equally affected by macroeconomic activity.[2] In fact, each industry can be viewed as operating in its own microeconomy. Although the national economy may be doing well, the industry in which the firm operates may be in a slump and firms in the industry may fail. When the macro- or microeconomy is in a slump, competition within an industry is generally heightened. Increased competition is often a key cause of business failures during a recession. The failure of a firm during an economic boom, on the other hand, is more often attributable to mismanagement.

Corporate maturity. Firms, like individuals, do not have infinite lives. A firm goes through the stages of birth, growth, maturity, and eventually decline. The idea that a business firm, such as IBM, may mature and then decline is hard for many people to comprehend, yet look what happened to the Penn-Central and many other railroads. Since our country can be considered industrially young, little more than 100 years having passed since the captains of industry began mastering capitalism, the opportunity to observe the failure of business firms due to old age has not been that profound. The life cycle of the firm, which is quite similar to a product's life cycle, is shown in Figure 26.1. Each stage of the firm's life is labeled in the figure. The firm's

---

[2]The success of some firms runs countercyclical to economic activity, and other firms are unaffected by economic activity. For example, the sale of sewing machines is likely to increase during a recession since people are more willing to make their own clothes and less willing to pay for the labor of others. The sale of boats and other luxury items may decline during a recession, while sales of staple items such as electricity are likely to be unaffected. In terms of "beta"—the measure of nondiversifiable risk developed in Chapter 16—negative beta stocks would indicate a firm whose behavior generally runs countercyclical to economic activity.

FIGURE 26.1 The life cycle of a firm

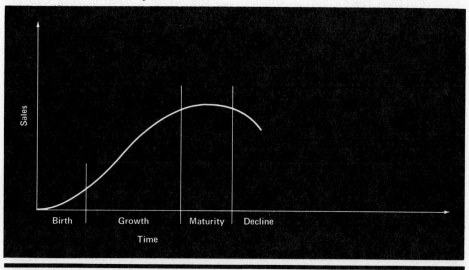

management should attempt to prolong the growth stage through acquisitions, research, and the development of new products. Once the firm has matured and begun to decline, it should seek to be acquired by another firm or liquidate before it fails. Good management planning should help the firm to postpone its decline and ultimate failure. Single-product firms that fail to diversify are the most likely candidates for eventual financial failure.

VOLUNTARY SETTLEMENTS

When a firm becomes either technically insolvent or bankrupt, it may arrange with its creditors an "out-of-court" settlement that leaves it in a position to continue operations. If the firm is technically insolvent, the voluntary settlement will probably permit the firm to continue operations, but if the firm is bankrupt the settlement may result in the liquidation of the firm. Regardless of whether the firm survives or is liquidated, a voluntary settlement enables it to bypass many of the costs involved in legal bankruptcy proceedings.

Initiating a voluntary settlement

A voluntary settlement is normally initiated by the debtor firm, since such a settlement may enable it to continue to exist or to be liquidated in a manner that gives the owners the greater chance of recovering some of their investment. The debtor, possibly with the aid of a key creditor, arranges a meeting of itself and all its creditors. Quite often the meeting is arranged by the adjustment bureau of the local credit managers' association or a trade association. The adjustment bureau or trade association will then act as the mediator of the settlement.

The first item of business at the meeting is to select a committee of creditors to investigate and analyze the debtor's situation and recommend a plan of action. If an adjustment bureau is involved, its investigators may gather the necessary information, leaving the creditor committee with only the analysis and recommendation chores. The recommendations of the committee are discussed with both the debtor and the creditors, and a plan for sustaining or liquidating the firm is made.

A voluntary settlement to sustain the firm

If the creditor committee recommends and the creditors agree to sustaining the firm's existence, a number of common plans may be used. The rationale for sustaining the firm is normally that it is reasonable to believe that the firm's recovery is feasible and that by sustaining the firm the creditors can continue to receive business from it. Common strategies for sustaining the firm include extension, composition, creditor control, and a combination of these approaches.

Extension.   An *extension* is an arrangement whereby the creditors receive payment in full, although, as one might imagine, not immediately. Extensions are arranged when the creditors feel that it is quite likely that the firm can overcome its problems and resume successful operations. Normally, when creditors give an extension, they will agree *not* to grant additional credit to the debtor until their claims have been satisfied; instead, they require cash payments for purchases until the past debts have been satisfied. Occasionally a creditor may agree to subordinate its claims to those of new creditors. This is done to permit the firm to get back on its feet so that repayment is more likely to be forthcoming. Quite often the creditor committee will insist on certain controls over the creditor. It may take legal control of the firm's assets or common stock, take a security interest in certain assets, or reserve for itself the right to approve all disbursements.

When the creditor committee makes its recommendations to the creditors, some creditors may dissent. In order to keep the firm from bankruptcy, a plan providing for the immediate repayment of the dissenting creditors may be arranged. If a large enough number of creditors dissent to the committee's recommendations and no acceptable solution can be reached, liquidation may be the only alternative. To prevent this situation, the creditor committee is normally made up of representatives of both large and small creditors.

Composition.   A *composition* is a pro rata cash settlement of creditor claims. Instead of receiving full payment of their claims, as in the case of an extension, creditors receive only a partial payment of their claims. A uniform percentage of each dollar owed is paid in satisfaction of each creditor's claim. The willingness of creditors to accept a composition arrangement depends greatly on their general evaluation of the effects of liquidation. The creditors must weigh their estimate of the amount they would recover in the event of liquidation against the composition and the prospect of future profits from the firm's continued existence. A composition arrangement is quite similar to a reorganization in the event of bankruptcy except that many of the legal and administrative procedures and expenses are bypassed. As in the case of an extension, there may be dissenting creditors, in which case the primary alternatives are to pay them the full amount they are owed, let them recover a higher percentage of their claims, or liquidate the firm.

Creditor control. Occasionally, the creditor committee's investigation results in the general finding that the current management cannot operate the firm so that it will have a reasonable chance for survival. In this case, the committee may decide that the only circumstance in which maintaining the firm is feasible is if the operating management is replaced. The committee may then take control of the firm and operate it until all claims have been settled. Once the claims have been settled, it may recommend that a new management be installed prior to the extension of additional credit. The real danger of attempting to sustain a failing corporation through creditor control is the opportunity it provides for mismanagement suits by stockholders.[3] For this reason creditors hesitate to take over the management of a failed corporation.

A combination of approaches. If the creditor committee recommends one of the preceding plans to the creditors and the creditors do not find the plan acceptable, it is likely that, through negotiations, a plan involving some combination of extension, composition, and creditor control will result. An example would be a settlement whereby the debtor agrees to pay 75 cents on the dollar in three equal annual installments of 25 cents on the dollar while the creditors agree to sell additional merchandise to the firm on 30-day terms if the existing management is replaced by a new management acceptable to them. Numerous variations and combinations of the plans mentioned here are possible; the important point for creditors to consider is the likelihood and amount of long-run returns expected from sustaining the firm. If a greater return is expected from liquidation proceedings, attempts to sustain the firm are unnecessary.

A voluntary settlement resulting in private liquidation

After the situation of the firm has been investigated by the creditor committee, recommendations have been made, and talks between the creditors, the adjustment bureau, and the debtor have been held, the only acceptable course of action may be the liquidation of the firm. Liquidation can be carried out in either of two ways—privately or through the legal procedures provided by bankruptcy law. If the debtor is willing to accept liquidation, legal procedures may not be required. Generally, the avoidance of litigation enables the creditors to obtain *quicker* and *higher* settlements. However, all the creditors must agree to a private liquidation for it to be feasible. Thus firms with a small number of creditors are more likely to be

---

[3]The existing ownership can sue creditors who are running the company and are unable to sustain the firm. In other words, if the creditor committee is in control when the firm fails, it can be held responsible instead of the firm's original management that placed the firm in technical insolvency or bankruptcy. Even if the creditor committee is assured of winning a mismanagement suit, the time and cost of the litigation are a serious drawback to such a course of action.

liquidated in this way. Two aspects of private liquidation that should be highlighted are its objective and organization.

Objective of liquidation.   The objective of the voluntary liquidation process is to recover as much per dollar owed as possible. From management's standpoint, the objective is to recover as much of the shareholders' original investment as possible. The common stockholders, who are the true owners, cannot of course receive any funds until the claims of all other parties have been satisfied. It is the financial manager's responsibility to make sure that the liquidation process is carried out in a manner that is in the best interest not only of creditors but also of the owners. Liquidation procedures aimed at just satisfying creditors' claims are not consistent with the manager's objective—maximization of the owners' wealth.

Organization for liquidation.   Liquidation procedures are generally carried out through the adjustment bureau or trade association initially used to organize a voluntary settlement. A common procedure is to have a meeting of the creditors at which they sign a legal contract *assigning* the power to liquidate the firm's assets to the adjustment bureau, the trade association, or a third party, which becomes the *assignee*. The assignee's job is to liquidate the assets, obtaining the best price possible. It may sell the assets at auction, piece by piece, or in bulk. This process of passing title to the firm's assets to a third party, which then liquidates them, is known as *assignment*. There are certain legal procedures that must be followed when assets are assigned. The *assignee* is sometimes referred to as the *trustee,* since it is entrusted with the title to the assets and the responsibility to liquidate them efficiently. Once the trustee has liquidated the firm's assets, it distributes the recovered funds to the creditors and owners (if any funds remain for the owners). The final action in a private liquidation is for the creditors to sign a release attesting to the satisfactory settlement of their claims. If the creditors do not sign the release, the case may go into bankruptcy court.

REORGANIZATION IN BANKRUPTCY[4]

If a voluntary settlement of a failed firm cannot be agreed upon, the firm can be forced into bankruptcy by its creditors. As a result of bankruptcy proceedings, the firm may be either reorganized or liquidated. This section of the chapter is concerned primarily with reorganization in the event of bankruptcy; the following section is devoted to liquidation procedures when bankruptcy is filed.

Bankruptcy

Bankruptcy in the legal sense occurs when the firm cannot pay its bills or when its liabilities exceed the fair market value of its assets. In either of these situations, a firm may be declared legally bankrupt. Generally, creditors

---

[4]For a more detailed discussion of the materials presented in this and the following section, the reader is referred to a business law text. One excellent text for example, is Rate A. Howell, John R. Allison, and Gaylord A. Jentz, *Business Law: Text and Cases* (Hinsdale, Ill.: Dryden, 1978), Chapter 43.

attempt (if at all possible) to avoid forcing a firm into bankruptcy if it appears to have opportunities for future success. Although bankruptcy proceedings do not necessarily result in liquidation, there is a certain stigma associated with firms that have been reorganized through bankruptcy proceedings. Voluntary settlements permitting the firm to continue to exist are generally preferable.

Bankruptcy legislation. The first bankruptcy legislation in the United States was the American Bankruptcy Act of 1800. After a number of repeals and reenactments of this initial act, the Bankruptcy Act of 1898 was passed. The Bankruptcy Act of 1898 is the backbone of the current bankruptcy statute, the *Chandler Act of 1938.* This piece of legislation has two primary objectives. The first is to provide for an equitable distribution of a bankrupt debtor's properties and the second is to discharge the debtor's debts and give him or her a chance at rehabilitation through making a fresh start. It establishes legal procedures for both the liquidation and the reorganization of a bankrupt firm. Although the Chandler Act contains fifteen separate chapters, the ones most commonly cited in cases of corporate bankruptcy are Chapters X and XI. Each is briefly described below.

Chapter X. Chapter X of the Chandler Act is concerned with corporate reorganizations. It outlines the various legal procedures to be followed in order to reorganize a bankrupt corporation.

Chapter XI. Chapter XI of the Chandler Act is concerned with *arrangements* that leave bankrupt firms in a state of limbo. These arrangements are quite similar to the extension or composition alternatives discussed earlier. They must be initiated by the debtor and agreed to by the creditors. Chapter XI applies to both individuals and corporations.

Chapters X and XI of the Chandler Act deal with corporate bankruptcies. The key legislation on ordinary bankruptcies is Chapters I–VII of the Chandler Act. These chapters describe the procedures for the liquidation and termination of a failed firm. The reason Chapters X and XI of the Chandler Act receive a great deal of attention is that they contain reorganization and arrangement provisions that may allow the firm to remain in business.

Types of bankruptcy. There are two basic types of bankruptcy—voluntary and involuntary.

Voluntary. Any firm that is not a municipal or financial institution or a railroad can file a petition of bankruptcy on its own behalf. Insolvency is not required in order to file for voluntary bankruptcy, nor does the company have to have committed one of the legal acts of bankruptcy (defined below).

Involuntary. Involuntary bankruptcy is initiated by an outside party, usually a creditor. An involuntary petition of bankruptcy against a firm can be filed if one of the following three conditions is met:

1. The firm has past-due debts of $1000 or more.
2. Three or more creditors can prove that they have aggregate unpaid claims of $500 against the firm. If the firm has fewer than 12 creditors, any creditor who is owed more than $500 can file the petition.
3. The firm has committed an *act of bankruptcy* within four months prior to filing the bankruptcy petition.

Six *acts of bankruptcy* are described in the Chandler Act:

1. *Fraudulent conveyance*—Permitting any part of the debtor's property to be concealed or removed in order to hinder, delay, or defraud creditors.
2. *Preference*—Transferring a portion of the insolvent firm's property to one or more of its creditors in order to favor those creditors over other creditors.
3. *Permitting a creditor to obtain a lien*—Allowing a creditor to obtain a lien on the firm's property when it is insolvent and not discharging the lien within 30 days.
4. *General assignment*—If a debtor assigns assets for the benefit of creditors, an act of bankruptcy has been committed.
5. *Permitting the appointment of a receiver*—If an insolvent firm permits the appointment of a receiver or trustee to take charge of its property, an act of bankruptcy has been committed.
6. An *admission in writing*—A debtor, by admitting in writing its inability to pay its debts and its willingness to be judged bankrupt commits an act of bankruptcy.

Whenever a debtor enters into a voluntary settlement resulting in the assignment of assets or the appointment of a trustee, it has committed an act of bankruptcy. The first three acts of bankruptcy are self-explanatory; the fourth and fifth result from voluntary settlement procedures, and the sixth gives the firm an opportunity to become involuntarily bankrupt. This is often preferable to voluntary bankruptcy since it does not carry with it the stigma of attempting to escape financial obligations; rather, it suggests an inescapable failure.

Reorganization procedures

The procedures for the reorganization of a corporation that has become bankrupt, either voluntarily or involuntarily, are quite easily implemented. In the reorganization process, there are certain standard procedures that must be employed in order to provide an acceptable solution. The procedures for the initiation and execution of corporate reorganizations under the Chandler Act entail five separate steps—filing, the appointment of a trustee, the development of a reorganization plan, the approval of the plan, and the payment of expenses.

Filing. A reorganization petition must be filed in a federal district court. Either a petition for an arrangement under Chapter XI of the Chandler Act or a reorganization under Chapter X can be filed.

Filing for arrangements under Chapter XI. A modest-sized corporation in which the relationship between the owners and the management is a close one may file a petition for an arrangement for the settlement of *unsecured debts* only. An *arrangement* here is a special type of reorganization in which the management of the firm may be placed in the hands of a receiver or left in the hands of the existing management. The debtor proposes an arrangement, or a plan, by which it will discharge its creditors' claims. The plan must be accepted by all the creditors, and the court must also judge the reasonableness of the arrangement in light of the creditors' interests. If the arrangement is not accepted by the courts or if the Securities and Exchange Commission exercises its privilege of intervening, the firm may be declared bankrupt, in which case it must file for reorganization under Chapter X or be liquidated. If an arrangement can be worked out, it prevents a great deal of litigation. An arrangement under Chapter XI is quite similar to the voluntary settlements for sustaining a firm discussed earlier.

Filing for reorganization under Chapter X. Arrangements are the exception rather than the rule since they relate only to unsecured debts and must be acceptable to all creditors. A petition for reorganization under Chapter X may be initiated either by the debtor corporation (voluntary reorganization) or by three or more creditors having total claims of $5000 or more (involuntary reorganization). Shareholders do not have the right to file a petition for reorganization under Chapter X.

The appointment of a trustee. The judge before whom the reorganization petition is submitted will evaluate it and, if he or she finds it in order, enter an order approving it. If it is approved, the judge will appoint a trustee for the assets or permit the debtor to remain in possession of the assets. If the debtor's liabilities exceed $250,000, the judge is required to appoint a trustee. Since the duties of the trustee are quite important, they will be discussed in a separate section.

The reorganization plan. The trustee, after investigating the firm's situation, submits a plan of reorganization to the court. The plan is filed and a hearing is held to determine whether it should be approved. The main requirement is that the plan be *fair, equitable, and feasible.* The court's approval or disapproval is based on its evaluation of the plan in light of these standards. A brief definition of these standards is given below.

Fair and equitable. A plan is considered fair and equitable if it *maintains the priorities* of the respective contractual rights of the creditors, preferred stockholders, and common stockholders. For example, holders of first mortgage bonds must be given priority over common stockholders. It would also be unfair to eliminate the original common stockholders as owners if the valuation of the firm indicates that some equity still exists.

Feasible. The court must find the reorganization plan not only fair and equitable, but feasible, meaning it must be *workable.* The reorganized corporation must have sufficient working capital, sufficient funds to cover fixed charges, sufficient credit prospects, and a sufficient ability to service debt to retire or refund debts as proposed by the plan. This requirement is intended to ensure that the reorganized firm can operate efficiently, compete with other companies in the industry, and avoid future reorganization or liquidation.

The approval of the plan. Once the court has determined that the reorganization plan is fair, equitable, and feasible, the plan, along with a summary, is given to the firm's creditors and shareholders for their acceptance. If the firm's indebtedness exceeds $3 million, the plan must first be submitted to the Securities and Exchange Commission, which makes an advisory report that is attached to the plan before it is reviewed by the creditors and shareholders. The SEC may advise or suggest the rejection of the plan, but it is the creditors and shareholders who make the accept-reject decision. For the plan to be approved, written acceptances from creditors holding two-thirds of the amount of the claims filed are necessary. When the firm is not insolvent, written acceptances from the majority of both the preferred and the common stockholders is also required. The plan, once approved, is put into effect as soon as possible.

The payment of expenses. After the reorganization plan has been approved or disapproved, the trustee and all parties to the proceedings whose services were beneficial or contributed to the approval or disapproval of the plan file a statement of expenses. If the court finds these claims acceptable, the debtor must pay these expenses within a reasonable period of time.

The trustee's responsibilities

Since reorganization activities are placed largely in the hands of the court-appointed trustee, it is useful to understand the trustee's responsibilities. His or her three key responsibilities are the valuation and recapitalization of the firm and the exchange of outstanding obligations for new securities.

The valuation of the firm. The trustee's first responsibility is the valuation of the firm in order to determine whether reorganization is appropriate. In order to determine this, the trustee must estimate both the *liquidation value* of the enterprise and its value as a *going concern*. If the trustee finds that its value as a going concern is less than its liquidation value, he or she will recommend liquidation; if the trustee finds the opposite to be true, he or she will recommend reorganization. The procedure used to determine the liquidation value of the firm is similar to that described in the discussion of valuation in Chapter 18. Estimating the value of the reorganized firm as a going concern involves forecasting its sales and the earnings from those sales. By applying an appropriate *capitalization rate,* the present value of forecast earnings can be transformed into the value of the firm as a going concern. An example will clarify this approach.

EXAMPLE

Creditors of the Weak Company recently filed and had accepted a petition for the reorganization of the firm under Chapter X of the Chandler Act. The court assigned a trustee, who upon investigation found the firm's liquidation value (after expenses) to be $5 million. The trustee further investigated the firm's past operations and expected industry trends in order to estimate its future sales. On the basis of his estimate of future sales, the trustee felt safe in expecting the reorganized firm to generate after-tax earnings of $600,000 annually. In view of the firm's changed capital structure and prevailing capital market conditions, a capitalization rate of 10 percent was used to evaluate the estimated earnings. Assuming the $600,000 annual earnings would continue indefinitely and using the procedure for capitalizing an infinite-lived stream of earnings (Equation 13.26), a value was found for the Weak Company as a going concern—$6 million [$600,000 $\cdot$ (1 ÷ .10)]. Since the firm's value as a going concern was estimated to be greater than its liquidation value ($6 million vs. $5 million), the trustee recommended the reorganization of the company. If this situation had not resulted, the trustee would have recommended liquidation of the firm. ●

Recapitalization. If reorganization of the firm is recommended by the trustee, he or she must draw up a plan of reorganization. The key portion of the reorganization plan generally concerns the firm's capital structure. Since most firms' financial difficulties result from high fixed charges, the capital structure is generally altered in order to reduce the fixed charges. Generally, debts are exchanged for equity or the maturities of debts are extended. Sometimes *income bonds* are exchanged for debentures and mortgage bonds. An income bond requires the payment of interest only when sufficient earnings are available from which to pay it.[5] The trustee, in recapitalizing the firm, places a great deal of emphasis on building a mix of debt and equity that allows the firm to service its debts and provide a reasonable level of earnings for its owners. It is important to recognize that the valuation of owners' returns after the recapitalization is one of the bases for the reorganization decision. An example will clarify the recapitalization process.

EXAMPLE

The Weak Company's current (i.e., before recapitalization) capital structure, according to its books, is as follows:

Debentures	$ 2,000,000
Mortgage bonds	4,000,000
Preferred stock	1,000,000
Common stock	3,000,000
Total Capital	$10,000,000

The high leverage of this plan is obvious from the debt-equity ratio of 1.50 ($6 million ÷ $4 million). Since the firm as a going concern was found to be worth only

---

[5]Although income bonds are generally considered not very desirable investments because of the high degree of uncertainty associated with the interest payment, they are very commonly used in corporate reorganizations. Since income bonds are a form of debt, their holders have preference over equity holders with respect to the receipt of interest and the recovery of principal in liquidation.

$6 million, the trustee created a less highly levered capital structure with total capital of $6 million.

Debentures	$1,000,000
Mortgage bonds	1,000,000
Income bonds	2,000,000
Preferred stock	500,000
Common stock	1,500,000
Total Capital	$6,000,000

Since interest on an income bond does not have to be paid unless earnings are available to pay it, it can be treated like equity in evaluating the firm's leverage. The new debt-equity ratio is 0.50 ($2 million ÷ $4 million), which indicates a considerably safer capital structure for the recapitalized Weak Company. ●

The exchange of obligations. Once the best capital structure has been established in accordance with the firm's value as a going concern, the trustee must establish a plan for exchanging outstanding obligations for new securities. The guiding principle is to *observe priorities*. Senior claims must be satisfied prior to settling junior claims. In order to comply with this principle, senior suppliers of capital must receive a claim on new capital equal to their previous claims. The common stockholders are the last to receive any new securities. It is not unusual for them to receive nothing. Security holders do not necessarily have to receive the same type of security they held before. Quite often they receive a combination of securities. An example will clarify this process.

EXAMPLE
The exchange of securities involved in the reorganization of the Weak Company were as follows:

1. The $2 million in debentures were exchanged for $1 million in new debentures and $1 million in mortgage bonds.
2. The $4 million in mortgage bonds were exchanged for $2 million in income bonds, $500,000 of preferred stock, and $1.5 million of common stock.
3. The preferred stockholders received nothing.
4. The common stockholders received nothing.

Since the valuation of the firm allowed a total capitalization of only $6 million, only the claims of the original debenture and mortgage bond holders were satisfied through the exchange process. The original preferred and common stockholders were virtually eliminated, and the original mortgage bondholders became the firm's new owners. ●

The Weak Company example should make clear the priorities in reorganization and the close relationship between the value of the firm as a going concern, the recapitalization process, and the ultimate exchange process. In many cases, the original common stockholders will retain some ownership in the firm, although there is no guarantee of this. Once the trustee has determined the new capital structure and distribution of capital, he or she will submit recommendations to the court as described in the preceding section. The trustee plays a major role in the reorganization process and must be certain to present a fair, equitable, and feasible plan.

LIQUIDATION IN BANKRUPTCY

A company that has been declared legally bankrupt, voluntarily or involuntarily by committing one of the acts of bankruptcy, may be liquidated. The liquidation of a bankrupt firm usually occurs once the courts have determined that reorganization is not feasible. A petition for reorganization must normally be filed by the creditors or managers of the bankrupt firm. If no petition for reorganization is filed, if a petition is filed and denied, or if the reorganization plan is denied, the firm must be liquidated. Three important aspects of liquidation in bankruptcy are discussed in this section—the legal aspects, the priority of claims, and the discharge of the firm.

Legal aspects

When a firm is adjudged bankrupt, the judge may appoint a *referee* to perform the many routine duties required in administering the bankruptcy. The judge (in involuntary bankruptcies) or the referee (in voluntary bankruptcies) may appoint *receivers* to take charge of the property of the bankrupt firm and protect the interest of creditors during the period between the filing of the bankruptcy petition and either the appointment of a trustee or the dismissal of the petition. A receiver is needed since much time often elapses between the petition for bankruptcy and the appointment of a trustee. The receiver protects the creditors' interests during this period of litigation.

Once the firm has been adjudged bankrupt, a meeting of creditors must be held between 10 and 30 days thereafter. At this meeting, creditors make their claims. The meeting is presided over by the judge or referee. The creditors appoint a *trustee*, who not only takes over the receiver's function but is responsible for liquidating the firm, disbursing money, keeping records, examining creditor claims, furnishing information as required, and making final reports on the liquidation. The trustee in essence is responsible for the liquidation of the firm. Often three trustees are appointed and (or) an advisory committee of three or more creditors is formed. Occasionally the court will call subsequent creditor meetings, but only a final meeting for closing the bankruptcy is required.

The priority of claims

It is the trustee's responsibility to liquidate all the firm's assets and to distribute the proceeds to the holders of *provable* claims. The courts have established certain procedures for determining the provability of claims.[6] The

---

[6]In order for a claim to be considered provable, the creditor must file in bankruptcy court within six months of the first creditor's meeting a signed statement specifying (1) the nature of the claim, (2) the amount of the claim, (3) whether any security is held against the claim, (4) whether and in what amount any payments have been made against the claim, and (5) that the claim is justly owed by the bankrupt to the creditor. Written evidence of the claim must be filed with the creditor's statement.

priority of claims, which is specified in the bankruptcy act, must be maintained by the trustee in distributing the funds from liquidation. The order of priority is as follows:

1. The expenses of *administering* the bankrupt firm.
2. *Wages* of not more than $600 per worker that have been earned by workers in the three-month period immediately preceding the commencement of bankruptcy proceedings.
3. *Taxes* legally due and owed by the bankrupt firm to the federal government, a state government, or any other governmental subdivision.
4. *Debts* for services received within three months before the date of bankruptcy. Rent payments fall in this category.
5. *Claims of secured creditors*, who receive the proceeds from the sale of the collateral held. If the proceeds from the liquidation of the collateral are insufficient to satisfy the secured claims, the secured creditors become general creditors for the unpaid amount.
6. *Claims of general and subordinated creditors*. The claims of unsecured, or general, creditors, unsatisfied portions of secured creditors' claims, and the claims of subordinated creditors are all treated equally. Subordinated creditors must pay the amount required (if any) to senior creditors.
7. *Preferred stockholders*, who receive an amount up to the par or stated value of the preferred stock.
8. *Common stockholders*, who receive any remaining funds, which are distributed on an equal per share basis. If the common stock has been classed, priorities may exist.

It can be seen from this list that the claims of certain nondebt holders have a higher priority than the claims of the secured creditors. The expenses of administering the bankruptcy proceedings, wages, taxes, and fees for recent services are paid first. The secured creditors then receive the liquidated value of their collateral. The claims of general and subordinated creditors, including the unpaid claims of secured creditors, are satisfied next and, finally, the claims of preferred and common stockholders. The application of these priorities by the trustee in bankruptcy liquidation proceedings can be illustrated by a simple example.

EXAMPLE

The Failed Company has the balance sheet presented in Table 26.2. The trustee, as was her obligation, has liquidated the firm's assets, obtaining the highest amounts she could get. She managed to obtain $2.3 million for the firm's current assets and $2 million for the firm's fixed assets. The total proceeds from the liquidation were therefore $4.3 million. It should therefore be clear that the firm is legally bankrupt since the firm's $5.6 million dollars of liabilities exceeds the 4.3 million dollar fair value of its assets.

The next step in the liquidation process is to distribute the proceeds to the various creditors. The only liability not shown on the balance sheet is an $800,000 expense for administering the bankrupt estate. The distribution of the $4.3 million among the firm's creditors is shown in Table 26.3. It can be seen from the table that

TABLE 26.2 The Failed Company's balance sheet

Assets		Liabilities and stockholders' equity	
Cash	$ 10,000	Accounts payable	$ 200,000
Accounts receivable	1,090,000	Notes payable—bank	1,000,000
Marketable securities	5,000	Accrued wages[a]	400,000
Inventory	3,100,000	Accrued rent[b]	100,000
Prepaid expense	5,000	Taxes payable	300,000
Total current assets	$4,210,000	Total current liabilities	$2,000,000
Land	$2,000,000	First mortgage[c]	$1,800,000
Net plant	1,810,000	Second mortgage[c]	1,000,000
Net equipment	80,000	Subordinated debentures[d]	800,000
Total fixed assets	$3,890,000	Total long-term debt	$3,600,000
		Preferred stock (5,000 sh.)	$ 400,000
		Common stock (10,000 sh.)	500,000
		Paid-in capital in excess	1,500,000
		Retained earnings	100,000
		Stockholders' equity	$2,500,000
Total	$8,100,000	Total	$8,100,000

[a]Represents wages of $400 per employee earned within three months of filing bankruptcy for 1,000 of the firm's employees.
[b]Rent owed for the use of machinery received within three months preceding the filing of bankruptcy.
[c]Mortgages on the firm's total fixed assets.
[d]Subordinated to the notes payable to the bank.

once all prior claims on the proceeds from liquidation have been satisfied, the general creditors get to divide the remaining funds on a pro rata basis. The distribution of the $700,000 between the general creditors is given in Table 26.4. The disposition of funds in the Failed Company liquidation should be clear from Tables 26.3 and 26.4. Since the claims of the unsecured creditors have not been fully satisfied, the preferred and common stockholders receive nothing.

TABLE 26.3 The distribution of the liquidation proceeds of the Failed Company

Proceeds from liquidation	$4,300,000
− Expense of administering bankruptcy	$ 800,000
− Wages owed workers	400,000
− Taxes owed governments	300,000
− Rent owed lessor	100,000
Funds available for creditors	$2,700,000
− First mortgage, paid from the $2 million proceeds from the sale of fixed assets	$1,800,000
− Second mortgage, partially paid from the remaining $200,000 of fixed-asset proceeds	200,000
Funds Available for General Creditors	$ 700,000

TABLE 26.4 The distribution of funds among general creditors of the Failed Company

General creditors' claims	Amount	Settlement @ 25 percent[a]	After subordination adjustment[b]
Unpaid balance of second mortgage	$ 800,000[c]	$200,000	$200,000
Accounts payable	200,000	50,000	50,000
Notes payable—bank	1,000,000	250,000	450,000
Subordinated debentures	800,000	200,000	0
Total	$2,800,000	$700,000	$700,000

[a]The 25-percent rate is calculated by dividing the $700,000 available for general creditors by the $2.8 million owed the general creditors. Each is entitled to a pro rata share.

[b]The subordination adjustment concerns the notes payable to which certain debentures are subordinated. The debenture holders must pay what they can from their proceeds *up to* an amount sufficient to satisfy fully the claims of the holder of the notes payable (the bank).

[c]This figure represents the difference between the $1-million second mortgage and the $200,000 payment on the second mortgage from the proceeds from the sale of the collateral remaining after satisfying the first mortgage.

It is interesting to note that of the unsecured creditors the bank holding the notes payable fares the best, thanks to the debentures that are subordinated to these notes. As a result of the subordination, the bank receives 45 percent of its claims ($450,000 ÷ $1,000,000) while the other unsecured creditors receive only 25 percent of their claims. Of course, the subordinated debenture holders receive nothing as a result of their obligation to the bank. The consequences in liquidation of subordinated debt for both the subordinated debt holders and the holders of debts to which other debts have been subordinated should be clear from this example. It is understandable that the firm must normally pay a higher interest rate in order to raise funds through sale of subordinated debts. They are simply more risky. •

The discharge of the firm

After the trustee has liquidated all the assets, distributed the proceeds to satisfy all provable claims in the appropriate order of priority, and made a final accounting of these proceedings, he or she may apply for the discharge of the bankrupt corporation. A *discharge* means that the court releases the bankrupt firm from all provable debts in bankruptcy except for certain debts that are immune to a discharge. If no objections to the discharge are filed, the court will discharge the firm. If objections are filed, the court will hear these objections and make the necessary decisions. If the debtor has not been discharged within the previous six years and did not become bankrupt because of fraudulent actions, he or she is free to enter into business again.

SUMMARY

This chapter has been devoted to the important but unpleasant topic of business failure. The financial manager should be aware of the causes and possible remedies for failure. This information is important not only in preventing or dealing with the firm's own failure but also applies when the firm is a creditor of a failed business. The firm's owners and management may consider low or negative earnings a form of business failure, but these do not necessarily result in the reorganization or liquidation of the firm. Technical insolvency or bankruptcy are more commonly considered indicators of business failure. The technically insolvent firm cannot pay its bills; the bankrupt firm's liabilities exceed the fair market value of its assets. Both technical insolvency and bankruptcy are considered legal forms of bankruptcy. The major causes of business failure are a lack of managerial skill, economic activity, and corporate maturity.

The financially failed firm has three basic alternatives. One alternative is to arrange a voluntary settlement with its creditors. Voluntary settlements are initiated by the debtor and can take one of a number of forms. In order to sustain the firm, an extension, a composition, creditor control of the firm, or a combination of these strategies can be arranged. An extension is an arrangement in which creditors eventually receive full payment. Composition involves paying off debts on a pro rata basis. Creditor control involves the management of the firm by the creditors until their claims have been satisfied. Often a combined strategy using extension, composition, and creditor control is implemented. The creditors must agree to any of these plans. If they do not, they may recommend voluntary liquidation, which bypasses many of the legal requirements of bankruptcy. If the firm is liquidated, its assets are assigned to a trustee.

A failed firm that cannot or does not want to arrange a voluntary settlement can voluntarily or involuntarily become bankrupt by petitioning for bankruptcy or committing an act of bankruptcy. There are six acts of bankruptcy, one of which is a written statement of bankruptcy by the debtor. The major legislation with respect to bankruptcy is the Chandler Act of 1938. Chapters X and XI provide for the reorganization of the firm either through the courts (Chapter X) or through an arrangement (Chapter XI) similar to that in a voluntary settlement. A bankrupt firm must file a petition for reorganization, which, if it is accepted, results in the appointment of a trustee. The trustee must determine the feasibility of reorganization by estimating the liquidation value of the firm and its value as a going concern. If he or she finds reorganization suitable, the trustee will draw up a plan of reorganization that is fair, equitable, and feasible. The plan generally involves a recapitalization and exchange of capital. In certain instances, the SEC makes an advisory report that is included with the reorganization plan. The plan must be acceptable to the courts, the creditors, and the firm's owners in order to be implemented.

A firm that cannot be reorganized or does not petition for reorganization is liquidated. The responsibility for liquidation is placed in the hands of a creditor-appointed trustee, whose responsibilities include the liquidation of assets, the distribution of the proceeds, and an accounting of all his or her actions. The proceeds must be distributed in accordance with the priority of claims established by the Chandler Act. If all claims are properly handled by the trustee and no objections are filed, the firm is discharged from all unpaid debts and if it has not been discharged within the previous six years, the firm is free to enter into business again.

QUESTIONS

26-1 How can a business firm that meets all its debt obligations technically be considered to have failed? Are firms that just break even each period considered failures? Why or why not?

26-2 What is the difference between *technical insolvency* and *bankruptcy*? How do the courts view these two situations?

26-3 Are poor returns recognized as a form of business failure by the courts? What is the primary purpose of the laws relating to business failure?

26-4 What are the primary causes of business failure? What types of actions commonly cause business failure?

26-5 What is a voluntary settlement? What probable actions will result from a voluntary settlement of the technically insolvent or bankrupt firm? What is the advantage of a voluntary as opposed to a legal settlement?

26-6 Who initiates a voluntary settlement? What are the procedures for the first meeting? Why is the voluntary settlement initiated in the fashion it is?

26-7 What is meant by an extension? What type of settlement, if any, do creditors receive under this arrangement? What is normally done when creditors disagree with a proposed extension?

26-8 What is meant by composition? What type of settlement, if any, do creditors receive under this arrangement? What happens if creditors dissent to a proposed composition?

26-9 How may an extension and composition be combined to form a settlement plan that permits the continued existence of the firm?

26-10 What is the objective of voluntary liquidation? How is the voluntary liquidation process organized? What are (1) an assignment, (2) an assignee, and (3) a trustee?

26-11 In what conditions would legal bankruptcy action be taken? What is the Chandler Act? What do Chapters X and XI of this act say?

26-12 How are *voluntary* and *involuntary bankruptcy* different? In order to file involuntary bankruptcy, what are the three key conditions?

26-13 What are the key acts of bankruptcy? Can a failed firm initiate involuntary bankruptcy proceedings? Why or why not?

26-14 How is the trustee involved in (1) the valuation of the firm, (2) the recapitalization of the firm, and (3) the exchange of securities using the priority rule in the reorganization of a bankrupt firm?

26-15 What are the characteristics of an income bond? Why is an income bond often viewed as equity in evaluating a firm's leverage?

26-16 In what conditions is a firm liquidated in bankruptcy? What legal procedures are associated with liquidating the bankrupt firm? What roles do the *referee*, the *receiver*, and the *trustee* play in the liquidation process?

26-17 In what order would the following claims be settled in bankruptcy proceedings?

a Claims of preferred shareholders.

b Claims of secured creditors.

c Expenses of administering the bankruptcy.

d Claims of common stockholders.

e Claims of general and subordinated creditors.

f Taxes legally due.

g Debt incurred within three months of the bankruptcy.

h Certain eligible wages.

PROBLEMS

26-1 Classify each of the following voluntary settlements as an extension, a composition, or a combination of the two.

a Paying all creditors 30 cents on the dollar in exchange for complete discharge of the debt.

b Paying all creditors in full in three periodic installments.

c Paying a group of creditors with claims of $10,000 in full over two years, and immediately paying the remaining creditors 75 cents on the dollar.

26-2 For a firm with outstanding debt of $125,000, classify each of the following voluntary settlements as an extension, a composition, or a combination of the two.

a Paying a group of creditors in full in four periodic payments, and paying the remaining creditors in full immediately.

b Paying a group of creditors 90 cents on the dollar immediately, and paying the remaining creditors 80 cents on the dollar in two periodic payments.

c Paying all creditors 15 cents on the dollar.

d Paying all creditors in full in 180 days.

26-3 The Peachtree Business Forms Company recently ran into certain financial difficulties that have resulted in the initiation of voluntary settlement procedures. The firm currently has $150,000 in outstanding debts and approximately $75,000 in liquidable short-term assets. Indicate, in each plan below, whether the plan is an extension, a composition, or a combination of the two. Also, indicate the cash payments and timing of those payments required of the firm under each plan.

a Each creditor will be paid 50 cents on the dollar immediately, and the debts will be considered fully satisfied.

b Each creditor will be paid 80 cents on the dollar in two quarterly installments of $.50 and $.30. The first installment is to be paid in 90 days.

c Each creditor will be paid the full amount of its claims in three installments of $.50, $.25, and $.25 per dollar. The installments will be made in 60-day intervals beginning in 60 days.

d A group of creditors having claims of $50,000 will be immediately paid in full, the remainder will be paid 85 cents on the dollar, payable in 90 days.

26-4 The following table summarizes the earnings after taxes, capitalization rate, and liquidation value of the six firms indicated. Earnings are expected to remain constant over an infinite time horizon.

Firm	Earnings after taxes	Capitalization rate	Liquidation value
A	$ 25,000	9%	$ 250,000
B	$140,000	12%	$1,200,000
C	$200,000	12%	$1,500,000
D	$ 40,000	10%	$ 500,000
E	$ 60,000	14%	$ 400,000
F	$150,000	8%	$1,875,000

a Calculate the value of the firm as a going concern in each case.

b If you were a trustee attempting to maximize the shareholders' wealth, would you recommend reorganization or liquidation in each case?

26-5   Wrightsman Supply is in financial difficulty. The firm has a liquidation value of $1,000,000 and has estimated after-tax earnings of $150,000 per year indefinitely. The firm has a capitalization rate of 12 percent. The trustee in reorganizaton has recommended the following proposed capital structure based on his valuation of the firm's worth.

	Amount	
Type of capital	Current	Proposed
Debentures	$ 500,000	$ 250,000
Mortgage bonds	1,250,000	250,000
Income bonds	0	500,000
Preferred stock	250,000	0
Common stock	500,000	750,000
Total	$2,500,000	$1,750,000

   a Calculate the value of Wrightsman as a going concern. Would you recommend liquidation or reorganization? Why?
   b Calculate and discuss the degree of leverage in the current and proposed capital structures.
   c Discuss the exchanges that would result from the proposed recapitalization. Indicate what amount, if any, and what type of capital each of the original suppliers of funds would receive.
   d Briefly discuss the requirements of a reorganization plan and indicate the role of priorities in the exchange process.

26-6   The Cannon Paper Company has an estimated liquidation value of $1,000,000. The firm's earnings are expected to remain at approximately $125,000 indefinitely, and its cost of capital is estimated to be 8 percent. The firm's current and proposed capital structures are given:

	Amount	
Type of capital	Current	Proposed
Debentures	$ 500,000	$ 100,000
Mortgage bonds	450,000	200,000
Income bonds	0	400,000
Preferred stock	25,000	0
Common stock	925,000	300,000
Total	$1,900,000	$1,000,000

   a Calculate the value of the firm as a going concern. Would you recommend liquidation or reorganization? Why?
   b Calculate and discuss the financial leverage in the current and proposed capital structures.
   c Discuss the exchanges that would result from the proposed recapitalization. Be sure to indicate what amount, if any, and type of capital each of the original fund suppliers would receive.

    d Discuss the requirements of a reorganization plan and the role of priorities in the exchange process.

26-7 The current capital structure and five proposed capital structures for the Ralston Company are presented:

	Amount		
Type of capital	**Current**	**A**	**B**
Debentures	$2,000,000	$ 500,000	$ 0
Mortgage bonds	3,000,000	2,000,000	0
Income bonds	0	1,000,000	3,000,000
Preferred stock	1,000,000	0	0
Common stock	2,000,000	1,500,000	2,000,000
Total	$8,000,000	$5,000,000	$5,000,000

	Amount		
Type of capital	**C**	**D**	**E**
Debentures	$1,000,000	$1,500,000	$1,000,000
Mortgage bonds	0	0	1,000,000
Income bonds	2,000,000	0	1,000,000
Preferred stock	500,000	0	1,000,000
Common stock	1,500,000	3,500,000	1,000,000
Total	$5,000,000	$5,000,000	$5,000,000

    a Calculate the degree of leverage in the current and each of the proposed plans. Compare the plans' leverage.

    b Indicate, for each of the proposed plans, the exchanges that would result from the recapitalization. Indicate what amount, if any, and type of capital each of the original fund suppliers would receive.

    c Viewing the proposals from both the creditors' and the current owners' viewpoints, indicate which reorganization plan you believe to be the most fair, equitable, and feasible. Explain your answers.

26-8 The Langston Company recently failed and was left with the following balance sheet.

    a The trustee liquidated the firm's assets, obtaining net proceeds of $2,200,000 from the current assets and $2,500,000 from the fixed assets. In the process of liquidating the assets, the trustee incurred expenses totaling $400,000.

       (1) Prepare a table indicating the amount, if any, to be distributed to each claimant except the general creditors. Indicate the amount to be paid, if any, to the group of general creditors.

       (2) After all claims other than those of the general creditors have been satisfied, how much, if any, is still owed the second mortgage holders? Why?

       (3) Prepare a table showing how the remaining funds, if any, would be distributed to the firm's general creditors.

       (4) Discuss what effect, if any, the presence of subordinated debentures has on the payment to the holders of the notes payable.

    b Rework **a** (1) through **a** (4) assuming the trustee liquidated the firm's assets for \$4,200,000—\$2,200,000 from the current assets and \$2,000,000 from the fixed assets.

    c Compare, contrast, and discuss your findings in **a** and **b**

Assets		Liabilities and stockholders' equity	
Cash	\$ 80,000	Accounts payable	\$ 400,000
Accounts receivable	1,090,000	Notes payable—bank	800,000
Marketable securities	10,000	Accrued wages[1]	600,000
Inventory	2,300,000	Accrued rent[2]	50,000
Prepaid expenses	20,000	Taxes payable	250,000
Total current assets	\$3,500,000	Total current liabilities	\$2,100,000
Land	\$1,000,000	First mortgage[3]	\$2,000,000
Net plant	2,000,000	Second mortgage[3]	800,000
Net equipment	1,500,000	Subordinated debentures[4]	500,000
Total fixed assets	\$4,500,000	Total long-term debt	\$3,300,000
		Preferred stock (10,000 sh.)	\$ 300,000
		Common stock (5,000 sh.)	300,000
		Paid-in capital in excess	1,500,000
		Retained earnings	500,000
		Stockholders' equity	\$2,600,000
Total	\$8,000,000	Total	\$8,000,000

[1]Represents wages of \$300 per employee earned within three months of filing bankruptcy for 2,000 of the firm's employees.
[2]Rent owed for the use of machinery received within three months preceding the filing of bankruptcy.
[3]The first and second mortgages are on the firm's total fixed assets.
[4]Subordinated to the notes payable to the bank.

26-9 A firm has \$450,000 in funds to distribute to its general creditors. Three possible sets of general creditor claims are presented below.

General creditors' claims	Case I	Case II	Case III
Unpaid balance of second mortgage	\$300,000	\$200,000	\$ 500,000
Accounts payable	200,000	100,000	300,000
Notes payable	300,000	100,000	500,000
Subordinated debentures[1]	100,000	200,000	500,000
Total	\$900,000	\$600,000	\$1,800,000

[1]Subordinated to notes payable.

    a Calculate the settlement, if any, to be received by each creditor in each case *ignoring* the subordination.

    b Determine the settlement, if any, to be received by each creditor in each case after adjusting for subordination.

    c Discuss the effect of subordination on the settlement to be received by the senior issue, or notes payable, in each case.

26-10 The Mindy Corporation recently failed and was liquidated by a court-appointed trustee who charged $300,000 for its services. The pre-liquidation balance sheet is given:

Assets		Liabilities and stockholders' equity	
Cash	$ 40,000	Accounts payable	$ 200,000
Accounts receivable	620,000	Notes payable—bank	300,000
Marketable securities	30,000	Accrued wages[1]	50,000
Inventory	1,200,000	Accrued rent[2]	30,000
Prepaid expenses	10,000	Taxes payable	20,000
Total current assets	$1,900,000	Total current liabilities	$ 600,000
Land	$ 300,000	First mortgage[3]	$ 700,000
Net plan	400,000	Second mortgage[3]	400,000
Net equipment	400,000	Subordinated debentures[4]	300,000
Total fixed assets	$1,100,000	Total long-term debt	$1,400,000
		Preferred stock (15,000 sh.)	$ 200,000
		Common stock (10,000 sh.)	200,000
		Paid-in capital in excess	500,000
		Retained earnings	100,000
		Stockholders' equity	$1,000,000
Total	$3,000,000	Total	$3,000,000

[1]Represent wages of $500 per employee earned within three months of filing bankruptcy for 100 of the firm's employees.
[2]Rent owed for use of machinery received two months prior to filing bankruptcy.
[3]The first and second mortgages are on the firm's total fixed assets.
[4]The debentures have been subordinated to the notes payable of the bank.

    a If the trustee liquidated the assets for $2,500,000—$1,300,000 from current assets and $1,200,000 from fixed assets,

        (1) Prepare a table indicating the amount to be distributed to each claimant. Indicate if the claimant is a general creditor.

        (2) Prior to satisfying the general creditor claims, how much is owed to first-mortgage holders and second-mortgage holders?

        (3) Do the firm's owners receive any distribution of funds? If so, in what amounts?

        (4) What effect, if any, does the presence of the subordinated debentures have on the payments to the holders of the notes payable?

    b If the trustee liquidated the assets for $1,800,000—$1,200,000 from current assets and $600,000 from fixed assets—answer questions a-(1) through a (4).

    c Compare, contrast, and discuss your findings in a and b.

SELECTED REFERENCES

Altman, Edward I., *Corporate Bankruptcy in America* (Lexington, Mass.: Heath, 1971).

———, "Corporate Bankruptcy, Potential Stockholder Returns and Share Valuation," *Journal of Finance 24* (December 1969), pp. 887–900.

———, "Financial Ratios, Discriminant Analysis and the Prediction of Corporate Bankruptcy," *Journal of Finance 23* (September 1968), pp. 589–609.

Beaver, William H., "Financial Ratios as Predictors of Failure," *Empirical Research in Accounting: Selected Studies, Journal of Accounting Research* supplement (1966), pp. 71–111.

———, "Market Prices, Financial Ratios, and the Prediction of Failure," *Journal of Accounting Research 6* (Autumn 1968), pp. 179–192.

Bogen, Jules I., Ed., *Financial Handbook*, 4th ed. (New York: Ronald, 1968), sects. 21 and 22.

Calkins, F. J., "Feasibility in Plans of Corporate Reorganizations Under Chapter X," *Harvard Law Review 61* (May 1968), pp. 763–781.

Deakin, E. B., "A Discriminant Analysis of Predictors of Business Failure," *Journal of Accounting Research 10* (Spring 1972), pp. 167–169.

DeWitt, N. P., "How to Survive a Corporate Financial Crisis," *Corporate Financing* (March-April 1973), pp. 25–29, 76–77.

Donaldson, Gordon, "Strategy for Financial Emergencies," *Harvard Business Review* (November-December 1969), pp. 67–79.

Edmister, Robert O., "An Empirical Test of Financial Ratio Analysis for Small Business Failure Prediction," *Journal of Financial and Quantitative Analysis 7* (March 1972), pp. 1477–1493.

Gordon, Myron J., "Towards a Theory of Financial Distress," *Journal of Finance 26* (May 1971), pp. 347–356.

Green, Steven J., "Bankruptcy: Help or Hindrance?," *Financial Executive 43* (December 1975), pp. 30–35.

Higgins, Robert C., and Lawrence D. Schall, "Corporate Bankruptcy and Conglomerate Merger," *Journal of Finance 30* (March 1975), pp. 93–113.

Howell, Rate A., John R. Allison, and Gaylord A. Jentz, *Business Law: Text and Cases* (Hinsdale, Ill.: Dryden, 1978), chap. 43.

Johnson, Craig G., "Ratio Analysis and the Prediction of Firm Failure," *Journal of Finance 25* (December 1970), pp. 1166–1168.

Krause, Sidney, "Chapters X and XI—A Study in Contrasts," *Business Lawyer 19* (January 1964), pp. 511–526.

Moyer, R. Charles, "Forecasting Financial Failure: A Re-examination," *Financial Management 6* (Spring 1977), pp. 11–17.

Murray, Roger F., "The Penn Central Debacle: Lessons for Financial Analysis," *Journal of Finance 26* (May 1971), pp. 327–332.

Scott, James H., Jr., "Bankruptcy, Secured Debt, and Optimal Capital Structure," *Journal of Finance 32* (March 1977), pp. 1–20.

Stanley, David T., and Marjorie Girth, *Bankruptcy: Problem, Process, Reform* (Washington, D.C.: Brookings Institution, 1971).

Walter, James E., "Determination of Technical Insolvency," *Journal of Business 30* (January 1957), pp. 30–43.

Weston, J. Fred, "The Industrial Economics Background of the Penn Central Bankruptcy," *Journal of Finance 26* (May 1971), pp. 311–326.

APPENDIX A
Financial Tables

TABLE A–1 Compound-value interest factors for one dollar, CVIF

Year	1%	2%	3%	4%	5%	6%	7%	8%	9%	10%
1	1.010	1.020	1.030	1.040	1.050	1.060	1.070	1.080	1.090	1.100
2	1.020	1.040	1.061	1.082	1.102	1.124	1.145	1.166	1.188	1.210
3	1.030	1.061	1.093	1.125	1.158	1.191	1.225	1.260	1.295	1.331
4	1.041	1.082	1.126	1.170	1.216	1.262	1.311	1.360	1.412	1.464
5	1.051	1.104	1.159	1.217	1.276	1.338	1.403	1.469	1.539	1.611
6	1.062	1.126	1.194	1.265	1.340	1.419	1.501	1.587	1.677	1.772
7	1.072	1.149	1.230	1.316	1.407	1.504	1.606	1.714	1.828	1.949
8	1.083	1.172	1.267	1.369	1.477	1.594	1.718	1.851	1.993	2.144
9	1.094	1.195	1.305	1.423	1.551	1.689	1.838	1.999	2.172	2.358
10	1.105	1.219	1.344	1.480	1.629	1.791	1.967	2.159	2.367	2.594
11	1.116	1.243	1.384	1.539	1.710	1.898	2.105	2.332	2.580	2.853
12	1.127	1.268	1.426	1.601	1.796	2.012	2.252	2.518	2.813	3.138
13	1.138	1.294	1.469	1.665	1.886	2.133	2.410	2.720	3.066	3.452
14	1.149	1.319	1.513	1.732	1.980	2.261	2.579	2.937	3.342	3.797
15	1.161	1.346	1.558	1.801	2.079	2.397	2.759	3.172	3.642	4.177
16	1.173	1.373	1.605	1.873	2.183	2.540	2.952	3.426	3.970	4.595
17	1.184	1.400	1.653	1.948	2.292	2.693	3.159	3.700	4.328	5.054
18	1.196	1.428	1.702	2.026	2.407	2.854	3.380	3.996	4.717	5.560
19	1.208	1.457	1.753	2.107	2.527	3.026	3.616	4.316	5.142	6.116
20	1.220	1.486	1.806	2.191	2.653	3.207	3.870	4.661	5.604	6.727
21	1.232	1.516	1.860	2.279	2.786	3.399	4.140	5.034	6.109	7.400
22	1.245	1.546	1.916	2.370	2.925	3.603	4.430	5.436	6.658	8.140
23	1.257	1.577	1.974	2.465	3.071	3.820	4.740	5.871	7.258	8.954
24	1.270	1.608	2.033	2.563	3.225	4.049	5.072	6.341	7.911	9.850
25	1.282	1.641	2.094	2.666	3.386	4.292	5.427	6.848	8.623	10.834
30	1.348	1.811	2.427	3.243	4.322	5.743	7.612	10.062	13.267	17.449
35	1.417	2.000	2.814	3.946	5.516	7.686	10.676	14.785	20.413	28.102
40	1.489	2.208	3.262	4.801	7.040	10.285	14.974	21.724	31.408	45.258
45	1.565	2.438	3.781	5.841	8.985	13.764	21.002	31.920	48.325	72.888
50	1.645	2.691	4.384	7.106	11.467	18.419	29.456	46.900	74.354	117.386

TABLE A-1 Compound-value interest factors for one dollar, CVIF (continued)

Year	11%	12%	13%	14%	15%	16%	17%	18%	19%	20%
1	1.110	1.120	1.130	1.140	1.150	1.160	1.170	1.180	1.190	1.200
2	1.232	1.254	1.277	1.300	1.322	1.346	1.369	1.392	1.416	1.440
3	1.368	1.405	1.443	1.482	1.521	1.561	1.602	1.643	1.685	1.728
4	1.518	1.574	1.630	1.689	1.749	1.811	1.874	1.939	2.005	2.074
5	1.685	1.762	1.842	1.925	2.011	2.100	2.192	2.288	2.386	2.488
6	1.870	1.974	2.082	2.195	2.313	2.436	2.565	2.700	2.840	2.986
7	2.076	2.211	2.353	2.502	2.660	2.826	3.001	3.185	3.379	3.583
8	2.305	2.476	2.658	2.853	3.059	3.278	3.511	3.759	4.021	4.300
9	2.558	2.773	3.004	3.252	3.518	3.803	4.108	4.435	4.785	5.160
10	2.839	3.106	3.395	3.707	4.046	4.411	4.807	5.234	5.695	6.192
11	3.152	3.479	3.836	4.226	4.652	5.117	5.624	6.176	6.777	7.430
12	3.498	3.896	4.334	4.818	5.350	5.936	6.580	7.288	8.064	8.916
13	3.883	4.363	4.898	5.492	6.153	6.886	7.699	8.599	9.596	10.699
14	4.310	4.887	5.535	6.261	7.076	7.987	9.007	10.147	11.420	12.839
15	4.785	5.474	6.254	7.138	8.137	9.265	10.539	11.974	13.589	15.407
16	5.311	6.130	7.067	8.137	9.358	10.748	12.330	14.129	16.171	18.488
17	5.895	6.866	7.986	9.276	10.761	12.468	14.426	16.672	19.244	22.186
18	6.543	7.690	9.024	10.575	12.375	14.462	16.879	19.673	22.900	26.623
19	7.263	8.613	10.197	12.055	14.232	16.776	19.748	23.214	27.251	31.948
20	8.062	9.646	11.523	13.743	16.366	19.461	23.105	27.393	32.429	38.337
21	8.949	10.804	13.021	15.667	18.821	22.574	27.033	32.323	38.591	46.005
22	9.933	12.100	14.713	17.861	21.644	26.186	31.629	38.141	45.923	55.205
23	11.026	13.552	16.626	20.361	24.891	30.376	37.005	45.007	54.648	66.247
24	12.239	15.178	18.788	23.212	28.625	35.236	43.296	53.108	65.031	79.496
25	13.585	17.000	21.230	26.461	32.918	40.874	50.656	62.667	77.387	95.395
30	22.892	29.960	39.115	50.949	66.210	85.849	111.061	143.367	184.672	237.373
35	38.574	52.799	72.066	98.097	133.172	180.311	243.495	327.988	440.691	590.657
40	64.999	93.049	132.776	188.876	267.856	378.715	533.846	750.353	1051.642	1469.740
45	109.527	163.985	244.629	363.662	538.752	795.429	1170.425	1716.619	2509.583	3657.176
50	184.559	288.996	450.711	700.197	1083.619	1670.669	2566.080	3927.189	5988.730	9100.191

TABLE A–1 Compound-value interest factors for one dollar, CVIF (continued)

Year	21%	22%	23%	24%	25%	26%	27%	28%	29%	30%
1	1.210	1.220	1.230	1.240	1.250	1.260	1.270	1.280	1.290	1.300
2	1.464	1.488	1.513	1.538	1.562	1.588	1.613	1.638	1.664	1.690
3	1.772	1.816	1.861	1.907	1.953	2.000	2.048	2.097	2.147	2.197
4	2.144	2.215	2.289	2.364	2.441	2.520	2.601	2.684	2.769	2.856
5	2.594	2.703	2.815	2.932	3.052	3.176	3.304	3.436	3.572	3.713
6	3.138	3.297	3.463	3.635	3.815	4.001	4.196	4.398	4.608	4.827
7	3.797	4.023	4.259	4.508	4.768	5.042	5.329	5.629	5.945	6.275
8	4.595	4.908	5.239	5.589	5.960	6.353	6.767	7.206	7.669	8.157
9	5.560	5.987	6.444	6.931	7.451	8.004	8.595	9.223	9.893	10.604
10	6.727	7.305	7.926	8.594	9.313	10.086	10.915	11.806	12.761	13.786
11	8.140	8.912	9.749	10.657	11.642	12.708	13.862	15.112	16.462	17.921
12	9.850	10.872	11.991	13.215	14.552	16.012	17.605	19.343	21.236	23.298
13	11.918	13.264	14.749	16.386	18.190	20.175	22.359	24.759	27.395	30.287
14	14.421	16.182	18.141	20.319	22.737	25.420	28.395	31.691	35.339	39.373
15	17.449	19.742	22.314	25.195	28.422	32.030	36.062	40.565	45.587	51.185
16	21.113	24.085	27.446	31.242	35.527	40.357	45.799	51.923	58.808	66.541
17	25.547	29.384	33.758	38.740	44.409	50.850	58.165	66.461	75.862	86.503
18	30.912	35.848	41.523	48.038	55.511	64.071	73.869	85.070	97.862	112.454
19	37.404	43.735	51.073	59.567	69.389	80.730	93.813	108.890	126.242	146.190
20	45.258	53.357	62.820	73.863	86.736	101.720	119.143	139.379	162.852	190.047
21	54.762	65.095	77.268	91.591	108.420	128.167	151.312	178.405	210.079	247.061
22	66.262	79.416	95.040	113.572	135.525	161.490	192.165	228.358	271.002	321.178
23	80.178	96.887	116.899	140.829	169.407	203.477	244.050	292.298	349.592	417.531
24	97.015	118.203	143.786	174.628	211.758	256.381	309.943	374.141	450.974	542.791
25	117.388	144.207	176.857	216.539	264.698	323.040	393.628	478.901	581.756	705.627
30	304.471	389.748	497.904	634.810	807.793	1025.904	1300.477	1645.488	2078.208	2619.936
35	789.716	1053.370	1401.749	1861.020	2465.189	3258.053	4296.547	5653.840	7423.988	9727.598
40	2048.309	2846.941	3946.340	5455.797	7523.156	10346.879	14195.051	19426.418	26520.723	36117.754
45	5312.758	7694.418	11110.121	15994.316	22958.844	32859.457	46897.973	66748.500	94739.937	134102.187
50	13779.844	20795.680	31278.301	46889.207	70064.812	104354.562	154942.687	229345.875	338440.000	497910.125

TABLE A–1 Compound-value interest factors for one dollar, CVIF (continued)

Year	31%	32%	33%	34%	35%	36%	37%	38%	39%	40%
1	1.310	1.320	1.330	1.340	1.350	1.360	1.370	1.380	1.390	1.400
2	1.716	1.742	1.769	1.796	1.822	1.850	1.877	1.904	1.932	1.960
3	2.248	2.300	2.353	2.406	2.460	2.515	2.571	2.628	2.686	2.744
4	2.945	3.036	3.129	3.224	3.321	3.421	3.523	3.627	3.733	3.842
5	3.858	4.007	4.162	4.320	4.484	4.653	4.826	5.005	5.189	5.378
6	5.054	5.290	5.535	5.789	6.053	6.328	6.612	6.907	7.213	7.530
7	6.621	6.983	7.361	7.758	8.172	8.605	9.058	9.531	10.025	10.541
8	8.673	9.217	9.791	10.395	11.032	11.703	12.410	13.153	13.935	14.758
9	11.362	12.166	13.022	13.930	14.894	15.917	17.001	18.151	19.370	20.661
10	14.884	16.060	17.319	18.666	20.106	21.646	23.292	25.049	26.924	28.925
11	19.498	21.199	23.034	25.012	27.144	29.439	31.910	34.567	37.425	40.495
12	25.542	27.982	30.635	33.516	36.644	40.037	43.716	47.703	52.020	56.694
13	33.460	36.937	40.745	44.912	49.469	54.451	59.892	65.830	72.308	79.371
14	43.832	48.756	54.190	60.181	66.784	74.053	82.051	90.845	100.509	111.119
15	57.420	64.358	72.073	80.643	90.158	100.712	112.410	125.366	139.707	155.567
16	75.220	84.953	95.857	108.061	121.713	136.968	154.002	173.005	194.192	217.793
17	98.539	112.138	127.490	144.802	164.312	186.277	210.983	238.747	269.927	304.911
18	129.086	148.022	169.561	194.035	221.822	253.337	289.046	329.471	375.198	426.875
19	169.102	195.389	225.517	260.006	299.459	344.537	395.993	454.669	521.525	597.625
20	221.523	257.913	299.937	348.408	404.270	468.571	542.511	627.443	724.919	836.674
21	290.196	340.446	398.916	466.867	545.764	637.256	743.240	865.871	1007.637	1171.343
22	380.156	449.388	530.558	625.601	736.781	866.668	1018.238	1194.900	1400.615	1639.878
23	498.004	593.192	705.642	838.305	994.653	1178.668	1394.986	1648.961	1946.854	2295.829
24	652.385	783.013	938.504	1123.328	1342.781	1602.988	1911.129	2275.564	2706.125	3214.158
25	854.623	1033.577	1248.210	1505.258	1812.754	2180.063	2618.245	3140.275	3761.511	4499.816
30	3297.081	4142.008	5194.516	6503.285	8128.426	10142.914	12636.086	15716.703	19517.969	24201.043
35	12719.918	16598.906	21617.363	28096.695	36448.051	47190.727	60983.836	78660.188	101276.125	130158.687
40	49072.621	66519.313	89962.188	121388.437	163433.875	219558.625	294317.937	393684.687	525508.312	700022.688

TABLE A-2 Compound-value interest factors for a one-dollar annuity, CVIFA

Year	1%	2%	3%	4%	5%	6%	7%	8%	9%	10%
1	1.000	1.000	1.000	1.000	1.000	1.000	1.000	1.000	1.000	1.000
2	2.010	2.020	2.030	2.040	2.050	2.060	2.070	2.080	2.090	2.100
3	3.030	3.060	3.091	3.122	3.152	3.184	3.215	3.246	3.278	3.310
4	4.060	4.122	4.184	4.246	4.310	4.375	4.440	4.506	4.573	4.641
5	5.101	5.204	5.309	5.416	5.526	5.637	5.751	5.867	5.985	6.105
6	6.152	6.308	6.468	6.633	6.802	6.975	7.153	7.336	7.523	7.716
7	7.214	7.434	7.662	7.898	8.142	8.394	8.654	8.923	9.200	9.487
8	8.286	8.583	8.892	9.214	9.549	9.897	10.260	10.637	11.028	11.436
9	9.368	9.755	10.159	10.583	11.027	11.491	11.978	12.488	13.021	13.579
10	10.462	10.950	11.464	12.006	12.578	13.181	13.816	14.487	15.193	15.937
11	11.567	12.169	12.808	13.486	14.207	14.972	15.784	16.645	17.560	18.531
12	12.682	13.412	14.192	15.026	15.917	16.870	17.888	18.977	20.141	21.384
13	13.809	14.680	15.618	16.627	17.713	18.882	20.141	21.495	22.953	24.523
14	14.947	15.974	17.086	18.292	19.598	21.015	22.550	24.215	26.019	27.975
15	16.097	17.293	18.599	20.023	21.578	23.276	25.129	27.152	29.361	31.772
16	17.258	18.639	20.157	21.824	23.657	25.672	27.888	30.324	33.003	35.949
17	18.430	20.012	21.761	23.697	25.840	28.213	30.840	33.750	36.973	40.544
18	19.614	21.412	23.414	25.645	28.132	30.905	33.999	37.450	41.301	45.599
19	20.811	22.840	25.117	27.671	30.539	33.760	37.379	41.446	46.018	51.158
20	22.019	24.297	26.870	29.778	33.066	36.785	40.995	45.762	51.159	57.274
21	23.239	25.783	28.676	31.969	35.719	39.992	44.865	50.422	56.764	64.002
22	24.471	27.299	30.536	34.248	38.505	43.392	49.005	55.456	62.872	71.402
23	25.716	28.845	32.452	36.618	41.430	46.995	53.435	60.893	69.531	79.542
24	26.973	30.421	34.426	39.082	44.501	50.815	58.176	66.764	76.789	88.496
25	28.243	32.030	36.459	41.645	47.726	54.864	63.248	73.105	84.699	98.346
30	34.784	40.567	47.575	56.084	66.438	79.057	94.459	113.282	136.305	164.491
35	41.659	49.994	60.461	73.651	90.318	111.432	138.234	172.314	215.705	271.018
40	48.885	60.401	75.400	95.024	120.797	154.758	199.630	259.052	337.872	442.580
45	56.479	71.891	92.718	121.027	159.695	212.737	285.741	386.497	525.840	718.881
50	64.461	84.577	112.794	152.664	209.341	290.325	406.516	573.756	815.051	1163.865

TABLE A–2 Compound-value interest factors for a one-dollar annuity, CVIFA (continued)

Year	11%	12%	13%	14%	15%	16%	17%	18%	19%	20%
1	1.000	1.000	1.000	1.000	1.000	1.000	1.000	1.000	1.000	1.000
2	2.110	2.120	2.130	2.140	2.150	2.160	2.170	2.180	2.190	2.200
3	3.342	3.374	3.407	3.440	3.472	3.506	3.539	3.572	3.606	3.640
4	4.710	4.779	4.850	4.921	4.993	5.066	5.141	5.215	5.291	5.368
5	6.228	6.353	6.480	6.610	6.742	6.877	7.014	7.154	7.297	7.442
6	7.913	8.115	8.323	8.535	8.754	8.977	9.207	9.442	9.683	9.930
7	9.783	10.089	10.405	10.730	11.067	11.414	11.772	12.141	12.523	12.916
8	11.859	12.300	12.757	13.233	13.727	14.240	14.773	15.327	15.902	16.499
9	14.164	14.776	15.416	16.085	16.786	17.518	18.285	19.086	19.923	20.799
10	16.722	17.549	18.420	19.337	20.304	21.321	22.393	23.521	24.709	25.959
11	19.561	20.655	21.814	23.044	24.349	25.733	27.200	28.755	30.403	32.150
12	22.713	24.133	25.650	27.271	29.001	30.850	32.824	34.931	37.180	39.580
13	26.211	28.029	29.984	32.088	34.352	36.786	39.404	42.218	45.244	48.496
14	30.095	32.392	34.882	37.581	40.504	43.672	47.102	50.818	54.841	59.196
15	34.405	37.280	40.417	43.842	47.580	51.659	56.109	60.965	66.260	72.035
16	39.190	42.753	46.671	50.980	55.717	60.925	66.648	72.938	79.850	87.442
17	44.500	48.883	53.738	59.117	65.075	71.673	78.978	87.067	96.021	105.930
18	50.396	55.749	61.724	68.393	75.836	84.140	93.404	103.739	115.265	128.116
19	56.939	63.439	70.748	78.968	88.211	98.603	110.283	123.412	138.165	154.739
20	64.202	72.052	80.946	91.024	102.443	115.379	130.031	146.626	165.417	186.687
21	72.264	81.698	92.468	104.767	118.809	134.840	153.136	174.019	197.846	225.024
22	81.213	92.502	105.489	120.434	137.630	157.414	180.169	206.342	236.436	271.028
23	91.147	104.602	120.203	138.295	159.274	183.600	211.798	244.483	282.359	326.234
24	102.173	118.154	136.829	158.656	184.166	213.976	248.803	289.490	337.007	392.480
25	114.412	133.333	155.616	181.867	212.790	249.212	292.099	342.598	402.038	471.976
30	199.018	241.330	293.192	356.778	434.738	530.306	647.423	790.932	966.698	1181.865
35	341.583	431.658	546.663	693.552	881.152	1120.699	1426.448	1816.607	2314.173	2948.294
40	581.812	767.080	1013.667	1341.979	1779.048	2360.724	3134.412	4163.094	5529.711	7343.715
45	986.613	1358.208	1874.086	2590.464	3585.031	4965.191	6879.008	9531.258	13203.105	18280.914
50	1668.723	2399.975	3459.344	4994.301	7217.488	10435.449	15088.805	21812.273	31514.492	45496.094

TABLE A–2 Compound-value interest factors for a one-dollar annuity, CVIFA (continued)

Year	21%	22%	23%	24%	25%	26%	27%	28%	29%	30%
1	1.000	1.000	1.000	1.000	1.000	1.000	1.000	1.000	1.000	1.000
2	2.210	2.220	2.230	2.240	2.250	2.260	2.270	2.280	2.290	2.300
3	3.674	3.708	3.743	3.778	3.813	3.848	3.883	3.918	3.954	3.990
4	5.446	5.524	5.604	5.684	5.766	5.848	5.931	6.016	6.101	6.187
5	7.589	7.740	7.893	8.048	8.207	8.368	8.533	8.700	8.870	9.043
6	10.183	10.442	10.708	10.980	11.259	11.544	11.837	12.136	12.442	12.756
7	13.321	13.740	14.171	14.615	15.073	15.546	16.032	16.534	17.051	17.583
8	17.119	17.762	18.430	19.123	19.842	20.588	21.361	22.163	22.995	23.858
9	21.714	22.670	23.669	24.712	25.802	26.940	28.129	29.369	30.664	32.015
10	27.274	28.657	30.113	31.643	33.253	34.945	36.723	38.592	40.556	42.619
11	34.001	35.962	38.039	40.238	42.566	45.030	47.639	50.398	53.318	56.405
12	42.141	44.873	47.787	50.895	54.208	57.738	61.501	65.510	69.780	74.326
13	51.991	55.745	59.778	64.109	68.760	73.750	79.106	84.853	91.016	97.624
14	63.909	69.009	74.528	80.496	86.949	93.925	101.465	109.611	118.411	127.912
15	78.330	85.191	92.669	100.815	109.687	119.346	129.860	141.302	153.750	167.285
16	95.779	104.933	114.983	126.010	138.109	151.375	165.922	181.867	199.337	218.470
17	116.892	129.019	142.428	157.252	173.636	191.733	211.721	233.790	258.145	285.011
18	142.439	158.403	176.187	195.993	218.045	242.583	269.885	300.250	334.006	371.514
19	173.351	194.251	217.710	244.031	273.556	306.654	343.754	385.321	431.868	483.968
20	210.755	237.986	268.783	303.598	342.945	387.384	437.568	494.210	558.110	630.157
21	256.013	291.343	331.603	377.461	429.681	489.104	556.710	633.589	720.962	820.204
22	310.775	356.438	408.871	469.052	538.101	617.270	708.022	811.993	931.040	1067.265
23	377.038	435.854	503.911	582.624	673.626	778.760	900.187	1040.351	1202.042	1388.443
24	457.215	532.741	620.810	723.453	843.032	982.237	1144.237	1332.649	1551.634	1805.975
25	554.230	650.944	764.596	898.082	1054.791	1238.617	1454.180	1706.790	2002.608	2348.765
30	1445.111	1767.044	2160.459	2640.881	3227.172	3941.953	4812.891	5873.172	7162.785	8729.805
35	3755.814	4783.520	6090.227	7750.094	9856.746	12527.160	15909.480	20188.742	25596.512	32422.090
40	9749.141	12936.141	17153.691	22728.367	30088.621	39791.957	52570.707	69376.562	91447.375	120389.375
45	25294.223	34970.230	48300.660	66638.937	91831.312	126378.937	173692.875	238384.312	326686.375	447005.062

TABLE A-2   Compound-value interest factors for a one-dollar annuity, CVIFA (continued)

Year	31%	32%	33%	34%	35%	36%	37%	38%	39%	40%
1	1.000	1.000	1.000	1.000	1.000	1.000	1.000	1.000	1.000	1.000
2	2.310	2.320	2.330	2.340	2.350	2.360	2.370	2.380	2.390	2.400
3	4.026	4.062	4.099	4.136	4.172	4.210	4.247	4.284	4.322	4.360
4	6.274	6.362	6.452	6.542	6.633	6.725	6.818	6.912	7.008	7.104
5	9.219	9.398	9.581	9.766	9.954	10.146	10.341	10.539	10.741	10.946
6	13.077	13.406	13.742	14.086	14.438	14.799	15.167	15.544	15.930	16.324
7	18.131	18.696	19.277	19.876	20.492	21.126	21.779	22.451	23.142	23.853
8	24.752	25.678	26.638	27.633	28.664	29.732	30.837	31.982	33.167	34.395
9	33.425	34.895	36.429	38.028	39.696	41.435	43.247	45.135	47.103	49.152
10	44.786	47.062	49.451	51.958	54.590	57.351	60.248	63.287	66.473	69.813
11	59.670	63.121	66.769	70.624	74.696	78.998	83.540	88.335	93.397	98.739
12	79.167	84.320	89.803	95.636	101.840	108.437	115.450	122.903	130.822	139.234
13	104.709	112.302	120.438	129.152	138.484	148.474	159.166	170.606	182.842	195.928
14	138.169	149.239	161.183	174.063	187.953	202.925	219.058	236.435	255.151	275.299
15	182.001	197.996	215.373	234.245	254.737	276.978	301.109	327.281	355.659	386.418
16	239.421	262.354	287.446	314.888	344.895	377.690	413.520	452.647	495.366	541.985
17	314.642	347.307	383.303	422.949	466.608	514.658	567.521	625.652	689.558	759.778
18	413.180	459.445	510.792	567.751	630.920	700.935	778.504	864.399	959.485	1064.689
19	542.266	607.467	680.354	761.786	852.741	954.271	1067.551	1193.870	1334.683	1491.563
20	711.368	802.856	905.870	1021.792	1152.200	1298.809	1463.544	1648.539	1856.208	2089.188
21	932.891	1060.769	1205.807	1370.201	1556.470	1767.380	2006.055	2275.982	2581.128	2925.862
22	1223.087	1401.215	1604.724	1837.068	2102.234	2404.636	2749.294	3141.852	3588.765	4097.203
23	1603.243	1850.603	2135.282	2462.669	2839.014	3271.304	3767.532	4336.750	4989.379	5737.078
24	2101.247	2443.795	2840.924	3300.974	3833.667	4449.969	5162.516	5985.711	6936.230	8032.906
25	2753.631	3226.808	3779.428	4424.301	5176.445	6052.957	7073.645	8261.273	9642.352	11247.062
30	10632.543	12940.672	15737.945	19124.434	23221.258	28172.016	34148.906	41357.227	50043.625	60500.207

TABLE A–3 Present-value interest factors for one dollar, PVIF

Year	1%	2%	3%	4%	5%	6%	7%	8%	9%	10%
1	.990	.980	.971	.962	.952	.943	.935	.926	.917	.909
2	.980	.961	.943	.925	.907	.890	.873	.857	.842	.826
3	.971	.942	.915	.889	.864	.840	.816	.794	.772	.751
4	.961	.924	.888	.855	.823	.792	.763	.735	.708	.683
5	.951	.906	.863	.822	.784	.747	.713	.681	.650	.621
6	.942	.888	.837	.790	.746	.705	.666	.630	.596	.564
7	.933	.871	.813	.760	.711	.665	.623	.583	.547	.513
8	.923	.853	.789	.731	.677	.627	.582	.540	.502	.467
9	.914	.837	.766	.703	.645	.592	.544	.500	.460	.424
10	.905	.820	.744	.676	.614	.558	.508	.463	.422	.386
11	.896	.804	.722	.650	.585	.527	.475	.429	.388	.350
12	.887	.789	.701	.625	.557	.497	.444	.397	.356	.319
13	.879	.773	.681	.601	.530	.469	.415	.368	.326	.290
14	.870	.758	.661	.577	.505	.442	.388	.340	.299	.263
15	.861	.743	.642	.555	.481	.417	.362	.315	.275	.239
16	.853	.728	.623	.534	.458	.394	.339	.292	.252	.218
17	.844	.714	.605	.513	.436	.371	.317	.270	.231	.198
18	.836	.700	.587	.494	.416	.350	.296	.250	.212	.180
19	.828	.686	.570	.475	.396	.331	.277	.232	.194	.164
20	.820	.673	.554	.456	.377	.312	.258	.215	.178	.149
21	.811	.660	.538	.439	.359	.294	.242	.199	.164	.135
22	.803	.647	.522	.422	.342	.278	.226	.184	.150	.123
23	.795	.634	.507	.406	.326	.262	.211	.170	.138	.112
24	.788	.622	.492	.390	.310	.247	.197	.158	.126	.102
25	.780	.610	.478	.375	.295	.233	.184	.146	.116	.092
30	.742	.552	.412	.308	.231	.174	.131	.099	.075	.057
35	.706	.500	.355	.253	.181	.130	.094	.068	.049	.036
40	.672	.453	.307	.208	.142	.097	.067	.046	.032	.022
45	.639	.410	.264	.171	.111	.073	.048	.031	.021	.014
50	.608	.372	.228	.141	.087	.054	.034	.021	.013	.009

TABLE A–3 Present-value interest factors for one dollar, PVIF (continued)

Year	11%	12%	13%	14%	15%	16%	17%	18%	19%	20%
1	.901	.893	.885	.877	.870	.862	.855	.847	.840	.833
2	.812	.797	.783	.769	.756	.743	.731	.718	.706	.694
3	.731	.712	.693	.675	.658	.641	.624	.609	.593	.579
4	.659	.636	.613	.592	.572	.552	.534	.516	.499	.482
5	.593	.567	.543	.519	.497	.476	.456	.437	.419	.402
6	.535	.507	.480	.456	.432	.410	.390	.370	.352	.335
7	.482	.452	.425	.400	.376	.354	.333	.314	.296	.279
8	.434	.404	.376	.351	.327	.305	.285	.266	.249	.233
9	.391	.361	.333	.308	.284	.263	.243	.225	.209	.194
10	.352	.322	.295	.270	.247	.227	.208	.191	.176	.162
11	.317	.287	.261	.237	.215	.195	.178	.162	.148	.135
12	.286	.257	.231	.208	.187	.168	.152	.137	.124	.112
13	.258	.229	.204	.182	.163	.145	.130	.116	.104	.093
14	.232	.205	.181	.160	.141	.125	.111	.099	.088	.078
15	.209	.183	.160	.140	.123	.108	.095	.084	.074	.065
16	.188	.163	.141	.123	.107	.093	.081	.071	.062	.054
17	.170	.146	.125	.108	.093	.080	.069	.060	.052	.045
18	.153	.130	.111	.095	.081	.069	.059	.051	.044	.038
19	.138	.116	.098	.083	.070	.060	.051	.043	.037	.031
20	.124	.104	.087	.073	.061	.051	.043	.037	.031	.026
21	.112	.093	.077	.064	.053	.044	.037	.031	.026	.022
22	.101	.083	.068	.056	.046	.038	.032	.026	.022	.018
23	.091	.074	.060	.049	.040	.033	.027	.022	.018	.015
24	.082	.066	.053	.043	.035	.028	.023	.019	.015	.013
25	.074	.059	.047	.038	.030	.024	.020	.016	.013	.010
30	.044	.033	.026	.020	.015	.012	.009	.007	.005	.004
35	.026	.019	.014	.010	.008	.006	.004	.003	.002	.002
40	.015	.011	.008	.005	.004	.003	.002	.001	.001	.001
45	.009	.006	.004	.003	.002	.001	.001	.001	.000	.000
50	.005	.003	.002	.001	.001	.001	.000	.000	.000	.000

TABLE A–3 Present-value interest factors for one dollar, PVIF (continued)

Year	21%	22%	23%	24%	25%	26%	27%	28%	29%	30%
1	.826	.820	.813	.806	.800	.794	.787	.781	.775	.769
2	.683	.672	.661	.650	.640	.630	.620	.610	.601	.592
3	.564	.551	.537	.524	.512	.500	.488	.477	.466	.455
4	.467	.451	.437	.423	.410	.397	.384	.373	.361	.350
5	.386	.370	.355	.341	.328	.315	.303	.291	.280	.269
6	.319	.303	.289	.275	.262	.250	.238	.227	.217	.207
7	.263	.249	.235	.222	.210	.198	.188	.178	.168	.159
8	.218	.204	.191	.179	.168	.157	.148	.139	.130	.123
9	.180	.167	.155	.144	.134	.125	.116	.108	.101	.094
10	.149	.137	.126	.116	.107	.099	.092	.085	.078	.073
11	.123	.112	.103	.094	.086	.079	.072	.066	.061	.056
12	.102	.092	.083	.076	.069	.062	.057	.052	.047	.043
13	.084	.075	.068	.061	.055	.050	.045	.040	.037	.033
14	.069	.062	.055	.049	.044	.039	.035	.032	.028	.025
15	.057	.051	.045	.040	.035	.031	.028	.025	.022	.020
16	.047	.042	.036	.032	.028	.025	.022	.019	.017	.015
17	.039	.034	.030	.026	.023	.020	.017	.015	.013	.012
18	.032	.028	.024	.021	.018	.016	.014	.012	.010	.009
19	.027	.023	.020	.017	.014	.012	.011	.009	.008	.007
20	.022	.019	.016	.014	.012	.010	.008	.007	.006	.005
21	.018	.015	.013	.011	.009	.008	.007	.006	.005	.004
22	.015	.013	.011	.009	.007	.006	.005	.004	.004	.003
23	.012	.010	.009	.007	.006	.005	.004	.003	.003	.002
24	.010	.008	.007	.006	.005	.004	.003	.003	.002	.002
25	.009	.007	.006	.005	.004	.003	.003	.002	.002	.001
30	.003	.003	.002	.002	.001	.001	.001	.001	.000	.000
35	.001	.001	.001	.001	.000	.000	.000	.000	.000	.000
40	.000	.000	.000	.000	.000	.000	.000	.000	.000	.000
45	.000	.000	.000	.000	.000	.000	.000	.000	.000	.000
50	.000	.000	.000	.000	.000	.000	.000	.000	.000	.000

TABLE A-3 Present-value interest factors for one dollar, PVIF (continued)

Year	31%	32%	33%	34%	35%	36%	37%	38%	39%	40%
1	.763	.758	.752	.746	.741	.735	.730	.725	.719	.714
2	.583	.574	.565	.557	.549	.541	.533	.525	.518	.510
3	.445	.435	.425	.416	.406	.398	.389	.381	.372	.364
4	.340	.329	.320	.310	.301	.292	.284	.276	.268	.260
5	.259	.250	.240	.231	.223	.215	.207	.200	.193	.186
6	.198	.189	.181	.173	.165	.158	.151	.145	.139	.133
7	.151	.143	.136	.129	.122	.116	.110	.105	.100	.095
8	.115	.108	.102	.096	.091	.085	.081	.076	.072	.068
9	.088	.082	.077	.072	.067	.063	.059	.055	.052	.048
10	.067	.062	.058	.054	.050	.046	.043	.040	.037	.035
11	.051	.047	.043	.040	.037	.034	.031	.029	.027	.025
12	.039	.036	.033	.030	.027	.025	.023	.021	.019	.018
13	.030	.027	.025	.022	.020	.018	.017	.015	.014	.013
14	.023	.021	.018	.017	.015	.014	.012	.011	.010	.009
15	.017	.016	.014	.012	.011	.010	.009	.008	.007	.006
16	.013	.012	.010	.009	.008	.007	.006	.006	.005	.005
17	.010	.009	.008	.007	.006	.005	.005	.004	.004	.003
18	.008	.007	.006	.005	.005	.004	.003	.003	.003	.002
19	.006	.005	.004	.004	.003	.003	.003	.002	.002	.002
20	.005	.004	.003	.003	.002	.002	.002	.002	.001	.001
21	.003	.003	.003	.002	.002	.002	.001	.001	.001	.001
22	.003	.002	.002	.002	.001	.001	.001	.001	.001	.001
23	.002	.002	.001	.001	.001	.001	.001	.001	.001	.000
24	.002	.001	.001	.001	.001	.001	.001	.000	.000	.000
25	.001	.001	.001	.001	.001	.000	.000	.000	.000	.000
30	.000	.000	.000	.000	.000	.000	.000	.000	.000	.000
35	.000	.000	.000	.000	.000	.000	.000	.000	.000	.000
40	.000	.000	.000	.000	.000	.000	.000	.000	.000	.000
45	.000	.000	.000	.000	.000	.000	.000	.000	.000	.000
50	.000	.000	.000	.000	.000	.000	.000	.000	.000	.000

TABLE A–4 Present-value interest factors for a one-dollar annuity, PVIFA

Year	1%	2%	3%	4%	5%	6%	7%	8%	9%	10%
1	.990	.980	.971	.962	.952	.943	.935	.926	.917	.909
2	1.970	1.942	1.913	1.886	1.859	1.833	1.808	1.783	1.759	1.736
3	2.941	2.884	2.829	2.775	2.723	2.673	2.624	2.577	2.531	2.487
4	3.902	3.808	3.717	3.630	3.546	3.465	3.387	3.312	3.240	3.170
5	4.853	4.713	4.580	4.452	4.329	4.212	4.100	3.993	3.890	3.791
6	5.795	5.601	5.417	5.242	5.076	4.917	4.767	4.623	4.486	4.355
7	6.728	6.472	6.230	6.002	5.786	5.582	5.389	5.206	5.033	4.868
8	7.652	7.326	7.020	6.733	6.463	6.210	5.971	5.747	5.535	5.335
9	8.566	8.162	7.786	7.435	7.108	6.802	6.515	6.247	5.995	5.759
10	9.471	8.983	8.530	8.111	7.722	7.360	7.024	6.710	6.418	6.145
11	10.368	9.787	9.253	8.760	8.306	7.887	7.499	7.139	6.805	6.495
12	11.255	10.575	9.954	9.385	8.863	8.384	7.943	7.536	7.161	6.814
13	12.134	11.348	10.635	9.986	9.394	8.853	8.358	7.904	7.487	7.103
14	13.004	12.106	11.296	10.563	9.899	9.295	8.746	8.244	7.786	7.367
15	13.865	12.849	11.938	11.118	10.380	9.712	9.108	8.560	8.061	7.606
16	14.718	13.578	12.561	11.652	10.838	10.106	9.447	8.851	8.313	7.824
17	15.562	14.292	13.166	12.166	11.274	10.477	9.763	9.122	8.544	8.022
18	16.398	14.992	13.754	12.659	11.690	10.828	10.059	9.372	8.756	8.201
19	17.226	15.679	14.324	13.134	12.085	11.158	10.336	9.604	8.950	8.365
20	18.046	16.352	14.878	13.590	12.462	11.470	10.594	9.818	9.129	8.514
21	18.857	17.011	15.415	14.029	12.821	11.764	10.836	10.017	9.292	8.649
22	19.661	17.658	15.937	14.451	13.163	12.042	11.061	10.201	9.442	8.772
23	20.456	18.292	16.444	14.857	13.489	12.303	11.272	10.371	9.580	8.883
24	21.244	18.914	16.936	15.247	13.799	12.550	11.469	10.529	9.707	8.985
25	22.023	19.524	17.413	15.622	14.094	12.783	11.654	10.675	9.823	9.077
30	25.808	22.397	19.601	17.292	15.373	13.765	12.409	11.258	10.274	9.427
35	29.409	24.999	21.487	18.665	16.374	14.498	12.948	11.655	10.567	9.644
40	32.835	27.356	23.115	19.793	17.159	15.046	13.332	11.925	10.757	9.779
45	36.095	29.490	24.519	20.720	17.774	15.456	13.606	12.108	10.881	9.863
50	39.197	31.424	25.730	21.482	18.256	15.762	13.801	12.234	10.962	9.915

TABLE A-4 Present-value interest factors for a one-dollar annuity, PVIFA (continued)

Year	11%	12%	13%	14%	15%	16%	17%	18%	19%	20%
1	.901	.893	.885	.877	.870	.862	.855	.847	.840	.833
2	1.713	1.690	1.668	1.647	1.626	1.605	1.585	1.566	1.547	1.528
3	2.444	2.402	2.361	2.322	2.283	2.246	2.210	2.174	2.140	2.106
4	3.102	3.037	2.974	2.914	2.855	2.798	2.743	2.690	2.639	2.589
5	3.696	3.605	3.517	3.433	3.352	3.274	3.199	3.127	3.058	2.991
6	4.231	4.111	3.998	3.889	3.784	3.685	3.589	3.498	3.410	3.326
7	4.712	4.564	4.423	4.288	4.160	4.039	3.922	3.812	3.706	3.605
8	5.146	4.968	4.799	4.639	4.487	4.344	4.207	4.078	3.954	3.837
9	5.537	5.328	5.132	4.946	4.772	4.607	4.451	4.303	4.163	4.031
10	5.889	5.650	5.426	5.216	5.019	4.833	4.659	4.494	4.339	4.192
11	6.207	5.938	5.687	5.453	5.234	5.029	4.836	4.656	4.487	4.327
12	6.492	6.194	5.918	5.660	5.421	5.197	4.988	4.793	4.611	4.439
13	6.750	6.424	6.122	5.842	5.583	5.342	5.118	4.910	4.715	4.533
14	6.982	6.628	6.303	6.002	5.724	5.468	5.229	5.008	4.802	4.611
15	7.191	6.811	6.462	6.142	5.847	5.575	5.324	5.092	4.876	4.675
16	7.379	6.974	6.604	6.265	5.954	5.669	5.405	5.162	4.938	4.730
17	7.549	7.120	6.729	6.373	6.047	5.749	5.475	5.222	4.990	4.775
18	7.702	7.250	6.840	6.467	6.128	5.818	5.534	5.273	5.033	4.812
19	7.839	7.366	6.938	6.550	6.198	5.877	5.585	5.316	5.070	4.843
20	7.963	7.469	7.025	6.623	6.259	5.929	5.628	5.353	5.101	4.870
21	8.075	7.562	7.102	6.687	6.312	5.973	5.665	5.384	5.127	4.891
22	8.176	7.645	7.170	6.743	6.359	6.011	5.696	5.410	5.149	4.909
23	8.266	7.718	7.230	6.792	6.399	6.044	5.723	5.432	5.167	4.925
24	8.348	7.784	7.283	6.835	6.434	6.073	5.747	5.451	5.182	4.937
25	8.422	7.843	7.330	6.873	6.464	6.097	5.766	5.467	5.195	4.948
30	8.694	8.055	7.496	7.003	6.566	6.177	5.829	5.517	5.235	4.979
35	8.855	8.176	7.586	7.070	6.617	6.215	5.858	5.539	5.251	4.992
40	8.951	8.244	7.634	7.105	6.642	6.233	5.871	5.548	5.258	4.997
45	9.008	8.283	7.661	7.123	6.654	6.242	5.877	5.552	5.261	4.999
50	9.042	8.305	7.675	7.133	6.661	6.246	5.880	5.554	5.262	4.999

TABLE A–4 Present-value interest factors for a one-dollar annuity, PVIFA (continued)

Year	21%	22%	23%	24%	25%	26%	27%	28%	29%	30%
1	.826	.820	.813	.806	.800	.794	.787	.781	.775	.769
2	1.509	1.492	1.474	1.457	1.440	1.424	1.407	1.392	1.376	1.361
3	2.074	2.042	2.011	1.981	1.952	1.923	1.896	1.868	1.842	1.816
4	2.540	2.494	2.448	2.404	2.362	2.320	2.280	2.241	2.203	2.166
5	2.926	2.864	2.803	2.745	2.689	2.635	2.583	2.532	2.483	2.436
6	3.245	3.167	3.092	3.020	2.951	2.885	2.821	2.759	2.700	2.643
7	3.508	3.416	3.327	3.242	3.161	3.083	3.009	2.937	2.868	2.802
8	3.726	3.619	3.518	3.421	3.329	3.241	3.156	3.076	2.999	2.925
9	3.905	3.786	3.673	3.566	3.463	3.366	3.273	3.184	3.100	3.019
10	4.054	3.923	3.799	3.682	3.570	3.465	3.364	3.269	3.178	3.092
11	4.177	4.035	3.902	3.776	3.656	3.544	3.437	3.335	3.239	3.147
12	4.278	4.127	3.985	3.851	3.725	3.606	3.493	3.387	3.286	3.190
13	4.362	4.203	4.053	3.912	3.780	3.656	3.538	3.427	3.322	3.223
14	4.432	4.265	4.108	3.962	3.824	3.695	3.573	3.459	3.351	3.249
15	4.489	4.315	4.153	4.001	3.859	3.726	3.601	3.483	3.373	3.268
16	4.536	4.357	4.189	4.033	3.887	3.751	3.623	3.503	3.390	3.283
17	4.576	4.391	4.219	4.059	3.910	3.771	3.640	3.518	3.403	3.295
18	4.608	4.419	4.243	4.080	3.928	3.786	3.654	3.529	3.413	3.304
19	4.635	4.442	4.263	4.097	3.942	3.799	3.664	3.539	3.421	3.311
20	4.657	4.460	4.279	4.110	3.954	3.808	3.673	3.546	3.427	3.316
21	4.675	4.476	4.292	4.121	3.963	3.816	3.679	3.551	3.432	3.320
22	4.690	4.488	4.302	4.130	3.970	3.822	3.684	3.556	3.436	3.323
23	4.703	4.499	4.311	4.137	3.976	3.827	3.689	3.559	3.438	3.325
24	4.713	4.507	4.318	4.143	3.981	3.831	3.692	3.562	3.441	3.327
25	4.721	4.514	4.323	4.147	3.985	3.834	3.694	3.564	3.442	3.329
30	4.746	4.534	4.339	4.160	3.995	3.842	3.701	3.569	3.447	3.332
35	4.756	4.541	4.345	4.164	3.998	3.845	3.703	3.571	3.448	3.333
40	4.760	4.544	4.347	4.166	3.999	3.846	3.703	3.571	3.448	3.333
45	4.761	4.545	4.347	4.166	4.000	3.846	3.704	3.571	3.448	3.333
50	4.762	4.545	4.348	4.167	4.000	3.846	3.704	3.571	3.448	3.333

TABLE A-4 Present-value interest factors for a one-dollar annuity, PVIFA (continued)

Year	31%	32%	33%	34%	35%	36%	37%	38%	39%	40%
1	.763	.758	.752	.746	.741	.735	.730	.725	.719	.714
2	1.346	1.331	1.317	1.303	1.289	1.276	1.263	1.250	1.237	1.224
3	1.791	1.766	1.742	1.719	1.696	1.673	1.652	1.630	1.609	1.589
4	2.130	2.096	2.062	2.029	1.997	1.966	1.935	1.906	1.877	1.849
5	2.390	2.345	2.302	2.260	2.220	2.181	2.143	2.106	2.070	2.035
6	2.588	2.534	2.483	2.433	2.385	2.339	2.294	2.251	2.209	2.168
7	2.739	2.677	2.619	2.562	2.508	2.455	2.404	2.355	2.308	2.263
8	2.854	2.786	2.721	2.658	2.598	2.540	2.485	2.432	2.380	2.331
9	2.942	2.868	2.798	2.730	2.665	2.603	2.544	2.487	2.432	2.379
10	3.009	2.930	2.855	2.784	2.715	2.649	2.587	2.527	2.469	2.414
11	3.060	2.978	2.899	2.824	2.752	2.683	2.618	2.555	2.496	2.438
12	3.100	3.013	2.931	2.853	2.779	2.708	2.641	2.576	2.515	2.456
13	3.129	3.040	2.956	2.876	2.799	2.727	2.658	2.592	2.529	2.469
14	3.152	3.061	2.974	2.892	2.814	2.740	2.670	2.603	2.539	2.477
15	3.170	3.076	2.988	2.905	2.825	2.750	2.679	2.611	2.546	2.484
16	3.183	3.088	2.999	2.914	2.834	2.757	2.685	2.616	2.551	2.489
17	3.193	3.097	3.007	2.921	2.840	2.763	2.690	2.621	2.555	2.492
18	3.201	3.104	3.012	2.926	2.844	2.767	2.693	2.624	2.557	2.494
19	3.207	3.109	3.017	2.930	2.848	2.770	2.696	2.626	2.559	2.496
20	3.211	3.113	3.020	2.933	2.850	2.772	2.698	2.627	2.561	2.497
21	3.215	3.116	3.023	2.935	2.852	2.773	2.699	2.629	2.562	2.498
22	3.217	3.118	3.025	2.936	2.853	2.775	2.700	2.629	2.562	2.498
23	3.219	3.120	3.026	2.938	2.854	2.775	2.701	2.630	2.563	2.499
24	3.221	3.121	3.027	2.939	2.855	2.776	2.701	2.630	2.563	2.499
25	3.222	3.122	3.028	2.939	2.856	2.776	2.702	2.631	2.563	2.499
30	3.225	3.124	3.030	2.941	2.857	2.777	2.702	2.631	2.564	2.500
35	3.226	3.125	3.030	2.941	2.857	2.778	2.703	2.632	2.564	2.500
40	3.226	3.125	3.030	2.941	2.857	2.778	2.703	2.632	2.564	2.500
45	3.226	3.125	3.030	2.941	2.857	2.778	2.703	2.632	2.564	2.500
50	3.226	3.125	3.030	2.941	2.857	2.778	2.703	2.632	2.564	2.500

APPENDIX B
Answers to Selected End - of - Chapter Problems

The following list of answers to selected problems (and portions of problems) is included in order to provide "check figures" for use in preparing detailed solutions to end-of-chapter problems requiring calculations. For problems that are relatively straightforward, the key answer is given, while for more complex problems answers to a number of parts of the problem are included. Detailed calculations are not shown—only the final and, in some cases, intermediate answers, which should help to confirm whether or not the correct solution is being developed. For problems containing a variety of cases for which similar calculations are required, the answers for only one or two cases have been included. The only verbal answers included are simple "Yes or No" or "Choice-of-Best Alternative" responses; answers to problems requiring detailed explanations or discussions are not given.

The problems (and parts of problems) for which answers have been included were selected randomly; therefore there is no discernible pattern to the choice of problem answers given. It is important to recognize that the answers given are based on what are believed to be the most obvious and reasonable assumptions related to the given problem; in a number of cases, other reasonable assumptions could result in equally correct answers.

2-1	(a)	$60,000; (c) $0.00	
2-2	$80,000		
2-3	(a)	DDB, yr. 1 = $60,000; DDB, yr. 3 = $21,600; SYD, yr. 1 = $50,000; SYD, yr. 3 = $30,000	
2-4	(b)	$14,000	
2-5	(a)	Rex, $4442; Bob, $2040	
2-6	(b)	$34,638	
2-7	(a)	Tax liability for $100,000 = $34,500	
2-9	(a)	$133,000; (c) $38,000	
2-10	(b)	(1) Only 1975 affected: operating income: $200,000; ordinary tax: $80,000	
		(2) No tax relief	
2-11	(c)	(1) $100,000	
		(2) $62,500	

3-1   (a) Current ratio: 1975 = 1.88, 1976 = 1.74, 1977 = 1.79, 1978 = 1.55
3-2   (a) Inventory turnover = 3.69
3-3   (b) Average age of accounts receivable = 45 days
3-4   (a) Debt to total capital = .60
           Total debt coverage = 1.29
3-5   (a) 1977 = 22.18% Raimer; 16.97% Industry
3-6   Current ratio = 1.67
           Average age of accounts receivable = 29.7 days
           Inventory turnover = 7.89
           Debt-equity ratio = .38
           Total asset turnover = .83
           Net profit margin = 6.6%
           Return on common equity = 8.97%
           Earnings per share = $15.25
           Total debt coverage = 3.54

4-1   (a) 20,000 books;   (c)   16,000 books
4-2   (a) R = 4000 units;   (b)   S = $56,000; T = $125,000
4-3   (a) $20,000
4-4   (a) $254,000;   (c)   Units 10%; EBIT 50%
4-5   (d) 60,000/0
4-6   (a) $0.375
4-7   (a) $10,000;   (c) $20,000
4-8   (a) DFL = 1.5
4.9   (a) Stock plan DFL = 1.25
4-10 (c) 5000 units
4-11 (a) Operating = 175,000 units; Total = 233,333 units
      (d) DTL = 2.4
4-12 (a) DTL of A = 2.14
      (b) DTL of B = 2.14

5-1   Five are sources.
      Seven are uses.
5-2   (a) $2000 = use
5-3   (a)   Total sources = $3600
      (b)   Total sources = $3000
5-4   (a)   Total sources = $90,800
      (b)   Total sources = $72,900
5-5   Expected cash receipts for July = $82,500
5-6

	May	June	July
Net cash flow	$3000	-$19000	-$13,000
Loans (investments)	X	X	$24,000

5-7   (a)   Nov. = $33,000,   Dec. = $14,000,   Jan. = -$7000,   Feb. = $37,000
            Mar. = $65,000,   Apr. = $154,000
5-8   (a)   First month = $5000
      (b)   First month—pessimistic = -$14,000
            First month—optimistic = $24,000

6-1   (a)   Pro forma income A/T = $67,500
      (b)   Total assets = $697,500
6-2   (a)   Total assets = $9,080,000
6-3   (a)   Labor per unit = P_1, 2 hrs.; P_2, 1.2 hrs.
      (b)   Overhead allocation for P_1 = $6.12 per unit
      (c)   Total cost/unit for P_2 = $19.68

6-4   (a)   Production of product X = 4600 units
        (c)   Cost per unit of product X = $22.89
6-5   Pro forma income after taxes = $69,491
6-6   Accounts receivable = $21,375
       Inventory = $39,038
       Total assets = $285,062

7-1   (a)   Profits on total assets = $2700
             Financing costs = $1920
             Net profits = $780
             Current ratio = 3.0
             ROI = 3.9%
7-2   (a)   (1)   Net profit = $1950
                Current ratio = 2.0
                ROI = 1.6%
7-3   Annual loan cost = $640
7-4   (a)   (1)   Aggressive plan financing cost = $440,000
            (2)   Conservative plan financing cost = $1,120,000
7-5   (a)   Conservative plan financing cost = $288,000
        (b)   Aggressive plan financing cost = $54,000
7-7   (a) $10,000
        (b)   Aggressive plan financing cost = $880
7-8   (a)   Conservative plan financing cost = $20,000

8-1   (a)   Cash cycle = 120 days
8-2   (c) $97,000
8-3   Current cash cycle = 120 days
       (b)   Cash cycle = 105 days
8-5   Annual savings = $70,000
8-6   (a) $3,000,000
8-7   (b)   −$6300
8-8   Yes
8-10   Savings = $4800
8-11   (a)   No
       (c)   Yes
8-12   (2)   Expected rate of return = 7.5%
       (4)   Expected rate of return = 4.04%

9-1   (b) $102,000
       (c) $120,000
9-2   (a) $125,000
9-3   (a)   Fixed costs, without = $180,000,000
9-4   (a) $5000
9-5   Yes
9-6   No
9-7   (b) $28,000
       (c)   No
       (d)   Yes
9-8   (a) $11,900
       (b) $11,183.33
9-9   Don't ease collection.

10-1   Approx. four A items
       Approx. five B items
       Approx. seven C items
10-2   (b) $33,333

10-3 (a) $43,750
10-4 (a) $2857
10-5 Recommend no change.
10-6 Addition to profits = $20,000
10-7 (a) For 1000 units: Annual order cost = $2000, carrying cost = $125, and total cost = $2125
For 5000 units: Annual order cost = $400, carrying cost = $625, and total cost = $1025
10-8 (a) (1) EOQ = 5000 units; average level of inventory = 2500 units; number of orders = 20; total cost of inventory = $1000
10-9 Level = 150 tons
10-10 (a) 200 units
(c) 33.33 units

11-1 (a) Dec. 25; (c) Jan. 15; (e) Nov. 25
11-2 (b) 18.18%; (d) 31.81%; (f) 55.67%
11-4 Annual savings = $18,000
11-6 (a) 13.75%; (b) 13.75%
11-7 (a) 6%
11-8 14.29%

12-1 (a) Acceptable accounts are D, E, F, H, J, K; (b) $152,000
12-2 (a) $80,000
12-4 (a) $1173.30
(c) 16.22%
12-5 (a) $328,482
(c) 12.12%
12-6 (a) Effective interest rate under pledging = 15%
12-7 (a) Plan 2 = $666.67
(b) Plan 1
(c) No

13-1 A = $530.60; C = $23,670; E = $62,345
13-2 (b) $338
13-3 (a) Annual = $7347
(b) Semiannual = $8954
(c) Quarterly = $12,935
13-4 (b) $12,650
13-6 $17.63
13-7 (b) Take $2000 in three years.
13-8 (b) $4467
13-9 $370
13-11 $4424.38
13-12 C = $698.84
13-13 He should take projects A and C.
13-14 (a) B = 4.75%
(b) C = 2.5%
13-16 $1087.97
13-17 (a) A, present-value interest factor = 12.5
(b) C, present value of perpetuity = $50,000
13-18 (b) He should take loan B.

14-1 Five capital expenditures
Three current expenditures
14-2 (b) Total taxes = $20,700
(d) Total taxes = $0.00

14-3   (a)   Cash flows: Yr. 0 = −$120,000;
              yrs. 1–18 = $20,000

14-4   (a) $9000;   (c) $9600;   (e) $13,200

14-5   (b)   Increases cash inflows by $4800 per year

14-6   (a)   With the new machine: Yr. 1 = $6160; yr. 2 = $6680; yr. 3 = $7200;
              yr. 4 = $7720; yr. 5 = $8240; yr. 6 = $8760.

14-8   (c) $148,000

14-9   (a)   Hoist A = $29,200
       (b)   Hoist B: Yr. 1 = $7600; yr. 2 = $8800; yr. 3 = $10,000; yr. 4 = $10,000;
              yr. 5 = $15,000

15-1   (a)   40%

15-2   (b)   Asset B

15-3   (b)   Yes

15-4   (b)   Yr. 1 = $10,000; yr. 2 = $10,000; yr. 3 = $10,000; yr. 4 = $10,000; yr. 5
              = $10,000.

15-5   (c)   Accept the first machine.

15-6   (a)   Net present value = $840
       (c)   Reject.

15-7   (a)   9%
       (c)   .975

15-8   (b)   NPV = $5131; B/C ratio = .795.

15-9   (c)   12%

15-10   (b)   18.3 yrs.; (c) $12,243

15-11   (a)   Project A = 26.67%
       (b)   Project B = 3.175 yrs.
       (c)   Project C = $4302.50
       (d)   Project A = 19.87%

15-12   (c)   Change in A/T cash inflows, yrs. 1–25 = $275,200
       (f)   Accept.

15-13   (a)   Yr. 0 = −$1,019,000; yrs. 1–10 = $154,000
       (d)   Reject.

15-14   (b)   Optimal group contains F, C, G.

16-1   (a)   Project A, range = $1600
       (b)   Project B, range of NPV = $1702.80
       (d)   Recommend project B.

16-2   (b)   Camera R, expected cash inflow = $750

16-3   (b)   Line B, expected cash inflow = $835

16-4   (b)   Project X, expected NPV = $33,450

16-5   (b)   Project A, expected cash inflow = $300
       (c)   Project B, std. dev. of cash inflows = $89.44

16-6   (a)   Project I, coefficient of variation = 1.5

16-7   (a)   (3) Project 473, std. dev. = $106.10
           (4) Project 297, coef. of var. = .367
       (d)   Project 473

16-8   (a)   A and B, B and D—projects positively correlated
           A and D—project negatively correlated
           A and D, B and C, C and D—projects not correlated
       (b)   Project A, std. dev. = $1000
           Project C, std. dev. = $0
       (c)   Project AB, std. dev. = $1899.80

16-9   (a)   Project B, rate of return = 10.25%
           Project D, rate of return = 5.0%

16-10   (b)   Recommended game is Signs Away.

16-12   (b)   −$4501

16-13   (a)   Yes

16-14 (b) (1) Project II, std. dev. = $1387
  (b) (2) Project I, risk-adjusted discount rate = 13.5%

17-1 (a) 11%
17-2 (a) Bond B = 6.23%, Bond D = 3.67%
  (b) Bond A = 5.05%, Bond C = 4.48%
17-4 B = 8.37%; C = 7.04%
17-5 (a) 3.0%
  (c) 6.48%
17-6 Firm A, cost of retained earnings = 10.25%
  Firm B, cost of new common stock equity = 6.63%
17-7 (b) 12%
17-8 (a) 6.86%
17-9 (b) 8.014%
17-10 (a) Cost of debt = 4%; cost of retained earnings = 11.54%
  (b) $5,600,000
  (c) 8.20%
17-11 (a) Common equity breaking points = $200,000, $750,000, $1,000,000
  (b) Levels of total financing = $200,000, $500,000, $750,000, $1,000,000
  (c) Weighted average cost for 1st range, $0.00 to $200,000 = 8.4%
  (e) Accept investments E, C, G, A, H.

18-1 (a) A = $1,477,612; C = $2,837,837.80
  (b) B = $1,222,222; D = $14,117,647
18-3 (a) $1,068,000
  (c) .508
  (d) No
18-4 (b) 8.46%
  (d) Yes
18-5 (a) A = $1,037,500; C = $1,029,412
  (b) B, Debt-equity structure = .236
    D, Overall capitalization rate = 8.18%
  (e) Capital structure B
18-6 (a) For EBIT of $80,000, eps = $8.50
  (b) $51,667
18-7 (b) Plan A = $46,000
  (f) Plan B
18-8 (a) Plan B = $12,000
  (e) Plan A
18-9 (a) Plan C = $20,400
  (c) Plan A, coverage ratio = $50,000/$0
18-11 (b) (2) $20.025 per share
18-12 (a) $180 per share
18-13 B = $54; D = $28.80 per share
18-14 A = 9%; C = 4.8%
18-15 $37.75 per share
18-16 (a) $73.60 per share
  (b) (2) Value = $92 per share

19-1 (a) Mon., June 12; (b) NCR = $57.75 per share
19-2 A = $1278.75; C = $50,760
19-3 (a) B = $570; D = $4176.57
  (b) A = $50; C = $29.80
19-4 (b) $411.53
  (d) 22.18%

19-5   (a)   A = $6045;   C = $5156.25
        (b)   B = $253.13
        (c)   C = $771.87
        (d)   B = −28.67%
        (e)   A = $1814.68
        (f)   B = −13.07%
19-6   (a)   (1)   400 shares
19-7   (a)   A = −$500;   C = −$2512.50
        (b)   B = $6720
19-8   (b)   −$1200
19-9   Three long positions
        One short position
19-10 $3.60 per share
19-11   (b) $94,750,000
        (c)   Selling group receives $750,000.

20-1   Yr. 0 = $40,000;   yrs. 1-11 = $24,000;   yr. 12 = −$16,000
20-2   A: Yr. 0 = $100,000;   yrs. 1-3 = $60,000;   yr. 4 = −$40,000
        C: Yr. 0 = $150,000;   yrs. 1-7 = $90,000;   yr. 8 = −$60,000
20-3   B = $147,930;   D = $430,696
20-4   A = $47,807;   C = $26,019
20-5   (a) $270,120
        (c)   Yr. 0 = $46,798;   yrs. 1-9 = $28,079;   yr. 10 = −$11,921
20-6   (a)   S = $110,340
        (b)   R = $32,540
20-7   (a)   (1)   Profit after taxes = $6000
               (2)   Profit after taxes = $7620
        (b)   (1)   Total assets = $210,000
               (2)   Total assets = $150,000
        (c)   (1)   Leasing = .6251
               (2)   Borrowing = 1.48
               (3)   Leasing = 1.867
               (4)   Borrowing = 2.85%
20-8   (a)   Yr. 0 = $20,000;   yrs. 1-14 = $12,000;   yr. 15 = −$8000
        (b)   (2)   2.667
        (d)   Total assets = $639,640
20-9   B = $667,680
        D = $44,144
20-10   Annual payment = $27,653.04
        Interest, yr. 1 = $12,870;   yr. 4 = $7435.30
20-11   A, rate = 8%;   C, rate = 8%
        B, interest, yr. 2 = $5622;   yr. 4 = $2037
        D, interest, yr. 3 = $5480
20-12 X_2, payment = $9679.20; X_4, payment = $14,232
        X_1, interest, yr. 2 = $1098;   yr. 4 = $401
        X_3, interest, yr. 2 = $220.45
20-13   (a)   (1) $5548
               (2)   Yr. 2 = $2022;   yr. 4 = $1125
               (3)   Yr. 0 = $0.00;   yr. 1 = $2988;   yr. 3 = $3308
               (4) $14,760
        (b)   (1)   Yr. 0 = $5000;   yrs. 1-4 = $3000;   yr. 5 = −$2000
20-14   (a)   Purchase alternative, yr. 0 = $0.00;   yr. 1 = $13,362;   yr. 2 = $13,954;   yr. 3 = $14,592
        (b)   P.V. of lease cash outflows = $38,812
        (c)   Borrow

20-15　(a)　$19,810
　　　　(c)　P.V. purchase cash outflows = $59,772
　　　　(d)　Lease

21-1　(a)　Debentures get $9,375,000; general creditors get $5,625,000; and
　　　　　　subordinated debt holders get nothing.
　　　　(b)　Debentures get 62.5%; general creditors get 37.5%; and subordinated
　　　　　　debt holders get 0.0%.
21-2　(a)　Debenture B would get $1,500,000.
　　　　(b)　General creditors get $500,000.
　　　　　　Debenture B gets $2,500,000.
　　　　(c)　General creditors get 50%.
　　　　　　Debenture B gets 83.3%.
21-3　A, Interest = $30,000;　C, Interest = $1,000,000
　　　　B, Tax shield = $640,000;　D, Tax shield = $113,333.33
21-4　(a)　A at discount;　C at face value
　　　　(b)　B = $280,000;　D = $450,000
　　　　(c)　B = $14,000;　D = $15,000
　　　　(d)　A = $320,000;　C = $0.00
　　　　(e)　A = $128,000;　B = $67,200
21-5　B = $360,000
　　　　D = $90,000
21-6　(a)　A = $16,667
　　　　　　C = $1600
　　　　(b)　B = $20,000
　　　　　　D = $8,000
21-7　(a)　$80,000
　　　　(c)　$1,080,000
　　　　(d)　$1,400,000
　　　　(e)　$364,000
　　　　(f)　Yes
21-8　(a)　$704,000
　　　　(b)　$178,933
　　　　(c)　Yes
21-9　(a)　$1,136,400
　　　　(b)　(1)　$128,400
　　　　(c)　(2)　At 8.5% coupon, $336,220
　　　　(e)　Yes

22-1　(a)　Annual dividend = $8.80 per share
　　　　(c)　$35.20 per share
22-2　A = $15.00 per share
　　　　C = $11.00 per share
22-3　(a)　Preferred stock = $14.875 per-share dividend
　　　　(c)　Common stock = $0.00 per-share dividend
22-4　(a)　8.5%
　　　　(b)　6.5%
　　　　(d)　9.0%
22-5　(b)　20.28%
22-6　(a)　Common stock = $10,000; capital surplus = $120,000
　　　　(c)　Common stock = $8,000,000
22-7　(b)　Majority, 3; minority, 2
22-8　(a)　B = 0;　D = 0
　　　　(b)　A = 0;　C = 1
22-9　(a)　A = .033 shares;　C = .05 shares
　　　　(b)　B = 5 shares;　D = 240 shares

22-10 (a) 40,000 shares
      (b) .08 shares
      (d) Ex rights = $.148
22-11 (a) B = $1.50;   D = $1.67
      (b) A = $.50;   C = $1.57
22-12 (b) 12.5 rights
      (d) (1) Rights on = $.296
      (f) (2) Tuesday, March 9 and thereafter.

23-1 (a) $50 per share
     (b) $8 per share
23-2 (b) 40 shares
     (c) 16 shares
23-4 (a) After first year = 2 shares
     (b) First year = $50 per share
23-5 (b) $87.50
     (d) At $85 per share = $1062.50
23-6 A, Conversion value = $1056.25
     B, Conversion premium percentage = 0.0%
23-7 (a) Earnings per share = $3.39
     (b) Number of shares of common outstanding = 150,000
     (c) Earnings per share = $3.49
23-8 (a) (3) $1.26 per share
     (b) Convertible bonds
23-9 Preferred R = $71.11
     Bond B = $681.90
23-10 (a) At $25 = $1000
           At $35 = $1400
      (b) $830.12
23-11 (a) At $11 = $44
           At $13 = $52
      (c) At $15 = $60
23-12 (a) At $46 = −$12; at $58 = $24
23-13 (a) Number of warrants = 400
      (b) Return on investment = 20%
23-14 (b) 6.67%
      (c) (1) For warrants, rate of return = −42.85%

24-1 (b) Cash = $500,000, dividends payable = $330,000, R/E = $2,170,000
     (c) Cash = $170,000
24-2 (b) $.40 per share
24-4 (a) 1970 = $0.00;   1974 = $1.28
     (b) 1973 = $1.00;   1977 = $1.40
     (c) 1972 = $ .50;   1978 = $1.30
24-5 (a) 1973 = $ .30;   1977 = $ .78
     (b) 1975 = $ .50;   1978 = $ .74
     (c) 1971 = $ .50;   1976 = $ .50
     (d) 1974 = $ .53;   1978 = $ .78
24-6 (a) Retained earnings = $85,000
     (b) (2) Common stock = $24,000
24-7 (a) $.05 per-share cash dividend, retained earnings = $3,000,000
     (b) 10% stock dividend, common stock = $440,000
24-8 (a) $2 per share
     (d) $20 per share
24-9 (a) $2.40 per share
     (b) Ownership proportion under 5% stock dividend plan = 1%

    (d)   eps under 10% stock dividend plan = $2.18

24-10 (b)   Common stock = $1,800,000 (400,000 shares at $4.50 par)

    (d)   Common stock = $1,800,000 (3,600,000 shares at $.50 par)

24-11 (a)   Common stock = $300,000 (150,000 shares at $2 par)

    (c)   After split = $66.67 per share

24-12 (a)   19,047 shares

    (c) $21.00 per share

24-13 (a)   Price-earnings multiple = 15

    (c) $4.13 per share

25-1   (a)   Yr. 1 = $112,000; yr. 3 = $112,000

    (b)   Yr. 2 = $ 24,000; yr. 4 = $112,000

25-2   (a)   Yr. 2 = $160,000; yr. 4 = $240,000

    (b)   Yr. 1 = $0.00;   yr. 3 = −$60,000

    (c) $620,000

25-3   (b)   Yr. 1 = $32,000; yr. 2 = $48,000

    (c)   Stud Duds, maximum cash price = $228,400

25-4   (a) $85,000

    (c)   Acquire Multi-Color.

25-5   (a)   Desirable

25-6   (a)   Yes

    (b)   Yes

25-7   (a) $1.029 per share Flannagans; $1.853 per share Moon Bar

25-8   (a)   8000 shares

    (c) $1.72 per share

25-9   A,   Ratio of exchange of shares = .6

    C,   Ratio of exchange of shares = 1.75

    B,   Ratio of exchange of market price = 1.25

    D,   Ratio of exchange of market price = 1.25

25-10 (a)   Yr. 1 = $2.10 per share; yr. 3 = $2.315 per share

    (b)   Yr. 2 = $2.157 per share; yr. 4 = $2.406 per share

    (c)   Yr. 3 = $2.328 per share; yr. 4 = $2.459 per share

25-11 (a)   Yr. 2 = $2.29 per share; yr. 4 = $2.62 per share

    (b)   (1) Yr. 1, ratio of .6 = $2.395 per share

              Yr. 3, ratio of .6 = $2.58 per share

        (2) Yr. 2, ratio of .8 = $3.079 per share

              Yr. 4, ratio of .8 = $3.32 per share

25-12 (a)   1.125

    (b)   Merwin Company, eps = $2.50

          Lyle Company, P/E Ratio = 15

    (d) $2.529 per share

    (e) $45.52 per share

25-13 (a)   2.5%

    (d)   For (a), equity as a percent of total assets = 1.37%

          For (b), equity as a percent of total assets = .206%

26-3   (a)   Cash payment = $75,000 at present

    (c)   Cash payment = $75,000 in 60 days, $37,500 in 120 days, $37,500 in 180 days

26-4   (a)   B = $116,667; D = $400,000

    (b)   A, reorganize; C, reorganize

26-5   (a)   Reorganization

    (c)   Debenture holders get $250,000.

          Common stockholders get $0.00.

26-6   (a)   Reorganization

        (c)   Mortgage bondholders get $200,000 in income bonds and $250,000 in common stock.

26-7   (b)   A, Debenture holders get $500,000 in debentures and $1,500,000 in mortgage bonds.
A, Preferred stockholders get $0.00.
C, Mortgage bondholders get $1,000,000 in bonds, $500,000 in preferred stock, and $1,500,000 in common stock.
C, Common stockholders get $0.00.

        (c)   All plans are fair, equitable, and feasible.

26-8   (a)   (1)   Employees get $600,000.
                 First mortgage holders get $2,000,000.
            (2) $300,000
            (3)   Subordinated debenture holders get $0.00.

        (b)   For (a),   (1)   Government (taxes) gets $250,000.
                             Second mortgage holders get $0.00.
            For (a),   (2) $800,000
            For (a),   (3)   Senior debt holder gets $276,800.

26-9   (a)   Case I, accounts payable get $100,000.
Case II, notes payable get $75,000.
Case III, subordinated debentures get $125,000.

        (b)   Case I, notes payable get $200,000.
Case II, subordinated debentures get $125,000.
Case III, Accounts payable get $75,000.

26-10   (a)   (1)   Lessors (rent) get $30,000.
                 First mortgage gets $700,000.
            (2)   Second-mortgage holder is owed $0.00.
            (3)   Yes

        (b)   For (a), (1)   Government (taxes) gets $20,000.
                          First mortgage holder gets $600,000.
            For (a), (2)   First mortgage holder is owed $100,000.
            For (a), (3)   No

GLOSSARY

ABC Inventory Control System A system of dividing a firm's inventory into three groups—A, B, and C—according to the contribution of the items to the firm's overall investment in inventory. A items are those requiring the largest investment, B items are those requiring the second largest investment, and C items are those requiring the smallest investment. Inventory control techniques can be applied in light of this breakdown.

Accelerated Depreciation Methods of depreciation that write off the value of a firm's assets at a faster rate than straight-line depreciation. The two most common approaches are the *double-declining-balance* and *sum-of-the-years' digits* methods. Both effectively increase the firm's early-year cash flows from the tax treatment of depreciation.

Accept-Reject Approach Evaluating capital expenditure proposals to determine whether the projects meet the minimum acceptance criteria established by the firm.

Accrual Basis The basis on which an accountant typically views the revenues and expenses of a business firm. Generally, revenues are recognized at the point of sale and expenses when they are incurred, although, in actuality, since sales and purchases are often made on credit, cash flows may not occur at these points.

Accruals A current liability commonly found on balance sheets. Accruals represent obligations of the firm for certain services received for which payment is not yet due. The most common accruals are accrued wages, accrued rent, and accrued taxes. Accruals are an inexpensive form of financing for the business firm.

Acid-Test Ratio A measure of liquidity used when a firm is believed to have illiquid inventories. It is calculated by dividing the firm's current assets minus its inventory by its current liabilities. The higher this ratio is, the more liquid the firm is considered.

Adjusted Gross Income The balance remaining after subtracting *deductions from gross income* from *gross income* in the process of calculating personal taxes.

Aggressive Approach Financing a firm's short-term outlays (seasonal needs) with short-term funds and its long-term outlays (permanent needs) with long-term funds. A high-profit–high-risk approach to financing.

Aging of Accounts The evaluation of a firm's accounts receivable or accounts payable to determine the percentages that are current and the percentages that are past due.

Allocation of Factory Overhead In preparing pro forma statements, it is necessary to allocate the budgeted overhead expenses on the basis of some factor; generally the most common are labor cost per unit, the labor hours per unit, or the floor space utilized.

Amortization   The process of allocating an expense or a loan payment to certain periods of time. An amortized loan schedule is one that requires equal loan payments in each period over the life of the loan, using a specified rate of interest.

Annual Cleanup   A provision normally included in a line of credit agreement. It requires the borrower to "clean up" its loans (have a zero loan balance) for a specified time during one or more periods a year. This requirement ensures that funds obtained by borrowing against a line of credit will be kept only for the short term.

Annuity   A pattern of cash flows that are equal in each year; often referred to as an equal annual pattern of cash flows.

Arrangement   A special type of reorganization of a failed firm in which the management of the firm may be placed in the hands of a *receiver* or left in the hands of the existing management. The debtor proposes a plan to discharge the creditors' claims, and the court determines whether the arrangement is acceptable.

Asset Structure   The mix and types of assets on a firm's balance sheet. The mix of assets depends on the current–fixed-asset breakdown; the type of assets depends on which current and fixed assets are best for a given firm. The management of the firm's asset structure is an important function of the financial manager.

Assignment   The process of passing title to a firm's assets to a third party, a *trustee*, who liquidates them to satisfy creditors' claims.

Average Age of Accounts Payable   A ratio indicating the average amount of time taken by a firm to pay its accounts payable. The credit-worthiness of a firm can be evaluated by comparing the average age of its payables to the credit terms extended to it.

Average Age of Accounts Receivable   The average amount of time required to collect an account receivable. A useful measure for evaluating the firm's credit and collection policies in light of the credit terms extended by it.

Average Investment in Accounts Receivable   The actual amount of dollars a firm has tied up in its receivables. This is a function of the average cost per unit of product, the annual credit sales, and the average amount of accounts receivable on the firm's books.

Average Investment in Inventory   The average amount of money a firm has tied up in its inventory. This is a function of the cost of goods sold and inventory turnover.

Average Rate of Return   A measure for evaluating proposed capital expenditures. It is calculated by dividing the average profits after taxes expected from a project by the average investment required by the project.

Average Tax Rates   The quotient found by dividing the amount of taxes owed by the related amount of taxable income. For individuals, including sole proprietors and partnerships, the average tax rate will increase with increasing levels of taxable income due to the progressive nature of the federal income tax structure.

Bad Debt Expense   The percentage of credit sales for which payment was not received or is not expected to be received. Bad debt expenses are often estimated as a percentage of sales, and a reserve is established to cover them.

Balloon Payment   A large final payment on a loan. Often the balloon payment consists of the entire principal; in other cases, it is only a disproportionately large final payment.

Banker's Acceptance   A short-term instrument arising through international trade transactions. A safe security because a number of parties become liable for its payment at maturity. Yields on banker's acceptances are similar to yields on negotiable certificates of deposit.

Bankruptcy   A situation in which a firm's liabilities exceed the fair value of its assets. A bankrupt firm therefore has a negative stockholders' equity unless it can somehow liquidate its assets for more than their fair market value. Formal bankruptcy may be *voluntarily* declared or result *involuntarily* from actions by the firm's creditors.

Benefit-Cost Ratio (B-C Ratio) Sometimes called a *profitability index*. B-C ratios are used to evaluate capital expenditure proposals. They are calculated by dividing the present value of cash inflows from a project by the initial investment in it. If the B-C ratio is greater than one, a project is acceptable; otherwise, it should be rejected.

Beta Coefficient, *b* A measure of *nondiversifiable risk*. It is an index of the degree of responsiveness or comovement of the asset return with the market return. The beta for the market portfolio is equal to one; all other betas are viewed relative to this value. They may be positive or negative; positive betas are much more common. The higher the beta, the more responsive the assets return, and therefore the greater the nondiversifiable risk and vice versa.

Bond A certificate indicating that a corporation has borrowed a certain amount of money, which it has promised to repay in the future. Bonds are long-term debt instruments that can be used to raise large sums of money from a diverse group of lenders. Semiannual interest payments over a 10-to 30-year life are generally required.

Bond Discount or Premium If a bond is sold at a *discount,* it is sold for less than its face value; if it is sold at a *premium,* it is sold for more than its face value. A firm must amortize bond discounts and premiums over the bond's life. A discount is treated as an expense, while a premium is treated as income.

Bond Indenture A legal document that specifically states the conditions under which a bond has been issued, the rights of the bondholders, and the duties of the issuing corporation. An indenture normally contains a number of standard and restrictive provisions, including a sinking-fund requirement, and a statement of the security if the bond is secured.

Bond Rating The riskiness of publicly traded bonds is assessed by certain financial services such as *Moody's* and *Standard & Poor's.* Their ratings are based on the overall quality of the bonds, which depends on the *safety of principal* and interest.

Bond Refunding The process of retiring outstanding bonds—typically in order to issue new securities at a lower interest rate than those retired. Bonds may be refunded through a preplanned arrangement involving the sale of *serial bonds* or by the exercise of a *call* privilege. Quantitative procedures are available for making bond refunding-reissue decisions.

Bond Value The current worth of a bond, which can be estimated by calculating the present value of all the cash inflows associated with it. The present value is found by discounting the cash inflows at a specified rate or at the prevailing rate of interest for a similar-risk instrument.

Book Value The accounting value of an asset, a liability, or an equity. The *book value per share* of common stock is equal to the per-share equity plus any retained earnings.

Breakeven Analysis A technique for evaluating the relationship between a firm's fixed costs, variable costs, profits, and sales. The *breakeven point* is the volume of sales at which the firm's revenues just equal its total operating costs. It can be measured in terms of either units or dollars.

Breaking Points The level of *total* new financing at which the cost of various capital components (i.e., debt, preferred stock, and common stock equity) changes. They are calculated by dividing the level of total new financing from a given source at the breaking point by the capital structure proportion—historic or target—for the given type of financing. At each breaking point, the firm's *weighted marginal cost of capital (WMCC)* function increases.

Call Feature Included in most bond issues, it gives the issuer the opportunity to repurchase the bonds at a stated price prior to their maturity. Some preferred stock is callable. The *call price* may vary over time; it is set above the face value. Securities are often called in order to force their conversion.

Capital Asset Property owned and used by a taxpayer for personal reasons, pleasure, or investment. The most common types of capital assets for individuals are securities and real estate.

Capital Asset Pricing Model (CAPM) A model that links together the risk and return for all assets. It provides a mechanism whereby the required return on an asset, j, k_j, can be estimated as a function of the *risk-free rate*, R_F, its *beta coefficient*, b_j, and the *required return on the market portfolio*, k_m. The basic relationship is $k_j = R_F + b_j (k_m - R_F)$. The model concerns itself only with *nondiversifiable risk* since it is assumed that the investor can diversify away any diversifiable risk. When depicted graphically, the function is referred to as the *security market line (SML)*.

Capital Budgeting The total process of generating, evaluating, selecting, and following up on capital expenditure alternatives.

Capital Expenditure An outlay made by a firm for a fixed or an intangible asset from which benefits are expected to be received over a period greater than a year.

Capital Gain A gain from the sale of an asset for more than the initial purchase price. It equals the amount by which the sale price exceeds the initial purchase price. *Long-term capital gains* are received on assets held for more than one year; *short-term capital gains* are received on assets held for one year or less. Long-term corporate capital gains are taxed at the firm's ordinary tax rate or 30 percent; short-term corporate capital gains are taxed as ordinary income. Long-term capital gains for individuals are taxed at one-half their ordinary tax rate; short-term personal capital gains are taxed as ordinary income.

Capital Loss A loss resulting from the sale of an asset for less than its book value. It equals the amount by which the sale price is below the cost or book value of the asset. A capital loss can be used to offset current, past, and future capital or operating gains for tax purposes depending on certain factors.

Capital Market A structure created by a number of institutions and arrangements whereby the suppliers and demanders of long-term funds make transactions. Participants in this market include individuals, business, and the government. The backbone of the capital market is the organized *security exchanges*.

Capital Rationing The allocation of a limited amount of funds to a group of competing capital budgeting projects.

Capital Structure The mix of the various types of debt and equity capital maintained by a firm. The more debt capital a firm has in its capital structure, the more highly *levered* the firm is considered to be. There are conflicting views on whether an *optimal capital structure* that maximizes the firm's value exists.

Captive Finance Company A wholly owned subsidiary of a manufacturer that often makes inventory loans on a *floor planning* basis, using inventory as collateral. Such companies typically finance inventory sold by the manufacturer who owns them.

Carryback or Carryforward For tax purposes, ordinary losses can be carried back three years and forward seven years; capital losses can be carried back three years and forward five years. Ordinary losses can be used to offset operating income, but capital losses can only be used to offset capital gains. If a loss cannot be fully written off by carrying it back three years and forward the allowable number of years, its use to the firm expires.

Cash Breakeven Analysis An approach for finding a firm's breakeven point recognizing that it is cash—not accounting profits—that is most important in meeting the firm's obligations. It is calculated using fixed *cash* costs, which are found by subtracting any noncash charges from the firm's fixed costs prior to calculating the breakeven point.

Cash Budget A statement of various cash receipts and disbursements expected by a firm during the coming year, generally on a month-by-month basis. It is a short-term financial planning tool. By determining the *net cash flows* for each period and adjusting for any beginning cash, the firm can determine when financing will be required and when surpluses will occur. If a surplus is expected, the firm can arrange certain short-term investments. The cash budget is sometimes called a *cash forecast.*

Cash Cycle The period of time from the point a firm makes an outlay to purchase raw materials to the point cash is collected from the sale of the associated finished good. The cash cycle represents the amount of time the firm's cash is tied up.

Cash Discount A feature often included in a firm's credit terms. It allows a firm's customers to pay less than the sale price of merchandise if payment is made within a certain number of days after the beginning of the credit period.

Cash Discount Period The number of days between the beginning of the credit period and the last day on which a customer can take a cash discount.

Cash Flows The actual payment or receipt of dollars by the firm. Cash flows do not necessarily occur at the point at which an obligation is incurred or an item is sold. The financial manager operates using a cash-flow point of view, since cash is the lifeblood of the firm.

Cash Turnover The number of times each year a firm's cash is turned over. It can be calculated by dividing the firm's cash cycle in days into the number of days in the year. The higher a firm's cash turnover, the more efficiently cash is being used, and vice versa.

Certainty Equivalents One of the most direct and preferred approaches for project risk adjustment. The certainty equivalent associated with each forecast cash inflow reflects the percent of that cash inflow that the financial decision maker would accept in exchange for the expected cash inflow. Multiplying the expected cash inflow by the certainty equivalent results in a certain cash inflow, which when discounted at the *risk-free rate* results in its certain present value.

Clientele Effect The effect on the value of a firm of the fact that a firm will attract stockholders whose preferences with respect to the pattern and stability of dividends corresponds to that of the firm. The existence of a clientele effect is part of an argument used by Modigliani and Miller to support their *dividend irrelevance theory.*

Coefficient of Variation A relative measure of the variability of the outcomes associated with an event. It is calculated by dividing the standard deviation of outcomes by the mean, and makes it easy to compare the risk associated with projects of different size.

Collateral Trust Bond A bond secured with stocks or bonds of other companies. *Holding companies* are the primary issuers of these types of bonds.

Collection Policies The procedures followed by a firm in attempting to collect accounts receivable as promptly as possible once they are due. Collection letters, telephone calls, personal visits, the use of collection agencies, and legal action are all possible collection techniques. A firm's bad-debt expense reflects the effectiveness of its collection policy.

Comaker Loan A loan secured by another, more credit-worthy party (the *cosigner,* or *comaker*). Cosigners generally have some interest in the borrowers for whom they do cosign.

Commercial Finance Company A financial institution without a bank charter that makes business loans secured with accounts receivable, inventory, or chattel mortgages. Commercial finance companies accept much higher risks than commercial banks.

Commercial Paper Short-term, unsecured promissory notes issued by corporations with a high credit standing. Its maturity ranges to 270 days, and its yield is often higher than that of any other marketable security. Sometimes this method of financing is cheaper for the issuer than borrowing from a bank at the prime rate.

Commercial Paper House A financial institution that markets commercial paper for its issuers. These houses receive fees for their services.

Commitment Fee A fee charged on the average unused balance, if any, under a revolving credit agreement. This fee is typically about one-half percent of the average unused balance.

Common Stock   Stock held by the "true owners" of the business firm, who are the last to receive any distribution of earnings or assets. The common stockholder is the "residual owner" of the firm's assets since he or she, in essence, takes what is left. Most common stockholders have voting rights.

Compensating Balance   A requirement commonly found in a line of credit or other short-term borrowing arrangement with a bank. The borrower is required to maintain a checking account balance of between 10 and 20 percent of the outstanding loan. A compensating balance requirement may raise the effective cost of borrowing.

Composition   A plan for the pro rata cash settlement of creditors' claims by the failed business firm. This plan generally allows the firm to continue to operate and is similar to a formal reorganization in bankruptcy.

Compound Interest   Interest that is paid both on the initial principal deposited in an account and on interest earned on the initial principal in previous periods. The interest earned in one period becomes, in effect, part of the principal in a following period.

Compound Value of an Annuity   The future amount accumulated at a certain point, assuming that an equal annual deposit into a medium earning at a specified rate is made.

Concentration Banking   The use of geographically dispersed collection centers to speed the collection of receivables and reduce the firm's need for cash.

Conglomerate   A firm that grows by acquiring virtually unrelated firms is considered a conglomerate. The key benefit claimed for this type of firm is the diversification of risk across various industries.

Conservative Approach   In financing, the use of long-term funds to cover all expected financing requirements and the use of short-term funds to cover only unexpected financial needs. A low-profit–low-risk approach.

Consolidation   The combination of two or more companies to form a completely new corporation. The new corporation absorbs the assets and liabilities of the companies from which it is formed.

Contribution Margin   The percent of each sales dollar that remains after satisfying all variable costs. This percentage represents the proportion of each sales dollar available for meeting fixed costs and profits.

Conventional Cash-Flow Pattern   A pattern of cash flows in which an initial outlay is followed by a series of inflows. Other, *nonconventional* patterns do exist, but traditional capital budgeting deals primarily with a conventional cash-flow pattern.

Conversion Feature   A feature often included in a bond or preferred stock issue that allows the holder to convert the security into another type of security (usually common stock) at a specified price over a specified period of years. Conversion is generally attractive when the market price of the alternate security exceeds the conversion price.

Conversion Premium   The percentage by which the issuance price of a security exceeds the conversion price. Usually the conversion premium is in the 10- to 20-percent range.

Conversion Price   The price effectively paid for common stock as a result of conversion. It can be found by dividing the *conversion ratio* into the face or stated value. In some cases, it may be stated directly.

Conversion Ratio   The ratio in which a convertible security can be converted into common stock. It represents the number of shares of common stock the convertible can be exchanged for.

Conversion Value   The value of a security in terms of the market value of the securities into which it may be converted. In most cases, it equals the conversion ratio times the current market price of common stock. Sometimes this is referred to as the *stock value*.

Convertible Security   A bond or preferred stock that may be converted into a lower form of security, typically common stock, at the option of the holder at a specified price over a specified period of time.

Corporation   A form of business organization in which all the owners, or shareholders, have *limited liability* and have their earnings taxed at a special corporate tax rate. Payments to the owners in the form of dividends are taxed as personal income. In terms of business receipts and net profits, the corporation is the dominant form of business organization.

Correlation   A statistical relationship between series of numbers representing anything from cash flows to test data. If series move together, they are *positively correlated;* if they move in opposite directions, they are *negatively correlated.*

Correlation Coefficient   A statistical measure of correlation. It ranges from +1 for perfectly positively correlated series to −1 for perfectly negatively correlated series.

Cost of Capital   The discount rate used in capital budgeting that causes the firm to accept projects which will increase the value of the firm. Accepting projects earning exactly the cost of capital should leave the value of the firm unchanged. The cost of capital is determined by the cost of the various types of debt and equity capital.

Coupon Rate   The stated rate of interest on a bond. The annual interest payment is the product of the coupon rate and the face value of the bond.

Coverage Ratios   Ratios, such as the times interest earned, total debt coverage, and overall coverage ratio, that measure the ability of a firm to meet its fixed financial obligations. The higher these ratios, the better.

Credit Analysis   The process of determining whether a credit applicant meets the firm's credit standards and what amount of credit it should receive.

Credit Interchange Bureaus   A network of suppliers and demanders of credit information. By supplying credit information on a firm's customers and paying a nominal administrative fee, the firm can obtain credit information on its existing and prospective customers.

Credit Period   The amount of time given a credit purchaser to remit the full payment for credit purchases. Accounts not paid by the end of the credit period are considered past due.

Credit Policy   Guidelines for determining whether to extend credit to a customer and how much credit to extend. Credit standards, credit information, and credit analyses are the important components of credit policy.

Credit Standards   The minimum criteria for the extension of credit to a customer. Credit ratings, credit references, and the like are used in setting credit standards.

Credit Terms   The repayment terms extended by a firm to its credit customers. They include the cash discount and cash discount period, if any, the net period, and the beginning of the credit period.

Cumulative Preferred Stock   Most preferred stock is cumulative, which means that all dividends in arrears must be paid prior to distributing any dividends to common stockholders. *Noncumulative preferred stock* does not entitle the holder to the eventual receipt of "passed" dividends, but requires the issuer to pay only the current dividend prior to paying common stockholders.

Cumulative Voting   A voting system in which each share of stock entitles the holder to as many votes as there are directors to be elected. This system gives minority shareholders an opportunity to elect some directors.

Current Ratio   A measure of liquidity calculated by dividing a firm's current assets by its current liabilities. The higher this ratio is, the more liquid the firm is considered.

Date of Record   The date on which holders of record in a firm's stock ledger are designated as the recipients of either dividends or stock rights. Stock usually sells *ex dividend* or *ex rights* beginning the fourth business day before the date of record; it generally sells *cum dividends* (with *dividends on*) or *cum rights* (with *rights on*) prior to the fourth business day preceding the date of record.

Debenture An unsecured bond whose holders have a claim on a firm's assets after the claims of all secured creditors have been satisfied. Unsecured bonds subordinated to these bonds become *subordinated debentures.*

Debt Capital Any type of *long-term* debt. Debt capital can be obtained by negotiated borrowing or through the sale of bonds.

Debt-Equity Ratio A measure of a firm's financial leverage, calculated by dividing the firm's long-term debt by its equity. The higher this ratio, the more highly levered the firm.

Decision Trees An expected-value-based approach commonly used when making capital budgeting decisions. They are diagrams that permit the various decision alternatives and payoffs as well as their probabilities of occurrence to be mapped out in a clear and easy-to-analyze fashion. They are not especially sophisticated since they use expected value as a substitute for the measurement of risk.

Deductions from Gross Income In the calculation of personal taxes, this item includes a variety of trade and business expenses that may have been incurred by the individual, sole proprietorship, or partnership during the tax year.

Degree of Financial Leverage (DFL) A measure of a firm's *financial leverage;* the higher the DFL, the greater the financial leverage and therefore the greater the *financial risk.*

Degree of Operating Leverage (DOL) A measure of a firm's *operating leverage;* the higher the DOL, the greater the operating leverage and therefore the greater the *operating risk.*

Degree of Total Leverage (DTL) A measure of a firm's *total leverage;* the higher the DTL, the greater the total leverage and therefore the greater the *total risk.*

Demand Deposit A checking account in a commercial bank.

Depreciable Value The amount of an asset's cost that is subject to depreciation. Depreciable value is calculated as the difference between cost and *salvage value.*

Depreciation A charge against current income for a portion of the historical cost incurred with the acquisition of fixed assets. The three most common approaches for depreciating an asset are *straight-line, double-declining-balance,* and *sum-of-the-years' digits.*

Dilution A decrease in the proportional share of various owners in a firm. Dilution may result from new issues of stock. The dilution of ownership usually results in the dilution of earnings, although the long-run effect may be to increase per-share earnings.

Direct Placement The sale of a bond or other security directly to one or a group of purchasers, normally large financial institutions such as life insurance companies and pension funds.

Discount Rate The rate at which a series of future cash flows are discounted in order to determine their present value. The *opportunity rate* or *cost of capital* used in capital budgeting.

Diversifiable Risk A risk representing the portion of an asset's risk that can be eliminated through diversification. It results from the occurrence of uncontrollable or random events such as labor strikes, lawsuits, regulatory actions, loss of key account, and so forth. The events generating this type of risk vary from firm to firm. It is assumed that any investor can create a portfolio in which this risk, sometimes called *unsystematic risk,* is completely eliminated through diversification.

Dividends Payments made by a firm to its owners. Dividends may be paid either in *cash* or in *stock.* The firm's directors periodically meet in order to decide whether to pay dividends and to determine the amount and form of the dividend payment. An effect similar to a stock dividend is often achieved through a *stock split.* A variety of types of *dividend policies* are commonly used by firms.

Dividend Yield   The annual dividend on a share of stock divided by its prevailing per-share market price. The first term of the *Gordon model* represents its dividend yield.

Double-Declining-Balance Depreciation   An accelerated depreciation method by which the annual depreciation charge is found by taking twice the straight-line rate times the asset's book value at the beginning of the period. The asset under this method is depreciated down to its salvage value. Firms are permitted by the IRS to switch from this method to straight-line depreciation.

Dun and Bradstreet, Inc.   The nation's largest mercantile credit-reporting agency. It provides a variety of types of credit information on any of millions of firms to its subscribers. It also publishes a variety of industry statistics, including industry-average financial ratios.

DuPont Formula   A formula relating a firm's net profit margin and total asset turnover to its *return on investment (ROI)*. The return on investment is equal to the product of the net profit margin and total asset turnover.

EAC   Earnings available for common stockholders.

Earned Income   The income earned by individuals, sole proprietors, and partnerships, including salaries, wages, and other income directly attributable to the personal services provided by the proprietor or partner. If personal income is not earned, it is called *unearned* or *passive* income, which should include items such as dividends and interest. The maximum tax on earned income is 50 percent, while on unearned income the maximum tax rate is 70 percent.

Earning Assets   A term commonly used to describe fixed assets since they generally provide the basis for a firm's earning power. Without plant and equipment, a firm could not produce a product.

EBIT   Earnings before interest and taxes.

EBIT-eps Analysis   A technique used to evaluate various capital structures in order to select the one that best maximizes a firm's *earnings per share* (eps), which is assumed to be consistent with the maximization of the owner's wealth. The financing plans are often shown graphically on a set of EBIT (*x*-axis)–eps (*y*-axis) axes.

Economic Order Quantity (EOQ) Model   A technique for determining the optimum quantity of items to order or produce based on the trade-off between inventory ordering and carrying costs. The optimum quantity is that which *minimizes* the total cost of inventory or the sum of the ordering and carrying cost.

Effective Rate of Interest   The true rate of interest on a loan, expressed as an annual percentage applicable for the life of the loan.

Efficient Markets   A marketplace in which all investors are assumed to have the same information with respect to securities. It is further assumed that this information is accurate. All investors view securities in light of a common holding period; there are no restrictions on investment, no taxes, and no transaction costs. None of the investors is large enough to impact the market significantly. The existence of efficient markets underlies the *capital asset pricing model (CAPM)*.

Efficient Portfolio   A portfolio that provides a maximum return for a given level of risk or a minimum risk for a given level of return.

eps   Earnings per share, which are found by dividing the earnings available for common stockholders (EAC) by the number of shares of common stock outstanding.

Equipment Trust Certificate   Certificates used by railroads, airlines, truck lines, and barge lines to finance the purchase of "rolling stock." A type of installment purchase arrangement that allows the firm to obtain the secured long-term financing necessary to finance fixed assets.

Equity Capital   Long-term funds provided by a firm's owners that do not mature at a future date, but have an infinite life. The basic sources of equity capital are preferred stock, common stock, and retained earnings.

Estimated Tax Payments   Self-employed persons, employed persons with outside income from which taxes are not withheld, and corporations are required to make estimated tax payments on a scheduled basis to the IRS. The specific *tax payment dates* differ depending upon whether the taxpayer is an individual or a corporation.

Excess Itemized Deductions   For persons itemizing their nonbusiness expenses when calculating taxable personal income, the amount (if any) by which these itemized expenses exceed the *zero-bracket amount.* An adjustment for any excess itemized deductions is required to determine *tax-table income.*

Excess Profits Tax   A tax levied by the IRS on a firm's retained earnings when the IRS has reason to believe that the firm has retained earnings not for internal investments, but to avoid the payment of taxes on dividends.

Ex Dividend or Ex Right   Phrases used to indicate that a stock is selling without a recently declared dividend or right. The ex dividend or ex right date is generally four business days prior to the *date of record.* If a stock is not selling ex dividend or ex rights, then it is selling *cum dividend* or *cum rights.*

Exemptions   In the calculation of personal taxes, an exemption of income in the amount of $750 is allowed for the taxpayer and each of his or her dependents. Exempt income is therefore not subject to federal income taxes.

Exercise Price   The price at which holders of *warrants* can purchase the number of shares on which they have an option. This price, which is set above the marked price when issued, is sometimes called the *option price.*

Expected Value   A measure of central tendency. It can be found by calculating the average value of the expected outcomes. If probabilities are attached to expected outcomes, the expected value can be calculated as the weighted average return, in which the weights used are the probabilities of the various outcomes.

Extension   An arrangement whereby, in order to sustain a failed firm, its creditors agree, under certain conditions, to allow it to continue to operate.

Factor   A financial institution that purchases accounts receivable from business firms. The purchase is made at a discount from the accounts' value. Most *factoring* is on a *notification* basis. Normally, the factor accepts all the credit risks associated with the accounts by purchasing them on a *nonrecourse basis,* which means it must absorb any losses from uncollectible accounts. Some banks and commercial finance companies factor accounts receivable.

Federal Agency Issue   An issue of an agency of the federal government, such as the Federal Home Loan Bank or the Federal National Mortgage Assocation. It is generally a short-term security with a higher yield than treasury issues.

Financial Accounting Standards Board (FASB)   Formerly the *Accounting Principles (APB),* it is the body of the *American Institute of Certified Public Accountants (AICPA)* that is responsible for establishing standards to be used in accounting for all types of transactions. It is the rule-making body of the AICPA.

Financial Analysis and Planning   A function of the financial manager. The use and transformation of financial data into a form that can be used to monitor and evaluate a firm's financial position, to plan future financing, and to evaluate the need for increased capacity.

Financial Breakeven Point   The level of EBIT necessary for a firm to be just able to meet its fixed financial obligations. In other words, the level of EBIT at which the eps just equals zero. The higher the financial breakeven point, the more financially risky the firm is considered.

Financial Intermediary   An institution that channels the savings of various parties into loans or investments. Some financial institutions primarily lend money, while others primarily invest money in other types of earning assets such as real estate, stocks, or bonds. The key financial institutions are commercial banks, mutual savings banks, savings and loan associations, credit unions, life insurance companies, and pension funds.

Financial Leverage   The ability of fixed financial charges such as interest and preferred stock dividends to magnify the effect of changes in EBIT on the firm's earnings per share (eps). The more fixed financial charges a firm must meet, the higher its financial leverage is.

Financial Markets The markets for short-term and long-term loans and investments. The two key financial markets are the *money market* and the *capital market.*

Financial Risk The risk of being unable to cover financial costs. The greater a firm's *financial leverage* is, the higher its financial risk is.

Financial Structure The mix and type of financing on the firm's balance sheet. The mix is determined by the amount of short-term as opposed to long-term financing; the type of financing is determined by the specific instruments used. The management of a firm's financial structure is an important function of the financial manager.

Fixed Costs Costs that are a function of time, not the volume of production or sales.

Float The amount of money tied up in checks that have been written but not yet collected. Float exists because of the banking system's check-clearing procedures. Many firms are known to "play the float," which involves writing checks against nonexistent deposits and depositing the money to "cover" the checks sometime prior to their presentation for payment.

Floor Planning A *trust receipt lending* arrangement whereby the inventory of a seller of large, relatively expensive items finances these items. Floor planning is most common among retailers of autos, trucks, and boats. The borrower is required to remit the payment from a sale on its receipt to the lender.

Flotation Costs Sometimes called *issuance costs.* The costs of preparing, consulting, underwriting, and selling a new security issue. These costs are amortized over a security's life.

Gordon Model A commonly cited *valuation model* in which the value of the firm is equal to the present value of all future dividends expected over the firm's infinite life. The dividends are discounted at the firm's cost of equity capital.

Gross Income In the calculation of personal taxes, all income that is subject to federal taxes.

Gross Profit Margin The percentage of each sales dollar remaining after a firm has paid for its goods. It is calculated by dividing gross profits by net sales.

Growth Rate The compond annual rate (stated as a percentage) at which a stream of cash inflows such as earnings or dividends grows over a period of years.

Holders of Record Owners of a firm's shares on the *date of record* indicated on the firm's stock ledger. Holders of record receive stock rights or dividends when they are announced.

Holding Company A corporation having a controlling interest in (voting control of) one or more other corporations. To hold a controlling interest in a corporation quite often requires ownership of only 10 to 20 percent of the outstanding stock.

Horizontal Integration The combination of firms in the same line of business.

Income Bonds A bond on which the payment of interest is required only when earnings are available from which to make the payment. Commonly used during the reorganization of a failing or failed business firm.

Independent Projects Capital expenditure alternatives that compete with each other, but in such a way that the acceptance of one project does not eliminate the other projects from further consideration.

Industry Capitalization Approach A valuation technique whereby the expected per-share earnings of the firm are capitalized at the *earnings-price ratio,* which is commonly referred to as the industry capitalization rate.

Initial Investment The *relevant* cash outflow that should be considered in evaluating a prospective capital expenditure. It is found by netting all inflows and outflows occurring at time zero for a proposed project.

Integer Programming A mathematical programming technique for optimizing an objective function given certain constraints, one of which is that all solutions be integer values. This technique is often used in *capital rationing* in order to select the best group of projects.

Interest Payments made on money borrowed or received on money lent. The amount of interest depends on the amount of principal borrowed or lent.

Intermediation The process by which savings are accumulated in financial institutions and then lent out or invested. The reverse of this process, *disintermediation,* often occurs during inflationary periods since the high interest rates available from other financial media causes the movement of funds out of financial institutions and into these media.

Internal Rate of Return (IRR) A sophisticated way of evaluating capital expenditure proposals. The discount rate that causes the net present value of a project to just equal zero. If a project's IRR is greater than the cost of capital, the project is acceptable; otherwise, it should be rejected. The IRR is often referred to as the *yield* on a project.

Inventory Turnover A ratio calculated by dividing the cost of goods sold by the average inventory. The number of times per year an item of inventory is sold. In general, a high inventory turnover is preferred.

Investment Banker A financial institution that acts as a middleman between the issuer and purchaser of new securities. It purchases securities from the government and business and sells them to the public. Its functions include *underwriting, advising clients,* and *risk bearing.*

Investment Company A financial organization that pools the funds of a large number of investors and invests them in a portfolio of securities. By purchasing a share in an investment company, a shareholder gets an interest in a diversified portfolio. A *mutual fund* is a type of investment company.

Investment Opportunities Schedule (IOS) A schedule (or graph) that lists the best (i.e., highest *internal rate of return [IRR]*) to the worst (i.e., lowest IRR) investment opportunities available to the firm at a given time. When used in combination with the firm's *weighted marginal cost of capital (WMCC),* the optimal level of total financing can be determined.

Investment Tax Credit In order to stimulate capital expenditures by business firms, the Internal Revenue Service has from time to time permitted an investment tax credit, which allows purchasers of both new and used capital equipment to deduct a certain amount from their *tax liability.* The amount of the deduction depends on various characteristics of the assets acquired. This credit can be carried back three years and forward seven years.

Itemized Nonbusiness Expenses Deductions from *adjusted gross income* available to individuals, sole proprietorships, and partnerships in calculating taxable personal income. They include interest expenses, medical expenses, property taxes, and so forth. These expenses may be itemized or the taxpayer may instead take the *zero-bracket amount.*

Key Man Life Insurance An insurance policy on the life of a key executive of a firm. Since the executive is of key importance, the firm must view his or her life as an asset, the removal of which would result in damages. Many lenders require a firm to maintain "key man" insurance on the lives of certain executives as part of the loan agreement.

Lead Time The amount of time that elapses between the placement of an order and the actual receipt of an order. To allow for the uncertainty that surrounds an expected lead time, most firms maintain a *safety stock* of inventory.

Leasing Obtaining the use of specific fixed assets without actually taking title to them. The *lessee* receives the services of the assets *leased* to it by the *lessor,* which owns the assets. A periodic tax-deductible lease payment is required. An *operating lease* is generally a short-term cancelable arrangement, while a *financial* or *capital lease* is a long-term noncancelable agreement.

Leverage   A term commonly used in finance to describe the ability of fixed costs to magnify returns to a firm's owners resulting from changes in the firm's revenues.

Lien   A legal term meaning "a claim on the property of another," such as a security interest obtained as collateral for the payment of a legal debt. A *floating lien* is a general claim on a group of assets that can not easily or economically be identified by serial numbers.

Limited Liability   A type of liability that protects owners of a business firm from losing more than their initial investment in the business. Owners of sole proprietorships and partnerships generally do not have limited liability, while shareholders in corporations do. If the liability of owners is not limited, then it is unlimited.

Line of Credit   The maximum amount of money or merchandise a lender or supplier, respectively, will extend to a firm without performing a further credit analysis. The firm can borrow or purchase on credit against the line as long as the amount owed is current and does not exceed the amount of the line.

Liquidation Value   The value of a firm if all its assets are valued at their liquidation price and the resulting proceeds are reduced by the firm's debts and obligations to preferred stockholders. Also, the price at which a useable asset can currently be sold.

Liquidity   The ability to pay bills as they come due. The liquidity of a firm is directly related to the level of cash, marketable securities, and other current assets it holds.

Liquidity Crisis   A situation in which a firm is unable to meet due bills, a period of "technical insolvency."

Lock-Box System   An arrangement whereby a firm has its customers mail their payment to geographically dispersed post office boxes, which are opened by its bank. The receipts are deposited in the firm's account, and any other enclosures are forwarded to the firm. This system speeds the collection process by reducing the time needed to mail, deposit, and clear checks.

Long Term   In finance, a period greater than one year. Fixed assets, noncurrent liabilities, and equity are the long-term assets, liabilities, and equities of the firm, respectively. Assets and liabilities with maturities of one to seven years are sometimes referred to as intermediate-term items.

Majority Voting   A voting system in which each stockholder may cast one vote for each director for each share of stock held. This system is to the advantage of the majority shareholders.

Marginal Analysis   A type of analysis that is the heart of microeconomics and is frequently used in the financial decision-making process. It involves comparing the relative costs and benefits of various financial strategies in order to take actions consistent with the goal of maximizing the firm's overall profitability. This type of analysis is sometimes referred to as *cost-benefit* or *trade-off analysis*.

Marginal Weights   Weights sometimes used in calculating the firm's weighted average cost of capital. *Marginal weights* reflect the percentage of each type of financing that will actually be raised. Since they do not reflect the firm's long-run capital proportions, their use is not viewed as a theoretically sound method for estimating the firm's cost of capital.

Margin Purchases   Purchases of securities made by borrowing a portion of the purchase price. The *margin requirement* set by the Federal Reserve System indicates the minimum percentage of the purchase price the purchaser must put up; the remainder may be borrowed. Brokers typically lend on margin, but they often require a higher margin than that established by the Fed.

Marketable Securities   Short-term debt securities that can be readily converted into cash without sustaining a loss of principal. They include treasury bills, tax-anticipation bills, treasury notes, federal agency issues, negotiable certificates of deposit, commercial paper, banker's acceptances, and repurchase agreements.

Market Makers   In the over-the-counter market, individuals or firms that *make markets* in certain securities by offering to buy or sell them at a stated price. The *bid* and *ask* prices represent, respectively, the highest price offered to purchase a given security and the lowest price at which the security is offered for sale.

Market Premium   The amount by which the market price of a convertible security exceeds its *straight value*. The market premium is larger the closer the straight value is to the conversion value.

Market Return   The expected rate of return on the market portfolio of assets that can be viewed as the average rate of return on all securities. Standard & Poors' 500 Stock Composite Index or some other stock index is commonly used to measure the market return. The *beta* associated with the market return is equal to one; it acts as the basis for measuring the amount of *nondiversifiable risk* associated with various assets.

Market Risk Premium   Represents the amount of return the investor must receive for taking the average amount of risk that would be associated with holding the market portfolio of assets. In terms of the *capital asset pricing model (CAPM)*, it is the difference between the required return on the market portfolio and the risk-free rate.

Merger   A combination of two or more firms in which one of the firms retains its initial identity and merely absorbs the other firms. Mergers are generally confined to the combination of two unequally sized firms. The term "merger" is often used to describe what technically is a *consolidation*.

Minimum Operating Cash   A firm's minimum operating cash can be estimated by dividing the firm's annual cash outlays by its cash turnover. The resulting value represents the minimum amount of cash or liquidity the firm is estimated to need during the year, assuming that there is a small degree of seasonality in the business.

Mixed Stream of Cash Inflows   A stream of cash inflows that does not reflect any particular pattern. Any pattern of cash inflows other than an *annuity* is considered a mixed stream.

Modified DuPont Formula   A formula relating the firm's *return on investment (ROI)* to the *return on equity (ROE)*. The return on equity is calculated by dividing the return on investment, which can be found using the DuPont formula, by one minus the *debt ratio*, which is equal to the total liabilities divided by the total assets.

Money Market   An intangible market created by the suppliers and demanders of short-term funds. Not an organized exchange, but a communications network through which marketable security transactions are made. Key money market instruments include treasury bills, tax-anticipation bills, treasury notes, federal agency issues, negotiable certificates of deposit, commercial paper, banker's acceptances, and repurchase agreements.

Mortgage Bonds   A bond secured with a lien on real property or buildings. Under a *blanket mortgage*, all assets are held as collateral. A *first-mortgage bond* gives the holder the first claim on secured assets; a *second-mortgage bond* gives the holder a secondary claim on the assets already secured by the first mortgage.

Mutually Exclusive Projects   A group of capital budgeting projects that compete with one another in such a way that the acceptance of one eliminates all the others in the group from further consideration.

Negotiable Certificates of Deposit (CD's)   Negotiable instruments representing the deposit of a certain number of dollars in a commercial bank. Negotiable CD's have a good secondary market and a relatively high yield. The face value and maturity of a negotiable CD is usually tailored to the investors' needs.

Net Present Value (NPV)   The most common of the sophisticated tools for evaluating capital expenditure proposals. It is calculated by subtracting the initial investment required by a project from the present value of the projected cash inflows. If a project's NPV is greater than zero, the project is acceptable; otherwise, it should be rejected.

Net Present-Value Profile   A graph or schedule that depicts the net present value of a project (*y*-axis) for various discount rates (*x*-axis). This graph clearly depicts the project's *internal rate of return* as the *x*-axis intercept.

Net Working Capital   A measure of a firm's liquidity that is useful in time-series comparisons. It is calculated by taking the difference between the firm's *current assets* and *current liabilities*. It is sometimes defined as the portion of a firm's current assets financed with long-term funds.

Noncash Charges   Items that are deducted for tax purposes on a firm's income statement, but which require no actual cash outlay. Depreciation, amortization, and depletion charges are the most common noncash charges.

Nondiversifiable Risk   A risk that is not diversifiable and is attributed to forces that affect all firms and therefore is not unique to the given firm. Factors such as war, inflation, international incidents, and political events account for an asset's nondiversifiable risk. This risk, which is often called *systematic* or *relevant risk*, cannot be eliminated through diversification. It is measured by *beta, b*.

Note   A paper representing a single-payment or installment loan received by the firm. A note generally represents a single-payment short-term loan.

Operating Leverage   The power of fixed operating costs to magnify the effects of changes in a firm's sales revenue on its earnings before interest and taxes (EBIT). The greater a firm's fixed operating costs are, the higher its operating leverage is.

Operating Loss   Occurs when a firm has negative before-tax profits. The firm is permitted to apply this loss against past or future operating gains, or both.

Operating Risk   The risk of being unable to cover operating costs. Increased *operating leverage* increases a firm's operating risk, which is sometimes called *business risk*.

Opportunity Cost   The return a firm can earn on the best similar-risk investment opportunity available at a given time. In some cases, the cost of borrowing or the savings that would result from repayment of an existing debt.

Ordinary Loss   For tax purposes, both losses from operations and losses on the sale below their book value of depreciable assets used in the business or trade are treated as *ordinary losses*, which can be deducted from current, future, or past operating income.

Organized Security Exchange   A tangible organization that provides facilities for transactions between suppliers and demanders of various types of securities. The exchanges are auction houses where listed securities are traded. The New York Stock Exchange is the largest of these exchanges.

Overhanging Issues   Convertible securities that are not converted because the market price of the associated securities does not reach a level sufficient to stimulate conversion.

Over-the-Counter Exchange   An intangible market for purchasers and sellers of unlisted stocks and bonds, linked by a sophisticated telecommunications network.

Par Value   The stated or face value of stocks or bonds. A relatively useless value except for bookkeeping purposes. Often, *no par* stock is issued.

Participating Preferred Stock   Preferred stock whose holders receive more than the stated dividends by participating with common stockholders in dividend distributions beyond a certain level. Most preferred stock is *nonparticipating*.

Partnership   A business organization owned by two or more individuals. Partnerships are the least common form of business organization. The partners' income is taxed as personal income, and the partners generally have *unlimited liability,* although certain partners in a *limited partnership* may have limited liability.

Pay-As-You-Go Basis   The basis on which the federal tax system operates. At the personal level, both *withholding taxes* and *estimated tax payments* are used to force the taxpayer to pay as he or she goes. Corporations make estimated tax payments in order to allow for a pay-as-you-go basis of taxation.

Payback Period   The number of years required for a firm to recover the initial investment required by a project from the cash inflows it generates. Short payback periods are preferred.

Payoff Matrix   A table indicating the payoff associated with each of a number of possible *states of nature,* or outcomes.

Payout Ratio   A firm's cash dividend per share divided by it's earnings per share. This ratio indicates the percentage of each dollar earned that is distributed to the owners in the form of cash.

Percentage Income Statement   An income statement in which each item is shown as a percentage of net sales. The firm's *gross profit margin, operating profit margin,* and *net profit margin* are readily available from this statement. It is useful for both time-series and cross-sectional comparisons.

Perpetuity   An annuity with an infinite life; in other words, an annuity that never stops providing the holder with x dollars at the end of each year.

Pledge of Accounts Receivable   Another term for the *assignment of accounts receivable.* The securing of a short-term loan with certain of the firm's accounts receivable, generally on a "trust" basis.

Portfolio   A combination of investments that may consist of securities or fixed assets, or a mixture of both.

Preemptive Right   Stock rights extended to most common stockholders that allow them to purchase new issues in order to maintain their proportionate ownership in the firm. This allows the existing owners to prevent the dilution of their interest in the firm. These stock rights are often sold rather than exercised.

Preferred Stock   A type of equity whose holders are given certain privileges, chiefly the right to receive a fixed periodic dividend. The claims of preferred stockholders are senior to those of the common stockholders in liquidation. Preferred stock is sometimes considered a form of *quasi-debt* since it has a fixed periodic dividend associated with it. Preferred stockholders normally do not receive voting rights.

Present Value   The value of a future sum or stream—annuity or mixed—of dollars discounted at a specified rate. The process of finding present values is actually the inverse of the compounding process.

Price-Earnings (P/E) Ratio   The ratio of the market price of a share of stock to the annual per share earnings. It is suggested that the higher this ratio the more optimistic investors are, and vice versa.

Prime Interest Rate   The rate of interest charged by the nation's leading banks on business loans to the best business borrowers. The prime rate is used as a reference point for lending rates and is known to fluctuate widely with changes in the supply of and demand for short-term unsecured loans.

Principal   The amount of money on which interest is earned by a depositor or an investor or the amount of money on which interest is paid by a borrower.

Probability   The percentage chance of a certain outcome occurring. If an outcome is expected to occur seven out of ten times, the probability associated with that outcome is .7, or 70 percent.

Profitability-Risk Trade-off   A trade-off common to many financial decisions. The most common area of concern is in the management of working capital. The lower a firm's liquidity is, the greater the risk of *technical insolvency* and the higher the expected profits. This relationship between the profitability and risk works both ways.

Pro Forma Statements   *Projected* financial statements. Pro forma income statements and balance sheets are typically prepared for the coming year. The cash budget and pro forma income statement act as inputs to the pro forma balance sheet. The sales forecast is the key input to all these statements.

Progressive Tax Rates Tax rates that increase with increasing levels of taxable income, and vice versa. The federal income tax structure applicable to individuals as well as sole proprietorships and partnerships are subject to a progressive tax-rate schedule.

Prospectus A portion of a security registration statement that may be issued to potential buyers of a security. A "red herring" or stamp indicating the tentative nature of the offer is placed on the prospectus during the period in which it is being reviewed for fraudulent or misleading statements by the *Securities and Exchange Commission (SEC)*.

Proxy A statement in which the holder of stock transfers his voting rights to another party. Sometimes *proxy battles* erupt when outside groups attempt to gain control of a firm's management.

Pyramiding The control by one holding company of other holding companies.

Range The most basic statistical measure of risk or variability. It is calculated by subtracting the lowest (i.e., worst or pessimistic) outcome from the highest (i.e., best or optimistic) outcome. The larger the range of a project, the more variability, or risk, it is said to have.

Ranking Approach Evaluating the relative attractiveness of capital projects on the basis of some predetermined criterion.

Ratio Analysis The use of various financial ratios for measuring various aspects of a firm's performance. Commonly grouped into liquidity and activity ratios, debt ratios, and profitability ratios. The key inputs to ratio analysis are the firm's income statement and balance sheet.

Ratio Comparisons The most common types of ratio comparisons are *time-series* and *cross-sectional* comparisons. Time-series comparisons evaluate the same firm's performance over time; cross-sectional comparisons compare the performance of similar firms at the same point in time. Sometimes industry averages are used in cross-sectional comparisons.

Ratio of Exchange In a merger or an acquisition, the ratio of the number of shares of the acquiring firm given for each share of the acquired firm. This ratio depends on the price paid for each share of the acquired firm and the market price of stock in the acquiring firm. The ratio of exchange is sometimes stated in terms of *market values*.

Recapitalization The process of changing a firm's capital structure by altering the mix of debt and equity capital without increasing the total amount of capital. This often occurs as part of a reorganization under the bankruptcy laws.

Recaptured Depreciation When a firm sells a depreciable asset used in business or trade for an amount greater than its book value, the premium over the book value and less than the initial purchase price is viewed as recaptured depreciation, which is taxable at the firm's ordinary tax rates.

Receiver A party appointed by the judge or referee in bankruptcy to take charge of the property of a bankrupt firm and protect the interests of the creditors during the period between the filing for bankruptcy and the appointment of a *trustee* or the dismissal of the petition.

Refunding The process of selling a new security in order to retire an existing security with the proceeds. This is often done in order to lower financial costs or to change a firm's capital structure.

Relevant or Incremental Cash Flows The incremental after-tax cash flows associated with a proposed capital expenditure. These cash flows are referred to as the *relevant cash flows* since they are the only cash flows relevant to the capital expenditure decision.

Reorder Point   The level of inventory at which the firm places an order. It may be stated as a specific number of items or as a certain level of items in a bin.

Reorganization   When a failed firm is reorganized, both its asset structure and its financial structure are changed to reflect their true value and an equitable settlement of claims is made. The reorganized firm then continues in existence, possibly with new owners who were previously creditors.

Repurchase Agreements   An agreement whereby a bank or government security dealer sells specific marketable securities to a firm agreeing to repurchase the securities at a specified price at a specific time.

Residual Theory of Dividends   A theory that suggests that a firm pay cash dividends if and only when acceptable investment opportunities for these funds are currently unavailable. In other words, cash dividends are viewed as residual funds that cannot be used in some acceptable investment opportunity.

Restrictive Loan Provisions   Provisions that place constraints on the operations of term borrowers, such as restrictions on working capital, fixed assets, future borrowing, combinations, salaries, security investments, the use of loan proceeds, and the payment of dividends. Sometimes called "restrictive covenants."

Retained Earnings   The portion of after-tax earnings not paid out as dividends. The balance sheet entry for retained earnings represents the earnings retained through the balance sheet date.

Return on Common Stock Equity   A ratio calculated by dividing the earnings available to common stockholders by the common stock equity. This ratio measures the rate of return earned on the owners' book investment.

Return on Equity (ROE)   A ratio measuring the return earned on the owners' (both preferred and common stockholders) investment. It is calculated by dividing net profit after taxes by stockholders' equity. It represents the end result of the *Modified DuPont formula*.

Return on Investment (ROI)   Sometimes called the *return on total assets*. It can be calculated by dividing the firm's net profits after taxes by its total assets or by multiplying its net profit margin by the total asset turnover. The relationship between the net profit margin, total asset turnover, and return on investment is often referred to as the *DuPont formula*.

Revolving Credit Agreement   A guaranteed line of credit arrangement in which the bank guarantees that, regardless of economic conditions, it will make available the amount of the line at any time during the term of the agreement. Often these agreements are written for two-year terms; they are more expensive than a simple line of credit.

Rights Offering   An offering of a new issue of common stock to the firm's shareholders on a pro rata basis in accordance with their *preemptive rights*.

Risk   Used interchangeably with the term *uncertainty* to refer to the variability of returns associated with a project or forecast values of the firm. In a statistical sense, risk exists when a decision maker can estimate the probabilities associated with various outcomes.

Risk-Adjusted Discount Rate   A discount rate used in capital budgeting decisions that has been adjusted for the firm or the project's risk. The risk-adjusted rate is determined by adding an appropriate *risk premium* to the *risk-free rate of return*.

Risk Class   A term used to describe the relative overall *risk* of a firm.

Risk-Free Rate   The rate of return commonly required on a risk-free security. It is usually measured by the yield on a U.S. government security such as a treasury bill. The *beta* for a risk-free security is equal to zero.

Risk Premium   The amount by which the required return on an asset or security j, k_j, exceeds the risk-free rate, R_F. In terms of the *capital asset pricing model (CAPM)*, it can be expressed as $b_j \cdot (k_m - R_F)$, where b_j is the assets beta coefficient and k_m is the required return on the market portfolio. The higher this premium, the more risky the asset and vice versa.

Risk-Return Function Often called the *market indifference curve.* A schedule of the discount rates associated with each level of project or firm risk. Estimation of this function is useful in adjusting discount rates for risk.

Safety of Principal The risk that the market value of a security will drop below the amount paid to purchase it. Concern over the safety of principal is especially important when making *marketable securities* investments. It can be viewed as the likelihood of loss in principal.

Safety Stock An amount of inventory maintained in excess of that needed to meet expected usage in view of the expected *lead times* to receive orders. It provides a cushion for fulfilling demand in the event that the actual usage exceeds expected usage or a delay in receipt of orders occurs.

Sale-Leaseback Arrangement An arrangement whereby a firm sells its existing assets to a leasing company, which then leases them back to the firm. This is often done to generate cash. This arrangement differs from a *direct lease* of assets originally owned by the lessor.

Sales Forecast Sales forecasts are an important input to the firm's financial planning process. *Internal sales forecasts* are obtained from the sales force; *external sales forecasts* are based on regression analysis and the consideration of certain macroeconomic factors.

Salvage Value The expected value of a depreciable asset at the end of the asset's usable life. For depreciation purposes, salvage values must be estimated.

Seasonal Dating A technique used by suppliers in seasonal businesses to escape inventory carrying costs. Goods are shipped to customers in advance of the selling season, but the credit period does not begin until the selling season arrives. Seasonal dating is a type of credit term.

Secondary Market A market for used securities (i.e., those that are not new issues). If a security has a secondary market, the holder should be able to sell it prior to its maturity.

Securities and Exchange Commission (SEC) The federal agency having the responsibility of regulating the listing and disclosure of information relative to publicly traded securities. The SEC is also charged with the regulation of the organized *securities exchanges.*

Security Used interchangeably with the term *collateral* to refer to the specific items used by a borrower to back up a loan.

Security Exchanges There are a number of organized security exchanges, as well as the intangible over-the-counter exchange. The organized exchanges include the New York Stock Exchange, the American Stock Exchange, and other, smaller organizations. These organized exchanges have certain *membership* and *listing* requirements. The suppliers and demanders of various debt (bond) and equity (stock) issues are brought together through an auction process.

Security Market Line (SML) The name given to the graphical depiction of the *capital asset pricing model (CAPM).* It is a straight line that reflects for each beta (*x*-axis) the associated required return (*y*-axis). As traditionally shown, the SML presents the required or expected returns associated with all positive betas.

Selling Group A group of investment bankers and stock brokerage firms formed to sell securities underwritten by an underwriter or underwriting syndicate. Members of the selling group are paid a certain amount for each security sold.

Semivariable Costs Costs that are fixed over a certain range of volume and change to a different level beyond that volume.

Sensitivity Analysis The analysis of the effect of changes in certain variables on an outcome in order to get a feel for the variability of outcomes, or risk, associated with a cash budget, a project, or other risky situations.

Serial Bonds Bonds issued in such a fashion that a certain proportion of them come due each year. Serial bonds allow the issuer to gradually refund debt.

Short Sale A stock transaction made in anticipation of a drop in a security's price.

The short seller sells stock belonging to another person or firm, promising to buy it back in order to replace it in the future. The idea is to sell high and buy low, so that the initial sale proceeds exceed the outlay required to repurchase the securities. Stockbrokers arrange short-sale transactions.

Short Term A period of time less than a year. Current assets are short-term assets, and current liabilities are short-term liabilities.

Simulation The process of generating outcomes of specific events using predefined probability distributions and random numbers. *Computer simulation* is commonly used to develop probability distributions associated with various decision outcomes.

Sinking Fund A deposit or investment account into which borrowers are required to make periodic payments to provide funds for the retirement of their debt. A sinking fund is normally established in such a way that the deposits accumulate to the maturity value of the debt.

Sole Proprietorship A business owned by one person, who operates it for his or her own profit. This is the most common form of business organization. The earnings of the sole proprietor are taxed as ordinary income, and the proprietor's liability is unlimited.

Source and Use of Funds Statement A statement of the various sources and uses of funds for a firm over a certain period. The inputs to this statement are balance sheets for the beginning and end of the period and an income statement covering the period. It can be prepared using either cash or net working capital as the pivotal value. This statement is sometimes referred to as a *source and application of funds statement*. It is often useful to present the statement on a *percentage basis*, in which each item is expressed as a percentage of the total sources or uses.

Sources of Funds Sources of funds for a firm include a decrease in an asset, an increase in a liability, net profits after taxes, depreciation and other noncash charges, and the sale of stock.

Spread The difference between the price paid for a security by an investment banker and the sale price; the difference in interest rates between various debt instruments.

Standard Deviation A statistical measure of the variability of the historical or expected outcomes associated with a specified event; the square root of the average squared deviations from the mean. It is used as a measure of risk.

Standard Loan Provisions Provisions normally included in a term-loan agreement. Generally, they require the firm to operate in a respectable and businesslike manner. They deal with the accurate disclosure of financial data, the payment of bills, the protection of assets used for collateral, and the adequate repair and maintenance of assets.

Standby Arrangement An arrangement whereby an underwriter agrees to purchase shares not subscribed to as a result of a rights offering. An issue of shares that is not fully subscribed is said to be *undersubscribed*.

Stock Dividend A payment of stock to a firm's existing owners. It actually represents the distribution of something the owners already have. The effect of this action is merely to capitalize a portion of the firm's retained earnings.

Stock Options Options generally extended to members of a firm's management that permit them to purchase a certain number of shares at a stated price over a specified period. They are intended to motivate the management to perform well.

Stock Power or Bond Power A power of attorney that allows a lender to obtain a security interest in stocks or bonds held by a borrower that wishes to use these items as collateral. This power allows the lender to liquidate the stocks or bonds if the borrower defaults on the loan.

Stock Purchase Plans Fringe benefits occasionally offered to employees that allow them to purchase their firm's stock at a discount or on a matching basis with the firm absorbing part of the cost. These plans do provide the firm with an "internal source" of new equity capital.

Stock Repurchases   The act of buying back the firm's own shares of common stock. The repurchased shares are called *treasury stock,* which represent the difference between the number of shares *issued* and the number of shares *outstanding.* Stock repurchases are sometimes used in lieu of paying cash dividends. The repurchase can be made by purchase in the open market, through *tender offers,* or on a negotiated basis from a group of large shareholders.

Stock Split   A method of either increasing or decreasing (by a reverse split) the number of shares of stock outstanding while lowering or raising the market price per share. Stocks are split in order to stimulate trading activity.

Straight-Line Depreciation   A depreciation method in which the annual depreciation is calculated by dividing the *depreciable value* by its depreciable life.

Straight Value   The value of a *convertible security* when viewed solely on the basis of the interest or dividends it provides. This value is found by discounting the stream of interest or dividends at the rate that would be earned on a similar-risk security not having the conversion feature.

Stretching Accounts Payable   A strategy of paying bills as late as possible as long as the firm's credit rating is not damaged, taking into consideration any cash discounts offered. By stretching its accounts payable, a firm "leans on the trade" and thereby reduces the amount of operating cash it requires.

Subchapter S Corporations   Certain corporations with fifteen or fewer stockholders are permitted by the Internal Revenue Service to be taxed as a partnership instead of a corporation. These corporations are referred to as Subchapter S Corporations.

Subordinated Debt   Debt whose holders have a claim on the firm's assets only after the claims of holders of *senior debt* (the debt to which the subordinated debt is subordinated) have been satisfied. The subordinated debt holder is in a much riskier position than the senior debt holders.

Subscription Price   The price at which the holder of stock rights can purchase a share of common stock. To make the rights attractive the subscription price is generally set below the prevailing market price at the time of the rights offering.

Sum-of-the-Years' Digits Depreciation   An accelerated depreciation method under which a formula is used to determine each year's depreciation rate, which can be multiplied by the asset's depreciable value in order to calculate the annual depreciation charge. The depreciation rate for each year represents the quotient of the number of years remaining in the asset's depreciable life divided by the sum of all integers between zero and the number of years in the asset's depreciable life.

Syndication   The process whereby an investment banker or a commercial bank diversifies the risk associated with a security issue or a loan by forming a group to share both the profits and the risk of the transaction.

Synergistic Effects   The results of certain economies of scale that cause the total value of an organization to be greater than the value of the components summed. Synergistic effects often act as an impetus for business combination.

Target Weights   Capital structure proportions often used in calculating a firm's *weighted average cost of capital (WACC).* The target weights are usually based upon certain desired capital structure proportions that in turn are typically based upon what is believed to be an "optimal capital structure." The target weights therefore represent the capital structure that is expected to be consistent with the firm's goal of owner wealth maximization.

Tax Anticipation Bill   A short-term debt instrument issued by a governmental unit such as the United States Treasury in order to raise funds to cover shortages prior to the receipt of taxes. Tax anticipation bills have a low risk and a low return.

Tax Credit   A deduction allowed for any of a variety of reasons from one's *tax liability*. For personal income taxation, tax credits are given for each exemption claimed, for child care, and so forth. For corporate tax purposes, the most common tax credit is the *investment tax credit.*

Tax Payment Dates   Individuals must pay taxes by April 15 following the tax year. They must also make estimated payments on a quarterly basis on any income expected against which taxes are not withheld. Corporations typically pay estimated taxes for the calendar year on April 15, June 15, September 15, and December 15. Any additional tax payments or refunds must be settled by March 15 of the following year.

Tax Rates   Individual income is taxed subject to a progressive schedule of tax rates. Corporate tax rates on ordinary income currently are 20 percent on the first $25,000, 22 percent on the next $25,000, and 48 percent on earnings beyond $50,000. On *capital gains*, individuals are taxed on only one-half of such gains, while the corporate tax rate on these gains is 30 percent.

Tax-Table Income   The amount of taxable income calculated by an individual, sole proprietor, or partnership in the process of determining their federal income taxes. Using tax-table income in conjunction with the tax tables, one can determine his or her tax liability.

Technical Insolvency   A firm is technically insolvent if it is unable to pay its bills as they come due. Technical insolvency normally precedes *bankruptcy*. A firm can overcome technical insolvency through borrowing in many cases.

Tender Offer   A formal offer by a firm to purchase a given number of its own shares or the shares of another company at a specified price. The price at which a tender offer is made is usually set above the prevailing market price in order to attract sellers. Tender offers are used to repurchase the firm's own stock or in takeover attempts in which management negotiations have failed.

Term Lenders   The most common suppliers of long-term loans to business are commercial banks, insurance companies, pension funds, regional development companies, the Small Business Administration, small business investment companies, commercial finance companies, and equipment manufacturers.

Term Loan   A loan having an initial maturity greater than one year; a *long-term loan.*

Thin Market   A situation in which a firm's stock is not actively traded either due to the small number of owners or because of the small size of the firm. Most stocks with a thin market are traded over the counter.

Total Asset Turnover   A ratio indicating the efficiency with which a firm uses its assets. It is calculated by dividing annual sales by total assets. The higher this ratio is, the more efficient the firm's use of assets is assumed to be.

Total Leverage   The power of fixed costs—both operating and financial—to magnify the effects of changes in a firm's sales revenue on its earnings per share (eps). The greater the firm's fixed costs, the higher its total leverage. It reflects the combined effect of *operating leverage* and *financial leverage* on the firm's risk.

Total Risk   The risk that a firm will be unable to meet its operating and financial costs. The higher a firm's operating and financial *leverage,* the greater its total risk.

Trade Credit   Credit obtained through open-account purchases, represented by an *account payable* by the recipient and an *account receivable* by the grantor.

Trade-Off Approach   A financial strategy in which the firm finances a portion of its forecast seasonal funds need with long-term funds. This strategy represents a trade-off between the high-profit–high-risk *aggressive approach* and the low-profit–low-risk *conservative approach*. The exact trade-off used depends largely on the decision maker's attitude toward risk.

Treasury Bill   A short-term obligation of the United States Treasury. Treasury bills are issued weekly. They have virtually no risk and therefore provide a low yield.

Treasury Notes   United States treasury notes having maturities of one to seven years and a relatively low return.

Treasury Stock Shares of stock that have been *issued* and then *repurchased* by a firm. Often stock is repurchased because all *authorized* shares are *outstanding* and the firm needs shares for stock options or employee incentive plans. Occasionally, shares are repurchased as a way of paying dividends.

Trustee in Bankruptcy A third party to a bankruptcy proceeding whose function it is to value and recapitalize the firm if it is to be reorganized or take charge of all aspects of its liquidation if the firm is to be liquidated.

Trustee (Bond) The third party to a bond indenture. Typically a trust department of a commercial bank, whose responsibility it is to make sure the issuer lives up to the numerous conditions in the bond indenture. The trustee is paid a fee and acts to protect the interests of the bondholders.

Trust Receipt A loan made against specific collateral that remains in the hands of the borrower, but which can usually be identified by serial numbers. Trust receipt loans involving inventory are referred to as *floor-planning* arrangements.

Uncertainty Commonly used interchangeably with the term *risk* to refer to the variability of outcomes associated with a specific project or event. In a statistical sense, uncertainty exists when a decision maker has no historical data from which to develop a probability distribution.

Underpricing The act of selling a new security issue at a price below the prevailing market price, thereby reducing the proceeds below the current market price. Underpricing is usually necessary in order to create additional demand for shares when the market is in equilibrium (at the current price).

Underwriting The investment banker's function of guaranteeing the issuer of a security that it will receive at least a specified minimum amount for the issue. The underwriter of an issue accepts the risk that it will not sell. Often an investment banker will aid in the *private placement* of an issue or agree only to a *best-efforts* offering whereby the risk of selling the issue is avoided.

Unlisted Securities Securities not listed on an organized security exchange, but traded in the *over-the-counter market*.

Uses of Funds Uses of funds by a firm include increases in assets, decreases in liabilities, a net loss, the payment of cash dividends, and the repurchase or retirement of stock.

Utility Function A distribution indicating the risk-return preferences of a decision maker.

Valuation The process of measuring the value of an asset or liability. A term typically used to describe the overall process of estimating the worth of a business firm using its *book value, liquidation value, market value,* the *industry capitalization* rate, or the *Gordon model.*

Variable Costs Costs that vary directly with a firm's sales. These costs are a function of volume, not time.

Vertical Integration The combination of a firm with suppliers of its raw materials or purchasers of its finished product. Vertical integration involves expansion either backward or forward through a channel of distribution or production. A firm controlling the entire production process is considered *totally integrated* vertically.

Voluntary Settlement An out-of-court settlement between a failed firm and its creditors with the purpose of avoiding the cost and inconvenience of bankruptcy proceedings.

Warehouseman The agent of a warehousing company whose responsibility it is to guard inventory held as loan collateral and to release it only upon the written request of the lender.

Warehouse Receipt Loan A loan secured with inventory that is controlled by the lender and can be removed for sale only with the lender's approval. Both *ter-*

minal and *field* warehousing arrangements are used. A *warehouse receipt* is issued by the *warehouseman* to the lender; it describes the various items of collateral under his control.

Warrant A certificate giving its holder the right to purchase a certain number of shares of common stock at a specified per-share price. A warrant is usually detachable, which means that the recipient can sell it without selling the security to which it was attached. Quite often, warrants are used to "sweeten" a debt or preferred stock issue, or are used in the merger process. Warrants are traded on the security exchanges and may or may not have limited lives.

Warrant Premium The difference between the market value and the theoretical value of a *stock purchase warrant*. The amount of the warrant premium typically depends upon the investors' expectations as well as their ability to get more leverage from the warrants than the underlying stock. This premium is typically largest when the market price of the stock and the warrant *exercise price* are close together.

Wealth Maximization A long-run strategy of maximizing the value of the owners' investment in a firm, which is generally measured by the market value of the firm's stock. This strategy does not permit the sacrifice of long-run returns for current earnings and is therefore not necessarily consistent with a strategy of profit maximization.

Weighted Average Cost of Capital (WACC) A measure of the cost of capital calculated by weighting the cost of each type of capital (debt, preferred stock, common stock, and retained earnings) by the proportion of that type of capital in the firm's capital structure, using *book, market, target,* or *marginal* weights, and aggregating the results.

Weighted Marginal Cost of Capital (WMCC) A schedule or graph relating the firm's *weighted average cost of capital (WACC)* to the level of new financing. The WMCC is an increasing function of the level of total new financing. In combination with the *investment opportunities schedule (IOS)*, the WMCC provides a mechanism for finding the optimal level of total new financing. The WMCC reflects the fact that the firm's raising more than a certain amount of a given type of financing also raises the specific cost of that type of financing, thereby raising the weighted average cost of capital for all amounts of financing.

Withholding Taxes Tax payments that are deducted from the wages and salaries of employees and are paid in to the IRS by the employer.

Working Capital Management An area of finance concerned with the management of a firm's current accounts, which include its *current assets* and *current liabilities*. The management of working capital is quite important, since if the firm cannot maintain a satisfactory working capital position it may become technically insolvent and may be forced into bankruptcy.

Yield The actual return received by an investor in a security. It depends on the price paid for the security and the annual interest or dividend payment expected. It is sometimes viewed as the internal rate of return on an investment. The phrase *yield to maturity* is used to refer to bond yields.

Zero-Bracket Amount A type of blanket deduction from adjusted gross income available to taxpayers not wishing to itemize their nonbusiness expenses in the process of calculating taxable personal income.

INDEX

A

ABC inventory system, 278–279
Accelerated depreciation, 31–34
Accept-reject capital budgeting decisions, 382. *See also* Capital budgeting
  using benefit-cost ratios, 408–410
  using internal rate of return, 400–416
  using net present value, 401, 402–407
Accounting and finance, 7–9
Accounting Principles Board (APB), 581–582
Accounts payable, 219
  aging of, 70–71
  average age of, 70
  as source of short-term financing, 293–304
  turnover ratio, 69–70, 248–249, 276–278
Accounts receivable. *See also* Accounts receivable management
  aging of, 70–71
  average age of, 69
  as collateral. *See* Pledging of accounts receivable; Short-term financing
  pledges of, 323–327
  speeding collection of, 219, 229–231
Accounts receivable management, 223–228, 245–264
  collection policy, 219, 225–228, 229–231,

261–264
  computerized collection, 263–264
  types of collection procedures, 229, 231
  credit policies, 226, 245–252
  credit analysis, 252–256
  credit standards, 246–252
Accounts receivable turnover ratio, 68
Accruals, 6–7
  in cash management, 232–233
  as source of financing, 303–304
Acid-test ratio, 64, 65–66
Acquisitions. *See* Consolidations; Holding companies
Aggressive approach to financing current assets, 205–208
Almanac of Business and Industrial Financial Ratios, 58
American Bankruptcy Act (1800), 759
American Stock Exchange (AMEX), 556
Annual clean-up, 307, 308
Annuities, 354–357, 361–364
  present value of, 362–364
Asset mix
  cash-marketable security decision, 235
  role of financial manager, 10
Assets. *See also* Capital budgeting; Fixed assets; Leased assets

earning power of, 199
Assignment
  of accounts receivable. *See* Pledging accounts receivable
  in liquidation, 758
Authorized, issued, and outstanding stock, 643

B

Bad debt expense, 251–252, 257, 347
Balance sheet, 10, 72, 512
Balloon payments, 611, 615
Banker's acceptances, 238
Bank loans
  long term, 612
  short term, secured, 318–322
  short term, unsecured, 304–309
Bankruptcy, 753, 758–768
  claims of lessors, 592
Banks. *See* Commercial banks; Savings and loan associations
Barrons, 686
Bearer bonds, 335
Benefit-cost (B/C) ratio, 408–410
Blue sky laws, 564
Bonds
  baby bonds, 614
  bearer, 335
  convertible, 660
  corporate. *See* Corporate bonds
    general features, 615–616, 622

Bonds (*continued*)
the conversion feature, 660–667. *See also* Conversion feature
stock purchase warrants, 611, 671–675
legal aspects, 614–615
ratings of, 618
refunding process, 603, 622–625
selling a bond, 616–618, 623
types of, 603, 618–622
use as loan collateral, 335–338
yield-to-maturity, 477
Bond value, determination, 367
Book value per share, 82, 84, 528–529, 725, 736
Breakeven analysis, 100–111
algebraic approach, 102–103
cash, 108–109
costs, types of, 100–106
graphical approach, 103–104
weaknesses of traditional approach, 109–111
Breakeven point, 101–102. *See also* Breakeven analysis
Broker-dealers, 559
Business, role of finance in, 9–10
Business combinations, 719–725. *See also* Consolidations; Holding companies; Mergers
motives for combination, 719, 721–724
relevant variables, 719, 724–726
restrictions in a long-term loan agreement, 605–608
restrictions in preferred stock agreements, 637–638
use of preferred stock, 637
Business failures, 751–768
bankruptcy, 753, 758–768
liquidation, 757–758, 765–768
reorganization, 751, 758–765
types and causes of failure 751, 752–755
voluntary settlements, 751, 755–758
Business organization forms
corporations, 22, 26–29

taxes on income, 40–42. *See also* Corporate taxes
treatment of income, 29–35
partnerships, 22, 24–26
sole proprietorships, 22–24
Business risk, 472. *See also* Operating risks
in mergers, 736–737

C

Call features, 616, 622, 639
in a bond agreement, 616, 622
for forcing conversion, 665–667
in perferred stock, 639
Call premiums, 623
Capital, 511–514, 633–635. *See also* Capital budgeting; Capital structure; Cost of capital
Capital asset pricing model (CAPM). *See* CAPM
Capital budgeting, 376. *See also* Capital budgeting under risk; Mathematics of finance
under capital rationing, 381, 401, 417–420
developing the relevant data, 383–395
fundamental concepts, 380–385
sophisticated techniques, 401, 407–417
benefit cost (B/C) ratios, 408–410
internal rate of return (IRR), 417–418, 454–457
net present value (NPV), 401, 402–407, 418–419
unsophisticated techniques, 402, 403–406
average rate of return, 404–405
payback period, 402, 405–407
Capital budgeting under risk, 429–457. *See also* Risk and return function
adjusting for project risk, 449–457
certainty equivalents, 453–454
basic risk concepts, 430–433

measuring project risk, 433–439
portfolio risk, 440–444
relationship to time, 439–440
Capital expenditures, 376–380
authorization of, 378
proposals for, 376–380
Capital gains, 36–37, 42–43
tax treatment, 42–43
Capital intensive, 375
Capital losses, 36–37, 44–46
Capital market, 554–561
functions and characteristics of securities exchanges, 554–559
investment companies, 560–561
special stock transactions, 559–560
Capital rationing, 381, 401–416, 417–420
present-value approach, 418–419
using integer programming, 419–420
Capital structure, 512–528
the EBIT-eps approach to, 522–528
measures of, 514–416
theory of, 516–522
types of capital, 511–514
CAPM (Capital asset pricing model), 444–449
Carryback and carryforward of taxes, 44–45
Cash
net losses, 134
net profits after taxes and noncash charges, 133
sources and uses of, classified, 132–134
Cash balance, 133
Cash budget, 131, 143–152
interpretation of, 148–149
net cash flow, 148
reducing uncertainty in, 150
sales forecast, 131, 144
statement format, 132, 145–148
statement preparation, 140–141
use in pro forma preparation, 179–183
Cash cycle. *See* Cash management
Cash disbursements, 146–147

Cash discount, 257–259, 296
Cash discount period, 259, 296–297
Cash dividends. *See* Dividends, cash
Cash flow, 29, 30. *See also* Cash budget
  and capital expenditures, 376–380
  and cash management, 220–221
  types of, 383–385
  within the month, 150
Cash forecast. *See* Cash budget
Cash inflows, 389–395
Cash management, 220–228
  accruals as a tool of, 232–233
  cash cycles and turnovers, 220–222
  collection procedures, 229
  disbursement procedures, 231, 232
  float, 232–233
  minimum operating cash, 219, 222–227
  opportunity cost concept, 223
  refinements in, 229–233
  strategies of efficient, 220–229
Cash statements, 140–153
Chandler Act (1938), 759, 761, 763
Chapters X and XI. *See* Bankruptcy; Chandler Act
Check cashing analysis, 232
Clientele effect, 14, 686
Coefficient of variation, 437–439
Collateral. *See* Security interest
Collateral trust bond, 621
Collection policies, 227–228, 261–264
  use of the computer, 263–264
Collection procedures. *See also* Accounts receivable
  basic strategy, 229–231, 262–263
  types of, 263–264
Comaker loans, 338
Commerical banks, 322, 549–551
  and secured short-term loans, 318–322
  and long-term loans, 612

and unsecured short-term loans, 304–309
Commercial finance companies, 322, 613–614
Commercial paper, 238, 309–311
Commerical paper house, 293, 309–311
Commitment fee on revolving credit agreement, 308–309
Common-size statement. *See* Percent income statement
Common stock, 82, 633, 642–651
  advantages and disadvantages of, 650–651
  basic values, 650. *See also* Valuation of corporate stock
  characteristics of, 642–646
  cost of, 480–487
  dividends on, 645–646. *See also* Dividends, cash; Dividends, noncash
  repurchases of, 646. *See also* Stock repurchases
  sale of new issues of, 649–650. *See also* Conversion feature; Investment bankers; Warrants
  stock rights, 646–649. *See also* Rights, stock purchase
  stock splits, 702–704
  voting rights, 643–645
Compensating balance, 307–308
Competitive bidding, 563
Compound interest, 347, 348–357
  annual compounding, 348–350
  compound sum of an annuity, 354–355
  deposit to accumulate a future sum, 364–365
  intrayear compounding, 351, 353–354
  relationship to present value, 359–360, 364–368
  using the tables, 349–350, 354
Computers in collecting receivables, 263–264

Concentration banking, 230
Conflicting rankings in capital budgeting, 415–416, 417–418
Conservative approach to financing current assets, 208–210
Consolidations, 719–720. *See also* Mergers
Constraints in long-term loan agreements, 606
Contribution margin, 107
Conversion feature, 660
  in bonds, 616, 660
  comparison to a warrant, 672–673
  forcing conversion, 665–667
  motives for use of convertibles, 663–665
  overhanging issues, 667
  in preferred stock, 639, 660
  the value of convertibles. *See* Valuation of convertible securities
Conversion period, 662
Conversion premium, 662
Conversion ratio, 661–662
Conversion value, 662
Convertible securities, 659, 660–667
  determining value of. *See* Valuation of convertible securities
Corporate bonds, 603, 614–615
Corporate income, treatment of, 29–35
Corporate stock. *See* Valuation of corporate stock
Corporate taxes, 40–47
  and business combinations, 723–724
  carryback and carryforward, 44–45
  investment tax credit, 46–47
  and losses, 43
  payment dates, 47
  rate on capital gains, 42–43
  rate on ordinary income, 40–41
  Subchapter S corporations, 47
Corporations, 22, 26–29. *See also* Business organization forms
  under Subchapter S, 40

Correlation, 441
  coefficient of, 441
  and portfolio risk, 441–444
Cost of capital, 357, 407,
      471–501. *See also* Capital structure; Weighted average cost of capital; Weighted marginal cost of capital
  cost of specific sources, 471, 475–488
  and the internal rate of return, 408
  key factors affecting financing costs, 474–475
  overall cost of capital, 471–475, 489–494
  and risk, 472–473
  taxes, 473–474
Cost of common stock, 480–488
  cost of equity, 482–484
  cost of new issues, 482
  and the theory of capital structure, 516–522
Cost of equity capital. *See* Cost of common stock; Gordon model
Cost of long-term debt, 476–479, 608–610
Cost of preferred stock, 479–482, 641–642
Cost of retained earnings, 487–488
Costs, types of. *See* Breakeven analysis
Cost-volume-profit analysis. *See* Breakeven analysis
Coverage ratios, 74–77
Credit analysis. *See* Credit policies
Credit interchange bureaus, 255
Creditor control of failed firms, 757
Credit policies, 226, 245–246
  credit analysis, 252–256
  credit standards, 226–228, 247–252
Credit standards. *See* Credit policies
Credit terms, 226, 256–261, 295
  beginning of credit period, 297–298
  cash discount period, 259, 296–297

cash discounts, 257–259
  credit period, 259–261, 295
Credit unions, 550
Cross-sectional ratio comparisons, 58–59
Cum dividends or cum rights, 647–648, 687
Cumulative voting system, 644–645
Current assets,
  discussed, 201, 203
  and current liabilities, 203. *See also* Working capital management
Current liabilities
  discussed, 202–203
  and current assets, 203. *See also* Working capital management
Current ratio, 64–65

D

Date of record, 647, 686
Debentures, 618–619. *See also* Bonds; Long-term debt financing
Debt. *See also* Long-term debt financing; Short-term financing
  measures of, 71
  servicing of, 73–74
Debt capital, 511–512, 513, 603–625
Debt-equity ratio, 72–73, 514
Debt ratio, 62, 72
Debt-to-total-capitalization ratio, 72, 514
Decision trees, 450
Deferred common stock financing, 663–664
Degree of financial leverage (DFL), 117–118
Degree of operating leverage (DOL), 113–114
Degree of total leverage (DTL), 122–124
Deposit to accumulate a future sum, 304–305
Depreciation, 29–34
  accelerated methods, 31–34
  and cash flows, 29, 30–31, 389–391
  of land with leasing, 591
  method of, 31–34
  recapture of, 43

straight-line method, 31, 32, 33, 34
DFL (Degree of financial leverage), 117–118, 124
Dilution, 646–647, 651, 694–695
Direct placement
  of bonds, 616–617
  of commercial paper, 311
  of security issue, 565–566
  of stock, 555, 649–650
Discharge of bankrupt firm, 768
Discount rate, 357, 407
Distribution of earnings and assets, 646
Diversification. *See* Portfolio risk and correlation
Dividend policies, 683, 690–706
  factors affecting, 683, 690–696
  objectives of, 683, 696–697
  types of policies, 683, 697–700
    constant payout ratio, 695, 698
    regular-and-extra, 698–700
Dividends, cash, 683. *See also* Common stock, dividends on
  and interest, 34–35
  payment procedures, 136–137, 686–687
  policy, 690–706. *See also* Dividend policies on preferred stock, 479, 637
  restrictions in term loans, 605–608
  restrictions on preferred stock, 638
  tax treatment, 29
  theoretical viewpoints, 683, 688–690
Dividends, noncash, 700–706
  repurchases of stock, 638, 646. *See also* Stock repurchases
  stock dividends, 700–702
  stock splits, 702–704
Dividends on and rights on, 647, 687
Dividends per share, 84, 725, 726
DOL (Degree of operating leverage), 118–119, 124

Double-declining balance depreciation method, 31, 32
DTL (Degree of total leverage), 122–124
Dun & Bradstreet, Inc., 58, 60–61, 252–255
DuPont formula, 80–81, 83

E
Earnings assets, 375
Earnings before interest and taxes (EBIT), 110, 118
and leverage, 99–100. See also Financial leverage; Operating leverage
Earnings per share, 83, 725
effect of mergers on, 725, 730–733
and financial leverage, 99–100
Earnings, retained. See Retained earnings
EBIT. See Earnings before interest and taxes
EBIT-eps approach to capital structure, 522–528
Economic order quantity model. See EOQ model
Economics and finance, 5–6
Efficiency
in markets, 445
as related to portfolios, 441–444
End of month credit period. See EOM credit period
EOM (end of month) credit period, 297
EOQ model, 279–285
Eps, 117. See also Earnings per share
Equipment trust certificate, 622
Equity capital, 511, 512–513, 633–635. See also Common stock; Preferred stock
claims in income and assets, 634–635
cost of, 512–513
maturity, 635
ownership rights, 634
Excess profits tax, 692
Ex dividend or ex rights, 647, 648, 686–687

Exercise or option price of warrant, 672
Extensions of failed firms, 756

F
Factor, 327
Factoring accounts receivable, 317, 323, 327–331. See also Accounts receivable
advantages and disadvantages of, 331
costs of, 330
factoring agreement, 328–330
Failures. See Business failures
FASB (Financial Accounting Standards Board), 581–585
Federal agency issues, 237
Federal funds, 549
Field warehouses, 320. See also Warehouse receipt loans
Finance
and accounting, 7–9
and economics, 5–6
mathematics of, 358–368. See also Compound interest; Present value
role in the business firm, 9
Financial Accounting Standards Board (FASB), 581–585
Financial breakeven point, 120
Financial institutions. See Financial intermediaries
Financial intermediaries, 548–551
key intermediaries described, 549–551
participants in, 548–549
relationship to financial markets, 551–552
Financial leases, 575. See also Leasing
Financial leverage, 99–100, 116–122
and capital structure, 513–514, 517–518
consideration in business combinations, 725
and the financial breakeven point, 101–102
illustrations, 116–117, 119–120

industry differences in, 515–516
and risks, 99
Financial managers, 6, 7–8
functions of, 10–11
goals of, 11
Financial markets, 551–552
the capital market, 554–561
and financial intermediaries, 551–552
the money market, 552–554
Financial ratios, 57–88
cautions in use of, 59
coverage measures, 62
debt measures, 71–75
interested parties, 58
and leasing, 582–585, 591
liquidity and activity measures, 62–71
profitability measures, 62, 77–84
types of comparisons, 58–59
Financial risk, 121, 472–473
in long-term borrowing, 609–610
in mergers, 736–737
Financial statement analysis. See Financial ratios
Financial statements, 252–255. See also Financial ratios
Financial structure. See Capital structure
Financing. See also Long-term debt financing; Short-term financing
cost of, 200
Financing mix, determination of, 10, 204–213
and capital structure. See Capital structure
cost considerations, 206–207
in working capital management, 204–213
Financing plan
and financial leverage, 118–121, 513–514
graphical presentation of, 118–121, 523–526
Finished goods, inventory of, 272
First mortgage, 619–620
Fixed-asset management, 375–380. See also Capital budgeting
restrictions in loan agreements, 606

Fixed assets, changes in, 135–136
Fixed operating costs, 99, 104–105
and operating leverage, 114
in breakeven analysis, 100–101, 104–105
Float, playing the, 232
Floating lien, 319, 320, 323, 332–333
Floor planning, 319
Flotation cost
in calculating cost of common stock, 480–481
in issuing bonds, 623–625
Forcing conversion, 665–667
Forecasts. See Sales forecasts
Forms of business organization. See Business organization forms
Fund raising, 722–723
Funds, use of, 132–134

G

Gordon, Myron J., 690
Gordon model
determining cost of common stock, 482–487, 528, 531–533
use in valuation, 531–533
Government
in financial transactions, 549
in the money market, 549
securities issued, 236
Gross income, 38
Gross profit margin, 78
Growth, types of, 721–722
Growth rate determination, 366. See also Gordon model

H

Holders of record, 687
Holding companies, 719, 720, 738–741
advantages and disadvantages, 739–741

I

Income, gross, 38
Income bond, 619
Incremental cash inflows, 391
Indebtedness, measuring degree of, 72
Indenture, bond, 614–615

Independent projects, 381. See also Capital budgeting
Industry capitalization approach to valuation, 531
Insolvency, technical, 198–199, 691, 753
Installation cost of fixed assets, 376–377
Insurance companies, term loans, 612
Integer programming in capital rationing, 419–420
Interest, 34, 35. See also Interest rate
and compounding, 366–367
tax treatment of, 29
Interest rate
on comaker loans, 338
on commercial paper, 310–311
computations of, 306–307
effective rate, 306
on factored receivables, 330
and fees, 321–322
on a floating inventory lien, 332, 333
on a lease, 587, 589, 593
on a line of credit, 305–308
on a long-term debt, 608–610
on a note, 304–305
on a pledge of receivables, 323–327
the prime interest rate, 305–306
on stock and bond collateral, 337–338
on a trust receipt loan, 333
on a warehouse receipt loan, 335
Intermediate-term financing. See Long-term debt financing
Internal rate of return (IRR), 408, 410–416
approach for calculating, 411–414
capital rationing approach, 417–418
decision criterion, 411
and present-value profiles, 414–416
yield-to-maturity, 477
Internal Revenue Code, 29, 47, 577
Internal Revenue Service. See IRS

Inventory, 269. See also Inventory management
average age of, 68
characteristics of, 269–278, 332
use as loan collateral, 331–335
types of, 270–272
Inventory management, 219, 269–285
basic costs of, 280–281
characteristics of, 331–332
functional viewpoints in, 273–275
as an investment, 275–276
relationship with accounts receivable, 276–278
techniques of, 278–285
reorder point, 285
Inventory turnover ratio, 67–68
Investment bankers, 561, 565–566, 617
cost of services of, 565
functions of, 561–562
organization of, 562–565
in rights offerings, 565–566
in sale of bonds, 617
in sale of stock, 565–566
Investment companies, 560–565
Investment in accounts receivable, 248–251
Investment in inventory, 275–276
Investment tax credit, 46–47
IRR. See Internal rate of return
IRS (Internal Revenue Service), 38–40, 46–47, 577, 691–692

J

Joint and several liability, 25

L

Labor intensive, 375
Leased assets, acquisition of, 575–576
Leasing, 573–594
advantages and disadvantages of, 590–594
characteristics of, 573, 574–578
contract for, 578

the lease-purchase decision, 574, 585–590
  borrowing cash inflows, 587–588
  comparing alternatives, 589–590
  leasing cash inflows, 586–587
legal requirements of, 577
as a long-term loan provision, 607
as a source of financing, 573, 574, 578–585
  the lease cost, 579–581, 593
Legal aspects of business operation, 21–47
Leverage, 99
  and breakeven analysis, 100–111
  effect of holding companies, 739–740
  financial. See Financial leverage
  income statement approach to, 99–100
  operating. See Operating leverage
  provided by preferred stock, 640–641
  relationship between types of, 124
  and risk, 99, 121–125
  total leverage. See Total leverage
Liability, types of, 24, 25, 27
Life insurance companies, 550–551
  and term lending, 612
Limited liability, 27
Limited partnership, 25
Linearity, assumption of, 109
Line of credit, 252, 305–308
  amount of a line, 307
  interest rate, 306
  restrictive provisions, 309–310
Liquidation of a failed firm, 757–758
  in legal bankruptcy, 765–768
  voluntary, 757–758
Liquidity, 64–66, 196–197
  increased ownership, 724
  of loan collateral, 321
  ratios of, 62–71
  trade-off with profitability, 198–204

Loan amortization, 365–366
Loans. See Long-term debt financing; Short-term financing
Lock-box system, 230–231
Long-term debt financing, 603–632
  characteristics and provisions, 604–610
  corporate bonds, 603. See also Bonds
  cost of, 476–479, 608–610
  long-term loans, 610–614
Long-term financing. See Common stock; Leasing; Long-term debt financing; Preferred stock; Retained earnings

M
Macroeconomics and finance, 56
Majority voting system, 644
Management. See Accounts receivable management; Cash management; Fixed asset management; Inventory management
Managerial skills, increased, 723
M and M. See Modigliani and Miller
Marginal analysis, 6
Marginal weights. See Weighted-average cost of capital
Margin purchase of stock, 559–560
Market, 445. See also Capital market; Money market
Marketability
  of loan collateral, 332
  related to securities, 219
Marketable securities, 219, 233–238. See also Money market
  characteristics of, 233, 234
  description of common types, 234, 236–237
  management of, 219, 235–238
  motive for holding, 219, 233
  optimum proportion of, 219, 235
Market debt-equity ratio, 514–515

Market indifference curve, 455–460
Market premium on convertibles, 670
Market value weights. See Weighted-average cost of capital
Mathematics of finance, 358–368. See also Compound interest; Present value
Mergers, 719, 720
  analyzing cash purchases, 726–728
  analyzing going concern mergers, 728
  analyzing prospective mergers, 726–738
  the negotiation process, 737–738
  stock exchange acquisitions, 729–737
    operating and financial risk, 736–737
    market price effect, 725, 734
    ratio of exchange, 729–730
Microeconomics and finance, 5, 6–7
Minimum operating cash. See Cash mangement
Mixed streams of cash flow, 360–361, 384–385
Modernization of fixed assets, 377–378
Modigliani and Miller (M and M), 517–518, 688–690
MOM (middle of month) credit period, 297
Money market, 552–554. See also Marketable securities
  instruments, operation, and participants, 552–554
Mortgage bonds, 619–621
Mortgages, 619–621. See also Mortgage bonds
  types of, 619–621
Most likely estimate. See Sensitivity analysis of risk
Mutual funds, 561
Mutually exclusive projects, 381. See also Capital budgeting
Mutual savings banks, described, 550

N

Negotiable certificates of deposit, 237
Negotiated offering, 563
Net cash flow. *See* Cash budget
Net present value (NPV), 408, 414–417
  for capital rationing, 415, 417–420
  the decision criterion, 408
Net profit margin, 79–80
Net working capital, 64, 195, 196, 197–198
  comparison with current ratio, 64, 65
  and risk of insolvency, 195
New York Stock Exchange (NYSE), 556–558, 687
Notification, accounts receivable financing
  in factoring, 328
  in pledging, 326
NPV. *See* Net present value

O

Odd lot, 557
Operating costs, types, 100–101
  and operating leverage, 114–115
Operating leases, 574, 576. *See also* Leasing
Operating leverage, 99–100, 111–117
  in breakeven analysis, 100
  illustration of concept, 99–100
  and operating risk, 115–116
  relationship to fixed and variable costs, 114–115
Operating profit margin, 78–79
Operating risk, 115–116, 481
Opportunity cost, 407
Optimistic estimate. *See* Sensitivity analysis of risk
Overall cost of capital. *See* Weighted average cost of capital
Overall coverage ratio, 75–77
Overhanging bond issue, 667
Oversubscribed security issue, 565, 649
Over-the-Counter (OTC) exchange, 559
Ownership rights, in equity capital, 634

P

Partnership, 22, 24–26. *See also* Business organization forms
Par value, 635, 642–643
Payback period, 402–403, 405–407
Pension funds, 551
  in term lending, 612
Percent income statement, 78
Perpetuity, 367–368
Personal taxes, 35–37
  determining taxable income, 38–39
Pessimistic estimate. *See* Sensitivity analysis of risk
Pledging accounts receivable, 323–327. *See also* Accounts receivable
  cost of pledges, 326–327
  types of pledges, 323–324
Portfolio risk and correlation, 441–444
Preemptive right, 646–647
Preferred stock, 633, 635–642
  advantages and disadvantages of, 640–642
  basic rights of stockholders, 635–636
  characteristics of equity capital, 633–635
  convertible, 660
  cost of, 479–482, 641–642
  sale of new issues, 637
  special features of, 637–640
Present value, 347, 357–364
  of an annuity, 361–364
  applied to bond refunding, 622–625
  applied to leasing decisions, 589–590
  applied to merger evaluation, 726–728
  in bond value determination, 367
  calculations, 347
  growth and interest rate determination, 366
  interest factor for one dollar, 358–359
  in loan amortization, 365–366
  mathematical expression for, 358
  of a mixed stream of cash flows, 360–361
  and perpetuities, 367–368

relationship to compound interest, 359–360, 364–368
  of a single amount, 357–358
  in straight convertible value determination, 668–670
  tables, 358–359, 362–364
Present value profiles, 415
Price-earnings (P/E) ratio, 531
  consideration in mergers, 726, 731–733
Price-pegging, 565
Prime interest rate, 305–306
Priority of claims in liquidation, 765–768
Private placement of securities, 562. *See also* Direct placement
Probability, 432, 433
  types of distributions of, 432, 434–436
Profitability, 62
  and the financing mix, 204–213
  measures of, 77–84
  ratios of, 62
  and trade-off with risk, 198–204. *See also* Working capital management
Profit maximization vs. wealth maximization, 11–15
Pro forma statements, 159–183
  balance sheet preparation, 165–167, 178–183
  budgeting inputs, 159–161, 168–175, 178, 179–183
  income statement preparation, 163–165, 176–178
  long approach to, 168–175
  sales forecasts, 162–163
  short-cut approach to preparation of, 161–168, 178, 183
Prospectus, 563
Proxy, 644
Public offerings, 617
Purchase syndicate, 563

Q

Quick ratio. *See* Acid-test ratio

R

Ranking approach, 382. *See also* Capital budgeting; Capital rationing
  using benefit-cost ratios, 416

using internal rate of return, 415–416
using net present value, 415–416
Rate of return, 402, 403–405
Ratio analysis. *See* Financial ratios
Ratio of exchange, 729–730
of market price, 734–736
Raw materials, inventory of, 270–271
Recapitalization, refinancing, and retirement, 639–640
of a failed business firm, 763–764
of securities, 528, 622
Recaptured depreciation, 43. *See also* Corporate taxes
Receipt of goods (ROG) credit terms, 298
Receiver in bankruptcy, 765
Red herring, 563–564
Referee in bankruptcy, 765
Regional development companies, 613
Relevant cash flow, 383, 391. *See also* Capital budgeting
Reorganization in bankruptcy, 760–761
procedures of, 760–765
Replacement costs, fixed assets, 377, 379–380
Repurchase agreements, 238
Repurchase, stock, 704–706
Residual owner, 642
Restrictive provisions
in a bond issue, 614
on a line of credit, 307–308
on a long-term loan, 605–608
in preferred stock issues, 637–638
Retained earnings, 683
as a source of financing, 684–686
Return on assets, 80–81
Return on common stock equity, 11, 82
Return on equity (ROE) and the Modified DuPont formula, 83 (table), 84–85
Return on investment (ROI), 80–81
and the DuPont formula, 80–81

Revolving credit agreements, 308–309
Rights, stock purchase
comparison with warrants, 673
management decisions, 647–648
market behavior of, 649
mechanics of offering, 565, 647
non-rights sale of new common stock, 649–650
preemptive rights, 646–647
under- and oversubscription, 649
value of, 648–649
Risk, 13
in capital budgeting, 429–457. *See also* Capital budgeting under risk
and cost of capital, 472–473
financial, 121
and financing mix decision, 207–208, 209
and leverage, 99, 121–125
operating, 115–116
total. *See* total risk
and working capital management, 198–204
Risk-adjusted discount rate, 454–457
Risk and return function. *See also* Capital budgeting under risk; Market indifference curve
CAPM (Capital Asset Pricing Model), 444–449
types of risk, 445–446
and uncertainty, 430
Risk classes, 481
Risk diversification, 445–446
Risk premium, 456
ROG. *See* Receipt of goods
ROI. *See* Return on investment
Round lot, 557

S
Safety motive, 233, 234
Sale price per unit, 105–106
Sales forecasts, 144
in cash budget, 144–145
internal and external methods of, 144
in pro forma statements, 162–163

Savings and loan associations, 550
Seasonal dating, 295–296
Second mortgage, 620–621
Secured loans. *See* Bonds; Long-term debt financing; Short-term financing
Securities. *See* Bonds; Common stock; Marketable securities; Preferred stock
Securities Exchange Act (1934), 563, 564
Securities Exchange Commission (SEC), 563–566
Securities exchanges
functions and characteristics, 554–559
organized exchanges, 556–559
over-the-counter exchange, 559
Security interest
acceptable short-term collateral, 319–321
in a bond, 615
collateral, stocks and bonds, 335–338
the floating lien, 319, 320, 323
in a long-term loan, 611
the trust receipt, 319–320, 333
Selling group, securities, 563
Semivariable costs, 101
Senior securities, sale of, 637
Sensitivity analysis of risk, 431–432
Serial issues, 622
Short sale of stock, 559
Short-term financing, 293–311, 317–338
bank loans, 304–309
characteristics of, 318–323
estimating requirements. *See* Cash budget
institutions extending loans, 322–323
non-bank sources of, 293, 309–311
secured sources
pledge of accounts receivable, 323–327
stock and bond collateral, 335–338

Short-term financing (*continued*)
  spontaneous sources, 293, 294–304
  unsecured, 293, 304–309, 317
Short-term loans. *See* Short-term financing
Simulation, use of, 452–453, 611
Sinking funds, 74–75, 614–615
Small Business Administration (SBA), 612–613
Small Business Invesment Company (SBIC), 613
SML (security market line), 448–449
Sole proprietorship, 22–24. *See also* Business organization forms
Sources and uses of funds statements, 131–143
  assets, 134
  the cash statement, 140–143
  classifying sources and uses, 132–134, 138
  interpreting the statement, 142–143
  liabilities, 134
  net working capital statement, 141–142
  percentage basis, 142
  preliminaries to preparation, 138
  special adjustments required, 135
  stockholders' equity, 134–135
Sources of funds, 132–134
  leasing as a source, 578–585
Speculative motive, 233, 234
Spread, 565
Standard & Poor's Industrial Ratios, 531, 618
Standard deviation, 436–438
  and coefficient of variation, 439
Standard loan provisions, 604–605
Standby arrangment, 649
Stock. *See also* Common stock; Preferred stock
  as loan collateral, 335–338
  market for. *See* Capital market; Securities exchanges

special types of transactions, 559–560
  warrants for, 671–675. *See also* Warrants
Stock dividends, 700–702
Stockholders, rights of, 26. *See also* Common stock; Preferred stock
  dividends. *See* Dividends, cash; Dividends, non-cash
  voting procedures, 636, 644–645
Stock options, 566
Stock purchase options. *See* Warrants
Stock purchase plans, 566, 650, 704–706
Stock repurchases, 638, 646
  accounting entries, 704
  motives for, 704–706
  repurchase process, 706
Stock rights. *See* Rights, stock purchase
Stock splits, 702–704
Straight-line depreciation method, 31, 32, 33
Straight value, bonds and preferred stocks, 668–669
Subchapter S corporations, 47
Subordinated debentures, 618–619
  restrictions in loan agreements, 606–607
Subsidiaries. *See* Holding companies
Sum of an annuity, 354–357
  using the table, 355, 356
Sum of one dollar, 349–357
  using the table, 350–351, 356
Sum-of-the-years' digits depreciation method, 31, 32
Sweeteners
  for financing, 664
  warrants as, 671–672
Synergistic effects of growth, 722

T

Tax anticipation bills, 236–237
Tax considerations, 723–724
Taxes. *See* Corporate taxes; personal taxes

Tax losses, 43–46
  carryback and carryforward of, 44–46
Tax rates. *See* Corporate taxes; Personal taxes
Tender offers, 708, 738
Terminal warehouses, 334. *See also* Warehouse receipt loans
Term loans. *See* Long-term debt financing
Theory of capital structure. *See* Capital structure
Time-series ratio comparison, 59
Times-interest-earned ratio, 74, 514
Total asset turnover ratio, 80
Total capitalization, 73, 514
Total debt coverage ratio, 74–75, 514
Total interest coverage, 74, 514
Total leverage, 99, 122–125
  illustrated, 122
  measuring (DTL), 122–124
Total revenue function curved, 109
Total risk, 124–125
Trade credit, 295
  cost of, 299–303
Trade-off approach to financing current assets, 198–204. *See also* Working capital management
Trade-off between aggressive and conservative approaches, 210–212
  cost considerations, 211
  risk considerations, 211
  summary comparison, 212
Transactions motive, 233–234
Treasury bills, 236
Treasury notes, 237
Treasury stock, 643, 647, 704
  and stock repurchases, 646, 704–706
Trustee
  in bankruptcy, 761, 762–765, 766, 768
  of a bond, 615
Trust receipt loans, 319–320
  on inventory, 333
  pledges of accounts receivable, 319–320

U

Uncertainty. *See* Risk
Undersubscribed security issues, 565, 649
Underwriting, 561–562. *See also* Investment bankers
Unlimited liability, 24, 25
Unsecured loans. *See* Short-term financing
Uses of funds, 132–134

V

Valuation of convertible securities, 667–671
 bond and preferred stock values, 667–668
 market value, 670
 special considerations, 670–671
 stock or conversion value, 669
Valuation of corporate stock, 511, 528–533, 650. *See also* Valuation of convertible securities
 book value, 528–529
 comparing valuation techniques, 533
 the Gordon model, 531–533
 industry capitalization, 531
 liquidation value of stock, 529–530
 market value, 530–531
Valuation of warrants, 673–675
 market value, 674
 theoretical value, 673–674
 warrant premium, 673, 674–675
Variable operating costs, 101
 in breakeven analysis, 101

Variable operating cost per unit
 changes in, 106, 109
Voluntary settlements of failed firms, 755–758
Voting rights
 of common stock, 643–645
 of preferred stock, 636

W

Wall Street Journal, 531, 558, 686
Warehouse receipt. *See*, Warehouse receipt loans
Warehouse receipt loans, 320, 333–334
 cost of, 320, 335
 lending procedure, 333–335
  field warehouses, 334
  terminal warehouses, 334
 loan agreement, 334–335
Warrant premium, 673, 674–675
Warrants, 671–675
 in bond agreements, 616
 characteristics, 671–673
  exercise or option price, 611, 672
 compared to convertibles, 672–673
 compared to rights, 673
 life of, 672
 market value, 674
 premium, 674
 theoretical value, 673–674
 trading, 672
 use in mergers, 737–738
 valuation of. *See* Valuation of warrants
 value, 673

Wealth maximization vs. profit maximization, 11–15
Weighted average cost of capital, 488–495
 cost of specific types of capital. *See* Cost of capital
 target weights, 491–492
 use of historical weights, 489–490
  book value, 489
  market value, 490
 use of marginal weights, 492–494
Weighted marginal cost of capital (WMCC), 494–501
 calculation of, 495–499
 use of for decision making, 499–501
WMCC (Weighted marginal cost of capital), 494–500
Working capital. *See also* Net working capital; Working capital management
 requirements of, 638
Working capital mangement, 195–213
 determination of financing mix, 204–213
 net working capital, 197
 profitability-risk trade-off, 198–200
  assumptions, 199–200
  profitability, 198
  risk, 198–199

Y

Yield to maturity, 477

Z

Zero-bracket amount, 38

79 80 81 7 6 5 4 3 2

PRESENT-VALUE INTEREST FACTORS FOR A ONE-DOLLAR ANNUITY, PVIFA

Year	1%	2%	3%	4%	5%	6%	7%	8%	9%	10%
1	.990	.980	.971	.962	.952	.943	.935	.926	.917	.909
2	1.970	1.942	1.913	1.886	1.859	1.833	1.808	1.783	1.759	1.736
3	2.941	2.884	2.829	2.775	2.723	2.673	2.624	2.577	2.531	2.487
4	3.902	3.808	3.717	3.630	3.546	3.465	3.387	3.312	3.240	3.170
5	4.853	4.713	4.580	4.452	4.329	4.212	4.100	3.993	3.890	3.791
6	5.795	5.601	5.417	5.242	5.076	4.917	4.767	4.623	4.486	4.355
7	6.728	6.472	6.230	6.002	5.786	5.582	5.389	5.206	5.033	4.868
8	7.652	7.326	7.020	6.733	6.463	6.210	5.971	5.747	5.535	5.335
9	8.566	8.162	7.786	7.435	7.108	6.802	6.515	6.247	5.995	5.759
10	9.471	8.983	8.530	8.111	7.722	7.360	7.024	6.710	6.418	6.145
11	10.368	9.787	9.253	8.760	8.306	7.887	7.499	7.139	6.805	6.495
12	11.255	10.575	9.954	9.385	8.863	8.384	7.943	7.536	7.161	6.814
13	12.134	11.348	10.635	9.986	9.394	8.853	8.358	7.904	7.487	7.103
14	13.004	12.106	11.296	10.563	9.899	9.295	8.746	8.244	7.786	7.367
15	13.865	12.849	11.938	11.118	10.380	9.712	9.108	8.560	8.061	7.606
16	14.718	13.578	12.561	11.652	10.838	10.106	9.447	8.851	8.313	7.824
17	15.562	14.292	13.166	12.166	11.274	10.477	9.763	9.122	8.544	8.022
18	16.398	14.992	13.754	12.659	11.690	10.828	10.059	9.372	8.756	8.201
19	17.226	15.679	14.324	13.134	12.085	11.158	10.336	9.604	8.950	8.365
20	18.046	16.352	14.878	13.590	12.462	11.470	10.594	9.818	9.129	8.514
21	18.857	17.011	15.415	14.029	12.821	11.764	10.836	10.017	9.292	8.649
22	19.661	17.658	15.937	14.451	13.163	12.042	11.061	10.201	9.442	8.772
23	20.456	18.292	16.444	14.857	13.489	12.303	11.272	10.371	9.580	8.883
24	21.244	18.914	16.936	15.247	13.799	12.550	11.469	10.529	9.707	8.985
25	22.023	19.524	17.413	15.622	14.094	12.783	11.654	10.675	9.823	9.077
30	25.808	22.397	19.601	17.292	15.373	13.765	12.409	11.258	10.274	9.427
35	29.409	24.999	21.487	18.665	16.374	14.498	12.948	11.655	10.567	9.644
40	32.835	27.356	23.115	19.793	17.159	15.046	13.332	11.925	10.757	9.779
45	36.095	29.490	24.519	20.720	17.774	15.456	13.606	12.108	10.881	9.863
50	39.197	31.424	25.730	21.482	18.256	15.762	13.801	12.234	10.962	9.915